Environmental Systems and Societies

for the IB Diploma Programme

3rd edition

Andrew Davis and Garrett Nagle

Published by Pearson Education Limited, 80 Strand, London, WC2R 0RL.
www.pearson.com/international-schools

Text © Pearson Education Limited 2024
Development edited by Pen Lyons
Copy edited by Sarah Binns
Proofread by Katharine Godfrey-Smith, Sarah Binns and Sarah Ryan
Indexed by Georgina Bowden
Designed by Pearson Education Limited 2024
Typeset by Straive Ltd
Picture research by Straive Ltd
Original illustrations © Pearson Education Limited 2024
Cover design © Pearson Education Limited 2024

Inside front cover: **Shutterstock.com**/Dmitry Lobanov

The right of Andrew Davis and Garrett Nagle to be identified as the authors of this work has been asserted by them in accordance with the Copyright, Designs and Patents Act 1988.

First published 2024

26 25 24
10 9 8 7 6 5 4 3 2 1

British Library Cataloguing in Publication Data
A catalogue record for this book is available from the British Library

ISBN 978 1 292 72954 1

Printed in Slovakia by Neografia

The "In cooperation with IB" logo signifies the content in this textbook has been reviewed by the IB to ensure it fully aligns with current IB curriculum and offers high-quality guidance and support for IB teaching and learning.

Dedication
Andrew Davis:
In memory of Fred Tao - a wonderful educator and friend.
Garrett Nagle:
To Angela, Rosie, Patrick and Bethany - for their continued support, help and patience.
To Adam Griffiths and Joe Cazabon for their help in producing this book.
Andrew Davis and Garrett Nagle:
Our thanks to Catherine Barber and Ellie Sorell, who coordinated the complex process or editing, reviewing, and proofreading with expertise and good humour. We are extremely grateful for the time and care they put into the production of this book, and for guiding it through to completion. We are also grateful to Penelope Lyons, who has edited not only this book but also the first two editions, and set the standard for the publication early on. We would like to thank our reviewer for the IB for their extensive work on this project, and whose feedback throughout the process has been both supportive and constructive – they went above and beyond what we could have wished for, and their perceptive, detailed and helpful comments have greatly improved the book.

Acknowledgments
Text:
African Studies Association: History in Africa, Volume 17, © 1990.

All Credits

The author and publisher would like to thank the following individuals and organizations for permission to reproduce photographs.

(key: b-bottom; c-centre; l-left; r-right; t-top)

Prominent Image Credit(s):

Front Cover: chinaface/Getty Images

Non-Prominent Image Credit(s):

123RF: 7activestudio 280, abbphoto 051t, Alexander Petrenko 206b R, andesign101 880c, aoosthuizen 089, casaltamoiola 880t, crystalart 841, designua 087, 247b, elnur 852, federico rostagno 460t, Feng Yu 854, Fernando Gregory Milan 273t, francoillustration 145, frankfichtmueller 222m R, Jane McLoughlin 133, Joshua Abbas 249t, lightwise 867, Mauro Rodrigues 123, max5128 284, normaals 365b, 352, nuttaya 470, PaylessImages 820, Peter Hermes Furian 356, phil_bird 181t, Prapan Ngawkeaw 447, Sander Meertins 220t, softlight69 323b, thewet 095b L, Wan Rosli Wan Othman 220c, wetzkaz 808, wrangel 254t; **Alamy Images:** Aas/Associated Press 012, ajsissues 697, Alexandre Rotenberg 759, Associated Press 018c, Avalon/Bruce Coleman Inc 017t R, blickwinkel/McPHOTO/I. Schulz 235 R, Boaz Rottem 298, Bruce J. Lichtenberger/Design Pics Inc 042, Christian Handl/imageBROKER.com GmbH & Co. KG 461, Christian Kober 1 361b, Christoph Soeder/dpa picture alliance 580, Claudia Thaler/dpa picture alliance 615, Czychowski/Timeline Images/Sueddeutsche Zeitung Photo 537, David Cherepuschak 776 L, Dino Fracchia 756, Dinodia Photos 020b, dpa picture alliance archive 837, Emmanuel LATTES 428, Farlap 510, Federico Magonio 368t, frans lemmens 432, guy oliver 677c, Hugh Threlfall 453, Ian Dagnall 030, Irena Mora/VWPics 414, Jasper Chamber 017t L, Jens Büttner/dpa picture alliance 116 R, Jim West 524, Jim West/imageBROKER.com GmbH & Co. KG 763, Joerg Boethling 543, John Wollwerth 754, KEVIN ELSBY 116L, Laszlo Mates 299, Lizzie Noble/ProAves/UPI 875cr, Lloyd 526, LOOK-foto/Image Professionals GmbH 575b, Manfred Bail/imageBROKER.com GmbH & Co. KG 460b, Maniglia Romano/Pacific Press Media Production Corp. 700, 704, Mark Stevenson/UIG/Universal Images Group North America LLC 556, Martin Bond 019t, Martin Shields 422, 874b, Matthew Hart 279t, Michael Seleznev 874t, Michel & Gabrielle Therin-Weise 279b, Mint Images Limited 241, Nathaniel Noir 517, Nature Picture Library 235 L, Panther Media GmbH 314, pawopa3336/Panther Media GmbH 672, 677b, Photo Researchers/Science History Images 120, Photoshot/Avalon.red 278b, Pictorial Press Ltd 017t C, 096b, Prisma by Dukas Presseagentur GmbH 876b, Raf Makda-VIEW 684, Reinhard Dirscherl/mauritius images GmbH 278t, Richard Ellis 800, Richard Vogel/Associated Press 738, Science History Images 148, Stephen Dwyer 786, Steve Morgan 078t, The Natural History Museum 281t, Travel Wild 292, Tuomas Lehtinen 745 L, USFWS Photo 419, Volodymyr Burdiak 222t C, Washington Imaging 365t, Zoonar/Kitch Bain 085; **Andrew J Davis:** 201, 204, 304, 305t, 305c, 305b, 321, 393t, 870cl, 870br, 871, 091b, 107, 108, 180, 200, 237t, 242, 255b, 274t, 307, 309, 310, 323t; **Arthur Chung:** 244b1, 244b2; **Bridgeman Images:** Paleolithic 649; **Cartoon Movement:** Tjeerd Royaards 060; **Chien C. Lee:** © Chien C. Lee 274b; **Children's Investment Fund Foundation:** © 2016 Cognitive www.wearecognitive.com/Children's Investment Fund Foundation (CIFF) www.ciff.org 864; **Dr Zainal Adlin Bin Tengku Mahamood:** 018b; **Garrett E Nagle:** 337, 361t, 366, 367, 369, 370, 384, 392, 404, 417, 637, 640, 641t, 641b, 647, 655 L, 655 R, 698, 707, 452 R, 452 L, 456, 458t, 458b, 463, 468, 473, 479t, 482, 484, 506, 507, 513, 529t, 529c, 750 R, 750 L, 753, 764, 772, 774, 782, 783, 793t, 793b, 092, 093, 096t, 106, 206b L, 701, 706 L, 574, 706 R, 745 C; **Getty Images:** 7postman 869, alvaher/iStock 095t, ANGELA WEISS/AFP 529b, Bettmann 057, CARL DE SOUZA/

AFP 590, CRIS BOURONCLE/AFP 017b, DEA/V. GIANNELLA/De Agostini 502, Fotosearch 199, Fuse/Corbis 237b1, Hubert Stadler/Corbis Documentary 279c, JIJI PRESS/AFP 020t, John van Hasselt/Corbis Historical 554, JUNIOR KANNAH/AFP 691, Kelvinyam/iStock/Getty Images Plus 311, Library of Congress/Corbis Historical/VCG 858, Natural Selection David Ponton/Design Pics 237b2, Orjan F. Ellingvag/Dagens Naringsliv/Corbis 676, Peter Chadwick/ Gallo Images ROOTS RF 257, pop_jop/DigitalVision Vectors 811 L, PORNCHAI KITTIWONGSAKUL/AFP 009, Richard Hamilton Smith 045t, Rubberball/Mike Kemp 881, Sean Gallup 004t, SHONE/GAMMA/Gamma-Rapho 021t, Smith Collection/Gado/Archive Photos 575c, Stephanie Keith/ Getty Images News 579, Stephanie Maze 216t, Stockbyte 877, The Asahi Shimbun 022, vlbentley/iStock/Getty Images Plus 373, Wendy Stone/Corbis Historical 018t; **Government of Western Australia:** © State of Western Australia (Department of Primary Industries and Regional Development, WA) 479b, 481; **Greenpeace:** Jean Paul Ferrero 014; **International Institute for Sustainable Development:** Photo courtesy of IISD Experimental Lakes Area (IISD-ELA). 427t, 427b; **National Aeronautics and Space Administration:** Joshua Stevens/NASA Earth Observatory 627, NASA/ NOAA GOES Project 581; **National Oceanic and Atmospheric Administration:** National Oceanic and Atmospheric Administration (NOAA) 406, 636, Garbage Patches 286; **Newscom:** archivo perticular/GDA Photo Service 053; **Oxford Designers & Illustrators Ltd:** 360, 247t, 248c, 248b, 261 L; **PaleoScene:** "Photos © 1984, by Glen J Kuban" 872 L, 872 R; **Science Photo Library:** ALEX HYDE 206t, BOB GIBBONS 215, BRITISH ANTARCTIC SURVEY 037, CHRISTIAN JEGOU 213t, DAVID M. SCHLESER/NATURE'S IMAGES 032, DAVID PARKER 091t, DIGITAL GLOBE 021b, DR JEREMY BURGESS 168, GEORGETTE DOUWMA 135, KJELL B. SANDVED 095b R, NASA 003, NATURAL HISTORY MUSEUM, LONDON 086, PATRICK LANDMANN 104, SINCLAIR STAMMERS 031, 098; **Shutterstock:** 151171 183, A_Lesik 418, AB Photographie 814, Abinieks 222b L, alexmillos 019b, Alison Hancock 787, Amelandfoto 221 C, Andrzej Gibasiewicz 882, Andrzej Jablonski 326b, Andy Rain/EPA 234, arenysam 222b R, arousa 393b, Atomazul 762, avkost 087, avoferten 341, AY Amazefoto 758, BMJ 283, Borisoff 111b L, Bukhta Yurii 134, Callums Trees 166, Charles Amundson 521, chayanuphol 862b, Christian Musat 152, coxy58 760, Crystal Eye Studio 387, Daniel J. Rao 216b R, davemhuntphotography 229, David Dirga 232, Designua 549, Dina Rogatnykh 087, DJ Sudermann 221 L, Dmussman 111t, EcoPrint 301, Edwin Butter 303, Ekaterina Pokrovsky 181b, elenabsl 862t, EMILIA 078b, Eric Isselee 087, 653, Eugene Troskie 272b, Everett Historical 269, fasphotographic 606, feathercollector 255t, Fedor Selivanov 082, feiyuezhangjie 747, fivepointsix 619, fotocraft 744, Freedom_wanted 692, fromshutter 745 R, Grigorii Pisotsckii 775, GUDKOV ANDREY 254b, 326t, Helen Hotson 273b, Helen18255 067, herle_catharina 561, hramovnick 111c, 620, Inger Anne Hulbí_kdal 169R, isak55 833, Ivan Marc 836, jan kranendonk 827, Janne Hamalainen 111b R, Jim Cumming 222m C, jo Crebbin 294, Joe Mercier 272t, John Wreford 568, Jon Benedictus 423 L, Jon Varsano 779t, Katarina Christenson 876 t R, Katia Titova 776 R, Katrevich Valeriy 822t, Kelly Marken 169t, kenary820 819, Kirk Fisher 789, Kuttelvaserova Stuchelova 087, Lane V. Erickson 834, Larsek 875t, Lasse Johansson 087, lavizzara 196, lewan 001, LifeCollectionPhotography 122, Linda Marie Caldwell 213b, Luriya Chinwan 748, Maceofoto 534b, MalikMirHadi 221 R, Marek R. Swadzba 275b, Mario Lopes 806t, Martin Good 282, Martina Badini 285, Matthijs Wetterauw 564, Mayabuns 773, MC MEDIASTUDIO 547, Merkushev Vasiliy 087, Michael Potter11 824, mikeledray 779b, Ministr-84 878, M-SUR 822b, Nathan Mortimer 335, Natursports 873, nechaevkon 876c, Nelson Beam 368b, NotionPic 132, Oleg Znamenskiy 110, Ondrej Prosicky 281b, Paolo Gallo 231b, Papaca Go 308, Paul Loewen 222m L, People Image Studio 385, petovarga 845, Photodigitaal.nl 216b L, Pichugin Dmitry 253, pio3 806b, Powerhouse Productions 523, Prasetyo tiyut 876 t L, Rawpixel.com 087, reisegraf.ch 329, Rich Carey 045b, Richard Griffin 087, Richard Whitcombe 276, saranya33 788, Sarfaraj sk 220b, Scharfsinn 503b, Sean Xu 182, ssguy 714, steph photographies 244t, Steve Bramall 583, STILLFX 231t, studio23 548, Tarcisio Schnaider 038, Tetyana Kochneva 051b, trevor kittelty 817, trgrowth 164, TristanBM 087, Trixcis 423 R, udaix 259, urosr 825, Ursula Perreten 838, valda butterworth 275t, Valentyn Volkov 087, 534t, ViDI Studio 004b, visdia 599, Vitalii Hulai 087, Vladimir Melnikov 222t L, Vladimir Wrangel 875cl, Volodymyr Burdiak 222t R, Weerawit Thitiworasith 163 R, WindVector 412, Yulia_B 169L, Zoran Milosavljevic 163 L; **SkyCool Systems:** 633; **THOMSON REUTERS CORPORATION:** Ben Nelms/ Reuters 498; **U.S. Environmental Protection Agency:** "Size comparisons for PM particles, " in Particulate Matter (PM) Basics. United States Environmental Protection Agency (EPA). https: //www.epa.gov/pm-pollution/particulate-matter-pm-basics 780; **Underwater Earth:** © Underwater Earth/XL Catlin Seaview Survey 567b, © Underwater Earth/XL Catlin Seaview Survey/Christophe Bailhache 567t; **United States Department of Agriculture:** 222b C, 503t; **United States National Park Service:** William Elder 553

Non-Prominent Text Credit(s):

ACTP eV: ACTP. ACTP responds to the commentary concerning conservation measures required for the endangered Amazon parrots of the Commonwealth of Dominica. 2018 Available at: https://www.act-parrots.org/wp-content/uploads/2018/04/Dominica-Statement.pdf 227; **American Association for the Advancement of Science:** "Used with the permission of American Association for the Advancement of Science from Ivory poaching and the rapid evolution of tusklessness in African elephants, Zapovednik, Campbell-Staton, S. C., et al., Science 374 (6566), 483-487, © 2021; permission conveyed through Copyright Clearance Centre, Inc." 258; **Antonio Guterres:** Quoted by Antonio Guterres 577, 589; **ASEAN Secretariat:** Priority Areas of Cooperation, https://asean.org/our-communities/asean-socio-cultural-community/haze-2/priority-areas-of-cooperation/ 820; **Barack Obama:** Barack Obama victory speech, 7 November 2012 197; **Benjamin Henley:** Ben Henley & Nerilie Abram "The three-minute story of 800, 000 years of climate change with a sting in the tail," The Conversation (12 June 2017). https://theconversation.com/the-three-minute-story-of-800-000-years-of-climate-change-with-a-sting-in-the-tail-73368 563; **Berkeley Earth:** "Temperature Distribution in 2020," in Robert Rohde (14 Jan 2021) Global Temperature Report for 2020. Berkeley Earth. https://berkeleyearth.org/global-temperature-report-for-2020/ 588; **BioNinja:** "Proportion of Greenhouse Gases (Natural vs Anthropomorphic)," BioNinja. https://ib.bioninja.com.au/standard-level/topic-4-ecology/44-climate-change/greenhouse-gases.html 565; **Bradbury and Evans:** Charles Dickens (1853) Bleak House. London: Bradbury and Evans. 785; **BYJU'S:** "Environmental Impact Assessment (EIA) Process," in Environmental Impact Assessment (EIA) - UPSC Notes. BYJU'S. https://byjus.com/free-ias-prep/eia/ 659; **Cambridge University Press:** Based on data in Wild, A., 1993, Soils and the environment, Cambridge, p. 116 471, Bridges, E., 1978, World soils, Cambridge University press, p. 18, Figure 2.6 457, Wild, A., 1993, Soils and the environment, Cambridge, p. 123, Table 7.5 464, Wild, A., 1993, Soils and the environment, Cambridge, p. 28, Table 2.5 468, Wild, A., 1993, Soils and the environment, Cambridge, p. 69, Table 5.1 472; **Carbon Brief:** Q&A: How do climate models work? Carbon Brief 15 January 2018. https://www.carbonbrief.org/qa-how-do-climate-models-work/. 585, Zeke Hausfather "Explainer: What climate models tell us about future rainfall," Carbon Brief (19 Jan 2018). https://www.carbonbrief.org/explainer-what-climate-models-tell-us-about-future-rainfall/ 589; **Carbon Streaming:** Visualizing Carbon Storage in Earth's Ecosystems, Visual Capitalist. Used by permission of Carbon Streaming Corporation. Retrieved from https://www.visualcapitalist.com/sp/visualizing-carbon-storage-in-earths-ecosystems/ 163; **CEDARS Communications Co., Ltd:** CEDARS Communications Co., Ltd 326; **Center for Sustainable Systems:** "U.S. ENERGY CONSUMPTION BY SOURCE, 2021," in U.S. Energy System Factsheet. Center for Sustainable Systems. https://css.umich.edu/publications/factsheets/energy/us-energy-system-factsheet 686; **Central Intelligence Agency:** "Niger," in The World Factbook. CIA. https://www.cia.gov/the-world-factbook/countries/niger/#people-and-society 804, Based on CIA data 716, By avis28 at English Wikipedia - Transferred from en.wikipedia to Commons., Public Domain 542, Data from CIA Worldfactbook 687, **Clear Seas:** "Black Carbon 101: How Black Carbon Behaves in the Arctic" was created by Clear Seas to provide independent fact-based information to enable governments, industry, and the public to make informed decisions on marine shipping issues." 551; **Climate Policy Watcher:** "The Global Thermohaline Conveyor," Climate Policy Watcher (9 Aug 2023). https://www.climate-policy-watcher.org/ocean-circulation-2/the-global-thermohaline-conveyor.html 356; **Congress for the New Urbanism:** The Charter of the New Urbanism, Retrieved from https://www.cnu.org/who-we-are/charter-new-urbanism 757; **Copernicus Publications:** Wunderling, N., et al. (2021). Interacting tipping elements increase risk of climate domino effects under global warming. Earth System Dynamics, 12(2), 601-619. 591; **Development Policy Centre:** Curtain, C. & Dornan, M. 2019, 'A pressure release valve? Migration and climate change in Kiribati, Nauru and Tuvalu', Report, Development Policy Centre, Crawford School of Public Policy, Australian National University. 738; **Donald Trump:** Quoted by Donald Trump 580; **Doughnut Economics Action Lab:** Doughnut Economics Action Lab. (2023). The embedded economy. https://doughnuteconomics.org/tools/65 850; **Earth.Org:** The three phases of the El Niño–Southern Oscillation (ENSO)https://earth.org/data_visualization/what-are-el-nino-and-la-nina/ 194, 195; **Eatforum:** The Planetary Health Diet, https://eatforum.org/eat-lancet-commission/the-planetary-health-diet-and-you/ 530; **Ellen MacArthur Foundation:** "Towards the circular economy Vol 1: an economic and business rationale for an accelerated transition," Ellen MacArthur Foundation, Figure 9, p.33. https://emf.thirdlight.com/link/x8ay372a3r11-k6775n/@/preview/1?o 708, Advancing vehicle remanufacturing in China – the role of policy 12 September 2022 https://ellenmacarthurfoundation.org/circular-examples/advancing-vehicle-remanufacturing-in-china-the-role-of-policy 074, Circular economy butterfly diagram https://emf.thirdlight.com/link/7kvazph93afk-owveai/@/preview/1?o; https://ellenmacarthurfoundation.org/circular-economy-diagramhttps://ellenmacarthurfoundation.org/circular-examples/advancing-vehicle-remanufacturing-in-china-the-role-of-policy 074; **Elsevier, Inc.:** "This article was published in One Earth, 4(6), Stringer, L. C., et al., Climate change impacts on water security in global drylands, 851-864, © Elsevier 2021". 360, "Used with the permission of Elsevier Inc from A review of water quality index models and their use for assessing surface water quality, Quinlivan, Uddin, M. G., Nash, S., & Olbert, A. I, Ecological Indicators, 122, 107218, © 2021; permission conveyed through Copyright Clearance Centre, Inc." 442, "Used with the permission of Elsevier Inc from Validating citizen science monitoring of ambient water quality for the United Nations sustainable development goals, Quinlivan, L., Chapman, D. V., & Sullivan, T, Science of the Total Environment, 699, 134255, no. 136, © 2020; permission conveyed through Copyright Clearance Centre, Inc." 377; "Used with the permission of Elsevier Inc Application of ultraviolet, visible, and infrared light imaging in protein-based biopharmaceutical formulation characterization and development studies, Marieke E. Klijn and Jürgen Hubbuch, European Journal of Pharmaceutics and Biopharmaceutics 165, 319-336, © 2021; permission conveyed through Copyright Clearance Centre, Inc." 623, "Used with the permission of Elsevier Inc from Prospects and Challenges for Solar Fertilizers, Benjamin M. Comer, Porfirio Fuentes, Christian O. Dimkpa, Yu-Hsuan Liu, Carlos A. Fernandez, Pratham Arora, Matthew Realff, Upendra Singh, Marta C. Hatzell, Andrew J. Medford, Prospects and Challenges for Solar Fertilizers, Joule, Volume 3, Issue 7, 2019, Pages 1578-1605, © 2019; permission conveyed through Copyright Clearance Centre, Inc." 519, Based on Ragheb, A., El-Shimy, H., & Ragheb, G. (2016). Green architecture: A concept of sustainability. Procedia-Social and Behavioral Sciences, 216, 778-787. 773; **Encyclopædia Britannica:** "Activated sludge process," Encyclopædia Britannica, Inc. https://www.britannica.com/technology/wastewater-treatment/Primary-treatment "Reprinted with permission from Encyclopædia Britannica, © 2024 by EncyclopædiaBritannica, Inc." 436; **Energy & Climate Intelligence Unit:** Net Zero Tracker 2021 Scorecard (Net Zero Emissions Race – Energy & Climate Intelligence Unit) | bluesyemre 595; **European Investment Bank:** Jonas Byström "The 15 circular steps for cities," European Investment Bank (2018), p. 5. https://www.eib.org/attachments/thematic/circular_economy_15_steps_for_cities_en.pdf 770, Jonas Byström "The 15 circular steps for cities," European Investment Bank (2018), p. 7. https://www.eib.org/attachments/thematic/circular_economy_15_steps_for_cities_en.pdf 770; **European Union:** Why do we need carbon capture, use and storage? https://climate.ec.europa.eu/eu-action/carbon-capture-use-and-storage/overview_en 165; **Faber & Faber:** Ebenezer Howard (1902) Garden Cities of To-morrow. London: Faber & Faber. 756; **FACTS Research & Analytics:** Department of Energy; Economic Survey FY 2016/17; Ministry of Finance Nepal's Energy Consumption. Retreived from https://twitter.com/FACTSNepal/status/954951647377031168 682; **Floating Press:** Charles Darwin (1839) "The Voyage of the Beagle". Auckland: Floating Press 235; **Florida International University:** Paul R. Reillo, Ph.D., President, Rare Species Conservatory Foundation, Director, Tropical Conservation Institute, Research Professor, Institute of the Environment, Florida International University. 227; **Food and Agriculture Organization of the United Nations:** FAO, Fishery and aquaculture statistics yearbook, 2019, Table A2 (adapted) 404, Food and Agriculture of the United Nations (2022) State of the world's fisheries and aquaculture. p. 104, Figure 55. 392, Food and Agriculture of the United Nations (2022) The state of the world's fisheries and aquaculture, Table 1 (adapted). 394, Food and Agriculture of the United Nations, State of the world's fishing and aquaculture, page 4, Figure 1 394, Food and Agriculture Organization of the United Nations, 2016, FAO, The State of World Fisheries and Aquaculture. Contributing to food security and nutrition for all, http: //www.fao.org/3/a-i5555e.pdf. 865, Lipinski, B., Hanson, C., Lomax, J., Kitinoja, L., Waite, R. & Searchinger, T. 2013. Reducing food loss and waste. Installment 2 of "Creating a Sustainable Food Future". Working Paper. Washington, DC, WorldResources Institute (http: //www.unep.org/pdf/WRI-UNEP_Reducing_Food_Loss_and_Waste.pdf). 516, The State of Food Security and Nutrition in the World 2022, retrieved from https://www.fao.org/3/cc0639en/cc0639en.pdf 497; **Frontier Economics:** Figure 1 in Tom Ovington & George Houpis "How Smart Cities can help tackle climate change," Frontier Economics. https://www.frontier-economics.com/uk/en/news-and-articles/articles/article-i4604-how-smart-cities-can-help-tackle-climate-change/# 613; **Frontiers Media S.A:** Moland E, et al., (2021) Restoration of Abundance and Dynamics of Coastal Fish and Lobster Within Northern Marine Protected Areas Across Two Decades. Front. Mar. Sci. 8: 674756. Fig. 2A 412; **Global Carbon Project:** Global Carbon Project 603; **Global Footprint Network:** "Source: Global Footprint Network, www.footprintnetwork.org." 079, © 2017 Global Footprint Network National Footprint Accounts from http: //data.footprintnetwork.org 846, Global Footprint Network National Footprint Accounts, 2018 Edition Dowloaded 7 July 2018 from http: //data.footprintnetwork.org 080, Global Footprint Network, n.d. Free public data set. [online]. Data used to create ecological footprint and biocapacity graph. Available at: https:// www.footprintnetwork.org/licenses/public-data-package-free/. Under copyright and licensed under a Creative Commons Attribution-ShareAlike 4.0 International License. https://creativecommons.org/licenses/by-sa/4.0/ 077; **Global Software:** Diane Rich "Air Conditioning Around the World," Mekko Graphics (14 Aug 2019). https://www.mekkographics.com/air-conditioning-around-the-world 634; **Google:** Map of Doha, Qatar. Google Maps. https://www.google.com/maps/@25.3709718, 51.4482694, 11z?hl=en-GB&entry=ttu 811; **Government of Canada:** "The formation of the ozone layer," in About the ozone layer. https://www.canada.ca/en/environment-climate-change/services/air-pollution/issues/ozone-layer/depletion-impacts/about.html 554; **Greenstone+ Ltd:** "What is Natural Capital and how does it link to materiality?," Greenstone+. https://www.greenstoneplus.com/blog/what-is-natural-capital-and-how-does-it-link-to-materiality#_ftn2 640; **Greta Thurnberg:** "Transcript: Greta Thunberg's Speech At The U.N. Climate Action Summit," NPR (26 Sept 2019). https://www.npr.org/2019/09/23/763452863/transcript-greta-thunbergs-speech-at-the-u-n-climate-action-summit 579; **GRID-Arendal:** GRID-Arendal, https://www.grida.no/resources/6067 055;

Acknowledgments are continued on page 926

Contents

Contents

Authors' introduction to third edition

Welcome to Environmental Systems and Societies (ESS) for the IB Diploma Programme. We hope you enjoy the course. This book is designed to be a comprehensive coursebook, covering all aspects of the syllabus at both Standard Level (SL) and Higher Level (HL). It will help you prepare for your ESS examinations in a thorough and methodical way as it follows the syllabus outline section by section, explaining and expanding on the material in the course subject guide. Links between different parts of the syllabus are emphasized, and key facts essential to your understanding are highlighted throughout.

Each chapter covers one topic from the syllabus and, within each chapter, each subtopic and piece of content is named and numbered following the ESS subject guide. This makes the book readily accessible for use and reference throughout the course. There are also short chapters offering advice on completing the Internal Assessment (IA), writing the Extended Essay (EE), Theory of Knowledge (TOK) as applied to ESS and developing examination strategies. In addition, there is an appendix in the eBook covering basic statistics and data analysis, along with additional skills content.

At the end of each subtopic, you will find questions to test your knowledge and understanding of that part of the course. At the end of each chapter, there are practice exam-style questions so that you can test yourself against the type of questions you will find in your external assessments. You can self-assess your answers using the mark-schemes that can be found in the eBook.

The nature of ESS

The ESS course recognizes that to understand the environmental issues of the 21st century, and suggest suitable management solutions, both the human and environmental aspects must be studied. The issues you will cover are complex and include the actions required for the fair and sustainable use of shared resources.

ESS is an interdisciplinary course that is now offered at both SL and HL and is included in two subject groups in the IB Diploma Programme: 'Individuals and societies' and the 'Sciences'. Various disciplines from the sciences and social sciences come together in ESS. These include biology, ecology, chemistry, economics, geography, psychology, physics, philosophy, anthropology and sociology. The ESS course therefore combines a mixture of methodologies, techniques and knowledge associated with individuals and societies and the sciences.

It is a multifaceted course that will require you to develop a diverse set of knowledge and skills, enabling you to explore the cultural, economic, political and social interactions of societies with the environment. It demands the scientific rigour expected of an experimental science.

The individuals and societies approach balances a scientific approach with a human-centred perspective that examines environmental issues from a social and cultural viewpoint. Throughout this book you will look at the environment from the perspective of human societies and assess their response in light of the scientific framework used in environmental sciences. As a result of studying this course you will become equipped with the ability to recognize and evaluate the impact of societies on the natural world. This book therefore looks at environmental issues from economic, historical, cultural and socio-political viewpoints, as well as a scientific one, to provide a holistic understanding from the various topics studied.

The aims of the ESS course and this book are to enable you to:

- develop an understanding of your own environmental impact, in the broader context of the impact of humanity on the Earth and its biosphere
- develop knowledge of diverse perspectives to address issues of sustainability
- engage and evaluate the tensions around environmental issues using critical thinking
- develop a systems approach to provide a holistic lens for the exploration of environmental issues
- be inspired to engage in environmental issues across local and global contexts.

A conceptual approach

Concepts allow you to network knowledge across the course, providing a framework for integrated thinking. Concepts allow you to see patterns and connections of knowledge across the syllabus. A conceptual approach allows you to apply ideas across different situations and will strengthen your fundamental understanding of ESS.

The ESS syllabus is structured around three key concepts: perspectives, systems and sustainability:

- *Perspectives* are how particular situations are viewed and understood by an individual. Personal perspectives give rise to a wide range of different positions on environmental and social issues. Perspectives also influence people's choices and actions, and these can have a real-world impact. By understanding this complexity, you will be able to consider how to make effective progress on complex issues such as the sustainable use of natural resources.
- A *system* is a collection of parts and the relationships between them, which together constitute an entity or whole. The interdependent components of systems are connected through the transfer of energy and matter, with all parts linked together and affecting each other. Examples of systems, with increasing levels of complexity, include particles, atoms, molecules, cells, organs, organ systems, communities, ecosystems, biomes and the Earth. The systems approach used in ESS is discussed further later in this section.
- *Sustainability* refers to the use of natural resources in ways that do not reduce or degrade them so that they are available for future generations. This is central to an understanding of the nature of interactions between environmental systems and societies. Social, cultural and political issues related to sustainability are covered in the course, for example, the value and conservation of traditional ecological knowledge. Throughout the book, we look at resource management issues and show that these are essentially issues of sustainability.

The ESS key concepts are embedded throughout the course.

Distinction between SL and HL

Both SL and HL students gain an understanding of the complexities of environmental issues, solutions and management during the ESS course. Common features of the course at both SL and HL include:

- a concept-based syllabus that promotes holistic thinking about strategies to address environmental issues
- a foundation topic (Topic 1) that introduces and explores the three key concepts
- a common internal assessment (IA)
- the collaborative sciences project, where you work with other students across all the IB Sciences to explore a real-world problem.

The SL course provides a fundamental understanding of ESS and experience of the associated skills. The HL course requires additional breadth and depth, underpinned by an exploration of ethical, legal and economic issues relating to the environment (HL lenses). Suggested connections between the HL lenses and Topics 1–8 are made throughout the course and this book. Lenses provide added dimensions when studying ESS.

Approaches to ESS

The systems approach

The central concept of the ESS course is the systems approach to environmental understanding and problem solving. The systems approach is explained in detail in Topic 1 and is used throughout the book. Science often uses a reductionist approach to examine phenomena, breaking a system down into its components and studying them separately. Environmental science cannot work in this way, as understanding the functioning of the whole topic, for example an ecosystem, is essential. Therefore, a holistic approach is needed. The traditional reductionist approach of science tends to overlook or understate this important holistic quality. Furthermore, the systems approach is common to many disciplines including economics, geography, politics and ecology. The approach emphasizes the similarities between all these disciplines in the ways in which matter, energy and information flow, and allows common terminology to be used when discussing different systems and disciplines. This approach, therefore, integrates the perspectives of different subjects. Throughout this book, the integrated nature of the approach is stressed by examining the links between different areas of the syllabus and between different disciplines.

Local and global approaches

Appreciation of your local environment will enable you to understand these issues from a local perspective, through carrying out fieldwork in nearby ecosystems and research on local issues. Certain issues, such as resource and pollution management, require a national or regional perspective, whereas others, such as global warming, require an international perspective. This book explores all these perspectives in detail. On a broader scale, the ESS course naturally leads us to appreciating the need for a global perspective, since the resolution of the major environmental issues rests heavily on international relationships and agreements.

Real-world examples and key facts are used throughout the course to illustrate how the course content applies to the real world. These examples illustrate information being tied to a specific time and place. Examples provide you with authentic illustrations of environmental issues which underpin the content and concepts of the course. By doing so, they deepen your understanding of the complexities that are being studied.

The application of skills

There are many skills needed to study the ESS course successfully. These skills include experimental techniques, technology, mathematical and inquiry skills, and the constructing and interpretation of systems diagrams. Skills are at the heart of the ESS syllabus and emphasize the practical nature of the subject. By actively applying these skills in context you are more likely to develop and retain an understanding of how these skills can be realized.

Holistic evaluation and human impact

The systems approach, along with the interaction between environmental systems and societies, encourages a holistic appreciation of the complexities of environmental issues. This course requires you to consider the costs and the benefits of human activities to the environment and to societies, over the short and long term, as well as on a local and global scale. In doing so, you will arrive at informed personal viewpoints. This book explains how you can justify your own position and appreciate the views of others.

Key to boxes

In the book you will see a number of coloured feature boxes. Each type provides different information and stimulus, as you can see in the following examples.

Guiding questions are listed at the beginning of each section. These are the overarching ideas that define and encapsulate the learning within each subtopic.

Guiding Question

How can the systems approach be used to model environmental issues at different levels of complexity and scale?

Each subtopic is divided into numbered **understandings**, which contain **content statements**. Each topic follows these numbered understandings in order.

1.2.1 Systems are sets of interacting or interdependent components.
1.2.2 A systems approach is a holistic way of visualizing a complex set of interactions, and it can be applied to ecological or societal situations.
1.2.3 In system diagrams, storages are usually represented as rectangular boxes and flows as arrows, with the direction of each arrow indicating the direction of each flow.
1.2.4 Flows are processes that may be either transfers or transformations.

The green **key fact** boxes highlight the key information in the section you are reading. This makes them easily identifiable for quick reference. The boxes also enable you to identify the core learning points within each section.

Biosphere refers to the part of the Earth inhabited by organisms, that extends from upper parts of the atmosphere to deep in the Earth's crust.

Weblink boxes direct you to relevant website(s) using QR codes. On these web pages, you will find additional information to support the topic such as video simulations and background reading recommendations.

To learn more about conservation of the Antarctic Ocean ecosystem, go to the CCAMLR website.

Hints for success provide insights into what you need to know or how to answer a question. These boxes also identify common pitfalls when answering questions and suggest approaches that examiners like to see. These boxes highlight the applications and skills you are expected to have covered, so you know what you need to revise for exams.

You are expected to be able to construct a system diagram or a model from a given set of information.

The central concepts of the ESS course are *perspectives*, *systems* and *sustainability*. **Concept** boxes highlight appropriate places in each chapter where these concepts are especially relevant, to put these central ideas into context. Issues encountered in the course, such as resource management, conservation, pollution, globalization and energy security, are linked to these concepts.

An EVS might be considered as a *system* in the sense that it may be influenced by education, experience, culture and media (inputs) and involves a set of interrelated assumptions, values and arguments that can generate judgements, positions, choices and courses of action (outputs).

In what ways do values affect the production of knowledge?

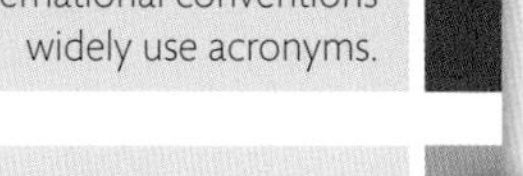

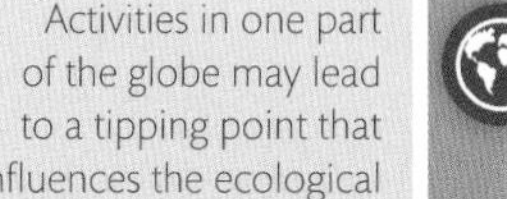

Acronyms are formed from the first letter or first few letters of each word in a phrase or title. Using such shortened forms can speed up communication. International conventions widely use acronyms.

Activities in one part of the globe may lead to a tipping point that influences the ecological equilibrium elsewhere on the planet. For example, fossil fuel use in industrialized countries can contribute to global warming, the impacts of which may be seen elsewhere, such as the desertification of the Amazon basin.

In addition to the Theory of Knowledge (TOK) chapter, there are **TOK** boxes throughout the book. These boxes are there to stimulate thought and consideration of any TOK issues as they arise in context. Many TOK boxes are focused on a knowledge question (in bold text), which your TOK exhibition and TOK essay are centred on. Often, TOK boxes will also contain other questions to stimulate your thoughts and discussion.

Interesting fact boxes contain additional background information that will add to your wider knowledge of the issues being discussed.

International-mindedness is important to the IB. **Global context** boxes indicate examples of international contexts within the area of study. The information given offers you the chance to think about how ESS fits into the global landscape.

Examples are self-contained real-world situations that enable you to apply understandings to a specific context.

Example – Biosphere 2

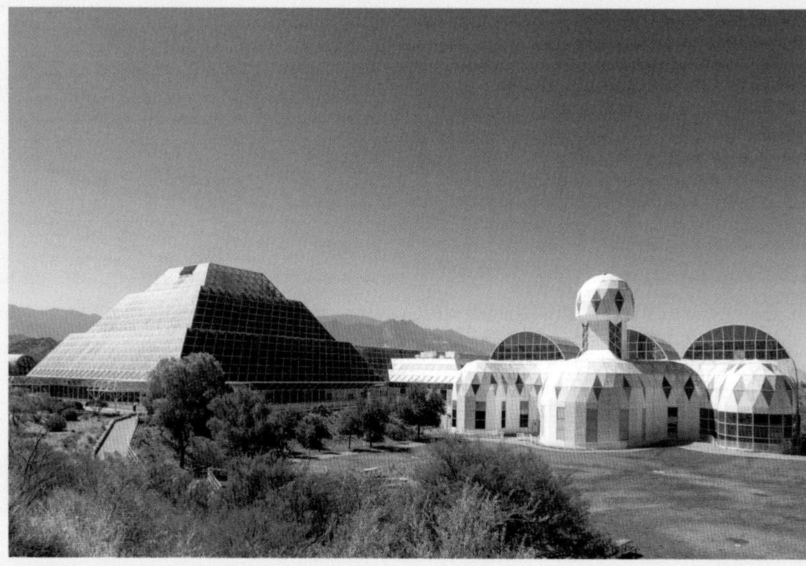

Biosphere 2 is an experiment modelling the Earth as a closed system. It was constructed in Arizona between 1987 and 1991 and enables scientists to study the complex interactions of natural systems such as the constantly changing chemistry of the air, water and soil within the greenhouses and the possible use of closed biospheres in space colonization. It allows the study and manipulation of a biosphere without harming the Earth. The project is still running and has resulted in numerous scientific papers. Results have shown that small, closed ecosystems are complex and vulnerable to unplanned events, such as fluctuations in CO_2 levels experienced during the experiment, a drop in O_2 levels due to soils over-rich in soil microbes and an over-abundance of insect pests that affected food supply.

Skills boxes allow you to learn about the techniques and methodologies that are used in ESS and encourage you to apply these skills in context. These skills and techniques must be experienced through the ESS course and are encompassed within the tools and inquiry process in the IB ESS subject guide. These skills will be useful when you carry out your IA.

Use diagrams representing examples of negative feedback

Diagrams can be used to show negative feedback in systems. Consider the figure below. If high winds blow down a tree in the rainforest, a gap is left in the canopy and more light reaches the forest floor. This encourages new growth. The rates of growth are rapid as light levels are high, so new saplings compete to take the place of the old tree in the canopy and equilibrium is restored. In this way, negative feedback and succession have closed the gap.

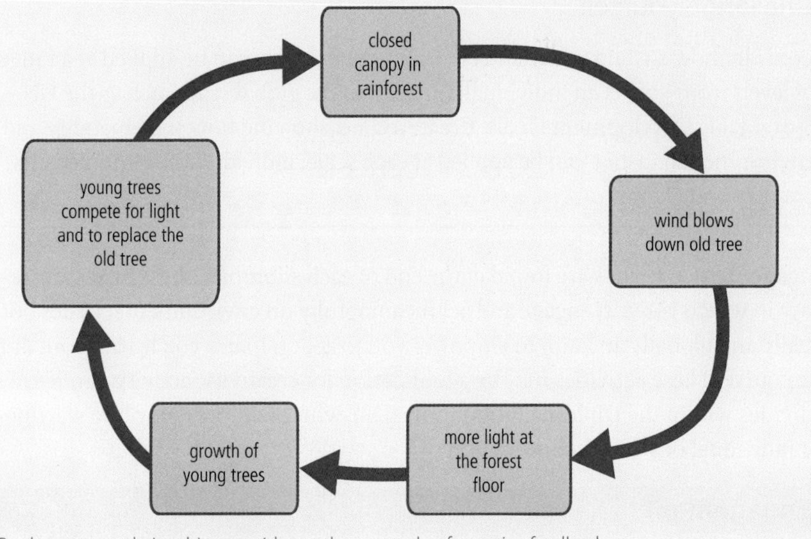

Predator–prey relationships provide another example of negative feedback.

Activity boxes provide opportunities for you to actively explore the subject of ESS and to develop your own answers to key questions. By learning through action, you are more likely to develop and remember both skills and understandings from the course and, as a result, be more able to apply your knowledge in novel situations.

Activity

Find out about another example of ecosystem collapse caused by the unsustainable use of natural resources. Produce a presentation to show to the rest of your class. What were the causes of the collapse and what solutions were used to reverse the decline? Did the solutions work?

Connection boxes make links between the topic you are studying and other parts of the course. This enables you to network your knowledge of ESS and form a holistic understanding of the course.

Some connection boxes refer to the **HL lenses**, enabling you to make links to material in Topics 1–8 if you are studying the HL course.

HL boxes include information relevant to HL students.

2.1 Individuals, populations, communities, and ecosystems
2.5 Zonation, succession and change in ecosystems
6.2 Climate change – causes and impacts
7.2 Energy resources, use and management
8.3 Urban air pollution

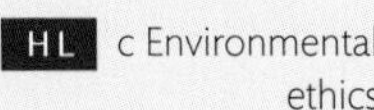

c Environmental ethics

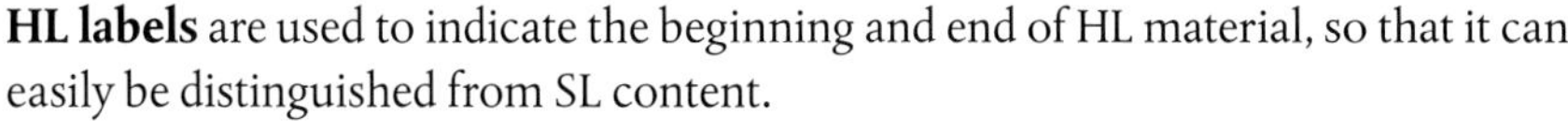

HL labels are used to indicate the beginning and end of HL material, so that it can easily be distinguished from SL content.

Throughout the IB ESS course, you will use quantitative data to discover when and if boundaries have been crossed.

HL

Challenge yourself boxes offer you opportunities to extend your knowledge and understanding of the subject.

Challenge yourself

Consider how sustainability and environmental justice can be applied at a range of levels from you as an individual, through to the global scale such as the UN Sustainable Development Goals. Create a chart showing how sustainability and environmental justice can be applied at each scale: individual, community, city, country and global.

Engagement activities are found at the end of each subtopic. These boxes suggest ways in which you can engage and act meaningfully on environmental issues both locally and globally and aim to empower you to act on issues you learn about during the course. These activities may be a foundation for creativity, activity, service (CAS) activities within the Diploma Programme (DP), whereas others may be a starting point for individual or whole-school action.

Engagement

- Within your class, select an environmental issue. Divide yourselves into three groups – one group discusses technocentric solutions to the issue, another group discusses anthropocentric solutions and the third group discusses ecocentric solutions. Each group should develop arguments to support their perspective. Now debate the environmental issue within your class, from each of the different perspectives. You may want to select one person, or your teacher, to mediate the debate.

Questions

Exercise questions are also found at the end of each subtopic. These questions allow you to apply your knowledge and test your understanding of what you have just been reading. All the answers to these questions can be found in the eBook.

Exercise

Q1. **Distinguish** between perspectives, values and worldviews.

Q2. **(a)** **State** what is meant by an *environmental value system (EVS).*

(b) **List** three inputs and three outputs to an EVS.

Exam-style **practice questions** are found at the end of each topic. They are mostly taken from previous years' IB examination papers. The answers to these questions can be found in the eBook. These questions, along with the exercises, can be used to help you revise and prepare for your exams.

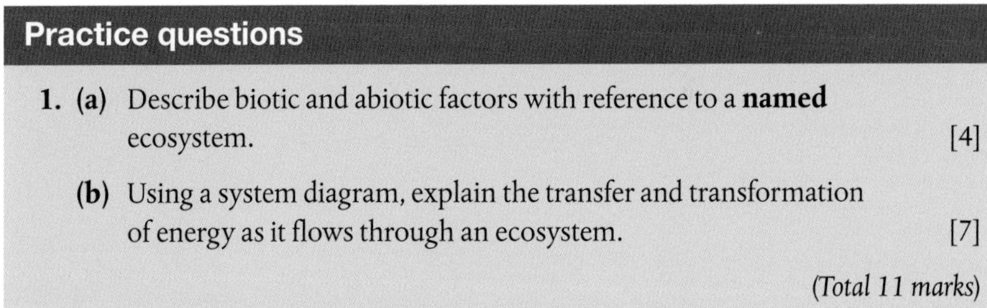

Practice questions
1. (a) Describe biotic and abiotic factors with reference to a named ecosystem. [4]
(b) Using a system diagram, explain the transfer and transformation of energy as it flows through an ecosystem. [7]
(Total 11 marks)

The eBook

You can find the following resources in the eBook or online:

- worksheets including extension exercises, suggestions for the IA, revision, or other sources of information
- answers to all of the exercise and practice questions in the book
- a glossary that includes definitions of all of the keywords printed in bold in the book.
- interactive quizzes, which can be used to help test your understanding and give you the change to practice answering exam style questions can be found on the Exercise tab of your eBook (see screenshot below)

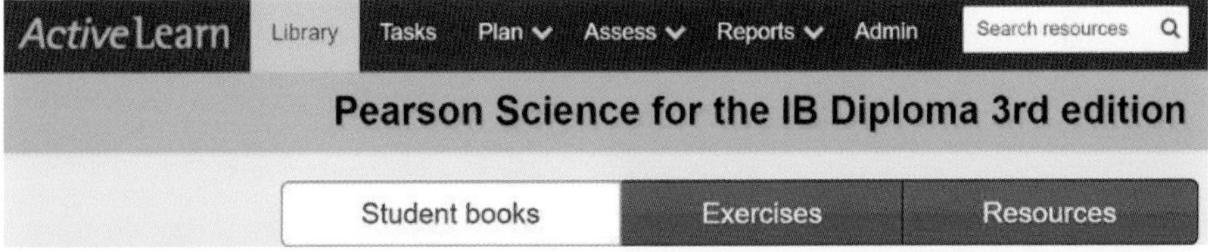

The journey ahead

The ESS is a unique course that will enable you to understand and make decisions regarding the pressing environmental issues faced by humanity. A conceptual and interdisciplinary approach is essential to problem-solving in ESS and this course and book will enable you to use truly holistic thinking in order to address environmental and societal challenges faced in the 21st century.

Now you are ready to start. Good luck with your studies.

Andrew Davis and Garrett Nagle

1 Foundation

Topic 1.1 Perspectives

Guiding Questions

How do different perspectives develop?

How do perspectives affect the decisions we make concerning environmental issues?

1.1.1 A perspective is how a particular situation is viewed and understood by an individual. It is based on a mix of personal and collective assumptions, values and beliefs.
1.1.2 Perspectives are informed and justified by sociocultural norms, scientific understandings, laws, religion, economic conditions, local and global events, and lived experience, among other factors.
1.1.3 Values are qualities or principles that people feel have worth and importance in life.
1.1.4 The values that underpin our perspectives can be seen in our communication and actions with the wider community. The values held by organizations can be seen through advertisements, media, policies and actions.
1.1.5 Values surveys can be used to investigate the perspectives shown by a particular social group towards environmental issues.
1.1.6 Worldviews are the lenses shared by groups of people through which they perceive, make sense of and act within their environment. They shape people's values and perspectives through culture, philosophy, ideology, religion and politics.
1.1.7 An environmental value system is a model that shows the inputs affecting our perspectives and the outputs resulting from our perspectives.
1.1.8 Environmental perspectives (worldviews) can be classified into the broad categories of technocentric, anthropocentric and ecocentric.
1.1.9 Perspectives and the beliefs that underpin them change over time in all societies. They can be influenced by government or non-governmental organization (NGO) campaigns or through social and demographic change.
1.1.10 The development of the environmental movement has been influenced by individuals, literature, the media, major environmental disasters, international agreements, new technologies and scientific discoveries.

1.1.1 A perspective is how a particular situation is viewed and understood

Perspectives are how particular situations are viewed and understood by an individual. *Perspectives* are based on a mix of personal and collective assumptions, values and beliefs.

Before the photo in Figure 1.1 was taken, the Earth had seemed vast, with almost limitless resources. But once people saw the image of Earth suspended in space, with the Moon much larger in the foreground, they gained an appreciation of the vulnerability of the planet and its uniqueness in the Solar System and the Universe beyond.

Activity

The NASA missions of the 1960s and 1970s produced memorable images of the Earth that had never been seen before.

Few photos can have had a greater impact than the one shown in Figure 1.1, which was taken by NASA's Apollo 8 mission on 24 December 1968.

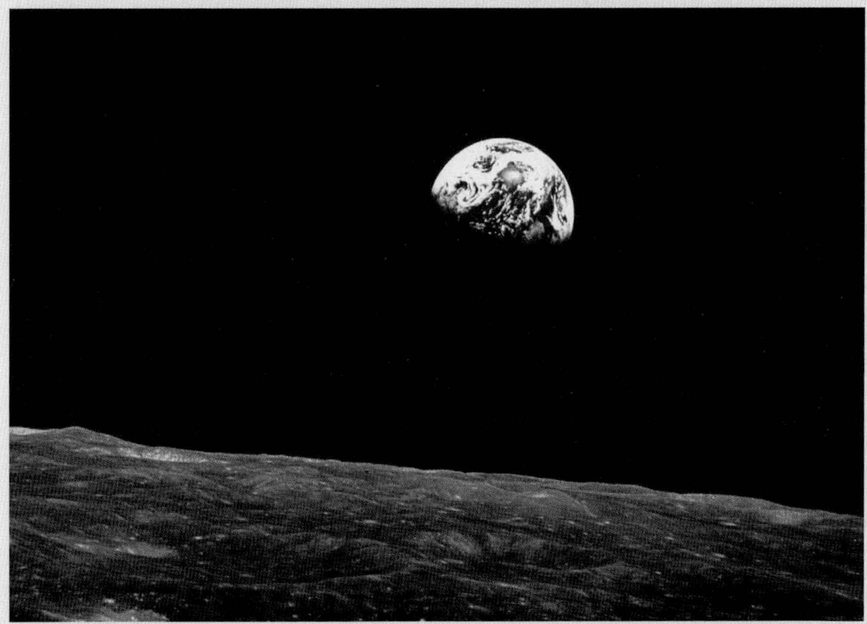

Figure 1.1 Earthrise from the Moon. This photograph was taken during the Apollo 8 mission of 21–27 December 1968.

What thoughts and ideas does this image inspire? Take a moment to write down your thoughts.

Now think about the following questions:

1. How might the image shown in Figure 1.1 have affected the public viewpoint or perspectives for the people who first saw it?
2. The Earth is known as a 'Goldilocks planet'. Why do you think this may be so? Find out why the terms 'Goldilocks planet' or 'Goldilocks zone' are used.
3. What issues are being caused by humanity on planet Earth?
4. Are these issues being solved? If not, why not?

The image changed peoples' **perspectives** of the Earth and the life that exists on it. A perspective is the way in which an individual views and understands a particular situation. Perspectives are based on a range of personal and collective assumptions, values and beliefs. The image in Figure 1.1, along with other images taken of the Earth from space, led to a greater understanding of its fragility and the limitation of natural resources and were instrumental in the development of the environmental movement (this topic, Section 1.1.10). Personal perspectives give rise to a wide range of different positions on environmental issues and on social ones. Perspectives also influence people's choices and actions.

TOK

What challenges are raised by the dissemination of knowledge?

The nineteenth-century British fairy tale *Goldilocks and the Three Bears* has become associated with the concept of ideal conditions.

Liquid water is one of the necessities for life. The metaphor 'Goldilocks planet' or 'Goldilocks zone' describes a planet or region in which the temperatures are neither too hot nor too cold for liquid water to exist. These conditions are determined by the distance between the planet and its nearest star.

Metaphors are often used to explain complex scientific ideas in a simple way. Scientists also use metaphors to develop hypotheses, interpret results and discuss scientific phenomena. Metaphors are only effective in communities where their meaning is understood. One of the challenges of disseminating knowledge is using language and contexts that are understood by all. Western nations will know *Goldilocks and the Three Bears* and the idea of conditions that are 'just right' but is it truly worldwide knowledge?

Figure 1.2 Coal mine near Gillette, Wyoming, USA.

1.1.2 Informing and justifying perspectives

Perspectives are informed and justified by sociocultural norms, scientific understandings, laws, religion and economic conditions. Perspectives are also affected by local and global events and lived experience, among other factors. Take, for example, someone who is brought up in a coal-mining town in the United States of America (USA). Coal continues to be a major source of energy in the USA (Figure 1.2), despite many alternative energy resources being available and the known impact of burning fossil fuels on the environment. The two largest coal mines in the USA are the North Antelope Rochelle and Black Thunder mines in Wyoming. Together, these two mines produced 22% of total coal production in the USA in 2022. The nearest city to North Antelope Rochelle mine is Gillette, Campbell County, the so-called 'Energy Capital of the Nation'. There are other mines near Gillette, including the Eagle Butte mine that is located 11 km north of Gillette. One in three households in Campbell County includes a household member who works in the coal mine or support services and therefore relies either directly or indirectly on the coal industry for income. A person from Gillette may see the role of the mine as an important employment opportunity for the local population. They would also be concerned about the reduction in coal use throughout the USA, which has led to a decline in the local economy.

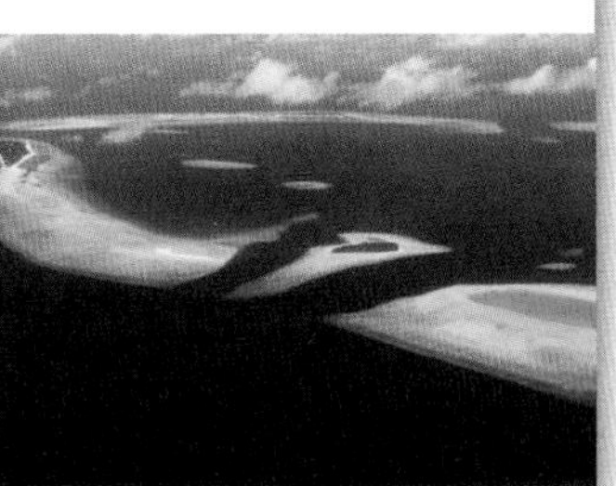

Figure 1.3 Tropical islands and atolls in the Maldives, Indian Ocean.

Now take, in contrast, an individual island from the Maldives (Figure 1.3). The islands that make up the country extend more than 820 km from north to south and 130 km from east to west. The islands have an average elevation of only 2 m above sea level and so the Maldives is one of the lowest-lying countries in the world. No ground surface is higher than 3 m above sea level and 80% of the land area is less than 1 m above the average sea level. Due to climate change, the sea level in and around the Maldives has been rising at a rate of 0.8–1.6 mm per year since 1950. Because most of the land mass is only slightly above sea level, small changes in sea level can have extensive effects, leading to flooding and loss of land. Rising seas threaten homes and industries near the coast. More than 90 of the 187 inhabited Maldives islands experience annual floods.

It is important to distinguish between a perspective and an **argument**. An argument is different from a perspective. Arguments are made to support a personally held perspective or to counter a different one.

The life experience of a person whose home is regularly flooded due to rising tides is going to have an effect on their perspective on the use of fossil fuels that is very different to that of a person from a mining town in the USA. The combustion of fossil fuels such as coal results in the emission of greenhouse gases such as carbon dioxide (CO_2) (Topic 6, Section 6.2.2). These greenhouse gases contribute to global warming and climate change. A person from the Maldives, who has direct knowledge and experience of the effects of climate change, may have the perspective that climate change is an important factor that is affecting the way they live their daily life and that urgent action is needed to mitigate the effects of global warming.

1.1.3 Values

Values are deeply held beliefs focused on the things that people see as important or desirable in life. Values can be moral, cultural, economic or environmental. Values affect people's priorities, judgements, perspectives and choices. Values are individually held but are shared with, and shaped by, others in a community.

Values are qualities or principles that people feel have worth and importance in life.

1.1.4 Showing values

A person who has had direct experience of climate change, such as rising sea levels and flooding of their home or business, may form personal values that reflect this lived experience. They may see the decisions about action needed to tackle climate change through the reduction of fossil fuels use and a move to more sustainable generation of energy as an important priority. In contrast, someone who has a family member who has lost their job due to a reduction in coal mining may have different values that are instead centred around the ongoing use of fossil fuels to maintain the local economy.

Your perspectives affect the philosophy of your life through which you perceive and make sense of the world. They structure your beliefs, which in turn form the foundations of your values. Your values then influence the judgements and choices you make, which in turn affect the actions you take.

The values that underpin our perspectives can be seen in our communication and actions with the wider community. For example, an individual in the Maldives may be involved with local action to promote the threat from climate change and the need to move to renewable energy resources away from fossil fuels. The values held by businesses and other organizations can be seen through advertisements, media, policies and actions. For example, businesses that value sustainable development (this topic, Section 1.3.6) will promote their use of sustainable products.

Different values often lead to **tensions** between individuals and organizations.

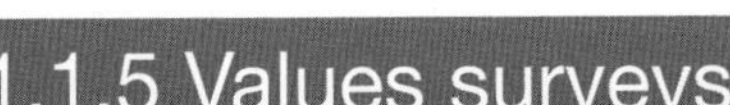

1.1.5 Values surveys

Values surveys can be used to investigate the values underpinning the perspectives shown by a particular social group. They can be used to recognize the values underpinning the perspectives toward a particular environmental issue and assess how these values are likely to impact the issue.

You need to know how to design surveys that can be used with a particular social group to investigate the values underpinning their perspectives toward a particular environmental issue and assess how these values are likely to impact the issue.

A **questionnaire** is a document that asks the same questions of all individuals in the sample. A questionnaire is a very useful tool for investigating patterns, trends and attitudes. It is often used to complement information obtained by other techniques such as observation. Questionnaire surveys involve both setting questions and obtaining answers.

Questionnaires can be used to correlate worldviews/perspectives with attitudes toward any particular environmental or sustainability issues.

HL c Environmental ethics

Design and carry out questionnaires, surveys and interviews

The questionnaire survey is probably the most popular method of obtaining primary data in human geography. In the wider world, questionnaires are used for a variety of purposes, including market research by manufacturing and retail companies and testing public opinion prior to political elections. Questionnaires may contain:

- closed questions with a fixed choice of answers to generate data for easy analysis
- open questions with space to give any answer for more detailed individual answers
- scale questions that are used to ask respondents whether they agree or disagree with several statements, to rate items on a scale or to rank items in order of importance or preference.

One of the most important decisions is the number of questionnaires you are going to use in your sample. Remember, if you do not have a high enough number of questionnaire responses, you will not be able to draw reliable conclusions. For extensive studies, such as those used for an Internal Assessment (IA), 25 questionnaires is probably the minimum you would need to draw reasonable conclusions, as this enables you to assess variation in the data. On the other hand, in larger studies, it is unlikely you would have time to carry out more than 100 questionnaires unless you were collecting data as part of a group.

A good questionnaire:

- has a limited number of questions that take no more than a few minutes to answer
- is clearly set out so the questioner can move quickly from one question to the next as people do not like to be kept waiting; careful use of tick boxes can help meet this objective
- is carefully worded so that the respondents are clear about the meaning of each question
- follows a logical sequence so that respondents can see 'where the questionnaire is going'; if a questionnaire is too complicated and long-winded people may decide to stop halfway through
- avoids questions that are too personal
- begins with the quickest questions to answer and leaves the longer/more difficult questions to the end
- reminds the questioner to thank respondents for their cooperation.

Questionnaires have some disadvantages. For example:

- The response rate may be lower than you anticipate. Many people may not want to cooperate for a variety of reasons. Some people will simply be too busy, others may be uneasy about talking to strangers, while some people may be concerned about the possibility of identity theft.
- Research has indicated that people do not always provide accurate answers in questionnaires. Some people are tempted to give the answer that they think the questioner wants to hear or the answer they think reflects well on them.
- Questionnaires are not suitable to investigate long and complex issues.

Do not work alone when collecting data by approaching people in a public place, even if you are working on an individual ESS project. Always work in small groups when carrying out questionnaires or interviews or at least have one of your classmates visible. Always make sure you are carrying a fully charged cell phone so you can contact other people if needed.

As with other forms of data collection, it is advisable to carry out a brief pilot survey first. It could be that some words or questions that you find easy to understand cause problems for other people. Amending the questionnaire in the light of the pilot survey before you begin the questionnaire in full will make everything go much more smoothly.

Traditionally, questionnaires were delivered using the following methods:

- Approaching people in the street or in another public place.
- Posting questionnaires to people. This method is costly and experience shows that response rates are rarely above 30%. Another disadvantage of this method is that it is not possible to ask for clarification if some responses are unclear.

Today, **online collaborative survey tools** exist to devise and collect data from questionnaires. Examples include SurveyMonkey, SmartSurvey and Google Forms, among others. These tools support group collaboration and allow users to work together effectively and collate data. Features of these tools focus on collaboration, coordination and communication. To create an online questionnaire, you must first decide on your research goals: what are your survey objectives and the expected outcomes? You then create a list of questions, invite participants (via email), gather the responses from those who have taken part, analyse the results and form a conclusion for your final report.

Environmental attitudes: Shades of green

Attitudes towards the environment can vary a great deal depending on age, gender, place in **society**, upbringing, education and many other factors. Showing different environmental values visually in graph or chart form can summarize complex information in a simple yet effective way. A good way of illustrating different attitudes to the environment is by using different shades of green to represent different environmental values, with a pale shade indicating less awareness and a darker shade indicating greater engagement. This was done in an online survey of homeowners in the USA (Figure 1.4).

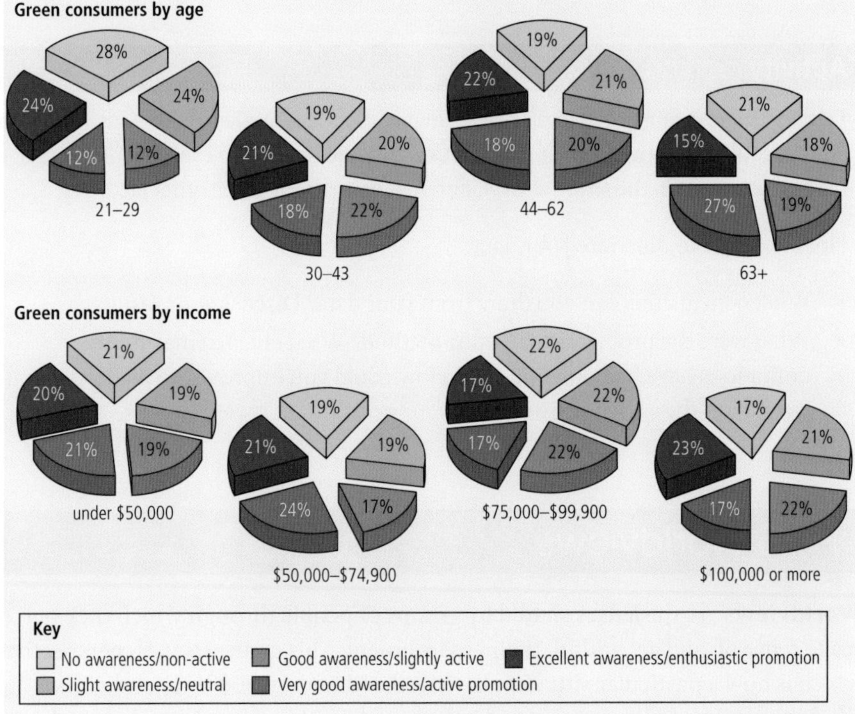

Figure 1.4 Pie charts with different shades of green to represent different environmental values.

The survey shows that those homeowners represented by the darker shades make up a minority of the total population meaning that environmental concerns are limited and not yet a compelling driver of green choices. Dividing personal value systems into shades of green provides a visual way of summarizing the views of society in relation to the environment.

Sample questionnaire

The questionnaire accessed from this page of your eBook can be used to explore the environmental attitudes of different groups in your school or community.

You can also use and develop 'behaviour-over-time' graphs to show lifestyle changes (this topic, Section 1.1.9, page 16).

Interviews

Interviews consist of a series of pre-planned oral questions by the interviewer and oral responses by the research participant. Interviews involve more detailed interactions than questionnaires, so will generally involve talking to a relatively small number of people. For example, a study aiming to find out why six different companies chose to locate on a specific industrial estate might involve interviews with the directors of those six companies. An interview involves a greater depth of discussion than a questionnaire, although you should still have pre-planned questions. Interviews enable you to ask open-ended questions that generate data that is more detailed than those generated by questionnaires. Interviews are thus more likely to produce unexpected responses than questionnaires.

A good interview will be based on preparatory stages like those used for a questionnaire. As the number of people interviewed will be relatively small, it is even more important that you are able to justify your choice of sample. For example, if you are investigating a controversial issue where there are three obvious interest groups, you will need to ensure that your interviews give equal coverage to each group. It can be a good idea to record interviews but make sure that you always ask the interviewee's permission first. It might be the case that a potential respondent may not be able to offer a face-to-face interview but is instead willing to offer a telephone/online interview. This should not present a problem, although it will be important to state that this was a telephone interview in your analysis and to note any limitations that this mode of communication created compared to your face-to-face interviews.

Activity

Develop a questionnaire to explore the environmental attitudes of different groups in your school or community. The questionnaire could be used to examine different age ranges (as shown in the study above), different genders, or some other factor.

Plot pie charts to illustrate your data.

- What conclusions can you draw from your data? Discuss your results.
- What were the problems with your method? What effect(s) may these limitations have had on your data? How could you improve the method if you were to do the survey again?

1.1.6 Worldviews

Worldviews are the lenses shared by groups of people through which they perceive, make sense of, and act within, their environment. This contrasts with perspectives, which is how a particular situation is viewed and understood by an individual. Worldviews refer to how societies see the world and how people's values and perspectives are shaped through culture, philosophy, ideology, religion and politics.

A worldview or **paradigm** shapes the way a group of people perceive and evaluate environmental issues. It is influenced by the cultural, religious, economic and sociopolitical context.

In the past, perspectives would have been influenced by a worldview that was established within a local community or context. With the development of the internet and social media, a person's perspective can be influenced by a far greater variety of worldviews than just those of the local community. Consequently, models that attempt to classify perspectives, though helpful, are invariably inaccurate as individuals often have a complex mix of positions.

Different types of society have different worldviews.

Example – Abrahamic and Buddhist societies

The view of the environment in Abrahamic religions is one of stewardship, where humans have a role of responsibility towards the Earth. For example, the Genesis story suggests that God gave the planet to humans as a gift. Other biblical stories indicate that humanity should make the most of this gift as stewards.

This contrasts with the Buddhist approach to the environment, which sees the human being as an intrinsic part of nature rather than a steward. Buddhism is sometimes seen as an ecological philosophy. This is because of its worldview rather than anything that appears in its writings, which are not explicitly environmental. Buddhism emphasizes human interrelationships with all other parts of nature and supports the belief that considering ourselves as isolated from the rest of nature is unrealistic.

Reincarnation, the belief that human consciousness (or spirit) is immortal and can be reborn after death in either human or animal form, emphasizes humanity's interconnectedness with nature. Buddhists believe that nothing has a fixed and independent existence; all things are without self-existence and are impermanent. From this perspective, humans are intimately related to their environment and cannot exist separately from the rest of the world. Recognizing this principle of interdependence inspires an attitude of humility and responsibility towards the environment.

In what ways do values affect the production of knowledge?

Different societies have different worldviews. Individual and societal understanding and interpretation of data regarding environmental issues is influenced by the perspectives and values of individuals within society. Can there be such a thing as an unbiased view of the environment? Can we ever expect to establish a balanced view of global environmental issues?

Differences in worldviews are influenced by differences in culture and society. A society's worldview influences the actions taken by its citizens in response to environmental issues. Buddhist monks in Thailand, for example, are part of a growing environmental movement (Figure 1.5). They are involved in ecological conservation projects and teach ecologically sound practices among Thai farmers. Unsustainable development based on rapid economic development is seen to be one of the primary causes of Thailand's environmental crisis. The respect in which Buddhist monks are held means that their views are listened to and can have a profound effect on the population.

HL c Environmental ethics

Figure 1.5 Buddhist monks are frequently active in a range of campaigns including forest conservation in Thailand.

What is the relationship between personal experience and knowledge?

Assumptions, values and beliefs and worldviews can affect the way in which we view the world. These are influenced by the way we were raised by our parents, by education, by our friends and by the society in which we live.

1.1.7 Environmental value systems

An EVS might be considered as a *system* in the sense that it may be influenced by education, experience, culture and media (inputs) and involves a set of interrelated assumptions, values and arguments that can generate judgements, positions, choices and courses of action (outputs).

An **environmental value system (EVS)** is a model (this topic, Section 1.2.13 and 1.2.14) showing the **inputs** affecting our perspectives and the **outputs** resulting from our perspectives.

The systems approach is explained in detail in this topic in Sections 1.2.1–1.2.5. An EVS, like all systems, is an assembly of parts and the relationships between them, which together constitute a whole. Systems have inputs, outputs and storages. The outputs are determined by the processing of inputs and generate decisions and evaluations.

EVS inputs are:

- education
- worldviews
- the media
- cultural influences
- economic factors
- sociopolitical factors (the interaction of social and political factors; for example, communism or capitalism)
- religious texts and doctrine.

EVS outputs are:

- judgements
- positions
- choices
- courses of action on how to act regarding environmental issues.

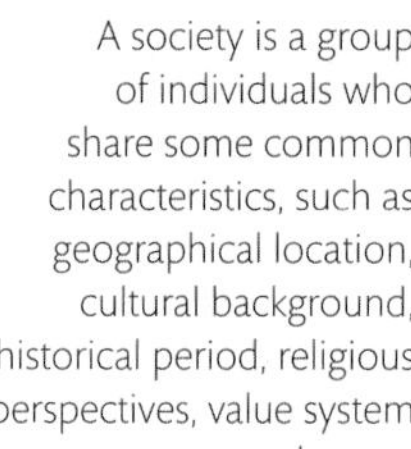

A society is a group of individuals who share some common characteristics, such as geographical location, cultural background, historical period, religious perspectives, value system and so on.

Inputs of information to individuals within societies are processed or transformed into changed perceptions of the environment and altered decisions about how best to act on environmental matters. At their strongest, such information flows cause people to take direct action to alleviate environmental concerns. It is possible that inputs transfer through the individual or group without processing but it is unlikely that an input has no effect at all.

EVSs act within **social systems**. Social systems are more general than **ecosystems**. There are lots of different types of social system: class-based; democratic or authoritarian; patriarchal (male dominance) or matriarchal (female dominance); religion-based; industrial (technology-based) or agrarian (agriculture-based); capitalist or communist. Rather than the flows of energy and matter we see in ecosystems (Topic 2, Section 2.1.21 (Figures 2.41 and 2.42) and Sections 2.2.8–2.2.12) social systems have flows of information, ideas and people. Both ecosystems and social systems exist at different scales and have common features such as **feedback** and equilibrium (this topic, Section 1.2.9–1.2.11). Trophic levels exist in ecosystems, while in social systems there are social levels within society. Both systems contain consumers and producers. Producers in social systems are responsible for new input such as ideas, films, books and documentaries. Consumers absorb and process this information.

1.1.8 Environmental perspectives (worldviews) and their categories

HL a Environmental law

HL c Environmental ethics

Environmental perspectives (worldviews) can be classified into the broad categories of **technocentric**, **anthropocentric** and **ecocentric** (Figure 1.6).

Figure 1.6 The range of environmental value systems.

Environmental Value System

Ecocentrism (nature-centred)

An ecocentric viewpoint integrates social, spiritual and environmental dimensions into a holistic ideal. It puts ecology and nature as central to humanity, and emphasizes a less materialistic approach to life with greater self-sufficiency of societies. An ecocentric viewpoint prioritizes biorights, emphasizes the importance of education and encourages self-restraint in human behaviour.

Anthropocentrism (people-centred)

An anthropocentric viewpoint believes humans must sustainably manage the global system. This might be through the use of taxes, environmental regulation and legislation. Debate would be encouraged to reach a consensual, pragmatic approach to solving environmental problems.

Technocentrism (technology-centred)

A technocentric viewpoint believes that technological developments can provide solutions to environmental problems. This is a consequence of a largely optimistic view of the role humans can play in improving the lot of humanity. Scientific research is encouraged in order to form policies and understand how systems can be controlled, manipulated or changed to solve resource depletion. A pro-growth agenda is deemed necessary for society's improvement.

Deep ecologists

1 Intrinsic importance of nature for the humanity of man.

2 Ecological (and other natural) laws dictate human morality.

3 Biorights – the right of endangered species or unique landscapes to remain unmolested.

Self-reliance soft ecologists

1 Emphasis on smallness of scale and hence community identity in settlement, work and leisure.

2 Integration of concepts of work and leisure through a process of personal and communal improvement.

3 Importance of participation in community affairs and of guarantees of the rights of minority interests. Participation seen as both a continuing education and a political function.

4 Lack of faith in modern large-scale technology and its associated demands on elitist expertise, central state authority and inherently anti-democratic institutions.

5 Implication that materalism for its own sake is wrong and that economic growth can be geared to providing for the basic needs of those below subsistence levels.

Environmental managers

1 Belief that economic growth and resource exploitation can continue assuming:
a suitable economic adjustments to taxes, fees, etc.
b improvements in the legal rights to a minimum level of environmental quality
c compensation arrangements satisfactory to those who experience adverse environmental and/or social effects.

2 Acceptance of new project appraisal techniques and decision review arrangements to allow for wider discussion or genuine search for consensus among representative groups of interested parties.

Cornucopians

1 Belief that people can always find a way out of any difficulties, whether political, scientific or technological.

2 Acceptance that pro-growth goals define the rationality of project appraisal and policy formulation.

3 Optimism about the ability of humans to improve the lot of the world's people.

4 Faith that scientific and technological expertise provides the basic foundation for advice on matters pertaining to economic growth and public health and safety.

5 Suspicion of attempts to widen basis for participation and lengthy discussion in project appraisal and policy review.

6 Belief that all impediments can be overcome given a will, ingenuity and sufficient resources arising out of growth.

The categories of EVSs outlined here are not exclusive and a variety of alternative schemes exist. There are many ways to classify our perspectives. Although these models are useful, they are also imperfect because individuals often have a complex range of positions that change over time and context.

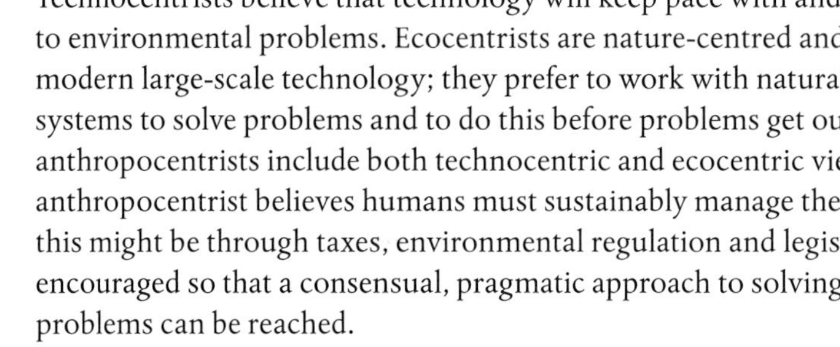

Technocentrists believe that technology will keep pace with and provide solutions to environmental problems. Ecocentrists are nature-centred and distrust modern large-scale technology; they prefer to work with natural environmental systems to solve problems and to do this before problems get out of control. The anthropocentrists include both technocentric and ecocentric viewpoints. An anthropocentrist believes humans must sustainably manage the global system and this might be through taxes, environmental regulation and legislation. Debate is encouraged so that a consensual, pragmatic approach to solving environmental problems can be reached.

In the ESS course, anthropocentrism is considered as 'humans sustainably managing the global system' (through regulations, policies, incentives and so on). The common dictionary definition is simply 'humans are the central/most significant entities in the world'. This could lead to an understanding of anthropocentrism as cornucopian, which is not necessarily true.

The technocentrist approach is sometimes termed a **cornucopian** view – a belief in the unending resourcefulness of humans and their ability to control their environment. This leads to an optimistic view about the state of the world. Ecocentrists, in contrast, see themselves as subject to nature rather than in control of it. Ecocentrists see a world with limited resources where growth needs to be controlled so that only beneficial growth occurs. At one end of the ecocentrist worldview are the self-reliance soft ecologists – those who reject materialism and have a conservative view regarding environmental problem-solving. At the other end are the **deep ecologists**, such as Norwegian philosopher Arne Næss (Figure 1.7), who put more value on nature than humanity.

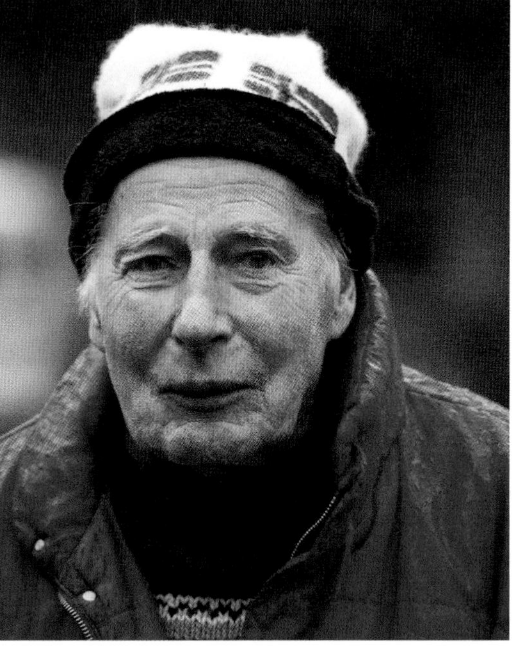

Figure 1.7 Norwegian philospher Arne Næss pioneered and first named the ecocentrist EVS known as deep ecology.

Although there are extremes at either end of this range (i.e. deep ecologists at the ecocentric end of the spectrum and cornucopians at the technocentric end), in practice EVSs vary greatly with culture and time and rarely fit simply or perfectly into any single classification.

The ESS course has many keywords that you need to know. Create your own glossary, using the worksheet in the eBook to help you.

Example – A technocentrist approach to reducing carbon dioxide emissions

Energy and gasoline companies have been developing technological solutions to CO_2 emissions to alleviate global warming. Carbon capture and storage (CCS) techniques involve taking the CO_2 produced from industrial processes and storing it in various ways (Figure 1.8). This means CO_2 is not released into the atmosphere and does not contribute to global warming. A BP project at In Salah in Algeria aims to store 17 million tonnes of CO_2 – an emission reduction equivalent to removing 4 million cars from the road. Such projects have yet to be made available on a large-scale commercial basis because of the costs involved.

Ecosystems often cross national boundaries and conflict may arise from the clash of different value systems about exploitation of resources. For example, the migration of wildlife across borders in southern Africa may lead to conflict due to the differing attitudes towards culling in different southern African countries. This is discussed further in Topic 2.

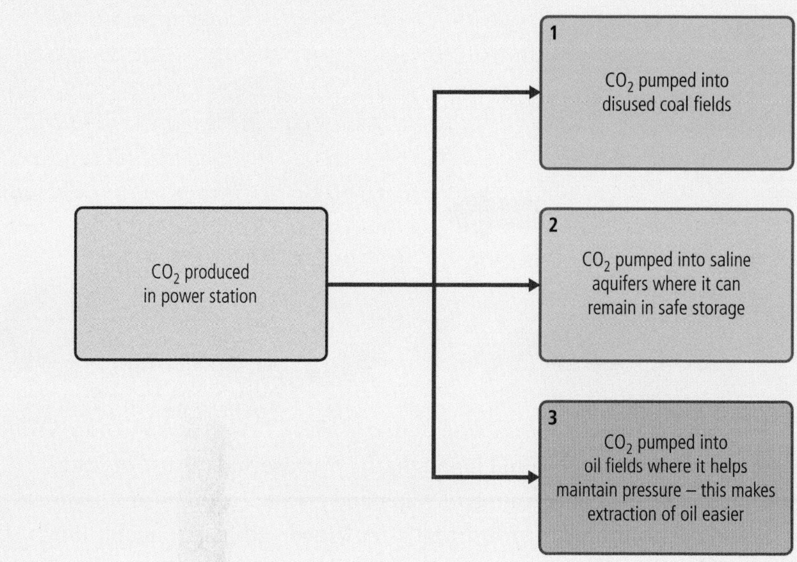

Figure 1.8 Options for carbon capture and storage.

Decision-making and EVSs

EVSs influence our decision-making processes. Let's consider the contrasting perspectives of ecocentrism and technocentrism in relation to two specific cases.

Technocentrism assumes all environmental issues can be resolved through technology. Anthropocentrism splits into a wide variety of views but generally views humankind as being the central, most important element of existence. Ecocentrism sees the natural world as having pre-eminent importance and intrinsic value.

Environmental challenges posed by the extensive use of fossil fuels

Fossil fuels have problems associated with their use. The gases produced during their combustion can contribute to global warming. The cornucopian belief in the resourcefulness of humans and their ability to control their environment would lead to a technocentric solution, where science is used to find a useful alternative, for example hydrogen fuel cells. As *technocentrists*, cornucopians would see this as a good example of resource replacement as an environmentally damaging industry can be replaced by an alternative one. Rather than changing their lifestyles to reduce the use of fuel, cornucopians would look to develop technology to reduce the output of CO_2 from fossil fuel use. A cornucopian would say that economic systems have a vested interest in being efficient so the existing problems will self-correct given enough time, and that development (which requires energy) will increase standards of living thus increasing demands for a healthy environment. They believe that scientific efforts should be devoted to removing CO_2 from the atmosphere and reducing its release, rather than curtailing economic growth. A technocentrist would predict that market pressure would eventually result in the lowering of CO_2 emission levels. An *ecocentrist* approach to the same problem would call for the reduction of greenhouse gases through curtailing existing gas-emitting industry, even if this restricts economic growth.

Approaches to increasing demand for water resources

The *technocentric* resource manager would suggest that future needs can be met by technology, innovation and the ability to use untapped reserves. They would support such measures as the removal of freshwater from seawater (desalination) if they were near an ocean, iceberg capture and transport, wastewater purification, synthetic water production (water made through chemical reactions or hydrogen fuel cell technology), cloud seeding (Figure 1.9) and extraction of water from deep aquifers. They would also look at innovative ways to reduce the use of water, both in industry and at a domestic level.

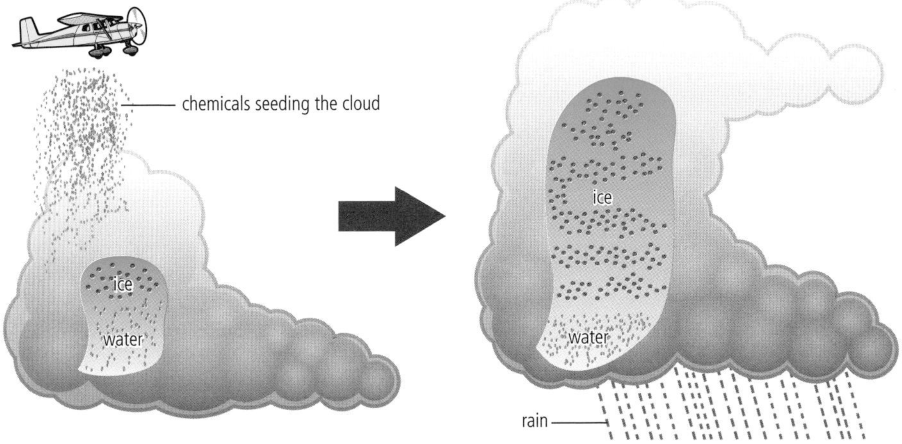

Figure 1.9 Chemicals such as silver iodide or frozen CO_2 are released into clouds. They offer surfaces around which water and ice crystals form. When they are large enough, they fall out of the cloud and become rain.

The *ecocentric* resource manager would highlight the overuse and misuse of water. They would encourage the conservation of water and greater recycling and say that water use should be monitored to ensure that it remained within sustainable limits. An ecocentrist would encourage water use that had few detrimental impacts on habitat, wildlife and the environment.

1.1.9 Change in perspectives

Perspectives, and the beliefs that underpin them, change over time in all societies. Protests about environmental disasters and concern about the unsustainable use of the Earth's resources have led to the formation of pressure groups, both local and international. All these groups have at their centre the belief that every person has a responsibility to look after the planet, for themselves and for future generations, through wise management of natural resources. The action of such groups has resulted in increased media coverage, which in turn has raised public awareness about these issues. One of the most influential of these groups is Greenpeace. Greenpeace is a non-governmental organization (NGO). NGOs are not run, funded or influenced by the governments of any country. Greenpeace was founded in the early 1970s and was made famous in 1975 by mounting an anti-whaling campaign. The campaign actively confronted Soviet whalers in the Pacific Ocean off the Californian coast and eventually developed into the 'Save the Whale' campaign (Figure 1.10), which made news headlines around the world and became the blueprint for future environmental campaigns. This campaign, among others, changed the public's perception of whale hunting and led to its eventual ban.

Figure 1.10 The crew of Greenpeace's flagship, the *Rainbow Warrior*, holding a 'Save the Whales' banner, 1978.

Perspectives and beliefs can also alter through the role of demographic change. Demographic change describes the changes in human population size and structure caused by changes in birth rates, death rates, differences in the economic factors, urbanization and patterns of migration. In the USA, for example, Millennials (young adults born from 1981 to 1996) became the largest adult generation in 2019. Recent studies have shown that 75% of Millennials are environmentally conscious, are notable for high levels of engagement with the issue of climate change and are willing to change their buying habits to favour environmentally-friendly products. 90% of Millennials are interested in pursuing sustainable investments. These figures contrast with preceding generations, who are less likely to have such a high engagement with environmental issues. Increased vegetarianism and a move away from meat in the diet (Topic 5, Section 5.2.10) is another indicator of the role that demographic change has in changing perspectives and beliefs.

Figure 1.11 shows the results of a study that indicate that younger generations are more engaged with global warming than older generations. The generations are categorized as: Millennials (born between 1981 and 1996), Generation X (born between 1965 and 1980), Baby Boomers (born between 1946 and 1964) and Silent (born between 1928 and 1945).

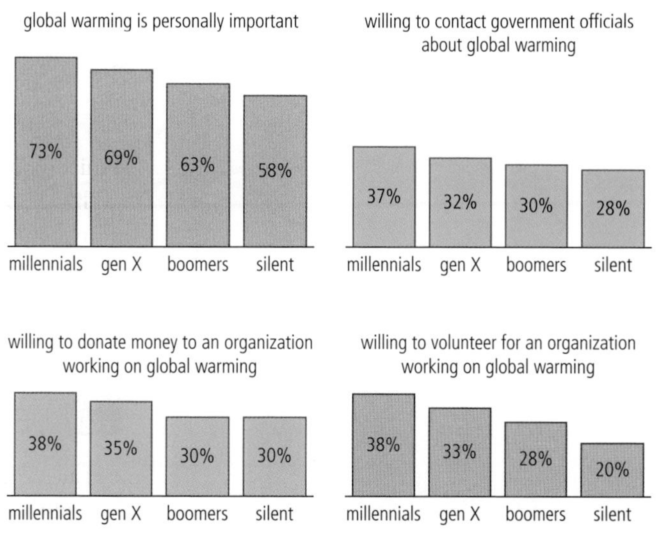

Figure 1.11 Generational changes in attitudes towards the environment.

Activity

Study the data presented in Figure 1.11. Summarize the findings of the study. What do the data reveal about how perspectives and the beliefs that underpin them have changed over time in society?

What are the environmental attitudes of the most recent generations, Generation Z (born between 1997 and 2012) and Generation Alpha (born between 2013 and 2025)? Can you find data on these generations, to compare with the outcomes shown in Figure 1.11?

Perspectives, and the beliefs that underpin them, change over time in all societies. These can be influenced by government or NGO campaigns or through social and demographic change.

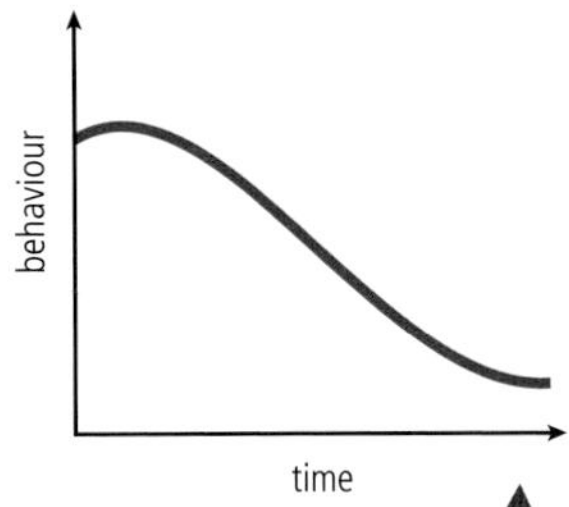

Figure 1.12 A behaviour-over-time graph.

SKILLS

Interpret behaviour-time graphs

Behaviour-over-time graphs (BoTGs) are line graphs that show how a factor changes over time. Time is plotted along the horizontal axis and the 'behaviour' (the factor that changes over time) is plotted on the vertical axis (Figure 1.12). Examples could include specific changes such as smoking, littering and eating meat, or how traditional lifestyles in Indigenous cultures are being replaced by modern ones.

Data concerning behavioural changes can be complex and the big picture can sometimes be lost in the detail. BoTGs enable overall trends to be clearly seen and interpreted. These graphs help you focus on patterns of change over time rather than on single events.

BoTGs do not require special equipment. They are drawn freehand using pencil and paper, or on a tablet or laptop. If you have access to data (figures relating to a specific factor) then graph paper may be needed. It is important to avoid getting caught up on lots of detail. The aim of these graphs is to focus on patterns of change rather than on isolated events or small details.

In BoTGs, the change may be linear or exponential (increasing or decreasing), or the pattern may fluctuate.

Once a BoTG has been constructed, the following questions can be asked:

1. What is changing? What is the variable being graphed?
2. How is it changing? How is the trend described?
3. Why is it changing? What are the causes driving the behavioural changes shown in the graph?
4. What is the significance? Why is the change important?

Figure 1.13 shows changing attitudes in the USA towards top priorities for the country.

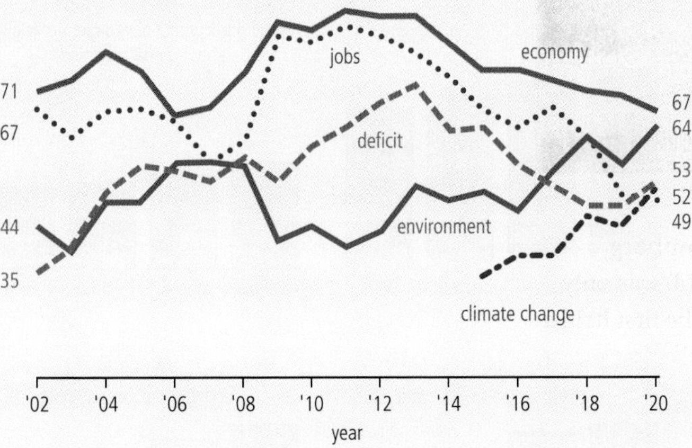

Figure 1.13 Behaviour-over-time graph for attitudes in the USA towards the economy, jobs and the environment, between 2002 and 2020.

The graph shows trends for the percentage of individuals who said that the economy, jobs, the environment or climate change should be a top priority for the President and Congress. In 2020, the American public placed a lower priority on economic and job concerns than it did a few years previously. While at the same time, environmental protection and global climate change increased in priority on the public's agenda for the President and Congress. These changes coincided with a strengthening economy and the visibility of the impacts of climate change within the country, such as an increase in the incidence of tornados and flooding.

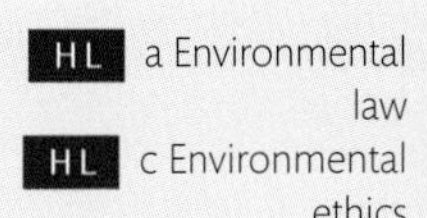

HL a Environmental law

HL c Environmental ethics

Significant historical influences on the development of the environmental movement have come from individuals, literature, the media, major environmental disasters, international agreements, new technologies and scientific discoveries. You need to know at least one example of each of the different influences.

1.1.10 The development of the environmental movement

Some people think that the photo from NASA's Apollo 8 mission of the Earth suspended in space (this topic, Section 1.1.1) was the beginning of the **environmental movement** – the worldwide campaign to raise awareness and coordinate action, to tackle the negative effects that humans are having on the planet. But although the image was pivotal in helping to highlight environmental issues, the environmental movement existed before this milestone photograph.

The environmental movement advocates sustainable development through changes in public policy and individual behaviour. The modern movement owes much to developments in the latter part of the 20th century, although its history stretches back for as long as humans have been faced with environmental issues. Some significant moments in the environmental movement are outlined in the following section.

HL c Environmental ethics

'To advocate' means to speak for, support, represent or publicly recommend someone or a particular issue.

Individuals

'Be the change you want to see in the world' is a quote often used to encourage people to act in a sustainable and environmentally friendly way. It is based on a statement made by former Indian Prime Minister, Mahatma Gandhi, *'We but mirror the world...If we could change ourselves, the tendencies in the world would also change.'* There are many individuals who have lived by this advice and have played a significant role in the development of the environmental movement.

Figure 1.14

Greta Thunberg (Figure 1.14) was only 15 when she first held a 'school strike to protect the climate'. This then became a global movement.

Figure 1.15

Rachel Carson (Figure 1.15), a pioneering marine scientist, was first to highlight the environmental hazards posed by insecticides.

Figure 1.16

Jane Goodall (Figure 1.16) was the first person to study chimpanzees in the wild and has set up a global community conservation organization that advances her vision.

Figure 1.17

Maxima Acuña de Chaupe (Figure 1.17), a subsistence farmer in Peru's northern highlands, is well known throughout Latin America for standing up against a multinational mining company that tried to remove her from her land. The mining company planned to mine two lakes on her land for copper and gold, and to drain two other lakes. One of the lakes would have been turned into a waste storage pit, threatening the water supply to any land downstream, including a high-altitude biologically diverse wetland. Despite intimidation and threats, Maxima stood her ground and refused to give up her land. She was awarded the Goldman Environmental Prize in 2016.

Read more about Maxima Acuña's activism on the Goldman Prize website.

Figure 1.18

Wangari Maathai (Figure 1.18) was an environmentalist from Kenya. She founded the Green Belt Movement. By the early 2000s this movement had resulted in 30 million trees being planted and had provided jobs and secured firewood for rural communities. She targeted women-led groups, ensuring that trees were planted on their farms and in school and church compounds conserving their environment and improving their quality of life. She was awarded the Nobel Peace Prize in 2004.

Visit the Bullard Centre (see 'Our founder' in the 'About' section) to read more about Robert D. Bullard's work.

Figure 1.19

Robert D. Bullard (Figure 1.19) is known as the 'Father of Environmental Justice' and has spent four decades acting as an advocate of environmental and racial justice across the USA. He has published 18 books including books on sustainable development.

Figure 1.20

Dato' Seri Tengku Dr Zainal Adlin Bin Tengku Mahamood (Figure 1.20) has initiated several conservation programs, including in biodiverse regions in East Malaysia. He was involved with the conception and creation of the 'Heart of Borneo: Three Countries One Conservation Vision', which seeks to preserve the central, pristine ecosystems in the centre of Borneo. It unites Malaysia, Indonesia and Brunei in protecting one of the largest transboundary rainforests remaining in the world.

Literature

In 1962, American biologist Rachel Carson's influential book *Silent Spring* was published. It remains one of the most influential books of the environmental movement. The case against chemical pollution was strongly made as Carson documented the harmful effects of pesticides along food chains to top predators. The book led to widespread concerns about the use of pesticides and the pollution of the environment.

Many other significant publications have also contributed to the environmental movement (Figure 1.21). In 1972, the Club of Rome – a global think tank of academics, civil servants, diplomats and industrialists that first met in Rome – published *The Limits to Growth*. This report examined the consequences of a rapidly growing world population on finite natural resources. It has sold 30 million copies in more than 30 translations and has become the best-selling environmental book in history.

James Lovelock's book *Gaia* (1979) proposed the hypothesis that the Earth is a living **organism**, with self-regulatory mechanisms that maintain climatic and biological conditions (this topic, Section 1.2.6). He saw the actions of humanity upsetting this balance with potentially catastrophic outcomes. Subsequent books, up to the present day, have developed these ideas.

Figure 1.21 A selection of books on environmental issues, including some that have influenced the Green movement.

Popular books such as *Silent Spring* and films such as Al Gore's *An inconvenient truth*, can provide knowledge about environmental issues on a global scale. People who previously had limited understanding of the environment are given the information to enable them to make their own minds up about global issues. But do they have enough information to see all sides of the argument? A good education would certainly put these arguments in a wider context. Is it a problem that many people receive only one side of the argument?

Mark Lynas is a leading environmentalist, who has written five major books on the environment: *High Tide* (2004), *Six Degrees* (2008), *The God Species* (2011), *Seeds of Science* (2018) and *Our Final Warning* (2020). His books discuss the impact of humanity on planet Earth and rapid changes that are needed to avoid irreversible tipping points.

Kate Raworth's book, *Doughnut Economics: seven ways to think like a 21st century economist*, presents a radical rethinking of economics. The 'doughnut' represents a safe space for humanity, between social and planetary boundaries (this topic, Section 1.3.20). Her book presents how doughnut economics can result in a sustainable future for humans and the planet.

The book *This Changes Everything: Capitalism vs. the Climate*, by Naomi Klein, explains why market-driven capitalism cannot fix the climate crises and that fundamental economic and social changes are needed.

The media

In 2006, the film *An Inconvenient Truth* examined the issues surrounding climate change and increased awareness of environmental concerns. The publicity surrounding the film meant that more people than ever became aware of global warming. The film's message was spread widely and rapidly through the internet making the arguments about global warming very accessible to a wider audience and raising the profile of the environmental movement worldwide. The film was supported by a book of the same title that included hard scientific evidence to support its claims.

The 2019 film *Dark Waters* tells the real-life story of Rob Bilott, a lawyer who took on one of the world's largest chemical corporations after discovering that the company was polluting drinking water with a harmful chemical.

Earth Day is marked each year on 22 April, coordinated globally via the internet and other media (Figure 1.22). It was founded in 1970 by Gaylord Nelson, a US Senator from Wisconsin, after he had seen the effects of a massive oil spill in Santa Barbara, California during 1969. The purpose of Earth Day is to highlight and promote the role of responsible consumption in achieving sustainability. By creating a day that celebrated the Earth, he saw a way of moving environmental protection more centrally onto the national political agenda.

Figure 1.22 Earth Day is celebrated simultaneously around the world, encouraging people to participate in environmental campaigns both locally and globally.

To learn more about Earth Day, go to their website:

Figure 1.23 Japanese Environment Minister Nobuteru Ishihara (R) and Achim Steiner (L), UN Environment Programme (UNEP) Executive Director, lay flowers on the memorial for the victims of 1950s mercury poisoning at Minamata city on 9 October, 2013.

Major environmental disasters

In 1956, a new disease was discovered in Minamata City in Japan. It was named **Minamata disease** and was found to be linked to the release of methyl mercury into the wastewater produced by the Chisso Corporation's chemical factory. The mercury accumulated in shellfish and fish along the coast. The contaminated fish and shellfish were eaten by the local population and caused mercury poisoning. The symptoms were neurological, including numbness of the hands, muscle weakness and damage to hearing, speech and vision. In extreme cases, Minamata disease led to insanity, paralysis and death. The pollution also led to birth defects in newborn children (Figure 1.23).

The Minamata Convention on mercury is a global treaty to protect the environment and human health from the harmful effects of mercury. It is a legally binding UN agreement adopted in 2013 and brought into force on 16 August 2017.

At midnight on 3 December 1984, the Union Carbide pesticide plant (owned by Dow) in the Indian city of Bhopal released 42 tonnes of the toxic gas methyl isocyanate. This happened because one of the tanks involved with processing the gas had overheated and burst. Some 500,000 people were exposed to the gas. It has been estimated that between 8,000 and 10,000 people died within the first 72 hours following the exposure and that up to 25,000 have died since from gas-related diseases (Figure 1.24).

Figure 1.24 The Bhopal disaster made headlines around the world. Despite protests, little has been done for the families of the victims.

Early in the morning of 26 April 1986, reactor number four at the **Chernobyl** plant in Ukraine (then part of the Soviet Union) exploded. A plume of highly radioactive dust (fallout) was sent into the atmosphere and fell over an extensive area (Figure 1.25). Large areas of Ukraine, Belarus and Russia were badly contaminated. The disaster resulted in the evacuation and resettlement of over 336,000 people. The fallout caused an increased incidence of cancers in the most exposed areas.

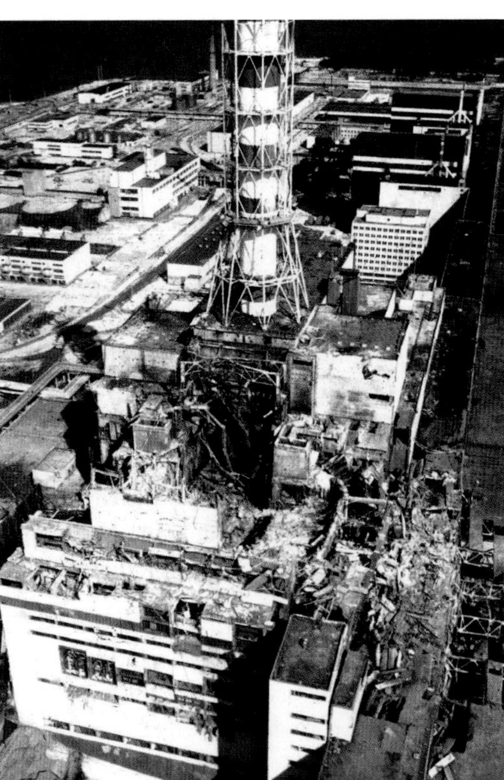

Figure 1.25 View of the Chernobyl power plant three days after the explosion.

The area immediately surrounding the plant, covering approximately 2600 km^2, remains under exclusion due to the high levels of radiation still present. The incident raised issues concerning the safety of Soviet nuclear power stations, but also the general safety of nuclear power. These worries remain to this day.

For many years, the Chernobyl disaster was the only major nuclear incident. That changed on 11 March 2011 when an earthquake in northern Japan caused a tsunami that hit the coastal **Fukushima** nuclear power plant, causing a meltdown in three of the six nuclear reactors (Figure 1.26). The damage resulted in radioactive material escaping into the sea. Following the incident, all 48 of the country's reactors were closed so that new safety checks could be done, leading to an increased dependence on fossil fuels. Before the Fukushima incident, the nuclear power plant had provided 30% of Japan's energy needs. Although the disaster at Fukushima was caused by specific local issues–the coastal location of the plant and the inadequacy of defenses for extreme tidal events such as tsunamis–the move away from nuclear power was replicated around the world. Germany, in particular, backtracked on its nuclear ambitions.

Figure 1.26 Satellite image of the Fukushima Daiichi nuclear power plant in Okuma, Japan, taken after the 2011 earthquake and tsunami.

On 15 January 2022, a leak from a pipeline during the discharge of oil at the La Pampilla Refinery, off the coast of Peru, resulted in nearly 12,000 barrels of crude oil spilling into one of the world's most diverse marine ecosystems. The oil slick affected 25 beaches, polluted three protected marine reserves and covered 1187 km^2 of sea and 1740 km^2 of coastal land. The oil spill killed invertebrates, fish and seabirds, left more than 1000 seabirds coated with oil and impacted marine mammals such as endangered sea otters. More than 700,000 people are thought to have been affected by the spill and at least 5000 people are thought to have lost their livelihoods. The refinery was owned by the Spanish company Repsol, who have been fined for the way they dealt with the spill and for damages done to people and the environment.

International agreements

In 1972, the United Nations (UN) held its first major conference on international environmental issues in Stockholm, Sweden – the **UN Conference on the Human Environment**, also known as the **Stockholm Conference**. It examined how human activity was affecting the global environment. Countries needed to think about how they could improve the living standards of their people without adding pollution, habitat destruction and species extinction. The conference led to the **Stockholm Declaration**, which played a pivotal role in setting targets and shaping action at both an international and local level. These early initiatives ultimately led to the **Rio Earth Summit** in 1992, coordinated by the UN (Figure 1.27), producing **Agenda 21** and the **Rio Declaration**. The Stockholm Declaration and subsequent global summits have played a leading role in shaping attitudes to sustainability.

In 1987, a report by the **UN World Commission on Environment and Development (WCED)** was published, intended as a follow-up to the Stockholm Conference. The report, titled *Our Common Future*, took the ideas from Stockholm and developed them further. It linked environmental concerns to development and sought to promote sustainable development through international collaboration. It also placed environmental issues firmly on the political agenda. *Our Common Future* is also known as the **Brundtland Report** after the Chair of the WCED, former Norwegian Prime Minister, Gro Harlem Brundtland.

The publication of *Our Common Future*, along with the work of the WCED, provided the groundwork for UN's Earth Summit at Rio in 1992. The conference was unprecedentedly large for a UN conference – it was attended by 172 nations. The wide uptake and international focus meant that its impact was likely to be felt across the world. The summit's radical message was that nothing less than a transformation of our attitudes and behaviour towards environmental issues would bring about the necessary changes. The conference led to the adoption of Agenda 21 – a blueprint for action to achieve sustainable development worldwide (21 refers to the 21st century).

Figure 1.27 UN Conference on Environment and Development, Rio de Janeiro, Brazil, 3–14 June 1992. The platform: L to R: Deputy Secretary-General of the Conference Nitin Desai, Secretary-General Maurice Strong, UN Secretary General Boutros Boutros Ghali, Brazilian President Fernando Collor de Mello.

Agenda 21 is a comprehensive plan of action to be taken globally, nationally and locally by organizations of the UN, governments and environmental groups in every area in which humans affect the environment. It was adopted by more than 178 governments at the Earth Summit.

The Earth Summit changed attitudes to sustainability on a global scale and changed the way in which people perceived economic growth. It encouraged people to move away from the idea that economic growth should occur at the expense of the environment and encouraged them to think of the indirect values of ecosystems, such as ecosystem services. It also was important for emphasizing the relationships between human rights, population, social development, women and human settlements and the need for environmentally sustainable development. The summit's emphasis was on change in attitude affecting all economic activities, ensuring that its impact could be extensive. The conference meant that environmental issues came to be seen as mainstream rather than the preserve of a few environmental activists. Achievements made included steps being made towards preserving the world's biodiversity through the **Convention on Biological Diversity** (**CBD**) and steps to address the enhanced greenhouse effect via the **UN Framework Convention on Climate Change** (**UNFCCC**). These steps in turn led to the establishment of the **Kyoto Protocol** and the **Paris Agreement**.

Acronyms are formed from the first letter or first few letters of each word in a phrase or title. Some examples include the Convention on Biological Diversity (CBD), the UN Framework Convention on Climate Change (UNFCCC) and the Conference of the Parties (COP). Using such shortened forms can speed up communication. International conventions widely use acronyms.

Both the CBD and UNFCCC are legally binding conventions and both are governed by the **Conference of the Parties (COP)**, which meets either annually or biennially to assess the success and future directions of the Convention. For example, COP15 of the CBD took place over a two-year period with part 1 being held in Kunming, China (October 2021) and part 2 being held in Montreal, Canada (December 2022). COP16 is scheduled to be held in Turkey in 2024. COP15 of the UNFCCC took place in Copenhagen, Denmark in December 2009 and COP28 of the UNFCCC took place in Dubai, United Arab Emirates (UAE) in December 2023. The **Copenhagen Accord** was a document produced at COP15 of the UNFCCC, in which attending parties were asked to 'take note' of the concerns raised about climate change. However, this document was not legally binding.

Activity

Details of the COPs for both the CBD and UNFCCC can be found by searching for 'COP' on the following websites:

CBD: 

UNFCCC: 

Select one COP for the CBD and one for the UNFCCC.

1. What were the major themes at these meetings of the COP?
2. What were the outcomes of the meetings?
3. How did the outcomes impact the subsequent COP?

Discuss your findings with others in your class. Which COPs did they research? Were any of the COPs especially significant in terms of their discussion and outcomes?

Read more about the IPCC and access the latest synthesis report on the IPCC website.

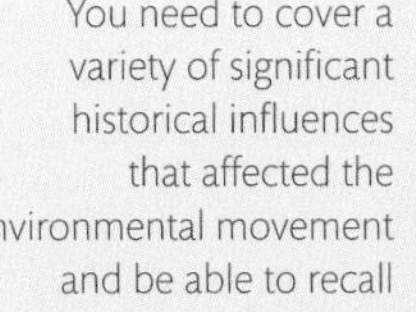

Some national and state governments have legislated or advised that local authorities take steps to implement Agenda 21. Known as '**Local Agenda 21**' (LA21), these strategies apply the philosophy of the Earth Summit at the local level. Each country is urged to develop an LA21 policy, with the agenda set by the community itself rather than by central or local government, as ownership and involvement of any initiatives by society at large is most likely to be successful.

The 1992 Earth Summit was followed up 10 years later by the **Johannesburg World Summit on Sustainable Development**. The Johannesburg meeting looked mainly at social issues. Targets were set to reduce poverty and increase people's access to safe drinking water and sanitation (problems that cause death and disease in many developing countries).

In 2012, the UN Conference on Sustainable Development (UNCSD, or **Rio+20**) took place to commemorate the 20th anniversary of the Earth Summit. Rio+20 again brought governments, international institutions and major groups together to agree on a range of measures to reduce poverty while promoting good jobs, clean energy and a more sustainable and fair use of resources.

Major landmarks in the modern environmental movement include: Minamata, Rachel Carson's *Silent Spring*, the 'Save the Whale' campaign, the Bhopal and Chernobyl disasters. These led to environmental pressure groups, both locally and globally; the concept of stewardship; and increased media coverage raising public awareness.

New technologies

The **Green Revolution** refers to a time between the 1940s and the late 1960s when developments in scientific research and technology in farming led to increased agricultural productivity worldwide. The Club of Rome (this topic, Section 1.1.10, page 18) claimed in their report *The Limits to Growth* that within a century a mixture of human-made pollution and resource depletion would cause widespread population decline. But the intervention of the Green revolution meant that by 2000, world population had reached six billion and is predicted to rise to nearly nine billion by 2050. The intensification of agriculture raised many questions for the environmental movement (Topic 5, Section 5.2.7), as has the increase in human population (Topic 8, Section 8.1.6).

You need to cover a variety of significant historical influences that affected the environmental movement and be able to recall a minimum of one example from each of the categories above. It is a good idea to select a range of influences that includes both local and global examples. Examples may also be recent.

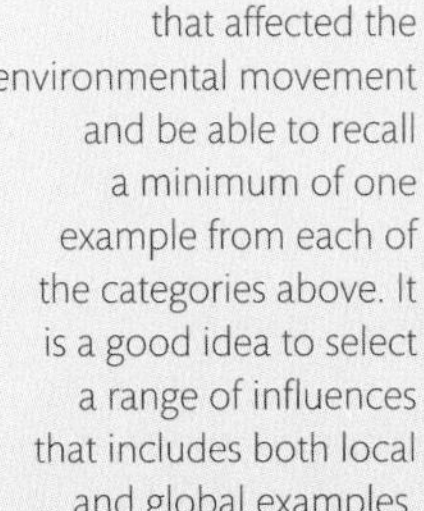

Other technological innovations have created alternatives to fossil fuels such as solar panels and wind turbines. These make the arguments proposed by environmentalists, that is, the need for a switch to more sustainable energy resources, a real possibility and drives the environmental movement forward.

Scientific discoveries

Rachel Carson's work on pesticide toxicity, culminating in her book *Silent Spring* (this topic, Section 1.1.10, page 18), led to a reassessment of the effect of human-made chemicals on the environment. Biodiversity loss has also shown the impact that humanity is having on the planet, promoting moves to conserve and protect species. In 2019, the UN's Intergovernmental Science-Policy Platform on Biodiversity and Ecosystem Services reported that approximately one million animal and plant species were threatened with extinction, including more than 40% of amphibian species, nearly 33% of sharks, shark relatives and reef-forming corals and at least 33% of all marine mammals.

Challenge yourself

Think about your own perspectives and how they might influence your behaviour. What environmental issues affect you locally? What are your views on these issues? What has affected your perspectives and how does this influence how you act on a given issue?

List the factors that have affected your perspectives and how these influence the way you respond to environmental issues. Now create a systems diagram to summarize this information – you may want to focus on your response to one environmental issue to help focus your ideas.

Engagement

- Within your class, select an environmental issue. Divide yourselves into three groups – one group discusses technocentric solutions to the issue, another discusses anthropocentric solutions and the third discusses ecocentric solutions. Each group should develop arguments to support their perspective. Now debate the environmental issue within your class, from each of the different perspectives. You may want to select one person, or your teacher, to mediate the debate.
- Design appropriately persuasive materials to advocate for an environmental or social cause within your school or college. Research the issue and develop arguments that promote the cause. Develop posters and information leaflets to disseminate the information within your community.
- Using the knowledge acquired in this topic, advocate to show how personal actions can create change towards a more sustainable society.
- Engage in discussing the role of politics, intergovernmental organizations (IGOs), NGOs and individuals (through social media) in solving an environmental problem. This could be through participating in a Model UN (MUN) group.

  You can find details of Model UN on the UN website.

The concept of *perspectives* provides a deeper understanding of worldviews and individual *perspectives* and their related value systems. Our value systems interact in complex ways with our decision-making abilities and actions with a real-world impact. Through understanding perspective and value systems, we are better positioned to consider how to make effective progress on complex sustainability issues.

Exercise

Q1. Distinguish between perspectives, values and worldviews.

Q2. (a) **State** what is meant by an *environmental value system (EVS)*.

(b) **List** three inputs and three outputs to an EVS.

Q3. Distinguish between ecocentric, anthropocentric and technocentric EVSs.

Q4. Perspectives, and the beliefs that underpin them, change over time in all societies. **Outline** how these changes can be shown.

Q5. Explain how the development of the environmental movement has been influenced by individuals, literature, the media, major environmental disasters, international agreements, new technologies and scientific discoveries.

1.2 Systems

Guiding Question

How can the systems approach be used to model environmental issues at different levels of complexity and scale?

1.2.1 Systems are sets of interacting or interdependent components.
1.2.2 A systems approach is a holistic way of visualizing a complex set of interactions, and it can be applied to ecological or societal situations.
1.2.3 In system diagrams, storages are usually represented as rectangular boxes and flows as arrows, with the direction of each arrow indicating the direction of each flow.
1.2.4 Flows are processes that may be either transfers or transformations.
1.2.5 Systems can be open or closed.
1.2.6 The Earth is a single integrated system encompassing the biosphere, the hydrosphere, the cryosphere, the geosphere, the atmosphere and the anthroposphere.
1.2.7 The concept of a system can be applied at a range of scales.
1.2.8 Negative feedback loops occur when the output of a process inhibits or reverses the operation of the same process in such a way as to reduce change. They are stabilizing as they counteract deviation.
1.2.9 As an open system, an ecosystem will normally exist in a stable equilibrium, either in a steady-state equilibrium or in one developing over time (for example, succession) and will be maintained by stabilizing negative feedback loops.
1.2.10 Positive feedback loops occur when a disturbance leads to an amplification of that disturbance, destabilizing the system and driving it away from its equilibrium.
1.2.11 Positive feedback loops will tend to drive the system toward a tipping point.
1.2.12 Tipping points can exist within a system where a small alteration in one component can produce large overall changes, resulting in a shift in equilibrium.
1.2.13 A model is a simplified representation of reality; it can be used to understand how a system works and to predict how it will respond to change.
1.2.14 Simplification of a model involves approximation and, therefore, loss of accuracy.
1.2.15 Interactions between components in systems can generate emergent properties.
1.2.16 The resilience of a system, ecological or social, refers to its tendency to avoid tipping points and maintain stability.
1.2.17 Diversity and the size of storages within systems can contribute to their resilience and affect their speed of response to change (time lags).
1.2.18 Humans can affect the resilience of systems through reducing these storages and diversity.

A systems approach is a way of visualizing a complex set of interactions which may be ecological or societal.

1.2.1 and 1.2.2 Systems

System components are organized to create a functional whole.

A **system** is an assemblage of parts and the relationships between them, which together constitute an entity or whole.

There are different ways of studying systems. A reductionist approach divides systems into parts, or components, and each part is studied separately. This is the way of traditional scientific investigations. But a system can also be studied as a whole, with patterns and processes described for the whole system. This is the **holistic** approach and is usually used in modern ecological investigations. The advantage of using the systems method is that it can show how components within the whole system relate to one another. A systems approach is a way of visualizing a complex set of interactions that can be applied across a wide range of different disciplines. This course focuses on systems as they relate to ecosystems and society, although the systems approach can equally be applied to other subjects such as economics or politics.

The interdependent components of systems are connected through the transfer of energy and matter, with all parts linked together and affecting each other. Examples of systems, with increasing levels of complexity, include particles, atoms, molecules, cells, organs, organ systems, communities, ecosystems, biomes, the Earth, the Solar System, galaxies and the Universe.

The concept of *systems* has been used in science for many years. This is especially true in biology where the functioning of the whole organism can be understood in terms of the interactions between various systems, such as the respiratory and circulatory systems. The reductionist approach often used in traditional science tends to look at the individual parts of a system, rather than the whole, so that the 'big picture' is missed. The nature of the environment and how we relate to it demands holistic treatment. A systems approach emphasizes the ways in which matter, energy and information flow, and can be used to integrate the perspectives of different disciplines to better represent the complex nature of the environment.

A systems approach

A system consists of storages and flows. **Storages** are places where matter or energy is kept in a system and **flows** provide inputs and outputs of energy and matter.

The systems approach emphasizes similarities in the ways in which matter, energy and information link together in a variety of different disciplines. This approach, therefore, allows different subjects to be looked at in the same way and for links to be made between them. Although the individual parts of a complex system can be looked at using the reductionist approach, this ignores the way in which such a system operates. A holistic approach is necessary to fully understand the way in which the parts of a complex system operate together. These interactions produce the emergent properties of the system (this topic, Section 1.2.15).

A system has storages and flows, with flows providing inputs and outputs of energy and matter.

1.2.3 Systems diagrams

2 Ecology
4.1 Water systems
5.1 Soil
8.2 Urban systems and urban planning

Systems can be represented as diagrams. In these **system diagrams**, storages are usually represented as rectangular boxes and flows as arrows with the arrowhead indicating the direction of the flow. Figure 1.28 shows flows and storage for the social system discussed in this topic, Section 1.1.7.

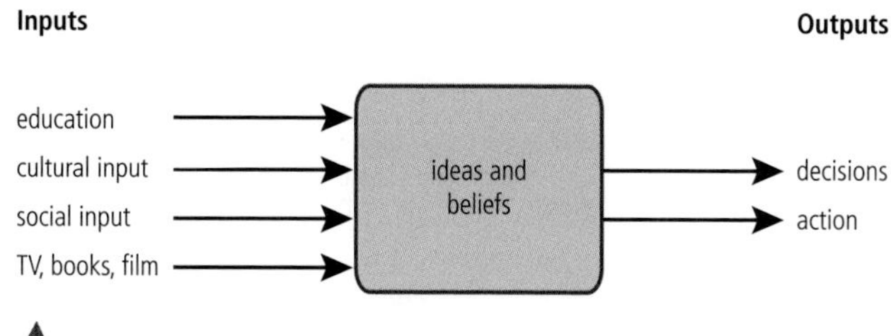

Figure 1.28 A social system, showing flows and storage. Flows are inputs and outputs and storage is the ideas and beliefs of the society.

A diagram can show several storages and the flows between them, and show the relationship between the parts of a complex system.

Throughout the course there are multiple opportunities for a systems approach. Make sure you are able to interpret system diagrams and use data to construct your own system diagrams for a variety of examples such as carbon cycling, food production and soil systems. These ideas are explored in subsequent topics.

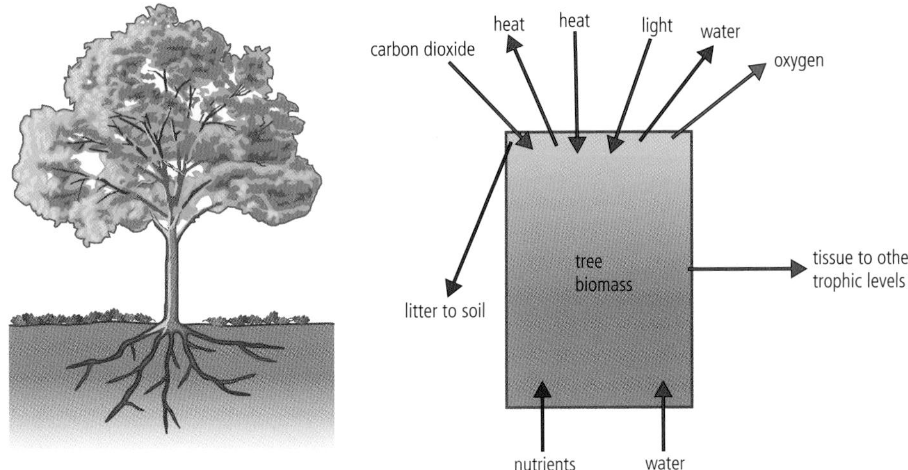

Figure 1.29 Tree system showing storage, inputs and outputs.

Using the systems approach, a tree can be summarized as shown in Figure 1.29.

The arrows flowing into and out of the tree systems diagram indicate the inputs and outputs. In addition, the diagram could be labelled with processes on each arrow. Processes in this example would include:

- **photosynthesis** – transforming CO_2, water (H_2O) and light into **biomass** and oxygen (O_2)
- **respiration** – transforming biomass into CO_2 and H_2O
- **diffusion** – allowing the movement of nutrients and H_2O into the tree
- **consumption** – transferring tissue (i.e. biomass) from one **trophic level** to another.

You need to be able to create systems diagrams representing the storages and flows, inputs and outputs of systems. These can be done, for example, for a lab-based or local natural ecosystem. The size of the boxes and the arrows may be representative of the size/magnitude of the storage or flow.

SKILLS

Create systems diagrams representing the storages and flows, inputs and outputs of systems

Figure 1.30 shows a systems diagram for the movement of energy and matter in a forest ecosystem.

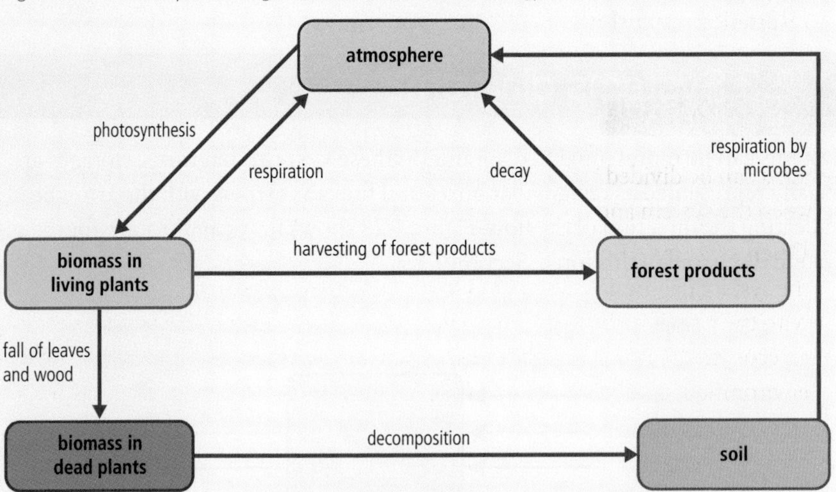

Figure 1.30 A forest ecosystem shown as a systems diagram.

Boxes in Figure 1.30 show storages, such the atmosphere and biomass (i.e. biological matter). Arrows show flows – inputs to and outputs from storages. The arrows are labelled with different processes, either transfers or transformations.

The size of boxes and arrows in systems diagrams can be drawn to represent the size (i.e. magnitude) of the storage or flow. The system diagrams in Figure 1.31 offer information about the different systems by drawing flows and stores proportionally (e.g. biomass store is larger in the woodland; litter store is larger in the woodland and there is a large output in mixed farming due to the harvested crops and livestock). The diagrams also show that legumes and fertilizers are additional inputs in mixed farming. Extra value can be given to systems diagrams, even simple ones, by showing data quantitatively.

(a) **Temperate deciduous woodland**

input dissolved in rain
biomass
leaf fall, tissue decay
litter
run-off
uptake by plants
mineralization, humification, and degradation
soil
weathering of rocks

(b) **Mixed farming**

input from rain and irrigation
harvesting crops, livestock manure
biomass
legumes
litter
soil
run-off
fertilizers
weathering of rocks

Figure 1.31 Nutrient cycles for **(a)** a temperate deciduous woodland and **(b)** an area nearby where the woodland has been cleared for mixed farming. Biomass is all the living material in the ecosystem. Arrows are proportional to the amount of energy present so larger arrows show a greater energy flow than smaller ones.

1.2.4 Flows are transfers or transformations

2.3 Biogeochemical cycles
4.1 Water systems
5.1 Soil

Flows are processes that may be either **transfers** (a change in location) or **transformations** (a change in the chemical nature, a change in state or a change in energy).

Transfers involve a change in the location of energy or matter.
Transformations involve a change in the chemical nature, a change in state or a change in energy.

Using the tree system (Figure 1.29) as an example, transfers include:

- harvesting of forest products
- the fall of leaves and wood to the ground.

Transformations include:

- photosynthesis – transforming CO_2, H_2O and light into biomass and O_2
- respiration – transforming biomass into CO_2 and H_2O.

1.2.5 Systems can be open or closed

An open system exchanges both energy and matter across its boundary, while a closed system exchanges only energy across its boundary. Biosphere 2 is an example of a closed system. An ecosystem is an example of an open system.

Systems can be divided into two types, depending on the flow of energy and matter between the system and the surrounding environment.

- **Open systems** – Both matter and energy are exchanged across the boundaries of the system (Figure 1.32a). Open systems are **organic** (i.e. living) and so must interact with their environment to take in energy and new matter and to remove wastes (e.g. an ecosystem). People are also open systems in that they must interact with their environment to take in food and water, obtain shelter and produce waste products.

(a)

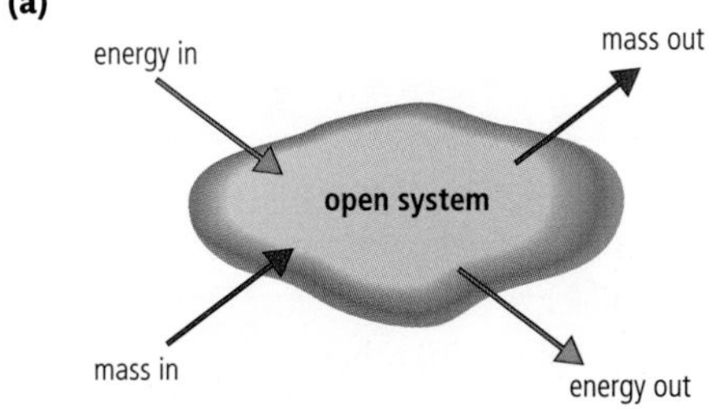

(b)

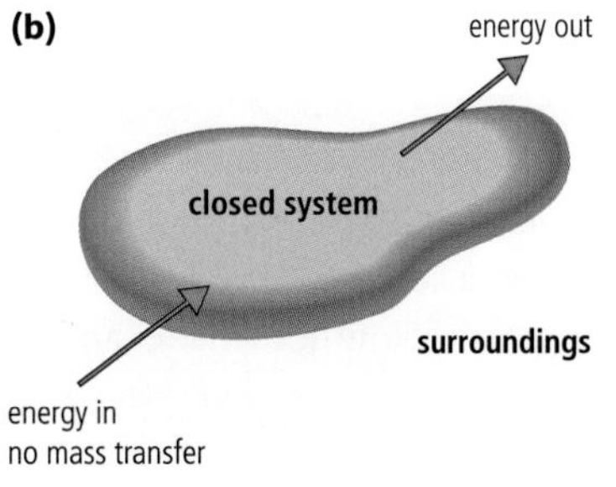

Figure 1.32 The exchange of matter (mass) and energy across the boundary of different systems. Open systems **(a)** exchange both mass and energy. Closed systems **(b)** exchange only energy.

- **Closed systems** – Energy but not matter is exchanged across the boundaries of the system (Figure 1.32b). Examples are atoms and molecules and mechanical systems. The Earth can be seen as a closed system: input = solar radiation (Sun's energy or light) and output = heat energy. Matter is recycled within the system. Although spaceships and meteorites can be seen as moving a small amount of matter in and out of the Earth system, they are generally discounted. Strictly, closed systems do not occur naturally on Earth. However, all the global cycles of matter, including the water cycle and nitrogen cycles, approximate to closed systems. Closed systems can also exist experimentally. An example of such a system is seen in Biosphere 2.

Almost all systems are open, only the global geochemical cycles (Topic 2, Sections 2.3.1 and 2.3.2) approximate to closed systems.

Example – Biosphere 2

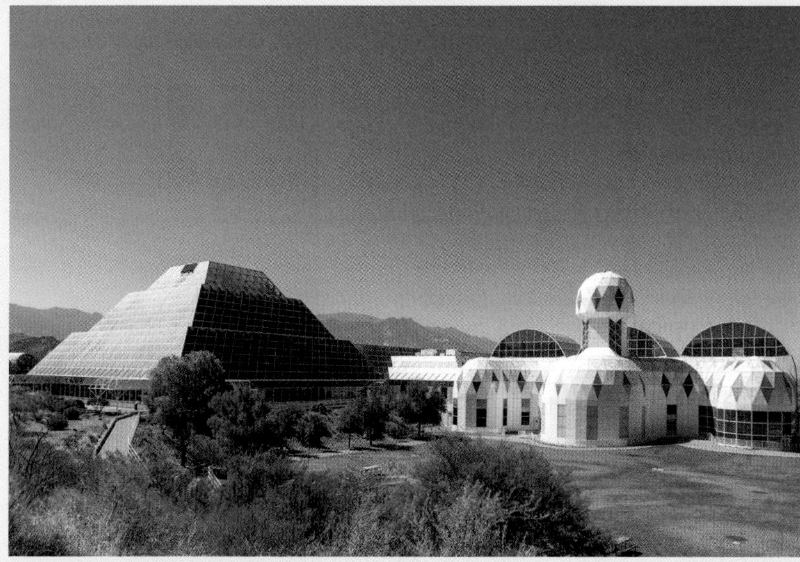

Figure 1.33 Biosphere 2 encloses an area equivalent to two and a half football pitches and contains five different biomes (ocean with coral reef, mangrove, rainforest, savannah and desert). Further areas explore agricultural systems and human impact on natural systems.

Biosphere 2 is an experiment modelling the Earth as a closed system (Figure 1.33). It was constructed in Arizona between 1987 and 1991 and enables scientists to study the complex interactions of natural systems such as the constantly changing chemistry of the air, water and soil within the greenhouses and the possible use of closed biospheres in space colonization. It allows the study and manipulation of a biosphere without harming the Earth. The project is still running and has resulted in numerous scientific papers. Results have shown that small, closed ecosystems are complex and vulnerable to unplanned events, such as fluctuations in CO_2 levels experienced during the experiment, a drop in O_2 levels due to soils over-rich in soil microbes and an over-abundance of insect pests that affected food supply.

TOK

How does the way that we organize or classify knowledge affect what we know?

Systems are hierarchical and what may be seen as the whole system in one study may be seen as only part of another system in a different study. For example, a human can be seen as a whole system, with inputs of food and water and outputs of waste or as part of a larger system such as an ecosystem or social system. Difficulties may arise as to where the boundaries are placed and how this choice is made.

2.3 Biogeochemical cycles
4.1 Water systems

Activity

Consider an ecosystem in your local environment, such as a temperate or tropical rainforest, a desert or grassland. In what ways can this ecosystem be considered an open system? How does matter and energy enter and leave the ecosystem? Draw a diagram to summarize your ideas and share your thoughts with others in your class.

The NASA missions of the 1960s and 1970s produced memorable images of the Earth from space. Prior to these images being published people had not seen the Earth in this way. The photos gave the public a greater appreciation of the vulnerability of the planet and its uniqueness both within the Solar System and more widely within the Universe beyond. These photos also prompted Lovelock to formulate his Gaia Hypothesis, named after the Greek supreme goddess of the Earth.

1.2.6 The Earth as a single integrated system

The photos of the Earth in space, taken on NASA's Apollo 8 mission (Figure 1.1), prompted English scientist James Lovelock to formulate his Gaia hypothesis in the mid-1960s. The Gaia hypothesis, named after the Greek supreme goddess of the Earth, was co-developed with Lynn Margulis and compares the Earth to a living organism in which feedback mechanisms maintain equilibrium. The hypothesis states that the Earth is a global control system of surface temperature, atmospheric composition and ocean salinity. It proposes that all parts of the Earth, including the water, soil, rock, atmosphere and the living components or **biosphere**, are closely integrated to form a complex interacting system. This system maintains the climatic and biogeochemical conditions on Earth in a preferred homeostasis. This means that the Earth has a balance that best provides the conditions for life on Earth and therefore functions as a single living organism.

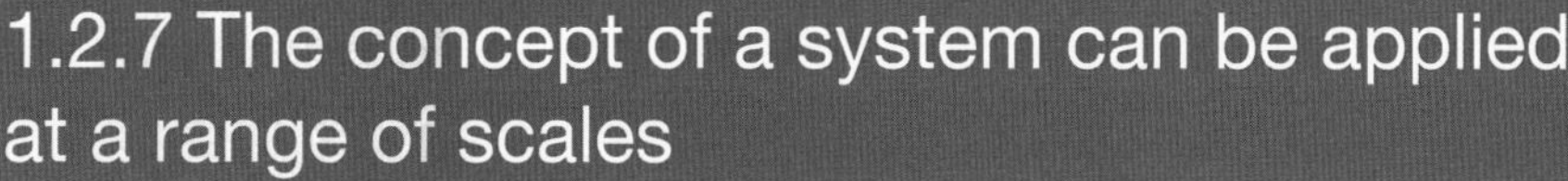

1.2.7 The concept of a system can be applied at a range of scales

James Lovelock's Gaia hypothesis is a model of the Earth as a single integrated system. Lovelock's Gaia theory was introduced to explain how atmospheric composition and temperatures are interrelated through feedback control mechanisms. There are many variations of the Gaia theory as further developed by Lovelock and Margulis.

Biosphere refers to the part of the Earth inhabited by organisms, that extends from upper parts of the atmosphere to deep in the Earth's crust.

An ecosystem is a community of interdependent organisms and the physical environment they inhabit. Different ecosystems exist where different species and physical or climatic environments are found. An ecosystem may, therefore, be of any size up to global.

For example, a tropical rainforest contains lots of small-scale ecosystems, such as the complex web of life that exists within a single bromeliad in the canopy (Figure 1.34). Systems have inputs, outputs and storages. The rainforest can be viewed as an ecosystem with inputs such as sunlight energy, nutrients and water; outputs such as oxygen, soil litter and water and finally, storages such as biomass within trees and plants or nutrients within soil. Such ecosystems can be viewed within one country on the local scale or more widely across many different countries where the same climatic conditions apply. On the global scale, ecosystems with similar climatic conditions in different parts of the world are called **biomes**. Examples of different biomes include tundra, tropical rainforest and desert (Topic 2, Sections 2.4.2–2.4.4).

On the largest scale, our entire planet can be seen as an ecosystem, with specific energy inputs from the Sun and with particular physical characteristics. The Gaia hypothesis proposes that our planet functions as a single living organism.

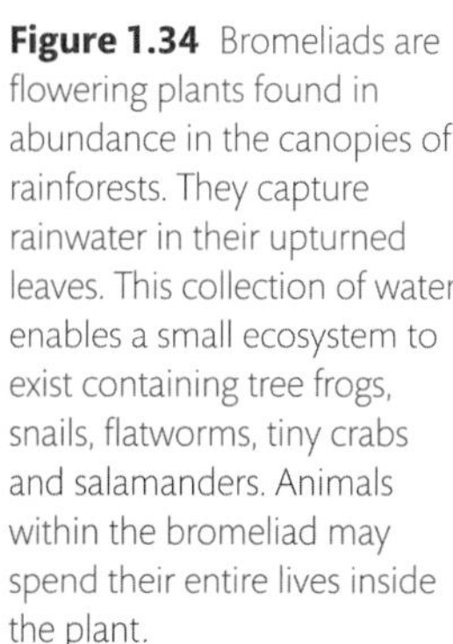

Figure 1.34 Bromeliads are flowering plants found in abundance in the canopies of rainforests. They capture rainwater in their upturned leaves. This collection of water enables a small ecosystem to exist containing tree frogs, snails, flatworms, tiny crabs and salamanders. Animals within the bromeliad may spend their entire lives inside the plant.

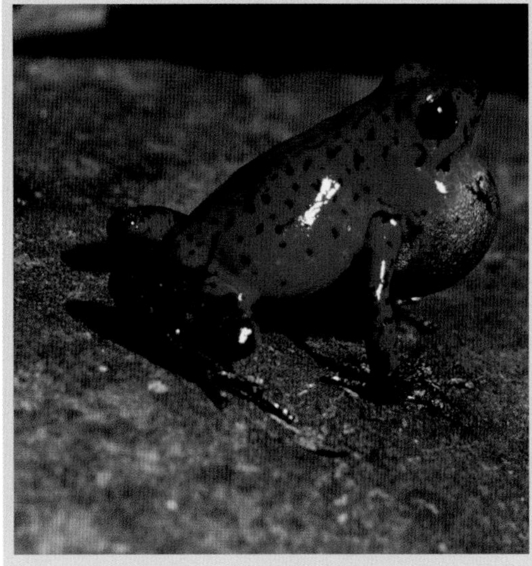

Figure 1.35 Strawberry poison-dart frog.

Dendrobates pumilio, the strawberry poison-dart frog, is common in the Atlantic lowland tropical forests of Central America, especially in Costa Rica (Figure 1.35). The female typically lays 3–5 eggs on the forest floor in a jelly-like mass that keeps them moist. Once the eggs are ready to hatch, one of the parents steps into the jelly surrounding the eggs: the tadpoles respond to the movement and climb onto the parent's back, where they stick to a secretion of mucus. The parent carries the tadpoles up to the canopy where they are deposited in water caught by the upturned leaves of a bromeliad. Each tadpole is put in a separate pool to increase the likelihood that some offspring will survive predation. The bromeliad ecosystem is a vital part of the frog's lifecycle.

How might the context in which knowledge is presented influence whether it is accepted or rejected?

The holistic approach and the reductionist approach used by conventional science use almost identical methodologies. Therefore, the difference between them may only be one perspective.

1.2.8 Negative feedback loops

'Feedback' refers to changes to the processes in a system that cause changes in the level of output. This feeds back to affect the level of input (Figure 1.36).

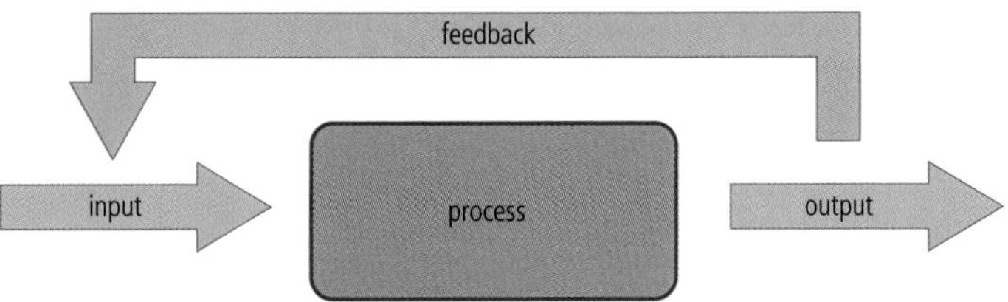

Figure 1.36 Feedback in a system.

What makes a good explanation?

The systems approach gives a holistic view of the issues, whereas the reductionist approach of conventional science breaks the system down into its components and describes the interrelations between them. The former describes patterns and models of the whole system, whereas the latter aims at explaining cause-and-effect relationships within it.

Feedback can be positive or negative.

Negative feedback can be defined as feedback that counteracts any change away from equilibrium, contributing to stability. Negative feedback is a method of control that regulates itself. For example, an ecosystem normally exists in a stable equilibrium, either a steady-state equilibrium or one developing over time (e.g. succession, Topic 2, Sections 2.5.3–2.5.7), because it is maintained by stabilizing negative feedback loops. Steady-state equilibrium in the human body is also maintained by negative feedback. For example, in temperature control, an increase in the temperature of the body results in increased sweat release and vasodilation, thus increasing evaporation of sweat from the skin, cooling the body and returning the temperature to its original equilibrium level. On a larger scale, an increased release of CO_2 through the burning of fossil fuels leads to enhanced plant growth through increased photosynthesis. This reduces atmospheric levels of CO_2. Negative feedback mechanisms are stabilizing forces within systems. They counteract deviation.

Systems occur at a range of scales including small-scale local ecosystems such as a bromeliad in rainforest, large ecosystems such as a rainforest and global systems such as the Gaia hypothesis or atmospheric circulation.

SKILLS

Use diagrams representing examples of negative feedback

Diagrams can be used to show negative feedback in systems. Consider Figure 1.37. If high winds blow down a tree in the rainforest, a gap is left in the canopy and more light reaches the forest floor. This encourages new growth. The rates of growth are rapid as light levels are high, so new saplings compete to take the place of the old tree in the canopy and equilibrium is restored. In this way, negative feedback and succession (Topic 2, Section 2.5.6) have closed the gap.

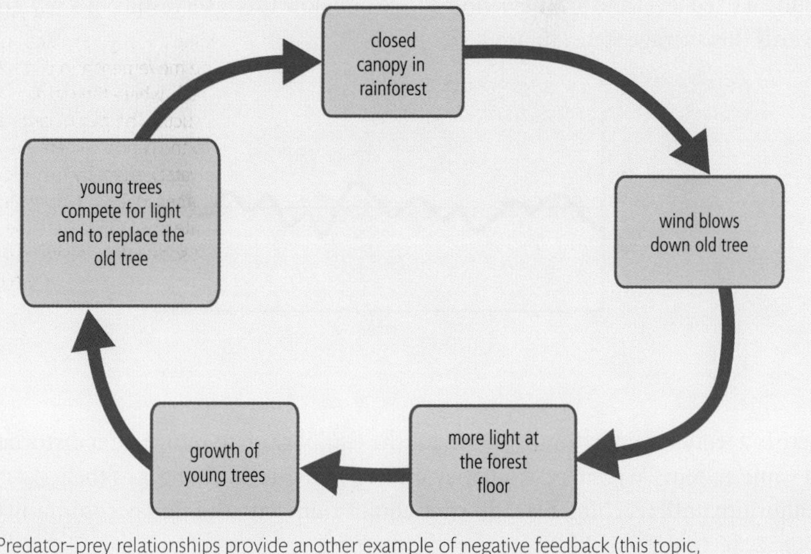

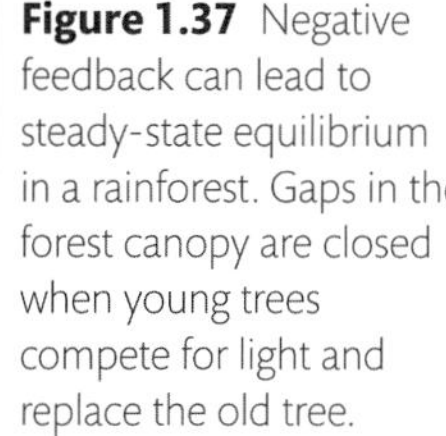

Figure 1.37 Negative feedback can lead to steady-state equilibrium in a rainforest. Gaps in the forest canopy are closed when young trees compete for light and replace the old tree.

Predator–prey relationships provide another example of negative feedback (this topic, Section 1.2.15).

2.1 Individuals, populations, communities and ecosystems
2.5 Zonation, succession and change in ecosystems
6.2 Climate change – causes and impacts
7.2 Energy resources, use and management
8.3 Urban air pollution

The DaisyWorld model

The DaisyWorld model, a computer simulation developed by James Lovelock and Andrew Watson, explains negative feedback loops.

The model shows how the Gaia hypothesis (this topic, Section 1.2.6) could regulate life on Earth. DaisyWorld is a simple model for a worldwide ecosystem and proposes that:

- The only life on DaisyWorld is black and white daisies. The rest of the planet is bare earth.
- The temperature of the planet is determined by the balance between the amount of light absorbed by the surface of the planet and heat radiated into space.
- The heat output from a nearby star is gradually increasing.
- Black daisies absorb more starlight energy and warm the planet – they will be abundant in the early history of DaisyWorld when the star is cooler.
- White daisies reflect more of the star's energy – these will become more abundant as the star's heat energy increases.
- The temperature of the planet remains the same within narrow limits.
- The temperature of the planet is therefore self-regulating.

The DaisyWorld model shows how temperature regulation can occur due to the presence of life on a planet in contrast with a planet on which no life is present.

1.2.9 Equilibrium

Open systems tend to have a state of balance among the components of a system – they are in a state of **equilibrium**. This means that although there may be slight fluctuations in the system, there are no sudden changes and any fluctuations tend to occur only between closely defined limits. Equilibrium allows systems to return to their original state following disturbance.

2.5 Zonation, succession and change in ecosystem
3.3 Conservation and regeneration

A steady-state equilibrium is the condition of an open system in which flows are still occurring but inputs are constantly balanced with outputs; there are no changes over the longer term, but there may be oscillations in the very short term.

Steady-state equilibrium

A **steady-state equilibrium** is the common property of most open systems in nature. Despite constant inputs and outputs of energy and matter, the overall stability of the system remains. In a steady-state equilibrium there is no change over the longer term but there may be oscillations in the very short term. Fluctuations in the system occur around a fixed level and any deviation above or below this level results in a return towards this average state (Figure 1.38).

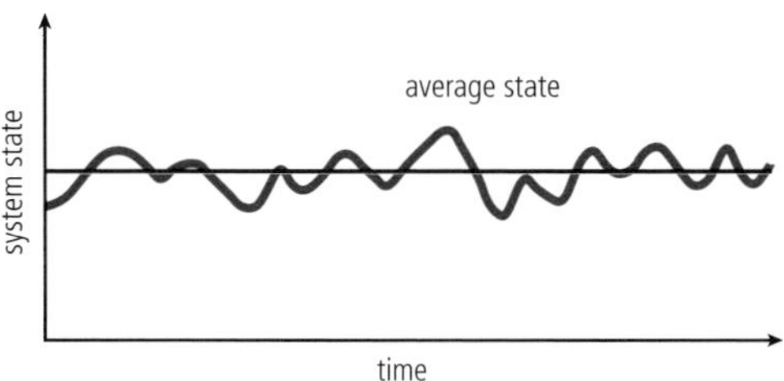

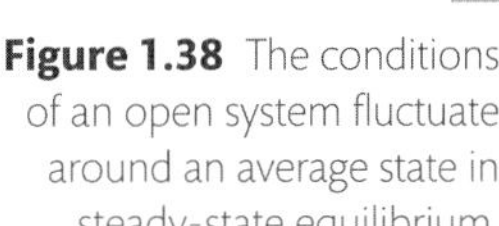

Figure 1.38 The conditions of an open system fluctuate around an average state in steady-state equilibrium.

Most open systems have a steady-state equilibrium, where any changes to a stable system result in a return to the original equilibrium after the disturbance. Negative feedback mechanisms (this topic, Section 1.2.8) return the system to the original state. This is because there are inputs and outputs of energy and matter to the system that allow this to happen. Static equilibrium is when there is no input or output from the system and no change occurs – this does not apply to any natural system.

There is a tendency in natural systems for the equilibrium to return after disturbance, but some systems (e.g. succession) may undergo long-term changes to their equilibrium until reaching a steady-state equilibrium with the climax community (Topic 2, Section 2.5.3–2.5.4).

The stability of steady-state equilibrium means that the system can return to the steady state following disturbance. For example, the death of a canopy tree in the rainforest leaves a gap in the canopy, which eventually closes again through the process of succession (Figure 1.37 and Topic 2, Section 2.5.6). Homeostatic mechanisms in animals maintain body conditions at a steady state – a move away from the steady state results in a return to equilibrium. (You may come across the term 'dynamic equilibrium' to describe this phenomenon but it is not used in this course.)

A stable equilibrium is the condition of a system in which there is a tendency for it to return to the previous equilibrium following disturbance.

Stable and unstable equilibrium

If a system returns to the original equilibrium after a disturbance, it is a **stable equilibrium** (Figure 1.39a and b). A system that does not return to the same equilibrium but instead forms a new equilibrium is an **unstable equilibrium** (Figure 1.40a and b). Positive feedback mechanisms (this topic, Section 1.2.10 and 1.2.11) can lead to a system moving away from its original equilibrium.

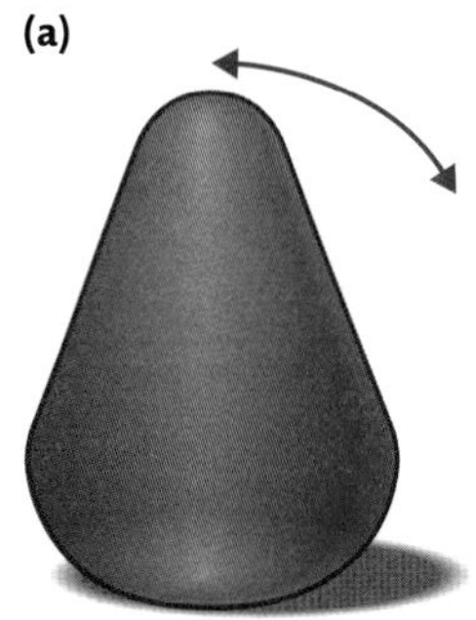

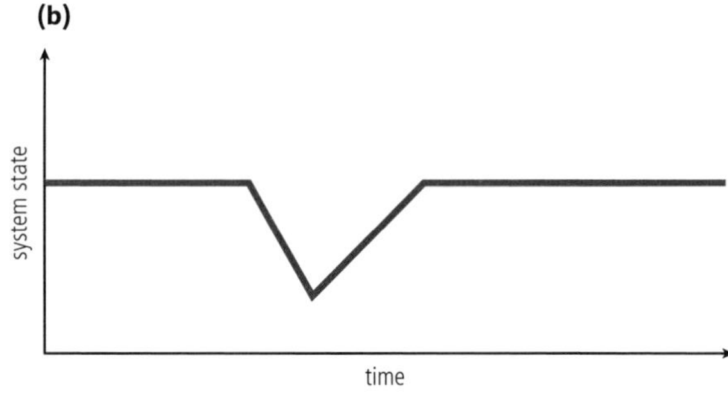

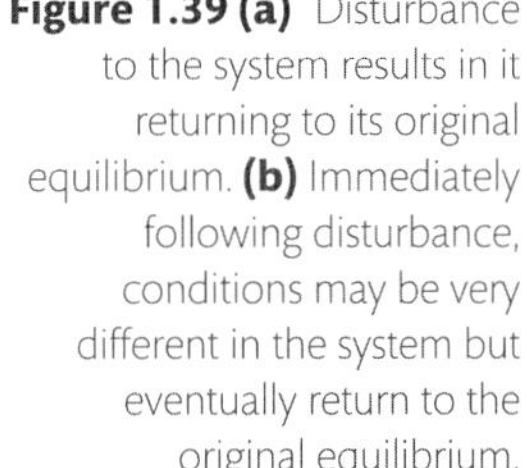

Figure 1.39 (a) Disturbance to the system results in it returning to its original equilibrium. **(b)** Immediately following disturbance, conditions may be very different in the system but eventually return to the original equilibrium.

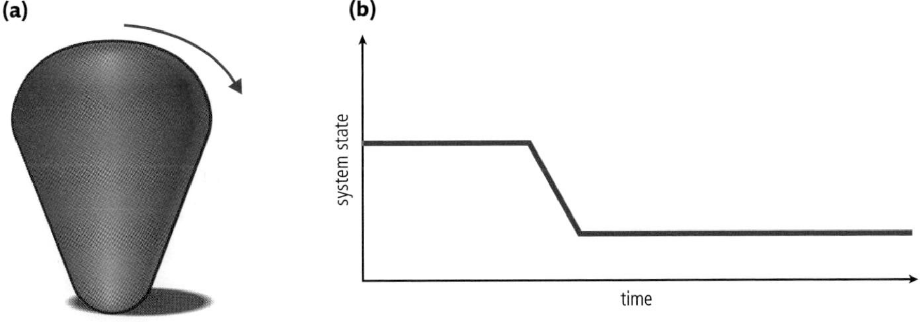

Figure 1.40 **(a)** Disturbance results in a new equilibrium very different from the first (in this case the object lying horizontally rather than standing vertically).
(b) Scientists believe that the Earth's climate may reach a new equilibrium following the effects of global warming, with conditions on the planet dramatically altered.

1.2.10 and 1.2.11 Positive feedback loops

Positive feedback loops have amplifying roles. Positive feedback occurs when a change in the state of a system leads to additional and increased change. Thus, an increase in the size of one or more of the system's outputs feeds back into the system and results in self-sustained change that alters the state of a system away from its original equilibrium towards instability (Figure 1.41). For example, increased temperature through global warming melts more of the ice in the polar ice caps and glaciers, leading to a decrease in the Earth's **albedo** (reflection from the Earth's surface). This means that Earth absorbs more of the Sun's energy, causing the temperature to increase further, melting more ice (Topic 6, Section 6.2.7). Exponential population growth is also an example of positive feedback (see Example).

Positive feedback can lead to an increase or a decrease in a system component. For example, as a population declines, the reproductive potential decreases, leading to further decrease.

SKILLS

Use diagrams representing examples of positive feedback

Diagrams can be used to show positive feedback in systems.

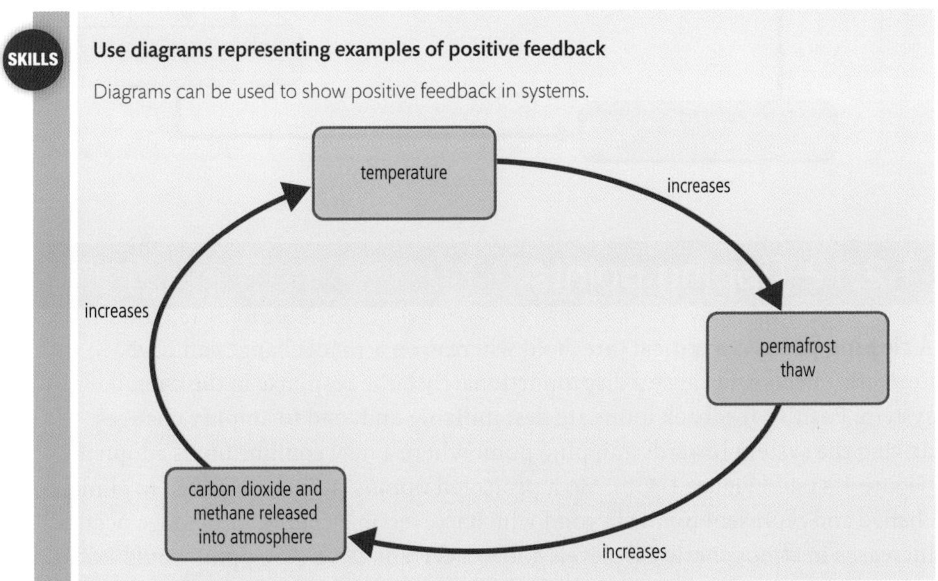

Figure 1.41 A positive feedback mechanism enhancing climate change. Such mechanisms are often linked to tipping points when the system becomes unstable and forms a new equilibrium (this topic, Section 1.2.12, page 36).

Feedback refers to the return of part of the output from a system as input, to affect succeeding outputs. There are two types of feedback. *Negative feedback* tends to reduce, neutralize or counteract any deviation from an equilibrium and promotes stability. *Positive feedback* amplifies or increases change, which leads to exponential deviation away from an equilibrium.

Example – Humans, resources and space

The population of humans on Earth is growing at an ever-increasing rate. A higher number of people on the planet leads to a higher number of children in a positive feedback loop. The rate will continue to increase if there are sufficient resources available to support the population. The human population has been growing exponentially. Some 2000 years ago, the Earth's population was about 300 million people. It took the human population thousands of years to reach one billion, which it did in 1804. However, it took only 123 years for this to double, reaching two billion in 1927. The population doubled again to four billion in 1974 (after only 47 years). In 2023, it reached eight billion. It is estimated that the population will reach nine billion in 2037. While it took the global population 12 years to grow from seven to eight billion, it will take approximately 15 years for it to reach nine billion, which suggests that the overall growth rate of the global population is beginning to decrease.

A system may contain both negative and positive feedback loops resulting in different effects within the system (Figure 1.42).

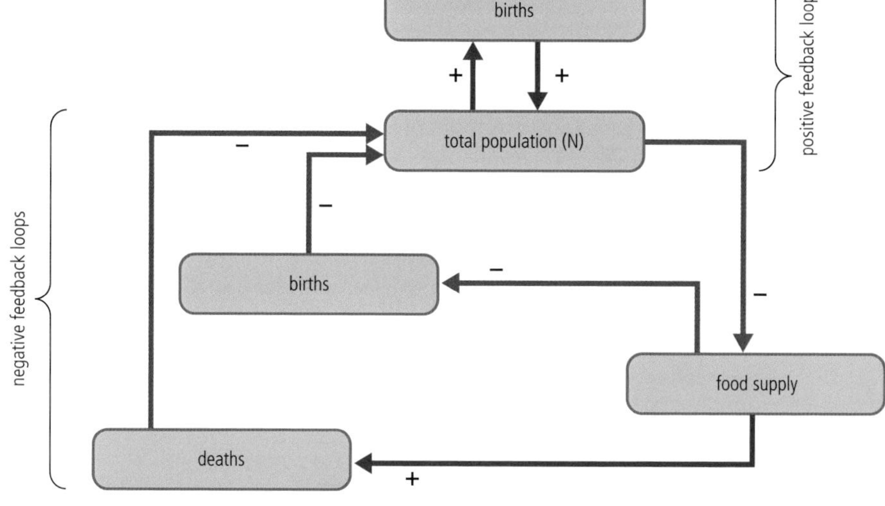

Figure 1.42 Population control in animal populations contains both negative and positive feedback loops.

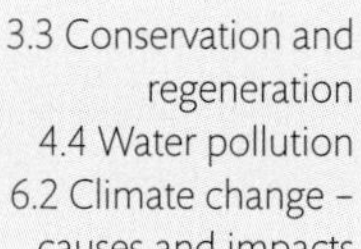

3.3 Conservation and regeneration
4.4 Water pollution
6.2 Climate change – causes and impacts

1.2.12 Tipping points

Positive feedback loops (destabilizing) will tend to amplify changes and drive the system towards a tipping point where a new equilibrium is adopted.

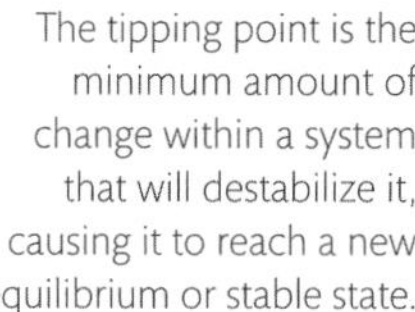

The tipping point is the minimum amount of change within a system that will destabilize it, causing it to reach a new equilibrium or stable state.

A **tipping point** is a critical threshold where even a small change can have dramatic effects and cause a disproportionately large response in the overall system. Positive feedback loops are destabilizing and tend to amplify changes, driving the system towards a tipping point where a new equilibrium is adopted (Figure 1.41 and Figure 1.43b). Most projected tipping points are linked to climate change and represent points beyond which irreversible change or damage occurs. Increases in atmospheric CO_2 levels above a certain value (450 ppm) would lead to an increase in global mean temperature, causing melting of the ice sheets and permafrost (Topic 6, Section 6.2.13). Reaching such a tipping point would, for example, cause the melting of Himalayan mountain glaciers, a lack of freshwater and long-term damage to many Asian societies.

If external conditions in the environment, such as nutrient input or temperature, change gradually, then the ecosystem state may respond gradually (Figure 1.43a) and no tipping points would be involved. In other cases, there may be little response below a certain threshold. However, fast changes in the system can occur once the threshold is reached (Figure 1.43b), even though a small change in environmental conditions has occurred. In such cases, a tipping point has been reached (see Example).

2.1 Individuals, populations, communities and ecosystems
2.5 Zonation, succession and change in ecosystems

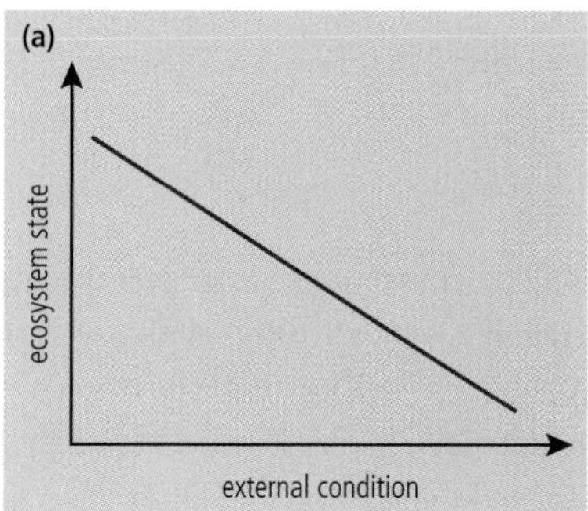

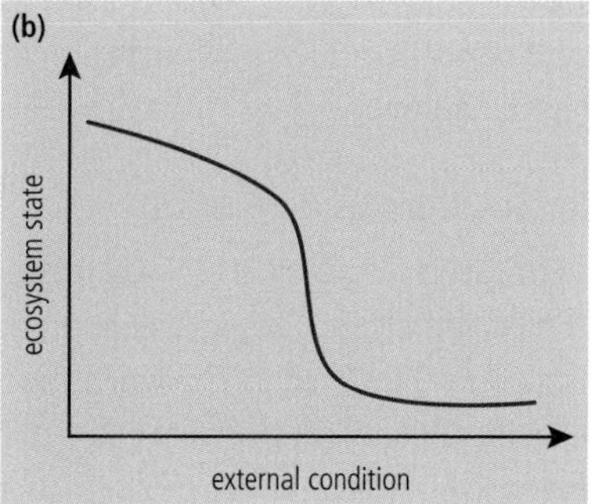

Figure 1.43 The ways in which different types of ecosystems may respond to changing external conditions.

Example – Krill harvesting in the Southern Ocean

Krill are small shrimp-like crustaceans that are a food source for seals, whales, penguins and other seabirds (Figure 1.44). Krill are harvested to produce food for farmed fish and nutritional supplements for people. Research into the effects of Antarctic krill in the seas near South Georgia have indicated a level of fishing that is sustainable. Beyond this level a tipping point would be reached, leading to rapid change in the southern ocean ecosystem. Krill form the basis of the food chain and so a significant reduction in their population density severely affects other animals (e.g. gentoo penguins, macaroni penguins and the Antarctic fur seal). The study showed that animals that feed on the krill began to suffer when the krill population declined below a critical level of 20 g m^{-2}, which is approximately one-third of the maximum measured number of krill available (Figure 1.45). This critical level is also shown throughout seabird species around the world that rely on krill, from the Arctic to the Antarctic and from the Pacific to the Atlantic.

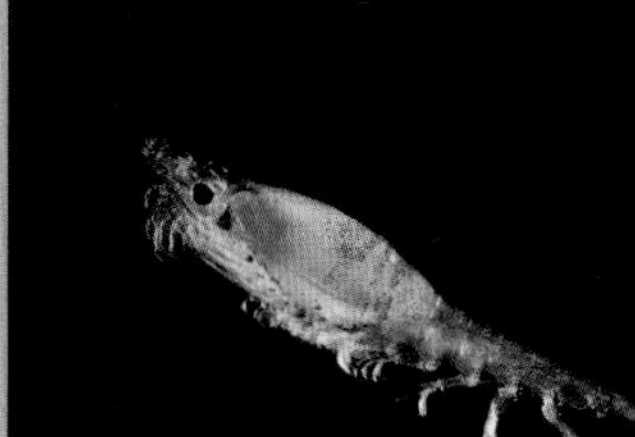

Figure 1.44 Krill live in huge swarms which can measure several kilometres across and reach densities of 10,000 individuals per cubic metre. Each individual has a maximum length of 6 cm. They feed on algae. Krill are a major food species for a wide array of oceanic creatures.

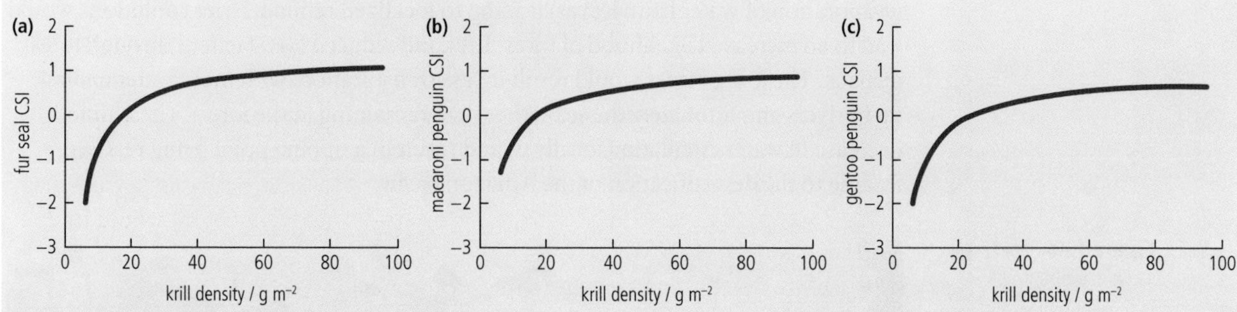

Figure 1.45 Graphs showing the effect of changes in krill density on upper trophic level predators (fur seals, macaroni penguins and gentoo penguins). The combined standardized index (CSI) uses a range of variables to assess the health of predator populations, including population size, breeding performance, offspring growth rate, foraging behaviour and diet. Data show that a tipping point is reached at a population of 20 g m^{-2} of krill.

To learn more about conservation of the Antarctic Ocean ecosystem, go to the Commission for the Conservation of Antarctic Marine Living Resources (CCAMLR) website.

Search online for the Met Office's webpage on climate change.

2.1 Individuals, populations, communities and ecosystems
3.3 Conservation and regeneration
4.4 Water pollution
6.2 Climate change – causes and impacts
8.3 Urban air pollution

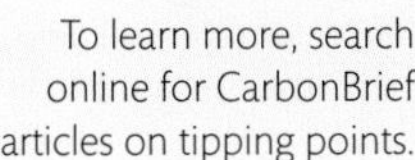

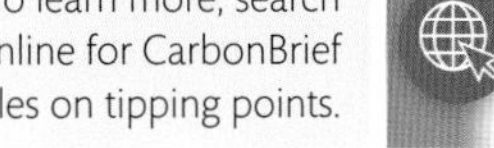

To learn more, search online for CarbonBrief articles on tipping points.

Shifts in equilibrium

Tipping points result in regime shifts between alternative stable states.
Systems at threat from tipping points include the Antarctic sea ecosystems, Arctic sea-ice, Greenland ice sheet, West Antarctic ice sheet, El Niño Southern Oscillation (ENSO), West African monsoon, Amazon rainforest, Boreal forest, thermohaline circulation (THC) (Topic 2, Section 2.4.6 and Topic 4, Section 4.1.14), and nitrate/phosphate concentrations and eutrophication (Topic 4, Section 4.4.5). Some of these are discussed below.

El Niño Southern Oscillation

El Niño Southern Oscillation (ENSO) refers to fluctuations in sea surface temperatures across the Pacific Ocean (Topic 2, Section 2.4.10 and 2.4.11, HL only), with oscillations occurring every 3 to 7 years. The warming and cooling oscillations of the tropical eastern Pacific Ocean, off the west coast of South America, are known as El Niño and La Niña, respectively. Because ocean circulation has a global extent, ENSO can have large-scale effects on the global climate system and cause extreme weather such as droughts and floods. El Niño events, for example, can lead to warm and very wet weather in the months of April to October with flooding occurring along the western coast of South America (in countries such as Peru and Ecuador). At the same time, drought occurs in Australia, Malaysia, Indonesia and the Philippines; warmer-than-normal winters occur in northern USA and Canada; greater rainfall occurs in south-west USA and droughts occur in Africa and India. Developing countries bordering the Pacific Ocean, on both its eastern and western extremes, are particularly affected by ENSO events.

West African monsoon

The heavy rains that occur in West Africa are affected by sea surface temperature. A change in global mean temperature of 3–5 °C could lead to a collapse of the West African monsoon. With reduced rainfall in western Africa, more moisture would reach areas such as the Sahara, which could lead to increased rainfall and 'greening' as more vegetation grows.

Amazon rainforest

Increased temperatures, due to climate change and the effects of deforestation through logging and land clearance (Figure 1.46), could lead to a tipping point in the Amazon. Rainforests create their own weather patterns, with high levels of **transpiration** (evaporation of water from leaves) leading to localized rainfall. Drier conditions would lead to an increased likelihood of forest fires and reduced forest extent through forest dieback. The loss of trees would result in less transpiration, with more water ending up in rivers and ultimately the sea rather than remaining in the forest. The ultimate decrease in water circulating locally would result in a tipping point being reached, leading to the desertification of the Amazon basin.

Figure 1.46 Illegal deforestation in the Brazilian Amazon.

Boreal forest

Boreal forest, or Taiga (Topic 2, Section 2.1.20, Figure 2.38), is characterized by coniferous trees such as pines. It is the Earth's most extensive biome and is found throughout the northern hemisphere. Research suggests that a 3 °C increase in mean global temperature may be the threshold for loss of the boreal forest because of increased water stress, decreased tree reproduction rates, increased vulnerability to disease and fire.

The likelihood and possible impacts of these tipping points are shown in Figure 1.47.

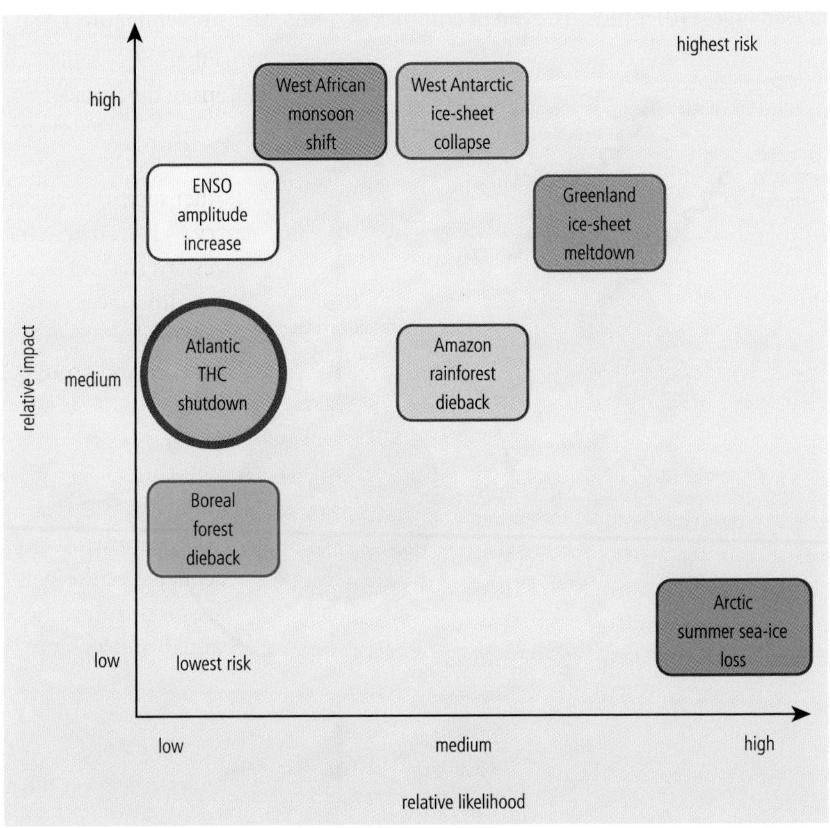

Figure 1.47 Possible likelihoods and impacts of tipping points resulting from climate change.

Models are used to predict tipping points and such models have strengths and limitations (this topic, Section 1.2.13 and 1.2.14, page 41). The delays involved in feedback loops make it difficult to predict tipping points and add to the difficulty of modelling systems.

Accurate predictions are critical as the costs of tipping points, both from environmental and economic perspectives, could be severe. Models that predict tipping points are, therefore, essential and have alerted scientists to the potential of large events. Continued monitoring, research and modelling is required to improve predictions.

Activities in one part of the globe may lead to a tipping point that influences the ecological equilibrium elsewhere on the planet. For example, fossil fuel use in industrialized countries can contribute to global warming, the impacts of which may be seen elsewhere, such as the desertification of the Amazon basin.

1.2.13 and 1.2.14 Models

A model is a simplified description designed to show the structure or workings of an object, system or concept. A model may take many forms including a graph, a diagram, an equation, a simulation or words.

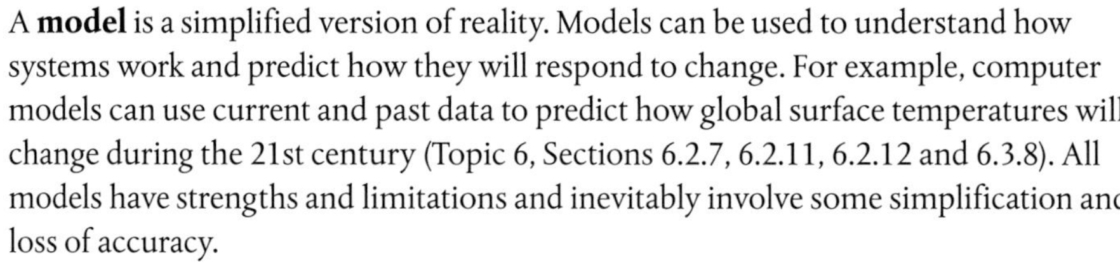

A **model** is a simplified version of reality. Models can be used to understand how systems work and predict how they will respond to change. For example, computer models can use current and past data to predict how global surface temperatures will change during the 21st century (Topic 6, Sections 6.2.7, 6.2.11, 6.2.12 and 6.3.8). All models have strengths and limitations and inevitably involve some simplification and loss of accuracy.

Some models are complex, such as the computer models that predict the effect of climate change. Other models, even of complex systems, are simpler (Figure 1.48).

Figure 1.48 A model of the climatic system.

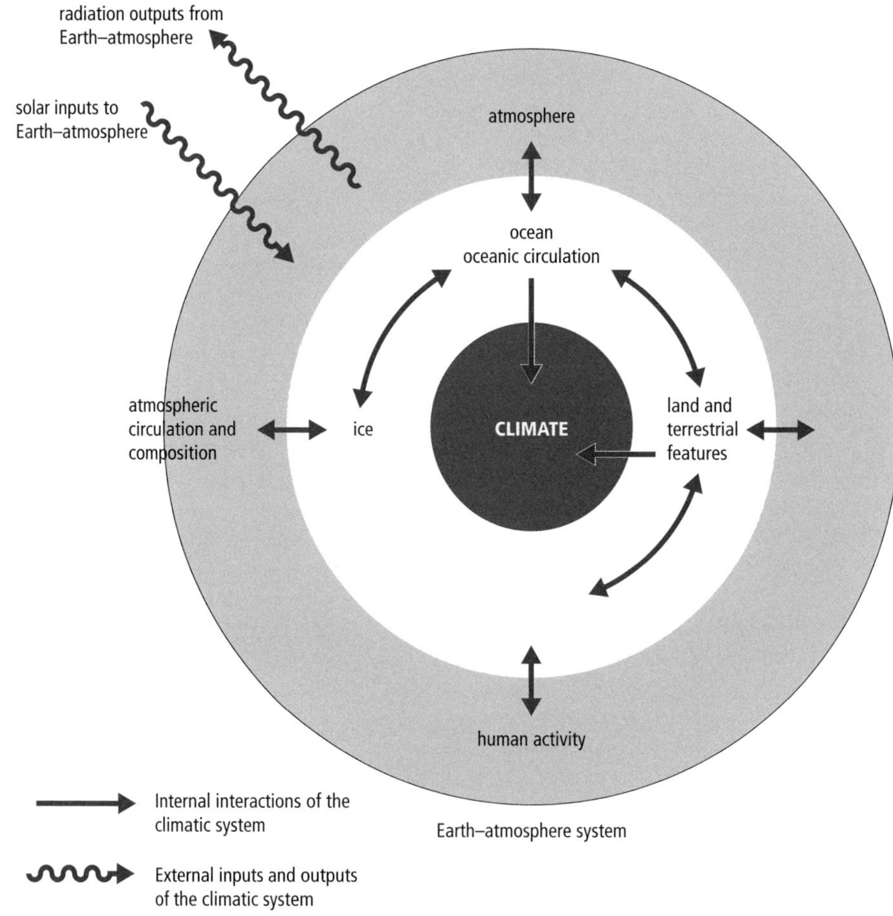

You are expected to be able to construct a system diagram or a model from a given set of information.

Models can be used to show the flows, storages and linkages within systems, using the diagrammatic approach (this topic, Section 1.2.3). For example, Figure 1.49 shows a model of an ecosystem. While unable to show much of the complexity of the real system, Figure 1.49 still helps us to understand basic ecosystem function.

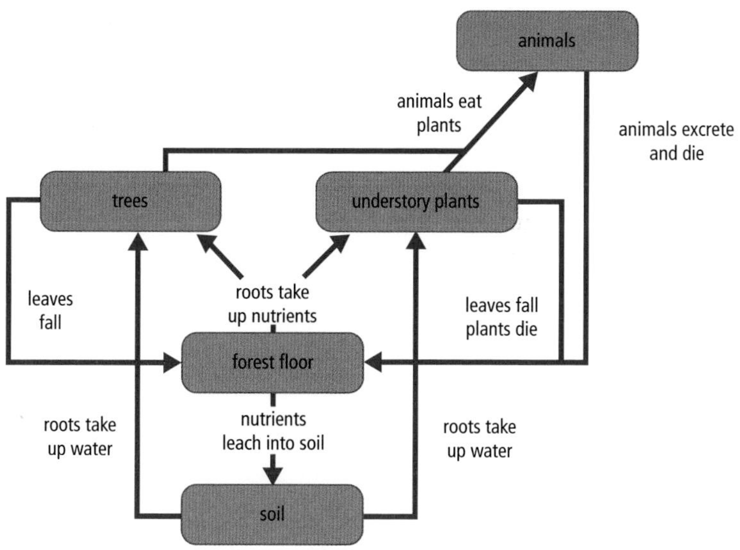

Figure 1.49 Models are simplified versions of reality. They can show much about the main processes in an ecosystem and show key linkages. This is a model of a forest ecosystem.

Models are used throughout the course to represent systems and processes, for example 1.1 Perspectives (modelling EVSs) and 2.1 Individuals, populations, communities and ecosystems (modelling population interactions).

6.2 Climate change – causes and impacts
8.1 Human populations

A model involves approximation and therefore loss of accuracy

The simplification of a model can make it less accurate. Different models may give very different results.

Strengths of models

- Models allow scientists to simplify complex systems and use them to predict what will happen if there are changes to inputs, outputs or storages.
- Models allow inputs to be changed and outcomes to be examined without having to wait a long time, as we would have to if studying real events.
- Models allow results to be shown to other scientists and to the public and are easier to understand than detailed information about the whole system.

Limitations of models

- Environmental factors are very complex with many interrelated components and it may be impossible to take all variables into account.
- Different models may show different effects using the same data. For example, models used to predict the effect of climate change can give very different results.
- Models themselves may be very complex and when they are oversimplified, they may become less accurate. For example, there are many complex factors involved in atmospheric systems.
- Because many assumptions must be made about these complex factors, models such as climate models may not be accurate.
- The complexity and oversimplification of climate models, for example, has led some people to criticize these models.
- Different models use slightly different data to calculate predictions.
- Any model is only as good as the data used. The data put into the model may not be reliable.
- Models rely on the expertise of the people making them and this can lead to impartiality.
- As models predict further into the future, they become more uncertain.
- Different people may interpret models in different ways and so come to different conclusions. People who would gain from the results of the models may use them to their advantage.

The need for models to summarize complex systems requires approximation techniques to be used and these can lead to loss of information and oversimplification. A model inevitably involves some approximation and therefore loss of accuracy. The advantage of models is that they can clearly illustrate links between parts of the system and give a clear overview of complex interrelationships.

1.2.15 Emergent properties

Interactions between components of a system can generate **emergent properties**. An emergent property is a property that a system has but which the individual components do not have. Predator-prey oscillations (Figures 1.50, 1.51 and 1.52) and trophic cascades (Figure 1.53) give examples of emergent properties where patterns of change occur that would not occur in isolated components.

Predator-prey relationships

Predation occurs when one organism hunts and eats another organism.

Figure 1.50 Female snowy owl swoops down to catch a lemming on top of the snow.

Predator–prey relationships are seen, for example, in lemming and snowy owl populations in the northern polar regions. The graph in Figure 1.51 shows fluctuations in the population sizes of lemmings (the prey) and snowy owls (the **predator**) over several years.

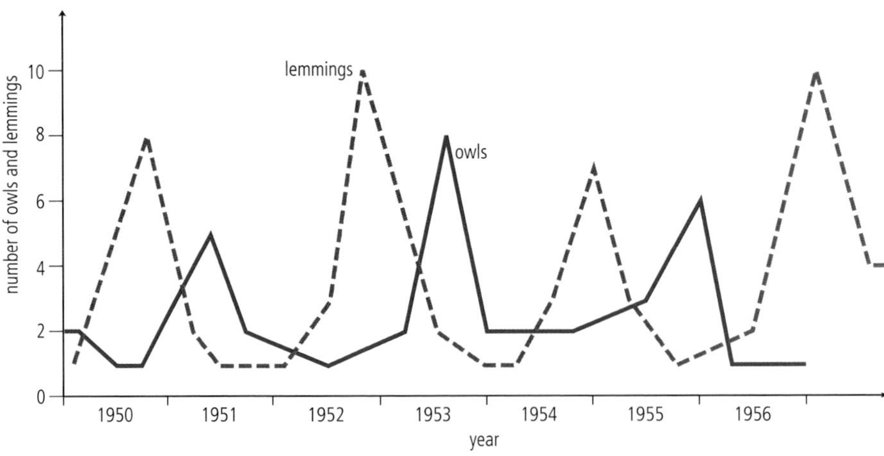

Figure 1.51 Variations in the populations of lemmings and snowy owls.

These predator–prey interactions are often controlled by negative feedback mechanisms that control population densities (Figure 1.52). In the relative absence of the predatory snowy owl (due to a limited prey population), the population of lemmings begins to increase in size. As the availability of prey increases, there is an increase in predator numbers, after a time lag. As the number of predators increases, the population size of the prey begins to decrease, again after a time-lag. With fewer prey, the number of predators decreases again. With fewer predators, the number of prey may begin to increase again and the cycle continues. Nevertheless, predation may be good for the prey. It removes old and sick individuals first as these are easier to catch. Those individuals remaining are healthier and form a superior breeding pool. This is an example of emergent properties because it shows how interactions between two different species lead to fluctuations in population size that are determined by interactions between different components of the overall system.

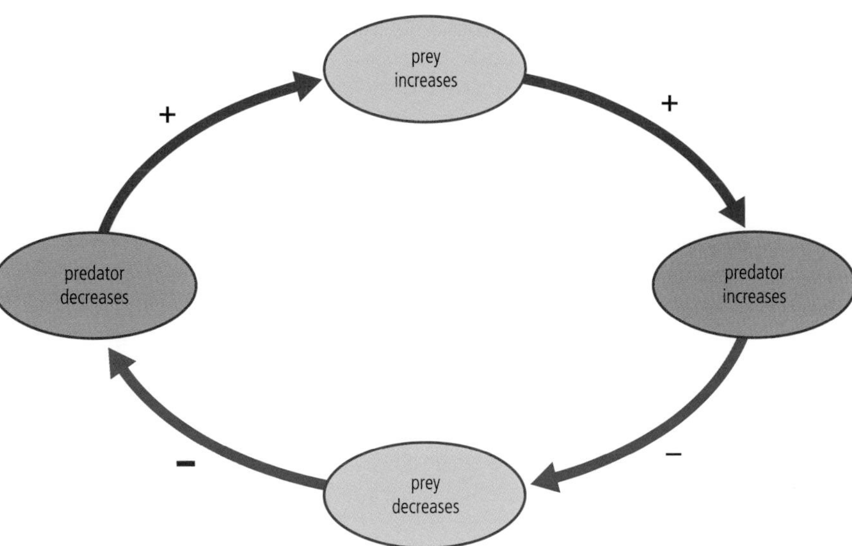

Figure 1.52 Predator–prey relationships show negative feedback.

Trophic cascades

A trophic level is the position that an organism occupies in a food chain (Topic 2, Section 2.2.10 and 2.2.11). Producers, for example, form the first trophic level in a food chain. 'Trophic cascade' refers to the impact that a top consumer has on the trophic level beneath it (i.e. its prey) and in turn the knock-on effect this has on lower trophic levels in the food chain. Trophic cascades occur when predators limit the population size of their prey, which in turn enhances the chance of survival of the individuals in the next lower trophic level in the food chain. Complex interactions between different trophic levels create emergent properties of the overall system. Adding or removing top predators, either deliberately or indirectly through human activities, can lead to associated changes in the relative populations of predator and prey through a food chain. This can result in dramatic changes in ecosystem structure and nutrient cycling.

Figure 1.53 Trophic cascade caused by removal of the top predator (wolf). When the top predator is removed, the population of deer is able to grow unchecked, which causes over-consumption of the primary producers.

3.3 Conservation and regeneration
5.2 Agriculture and food
6.3 Climate change – mitigation and adaptation
8.2 Urban systems and urban planning

Before removal of the top carnivore (Figure 1.53), the ecosystem would have:

- few large herbivores
- a diverse plant community, as the top predator limited the population of herbivores
- a mix of large and small predators
- a diverse community of birds, supported by the plant community and a complex environment, with plenty of food.

After removal of the top carnivore, the ecosystem would have:

- a large population of herbivores, due to lack of predation
- a simplified plant community, due to feeding by herbivores
- a simplified bird community
- an absence of large predators but a dominance of small predators, such as the fox, due to lack of competition with large predators.

1.2.16 The resilience of a system

The resilience of a system is the capacity to resist damage and recover from or adapt efficiently to disturbance.

The **resilience** of a system, ecological or social, refers to its tendency to avoid tipping points and maintain stability through a steady-state equilibrium. Resilience is the capacity to resist damage and recover from or adapt efficiently to disturbance.

3.3 Conservation and regeneration
6.2 Climate change – causes and impacts
6.3 Climate change – mitigation and adaptation

You need to be able to discuss resilience in a variety of systems.

Diversity and the size of storages within systems can contribute to their resilience and affect the speed of response to change. Large storages, or high diversity, will mean that a system is less likely to reach a tipping point and move to a new equilibrium. Humans can affect the resilience of systems through reducing these storages and diversity. Tropical rainforests, for example, have high **diversity** (i.e. large numbers and proportions of species present) but catastrophic disturbance through logging (i.e. rapid removal of tree biomass storages) or fires can lower its resilience and can mean it takes a long time to recover. Natural grasslands, in contrast, have low diversity but are very resilient, because a lot of nutrients are stored below ground in root systems. Therefore, they can recover quickly after fires (see Example).

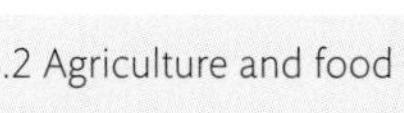

5.2 Agriculture and food

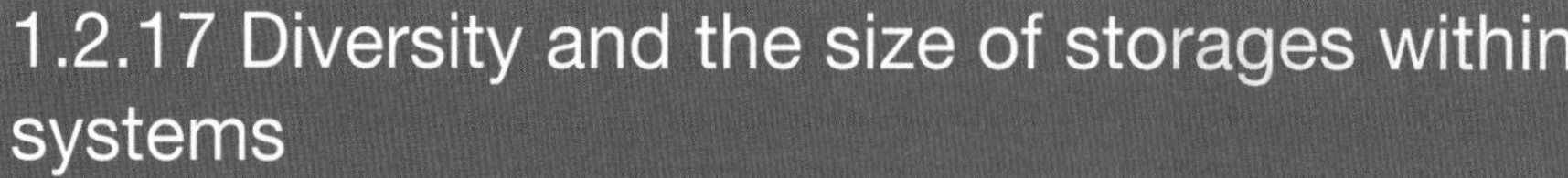

1.2.17 Diversity and the size of storages within systems

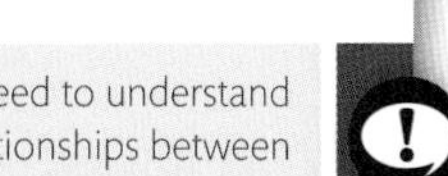

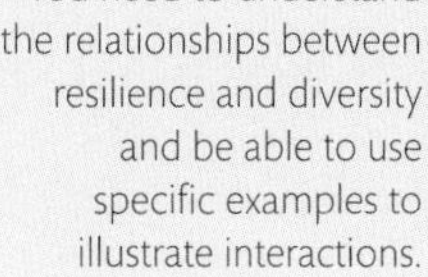

You need to understand the relationships between resilience and diversity and be able to use specific examples to illustrate interactions.

Diversity and the size of storages within systems can contribute to their resilience and affect their speed of response to change or time lags.

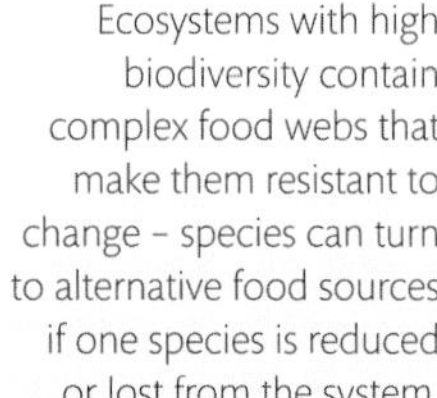

Ecosystems with high biodiversity contain complex food webs that make them resistant to change – species can turn to alternative food sources if one species is reduced or lost from the system.

Example – Disturbance of tall grass prairie

Tall grass prairie is a native ecosystem to central USA (Figure 1.54). High diversity, complex food webs and nutrient cycles in this ecosystem maintain stability. The grasses are between 1.5 and 2 m in height, with occasional stalks as high as 2.5 or 3 m. Due to the build-up of organic matter, these prairies have deep soils and recover quickly following periodic fires that sweep through them, meaning they can quickly return to their original equilibrium. Plants have a growth point below the surface that protects them from fire and enables a swift recovery.

North American wheat farming has replaced native ecosystems (e.g. tall grass prairie) with a monoculture (a one-species system). Such systems are prone to the outbreak of crop pests and damage by fire – low diversity and low resilience combined with soils that lack structure and need to be maintained artificially with added nutrients lead to poor recovery following disturbance.

Figure 1.54 Tall grass prairie.

1.2.18 Humans can affect the resilience of systems

Large storages and high diversity, such as those found in forests, mean that a system is less likely to reach a tipping point and move to a new equilibrium. A resilient ecosystem can maintain its structure, ecological functions and processes. Humans can affect the resilience of systems through reducing these storages and diversity. Tropical rainforests, for example, have high diversity and large storage of carbon in the trees. Any disturbance through removal of tree biomass storages can lower its resilience (Figure 1.55). For example:

- deforestation and reduction in the size of storages leads to decreased productivity through the removal of primary producers (the trees)
- reduction in producers leads to reduced habitat diversity and fewer niches, which threatens more specialized species
- changed conditions and a less complex ecosystem can lead to species extinction, resulting in shorter food webs and decreased stability.

A useful way of remembering how the resilience of a system depends on the size of storages is to think about the differences between a puddle and a lake. Both are comprised of water and a community of organisms (although in a puddle this may be very limited). The lake is much larger than the puddle and so fluctuations in the quantity of water in the lake, temperature and other abiotic variables will be less noticeable than those of a puddle. Loss of water in the puddle, for example, due to evaporation, can lead to the puddle disappearing completely. The size of storage affects the relative stability of the puddle compared to the lake, with knock-on effects for the organisms living within it.

Figure 1.55 Deforestation: logging in Malaysian rainforest.

In addition to the loss of storage when trees are removed, the deforestation of tropical rainforests leads to a loss of nutrients. Rainforests have thin soils and although storage of biomass in trees is high, the nutrient storage in soils is low. Nutrients are locked up in decomposing plant matter on the surface of the soil and in rapidly growing plants. When the forest is disturbed, nutrients are quickly lost when the leaf layer and topsoil are washed away and when tree biomass is harvested.

Complex ecosystems, such as rainforests, have complex food webs that allow animals and plants many ways to respond to disturbance of the ecosystem and thus maintain stability. They also contain long-lived species and dormant seeds and seedlings that promote a steady-state equilibrium. Nutrients are locked-up in decomposing plant matter on the surface of the soil and in rapidly growing plants within the forest, so when the forest is disturbed, nutrients are quickly lost.

The concept of *systems* provides a useful tool for holistic analysis and gives insight into understanding the mechanics and purpose of human constructed systems and the function of natural ones. Systems theory uses conceptual models that provide essential analytical tools for understanding socio-ecological systems. Models allow analysis of tipping points that could lead to undesirable change and leverage points that could help to manage systems behaviour.

2.5 Zonation, succession and change in ecosystems
5.2 Agriculture and food

Engagement

- Build a bottle ecosystem (Topic 2, Section 2.1.20), aquarium, terrarium, compost heap or another school-based ecosystem and use it to construct a systems diagram. Compare variables of the system. For example, with and without one organism or with different levels of water/nutrients.
- Use your skills in system analysis to help solve a whole school problem. To do this, select one school problem, such as food waste. What inputs are there to this system and what outputs are there? How can the inputs be changed so that the outputs are also altered? For example, inputs to food waste may be the food selected by your school canteen and the way in which students select the food they eat. Outputs may be the quantity of food that is selected but that is not eaten, as well as the food that is consumed. Produce a poster that summarizes the information – there could be two diagrams, one representing the current situation and a second that shows how alterations to the inputs could alter the outputs, thereby addressing the whole school problem.
- Advocate to peers to educate them about the importance of tipping points. The information you produce (in the form of a presentation, poster, leaflet, podcast or webinar) should explain the concept of tipping points and then explain several potential tipping points that may affect Earth systems in the future (this topic, Section 1.2.12). How can these tipping points be avoided?

Exercise

Q6. **Outline** how the holistic approach to systems differs from the reductionist approach of conventional science.

Q7. **Compare and contrast** open and closed systems.

Q8. **Distinguish** between transfers and transformations within a system.

Q9. **Draw** a systems diagram showing the inputs, outputs and storages of a forest ecosystem.

Q10. **Describe** the Gaia hypothesis.

Q11. **Distinguish** between negative and positive feedback, using examples of each.

Q12. **Describe** how tipping points can result in regime shifts between alternative stable states. Use examples to support the explanation.

Q13. **Explain** why an ecosystem's capacity to survive change depends on diversity and resilience.

Q14. **Evaluate** the use of models in studying environmental systems.

Q15. **Explain** how interactions between components in systems can generate emergent properties.

1.3 Sustainability

Guiding Questions

What is sustainability and how can it be measured?

To what extent are challenges of sustainable development also ones of environmental justice?

1.3.1 Sustainability is a measure of the extent to which practices allow for the long-term viability of a system. It is generally used to refer to the responsible maintenance of socio-ecological systems such that there is no diminishment of conditions for future generations.
1.3.2 Sustainability is comprised of environmental, social and economic pillars.
1.3.3 Environmental sustainability is the use and management of natural resources that allows replacement of the resources, and recovery and regeneration of ecosystems.
1.3.4 Social sustainability focuses on creating the structures and systems, such as health, education, equity, community, that support human well-being.
1.3.5 Economic sustainability focuses on creating the economic structures and systems to support production and consumption of goods and services that will support human needs into the future.
1.3.6 Sustainable development meets the needs of the present without compromising the ability of future generations to meet their own needs. Sustainable development applies the concept of sustainability to our social and economic development.
1.3.7 Unsustainable use of natural resources can lead to ecosystem collapse.
1.3.8 Common indicators of economic development, such as gross domestic product (GDP), neglect the value of natural systems and may lead to unsustainable development.
1.3.9 Environmental justice refers to the right of all people to live in a pollution-free environment, and to have equitable access to natural resources, regardless of issues such as race, gender, socio-economic status, nationality.
1.3.10 Inequalities in income, race, gender and cultural identity within and between different societies lead to disparities in access to water, food and energy.
1.3.11 Sustainability and environmental justice can be applied at the individual to the global operating scale.
1.3.12 Sustainability indicators include quantitative measures of biodiversity, pollution, human population, climate change, material and carbon footprints, and others. These indicators can be applied on a range of scales, from local to global.
1.3.13 The concept of ecological footprints can be used to measure sustainability. If these footprints are greater than the area or resources available to the population, this indicates unsustainability.
1.3.14 The carbon footprint measures the amount of greenhouse gases (GHGs) produced, measured in carbon dioxide equivalents (in tonnes). The water footprint measures water use (in cubic metres per year).
1.3.15 Biocapacity is the capacity of a given biologically productive area to generate an ongoing supply of renewable resources and to absorb its resulting wastes.

1.3.16 Citizen science plays a role in monitoring Earth systems and whether resources are being used sustainably.
1.3.17 There are a range of frameworks and models that support our understanding of sustainability, each with uses and limitations.
1.3.18 The UN Sustainable Development Goals (SDGs) are a set of social and environmental goals and targets to guide action on sustainability and environmental justice.
1.3.19 The planetary boundaries model describes the nine processes and systems that have regulated the stability and resilience of the Earth system in the Holocene epoch. The model also identifies the limits of human disturbance to those systems and proposes that crossing those limits increases the risk of abrupt and irreversible changes to Earth systems.
1.3.20 The doughnut economics model is a framework for creating a regenerative and distributive economy in order to meet the needs of all people within the means of the planet.
1.3.21 The circular economy is a model that promotes decoupling economic activity from the consumption of finite resources. It has three principles: eliminating waste and pollution, circulating products and materials, and regenerating nature.

Sustainability is the use of natural resources in ways that do not reduce or degrade the resources, so that they are available for future generations. The concept of sustainability is central to an understanding of the nature of interactions between environmental systems and societies. Resource management issues are essentially issues of sustainability.

Sustainability is the use and management of resources that allows full natural replacement of the resources exploited and full recovery of the ecosystems affected by their extraction and use.

1.3.1 and 1.3.2 Sustainability

Sustainability means using global resources at a rate that allows natural regeneration and minimizes damage to the environment. If continued human well-being is dependent on the goods and services provided by certain forms of **natural capital** (Topic 7, Section 7.1.2), then long-term harvest (and pollution) rates should not exceed rates of capital renewal. For example, a system harvesting renewable resources at a rate that enables replacement by natural growth shows sustainability. Sustainability is living within the means of nature (i.e. on the 'interest' or sustainable income generated by natural capital) and ensuring resources are not degraded (i.e. natural capital is not used up) so that future generations can continue to use the resource. The concept can be applied throughout our everyday lives.

Deforestation can be used to illustrate the concept of sustainability and unsustainability: if the rate of forest removal is less than the annual growth of the forest (i.e. the **natural income**), then the forest removal is sustainable. If the rate of forest removal is greater than the annual growth of the forest, then the forest removal is unsustainable (see this topic, Section 1.3.7, for another example of the unsustainable use of natural resources).

When processing a natural resource to create income, sustainability needs to be applied at every level of the supply chain (Figure 1.56).

Sustainability can be encouraged though careful application of:

- ecological land use to maintain habitat quality and connectivity for all species
- sustainable material cycles (e.g. carbon, nitrogen and water cycles) to prevent the contamination of living systems
- social systems that contribute to a culture of sufficiency that eases the consumption pressures on natural capital.

All activity is embedded in a system and, in general, enhancing system resilience enhances sustainability (this topic, Section 1.2.16).

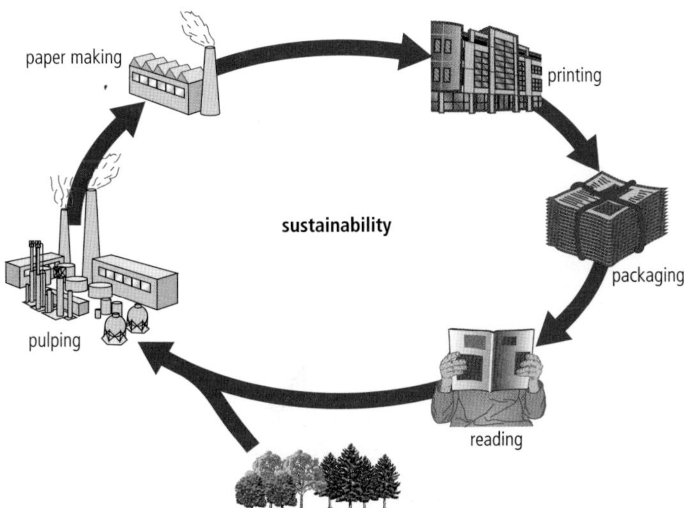

Figure 1.56 Sustainability applies to harvesting natural capital, to the generation of energy to process the product, and to how the product is packaged and marketed.

Humans often use resources beyond sustainable limits through over-population (unrealistic demand for limited resources), financial motives (exploitation of resources for short-term financial gain), or ignorance (lack of knowledge of the resource's sustainable level). For example, unsustainable practice regarding soils includes:

- overgrazing (trampling and feeding by livestock lead to loss of vegetation and exposure of the underlying soil)
- overcultivation (loss of soil fertility and structure leave topsoil vulnerable to erosion by wind and water).

Sustainability is a measure of the extent to which practices allow for the long-term viability of a system. It is generally used to refer to the responsible maintenance of socio-ecological systems such that there is no diminishment of conditions for future generations.

Local or global?

A global perspective for managing resources sustainably is desirable because many problems, such as global warming (Topic 6, Section 6.2.4) have a worldwide impact. Such a perspective allows for understanding the knock-on effects of environmental problems beyond national boundaries and helps governments to be more responsible. Ecosystems are affected by global processes, so sustainability needs to be understood as a global issue. An example of this is the atmospheric system regarding the effects on climate change. A global perspective also helps us to understand that our actions have an impact on others, which is useful for getting societies to think about impacts on different generations, as well as different countries. A worldview stresses the interrelationships between systems so knock-on effects are reduced. But because ecosystems exist on many scales, a more local perspective is sometimes appropriate. Human actions are often culturally specific (e.g. traditional farming methods) and so global solutions may not be locally applicable.

1.2 Systems

Often local methods have evolved to be more sustainable and appropriate for the local environment. It is also often the case that individual and small-scale community actions, such as local recycling schemes, can be very effective for managing resources sustainably. Sometimes a global approach is not appropriate because environmental problems are local in nature as, for example, point-source pollution.

Sustainability is comprised of environmental, social and economic domains

One of the most common diagrams used to represent sustainability is the overlapping circles model (Figure 1.57). In this model, the environment, society and the economy are shown as equal and independent, with sustainability at the point where they intersect. However, the model underestimates the complexity of the socio-ecological system and is referred to as 'weak' sustainability.

HL b Environmental economics

Figure 1.57 Sustainability: overlapping circles model.

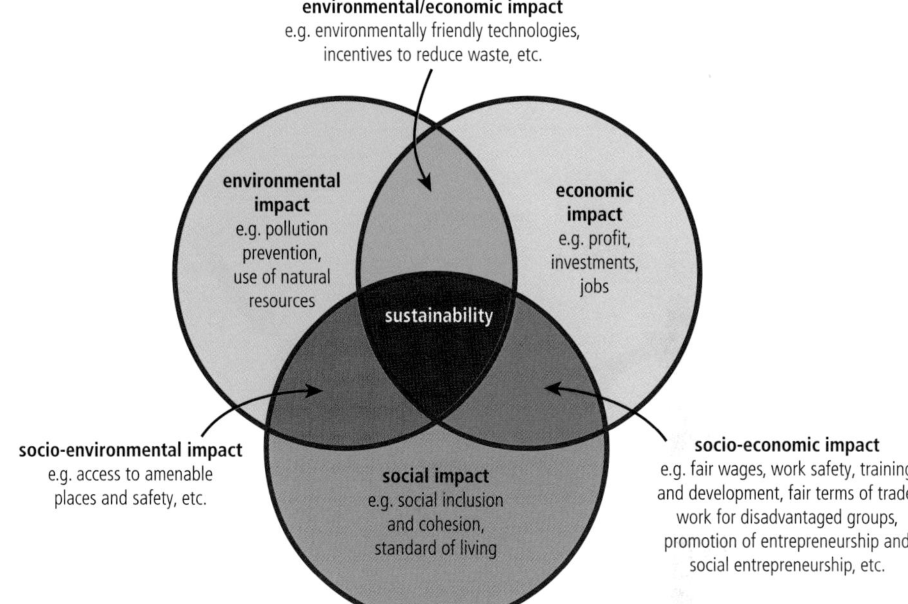

Diagrams show how environmental, social and economic sustainability interact. Strong sustainability models show the economy embedded in society and both society and economy embedded in the natural environment. Weak sustainability models only show an overlap in the three domains.

Figure 1.58 Sustainability: nested circle model.

A more accurate conceptualization is a model that shows the economy, society and the environment in systems nested in one another (Figure 1.58). This comes from the understanding that the economy is a subsystem of human society, which is in turn a subsystem of the environment or biosphere. The economy cannot satisfy its own needs for resources without considering the consequences for both society and the environment. The nested circle model recognizes that social and economic activity occurs within ecological limits. This is referred to as 'strong' sustainability. Therefore, the economy must adapt to the environment it finds itself in, both social and natural. There would not be an economy without society and no society without the biosphere. This model of sustainability emphasizes that no subsystem can overgrow the system it is part of. This concept of sustainability contrasts with the overlapping circles model, which was based on the principle that the social, ecological and economic spheres are equally important.

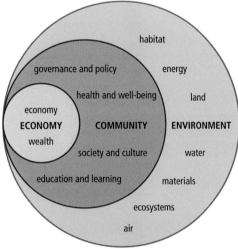

Definitions of *sustainability* begin with the idea that development should meet the needs of the present without compromising the ability of future generations to meet their needs. It refers to limiting the degree to which the current generation's activities create harmful environmental outcomes involving resource depletion or degradation that will negatively affect future generations. Sustainability has three integrated aspects: environmental, societal and economic.

1.3.3 Environmental sustainability

Environmental sustainability focuses on resource depletion, pollution and conserving biodiversity. Active regeneration of ecosystems is also considered a component of environmental sustainability.

Resource depletion

Resources from the Earth can be **renewable** or **non-renewable** (Topic 7, Section 7.1.6). There are different timescales in replacement of natural resources. Non-renewable resources, such as fossil fuels and rare earth metals (Figure 1.59) can only be replaced at a rate far slower than the rate at which they are being used. Non-renewable resources will eventually run out if they are not replaced. Using economic terms, these resources can be considered as equivalent to those forms of economic capital that cannot generate wealth or income without liquidation of the estate. In other words, the capital in the bank account is spent. Predictions about how long many of Earth's minerals and metals will last before they run out are usually basic. They may not consider any increase in demand due to new technologies and they may assume that production equals consumption. Accurate estimates of global reserves and precise figures for consumption are needed for more exact predictions. However, key non-renewable natural resources are limited and there is a need to minimize waste, recycle, reuse and, where possible, replace rare elements with more abundant ones.

HL a Environmental law
HL b Environmental economics

Figure 1.59 A Norwegian oil rig. Oil is a non-renewable resource, the use of which has been a key feature of the 20th century and continues to be so into the 21st century.

3.1 Biodiversity and evolution
3.2 Human impact on biodiversity
4.2 Water access, use and security
4.4 Water pollution
7.2 Energy resources, use and management
7.3 Solid waste
8.2 Urban systems and urban planning
8.3 Urban air pollution

Renewable resources, in contrast, can be replenished at a rate that is equal to or greater than the rate at which they are used (Figure 1.60). This may be through natural growth or reproduction, such as food, crops or timber, or through other repeated processes, such as freshwater production. Sustainable use of these renewable resources depends on the rate at which they are extracted and, in terms of logging, the type of forest the wood is taken from.

How can we distinguish between knowledge, belief and opinion?

The idea of environmental sustainability suggests that people should avoid destroying resources today so as not to penalize future generations.
Is it possible to have knowledge of the future? How is an understanding of future sustainability one of knowledge, rather than belief or opinion?

Figure 1.60 Renewable natural resources include timber.

Environmental sustainability depends on the increasing use of renewable, rather than non-renewable, resources. Resource depletion occurs when extraction of natural resources exceeds the rate at which they can be replaced.

Pollution is the addition of a substance or an agent to an environment by human activity, at a rate greater than that at which it can be rendered harmless by the environment and which has an appreciable effect on the organisms within it.

Pollution

Pollution is the contamination of the Earth and atmosphere to such an extent that normal environmental processes are adversely affected. Polluted elements are disagreeable, toxic and harmful.

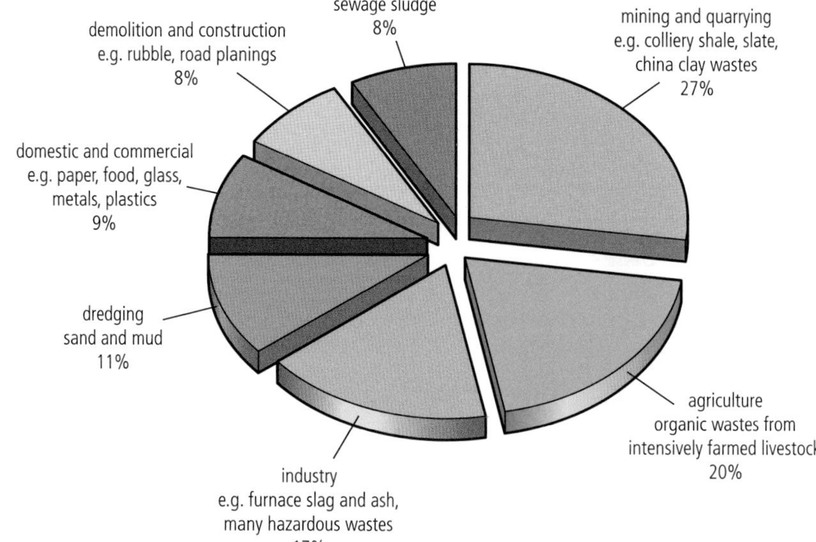

Figure 1.61 The major sources of pollution include the combustion of fossil fuels, domestic and industrial waste, manufacturing and agricultural systems.

Most industrial nations adopt a Cornucopian approach to the environment. This means that they believe that people can find a solution to the problems created by human use or misuse of the environment, such as those caused by pollution, through a technocentric *perspective*.

TOK

Does all knowledge impose ethical obligations on those who know it?

Many rich countries have knowingly polluted the environment, in return for the economic benefits they gain. An example of this is energy production. Much of the cost of this pollution is borne by other countries – is this moral?

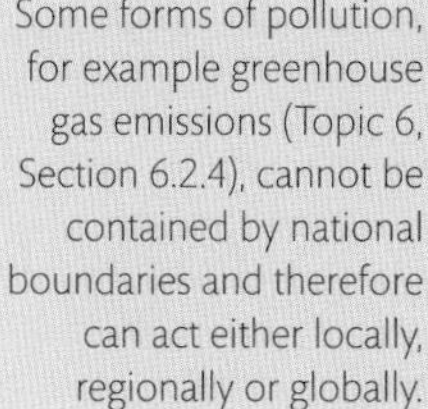

Some forms of pollution, for example greenhouse gas emissions (Topic 6, Section 6.2.4), cannot be contained by national boundaries and therefore can act either locally, regionally or globally.

Biodiversity refers to the variety of life on Earth. Conservation biologists first used the word to highlight the threat to species and ecosystems and it is now widely used in international agreements concerning the sustainable use and protection of natural resources.

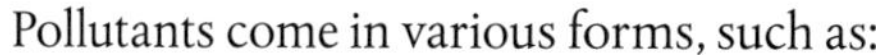

Pollutants come in various forms, such as:

- organic or **inorganic** substances, such as pesticides and plastics
- light, sound or heat energy
- those derived from a wide range of human activities including the combustion of fossil fuels (Figure 1.61).

It is difficult to define the levels that constitute pollution. Much depends on the nature of the environment. For example, decomposition is much slower in cold environments – so oil slicks pose a greater threat in Arctic areas than they do in tropical ones. Similarly, levels of air quality that do not threaten healthy adults may affect young children, the elderly or people with lung diseases such as asthma.

Pollution costs

The costs of pollution are widespread and difficult to quantify. They include death, decreased levels of health, declining water resources, reduced soil quality and poor air quality. It is vital to control and manage pollution. To be effective, pollution treatment must be applied at the source. However, unless point sources can be targeted, this may be impossible. There is no point treating symptoms if the cause is not tackled. For example, treatment of acidified lakes with lime will not be effective if the emission of acidic materials continues.

Conserving biodiversity

Biodiversity refers to the variety of life on Earth (Topic 3, Section 3.1.1, page 231). The term can be used to evaluate both the complexity of an area and its health.

Active regeneration of ecosystems is a component of environmental sustainability (Topic 3, Section 3.3.8). Re-establishing biodiversity through management, such as rewilding schemes (Topic 3, Sections 3.3.7 and 3.3.11), ensures the ongoing survival of natural systems.

1.3.4 Social sustainability

HL c Environmental ethics

Social sustainability focuses on the survival of societies and their cultures and may include consideration of the continued use of language, belief or spiritual practices in a society.

Example – The Dongria Kondh of India

In 2003, the mining company Vedanta Resources applied to dig an open pit containing the aluminium ore bauxite on Niyamgiri Mountain in Orissa, India, to provide material for the aluminium refinery at Lanjigarh, Odisha. The mountain is home to the Dongria Kondh, who farm the hill slopes, carry out shifting cultivation to grow crops in the forest (Topic 5, Section 5.2.6) and collect wild fruit and leaves to sell. There are over 8000 members of the tribe, living in villages scattered throughout the area. The mine would destroy forests on which the Dongria Kondh people depend and would seriously affect the lives of thousands of other Kondh tribal people living in the area. In 2008, India's Supreme Court gave permission for the mine to be built. This led to local protests against the mine (Figure 1.62).

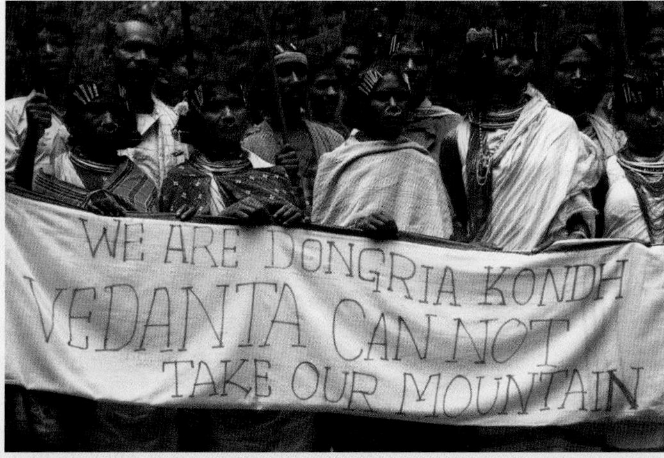

Figure 1.62 Dongria Kondh protest against Vedanta Resources, Niyamgiri, India.

In late August 2010, India's Environment Minister Jairam Ramesh blocked plans to develop the mine. Mr Ramesh said Vedanta had shown a 'shocking and blatant disregard for the rights of the tribal groups'. The minister also questioned the legality of the massive refinery Vedanta has already built below the hills. This decision should ensure the survival of the Dongria Kondh and their ancestral homeland.

Activity

The Dongria Kondh example leads to many issues to discuss within your class:

1. To the Dongria Kondh, Niyam Dongar hill is their home and seat of their god, Niyam Raja. To Vedanta it is just a deposit of bauxite worth $2 billion. How does this case study highlight problems with the way that humanity values its natural resources?
2. In your view, which perspective played the most important role in leading to the rejection of Vedanta's mine – the local government, the national government, protests organized by the Indigenous people, or campaigns organized by international non-governmental organizations (NGOs)?

Read more about the Dongria Kondh, using the Survival International website as a starting point.

The case of the Dongria Kondh is one of many examples of traditional ways of life being threatened by outside organizations seeking land or resources.

Find another example using research from the internet and books. Write a report about the threats faced by the local people and the way in which local and international campaigns are highlighting the issues and trying to resolve the problems.

In terms of resource use to meet human needs, there is no economic sustainability without environmental sustainability.

HL b Environmental economics

Ultimately, the choices people make depend on their *perspectives*. People with a technocentric worldview see the technological possibilities as central to solving environmental problems. An ecocentric worldview leads to greater caution and a drive to use Earth's natural resources in a sustainable way, rather than rely on technology to solve the problems.

1.3.5 Economic sustainability

Economic sustainability refers to the ability of the present generation to meet its needs without compromising the ability of future generations to meet their own needs. It refers to limiting the damage to the environment caused by the economic activity of the current generation, such as resource depletion or degradation that will negatively affect future generations.

Sometimes governments must intervene with the workings of markets. Markets are generally considered the most efficient mechanism to use to organize economic activity, although they may fail to achieve societal goals, such as **equity**, economic well-being or sustainability. Failure to achieve such goals can lead to government intervention. There is often disagreement among economists and policymakers on the need for, and extent of, government intervention and there is some debate about the merits of intervention versus the free market.

Current economic models, such as gross domestic product (this topic, Section 1.3.8), were not developed with sustainability in mind. To ensure **sustainable development** (this topic, Section 1.3.6), economic models need to be devised which consider the replenishment of natural resources and factors that impact the environment in a negative way, such as pollution and habitat loss. Sustainability needs to be a central component of economic models if the equilibrium of Earth systems is to be maintained into the future (this topic, doughnut economics, Section 1.3.20 and the circular economy, Section 1.3.21).

Sustainable development is a framework guiding further development of human civilization while maintaining economic stability, social equity and ecological integrity.

The Brundtland report in 1987 introduced the social and economic aspects of sustainability to sustainable development.

1.3.6 Sustainable development

Sustainable development means 'meeting the needs of the present without compromising the ability of future generations to meet their own needs'. Sustainable development consists of three pillars: economic development, social development and environmental protection (Figure 1.63). Sustainable development was first clearly defined in 1987 in the Brundtland Report, *Our Common Future*, produced by the UN World Commission on Environment and Development (this topic, Section 1.1.10, page 22).

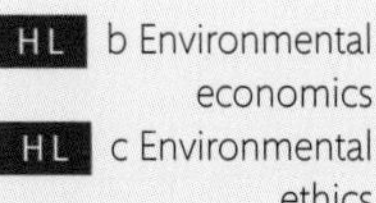

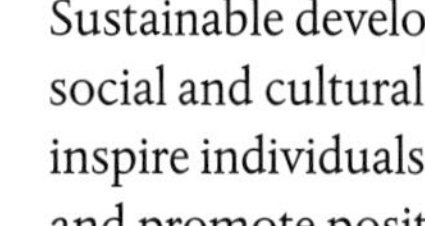

HL b Environmental economics

HL c Environmental ethics

Sustainable development focuses on the quality of environmental, economic and social and cultural development. The concept encompasses ideas and values that inspire individuals and organizations to become better stewards of the environment and promote positive economic growth and social objectives.

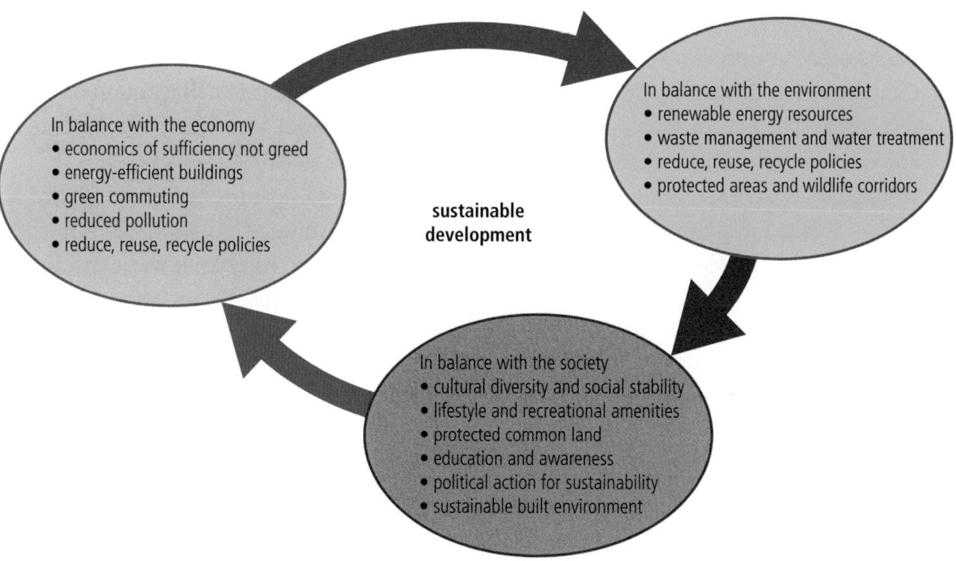

Figure 1.63 Sustainable development focuses on the quality of environmental, economic and social and cultural development. The concept encompasses ideas and values that inspire individuals and organizations to become better stewards of the environment and promote positive economic growth and social objectives.

1.3.7 Unsustainable use of natural resources

Overexploitation of the environment due to human activities can lead to ecosystem collapse.

World fish stocks have rapidly declined and some species have become extinct. Nearly 70% of the world's stocks need management. Populations of cod have been particularly affected by overfishing in the North Atlantic (this topic, Section 1.3.8). Cod stocks in the North Sea are less than 10% of the 1970 levels. Fishing boats from the EU now regularly fish in other parts of the world such as Africa and South America, to make up for the shortage of fish in EU waters. More than half the fish consumed in Europe is now imported.

If resource use is to be *sustainable*, natural resources should be replenished at or above the rate at which they are extracted. The declining global marine catch over the last few years, together with the increased percentage of over-exploited fish stocks and the decreased proportion of non-fully exploited species, suggests that the state of world marine fisheries is worsening and has had a negative impact on fishery production. Over-exploitation and unsustainable use of resources not only causes negative ecological consequences but also reduces fish production, which further leads to negative social and economic consequences.

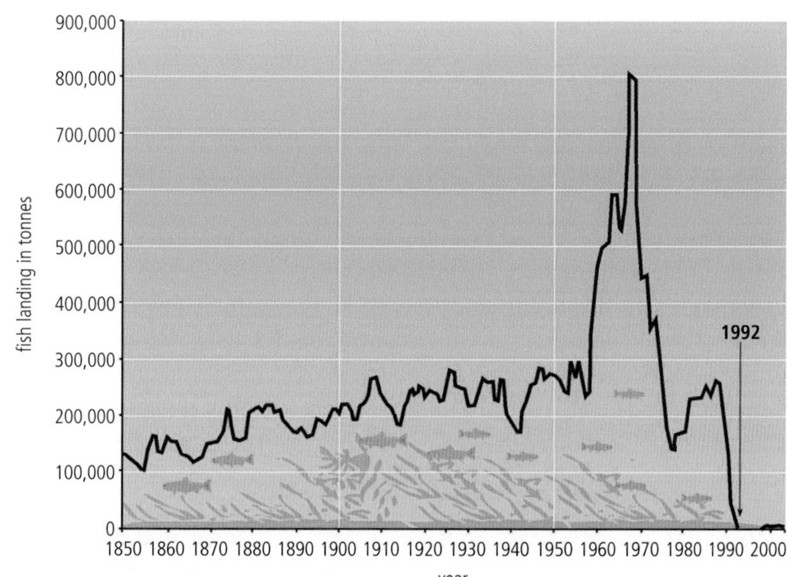

Figure 1.64 The collapse of the Newfoundland cod fisheries. The numbers of cod caught by Canadian firms rapidly increased in the 1960s, crashed in the 1970s, recovered slightly in the 1980s, and crashed to close to zero in the early 1990s.

Once a fish stock has been overfished, it is very difficult for it to recover. The Grand Banks off Newfoundland (a series of underwater plateaus off the north-east coast of Canada) were once the world's richest fishery. Overfishing and mismanagement of fish stocks in the second half of the 20th century led to a rapid decline in cod numbers and ultimately to their collapse (Figure 1.64). The collapse of fish stocks and the fishing industry led to serious economic problems and significant social issues for the people of Newfoundland, who had come to rely on cod fishing as a major part of their economy. In 1992, the area had to be closed to allow stocks to recover. It was expected to be closed for three years but fish populations, especially cod, have not yet recovered and the area is still closed. However, the decline in cod population had led to collapse of the ecosystem, with the cod's niche in the ecosystem taken over by other species, such as shrimp and langoustines.

1.2 Systems
4.3 Aquatic food production systems

HL a Environmental law
HL b Environmental economics

Activity

Find out about another example of ecosystem collapse caused by the unsustainable use of natural resources. Produce a presentation to show to the rest of your class. What were the causes of the collapse and what solutions were used to reverse the decline? Did the solutions work?

1.3.8 Unsustainable development

Gross domestic product (GDP) is a measure of national output. It was a concept developed in the 1930s that rapidly became the overriding goal of policymaking within national governments. GDP is the total money value of all final goods and services produced in an economy over a given period, usually one year. Other terms relating to GDP include:

- real GDP, which is the total money value of all final goods and services produced in an economy in a given period, usually one year, adjusted for inflation
- real GDP per person (per capita), which is given as the sum of the real GDP divided by the population of the country.

GDP is a measure of the monetary value of final goods and services produced and sold by a country over a given period. Focusing on GDP as a measure of economic progress may cause unsustainable development.

Economic growth, as currently measured, is the growth of the real value of output in an economy over time and is usually measured as growth in real GDP.

Today, the governments of the richest countries on Earth think that the solutions to economic problems lie in more growth. In its most developed stages, a country's GDP allows its citizens to buy any consumer goods they want. Growth in GDP has led to the era of mass consumption, where consumption must continue to follow an upward trajectory to allow continued growth in GDP. Economies have come to expect, demand and depend upon continued growth. Societies are politically, socially and financially dependent on continued growth in GDP. The current financial system is designed to pursue the highest rate of monetary return, for example by growing market share, growing sales and growing profits. Politically, growing GDP appeals to politicians because they do not want to put up taxes, and growth in the economy is an attractive alternative for the electorate. Psychologically and socially, societies have been encouraged to believe that consumerism is transformative and leads to happiness by acting as a form of 'retail therapy' that improves the buyer's mood or how they feel about themselves. Global GDP is now 10 times bigger than it was in 1950, leading to prosperity for many people in many countries. However, this growth in GDP has been very divisive. An increase in wealth has occurred for only a small fraction of the global population, with returns not distributed evenly. The global economy has also become very degenerative (this topic, Section 1.3.20, page 72), meaning that it has destabilized planetary equilibrium, through overexploitation of limited resources, pollution and biodiversity loss (this topic, Section 1.3.19, page 68).

Another measure of gross domestic product, per capita GDP (i.e. per person or per head of the population), takes inequalities of income distribution into account. Higher levels of inequality can reduce GDP per capita.

Read more about green GDP by searching the System of Environmental Economic Accounting (SEEA) website.

The goal of societies in the 21st century should be to meet the needs of all people within the means of planet Earth, so that humans and the rest of nature can thrive. A new model of economic, environmental and social sustainability is needed (this topic, doughnut economics, Section 1.3.20 and the circular economy, Section 1.3.21). Green GDP measures environmental costs and subtracts these from GDP. Green GDP is also known as environmentally adjusted domestic product and quantifies the costs of climate change, biodiversity loss, carbon emissions and other environmental factors.

1.3.9 Environmental justice

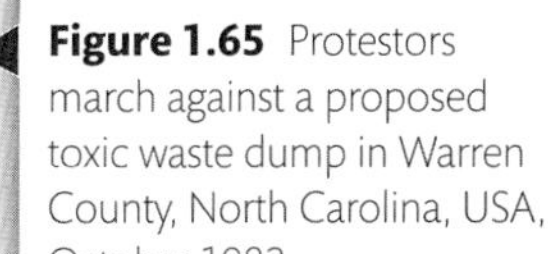

HL b Environmental economics

People in all societies should have an equal right to natural resources and freedom from pollution and other causes of environmental harm, although this is often not the case. Inequalities in wealth, race, gender and indigeneity within and between different societies lead to disparities in access to water, food and energy (Figure 1.65).

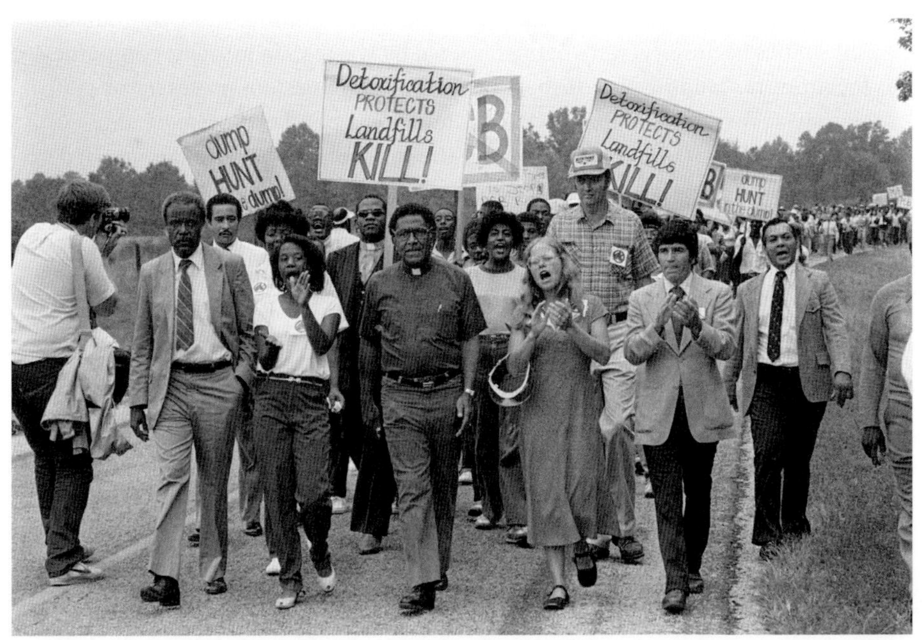

Figure 1.65 Protestors march against a proposed toxic waste dump in Warren County, North Carolina, USA, October 1982.

Environmental justice means the fair treatment and meaningful involvement of all people with respect to the development, implementation and enforcement of environmental laws, regulations and policies. Considerations include:

- it is the rights of all people to live in an unpolluted environment and have equal access to natural resources
- it should result in the development, implementation and enforcement of environmental policies and laws to ensure that no group or community is made to bear a disproportionate share of the harmful effects of pollution or environmental hazards from a lack of economic or political influence
- any model of sustainable development failing to incorporate equity is not a sustainable model
- any promotion of environmental justice that does not take account of the principles of sustainability will not be able to achieve its objectives on a large scale.

The aim of environmental justice is equitable access to resources for all societies. Justice can be achieved both voluntarily and by national or international legislation. Environmental justice should be a right both for those alive today and for future generations.

Environmental justice means that communities affected by, for example, pollution or site contamination should be able to participate as equal stakeholders in environmental regulation processes.

HL a Environmental law

HL c Environmental ethics

Environmental justice aims to address the various impacts of industrial pollution and ecological damage on minority and low-income communities. To address issues of inequity, these communities need to be empowered to resist any unwanted development or be able to negotiate some form of compensation for the real or potential harm a development may cause.

Search for and read the following article on the PNAS website: 'Inequity in consumption of goods and services adds to racial-ethnic disparities in air pollution exposure'.

Example – Racial-ethnic disparities in air pollution exposure in Houston, Texas, USA

In 1979, residents in Houston, Texas were resisting the situating of a landfill in their neighbourhood. The residents felt that their community, and other Black communities in the city, were being targeted by waste management companies as locations for landfill sites. Robert Bullard was an assistant professor of sociology at Texas Southern University and the husband of attorney Linda McKeever Bullard who was representing the residents. Robert Bullard carried out a demographic study on the location of waste management sites in Houston and found that, between the 1920s and 1978, more than 80% of the city's household landfills and incinerators were in mostly Black neighbourhoods, even though Black residents made up only 25% of Houston's population. A lawsuit was subsequently brought against the waste management company. Although the residents lost the lawsuit and the landfill was still built in their area, this case formed a foundation for the environmental justice movement, which demands that all people have equal protection from environmental laws. Bullard eventually became Professor of Urban Planning and Environmental Policy at Texas Southern University and is now a leading figure in the environmental justice movement (this topic, Section 1.1.10, page 18).

1.1 Perspectives
3.3 Conservation and regeneration
4.2 Water access, use and security
4.3 Aquatic food production systems
5.2 Agriculture and food
6.3 Climate change – mitigation and adaptation
7.2 Energy resources, use and management
8.2 Urban systems and urban planning

In 1919, a report published by Proceedings of the National Academy of Sciences (PNAS) concluded that 'pollution inequity is driven by differences among racial-ethnic groups in both exposure and the consumption that leads to the exposure.' The study found that members of the community who were white experienced 17% less pollution caused by their consumption of goods and services, whereas Black people and Hispanics experienced 56% and 63%, respectively, more pollution than their consumption would generate. The environmental justice movement continues to campaign against these types of unjust, unfair and illegal land-use policies, which affect communities of low wealth and people of colour.

Activity

1. Discuss the Athabasca tar sands project with your class. Do the environmental costs outweigh the financial benefits, or vice versa?
2. What other examples of environmental injustice are there? Research one local and one global example and produce a summary poster on each. Examples could include the Deepwater Horizon oil spill, Gulf of Mexico (2010); Union Carbide Gas Release in Bhopal, India (1984); Maasai land rights in Kenya and Tanzania; plastic waste disposal by developed to developing countries.

1.1 Perspectives
3.3 Conservation and regeneration
4.2 Water access, use and security
4.3 Aquatic food production systems
5.2 Agriculture and food
6.3 Climate change – mitigation and adaptation
7.2 Energy resources, use and management
8.2 Urban systems and urban planning

1.3.10 Inequalities lead to disparities in access to water, food and energy

Globally, there are inequalities in access to, and consumption of, clean freshwater, adequate food supplies and reliable energy. An example of such inequality is the inability to afford electricity supply or the privatization of water sources. The Earth has sufficient quantities of food, fresh water and energy resources for everyone on our planet but these resources are not evenly distributed or shared. In general, people in developed countries consume higher levels of resources than people in developing countries.

HL c Environmental ethics

Reasons for varying consumption of food, water and energy include:

1. **Access**: some countries have easy access to more natural resources than others.
2. **Quantity**: there is inequality in the quantity of resources available to different countries. Some countries have abundant resources and others do not.
3. **Wealth**: the greater the wealth of a country the more options it has. If a wealthy country does not have direct access to, or sufficient quantities of, a resource then it can import or develop technological solutions, whereas less wealthy countries may not have these options.
4. **Technology and infrastructure**: the ability of a country to develop technological solutions and to deliver food, water and energy throughout its population will affect direct access to key resources.

Issues of food security are covered in Topic 5.2 and issues of water security are covered in Topic 4.2.

Issues concerning food inequality:

- over 900 million people suffer from hunger
- two billion more face serious health risks from undernourishment
- 1.5 billion people overeat
- over one-third of all food is lost or wasted
- demand for food and fibre is projected to increase by 70% by 2050
- feeding over nine billion people by 2050 is possible but there is a cost to the environment in terms of water withdrawals and land resources.

Activity

Figure 1.66 Access to water: A cartoon for World Water Day (22 March).

The cartoon in Figure 1.66 was produced for World Water Day, 22 March, in 2021.

- What is the message of the cartoon?
- What does the cartoon say about the issue of water inequality?
- How do inequalities lead to disparities in access to water?

Produce your own illustration, mind map or video about water inequality to show the issues to others in your community.

> Saving water by reducing food waste, increasing productivity, plant breeding and wastewater recycling are critical to everyone. Over 25% of all the water we use worldwide is taken to grow over one billion tonnes of food that nobody eats.
>
> Throughout the world, 2.6 billion small-scale producers till the land, raise animals and fish. They are the main providers of food in the developing world. Agriculture holds the key to sustainable water use.

As with water and food, there are significant differences in energy consumption between countries, with the wealthiest 10% of the world's population consuming about 20 times more energy than the poorest 10%. Energy security for a country means access to affordable and reliable sources of energy.

For more about energy security, see Topic 7, Section 7.2.7.

1.3.11 Sustainability and environmental justice

Sustainability and environmental justice issues can be applied at different operating scales. Different operating scales include:

- an individual with individual decisions on how to live and work
- a business
- a community such as religious, cultural, political or Indigenous
- a city
- a country with different policies, laws and socio-economic systems
- globally, for example UN Sustainable Development Goals.

Challenge yourself

Consider how sustainability and environmental justice can be applied at a range of levels from you as an individual, through to the global scale such as the UN Sustainable Development Goals. Create a chart showing how sustainability and environmental justice can be applied at each scale: individual, community, city, country and global.

- What are the similarities that apply to each level?
- How do the ways these issues are addressed vary between levels? What are the distinctions between each level?
- How does the implementation of sustainability and environmental justice at the global scale depend on individuals and societies at the local scale?

Once you have created your chart, draw a Venn diagram showing the distinctions and overlaps between each level, to summarize the information you have developed.

1.1 Perspectives

HL a Environmental law
HL b Environmental economics
HL c Environmental ethics

1.3.12 Sustainability indicators

There are a variety of different environmental indicators that can be used to assess sustainability. Sustainability indicators include quantitative measures of biodiversity, pollution, human population, climate change, material and carbon footprints and others. These indicators can be applied on a range of scales, from local to global.

- Ecological footprints (this topic, Section 1.3.13), along with carbon and water footprints (this topic, Section 1.3.14), can be used to assess whether individuals or societies are acting in a sustainable way.
- Some species are sensitive to pollutants or are adapted to polluted waters, so can be used as indicator species (Topic 4, Section 4.4.13 and Topic 8, Section 8.3.2). A biotic index, such as the Trent Biotic Index (Topic 4, Section 4.4.14), can provide an indirect measure of water quality based on the tolerance to pollution, relative abundance and diversity of species in the community.
- Quantitative measures of biodiversity, known as diversity indices, can be used to establish the effects of human activity on natural communities. One such index is Simpson's reciprocal index, which is used to provide a quantitative measure of species diversity, allowing different ecosystems to be compared, and change in a specific ecosystem over time to be monitored (Topic 3, Sections 3.1.7–3.1.8).
- Changes in human populations can be explored by correlating a socio-economic indicator with a demographic factor (Topic 8, Sections 8.1.1–8.1.3).

Activity

The AtKisson sustainability compass is a tool that can be used to teach and promote sustainability and sustainable development in a clear and simple way.

The compass takes the four points of the compass (North (N), East (E), South (S), West (W)) and renames them Nature (N), Economy (E), Society (S) and Well-being (W). The compass provides a unifying symbol for sustainability and sustainable development. It also encourages organizations to manage sustainability initiatives, develop sustainability indicators and perform sustainability assessments.

3.3 Conservation and regeneration
6.3 Climate change – mitigation and adaptation
8.2 Urban systems and urban planning

Visit this website to read more about the Sustainability Compass.

This YouTube video explains the Sustainability Compass and how it can be used.

4.2 Water access, use and security
6.3 Climate change – mitigation and adaptation
8.2 Urban systems and urban planning

HL b Environmental economics

1.3.13 Ecological footprints

An **ecological footprint (EF)** focuses on a given population and its current rate of resource consumption and estimates the area of environment necessary to sustainably support that population. How great this area is, compared to the area available to the population, gives an indication of whether the population is living sustainably. If the EF is greater than the area available to the population, the population is living unsustainably.

An **ecological footprint** (**EF**) is the area of land and water required to sustainably provide all resources at the rate of consumption and assimilate all wastes at the rate of production by a given population.

SKILLS

Use footprint calculators to establish your own ecological footprint

There are many websites available to help you calculate your EF.

Use the online WWF Footprint Calculator to calculate your ecological footprint.

The concept of ecological footprint gives you a sense of your own impact on the planet.

- How many planets would we need if everyone lived the same lifestyle as you?
- What issues are considered when calculating EF?
- What can you do to reduce your EF, or that of your school or college, based on the information you are given?

You need to be able to use footprint calculators to establish your own footprint. Comparative data on footprints can be presented graphically, using a spreadsheet and graph plotting software.

1.3.14 Carbon and water footprints

As well as the ecological footprint, specific indicators for carbon and water can be calculated.

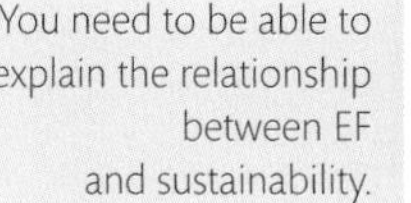

You need to be able to explain the relationship between EF and sustainability.

Carbon footprint

Whereas an ecological footprint is a general measure of an individual's or group's impact on the planet, a **carbon footprint** relates specifically to the quantity of greenhouse gases produced by human activities. Greenhouse gases (GHG) heat the planet, with increasing quantities warming the planet still further (Topic 6, Section 6.2.4). An increase in GHGs provides a key measurement of humanity's impact on the planet, specifically relating to climate change. The measure is known as the 'carbon footprint' because CO_2 is a significant contributor to global warming. However the measure also includes other greenhouse gases, including methane (CH_4, which also contains carbon), CFCs and HFCs (Topic 6, Section 6.4.12) and nitrous oxide (N_2O). The carbon footprint measures the amount of greenhouse gases produced and is measured in CO_2 equivalents (in tonnes).

4.2 Water access, use and security
6.2 Climate change – causes and impacts

Activity

Work out your own carbon footprint using a carbon footprint calculator such as the one on the Carbon Footprint website.

- How large is your footprint compared to others in your class?
- Why do some people have larger carbon footprints than others?
- What are realistic and effective ways of reducing your carbon footprint?
- What is meant by the phrase 'carbon offset' and do you think this is an effective way of lowering a carbon footprint?

A standard unit for measuring carbon footprints is carbon dioxide equivalent, or 'CO_2e'. Burning fossil fuels releases mainly CO_2, but other greenhouse gases are also emitted such as CH_4 and nitrous oxide (N_2O). This unit allows a single number to be used rather than a carbon footprint consisting of lots of different greenhouse gases. It measures the impact of each different greenhouse gas in terms of the amount of CO_2 that would create the same amount of warming.

There are many ways of reducing a carbon footprint (Figures 1.67 and 1.68).

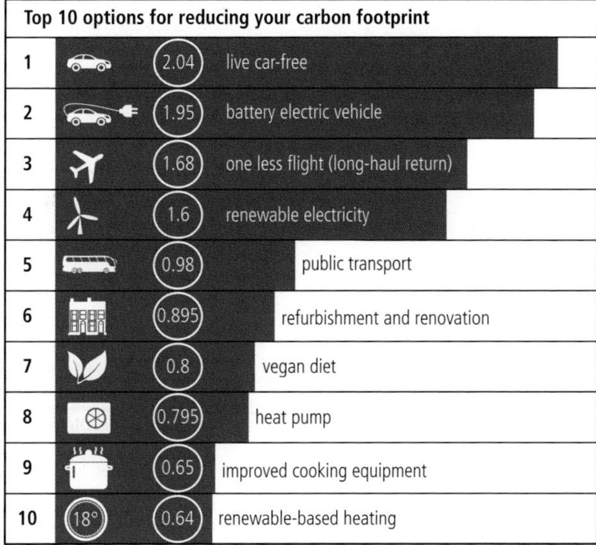

Figure 1.67 Options for reducing a carbon footprint. Data show average reduction per person per year in tonnes of carbon dioxide equivalents (CO_2e).

Do not confuse nitrous oxide (N_2O) with nitrogen oxides (NOx). Nitrous oxide is a 'direct' greenhouse gas produced during combustion. NOx are 'indirect' greenhouse gases that are involved in urban air pollution (Topic 8, Section 8.3.1).

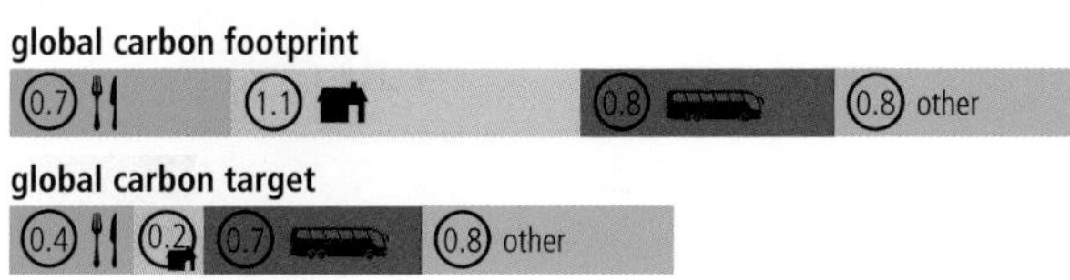

Figure 1.68 Breakdown of global carbon footprint by sector, showing annual consumption per person globally, in tonnes of carbon dioxide equivalents (CO_2e). The top diagram shows current data. The lower diagram shows the target for the global carbon footprint. Blue-green = food, yellow = home, red = transport, green = other sources. Data includes direct and indirect emissions, such as those from global supply chains.

Water footprint

Water is an important molecule for the functioning of organisms and ecosystems. Water forms a large proportion of living organisms, with between 65% and 95% of the mass of most plants and animals consisting of water. Approximately 71% of the Earth's surface is water, with 97% found in oceans and only 3% as freshwater. Water is a key component of photosynthesis (Topic 2, Sections 2.2.3–2.2.7, page 130), the process by which plants produce sugars which form the basis of food chains (Topic 2, Sections 2.2.10 and 2.2.11). Because so little of the Earth's water is found as freshwater, which is the form in which organisms need to obtain this vital ingredient of life, water shortage is a significant issue. Assessment of the use of water by humans is therefore another important measure of sustainability.

The **water footprint** measures water use in cubic metres per year. It measures the volume of water used to produce goods and services. The water footprint can indicate how much water is being consumed by an individual, company or country.

Activity

Read more about the water footprint at the website of the Water Footprint Network.

Use the 'Extended Water Footprint Calculator' on the website to calculate your water footprint.

- What lifestyle choices increase the footprint?
- What aspects of the footprint are associated with the level of development in your country?
- Are there realistic ways in which you can reduce your water footprint?
- Why is it important to limit a water footprint to a sustainable level?
- How can the concept of water footprint be used to promote sustainable, fair and efficient use of freshwater?

Produce a poster summarizing your findings, to educate other people in your school or college about the water footprint and its application.

Activity

Figure 1.69 shows the volume of water needed to produce various food products. Analyse the data carefully, then answer the questions below.

Figure 1.69 Water footprint of different food and drink products.

Measurements for food products are: litres of water to produce 500 g of product; tea and coffee: litres of water for one 750 ml pot; milk: litres of water to produce one litre of milk

WATER footprint

one drop = 50 l of water

650 Barley

650 Wheat

1400 Sorghum

2500 Millet

650 Toast

750 Cane Sugar

90 Tea

840 Coffee

2500 Burger

4650 Beef

1000 Milk

2500 Cheese

1. Which products have the highest levels of water usage?
2. Why do some products require a much larger volume of water than others?
3. How could this knowledge be used to reduce the water footprint of an individual or society?
4. How realistic is it to expect an individual or society to reduce their water footprint by changing food and drink consumption? What are the strengths and limitations of this approach?

1.3.15 Biocapacity

2.2 Energy and biomass in ecosystems
2.5 Zonation, succession and change in ecosystems
8.2 Urban systems and urban planning

Biocapacity is the capacity of a given biologically productive area to generate an on-going supply of renewable resources and to absorb its resulting wastes. Unsustainability occurs if the area's ecological footprint exceeds its biocapacity (see Figure 1.70).

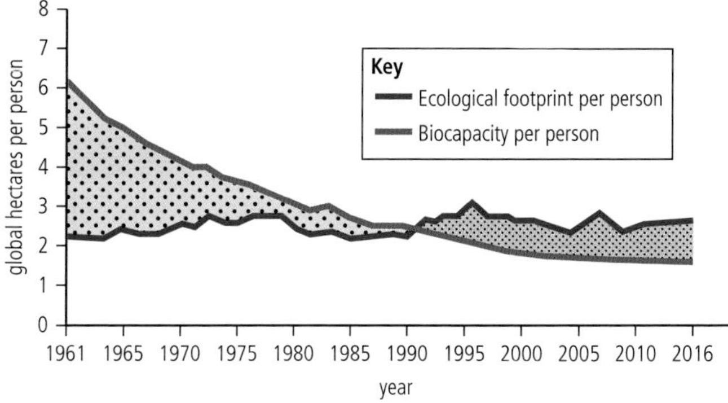

Figure 1.70 Ecological footprint and biocapacity per person in Costa Rica (1961–2016).

Figure 1.70 shows how sustainability in Costa Rica changed between 1961 and 2016. The EF must be lower than biocapacity to be sustainable. If the EF is above biocapacity, it is not sustainable. Overall sustainability declined over time as EF increased and biocapacity declined. Until around 1990/1991, Costa Rica was sustainable as its EF was lower than its biocapacity. After 1990/1991, the EF was greater than biocapacity and therefore Costa Rica was no longer sustainable.

1.3.16 Citizen science

Citizen science is the involvement of the public in scientific research (Figure 1.71). Citizen science plays a role in the larger picture of scientific research on environmental systems and includes monitoring Earth systems and whether resources are being used sustainably. Information gathered is relevant to local problems and can be used in research on global issues such as climate change.

Scientific research, especially that relating to study of the environment, involves the gathering of large quantities of complex data. To understand an ecosystem, and therefore be able to comprehend how human actions are impacting it, all aspects of the environment must be studied, both biotic or living factors and abiotic or non-living factors such as water, temperature and other climate measurements. The higher the number of people involved with gathering this data the better, so this is where citizen science plays an important role. Interactions between citizens and scientists, in the quest for large quantities of accurate environmental data, are shown in Figure 1.71.

Information for citizen science projects can be gathered through crowdsourcing. Crowdsourcing involves obtaining information from a large group of people who submit their data via the internet and/or social media.

Figure 1.71 Bidirectional communication between the citizens and scientists for a citizen science project. Even though the citizens are responsible for providing data to the scientists, the rest of the research phases must be based on the interaction between both groups.

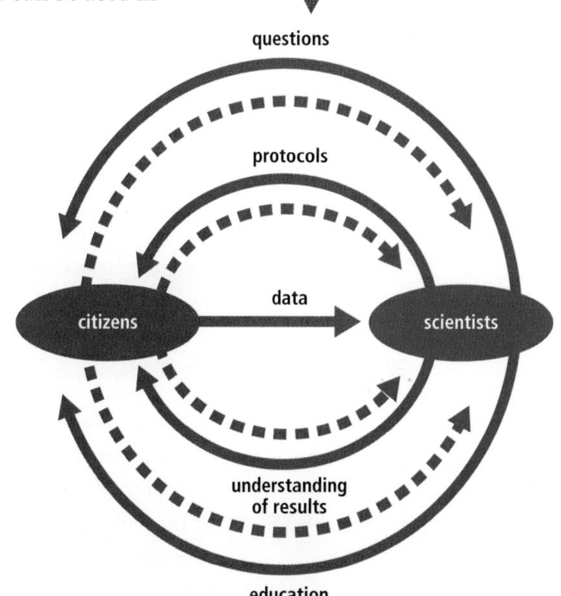

Citizen science and other open-source data gathering projects are applicable to many parts of the ESS course.

2.1 Individuals, populations, communities, and ecosystems
3.1 Biodiversity and evolution
3.2 Human impact on biodiversity
4.2 Water access, use and security
6.1 Introduction to the atmosphere
7.2 Energy sources–uses and management
8.3 Urban air pollution

HL c Environmental ethics

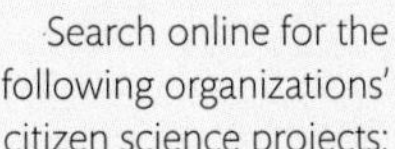

Search online for the following organizations' citizen science projects:

The Wildlife Trusts

Metode

US Environmental Protection Agency

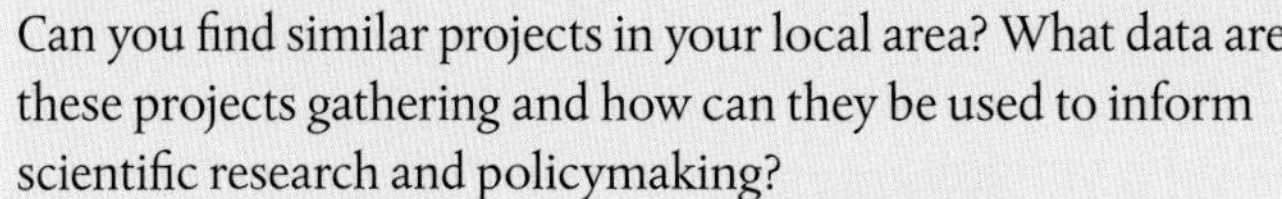

Activity

Project BudBurst is obtaining data on seasonal changes to flowering in spring and leaf fall in autumn, using crowdsourced information. Scientists have observed earlier blooming and later leaf fall. Find out more about BudBurst on their website.

Can you find similar projects in your local area? What data are these projects gathering and how can they be used to inform scientific research and policymaking?

Activity

Search for and read the following article on ScienceDirect: 'Success factors for citizen science projects in water quality monitoring'.

Now answer the following questions:

1. How can citizen science overcome data gaps in monitoring SDG indicators?
2. What factors are likely to influence the success of citizen science projects globally? (Hint: there are nine mentioned in the report.)
3. What success factors relate to specific attributes of citizens, institutions and their interactions?
4. To what extent do success factors depend on the regional context?

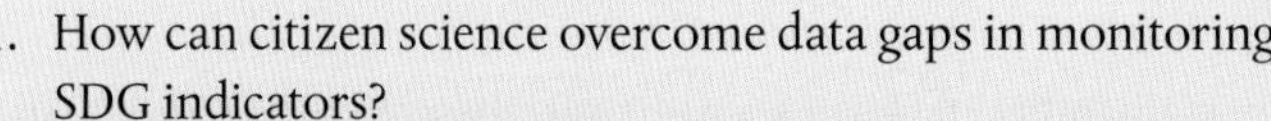

1.3.17 A range of frameworks and models support understanding of sustainability

There are a range of frameworks and models that support our understanding of sustainability, each with their own uses and limitations.

Frameworks and models include:

- the UN **Sustainable Development Goals (SDGs)**
- the planetary boundaries model
- the doughnut economics model.

These frameworks and models are explored in the following sections.

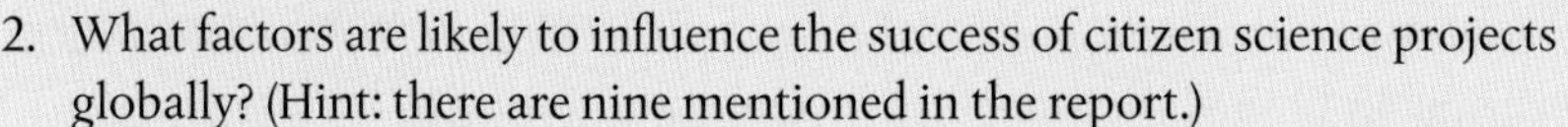

1.3.18 The UN Sustainable Development Goals (SDGs)

The Sustainable Development Goals (SDGs) were developed through decades of work by countries and the UN (this topic, Section 1.1.10, pages 22–23), concluding in the adoption of the 2030 Agenda for Sustainable Development, with the SDGs at its core, at the UN Sustainable Development Summit in September 2015. There are 17 SDGs (Figure 1.72) with 169 targets. All UN member states adopted the SDGs in 2015 with the intention of implementing them by 2030.

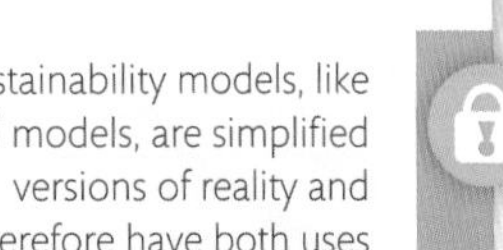

Sustainability models, like all models, are simplified versions of reality and therefore have both uses and limitations.

The SDGs provide a framework for sustainable development and address the global challenges faced by humanity, including those related to poverty, inequality, climate, environmental degradation, prosperity and peace and justice.

The SDGs relate to both developed and developing countries and their uses include:

- setting of a common ground for policymaking
- galvanizing the international community into addressing economic and social inequality.

Limitations of the SDGs include:

- not going far enough
- being top down and bureaucratic
- tending to ignore local contexts
- lacking supportive data.

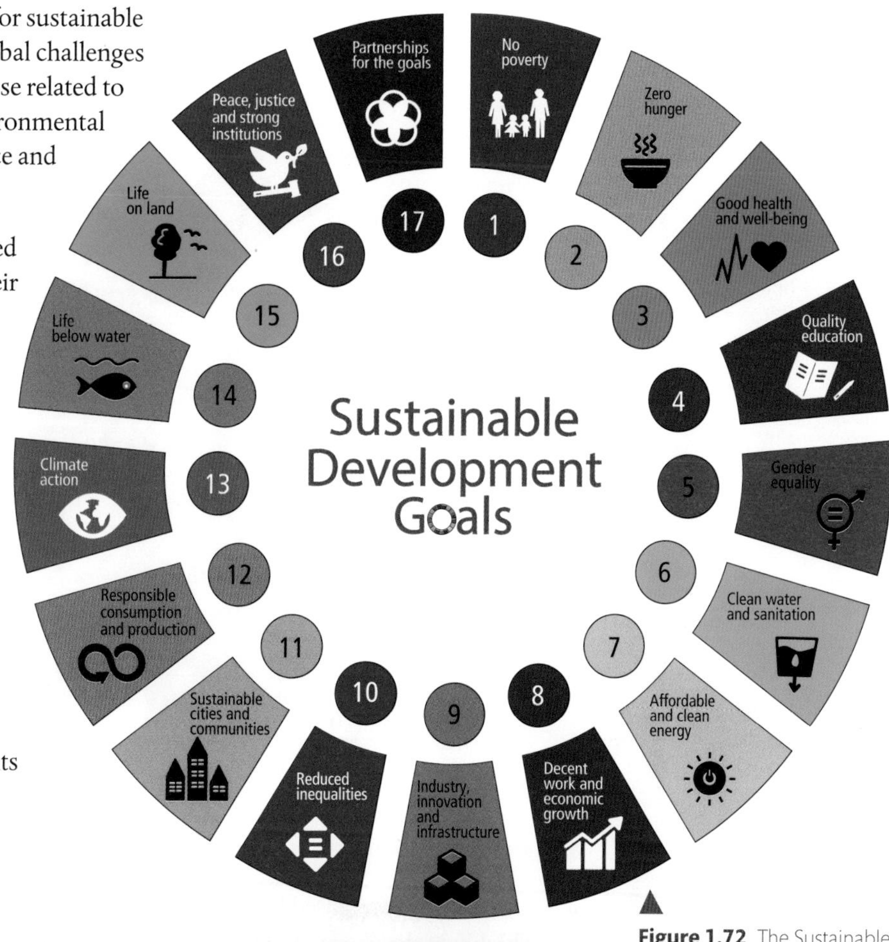

Figure 1.72 The Sustainable Development Goals.

The UN Sustainable Development Goals (SDGs) are a set of social and environmental goals and targets to guide action on sustainability and environmental justice.

Activity

Find out more about the SDGs on the UN's SDGs website.

Select one of the 17 SDGs. How does it relate to the ESS syllabus? Which of the eight topics is it particularly relevant to? Produce a presentation on your chosen SDG to show the rest of your class how it links to the ESS course.

4.2 Water access, use and security
5.2 Agriculture and food
7.2 Energy resources, use and management
8.2 Urban systems and urban planning

HL a Environmental law
HL b Environmental economics
HL c Environmental ethics

1.3.19 The planetary boundaries model

The **planetary boundaries model** (Figure 1.73) was developed by a group of 28 Earth system and environmental scientists in 2009. The team was led by Johan Rockström from the Stockholm Resilience Centre and Will Steffen from the Australian National University. They proposed nine quantitative planetary boundaries, shown in Figure 1.73, that have regulated the stability and resilience of the Earth system throughout the Holocene epoch (the geological epoch in which all of recorded human history has occurred), within which humanity can continue to develop and thrive for generations to come. The model identifies the limits of human disturbance to those systems and proposes that crossing these boundaries increases the risk of creating sudden, extensive or irreversible environmental changes. The planetary boundaries framework has generated enormous interest within science, policy and practice.

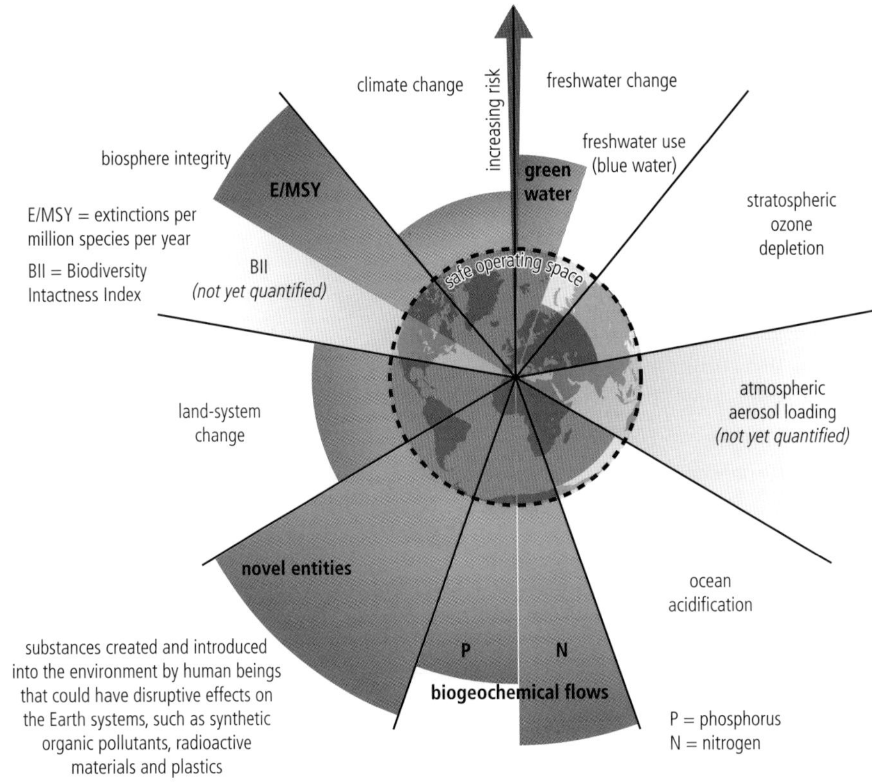

Figure 1.73 The planetary boundaries model, from April 2022.

The planetary boundaries model relates to Earth system processes, each containing environmental boundaries.

The planetary boundaries represent the environmental ceiling beyond which lie unacceptable environmental degradation and potential tipping points in Earth systems.

You need to consider the planetary boundaries model and select which planetary boundaries appear to have been crossed and what factors have led to this.

Find and read the original paper which first proposed the planetary boundaries model: *Ecology and Society*, volume 14, issue 2, 2009, 'Planetary Boundaries: Exploring the Safe Operating Space for Humanity'.

The planetary boundaries model is used to:

- identify science-based limits to human disturbance of Earth systems
- highlight the need to focus on more than just climate change, which dominates discussion on the environmental impacts of human activities
- alert the public and policymakers to the urgent need for action to protect Earth systems.

As with all models, there are limitations. These include:

- the focus of the model is only on ecological systems and does not consider the human dimension necessary to act for environmental justice
- the model is a work in progress and assessments of the boundaries change as new data becomes available
- the focus on global boundaries may not be a useful guide for local and country-level actions.

Crossing the boundaries

In 2015, an article published in the journal *Science* stated that society's activities had pushed several of the planetary boundaries beyond their safe limits. These activities were:

- climate change
- biodiversity loss
- shifts in nutrient cycles (nitrogen and phosphorus)
- land use.

Assessment that these planetary boundaries had been crossed was based on the data shown in Table 1.1.

Planetary boundary	Quantitative measurement	Planetary boundary (safe limit)	Current value (2015)
Climate change	Atmospheric CO_2 concentration (parts per million/ppm)	350 ppm (at most)	400 (in 2015)
Biodiversity loss	Rates of species extinction per million species per year	10 per year (at most)	Approximately 100–1000 and rising (i.e. extinction rate increasing)
Nitrogen and phosphorus loading	Phosphorus and nitrogen applied to land as fertilizer, millions of tonnes per year	phosphorus – 6.2 million tonnes per year nitrogen – 62 million tonnes per year	phosphorus –14 million tonnes per year and rising nitrogen – 150 million tonnes per year and rising
Land conversion	Area of forested land as a proportion of forest-covered land prior to human alteration	At least 75%	62% and decreasing through, for example, intensifying deforestation

Table 1.1 Planetary boundaries that have been crossed.

The planetary boundaries model is a concept relating to Earth system processes, each containing environmental boundaries. *Sustainable* development is possible within the boundaries but not if they are crossed.

2.3 Biogeochemical cycles
3.2 Human impact on biodiversity
4.2 Water access, use and security
4.4 Water pollution
5.2 Agriculture and food
6.2 Climate change – causes and impacts
6.4 Stratospheric ozone
7.2 Energy resources, use and management
8.3 Urban air pollution

In January 2022, 14 scientists concluded in the scientific journal *Environmental Science and Technology* that humanity has exceeded the planetary boundary related to environmental pollutants and other 'novel entities', including plastics.

In April 2022, a reassessment of the freshwater planetary boundary, published in the journal *Nature Reviews Earth & Environment*, indicated that it has been crossed. This conclusion was due to the inclusion of 'green water', which is the water available to plants, into the boundary assessment for the first time. The new assessment was based on evidence of widespread changes in soil moisture relative to mid-Holocene and pre-industrial conditions. It was also based on destabilization of ecological, atmospheric and biogeochemical processes driven by changes to green water.

HL a Environmental law

HL b Environmental economics

HL c Environmental ethics

1.3.20 The doughnut economics model

It is clear that progress towards the goal of meeting the needs of all people within the means of planet Earth cannot be achieved using the metric of money (see GDP, this topic, Section 1.3.8). An array of indicators is needed. A model that addresses the challenges of meeting environmental and social sustainability is the **doughnut economics model** (Figure 1.74). The outer ring of the doughnut represents the planetary boundaries of humanity's resource use, radiating outwards. The inner ring represents the social foundation for the safe and just space for humanity. The hole in the middle is where people are falling short of life's essentials. Between the social and planetary boundaries lies an environmentally safe and socially just space in which humanity can thrive.

Throughout the IB ESS course, you will use quantitative data to discover when and if boundaries have been crossed.

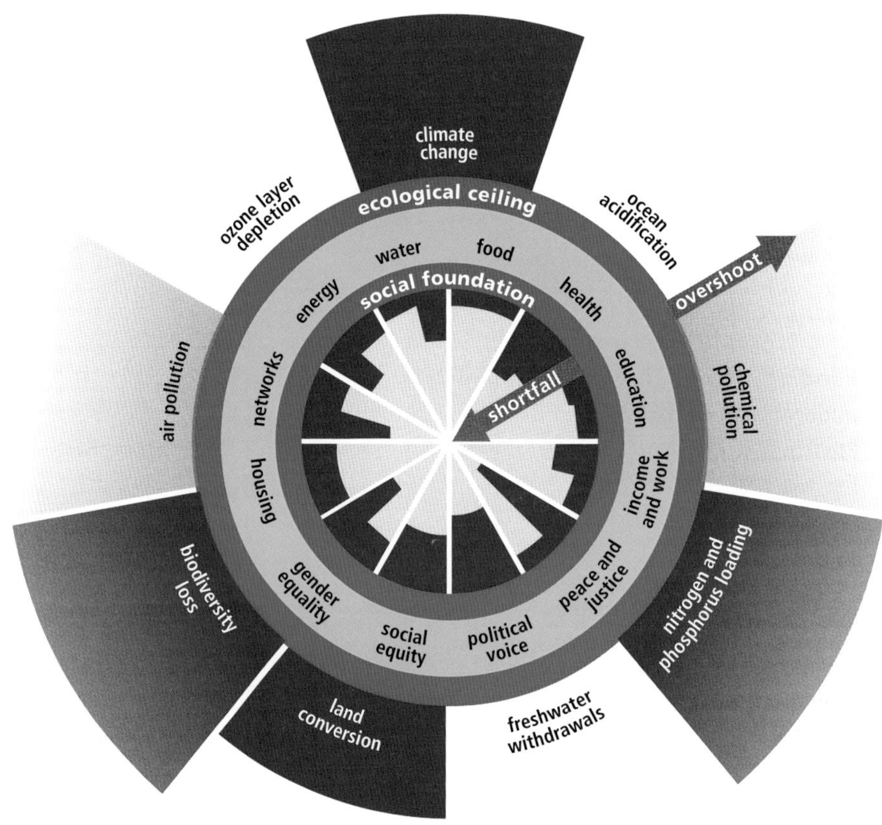

Figure 1.74 The doughnut economics model.

The twelve aspects of the social foundation are derived from internationally agreed minimum social standards, identified by the world's governments in the SDGs in 2015 (this topic, Section 1.3.18).

Today, billions of people fall short of the social foundation, while humanity has already exceeded some of the planetary boundaries. Hence, the goal is to move into the 'doughnut' and create an economy that enables humanity to thrive in balance with the rest of the living world. The doughnut (green section of the diagram in Figure 1.74) represents an optimal place for an action, where humanity can thrive in dynamic balance between the foundation and the ceiling.

The doughnut economics model incorporates the concepts of regenerative and distributive design. A **regenerative economy** works with and within the cycles and limits of the living world. A **distributive economy** shares value and opportunity far more equitably among all stakeholders.

Creating an economy that enables humanity to thrive in balance with the rest of the living world can only be achieved by making economies become regenerative and distributive by design.

In nature, materials are recycled through nutrient cycles such as the carbon, nitrogen and water cycles. Similarly, a regenerative economy reuses and recycles valuable resources. By the appropriate distribution of these resources, an economy meets the needs of environmental justice.

There are many advantages to the doughnut economics model, including:

- it challenges the traditional story of economics and the goal of GDP, in favour of a regenerative and distributive approach
- it has reached popular awareness and is being used at different scales (countries, cities, neighbourhoods, businesses and so on) to support action on sustainability
- it includes both ecological and social elements and so supports the concept of environmental justice.

Limitations of the model include:

- it is a work in progress, with different groups trying to apply the model for concrete action
- while it advocates broad principles of regenerative and distributive practice, the model does not propose specific policies or solutions.

The ecological ceiling of the planetary boundaries has been discussed in this topic, Section 1.3.19. In terms of the social foundation of the model, data suggest that humanity is falling short in all 12 aspects:

- **Food**: Between 2014 and 2016, the percentage of the population that was undernourished was 11%.
- **Health**: The population in countries where the mortality rate for children below five years old exceeded 25 per 1000 live births was 45% in 2015. The population in countries where the life expectancy at birth was less than 70 years was 39% in 2013.
- **Education**: Adult population, those aged 15 years or older, who are illiterate was 15% in 2013. The population of children who were not in education between the ages of 12 and 15 years was 17% in 2013.
- **Income and work**: The population living on less than the international poverty limit of $3.10 per day was 29% in 2012. The proportion of young people aged 15–24 years who were seeking but not able to find work was 13% in 2014.
- **Peace and justice**: In 2014, the population of countries scoring 50 or less out of 100 in the Corruption Perception Index was 85%. The population in countries with a homicide (murder) rate of 10 or more per 10,000 was 13% between the years of 2008 and 2013.
- **Political voice**: In 2013, the population in countries scoring 0.5 or less out of 1.0 in the Voice and Accountability Index was 52%.
- **Social equity**: The population living in countries with a Palma ratio (the ratio of the income share of the top 10% of people to that of the bottom 40%) was 39% between the years 1995 and 2012.
- **Gender equality**: The representation gap between women and men in national parliaments was 56% in 2014 and the worldwide earnings gap between women and men in 2009 was 23%.
- **Housing**: In 2012, the global urban population living in slum housing in developing countries was 24%.
- **Networks**: In 2015, the population who said they did not have someone to count on for help in times of trouble was 24% and 57% of the population were without access to the internet.
- **Energy**: In 2013, 17% of the population lacked access to electricity and 38% lacked access to cooking facilities.
- **Water**: In 2015, 9% of the population were lacking access to improved drinking water and 32% lacked access to improved sanitation.

Humanity is currently, therefore, both falling short of and overshooting these planetary boundaries. Billions of people globally still fall short of their basic needs and we have currently overshot at least four of the planetary boundaries, risking escalating climate change and ecosystem collapse. Global economies need to move away from a degenerative 'take–make–use–waste' model where industries take raw

In the doughnut economics model, the social foundation (inner boundary of the doughnut) is based on the social SDGs. The ecological ceiling (outer boundary of the doughnut) is based on planetary boundaries science, consisting of the Earth's environmental limits. Beyond these limits humanity will inflict dangerous levels of climate change, chemical pollution, ocean acidification, shifts in the hydrological system, land system change, loss of species and alterations to biogeochemical cycles. Together, the social foundation and the ecological ceiling represent the minimum conditions for an economy that is ecologically safe and socially just – thus, the doughnut is the 'safe and just space for humanity'.

materials, make them into items we want, use these items for a while (often only once) and then throw them away. Economies need to move to models that are instead regenerative (Figure 1.75).

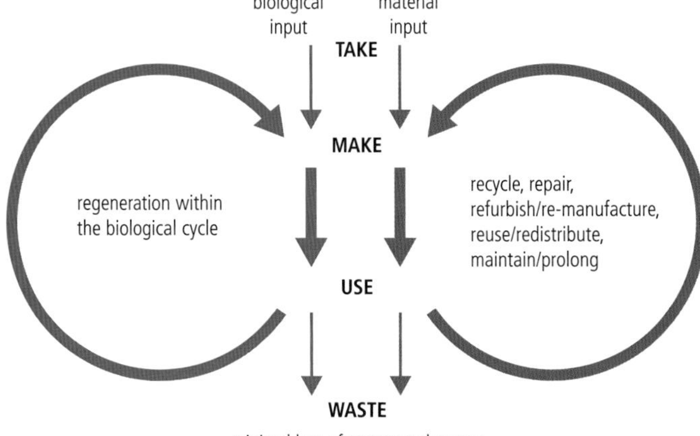

Figure 1.75 Moving from a degenerative ('take-make-use-waste') to a regenerative economic model.

These economic models also need to be distributive (Figure 1.76). Modern technologies and institutions can distribute wealth, knowledge and empowerment away from a small minority to the global majority population.

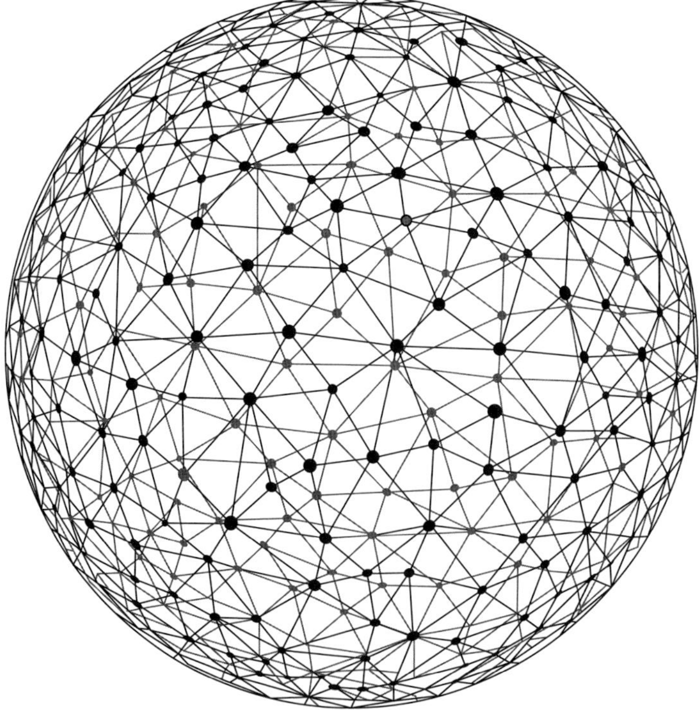

Figure 1.76 Distributive economic model.

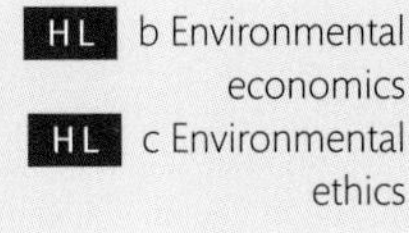

Activity

Find the animations in the Menu on the Kate Raworth website.

Choose one of the animations and write a script that summarizes the content and covers all of the main points. Show the animation to others in your class, muting the narration and using your own script to discuss the contents of the animation.

1.3.21 The circular economy model

The **circular economy model** promotes decoupling economic activity from the consumption of finite resources. It has three principles: eliminating waste and pollution, circulating products and materials, and regenerating nature.

The circular economy model is different from the linear economic model (take-make-use-waste).

The linear economy does not usually consider waste, pollution and issues that lead to environmental degradation.

The circular economy model aims to reduce waste and pollution, keep materials and products in use and lead to the regeneration of natural systems.

The circular economy model is an economic system that provides a sustainable alternative to the linear 'take–make–use–waste' model (this topic, Section 1.3.20, page 72). In the current economic model, materials are taken from the Earth, made into products, used (often only briefly) and eventually thrown away as waste – the process is linear. In a circular economy, by contrast, waste is not produced in the first place or is recycled.

The circular economy model is based on three principles, driven by design:

- eliminate waste and pollution
- keep products and materials in use
- regenerate natural systems.

It is supported by a move away from non-renewable energy resources such as coal, oil and gas and instead towards renewable energy resources and materials. A circular economy separates economic activity from the consumption of finite resources and it is therefore a resilient system that is good for business, people and the environment.

Uses of the circular economy model include:

Search for 'Explaining the Circular Economy and How Society Can Re-think Progress' on the Ellen MacArthur YouTube channel.

- regeneration of natural systems
- reduction of greenhouse emissions
- improvement of local food networks and support for local communities
- reduction of waste by extending product lifecycle
- changing consumer habits.

Limitations of the circular economy model include:

HL b Environmental economics
HL c Environmental ethics

- lack of environmental awareness by consumers and companies
- lack of regulations enforcing recycling of products
- some waste is not recyclable and technical limitations
- lack of finance to implement the model.

The circular economy is intended to result in a more intelligent use of resources that aims to create more from less and has benefits for the economy, society and the environment.

The butterfly diagram

The **butterfly diagram** is the visual representation of the circular economy and shows the different ways in which materials can be kept in use (Figure 1.77). It was developed by the Ellen MacArthur Foundation.

The butterfly diagram shows the continuous flow of materials in a circular economy.

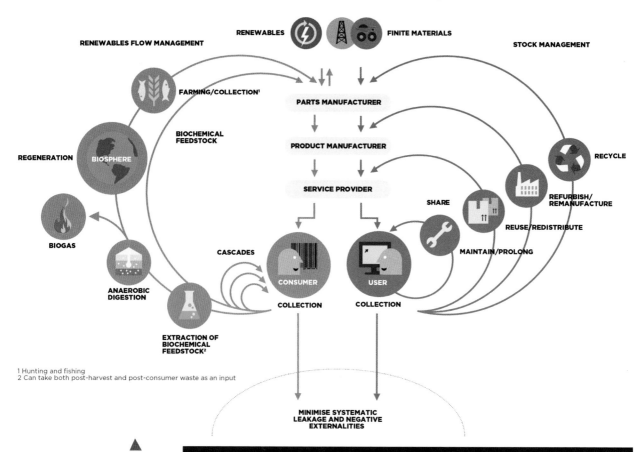

Figure 1.77 The butterfly diagram.

Activity

Search for 'Butterfly diagram animation' on the Ellen MacArthur YouTube channel.

Summarize the main points made in the video. Why is it called the 'butterfly' diagram? What do the wings of the butterfly represent? How does the diagram demonstrate the circular economy?

The Example – Vehicle remanufacturing in China shows how the circular economy has been applied to the production of one commodity.

The Ellen MacArthur Foundation is a charity committed to creating a circular economy.

Example – Vehicle remanufacturing in China

China has adopted the circular economy as a national priority since the late 2000s. Vehicle remanufacturing has been highlighted as a key part of the economy where these principles can be applied.

Remanufacturing uses approximately 60% less energy and 70% less material than making new products. China has an existing stock of 365 million vehicles and an automotive repair and maintenance market worth 1 RMB trillion (USD 157 billion) annually. Policy changes in China have increased the growth of the vehicle remanufacturing sector. Financial incentives have been put forward to encourage participation, with subsidies for businesses that collect vehicles and component parts and consumers being offered a 10% discount on remanufactured components. The State Council of the Chinese government has set a target of 100 industrial zones to enable businesses to exchange information and best practice.

Activity

Carefully analyse the diagram in Figure 1.78, then answer the questions.

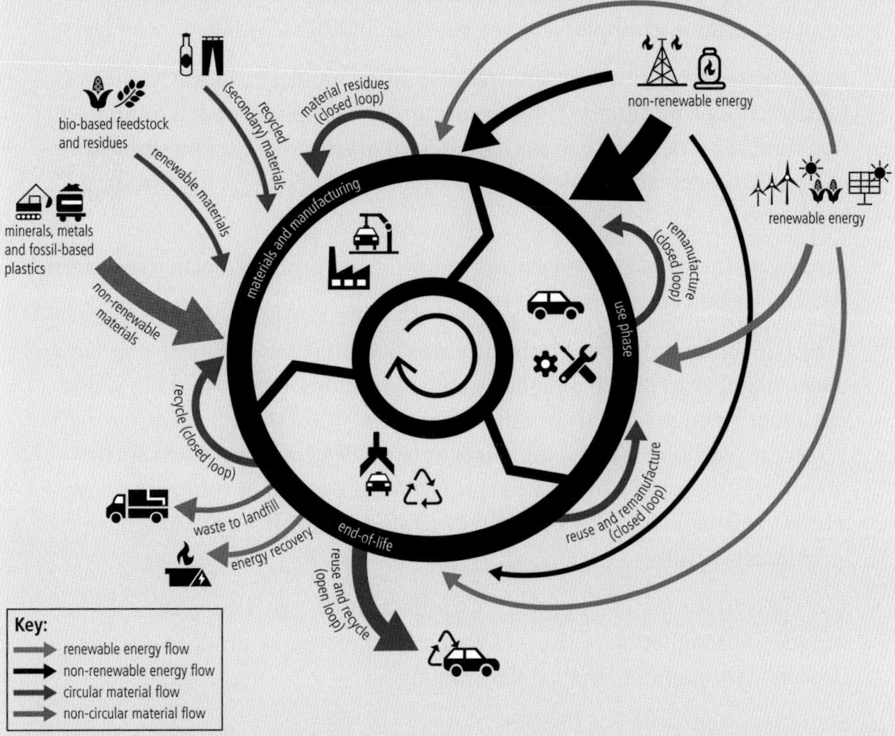

Figure 1.78 The current circular economy model for cars. Arrow widths approximately indicate the relative magnitudes of flows but do not represent specific values. Energy and material flows are not on a uniform scale.

1. (a) (i) To what extent do circular flows dominate across the vehicle life cycle?
   (ii) To what extent do non-circular flows dominate across the vehicle life cycle?
   (b) To what extent does the circular economy model apply to the vehicle manufacture process?
2. Materials and energy resources, including renewable energy resources, use some fossil energy upstream. What effect does this have on the way the diagram is interpreted?
3. What changes could be made to the model to make the processes more sustainable?

Activity

1. Discuss in groups the following questions:
   (a) How can justice issues be addressed through considering the social foundation, the inner ring of the doughnut?
   (b) How can the doughnut economics model expand understanding of environmental justice?
2. Feedback the outcomes of your discussion to the rest of your class.

Engagement

- Present research on examples of environmental injustice and inequalities leading to problems of access to resources. Focusing on causes and effects, summarize these examples and present your findings to others in your class.
- Promote the doughnut economic model and/or circular economy strategies for the school community. How do sustainable economic models differ from traditional approaches, such as GDP? Design posters that explain sustainable economic models and display these in your school or college to promote awareness.
- Investigate the whole school carbon footprint and produce a plan to reduce the school's carbon emissions.
- A sustainability walk showcases sustainability initiatives in a local area. Design a sustainability walk to highlight sustainable options locally. To do this, find out about locations that show different aspects of sustainability, such as zero carbon/no carbon emission initiatives, renewable energy resources such as solar power, recycling and conservation areas. Produce a map of your route, with a brief explanation of each site. Prepare to guide small groups through your sustainability walk.
- Use SDGs (this topic, Section 1.3.18) to advocate for a particular issue. Either produce a presentation to show in your school/college or produce a poster to distribute throughout your local community.

Exercise

Q16. **State** what is meant by the term *sustainability*.

Q17. **Compare** and **contrast** environmental, social and economic sustainability.

Q18. **Discuss** the concept of sustainable development.

Q19. **Outline** the difference between sustainability and sustainable development.

Q20. **Explain**, using an example, how unsustainable use of natural resources can lead to ecosystem collapse.

Q21. **Outline** the role of environmental justice in sustainable development.

Q22. **Distinguish** between ecological footprint and biocapacity.

Q23. **List** three frameworks or models that support an understanding of sustainability.

Q24. **Discuss** the effectiveness of the UN Sustainable Development Goals (SDGs) in guiding action on sustainability and environmental justice.

Q25. **Evaluate** the planetary boundaries model.

Q26. **Outline** the doughnut economics model.

Q27. **Distinguish** between a linear and circular economy.

Practice questions

1. Review Figure 1.79 before answering the questions.

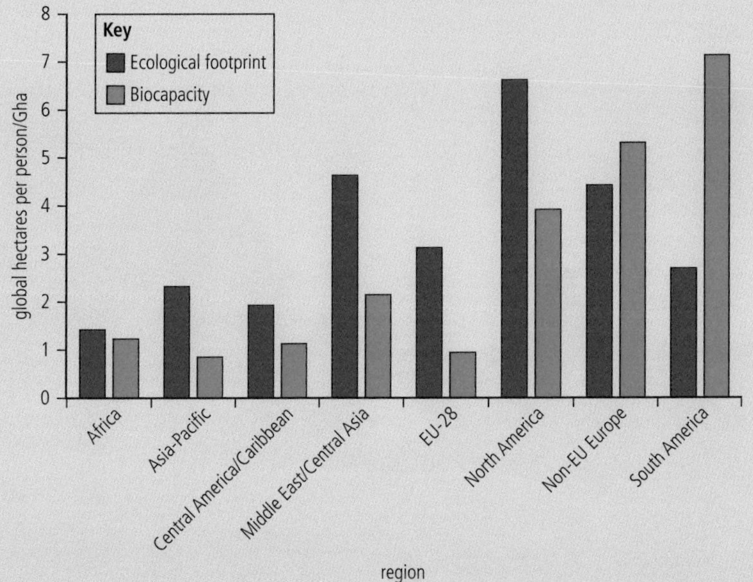

Figure 1.79 The ecological footprint and biocapacity for selected world regions, 2016.

(a) Identify **one** region shown in Figure 1.79 that has an ecological footprint that is lower than its biocapacity. [1]

(b) Outline **one** reason a region whose ecological footprint is greater than its biocapacity is considered unsustainable. [1]

(c) Evaluate the use of the ecological footprint as a model. [4]

(Total 6 marks)

2. Identify **one** transfer process and **one** transformation process shown in Figure 1.80. [2]

(Total 2 marks)

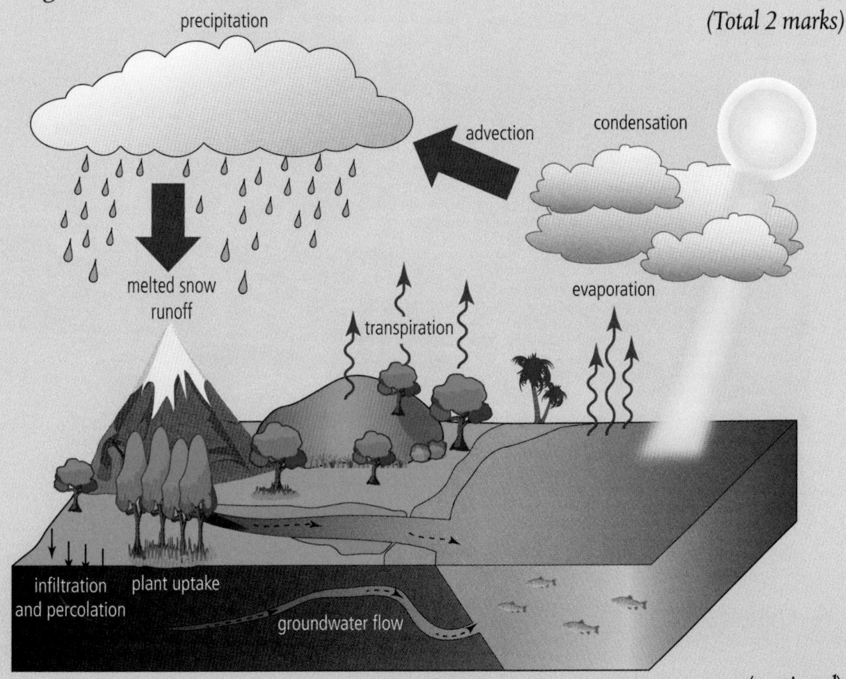

Figure 1.80 Representation of the water cycle.

(continued)

3. The Chukchi are Indigenous nomadic deer herders who live in yarangas. The yaranga is made from poles of local wood covered in tree bark and animal skins. In winter, a deer skin canopy is added to the yaranga to improve insulation (Figure 1.81).

Figure 1.81 A family of Chukchi outside their yaranga in Siberia.

This modern house is made mostly from wood, according to local tradition, but with some brickwork and concrete foundations (Figure 1.82).

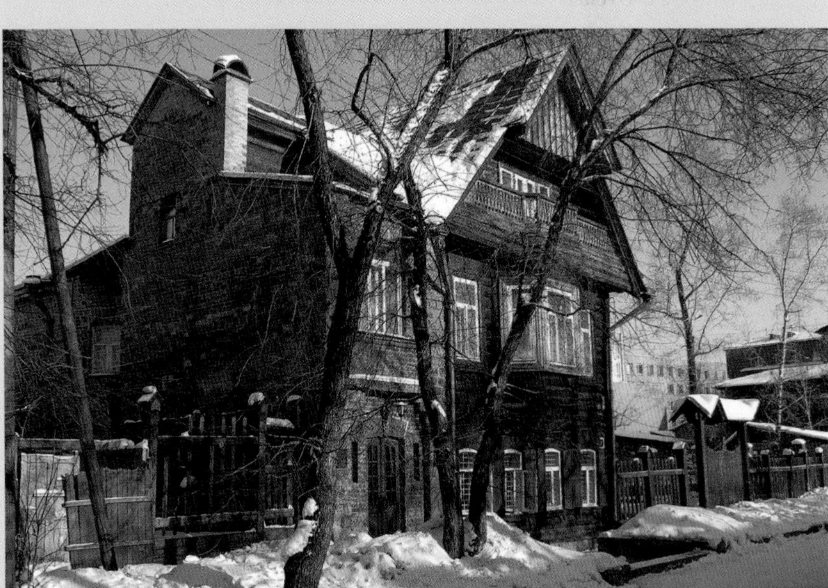

Figure 1.82 A modern wooden house in an industrial city in Siberia.

With reference to Figures 1.81 and 1.82, outline **three** reasons why the yaranga is more sustainable than the modern city house. [3]

(Total 3 marks)

4. Outline how a positive feedback loop can impact an ecosystem. [4]

(Total 4 marks)

5. To what extent would different environmental value systems be successful in reducing a society's ecological footprint? [9]

(Total 9 marks)

6. Review Figure 1.83 before answering the questions.

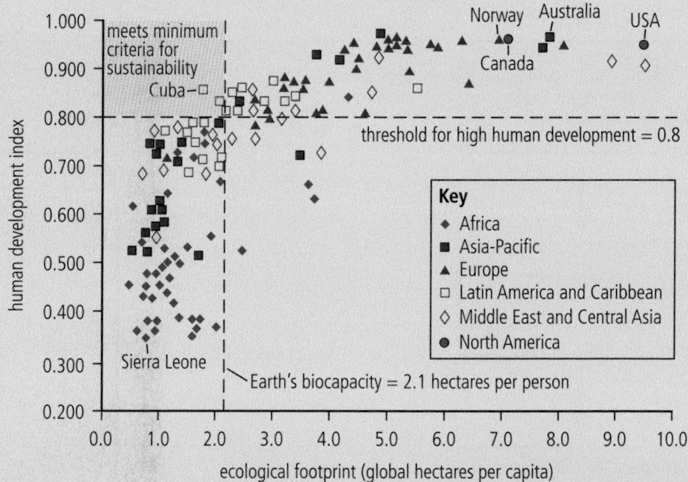

Figure 1.83 A measure of the sustainability of individual countries from a comparison of their ecological footprint and their standard of living.

(a) Using Figure 1.83, identify the country that is above the threshold for high human development and below the Earth's biocapacity. [1]

(b) Outline the relationship between carrying capacity and ecological footprint. [2]

(Total 3 marks)

7. Explain how environmental indicators are used to assess sustainability. [7]

(Total 7 marks)

8. Explain why the ecological footprint of two populations consuming the same quantity of food and energy may be different. [7]

(Total 7 marks)

9. Outline the factors that lead to different environmental value systems in contrasting cultures. [4]

(Total 4 marks)

10. Outline how feedback loops are involved in alternate stable states and the tipping points between them. [4]

(Total 4 marks)

(continued)

11. Outline how the model shown in Figure 1.84 demonstrates positive feedback. [2]

(Total 2 marks)

Figure 1.84 Tourism multiplier effect.

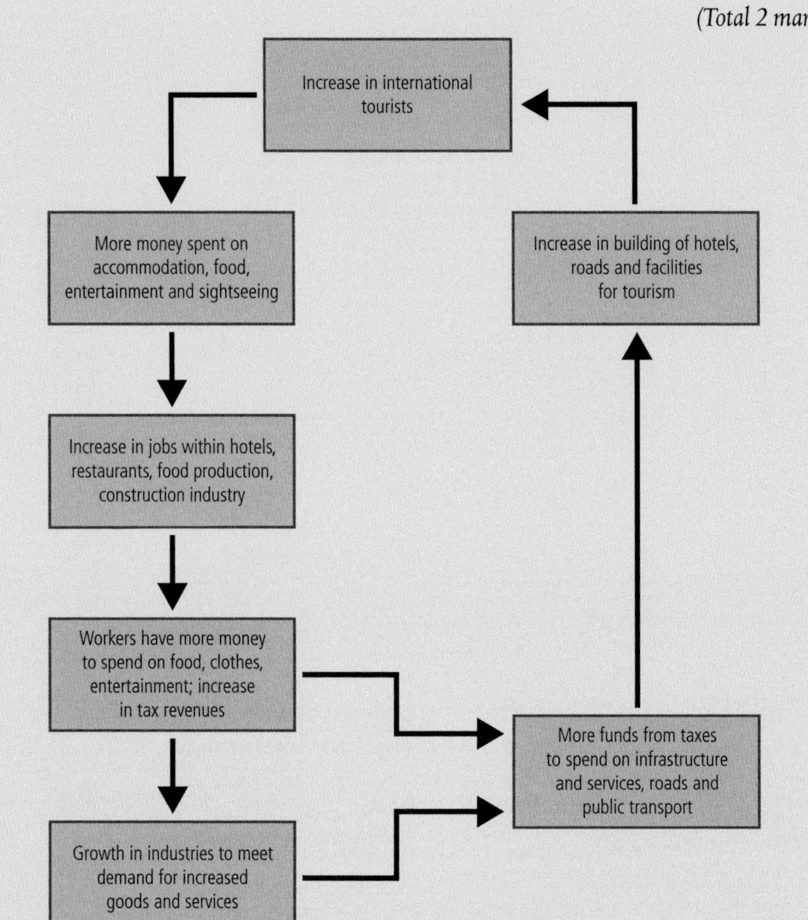

12. Review Figure 1.85 before answering the questions.

Figure 1.85 Ecological footprint and biocapacity per person in Madagascar.

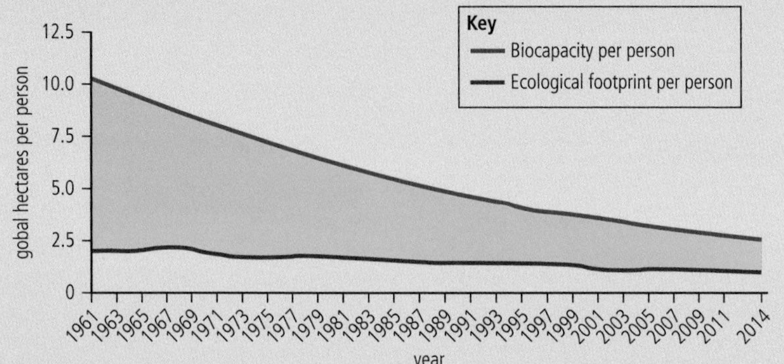

(a) Describe the trend in the ecological footprint over the period shown in Figure 1.85. [1]

(b) Outline why the ecological footprint for the total population of Madagascar has increased during the period shown in Figure 1.85. [2]

(c) Outline **one** reason for the trend in biocapacity during the period shown in Figure 1.85. [1]

(Total 4 marks)

13. (a) Outline how **four** different factors influence the resilience of an ecosystem. [4]

(b) Explain how a community of trees in a woodland may be considered a system. [7]

(Total 11 marks)

14. Explain the role of **two** historical influences in shaping the development of the environmental movement. [7]

(Total 7 marks)

15. With reference to Figure 1.86, suggest what conclusions can be drawn regarding the sustainability of the Brazilian population over the period shown. [2]

(Total 2 marks)

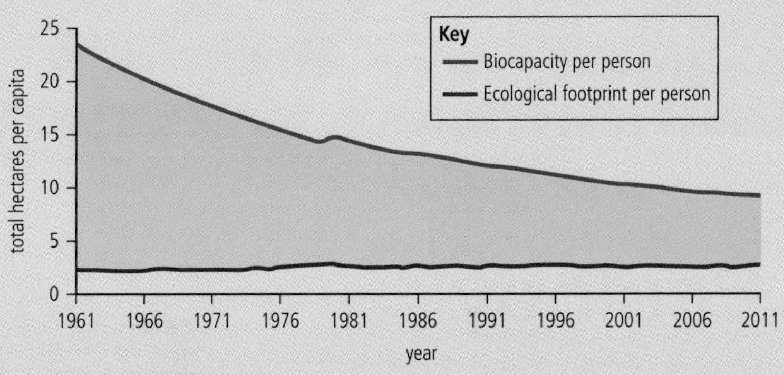

Figure 1.86 Ecological footprint and biocapacity per person in Brazil.

16. You will find an additional Paper 1 question on this page of your eBook.

2

Ecology

2.1 Individuals, populations, communities and ecosystems

Guiding Question

How can natural systems be modelled, and can these models be used to predict the effects of human disturbance?

2.1.1 The biosphere is an ecological system composed of individuals, populations, communities and ecosystems.
2.1.2 An individual organism is a member of a species.
2.1.3 Classification of organisms allows for efficient identification and prediction of characteristics.
2.1.4 Taxonomists use a variety of tools to identify an organism.
2.1.5 A population is a group of organisms of the same species living in the same area at the same time, and which are capable of interbreeding.
2.1.6 Factors that determine the distribution of a population can be abiotic or biotic.
2.1.7 Temperature, sunlight, pH, salinity, dissolved oxygen and soil texture are examples of many abiotic factors that affect species distributions in ecosystems.
2.1.8 A niche describes the particular set of abiotic and biotic conditions and resources upon which an organism or a population depends.
2.1.9 Populations interact in ecosystems by herbivory, predation, parasitism, mutualism, disease and competition, with ecological, behavioural and evolutionary consequences.
2.1.10 Carrying capacity is the maximum size of a population determined by competition for limited resources.
2.1.11 Population size is regulated by density-dependent factors and negative feedback mechanisms.
2.1.12 Population growth can either be exponential or limited by carrying capacity.
2.1.13 Limiting factors on the growth of human populations have increasingly been eliminated, resulting in consequences for sustainability of ecosystems.
2.1.14 Carrying capacity cannot be easily assessed for human populations.
2.1.15 Population abundance can be estimated using random sampling, systematic sampling or transect sampling.
2.1.16 Random quadrat sampling can be used to estimate population size for non-mobile organisms.
2.1.17 Capture–mark–release–recapture and the Lincoln index can be used to estimate population size for mobile organisms.
2.1.18 A community is a collection of interacting populations within the ecosystem.

2.1.19 Habitat is the location in which a community, species, population or organism lives.
2.1.20 Ecosystems are open systems in which both energy and matter can enter and exit.
2.1.21 Sustainability is a natural property of ecosystems.
2.1.22 Human activity can lead to tipping points in ecosystem stability.
2.1.23 Keystone species have a role in the sustainability of ecosystems.
2.1.24 The planetary boundaries model indicates that changes to biosphere integrity have passed a critical threshold.
2.1.25 To avoid critical tipping points, loss of biosphere integrity needs to be reversed.
HL 2.1.26 There are advantages of using a method of classification that illustrates evolutionary relationships in a clade.
HL 2.1.27 There are difficulties in classifying organisms into the traditional hierarchy of taxa.
HL 2.1.28 The niche of a species can be defined as fundamental or realized.
HL 2.1.29 Life cycles vary between species in reproductive behaviour and lifespan.
HL 2.1.30 Knowledge of species' classifications, niche requirements and life cycles help us to understand the extent of human impacts upon them.

2.1.1 The biosphere

The term biosphere refers to all the parts of the Earth where life exists, from the deep sea to the tops of mountains. Conditions in these areas must be suitable for life. This means that they should contain water, the correct nutrients needed by living organisms and an input of energy. The range of **environments** that support life ranges from hydrothermal vents in the deep ocean to hot deserts such as the Sahara (this topic, Section 2.4.4). In hydrothermal vents, the temperature can reach over 400 °C and a lack of sunlight means that organisms must derive their energy from other sources. The conditions in hot deserts are dry and arid.

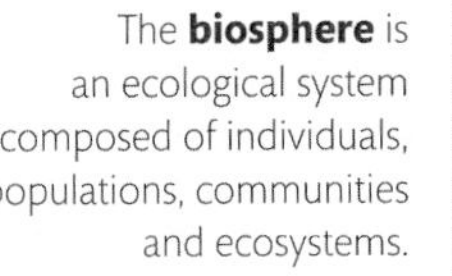

The **biosphere** is an ecological system composed of individuals, populations, communities and ecosystems.

1.2 Systems

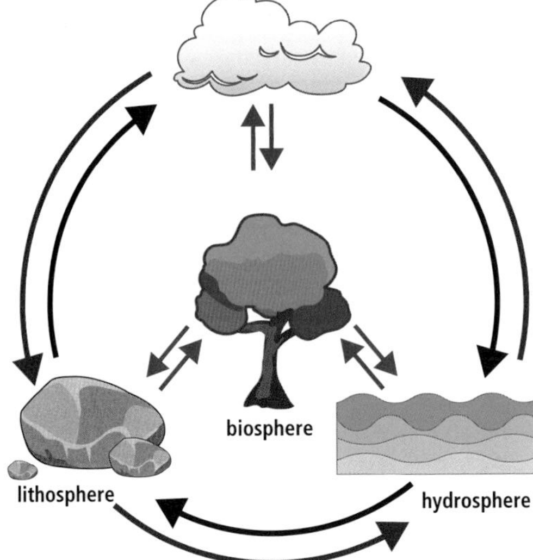

Figure 2.1 The biosphere.

The biosphere is supported by interactions between the **lithosphere** (rocks that degrade to form soils), the **atmosphere** (gases such as carbon dioxide, (CO_2), which is used in the process of photosynthesis) and the **hydrosphere** (water resources) (Figure 2.1).

2.1.2 Species

An individual organism is a member of a **species**. According to the **biological species concept**, a species is a group of organisms that can interbreed and produce fertile offspring (Figure 2.2). Sometimes, two species breed together to produce hybrid offspring. A hybrid may survive to adulthood but cannot produce viable gametes and so is sterile. For example, a horse (*Equus caballus*) can breed with a donkey (*Equus asinus*) to produce a mule, but mules are sterile and cannot produce offspring of their own.

The species concept cannot:

- clarify whether geographically isolated populations belong to the same species
- classify species in extinct populations
- account for asexually reproducing organisms
- clearly define species when barriers to reproduction are incomplete (Figure 2.3).

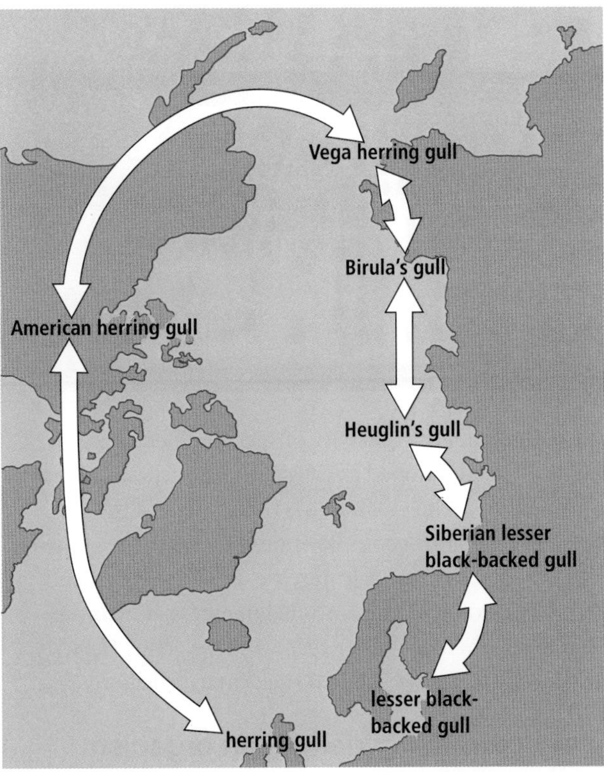

Figure 2.3 Gulls interbreeding in a ring around the Arctic are an example of ring species. Neighbouring species can interbreed to produce viable hybrids but herring gulls and lesser black-backed gulls, at the ends of the ring, cannot interbreed.

Figure 2.2 A snow leopard (*Panthera uncia*) – an example of a species. Species names have two parts – the genus name (*Panthera*) and a specific name (*uncia*). Species names are always written in italics or underlined.

TOK

How does the way that we organize or classify knowledge affect what we know?

The species concept is sometimes difficult to apply. For example, can it be used to accurately describe extinct animals and fossils? The term is also sometimes loosely applied to what are, in reality, sub-species that can interbreed. This is an example of an apparently simple term that is difficult to apply in practical situations.

When discussing examples of species, habitat, niche and so on, make sure that you use specific examples. For example, when referring to species, use Atlantic salmon rather than fish, use Kentucky Bluegrass rather than grass and use silver birch rather than tree.

2.1.3 and 2.1.4 Classification of organisms

The natural history museums of the world are treasure troves of species (Figure 2.4). There are 1.8 million known species to date, with many more still to be discovered. Species are classified by a special group of scientists called taxonomists. The word 'taxon' means a group that is used to distinguish one type of organism from another. Taxonomic groupings range from species (the smallest unit of **classification**) to domain (the largest). **Taxonomy** therefore produces a hierarchy from small to large groupings. The classification of organisms allows for the identification and prediction of common characteristics. If the taxon of an organism is known, at any level of the taxonomic hierarchy, something of the biology of the organism can be predicted from previously classified organisms in the group.

Figure 2.4 Museums, such as the Natural History Museum (NHM) in London, hold a vast array of different species from around the globe. Here, a selection of beetles is shown in a display case at the NHM.

Classification is needed because of the immense diversity of species. Species are classified using the binomial system, first developed by Swedish scientist Carl Linnaeus in the 1700s. Binomial means 'two names'. The first name is the genus and the second name is the species. Species of the same genus have similar traits. The genus name is given a capital letter and the species name is lowercase. Both the genus and species names should be italicized. For example, the binomial name for humans is *Homo sapiens* (abbreviated to *H. sapiens*). There are other species of the genus *Homo*, which have now become extinct, such as *Homo erectus* and *Homo neanderthalensis*.

Taxonomists use a variety of tools to identify an organism

Identification in this context means determining the species of an individual organism. Methods used include use of **dichotomous keys**, comparison with specimens in reference collections by expert taxonomists and DNA surveys.

Ecology is the study of living organisms in relation to their environment. In any ecological study, it is important to correctly identify the organisms in question, otherwise the results and conclusions will be invalid. A dichotomous key is a tool used for the identification of an organism with which you are not familiar.

Dichotomous means 'divided into two parts'. The dichotomous key is written so that identification is done in steps. At each step, you have a choice of two options, based on different possible characteristics of the organism you are looking at. Sometimes, such keys are presented in written form, sometimes they are drawn as a tree diagram.

Suppose you want to identify one of the organisms or objects pictured in Figure 2.5.

You could use a written key such as the one found on this page of your eBook or a dichotomous key diagram such as the one shown in Figure 2.6.

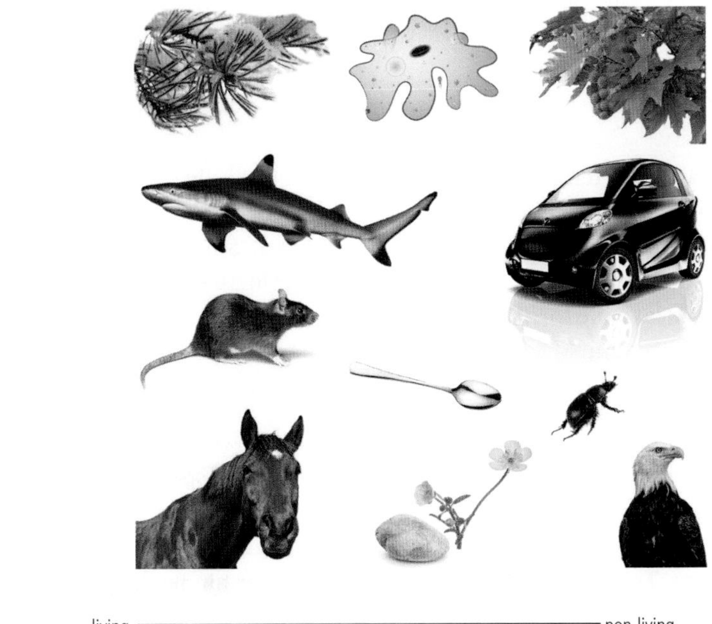

Figure 2.5 A random selection of animate and inanimate specimens. Organisms and objects are not drawn to scale and vary greatly in size, from microscopic (the amoeba, top centre) to much larger specimens, such as the sycamore tree (top right) and pine tree (top left).

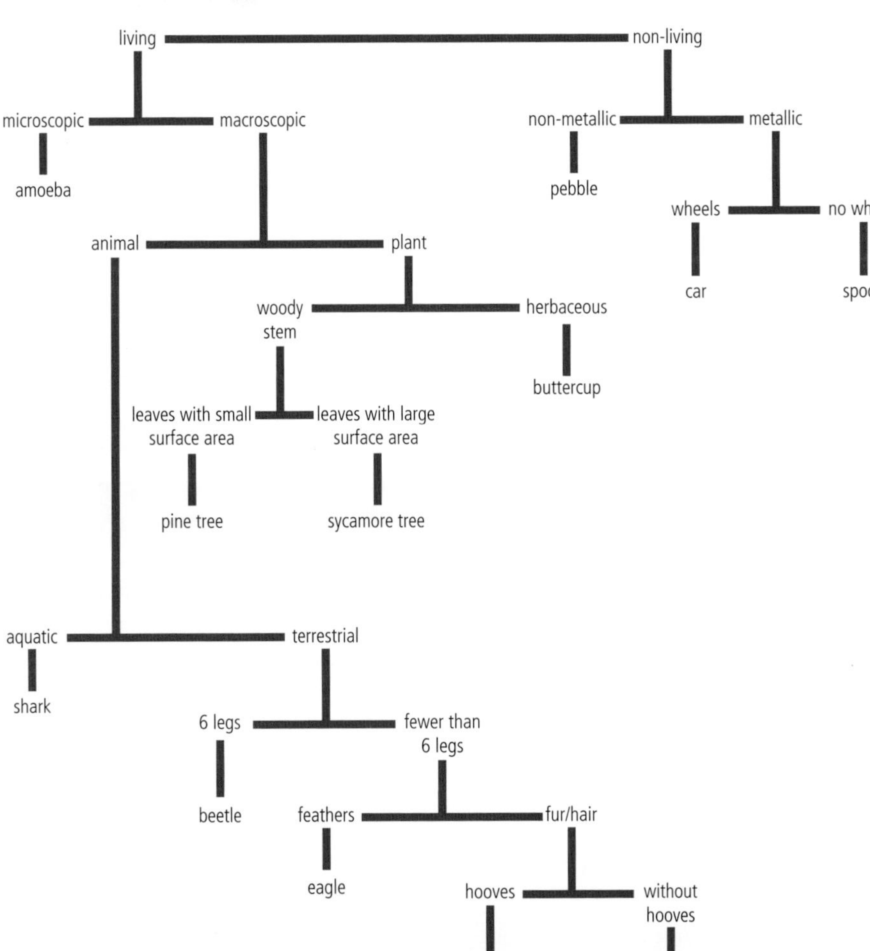

Figure 2.6 A dichotomous key for a random selection of animate and inanimate objects.

A **dichotomous key** is a stepwise tool used for identification of organisms where there are two different answers based on different characteristics at each step. The outcome of each choice leads to another pair of options. This continues until the organism is identified.

When constructing an identification key, do not use terms such as big or small – these are not useful. Make sure that you write quantitative descriptors (i.e. descriptions that allow numbers to be given to features, such as the number of legs) and the simple presence or absence of external features such as tails.

There are limitations to the use of dichotomous keys. These include:

- Only the physical characteristics of the organism can be used with dichotomous keys, rather than being able to use behaviours. Two species that have very similar physical characteristics may display very different behaviours.
- Some dichotomous keys use technical terms that only an expert would understand.
- There may not be a dichotomous key available for the type of organisms you are trying to identify.
- Some physical characteristics of organisms cannot be easily established in the field. For example, whether an animal has a placenta; whether an animal is endothermic or ectothermic (warm- or cold-blooded). Some organisms show significant changes in their body shape during their lifetime (e.g. frogs have an aquatic tadpole juvenile form that is very different from the adult), which keys must take into account. Many insects, for example, show differences between male and female individuals of the species that can cause difficulties when identifying the species.

Organisms in an ecosystem can also be identified by comparing specimens to those in a herbarium, comparing them to museum specimen collections or by using scientific expertise. Museums today often use DNA profiling techniques to identify differences between specimens. This can be a more accurate way of determining the identity of an organism than using only its physical appearance.

Know how to use dichotomous keys for the identification of species

Select eight objects that are linked in some way, for example shells from a beach or leaves from different species of tree. Carefully examine your specimens. What are the most significant structural features? In which specimens are these features present and in which are they absent? How can these specimens be arranged to make a dichotomous key?

Search online for the Online Visual Paradigm Dichotomous Key Maker.

Use this intuitive tool to construct a dichotomous key for your specimens. Each division point in the key should be labelled with the critical diagnostic feature used to distinguish specimens. You will also find example templates on this website.

A **population** is a group of organisms of the same species living in the same area at the same time and which are capable of interbreeding.

2.1.5 Population

A **population** is a group of organisms of the same species living in the same area at the same time and which are capable of interbreeding (Figure 2.7). There may be one or several different populations of the same species in different places.

Investigate a local ecosystem

What animal or plant populations exist in your local area? Populations exist within ecosystems (this topic, Section 2.1.20). How would you investigate a local ecosystem?

Design a plan to investigate a local ecosystem. What methodology will you use? Now carry out the investigation. You can use tools outlined in this topic to analyse your data.

Later in this topic, there are techniques for investigating ecosystems (this topic, Section 2.1.6 and 2.1.7, and Section 2.1.15–2.1.17).

Figure 2.7 A population of meerkats.

2.1.6 and 2.1.7 Abiotic and biotic factors

Abiotic factors include:
- temperature
- sunlight
- acidity/alkalinity (pH)
- rainfall (precipitation)
- salinity
- the soil (edaphic factors)
- topography (the landscape).

Species interact with their environment. The environment is the external surroundings that act on a species, influencing its survival and development. Factors that determine the distribution of a population can be living and non-living. **Biotic factors** are the living components of an ecosystem (animals, plants, algae, fungi and bacteria). The non-living, physical factors that influence the organisms and ecosystem are termed **abiotic factors**.

Abiotic factors

Examples of specific abiotic factors

Ecosystems can be broadly divided into three types (this topic, Section 2.1.20):

- marine – the sea, estuaries, salt marshes and mangroves, all characterized by the water having a high salt content
- freshwater – rivers, lakes and wetlands
- terrestrial – land-based.

Abiotic factors affect the distribution of species in ecosystems. Each ecosystem has its own specific abiotic factors as well as the common ones they share.

Abiotic factors of a marine ecosystem include:

- salinity
- pH
- temperature
- dissolved oxygen (O_2)
- soil texture.

All plants and animals need water to survive. For plants, water stress (too little water) may cause germination to fail, seedlings to die and seed yield to be reduced. Categories of water-tolerant plants include:

- hydrophytes – water-tolerant plants that can root in standing water
- mesophytes – plants that inhabit moist rather than wet environments
- xerophytes – plants that live in dry environments.

Estuaries are classified as marine ecosystems because they have high salt content compared to freshwater. Mixing of freshwater and oceanic seawater leads to a diluted salt content but one that is still high enough to influence the distribution of organisms within it. Salt-tolerant animals and plants have specific adaptations to help them cope with the osmotic demands of saltwater.

Only a small proportion of freshwater is found in ecosystems (Topic 4, Section 4.1.3). Abiotic factors of a freshwater ecosystem include:

- turbidity
- pH
- temperature
- dissolved O_2
- flow velocity
- light intensity.

4.2 Water access, use and security

Abiotic factors of a terrestrial ecosystem (such as Figure 2.8) include:

- temperature
- light intensity
- wind speed
- soil texture
- slope/aspect
- soil moisture
- drainage
- soil mineral content.

Temperature, sunlight, pH, salinity, dissolved O_2 and soil texture are examples of many abiotic factors that can affect species distributions in ecosystems.

Abiotic factors can be quantified to clarify the distribution of species.

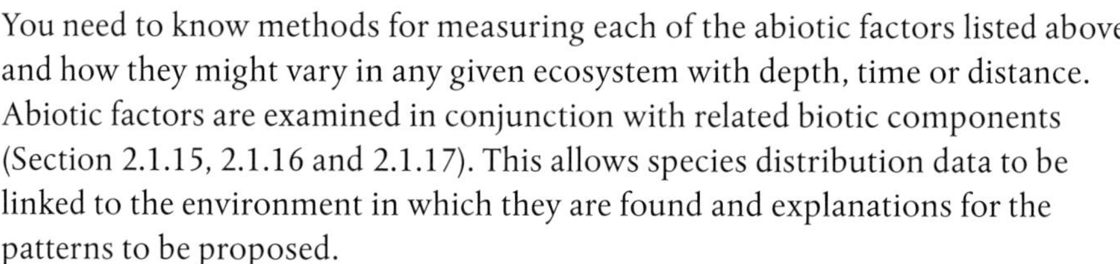

You need to know methods for measuring each of the abiotic factors listed above and how they might vary in any given ecosystem with depth, time or distance. Abiotic factors are examined in conjunction with related biotic components (Section 2.1.15, 2.1.16 and 2.1.17). This allows species distribution data to be linked to the environment in which they are found and explanations for the patterns to be proposed.

Abiotic factors that can be measured within an ecosystem include:

- marine environment: salinity, pH, temperature, dissolved O_2, wave action
- freshwater environment: turbidity, pH, temperature, dissolved O_2, flow velocity
- terrestrial environment: temperature, light intensity, wind speed, soil texture, slope, soil moisture, drainage, mineral content.

Evaluating measures for describing abiotic factors

Let's consider the techniques used for measuring abiotic factors. An inaccurate picture of an environment may be obtained if errors are made in sampling, so possible sources of error are examined.

Figure 2.8 The Nevada desert, USA. Water supply in terrestrial ecosystems can be extremely limited, especially in desert areas. Water is an important abiotic factor in controlling the distribution of organisms.

Make sure you are familiar with the measurement of at least three abiotic factors in an aquatic or terrestrial ecosystem, including the use of data-logging and other sensors.

Measurements should be repeated to increase the reliability of data. The number of repetitions required depends on the factor being measured.

Light

A light-meter can be used to measure the light intensity in an ecosystem (Figure 2.9). The light-meter should be held at a standard, fixed height above the ground and read when the value is steady and not fluctuating. Cloud cover and changes in light intensity during the day mean that values must be taken at the same time of day and same atmospheric conditions. This can be difficult if several repeat measurements are taken. The direction of the light-meter also needs to be standardized so it points in the same direction and at the same angle each time it is used. Care must be taken not to shade the light-meter during a reading being taken.

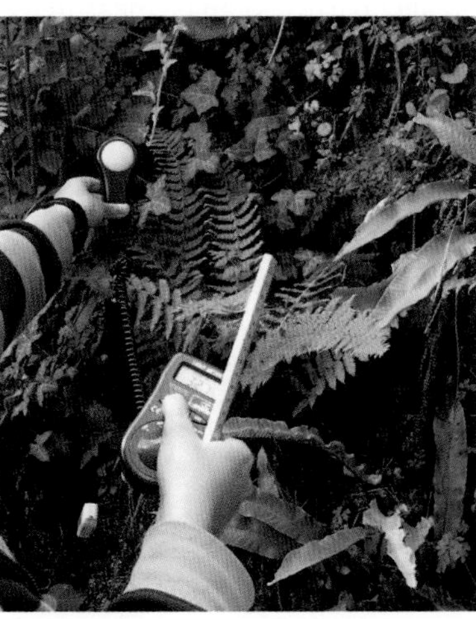

Figure 2.9 Using a light-meter to record light intensity falling on ivy.

Temperature

An electronic thermometer with probes (datalogger) allows the temperature to be accurately measured in air, water and at different soil depths. The temperature needs to be taken at a standard depth. Problems arise if the thermometer is not buried deeply enough so the depth needs to be checked each time it is used. Temperature can only be measured for a short period of time (i.e. seconds or minutes) using conventional digital thermometers. Dataloggers can be used to measure temperature over longer periods of time (i.e. days or years) and take any fluctuations in temperature into account.

Figure 2.10 An anemometer measuring wind speed. It works by converting the number of rotations made by three cups at the top of the apparatus into wind speed.

The percentage slope can be calculated as follows. For example, if the slope is 10 degrees:

percentage slope = tan(10) × 100 = 0.176 × 100 = 17.6%

pH

pH can be measured using a pH meter or datalogging pH probe. Values in freshwater range from slightly basic to slightly acidic depending on the pH of the surrounding soil, rock and vegetation. Seawater usually has a pH above 7 (alkaline). The meter or probe must be cleaned between readings and each reading must be taken at the same depth. Soil pH can be measured using a soil testing kit, where an indicator solution is added to the sample and the colour produced is compared to a coloured chart with known pH values.

Wind

Measurements can be taken by observing the effects of wind on objects and relating these to the Beaufort scale. Precise measurements of wind speed can be made with a digital anemometer, which can be mounted or hand-held (Figure 2.10). Some anemometers use cups to capture the wind, whereas other smaller devices use a propeller. Care must be taken not to block the exposure of the anemometer to the wind. Gusty conditions may lead to large variations in data.

Soil texture

Soil can be made up of large, small or intermediate particles. Particle size determines drainage and water-holding capacity (Topic 5, Section 5.1.3). Large particles (pebbles) can be counted and measured individually, and the average particle size calculated. Smaller particles can be measured by using a series of sieves with increasingly fine mesh sizes. The smallest particles can be separated by sedimentation. Optical techniques (examining the properties of light scattered by a suspension of soil in water) can also be used to study the smallest particles.

Slope

Surface run-off is determined by the angle of the slope, which can be calculated using a clinometer (Figure 2.11). The slope's aspect can be determined using a compass. Care must be taken in interpreting results as the slope may vary in angle over its distance.

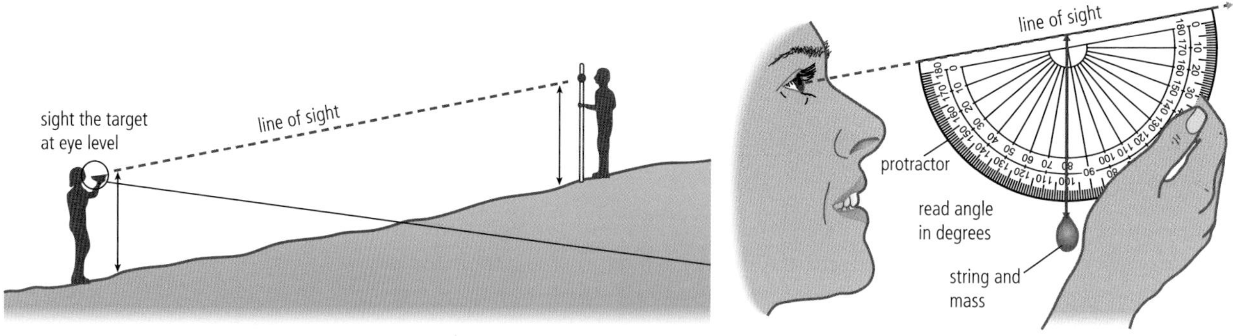

Figure 2.11 The slope angle is taken by sighting along the protractor's flat edge and reading the degree aligned with the string. Percentage slope can be calculated by determining the tangent of the slope using a scientific calculator and multiplying by 100.

Soil moisture

Soils contain water and organic matter. Measuring the mass of samples before and after heating in an oven gives the mass of water evaporated and therefore the moisture levels. If the oven is too hot when evaporating the water, organic content can also burn off. This further reduces soil mass and gives inaccurate readings. Repeated readings should be taken until no further mass loss is recorded – the final reading should be used. Loss of mass can be calculated as a percentage of the starting mass. Soil moisture probes are also available, which are simply pushed into the soil. These need to be cleaned between readings as they can be inaccurate.

Mineral content

The loss on ignition (LOI) test can determine mineral content. Soil samples are heated to high temperatures (500–1000 °C) for several hours to allow volatile substances (i.e. ones that can evaporate) to escape. The loss of mass is equivalent to the quantity of volatile substances present. The temperature and heating required may depend on the mineral composition of the soil, but there are no standard methods. The same conditions should be used when comparing samples.

Flow velocity

Surface flow velocity can be measured by timing how long it takes a floating object to travel a certain distance. More accurate measurements can be taken using a flow meter (a calibrated propeller attached to a pole) (Figure 2.12). The impeller is inserted into water just below the surface and pointed into the direction of the flow. Several readings (at least three to five) are taken to ensure accuracy. As velocity varies with distance from the surface, readings must be taken at the same depth. Results can be misleading if only one part of a stream is measured. Water flows can vary over time because of rainfall or glacial melting events.

Figure 2.12 A flow meter allows water velocity to be recorded at any depth.

Short-term and limited field sampling reduces the effectiveness of the measurement techniques because abiotic factors may vary from day to day and season to season. Most of these abiotic factors can be measured using datalogging devices. The advantage of dataloggers is that they can provide continuous data over a long period of time, making results more representative of the area. The reliability of the results can also be improved by taking many samples. Make sure you use a sample size that is large enough for data processing. For example, a sample size of less than five is usually considered too small to calculate standard deviation.

Each statistical test has an optimal sample size. For example, the t-test, which provides a way of measuring the overlap between two sets of data, may be applied to sample sizes of more than 15 and less than 30 taken from normally distributed data.

Salinity

Salinity can be measured using electrical conductivity (with a datalogger) or by the density of the water (the higher the salt content, the higher the density). Salinity is commonly expressed in parts per thousand (ppt), which means parts of salt per thousand parts of water. Seawater has an average salinity of 35 ppt, which is equivalent to 35 g dm^{-3} or 35‰.

Dissolved oxygen

Oxygen-sensitive electrodes connected to a meter can be used to measure dissolved O_2. Readings may be affected by O_2 in the air. Therefore, care must be taken when using an oxygen meter to avoid contamination with O_2 in the air. A more labour-intensive method is Winkler titration. This is based on the principle that O_2 in the water reacts with iodide ions and acid can be added to release iodine, the amount of which can be quantitatively measured.

Wave action

Areas with high wave action have high levels of dissolved O_2 due to the mixing of air and water in the turbulence. Wave action is measured using a dynamometer, which measures the force in the waves. Changes in tide and wave strength during the day and over monthly periods mean that average results must be used to take this variability into account.

Figure 2.13 A Secchi disc is mounted on a pole or line and is lowered into water until it is just out of sight. The depth is measured using the scale on the line or pole. The disc is raised until it is just visible again and a second reading is taken. The average depth calculated is known as the Secchi depth.

Turbidity

Cloudy water is said to have high turbidity and clear water has low turbidity. Turbidity affects the penetration of sunlight into water and therefore rates of photosynthesis. Turbidity can be measured using a Secchi disc (Figure 2.13). Problems may be caused by the Sun's glare on the water or the subjective nature of the measure (one person may see the disc at one depth but someone with better eyesight may see it at a greater depth). Errors can be avoided by taking measures on the shady side of a boat. More sophisticated optical devices can also be used (e.g. a nephelometer or a turbidimeter) to measure the intensity of light scattered at 90° as a beam of light passes through a water sample.

TOK

How important are material tools in the production or acquisition of knowledge?

Abiotic data can be collected using instruments that avoid issues of objectivity because they directly record quantitative data. Instruments can record data beyond the limits of unaided human perception.

Use methods for measuring at least three abiotic factors in an aquatic or terrestrial ecosystem, including the use of data logging

Compare abiotic variables in undisturbed and disturbed areas of a local ecosystem. For example, compare an area of forest that has not been affected by human activity with another area that has been (e.g. has been logged/had timber removed). Examples of abiotic factors you could investigate include wind speed, soil moisture, light intensity, temperature and humidity. Select at least three factors to measure. Use sensors to measure abiotic variables such as temperature, light intensity and soil pH or equipment shown in Section 2.1.6 and 2.1.7.

Were there any differences between the undisturbed and disturbed areas? Which abiotic factors were affected and why? What conclusions can you reach from your investigation?

2.1.8 Niche

A **niche** describes the particular set of abiotic and biotic conditions and resources on which an organism or a population depends.

An ecological niche is the role of a species in an ecosystem and can be described as where, when and how an organism lives. An organism's niche depends not only on where it lives (its habitat) but also on what it does. The niche comprises all biotic and abiotic interactions that influence the growth, survival and reproduction of a population, including how food is obtained. For example, the niche of an elephant includes everything that defines this species such as its habitat (forest and grasslands), interactions between members of the herd (touching each other with their trunks, rubbing their bodies against one another, calling to each other), what it feeds on (grasses, small plants, bushes, fruit and twigs), when it feeds (elephants can spend three quarters of the day eating) and so on. No two species can have the same niche because the niche completely defines a species.

2.1.9 Population interactions

Populations of different organisms interact with each other in ecosystems. There are a variety of different interactions: herbivory, predation, parasitism, mutualism, disease and competition. Each interaction has ecological, behavioural and evolutionary consequences.

Make sure you consider one example of each relationship and consider how the relationships influence the population dynamics of the interacting populations and the selective pressures involved.

Herbivory

Herbivory is an interaction where an animal feeds on a plant. The animal that eats the plant is called a **herbivore**. An example of herbivory is provided by the hippopotamus, which eats vegetation on the land during the coolness of the night (Figure 2.14). Hippopotamuses spend the day in rivers so they do not overheat.

Figure 2.14 A hippopotamus has a specialized stomach to enable it to eat vegetation – its four chambers are the same as those found in other herbivores such as cows and deer.

The **carrying capacity** of a herbivore's environment is affected by the quantity of the plant it feeds on. An area with more abundant plant resources has a higher carrying capacity than an area that has less plant material available as food for the herbivore.

Parasitism

A parasite is an organism that benefits at the expense of another (the host) from which it derives food. Ectoparasites live on the surface of their host (e.g. ticks and mites) (Figure 2.15). Endoparasites live inside their host (e.g. tapeworms).

Parasitism is a symbiotic relationship in which one species benefits at the expense of the other.

The carrying capacity of the host may be reduced because of the harm caused by the parasite. Some plant parasites draw food from the host via their roots (Figure 2.16).

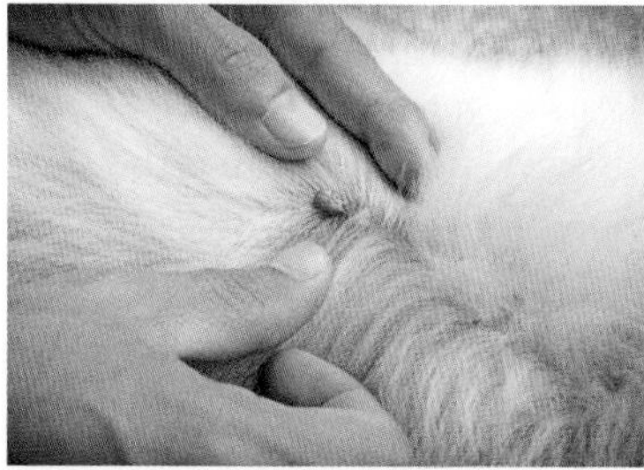

Figure 2.15 A tick feeding on a dog.

Figure 2.16 *Rafflesia* have the largest flowers in the world but have no leaves. Without leaves, these plants cannot photosynthesize, so they grow close by South-east Asian vines (*Tetrastigma* spp.) from which they draw the sugars they need for growth.

Mutualism is a symbiotic relationship in which both species benefit.

Figure 2.17 Lichens consist of a fungus and alga in a symbiotic relationship. The fungus is efficient at absorbing water but cannot photosynthesize, whereas the alga contains photosynthetic pigments and so can use sunlight energy to convert CO_2 and water into glucose. The alga therefore obtains water and shelter and the fungus obtains a source of sugar from the relationship. Lichens with different colours contain algae with different photosynthetic pigments.

Mutualism

Symbiosis is a relationship in which two organisms live together. Parasitism is a form of symbiosis where one of the organisms is harmed. **Mutualism** is a form of symbiosis where both species benefit from the relationship. Examples include coral reefs and lichens (Figure 2.17). Coral reefs show a symbiotic relationship between the coral animal (polyp) and zooxanthellae (unicellular brown algae or dinoflagellates) that live within the coral polyp. The polyp animal has a mouth and so can feed on organisms in the seawater. The algae photosynthesize and provide the polyps with an additional source of glucose. The polyp provides protection for the algae and a source of CO_2 for photosynthesis. Nematocysts are stinging cells located in the tentacles of the polyp and protect the coral from predators. Coral gets up to 90% of its organic nutrients from the zooxanthellae.

Disease

An organism that causes disease is known as a **pathogen**. Pathogens include bacteria, viruses, fungi and single-celled animals called protozoa. The disease-causing species may reduce the carrying capacity of the organism it is infecting. Changes in disease can also cause populations to increase and decrease around the carrying capacity (Figure 2.23, Section 2.1.12).

Dutch elm disease is caused by fungus (*Ascomycota*) that affects elm trees (Figure 2.18). The elm bark beetle spreads the fungus.

Figure 2.18 In Dutch elm disease, fungal infection causes the clogging of vascular tissues. This prevents the movement of water around the tree from the roots to the leaves and results in wilting and the death of the tree.

Competition

When resources are limited, populations compete to survive. **Competition** is the demand by individuals for limited environmental resources. It may be either within a species (**intraspecific competition**) or between different species (**interspecific competition**). Interspecific competition exists when the niches of different species overlap (Figure 2.19).

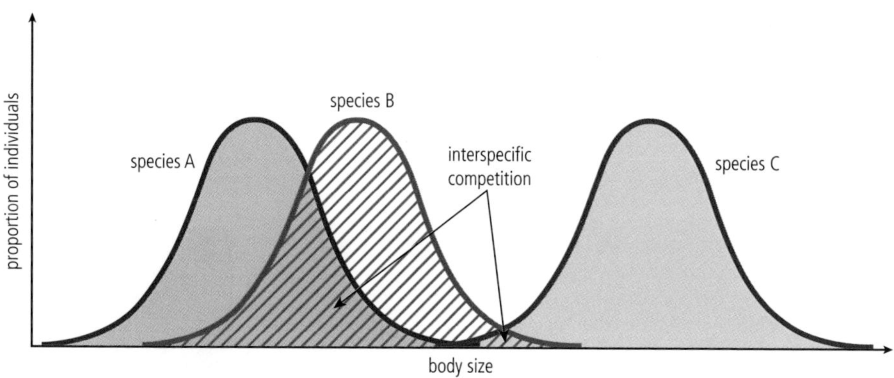

Figure 2.19 The niches of species A and species B, based on body size, overlap with each other to a greater extent than with species C. Strong interspecific competition will exist between species A and B but not with species C.

No two species can occupy the same niche, so the degree to which niches overlap determines the degree of interspecific competition. In this relationship, neither species benefit, although better competitors suffer less.

Experiments with single-celled animals have demonstrated the principle of competitive exclusion: if two species occupying similar niches are grown together, the poorer competitor will be eliminated (Figure 2.20).

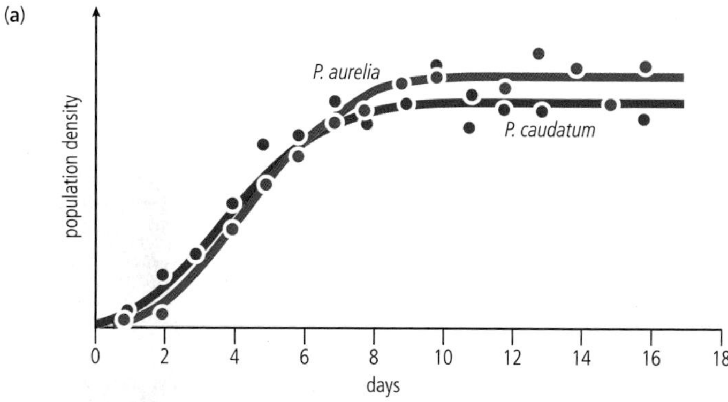

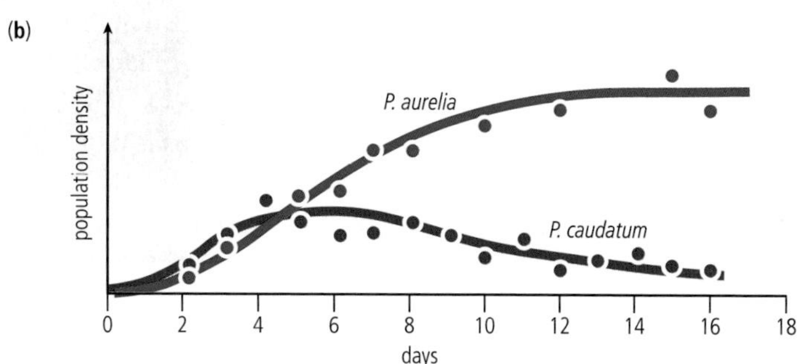

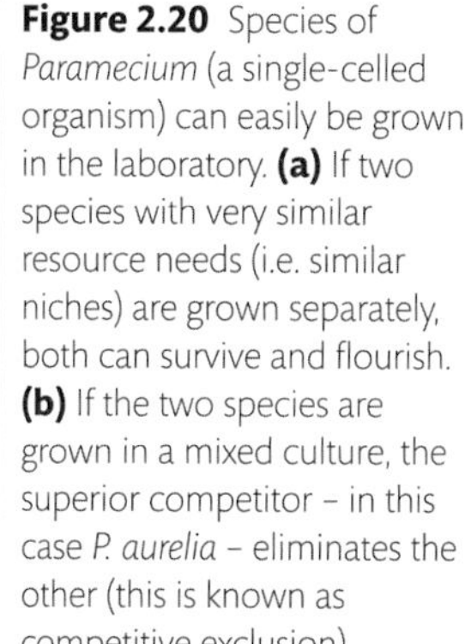

Figure 2.20 Species of *Paramecium* (a single-celled organism) can easily be grown in the laboratory. **(a)** If two species with very similar resource needs (i.e. similar niches) are grown separately, both can survive and flourish. **(b)** If the two species are grown in a mixed culture, the superior competitor – in this case *P. aurelia* – eliminates the other (this is known as competitive exclusion).

Individuals within the same species occupy the same niche. Thus, if resources become limiting for a population, intraspecific competition becomes stronger. In this interaction, the stronger competitor (i.e. the one better able to survive) will reduce the carrying capacity of the other's environment.

Make sure you know how to interpret graphical representations or models of factors that affect an organism's niche. Examples should include predator–prey relationships, competition and organism abundance over time.

Make sure you know how models can be used to show feeding relationships, such as the predator–prey relationship.

Use models that demonstrate feeding relationships

Predation occurs when one organism hunts and eats another organism. An example of predation is snowy owls feeding on lemmings (Topic 1, Section 1.2.15, page 42). Such interactions are controlled by negative feedback (Topic 1, Section 1.2.8). Predator–prey interactions are an example of a feeding relationship.

Not all predators are animals. Insectivorous plants, such as Venus fly traps and pitcher plants (Figure 2.21), trap insects and feed on them. Such plants often live in areas with nitrate-poor soils and obtain much of their nitrogen from animal protein. These plants still obtain energy from photosynthesis.

Figure 2.21 *Nepenthes rajah*, the largest pitcher plant.

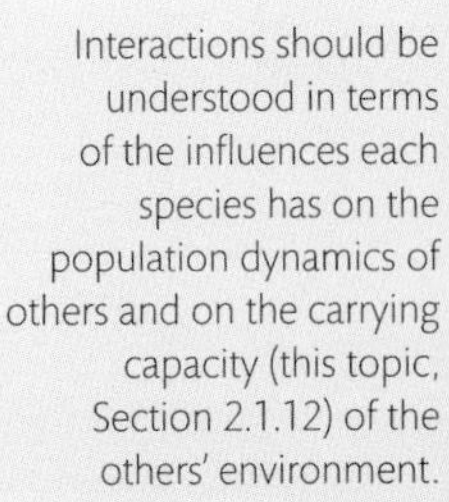

Interactions should be understood in terms of the influences each species has on the population dynamics of others and on the carrying capacity (this topic, Section 2.1.12) of the others' environment.

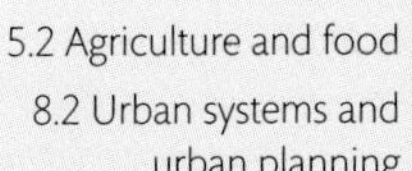

5.2 Agriculture and food
8.2 Urban systems and urban planning

2.1.10 Carrying capacity

Carrying capacity is the maximum size of a population determined by competition for limited resources.

Resources that may affect carrying capacity include both biotic and abiotic factors. Biotic factors are the living part of the environment. Interactions between organisms are also biotic factors. Ecosystems contain numerous populations with complex interactions between them. The nature of the interactions varies and can be broadly divided into specific types (predation, herbivory, parasitism, mutualism, disease and competition).

2.1.11 Regulation of population size

Some limiting factors are related to **population density**, such as competition for resources, space, disease, parasitism and predation. As a population increases, the availability of food per individual decreases. This can lead to a reduced birth rate and an increased death rate. As predators may be attracted to areas of high population density, the mortality rate may increase. Similarly, disease spreads more easily in denser populations. Other density dependent factors include the size of the breeding population and size of the territory. The larger the population size and the larger the territory, the greater the potential chance a species has for survival.

Density-dependent factors operate as negative feedback mechanisms regulating the population and leading to stability.

Predator–prey relationships are a good example of density-dependent control (example of lemmings and snowy owls, Topic 1, Section 1.2.15 page 42).

Density-independent factors are generally abiotic. The most important ones are extremes of weather (drought, fire, hurricanes) and long-term climate change. Others include geophysical and geological events such as earthquakes and volcanic eruptions and the tsunamis that can result from them. Their impacts include an increase in the death rate and a reduction in the birth rate, especially of smaller individuals. The response depends, in part, on the frequency and severity of the event. Density-independent factors can operate alongside density-dependent factors.

Density-dependent factors are those that lower the birth rate or raise the death rate as a population increases. In contrast, **density-independent** factors are those that affect a population irrespective of population density, notably environmental change.

Density-independent factors may have significant influence on population size, but it is the density-dependent factors that tend to regulate the population around the carrying capacity. In addition to competition for limited resources, these factors include the increased risk of predation and the transfer of pathogens in dense populations.

The introduction of the European rabbit to Australia resulted in a population increase to around 600 million individuals. In 1950, the Australian government sanctioned the release of the myxomatosis disease across the rabbit population – a density-independent factor – resulting in the population decreasing to 100 million. However, by 1991, genetic resistance had rebuilt the population to as many as 300 million individuals, prompting a second disease, the calicivirus, to be released. In areas where there was a greater density of rabbits, the virus was more lethal – illustrating features of density-dependent control.

Population size is regulated by density-dependent factors and negative feedback mechanisms.

2.1.12 Population growth

Limiting factors slow population growth as it approaches the carrying capacity of the system.

Limiting factors include:

- for plants: light, nutrients, water, CO_2 and temperature
- for animals: space, food, mates, nesting sites and water.

Populations have an upper level or extent to the number of individuals that can be sustained in each environment. Carrying capacity is the term used to describe the maximum number of individuals of a species that can be sustained by an environment. The carrying capacity represents the population size at which environmental limiting factors limit further population growth.

The term limiting factor was first used by the German agricultural chemist Justus von Liebig (1803–73), who noted that the growth of crops was limited by the shortage of certain minerals. Liebig established the 'law of minimum' – the idea that the productivity, reproduction and growth of organisms will be limited if one or more environmental factors is below its limiting level. Equally, there can be too much of a factor (i.e. there is an upper limit to how much of a particular nutrient plants can tolerate).

The carrying capacity of a population is affected by various limiting factors, such as:

- the availability of food and water
- territorial space
- predation
- disease
- availability of mates.

Population growth curves

Population growth can either be **exponential** or limited by carrying capacity. If a population is introduced into a new environment, such as that seen in the re-establishment of vegetation after the eruption of Krakatau in 1883 (this topic, Section 2.5.5) or the Mount St Helens eruption in 1980, specific population growth curves occur. Imagine rabbits are introduced into a new meadow. After an initial rapid (exponential) growth, the rabbit population will eat the vegetation faster than it can grow because of the large numbers of rabbits. Further increases in population will stop. In this situation, the food supply has become a **limiting factor** in the growth of the rabbit population. Eventually, the rabbit population will reach the carrying capacity of the meadow (i.e. the size of rabbit population that the meadow can support).

Limiting factors are the factors that limit the distribution or numbers of a particular population. Limiting factors are environmental factors that slow down population growth.

S-shaped population curve

When a graph of population growth for such species is plotted against time, an **S-shaped population curve** is produced. This is also known as a sigmoid growth curve. An S-shaped population curve shows an initial rapid growth (exponential growth) and then slows down as the carrying capacity is reached (Figure 2.22).

Figure 2.22 An S-shaped population growth curve.

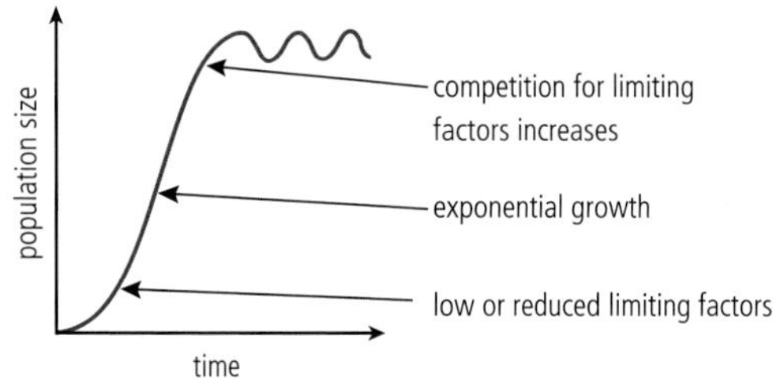

Make sure you know how to explain population growth curves in terms of numbers and rates.

The graph shows slow growth at first when the population is small and there is a lack of mature adults. Early in the population growth curve there are few limiting factors and the population can expand exponentially. Competition between the individuals of the same species increases as a population increases. Competition increases because individuals are competing for the same limited factors, such as resources (e.g. space on a rock for barnacles to attach to). The population eventually reaches its carrying capacity. Changes in the limiting factors cause the population size to increase and decrease (i.e. fluctuate) around the carrying capacity. Increases and decreases around the carrying capacity are controlled by negative feedback mechanisms.

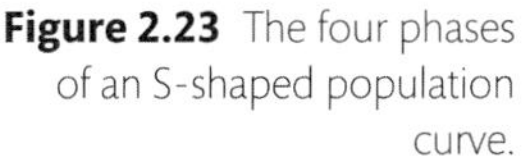

Figure 2.23 The four phases of an S-shaped population curve.

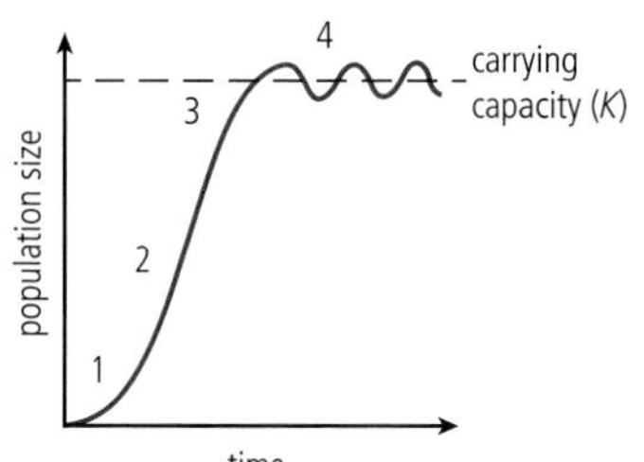

The S-shaped population curve can be divided into four phases (Figure 2.23 and Table 2.1).

Table 2.1 The four stages of an S-shaped population curve.

Phase number	Phase name	Description	Explanation
1	lag phase	low population numbers leading to low birth rates	• few individuals colonize a new area • because numbers of individuals are low, birth rates are also low
2	exponential growth phase	population grows at an increasingly rapid rate	• limiting factors do not restrict the growth of the population • there are favourable abiotic components, such as temperature and rainfall, and a lack of predators or disease • the number of individuals rapidly increases as does the rate of growth of population
3	transitional phase	population growth slows down considerably although continues to grow	• limiting factors begin to affect the population and restrict its growth • there is increased competition for resources • there is an increase in predators and an increase in disease and mortality due to increased numbers of individuals living in a small area • there is also a slowdown in growth rate of population
4	stationary phase	population growth stabilizes (the graph 'flattens') and then population fluctuates around a level that represents the carrying capacity	• limiting factors restrict the population to its carrying capacity (*k*) • changes in limiting factors, predation, disease and abiotic factors cause populations to increase and decrease around the carrying capacity

J-shaped population curve

Exponential growth is an increasing or accelerating rate of growth, sometimes referred to as a **J-shaped population curve** or a J-curve. Growth is initially slow but becomes increasingly rapid and does not slow down as population increases. Many populations show J-shaped rather than S-shaped population growth curves. Organisms showing J-shaped population curves tend to produce many offspring rapidly and have little parental care (e.g. insects such as locusts).

Exponential growth occurs when:

- limiting factors are not restricting the growth of the population
- there are plentiful resources such as light, space and food
- there are favourable abiotic components, such as temperature and rainfall.

Abiotic components can affect population growth (e.g. the carrying capacity of an environment for locusts can be raised due to rain). The sudden decrease in the population is called a population crash (Figure 2.24).

Populations showing J-shaped population curves are generally controlled by abiotic rather than biotic components, although a lack of food can also cause populations to crash.

S- and J-shaped population curves describe a generalized response of populations to a particular set of conditions (abiotic and biotic factors).

S-shaped population curves are population growth curves that show an initial rapid growth (exponential growth) and then slow down as the carrying capacity is reached. Population size fluctuates around a set point (carrying capacity) (Figure 2.23). In contrast, a **J-shaped population curve** is a population growth curve that shows only exponential growth. Growth is initially slow and becomes increasingly rapid; it does not slow down (Figure 2.24).

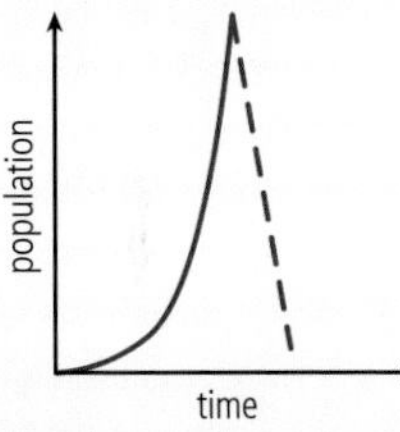

Figure 2.24 The J-shaped population growth curve.

Example – The introduction of reindeer to St Matthew Island, Alaska

Population growth curves can be studied in terms of numbers of individuals and rates of change, with populations showing a J-shaped population curve or a 'boom and bust' pattern.

One example was the introduction of reindeer to St Matthew Island, Alaska. The island, 128 square miles in area, is in the Bering Sea Wildlife Refuge in the north central Bering Sea.

Twenty-nine reindeer (*Rangifer tarandus*) were introduced to the island in 1944. By the summer of 1963, the population had increased to 6000. The density of reindeer had increased from 0.23 per square mile in 1944 to 46.88 per square mile in 1963. Studies showed that the body mass of the reindeer was larger than that of reindeer in domestic herds by 24–53% among females and 46–61% among males. The reindeer population benefited from the high quality and quantity of vegetation on the island, with the population responding by increasing rapidly due to a high birth rate and low mortality. However, the population crashed, undergoing a die-off in the winter of 1963, to 42 animals (Figure 2.25). Lichens, which had formed an important component of the winter diet, had been eliminated through excessive foraging by the reindeer, with other plants unsuitable for reindeer diets increasing in abundance. In the late

Some factors that limit the size of populations depend on the density of the population, whereas others do not. Density-dependent factors are those that lower the birth rate or raise the death rate as a population increases. In contrast, density-independent factors are those that affect a population irrespective of population density. Factors affected by population density include supply of food and water, predation, parasites and communicable disease (e.g. influenza). Factors not related to population density include climate (e.g. precipitation and humidity) and natural disasters (e.g. fire and flood).

winter of 1963–1964, virtually the entire population of 6000 reindeer died of starvation (Figure 2.25).

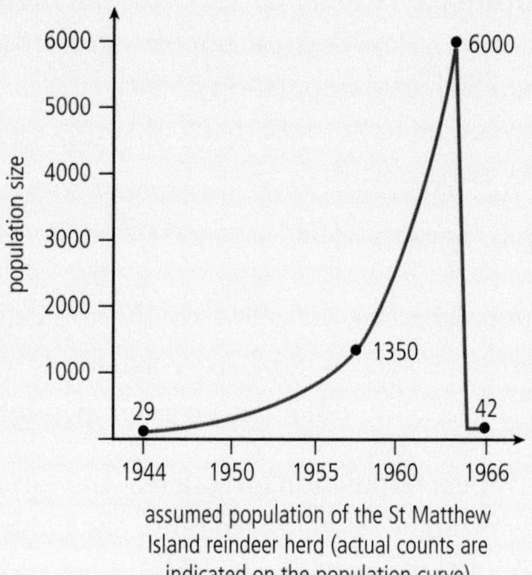

Figure 2.25 The introduction, increase and crash of a reindeer population on St Matthew Island.

If there are no limiting factors, population growth follows a J-shaped population curve (showing exponential growth). When density-dependent limiting factors start to operate, the curve becomes S-shaped.

Similar events to those seen on St Matthew's Island have been repeated around the globe. They occur when a population of one species is introduced to an island, where ecosystems have a limited food supply and regulating factors for populations are lacking (for example, natural predators for the introduced species).

5.2 Agriculture and food
8.2 Urban systems and urban planning

2.1.13 and 2.1.14 Limiting factors on the growth of human populations

Access to Earth resources, following technological advances, has encouraged a cornucopian *perspective*.

Populations of all organisms in ecosystems experience limiting factors that control their population size (this topic, Section 2.1.12, page 99). These limiting factors include food resources, access to water and space. The first human populations encountered the same limiting factors but as human populations grew and spread around the planet, they found ways to eliminate natural predators and develop technology and access to energy sources not available to the early humans. These innovations meant that the effect of limiting factors on the growth of human populations has become increasingly less important, leading ultimately (in many human populations) to the elimination of these factors.

5.2 Agriculture and food
8.1 Human populations
8.2 Urban systems and urban planning

Technological advances have enabled humans to access resources from every area of the biosphere. By removing limiting factors in this way, human populations have continued to grow, with far-reaching consequences for the sustainability of ecosystems. Excessive and unsustainable extraction of natural resources has led to degradation of the environment (Topic 1, Section 1.3.7).

Carrying capacity cannot be easily assessed for human populations

Estimating the carrying capacity of an environment for human populations is more complicated because of the broad and changing ecological niche of humans.

It is difficult to reliably estimate the environmental carrying capacity for human populations because:

- the variety of resources used is greater
- humans can substitute one resource for another when the first becomes depleted
- lifestyle affects resource requirement

- technological developments change resources required and available (e.g. developments in renewable energy could reduce demand for fossil fuels)
- resources can be imported.

The concept of niche has been discussed in Section 2.1.8. Humans have a broad and changing ecological niche. In natural ecosystems, species achieve equilibrium with their environment (this topic, Section 2.1.12, page 100), leading to fluctuating but stable populations that are controlled by limiting factors. Human populations, in contrast, are less limited due to the mobility of resources. The expansion of the human niche also takes place through technological advances and changes in consumption.

The rapidly changing human niche has implications for the measurement of human carrying capacity. Estimations of human carrying capacity can be disputed because of differing input data. Human carrying capacity can only be estimated for the current time (i.e. now) and not for the future. This is due to the lack of knowledge of how human populations will develop in the coming decades. Estimates of carrying capacity are a reciprocal (the inverse) of the ecological footprint, meaning that as ecological footprint (Topic 1, Section 1.3.13) increases, human carrying capacity decreases (Figure 2.26). When a population surpasses its carrying capacity, it enters a period of 'overshoot'. As carrying capacity is defined as the maximum population that an environment can maintain indefinitely, overshoot must, by definition, be temporary. With human populations, the overshoot can be sustained by technological innovations and substitution of resources but ultimately the degradation of natural systems that occur will led to a reduction in human carrying capacity.

An ecological footprint is the inverse of carrying capacity and provides a quantitative estimate of human carrying capacity.

8.1 Human populations

8.2 Urban systems and urban planning

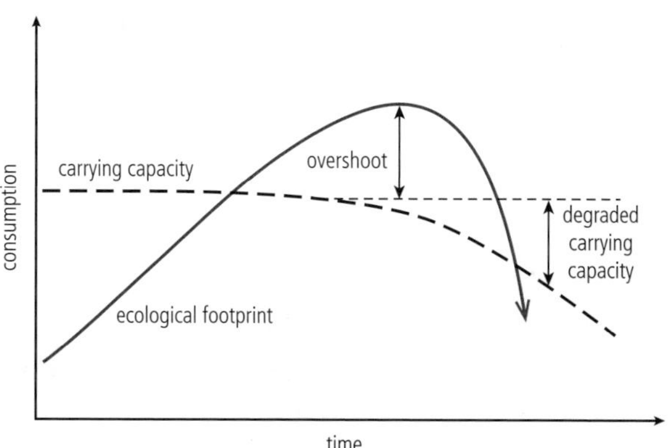

Figure 2.26 Increasing ecological footprint leads to reduction in carrying capacity.

2.1.15, 2.1.16 and 2.1.17 Estimating population abundance

HL b Environmental economics

Make sure you consider reasons for selecting the most appropriate technique for estimating population abundance. The information on the following pages will help you with this selection.

Ecosystems are highly complex systems. Abiotic factors such as temperature, **insolation** (a measure of the amount of sunlight) and precipitation define where ecosystems are found and how they influence the biotic components (i.e. the organisms found there – this topic, Section 2.1.6 and 2.1.7, page 89). Flows of energy and cycles of matter support ecosystems (this topic, Sections 2.2.1–2.2.9). Given the complexity of ecosystems, standardized methods are needed to compare ecosystems with one another. Such studies also allow ecosystems to be monitored, modelled and evaluated over time, with both

Population abundance can be estimated using **random sampling**, **systematic sampling** or **transect sampling**.

Make sure you know how to design and carry out ecological investigations. These make ideal studies for your Internal Assessment project. The study of an ecosystem requires that it be named and located (e.g. Deinikerwald, Baar, Switzerland, a mixed deciduous-coniferous managed woodland).

TOK

What constraints are there in the pursuit of knowledge?

The measurement of biotic factors is often subjective, relying on your interpretation of different measuring techniques to provide data. It is rare in environmental investigations to be able to provide ways of measuring variables that are as precise and reliable as those in the physical sciences. Will this affect the value of the data collected and the validity of the knowledge?

natural change and human impacts being measured. For human effects to be established, the undisturbed ecosystem must first be researched.

Let's now consider the biotic or living factors in an ecosystem and how their abundance can be estimated. Remember, when carrying out fieldwork you must follow the IB ethical practice guidelines and IB animal experimentation policy, that is, animals and the environment should not be harmed during your work.

Methods for estimating abundance of organisms

It is not possible to study every organism in an ecosystem, so limitations are put on how many plants and animals are studied. Trapping methods enable limited samples to be taken.

Trapping methods for organisms that can move around (are motile/mobile) include:

- pitfall traps – beakers or pots buried in the soil that animals walk into and cannot escape from
- nets – sweep, butterfly, seine and purse
- flight interception traps – fine-meshed nets that intercept the flight of insects – the animals fall into collecting trays where they can be collected (Topic 3, Section 3.1.8, page 242)
- small mammal traps – often baited, with a door that closes once an animal is inside (e.g. the Longworth trap).
- light traps – a UV bulb against a white sheet attracts certain night-flying insects (Figure 2.27)
- Tullgren funnels (Figure 2.28) – paired cloth funnels, with a light source at one end, a sample pot at the other end and a wire mesh between; invertebrates in soil samples placed on the mesh move away from the heat of the lamp and fall into the collecting bottle at the bottom.

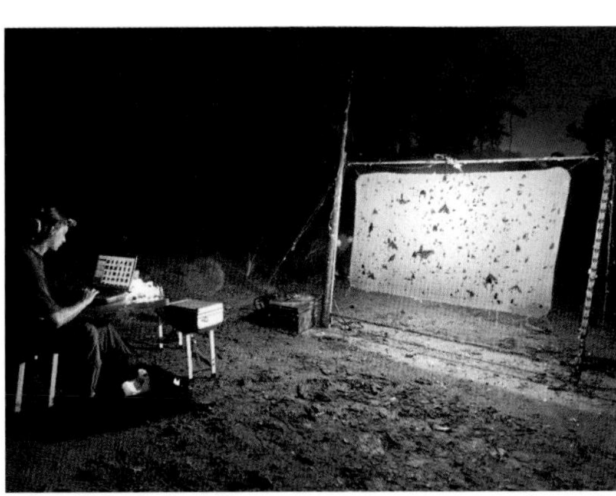

Figure 2.27 A light trap attracts nocturnal insects.

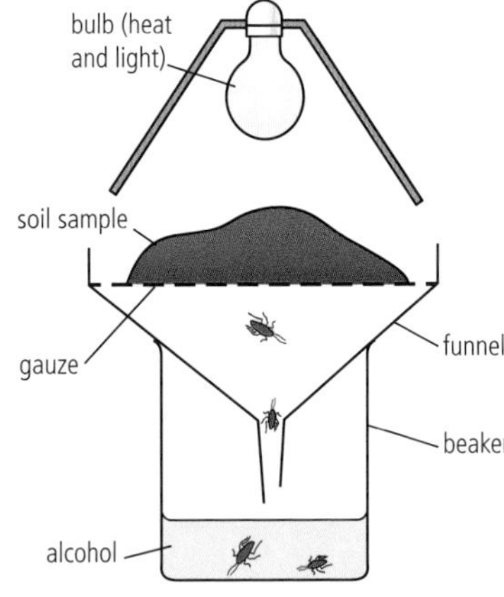

Figure 2.28 A Tullgren funnel.

Trapping methods for organisms that cannot move around (are non-motile) or have limited movement) include:

- quadrats – square frames of different sizes depending on the sample area being studied; frames can be divided into grids of smaller squares to quantify the numbers of organisms present more easily (later in this section, page 106)
- point frames.

Abundance, as used in ecology, refers to the relative representation of a species in an ecosystem. You can work out the number or abundance of organisms in various ways – either by directly counting the number or percentage cover of organisms in a selected area (for organisms that do not move or are limited in movement) or by indirectly calculating abundance using a formula such as the Lincoln index (for animals that are motile).

In the early 1980s, Terry Erwin, a scientist at the Smithsonian Institution collected insects from the canopy of tropical forest trees in Panama. He sampled 19 trees and collected 955 species of beetle. Using extrapolation methods, he estimated there could be 30 million species of arthropod worldwide. Although now believed to be an overestimation, this study started the race to calculate the total number of species on Earth before many of them become extinct.

Direct methods of estimating the abundance of motile animals

Direct methods of estimating abundance include actual counts and sampling. These methods give the relative abundance of different animals in a sample, rather than an estimation of absolute population size (which the Lincoln index does).

Technology now enables direct counts of animal populations using aerial photography. Photographs can be taken of animal herds and the number of individuals counted using a computer.

There are many ways to sample animal populations, such as those listed on the previous page, including pitfall traps (Figure 2.29).

Figure 2.29 A pitfall trap. A plastic pot is buried in the ground. A rain cover (e.g. a plastic plate) is placed over the pit to prevent rain from flooding the trap. The rain cover can be supported by stones or sticks that elevate it above the pit. Animals fall into the trap and cannot escape.

If the leaf litter on a forest floor is to be sampled, a standardized sample of leaf litter can be put in a tray and a pooter used to suck invertebrates into a small pot. Pooters can also be used to sample insects directly from vegetation. Pooters can be bought or made using a glass jar or plastic pot with tubes or straws (Figure 2.30).

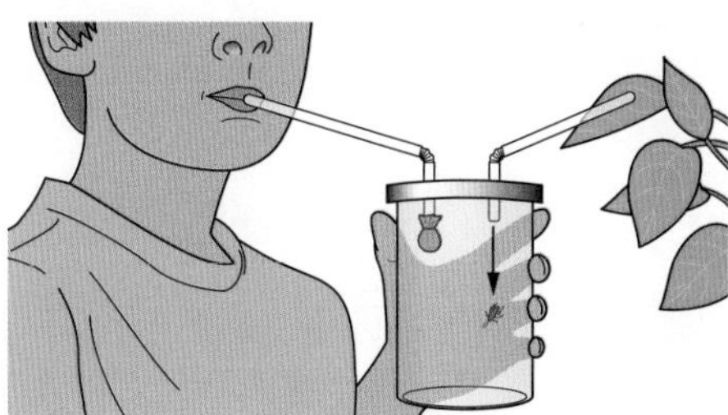

Figure 2.30 A home-made pooter. Plastic straws are attached to a glass jar or pot. One tube is put in the mouth: suction creates a lower pressure in the jar so that small animals are drawn into the jar. A fine mesh is wrapped around the end of the tube so that insects are not ingested when creating the suction.

To sample river organisms, the bed of the river is disturbed so that animals found there can be collected. The method involves agitating the riverbed with a boot and collecting disturbed animals downstream in a net. A fixed time is set for this 'kick sampling'. The catch is put in a shallow white tray with at least 2 cm depth of freshwater from the river and an identification key is used to sort the catch into different groups. Limitations to this method include the difficulty of standardizing the kick-action (different intensities of kicking will disturb different numbers of organisms) and some animals may remain stuck to rocks and so will not be sampled.

Sample methods must allow for the collection of data that is scientifically representative and appropriate and allow the collection of data on all species present. Results can be used to compare ecosystems.

Make sure you know how to evaluate methods for measuring or estimating populations of motile and non-motile organisms.

Random quadrat sampling

Use quadrat sampling estimates for abundance, population density, percentage cover and percentage frequency for non-mobile organisms

Quadrats are used to limit the sampling area when you want to measure the population size of non-mobile organisms (motile ones can move from one quadrat to another and so be sampled more than once thus making results invalid). Quadrats vary in size from 0.25 m square to 1 m square. The size of quadrat should be optimal for the organisms you are studying. To select the correct quadrat size, count the number of different species in several differently sized quadrats. Plot the number of species against quadrat size: the point where the graph levels off and no further species are added even when the quadrats gets larger, gives you the size of the quadrat you need to use.

If your sample area contains the same habitat throughout, **random sampling** is used. Quadrats should be located at random (use a random number generator). First, you mark out an area of your habitat using two tape measures placed at right angles to each other. Then you use the random numbers to locate positions within the marked-out area. For example, if the grid is 10 m by 10 m, random numbers are generated between 0 and 1000. The random number 596 represents a point 5 m 96 cm along one tape measure. The next random number is the coordinate for the second tape. The point where the coordinates cross is the location for the quadrat.

Random quadrat sampling can be used to estimate population size for non-mobile organisms.

If your sample area covers habitats very different from each other (e.g. an undisturbed and a disturbed area), you need to use **stratified random sampling**, so you take sets of results from both areas. If the sample area is along an environmental gradient, make sure you place quadrats at set distances (e.g. every 5 m) along a transect: this is called **systematic sampling**. In **continuous sampling**, samples are taken along the whole length of the transect.

Population density is the number of individuals of each species per unit area. It is calculated by dividing the number of organisms sampled by the total area covered by the quadrats, as shown below.

$$\text{population density} = \frac{\text{total number of a species in all quadrats}}{\text{area of one quadrat} \times \text{total number of quadrats}}$$

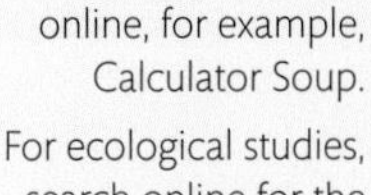

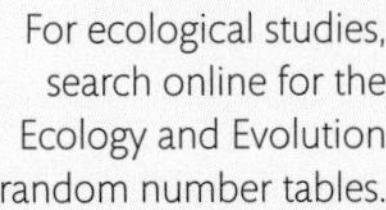

You can find random number generators online, for example, Calculator Soup.

For ecological studies, search online for the Ecology and Evolution random number tables.

Plant abundance is best estimated using **percentage cover** (Figure 2.31). This is an estimate of the area in each quadrat covered by the organism (usually a plant) in question.

Figure 2.31 Percentage cover is the percentage of the area within the quadrat covered by one species. Percentage cover is worked out for each species present. Dividing the quadrat into a 10 × 10 grid (100 squares) helps to estimate percentage cover (each square is 1% of the total area cover).

Percentage frequency is the number of *actual* occurrences divided by the number of *possible* occurrences, expressed as a percentage. For example, if a plant occurs in 7 out of 100 squares in a grid quadrat, its percentage frequency is 7%. If 8 quadrats out of 10 contain yellow-horned poppy on a transect across a shingle ridge (this topic, Section 2.5.3 and 2.5.4, page 204), their percentage frequency would be 80%. When using whole quadrats to estimate percentage frequency, results depend on the size of the quadrat and so these details need to be included in the conclusion (e.g. yellow-horned poppies occur at a frequency of 80% in a sample of 10 × 1 m^2 quadrats).

The quadrat method is subjective and different people will end up with different measures. There are many possible sources of error. One species may be covering another and so not be included and differences between species may be slight, so two or more organisms may be mistakenly identified as the same or different species. It is also difficult to use quadrats for very large or very small plants or for plants that grow in tufts or colonies. It is possible that plants that appear to be separate are joined by roots: this will affect calculation of population density. It is also difficult to measure the abundance of plants outside their main growing season when plants are largely invisible.

The sampling system used depends on the area being sampled:

- random sampling is used if the same habitat is found throughout the area
- stratified random sampling is used in two areas of different habitat quality
- systematic sampling is used along a transect where there is an environmental gradient (such as along a succession – this topic, Section 2.5.3 and 2.5.4, page 202).

Abundance scales

Another method of estimating the abundance of non-motile organisms is the use of abundance scales: these can be used to estimate the relative abundance of different organisms on, for example, a rocky shore. These are known as DAFOR scales, where each letter indicates a different level of abundance: D = dominant, A = abundant, F = frequent, O = occasional and R = rare. Quadrats are usually used to define the sample area. Different types of species are put in different categories, for example seaweeds will be in a different group to periwinkles (periwinkles are a type of mollusc). These scales allow for general comparison between different sampling sites. It is a qualitative scale used to judge the abundance of different organisms. Because it is qualitative, it is subjective and so different people may have different judgements of abundance. Also, there are no distinctions between different species in the same category (e.g. all seaweeds will be treated alike, irrespective of size or other differences). The lack of quantitative data makes statistical analysis difficult.

Percentage cover is an estimate of the area in each frame size (quadrat) covered by the plant or animal in question.

Percentage frequency is the number of occurrences divided by the number of possible occurrences. For example, if a plant occurs in 5 out of 100 squares in a grid quadrat, then the percentage frequency is 5%.

Percentage cover and frequency give an estimate of abundance but not actual population size.

Transects

SKILLS

Use quadrat sampling to measure change along a transect

Different types of quadrats can be used, depending on the type of organism being studied.

Frame quadrats (Figure 2.32) are empty frames of known area, such as 1 m^2.

Figure 2.32 A frame quadrat.

TOK

How can we judge whether evidence is adequate?

Applying the rigorous standards used in a physical science investigation would render most environmental studies unworkable. Whether this is acceptable or not is a matter of opinion, although it could be argued that by doing nothing, we would miss an opportunity to gain a useful understanding of the environment.

Environmental gradients are changes in environmental factors through space (e.g. decreasing temperature with increasing altitude up a mountain) or where an ecosystem suddenly ends (e.g. at forest edges). In these situations, both biotic and abiotic factors vary with distance and form gradients in which trends can be recorded. The techniques used in sampling such gradients are based on the quadrat method (earlier in this section, page 106) and, as such, are more easily carried out on vegetation and non-motile animals.

Grid quadrats are frames divided into 100 small squares with each square representing 1%. This helps in calculating percentage cover (earlier in this section, page 106).

Point quadrats (Figure 2.33) are made from a frame with 10 holes, which is placed into the ground by a leg. A pin is dropped through each hole in turn and the species touched are recorded. The total number of pins touching each species is converted to percentage frequency data; for example, if a species touched 6 out of the 10 pins it has 60% frequency.

Figure 2.33 A point quadrat.

Because environmental variables change along a gradient, random quadrat sampling is not appropriate. All parts of the gradient need to be sampled, so a transect is used. The simplest transect is a **line transect** – a tape measure laid out in the direction of the gradient (e.g. on a beach this would be laid out at 90° to the sea). All organisms touching the tape are recorded. Many line transects need to be taken to obtain valid quantitative data. Larger samples can be taken using a **belt transect** (Figure 2.34). This is a band of chosen width (usually between 0.5 and 1 m) laid along the gradient.

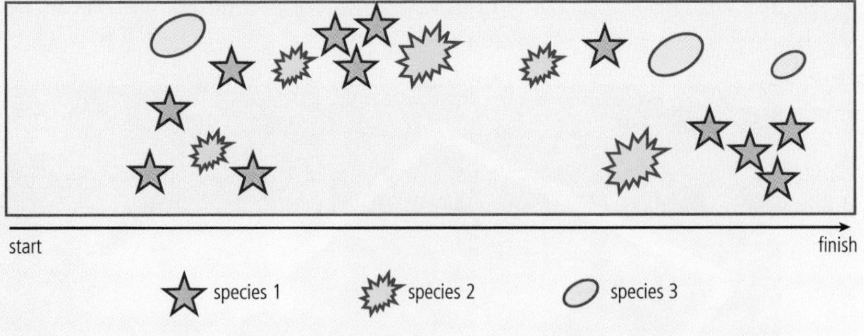

Figure 2.34 Belt transects sample a strip through the sample area. Replication of transects is needed to obtain valid quantitative data.

In both line and belt transects, the whole transect can be sampled (a **continuous transect**) or samples can be taken at points of equal distance along the gradient (an **interrupted transect**). If there is no discernible vertical change in the transect, horizontal distances are used (e.g. along a shingle ridge succession), whereas if there is a climb or descent then vertical distances are normally used (e.g. on a rocky shore).

It is important that transects are carried out, as far as possible, at the same time of day, so abiotic variables are comparable. Seasonal fluctuations also mean that samples should be taken either as close together in time as possible or throughout the whole year. Datalogging equipment allows the latter to take place, although this may be impractical in school studies.

So that data are reliable and quantitatively valid, transects should be repeated – at least three repeats is recommended. To avoid bias in placing the transects, a random number generator can be used (earlier in this section, page 106). A tape measure is laid at right angles to the environmental gradient and transects can be located at random intervals along the tape or at regular intervals (Figure 2.35).

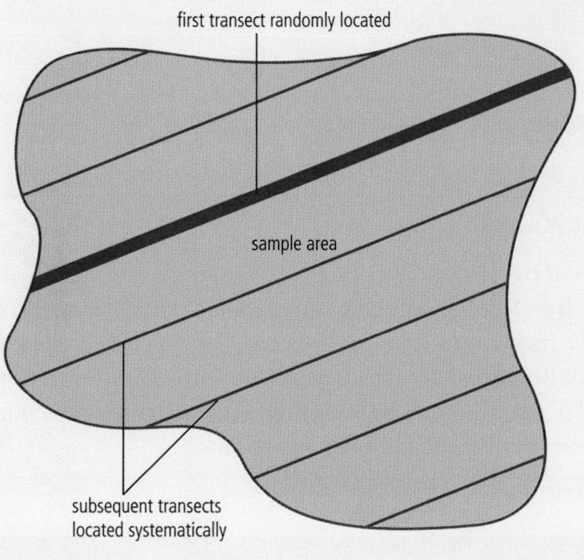

Figure 2.35 All transects can be located randomly or they can be systematically located following the random location of the first. So, for example, subsequent transects might be located every 10 m along a line perpendicular to the ecological gradient.

Capture–mark–release–recapture and the Lincoln index

Capture–mark–release–recapture and the Lincoln index can be used to estimate population size for mobile organisms.

The Lincoln index is used to estimate the total population size of mobile animals in a study area. In a sample taken using the methods outlined previously, it is unlikely that all the animals in a population are sampled, so a mathematical method is used to calculate the total numbers. The Lincoln index is an *indirect* way of estimating the abundance of an animal population because a formula is used to calculate abundance rather than counting the total number of organisms directly.

Using the Lincoln index involves collecting a sample from the population, marking the organisms in some way (paint can be used on insects or fur clipping on mammals), releasing them back into the wild, then resampling some time later and counting how many marked individuals you find in the second capture. It is essential that marking methods are ethically acceptable (non-harmful) and non-conspicuous (so that the animals are not more easily seen by predators).

Because of the procedures involved, this is called a 'capture–mark–release–recapture' technique. If all the marked animals are recaptured then the number of marked animals is assumed to be the total population size, whereas if half the marked animals are recaptured then the total population size is assumed to be twice as big as the first sample.

Capture-mark-release-recapture and use of the Lincoln index to estimate population size

The formula used in calculating population size is:

$$\text{Lincoln index} = \frac{(M \times N)}{R}$$

where M is the number caught and marked in the first sample, N is the number caught in the second sample and R is the number caught in the second sample that were previously marked.

There are several assumptions made when using the Lincoln index. It is assumed that animals do not enter or leave the study area and that there are no births or deaths of any of the sampled animals. It is also assumed that the method samples a representative portion of the total population.

Population size estimate = $\frac{(M \times N)}{R}$, where M is the number of individuals caught and marked initially, N is the total number of individuals recaptured and R is the number of marked individuals recaptured.

Make sure you know how to describe and evaluate direct and indirect methods for estimating the abundance of mobile organisms.

1.2 Systems

These assumptions mean that the Lincoln index method has limitations. Animals may move in and out of the sample area, making the capture–mark–release–recapture method less trustworthy and the data invalid. The density of the population in different habitats might vary or there may be many in one area, few in another. The assumption that they are equally distributed may not be true. Some individuals may be hidden by vegetation and therefore be difficult to find, hence they are not included in the sample. There may be seasonal variations in animals affecting population size. For example, animals may migrate in or out of the study area. In addition, sample animals may die and others may be born during the sample period.

Challenge yourself

Take a sheet of paper and divide it into 100 squares. Cut these squares out and put them into a tray. Select 20 of these squares and mark them with a cross. Put them back into the tray. Capture another 20 pieces of paper. Record how many of these are marked with a cross. Use the Lincoln index to estimate the population size of all pieces of paper. How closely does this agree with the actual number (100)? How could you improve the reliability of the method?

A **community** is a group of populations living and interacting with each other in an ecosystem.

2.1.18 Community

A **community** is a group of several populations living and interacting with each other in an ecosystem. A community is many species living together, whereas the term *population* refers to just one species. The savannah grasslands and lake ecosystems of Africa contain wildebeest, lions, hyenas, giraffes, elephants and zebras (Figure 2.36). Communities include all biotic parts of the ecosystem, both plants and animals.

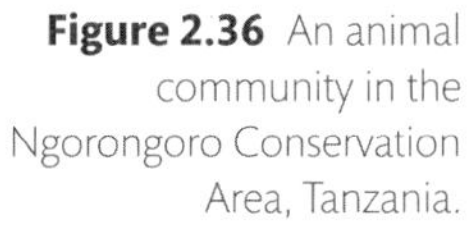

Figure 2.36 An animal community in the Ngorongoro Conservation Area, Tanzania.

A **habitat** is the location in which a community, species, population or organism lives.

2.1.19 Habitat

A **habitat** is the location in which a community, species, population or organism lives. A description of the habitat of a species can include both geographical and physical locations and the type of ecosystem required to meet all environmental conditions needed for survival.

The habitat of the African elephant includes savannahs, forests, deserts and marshes (Figure 2.37).

Figure 2.37 Elephant family in front of Mount Kilimanjaro, in the Amboseli National Park. These elephants live in an environment with open savannah grassland, acacia woodland, swamps and marshlands.

Make sure you are aware that for some organisms, habitats can change over time because of migration.

2.1.20 Ecosystems

An ecosystem is a community of interdependent organisms (the biotic component) and the physical environment (the abiotic component) with which it interacts. Ecosystems are open systems in which both energy and matter can enter and exit (Topic 1, Section 1.2.5).

Ecosystems can be divided into three types: terrestrial, marine and freshwater. Marine ecosystems include the sea, estuaries, salt marshes and mangroves. Terrestrial ecosystems (Figure 2.38) include all land-based ecosystems.

Figure 2.38 Taiga forest, the largest areas of which are located in Russia and Canada, is an example of a terrestrial ecosystem.

Marine ecosystems (Figure 2.39) all have a high concentration of salt in the water. Estuaries are included in the same group as marine ecosystems because they have high salt content compared to freshwater ecosystems.

Freshwater ecosystems (Figure 2.40) include rivers, lakes and wetlands.

Figure 2.39 A coral reef is an example of a marine ecosystem.

Figure 2.40 The Orinoco river, Venezuela, is an example of a freshwater ecosystem.

Ecosystems such as the northern coniferous forest Taiga, cross several countries and so their conservation and ecology have an international dimension.

Activity

Which ecosystem or ecosystems are found in your local area? What defines these ecosystems?

Produce a poster on one ecosystem and add details about the abiotic factors that determine why this ecosystem exists in your local area and how these determine the communities that are found there.

An **ecosystem** is a community and the physical environment with which it interacts.

Thinking back to the definitions of community and habitat in Section 2.1.18 and 2.1.19, add the following details to your poster:

Consider the concept of systems in this local ecosystem.
- What are inputs and outputs to the system?
- Can you produce a systems diagram of the ecosystem?

Consider the concept of community in this local ecosystem:
- What communities are found in the ecosystem?
- Add details of the communities to your poster.

1.2 Systems

Consider the concept of habitat in this local ecosystem:
- What habitats are found in the ecosystem and how are they defined?
- What abiotic and biotic factors distinguish one habitat from another?

Challenge yourself

See this page of your eBook for a bottle ecosystem activity.

The use of invertebrates in such experiments has ethical implications. You need to adhere to the IB ethical guidelines. IBO guidelines state that 'Any experimentation should not result in any pain or undue stress on any animal (vertebrate or invertebrate) or compromise its health in any way'. Animals must be handled with care and should only be used for brief periods of time, and returned to a safe environment once the experiment is completed.

2.1.21 Sustainability is a natural property of ecosystems

Inputs are balanced by outputs in a steady-state ecosystem.

In Topic 1, we saw how inputs are balanced by outputs in a steady-state system (Sections 1.2.8 and 1.2.9). The same is true of ecosystems that are in steady state.

Energy leaving an ecosystem as heat (as the ultimate product of **cellular respiration** – this topic, Sections 2.2.3 to 2.2.9) are balanced by input of solar energy (Figure 2.41). The input of CO_2 maintains the process of photosynthesis (this topic, Section 2.2.4, page 130). This produces glucose, which in turn is used to release energy during cellular respiration to support life processes. Matter cycles within ecosystems, with some minerals lost through leaching. Water enters an ecosystem through rainfall and leaves the ecosystem through evaporation. Water is needed for photosynthesis and is a basic requirement for life, so outputs of water need to be balanced by inputs. The internal cycling of matter within ecosystems, and the constant input of energy, sustains the ecosystem through time – there is evidence that some ecosystems, such as rainforests, have persisted for millions of years.

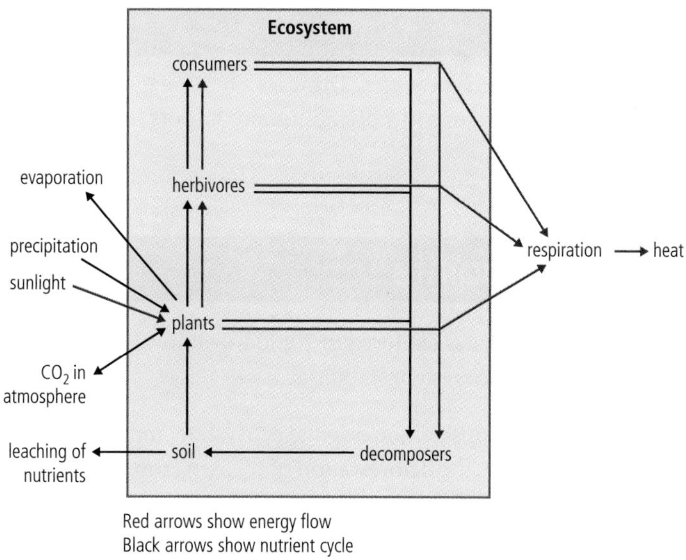

Figure 2.41 Input of energy and CO_2 from the atmosphere, and cycling of nutrients, maintain steady-state conditions in ecosystems.

Example – Systems diagram for a forest ecosystem

Balance of inputs and outputs can be considered in flow diagrams of specific ecosystems, for example, Figure 2.42 shows the inputs and outputs from a forest ecosystem.

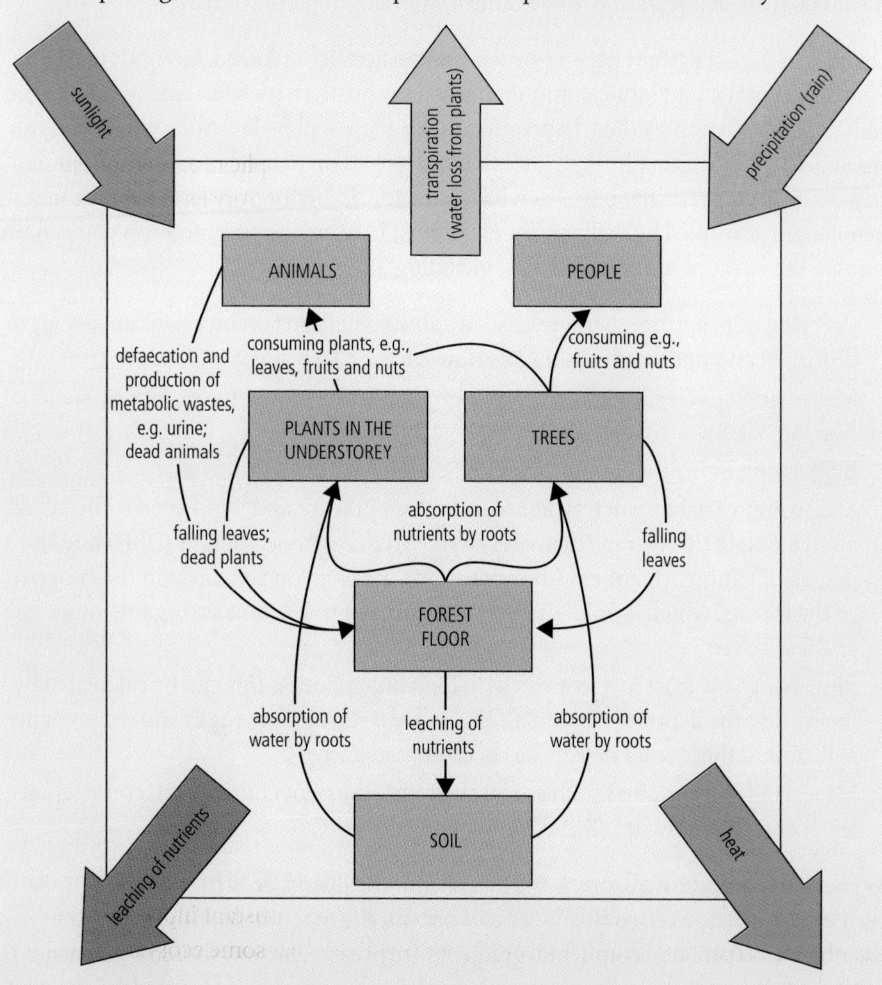

Figure 2.42 Inputs and output of a forest ecosystem.

1.3 Sustainability
7.2 Energy resources, uses and management

Activity

Select an ecosystem from your local area. Draw a systems diagram showing inputs and outputs from the ecosystem. How do inputs and outputs help achieve steady-state equilibrium?

2.1.22 Tipping points

1.2 Systems

5.1 Soil
6.2 Climate change - causes and impacts

The concept of tipping points was explored in Topic 1 (Section 1.2.12). Human activity can lead to tipping points in ecosystem stability.

Tipping points lead to the collapse of the original ecosystem and development of a new equilibrium. For example, the deforestation of the Amazon rainforest reduces generation of water vapour through transpiration and consequently reduces cooling and precipitation necessary for the maintenance of the remaining forest.

Measuring changes in an ecosystem due to human activity

Interesting studies can be made using historic maps or geographic information system (GIS) data to track land use change.

Human impacts on ecosystems include toxins from mining activity, landfills, eutrophication (Topic 4, Section 4.4.5), effluent, oil spills, overexploitation and change of land use (e.g. deforestation, use of land for development or tourism).

Greater awareness of environmental issues has caused *perspectives* to alter over time. What would not have been seen as a problem in the past (e.g. mining activity) is now understood to produce toxins and to lead to environmental damage. Greater understanding of scientific issues has influenced public perception of human effects on the environment and has changed worldviews.

Changes in the ecosystem depend on the human activity involved. Methods used for measuring abiotic and biotic components of an ecosystem must be appropriate to the human activity being studied. In your local area there will be locations where you can investigate the effect that human disturbance has had on natural ecosystems. These may be areas of forest that have been harvested for timber or grassland habitats that are regularly trampled by walkers, for example. There are various methods you can use to study the effect of human activities, including:

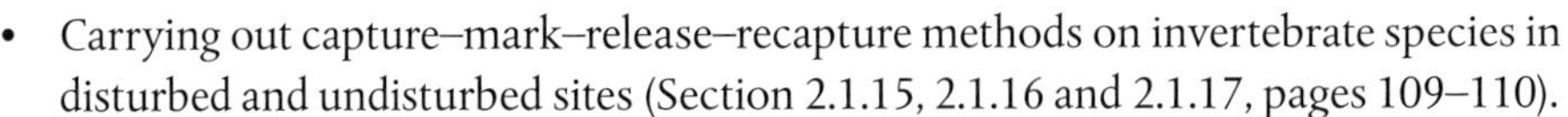

- Carrying out capture–mark–release–recapture methods on invertebrate species in disturbed and undisturbed sites (Section 2.1.15, 2.1.16 and 2.1.17, pages 109–110).
- Measuring species diversity using Simpson's reciprocal index (Topic 3, Section 3.1.8).
- HL Using indicator species (Topic 4, Section 4.4.13).
- Measuring variables such as light levels, temperature and wind speed. You could also calculate the average diameter of tree stems at breast height (DBH) and the degree of canopy openness (the amount of sky can you see through the canopy of the forest), which would give you measures of tree biomass (organic matter) and leaf cover.
- Measuring soil erosion – in areas with high precipitation this can be calculated by measuring the depth of soil remaining under free-standing rocks and stones, where soil around these solid objects has been eroded away.
- Measuring soil variables such as soil structure, nutrient content, pH, compaction levels and soil moisture (Topic 5.1, Section 5.1.3).

You need to compare measurements taken from the disturbed area with those from undisturbed areas, so that you can work out the magnitude and effect of the disturbance. Where environmental gradients are present, factors should be measured along the full extent of the gradient so that valid comparisons can be made.

Example – Studying the effects of deforestation

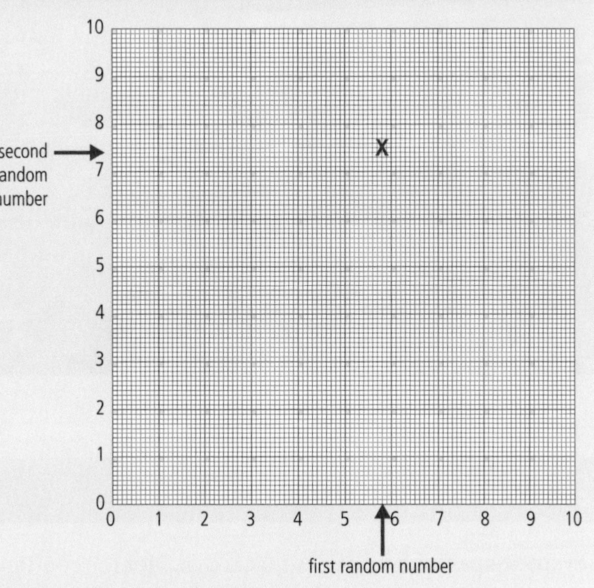

Figure 2.43 Locating a sampling point (X) using random numbers (see page 106 for details).

Both pristine and logged forest areas must be studied so comparisons can be made. Stratified random sampling is used in two areas because the pristine and logged forest areas are different in habitat quality. Sampling grids are established in both pristine and logged forest sites. Samples are collected from the grids using random sampling methods. For example, for a grid of 10 m by 10 m, a random number generator could be used to choose random points to sample within the grid. Numbers generated between 0 and 1000 would provide the sample points; for example 580 would represent a point 5 m 80 cm along the bottom of the grid and 740 a point 7 m 40 cm along the side of the grid (Figure 2.43).

Abiotic and biotic measurements can be made at each sample point. Abiotic measurements include wind, temperature and light intensity. Quadrats can be used to sample biotic measurements. Biotic factors include the species of plants and animals present and the population size of selected indicator species. Motile animals can be sampled using capture–mark–release–recapture methods.

Several samples are taken from each sampling grid. Sampling grids must be repeated in both pristine and logged forest areas so that data are reliable. At least five sampling grids from both pristine and logged forest are recommended. Abiotic and biotic components must be measured over a long period of time and any daily and seasonal variations considered to ensure data are valid.

Geographic information system (GIS) data can be used to track changes in ecosystems over time. One example of this is the use of satellite images (Figure 2.44).

An advantage of satellite images is that the visible nature of the photos is useful for motivating public opinion and action. A disadvantage is that they can be expensive to obtain and may not be available for the area being studied. Another disadvantage is that although some biotic measurements, such as plant productivity, can be measured, other biotic and abiotic components, such as species diversity and relative humidity, cannot. Satellite images are best used in conjunction with ground studies so that the images can be matched with abiotic and biotic data from the ground.

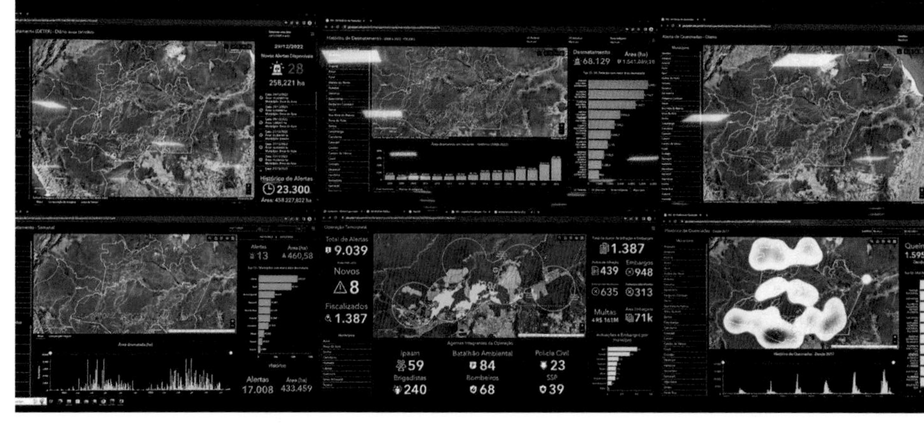

Figure 2.44 These images show deforestation in Brazil.

Figure 2.45 An agouti feeding on a Brazil nut in a forest.

A keystone is the central stone at the top of an arch. It enables the whole arch to support its mass, maintaining stability in the building it is part of.

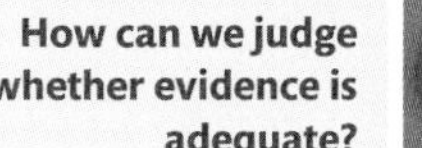

How can we judge whether evidence is adequate?

There are various approaches to the conservation of biodiversity. How can we know when we should act on what we know?

There is a disproportionate impact on community structure and the risk of ecosystem collapse if keystone species are removed.

1.2 Systems

3.3 Conservation and regeneration

2.1.23 Keystone species

Keystone species are species that are vital for the continuing function of the ecosystem: without them the ecosystem may collapse. Keystone species therefore have a role in the sustainability of ecosystems. An example is the agouti of tropical South and Central America, which feeds on the nuts of the Brazil nut tree (Figure 2.45).

The Brazil nut tree (*Bertholletia excelsa*) is a hardwood species that is found from eastern Peru, eastern Colombia and eastern Bolivia through Venezuela and northern Brazil. They are the tallest trees in the Amazon (they grow up to 50 m). The agouti is a large forest rodent and the only animal with teeth strong enough to open the Brazil nut tree's tough seed pods. The agouti buries many of the seeds around the forest floor, so it has access to food when the Brazil nuts are less abundant. Some of these seeds germinate and grow into adult plants. Without the agouti, the Brazil nut tree would not be able to distribute its seeds and the species would eventually die out. Without the Brazil nut tree, other animals and plants that depend on it would be affected; for example, harpy eagles use the trees for nesting sites. Brazil nuts are one of the most valuable non-timber products found in the Amazon as they are a protein-rich food source and their extracted oils are a popular ingredient in many cosmetic products. The sale of Brazil nuts provides an important source of income for many local communities.

Given the complexity of ecosystems, keystone species may be difficult to identify. In addition, many keystone species may be species that are yet unidentified. By conserving whole ecosystems (i.e. establishing protected areas), rather than attempting to conserve individual species, the complex interrelationships that exist there will be preserved, including the keystone species.

Activity

Find out about two further examples of keystone species, e.g. purple sea stars controlling mussel populations on the North Pacific coast that would otherwise overwhelm the ecosystem; elephants feeding on shrubs and trees and thus maintaining savannah grasslands. Write a summary of each example, explaining why each species is a keystone species and the potential impact on its ecosystem if it were removed.

2.1.24 and 2.1.25 Changes to biosphere integrity have passed a critical threshold

The planetary boundaries model (Topic 1, Section 1.3.19) is used to indicate the environmental ceiling beyond which lie unacceptable environmental degradation and potential tipping points in Earth systems. One of the planetary boundaries relates to biodiversity loss. The planetary boundaries model indicates that changes to biosphere integrity have passed a critical threshold.

The unit E/MSY (extinction per million species years) means that if there were a million species on Earth, one would go extinct every year, while if there was only one species it would go extinct in one million years. The average duration of mammalian species, for example, is estimated to be 10^6 years and so their background extinction rate is therefore 1 E/MSY, i.e. one extinction per million species per year or one extinction per 1000 species per century. The rate of natural extinctions is known as the 'background extinction rate' (Topic 3, HL Section 3.2.13). The background extinction range for most animal groups is between 0.1 and 1 E/MSY. Research indicates that the upper limit for species extinction rate (the rate at which species disappear) is less than 10 extinctions per million species-years (E/MSY).

The integrity and functioning of ecosystems, necessary for the ongoing maintenance of biodiversity and to minimize extinction, is measured using the biodiversity intactness index (BII). Biodiversity intactness can be defined as the average abundance of originally present species relative to an intact ecosystem, assessed geographically by biomes and major marine ecosystems (e.g. coral reefs).

- If the BII is 90% or more, the area has enough biodiversity to be a resilient and functioning ecosystem.
- If the BII is under 90%, biodiversity loss means ecosystems become less resilient.
- If the BII is 30% or less, the area's biodiversity has been depleted and the ecosystem could be at risk of collapse.

Estimates of BII are shown in Figure 2.46.

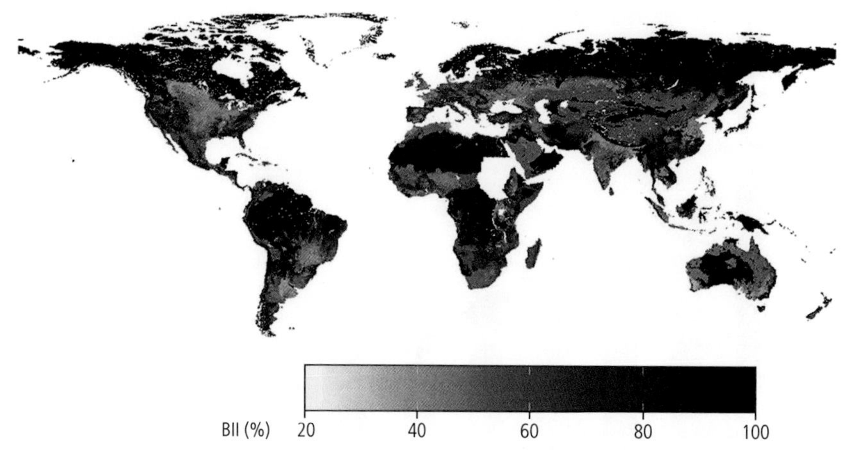

Figure 2.46 Estimated biodiversity intactness index (BII) in the year 2020. Only the darkest areas have retained enough natural biodiversity to be within the proposed planetary boundary for biosphere integrity, i.e. have a BII above 90%.

Activity

Find out about the Biodiversity Intactness Index on the Natural History Museum (NHM's) website.

How is the index measured? What are the assumptions and limitations of the model?

What are the BII measurements for different ecosystems? How has reduction in BII led to loss of species?

Correlate your findings with the map shown in Figure 2.46. Create a poster by annotating the map with the information you have found about the links between biosphere integrity and biodiversity.

Studies suggest that the current rate of extinction is 100–1000 E/MSY and so between 100 and 1000 times higher than the background rate of extinction. There is an interrelationship between ecosystems and species diversity. Disturbance of ecosystems due to human activity has led to loss of biosphere integrity. Extinction rates provide evidence that the planetary boundary for biosphere integrity has been crossed.

Example – IUCN Red List extinctions

One way of assessing the magnitude and patterns of current anthropogenic extinctions is the International Union for Conservation of Nature (IUCN) Red List of threatened species (Topic 3, Section 3.2.4, page 277). The list contains nearly 140,000 species, 900 of which have already become extinct since the year 1500 (Figure 2.47). Most of the recorded extinct species (86%) are animals with the remaining (14%) mostly flowering plants, except for a few fern and moss species.

Most extinctions took place in the Pacific islands (30%), the Americas (30%) and tropical Africa (20%). Other extinctions have taken place in Eurasia, Australia and the South-East Asian region (<10% of species). The causes for their extinction have mainly been due to human activities (i.e. anthropogenic), including overhunting, replacement by introduced species, habitat loss (e.g. deforestation), increased land use and introduction of alien pathogens.

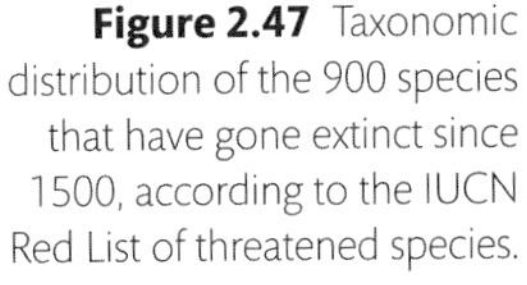

Figure 2.47 Taxonomic distribution of the 900 species that have gone extinct since 1500, according to the IUCN Red List of threatened species.

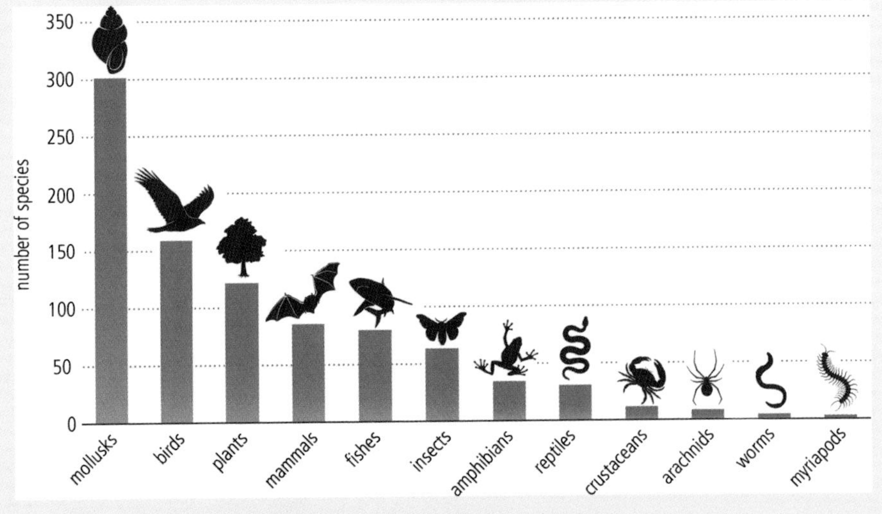

The Encyclopedia of Life (EOL) has recorded 1.9 million species on Earth and estimates a total of 8.7 million species. The 900 IUCN-documented extinct species would therefore represent 0.5% of the known species and 0.01% of Earth's estimated total biodiversity. A mass extinction is defined as the loss of 75% or more of the living species within a couple million years or less (Topic 3, HL Section 3.1.17, page 262). With the average rate estimated to be 180 extinctions per century, 75% of the total known species (1.4 million species) would be extinct in 800,000 years and 75% of the total estimated species (6.5 million species) would be extinct in 3.6 million years. The rate of the current biodiversity loss is therefore within the range of mass extinction. If unrecorded extinctions (which may be significant, especially in poorly recorded species such as insects) and prehistoric extinctions (where estimates are lacking) were added to the estimate, extinction rates would be greater and the time at which the 75% extinction boundary would be reached is sooner.

1.2 Systems
3.2 Human impact on biodiversity

To avoid critical tipping points, loss of biosphere integrity needs to be reversed

Ecosystem damage and loss of species can be slowed by protecting the integrity of ecosystems. Protecting ecosystems maintains the provision of niche requirements for the ongoing survival of a species.

Biosphere integrity refers to interdependence between different species in an ecosystem and the balance between organisms and the resources that support them. Each species has specific niche requirements (this topic, Section 2.1.8) and by protecting an ecosystem these are maintained. Preserving or restoring resources that support **food webs** will in turn preserve biodiversity. In ecosystems that have been disturbed by human activity, such as removal of timber from forests, restoring ecosystem structure (e.g. replanting trees) can go some way to restoring ecosystem integrity.

By studying ecological relationships between species and their environment (this topic, Section 2.1.5, 2.1.6 and 2.1.17), the niche requirements of species can be better understood. In areas where ecosystem integrity has been lost or reduced, knowledge of niche requirements can help restore ecosystems and provide the conditions needed for species to exist. Replanting forests, re-establishing apex predators and other techniques can be used to restore biosphere integrity and avoid critical tipping points that can lead to species extinction.

1.3 Sustainability
3.3 Conservation and regeneration

HL

2.1.26 Clades

Taxonomy is the science of describing, naming and classifying organisms. Taxa (singular, taxon) are the hierarchical divisions of organisms used by taxonomists, from species to kingdom (this topic, Section 2.1.27, page 121). In the past, classification was often based on the appearance of organisms (so-called artificial or superficial classification). Taxonomists now use evolutionary relationships when classifying organisms (so called 'natural' classification).

There are advantages of using a method of classification that illustrates evolutionary relationships in a clade.

A **clade** illustrates evolutionary relationships in which all the members of a taxonomic group have evolved from a common ancestor.

Diagrams can be drawn that show these evolutionary relationships, known as phylogenetic trees or cladograms. A **clade** is a group of organisms that has evolved from a common ancestor.

Cladograms have two important features:

- branch points in the tree – representing the time at which a divide between two taxa occurred
- the degree of divergence between branches – representing the differences that have developed between the two taxa since they diverged.

Taxonomists must decide which features are the more significant in a phylogenetic taxonomy, i.e. those that should receive the greater emphasis in devising a scheme. In cladistics, classification is based on an analysis of relatedness and the product is a cladogram.

A cladogram:

- shows patterns of shared characteristics
- is a diagram that shows the evolutionary relationships among a group of organisms
- classifies organisms according to the order in time at which branches arise along their phylogenetic tree.

Figure 2.48 shows the relationship between different vertebrate taxa. The cladogram shows the features used to define each branching point of the diagram. The bottom of the diagram is the furthest back in time. The lowest branch indicates that all vertebrates share a common ancestor at some point in the distant past. The first taxa to evolve were the sharks followed by ray-finned fish and amphibians. Primates and rodents are closely related, as are crocodiles and birds, and all have the most recent common ancestors (the branching points in the cladogram).

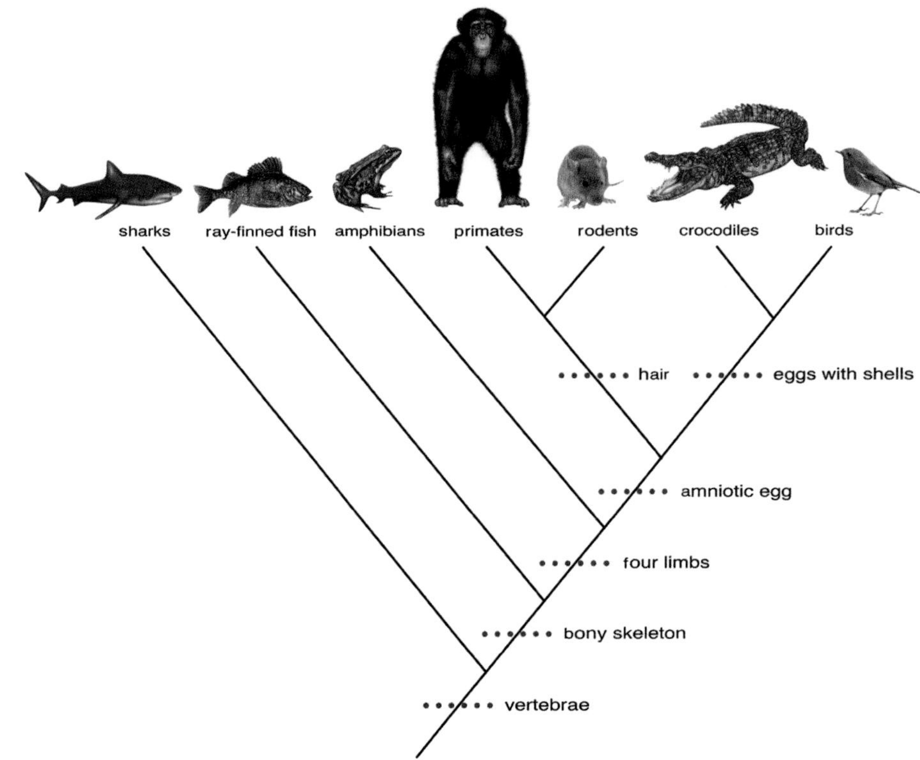

Figure 2.48 Cladogram showing the evolutionary relationship between different vertebrate animals.

Evolutionary relationships can be deduced from a cladogram. The points at which two branches form are called nodes. Close relationships are shown by a recent branching point (or 'fork') – the closer the fork in the branch between two organisms, the closer their relationship and evolutionary origin. The lowest part of the diagram indicates the ancestor common to all groups branching from it.

Construction of cladograms

The more derived structures that are shared by two organisms, the closer their evolutionary relationship (i.e. the more recently their common ancestor lived).

- Points at which two branches form are called nodes. They represent speciation events (Figure 2.48).
- Close relationships are shown by a recent fork – the closer the fork in the branch between two organisms, the closer their relationship.

Cladograms provide strong evidence for evolutionary relationships, although they cannot be regarded as absolute proof. They assume that the smallest number of mutations (changes in the genetic code) possible account for differences between species. If such assumptions are incorrect, errors may occur in cladograms, (this topic, Section 2.1.27). Using several different cladograms, derived independently from different data, can overcome such difficulties.

2.1.27 Difficulties in classifying organisms

HL

When classifying organisms, as many characteristics as possible are used when placing similar organisms together. Organisms are grouped in a hierarchy, with each level of the hierarchy sharing common features:

- similar species are grouped together into the same genus (plural, genera)
- similar genera are grouped together into families
- similar families are grouped together in orders
- similar orders are grouped together in classes.

This approach is extended from classes to phyla (singular, phylum) and kingdoms. This hierarchical scheme of classification means that each successive group contains more different kinds of organism.

Natural classifications help in identification of species and allow the prediction of characteristics shared by species within a group.

It is important to distinguish similarities that are based on shared ancestry (so-called homologous structure) from those based on structures that have evolved independently but under similar selective pressures and so appear the same or similar (so called analogous structures, such as human and octopus eyes). Species that are similar in appearance may not be closely related – their resemblance is due to analogous adaptations to very similar environments. Morphology (form and structure) of organisms can lead to mistakes in classification, due to misinterpreting whether structures are analogous or homologous. Base or amino acid sequences are more accurate ways of determining members of a clade because they represent true homology.

There are difficulties in classifying organisms into the traditional hierarchy of taxa. The traditional hierarchy of kingdom, phylum, class, order, family, genus and species does not always correspond with patterns of divergence generated by evolution.

Evidence from cladistics has shown that classification of some groups based on structure does not correspond with the evolutionary origins of a group or species. The use of base and amino acid sequences has made the study of phylogenetic trees more accurate. Traditional classification based on morphology does not always match the evolutionary origin of groups of species. Old cladograms, developed before molecular and computing techniques, have been replaced by revised ones. Reclassification has led to:

- some groups merging with others
- some groups being divided
- some species being transferred from one group to another.

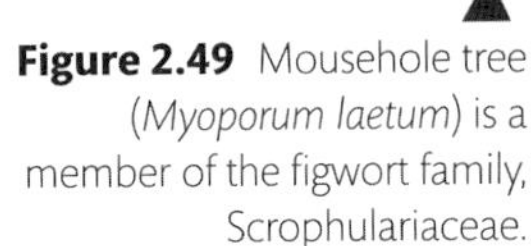

Figure 2.49 Mousehole tree (*Myoporum laetum*) is a member of the figwort family, Scrophulariaceae.

Example – Reclassification of the figwort family

The Scrophulariaceae (figwort family) is a large group of flowering plants (Figure 2.49). The flowering plant families were originally classified before biochemical studies were applied to plant taxonomy. Today, flowering plant classification is being revised following the development of biochemical techniques. Most evidence for plant evolutionary relationships now comes from a comparison of DNA sequences in only one to three genes found in the chloroplasts of the plant cells.

Many traditional plant families appear to be natural classifications, for example the rose family (Rosaceae) and the Cruciferae (which includes many economically important plants). However, biochemical techniques have shown other families have not been correctly classified.

In the reorganization of the figwort family, the genetic makeup of many species has been compared. This has resulted in the repositioning of several genera from the Scrophulariaceae into other families and the repositioning of other genera, previously in other families, into the Scrophulariaceae.

HL

2.1.28 Fundamental and realized niches

The **fundamental niche** describes the range of conditions and resources in which a species could survive and reproduce without any limiting factors. The **realized niche** of a species is the actual mode of existence, which results from its adaptations and competition with other species.

There are usually differences between the niche that a species can theoretically occupy and the one that it occupies. Factors affecting how a species disperses itself and interacts with other species can restrict the actual niche in which it lives. The niche of a species can be defined as fundamental or realized.

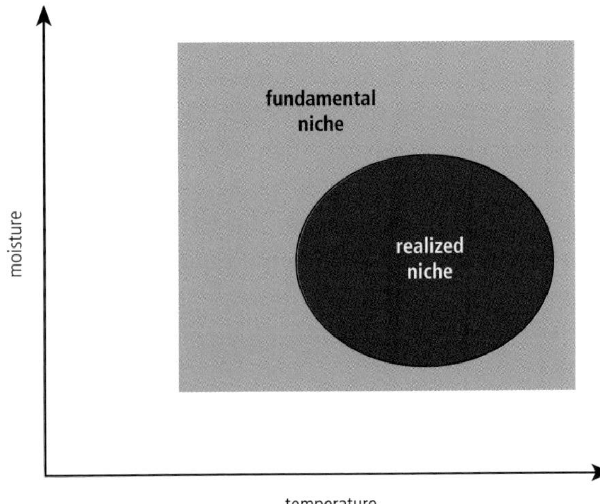

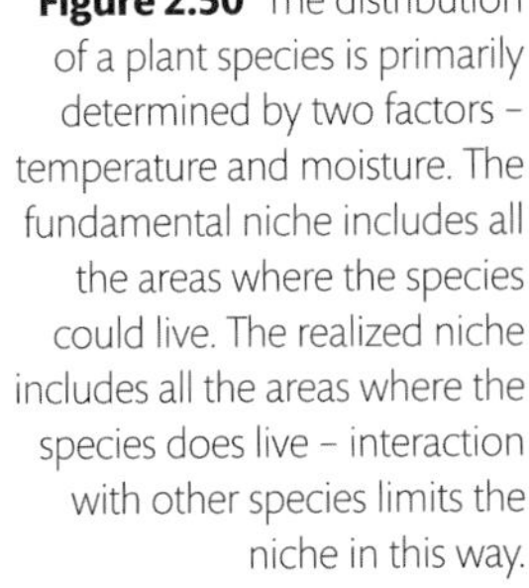

Figure 2.50 The distribution of a plant species is primarily determined by two factors – temperature and moisture. The fundamental niche includes all the areas where the species could live. The realized niche includes all the areas where the species does live – interaction with other species limits the niche in this way.

The **fundamental niche** can be defined as where and how an organism could live and includes the full range of conditions and resources in which a species could (theoretically) survive and reproduce.

The **realized niche** describes the conditions and resources in which an organism exists due to biotic interactions (Figure 2.50).

Example – Fundamental and realized niches of barnacles

American ecologist Joseph Connell investigated the realized and fundamental niches of two species of barnacle – a common animal on rocky shores in the UK (Figure 2.51). Connell had observed that one of the species, *Semibalanus (Balanus) balanoides*, was most abundant on the middle and lower intertidal area and that the other species, *Chthamalus stellatus*, was most common on the upper intertidal area of the shore (Figure 2.52). When he removed *Chthamalus* from the upper area of shore, he found that no *Semibalanus* replaced it. His explanation was that *Semibalanus* could not survive in an area that regularly dried out due to low tides. He concluded that the realized niche of *Semibalanus* was the same as its fundamental niche.

Figure 2.51 A colony of barnacles on the rocky shore.

In another experiment, he removed *Semibalanus* from the middle areas. He found that over time *Chthamalus* replaced it in the middle intertidal zone: his explanation was that *Semibalanus* was a more successful competitor in the middle intertidal zone and usually excluded *Chthamalus*. He concluded that the fundamental niche and realized niche for *Chthamalus* were not the same and that its realized niche was smaller due to interspecific competition (i.e. competition between species) leading to competitive exclusion (when one species outcompetes and excludes another when their niches overlap, this topic, Section 2.1.9, page 97).

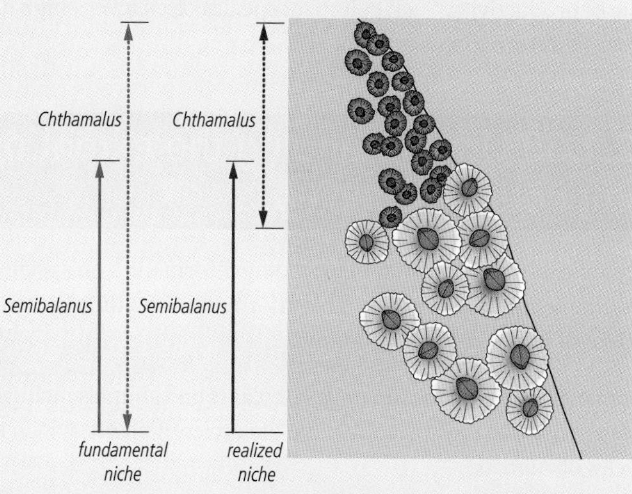

Figure 2.52 The fundamental and realized niches of two species of barnacle, *Chthamalus stellatus* and *Semibalanus balanoides*, showing distribution of species in intertidal zones (top to bottom in the figure is height relative to sea level, showing upper and middle/lower intertidal zones).

Make sure you know how to consider the fundamental and realized niche of a named species, e.g. Joseph Connell's study of barnacle species.

2.1.29 Life cycles of organisms

HL

Life cycles vary between species in reproductive behaviour and lifespan. Species can be classified according to how rapidly they reproduce and the degree to which they give parental care.

Species that are characterized by periods of rapid growth followed by decline, tend to inhabit unpredictable, rapidly changing environments (i.e. early **seral stages** – this topic, Section 2.5.3 and 2.5.4, page 202) and are termed opportunistic species. They have a high reproductive rate and high rate of development (*r*) and are called **r-strategists** or *r*-species. These species produce a high number of small offspring that mature rapidly and that receive little or no parental care. Species producing egg-sacs are a good example.

In contrast, slow-growing organisms tend to be limited by the carrying capacity of an environment (*K*) and so are known as **K-strategists** or *K*-species. They inhabit stable environments and have lower reproductive rates but better competitive ability. *K*-species have long life spans, large body size and develop slowly. *K*-species produce very few, often exceptionally large, offspring that mature slowly and receive a great

Species that are *r*-strategists grow and mature quickly and produce a high number of small offspring, whereas *K*-strategists are slow-growing and produce a few large offspring that mature slowly.

Many species lie in between these two extremes and are known as C-strategists or C-species.

A female cane toad spawns twice a year and produces up to 35,000 eggs each time.

Species can have traits of both *K*- and *r*-species. Studies showed that dandelions in a disturbed lawn had high reproduction rates whereas those on an undisturbed lawn produced fewer seeds but were better competitors.

deal of parental support. Elephants and whales are good examples. As a result of the low birth rate, *K*-species are vulnerable to high death rates and extinction.

r- and *K*-species have reproductive strategies that are better adapted to pioneer and climax communities respectively (this topic, Section 2.5.11).

In predictable environments – where the availability of resources does not fluctuate – there is little advantage to rapid growth. Instead, evolution favours species that can maximize the use of natural resources and that produce few young that have a high probability of survival.

In contrast, disturbed habitats with rapidly changing conditions favour species that can respond rapidly, develop quickly and have early reproduction. This leads to a high rate of productivity. Such colonizer species often have a high dispersal ability to reach areas of disturbance.

HL

2.1.30 Understanding the extent of human impacts on species

Ecological studies are vital in providing information on species' classifications, niche requirements and life cycles. This information can then be used to help understand the extent of human impacts on them.

Human impacts on the life cycles of plants and animals include temperature changes from climate change that affect the life cycles of plants, which in turn affect the life cycles of animals.

3.3 Conservation and regeneration

The life cycles of many species are synchronized with those of others and with the seasons. Human impacts contribute to climate change, which in turn may disrupt plant and animal life cycles.

HL end

Engagement

- Carry out an ecological investigation on natural and disturbed ecosystems, using the application of skills explored in this subtopic (e.g. Section 2.1.6 and 2.1.7: use methods for measuring at least three abiotic factors, page 90; Section 2.1.15, 2.1.16 and 2.1.17: random quadrat sampling, page 106 capture–mark–release–recapture and the Lincoln index, page 109). Secondary data can be used as a comparison. Produce a research poster to summarize your findings – make sure you include your research design, methodology, samples of your data, analysed data, tables and graphs and your conclusions.
- Advocate about reversing biodiversity loss by producing a presentation to present to the rest of your class or school community. 'To advocate' means to publicly recommend or support, and so you need to outline the issues of biodiversity loss and matters that can be taken to address this issue, such as preserving natural ecosystems, reducing pollution, and removing invasive species.

- Take part in citizen science projects (Topic 1, Section 1.3.16) that collect data on species distributions and abundance. Join a local group that is observing and collecting information on the presence or absence of a species in your area (such as birds or insects), which can then be used to determine a species' distribution.

Exercise

Q1. Define the terms *species, population, habitat* and *niche.*

Q2. Distinguish between a habitat and a niche.

Q3. Distinguish between mutualism and parasitism, using examples of each.

Q4. Describe and **explain** an S-shaped population curve.

Q5. The abundance of one species can affect the abundance of another.

(a) **State** one ecological example of this relationship.

(b) **Explain** how the predator affects the abundance of the prey and vice versa.

Q6. Explain the concepts of limiting factors and carrying capacity in the context of population growth.

Q7. The data below show rates of growth in ticklegrass (as above ground biomass in $g\ m^{-2}$) in soils with low or high nitrogen content and using high or low seed density.

Year	Low nitrogen, high seed density: above ground biomass / $g\ m^{-2}$	Low nitrogen, low seed density: above ground biomass / $g\ m^{-2}$	High nitrogen, high seed density: above ground biomass / $g\ m^{-2}$	High nitrogen, low seed density: above ground biomass / $g\ m^{-2}$
1	0	0	0	0
2	420	60	500	30
3	780	80	1050	100
4	0	70	0	90
5	50	100	160	80
6	180	110	600	70

(a) **Plot** the data showing the growth rates among ticklegrass depending on nitrogen availability and density of seeds.

(b) **Describe** the results you have produced.

(c) **Suggest** reasons for these results.

The values in Column 2 have been rounded to a whole number, but the real number for each generation has been multiplied by 1.2 to get the answer for the next generation (e.g. N4 has a population of 2073.6. This has been rounded up to 2074. However, to find N5, 2037.6 has been multiplied by 1.2 to make 2488.32, which is rounded down to 2488).

Q8. The table below shows population growth in a population with discrete generations, starting with a population of 1000 and increasing at a constant reproductive rate of 1.2% per generation.

Generation number	Population, N	Increase in population
N0	1000	–
N1	1200	200
N2	1440	240
N3	1728	288
N4	2074	346
N5	2488	414
N6	2986	498
N7	3583	597
N8		
N9		
N10		
N11		
N12		
N13		
N14		
N15		

(a) Complete the table by **calculating** total population (Column 2) and the increase in population size from generation to generation (column 3).

(b) **Plot** the graph of total population size.

(c) **Describe** the graph and identify the type of population growth that it shows.

Q9. **Define** the terms *community* and *ecosystem*.

Q10. **Explain** the role of producers, consumers and decomposers in the ecosystem.

Q11. **List** five abiotic factors you can think of. **Describe** how you would measure each of these factors in an ecological investigation.

Q12. **Evaluate** each of the methods you have listed in **Q11**. What are their limitations and how may they affect the data you collect?

Q13. **Outline** methods could you use to study **(a)** marine ecosystems, **(b)** freshwater ecosystems and **(c)** terrestrial ecosystems.

Q14. **Construct** a key for a selection of objects of your choice. **Explain** whether your key allows you to accurately identify each object.

Q15. **Describe** ethical considerations you must bear in mind when carrying out capture–mark–release–recapture exercises on wild animals.

HL

Q16. HL Distinguish between fundamental and realized niche, using an example to illustrate your answer.

Q17. HL **Explain** why there are advantages of using a method of classification that illustrates evolutionary relationships in a clade.

Q18. HL **Describe** how life cycles vary between species in reproductive behaviour and lifespan.

HL end

2.2 Energy and biomass in ecosystems

Guiding Questions

How can flows of energy and matter through ecosystems be modelled?
How do human actions affect the flow of energy and matter, and what is the impact on ecosystems?

2.2.1 Ecosystems are sustained by supplies of energy and matter.
2.2.2 The first law of thermodynamics states that as energy flows through ecosystems, it can be transformed from one form to another but cannot be created or destroyed.
2.2.3 Photosynthesis and cellular respiration transform energy and matter in ecosystems.
2.2.4 Photosynthesis is the conversion of light energy to chemical energy in the form of glucose, some of which can be stored as biomass by autotrophs.
2.2.5 Producers form the first trophic level in a food chain.
2.2.6 Cellular respiration releases energy from glucose by converting it into a chemical form that can easily be used in carrying out active processes within living cells.
2.2.7 Some of the chemical energy released during cellular respiration is transformed into heat.
2.2.8 The second law of thermodynamics states that energy transformations in ecosystems are inefficient.
2.2.9 Consumers gain chemical energy from carbon (organic) compounds obtained from other organisms. Consumers have diverse strategies for obtaining energy-containing carbon compounds.
2.2.10 Because producers in ecosystems make their own carbon compounds by photosynthesis, they are at the start of food chains. Consumers obtain carbon compounds from producers or other consumers, so form the subsequent trophic levels.
2.2.11 Carbon compounds and the energy they contain are passed from one organism to the next in a food chain. The stages in a food chain are called trophic levels.
2.2.12 There are losses of energy and organic matter as food is transferred along a food chain.
2.2.13 Gross productivity (GP) is the total gain in biomass by an organism. Net productivity (NP) is the amount remaining after losses due to cellular respiration.
2.2.14 The number of trophic levels in ecosystems is limited due to energy losses.
2.2.15 Food webs show the complexity of trophic relationships in communities.
2.2.16 Biomass of a trophic level can be measured by collecting and drying samples.
2.2.17 Ecological pyramids are used to represent relative numbers, biomass or energy of trophic levels in an ecosystem.

2.2.18 Pollutants that are non-biodegradable, such as polychlorinated biphenyl (PCB), dichlorodiphenyltrichloroethane (DDT) and mercury, cause changes to ecosystems through the processes of bioaccumulation and biomagnification.
2.2.19 Non-biodegradable pollutants are absorbed within microplastics, which increases their transmission in the food chain.
2.2.20 Human activities, such as burning fossil fuels, deforestation, urbanization and agriculture, have impacts on flows of energy and transfers of matter in ecosystems.
HL 2.2.21 Autotrophs synthesize carbon compounds from inorganic sources of carbon and other elements. Heterotrophs obtain carbon compounds from other organisms.
HL 2.2.22 Photoautotrophs use light as an external energy source in photosynthesis. Chemoautotrophs use exothermic inorganic chemical reactions as an external energy source in chemosynthesis.
HL 2.2.23 Primary productivity is the rate of production of biomass using an external energy source and inorganic sources of carbon and other elements.
HL 2.2.24 Secondary productivity is the gain in biomass by consumers using carbon compounds absorbed and assimilated from ingested food.
HL 2.2.25 Net primary productivity is the basis for food chains because it is the quantity of carbon compounds sustainably available to primary consumers.
HL 2.2.26 Maximum sustainable yields (MSYs) are the net primary or net secondary productivity of a system.
HL 2.2.27 Sustainable yields are higher for lower trophic levels.
HL 2.2.28 Ecological efficiency is the percentage of energy received by one trophic level that is passed on to the next level.
HL 2.2.29 The second law of thermodynamics shows how the entropy of a system increases as biomass passes through ecosystems.

2.2.1 Ecosystems are sustained by supplies of energy and matter

Ecosystems are open systems (Topic 1, Section 1.2.5) in which both energy and matter are exchanged. Energy enters the ecosystem from the Sun and is transformed to chemical energy through the process of photosynthesis (this topic, Section 2.2.4, page 131). Ecosystems depend on the constant input of energy to sustain them. Both matter and energy move through the ecosystem from one trophic level to the next (this topic, Section 2.2.8 and 2.2.9, page 132), with energy ultimately leaving as heat. Matter cycles through the ecosystem, with new matter arriving through precipitation, or with the movement of new organisms or nutrients into the system. Matter leaves the ecosystem when water evaporates, when organisms move to other areas or when nutrients leach out of the soil (this topic, Section 2.1.21, Figure 2.42).

1.2 Systems

Matter forms the building blocks from which new organisms are formed and the energy is needed to sustain life processes.

Use the worksheet in your eBook to explore why some ecosystems are more biodiverse than others.

2.2.2 The first law of thermodynamics and ecosystems

Energy exists in a variety of forms (light, heat, chemical, electrical and kinetic). It can only be changed from one form into another; it cannot be created or destroyed. Any form of energy can be converted to any other form, but heat can be converted to other forms only when there is a temperature difference between two bodies. The behaviour of energy in systems is defined by the laws of thermodynamics. There are two laws that relate to how energy moves through systems.

The **first law of thermodynamics** states that as energy flows through ecosystems, it can be transformed from one form to another, but it cannot be created or destroyed.

Energy transformations occur, such as light to chemical and from chemical to heat.

The **first law of thermodynamics** states that energy can be neither created nor destroyed, it can only change form. This means that the total energy in any system, including the entire Universe, is constant and all that can happen is a change in the form the energy takes. This law is known as the law of the conservation of energy. In ecosystems, energy enters the system in the form of sunlight, is transformed into biomass via photosynthesis, passes along **food chains** as biomass, is consumed and ultimately leaves the ecosystem in the form of heat. No new energy has been created – it has simply been transformed and passed from one form to another (Figure 2.53). Heat is released because of the inefficient transfer of energy (as in all other systems).

Available energy is used for growth, movement and the assembly of complex molecules. Although the total amount of energy in a system does not change, the amount of available energy does (Figure 2.53).

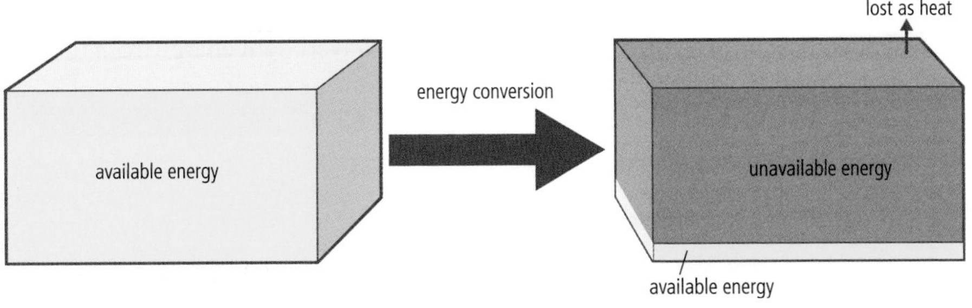

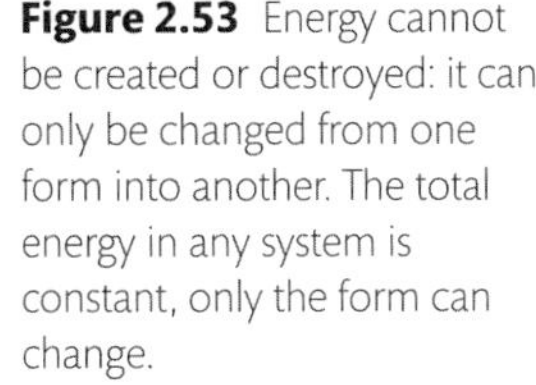

Figure 2.53 Energy cannot be created or destroyed: it can only be changed from one form into another. The total energy in any system is constant, only the form can change.

The available energy in a system is reduced through inefficient energy conversions. The total amount of energy remains the same, but less is available for work. An increasing quantity of unusable energy is lost from the system as heat (which cannot be recycled into usable energy).

1.2 Systems

The **second law of thermodynamics** is discussed in this topic, Sections 2.2.8 and 2.2.9, page 132.

2.2.3–2.2.7 Photosynthesis and cellular respiration transform energy and matter in ecosystems

Continual inputs of energy and matter are essential in the support of ecosystems. Two processes control the flow of energy through ecosystems: photosynthesis and cellular respiration. Cellular respiration is a chemical process that occurs in all cells. Photosynthesis converts light energy to chemical energy, which is stored as biomass. Cellular respiration releases this energy so that it can be used to support the life processes (e.g. movement) of organisms.

Cellular respiration and **photosynthesis** can be represented as systems diagrams, with inputs, outputs, storages and processes.

Cellular respiration and photosynthesis can be described as processes with inputs, outputs and transformations of energy and matter. Transformation of matter happens in chemical reactions and can be summarized using equations.

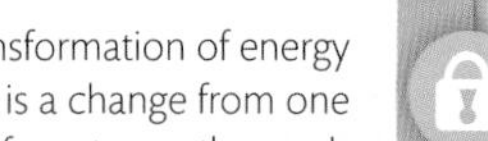

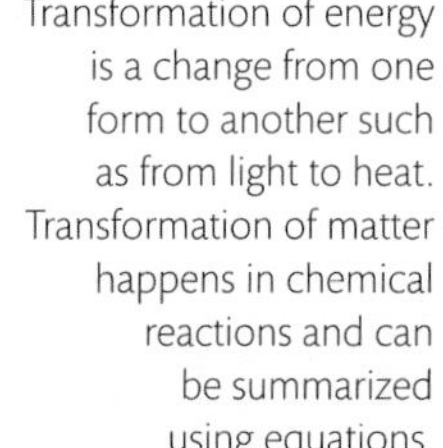

Transformation of energy is a change from one form to another such as from light to heat. Transformation of matter happens in chemical reactions and can be summarized using equations.

SKILLS

Make sure you know how to create system diagrams from a set of data of ecosystems showing transfers and transformations of energy and matter.

Challenge yourself

Carry out research to find data for a local ecosystem. The data should include measurements of energy and matter. Create a systems diagram from a set of data of ecosystems showing transfers and transformations of energy and matter.

Photosynthesis

Photosynthesis is the process by which green plants convert light energy from the Sun into usable chemical energy in the form of glucose, some of which can be stored as biomass (organic matter). It requires CO_2, H_2O, chlorophyll and light and is controlled by enzymes. O_2 is produced as a waste product in the reaction.

The photosynthesis reaction is:

$$\text{carbon dioxide} + \text{water} \xrightarrow[\text{chlorophyll}]{\text{light}} \text{glucose} + \text{oxygen}$$

Photosynthesis produces the raw material for producing biomass.

In terms of inputs, outputs and energy transformations, photosynthesis can be summarized as follows:

- Inputs – sunlight as energy source, CO_2 and H_2O.
- Outputs:
  - glucose – used as an energy source for the plant and as the basic starting material for other organic molecules (e.g. cellulose, starch)
  - O_2 – released to the atmosphere through stomata in leaves.
- Transformations – the energy change is from light energy into stored chemical energy; thus chemical energy is stored in organic matter (i.e. carbohydrates, fats and proteins). Chlorophyll is needed to capture certain visible wavelengths of sunlight energy and enable this energy to be transformed into chemical energy.

Once glucose is formed, it can be converted into other carbon compounds contained within biomass – for example, proteins and fats.

Organisms which can create their own glucose are known as **autotrophs** (meaning 'self-feeding'). This is explored further in the HL material in this topic, Section 2.2.21.

Photosynthesis is the process by which green plants convert light energy from the Sun into usable chemical energy in the form of glucose. Some of the glucose can be stored as biomass.

Producers

Certain organisms in an ecosystem convert abiotic components into living matter. These are the **producers** and they support the ecosystem by providing a constant input of energy and new biological matter (biomass) (Figure 2.54). Producers are also known as autotrophs. Producers typically include plants, algae and photosynthetic bacteria that produce their own food using photosynthesis and form the first trophic level in a food chain.

Producers form the first trophic level in a food chain.

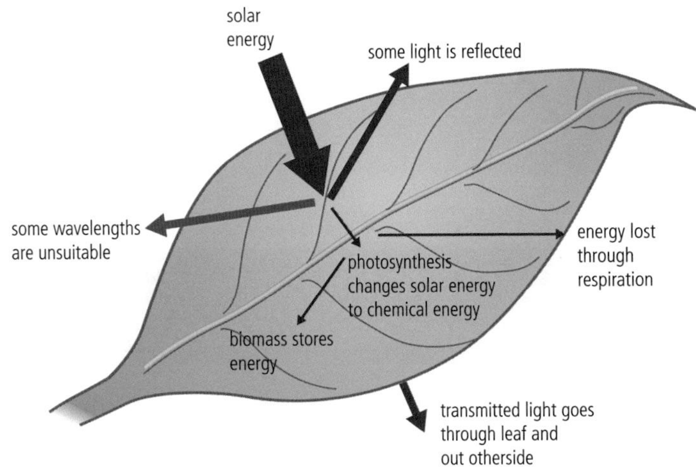

Figure 2.54 Producers such as plants convert sunlight energy into chemical energy using photosynthetic pigments (e.g. chlorophyll). The food produced supports the rest of the food chain.

Cellular respiration releases energy from glucose by converting it into a chemical form that can easily be used in carrying out active processes within living cells.

Cellular respiration

Cellular respiration releases energy from glucose and other organic molecules inside all living cells. The process is controlled by enzymes. The energy released is in a form available for use by living organisms but is ultimately lost as heat (Topic 1, Section 1.2.5, page 30).

Aerobic cellular respiration can simply be described as:

$$\text{glucose} + \text{oxygen} \rightarrow \text{carbon dioxide} + \text{water}$$

Cellular respiration (Figure 2.55) can be summarized as follows:

- Inputs – organic matter (glucose) and O_2.
- Processes – oxidation processes inside cells.
- Outputs – release of energy for work and heat.
- Transformations – the energy transformation is from stored chemical energy into kinetic energy and heat. Energy is released in a form available for use by living organisms, but much is also lost as heat (the second law of thermodynamics, this topic, Section 2.2.8, page 132).

Make sure you know how to construct system diagrams representing photosynthesis and cellular respiration.

During cellular respiration, large amounts of energy are dissipated as heat.

Photosynthesis involves the transformation of light energy into the chemical energy of organic matter. Cellular respiration is the transformation of chemical energy into kinetic energy with, ultimately, heat being lost from the system.

Chemical energy transformed into heat

Heat is generated by cellular respiration because it is not 100% efficient at transferring energy from substrates such as carbohydrates into the chemical form of energy used in

All organisms respire: bacteria, algae, plants, fungi and animals. Only plants, algae and cyanobacteria photosynthesize.

Some of the chemical energy released during cellular respiration is transformed into heat.

cells. Heat generated within an individual organism cannot be transformed back into chemical energy and is ultimately lost from the body.

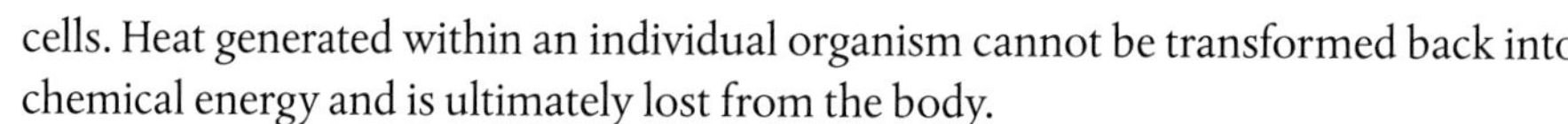

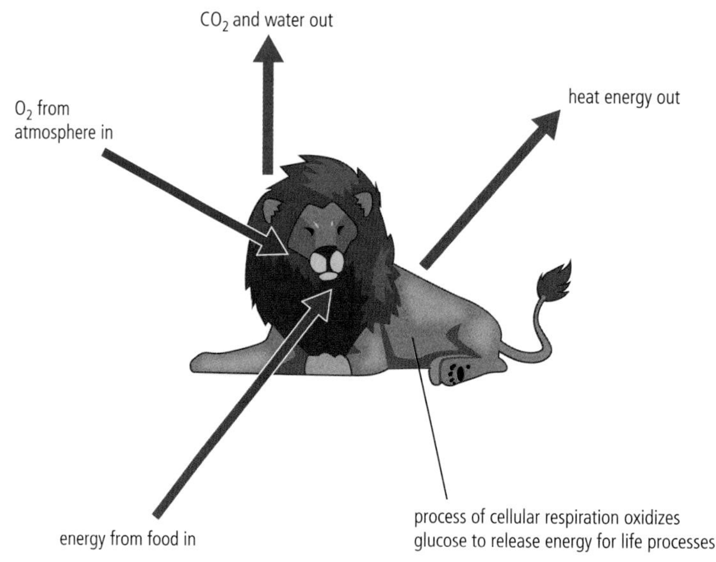

Figure 2.55 The inputs, outputs and processes involved in cellular respiration.

The first law of thermodynamics concerns the conservation of energy (i.e. energy can be neither created nor destroyed), whereas the second law of thermodynamics states that energy transformations in ecosystems are inefficient.

The first law of thermodynamics explains how some of the energy entering an ecosystem is lost as heat energy, because energy entering the system must equal energy remaining in the system plus energy leaving the system. The second law of thermodynamics explains how energy transformations in living systems can lead to loss of energy from the system. The order in living systems is only maintained by constant input of new energy from the Sun.

2.2.8 and 2.2.9 The second law of thermodynamics and ecosystems

The transformation and transfer of energy is not 100% efficient: in any energy conversion there is less usable energy at the end of the process than there is at the beginning (Figure 2.56). This means there is a dissipation of energy that is then not available for work. The second law of thermodynamics states that energy goes from a concentrated form (e.g. the Sun) into a dispersed form (ultimately heat) and that the availability of energy to do work therefore decreases.

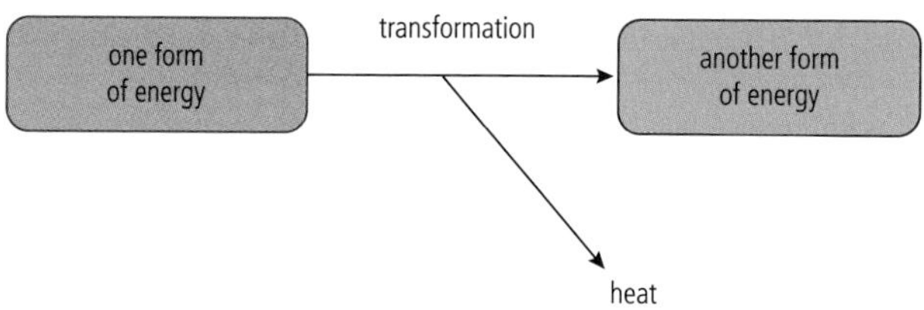

Figure 2.56 The second law of thermodynamics states that energy is converted into heat when energy is transformed from one form to another.

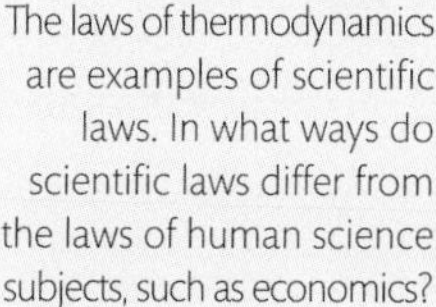

How does the way that we organize or classify knowledge affect what we know?

The laws of thermodynamics are examples of scientific laws. In what ways do scientific laws differ from the laws of human science subjects, such as economics?

The laws of thermodynamics and environmental systems

Natural systems can never actually be isolated because there must always be an input of energy for work (to replace energy that is dissipated). The maintenance of order in living systems requires a constant input of energy to replace available energy lost through inefficient transfers. Although matter can be recycled, energy cannot. Energy that has been lost from a system in the form of heat energy cannot be made available again.

One way energy enters an ecosystem is as sunlight energy. This sunlight energy is then changed into biomass by photosynthesis. This process captures sunlight energy and transforms it into chemical energy. Chemical energy in producers is passed along

Make sure you know how to explain the implications of the laws of thermodynamics for ecological systems.

food chains as biomass or transformed into heat during cellular respiration. Available energy is used to do work such as growth, movement and making complex molecules. As we know from the second law of thermodynamics, the transfer and transformation of energy is inefficient, with all energy ultimately being lost into the environment as heat (Figure 2.57). This is why food chains tend to be short.

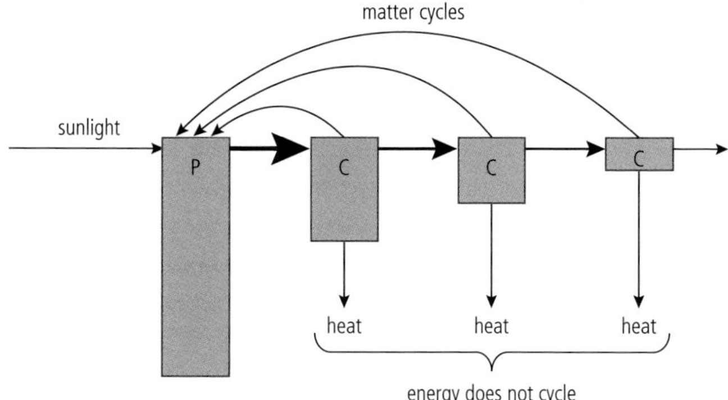

Figure 2.57 Energy flow through a food chain; P = producers, C = consumers. The boxes show energy available to do work at each feeding level. Energy decreases through the food chain as some is converted to heat. The '10% rule' indicates that on average only around 10% of the available energy is passed on to the next trophic level.

Consumers

Organisms that cannot make their own food eat other organisms to obtain energy and matter: they are **consumers.** Consumers do not contain photosynthetic pigments such as chlorophyll so they cannot make their own food. They must obtain their chemical energy by eating other organisms – they are **heterotrophs.** Herbivores feed on autotrophs, carnivores feed on other heterotrophs and omnivores feed on both.

Consumers pass energy and biomass from producers through to the top carnivores.

Consumers have a range of strategies for obtaining energy-containing carbon compounds:

- Herbivores eat plant material (this topic, Section 2.1.9, page 95) and contain bacteria in their gut which helps them to digest plant material. An example of a herbivore is a hippopotamus (Figure 2.14, Section 2.1.9, page 95).
- **Detritivores** eat dead organic matter such as dead leaves on the forest floor. They contain a digestive system and digest food within their bodies. An example of a detritivore is an earthworm (Figure 2.58).
- Predators are organisms that hunt prey. An example of a predator is a cheetah (Topic 3, Section 3.1.1, Figure 3.3, page 232).
- **Parasites** are organisms that benefit at the expense of another organism (the host) from which they derive food (Section 2.1.9, page 95). An example of a parasite is a tick (Figure 2.15, Section 2.1.9, page 95).
- **Saprotrophs** are fungi and bacteria that do not possess a digestive system. They secrete enzymes onto their food and absorb the digested products. This is known as saprotrophic digestion. Examples of saprotrophs are mushrooms (Figure 2.59) and toadstools.
- **Scavengers** are animals that feed on carrion (dead animal matter). An example of a scavenger is the hyena. While most carnivores hunt and kill their prey, scavengers usually consume animals that have either died of natural causes or been killed by another carnivore.
- **Decomposers** obtain their food and nutrients from the breakdown of dead organic matter. When they break down tissue, they release nutrients ready for

The second law of thermodynamics relates to the quality of energy and that when energy is transformed, some must be degraded into a less useful form e.g. heat. In ecosystems, the biggest losses occur during cellular respiration. The second law explains why energy transfers are never 100% efficient.

1.2 Systems
5.2 Agriculture and food

Figure 2.58 Earthworm feeding on detritus in soil.

Consumers gain chemical energy from carbon (organic) compounds obtained from other organisms.

Figure 2.59 Mushrooms (Honey fungus, *Armillaria mellea*) growing on a decaying tree in a woodland ecosystem.

reabsorption by producers. They form the basis of a decomposer food chain. Decomposers also contribute to the build-up of humus in soil. Humus is organic material in soil made by the decomposition of plant or animal matter. It improves the ability of soil to retain nutrients. Decomposers are essential for cycling matter in ecosystems. Matter that is cycled by decomposers in ecosystems includes elements such as carbon and nitrogen.

2.2.10 and 2.2.11 Food chains

The flow of energy and matter from organism to organism can be shown in a food chain (Figure 2.60). The position that an organism occupies in a food chain is called the trophic level (this topic, Section 2.2.12). 'Trophic level' can also mean the position in the food chain occupied by a group of organisms in a community. As producers in ecosystems make their own carbon compounds by photosynthesis, they are at the start of food chains. Consumers obtain carbon compounds from producers or other consumers so form the subsequent trophic levels.

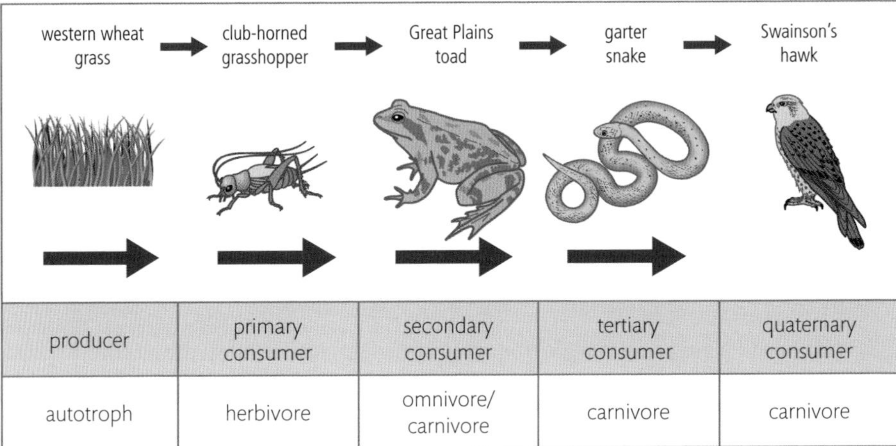

Figure 2.60 A food chain. Ecosystems contain many food chains.

In a food chain, organic matter flows from primary producers to primary consumers to secondary consumers and so on.

Create a food chain from given data

If you are asked to draw a food chain, you do not need to draw the animals and plants involved. You do need to give specific names for the different organisms (e.g. salmon rather than fish). Arrows show the flow of energy from one organism to the next and should be in the direction of energy flow.

Activity

Below is an account of some of the animals and plants found in the tropical rainforest of Borneo:

Sambar deer eat leaves from dipterocarp tree seedlings in the understory of the forest. Clouded leopards, the largest cats in the Borneo rainforest, are known to eat sambar deer. The Borneo python is also known to attack and consume deer, as well as other mammals. Crested serpent eagles can be seen catching and eating pythons and other snakes. Giant squirrels feed on the seeds of fig trees.

Using the information here or from other sources, create a food chain containing at least three species from the Borneo rainforest.

Trophic levels

Carbon compounds and the energy they contain are passed from one organism to the next in a food chain. The stages in a food chain are called trophic levels. Figure 2.61 shows the trophic levels in a food web.

The **trophic level** is the position that an organism occupies in a food chain, or a group of organisms in a community that occupy the same position in food chains.

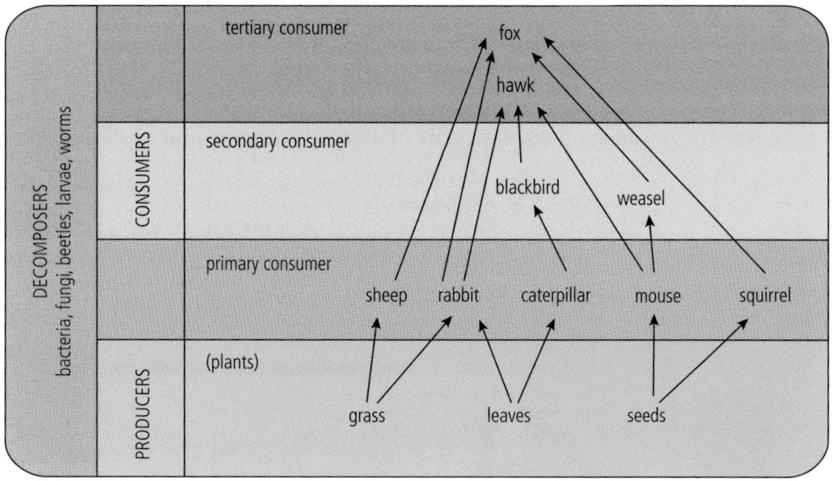

Figure 2.61 A food web showing its trophic levels.

Food chains always begin with the producers (usually photosynthetic organisms), followed by primary consumers (herbivores), secondary consumers (omnivores or carnivores) and then higher consumers (tertiary, quaternary). Decomposers feed at every level of the food chain.

Decomposers are important in energy transformation in food webs. However, decomposers are generally not included in food chains because they typically gain carbon compounds at each level of the food chain when organisms die and decay. Decomposers can be shown as a vertical column at the side of a food web, indicating that they can feed at each trophic level (Figure 2.61).

Find an example of a food chain from your local area, with named examples of producers, consumers, decomposers, herbivores, carnivores and top carnivores.

The earliest forms of life on Earth, 3.8 billion years ago, were consumers that fed on organic material formed by interactions between the atmosphere and the land surface. Producers, in the form of photosynthetic bacteria, appeared around 3 billion years ago (Figure 2.62). As O_2 is a waste product of photosynthesis, these bacteria eventually brought about a dramatic increase in the amount of O_2 in the atmosphere. The O_2 enabled organisms using aerobic cellular respiration to evolve and generate the large amounts of energy they needed. And eventually, complex ecosystems followed.

Figure 2.62 Stromatolites were the earliest producers on the planet and are still here. These large aggregations of cyanobacteria can be found in the fossil record and alive in locations such as Western Australia and Brazil.

2.2.12 Losses of energy and organic matter along a food chain

Open systems such as ecosystems are supported by continual input of energy, usually from the Sun (Topic 1, Section 1.2.5). Remember that the second law of thermodynamics (this topic, Section 2.2.8 and 2.2.9, page 132) states that transformations of energy are inefficient, so energy is lost from the system at each stage of a food chain, ultimately as heat energy (this topic, Section 2.2.8 and 2.2.9, page 134).

- Not all the food available to a given trophic level is harvested – for example, sheep eat the leaves of grass but not the roots.
- Not all that is harvested is consumed – for example, the bones and teeth of animals are not usually eaten.
- Not all that is consumed is absorbed – for example, some parts of the food cannot be digested such as the cellulose in plant matter.
- Not all that is absorbed is stored – for example, some is lost as heat through cellular respiration.

There are losses of energy and organic matter as food is transferred along a food chain.

There is never 100% transference of organic matter from one trophic level to the next.

Systems diagrams can be used to show the flow of energy through ecosystems (Figure 2.63). Stores of energy are usually shown as boxes (other shapes may be used) that represent the various trophic levels. Flows of energy are usually shown as arrows (with the amount of energy in joules or biomass per unit area represented by the thickness of the arrow).

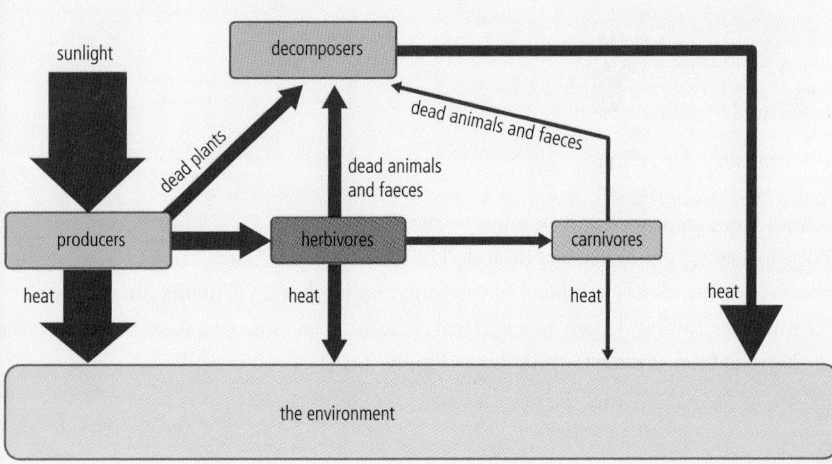

Figure 2.63 Energy flow in an ecosystem. The width of the arrows is proportional to the quantity of energy transferred. Producers convert energy from sunlight into new biomass through photosynthesis. Heat is released to the environment through cellular respiration.

Make sure you know how to analyse the efficiency of energy transfers through a system.

2.2.13 Gross productivity and net productivity

The term 'productivity' in ecology refers to the rate of accumulation of new biomass. Productivity can further be divided into **gross productivity (GP)** and **net productivity (NP)**, in the same way that monetary income can be divided into gross and net profits. 'Gross' refers to the whole of something, while 'net' refers to a part of the whole following a deduction of some sort. The terms 'gross' and 'net' are used in economics to indicate the total income a business makes (gross income) and the income a business makes once taxes, expenses and other payments are considered (net income). Gross income is the total monetary income and net income is gross income minus costs. Similarly, GP is the total gain in energy or biomass per unit area per unit time.

In ecology, **gross productivity (GP)** is the total gain in biomass by an organism. **Net productivity (NP)** is the amount of biomass (and therefore energy) remaining after losses due to cellular respiration.

NP is the gain in energy or biomass per unit area per unit time remaining after allowing for respiratory losses (R). NP represents the energy that is incorporated into new biomass and is therefore available for the next trophic level. NP is calculated by subtracting from GP the energy lost through cellular respiration (other metabolic processes may also lead to the loss of energy but these are minor and are ignored). Losses due to cellular respiration are typically greater in consumers than in producers as their bodies require more energy. The NP of any organism or trophic level is the maximum sustainable yield that can be harvested without diminishing the availability for the future.

Activity

Experiments can be carried out to estimate the GP and NP of plants. The worksheet on this page of the eBook has an example experiment.

The experiment uses light and dark bottles to estimate GP and NP, using algae or aquatic plants. Measuring dissolved O_2 concentration allows the rate of cellular respiration to be estimated. Photosynthesis and cellular respiration will occur in the plants in the light bottle but only cellular respiration can occur in the bottle stored in the dark. The decrease in dissolved O_2 in the dark bottle over time is a measure of the rate of cellular respiration.

Carry out the experiment on the worksheet and gather data for GP and NP. Evaluate the experiment – what are its strengths and weaknesses?

2.5 Zonation, succession and change in ecosystems

2.2.14 The number of trophic levels in ecosystems is limited due to energy losses

Energy released by cellular respiration and lost as heat by organisms is unavailable to organisms in higher trophic levels. Typically 10% or less of the energy flowing to a trophic level is available to the next level. The number of trophic levels in ecosystems is therefore limited due to energy losses.

4.3 Aquatic food production systems

5.2 Agriculture and food

Work out the efficiency of transfer between trophic levels

The efficiency of transfer between trophic levels can be calculated if the quantity of energy entering an organism, and the amount leaving the organism, are known (this topic, Section 2.2.28).

2.2.15 Food webs

Ecosystems contain many interconnected food chains that form food webs. Food webs show the complexity of trophic relationships in communities. Arrows in food chains and food webs indicate the direction of energy flow and transfer of biomass.

One species may occupy several different trophic levels depending on which food chains it occurs in. For example, in Figure 2.61, both foxes and hawks are both secondary and tertiary consumers depending on the food chains they are in. Decomposers feed on dead organisms at each trophic level.

Food webs show the complexity of trophic relationships in communities.

In a food web, species may feed at more than one trophic level.

Example – The effect of harvesting on food webs in the North Sea

Diagrams of food webs can be used to estimate the knock-on effects of changes to an ecosystem. Figure 2.64 shows a food web for the North Sea. In the figure, the producer is phytoplankton (microscopic algae), the primary consumers (herbivores) are zooplankton (microscopic animal life), the secondary consumers (carnivores) include jellyfish, sand eels and herring (each on different food chains) and the tertiary consumers (top carnivores) are mackerel, seals, seabirds and dolphins (again, on different food chains).

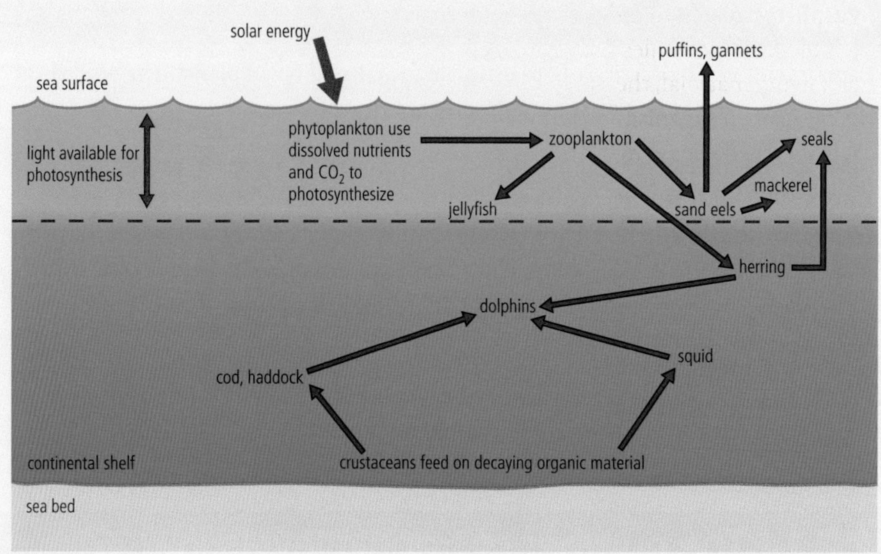

Figure 2.64 A simplified food web for the North Sea in Europe.

During the 1970s, sand eels were harvested and used as animal feed, for fishmeal and for oil and food on salmon farms. Figure 2.64 can be used to describe the effects that a dramatic reduction in the number of sand eels might have on the rest of the ecosystem. Sand eels are the only source of food for mackerel, puffin and gannet, so populations of these species may decline, or they may have to switch food source. Similarly, seals will have to rely more on herring, possibly reducing their numbers or they may also have to switch food source. The number of zooplankton may increase, improving food supply for jellyfish and herring.

An estimated 1000 kg of phytoplankton (plant plankton) are needed to produce 100 kg of zooplankton (animal plankton). The zooplankton is in turn consumed by 10 kg of fish, which is the amount needed by a person to gain 1 kg of body mass. Biomass and energy decline at each successive trophic level so there is a limit to the number of trophic levels which can be supported in an ecosystem. Energy is lost as heat (produced as a waste product of cellular respiration) at each stage in the food chain, so only energy stored in biomass is passed on to the next trophic level. Thus, after four or five trophic levels, there is not enough energy to support another level.

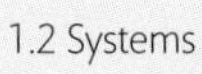
1.2 Systems

SKILLS

Create a food web from given data

You need to be able to create and interpret models representing feeding relationships. Find out about the organisms in a local ecosystem. Make a list of the species and research the feeding relationships – which organisms the different species feed on. Now construct a food web using your data.

Methods for estimating the biomass and energy of trophic levels in a community include measurement of dry mass, controlled combustion, and extrapolation from samples. Data from these methods can be used to construct ecological pyramids.

2.2.16 Measuring biomass

Biomass can be measured at each trophic level. Rather than measuring the mass of the total number of organisms at each trophic level (clearly impractical) an extrapolation method is used: the mass of one organism (or the average mass of a few organisms) is multiplied by the total number of organisms present to estimate total biomass.

Biomass is calculated to indicate the total energy within a living being or trophic level. Biological molecules are held together by bond energy, so the greater the mass of living material, the greater the amount of energy present. Biomass is taken as the mass of an organism minus water content (i.e. dry mass biomass). Water is not included in biomass measurements because the amount varies from organism to organism, it contains no energy and is not organic. Other inorganic material is usually insignificant in terms of mass, so dry mass biomass is a measure of organic content only.

Make sure you know how to evaluate methods for estimating biomass at different trophic levels in an ecosystem.

SKILLS

Carry out procedures for estimating biomass (dry weight)

To obtain quantitative samples of biomass, biological material is dried to constant mass. Only plant material should be used when estimating biomass, as it would be unethical to use animals. The mass of the sample is measured in a container of known mass. The specimens are put in a hot oven (not hot enough to burn tissue) – around 80 °C – and left for a specific length of time. The mass of the sample is measured again, and the sample is placed back into the oven. This process is repeated until a similar mass is obtained on two subsequent measurements (i.e. no further loss in mass is recorded as no further water is present). Biomass is usually stated per unit area (i.e. per metre squared) so that comparisons can be made between trophic levels. Biomass productivity is given as mass per unit area per period (usually per year).

To estimate the biomass of a primary producer within a study area, you would collect all the vegetation (including roots, stems and leaves) within a series of 1 m by 1 m quadrats and then carry out the dry-mass method outlined above. Average biomass can then be calculated.

Biomass of a trophic level can be measured by collecting and drying samples. The dry mass of the sample is approximately equal to the mass of its organic matter (biomass) since water represents most inorganic matter in most organisms.

Once dry biomass has been obtained, the combustion of samples under controlled conditions gives quantitative data about the amount of energy contained per unit sample (e.g. per gram) in the material. Organic matter can be burned in a calorimeter (Figure 2.65), where the heat released during combustion is measured to determine the energy content. Extrapolation from these samples, by estimating the total biomass of organisms and multiplying this by the energy content per unit mass, can be used to indicate the total energy per trophic level in an ecosystem. From such data, a **pyramid of energy** can be constructed.

Dry-mass measurements of quantitative samples can be extrapolated to estimate total biomass.

Energy in biomass can be measured by combustion of samples and extrapolation.

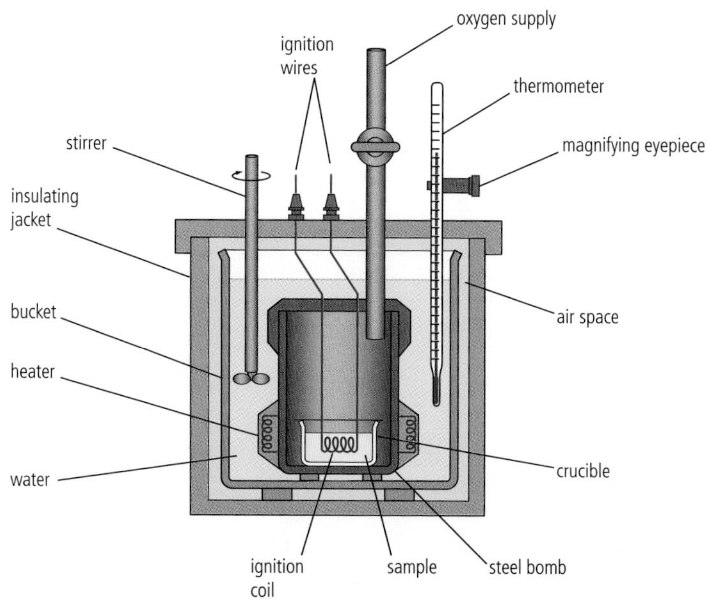

Figure 2.65 A calorimeter – used to calculate the energy content of biomass.

TOK

How can we judge when evidence is adequate?

Variables can be measured but not controlled while working in the field. Fluctuations in environmental conditions can cause problems when recording data. Standards for acceptable margins of error are therefore different from laboratory-based experiments. Is this acceptable?

Ecological sampling can at times involve the killing of wild organisms. For example, to help assess species diversity of poorly understood organisms, it may be necessary to take dead specimens back to the lab for identification; similarly, dead organisms may be needed to assess biomass. An ecocentric *perspective*, which promotes the preservation of all life, may lead you to question the value of such approaches. Does the end justify the means and what alternatives (if any) exist?

One criticism of this method is that it involves killing living organisms. It is also difficult to measure the biomass of very large plants, such as trees. There are further problems in measuring the biomass of roots and underground biomass because these are difficult to remove from the soil.

2.2.17 Ecological pyramids

Pyramids are graphical models of the quantitative differences (e.g. differences in numbers) that exist between the trophic levels of a single ecosystem and are usually measured for a given area and time. These models provide a better understanding of the workings of an ecosystem by showing the feeding relationships in a community. There are three types of pyramids: **pyramids of numbers**, **pyramids of biomass** and pyramids of energy.

Pyramids of number and pyramids of biomass show the standing crop per unit area at a particular time. Pyramids of energy (also known as 'pyramids of productivity') show the amount of energy flowing to each trophic level per unit area and per unit time (usually kJ m^{-2} $year^{-1}$).

Pyramids are graphical models showing the quantitative differences between the trophic levels of an ecosystem and are usually measured for a given area and time. There are three types.

- **Pyramids of numbers** record the number of individuals at each trophic level coexisting in an ecosystem. Quantitative data for each trophic level are drawn to scale as horizontal bars arranged symmetrically around a central axis.
- **Pyramids of biomass** represent the biological mass of the standing stock at each trophic level at a particular point in time measured in units such as grams of biomass per square metre (g m^{-2}). Biomass may also be measured in units of energy, such as J m^{-2}.
- Pyramids of energy show the flow of energy (i.e. the rate at which the stock is being generated) through each trophic level of a food chain over a period. Productivity is measured in units of flow (g m^{-2} yr^{-1} or J m^{-2} yr^{-1}).

Ecological pyramids are used to represent relative numbers, biomass or energy of trophic levels in an ecosystem.

Create pyramids of numbers, biomass and energy from given data

Some quantitative data for a food chain are shown in Table 2.2.

Table 2.2 Data for a terrestrial food chain.

Species	Number of individuals
leaves	40
caterpillar	20
blackbird	14
hawk	16

To construct a pyramid of numbers for these data, first draw two axes on graph paper. Draw the horizontal axis along the bottom of the graph paper and the vertical axis in the centre of the graph paper. Plot data from the table symmetrically around the vertical axis. As there are 40 leaves, the producer trophic level is drawn with 20 units to the left and 20 units to the right of the vertical axis. The height of the bars is kept the same for each trophic level. Each trophic level is labelled with the appropriate organism. Figure 2.66 shows the results.

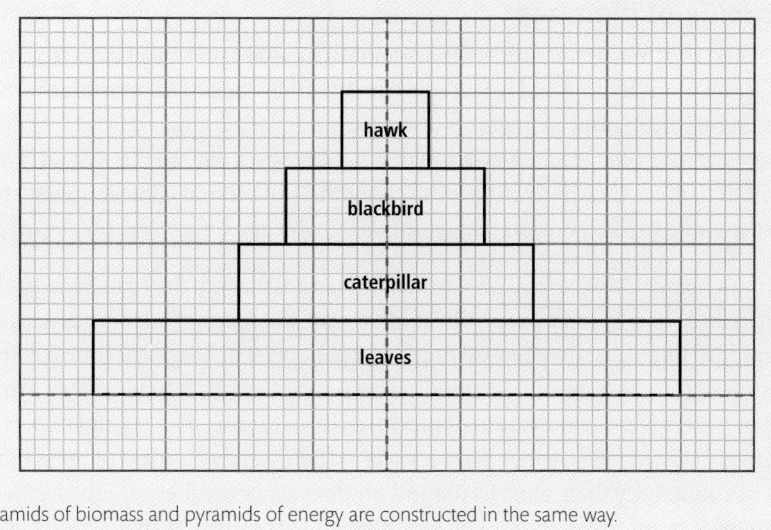

Pyramids of biomass and pyramids of energy are constructed in the same way.

Figure 2.66 Pyramid of numbers for given data.

Pyramids of numbers

The numbers of producers and consumers coexisting in an ecosystem can be shown by counting the numbers of organisms in an ecosystem and constructing a pyramid. Sometimes, rather than counting every individual in a trophic level, limited collections may be carried out in a specific area and this multiplied up to the total area of the ecosystem. In accordance with the second law of thermodynamics, there is a tendency for numbers to decrease along food chains and so graphical models tend to be pyramids – they are narrower towards the apex (Figure 2.67a). However, pyramids of numbers are not always pyramid-shaped. For example, in a woodland ecosystem with many insect herbivores feeding on trees, there are fewer trees than insects. This means the pyramid is inverted (upside-down) as shown in Figure 2.67b. This situation arises when the individuals at lower trophic levels are of a relatively large size. Pyramids of numbers, therefore, have limited use in representing the flow of energy through food chains.

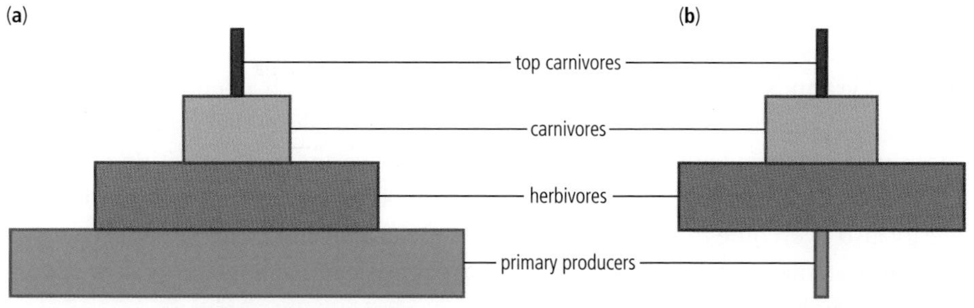

Figure 2.67 Pyramids of numbers. **(a)** A typical pyramid where the number of producers is high. **(b)** A limitation of number pyramids is that they are inverted when the producers are outnumbered by the herbivores.

Activity

A scientist is studying species interactions at a park in Singapore. They observe 10 slugs feeding on the leaves of the 16 sunflowers. A group of 6 orange-headed thrush regularly visits the park where the flowers are located. The scientist sees these birds feeding on the slugs. As the birds fly away, two pairs of Japanese sparrowhawks attack the flock and all six of the thrush are eaten.

Construct a pyramid of numbers for this food chain.

Pyramids of biomass

A pyramid of biomass quantifies the amount of biomass present at each trophic level at a certain point in time and represents the standing stock of each trophic level. Biomass may be measured in grams of biomass per metre squared (g m^{-2}) or units of energy, such as joules per metre squared (J m^{-2}). According to the second law of thermodynamics, there is a tendency for quantities of biomass (like numbers) to decrease along food chains, so the pyramids become narrower towards the top.

Pyramids of biomass can show greater quantities at higher trophic levels because they represent the biomass present at a given time, but there may be marked seasonal variations. For example, phytoplankton vary in productivity (and therefore biomass) depending on sunlight intensity. The biomass present in an area also depends on the quantity of zooplankton consuming the phytoplankton.

Although pyramids of biomass are usually pyramid-shaped, they can sometimes be inverted and show greater quantities at higher trophic levels. This is because, as with pyramids of numbers, they represent the biomass present at a given time (i.e. they are a snapshot of the ecosystem). The standing crop biomass (the biomass taken at a certain point in time) gives no indication of productivity over time. For example, a fertile intensively grazed pasture may have a lower standing crop biomass of grass but a higher productivity than a less fertile and ungrazed pasture (because the fertile pasture has biomass constantly removed by herbivores). This results in an inverted pyramid of biomass. In a pond ecosystem, the standing crop of phytoplankton (the major producers) at any given point will be lower than the mass of the consumers, such as fish and insects. This is because phytoplankton reproduce very quickly. Inverted pyramids sometimes result from marked seasonal variations.

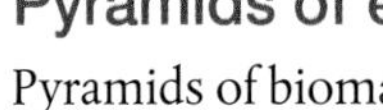

Pyramids of energy

Pyramids of energy show the flow of energy through a trophic level, indicating the rate at which that stock/storage is being generated.

Pyramids of biomass represent the momentary stock, whereas pyramids of energy show the rate at which that stock is being generated. You cannot compare the turnover of two shops by comparing the goods displayed on the shelves, because you also need to know the rates at which the goods are sold, and the shelves are restocked. The same is true of ecosystems.

Make sure you know how to explain the relevance of the laws of thermodynamics to the flow of energy through ecosystems.

Pyramids of energy also consider the rate of production over a period because each level represents energy per unit area per unit time. Productivity is measured in units of flow – mass or energy per metre squared per year (g m^{-2} yr^{-1} or J m^{-2} yr^{-1}). This is a more useful way of measuring changes along a food chain than looking at either biomass (measured in g m^{-2}) or energy (measured in J m^{-2}) at one moment in time. Pyramids of energy show the flow of energy through an entire ecosystem over a year. This means they invariably show a decrease along the food chain. There are no inverted pyramids of energy. The relative energy flow within an ecosystem can be studied and different ecosystems can be compared. Pyramids of energy also overcome the problem that two species may not have the same energy content per unit mass: in these cases, biomass is misleading, but energy flow is directly comparable.

1.2 Systems

Pyramids of biomass refer to a standing crop (i.e. at a fixed point in time) and pyramids of energy refer to the rate of flow of biomass or energy as shown in Table 2.3.

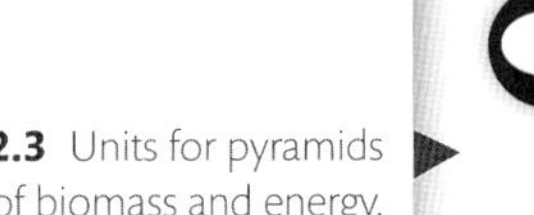

Table 2.3 Units for pyramids of biomass and energy.

Pyramid	Units
biomass (standing crop)	g m^{-2}
productivity (flow of biomass/energy)	g m^{-2} yr^{-1} J m^{-2} yr^{-1}

Challenge yourself

Find an app that explores pyramids of numbers, biomass and productivity. For example, search online for the BioInteractive Exploring Biomass Pyramids app.

Measure the biomass of primary producers in a defined area and extrapolate to calculate the amount of algal biomass in a river pool. Then use the '10% rule' to predict the amount of consumer biomass that can be supported by the primary producers. Produce a hypothesis for the relationship between biomass pyramids and pyramids of energy and then test those hypotheses with data. Explain the role of abiotic factors, such as sunlight, on pyramids of biomass.

How does the way that we organize or classify knowledge affect what we know?

Feeding relationships can be represented by different models (food chains, food webs and ecological pyramids). How can we decide when one model is better than another?

DDT is a synthetic **pesticide** with a controversial history. DDT exemplifies a conflict between the utility of a pollutant and its effect on the environment.

2.2.18 and 2.2.19 Non-biodegradable pollutants

Pollutants that are non-biodegradable such as polychlorinated biphenyls (PCBs), **DDT** and mercury cause changes to ecosystems through the processes of **bioaccumulation** and **biomagnification**.

In 1962, American biologist Rachel Carson published her hugely influential book *Silent Spring* (Topic 1, Section 1.1.10, pages 18–19) in which she claimed that the large-scale spraying of pesticides, including DDT, was killing wildlife. Top carnivores such as birds of prey were declining in numbers. Moreover, DDT could cause cancer in humans. Public opinion turned against DDT.

Bioaccumulation and biomagnification

DDT is a synthetic **pesticide**. DDT was used extensively during the Second World War to control the lice that spread typhus and the mosquitoes that spread malaria. Its use led to a huge decrease in both diseases. After the war, DDT was used as a pesticide in farming and its production soared.

In 1955, the World Health Organization (WHO) began a programme to eradicate malaria worldwide. This relied heavily on DDT. The programme was initially successful, but resistance evolved in many insect populations after only six years, largely because of the widespread agricultural use of DDT. In many parts of the world including Sri Lanka, Pakistan, Turkey and central America, DDT has lost much of its effectiveness.

Bioaccumulation is the build-up of persistent/non-biodegradable pollutants within an organism or trophic level because more are absorbed, and they cannot be broken down.
Biomagnification is the increase in concentration of persistent/non-biodegradable pollutants along a food chain (due to the loss of biodegradable biomass through cellular respiration and other processes).
Toxins such as DDT and mercury accumulate along food chains due to the decrease of biomass and energy.

Between 1950 and 1980, DDT was used extensively in farming and over 40,000 tonnes were used each year worldwide. Up to 1.8 million tonnes of DDT have been produced globally since the 1940s. About 4000–5000 tonnes of DDT are still produced and used each year for the control of malaria and other diseases. DDT is applied to the inside walls of homes, in a process known as indoor residual spraying (IRS), to kill or repel mosquitoes entering the home. India is the largest consumer of DDT but the main producers are India, China and North Korea.

Restrictions on the use of DDT

In the 1970s and 1980s, agricultural use of DDT was banned in most developed countries. DDT was first banned in Hungary (1968) followed by Norway and Sweden (1970), the USA in 1972 and the UK in 1984. The use of DDT in vector control has not been banned, but it has been largely replaced by less persistent alternative insecticides.

The Stockholm Convention banned several **persistent organic pollutants (POPs)** such as DDT and restricted the use of DDT to disease control. The Convention was signed by 98 countries and is endorsed by most environmental groups. Despite the

4.4 Water pollution

worldwide ban on agricultural use of DDT, its use in this context continues in India and North Korea.

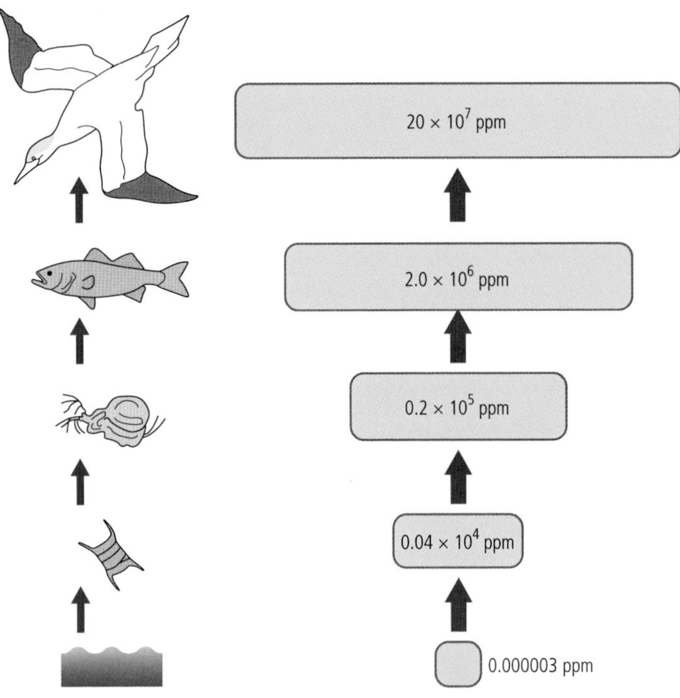

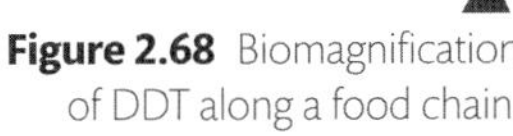

Figure 2.68 Biomagnification of DDT along a food chain.

Environmental impacts of DDT

DDT is a POP that is extremely hydrophobic and strongly absorbed by soils. DDT is not very soluble in water but is very soluble in lipids (fats). This means it can build up inside fatty tissue. Its soil half-life can range from 22 days to 30 years.

Bioaccumulation is the retention or build-up of non-biodegradable or slowly **biodegradable** chemicals in the body. Biomagnification or biological amplification is the process whereby the concentration of a chemical increases at each trophic level. The result is that top predators may have in their bodies concentrations of a chemical several million times higher than the same chemical's concentration in water and primary producers.

DDT and its breakdown products all biomagnify through the food chain (Figure 2.68). DDT is believed to be a major reason for the decline of the bald eagle in North America in the 1950s and 1960s. Other species affected included the brown pelican and the peregrine falcon. Recent studies have linked the thinning of the birds' eggshells with high levels of DDT, resulting in eggs being crushed by parents when incubating.

Effects on human health

The effects of DDT on human health are disputed and conflicting. For example, some studies have shown that:

- farmers occupationally exposed to DDT had an increased incidence of asthma and/or diabetes
- some people exposed to DDT had a higher risk of cancer of the liver, breast and/or pancreas
- DDT exposure is a risk factor for early pregnancy loss, premature birth and/or low birth mass
- a 2007 study found increased infertility among South African men from communities where DDT is used to combat malaria.

Use of DDT against malaria

Malaria remains a major public health challenge in many parts of the world. The WHO estimates that there are 250 million cases every year, resulting in almost 1 million deaths. About 90% of these deaths occur in Africa. In 2006, only 13 countries were still using DDT.

Nevertheless, the WHO is 'very much concerned with health consequences from use of DDT' and it has reaffirmed its commitment to eventually phase it out. In South America, malaria cases increased after countries stopped using DDT.

In Ecuador, between 1993 and 1995, the use of DDT increased and there was a 61% reduction in malaria rates.

Some donor governments and agencies have refused to fund DDT spraying or have made aid contingent on not using DDT. Use of DDT in Mozambique was stopped because 80% of the country's health budget came from donor funds and donors refused to allow the use of DDT.

Non-biodegradable pollutants are absorbed within microplastics

Plastics are used in an increasing number of disposable consumer products. **Microplastics** are tiny plastic particles up to 5 mm in diameter. Figure 2.69 shows how microplastic debris enters the marine environment and what happens to it subsequently.

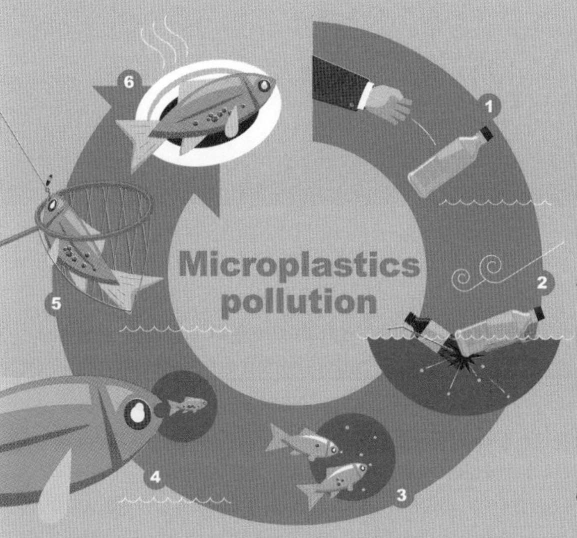

1. Plastic product is discarded into the environment.
2. Wave action and weathering break down product into microplastics.
3. Microplastics are consumed by aquatic organisms, such as fish.
4. Smaller organisms are eaten by larger animals, passing on the plastic contamination in the food chain.
5. Animals containing plastic contamination are caught.
6. Contaminated animals are eaten by humans.

Figure 2.69 Microplastic pollution.

Microplastic debris has accumulated in marine environments. Degradation of marine

Activity

Studies of southern fur seals have shown that seal scat (faeces) can contain plastic particles from the night-feeding myctophids (lanternfish), which are active near the sea surface and are consumed by the seals.

Pollution by microplastics can affect the food chain. Find out more about microplastics and their impacts using these and other sites:

NOAA National Ocean Service
United Nations Environment Programme (UNEP)

Use the QR code to access an article that reports scientific research on the bioaccumulation and biomagnification of microplastics in food chains.

This study suggests that the degree of biomagnification may depend on the feeding strategy of organisms in food chains. Read the report and summarize the findings. Give one example of how microplastics can affect a food chain.

4.3 Aquatic food production systems

2.2.20 Human activities have impacts on flows of energy and transfers of matter in ecosystems

Make sure you know how to discuss human impacts on energy flows and on the transfers of matter in ecosystems.

Energy flows

For thousands of years, humankind's only source of energy was radiation from the Sun. Sunlight energy, trapped by producers through photosynthesis, provided energy for food. This limited population growth as only limited amounts of food were available (i.e. that which occurred naturally). With the advent of industrial revolutions, which saw the rapid development of industry and the increased use of fossil fuels, industry was able to harness the sunlight energy trapped in coal and oil. Energy trapped by plants millions of years ago could be released so the amount of energy available to humans increased greatly. This enabled the use of machinery to increase, so industry and agricultural output both increased. Population growth increased rapidly due to increased food output. This change in the Earth's energy budget has ultimately led to many of the environmental issues covered in this course – habitat destruction, climate change, the reduction of non-renewable resources, acid deposition and so on.

Human activities such as burning fossil fuels, deforestation, urbanization and agriculture impact energy flows as well as the transfer of matter in ecosystems.

The combustion of fossil fuels has altered the way in which energy from the Sun interacts with the atmosphere and the surface of our planet. Increased CO_2 levels, and the corresponding increase in temperatures (Topic 6), have led to the reduction in Arctic land and sea ice. This reduces the amount of reflected sunlight energy (Topic 6, Section 6.1.3). Changes in the atmosphere through pollution (Topic 1, Section 1.3.3, page 51, Topic 6, Section 6.1.3 and Topic 8, Sections 8.3.1–8.3.3) have led to changes in reflection by scatter from tiny atmospheric particles and through absorption by molecules and dust. This in turn has led to increased interception of radiation from the Sun.

Energy flows and nutrient cycles occur at a global level – so human impacts have worldwide implications.

Matter cycles

Timber harvesting (i.e. logging) interferes with nutrient cycling. This is especially true in tropical rainforests, where soils have low fertility and nutrients cycle between leaf litter and tree biomass. Rapid decomposition, due to warm conditions and high rainfall, leads to the breakdown of the rich leaf litter throughout the year. Once the trees have been removed, the canopy no longer intercepts rainfall and the soil and leaf litter is washed away, along with many of the available nutrients. In South-East Asia, large areas of tree biomass have been cleared to grow oil palm. Oil palm is used in food production, in domestic products and as a source of biofuel. Once the original forest has been removed, natural nutrient recycling is also lost. The soils are generally nutrient poor (this topic, Section 2.4.4), so oil-palm trees require fertilizer to produce yields that return a reasonable profit. Fertilizers can have various negative environmental impacts. Adding fertilizers containing nitrates can cause eutrophication in nearby bodies of water (Topic 4, Section 4.4.5) due to run-off from soils causing disruption to ecosystems.

Increased agricultural land use leads to a reduction in native ecosystems, altering the nature of carbon storage. When crops are harvested, they are transported to be sold at markets away from the location where they are grown. The carbon storage present in crops is therefore transported to new locations, altering the carbon cycle on a local and global scale.

Urbanization leads to increased need for energy and therefore increased use of fossil fuels, which in turns leads to greater combustion of fossil fuels. Urbanization also leads to decreased land covered by vegetation, reducing photosynthesis. The concentration of the human population in cities has increased food requirements, leading to increased land use for agriculture. Increased transport of food into cities leads to greater energy requirements and increased fossil fuel use.

Burning fossil fuels increases the amount of CO_2 in the atmosphere, leading to global warming and climate change (Topic 6, Sections 6.2.2 and 6.2.4). Mining and burning of fossil fuels reduces the storages of these non-renewable energy resources and increases the storage of carbon in the atmosphere. Increased CO_2 levels in the atmosphere can lead to increased vegetation growth because there is more CO_2 available for photosynthesis, again altering the carbon cycle. Although burning fossil fuels may lead to increased CO_2 available for photosynthesis, the other pollutants produced and the impacts of global warming will reduce primary productivity.

6.2 Climate change – causes and impacts

8.2 Urban systems and urban planning

Deforestation, urbanization and agriculture all lead to loss of ecosystem biomass, disruption of food webs and the capacity for photosynthesis.

An autotroph is an organism that makes its own food – it is a producer. Heterotrophs cannot photosynthesize and so need to obtain carbon compounds from other organisms.

HL

HL

2.2.21 Autotrophs and heterotrophs

Autotrophs synthesize carbon compounds from inorganic sources of carbon and other elements. All autotrophs are producers, including plants, algae and photosynthetic bacteria. Heterotrophs are consumers that obtain carbon compounds from other organisms. All living organisms can be classified as autotrophs or heterotrophs.

HL

2.2.22 Photoautotrophs and chemoautotrophs

Plants, algae and some bacteria are producers. Organisms that use sunlight energy to create their own food are called **photoautotrophs**. All green plants are photoautotrophs but not all producers use sunlight to make food. For example, some bacteria use chemical energy rather than sunlight to make sugars. **Chemosynthetic** bacteria are part of the nitrogen cycle (this topic, Sections 2.3.17 to 2.3.21, page 168). Giant tube worms (*Riftia pachyptila*) (Figure 2.70) live on or near deep-sea hydrothermal vents (this topic, Section 2.1.1). They have a symbiotic relationship with chemosynthetic bacteria using hydrogen sulfide and CO_2 to produce sugars.

Figure 2.70 Giant tube worms (with a resident fish) at a hydrothermal vent.

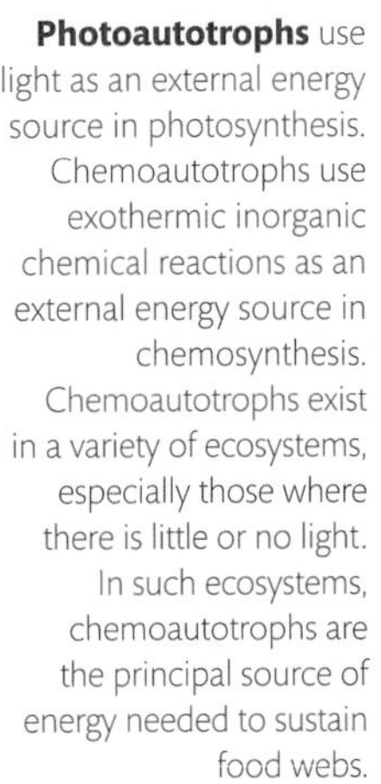

Photoautotrophs use light as an external energy source in photosynthesis. Chemoautotrophs use exothermic inorganic chemical reactions as an external energy source in chemosynthesis. Chemoautotrophs exist in a variety of ecosystems, especially those where there is little or no light. In such ecosystems, chemoautotrophs are the principal source of energy needed to sustain food webs.

HL

2.2.23, 2.2.24 and 2.2.25 Primary and secondary productivity

Productivity in ecosystems can be described as production of biomass per unit area per unit time. Productivity occurs at each level of a food chain and depending on where productivity occurs, it is referred to as **primary productivity** or **secondary productivity**.

- Primary productivity – the gain by producers (autotrophs) in energy or biomass per unit area per unit time.
- Secondary productivity – the biomass gained by heterotrophic organisms, through feeding and absorption, measured in units of mass or energy per unit area per unit time.

The conversion of energy into biomass for a given period is measured as **productivity**.

Primary productivity

Primary productivity is the rate of production of biomass using an external energy source and inorganic sources of carbon and other elements. The units usually used for productivity are kg carbon m^{-2} year $^{-1}$ (kilograms of carbon per square metre of ecosystem per year).

Primary productivity involves the conversion of solar energy into chemical energy in photosynthesis or the release of energy from oxidation of inorganic molecules in chemosynthesis to produce glucose. Secondary productivity involves feeding and absorption. Primary productivity depends on:

- the amount of sunlight
- the ability of producers to use energy to synthesize organic compounds
- the availability of other factors needed for growth (e.g. minerals and nutrients) (Figure 2.71).

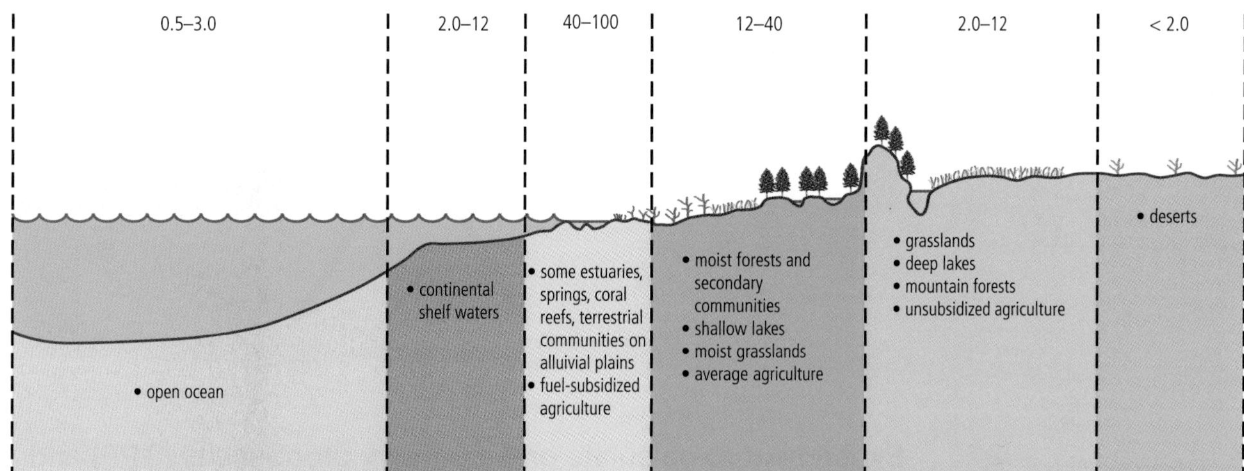

Figure 2.71 Comparison of biomes in terms of primary production / 10^3 kJ m^{-2} yr^{-1}.

Primary production is highest where conditions for growth are optimal, including high levels of insolation, a good supply of water, warm temperatures and high nutrient levels. For example, tropical rainforests have high rainfall and are warm throughout the year, so they have a constant growing season and high productivity. Deserts have little rain, so plant growth is limited. Estuaries are shallow, receive sediment containing nutrients from rivers and are light and warm so have high productivity. Deep oceans are dark below the surface and this limits productivity of plants (nutrients are the limiting factors at the surface). The productivity in different biomes is examined in detail later in this topic (this topic, Section 2.4.4). Productivity can further be divided into gross and net productivity (this topic, Section 2.2.13).

Activity

There are protocols for determining primary productivity in ecosystems. Estimates can be based on photosynthesizing samples within a lab or in the field measuring change in biomass of samples (of e.g. grassland) over time.

Methods for determining productivity are outlined later in this section on pages 150–153. Are there other methods you can find to determine primary productivity?

- **Net primary productivity (NPP)** is the basis for food chains. It is the quantity of carbon compounds sustainably available to primary consumers. Net primary production can be thought of as plant growth that is sustainably harvestable by primary consumers in natural ecosystems or by farmers and foresters in agricultural and silvicultural (where forests are maintained, harvested and regenerated) systems.
- **Gross primary productivity (GPP)** is equivalent to the mass of glucose created by photosynthesis per unit area per unit time in primary producers.

- NPP is the gain by producers in energy or biomass per unit area per unit time remaining after allowing for respiratory losses (R). This is potentially available to consumers in an ecosystem (Figure 2.72).

$$NPP = GPP - R$$

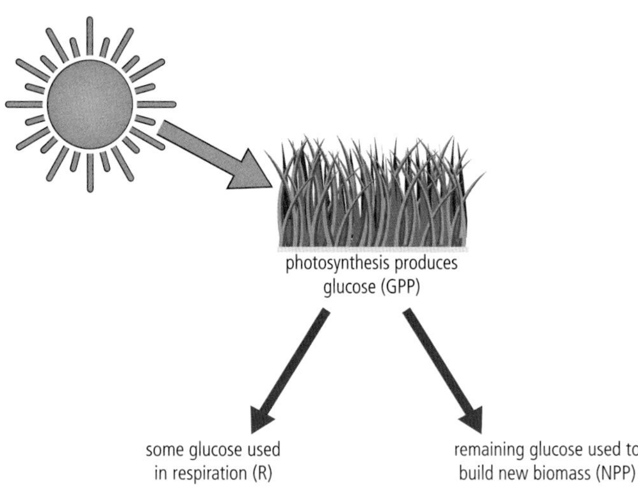
photosynthesis produces glucose (GPP)
some glucose used in respiration (R)
remaining glucose used to build new biomass (NPP)

Figure 2.72 NPP is the rate at which plants accumulate new dry mass in an ecosystem. It is a more useful value than GPP as it represents the actual store of energy contained in potential food for consumers rather than just the amount of energy fixed into sugar initially by the plant through photosynthesis. The accumulation of dry mass is more usually termed biomass and has a key part in determining the structure of an ecosystem.

Gross secondary productivity (GSP) is the total energy or biomass assimilated by consumers and is calculated by subtracting the mass of faecal loss from the mass of food consumed.

The term *assimilation* is sometimes used instead of *secondary productivity*.

Make sure you know how to calculate the values of both gross primary productivity (GPP) and net primary productivity (NPP) from given data.

Experiment to calculate gross primary productivity (GPP) and net primary productivity (NPP)

Values for GPP and NPP can be obtained from measurements taken during photosynthesis and cellular respiration in an aquatic plant placed in light and dark conditions. Photosynthesis produces O_2 and cellular respiration uses O_2. Measuring the amount of dissolved O_2 in water around aquatic plants before and after the plant was put in the light and in the dark will, therefore, give an indirect measurement of the amounts of photosynthesis and cellular respiration taking place. However, this will not provide a direct measure of the amount of energy fixed.

In this experiment, GPP and NPP are measured by using changes in dissolved O_2 in milligrams of O_2 per litre per hour.

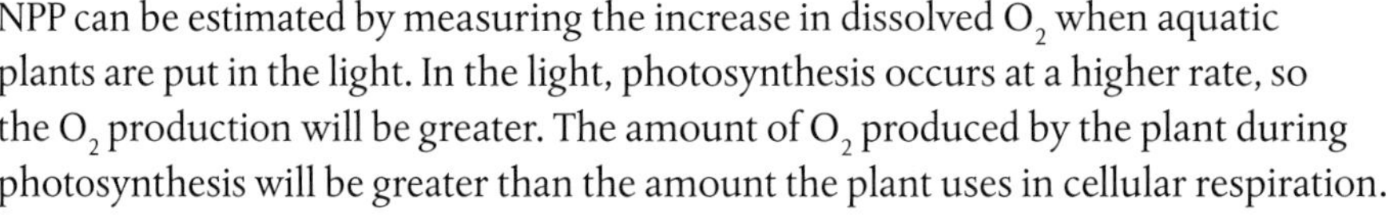

NPP can be estimated by measuring the increase in dissolved O_2 when aquatic plants are put in the light. In the light, photosynthesis occurs at a higher rate, so the O_2 production will be greater. The amount of O_2 produced by the plant during photosynthesis will be greater than the amount the plant uses in cellular respiration.

NPP can be calculated using the equation:

$$NPP = GPP - R$$

where R represents respiratory loss.

Net primary productivity (NPP) is calculated by subtracting respiratory losses (R) from **gross primary productivity (GPP)**.

Respiratory loss can be calculated by measuring the decrease in dissolved O_2 when aquatic plants are put in the dark. In the dark, only cellular respiration will occur and not photosynthesis. The equation can be rearranged to calculate GPP:

$$GPP = NPP + R$$

Aquatic plant placed in light conditions
Amount of dissolved O_2 at the start of the experiment = 10 mg of O_2 per litre
Amount of dissolved O_2 at the end of the experiment = 12 mg of O_2 per litre
Increase in dissolved O_2 = 2 mg of O_2 per litre
The increase in dissolved O_2 is a measure of NPP. The experiment lasted one hour and so the indirect measurement of NPP = 2 mg of O_2 per litre per hour (this could be used to estimate the amount of new biomass produced).
Aquatic plant placed in dark conditions
Amount of dissolved O_2 at the start of the experiment = 10 mg of O_2 per litre
Amount of dissolved O_2 at the end of the experiment = 7 mg of O_2 per litre
Loss of dissolved O_2 = 3 mg of O_2 per litre per hour
The loss of dissolved O_2 is a measure of respiratory loss (R)

$$NPP = GPP - R, \text{ so } GPP = NPP + R$$

Therefore, indirect estimation of GPP = 2 + 3 = 5 mg of O_2 per litre per hour (this could be used to estimate the amount of glucose produced).

The definitions of productivity must include units (i.e. the gain in biomass per unit area per unit time).

SKILLS

Use field techniques for measuring primary productivity

Primary productivity can be measured in field experiments. In terrestrial ecosystems, comparison plots can be set up, one covered in opaque plastic and the other left exposed to sunlight in the ecosystem being studied. Dry biomass is measured at the start and end of the experiment. Measurements can be compared from the open (i.e. with light) and covered (without light) plots. NPP is equivalent to the change in biomass in the open plot, whereas GPP is equivalent to the change in biomass plus the loss of biomass in the covered plot (due to cellular respiration). Measurements should be taken over a set period, for example one week.

It is relatively simple to isolate primary producers in an ecosystem sample, although it is difficult to collect all the biomass, which will affect the accuracy of measurements. Such studies also pose ethical problems because samples need to be killed to measure dry biomass. Productivity is easier to measure in simpler systems, for example grassland ecosystems, but is more difficult to measure where there are larger producers (such as trees and bushes).

Secondary productivity

Secondary productivity is the gain in biomass by consumers, using carbon compounds that are absorbed and assimilated from ingested food. Secondary productivity is ingested food minus faecal waste. The units are the same as those used for primary productivity. Faecal matter is not included as it is material that has remained undigested and unabsorbed.

Secondary productivity depends on the amount of food present and the efficiency of consumers in turning this into new biomass.

Secondary productivity can further be divided into gross and net secondary productivity:

Gross secondary productivity (GSP) is the total energy or biomass assimilated by consumers and is calculated by subtracting the mass of faecal loss from the mass of food consumed:

GSP = food eaten – faecal loss
GSP is the total energy gained through absorption in consumers (Figure 2.73).

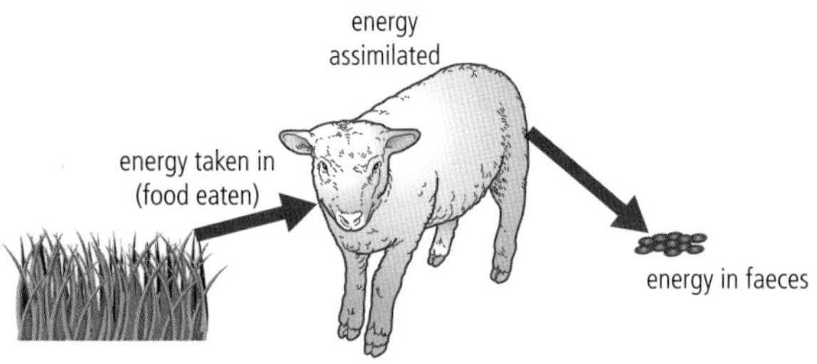

Figure 2.73 Animals do not use all the biomass they consume. Some of it passes out in faeces and excretion. Gross secondary productivity in animals (GSP) is the amount of energy or biomass assimilated minus the energy or biomass of the faeces (i.e. the amount of energy absorbed by the body).

Net secondary productivity (NSP) is calculated by subtracting respiratory losses (R) from GSP (Figure 2.74):

NSP = GSP – R.

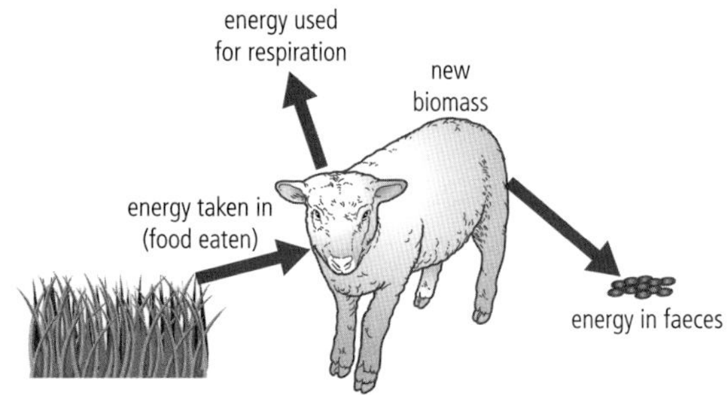

Figure 2.74 Some of the energy assimilated by animals is used in cellular respiration, to support life processes and the remainder is available to form new biomass. It is this new biomass that is then available to the next trophic level.

Experiment to calculate gross secondary productivity (GSP) and net secondary productivity (NSP)

You must know how to calculate the values of both GSP and NSP from given data.

A sample including 10 stick insects was fed privet leaves for five days (Figure 2.75). The mass of the leaves, stick insects and faeces produced were measured at the start and end of the experiment. The data recorded are shown in Table 2.4.

Figure 2.75 Stick insect on privet.

Table 2.4 Data collected from an experiment using stick insects.

	Start of experiment	End of experiment
Mass of leaves / g	29.2	26.3
Mass of stick insects / g	8.9	9.2
Mass of faeces / g	0.0	0.5

Calculating NSP

NSP can be calculated by measuring the increase in biomass in stick insects over a specific amount of time. The increase in the biomass of the 10 stick insects (NSP) is equal to the mass of food eaten minus biomass lost through cellular respiration and faeces.

In this experiment, NSP = mass of stick insects at end of experiment – mass of stick insects at start of experiment.

Over a five-day period: NSP = 9.2 – 8.9 = 0.3 g

Therefore, NSP = 0.3/5 = 0.06 g per day.

Calculating GSP

GSP can be calculated using the following equation:

$$\text{GSP} = \text{food eaten} - \text{faecal loss}$$

Food eaten = mass of leaves at start of the experiment – mass of leaves at end of the experiment.

Food eaten = 29.2 – 26.3 = 2.9 g

Also, faecal loss = mass of faeces at end of experiment = 0.5 g

Therefore, over a five-day period: GSP = 2.9 – 0.5 = 2.4 g

Therefore, GSP = 2.4/5 = 0.48 g per day.

GSP represents the amount of food absorbed by the consumer.

Calculating cellular respiration

Respiratory loss (R) (the loss of glucose as cellular respiration breaks it down) can be calculated by rearranging the equation:

$$\text{NSP} = \text{GSP} - \text{R}$$

to:

$$\text{R} = \text{GSP} - \text{NSP}$$

Therefore, R = 0.48 – 0.06 = 0.42 g per day.

2.2.26 Maximum sustainable yield (MSY)

HL

Sustainable yield (SY) means that a natural resource can be harvested at a rate equal to or less than its natural productivity, so the natural capital is not diminished. The annual sustainable yield for a given natural resource such as a crop is the annual gain in biomass or energy through growth and recruitment. **Maximum sustainable yield (MSY)** is the maximum flow of a given resource such that the stock does not decline over time. That is, the highest rate of harvesting that does not lead to a reduction in the original natural capital. In Topic 4, we will explore MSY as applied to fish stocks (Topic 4, Section 4.3.6).

Sustainable yield is the rate of increase in natural capital (i.e. natural income) that can be exploited without depleting the original stock or its potential for replenishment.

Maximum sustainable yields (MSYs) are the net primary or net secondary productivity of a system.

MSYs are equivalent to the NPP or NSP of a system. Net productivity is measured in the amount of energy stored as new biomass per year. So any removal of biomass at

Make sure you understand the link between *sustainable* yields and productivity.

1.3 Sustainability
4.3 Aquatic food production systems
7.1 Natural resources, uses and management

a rate greater than this rate means that NPP or NSP cannot replace the biomass that is extracted. Any harvesting that occurs above these levels is unsustainable and will lead to a reduction in the natural capital.

MSYs can be estimated for natural ecosystems and agricultural or silvicultural systems. Silviculture involves the treatment of forests to conserve and improve their productivity.

HL

2.2.27 Sustainable yields are higher for lower trophic levels

1.3 Sustainability
4.3 Aquatic food production systems
5.2 Agriculture and food

SY is calculated as the rate of increase in natural capital (i.e. natural income) that can be exploited without depleting the original stock or its potential for replenishment. Exploitation must not decrease long-term productivity. So, the annual SY for a given crop may be estimated as the annual gain in biomass or energy through growth and recruitment (in-migration of species).

SYs are higher for lower trophic levels. In terrestrial systems, most food is harvested from relatively low trophic levels (producer and herbivores). Systems that produce crops (arable) are more energy efficient than those that produce livestock. This is because crops are producers. They are at the start of the food chain and contain a greater proportion of the Sun's energy than subsequent trophic levels such as livestock.

Organisms in lower trophic levels contain a higher percentage of the energy that entered the food chain via producers (this topic, Section 2.2.8 and 2.2.9, page 133). This means that a given area of land can support a greater number of organisms if they consume organisms from lower trophic levels (either the plants themselves or herbivores that feed on the crops) because less energy has been lost from the food chain as heat, inedible parts and waste material. Sustainability in food production is therefore easier to achieve if humans consume organisms from lower trophic levels, especially plant-based foods.

HL c Environmental ethics

HL

2.2.28 Ecological efficiency

Ecological efficiency is the percentage of energy received by one trophic level that is passed on to the next level.

Once producers have converted energy into a chemical store, energy is available in a usable form both to the producers and to organisms higher up the food chain. Efficiencies of energy transfer are low, which results in a loss of chemical energy from one trophic level to another (Figure 2.76). The percentage of energy transferred from one trophic level to the next is called the ecological efficiency.

$$\text{ecological efficiency} = \left(\frac{\text{energy used for growth (new biomass)}}{\text{energy supplied}}\right) \times 100$$

The ecological efficiency varies between ecosystems, trophic levels and species. The percentage of energy transferred from one trophic level to the next is very variable and the value of 10% is neither a fixed amount nor a true average.

Consider Figure 2.76. If energy used for new growth is 0.1 J (converted to new biomass in the blackbird) and 1.0 J of energy is available (the amount of energy consumed by the blackbird) then the ecological efficiency = (0.1/1.0) × 100 = 10%.

Ecological efficiency varies between 5% and 20% with an average of 10%. This means that on average, one tenth of the energy available to one trophic level becomes available to the next.

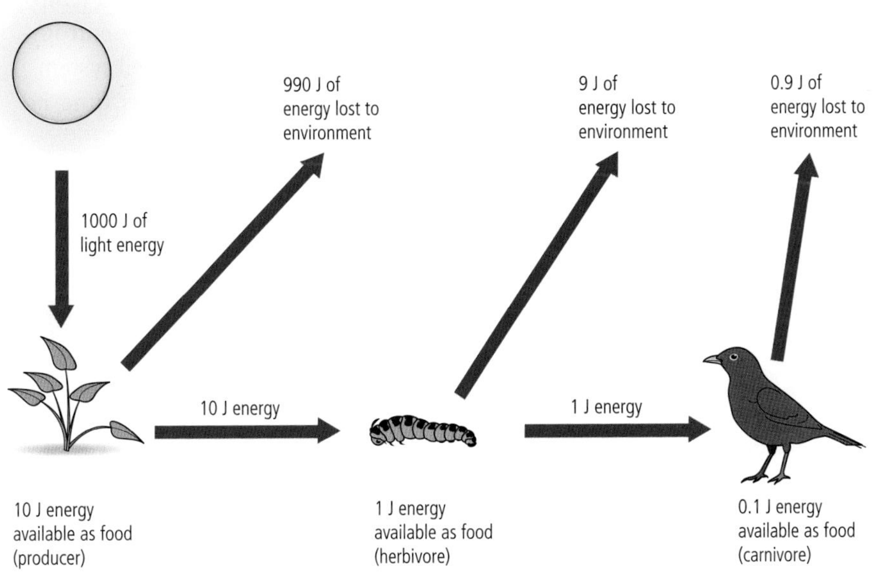

Figure 2.76 Loss of energy in food chains.

Make sure you understand the difference between storages and flows of energy. Storages of energy are shown as boxes that represent the trophic level. Storages are measured as the amount of energy or biomass per unit area. Flows of energy or productivity are given as rates, for example J m^{-2} day^{-1}.

Some pathways of energy through an ecosystem:

- conversion of light energy to chemical energy
- transfer of chemical energy from one trophic level to another with varying efficiency
- overall conversion of ultraviolet and visible light to heat energy by an ecosystem
- radiation of heat energy back out into the atmosphere.

Ultimately all energy lost from an ecosystem is in the form of heat, through the inefficient energy conversions of cellular respiration. This means that, overall, there is a conversion of light energy to heat energy by an ecosystem. Heat energy is radiated back into the atmosphere.

Systems diagrams showing energy flow through ecosystems need to show the progressive loss of energy in both storages and flows. Boxes show storages of energy and are drawn in proportion to the amount of energy they represent (Figure 2.77). Storages of energy are measured as the amount of energy or biomass in a specific area. The flows of energy are shown as arrows. Arrows also represent flows of productivity. Flows are measured as rates; for example, J m^{-2} day^{-1}.

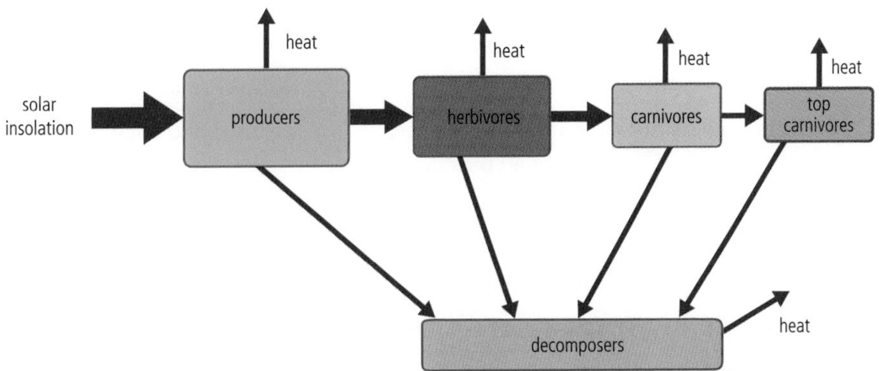

Figure 2.77 An energy-flow diagram showing the flow of energy through an ecosystem. Storages (boxes) and flows (arrows) vary in width and are proportional to the amount of energy being transferred.

2.2.29 Entropy

HL

Entropy is a measure of the amount of disorder in a system. An increase in entropy arising from energy transformations reduces the energy available to do work.

Energy is needed to create order (e.g. to hold complex molecules together). The second law of thermodynamics states that the disorder in a system increases over time. Disorder in a system is called **entropy**. The second law of thermodynamics shows how the entropy of a system increases as biomass passes through ecosystems. An increase in entropy arising from energy transformations reduces the energy

American scientist Howard Odum carried out the first complete analysis of a natural ecosystem (a spring-fed stream) at Silver Spring in Florida and constructed systems diagrams from the data gathered. He mapped out all the flow routes to and from the stream in detail and measured the energy and organic matter inputs and outputs. From these diagrams he calculated productivity for each trophic level and the flows between them. Such diagrams are useful as they give an indication of turnover in ecosystems by measuring energy flows per unit time as well as area.

available to do work. Therefore, as less energy becomes available, disorder (entropy) increases. In any isolated system, where there is no new input of energy, entropy tends to increase spontaneously. The universe can be seen as an isolated system in which entropy is steadily increasing so eventually, in billions of years' time, no available energy will be present.

Living systems can maintain a high degree of organization and low entropy through the net increase in entropy resulting largely from cellular respiration.

HL end

Engagement

- Using primary or secondary data, study the impact of pollution on an ecosystem and the effect on food chains – for example, the effect of a sewage overflow on aquatic communities. Health and safety and ethical issues should be considered. Produce a report of your research, including analysis of data and conclusions.
- Advocate for the planetary health diet in your community based on the second law of thermodynamics. Why is it better to eat food from shorter food chains? Produce a poster or blog to explain the issues to others in your community, using your knowledge of energy loss from food chains.
- Contribute to citizen science programs (Topic 1, Section 1.3.16) about microplastics. See if a local university is researching the effect of microplastics on the environment and whether they are asking for air, land or water samples to be sent to them. For example, the University of the West of England's (UK) Homes Under the Microscope project or the University of Portsmouth's (UK) Big Microplastic Survey.

Exercise

Q19. **Draw** a systems diagram for the process of photosynthesis, showing inputs, outputs and energy transformations. Now do the same for cellular respiration.

Q20. **Explain** why not all available light energy is transformed into chemical energy in biomass and not all the energy in biomass is made available to the next tropic level.

Q21. **Construct** an energy-flow diagram illustrating the movement of energy through ecosystems, including the productivity of the various trophic levels.

Q22. **Distinguish** between a pyramid of biomass and a pyramid of energy.

Q23. **Explain** the impact of a persistent/non-biodegradable pollutant on a named ecosystem.

Q24. **Define** the terms *gross productivity*, *net productivity*, *primary productivity* and *secondary productivity*.

HL

Q25. HL **Explain** how NPP is calculated from GPP and which measurement represents the biomass available to the next trophic level.

Q26. HL **Define** the terms *gross secondary productivity* (GSP) and *net secondary productivity* (NSP). **State** the formula for each.

Q27. HL NPP, mean biomass and NPP per kg biomass vary in different biomes, depending on levels of insolation, rainfall and temperature. Mean NPP for tropical rainforest is greater than it is for tundra because rainforest is hot and wet, so there is more opportunity to develop large biomass than there is in tundra. However, NPP per kg biomass is far lower in rainforest than in tundra because rainforest has a high rate of both photosynthesis and cellular respiration, so NPP compared to total biomass is low. Tundra are cold and dry and have low rates of photosynthesis and cellular respiration; plants are slow growing with a gradual accumulation of biomass but a relatively large growth in biomass per year.

The table below shows values for these parameters for different biomes.

Biome	Mean net primary productivity (NPP) / kg m^{-2} yr^{-1}	Mean biomass / kg m^{-2}	NPP per kg biomass per year
desert	0.003	0.002	
tundra	0.14	0.60	0.233
temperate grassland	0.60	1.60	0.375
savannah (tropical) grassland	0.90	4.00	0.225
temperate forest	1.20	32.50	0.037
tropical rainforest	2.20	45.00	0.049

(a) **Calculate** the NPP per kg of biomass per year for the desert biome.

(b) **Describe** how this value compares to those for other biomes.

Explain the value you have calculated in terms of NPP and NPP per kg biomass.

(c) **Compare and contrast** the values for NPP in temperate and tropical grassland. **Explain** the difference.

HL end

2.3 Biogeochemical cycles

Guiding Question

How do human activities affect nutrient cycling, and what impact does this have on the sustainability of environmental systems?

2.3.1 Biogeochemical cycles ensure chemical elements continue to be available to living organisms.
2.3.2 Biogeochemical cycles have stores, sinks and sources.

2.3.3 Organisms, crude oil and natural gas contain organic stores of carbon. Inorganic stores can be found in the atmosphere, soils and oceans.
2.3.4 Carbon flows between stores in ecosystems by photosynthesis, feeding, defecation, cellular respiration, death and decomposition.
2.3.5 Carbon sequestration is the process of capturing gaseous and atmospheric carbon dioxide and storing it in a solid or liquid form.
2.3.6 Ecosystems can act as stores, sinks or sources of carbon.
2.3.7 Fossil fuels are stores of carbon with unlimited residence times. They were formed when ecosystems acted as carbon sinks in past eras and become carbon sources when burned.
2.3.8 Agricultural systems can act as carbon stores, sources and sinks, depending on the techniques used.
2.3.9 Carbon dioxide is absorbed into the oceans by dissolving and is released as a gas when it comes out of a solution.
2.3.10 Increases in concentrations of dissolved carbon dioxide cause ocean acidification, harming marine animals.
2.3.11 Measures are required to alleviate the effects of human activities on the carbon cycle.
HL 2.3.12 The lithosphere contains carbon stores in fossil fuels and in rocks, such as limestone, that contain calcium carbonate.
HL 2.3.13 Reef-building corals and molluscs have hard parts that contain calcium carbonate that can become fossilized in limestone.
HL 2.3.14 In past geological eras, organic matter from partially decomposed plants became fossilized in coal, and partially decomposed marine organisms became fossilized in oil and natural gas held in porous rocks.
HL 2.3.15 Methane is produced from dead organic matter in anaerobic conditions by methanogenic bacteria.
HL 2.3.16 Methane has a residence time of about 10 years in the atmosphere and is eventually oxidized to carbon dioxide.
HL 2.3.17 The nitrogen cycle contains organic and inorganic stores.
HL 2.3.18 Bacteria have essential roles in the nitrogen cycle.
HL 2.3.19 Denitrification only happens in anaerobic conditions, such as soils that are waterlogged.
HL 2.3.20 Plants cannot fix nitrogen so atmospheric dinitrogen is unavailable to them unless they form mutualistic associations with nitrogen-fixing bacteria.
HL 2.3.21 Flows in the nitrogen cycle include mineral uptake by producers, photosynthesis, consumption, excretion, death, decomposition and ammonification.

HL 2.3.22 Human activities such as deforestation, agriculture, aquaculture and urbanization change the nitrogen cycle.
HL 2.3.23 The Haber process is an industrial process that produces ammonia from nitrogen and hydrogen for use as fertilizer.
HL 2.3.24 Increases in nitrates in the biosphere from human activities have led to the planetary boundary for the nitrogen cycle being crossed, making irreversible changes to Earth systems likely.
HL 2.3.25 Global collaboration is needed to address the uncontrolled use of nitrogen in industrial and agricultural processes and bring the nitrogen cycle back within planetary boundaries.

2.3.1 and 2.3.2 Biogeochemical cycles

Cycles of nutrients in ecosystems are called biogeochemical cycles. They include the carbon cycle (both SL and HL) and the nitrogen cycle (HL only). The cycling of nutrients is essential in the maintenance of ecosystems because nutrients provide the chemical elements needed for biological molecules. (Carbon is needed for carbohydrates, fats and proteins. Nitrogen is needed for proteins.)

Human impacts on these cycles can affect the sustainability of ecosystems (this topic, Section 2.3.9 and 2.3.10, and HL only Section 2.3.22–2.3.24).

Biogeochemical cycles have stores, sinks and sources

Whereas energy flows through ecosystems (it may enter as sunlight energy and leave as heat energy), matter cycles between the biotic and abiotic environments. **Stores** (storages) in biogeochemical cycles remain in equilibrium with the environment. **Sinks** indicate net accumulation of the element, whereas **sources** indicate net release of the element.

Nutrient cycles can be shown in systems diagrams that show stores and transfers of nutrients (Figure 2.78).

The factors that affect the store of nutrients and their transfer include:

- the amount and type of weathering
- overland run-off and soil erosion
- the amount of rainfall
- rates of decomposition
- the type of vegetation (woody perennial species hold onto nutrients for much longer than annuals)
- the age and health of plants
- plant density
- fire.

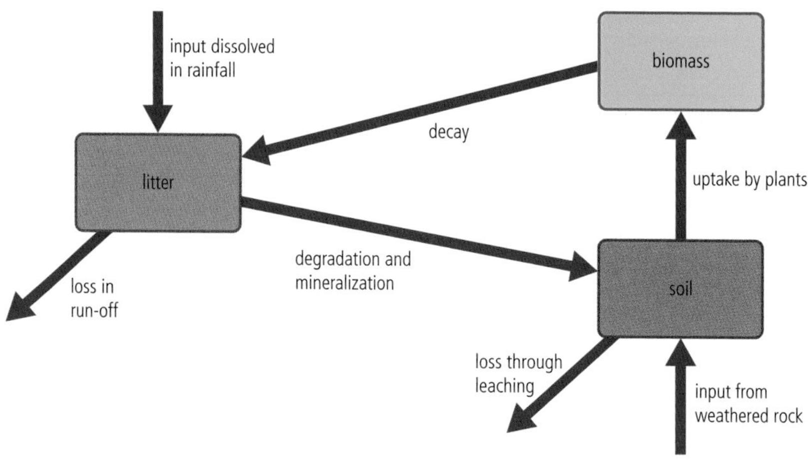

Figure 2.78 Systems diagram (developed by Gersmehl) showing nutrient cycles.

Explaining the differences between nutrient cycles in different ecosystems involves consideration of many processes.

Nutrients are circulated and re-used frequently. Natural elements are capable of being absorbed by plants, either as gases or as soluble salts. Only oxygen, carbon, hydrogen and nitrogen are needed in large quantities. These are known as macronutrients. The rest are trace elements or micronutrients and are needed only in small quantities (e.g. magnesium, sulfur and phosphorus). Nutrients are taken in by plants and are broken down and built up into new organic matter. When animals eat the plants, they absorb the nutrients. The nutrients eventually return to the soil when the plants and animals die and are broken down by the decomposers when animals defecate and excrete waste.

All nutrient cycles involve interaction between the soil and the atmosphere and many food chains. Nevertheless, there is great variety between the cycles. Some nutrient cycles are sedimentary-based, where the source of the nutrient is rocks (e.g. the phosphorus cycle). Others are atmosphere-based (e.g. the nitrogen cycle).

1.2 Systems 

Matter flows through and between ecosystems, linking them together. This flow of matter involves transfers and transformations.

2.3.3 and 2.3.4 The carbon cycle

Organic and inorganic stores of carbon

Unlike energy, nutrients are recycled and reused in ecosystems. Without this recycling, the Earth would be covered with detritus and the availability of nutrients would decline. Although decomposition is at the centre of these nutrient cycles, other processes play their part as well.

Carbon is an essential element in ecosystems because it forms the key component of biological molecules such as carbohydrates, fats and protein. Ecosystems form an important store of carbon (especially trees), but carbon is also stored in limestone and in fossil fuels such as coal, gas, peat and oil. Carbon can remain in these latter forms for very long periods of time.

Stores in the carbon cycle include organic stores such as living organisms (including trees) and inorganic stores such as the atmosphere, soil, oceans and fossil fuels.

Organic means made from living matter (e.g. plants and animals). Inorganic means made from non-living matter (e.g. rocks).

A store is in a state of equilibrium when the amount of carbon absorbed is balanced by the amount of carbon released. Historically, the carbon produced by the processes of cellular respiration and photosynthesis has been in balance. CO_2 is absorbed by plants during the process of photosynthesis (making glucose from sunlight energy). CO_2 is released during the process of cellular respiration, which provides energy for organisms. **Residence time** is the average period that a carbon atom remains in a store. Without human interference (i.e. mining) the residence time of carbon in fossil fuels, such as coal, could be measured in hundreds of millions of years.

6.2 Climate change – causes and impacts

Carbon flows between stores in ecosystems

Flows in the carbon cycle can be classed as transfers and transformations. Transfers involve a change in location of energy or matter, whereas transformations involve a change in the chemical nature, a change in state or a change in energy.

Organisms, soil, crude oil and natural gas contain organic stores of carbon. Inorganic stores include the atmosphere and oceans.

Transfers in the carbon cycle include:

- herbivores feeding on producers
- carnivores feeding on herbivores
- decomposers feeding on dead organic matter.

Transformations in the carbon cycle include:

- photosynthesis, involving the conversion of inorganic CO_2 and water into organic glucose using sunlight energy trapped by chlorophyll
- cellular respiration, involving the conversion of organic glucose into inorganic CO_2 and water
- dissolution of CO_2 from the atmosphere into the oceans
- conversion of organic biomass into CO_2 and water during combustion
- fossilization of organic matter in dead organisms into fossil fuels through incomplete decay and pressure.

CO_2 is fixed (i.e. converted from a simple inorganic molecule into a complex organic molecule – glucose) by autotrophs in either aquatic or terrestrial systems. These organisms respire and return some carbon to the atmosphere in the form of CO_2. They also assimilate the carbon into their bodies as biomass. When the organisms die, they are consumed by decomposers that use the dead tissue as a source of food. The decomposers return the carbon to the atmosphere in the form of CO_2 when they respire.

Oil and gas were formed millions of years ago when marine organisms died and fell to the bottom of the ocean, where anaerobic conditions slowed the decay process. The burial of these organisms, followed by pressure and heat over long periods of time, created these fuels. Coal was formed largely by similar processes acting on land vegetation. Limestone (calcium carbonate, $CaCO_3$) was formed by the shells of ancient organisms and corals being crushed and compressed into sedimentary rock. Weathering of limestone, acid rain and the burning of fossil fuels, returns carbon to the atmosphere.

Carbon flows between stores in ecosystems by photosynthesis, feeding, defecation, cellular respiration, death and decomposition.

SKILLS

Create a systems diagram of the carbon cycle

System diagrams can be made of the carbon cycle (Figure 2.79).

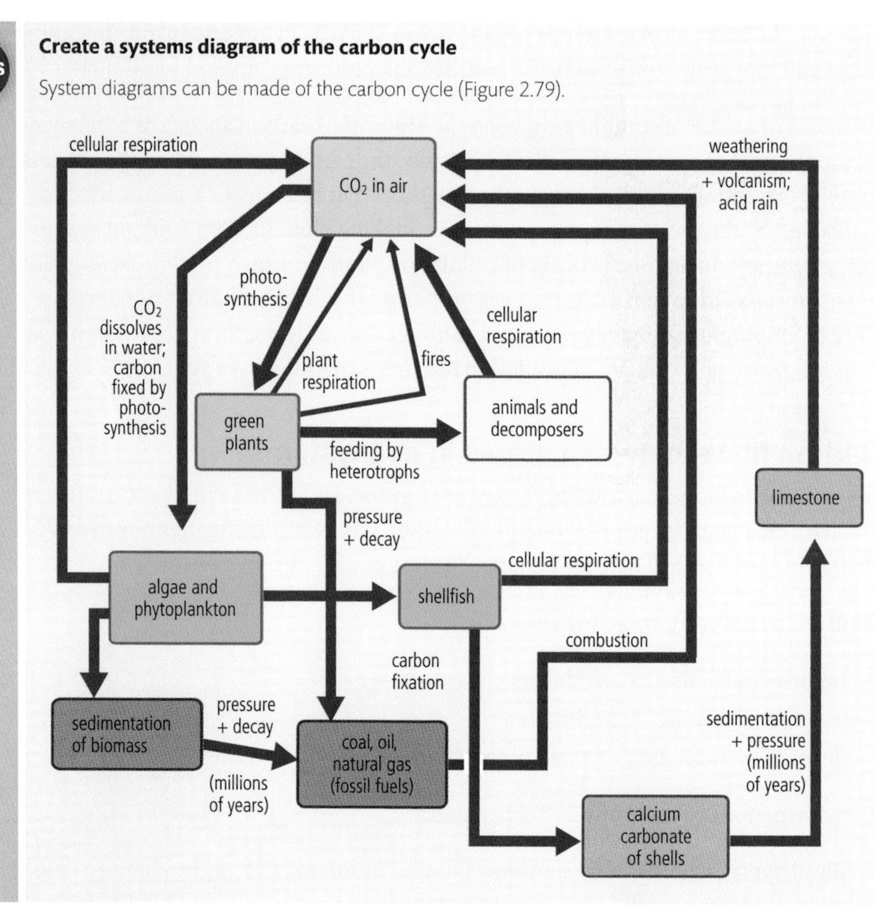

Figure 2.79 The carbon cycle.

6.2 Climate change – causes and impacts

2.3.5 Carbon sequestration

Carbon sequestration is the process of capturing gaseous and atmospheric CO_2 and storing it in a solid or liquid form.

Carbon sequestration is the natural capture and storage of CO_2 from the atmosphere by physical or biological processes such as photosynthesis.

Trees sequester carbon naturally by absorbing CO_2 and converting it into biomass. Organic matter is fossilized into coal, oil and natural gas.

2.3.6, 2.3.7 and 2.3.8 Ecosystems as stores, sinks or sources of carbon

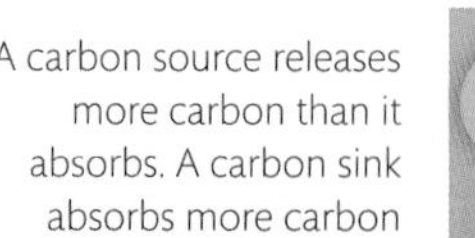

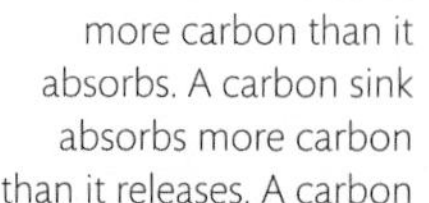

A carbon source releases more carbon than it absorbs. A carbon sink absorbs more carbon than it releases. A carbon store maintains a constant amount of carbon.

In ecosystems, carbon can accumulate in sinks or be released by sources. The difference between total inputs and outputs is the net accumulation or release of carbon. A carbon store maintains a constant amount of carbon.

If photosynthesis exceeds cellular respiration in an ecosystem there is a net uptake of CO_2. If cellular respiration exceeds photosynthesis there is a net release of CO_2. For example, a young forest will be accumulating biomass through the process of photosynthesis to grow and so will be a sink for carbon. In contrast, a forest that has been destroyed by fire will be a source of carbon, with CO_2 released from biomass in the process of combustion (Figure 2.80). A mature forest acts as a store, because overall there is no net uptake or release of carbon (photosynthesis and cellular respiration are in balance).

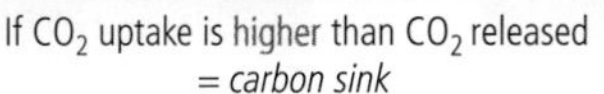
If CO_2 uptake is higher than CO_2 released
= *carbon sink*

If CO_2 uptake is lower than CO_2 released
= *carbon source*

Figure 2.80 Carbon sinks and sources.

1.2 Systems
5.1 Soil
6.2 Climate change – causes and impacts

Figure 2.81 Storage of carbon in ecosystems. Numbers are average stored carbon in tonnes per hectare.

Carbon is stored in the soil of an ecosystem, in the biomass (e.g. trunk, leaves and roots) and in dead biomass (e.g. woody debris and leaf litter). The largest storage of carbon is in the soil (Figure 2.81).

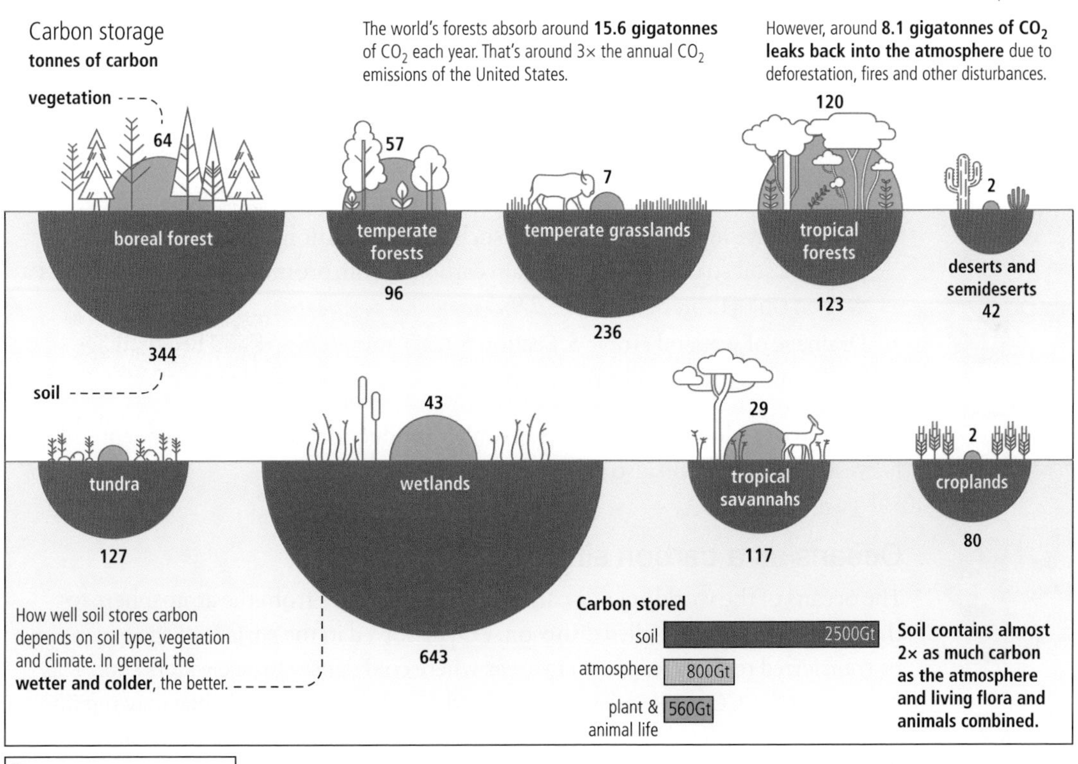

Fossil fuels as stores of carbon

Fossil fuels are non-renewable carbon resources and examples include oil, coal, natural gas, shale gas and tar sands (Topic 7, Sections 7.2.1 and 7.2.3). They were formed over geological time, millions of years ago (see Figure 2.82) and are known as fossil fuels because they are formed from the dead remains of ancient organisms. Fossil fuels contain carbon because the organisms they were formed from contained carbon in their biological molecules (carbohydrates, fat and proteins).

6.2 Climate change – causes and impacts

Fossil fuels are stores of carbon with unlimited residence times that were formed when ecosystems acted as carbon sinks in past eras. The occurrence of industrial revolutions around the globe resulted in coal being mined as a source of energy to power engines and machines, and more recently oil and gas reserves also being accessed as a source of energy. These fossil fuels, when burned to provide energy, became carbon sources.

Figure 2.82 Fossil fuels in geological history and in modern times, moving from stores to sources of carbon.

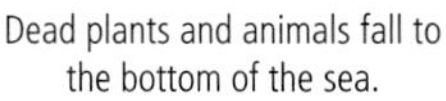

Dead plants and animals fall to the bottom of the sea.

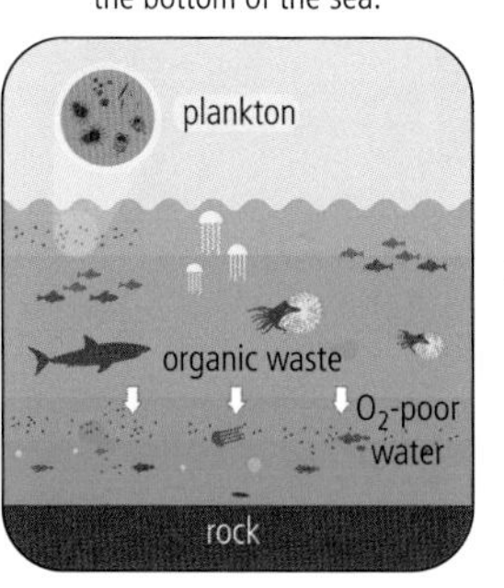

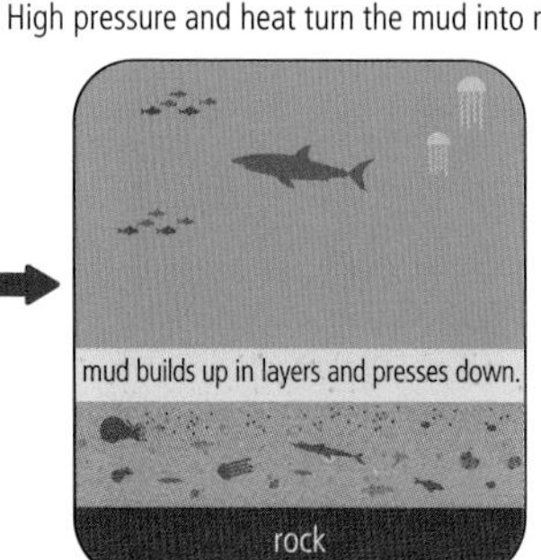

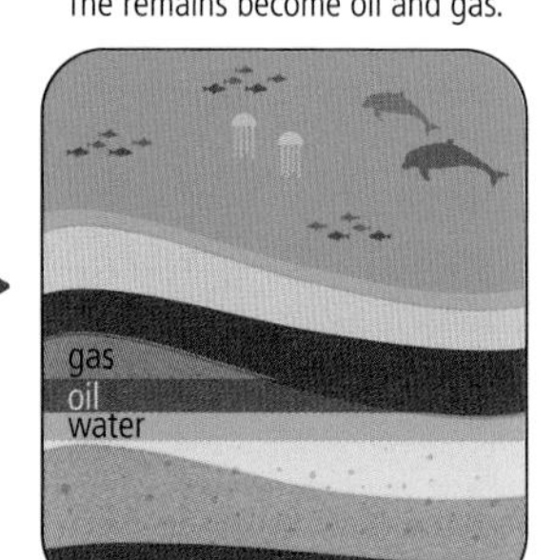

Mud builds up and presses down.
High pressure and heat turn the mud into rock.

The remains become oil and gas.

300 to 400 million years ago
50 to 100 million years ago

Agricultural systems

Agricultural systems can act as carbon stores, sources and sinks, depending on the techniques used:

- Regenerative agricultural methods such as crop rotation, cover crops and no till, preserve soil structure and maintain carbon in soil, promoting the role of soil as a carbon sink (Topic 5, Section 5.2.9).
- Drainage of wetland (Topic 5, Section 5.1.21), monoculture and heavy tillage will result in the agricultural system becoming a carbon source.

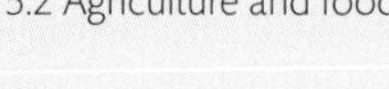

Cropping over a longer timescale (e.g. timber production) and the subsequent use of harvested products will also affect these roles.

Oceans as a carbon sink

CO_2 is absorbed into the oceans by dissolution and it is released as a gas when it comes out of solution.

The oceans of the world act as a carbon sink. CO_2 moves from the atmosphere to the ocean by a process called diffusion. CO_2 dissolved in the surface of the ocean can be transferred to the deep ocean in areas where cold dense surface waters sink. This process carries CO_2 molecules to great depths in the ocean where they may remain for centuries. The level of CO_2 diffusion also determines the acidity of the oceans (Section 2.3.9 and 2.3.10).

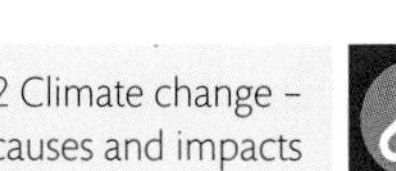

Although oceans act as a carbon sink, the human use of fossil fuels releases inorganic carbon at a faster rate than oceans can absorb it.

2.3.9 and 2.3.10 Ocean acidification

CO_2 dissolves in water to form hydrogencarbonate ions and hydrogen ions, which make the water more acidic. Increases in the concentration of dissolved CO_2, therefore, cause ocean acidification, which in turn harms marine animals.

Coral reefs are made of calcium carbonate ($CaCO_3$). A decrease in pH, meaning an increase in acidity, can lead to reduced calcification rates and destruction of coral reefs as the acid reacts with the alkali coral skeleton. Small decreases in pH can also interfere with calcium carbonate deposition in aquatic mollusc shells, which are also made from calcium carbonate.

2.1 Individuals and populations, communities and ecosystems

2.3.11 Alleviating the effects of human activities on the carbon cycle

Measures that are required to alleviate the effects of human activities on the carbon cycle include:

- Low carbon technologies. These are renewable energy resources (Topic 7, Section 7.2.1) such as solar heating, air-source heat pumps, ground-source heat pumps, biomass heating, solar panels, photovoltaics (PV), and wind turbines.
- Reduction in the use of fossil fuels. A reduced combustion of fossil fuels will reduce CO_2 emissions.
- Reduction in soil disruption. The majority of carbon in ecosystems is stored in soil (this topic, Section 2.3.6), so conserving soils is an important way of reducing carbon emissions.
- Reduction in deforestation. Trees are an important store and sink of carbon, so maintaining forest ecosystems maintains the equilibrium of the carbon cycle.
- **Carbon capture** through reforestation and artificial sequestration. Carbon capture is the process of capturing CO_2 and depositing it where it will not enter the atmosphere (see Topic 1, Section 1.1.8, page 13).

When fossil fuels are burned, CO_2 enters the atmosphere, where it may reside for decades or even centuries. A potential solution is to capture the CO_2 instead of allowing it to accumulate in the atmosphere. Two main ways to do this have been proposed. The first is to capture the gas at the site where it is produced (e.g. the power plant) and then to store it underground in a geologic deposit (e.g. an abandoned oil reservoir – Figure 2.83). The second is to allow the gas to enter

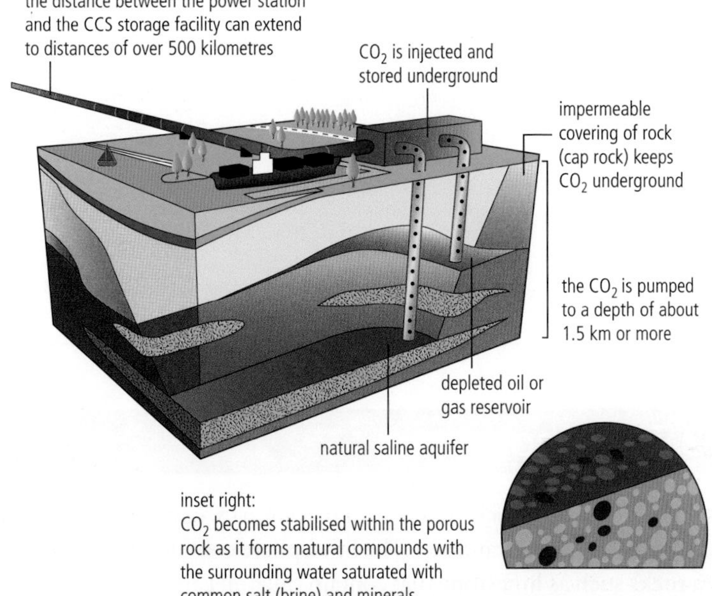
the distance between the power station and the CCS storage facility can extend to distances of over 500 kilometres
CO2 is injected and stored underground
impermeable covering of rock (cap rock) keeps CO2 underground
the CO2 is pumped to a depth of about 1.5 km or more
depleted oil or gas reservoir
natural saline aquifer
inset right:
CO2 becomes stabilised within the porous rock as it forms natural compounds with the surrounding water saturated with common salt (brine) and minerals

Figure 2.83 Carbon capture and storage.

the atmosphere but then to remove it directly from the atmosphere using specially designed removal processes (e.g. collecting the CO_2 with special chemical sorbents that attract it). This latter approach is called direct air capture of CO_2. Both techniques are examples of **artificial sequestration**.

There are many technical and policy issues about the feasibility and cost-effectiveness of large-scale carbon capture and storage (CCS) technologies. First, how costly will it be to capture CO_2 on a large scale? How costly will it be to ship the CO_2 by a pipeline network and then store it in some safe, underground geologic deposit? How certain are we that the CO_2 will stay underground, rather than returning to the surface and then into the atmosphere? Tens of billions of tonnes of CO_2 would have to be captured and stored each year for CCS technologies to play the leading role in addressing CO_2 emissions. Is there enough room for all this carbon? There is relatively little research and development underway to test the economic and geologic potential for large-scale CCS technologies.

Figure 2.84 Reforestation project.

Reforestation involves planting trees in deforested areas (Figure 2.84). New trees act as carbon sinks and can therefore help with climate change mitigation.

- The UN-REDD Programme, launched in 2008, is the United Nations Initiative on Reducing Emissions from Deforestation and Forest Degradation (REDD) in low-income countries (LICs). REDD provides incentives for developing countries to conserve their rainforests by placing a monetary value on forest conservation. This is an important example of successful global governance. REDD stresses the role of conservation, the sustainable management of forests and the increase of forest carbon stocks. By June 2014, total funding had reached almost US$ 200 million. Norway is the leading donor country.
- The UK Forestry Commission was established in 1919, following the end of the First World War, to increase timber supplies through a policy of land use changes, a rare early example of human action bringing a positive change in carbon storage. Marginal areas of grassland, heather and moorland were used to grow coniferous forest, for example in Bannau Brycheiniog (the Brecon Beacons, Wales) and the Isle of Arran (Scotland).
- New monoculture of commercial trees, such as coniferous plantations in the UK, can increase carbon storage if it replaces grassland. However, it may store less carbon than natural forest biome communities do. In addition, monoculture forest lacks biodiversity and provides few habitats for other plant and animal species to occupy.
- Individual citizens can play an active role in **afforestation** through the practice of carbon offsetting. This is a widely used mitigation strategy that aims to marry business principles with environmental goals. Our everyday actions such as driving, flying and heating buildings, consume energy and produce carbon emissions. Carbon offsetting is a way of compensating for your emissions, although the amount of carbon removed from the atmosphere is tiny compared to the emissions produced. For example, offsetting the UK's annual greenhouse gas emissions would require yearly planting of an area of forest the size of Devon and Cornwall combined and maintaining these forests forever. In addition, many argue that carbon stored in trees or biological carbon is not equivalent to fossil carbon because it will be released back into the atmosphere through fire, natural decay or harvesting.

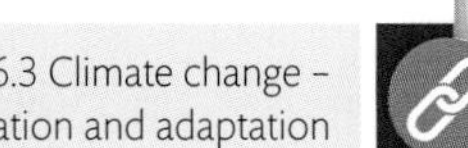

Reforestation is the restoration of forests to lands where they once existed whereas afforestation is the addition of forests to land that did not originally have them.

6.3 Climate change – mitigation and adaptation

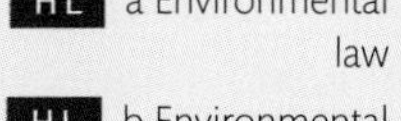

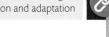

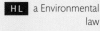

HL a Environmental law

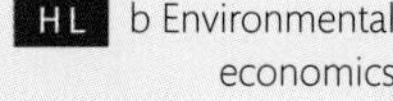

HL b Environmental economics

HL

HL

2.3.12 The lithosphere

The lithosphere is the solid, rocky outer layer of the Earth, consisting of the crust, the outermost layer of the mantle and soil. The lithosphere contains carbon stores in fossil fuels and in rocks such as limestone that contain calcium carbonate. Fossil fuels are formed by the decomposition and decay of dead organisms over millions of years (this topic, Section 2.3.7, page 163). Limestone is produced from shells and reef-building coral, which contain calcium carbonate (this topic, Section 2.3.3 and 2.3.4, page 160).

The residence time of carbon is the average length of time it remains in any carbon store. This ranges from long-term (millions/thousands of years) to short-term (tens/hundreds of years). For example, the residence time for carbon in the atmosphere and terrestrial biomass is short term. The residence time for carbon in limestone and fossil fuel stores is long term and can be hundreds of millions of years.

6.2 Climate change - causes and impacts

2.3.13 Reef-building corals and molluscs can become fossilized in limestone

HL

Corals are colonies of small animals (polyps) embedded in a skeleton that they secrete (this topic, Section 2.1.9, page 96). They form underwater structures, known as coral reefs, in warm, shallow water where sunlight penetrates.

The hard parts of reef-building corals (the coral skeleton) and molluscs contain calcium carbonate that can become fossilized in limestone. Limestone is the largest store of carbon in Earth systems. Not all limestone is formed by fossilization of animal remains. It can also be formed by both biological and non-biological processes.

6.2 Climate change - causes and impacts

2.3.14 Formation of coal, oil and gas

HL

In past geological eras, organic matter from partially decomposed plants became fossilized in coal. Organic matter from partially decomposed marine organisms became fossilized in oil and natural gas held in porous rocks (Figure 2.82, this topic, Section 2.3.7, page 164).

Formation of fossil fuels – coal, oil and gas – was greatest in specific geological eras when conditions were most suitable for the preservation of organic matter. The accumulation of significant stores took tens of millions of years.

6.2 Climate change - causes and impacts

2.3.15 and 2.3.16 Methane

HL

Methane (CH_4) is a colourless gas produced from dead organic matter in anaerobic conditions by methanogenic bacteria (i.e. bacteria which release CH_4 as a waste product). The production of CH_4 is known as methanogenesis.

Many coal seams also contain natural gas. What was once a byproduct of the coal industry, is becoming an increasingly important source of natural gas.

CH_4 accumulates in the ground in porous rocks, under permafrost in decomposing plant material or underwater, but may diffuse into the atmosphere. In air and light, CH_4 is oxidized to CO_2 and water.

Anaerobic conditions suitable for methanogenesis occur in swamps, rice paddies and the stomachs of cattle and other ruminants. Cattle alone emit between 65 and 85 million tonnes of CH_4 per year, produced by methanogenic bacteria in their stomachs. Natural wetlands and paddy fields are another important source – paddy

5.2 Agriculture and food

6.2 Climate change - causes and impacts

fields emit up to 150 million tonnes of CH_4 annually. As global warming increases, bogs trapped in permafrost will thaw and could emit vast quantities of CH_4.

6.1 Introduction to the atmosphere
6.2 Climate change - causes and impacts

Residence time of methane

Residence time is the average time it takes for a molecule to be removed from the atmosphere. CH_4 has a residence time of about ten years and is eventually oxidized to CO_2. CH_4 is a potent greenhouse gas and is the second largest contributor to global warming (Topic 6, Section 6.2.4).

HL

2.3.17–2.3.21 The nitrogen cycle

The nitrogen cycle contains organic and inorganic stores.

Nitrogen is an essential building block of amino acids (which link together to make proteins) and DNA. It is a vital element for all organisms.

Organic stores in the nitrogen cycle include proteins and other nitrogenous carbon compounds in living organisms and dead organic matter.

1.2 Systems
5.2 Agriculture and food

Inorganic stores in the nitrogen cycle include atmospheric nitrogen gas (N_2) and ammonia (NH_3) and other nitrogen compounds (nitrites and nitrates) in soil and water.

Bacteria have essential roles in the nitrogen cycle

The cycling of nitrogen is controlled by several different types of bacteria.

Nitrogen-fixing bacteria

Nitrogen-fixing bacteria are found either free-living in the soil (e.g. *Azotobacter*) or living within the root nodules of leguminous plants (*Rhizobium*).

Nitrogen (N_2) is the most abundant gas in the atmosphere (80%) but because it is very stable it is not directly accessible to animals or plants. Plants cannot fix nitrogen so atmospheric N_2 is unavailable to them unless they form mutualistic associations with specific bacteria. Only certain species of bacteria (**nitrogen-fixing bacteria**) can generate the energy needed to convert N_2 gas into ammonium ions (NH_4^+).

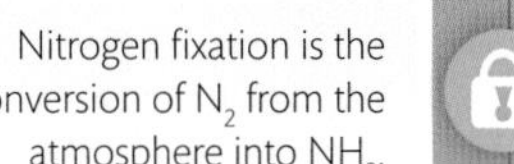

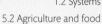

Nitrogen fixation is the conversion of N_2 from the atmosphere into NH_3.

Species of nitrogen-fixing bacteria found in root nodules have a symbiotic relationship with the plant – they derive the sugars they need for cellular respiration from the plant (a lot of energy is needed to split the N_2 molecule) and the plants gain a usable form of nitrogen. These bacteria fix atmospheric N_2 into NH_4^+ ions, which are then not only available to the plant that contains the nitrogen-fixing bacteria, but also benefit other plants when they enter the soil.

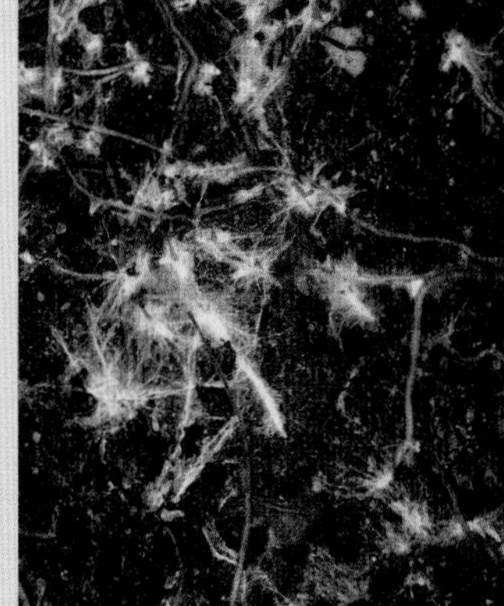

Figure 2.85 Mycorrhizae attached to plant roots form a thread-like network, extending beyond the roots. This extra network takes up additional water and nutrients and supplies them to the plant.

Nitrogen from the breakdown of amino acids and proteins in plant structures causes the build-up of nitrogen in the soil. The breakdown of organic matter is faster in tropical forest than in temperate woodland because high temperatures and year-round availability of water in tropical forests allow for continuous breakdown of nitrogen-containing compounds. This results in very rapid cycling and reabsorption. In temperate woodland, the breakdown of organic matter slows down significantly during winter months, causing slower cycling of nitrogen.

Some tropical forest trees have specific species of mycorrhizal fungi (Figure 2.85) associated with their roots that increase the rate of organic matter breakdown, leading to rapid reabsorption of nitrogen. This rapid recycling of nitrogen allows for rapid growth to occur in the nutrient-poor soils of tropical forests.

Example – Plants which form mutualistic associations with nitrogen-fixing bacteria

Many different species of plant form mutualistic associations with nitrogen-fixing bacteria.

Soybeans have the nitrogen-fixing bacteria *Sinorhizobium fredii* in their root nodules (Figure 2.86).

Clover (Figure 2.87) is another legume plant that has a mutualistic relationship with nitrogen-fixing bacteria. Farmers grow clover to provide a natural source of nitrogen for crops.

Birds-foot trefoil (Figure 2.88) is a member of the pea family. It is a small plant that is native to grasslands in North Africa and temperate Eurasia, but is also an invasive species (Topic 3, Section 3.2.3, page 275) found across many parts of North America and Australia.

Figure 2.86 Root nodules of soybean.

Figure 2.87 Flowering red clover.

Figure 2.88 Birds-foot trefoil.

In ecosystems where nitrogen is a limiting factor on plant growth, plants that have a mutualistic relationship with nitrogen-fixing bacteria have a competitive advantage over other plant species. This is why birds-foot trefoil, for example, became an invasive species. The plant could survive in areas that were low in nitrogen and once established it out-competed other native species.

2.1 Individuals and populations, communities and ecosystems

2.5 Zonation, success and change in ecosystems

Decomposers

Decomposers produce ammonia gas (NH_3) and ammonium ions (NH_4^+) from amino acids. NH_3 is also present in the excretory products of consumers.

Decomposition involves the conversion of amino acids into ammonium ions.

Nitrifying bacteria

Nitrifying bacteria found in the soil oxidize NH_4^+ ions first into nitrite ions (NO_2^-) and then into nitrate ions (NO_3^-). This process is known as **nitrification**. These chemosynthetic organisms (this topic, Section 2.2.22) convert inorganic materials into organic matter. The bacteria gain energy from this reaction to form food (glucose). NH_3 and NO_2^- ions are toxic to plants, but the NO_3^- ions are taken up with water into plant roots and used to create amino acids and other organic chemicals.

Nitrification is the conversion of NH_3 gas to NO_3^- ions.

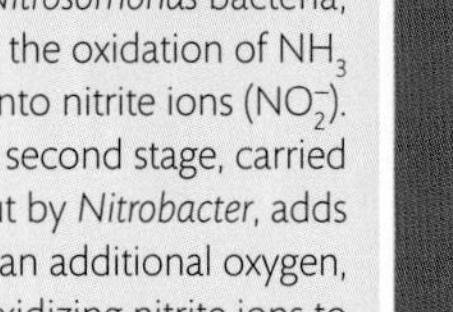

Nitrification is a two-stage process, carried out by different species of bacteria. The first stage, carried out by *Nitrosomonas* bacteria, is the oxidation of NH_3 into nitrite ions (NO_2^-). The second stage, carried out by *Nitrobacter*, adds an additional oxygen, oxidizing nitrite ions to nitrate ions (NO_3^-).

Denitrifying bacteria

N_2 is returned to the atmosphere by **denitrifying bacteria**, which remove O_2 from NO_3^- ions for use in cellular respiration. This process is known as **denitrification**. Denitrifying bacteria live in oxygen-poor soils where free O_2 is not readily available. Denitrification only happens in anaerobic conditions – for example, in soils that are waterlogged. N_2 gas is released as a by-product. Waterlogged soils are not good for farmers because denitrifying bacteria thrive in these conditions and dramatically reduce the quantity of NO_3^- ions available for crop growth. In waterlogged soils, plant growth and crop yield are reduced due to lack of available nitrogen.

In soils which lack NO_3^- ions, insectivorous plants can capture and digest insects and use them as a nitrogen source, e.g. pitcher plants and sundews.

You do not need to know the chemical details of the reactions in which the conversion of NH_4^+ ions and NO_2^- ions to NO_3^- ions take place.

Flows in the nitrogen cycle

Flows in the nitrogen cycle can be divided into transfers and transformations (Topic 1, Section 1.2.4).

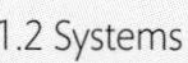

1.2 Systems

Transfers in the nitrogen cycle include:

- herbivores feeding on producers
- carnivores feeding on herbivores
- decomposers feeding on dead organic matter
- producers absorbing minerals (NO_3^- ions) through their roots
- removal of metabolic waste products from an organism (excretion).

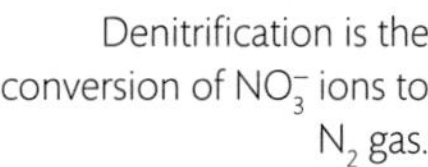

Denitrification is the conversion of NO_3^- ions to N_2 gas.

Transformations in the nitrogen cycle include:

- nitrogen fixation – lightning transforming atmospheric N_2 into nitrate ions (NO_3^-)
- ammonification – nitrogen-fixing bacteria transforming N_2 gas in the soil into NH_4^+ ions
- plants providing sugars from photosynthesis that are utilized by the nitrogen-fixing bacteria for the energy they require for nitrogen fixation
- nitrifying bacteria transforming NH_4^+ ions into NO_2^- ions and then into NO_3^- ions
- denitrifying bacteria transforming NO_3^- ions into N_2
- decomposers breaking down organic nitrogen (protein) into NH_3; the breakdown of organic nitrogen into NH_3 is called deamination
- assimilation – nitrogen from NO_3^- ions being used by plants to make amino acids and proteins.

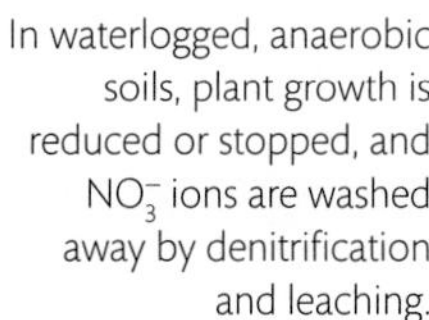

In waterlogged, anaerobic soils, plant growth is reduced or stopped, and NO_3^- ions are washed away by denitrification and leaching.

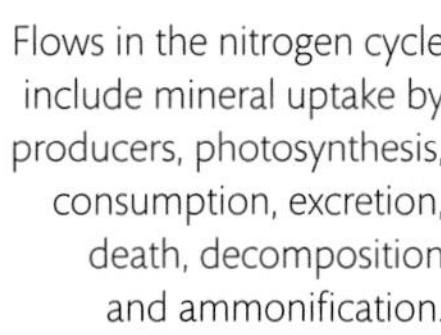

Flows in the nitrogen cycle include mineral uptake by producers, photosynthesis, consumption, excretion, death, decomposition and ammonification.

SKILLS

Create a systems diagram of the nitrogen cycle

System diagrams can be made of the nitrogen cycle (Figure 2.89).

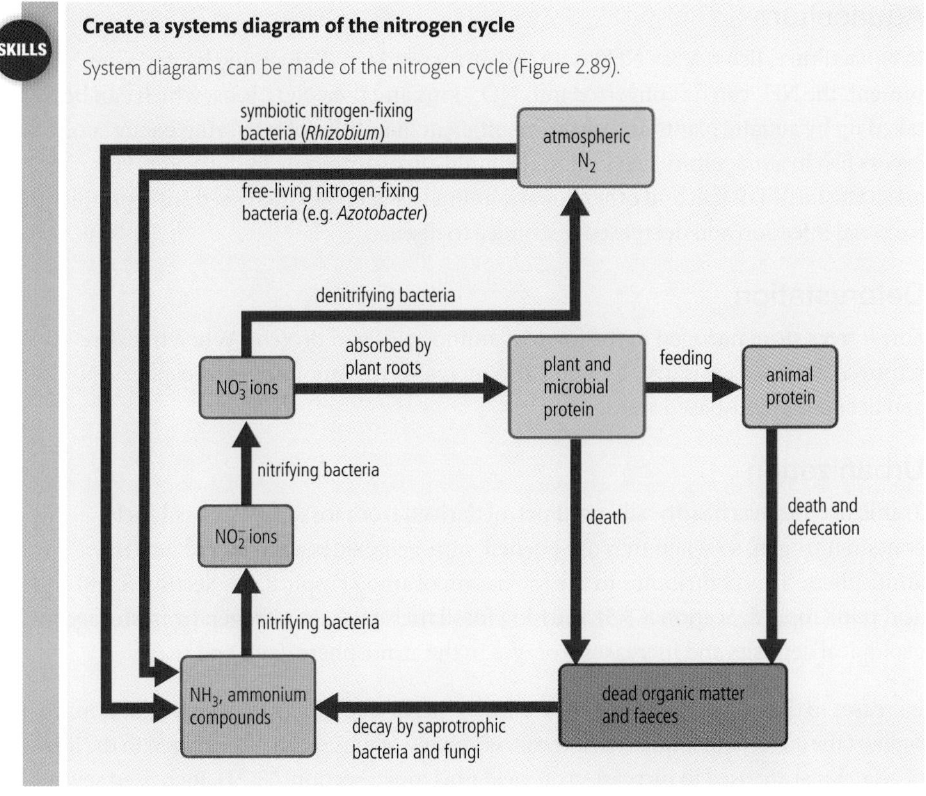

Figure 2.89 The nitrogen cycle.

2.3.22 Human activities change the nitrogen cycle

HL

Human activities such as agriculture, aquaculture, deforestation and urbanization all affect the nitrogen cycle.

Agriculture

Nitrogen fixation via industrial techniques, such as the Haber process (this topic, Section 2.3.23), has significantly increased the amount of global nitrogen fixation, leading to increased amounts of usable nitrogen in the form of fertilizers. Application of nitrate fertilizer increases the amount of biologically available nitrogen in an ecosystem. Nitrate fertilizer, used to increase crop yield, runs off or leaches into bodies of waters, such as rivers and lakes, causing eutrophication and disruption to ecosystems (Topic 4, Section 4.4.6). Eutrophication leads to low O_2 levels in aquatic ecosystems, changing food-web structure and resulting in habitat degradation. The addition of nitrogen can lead to changes in biodiversity and species composition that may lead to changes in overall ecosystem function.

Nitrogen in the biomass of crops is transferred from fields in one area to markets in other areas. These processes remove nitrogen from the cycle in one location and add it to another cycle at a different location. This alters the nitrogen cycle and can cause disruption to ecosystems.

Waterlogged soils on agricultural land leads to an increase in denitrifying bacteria, increasing the rate at which N_2 gas is returned to the atmosphere.

Aquaculture

In aquaculture, fish release NH_3 as an excretory product. If nitrifying bacteria are present, the NH_3 can be converted into NO_2^- ions and then NO_3^- ions, which can be taken up by aquatic plants and algae. Insufficient quantities of nitrifying bacteria or excess fish in aquaculture can lead to the build-up of ammonia in the water. This can affect the health of fish and other aquatic animals, leading to increased susceptibility to bacterial infection and decreased resistance to disease.

Deforestation

Forest trees store nitrogen in the form of amino acids and protein. When trees are removed, this storage is lost. Logging also increases the amount of atmospheric N_2 and decreases land-based storages.

Urbanization

Traffic in cities has historically used petrol derived from fossil fuels. Fossil fuels contain nitrogen, so when they are burned, nitrogen oxides are released into the atmosphere. This contributes to the formation of smog (Topic 8, HL Section 8.3.8) and acid rain (Topic 8, Section 8.3.5). Burning fossil fuels releases nitrogen from storage in geological deposits and increases storages in the atmosphere, land and sea.

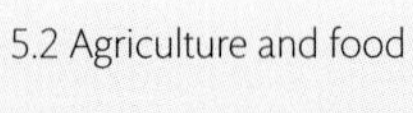
5.2 Agriculture and food

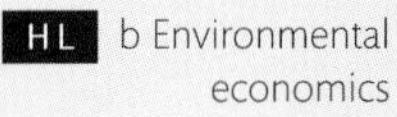
HL b Environmental economics

Increases in the human population have led to increased food needs and production. To support the increase in food needed, fertilizers (many of which contain nitrogen in the form of NO_3^- ions) are used to increase crop yield (this topic, Section 2.3.21). Increased sewage output leads to increased quantities of NH_4^+ and NO_3^- ions in rivers, lakes and the sea.

HL

2.3.23 The Haber process

The Haber process is an industrial process that produces NH_3 from N_2 gas and hydrogen gas (H_2) for use as fertilizer. The process takes place under high temperatures and pressures and the reaction between N_2 and H_2 is made possible by using an iron catalyst (Figure 2.90). The process was developed by Fritz Haber in 1909 and was later developed further by Carl Bosch for industrial use.

Figure 2.90 The Haber process.

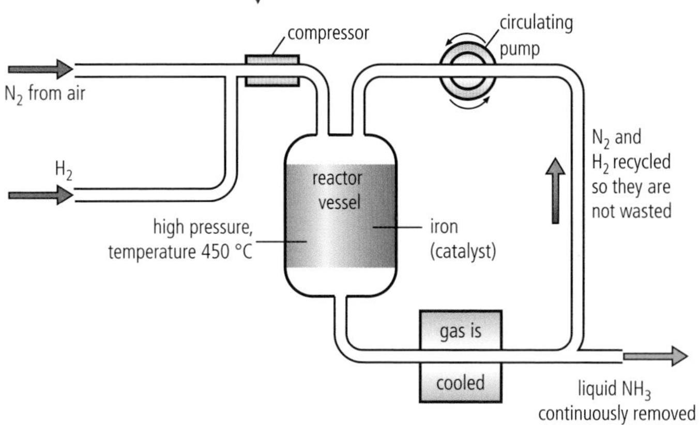

The benefit of the Haber process is that it provides NH_3 for fertilizers. Nitrogen-based fertilizers provide nitrogen, which plants need for growth. Using nitrogenous fertilizers can lead to increased crop yields. This has enabled sufficient food to be produced for the growing global human population. The NH_3 produced can also be used in other processes (Figure 2.91).

There are disadvantages of the Haber process. Soil fertilizers are easily soluble in water and are therefore easily transported from soil to bodies of water by land run-off and soil leaching. This leads to increased nitrogen in lakes, rivers and other water resources, which can lead to eutrophication (Topic 4, Section 4.4.5). Eutrophication leads to the reduction of biodiversity in aquatic systems. The Haber process also requires high levels of energy, derived from fossil fuels, which results in high greenhouse gas emissions (e.g. CO_2).

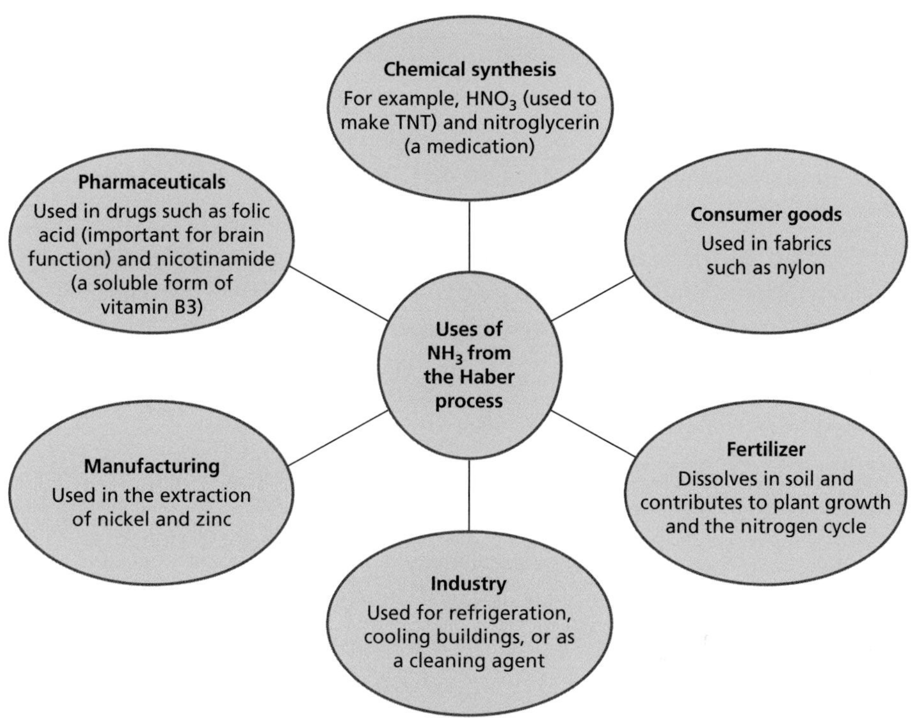

Figure 2.91 Uses of ammonia, produced by the Haber process.

6.2 Climate change – causes and impacts

HL b Environmental economics

Increases in nitrates in the biosphere from human activities have led to the planetary boundary for the nitrogen cycle being crossed, making irreversible changes to Earth systems likely.

HL

2.3.24 Evidence that the boundary for the nitrogen cycle has been crossed

Research has proposed a planetary boundary of 62 Tg N $year^{-1}$ for the eutrophication of aquatic ecosystems originating from industrial and intentional biological nitrogen-fixation. Research indicates that this planetary boundary for the biogeochemical cycle of nitrogen has been crossed (Topic 1, Section 1.3.19). The global dependence on inorganic fertilizers for crop production is the major cause of this. Figure 2.92 shows global environmental nitrogen levels. A few agricultural regions greatly exceed the safe regional limits for nitrogen.

One Tg (teragram) is equivalent to 10^9 kg.

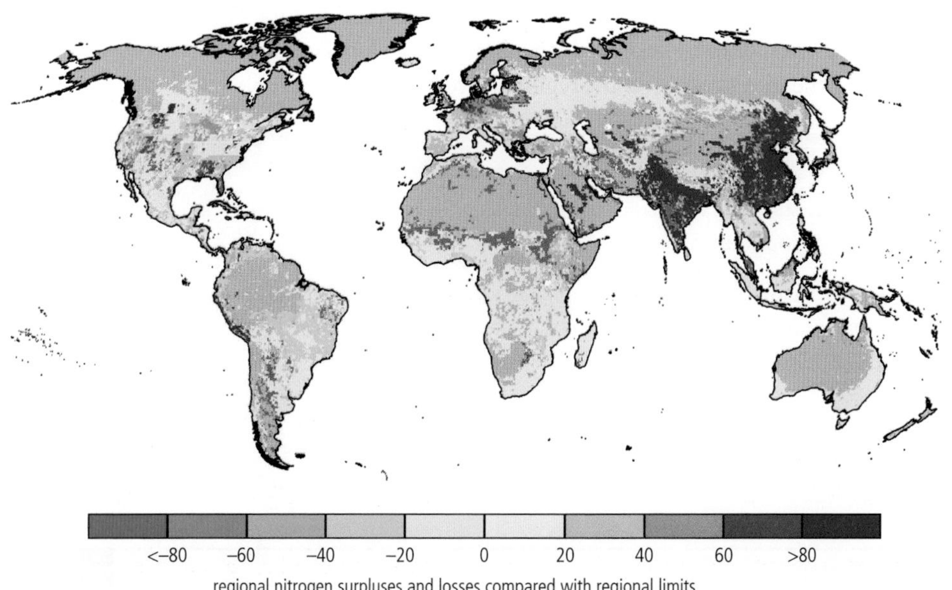

Figure 2.92 Global nitrogen levels. Colours indicate comparisons with safe regional limits for nitrogen. Values are in kg N ha^{-1} yr^{-1}. Grey areas indicate where N-fertilizers are not applied.

Activity

What is the evidence that the boundary for the biogeochemical cycle of nitrogen has been crossed?

The planetary boundary for nitrogen has been taken from the analysis of de Vries et al. (2013):

de Vries, W., Kros, J., Kroeze, C. and Seitzinger, S.P. (2013) Assessing planetary and regional nitrogen boundaries related to food security and adverse environmental impacts. *Current Opinion in Environmental Sustainability* 5, 392–402.

Access the full paper via your school or college library.

Also read the section of the following paper relating to the biogeochemical cycles:

Steffen, W., et al. (2015) Planetary boundaries: Guiding human development on a changing planet. *Science*, Vol 347, Issue 6223

Are there other sources you can find that provide data to support the assertion that the planetary boundary for nitrogen has been crossed? Evaluate the sources of information you find.

1.3 Sustainability
6.2 Climate change – causes and impacts

HL

2.3.25 Global collaboration is needed to bring the nitrogen cycle back within planetary boundaries

Global collaboration is needed to address the uncontrolled use of nitrogen in industrial and agricultural processes and bring the nitrogen cycle back within planetary boundaries.

Nitrogen in agriculture must be used more efficiently if the world is to provide enough food without exceeding regional and planetary nitrogen thresholds. Emissions from non-agricultural nitrogen sources such as sewage or industry must also be reduced.

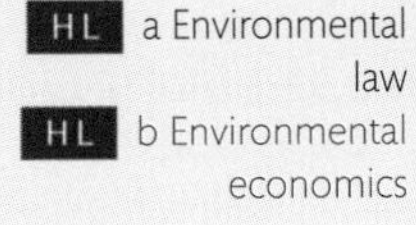

HL a Environmental law
HL b Environmental economics

Studies have indicated that, rather than every country of the globe being responsible, transgression of the boundary is due to a few main contributors. This suggests that a redistribution of nitrogen globally could increase global crop production while reducing the transgression at the regional level.

Activity

What measures are needed to bring the biogeochemical cycle of nitrogen back within planetary boundaries?

Discuss this with a partner. Have you thought of the same solutions? Write a list of the measures you have decided on. Now compare your notes with others in your class. Are there other solutions that you can add to your list?

Produce an informative poster outlining the issues relating to the planetary boundaries for the biogeochemical cycle of nitrogen and the solutions that can be applied to bring the nitrogen cycle back within planetary boundaries.

HL end

Engagement

- Provide advocacy about the use of organic fertilizers instead of inorganic ones around school or community green areas. If your school has a radio broadcast or magazine, prepare an article about the issues. Alternatively, produce an informative poster to distribute in your community.
- Explore issues of justice for local communities when the local environment is overexploited for financial gain. Produce a presentation and explore the issues with your class.

Exercise

Q28. Distinguish between the terms *store, sink* and *source.*

Q29. Draw a system diagram for the carbon cycle, showing stores, flows, transfers and transformations.

Q30. Outline the effect that human activities have had on matter cycles.

Q31. Explain why agricultural systems can act as carbon stores, sources and sinks, depending on the techniques used.

Q32. Outline how increases in concentrations of dissolved CO_2 cause ocean acidification, harming marine animals.

HL

Q33. HL **Define** the term *lithosphere.*

Q34. HL **Explain** how limestone is formed.

Q35. HL **Draw** a system diagram for the nitrogen cycle, showing stores, flows, transfers and transformations.

Q36. HL **Evaluate** the use of the Haber process to provide fertilizer for increased crop yield.

HL end

2.4 Climate and biomes

Guiding Questions

How does climate determine the distribution of natural systems?
How are changes in Earth systems affecting the distribution of biomes?

2.4.1 Climate describes atmospheric conditions over relatively long periods of time, whereas weather describes the conditions in the atmosphere over a short period of time.
2.4.2 A biome is a group of comparable ecosystems that have developed in similar climatic conditions, wherever they occur.
2.4.3 Abiotic factors are the determinants of terrestrial biome distribution.

Climate describes how the atmosphere behaves over relatively long periods of time whereas **weather** describes the conditions in the atmosphere over a short period of time.

2.4.4 Biomes can be categorized into groups that include freshwater, marine, forest, grassland, desert and tundra. Each of these groups has characteristic abiotic limiting factors, productivity and diversity. They may be further classed into many subcategories (for example, temperate forests, tropical rainforests and boreal forests).

2.4.5 The tricellular model of atmospheric circulation explains the behaviour of atmospheric systems and the distribution of precipitation and temperature at different latitudes. It also explains how these factors influence the structure and relative productivity of different terrestrial biomes.

2.4.6 The oceans absorb solar radiation and ocean currents distribute the resulting heat around the world.

2.4.7 Global warming is leading to changing climates and shifts in biomes.

HL 2.4.8 There are three general patterns of climate types that are connected to biome types.

HL 2.4.9 The biome predicted by any given temperature and rainfall pattern may not develop in an area because of secondary influences or human interventions.

HL 2.4.10 The El Niño Southern Oscillation (ENSO) is the fluctuation in wind and sea surface temperatures that characterizes conditions in the tropical Pacific Ocean. The two opposite and extreme states are El Niño and La Niña, with transitional and neutral states between the extremes.

HL 2.4.11 El Niño is due to a weakening or reversal of the normal east–west (Walker) circulation, which increases surface stratification and decreases upwelling of cold, nutrient-rich water near the coast of north-western South America. La Niña is due to a strengthening of the Walker circulation and reversal of other effects of El Niño.

HL 2.4.12 Tropical cyclones are rapidly circulating storm systems with a low-pressure centre that originate in the tropics and are characterized by strong winds.

HL 2.4.13 Rises in ocean temperatures resulting from global warming are increasing the intensity and frequency of hurricanes and typhoons because warmer water and air have more energy.

2.4.1 Climate

6.1 Introduction to the atmosphere

'Climate' is sometimes incorrectly used as an alternative term for 'weather'. These terms are have different meanings. Climate describes atmospheric conditions over relatively *long* periods of time, whereas weather describes the conditions in the atmosphere over a *short* period of time.

Climate plays a significant role in determining the distribution of organisms within the biosphere. The term climate refers to the average and extreme states of the atmosphere over approximately 30 years. It includes variables such as temperature, rainfall, winds, humidity, cloud cover and air pressure.

In contrast **weather** refers to the state of the atmosphere at any moment in time or over a short period. However, we usually look at the weather over a period of a few days to a week. The same variables are considered as for climate.

Climate and weather are affected by several factors such as atmospheric circulation, ocean circulation, latitude, altitude, distance from the sea, prevailing winds, aspect and human activities.

Until the end of 2020, the most current and widely used standard reference period for calculating climate statistics was the 30-year period between 1981 and 2010. The use of records covering a period of 30 years is considered adequate. However, there are several arguments against using a 30-year period:

- the database is too short
- 1981–2010 was a period of climate change and so is not a representative period
- it is impossible to create a 50-year maximum (the maximum size of event that would be expected once every 50 years) or a 100-year return event (the size of an event that would occur, on average, only once every 100 years) from a record set of 30 years.

2.4.2, 2.4.3 and 2.4.4 Biomes

A biome is a group of comparable ecosystems that have developed in similar climatic conditions wherever they occur.

Ecosystems developed in similar conditions in different parts of the world can have many parallel features. Precipitation, temperature and insolation are major influences on the distribution of terrestrial biomes.

Biomes are collections of ecosystems sharing similar climatic conditions. They can be grouped into five major classes – aquatic, forest, grassland, desert and tundra.

Biomes have distinctive abiotic factors and species that distinguish them from other biomes (Figure 2.93). Water (rainfall), insolation (sunlight) and temperature are the climate controls that determine how biomes are structured, how they function and where they are found round the world.

Abiotic factors are the determinants of terrestrial biome distribution

Abiotic factors are the determinants of terrestrial biome distribution. Water is needed for photosynthesis, transpiration and support (cell turgidity). Sunlight is needed for photosynthesis. Photosynthesis is a chemical reaction, so temperature affects the rate at which it progresses. Rates of photosynthesis determine the productivity of an ecosystem (NPP, this topic, HL Section 2.2.25, pages 149–150). The more productive a biome, the higher its NPP. Rainfall, temperature and insolation determine the rate of photosynthesis and this is what determines the structure, function and distribution of biomes. For any given temperature and rainfall pattern, one natural ecosystem type is likely to develop.

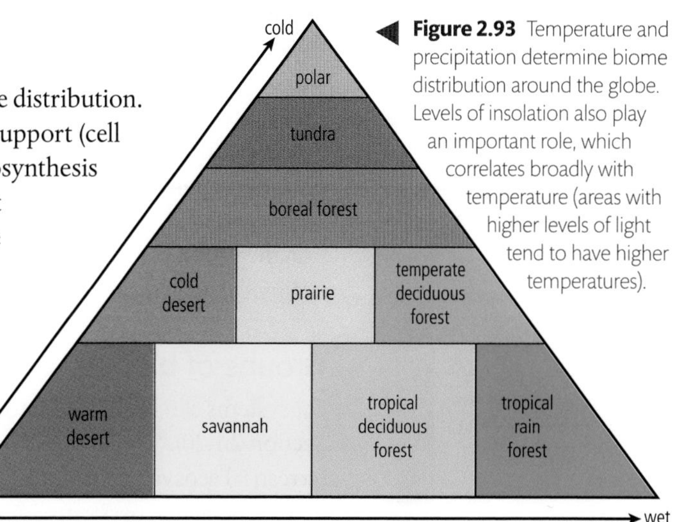

Figure 2.93 Temperature and precipitation determine biome distribution around the globe. Levels of insolation also play an important role, which correlates broadly with temperature (areas with higher levels of light tend to have higher temperatures).

SKILLS

Create climate graphs showing annual precipitation/average temperature for different biomes

A **climograph** is a graphical model that shows the relationship between temperature, precipitation and ecosystem type. Temperature and rainfall are two of the main limiting factors that affect plant growth. So, these abiotic factors can be used to model and predict the geographical distribution of different ecosystems around the planet.

Figure 2.94 on the next page shows Whittaker's climograph, a climograph that illustrates the distribution of major terrestrial ecosystems with respect to mean annual precipitation and temperature.

Although the climograph suggests that each ecosystem has a distinct 'edge', this may not actually be the case. There may be steady gradation from one ecosystem to another, rather than distinct boundaries. Tropical ecosystems, for example, graduate from a highly productive rainforest to a low-productive desert.

There are various forms of this graph, sometimes the axes are reversed or the temperature is plotted from lowest to highest. In some regions, distribution is determined by soils rather than climate. In savannah areas, for example, grasslands are found on well-drained sandy soil and forests are found on clay soils where water is retained.

Abiotic factors (insolation, precipitation and temperature) are the determinants of terrestrial biome distribution.

Climographs show the distribution of biomes with temperature on the horizontal axis and rainfall pattern on the vertical axis.

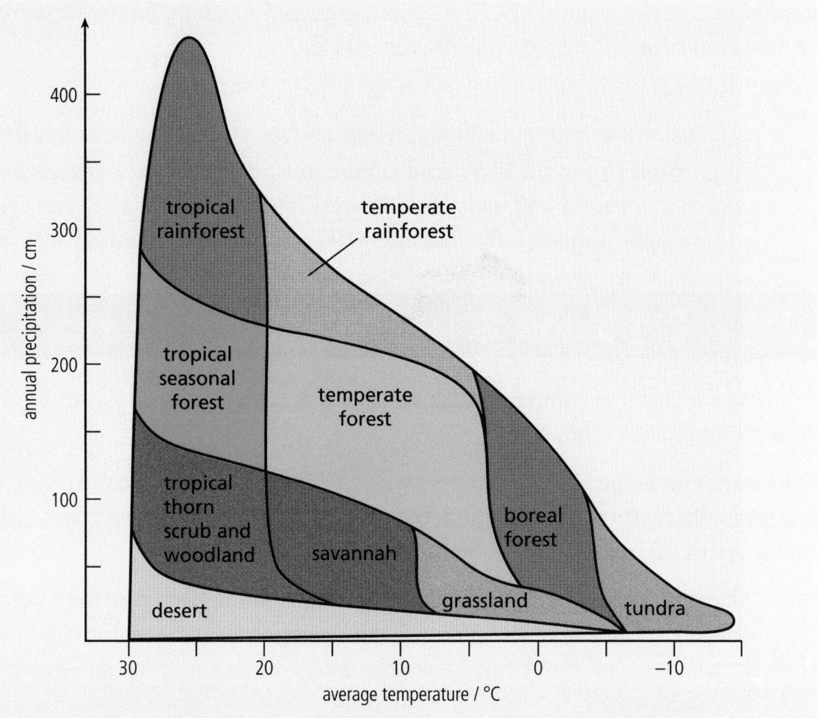

Figure 2.94 Whittaker's climograph.

The climograph was first developed by the plant ecologist R.H. Whittaker. It shows the likely stable ecosystems that are found under specific climatic conditions. Vegetation underpins communities found in all different geographical areas, so factors that affect plant growth also strongly influence the distribution of different ecosystems.

Activity

To create a climate graph, find the range of temperature and rainfall (annual precipitation) for each biome. The biomes to include in the graph are desert, tropical thorn-scrub and woodland, tropical seasonal forest, tropical rainforest, temperate rainforest, temperate forest, savannah, grassland, boreal forest and tundra. Construct a graph by putting mean annual temperature on the *x*-axis and annual precipitation on the *y*-axis. For each biome, define areas on the graph using temperature and rainfall data. Use different colours and a key to clearly show each biome.

Make sure you know the limiting factors, productivity and resulting biodiversity of tropical rainforests, hot deserts, tundra and at least two other biomes.
Make sure you can explain climate in terms of temperature, precipitation and insolation.

Groups of biomes

Ecosystems can be divided into terrestrial, freshwater and marine (this topic, Section 2.1.20). Similarly, biomes can be grouped into five major classes – the terrestrial ecosystems of forest, desert, tundra and grassland and the aquatic marine and freshwater ecosystems.

Each of these classes has the characteristic limiting factors of productivity and biodiversity. Insolation, precipitation and temperature are the main factors governing the distribution of biomes.

Biomes may be further classed into many subcategories, such as temperate forests, tropical rainforests and boreal forests.

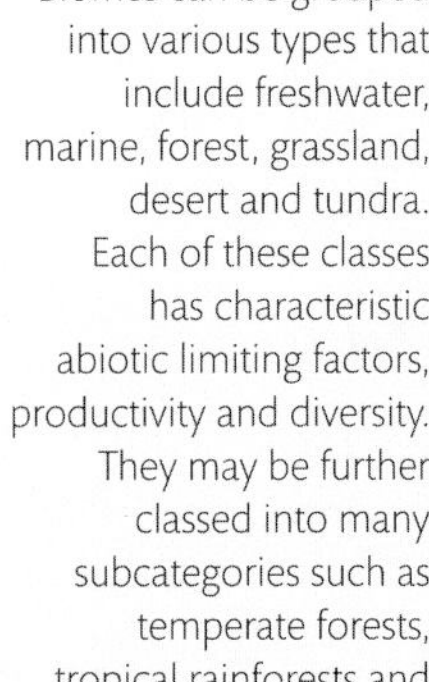

Biomes can be grouped into various types that include freshwater, marine, forest, grassland, desert and tundra. Each of these classes has characteristic abiotic limiting factors, productivity and diversity. They may be further classed into many subcategories such as temperate forests, tropical rainforests and boreal forests.

Tropical rainforest

Tropical rainforests have constant high temperatures (typically 26 °C) and high rainfall (over 2500 mm yr $^{-1}$) throughout the year. Because tropical rainforests, as their name implies, lie in a band around the equator within the tropics of Cancer and Capricorn (23.5° N and S) (Figure 2.95), they enjoy high light levels throughout the year. There is little seasonal variation in sunlight and temperature (although the monsoon period can reduce levels of insolation) providing an all-year growing season. Their position in low **latitudes**, with the Sun directly overhead, determines their climatic conditions and enables high levels of photosynthesis and high rates of NPP throughout the year. Tropical rainforests are estimated to produce 40% of the total NPP of all terrestrial ecosystems.

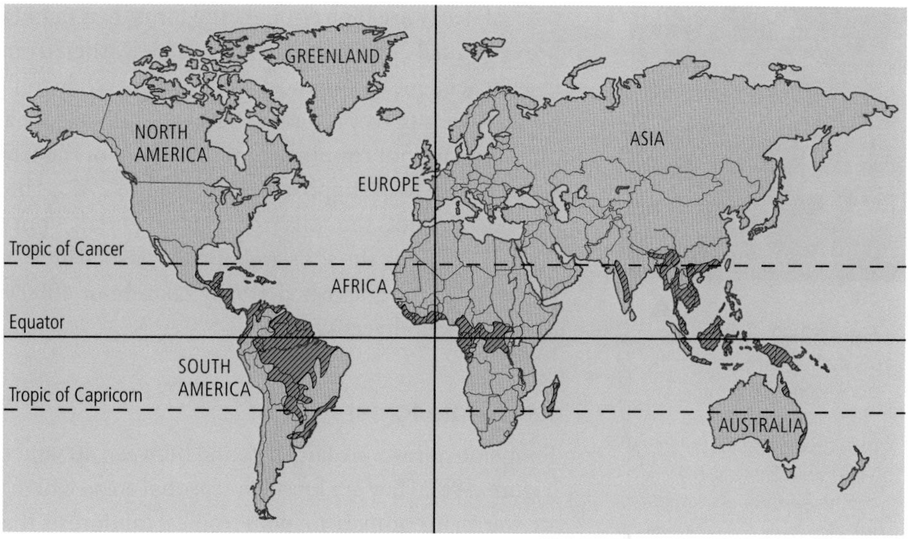

Figure 2.95 Tropical rainforest distribution around the globe.

Tropical rainforests are broad evergreen forests with a very high diversity of animals and plants. A rainforest may have up to 480 species of tree in a single hectare (2.5 acres), whereas temperate forest may only have six tree species making up most of the forest. The high diversity of plants is because of the high levels of productivity resulting from year-round high rainfall and insolation. The high diversity of animals follows from the complexity of the forests. Because the forests are multilayered and provide many different niches, they allow for an enormous variety of different organisms (Figure 2.96).

Figure 2.96 Tropical rainforests show a highly layered (stratified) structure. Emergent trees can be up to 80 m high, although overall structure depends on local conditions and varies from forest to forest. Only about 1% of light hitting the canopy layer reaches the floor, so the highest levels of NPP are found in the canopy – one of the most productive areas of vegetation in the world. High productivity in the canopy results in high biodiversity and it is believed that half of the world's species could be found in rainforest canopies.

Although tropical rainforests are highly productive, many of the inorganic nutrients needed for growth are locked up in the trees. The soil is low in nutrients. Trees obtain their nutrients from the rapid recycling of detritus that occurs on the forest floor. If

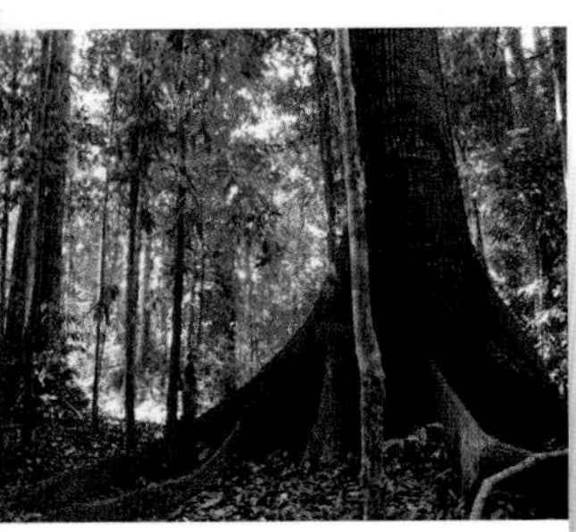

Figure 2.97 Buttress roots grow out from the base of the trunk, sometimes as high as 5 m above the ground and provide support for the tree on thin soils. These also allow roots to extend out from the tree increasing the area over which nutrients can be absorbed from the soil.

rates of decay are high enough, the forest can maintain levels of growth. However, heavy rainfall can cause nutrients to be washed from the soil (leaching) resulting in a consequent lack of inorganic nutrients that could limit primary production. Because soils in tropical rainforests are thin, trees have shallow root systems with one long tap root running from the centre of the trunk into the ground plus wide buttresses to help support the tree (Figure 2.97). The forest canopy provided by the trees protects the soils from heavy rainfall – but once areas have been cleared through logging, the soils are quickly washed away (eroded) making it difficult for forests to be re-established. It may take about 4000 years for a logged area to recover its original biodiversity.

Temperate forest

Temperate forests are largely found between 40° and 60° N of the equator (Figure 2.98). They are found in seasonal areas where winters are cold and summers are warm, in comparison with tropical rainforests that enjoy similar conditions all year round. Two different tree types are found in temperate forest – evergreen (which are in leaf all year round) and deciduous (which lose their leaves in winter). Evergreen trees have protection against the cold winters through thicker leaves or needles, whereas deciduous trees have leaves that would suffer frost damage, so they shut down in winter. Forests might contain only deciduous trees, only evergreens or a mixture of both. At these mid-latitudes, the amount of rainfall determines whether an area develops forest. If precipitation is sufficient, temperate forests form. If there is insufficient rainfall, grasslands develop. Rainfall in these biomes reaches between 500 and 1500 mm yr^{-1}.

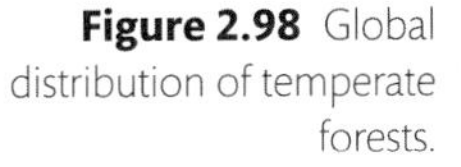

Figure 2.98 Global distribution of temperate forests.

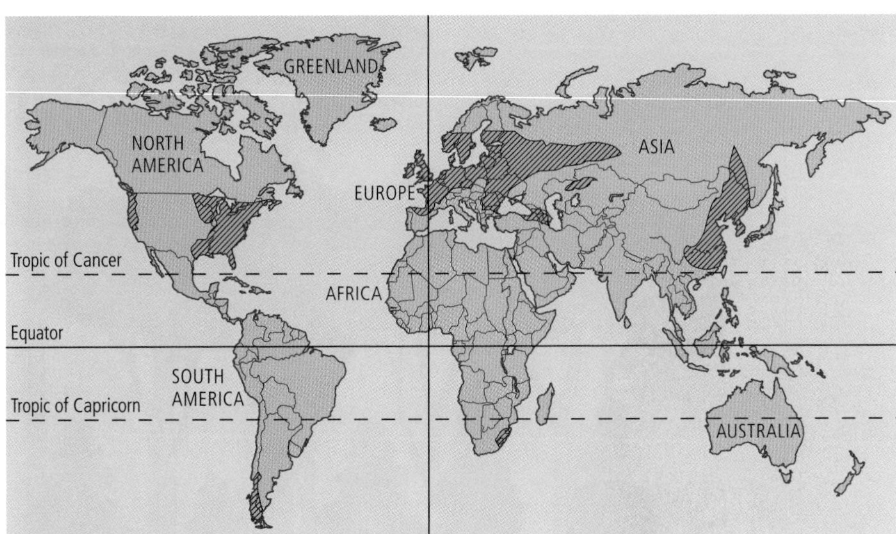

Biomes such as tropical rainforests and coral reefs are ecological *systems* which are found in equatorial areas with high light intensity all year round and warm temperatures, which enable high levels of NPP. High productivity leads to high levels of resources such as food, high complexity of habitats and niches and therefore high biodiversity.

Variation in insolation during the year is caused by the tilt of the Earth and its rotation around the Sun. This variation means that productivity is lower than in tropical rainforests because there is a limited growing season. The mild climate, with lower average temperatures and lower rainfall than are found at the equator, reduces levels of photosynthesis and productivity compared to tropical rainforest. However, temperate forests have the second highest NPP (after tropical rainforests) of all biomes. Diversity is lower than in tropical rainforest but the structure of temperate forest is simpler. Temperate forests are generally dominated by one species and 90% of the forest may consist of only six tree species. There is some layering of temperate forests, although the tallest trees generally do not grow more than 30 m, so vertical stratification is limited. The less complex structure of temperate forests, compared to tropical rainforests, reduces the number of available niches and therefore the amount of species diversity is lower. The forest floor has a reasonably thick leaf layer that is rapidly broken down when temperatures are higher and nutrient availability is, in general, not limiting. The lower and less dense canopy of temperate forests means that light levels on the forest floor are higher than they are in tropical rainforests, so the shrub layer can contain many plants such as brambles, grasses, bracken and ferns (Figure 2.99).

Figure 2.99 The loss of leaves from deciduous trees in temperate forests over winter allows increased insolation of the forest floor, enabling the seasonal appearance of species such as bluebells.

Hot deserts

Deserts are found in bands at latitudes of approximately 30° N and S (Figure 2.100 and Figure 2.101). They cover 20–30% of the land surface. It is at these latitudes that dry air descends, having lost water vapour over the tropics. Hot deserts are characterized by high temperatures at the warmest time of day (typically 45–49 °C) in the early afternoon and low precipitation (typically under 250 mm yr^{-1}). Rainfall may be unevenly distributed. The lack of water limits the rate of photosynthesis and so the rates of NPP are very low. Organisms also must overcome fluctuations in temperature (night temperatures, when skies are clear, can be as low as 10 °C, sometimes even as low as 0 °C), which make survival difficult.

Figure 2.100 The Sahara Desert in northern Africa is the world's largest desert. Covering more than 9 million square kilometres (3.5 million square miles), it is slightly smaller than the USA. However, it is not the site of the world's lowest rainfall – that occurs in Antarctica, which receives less than 50 mm of precipitation annually (and is therefore classified as a cold desert).

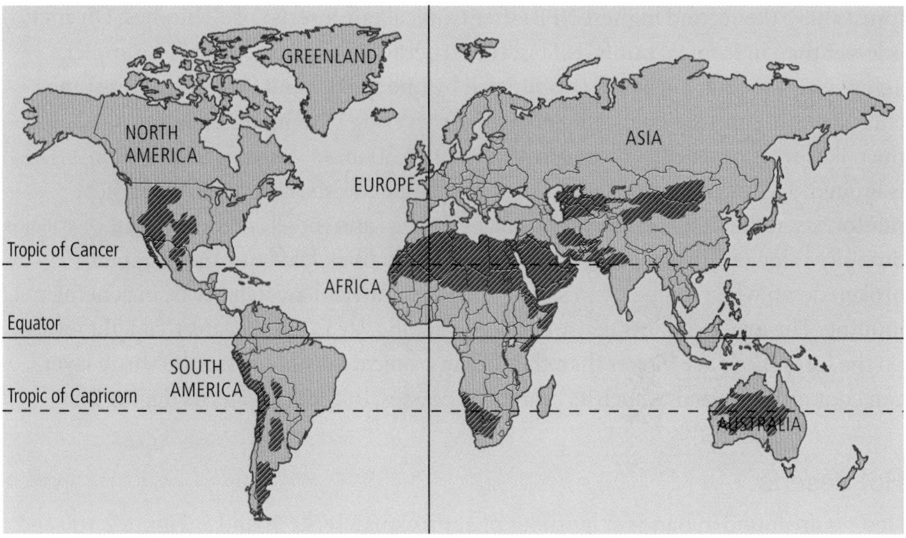

Figure 2.101 Global distribution of deserts.

Low productivity means that vegetation is sparse. Soils can be rich in nutrients because they are not leached away, this helps to support the plant species that can survive there. Decomposition levels are low because of the dryness of the air and lack of water. The species that can exist in deserts are highly adapted, showing many xerophytic adaptations (i.e. adaptations to reduce water loss in dry conditions). Cacti (a group restricted to the Americas) have reduced their surface area for transpiration by converting leaves into spines. They store water in their stems, which can expand enabling more water to be stored. Their surface area : volume ratio is decreased thus further reducing water loss from the surface. The spiny leaves deter animals from eating plants and accessing the water. Xerophytes also have a thick cuticle that further reduces water loss. Roots can be both deep (to access underground sources of water) and extensive near the surface (to quickly absorb precipitation before it evaporates).

Some animals have also adapted to desert conditions. Snakes and reptiles are the most common vertebrates. They are highly adapted to conserve water and their cold-blooded metabolism is ideally suited to desert conditions. Mammals are adapted to live underground and emerge at the coolest parts of day.

Figure 2.102 Elk crossing frozen tundra.

Tundra

Tundra is found at high latitudes where insolation is low (Figure 2.102 and Figure 2.103). Short day length also limits levels of sunlight. Water may be locked up in ice for months and this, combined with little rainfall, means that water is also a limiting factor. Low light intensity and rainfall mean that rates of photosynthesis and productivity are low. Temperatures are very low for most of the year. Temperature is a limiting factor because it affects the rate of photosynthesis, cellular respiration and decomposition (these enzyme-driven chemical reactions are slower in colder conditions). Soil may be permanently frozen (permafrost) and so water is limited. Low temperatures mean that the recycling of nutrients is low, leading to the formation of peat bogs where a high amount of carbon is stored. The vegetation consists of low scrubs and grasses.

Most of the world's tundra is found in the North Polar region (Figure 2.103) and so is known as Arctic tundra. There is a small amount of tundra in parts of Antarctica that are not covered with ice and in lower latitudes on high altitude mountains (alpine tundra).

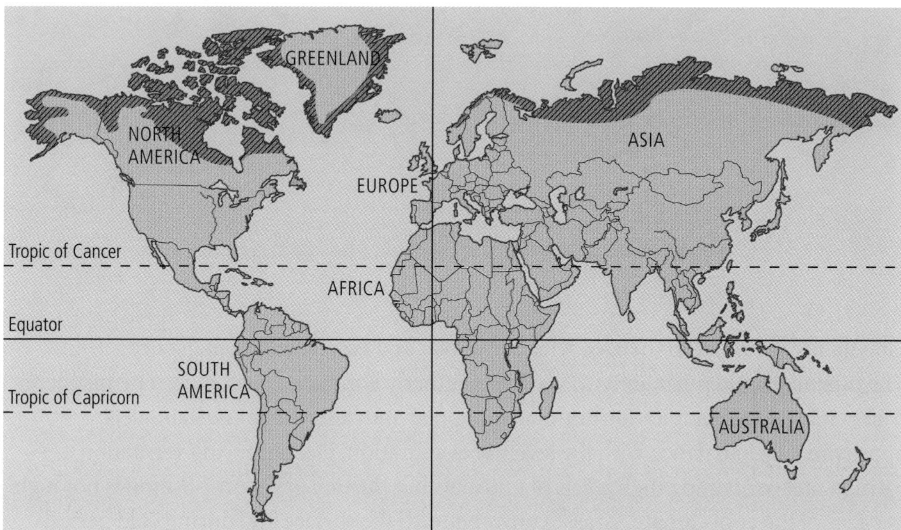

Figure 2.103 Map showing the global distribution of tundra.

During the winter months, temperatures in the tundra can reach −50 °C – all life activity is low in these harsh conditions. In summer, the tundra changes. The Sun is out for almost 24 hours a day, so levels of insolation and temperature both increase leading to plant growth. Only small plants are found in this biome because there is not enough soil for trees to grow. And even in the summer, the permafrost drops to only a few centimetres below the surface. In the summer, animal activity also increases, due to increased temperatures and primary productivity. The growing period is limited to 6 weeks of the year, after which the temperatures drop again and the hours of sunlight decline. Plants are adapted with leathery leaves or underground storage organs. Animals are adapted to the cold conditions with their thick fur. In general, Arctic animals are larger than their southerly relations. This decreases their surface area relative to their size and enables them to reduce heat loss (e.g. the Arctic fox is larger than the European fox).

Tundra is the youngest of all biomes because it was formed after the retreat of glaciers from 15,000 to 10,000 years ago.

Grasslands

Grasslands are found on every continent except Antarctica and cover about 16% of the Earth's surface (Figure 2.104, Figure 2.105). They develop where there is not enough precipitation to support forests, but enough to prevent deserts forming. There are several types of grassland. The Great Plains and the Russian Steppes are temperate grasslands, whereas the savannahs of east Africa are tropical grassland.

Figure 2.104 Bison roam on mixed grass prairie.

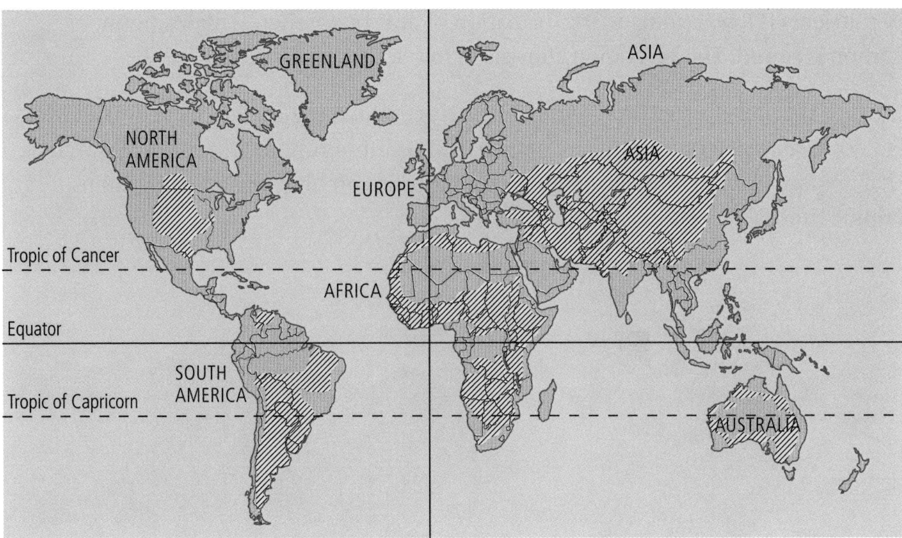

Figure 2.105 Global distribution of grasslands.

Explore the distribution and composition of different biomes using the BiomeViewer on the HHMI BioInteractive website.

Grasslands are found in the area where the Polar and Ferrel cells meet (Figure 2.106). The mixing of cold polar air with warmer southerly winds (in the northern hemisphere) causes increased precipitation compared to polar and desert regions. Rainfall is approximately in balance with the levels of evaporation. Decomposing vegetation forms a mat containing high levels of nutrients but the rate of decomposition is not high because of the cool climate. Grasses grow beneath the surface and during cold periods (more northern grasslands suffer a harsh winter) they can remain dormant until the ground warms.

Challenge yourself

Research a pair of contrasting biomes – for example, temperate bog and tropical mangrove forests – and produce fact sheets on each. Draw up a table comparing four pairs of contrasting biomes (the ones you have researched and the examples in this book). How do their structure, biodiversity and relative productivity compare?

Now research the values of NPP for all the biomes you have studied. How do the NPP values of different biomes compare? Why do these differences exist?

2.4.5 The tricellular model of atmospheric circulation

As well as the differences in insolation and temperature found from the equator to higher (more northern or more southern) latitudes, the distribution of biomes can be understood by looking at patterns of atmospheric circulation. Latitude is the angular distance from the equator (north or south of it) as measured from the centre of the Earth (usually in degrees). The **tricellular model** of atmospheric circulation is a way of explaining differences in atmospheric pressure belts, temperature and precipitation that exist across the globe (Figure 2.106).

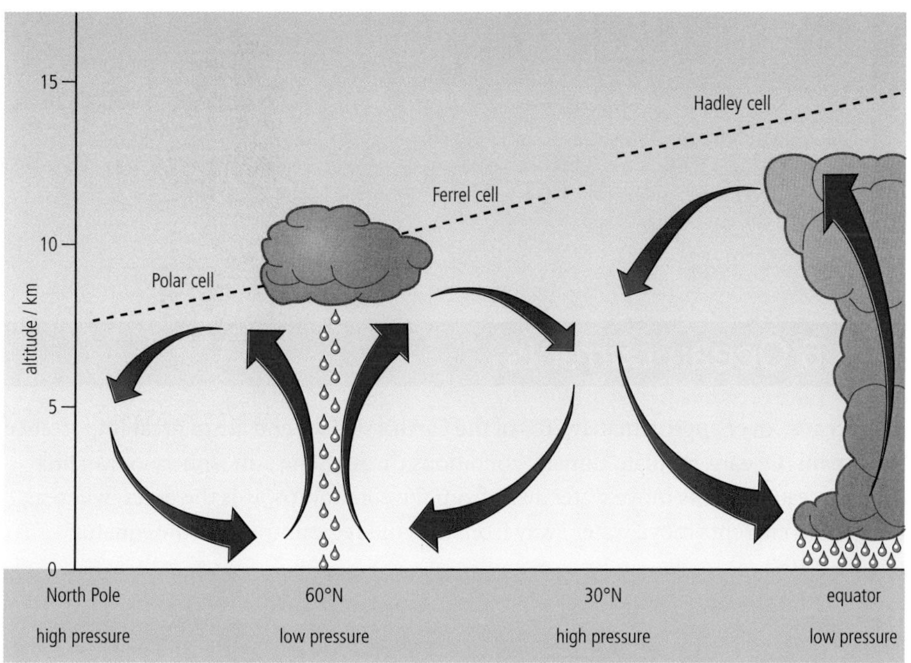

Figure 2.106 The tricellular model is made up of the Polar cell, the Ferrel cell in mid-latitudes and the Hadley cell in the tropics. Downward air movement creates high pressure. Upward air movement creates low pressure and cooling air that leads to increased cloud formation and precipitation.

Atmospheric movement can be divided into three major cells, Hadley, Ferrel and Polar, with boundaries coinciding with particular latitudes (although they move on a seasonal basis). The Hadley cell controls weather over the tropics, where the air is warm and unstable. The equator receives most insolation per unit area of Earth. This heats up the air, which then rises to create the Hadley cell. As the air rises, it cools and condenses, forming large cumulonimbus clouds that create the thunderstorms characteristic of tropical rainforests. These conditions provide the highest rainfall on the planet. The pressure at the equator is low as the air is rising. Eventually, the cooled air begins to spread out and descends at approximately 30° north and south of the equator. The pressure here is therefore high because air is descending. This air is dry, so the desert biome is found in these locations. Air then either returns to the equator at ground level or travels towards the poles as warm winds. Where the warm air travelling north and south hits the colder polar winds, at approximately 60° N and S of the equator, the warm air rises because it is less dense. This creates an area of low pressure. As the warm air rises it cools and condenses, forming clouds and resulting in precipitation. This is where temperate forest biomes are found. The model explains why rainfall is high at the equator and at 60° N and S of the equator.

The **tricellular model** of atmospheric circulation explains the behaviour of atmospheric systems and the distribution of precipitation and temperature at different latitudes. It also explains how these factors influence the structure and relative productivity of different terrestrial biomes.

SKILLS

Use the tricellular model of atmospheric circulation and link it to the planetary distribution of heat and biomes

Search online for the Met Office's webpage on global circulation patterns.

How is the tricellular model of atmospheric circulation linked to the planetary distribution of heat and biomes?

Summarize your findings as an annotated poster, with the tricellular model in the centre and an explanation of why specific biomes are found at particular latitudes around the outside.

Biomes cross national boundaries. In Borneo, for example, the rainforest crosses three countries – Indonesia, Malaysia and Brunei. Studying biomes may therefore require investigations to be carried out across national frontiers – this can sometimes be politically, as well as logistically, difficult.

In 1735, George Hadley described the operation of the Hadley cell to explain atmospheric circulation. He suggested that the direct heating of low latitudes forces air to rise by convection, the air then travels towards the poles but sinks at the sub-tropical anticyclone (high pressure belt). Hadley suggested that similar cells might exist in mid-latitudes and high latitudes. William Ferrel refined Hadley's ideas by suggesting that air in a Hadley cell rotates and interlinks with a mid-latitude cell, which is also rotating. These cells in turn rotate the Polar cell. The most recent models have refined the basic principles and include air motion in the upper atmosphere, in particular jet streams (very fast thermal winds).

1.2 Systems
6.1 Introduction to the atmosphere

2.4.6 Ocean currents

The oceans absorb solar radiation and ocean currents distribute the resulting heat around the world.

The oceans cover approximately 70% of the Earth's surface and are of great importance to humans. Oceans regulate climatic conditions through the atmosphere-ocean link. Warm ocean currents move water away from the equator towards the poles, whereas cold ocean currents move water away from the cold regions towards the equator (Figure 2.107).

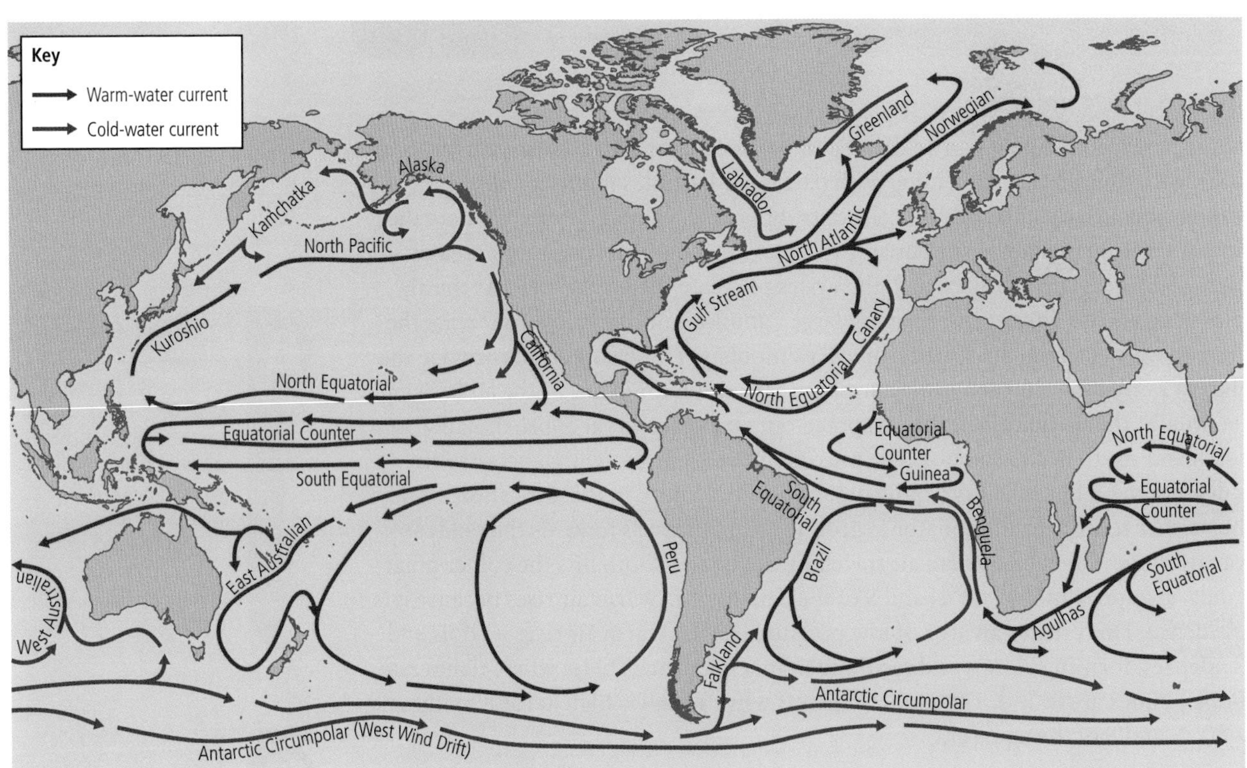

Figure 2.107 The world's main ocean currents.

The warm Gulf Stream, for instance, transports 55 million cubic metres of water per second from the Gulf of Mexico towards north-west Europe. Without it, the temperate lands of north-west Europe would be more like the sub-Arctic. The cold Peru current brings nutrient-rich waters dragged to the surface by offshore winds. In addition, there is the great ocean conveyor belt (HL only, later in this section). This deep, global-scale circulation of the ocean's waters effectively transfers heat from the tropics to colder regions.

Details of the great ocean conveyor belt and thermohaline circulation are HL only.

Warm ocean currents move water away from the equator, whereas cold ocean currents move water away from cold regions towards the equator (Figure 2.108). The major currents move huge masses of water over long distances.

The rotation of the Earth causes water in the oceans to push westward. This piles up water on the western edge of ocean basins rather like water slopping in a bucket. The return flow is often narrow, fast-flowing currents like the Gulf Stream.

The effect of surface ocean currents on temperatures depends on whether the current is cold or warm. Warm currents from equatorial regions raise the temperature of polar areas (with the aid of prevailing westerly winds). However, the effect is only noticeable in winter. For example, the North Atlantic Drift (the northern extension of the Gulf Stream) raises the winter temperatures of north-west Europe (Figure 2.108). Some areas are more than 24 °C warmer than the average for their line of latitude. By contrast, there are other areas that are made colder by ocean currents. Cold currents such as the Labrador Current off the north-east coast of North America may reduce summer temperatures, but only if the wind blows from the sea to the land (Figure 2.108).

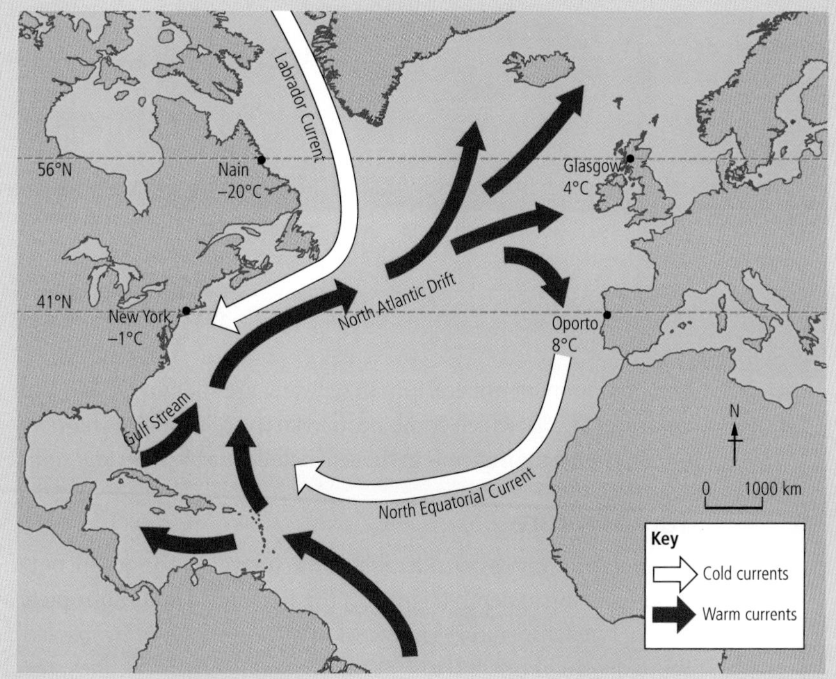

Figure 2.108 Warm and cold ocean currents in the North Atlantic Ocean.

4.1 Water systems
6.1 Introduction to the atmosphere

HL

Salinity

Oceanic water varies in salinity (Figure 2.109). Average salinity is about 35 parts per thousand (ppt). Concentrations of salt are higher in warm seas because of the high evaporation rates of the water. In tropical seas, salinity decreases sharply with depth. The runoff from most rivers is quickly mixed with ocean water by the currents and has little effect on reducing salinity. However, a large river such as the Amazon in South America may result in the ocean having little or no salt content for over a kilometre or more out to sea.

The freezing and thawing of ice also affects salinity. The thawing of large icebergs (made of frozen freshwater and therefore lacking salt) decreases salinity, while the freezing of seawater increases the salinity temporarily. Salinity levels increase with depth, in contrast with equatorial and tropical regions where salinity decreases with depth.

If you are studying ESS at HL, you need to know about details of the great ocean conveyor belt and thermohaline circulation (earlier in this section). This material is for HL only.

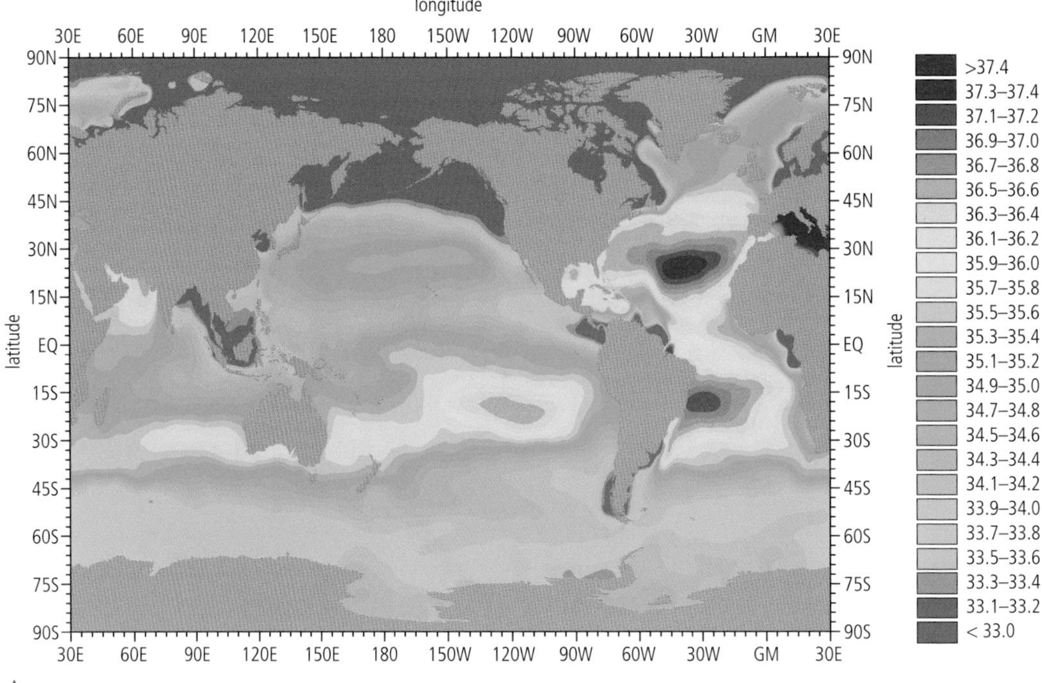

Figure 2.109 Global variations in oceanic salinity.

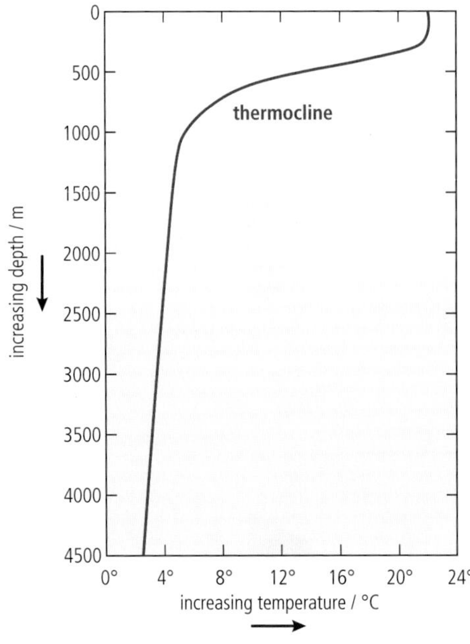

Figure 2.110 Ocean temperature and depth.

The predominant mineral ions in seawater are sodium (30.2%) and chloride (54.3%), which combine to form the salt sodium chloride. Other important minerals in the sea include magnesium and sulfate ions.

Temperature

Temperature varies considerably at the surface of the ocean, but there is little variation at depth (Figure 2.110). In tropical and subtropical areas, sea surface temperatures in excess of 25 °C are caused by insolation. From depths about 300 to 1000 m, the temperature declines steeply to about 8–10 °C. At ocean depths greater than 1000 m, the temperature decreases to a more uniform 2 °C.

The temperature profile is similar in the mid-latitudes (40–50° N and S), although there are clear seasonal variations. Summer temperatures may reach 17 °C, whereas winter sea temperatures are closer to 10 °C. There is a more gradual decrease in temperature with depth **(thermocline)**.

Density

Temperature, salinity and pressure affect the density of seawater. Large water masses of different densities are important in the layering of the ocean water (denser water sinks). As temperature increases, water becomes less dense. As salinity increases, water becomes denser. As pressure increases, water becomes denser. A cold, deep mass of water with a high salinity is very dense, whereas warm, surface water with a lower salinity is less dense. When large water masses with different densities meet, the denser water mass slips under the less dense mass. These responses to density are the reason for some of the deep ocean circulation patterns.

The great ocean conveyor belt

The oceanic conveyor belt is a global **thermohaline circulation**. It is driven by the formation and sinking of cold, salty water into deep water and is responsible for the large flow of upper ocean water (Figure 2.111). In addition to the transfer of energy by wind and the transfer of energy by ocean currents, there is also a transfer of energy by deep-sea currents. In the polar regions, cold water with a high salinity sinks to the depths and makes its way towards the equator. It then spreads into the deep basins of the Atlantic, the Pacific and the Indian Oceans. Surface currents bring warm water to the North Atlantic from the Indian and Pacific Oceans. These waters give up their heat to cold winds that blow from Canada across the North Atlantic. This water then sinks and starts the reverse convection of the deep ocean current. The amount of heat given up is about a third of the energy received from the Sun.

Ocean circulation systems are driven by differences in temperature and salinity that affect water density. The resulting difference in water density drives the ocean conveyor belt which distributes heat around the world, so affecting climate.

Because the conveyor operates in this way, the North Atlantic is warmer than the North Pacific, so there is proportionally more evaporation there. The water left behind by evaporation has a higher salinity and therefore is much denser, which causes it to sink. Eventually the water is transported into the Pacific where it mixes with warmer water and its density is reduced.

Figure 2.111 The great ocean conveyor belt.

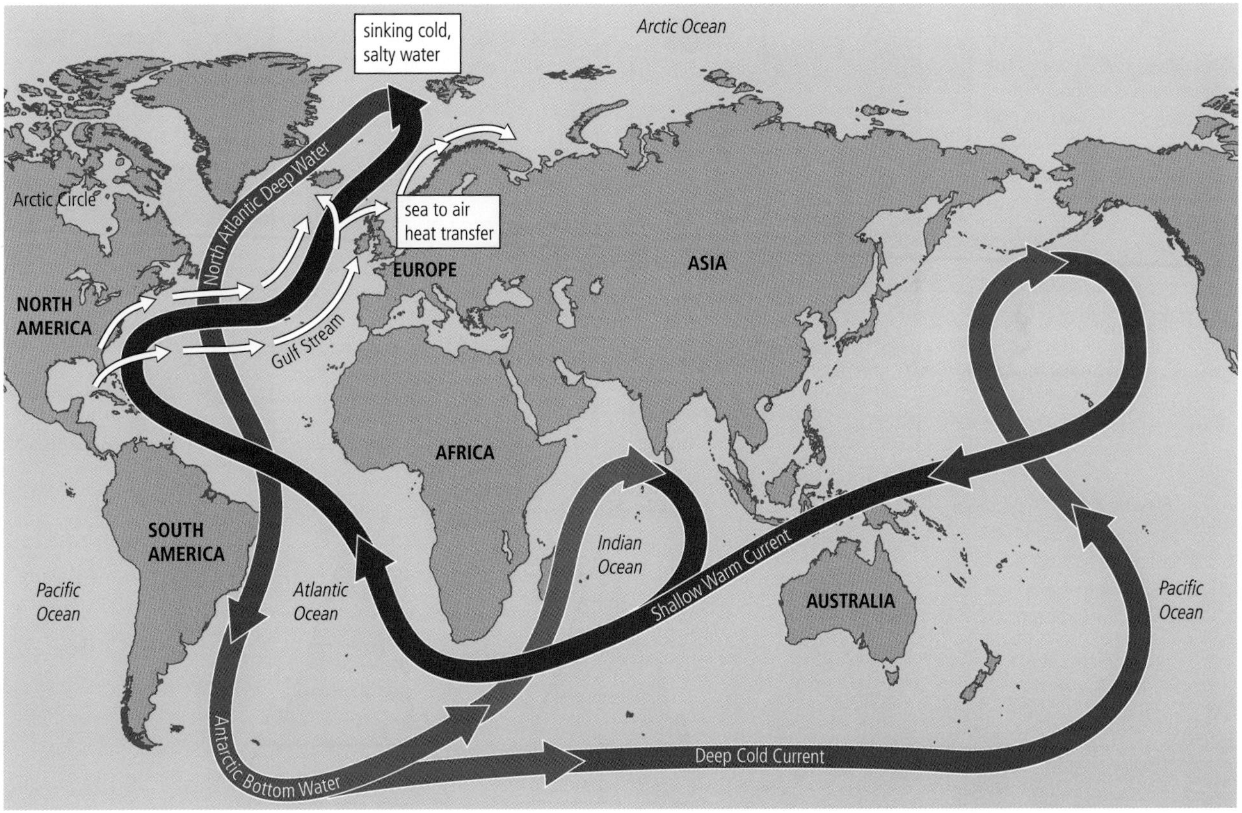

HL end

2.4.7 Global warming is leading to shifts in biomes

Global warming is leading to changing climates and shifts in biomes.

The distribution of biomes is controlled by a combination of temperature, insolation and precipitation. Increases in CO_2 and other greenhouse gases lead to an increase in mean global temperature (Topic 6), which in turn affects rainfall patterns. These changes in climate affect the distribution of biomes.

Climate change in the geological past can show how we might expect biomes to move with increases in global temperature in the future (Figure 2.112). Models suggest a north/south shift in biomes relative to the equator (a latitudinal shift). Biomes will also move up slopes (altitudinal shift) as on mountains (Figure 2.113). Low-lying biomes such as mangroves may be lost due to changes in sea level.

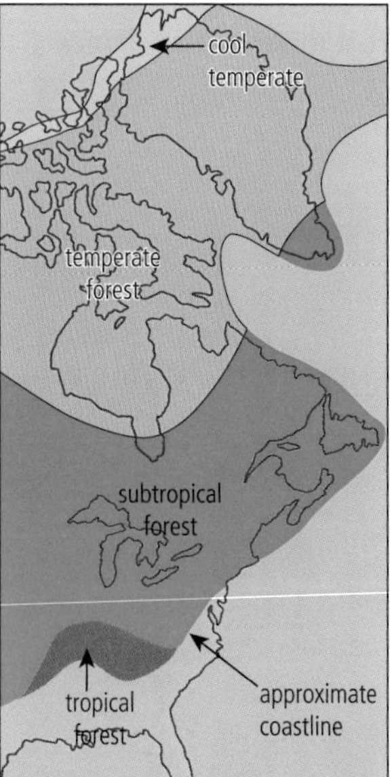

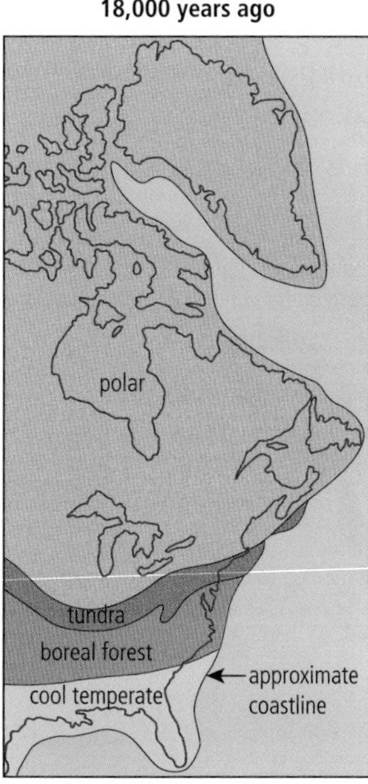

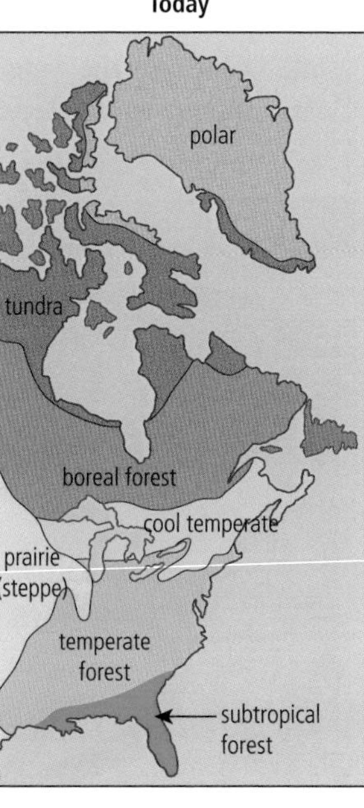

Figure 2.112 In the most recent globally warm period 50–60 million years ago, the Arctic was free of ice and subtropical forests extended northwards to Greenland. During the Pleistocene glaciations, 18,000 years ago, these areas were covered by ice sheets. In the last 18,000 years, temperatures have increased and the tundra and temperate forest biomes have shifted north. With further increases, all biomes are likely to move further toward the poles, with the probable disappearance of tundra and boreal forests.

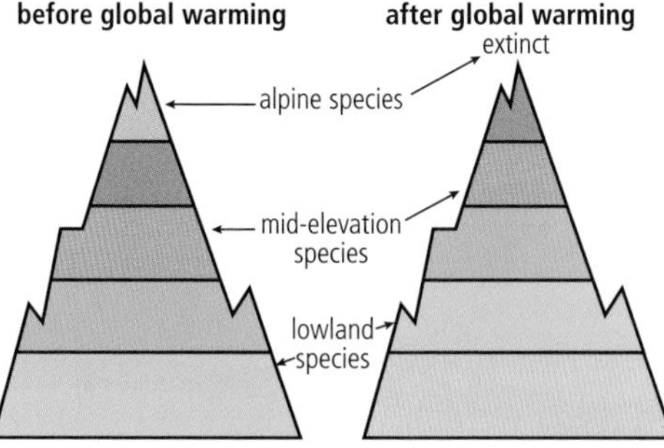

Figure 2.113 Alpine (mountain) species are particularly at risk, because zonation will move up the mountain.

The general trend is that biomes move poleward toward higher altitudes.

Species composition in *ecosystems* is also likely to change. Climate change in the past happened over long periods of time, and allowed the adaptation of animals to new conditions. Current increases in temperature are happening very rapidly so there is little time for organisms to adapt. Some organisms will be able to migrate to new areas where the conditions they need are found, but many face insurmountable obstacles to migration (e.g. rivers and oceans) or even no suitable habitat and will become extinct. Tropical diseases can be expected to spread as warmer conditions are found in higher latitudes.

6.2 Climate change – causes and impacts

Change in climate can lead to changes in weather patterns and rainfall (in both quantity and distribution). Climates may become more extreme and more unpredictable. An increase in more extreme weather conditions (e.g. hurricanes) can be expected as atmospheric patterns are disturbed.

Agriculture will be affected. Drought reduces crop yield and the reduction in water resources will make it increasingly difficult for farmers in many areas to irrigate fields. Changes in the location of crop-growing areas can be expected, with movements north and south from the equator. Recent models predict dramatic changes to the wheat-growing regions of the USA, with many becoming unviable by 2050 (Figure 2.114). This would have serious knock-on effects on the economy. Crop types may need to change and changing water resources will either limit or expand crop production depending on the region and local weather patterns.

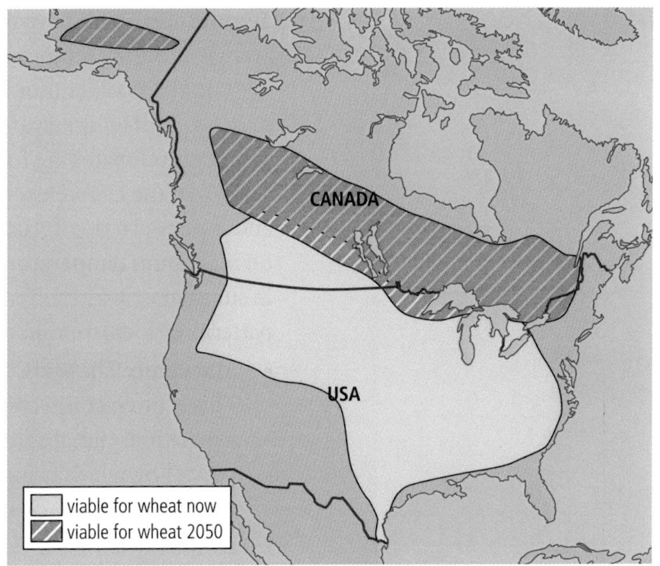

Figure 2.114 Scientists project a northward shift of wheat-growing in North America.

HL

2.4.8 Three general patterns of climate types

HL

The climate shows large variation around the globe. Distinct climate types, based on latitude (which in turn reflects temperature and rainfall), can be distinguished at different latitudes (Figure 2.115). There are three general patterns of climate types that are connected to biome types.

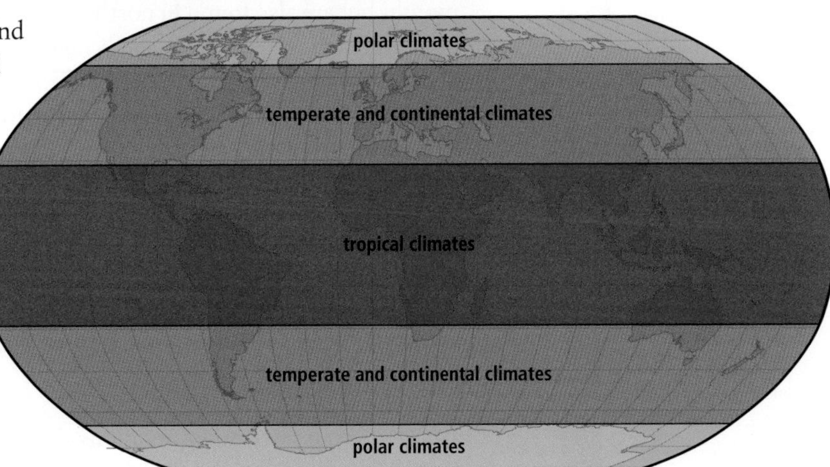

Figure 2.115 A simplified map of the world's climate zones.

Climate types include:

- **Tropical:** Close to the equator, between the Tropics of Cancer and Capricorn, with high temperatures and rainfall. Tropical rainforest climates are found in: South America, Africa, northern Australia and South-East Asia.
  - **Seasonal:** These receive, in general, high total rainfall, averaging more than 1000 mm per year but with a distinct dry season. Includes the forests of the Congo in Africa and a broad region of highland tropical forest which extends across the basin of the Congo River, Central American tropical forests in Panama and Nicaragua, the seasonal forests that predominate across much of the Indian subcontinent, Indochina and in northern Australia (Queensland).
  - **Equatorial:** These have a high average temperature all year round and high monthly precipitation (typically no less than 60 mm a month with annual precipitation tending to be over 2000 mm). The diurnal temperature range is greater than the annual temperature range. Although some parts of the year may be wetter than others, there are no distinct seasons.

- **Temperate:** These have relatively moderate mean annual temperatures, with average monthly temperatures above 10 °C in their warmest months and above −3 °C in their colder months. Most regions with a temperate climate have four seasons, with temperatures changing significantly between summer and winter. Temperate climates are found in most of western Europe, western and eastern regions of the USA, eastern China, parts of Argentina and south-eastern Brazil and the eastern tip of Australia. Different types of temperate climates are based on maximum temperatures and whether they have a distinct dry season (either in summer or winter). Temperate forest type is influenced by prevailing weather patterns or local topography.
  - **Maritime:** These are characterized by dry summers and mild, wet winters. This is often connected to weather patterns and prevailing winds. Areas with a maritime climate are often found on the western coasts of continents, where prevailing winds bring in wetter weather at certain times of the year.
  - **Continental:** These have greater temperature extremes than maritime temperate climates. Areas that have these climates are mostly found in the interior of continents, away from the effect of nearby oceans. Oceans store heat energy, which moderates temperate regions nearer the sea (allowing for more consistent temperature in e.g. maritime areas). Mostly found in Eurasia (mainly Russia) and North America (mainly Canada, with some in the northern USA).
- **Polar**: These are cold regions where most water is found as ice and the average temperature does not exceed 10 °C in any months of the year. Often windy, with very little precipitation and long cold winters. Dominated by the Arctic and Antarctic regions, where the average temperature does not exceed 0 °C in any months but are also found in northern Canada, Russia and Greenland. Small plants, such as mosses, algae and lichens (a symbiotic relationship between algae and fungi) can survive in these environments. Ice cap climates can also be found at high altitude, such as the highest peaks of the Himalaya.

There are many climate classification systems that define zones based on different climatic factors or on combinations of factors. Climate types that you need to know for your course are tropical (seasonal and equatorial), temperate (maritime and continental) and polar.

Tropical and temperate biomes are discussed in this topic, Section 2.4.2, 2.4.3 and 2.4.4. The soil in some polar climates is covered by ice throughout the year. Biomes at the North and South Poles contain animals that feed on aquatic organisms. For example, the North Pole has polar bears that feed on seals and the South Pole has penguins that feed on fish. Tundra is a cold-climate biome that is found at a high-latitude, in regions above the tree line but lower than the Arctic ice cap. Soil may be permanently frozen (permafrost), and nutrients are limiting.

Climate zones can track how conditions change in specific areas. They help us understand the ranges of plants and animals, including identifying species that may be under threat from habitat loss. Climate zones can even help farmers and gardeners understand which plants will grow best in their area.

HL

2.4.9 Secondary influences and human interventions

The biome predicted by any given temperature and rainfall pattern may not develop as predicted. This could be because of secondary influences or human interventions such as logging and other forms of habitat loss, agricultural use, loss of apex predators or pollution.

Activity

Think about your local area. Which biome would develop if there was interference from urban or agricultural development? Look at areas which have been undisturbed to give you an idea about the biome or biomes which would have once existed. How have secondary influences and human interventions affected the biotic environment? Have any abiotic factors been affected? What impact has disturbance had on food chains and food webs? Is it possible to restore these biomes?

Produce an illustrated summary of the information you have found. Add details of the climatic conditions needed for development of the biome and how human impacts have led to the loss of the biome.

2.4.10 and 2.4.11 The El Niño Southern Oscillation (ENSO)

HL

The **El Niño Southern Oscillation (ENSO)** is a naturally occurring climatic phenomenon. ENSO is the fluctuation in wind and sea surface temperatures that characterizes conditions in the tropical Pacific Ocean. The two opposite and extreme states are El Niño and La Niña, with transitional and neutral states between them (see *Weakening or strengthening of* ***Walker circulation*** below).

ENSO occurs every three to seven years and usually lasts for eighteen months. It occurs when the Walker circulation is altered with either strengthened or weakened trade winds.

El Niño, La Niña and the North Atlantic Oscillation are responsible for many short-term changes in weather.

Walker circulation

Air moves from the eastern to western Pacific Ocean before returning east – this is known as Walker circulation (Figure 2.116).

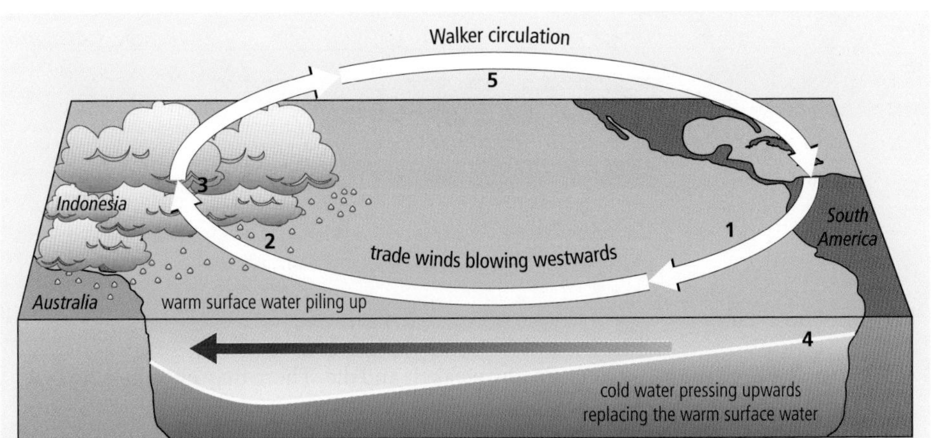

Figure 2.116 Walker circulation.

1. The trade winds blow Equator-wise and westwards across the tropical Pacific (Figure 2.116).
2. The trade winds blow towards the warm water of the western Pacific (near Australia and South-East Asia).

3. As the water heats the atmosphere in the western Pacific, air rises (known as convectional uplift).
4. Surface water moves west, and is replaced by cold, nutrient-rich deep water through upwelling along the west coast of Peru. Rising water causes the upwelling of nutrient-rich cold water, leading to optimum fishing conditions.
5. The Walker loop returns air to the eastern tropical Pacific (Figure 2.116).

The pressure of the trade winds results in sea levels in Australasia being 50 cm higher than on the west coast of Peru and sea temperatures being 8 °C higher.

Weakening or strengthening of Walker circulation

Figure 2.116 shows the differences in water temperature between the western and eastern Pacific ocean during normal years.

Walker circulation is the normal east–west circulation that El Niño interrupts (Figure 2.116). Normally, sea surface temperatures (SSTs) in the western Pacific are over 28 °C, creating an area of low pressure and producing high rainfall. By contrast, over coastal South America, SSTs are lower, high pressure exists and conditions are dry.

El Niño is due to a weakening or reversal of the normal east-west (Walker) circulation (Figure 2.117).

During El Niño episodes, this pattern is reversed.

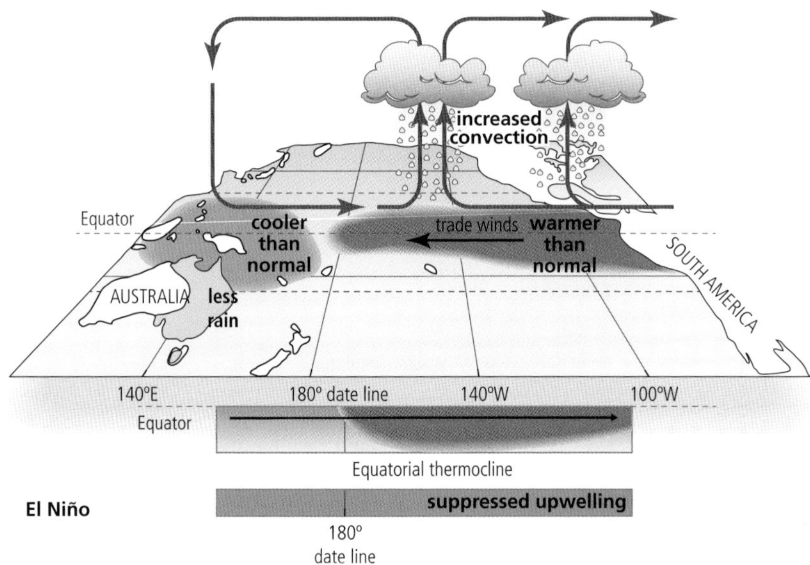

Figure 2.117 An El Niño event.

In an El Niño event:

- The trade winds in the western Pacific weaken and die. There may even be a reverse direction of flow.
- The piled-up water in the west moves back east, leading to a 30 cm rise in sea level in Peru.
- The region of rising air moves east with the associated convectional uplift.

- The eastern Pacific Ocean becomes 6–8 °C warmer.
- Low pressure develops over the eastern Pacific as water temperature rises, while high pressure takes hold over the western Pacific. Consequently, heavy rainfall occurs over coastal South America. In contrast, Indonesia and the western Pacific are now warm and dry.
- The El Niño effect overrides the cold northbound Humboldt Current, which normally carries plankton and other aquatic organisms northwards, breaking the food chain.
- Lack of phytoplankton results in a reduction in fish numbers, which in turn affects fish-eating birds such as those found on the Galapagos Islands.

Not all El Niño events are the same. There are stronger and weaker events, which may be linked to climate change.

In some other years, a phenomenon called La Niña (Figure 2.118) occurs instead. This is an intensification of the normal Walker circulation, whereby strong easterly winds push cold upwelling water off the coast of South America into the western Pacific. Its impact extends beyond the Pacific and has been linked with unusual rainfall patterns in the Sahel (just to the south of the Sahara desert) and in India, and with colder and wetter condition in western Canada.

La Niña is due to a strengthening of the Walker circulation.

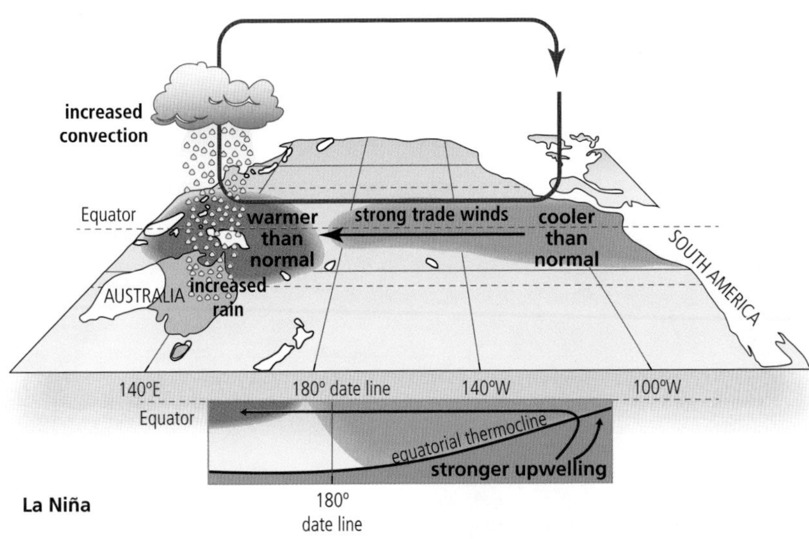

Figure 2.118 A La Niña event.

- El Niño is due to a weakening or reversal of the normal east-west (Walker) circulation, which increases surface stratification and decreases upwelling of cold, nutrient-rich water near the coast of north-western South America.
- La Niña is due to a strengthening of the Walker circulation and reversal of the effects of El Niño.

In a La Niña event:

- There are extremely strong trade winds.
- The trade winds push warm water westwards, giving a sea level up to 1 m higher in Indonesia and the Philippines.
- Low pressure develops with very strong convectional uplift as very warm water heats the atmosphere. This leads to heavy rain in southeast Asia.
- Very strong upwelling of cold water off Peru results in strong high pressure and extreme drought. This can be a major problem in the already semi-arid (dry) areas of northern Chile and Peru.

The frequency and intensity of both El Niño and La Niña events is irregular and hard to predict.

The climate system in the southern Pacific region is essentially stable and unchanging when a longer-term analysis of air and ocean circulation is made. Periodic El Niño and

ENSO affects conditions directly in the tropical Pacific Ocean and the climate of other regions in the tropics and subtropics indirectly.

6.1 Introduction to the atmosphere

La Niña reversals in circulation are part of the system's normal steady state. Moreover, local water cycles in those parts of South America most affected by ENSO cycles enjoy a steady state in the longer term, despite alternating years or longer periods of very low and very high rainfall. Water stores that were exhausted during La Niña years are replenished during El Niño years.

HL

2.4.12 Tropical cyclones

In areas of the Earth where surface water is heated, large storm events develop that draw heat from warm water at the ocean's surface and provide energy for horizontal, rotating winds.

Hurricanes, typhoons and cyclones are essentially the same weather phenomenon. The difference in name depends on the location in which they initially develop.

- Cyclones develop over the South Pacific Ocean and Indian Ocean, affecting countries from Australia to Mozambique (Figure 2.119).
- Hurricanes mainly develop over the North Atlantic Ocean, central North Pacific Ocean and eastern North Pacific Ocean, often affecting the Caribbean and east coast of the USA.
- Typhoons develop over the Northwest Pacific Ocean and frequently affect the Philippines and Japan.

Figure 2.119 Cyclone Idai heading towards Mozambique and Zimbabwe in 2019.

Tropical cyclones are rapidly circulating storm systems with a low-pressure centre that originate in the tropics and are characterized by strong winds. The names of the powerful storms that form in the waters of the Atlantic and Pacific (hurricane, cyclone or typhoon) depend on where they form. Tropical cyclones are commonly hurricanes over the North Atlantic Ocean and Northeast Pacific. Tropical cyclones that form in the West Pacific are called typhoons. The term cyclone is used for storms in the Indian Ocean and South Pacific.

They are all large tropical storm systems that revolve around an area of low pressure and produce heavy rain and wind speeds exceeding 119 kph. These tropical storms can have far-reaching effects, including impacts to marine fishing and agriculture, damage to infrastructure and human settlements and loss of life and property.

What is the difference between cyclones and tornadoes? The difference is one of scale. Tornadoes have a diameter of up to hundreds of metres, whereas tropical cyclones have a diameter of hundreds of kilometres.

2.4.13 Rises in ocean temperatures

HL

Rises in ocean temperatures resulting from global warming are increasing the intensity and frequency of cyclones, hurricanes and typhoons because warmer water and air have more energy.

'We want our children to live in an America that isn't burdened by debt, which isn't weakened by inequality, which isn't threatened by the destructive power of a warming planet.'

Barack Obama victory speech, 7 November 2012

On 6 November 2012 Barack Obama was re-elected as President of the USA. In his victory speech, made to supporters in his home city of Chicago, he referred to climate change, by stating that the children of America should not have to live in a country that is 'threatened by the destructive power of a warming planet'. The issue of climate change had largely been ignored during the election campaign but was brought into play in the final week. At this point, New York Mayor Michael Bloomberg connected Hurricane Sandy, which had reached the eastern seaboard of America on 29 October 2012, to climate change. This raised the issue of global warming as an electoral issue when Bloomberg endorsed President Obama, stating that he was the more likely of the two candidates to tackle global warming.

Could climate change have contributed to Hurricane Sandy? Warmer oceans make hurricanes more likely and more severe and a warmer atmosphere holds more moisture, increasing the maximum rainfall. Higher sea levels intensify storm surges. Scientists predict that with a warming planet, there will be an increased incidence of tropical cyclones.

TOK

What constraints are there on the pursuit of knowledge?

To what extent can scientists predict the effect of climate change on the incidence of cyclones, hurricanes and typhoons? Will climate change affect the frequency or magnitude? Will there be a longer season of severe tropical storms? To what extent are scientific predictions limited by available data and processing power?

Activity

Science predicts that increased average global temperatures (global warming) will lead to increased incidence of tropical cyclones, hurricanes and typhoons. What evidence can you find to support this claim? If you live in an area that is subject to tropical cyclones, find out about local incidences of tropical cyclones over the last 20 years. On a yearly basis, have they become more numerous? Is there evidence that this may be due to warmer ocean temperature?

If you do not live in an area that experiences these storm events, research an area of interest to you.

6.2 Climate change – causes and impacts

HL end

Engagement

- Explore the effect of climate change on a local or regional biome and produce a presentation to show to the rest of your class that explains the cause and effect of the shift.
- Raise awareness and fundraise for communities impacted by severe hurricanes or typhoons. For example, have a bake sale to raise money, or arrange a sponsored walk or other activity.

Exercise

Q37. **Distinguish** between weather and climate.

Q38. **Define** the term *biome*.

Q39. **Outline** how abiotic factors determine terrestrial biome distribution.

Q40. **Construct** a table listing the following biomes: tropical rainforest, temperate forest, hot desert and tundra. The table should include information about the levels of insolation (sunlight), rainfall (precipitation) and productivity for each biome.

Q41. **Describe** and **explain** which biome has the highest and lowest productivity.

Q42. **Explain** how global warming is leading to changing climates and shifts in biomes.

HL

Q43. HL **List** three general patterns of climate types that are connected to biome types.

Q44. HL **Explain** how the El Niño Southern Oscillation (ENSO) develops and its effect on wind and sea surface temperatures.

Q45. HL **Evaluate** evidence for increases in the incidence of hurricanes and typhoons.

HL end

2.5 Zonation, succession and change in ecosystems

Guiding Question

How do ecological systems change over time and over space?

2.5.1 Zonation refers to changes in community along an environmental gradient.
2.5.2 Transects can be used to measure biotic and abiotic factors along an environmental gradient to determine the variables that affect the distribution of species.
2.5.3 Succession is the replacement of one community by another in an area over time due to changes in biotic and abiotic variables.
2.5.4 Each seral community (sere) in a succession causes changes in environmental conditions that allow the next community to replace it through competition until a stable climax community is reached.
2.5.5 Primary successions happen on newly formed substratum where there is no soil or pre-existing community, such as rock newly formed by volcanism, moraines revealed by retreating glaciers, wind-blown sand or waterborne silt.

2.5.6 Secondary successions happen on bare soil where there has been a pre-existing community, such as a field where agriculture has ceased or a forest after an intense firestorm.
2.5.7 Energy flow, productivity, species diversity, soil depth and nutrient cycling change over time during succession.
2.5.8 An ecosystem's capacity to tolerate disturbances and maintain equilibrium depends on its diversity and resilience.
HL 2.5.9 The type of community that develops in a succession is influenced by climatic factors, the properties of the local bedrock and soil, geomorphology, together with fire and weather-related events that can occur. There can also be top-down influences from primary consumers or higher trophic levels.
HL 2.5.10 Patterns of net productivity (NP) and gross productivity (GP) change over time in a community undergoing succession.
HL 2.5.11 *r*- and *K*-strategist species have reproductive strategies that are better adapted to pioneer and climax communities, respectively.
HL 2.5.12 The concept of a climax community has been challenged, and there is uncertainty over what ecosystems would develop naturally were there no human influences.
HL 2.5.13 Human activity can divert and change the progression of succession leading to a plagioclimax.

2.5.1 Zonation

Zonation refers to changes in community along an environmental gradient.

Zonation is the arrangement or pattern of communities in bands in response to change in some environmental factor over a distance. For example, changes in ecosystems up a mountain as altitude increases.

Rocky shores can be divided into zones from the lower to the upper shore. Each zone is defined by the spatial patterns of animals and plants (Figure 2.120). Seaweeds in particular show distinct zonation patterns, with species more resilient to water loss being found on the upper shore (e.g. channel wrack) and those less resilient to water loss being found on the lower shore where they are not out of water for long (e.g. kelp).

Figure 2.120 Rocky shores provide an ideal location for studying zonation.

Zonation occurs on different scales. Rocky shores show local zonation whereas biome distribution is an example of zonation on a global scale.

Example – Zonation on rocky shores

Figure 2.121 shows how abiotic factors vary along an environmental gradient on rocky shore. Organisms that are high on the rocky shore, and that are exposed to the air for long periods of time, must withstand desiccation (drying out) and variations in temperature and salt concentration. Organisms that are lower on the shore are covered by seawater for much of the time and so are unlikely to dry out. They experience less variation in temperature and salt concentration in their environment, although wave action is greater.

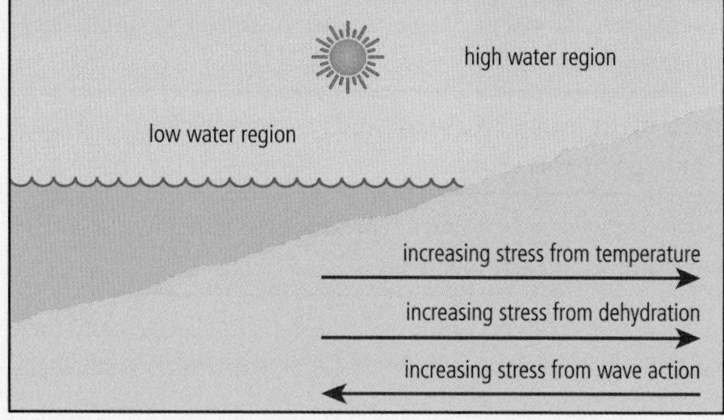

Figure 2.121 Variation in abiotic factors along a rocky shore.

Because of the varying conditions, organisms can be expected to show zonation depending on their adaptations to abiotic factors. Seaweeds show marked zonation (Figure 2.122, Figure 2.123).

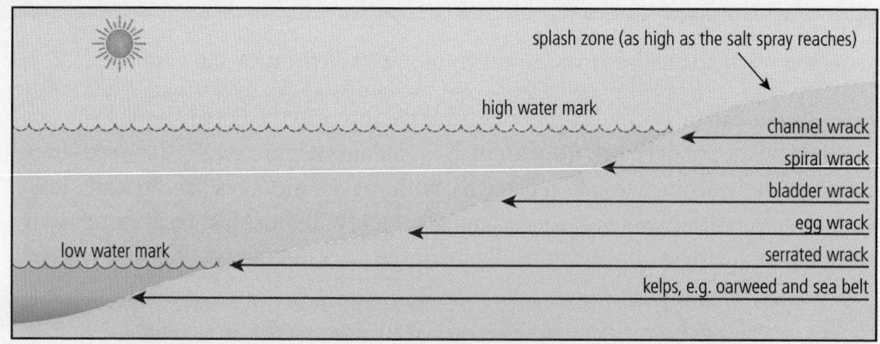

Figure 2.122 Zonation of seaweeds on a rocky shore.

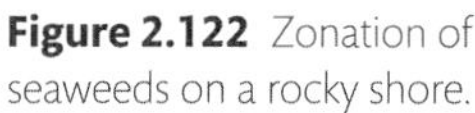

Zonation occurs due to a range of factors such as changes in elevation, latitude, tidal level, soil horizons or distance from a water source.

Figure 2.123 Variety of algae (seaweed) on a rocky shore. The area shown here is dominated by egg wrack, which has air bladders along its fronds that keep the seaweed afloat when the tide comes in, enabling them to obtain the maximum amount of sunlight for photosynthesis.

2.5.2 Transects

Transects are used to measure biotic and abiotic factors along an environmental gradient to determine the variables that affect the distribution of species (Section 2.1.15, 2.1.16 and 2.1.17, pages 107–109). Kite diagrams can be plotted to show distribution of species along a transect (this section, page 202).

Investigate zonation along an environmental gradient using transect sampling

Zonation can be measured by recording biotic and abiotic factors at fixed heights along a transect. A transect is set up using a long tape measure. The transect runs along the vertical gradient being studied (i.e. through the different zones). A cross staff is used to move a set distance (e.g. 0.6 m) vertically up the transect (Figure 2.124). The staff is set vertically at one sample location and a sighting point on the staff, at 0.6 m above the ground, is used to sight the next sampling point along the gradient. Biotic and relevant abiotic factors are measured at each height interval.

Figure 2.124 Using a cross staff to measure vertical distances along a zonation transect.

Create kite diagrams to show distribution

Kite diagrams are visual diagrams that are used to show changes in species abundance and distribution data along a transect. Distance along the transect is put on the *x*-axis, and abundance data (such as percentage frequency) on the *y*-axis. Points showing maximum and minimum abundance values are plotted along the transect, and these points then joined up with straight lines to form a 'kite' shape.

Online kite graph creators are available, for example, the Geography Fieldwork Kite Diagram Creator.

Example – Sand dune succession at Studland Beach

The following data were collected by students using 1 m^2 size quadrats along three parallel, 100 m, straight line transects through the dunes, on a field trip to Studland Beach on the south coast of England. The table shows a summary of slope angle, percentage cover of marram grass and percentage cover of heather. The students took three transects through the dunes. The average results are shown in Table 2.5.

Distance from the sea / m	Average slope angle / °	Percentage cover of marram grass / %	Percentage cover of heather / %
0	5	0	0
10	15	37	0
20	5	63	0
30	5	48	0
40	3	8	34
50	−7	0	43
60	3	0	100
70	−5	0	100
80	−2	10	35
90	0	0	68

Table 2.5 Data from Studland Beach showing slope angle, percentage cover of marram grass and percentage cover of heather.

The data in Table 2.5 can be used to plot the dune profile and kite diagrams for the percentage cover of marram and the percentage cover of heather (Figure 2.125).

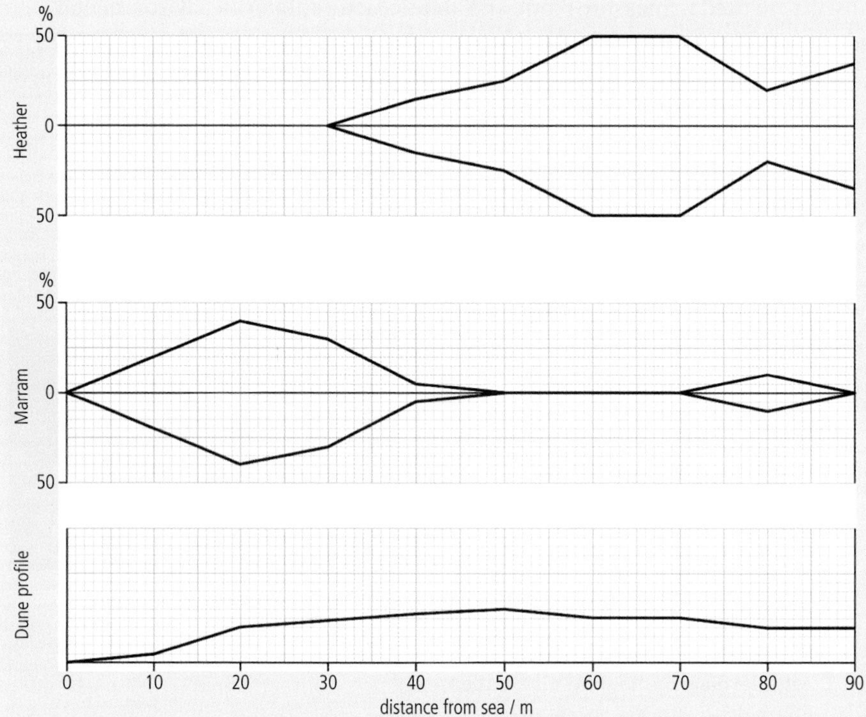

Figure 2.125 Kite diagrams showing the distribution of species and dune profile at Studland Beach.

Figure 2.125 shows that marram is located closer to the sea – this is because it is better able to cope with the windy, salty, arid conditions associated with the shoreline. In contrast, heather dominates away from the shoreline. There is one anomaly at 80 m where the proportion of heather falls and there is a slight increase in marram.

How useful are kite diagrams for showing distribution of vegetation?

Kite diagrams are very useful for showing the relative location/distribution of many species, although only two are shown here. There could be 8–10 different species shown on a single kite diagram. One disadvantage is that many people find the split scale (100% = 50% above the line and 50% below the line) difficult to interpret.

2.5.3 and 2.5.4 Succession

Succession is the replacement of one community by another in an area over time due to changes in biotic and abiotic variables.

As we saw in Section 2.5.2, communities can change along environmental gradients because of changes in factors such as altitude, latitude or distance from the sea on a rocky shore. These changes are a spatial phenomenon. Communities can also change through time. For example, an ecosystem changes as it develops from early stages to later ones. These changes are a temporal phenomenon.

The long-term change in the composition of a community is called succession (Figure 2.126). It explains how ecosystems develop from bare substrate over a period of time. Successions can be divided into a series of stages, with each distinct community in the succession called a seral stage. The first seral stage of a succession is called the **pioneer community**. A pioneer community can be defined as the first stage of an ecological succession that contains hardy species that are able to withstand difficult conditions. The later communities in a succession are more complex than those that appear earlier. The final seral stage of a succession is called the **climax community**. A climax community can be defined as the final stage of a succession, which is in equilibrium and is more stable than earlier seral stages.

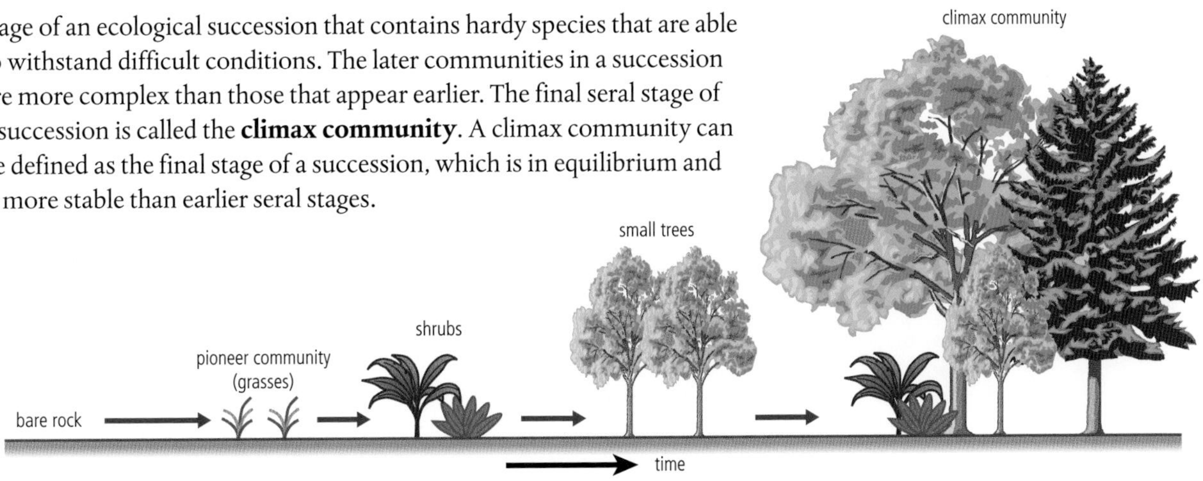

climax community
small trees
shrubs
pioneer community (grasses)
bare rock
time

Figure 2.126 A typical temperate forest succession pattern. Left undisturbed, uncolonized land will change from bare rock into a scrub community, then become populated by pines and small trees and ultimately by large hardwood trees such as oak.

There are various types of succession, depending on the type of environment occupied:

- succession on bare rock is a lithosere (Figures 2.127 and 2.128)
- succession in a freshwater habitat is a hydrosere
- succession in a dry habitat (e.g. sand) is a xerosere.

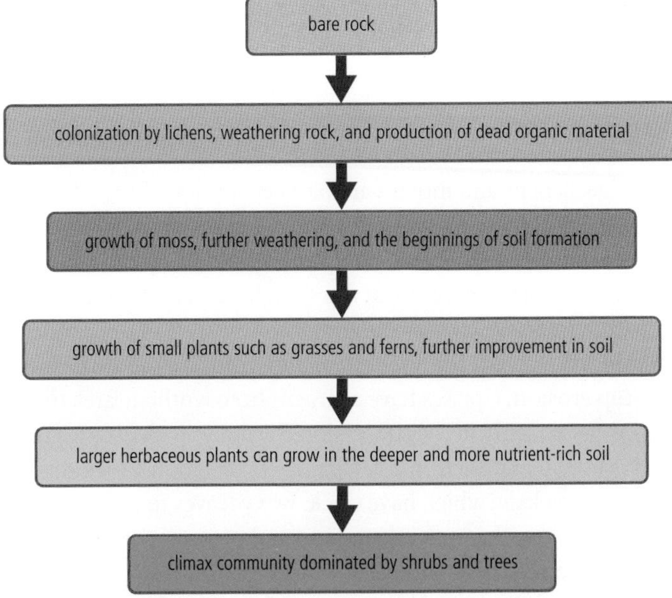
bare rock
colonization by lichens, weathering rock, and production of dead organic material
growth of moss, further weathering, and the beginnings of soil formation
growth of small plants such as grasses and ferns, further improvement in soil
larger herbaceous plants can grow in the deeper and more nutrient-rich soil
climax community dominated by shrubs and trees

Figure 2.127 A model of succession on bare rock.

Ecological *systems* change through time, such as seen in a succession. The final stage of a succession is the **climax community**. It tends to be in a state of equilibrium because it has large storages of biomass, complex food webs and the NPP is balanced by rates of cellular respiration. In a complex ecosystem, such as those represented by climax communities, the variety of nutrient and energy pathways contributes to its stability.

Succession occurring on a previously uncolonized substrate (e.g. rock) is called **primary succession. Secondary succession** occurs in places where a previous community has been destroyed (e.g. after forest fires). Secondary succession is faster than primary succession because of the presence of soil and a seed bank.

Succession occurs when species change the habitat they have colonized and make it more suitable for new species. For example, lichens and mosses are typical pioneer species. Very few species can live on bare rock because it contains little water and has few available nutrients. Lichens and mosses can photosynthesize and are good at absorbing water, so they need no soil to survive and are excellent pioneers. Once established, they trap particles blown by the wind. Their growth reduces wind speed and increases temperature close to the ground. When they die and decompose, they form a simple soil in which grasses can germinate. The growth of pioneers also helps to weather parent rock adding still further to the soil. Other species, such as grasses and ferns that grow in thin soil, are now better able to colonize.

The new wave of species are better competitors than the earlier species. For example, grasses grow taller than mosses and lichen, so they get more light for photosynthesis. Their roots trap substrate (the thin soil) thereby reducing erosion and they have a larger photosynthetic area, so they grow faster. The next stage involves the growth of herbaceous plants (e.g. dandelion and goosegrass). These require more soil to grow but out-compete the grasses. They have wind-dispersed seeds and rapid growth, so become established before larger plants. Shrubs then appear such as bramble, gorse and rhododendron. These larger plants grow in fertile soil and are better competitors than the pioneers.

The final stage of a succession is the climax community. In this community, trees produce too much shade for the shrubs, which are replaced by shade-tolerant forest floor species (see Example – Succession on a shingle ridge). The amount of organic matter present increases as succession progresses. This is because pioneer and subsequent species die out and their remains contribute to a build-up of litter from their biomass. Soil organisms, such as earthworms, move in and break down litter, leading to a build-up of organic matter in the soil and making it easier for other species to colonize. Soil traps water, so increasing amounts of moisture are available to plants in the later stages of the succession.

Figure 2.128 Succession on a shingle ridge in Devon, UK. The community changes from a pioneer community of lichens and mosses through to a climax woodland community containing sycamore and oak trees.

Make sure you know how to describe the process of succession in a named example and explain the general patterns of change in communities undergoing succession. Named examples of organisms from the pioneer, intermediate and climax communities should be provided.

Example – Succession on a shingle ridge

On a shingle ridge, lichens and mosses are pioneer species. Shingle has few available nutrients, but lichens can photosynthesize and are effective at absorbing water. Once established, lichens and mosses trap particles blown by the wind, reduce wind speed and increase temperature at the shingle surface. Their growth helps to weather the parent rock. When they die and decompose, thin soil results. Grasses that grow in thin soil, such as red fescue, can now colonize the area. Grass roots trap soil and stop erosion. Grasses have a larger photosynthetic area than pioneers and so can grow faster. Early in the succession, xerophytic plants (this topic, Section 2.1.6 and 2.1.7, page 90 and Section 2.4.4, page 182) are found, including the yellow-horned poppy and sea kale, which have thick, waxy leaves to prevent water loss and a bluish white colour that reflects sunlight and protects the plant. Plants with nitrogen-fixing bacteria in root nodules (this topic, HL Section 2.3.17 to 2.3.21, page 168), such as rest harrow and bird's foot trefoil, enter the succession. These new species are better competitors than the pioneer species.

The next stage of the succession involves the growth of larger plants such as sea radish, and then a shrub community dominated by bramble (*Rubus fruticosus*). The larger plants grow in deeper soil and are better competitors than the plants of the earlier seral stages.

The final stage of a succession is the climax community, a temperate forest ecosystem (this topic, Section 2.4.4, page 180). Here, trees block sunlight to the shrub community and the shrubs are replaced by shade-tolerant forest floor species (species that can survive in shady conditions) such as ferns.

The concept of succession must be carefully distinguished from the concept of zonation. Succession refers to changes over time, whereas zonation refers to spatial patterns. Rocky shores can be divided into zones from lower to upper shore, with each zone defined by the spatial patterns of animals and plants. Succession, in contrast, is the orderly process of change over time in a community. Changes in the community of organisms frequently cause changes in the physical environment that allow another community to become established and replace the former through competition. Often, but not inevitably, the later communities in such a sequence are more complex than those that appear earlier.

Succession occurs over time, whereas zonation refers to a spatial pattern.

Changes occur as one community changes the environmental conditions so another community can colonize the area and replace the first through competition. This process may continue for hundreds of years but pollen records in peat provide evidence of such changes.

Use secondary data and a mapping database to recreate or map the changes through succession in a given area

Data to show changes in communities, such as those demonstrated by succession, can be generated and mapped using a geographic information system (GIS) and remote sensing (RS), along with aerial photographs, for example, see: Çakir, G. *et al.* (2007) Mapping secondary forest succession with Geographic Information Systems: a case study from Bulanıkdere, Kırklareli, Turkey. *Turkish Journal of Agriculture and Forestry* 31, 71–81.

Online databases can provide extremely detailed information. For example, search for DEFRA's Magic Map online. Information covers rural, urban, coastal and marine environments across the UK. It is presented as an interactive map that can be explored using various mapping tools that are included (e.g. display habitat and species).

Produce an A4 guide about how mapping tools and databases can be used to track succession through time. Include the following information:

- What are GISs?
- What is RS?
- What is light detection and ranging (LIDAR) and how can it be used to map ecosystems?
- How can mapping tools and databases be used to record succession?

Zonation is a spatial phenomenon, whereas succession is a temporal phenomenon.

Succession is the process of change over time in an ecosystem involving pioneer, intermediate and climax communities.

Investigating succession

See the activity in the eBook.

Seral stages

Each seral community in a succession is called a **sere**. Each sere causes changes in environmental conditions that allow the next community to replace it through competition. Eventually, a stable climax community is reached.

For example, mosses start soil formation on bare rock allowing larger plants to colonize.

6.2 Climate change – causes and impacts

Climax communities

Ecosystem stability refers to how well an ecosystem can cope with changes. Most ecosystems are negative feedback systems – they contain inbuilt checks and balances without which they would spiral out of control and no ecosystem would be self-sustaining (Topic 1, Section 1.2.8). Ecosystems with more feedback mechanisms are more stable than simple ecosystems. Thus, ecosystems in the later stages of succession are likely to be more stable as food webs are more complex (because of high species diversity). This means that a species can turn to alternative food sources

A climax community is a community of organisms that is stable (i.e. in a steady-state equilibrium) and is also in equilibrium with natural environmental conditions such as climate. It is the endpoint of ecological succession.

Figure 2.129 Lowland tropical rainforest is a climax community in South-East Asia. Hardwood trees of the family Dipterocarpaceae are dominant. They are often very tall and provide a rich three-dimensional structure to the forest.

if its main food source is reduced. By late succession, large amounts of organic matter are available to provide a good source of nutrients. Nutrient cycles are more closed and self-sustaining. They are not dependent on external influences. This also contributes to stability.

In a climax community there are continuing inputs and outputs of matter and energy but the system remains in a more-or-less constant state (steady-state equilibrium).

The features of a climax community (compared to an early community) are:

- greater biomass
- higher levels of species diversity
- more favourable soil conditions (e.g. greater organic content and deeper soil)
- better soil structure (therefore greater water retention and aeration)
- taller and longer-living plant species
- greater community complexity and stability
- greater habitat diversity
- steady-state equilibrium.

There is no single climax community but rather a set of alternative stable states for a given ecosystem. These depend on the climatic factors, the properties of the local soil and a range of random events that can occur over time (Figures 2.129, 2.130, 2.131).

Figure 2.130 Temperate forests are often dominated by a single tree species, such as the oak.

Figure 2.131 Redwood forests along the Pacific coast of the USA contain some of the tallest trees in the world. The dominant species in terms of biomass is *Sequoia sempervirens*. Trees can reach heights up to 115.5 m (379.1 ft) and diameters up to 8 m (26 feet).

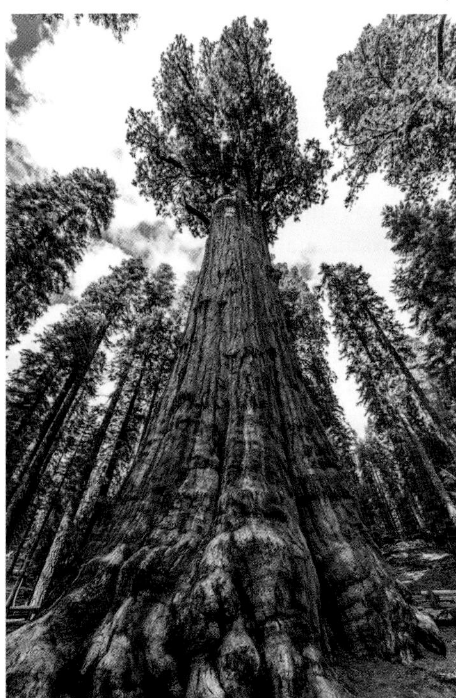

2.5.5 Primary succession

Primary successions happen on newly formed substratum where there is no soil or pre-existing community, such as rock newly formed by volcanism, moraines revealed by retreating glaciers, wind-blown sand or waterborne silt.

Example – Primary succession on Krakatau, Indonesia

Krakatau was a volcanic island to the west of Java in Indonesia, South-East Asia (Figure 2.132). A huge volcanic eruption took place on the island in 1883.

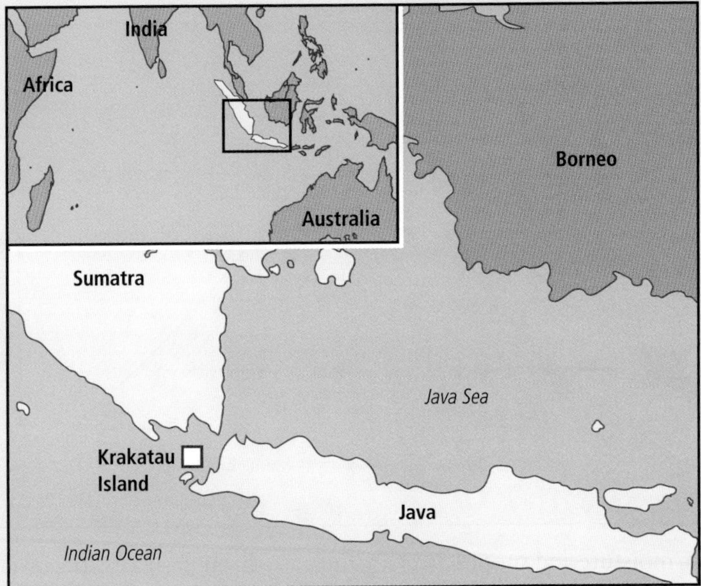

Figure 2.132 Krakatau is part of Indonesia, a band of islands on the equator.

Studies of the colonization of Krakatau, after the massive eruption in 1883, show that tropical rainforest ecosystems are capable of recovery from even extreme damage, given sufficient time. After the initial eruption, no living thing remained on what was left of the island, whereas today Krakatau is covered by tropical forest. On the islands left after the eruption, there are now over 400 species of vascular plants, thousands of species of arthropods, over 30 species of birds, 18 species of land molluscs, 17 species of bats and 9 reptiles.

Organisms can colonize isolated land using several mechanisms:

- air – by flying (birds, insects) or by passive transportation (spores or seeds with a lower mass)
- sea – by swimming or floating on a log
- animal – by travelling (or hitchhiking) inside or attached to animals that swim or fly (plant seeds and animal larvae).

The formation of an ecosystem from bare rock (as on Krakatau) is called a primary succession. The succession always follows the same sequence with the arrival of different organisms in turn (Figure 2.133).

- Pioneer species arrive (e.g. lichens, algae, bacteria) and colonize a bare or disturbed site.
- As these organisms die, soil is created.

Specific types of dispersal

Jump dispersal – long-distance dispersal to remote areas by one or a few individuals. This dispersal mechanism explains widely distributed species in geographically isolated areas. For example, the colonization of the Galápagos Islands by finches from mainland South America.

Diffusion – slower than jump dispersal and involves populations, rather than individuals. This method describes the spread of species at the edge of their ranges into new areas.

Secular migration – dispersal over geological timescales (thousands to millions of years). Dispersal takes place so slowly that the dispersing species undergoes evolutionary change during the process. For example, the evolution of South American llamas that are descended from the now extinct North American members of the camel family.

- Growth in plants causes changes in the physical environment (e.g. light, moisture).
- New species of plants arrive that need soil to survive. They displace the existing pioneer plants.
- The growth of roots enables soil to be retained and not washed away.
- Newly arriving species alter the physical conditions (e.g. increased shade, more minerals and nutrients in the soil as plants die and decay and nitrogen-fixing plants arrive), allowing other species to become established.
- Animals come in with or after the plants they need for food.
- Eventually, a stable climax community is established.
- Disturbances start the process of succession again.

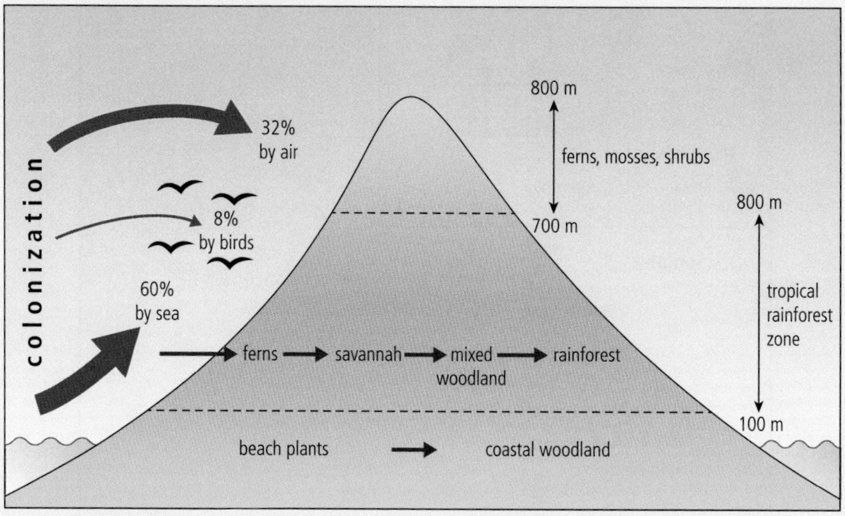

Figure 2.133 Succession on Krakatau began with blue-green bacteria and then ferns (the pioneer species) followed by grasses, shrubs and ferns. Next came mixed woodland (smaller trees) and finally the climax community of tropical rainforest (including tall hardwood trees).

A seral community (or sere) is an intermediate stage found in ecological succession.

Soil depth, moisture and species diversity increase through succession, reaching their maximum in the climax community (the last stage of the succession). Greater habitat diversity leads to greater species and genetic diversity.

Activity

Find out about a local example of primary succession. Alternatively, research the example of Surtsey Island – a volcanic island approximately 32 km from the south coast of Iceland. Surtsey is a new island formed by volcanic eruptions that occurred between 1963 and 1967.

Write a summary of your example. Use the terms seral communities or stages, pioneer and climax communities.

2.5.6 Secondary succession

Secondary succession occurs in an area that already contains soil. Human activities, such as forest clearance (logging or burning), can cause this type of succession, providing no further disturbance occurs.

Secondary successions happen on bare soil where there has been a pre-existing community, such as a field where agriculture has ceased or a forest after an intense fire.

Example – Secondary succession in the Broadbalk Wilderness, Rothamsted, UK

A well-documented example of secondary succession was recorded at Rothamsted in the UK. Areas that had previously been used for agriculture, such as the Broadbalk Wilderness, were fenced off in the 1880s and left to revert naturally to woodland through the process of secondary succession. The project is ongoing, and scientists continue to gather data about the succession. Figure 2.134 shows the changes in organic carbon in soil and tree biomass through time.

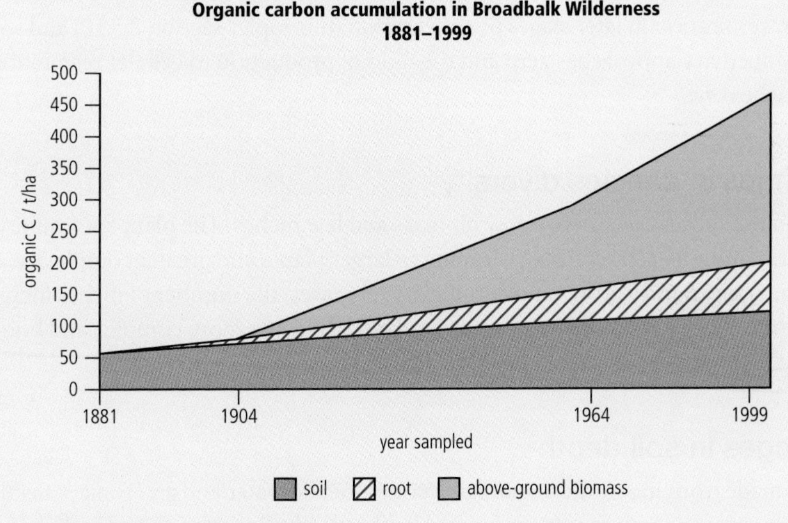

Figure 2.134 Data from Broadbalk Wilderness at Rothamsted, UK, showing changes through time in the mass of carbon stored in soil and tree biomass.

Activity

Find out about the Broadbalk Wilderness at Rothamsted Research (Harpenden, Hertfordshire, UK). Alternatively, find out about a local example of secondary succession.

Produce a fact sheet about the succession. What were the conditions before the succession began? What were the first colonizers and what is the climax community? Provide details about changes in the abiotic and biotic factors through time. How does the rate of change in the communities compare to primary succession?

2.5.7 Changes over time during succession

Energy flow, productivity, species diversity, soil depth and nutrient cycling change over time during succession.

Gross productivity, net productivity, diversity and mineral cycles change over time as an ecosystem goes through succession. During a succession, greater habitat diversity leads to greater species and genetic diversity.

Changes in energy flow, gross productivity and net productivity

In the early stages of a succession, the density of producers is low due to the lack of soil, water and nutrients. This results in a low gross productivity because the proportion of energy lost through community cellular respiration is relatively low and net productivity is high. When net productivity is high, the ecosystem is growing, and biomass is accumulating.

In later stages of a succession, the gross productivity is high in the climax community as there is an increased consumer community. The gross productivity is balanced by cellular respiration in later stages of a succession (this topic, Section 2.5.10) and so the net productivity approaches zero and the ratio of production to cellular respiration approaches one.

Changes in species diversity

Early in the succession, there is low biomass and few niches. The plant community changes through each seral stage, leading to larger plants and greater complexity. As the plant community grows and complexity increases, the number of niches increases. As the number of niches increases, the food webs become more complex and both habitat diversity and species diversity increase.

Changes in soil depth

Soil is made from inorganic and organic components, water and air (Topic 5, Section 5.1.2). Inorganic components are formed by the weathering of rock and include rock fragments, sand, silt and clay. Organic components include living organisms and material produced by the decay of organisms. At the beginning of a primary succession, there is no soil. As pioneer plants establish themselves, they help to break up the rock substrate and when they die, they create organic matter, both of which form soil. As the succession progresses, increased biomass results in increased soil formation. Deeper soils allow larger plants to establish themselves, as the plant roots can anchor themselves in the soil.

Changes in nutrient cycling

Mineral cycling forms an open system at the early stages of succession. Elements such as carbon and nitrogen are introduced to the system from the surrounding area and are also able to leave the system. Later in the succession, nutrient cycling forms a more closed system. Elements such as carbon and nitrogen can remain and cycle within the system. Minerals pass from the soil into living biomass. Minerals return to the soil when organisms die and decay.

Further changes in a succession are shown in Figure 2.135.

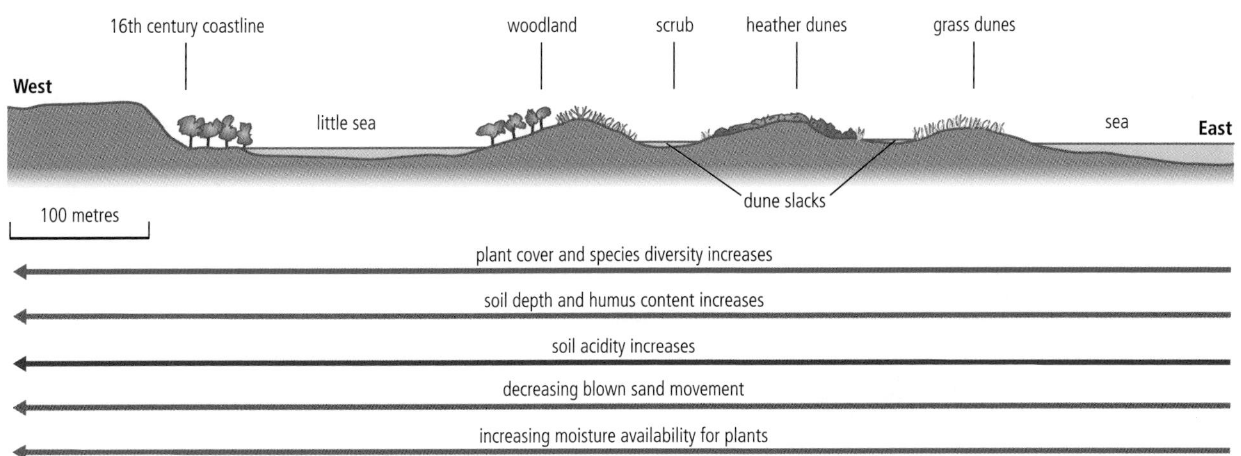

Figure 2.135 Changes in biotic and abiotic factors along a sand-dune succession.

Table 2.6 summarizes the differences in productivity, diversity and nutrient cycling between the early and late stages of succession.

Table 2.6 Features of early and late succession.

Feature	Pioneer community	Climax community
GPP	low	high
NPP	high	low
total biomass	low	high
niches	few	many
species richness	low	high
diversity	low	high
organic matter	small	large
soil depth	shallow	deep
minerals	external	internal
nutrient cycles	open system	closed system
mineral conservation	poor	good
role of detritus	small	large

2.5.8 An ecosystem's capacity to tolerate disturbances and maintain equilibrium

An ecosystem's capacity to tolerate disturbances and maintain equilibrium depends on its diversity and resilience (Topic 1, Section 1.2.16 and 1.2.17).

The resilience of a system refers to its tendency to avoid tipping points and maintain stability through a steady-state equilibrium. Diversity and the size of storages within systems can contribute to their resilience and affect the speed of response to change. Large storages or high diversity will mean that a system is less likely to reach a tipping point and move to a new equilibrium. Humans can affect the resilience of systems through reducing these storages and diversity. Tropical rainforests, for example, have a high diversity (i.e. a large number and proportion of species present).

Ecosystems with high biodiversity contain complex food webs which make them resistant to change – species can turn to alternative food sources if one species is reduced or lost from the *system*.

However, catastrophic disturbance through logging (i.e. rapid removal of tree biomass storages) or fires can lower rainforest resilience, so recovery takes a long time. Natural grasslands, in contrast, have a low diversity but are very resilient. This is because a lot of nutrients are stored below ground in root systems, so they can recover quickly after fire. Fires in savannah ecosystems keep tree cover low and prevent forests from encroaching on the grassland (elephants also allow grasslands to develop – see the Example in Section 2.5.9, page 213, this topic).

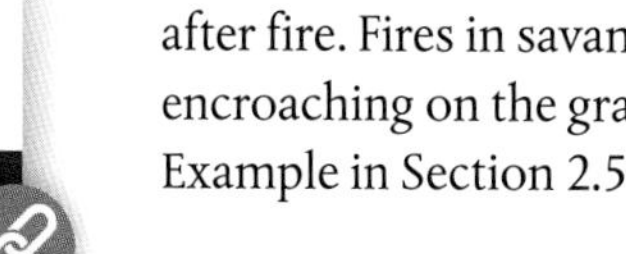
1.2 Systems
6.2 Climate change – causes and impacts

Succession increases diversity which adds to resilience and stability – though human interference can cause a reduction in these qualities.

HL

HL

2.5.9 Influences on the type of community that develops in a succession

The type of community that develops in a succession is influenced by bottom-up or top-down factors. Bottom-up factors affect the soil and producers. Top-down factors affect the organisms higher in the food chain (therefore causing downward effects on succession).

Bottom-up and top-down factors

Bottom-up factors include:

- steep slopes that restrict soil development
- lack of drainage that cause waterlogging
- underlying (parent) rock that may cause ultra-basic or other extreme soil types to develop.

Soils play an essential role in the development of plant communities and their structure and mineral content vary from one area to another (this topic, Section 2.5.3 and 2.5.4, page 204 and Section 2.5.7 page 211). Depending on edaphic (i.e. soil) factors, different communities will develop.

Top-down factors include:

- primary consumers
- higher trophic levels.

Living organisms therefore affect the structure of the final community in a succession.

Find out more about the impact of the grey wolf reintroduction by searching for 'Wolves of Yellowstone' at National Geographic Education.

Example – The ecology of Yellowstone National Park, USA

Historically, the grey wolf, a top carnivore, played an important role in the ecology of Yellowstone National Park in the USA. Human hunting and other pressures led to the extinction of the grey wolf 100 years ago. In 1995, the grey wolf was reintroduced into the ecosystem. Scientists have been studying the effect of the reintroduction on population dynamics in the park and on community structure.

Grey wolves are keystone species (this topic, Section 2.1.23, page 116) at Yellowstone. They cause a 'trophic cascade' within the ecosystem, where the effects on the animals they prey on have knock-on effects for the rest of the food web. All levels of the community are affected (Figure 2.136).

Figure 2.136 Yellowstone National Park ecosystem without (left) and with (right) the grey wolf.

Example – The role of elephants in savannah ecosystems

Elephants in the savannahs consume large amounts of vegetation. These large herbivores (the largest land animal) therefore contribute to the equilibrium of the savannahs and forested areas. As well as eating grass, the elephants feed on saplings (small trees) and trample ground preventing tree growth. They therefore reduce tree densities (Figure 2.137), allowing grasslands to develop (which are typical of the savannah biome – this topic, Section 2.4.4, page 183). Without elephants, many other plants and animals would not survive savannah ecosystems. Elephants also make pathways through dense forested habitat areas, allowing other animals to move easily through the ecosystem.

Figure 2.137 Elephant eating part of a tree on the savannah grasslands of the Maasai Mara, Kenya.

HL

2.5.10 Changes in net productivity and gross productivity in a community undergoing succession

Net and gross productivity change over time as a community progresses through succession.

Production : cellular respiration ratio

The early stages of a succession have low GPP but high NPP because of the low overall rates of cellular respiration. This relationship can be described as a production : cellular respiration ratio or a P : R ratio.

- If production is equal to rate of cellular respiration, the value of P/R is 1.
- Where P : R is greater than 1, biomass accumulates.
- Where P : R is less than 1, biomass is depleted.
- Where P : R = 1 a steady-state community is produced.

Figure 2.138 Difference in production : cellular respiration ratios between natural and agricultural systems.

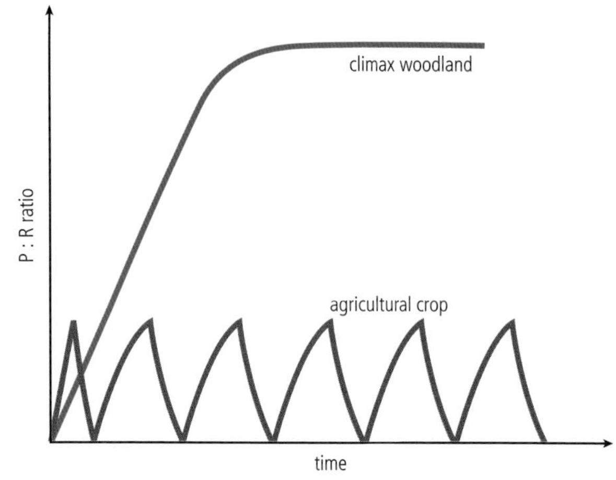

P : R ratio
climax woodland
agricultural crop
time

In the later stages of a succession, with an increased consumer community, rates of community cellular respiration are high. Gross productivity may be high in a climax community but because this is balanced by cellular respiration, the net productivity approaches zero (NPP = GPP – R) and the P : R ratio approaches 1.

If the production : cellular respiration ratios of a food production system are compared to a natural ecosystem with a climax community, clear differences can be seen. Figure 2.138 compares intensive crop production with deciduous woodland. Fields and woodland both have low initial productivity, which increases rapidly as biomass accumulates. Farmers do not want the P : R ratio to reach 1 because at that point, community cellular respiration negates the high rates of gross productivity. This means that yields are not increased. The wheat is therefore harvested before P : R = 1. Community cellular respiration is also controlled in the food production system by isolating herbivores and thereby increasing net productivity and growth. In natural woodland, the consumer community increases, so naturally high productivity is balanced by consumption and cellular respiration. The woodland reaches its climax community when P : R = 1 (i.e. all woodland productivity is balanced by cellular respiration).

Where P : R is greater than 1, biomass accumulates. Where P : R is less than 1, biomass is reduced. Where P : R = 1, a community in steady-state equilibrium is produced.

In the early stages of succession, gross productivity is low due to the unfavourable initial conditions and low density of producers. The proportion of energy lost through community cellular respiration is relatively low too, so net productivity is high. That means the system is growing and biomass is accumulating.

In the later stages of succession, with an increased consumer community, gross productivity may be high in a climax community. However, this is balanced by cellular respiration, so net productivity approaches zero and the production : cellular respiration ratio (P : R) ratio approaches 1.

2.2 Energy and biomass in ecosystems

HL

2.5.11 *r*- and *K*-strategist species

Species can have traits of both *K*- and *r*-species. Studies of dandelions in a disturbed lawn had high reproduction rates, whereas those on an undisturbed lawn produced fewer seeds but were better competitors.

r- and *K*-species (this topic, Section 2.1.29) have reproductive strategies that are better adapted to pioneer and climax communities, respectively.

r-species are those that produce large numbers of offspring so they can colonize new habitats quickly and make use of short-lived resources. *K*-species tend to produce a small number of offspring, which increases their survival rate and enables them to survive in long-term climax communities.

r- and K-selection theory

This theory states that natural selection (Topic 3, Section 3.1.4) may favour individuals with a high reproductive rate and rapid development (*r*-species) over those with lower reproductive rates but better competitive ability (*K*-species). Characteristics of the classes are shown in Table 2.7.

2.2 Energy and biomass in ecosystems

r-species	*K*-species
initial colonizers	dominant species
large numbers of a few species	diverse range of species
highly adaptable	generalists
rapid growth and development	slow development
early reproduction	delayed reproduction
short life	long living
small size	large size
very productive	not very productive

Table 2.7 A comparison of *r*- and *K*-species.

r- and *K*-species have adapted their life cycles to different environments and successional stages.

r-species colonize new habitats rapidly and make opportunistic use of short-lived resources by producing large numbers of offspring with more limited provision for the individual's survival.

K-species thrive in stable communities by producing a small number of offspring that have a high chance of survival, enabling them to survive in long-term climax communities.

In predictable environments – those in which resources do not fluctuate, such as climax communities – there is little advantage to rapid growth. Instead, natural selection favours species that can maximize use of natural resources, and which produce only a few young that have a high probability of survival. These *K*-species have long life spans, large body size and develop slowly. In contrast, disturbed habitats with rapidly changing conditions, such as those in pioneer communities, favour *r*-species that can respond rapidly, develop quickly and have early reproduction. This leads to a high rate of productivity. Such colonizer species often have a high dispersal ability to reach areas of disturbance.

2.5.12 Challenges to the concept of a climax community

HL

The concept of a climax community has been challenged and there is uncertainty over which ecosystems would develop naturally were there no human influences.

Make sure you know how to distinguish the roles of *r*- and *K*-species as selected species in a succession.

Historically, the generally accepted theory was that, without human impacts, closed-canopy forest would predominate in Central and Western Europe in all locations where trees can grow. An alternative hypothesis suggests that grazing by large ungulates, such as cattle and horses, would have created a dynamic landscape where forest and more open areas would alternate through time. This hypothesis was first proposed and published by Frans W.M. Vera and so is known as the 'Vera' wood–pasture hypothesis. In this scenario, the random movement of herbivores creates alternative stable states, rather than one definitive climax community.

Research suggests that Europe has not been totally covered by closed-canopy forest in places where trees can grow. In places where wild cattle and wild horses could live together with other large ungulates, such as deer, it was originally made up of dynamic wood-pasture (Figure 2.139).

Figure 2.139 Ancient wood-pasture, Estonia.

1.2 Systems

Activity

Read this article about the 'Vera' wood–pasture hypothesis: Vera, F. (2002) The dynamic European forest. *Arboricultural Journal* 26, 179–211.

Consider the debate over the 'Vera' wood–pasture hypothesis regarding the effects of primary consumers on the plant communities. You can use the European example outlined on this page or refer to a local example. Working with a partner, summarize the key points. Why would a climax community be unlikely to develop? What impacts do large herbivores have on the succession?

HL

2.5.13 Plagioclimax

Figure 2.140 Burning and deforestation of the Amazon forest to make grazing land leads to loss of large areas of rainforest. Continued burning and clearance, and the establishment of grasslands, prevents succession occurring.

Climatic and edaphic (i.e. relating to soil) factors determine the nature of a climax community. Human factors frequently affect this process through disturbance. The interference or disturbance halts the process of succession and diverts it so that a different stable state is reached rather than the climax community. This interrupted succession is known as **plagioclimax**. An example is the effect of footpath erosion caused by the continued trampling from feet. Or consider a sand dune ecosystem, where walkers might trample plants to the extent that they are eventually destroyed. Human activity can affect the climax community through agriculture, hunting, forest clearance, burning and grazing (Figures 2.140. 2.141 and 2.142). All of these activities divert the progression of succession to an alternative stable state so that the original climax community is not reached.

An ecosystem's capacity to survive change may depend on its diversity and resilience (Topic 1, Section 1.2.17).

Figure 2.141 Large parts of the UK were once covered by deciduous woodland. Some heather would have been present in the north, but relatively little. From the Middle Ages onward, forests were cleared to supply timber for fuel, housing, and the construction of ships (especially oak) and to clear land for agriculture. As a result, soil deteriorated and heather came to dominate the plant community. Sheep grazing and associated burning has prevented the regrowth of woodland by destroying young saplings.

Figure 2.142 Controlled burning of heather also prevents the re-establishment of deciduous woodland. The heather is burned after 15 years, before it becomes mature. If the heather matured, it would allow colonization of the area by other plants. The ash adds to the soil fertility and the new heather growth that results increases the productivity of the ecosystem.

Human activity is one factor that can divert the progression of succession to an alternative stable state, by modifying the ecosystem. Examples include the use of fire, agriculture, grazing pressure or resource use such as deforestation. The complete removal of top carnivores, such as the removal of grey wolves from Yellowstone National Park (this topic, Section 2.5.9), can also modify ecosystems. This diversion may be permanent depending on the resilience of the ecosystem.

Make sure you know how to discuss the factors that could lead to alternative stable states in an ecosystem and discuss the link between ecosystem stability, succession, diversity and human activity.

Human activity can divert and change the progression of succession leading to a **plagioclimax**.

Activity

Find out about other examples of plagioclimax. Use local examples, such as the complete removal of top carnivores and grazing by domesticated livestock. Produce a summary of the examples you find.

Deforestation is having a major impact on one of the most diverse biomes, tropical rainforest (Figures 2.143 and 2.144).

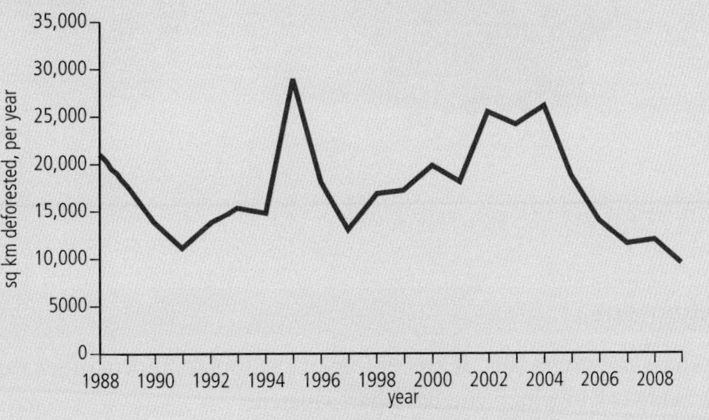

Figure 2.143 Deforestation in the Brazilian Amazon basin fluctuates but remains high, despite warnings about the consequences for the planet. The loss of the highly diverse climax community and its replacement by agricultural or grazing ecosystems affects global biodiversity, regional weather, the water cycle and sedimentation patterns.

An area of tropical rainforest the size of a football pitch is destroyed every four seconds. As well as the loss of habitat and destruction of a complex climax community, the CO_2 released when the trees are burned returns to the atmosphere. The amount of CO_2 is greater than that produced by the entire global transport sector.

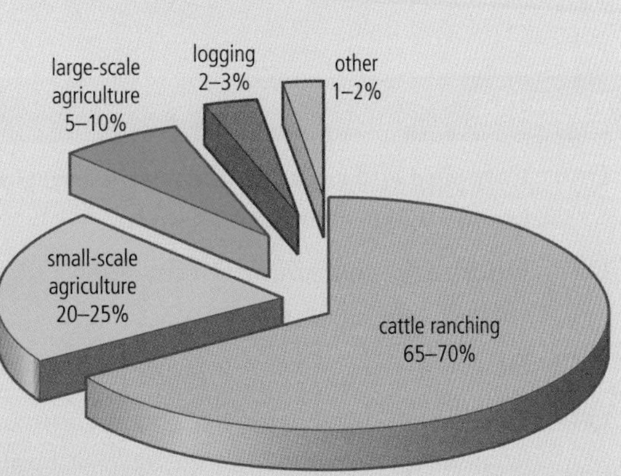

Figure 2.144 Pie chart showing causes of deforestation in the Brazilian Amazon basin, between 2000 and 2005. These human activities are affecting the ecology of the Amazon. The main reason for deforestation, cattle ranching, is a result of the high percentage of meat in Western diets and the increasing consumption of beef in developing countries.

Example – Deforestation in Borneo

Deforestation in Borneo has progressed rapidly in recent years (Figure 2.145). Deforestation affects people, animals and the environment. A recent assessment by the United Nations Environment Program (UNEP) predicts that the Bornean orangutan (endemic to the island) will be extinct in the wild by 2025 if current trends continue. Rapid forest loss and degradation threaten many other species, including the Sumatran rhinoceros and clouded leopard. The main cause of forest loss in Borneo is logging and the clearing of land for palm oil plantations.

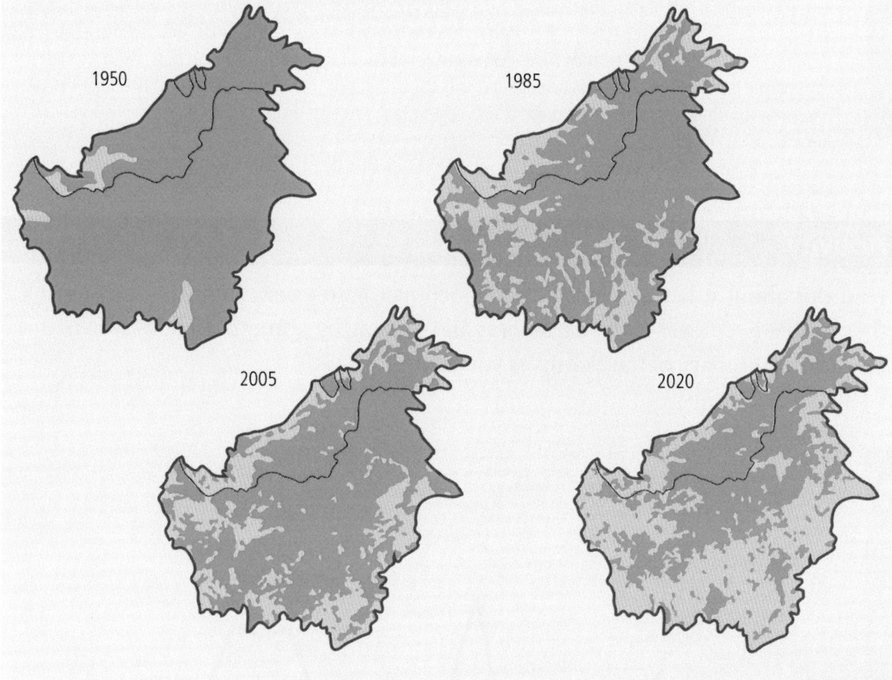

Figure 2.145 Loss of primary forest between 1950 and 2020.

1.2 Systems

HL end

Engagement

- Produce an infographic or poster for your school to inform other students about the fieldwork in which you have participated.

Exercise

Q46. **Compare and contrast** the processes of succession and zonation, using examples of each in your answer.

Q47. **Outline** the changes that occur along a succession. **Explain** the effect these changes have on biodiversity.

Q48. **Distinguish** between primary and secondary succession.

Q49. **Outline** the characteristics of climax communities. Your answer should include details of biomass levels, species diversity, soil conditions, soil structure, pH, community complexity, type of equilibrium and habitat diversity.

Q50. **Describe** methods for measuring changes in abiotic and biotic factors along an environmental gradient. **Evaluate** each method. What are the limitations of each and how will they affect the data you collect?

HL

Q51. HL **Explain** what the P : R ratio measures and how it changes from early to late succession.

Q52. HL **Define** the term *plagioclimax*. **Describe** two examples of how human activities divert the progression of succession to an alternative stable state, by modifying the ecosystem.

Q53. HL **Construct** a table with *r*-species in one column and *K*-species in the other. **List** the characteristics that apply to each.

Q54. HL **Evaluate** the term *climax community*.

HL end

Practice questions

1. The organisms shown in Figure 2.146 (not drawn to scale) were found in an aquatic ecosystem.

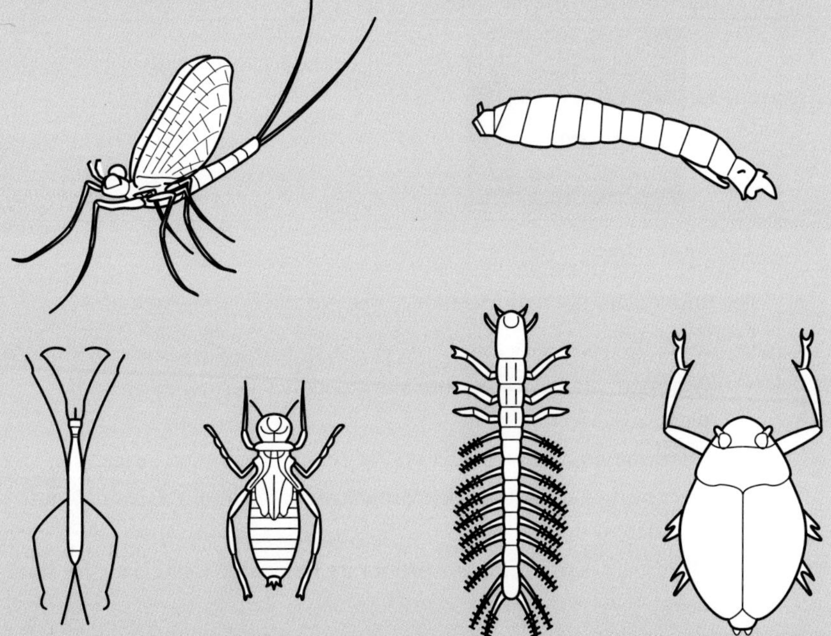

Figure 2.146 Organisms in an aquatic ecosystem.

(a) Suggest two visible characteristics of the organisms shown in Figure 2.146 that could be used to construct an identification key. [2]

(b) Identify one limitation of using a key to identify an organism. [1]

(Total 3 marks)

2. (a) Describe biotic and abiotic factors with reference to a **named** ecosystem. [4]

(b) Using a system diagram, explain the transfer and transformation of energy as it flows through an ecosystem. [7]

(Total 11 marks)

3. Outline the role of the atmospheric system in the distribution of biomes. [4]

(Total 4 marks)

(continued)

4. Review Figures 2.147, 2.148, 2.149 and 2.150 before answering the questions.

Figure 2.147 Fact file on deer species found in London.

Reeves' Muntjac (*Muntiacus reevesi*) (male)	
	• Native to Southeast Asia, introduced to UK when they escaped from a zoo • Lives throughout London • Eats grass, nuts and garden flowers • Breeds all year round • One of the smallest deer species; 0.44–0.52 m to shoulder
Red deer (*Cervus elaphus*) (male)	
	• Native to Europe, western Asia and northern Africa • Lives in Richmond Park • Eats grass and woody plants • Breeds once per year • One of the largest deer species; 1.00–1.20 m to shoulder
Fallow deer (*Dama dama*) (male)	
	• Native to Europe • Lives in Richmond Park • Eats grass and woody plants • Breeds once per year • Medium in size; 0.84–0.94 m to shoulder

Figure 2.148 Fact file on Richmond Park.

Richmond Park is a national nature reserve and Special Area of Conservation.

- Approximately 630 red and fallow deer live permanently in the park.
- There are no natural predators for deer in Richmond Park.
- Deer numbers in the park are managed to maintain a sustainable population.
- Deer meat is sold, and any profits are reinvested into caring for the deer.

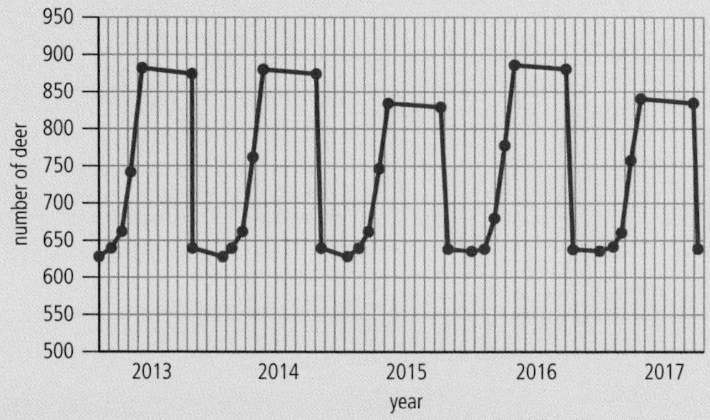

Figure 2.149 Population of deer in Richmond Park, 2013–2017.

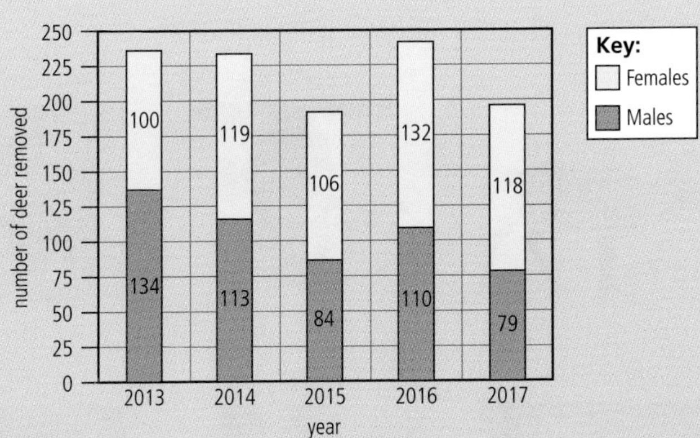

Figure 2.150 Number of deer removed from Richmond Park, 2013–2017.

(a) Using Figure 2.147, construct an identification key for the deer species found in London. [3]

(b) With reference to Figures 2.148, 2.149 and 2.150, predict how the ecosystem would be affected if the deer population in Richmond Park was not managed. [2]

(Total 5 marks)

5. Review Figure 2.151 before answering the questions.

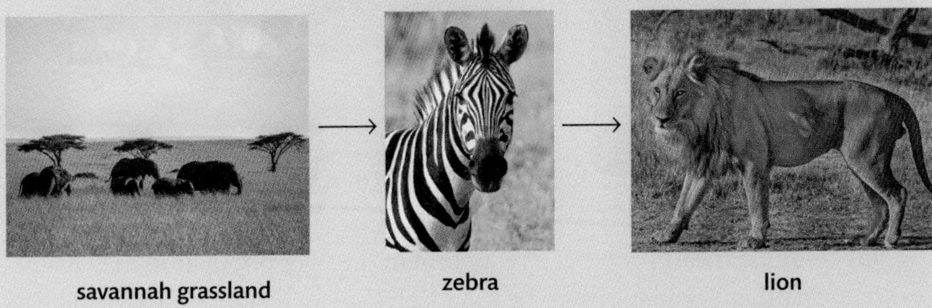

Figure 2.151 Savannah food chain.

(a) **(i)** State the trophic level of the zebra. [1]

(ii) Explain how the second law of thermodynamics applies to this food chain. [2]

Biting flies bite and drink the blood of zebras. They commonly carry diseases that can be fatal to zebras.

(b) State the type of relationship that exists between biting flies and the zebra. [1]

(Total 4 marks)

(continued)

6. Review Figure 2.152 before answering the questions.

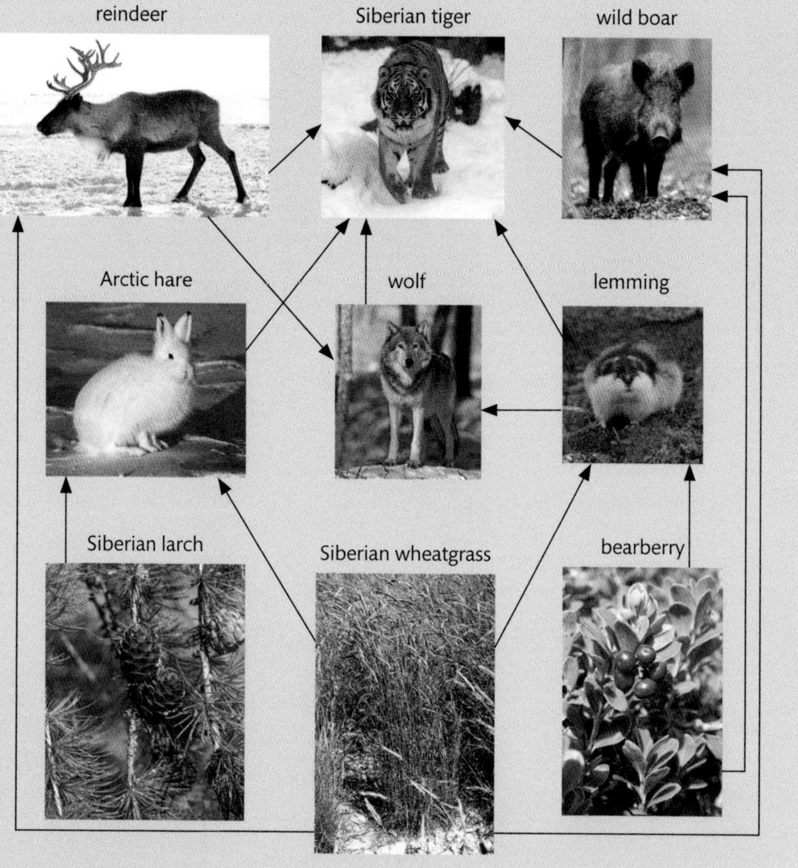

Figure 2.152 Example of a Siberian food web.

(a) Outline the impact that a reduction in the tiger population may have on other populations in the food web shown in Figure 2.152. [2]

(b) Outline why a reduction in the Siberian tiger's population may increase its probability of extinction. [2]

(Total 4 marks)

7. (a) Identify **four** ways to ensure reliability of the capture–mark–release–recapture method in estimating population size. [4]

(b) Explain how the interactions between a species and its environment give rise to an S-shaped population growth curve. [7]

(Total 11 marks)

8. (a) Distinguish between **two** named biomes and the factors that cause their distribution. [4]

(b) Evaluate **one** method for measuring primary productivity in a named ecosystem. [7]

(Total 11 marks)

9. Review Figures 2.153, 2.154, 2.155 and 2.156 before answering the questions.

- Opportunistic feeders that change their food sources with the seasons.
- Can live for up to 70 years.
- 40–50% of the beluga whale's body mass is made up of fat.
- Reaches sexual maturity between 5 and 9 years of age.
- The worldwide population of beluga whales is estimated at 150,000.
- The St Lawrence River estuary population (900 individuals):
  - is isolated from other beluga whales
  - is listed as endangered by the Canadian government
  - has been protected by law since 1983.

Figure 2.153 Fact file on the beluga whale (*Delphinapterus leucas*).

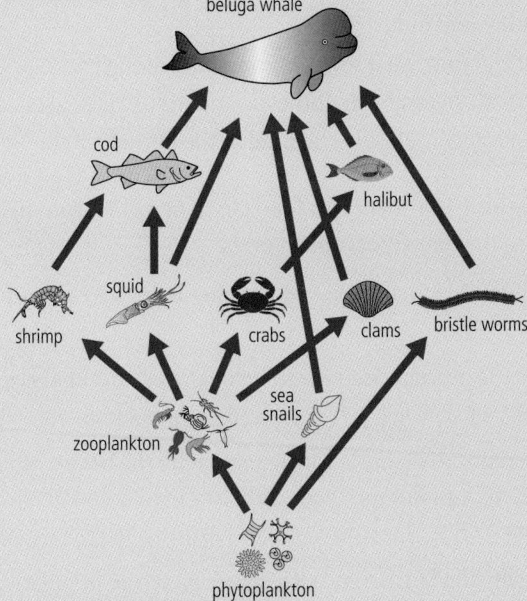

Figure 2.154 A simplified food web for the St Lawrence River beluga whale.

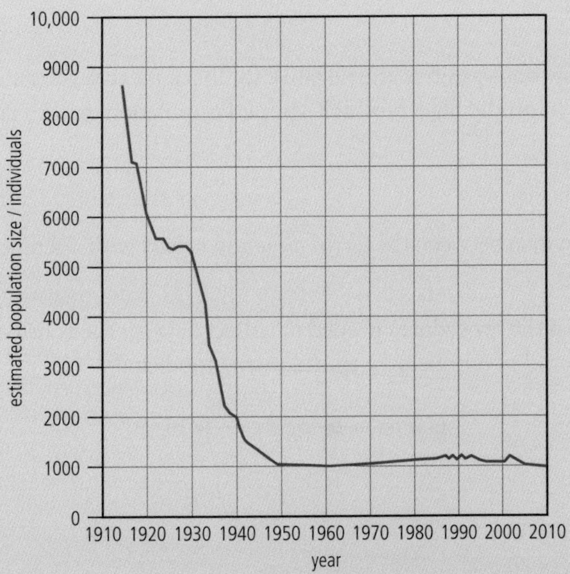

Figure 2.155 Estimated population of the St Lawrence River beluga whales.

(continued)

Figure 2.156 Threats to the St Lawrence River beluga whale.

Shipping and whale watching issues:

- The noise from ships disturbs feeding behaviour.
- Ships may separate young whales from their mothers.

Hunting:

- Until the 1980s, beluga whales were hunted because they competed with the commercial fishing industry.

Pollution:

- Heavy metals, such as lead (Pb), mercury (Hg) and cadmium (Cd) from industrial effluent.
- Persistent organic pollutants (POPs), such as DDT and PCBs, from agriculture and industry.
- Treated and untreated sewage from cities along the river.
- Microplastic beads from domestic and industrial waste.
- Pollutants accumulate in the mud at the bottom of the river.

(a) Using Figure 2.154, identify a food chain in the St Lawrence River ecosystem that has **five** trophic levels. [1]

(b) Using Figure 2.155, state the St Lawrence beluga whale population in 1920 and 1940. [1]

(c) Calculate the percent decrease in beluga whale numbers between 1920 and 1940. [1]

(d) With reference to Figure 2.156, explain why the beluga whale is more at risk from toxic pollutants, such as heavy metals and persistent organic pollutants (POPs), than most other organisms in its food web. [3]

(e) Suggest why the St Lawrence River beluga whale population has not recovered despite being given protected status in 1983. [4]

(Total 10 marks)

10. Explain how both positive and negative feedback mechanisms may play a role in producing a typical S-shaped population growth curve for a species. [7]

(Total 7 marks)

11. (a) Distinguish between the terms *niche* and *habitat* with reference to a named species. [4]

(b) Suggest the procedures needed to collect data for the construction of a pyramid of numbers for the following food chain:

plants ⟶ snails ⟶ birds [7]

(Total 11 marks)

12. Review Figure 2.157 before answering the questions.

Volcano	Latitude	Eruption date	Type of surface	Number of species (plants) recorded in three separate years		
				1930	1975	2015
Krakatau, Indonesia	6°S	1883	Ash and lava	24	243	397
Tarawera, New Zealand	38°S	1886	Lava	2	63	74

Figure 2.157 The number of plant species present on the slopes of two volcanoes, which erupted in the 1880s. Measurements were taken in 1930, 1975 and 2015.

(a) State the ecological processes illustrated by the data in Figure 2.157. [1]

(b) Describe a method for measuring the abundance of plant species in volcanic areas. [3]

(c) Suggest **two** reasons why there are differences in the number of plant species found on Krakatau and Tarawera. [4]

(Total 8 marks)

13. Figure 2.158 shows the concentration of DDT at different trophic levels of the food chain.

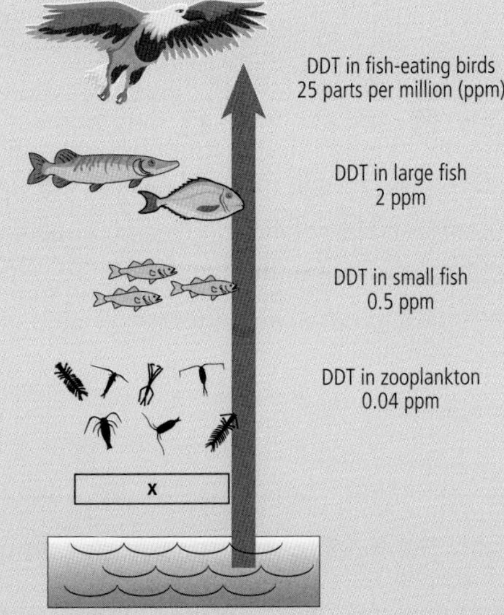

Figure 2.158 Levels of concentration of DDT in food chain.

(a) State the main source of energy for the food chain in Figure 2.158. [1]

(b) State the trophic level labelled **X** in Figure 2.158. [1]

(c) Identify **one** use of DDT that has led to its presence in the environment. [1]

(d) With reference to the concepts of bioaccumulation **and** biomagnification, outline how the concentration of DDT has changed along the food chain. [2]

(e) **(i)** State the relationship between large and small fish in Figure 2.158. [1]

(ii) Outline how this relationship may be of benefit to the populations of both species. [2]

(Total 8 marks)

(continued)

14. Review Figure 2.159 before answering the questions.

Figure 2.159 The gross and net productivity at different trophic levels within the Silver Springs, Florida, ecosystem.

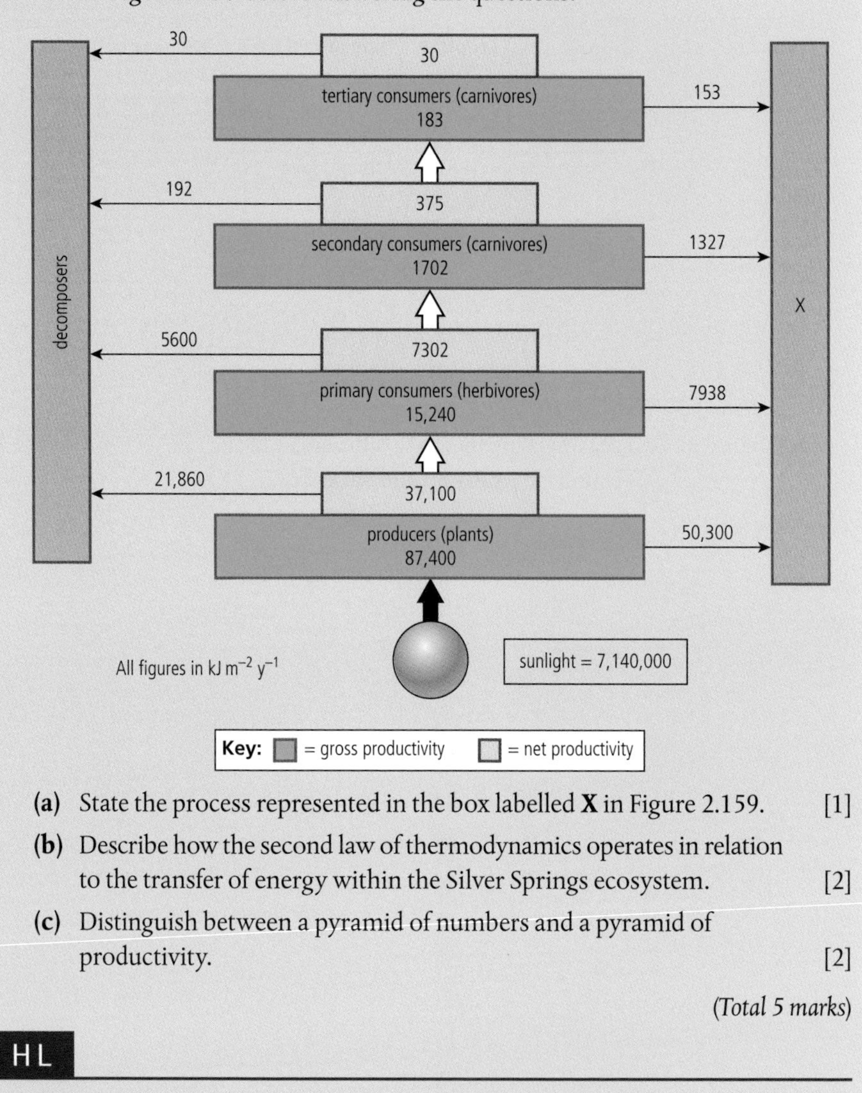

(a) State the process represented in the box labelled **X** in Figure 2.159. [1]

(b) Describe how the second law of thermodynamics operates in relation to the transfer of energy within the Silver Springs ecosystem. [2]

(c) Distinguish between a pyramid of numbers and a pyramid of productivity. [2]

(Total 5 marks)

HL

15. HL Review Figures 2.160 and 2.161 before answering the questions.

Figure 2.160 Fact file about the red-necked and imperial amazon parrots.

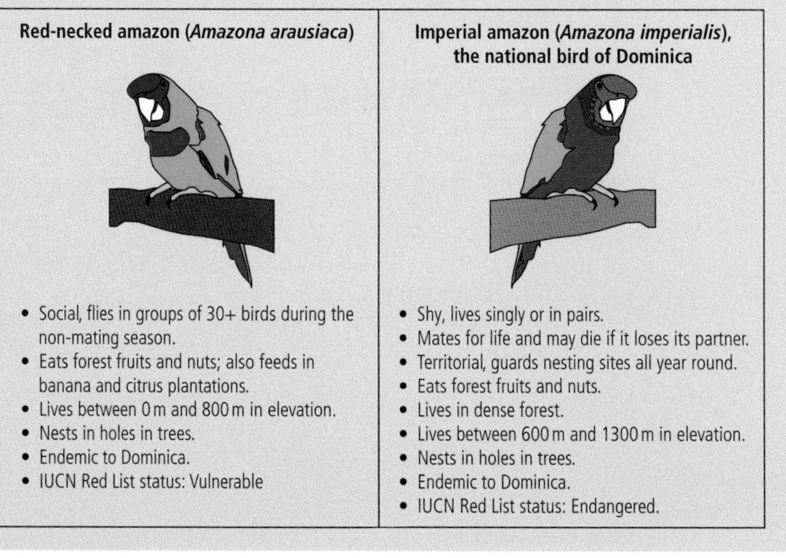

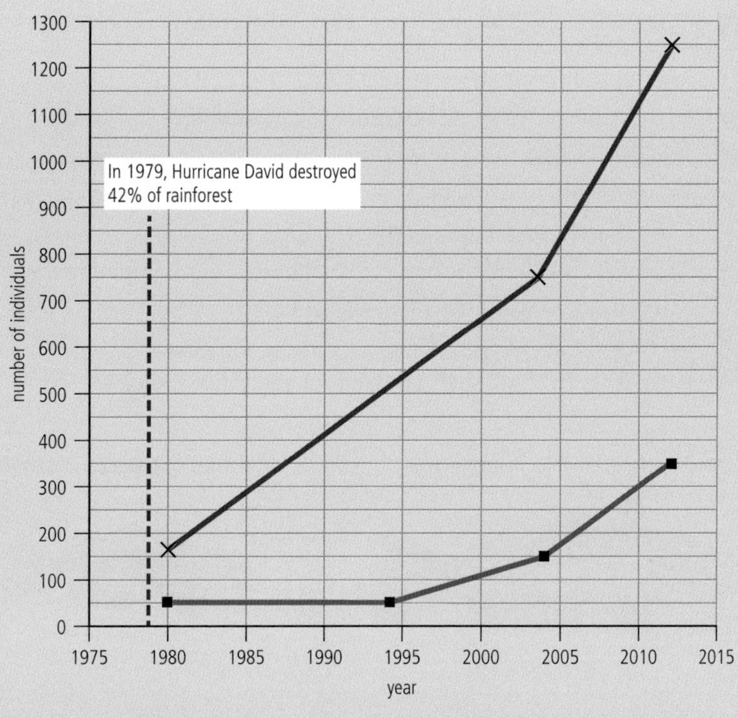

Figure 2.161 Changes in the numbers of individual imperial and red-necked amazon parrots.

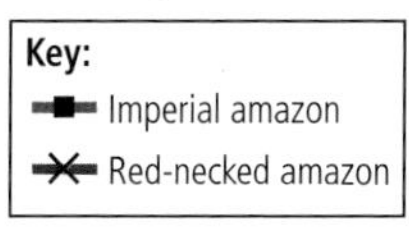

(a) Using Figure 2.160, state **one** physical characteristic that may be used to differentiate these two species from each other in an identification key. [1]

(b) With reference to Figure 2.160, state the type of biotic interaction that occurs between the imperial amazon and the red-necked amazon parrots. [1]

(c) Compare and contrast the realized niches of the two parrot species. [3]

(d) With reference to Figure 2.161, calculate the percent increase in red-necked amazon numbers between 1980 and 2012. [1]

(e) With reference to Figures 2.160 and 2.161, suggest **two** reasons why the red-necked amazon population has recovered more quickly than the imperial amazon population following Hurricane David in 1979. [2]

(Total 8 marks)

(continued)

16. HL Review Figures 2.162 and 2.163 before answering the questions.

Figure 2.162 Fact file on the round goby (*Neogobius melanostomus*).

- An invasive species from Asia.
- First discovered in the St Lawrence River in 1990.
- Females lay eggs three times a year; up to 5000 eggs at a time.
- Young fish mature quickly.
- Can eat up to 4000 eggs of other fish in 15 minutes.
- Aggressively defend the best egg-laying sites, out-competing the native mottled sculpin (*Cottus bairdii*).
- Eat invasive zebra mussels.
- Eaten by native fish, such as lake trout and yellow perch.

Figure 2.163 Picture of the round goby and mottled sculpin.

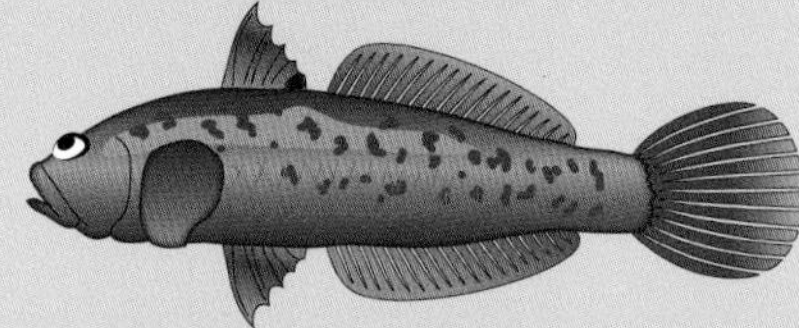

(a) Using Figures 2.162 and 2.163, identify **one** feature of the round goby that shows it is an *r*-selected species. [1]

(b) With reference to Figure 2.162, outline how the round goby both positively and negatively affects the St Lawrence River ecosystem. [3]

(c) With reference to Figure 2.162, explain why the realized niche of the mottled sculpin has changed in recent years. [3]

(Total 7 marks)

HL end

3 Biodiversity and conservation

3.1 Biodiversity and evolution

Guiding Questions

How can diversity be explained and quantified, and why is this important?

How does the unsustainable use of natural resources impact biodiversity?

3.1.1 Biodiversity is the total diversity of living systems and it exists at several levels.
3.1.2 The components of diversity contribute to the resilience of ecological systems.
3.1.3 Biodiversity arises from evolutionary processes.
3.1.4 Natural selection is the mechanism driving evolutionary change.
3.1.5 Evolution by natural selection involves variation, overproduction, competition for limited resources, and differences in adaptation that affect rates of survival and reproduction.
3.1.6 Speciation is the generation of new species through evolution.
3.1.7 Species diversity in communities is a product of richness and evenness.
3.1.8 Simpson's reciprocal index is used to provide a quantitative measure of species diversity, allowing different ecosystems to be compared and for change in a specific ecosystem over time to be monitored.
3.1.9 Knowledge of global and regional biodiversity is needed for the development of effective management strategies to conserve biodiversity.
HL 3.1.10 Mutation and sexual reproduction increase genetic diversity.
HL 3.1.11 Reproductive isolation can be achieved by geographical separation or, for populations living in the same area, by ecological or behavioural differences.
HL 3.1.12 Biodiversity is spread unevenly across the planet, and certain areas contain a particularly large proportion of species, especially species that are rare and endangered.
HL 3.1.13 Human activities have impacted the selective forces acting on species within ecosystems, resulting in evolutionary change in these species.
HL 3.1.14 Artificial selection reduces genetic diversity and, consequently, species resilience.
HL 3.1.15 Earth history extends over a period of 4.5 billion years. Processes that occur over an extended timescale have led to the evolution of life on Earth.
HL 3.1.16 Earth history is divided up into geological epochs according to the fossil record.
HL 3.1.17 Mass extinctions are followed by rapid rates of speciation due to increased niche availability.
HL 3.1.18 The Anthropocene is a proposed geological epoch characterized by rapid environmental change and species extinction due to human activity.
HL 3.1.19 Human impacts are having a planetary effect, which will be detectable in the geological record.

3.1.1 Biodiversity

Conflation means combining two or more separate things, such as words. The word *biodiversity* is a combination of 'biological' and 'diversity'.

The word *biodiversity* is a conflation of 'biological diversity' and was first made popular by ecologist E.O. Wilson in the 1980s. *Bio* makes it clear we are interested in the living parts of an ecosystem. *Diversity* is a measure of both the number of species in an area and their relative abundance (this topic, Section 3.1.7). Biodiversity is the total diversity of living systems and exists at several levels. It is a result of habitat diversity, species diversity and genetic diversity (Figure 3.1).

Figure 3.1 Rainforests are diverse. They are rich in resources, such as food and space and have many different niches available, so many species can co-exist.

Biodiversity is the total diversity of living systems. It is made up of **habitat diversity, species diversity** and **genetic diversity**.

Biodiversity refers to the variety of life on Earth. Conservation biologists first used the word to highlight the threat to species and ecosystems. It is now widely used in international agreements concerning the sustainable use and protection of natural resources.

Habitat diversity

Habitat diversity means the range of different habitats in an ecosystem or biome. It is often associated with the variety of ecological niches. For example, woodland has a high habitat diversity because it contains many different habitats, including rivers, soil, trees, shrubs, ground vegetation, leaf litter, fallen dead trees and so on. In contrast, a desert has a low habitat diversity because it only contains a few habitats such as sand and occasional vegetation (Figure 3.2).

Figure 3.2 Death Valley desert. Ecosystems such as deserts have low habitat biodiversity so there are fewer opportunities for species to co-exist.

A habitat is the environment in which a species normally lives.

Habitat diversity refers to the range of different habitats in an ecosystem or biome.

Species diversity

Species diversity refers to the variety of species per unit area. It includes both the number of species present and their relative abundance. The higher the species diversity of a community or ecosystem is, the greater the complexity. Areas of high species diversity, such as primary rainforest, are more likely to be undisturbed. Species diversity within a community is a component of the broader description of the biodiversity of an entire ecosystem.

A species is a group of organisms sharing common characteristics that interbreed and produce fertile offspring.

Species diversity in a community is the relative proportion of species within that community.

Genetic diversity

The term *genetic* refers to **genes**, which are sections of DNA found in the nucleus of all cells. Each gene contains the code for a specific **protein** (structural molecule of the body) or characteristic (Figure 3.17, this topic, Section 3.1.10). They are essentially the instructions from which a species is produced. The term **gene pool** refers to all the different types of gene found within every individual of a species. A large gene pool leads to high **genetic diversity** and a small gene pool leads to low genetic diversity. The term *genetic diversity* normally refers to the diversity within one species. However, it can also be used to refer to the diversity of genes in all species within an area.

Genes are sections of DNA found in the nucleus of all cells. They are essentially the instructions from which a species is produced. **Gene pool** refers to all the different types of gene found within every individual of a species.

Genetic diversity refers to the range of genetic material present in a population of a species.

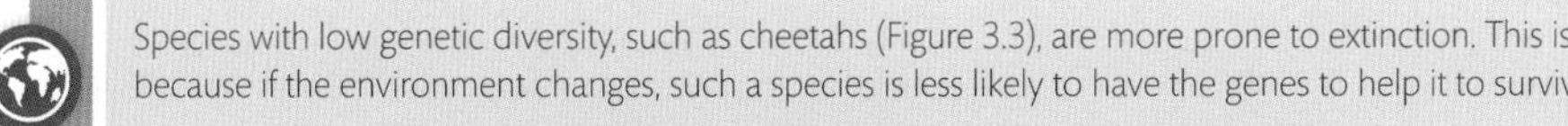

Species with low genetic diversity, such as cheetahs (Figure 3.3), are more prone to extinction. This is because if the environment changes, such a species is less likely to have the genes to help it to survive.

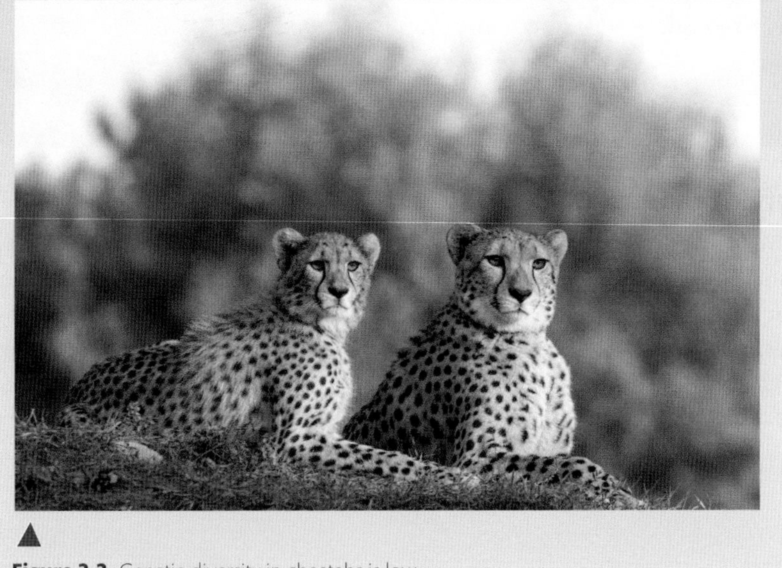

Figure 3.3 Genetic diversity in cheetahs is low.

TOK

How is current knowledge shaped by its historical development?

Early definitions of diversity have become limited as scientific knowledge has increased. Species diversity depends on the correct identification of different organisms and their distribution around the Earth. In the past, this identification was based on physical characteristics. However, we now know that this method can be unreliable because two different species may have similar physical characteristics but be completely unrelated. Genetic diversity allows for a more accurate way to describe species.

Overview of biodiversity

The term *biodiversity* is often used to refer to the heterogeneity (variability) of a community, ecosystem or biome, at the species, habitat or genetic level. The scientific meaning of diversity can become clear from the context in which it is used. For the meaning to be obvious, the full correct term – species diversity, habitat diversity or genetic diversity – should be used.

Of the three types of diversity, an increase in habitat diversity is the more likely to lead to an increase in the other two. This is because different habitats tend to contain different species and so a greater number of habitats will generally result in a greater variety of species. Similarly, different species tend to have different genes and so a greater number of species will generally result in a greater variety of genes. The conservation of habitat diversity will therefore usually lead to the conservation of species and genetic diversity.

Make sure you can distinguish between the terms *biodiversity, species diversity, genetic diversity* and *habitat diversity*.

Biodiversity is a broad concept encompassing the total diversity of living *systems*, which includes species diversity, habitat diversity and genetic diversity.

Conservation of habitat diversity usually leads to the conservation of species and genetic diversity.

Habitat diversity confers high species and genetic diversity, resulting in greater *sustainability* in ecosystems.

3.1.2 The components of diversity contribute to the resilience of ecological systems

Each component of biodiversity (species diversity, habitat diversity and genetic diversity) contributes to the resilience of living systems. *Resilience* refers to the ability of a system to maintain equilibrium and avoid tipping points (Topic 1, Section 1.2.16).

In communities with high species diversity, the food webs tend to be complex, so the loss of one species (unless it is a keystone species) does not adversely affect the community (Topic 2, Section 2.5.8).

Species diversity is reflected by habitat diversity. An ecosystem with many different habitats will enable many niches to co-exist, which enhances species diversity.

Species that are genetically diverse are more likely to survive than populations with low genetic diversity (Figure 3.3). One gene can have different versions, each of which has a slightly different genetic code – these different forms of the same gene are called **alleles**. Genetic diversity reflects the number of different alleles for different genes in a population. The greater the genetic diversity, the greater the ability of a population to survive periods of adversity. Genetically diverse populations therefore have greater resilience than ones that show a narrow range of alleles for any given characteristic.

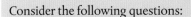

Activity

Why is biodiversity essential for limiting climate change?

Use the QR code to access the United Nations Climate Change article, *Biodiversity – our strongest natural defense against climate change.*

Consider the following questions:

- How does climate change impact biodiversity?
- How can biodiversity limit climate change?
- How does the resilience provided by biodiversity guard against the effects of global warming?

Produce a flow chart or mind map to indicate the relationships between diversity, the resilience of living systems and mitigation of the effects of climate change.

1.2 Systems
3.3 Conservation and regeneration
5.2 Agriculture and food
6.3 Climate change – mitigation and adaptation
7.2 Energy resources, use and management

3.1.3 Biodiversity arises from evolutionary processes

When we look at the great diversity of life on Earth, one important question to consider is how has this biodiversity arisen? The answer is that biodiversity arises from evolutionary processes.

The theory of evolution describes the cumulative changes in the genetic composition of a species over many successive generations and explains how these changes ultimately give rise to species that are completely different to the common ancestor. A *common ancestor* is the most recent species from which two or more now different species have evolved. For example, humans and chimpanzees share a common ancestor of some six million years ago.

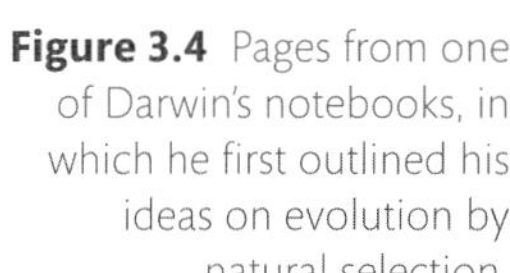

Evolution results from the cumulative changes in the **heritable** characteristics of a population or species. The term *heritable* means that characteristics can be passed on from parent to offspring through the genetic code.

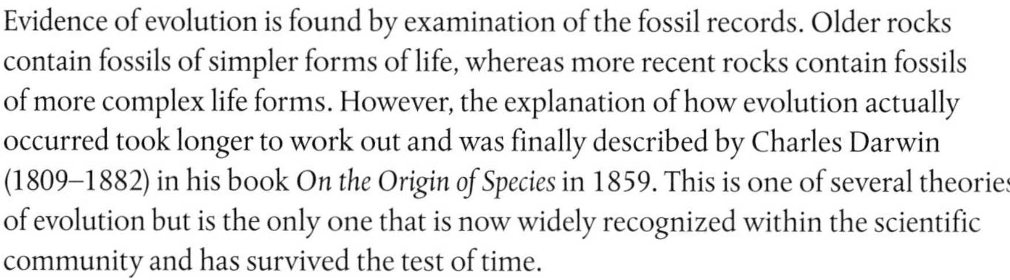

Evidence of evolution is found by examination of the fossil records. Older rocks contain fossils of simpler forms of life, whereas more recent rocks contain fossils of more complex life forms. However, the explanation of how evolution actually occurred took longer to work out and was finally described by Charles Darwin (1809–1882) in his book *On the Origin of Species* in 1859. This is one of several theories of evolution but is the only one that is now widely recognized within the scientific community and has survived the test of time.

3.1.4 Natural selection

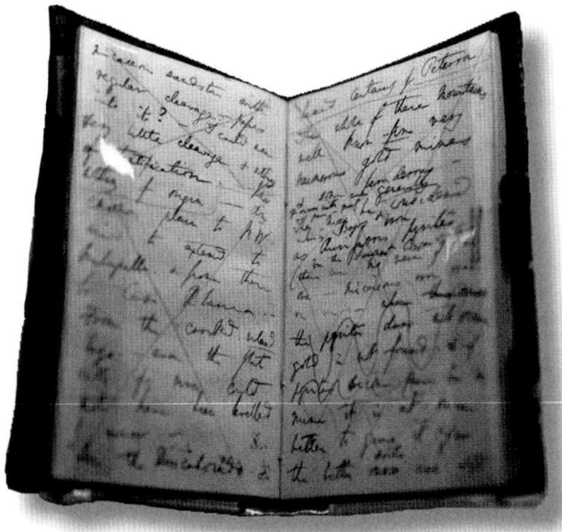

Figure 3.4 Pages from one of Darwin's notebooks, in which he first outlined his ideas on evolution by natural selection.

Darwin went on a five-year expedition on the HMS *Beagle* between 1831 and 1836. The aim of the expedition was to map the coasts and waters of South America and Australia. Darwin was on board as a companion to the captain, but Darwin was also a talented and curious naturalist. During the trip, he was exposed to some of the most diverse ecosystems on Earth, including the rainforests of South America and the Galápagos Islands off the west coast of South America. It was essentially the interrelationship between species and environment in the Galápagos Islands that stimulated Darwin to develop his theory of evolution by **natural selection** (Figure 3.4).

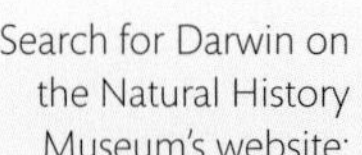

Search for Darwin on the Natural History Museum's website:

Search for Darwin in the University of Cambridge's ArchiveSearch:

Biogeography is the study of the geographical distribution of species and explains their current distribution using evolutionary history. Once the historical factors that have been involved in shaping biodiversity are understood, scientists can better predict how biodiversity will respond to climate change.

Search for Charles Darwin's library on the American Museum of Natural History website:

Darwin called the process natural selection because nature does the choosing, as opposed to **artificial selection**, also known as **selective breeding**. Selective breeding is a common practice in which humans choose animals or plants to breed together based on desirable characteristics. It is selective breeding that has led to all the varieties of domestic and agricultural animals we have today. Over millennia, natural selection has resulted in not only new varieties, but also entirely new species. The process of natural selection contributes to the changes in biodiversity over time.

Darwin collected huge numbers of animals, plants and fossils during his trip on HMS *Beagle*. Many of these specimens are now in the Natural History Museum, London. It

was after his return to the UK, and after he had time to examine his specimens, that Darwin began to develop his theory.

He was particularly influenced by specimens of three species of mockingbird from the Galápagos Islands. The mockingbirds are believed to have had a more important role in the development of Darwin's initial ideas than the famous Galápagos finches. In *The Voyage of the Beagle* (1839), Darwin wrote: 'My attention was first thoroughly aroused by comparing together the various specimens... of the mocking-thrush'.

Darwin noticed that each species of mockingbird was specifically adapted, in body size and beak shape, to the specific conditions on the three different islands. This led him to start to think that, rather than each species being created separately (as was widely thought at the time), perhaps all were related to a common ancestor from the South American mainland. Moreover, perhaps each had evolved through the process of natural selection to become adapted to different niches on the three different islands. Darwin also noted adaptations in species of giant tortoise on different islands (Figure 3.5), which also helped him formulate his ideas on natural selection.

Natural selection is the mechanism driving evolutionary change.

Natural selection operates continuously in natural *systems* and can take place over millions of years or over shorter time spans, resulting in the biodiversity of life on Earth.

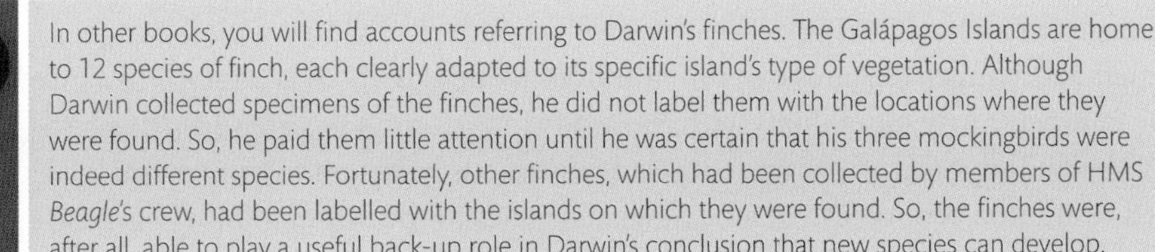

In other books, you will find accounts referring to Darwin's finches. The Galápagos Islands are home to 12 species of finch, each clearly adapted to its specific island's type of vegetation. Although Darwin collected specimens of the finches, he did not label them with the locations where they were found. So, he paid them little attention until he was certain that his three mockingbirds were indeed different species. Fortunately, other finches, which had been collected by members of HMS *Beagle*'s crew, had been labelled with the islands on which they were found. So, the finches were, after all, able to play a useful back-up role in Darwin's conclusion that new species can develop.

(a) (b)

Figure 3.5 Different species of giant tortoise are found on different islands of the Galápagos, each adapted to local conditions. **(a)** On islands with tall vegetation, saddle-shaped shell fronts enable the animals to stretch up and reach the plants. **(b)** Animals with domed-shaped shell fronts are found on islands where vegetation is common on the ground.

TOK

What is the relationship between personal experience and knowledge?

In 1858, Charles Darwin unexpectedly received a letter from a young naturalist, Alfred Russel Wallace (1823–1913). Wallace outlined a theory of natural selection that was remarkably similar to Darwin's own. Wallace had come up with the idea while travelling in South-East Asia. The men had developed the same theory independently. How was this possible? Common experiences seem to have been crucial and both had read similar books. For two individuals to arrive at one of the most important theories in science independently, and at the same time, is remarkable.

The first publication of the theory of evolution by natural selection was not in 1859 in Darwin's *On the Origin of Species*, but in 1858 in a joint publication by Darwin and Wallace in *Proceedings of the Linnaean Society of London*, following a presentation of their findings at the Society earlier that year.

The evidence for Darwin's theory is overwhelming. Despite this, some people, including creationists, do not accept it to be correct. Creationists believe that all life on Earth was created within six days. Scientific evidence strongly contradicts this version of events. Most religions accept Darwin's theory, while maintaining a belief in a creator God. What do you think? Ultimately you must weigh your *perspective* with scientific evidence and draw your own conclusions.

What makes a good explanation?

TOK

The theory of evolution by natural selection tells us that change in populations is achieved through the process of natural selection. Is there a difference between a convincing theory and a correct one?

3.1.5 Variation, overproduction, competition, and differences in adaptation

During his travels, Darwin noted that all species tended to over-reproduce and that this led to competition for limited resources (a 'struggle for existence'). He also noted that individuals of the same species showed variation where, rather than being alike, there were subtle differences in appearance or behaviour between individuals.

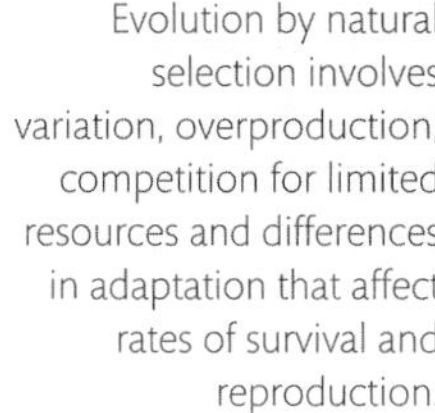

Evolution by natural selection involves variation, overproduction, competition for limited resources and differences in adaptation that affect rates of survival and reproduction.

From this, Darwin concluded that those individuals that were best adapted to their surroundings could survive and could then go on to reproduce and pass those adaptations on to their offspring.

Natural selection can occur because genetic diversity gives rise to variation within a population. Genetic diversity occurs because of sexual reproduction and changes in the genetic code known as genetic mutations. These genetic mutations happen randomly and can result in altered genes that can be beneficial, can cause damage or can have no impact on the survival of the individual with those genes. Beneficial changes to genes can provide an individual with an advantage in a given environment. Any individuals with those advantageous genes are more likely to survive and reproduce, passing those advantageous genes on to their offspring. As a result, the proportion of advantageous genes in the population will increase over many generations. Over time, this results in a change in the species' gene pool. Ultimately, such changes lead to new species.

Changes to the genetic code can lead to non-beneficial effects, for example the development of a genetic disease such as cystic fibrosis – a disease that affects the lungs and digestive system. These mutated genes can still be passed down through the generations, but they offer no adaptive advantage. If such genes are distinctly harmful, individuals with them may die before they can reproduce. Some variation has no effect on the survival of a species, so it is said to be neutral.

Natural selection occurs through the following mechanism.

- Within a population of any species there is genetic diversity. This is called natural variation.
- Natural variation means that some individuals will be better suited to their environment than others.
- The individuals that are better suited to the environment have an advantage and will reproduce more successfully.
- The offspring of these individuals inherit the advantageous genes and survive to reproduce and pass on the genes to subsequent generations.

A species is a group of organisms that interbreed and produce fertile offspring. **Speciation** is the generation of new species through evolution.

3.1.6 Speciation

Natural selection is not, on its own, sufficient to lead to **speciation. Reproductive isolation** is required, where populations become separated and isolated from each other so that genes cannot be exchanged between them (Figure 3.6). If the environments of the isolated populations are different, natural selection will work on each population so that, through evolution, speciation occurs, forming new species.

Figure 3.6 Mountains (like the Eiger, Munch and Jungfrau, in the Swiss Alps) form a physical barrier that isolates populations. The formation of these mountains leads to evolution and increased biodiversity. The altitude can also create new habitats, with an increase in biodiversity due to populations adapting to new habitats through natural selection.

Sometimes, two species breed together to produce a hybrid species. Hybrid organisms are sterile and cannot reproduce.

Speciation takes place when a population of a species becomes isolated and adapts in different ways to their environment. Over time, they become unable to interbreed with other populations of the original species and thus they evolve into a new species.

Example – Speciation in spotted owls

Populations of the spotted owl in Northern America have become geographically separated over time, forming two varieties or subspecies – the northern spotted owl and the Mexican spotted owl (Figure 3.7). The two species of owl inhabit geographically separate locations, each of which has a different climate and ecosystem. The northern area has a cooler climate than the south, causing the physiology and behaviour of owls in each ecosystem to differ. In addition, the hunting habits and selection of prey used by the southern owls vary to those used by the northern owls. The different adaptations to the two separate areas and the distance between them (owls are unlikely to fly long distances) meant that the populations became isolated. Given enough time, and continued isolation, populations are unable to interbreed and produce fertile offspring, so two separate subspecies evolve.

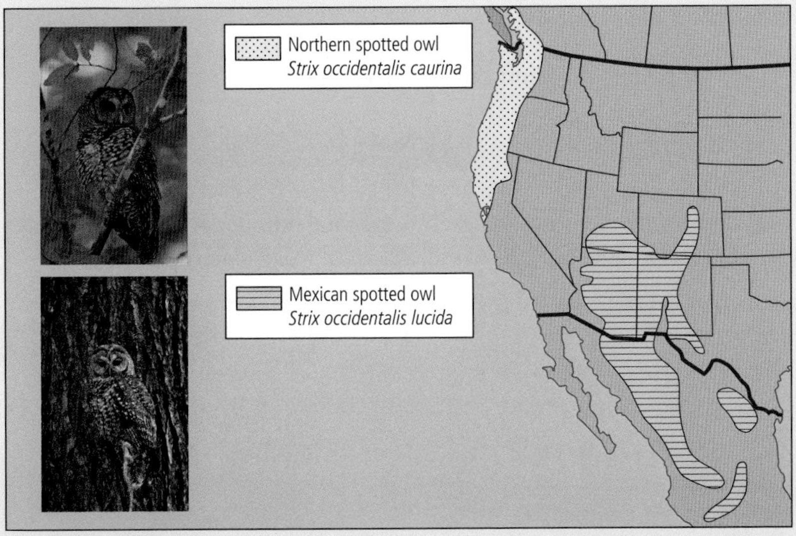

Northern spotted owl *Strix occidentalis caurina*

Mexican spotted owl *Strix occidentalis lucida*

Figure 3.7 The ranges of these two varieties of spotted owl do not overlap and they occupy different niches – geographical separation means there is little gene flow between the two varieties.

3.1.7 Species diversity

A **community** is a group of populations living and interacting with each other in a common habitat.

Species diversity is the number of species and their relative abundance in each area or sample. It is a product of richness and evenness in a community.

Richness is the number of species in a community and is a useful comparative measure.

Evenness is how similar the population sizes of each species are.

Richness and evenness are components of biodiversity. **Species richness** refers to the number of a species in an area and species **evenness** refers to the relative abundance of each species. A community with high evenness is one that has a similar abundance of all species – this implies a complex ecosystem where there are lots of different niches that support a wide range of different species. In contrast, in a community with low evenness, one or a few species dominate – this suggests lower complexity and a smaller number of niches that could support a range of species (Figure 3.8).

Figure 3.8 Richness and evenness in two different communities. Both communities have the same species richness with three species each. Community 1 has greater evenness, with all species being equally abundant, than Community 2, where one species dominates. Community 1 shows greater species diversity than Community 2.

3.1.8 Simpson's reciprocal index for diversity

Simpson's reciprocal index is used to provide a quantitative measure of species diversity, allowing different ecosystems to be compared, and change in a specific ecosystem over time to be monitored.

Species diversity is considered as a function of two components – the number of different species and the relative numbers of individuals of each species. It is different from species richness (the number of species in an area) because the relative abundance of each species is also considered.

There are many ways of quantifying diversity. You must be able to calculate diversity using **Simpson's reciprocal index for diversity**. This index can be used for both animal and plant communities.

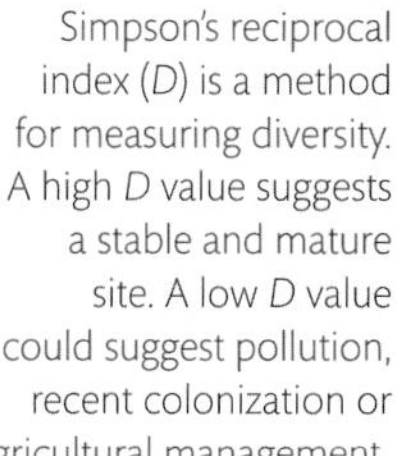

Simpson's reciprocal index (*D*) is a method for measuring diversity. A high *D* value suggests a stable and mature site. A low *D* value could suggest pollution, recent colonization or agricultural management.

The formula for calculating Simpson's reciprocal index is:

$$D = \frac{N(N-1)}{\sum n(n-1)}$$

where *D* is Simpson's reciprocal index, *N* is the total number of organisms of all species found and *n* is the number of individuals of a particular species.

Make sure you know how to calculate and interpret data for species richness and diversity.

There are many versions of diversity indices, but you are only expected to be able to apply and evaluate the result of Simpson's reciprocal index. You are not expected to memorize Simpson's reciprocal index, but make sure you know the meaning of the symbols.

Suppose you want to examine the diversity of beetles within a woodland ecosystem. You could use multiple pitfall traps to establish the number of species and the relative abundance of individuals present (Topic 2, Section 2.1.15). You could then use Simpson's reciprocal index to quantify the diversity.

Samples must be comprehensive to ensure all species are sampled (Figure 3.9). However, it is always possible that certain habitats are not sampled and therefore some species get missed. For example, canopy fogging does not knock down insects living within the bark of the tree, so these species would not be sampled.

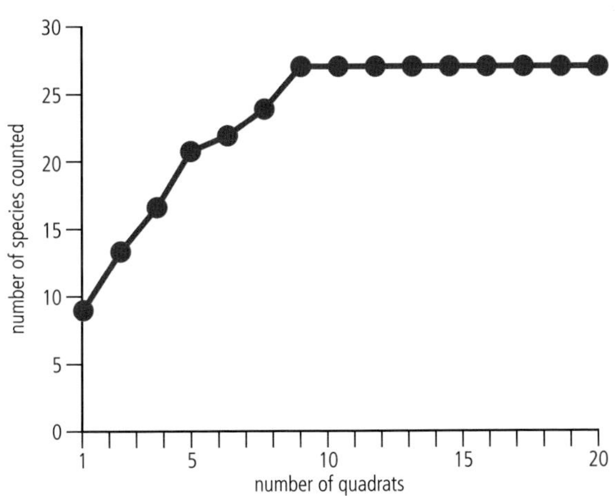

Figure 3.9 To make sure you have sampled all the species in your ecosystem, perform a cumulative species count. As a higher number of quadrats are added to sample size, any additional species are noted and added to species richness. The point at which the graph levels off gives you the best estimate of the number of species in your ecosystem.

Measures of diversity are relative, not absolute. They are relative to each other but not to anything else. This differs from other measurements, such as temperature, where values relate to an absolute scale. Comparisons can be made between communities containing the same type of organisms and within the same ecosystem, but not between different types of community or different ecosystems.

Communities with individuals evenly distributed between different species are said to have high 'evenness' and have high diversity. This is because many species can co-exist in many different niches within a complex ecosystem.

Communities with one dominant species have low diversity, which indicates an ecosystem is not able to support a great variety of organisms. Measures of diversity in communities with few species can be unreliable as relative abundance between species can misrepresent true patterns. For example, samples may contain unrepresentative numbers of certain species.

When comparing communities that are similar, low diversity could be evidence of pollution, eutrophication or recent colonization of a site. Number of species is often used to assess biodiversity in an area, although measurement of species richness alone can be a misleading measure of disturbance to ecosystems. Species diversity measurements give more meaningful data.

Measurements of species richness depend on sample size, especially when dealing with small organisms such as insects.

Dung beetles are scarab beetles that feed on a variety of food sources including faeces, carrion (dead animals) and decomposing plant material. Figure 3.10 shows

!

It is useful to be able to draw graphs to illustrate how the species diversity in a community changes over time or between communities. A line graph can be drawn when plotting changes in diversity over time, with values of D being shown on the y-axis (vertical axis) and values of time being shown on the x-axis (horizontal axis). A bar chart can be plotted when comparing communities, to show the values of D for each community.

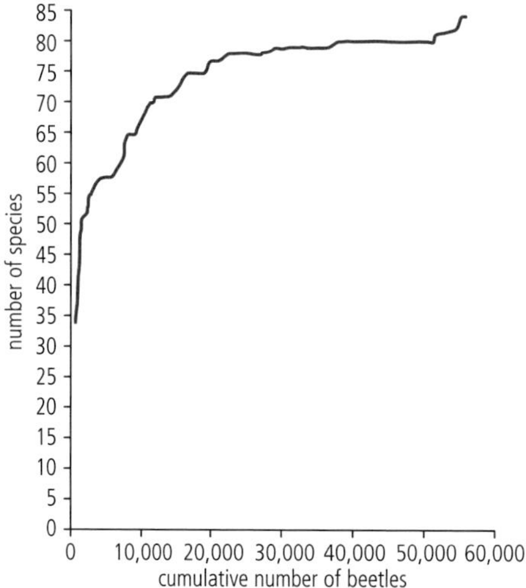

Figure 3.10 Species accumulation graph for beetles collected by pitfall trap in the Bornean lowland rainforest.

Make sure you know how to comment on the relative values of biodiversity data and explain, for example, why the value of *D* in one area is higher than that in another. Interpreting diversity is complex, low diversity can be present in natural, ancient and unpolluted sites such as desert ecosystems (Topic 2, Section 2.4.4).

the accumulated species richness of dung beetles in a rainforest ecosystem in Borneo. Accurate measurement of species richness was only possible after many beetles had been collected. Most species had been collected once a sample of 20,000 beetles had been accumulated, although some additional species were added after 55,000 beetles had been collected (Figure 3.10). Species accumulation curves can be used in this way to indicate appropriate sample sizes.

TOK

Does it matter that there are no absolute measurements for diversity indices?

Numbers can be used for comparison but on their own mean little. Are there other examples in science of similar relative rather than absolute measurement systems?

Example calculation of Simpson's reciprocal index

Table 3.1 shows the collated data from several quadrats in a woodland area.

Species	Number, n	$n(n-1)$
woodrush	2	2
holly (seedlings)	8	56
bramble	1	0
Yorkshire fog	1	0
sedge	3	6
Total (N)	15	64

Table 3.1 Data from woodland.

Putting the values into the formula for Simpson's reciprocal index:

$$D = \frac{N(N-1)}{\sum n(n-1)}$$

$N = 15$

$N - 1 = 14$

$N(N-1) = 15 \times 14 = 210$

$\sum n(n-1) = 64$

$D = 210/64 = 3.28$

The value of *D* will be higher where there is greater richness (number of species) and evenness (similar abundance), with 1 being the lowest possible value.

Suppose that Simpson's reciprocal index was calculated for a second woodland, where $D = 1.48$. A high value of *D* suggests a stable and mature site and a low value of *D* suggests pollution or agricultural management. The woodland where $D = 3.28$ could be an undisturbed ecosystem and the woodland where $D = 1.48$ could be a disturbed ecosystem. Some ecosystems have naturally low diversity, such as Arctic tundra (Topic 2, Section 2.4.4). Therefore, the reasons for *D* values must be attributed based on what is known about the ecosystem being studied. The higher *D* value in the woodland study suggests a more complex ecosystem where many species can co-exist. The lower *D* value suggests a simpler ecosystem where fewer species can co-exist. The woodland with the higher Simpson's reciprocal index is an area that would be better for conservation. The woodland with the lower Simpson's reciprocal index is an area that would not be as good for conservation.

Different habitats can be compared using *D* values. As a higher *D* value indicates a greater species diversity, a lower *D* value in one habitat may indicate human impact. Low values of *D* in the Arctic tundra, however, may represent stable and mature sites. This indication of diversity is only useful when comparing two similar habitats or the same habitat over time.

TOK

In what ways do values affect the production of knowledge?

The focus of conservation is often on rare species that are in danger of extinction. But is a focus on individual species, which may be very difficult to study due to their rareness, the most effective use of scarce conservation funds? Many common species also make important contributions to the functioning of ecosystems. Could it be argued that conservation efforts should be directed towards common species? Common species create habitat for other species, and so by protecting them it is possible to also protect the rare animals. Could it be argued that an area with a lower number of rare species might be more important for conservation than an area with a higher number of common species and if so, why? To what extent do the choices of conservation depend on the values of individuals or communities?

Do not confuse *species richness* with *diversity*. Diversity is the function of the number of different species and the relative numbers of individuals of each species. This is different from species richness, which refers only to the number of species in a sample or area.

Ecosystems can be immensely complex systems, as shown in Topic 2. How can the effects of human activities be assessed given such complexity? Topic 2 considers the ways in which the effects of human disturbance can be measured (Section 2.1.22, pages 114–116). Disturbance, or perturbation, takes ecosystems away from a steady-state equilibrium and can lead to new stable states after certain tipping points are reached (Topic 1, Section 1.2.12). Topic 2 explores the differences between fundamental and realized niches (Section 2.1.28, HL only). Perturbation can simplify ecosystems or change them so that the realized niche of species no longer exists in the area and the opportunities for the existence for many species are removed. Such changes may, for other species, provide an expansion of their usual range because their realized niche spreads into the disturbed area. For example, species found in the canopy and along riverbanks in a rainforest (rather than the forest interior) may spread into forest that has been logged where new conditions are now found (Figure 3.11).

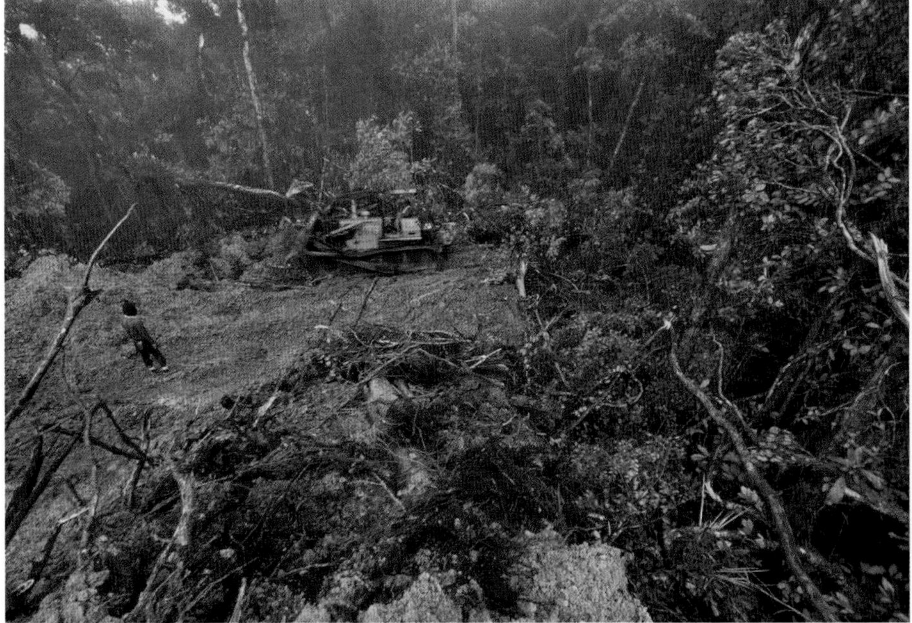

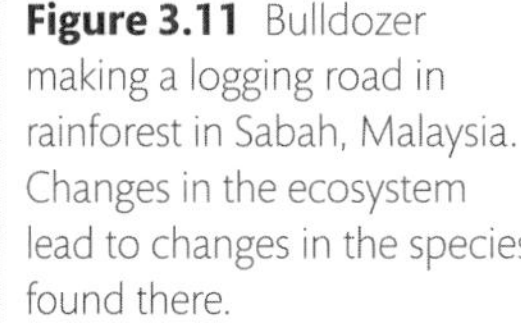

Figure 3.11 Bulldozer making a logging road in rainforest in Sabah, Malaysia. Changes in the ecosystem lead to changes in the species found there.

Disturbance moves ecosystems away from a steady-state equilibrium and can lead to new stable states if certain tipping points are reached. These changes move ecosystems away from *sustainability*.

Diversity indices can be used to assess whether the impact of human development on ecosystems is *sustainable* or not, over shorter or longer periods of time.

Diversity indices, such as Simpson's reciprocal index, are key tools used by conservation biologists to assess the effect of disturbance. Quantification of biodiversity in this way is important for conservation efforts to enable areas of high biodiversity to be identified and explored, and for appropriate conservation to be put in place where possible. Areas that are high in biodiversity are known as hotspots. They contain large numbers of **endemic** species (species not found anywhere else) and so measures of biodiversity are essential in identifying areas that should be protected against damaging human activities. An example of a biological hotspot is Tumbes-Chocó-Magdalena, an area that includes the forests of the South American Pacific coast, from Panama to Peru, and the Galápagos Islands.

Values of *D* are relative to each other and are not absolute. This is unlike measures of, for example, temperature that are on a fixed scale. This means that two different areas can be compared to each other using the index, but a *D* value on its own is not useful.

Measurements of species richness, on their own, are not sufficient to establish the impacts of human activities as the assessment of species richness can vary according to sampling technique. Some sampling techniques are suitable for certain species but not for others. For example, light traps can be used for insects that are drawn to a light bulb but not for those that are not. Sample size also affects the assessment of species richness – the bigger the sample, the higher the number of species collected. The relative abundance of species in a community must also be considered. Care must be taken when giving reasons for differences in species diversity, as measured by Simpson's reciprocal index. For comparisons to be made between different areas using a diversity index, the same sampling method must be used and a similar type of habitat should be investigated. An example of this could be investigating forest ecosystems in the same region.

The ability to assess changes to biodiversity in each community over time is important in assessing the impact of human activity in the community.

Diversity indices also work best when similar groups of organisms are compared rather than broader groups. For example, investigating dung beetle communities from undisturbed and perturbed forest sites (see Example below) rather than all of the animal species in one area.

Make sure you know how to discuss the usefulness of providing numerical values of species diversity to understanding the nature of biological communities and the conservation of biodiversity.

Individual values of *D* give an indication of the composition of the community being investigated. Low values of *D* indicate low evenness, meaning one species may dominate the community, but they cannot be used alone to help in the identification of areas of biodiversity that should be conserved.

Example – Species richness and diversity of beetle communities following logging

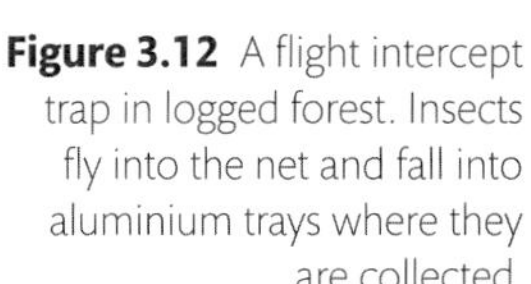

Figure 3.12 A flight intercept trap in logged forest. Insects fly into the net and fall into aluminium trays where they are collected.

A study was carried out in the tropical rainforests of Borneo in the 1990s to investigate the effects on dung beetle communities of logging and conversion to plantation forests. The aim of the investigation was to understand the nature of biological communities in these forest ecosystems, evaluate the effect of human activities and to establish the conservation value of these areas. Beetles were collected using a flight intercept net (Figure 3.12).

The results are shown in Table 3.2.

Trap location	Measurements of species richness and diversity		
	Species richness	Diversity	Evenness
primary forest	36	2.96	0.83
logged forest	42	2.24	0.60
plantation	14	2.05	0.78

Table 3.2 Results of investigation into the effect of human activity on beetles in Borneo rainforests.

Primary forests are forests that are pristine and have not been affected by human activities. Species richness is the number of species, diversity is measured using a diversity index and evenness is a measure of how evenly (equally) abundance is distributed between species. An evenness value of 1 would indicate that all species are equally abundant.

Evenness can be measured by calculating the ratio between the diversity index and a theoretical maximum diversity. Maximum diversity would be found in a situation where all species have equal abundance. Evenness measures therefore range between 0 and 1, with higher values indicating high evenness where all species are equally abundant.

The results showed that species richness was highest in logged areas of forest. This is because disturbed forests contain a variety of species, that are usually separated along environmental gradients and that are not found in one location in primary forest. For example, riverine species, and those found in the canopy, often move into logged areas. However, the low evenness measure from the logged areas show that the species diversity in logged areas is lower than that for primary forests. This indicates that the logged areas are simplified ecosystems where certain species dominate. Plantation forest had the lowest species richness and diversity overall, which indicates a loss of primary forest species and a much simpler ecosystem compared to primary rainforest. This study demonstrates the importance of using species diversity as well as species richness information to compare different areas. Species diversity is a much more robust and accurate method of indicating the health, and therefore conservation value, of ecosystems.

Quantification of biodiversity is important in conservation efforts so that areas of high biodiversity may be identified, explored and appropriate conservation measures put in place where possible.

SKILLS

Calculating Simpson's reciprocal index for diversity

Collect data to work out Simpson's reciprocal index for diversity. See the worksheet in your eBook.

3.1.9 Effective management strategies to conserve biodiversity

Knowledge of global and regional biodiversity is needed for the development of effective management strategies to conserve biodiversity.

Example – Management and conservation of the Kinabalu birdwing butterfly

At 4095 m, Mount Kinabalu is the tallest peak in South-East Asia (Figure 3.13). This mountain shows altitudinal zonation (Topic 2, Section 2.5.1), with tropical rainforest at its lowest elevations, then tropical montane (containing mixed broad-leaved and coniferous evergreen trees) higher up the mountain and alpine communities near the summit. Zonation is caused by changes in temperature, from 26 °C in the rainforest zone to 0 °C at the summit.

Figure 3.13 Mount Kinabalu, Sabah, Malaysia, with montane cloud forest, home of the endemic Kinabalu birdwing butterfly.

Mount Kinabalu is well known worldwide for its tremendous botanical and biological species diversity. For example, botanical studies of the mountain estimate a colossal 5000 to 6000 plant species. There are approximately 600 species of fern on the mountain, which is higher than the total of 500 species of fern found in the whole of Africa.

Because some of the upper communities are isolated from similar communities elsewhere, the mountain has many endemic species unique to its forests, these species are found only on Kinabalu and are not found anywhere else in the world. For example, five of its thirteen pitcher plant (Topic 2, Section 2.1.9, Figure 2.21) species are not found anywhere else on Earth.

Figure 3.14a Female Kinabalu (or Borneo) birdwing (*Troides andromache*), Mountain Valley Resort, Kiau Gap, Sabah, Malaysia.

Figure 3.14b Male Kinabalu birdwing (*Troides andromache*).

The large number of different ecosystems found on the mountain provides a huge variety of different habitats for species to live in. The mountain is therefore an important safe place for many species, and the conservation of the habitats on Kinabalu is essential if an important part of both regional and global biodiversity is to be preserved for the future.

One of the most striking endemic species on the mountain is the Kinabalu (or Borneo) birdwing butterfly (Figures 3.14a and b).

The Kinabalu birdwing is an attractive insect with restricted distribution, although it is found not only on Kinabalu but also on other peaks in Borneo. It is one of the largest butterflies on Earth with females having wingspans up to 185 mm (Figure 3.14a). The butterfly's native habitat is undisturbed cloud forest between 750 m and 2000 m above sea level. In its native habitat, the larvae feed only on the vine *Aristolochia foveolata*, which is found only in the cloud forest in Borneo and occurs in very few places. In forests, adults are rarely seen at ground level as they fly high up in the canopy, feeding on nectar from the flowers of trees and vines. Because the Kinabalu birdwing is only found at high altitude, in cloud forest, its distribution within Borneo is limited, as there are few areas on the island where these conditions are found (Figure 3.15).

Citizen science (Topic 1, Section 1.3.16) is helping to understand the largely unknown life history of the Kinabalu birdwing. The insect is of particular interest to scientists, amateur naturalists and entomotourists (tourists who have an interest in studying and photographing insects), who all record valuable information on new sites for the birdwing and life history information. For example, the first image of a Kinabalu birdwing laying eggs provided evidence that the vine *Aristolochia acuminata* is used as a host plant for the caterpillar of the Kinabalu birdwing.

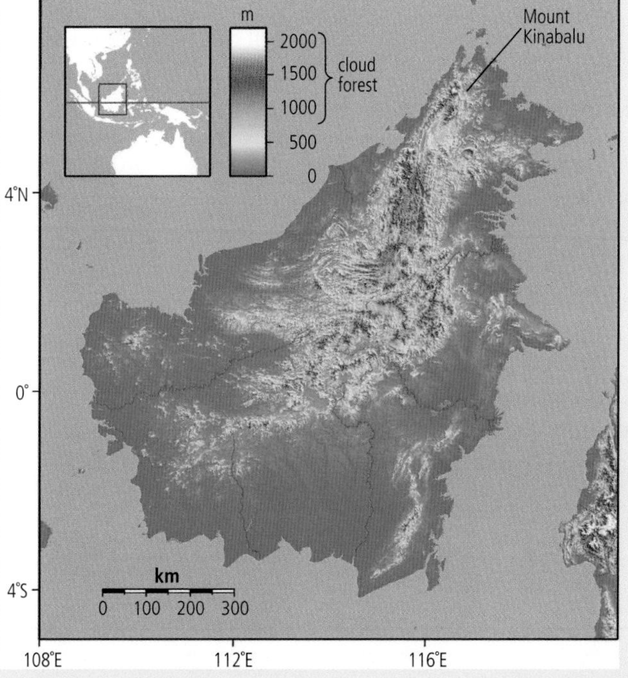

Figure 3.15 Elevation map of Borneo. The montane zone is located between 750 and 2000 m above sea level (the 'cloud forest' zone), which is the elevational niche of the Kinabalu birdwing butterfly (*Troides andromache*). The majority of mountainous terrain in Borneo lies below the 2000 m elevation mark, with only small areas exceeding this altitudinal limit around Mount Kinabalu, Mount Trus Madi and Mount Murud and the summits of a small number of other peaks.

The Kinabalu Birdwing is 'sexually dimorphic', meaning male and female can be easily distinguished by their differing size and colouration. Females have white forewings with a black band on the edge of the wings (Figure 3.14a). The males have black forewings with a number of white 'arrowheads' on the underside of the wings (Figure 3.14b). Both sexes have yellow and black hind wings.

The Mesilau Plateau is an elevated plateau found on the East Ridge of Mount Kinabalu, at approximately 2000 m above sea level, which has patches of forest mixed with vegetable plots and gardens. Although native to primary cloud forest, the Kinabalu birdwing has adapted to this mosaic of habitats on the Mesilau Plateau and finds nectar in the garden flowers, as well as in the forest canopy.

Another area where the birdwing is found is Kampung Kiau – a village that lies to the south-west of Kinabalu National Park. The people of the village are Kadazan-Dusun. Kadazan-Dusun is the largest Indigenous group in the state of Sabah, accounting for approximately 28% of the population. The village has an active homestay business that has helped to improve the socio-economic status of the villagers over the last few years. Homestay is a concept of local lodging where the guest is accommodated in the family's residence or in a separate house nearby. Above the kebuns (smallholdings) of the Kampung Kiau Homestays is a tract of montane forest, 1500 m above sea level. This montane forest is a conservation habitat for the birdwing. Voluntary and government-funded agencies are working with homestay operators in the village to grow the host plant of the Kinabalu birdwing caterpillar, so that paying visitors coming to photograph these giant butterflies can provide a new, sustainable income for villagers. By increasing the number of caterpillars on host plants, the number of adult butterflies will be increased. By helping to breed birdwing butterflies and raise an income, the project aims to conserve not only the birdwing butterfly, but also the montane forest above the village. The training of homestay owners to breed the birdwings has also been linked to more general nature tourism training in the field, such as bird guide training courses. In addition to conserving the Kinabalu birdwing, promoting public awareness of the project will help gain the attention of the state authorities and encourage them to consider whether deforestation should continue in the area.

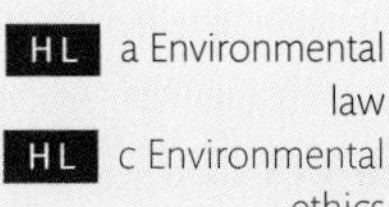

HL a Environmental law
HL c Environmental ethics

Loss of forest habitat is a serious concern for the Borneo birdwing butterfly. Because it is only found in restricted montane forest ecosystems, loss of this habitat could lead to the loss of this important species. Tourism is one of the sources of income for the state of Sabah. By taking urgent, mitigating steps to conserve their natural heritage, and promoting this 'icon' of the natural world to its visitors (over 3 million tourists per year), ecotourism could play a vital role in sustaining its existing ecosystems and biodiversity.

Knowledge of biodiversity is gathered in the local region by involving citizen science (Topic 1, Section 1.3.16) and the work of voluntary and government-funded agencies. Indigenous people and scientists such as parabiologists are also trained and used to gather information for use in conservation management.

You can read more about the Borneo birdwing project on the Swallowtail and Birdwing Butterfly Trust's website.

HL

HL

3.1.10 Mutation and sexual reproduction increase genetic diversity

Mutation

DNA, found in the nucleus of every cell in the body, is the molecule of inheritance. DNA forms **chromosomes**, which are lengths of DNA that carry genes in a linear sequence, forming the genetic code. Sections of chromosomes that code for particular characteristics in the body are known as genes (Figure 3.16a). Humans have 23 pairs of chromosomes in their DNA.

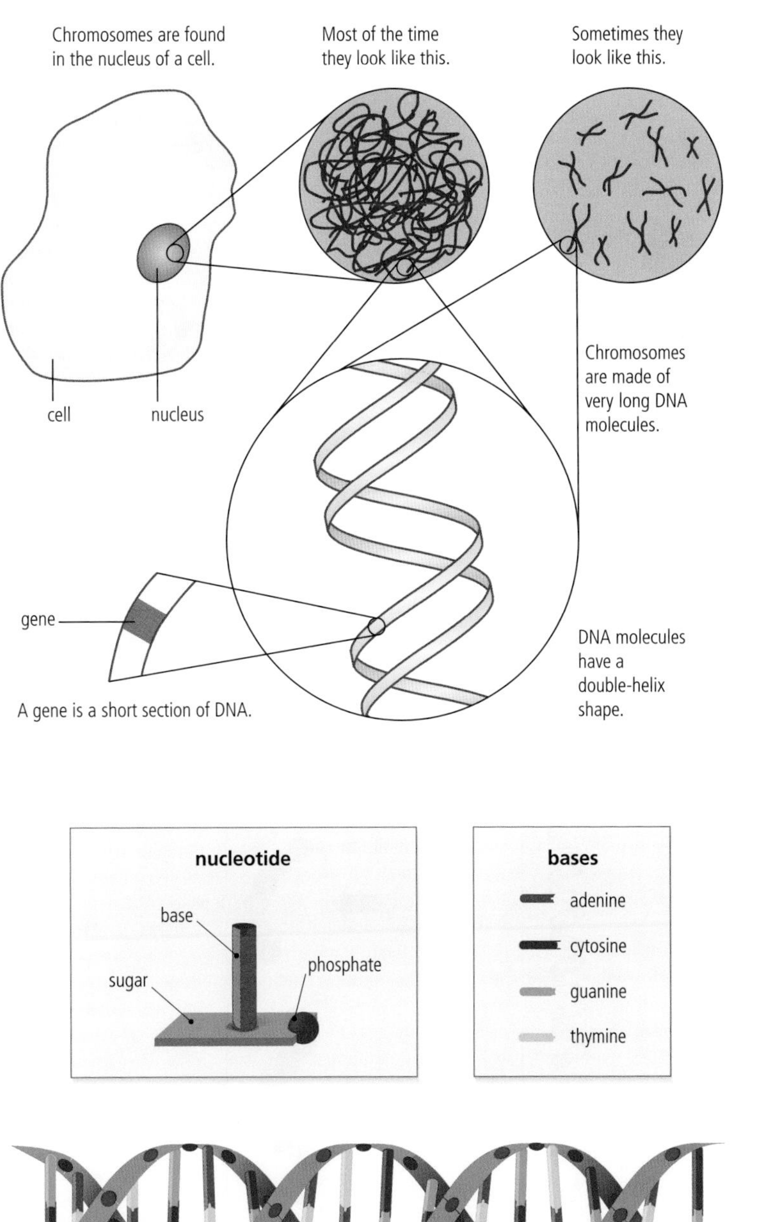
Chromosomes are found in the nucleus of a cell.
Most of the time they look like this.
Sometimes they look like this.
cell
nucleus
Chromosomes are made of very long DNA molecules.
gene
A gene is a short section of DNA.
DNA molecules have a double-helix shape.
nucleotide
base
sugar
phosphate
bases
adenine
cytosine
guanine
thymine
thymine
adenine
guanine
cytosine

Figure 3.16a DNA forms chromosomes in the nucleus of cells. Small lengths of DNA that code for particular characteristics are known as genes.

Figure 3.16b The structure of DNA.

DNA is a complex molecule made up of many repeating units. Each repeating unit of DNA is known as a nucleotide (Figure 3.16b). Each unit is made from a sugar (deoxyribose), a phosphate group and a nitrogenous base. There are four different bases: adenine (A), guanine (G), cytosine (C) and thymine (T).

Proteins are important molecules in the structure and functioning of organisms. Each protein is made from a long sequence of building blocks known as amino acids (Figure 3.17a). The order in which the bases appear in DNA determines the order in which amino acids are assembled to form proteins (Figure 3.17b). Because different genes contain different sequence of bases, each gene codes for a different protein (Figure 3.17c).

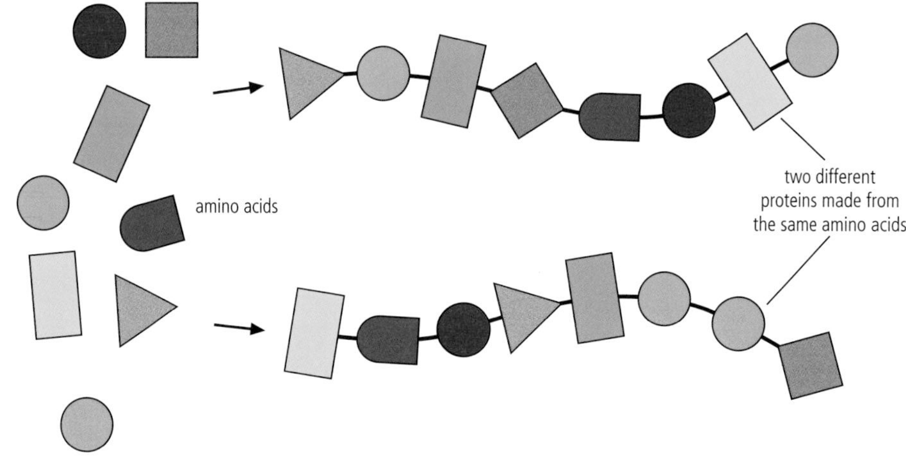

Figure 3.17a Amino acids are the building blocks of proteins. Proteins are a structural molecule of organisms. The order in which amino acids are joined together determines which proteins are made.

sequence of bases
C T A C G A A T T C C G C T A T T C
base
16 9 5 3 16 1
protein
amino acid

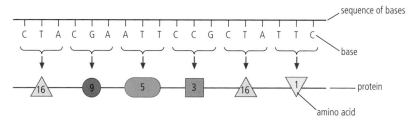

Figure 3.17b The genetic code (the sequence of bases) determines the assembly of proteins. The numbers represent different amino acids (there are 20 different naturally occurring amino acids).

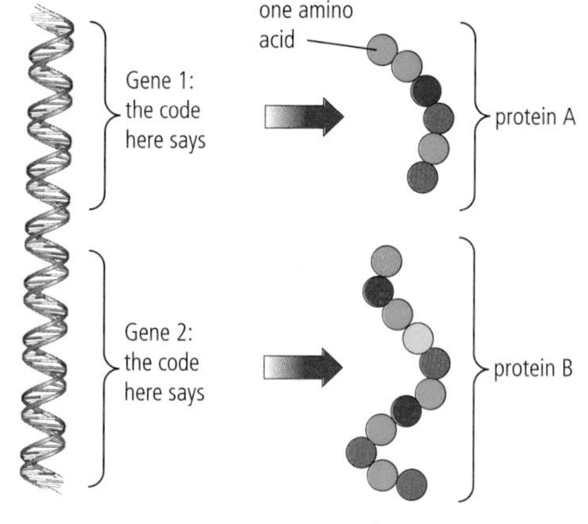

Figure 3.17c Different genes produce different proteins. This figure shows two genes in a section of DNA and the corresponding proteins they code for.

Mutation generates new variants of genes and sexual reproduction generates new combinations of genes.

Mutation occurs when the order of the bases in DNA changes. This can be caused by copying errors in DNA such as the genetic code being incorrectly copied during DNA replication or by external factors such as radiation or mutagenic chemicals. The genetic code therefore causes differences in the proteins assembled, which in turn can affect the structure and function of the organism.

Sections of DNA that code for particular proteins or characteristics are known as genes (this topic, Section 3.1.1). Mutations can alter a gene so they become a different version, or allele, of the gene (Figure 3.18). For example, the original eye colour in humans was brown, but a mutation led to an alteration in the gene for eye colour that reduced the amount of pigment (melanin) in the iris of the eye. Less melanin in the iris gives blue eyes.

Mutations can create different alleles and therefore increase variation. From this variation, natural selection can select alleles that give an individual, and therefore a population, a selective advantage.

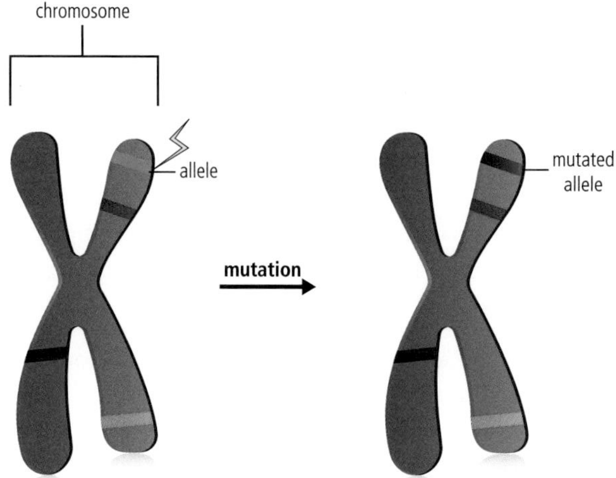

Figure 3.18 Mutations create variation.

Sexual reproduction

There are two types of reproduction – asexual and sexual. The first type of reproduction that evolved was **asexual reproduction**, which occurs in bacteria as well as in some plants and animals. In asexual reproduction there is only one parent. As all of the genetic material comes from this parent, the offspring are always genetically identical to the parent and no variation is produced.

In **sexual reproduction**, the genetic material in the gametes, or sex cells, from the two parents is combined during the process of fertilization. Each gamete produced by an individual is genetically different from every other gamete and so, depending on which gametes (sperm or pollen from the male organism and eggs/ova from the female) fuse together during fertilization, different offspring will be created. The combination of this DNA means that the offspring are genetically different to the parents and every offspring is genetically different from other offspring from the same parents. This results in variation (Figure 3.19).

There are two different types of cell division: mitosis and meiosis. Mitosis produces cells that are genetically identical to the parent cell (for growth and tissue repair), whilst meiosis results in the production of sex cells (gametes) that are genetically different from the original cell. Meiosis reorders alleles from the original cell (in a process called crossing over), with further genetic variation created in the way that maternal and paternal chromosomes separate into gametes (known as random orientation).

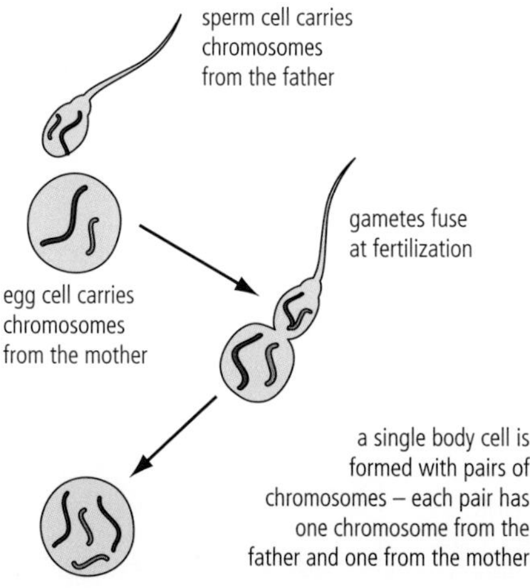

Figure 3.19 Sexual reproduction creates variation.

HL

3.1.11 Reproductive isolation

Natural selection, on its own, is insufficient for speciation to occur. The process of natural selection needs to act on isolated populations for evolution to occur.

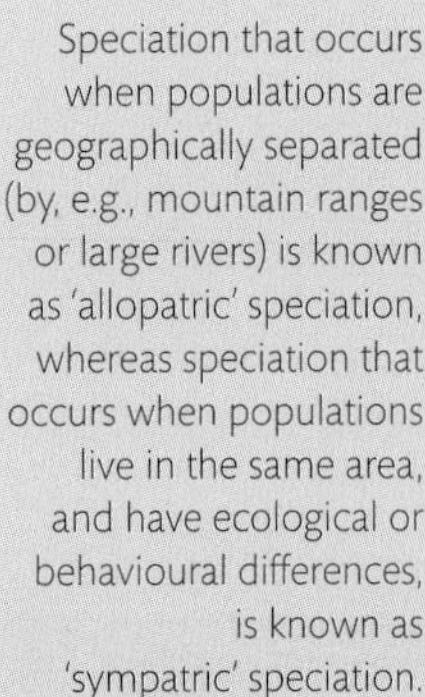

Speciation that occurs when populations are geographically separated (by, e.g., mountain ranges or large rivers) is known as 'allopatric' speciation, whereas speciation that occurs when populations live in the same area, and have ecological or behavioural differences, is known as 'sympatric' speciation.

Giraffes do not provide a suitable example of speciation due to reproductive isolation because they illustrate evolutionary change rather than speciation. The evolution of species on the Galápagos Islands, such as the finches, is a good example of speciation where individuals on separate islands become reproductively isolated.

The process of speciation requires separate populations to become reproductively isolated. This means that two or more populations become separated so that they can no longer mix and breed together. Over time, selective pressures, which will be different for each isolated population, lead to the isolated populations adapting to the different environmental conditions. This in turn leads to selection for particular alleles. Over many generations, changes to the gene pool of an isolated population leads the population to become genetically distinct from the other populations. The changes to the gene pool occur to such an extent that, should the isolated populations encounter each other, they would be unable to breed together to produce fertile offspring. Speciation has therefore occurred.

Reproductive isolation can be achieved by geographical separation or, for populations living in the same area, by ecological or behavioural differences.

Geographical separation

Altitudinal environmental gradients on mountains lead to different communities forming at different heights (Topic 2, Sections 2.4.7, 2.5.1, and Figure 3.6, this topic, Section 3.1.6). When mountains come into existence, they provide new environments for natural selection to act on. Sea level changes caused by climate change have led to higher altitude areas becoming isolated as sea levels rise or have provided land bridges for migration of species to new areas when sea levels drop and once-separated areas of land join up. Environmental change produces new challenges for species. Those that are suited survive and those that are not suited become extinct. The same process takes place whenever environmental change occurs, whether it is by barrier formation (e.g. mountains; sea level change), climatic change or the movement of tectonic plates (covered later in this section).

The islands of the Galápagos are quite widely separated and very different from each other (Figure 3.20). This means that animal and plant populations that arrived from mainland South America (ancestral populations) became geographically isolated from each other. For example, an ancestral population of mockingbirds arriving from the mainland would have spread onto several different islands. As local environmental and

Figure 3.20 The Galápagos Islands.

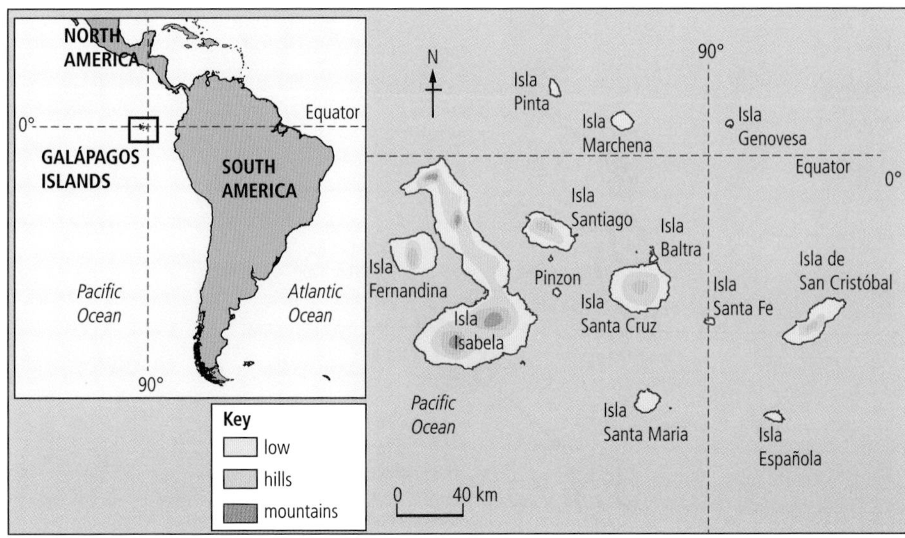

biological conditions were different on each island, different species evolved to fulfil different ecological niches. The islands are 1060 kilometres from the mainland and the distances between them are sufficiently large to make it difficult for the geographically isolated populations on different islands to interbreed. Thus 'gene flow', the exchange of genetic material through interbreeding, would be limited.

Geographical separation is caused by a physical barrier, such as a mountain range, which causes populations to become separated.

Geographical separation is essential in the formation of new species. Without it, interbreeding would cause the genes from two populations to continue to mix (Figure 3.21) and characteristics of the ancestral species to remain.

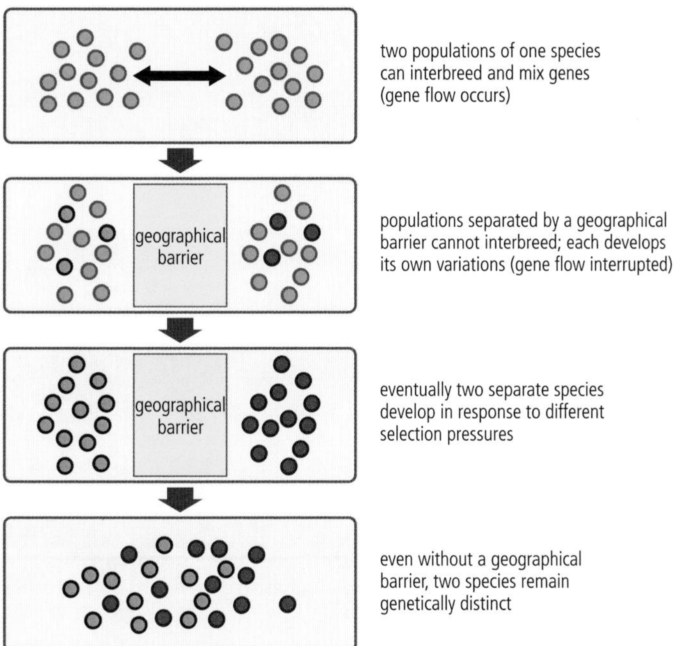

two populations of one species can interbreed and mix genes (gene flow occurs)
geographical barrier
populations separated by a geographical barrier cannot interbreed; each develops its own variations (gene flow interrupted)
geographical barrier
eventually two separate species develop in response to different selection pressures
even without a geographical barrier, two species remain genetically distinct

Figure 3.21 Geographical barriers include mountains, island formation, water (sea, river or lake) or a hostile environment.

Activity

Separation of bonobos and common chimpanzees is an example of speciation by geographical separation.

Find out about this example of geographical separation. What was the barrier that separated the populations? What selective forces led to the evolution of two distinct species – chimpanzees and bonobo?

Produce an A3 poster of this example of geographical separation.

The Pleistocene ice ages, which began 2.6 million years ago, caused a fall in sea levels due to a decrease in temperature and large amounts of water becoming locked up in ice caps and glaciers above sea level. This resulted in the formation of a land bridge (Beringia) between previously separated Alaska and eastern Siberia (Figure 3.22). It is possible that the earliest human colonizers of the Americas entered from Asia via this route. Between about 17,000 and 25,000 years ago, the Borneo, Java and Sumatra islands of South-East Asia were connected to the mainland of Asia to form one land mass, which we call Sundaland (Figure 3.23). This land bridge was also caused by a drop in sea levels due to climate change. In both cases, as sea levels rose again, the land bridges were lost and the areas became isolated once more.

i Two separate supercontinents had formed during the breakup of Pangaea (Earth's first land mass), Laurasia and Gondwana (see Figure 3.25, later in this section). The archipelago of islands, from Sumatra in the west to New Guinea in the east (see Figure 3.23) was formed from both Laurasian and Gondwanic elements. During his travels in South-East Asia, naturalist Alfred Russel Wallace (this topic, Section 3.1.4) noted differences in plants and animals between Gondwanic and Laurasian areas. He drew a line, now known as the 'Wallace Line', through the Lombok Strait (between the islands of Bali and Lombok) and northward through the Makassar Strait (between Borneo and Sulawesi). The line separates Sundaland from islands to the east, including Bali, as well as Australia. The Wallace line therefore separates species found in Australia and Papua New Guinea from those found in South-East Asia: differences that can be explained by the separate land masses on which they originated.

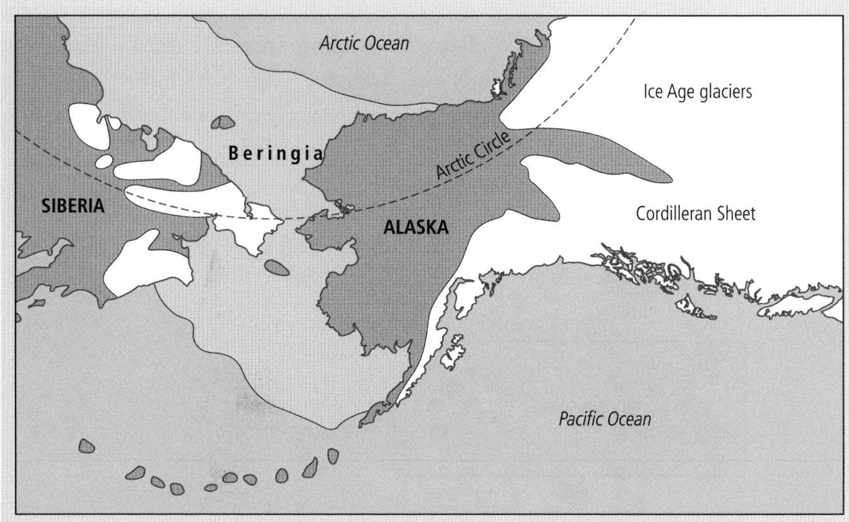

Figure 3.22 A land bridge formed between Siberia and Alaska during the Pleistocene ice age.

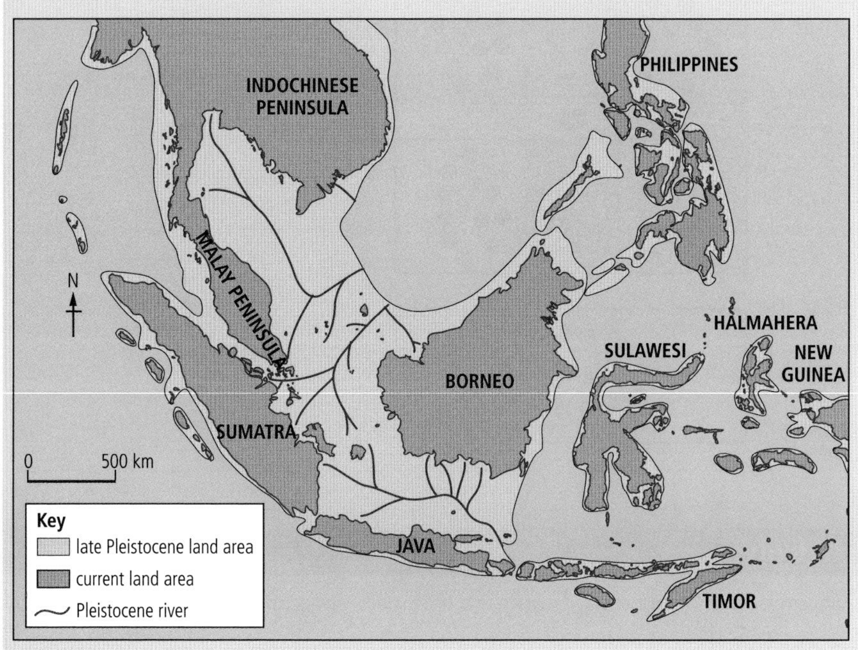

Figure 3.23 Lower sea levels during the late Pleistocene led to mainland Asia joining with the islands of Sumatra, Java and Borneo.

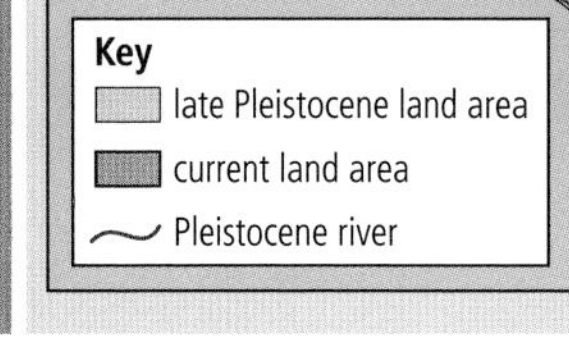

Isolation of populations can be caused by environmental change such as mountain formation, change in river courses, sea level change, climatic change or plate movements.

3.3 Conservation and regeneration

Plate tectonics

Let's now consider how movement of the Earth's tectonic plates creates mountains and other phenomena that lead to the isolation of populations and speciation.

The surface of the Earth is divided into tectonic plates, which have moved throughout geological time. This has led to the creation of both physical barriers and land bridges with evolutionary consequences.

The outer layer of the Earth, the crust (lithosphere), is divided into eight major and many minor plates (Figure 3.24), which vary in size and shape but which can move relative to each other. The plates are carried on the mantle (asthenosphere) beneath them, which can flow like a liquid on geological timescales. The edges of adjacent plates can move parallel to each other, be pushed one under the other or collide. Earthquakes, volcanoes and mountain-building occur at these boundaries. The movement and forming and reforming of these plates is known as **plate tectonics**.

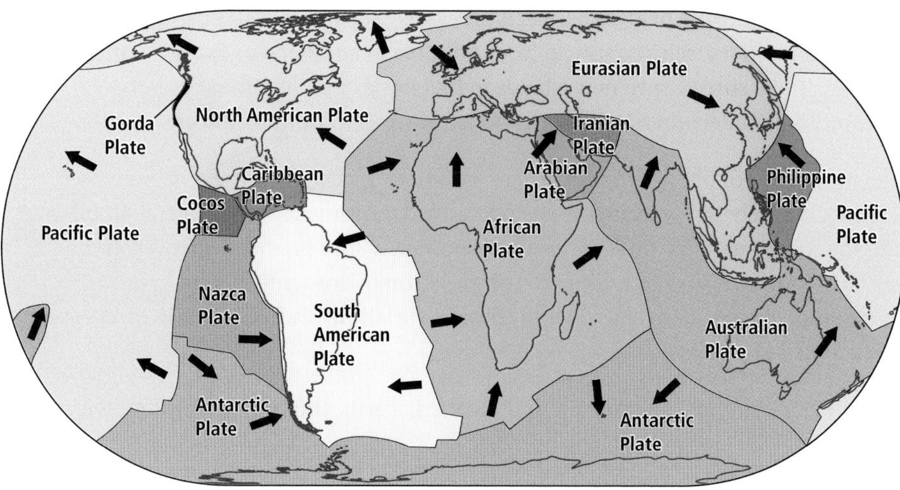

Figure 3.24 Earth's tectonic plates.

During the Paleozoic and Mesozoic eras (about 250 million years ago) all land mass on Earth existed as one supercontinent, Pangaea (Figure 3.25). This name is derived from the Greek for 'entire'. About 175 million years ago, the land mass split into two separate supercontinents, Laurasia and Gondwana. Laurasia contained the land that became North America, Eurasia (Europe and Asia) and Greenland. Gondwana contained the land that became South America, Africa, Australia, Antarctica and India. The distribution of all extinct and extant, still living, species found in these geographical areas today can be explained in terms of these ancient land masses.

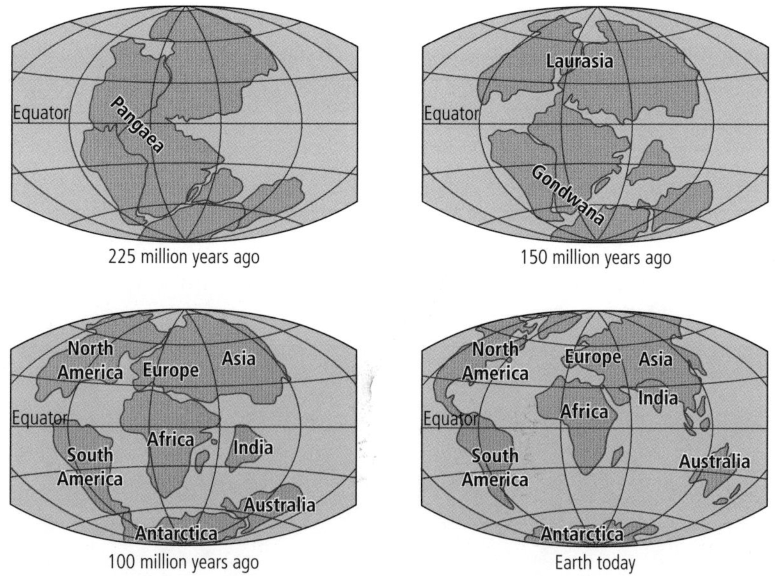

Figure 3.25 Continental drift from 225 million years ago to the present day.

Mount Everest (Figure 3.26), the world's tallest mountain at nearly 9000 metres, has been created over 40 million years by the collision between the Indian and Eurasian plates. The rocks on the summit are 50-million-year-old limestones that formed in the shallow waters of an ocean that once lay between India and Asia. The Himalayas are a physical barrier that has led to the separation of populations and the evolution of new species. This is also true of mountain-building in general.

Figure 3.26 Mount Everest.

Movement of the tectonic plates can produce barriers such as mountain ranges, oceans and rift valleys that lead to isolation of gene pools and then speciation. Separation of the plates can also lead to isolation and the development or preservation of unique species. For example, the separation of Australia led to the preservation of its distinctive flora and fauna, including eucalypts, monotremes and marsupials such as kangaroos. Similarly, Madagascar is the only place where lemurs are found today.

The movement of the Earth's plates has caused isolation of populations, climatic variations and variation in food supply, contributing to evolution of biological *systems* and new biodiversity.

TOK

What role do experts play in influencing our consumption or acquisition of knowledge?

Evidence for the role of plate tectonics in contributing to speciation can be interpreted from the fossil record and from the current distribution of organisms around the planet. Before the continental drift hypothesis, there was no satisfactory explanation of the distribution of life forms. Why, therefore, didn't scientists establish such a hypothesis earlier?

The formation of land bridges between previously separated plates can provide opportunities for species to spread from one area to another. For example, species from Australia spread onto new islands in Indonesia, and the similarity between caribou and reindeer (in Alaska and Siberia) suggests a common ancestry.

The movement of plates through different climatic zones allows new habitats to present themselves. For example, the northward movement of the Australian plate and the subsequent drying of much of the continent, has provided changes in the selective forces on species leading to the evolution of drought-tolerant species. The distribution of continents has caused climatic variations and variation in food supply, both contributing to evolution.

Plate movement can generate new and diverse habitats, thus promoting biodiversity

Endemism on isolated islands

The term **endemism** refers to species that are found in one geographical area and nowhere else. Islands have high levels of endemism. This is because populations of islands are geographically isolated and so cannot interbreed with populations elsewhere. Over time, selective pressures lead to changes in the genetic makeup and physical appearance of these populations, which results in speciation. The finches and other species of the Galápagos Islands are examples of endemic species evolving on isolated islands (as we saw earlier in this section).

Figure 3.27 Ring-tailed lemur in Madagascar.

Madagascar is a large island that has been isolated for almost 100 million years. Levels of endemism on Madagascar are some of the highest in the world, with all of the island's amphibians and terrestrial mammals, 83% of plant species and 86% of larger invertebrates found nowhere else. The lemurs are one of the best-known groups of endemic animals in Madagascar (Figure 3.27).

The Komodo dragon (Figure 3.28) is a large reptile that is endemic to five islands in Indonesia, South-East Asia. Four of those islands (Komodo, Nusa Kode, Gili Motang and Rinca) form the Komodo National Park. Island species are often larger than mainland species due to lack of predation or competition with other animals.

Figure 3.28 A Komodo dragon in the Komodo National Park.

Ecological and behavioural differences

As well as geographical separation, other separating mechanisms exist that cause speciation. Speciation can take place in populations that are not separated by geographical barriers and exist in the same location. For example, behavioural differences that emerge between populations can lead to reproductive isolation.

Differences in the courtship displays shown by birds of paradise (Figure 3.29) have led to the evolution of numerous species within the same forest. Male birds of paradise have bright and colourful feathers that they use to attract females and different species also have different dancing displays. Changes in the appearance or behaviour of populations may result in the males and females of those populations no longer being attracted to each other and therefore not breeding together.

Ecological differences can also emerge between populations. For example, species may become separated along environmental gradients. In the rainforests of Borneo, a group of dung beetles (Figure 3.30) have become adapted to living in the canopy, where environmental conditions are very different from those on the ground. This group are an example of isolation and speciation occurring within the same forest ecosystem as they are separate from ground-living dung beetles, which also live in the rainforest.

Figure 3.29 A male Raggiana bird of paradise displaying his plumage to a female. The male bird is brightly coloured but the female is plain. Alfred Russel Wallace was one of the first naturalists to observe these and other species of birds of paradise in the wild.

Visit the Birds of Paradise Project's website and search for 'dance' to watch videos of bird of paradise mating rituals.

Figure 3.30 These male and female dung beetles, which live in the canopy of the Borneo rainforest, are working together to make a ball from primate dung.

Activity

The apple maggot (*Rhagoletis pomonella*) is an example of behavioural separation.

Find out about the apple maggot.

- Where is it found?
- How has it become behaviourally isolated?
- What are the selective pressures that have acted on it and led to speciation?

Produce an A3 poster about the apple maggot and how it is an example of behavioural separation.

HL

3.1.12 Biodiversity hotspots

The Earth's biodiversity is being rapidly diminished through human action such as pollution, the introduction of invasive species, overharvesting of natural populations, habitat loss and fragmentation. Biodiversity is spread unevenly across the planet and certain areas contain a particularly large proportion of the Earth's biodiversity, especially species that are rare and endangered. Given limited time and resources to address environmental threats in all areas, scientists have proposed that these key **'biodiversity hotspots'** should be specifically targeted for protection. Conserving these biodiversity hotspots allows a significant proportion of existing species to be preserved for the future because these areas contain a significant proportion of the Earth's biodiversity (Figure 3.31).

Figure 3.31 Biodiversity hotspots – 36 areas have so far been designated.

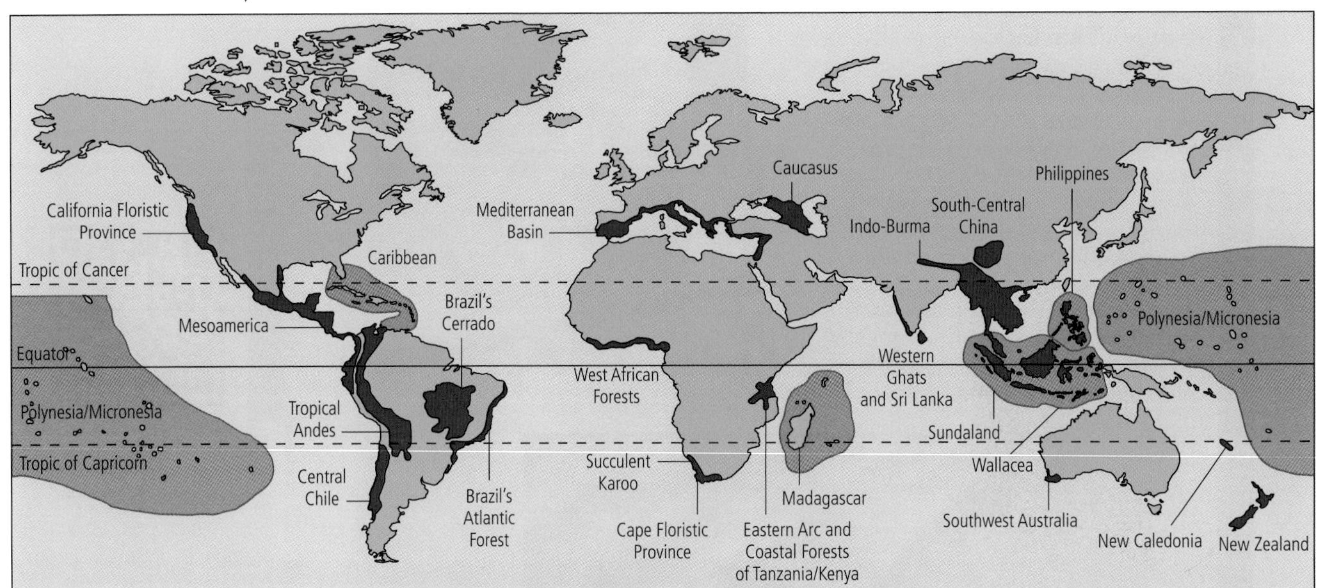

Activity

What are the criteria for defining an area as a 'biodiversity hotspot'?

Search for 'biodiversity hotspots defined' on the Critical Ecosystem Partnership Fund website:

- Summarize the two criteria used.

Research a biodiversity hotspot in your local or regional area, or one elsewhere that you find interesting, and create a fact file.

- How does it meet the criteria for a biodiversity hotspot?
- Is the designation helping to conserve habitats and species in the area?

Many biodiversity hotspots are found in tropical biomes. By being on or near the equator, tropical biomes receive the optimal conditions for photosynthesis – warm (but not too hot), plenty of rainfall and sunshine throughout the year – so productivity is high. This produces biomass that enables complex ecosystems to develop, which supports a large diversity of species. The high input of energy ensures enough food is supplied to support intricate food chains.

1.1 Perspectives

3.1.13 Human impacts on the selective forces acting on species

HL

Human activities have impacted the selective forces acting on species within ecosystems, resulting in evolutionary change in these species.

Example – The tuskless elephants in Gorongosa, Mozambique

Elephant populations contain a mix of tusked and non-tusked elephants. Tusks provide a selective advantage to elephants, providing a threat and defensive weapon that allows them to survive against predators. Tuskless elephants (Figure 3.32) are usually in a minority.

Figure 3.32 African elephant herd with tuskless matriarch.

In Mozambique, Africa, an elephant population has been studied in the Gorongosa National Park. A civil war took place in Mozambique between 1977 and 1992. Before the war, approximately 18.5% of female African elephants were naturally tuskless but this figure has risen to 33% among elephants born since the early 1990s (Figure 3.33).

Around 90% of Mozambique's elephant population was killed by fighters on both sides of the civil war. Poachers targeted tusked elephants for ivory, which they could sell to fund the conflict between government forces and anti-communist guerrillas. About 200 of an estimated 2500 elephants in Gorongosa survived the 15-year-long war. Tusklessness was therefore a selective advantage, as an individual was less likely to be killed by poachers if it did not have tusks. Because poachers were preferentially killing animals with tusks and leaving tuskless ones to survive, the tuskless individuals were breeding and producing more tuskless offspring. In this way, humans were artificially selecting tuskless animals (this topic, Section 3.1.14). After the civil war, the number of tuskless females tripled.

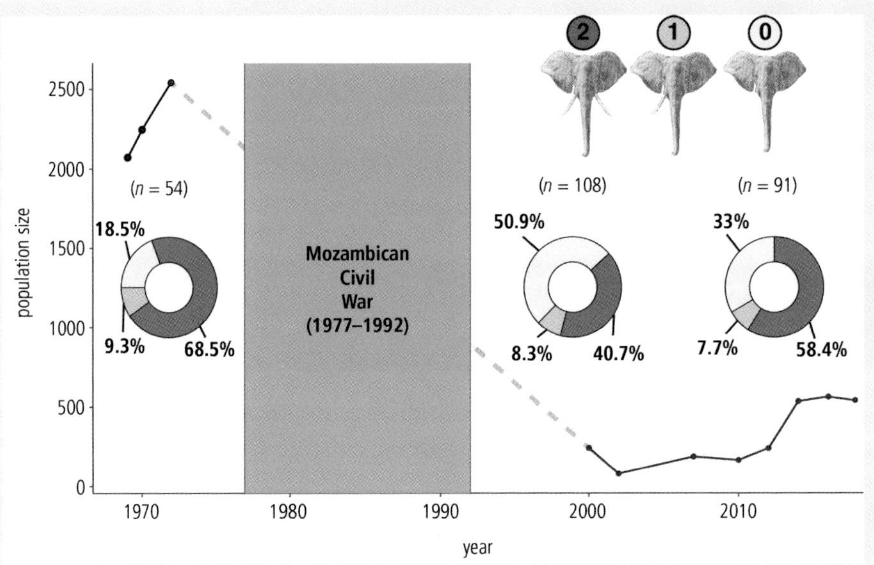

Figure 3.33 Change in population size and number of tusks of elephants in the Gorongosa National Park, Mozambique. The line shows the minimum elephant population size by year from an aerial census. The dashed line indicates a period for which no reliable census data are available. The pie charts show the proportion of two-tusked (dark blue), single-tusked (blue) and tuskless (light blue) females observed pre-war (sample size = 54 individuals), in survivors of the war (sample size = 108) and in the first generation born post-war (sample size = 91), based on recent surveys and historical photos.

Genes are responsible for whether elephants inherit tusks from their parents, in the same way that different alleles (variations of the same gene) determine eye colour and blood type in humans. Analysis of elephant DNA has indicated that the trend in tuskless elephants was linked to a mutation on the X chromosome that was fatal to males, who then did not develop properly in the womb, and dominant in females. Because the tuskless characteristic was fatal to male offspring, it was possible that fewer elephants would be born overall. This could slow the recovery of the species, whose population now stands at just over 700 in the park.

Another potential knock-on effect of this artificial selection is changes to the habitat in which the elephants live, with research indicating that tusked and tuskless animals eat different plant species. An increase in tuskless elephants may therefore change the vegetational mix of the ecosystem, resulting in shifts in plant species composition, reduced spatial heterogeneity and increased tree cover. Evolution in species that perform key ecological functions has had significant effects on food-web structure, community composition and nutrient transport. Therefore, changes to the elephant population can be expected to have similar impacts.

Read more about the selection for tuskless elephants by searching for 'Mozambique tuskless elephants' on the Mongabay website:

Read about the tuskless elephants of Gorongosa in the following research article: Campbell-Station, S.C. et al. (2021) Ivory poaching and the rapid evolution of tusklessness in African elephants. *Science*, Vol 374, Issue 6566, pp. 483–487.

3.2 Human impact on biodiversity

Activity

Find a local or regional example of how human activities have affected natural selection. Examples of selection pressures can include climate change due to burning fossil fuels, hunting, poaching, overharvesting and the creation of new habitats.

HL b Environmental economics
HL c Environmental ethics

- What selection pressure(s) have been created by humanity's actions?
- How have these selection pressures affected species populations?
- Will the new conditions lead to the evolution of new species over time?
- What effect will the impacts on natural selection have on the ecosystem?

Produce a presentation about your example, to show to the rest of your class.

3.1.14 Artificial selection

HL

Artificial selection, also known as selective breeding, is carried out deliberately by humans. Artificial selection has been used for thousands of years to modify the genetic makeup of species by selecting favourable characteristics (Figure 3.34), providing humans with improved crops and livestock. Artificial selection produces species with desired features such as disease resistance or improved milk yield.

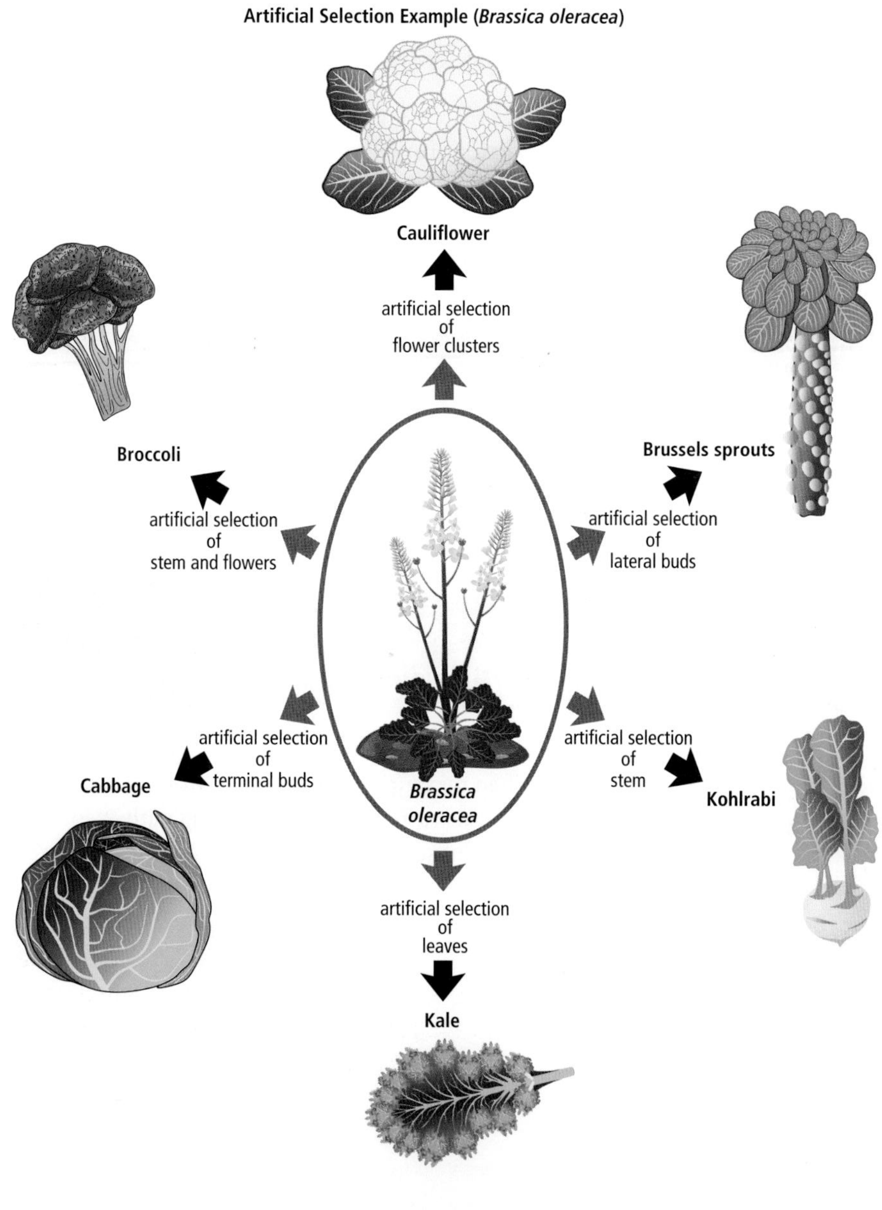

Artificial Selection Example (*Brassica oleracea*)

Figure 3.34 Artificial selection of wild mustard (*Brassica oleracea*) has created different types of vegetable.

Charles Darwin had observed that humans can select for different breeds of animals and that if this **artificial selection** could lead to new varieties then there was no reason, given sufficient amounts of time, that nature could not select for new species (hence natural selection). Selective breeding provided Darwin with evidence to support his theory of evolution by natural selection. Humans have created hundreds, if not thousands, of varieties of different species by selecting desirable characteristics in organisms and then cross breeding these organisms with similar individuals (Figure 3.34).

4.3 Aquatic food production systems
5.2 Agriculture and food

Selective breeding works in the following way.

- An animal or plant with a desired feature, for example disease resistance, is selected.
- This individual is bred with another individual that has similar desirable characteristics.
- The offspring that have inherited the desired gene are identified.
- These offspring are bred together.
- Selected offspring are continued to be bred together. Other individuals are not allowed to reproduce.
- This process increases the number of animals or plants with the desired feature.
- This process is continued over many generations.

Artificial selection reduces genetic diversity and consequently species resilience.

Natural selection can be distinguished from artificial selection in the following ways.

- Natural selection is not deliberate, whereas artificial selection is the deliberate act of choosing individual plants or animals for breeding.
- Natural selection results in new speciation, whereas artificial selection produces new varieties of the same species.

Organisms produced by artificial selection are often prone to diseases or other vulnerabilities. The vulnerability of artificially selected species (livestock or crops) highlights the importance of genetic diversity to preserve resilience within a population.

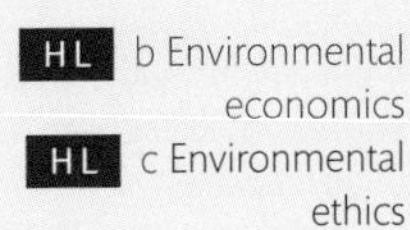

Activity

Using an example of artificial selection, consider the value of genetic diversity from both an economic and environmental perspective.

Produce an illustrated summary of your findings.

HL

3.1.15 and 3.1.16 The geological timescale – eons and epochs

The evolution of life on Earth has happened as a result of processes that occurred over a period of 4.5 billion years. When measuring time on a day-to-day basis, the use of days, hours, minutes and seconds is sufficient. When dealing with events that occurred over millions of years, a different set of measurements is needed. This set of measurements makes up the geological timescale (see the figure on this page of your eBook).

Fossils are used to explain the evolution of life over the geological timescale and have helped to define the different periods within it (Figure 3.35).

The movement and forming and reforming of the Earth's plates is known as plate tectonics (this topic, Section 3.1.11, pages 352–354). The theory was developed by Alfred Wegener (1880–1930), who used fossil evidence to support his 'continental drift' hypothesis. The fossils of these organisms looked similar but were found in areas that are now far apart. Wegener was able to use this fossil evidence to hypothesize what the land mass of the ancient Earth, millions of years ago, would have looked like compared to today (Figure 3.36).

The geological timescale is divided into **eons**, which are further classified into **eras**, **periods** and **epochs**. Changes in these time frames are marked by major geological and biological events (Figure 3.36). The division between one epoch and the next is marked by significant changes in the fossil record, which indicate that environmental changes have caused many extinctions and the evolution of new species.

Fossils are the remains or impressions of species preserved in rock. The rock is formed over millions of years, from sediments that covered and protected the organisms after they died allowing hard tissue, such as bones, teeth and shells, to be preserved and eventually replaced by minerals from the sediment. The soft parts of the organism, such as skin and muscle tissue, are generally not preserved. Footprints and other marks left by organisms can also fossilize.

Earth history is divided up into geological epochs according to the fossil record.

1. When an organism dies, such as this fish, it falls to the bottom of the sea bed and is buried by mud or sand.

2. Hard parts may be preserved, such as teeth and bones. The soft parts decay and so are not preserved. Further layers of sediment cover the fish.

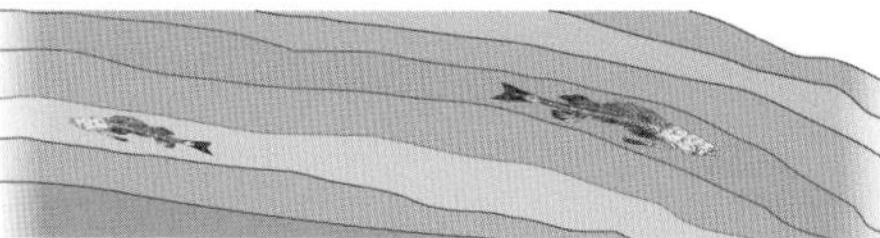

3. The sediments are compressed to form rocks, over millions of years.

4. Later, earth movements raise the rocks to above sea level. When the rock erodes, the fossil fish is exposed.

Figure 3.35 The process of fossilization, showing how a species of fish can become fossilized.

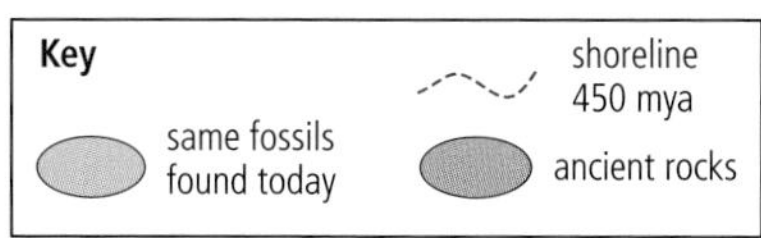

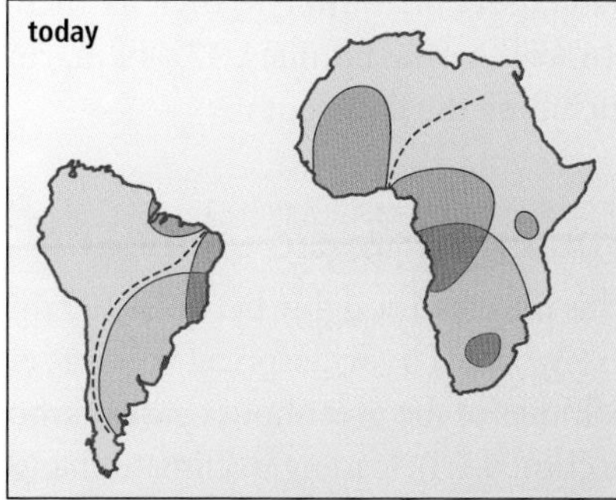

△ How the continents are today.

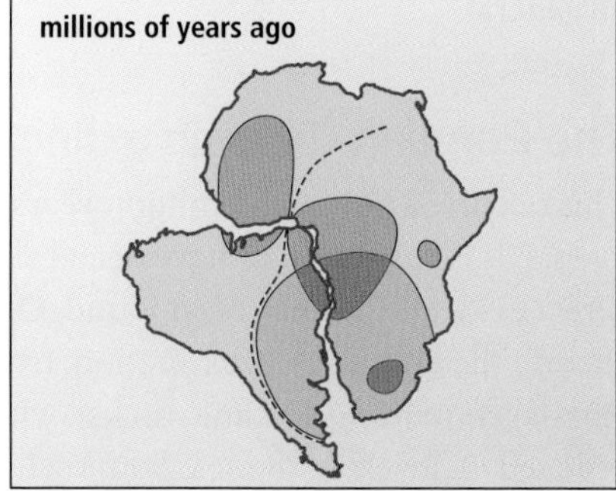

△ How Wegener thought the land must have been millions of years ago.

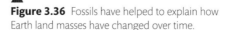

Figure 3.36 Fossils have helped to explain how Earth land masses have changed over time.

HL

3.1.17 Mass extinctions

A **mass extinction** is a period in which at least 75% of the total number of species on Earth at the time are wiped out.

Mass extinctions are followed by rapid rates of speciation due to increased niche availability.

A **mass extinction** is a period in which at least 75% of the total number of species on Earth at the time have been wiped out. The fossil record shows that over millions of years, there have been five mass extinctions, caused by natural physical (abiotic) phenomena. In mass extinctions, species disappear in a geologically short time period, usually between a few hundred thousand to a few million years. Mass extinctions of the past have been caused by factors such as tectonic movements, super-volcanic eruptions, climate change and meteorite impact.

The Cretaceous–Tertiary extinction

This occurred about 65 million years ago and was probably caused by the impact of a several-mile-wide asteroid that created a huge crater, which is now hidden beneath the Gulf of Mexico. Dust thrown into the atmosphere by the impact would have led to a reduction in the amount of sunlight reaching the Earth's surface, causing a drop in temperature. There may also have been flood-like volcanic eruptions of basalt lava from India's Deccan Traps, leading to climate change through the increased emission of greenhouse gases. It is also possible that tectonic plate movements caused a major rearrangement of the world's land masses, resulting in climatic changes that could have caused a gradual deterioration of dinosaur habitats, contributing to their extinction. The extinction killed 76% of all species (16% of marine families, 47% of marine genera and 18% of land vertebrate families, including the dinosaurs).

The End Triassic extinction

This occurred roughly between 199 million and 214 million years ago and was most likely caused by widespread volcanic eruptions, which resulted in the release of huge volumes of the greenhouse gases carbon dioxide (CO_2) and methane (CH_4) (Topic 6, Section 6.1.3), leading to climate change. The increase in CO_2 also caused acidification of the oceans. The extinction killed 80% of all species (23% of all families and 48% of all genera).

The Permian–Triassic extinction

This occurred about 251 million years ago and was the largest of these extinction events. It is suspected to have been caused by a comet or asteroid impact, although direct evidence has not been found. Others believe the cause was volcanic activity, as with the End Triassic extinction, from the Siberian Traps (a large area of Siberia, Russia, containing volcanic rocks), which destroyed algae and plants, and therefore reduced O_2 levels in the sea. Some scientists believe that plate movement may have contributed to the Permian extinction. The joining of all the land masses to create the supercontinent Pangaea (this topic, Section 3.1.11, Figure 3.25), which occurred sometime before the Permian extinction, would have led to environmental change on the new land mass, especially in the interior, which would have become much drier. The new land mass also decreased the quantity of shallow seas and exposed formerly isolated organisms of the former continents to increased competition.

Pangaea's formation would have altered oceanic circulation and atmospheric weather patterns, creating seasonal monsoons. However, Pangaea formed millions of years before the Permian extinction and the very gradual changes that are caused by continental drift are unlikely, on their own, to have led to the simultaneous loss of both terrestrial and oceanic life on the scale seen.

The Permian extinction wiped out 96% of all species (53% of marine families, 84% of marine genera and an estimated 70% of land species such as plants, insects and vertebrate animals. In total, 57% of all families and 83% of all genera were wiped out).

The Late Devonian extinction

This occurred about 364 million years ago and was caused by global cooling (followed by global warming). It was linked to the diversification of land plants, which resulted in a decrease in the volume of CO_2 in the atmosphere and therefore lower overall levels of greenhouse gases. The extinction killed 75% of all species (19% of all families and 50% of all genera).

The Ordovician–Silurian extinction

This occurred about 439 million years ago and was caused by a drop in sea levels as glaciers formed, then by rising sea levels as glaciers melted. The extinction killed 86% of all species (27% of all families and 57% of all genera).

Mass extinctions have led to initial massive reductions in the Earth's biodiversity. These extinction events have resulted in new directions in evolution of natural *systems* and therefore increased biodiversity in the long term.

The average time between these mass extinctions is around 100 million years. The exception is the gap between the Permian–Triassic and the End Triassic extinctions, which were approximately 50 million years apart. All mass extinctions resulted in new directions in evolution and, therefore, an eventual increase in biodiversity. Mass extinctions are followed by rapid rates of speciation due to increased niche availability.

Although the mass extinction events led to a massive loss of biodiversity, with less than 1% of all species that have ever existed still being alive today, they ultimately led to new biodiversity evolving (Figure 3.37). The large-scale loss of species led to new opportunities for surviving populations, with many groups undergoing **adaptive radiation** (where an ancestral species evolves to fill different ecological niches, leading to new species).

You need to be able to discuss the causes of mass extinctions.

A sixth mass extinction?

How can we distinguish between knowledge, belief and opinion?

We can never know for sure what has caused past extinctions. Scientists can only look at the fossil record and the geology of the Earth and draw conclusions from them. Does this lack of experimental evidence limit the validity of the conclusions drawn?

The Earth is believed to be currently undergoing a sixth mass extinction, caused by human activities (biotic factors). If this is the case, it is the first extinction event to have biotic, rather than abiotic causes. The difference between abiotic and biotic factors is important and represents a significant shift in the cause of extinction.

The sixth extinction can be divided into two discrete phases:

- phase 1 began when the first modern humans began to disperse to different parts of the world about 100,000 years ago
- phase 2 began about 10,000 years ago when humans turned to agriculture.

The development of agriculture and the clearance of native ecosystems accelerated the pace of extinction. Mass extinctions of the past took place over geological time, which allowed time for new species to evolve to fill the gaps left by the extinct species. Current changes to the planet are occurring much faster, over the period of human lifetimes. Over-population, invasive species, and over-exploitation are fueling extinction. Pollution and the advent of global warming (Topics 6 and 7) are also accelerating changes to the planet and increasing extinction rates in species that cannot adapt to the changing conditions or migrate to new areas. Some scientists have predicted that 50% of all species could be extinct by the end of the 21st century.

2.1 Individuals, populations, communities and ecosystems

Figure 3.37 The mass extinctions that have wiped out 99% of all species that have ever existed on Earth and the evolution of life that followed (lower part of figure).

The five mass extinctions in the past have been caused by various factors such as tectonic plate movements, super-volcanic eruption, climatic changes, sea level changes, and meteorite impact, in contrast with the current anthropogenic sixth mass extinction.

As well as the animal extinctions indicated in Figure 3.37, there is evidence for the global disruption of plant communities during mass extinction events. Scientists estimate that nearly 600 species of plant have gone extinct in the last 250 years, This figure is over double the number of extinct animals over this period.

HL

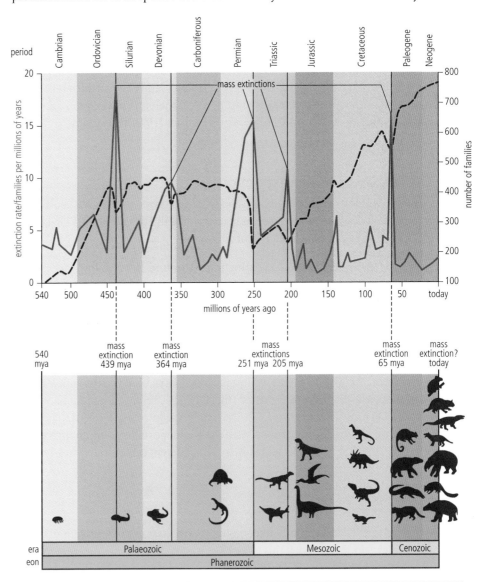

3.1.18 and 3.1.9 The Anthropocene

The most recent geological epoch, the **Holocene**, has been a relatively stable part of the Quaternary period. The Quaternary, which existed for about 2 million years, was distinguished by regular shifts into and out of glacial and inter-glacial phases. The Quaternary forms part of the 65 million-year Cenozoic era, distinguished by the opening of the North Atlantic, the rise of the Himalayas and the widespread presence of mammals and flowering plants. However, scientists believe that we have entered a new epoch called the **Anthropocene**.

The **Anthropocene** is a proposed geological epoch characterized by rapid environmental change and species extinction due to human activity.

In 2000, Paul Crutzen, an atmospheric chemist, claimed he no longer believed he was living in the Holocene. He was living in some other age, one shaped primarily by changes brought about by humans. These changes included global warming, ocean acidification, desertification, eutrophication, decline of biodiversity and changes to air quality. There appeared to be few places, if any, on Earth that were unaffected by humans.

The term **Great Acceleration** refers to a dramatic, continuous, approximately simultaneous and rapid increase of factors across a large range of measures of human activity, which were first recorded in the mid-20th century and continue to this day (Figure 3.38a and b). The Great Acceleration forms the basis for the Anthropocene as a new geological epoch in Earth history, where humans have caused fundamental changes to Earth systems.

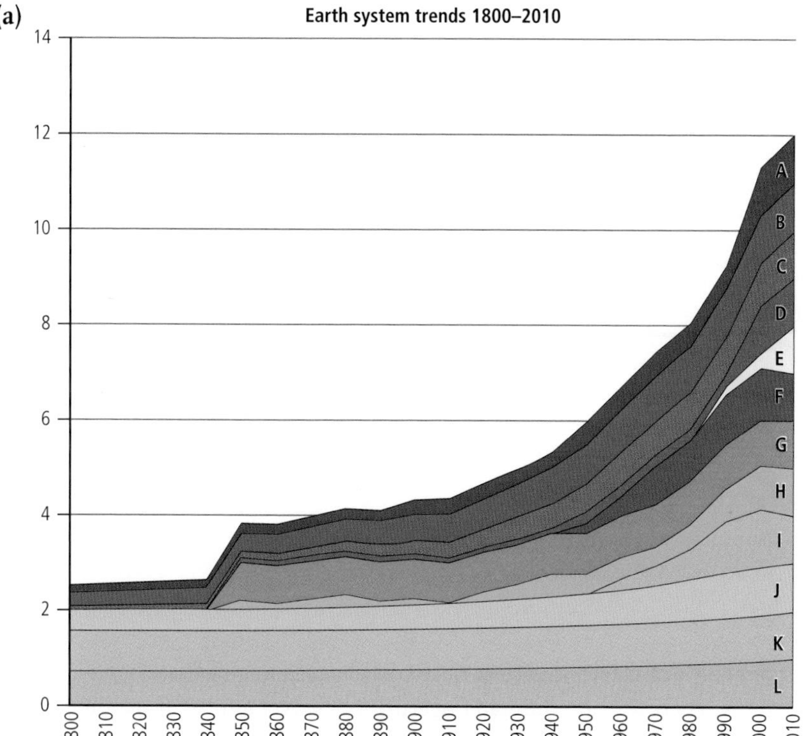

A – terrestrial biosphere degradation: 3.53–28.57% decrease of mean species abundance

B – domesticated land: 0.08–0.38% of total land area

C – tropical forest loss: 0.96–27.6% of total land area compared to 1700

D – coastal nitrogen: 0–79.7 megatonnes/year

E – shrimp aquaculture: 3.77 megatonnes/year

F – marine fish capture: 64.14 megatonnes/year

G – ocean acidification: 8.21 nmol kg^{-1}

H – temperature anomaly: 0.47 Celsius

I – O_3: 54.09% lost

J – CH_4: 705.34–1744.07 PPB

K – nitrous oxide: 271.39–322.46 PPB

L – CO_2: 276.81–384.27 PPM

Figure 3.38(a) Earth system trends category of the Great Acceleration of the Anthropocene from 1800 to 2010. The data graphically displayed is scaled for each subcategory's 2010 value.

Figure 3.38(b) Socio-economic trends of the Great Acceleration of the Anthropocene from 1800 to 2010.

(b)

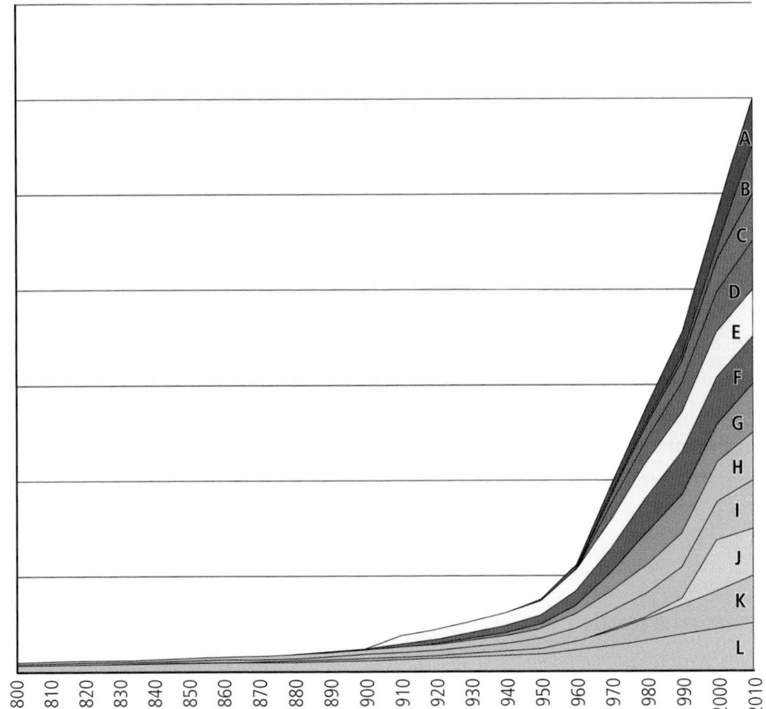

A – international tourism: 0–939.9 millions of arrivals

B – telecommunications: 0–6.48 billion landlines and subscriptions

C – transportation: 0–1281.35 million vehicles

D – paper production: 0–398.77 megatonnes/year

E – water use: 0–3.87 1000 km^3

F – large dams: 0.06–31.63 > 15 m height

G – fertilizer consumption: 171.46 megatonnes/year

H – primary energy use: 16–533.37 exajoule

I – urban population: 0.05–3.5 billions

J – foreign direct investment: 0–1.3 trillion (2013 USD)

K – real GDP: 0.35–50.15 trillion (2005 USD)

L – world population: 0.73–6.9 billions

TOK

What role do paradigm shifts play in the progression of scientific knowledge?

The Anthropocene epoch represents a 'paradigm shift' in how science views the world. For natural sciences to view human activities as central to the functioning of the Earth, marked a major shift in how scientists viewed the world. For many centuries, the study of people in the way the Earth functions was limited. In the 16th century Nicholas Copernicus (1473-1543) moved the Earth from the centre of the Universe and replaced it with the Sun. In the 18th century, James Hutton (1726-1797) revealed the extent of geological time, with humans appearing relatively insignificant on that timescale. Charles Darwin, writing in the 19th century, showed that humans were just one tiny part of the evolution of life on Earth. Thus, embracing the idea of the Anthropocene epoch means studying the Earth, not with humans as insignificant actors, but instead recognizing that human actions are central to the functioning of Earth processes.

The Anthropocene is characterized by widespread changes to global and local physical systems. There are now 'human fingerprints' all over almost everything in the natural world. In particular, it is the unprecedented rapid change in atmospheric CO_2 witnessed since the onset of the industrial revolution – and resulting carbon cycle changes – that underpins the Anthropocene argument.

For most of the history of Earth, the planet has been subject to natural forces, such as water and carbon cycling, which have influenced and shaped the life that inhabits it. Since the advent of modern humans, one species – *Homo sapiens* – has been the dominant influence on Earth's ecosystems.

Early humans lived as hunter–gatherers within natural Earth systems and had little impact on their environment. Populations were small and people lived off the land, rather than manipulating it towards their own ends. As these populations grew in size and spread away from Africa, there was an increase in the number of farmers and an increase in the amount of land being cleared to grow crops.

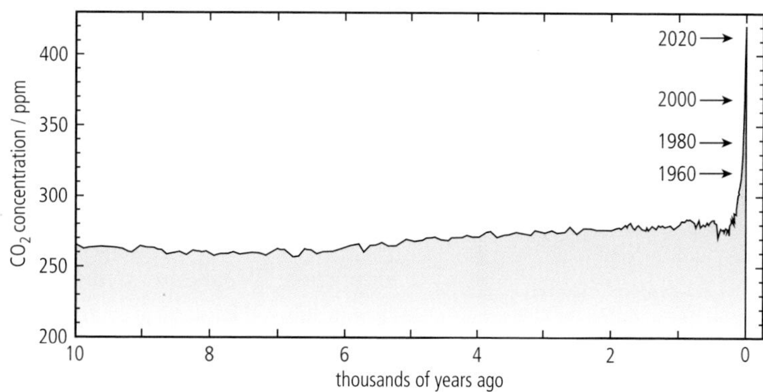

Pre-Anthropocene events:
Fire-stick farming, mega fauna extinctions, forest clearing

Anthropocene Stage 1 (ca 1800–1945)
Internal combustion engine, fossil fuel energy, science & technology

Anthropocene Stage 2 (1945–2010 or 2020)
The Great Acceleration, new institutions and vast global networks

Anthropocene Stage 3 (2010 or 2020–?)
Sustainability or collapse?

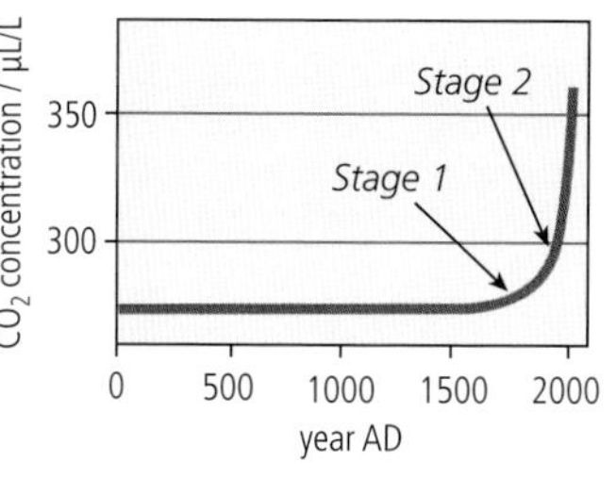

▲ **Figure 3.39** The stages of the 'Anthropocene.'

The development of settled agriculture represents one of the most significant changes in human history. The period known as the Neolithic ('new stone age') revolution began in the 'fertile crescent' in the Middle East about 10,000 years ago and changed forever the way that humanity interacts with the environment. The growth in agriculture led to significant land clearance and a significant transformation of the terrestrial biosphere.

For the majority of the time since *Homo sapiens* evolved in Africa, *c.* 250,000 years ago, the concentration of CO_2 in the atmosphere was below 200 ppm, which was low. 10,000 years ago, in the period of early agriculture, CO_2 concentrations were around 265 ppm (Figure 3.39). Early human activities that may have contributed to relatively small, elevated levels of CO_2 (with evidence provided by ice cores) included **fire-stick farming** and forest clearing, raising CO_2 levels to 280 ppm. Fire-stick farming is a technique used by Indigenous Australians to help them when hunting animals. The vegetation was set alight and the resulting fires herded animals into specific areas where they could be killed. Fire-stick farming also caused new vegetation to grow, which attracted new animals.

In recent times, the rapid growth in human population, from mere millions in the Neolithic period to over 8 billion today, along with its tremendous need for resources and land, has put even more pressure on Earth's natural systems. The discovery of coal and other fossil fuels as energy resources liberated humanity from the shackles of having to use horse-drawn equipment to farm the land and allowed much larger areas of land to be cleared and used to grow crops. Solar energy trapped by plants millions of years ago could be released, simultaneously releasing CO_2. Since the start of the Industrial Revolution in Europe, in the early part of the 19th century, CO_2 has been released at an increasing rate from the burning of coal and oil. We are now adding carbon that had been locked away for about 350 million years to our atmosphere. This is an entirely new development in geological history.

Studies suggest that a sixth mass extinction caused by humans will likely resemble the Permian–Triassic and Cretaceous–Tertiary extinctions. Analysis of the marine fossil record suggests that this will be the case and that recovery will take tens of millions of years.

The Quaternary period includes two epochs, the Pleistocene and the Holocene. The latter began *c.* 11,500 years ago and is signified by an interglacial period. The Holocene is, however, just one of a series of warmer periods that have occurred over the last 2 million years and is defined as an epoch simply because many of the soils and river deposits on which we live were formed during this time. Many argue that changes to the land, sea and air, including mass extinction events, warrant the addition of the Anthropocene as a third epoch to the Quaternary.

Changing CO_2 levels are recorded on Earth through geological history using ice cores drilled in the Antarctic and Greenland ice sheets. The ice there has formed from accumulation of layer upon layer of frozen snow, which has been deposited and compacted over thousands of years. Gases from the surrounding atmosphere, including CO_2, were trapped as the layers built up. Columns of ice are taken and analysed for CO_2 levels – the lower layers of ice are the oldest and those nearest the top of the column are the youngest.

Much of the coal and oil on Earth was formed from organisms deposited 350 million years ago.

The modification of biomes by humans over the recent past has led to some people terming them 'anthromes', that is human-modified biomes.

The Anthropocene encompasses the idea that there are no truly natural environments or processes and that human activities have modified physical systems by their carbon emissions, even in areas where there are relatively few people such as the oceans and areas at high latitudes. In other environments that are conducive to human habitation, such as river valleys, the impact of human activity has been considerable.

Activity

Evaluate the evidence for the onset of the Anthropocene in your local area. This could be a challenging but potentially rewarding investigation focus with many opportunities for a rigorous evaluation to be carried out that reflects critically on different aspects of the work.

In the first place, you would need to devise a programme of data collection that is fit for purpose. What criteria might this include? Possibilities include: changes in local climate caused by season changes, types of vegetation that grow and thrive in people's gardens and parks, and changes in local river flows or other environmental features.

A mixture of secondary and primary data sources can be used including old photographs and paintings as proxy data for what the local environment used to be like.

Interviews with older community members might focus on people's recollections about the climate, such as how much it used to snow, when Autumn began and so on.

A similar approach can be taken if you decide instead to evaluate evidence for changing carbon cycles in your local area.

There is debate about when the Anthropocene epoch began. Various start dates have been proposed for the epoch. **Golden spikes** are reference points that mark the beginnings of new stages in planetary history. The location that is finally selected for the start of the Anthropocene will become an important part of the final definition for the Geological Timescale. Suitable golden spikes in the geological strata marking the proposed beginning of the Anthropocene include:

- 1610 – when there was a dip in CO_2 caused by the arrival of Europeans in the Americas
- 1950 – observation of spherical fly ash particles produced during the process of combustion in coal-fired power stations
- 1964 – observation of carbon-14 markers linked to nuclear tests.

Human impacts are having a planetary effect, which can be recognized by designating a new epoch - the Anthropocene. To be defined as a separate geological epoch from the Holocene, evidence for the Anthropocene must be detectable in the geological record. This means that events that have occurred in the relatively recent past must be detectable not only in the next hundred, thousand or tens of thousands of years, but millions of years in the future (in the same way that the fossil record forms a record of Earth's past).

Changes to the geological record support the argument for the Anthropocene

There are several examples of evidence for the Anthropocene:

- signals from chemical pollution are currently accumulating in geological strata, with the potential to be preserved into the far future
- mixing of native and non-native species, which will be represented in the fossil record
- deposits from nuclear testing (Figure 3.40)
- modification of terrestrial and marine sedimentary systems
- minerals created solely or primarily from human activity.

The synthesis of chemicals that were not previously present on Earth, largely since the 1950s, is one signature of the Anthropocene. These chemicals include organic chemicals such as persistent organic pollutants (such as DDT) and inorganic chemicals, such as microplastics, and have the potential to be preserved in sediments long into the future. In the planetary boundaries model (Topic 1, Section 1.3.19), these chemicals are known as 'novel entities'.

Global trade led to the spread of species around the planet due to human activity. Pollen from maize, for example, only appears in European sediments in 1600 when the food crop was brought from central Mexico. Alien species (this topic, Section 3.2.3) introduced from one continent onto another show examples of the consequences of mixing of native and non-native species. The evidence of the global mixing of species, either intentionally or accidentally by humans, will be seen in the fossil record when some of these organisms are fossilized.

Global fallout from nuclear bomb testing, which rose between the late 1940s and 1950s and fell abruptly following the Partial Test Ban Treaty in 1963, has created a signal of radioactive versions of elements within ocean and lake sediments. Evidence of the fallout can also found in glacier ice, tree rings and other sources. Radioactive versions of elements include carbon-14 (detectable in tree rings), plutonium-239 (found in marine sediments) and iodine-129.

Figure 3.40 Nuclear testing in the Nevada desert, USA, in the 1950s.

Sedimentary records contain information that can be used to determine and quantify the impact of humans on the planet. Movement of sediment from land to aquatic systems, due to soil erosion, has increased greatly due to human activities such as agriculture, resource extraction and construction. Movement of sediment has increased from an average of approximately 5×10^9 tonnes per year to $100–120 \times 10^9$ tonnes per year.[1] Large quantities of sediment are trapped in reservoirs, such as the Three Gorges reservoir, China.

Geologists refer to a *golden spike* that indicates the beginning of the Anthropocene. This means an indicator, present in the geological record, that clearly shows traces of the Great Acceleration and could provide a marker for the new geological epoch.

Of the 5208 minerals recognized by the International Mineralogical Association, 208 have been created by humans (4 % of the total). These minerals include yttrium aluminium garnet (YAG) crystals (used in lasers), Portland cement, silicon chips for semi-conductors and minerals indirectly created in human-created environments such as mine tunnels.

Any of the examples outlined above could provide the golden spike that defines the start of this epoch.

Activity

Find out for yourself about the different examples of evidence for the Anthropocene described in this section.

Which would you choose as the golden spike that clearly provides a marker for the new geological epoch? Justify your answer.

Now produce a presentation or podcast to explain to others in your school or community the concept of the Anthropocene, your choice of the golden spike, and the implications of the new geological epoch for life on Earth.

HL end

Engagement

- Consider an example of how human activities have affected natural selection, such as the increase in abundance of tuskless elephants in regions undergoing civil conflict. Is there anything that can be done to address human activities? Promote the issues in your school or local community, using a poster campaign to raise awareness.

[1]Owens, P.N. Soil erosion and sediment dynamics in the Anthropocene: a review of human impacts during a period of rapid global environmental change. *J Soils Sediments* 20, 4115–4143 (2020).

- Investigate the impact of inequality on knowledge of biodiversity. What are the issues and how can they be addressed? How can individuals or communities improve the situation? Promote the ideas you have explored in your school community.
- Citizen science (Topic 1, Section 1.3.16) and voluntary agencies offer opportunities for students to participate in gathering knowledge of local and regional biodiversity. Find a local citizen science project and get involved with one of their projects. This can count towards the 'service' component of the CAS programme.
- If you are on the HL course, create a podcast exploring the epoch of the Anthropocene. What does this new geological epoch tell us about the impact that humans are having on the planet? Promote your podcast to inform others about environmental issues you have explored in the ESS course.

Exercise

Q1. **Define** the terms *habitat diversity, species diversity* and *genetic diversity.*

Q2. **Distinguish** between species diversity and species richness.

Q3. (a) **Outline** what high and low values of the Simpson reciprocal index indicate about an ecosystem.

(b) **Explain** how diversity indices can be used to measure the impact of human activities.

(c) **Discuss** the usefulness of providing numerical values of species diversity to understanding the nature of biological communities and the conservation of biodiversity.

Q4. Darwin's theory of evolution is explained in terms of natural selection. **Describe** the process of natural selection, and how it leads to the generation of new species.

Q5. Isolation mechanisms are essential for the generation of new species. **Explain** how the isolation of populations leads to speciation.

HL

Q6. HL **Explain** how mutation and sexual reproduction increase genetic diversity.

Q7. HL **Compare and contrast** two different causes of reproductive isolation.

Q8. HL **State** how many mass extinctions there have been in the past. What was the cause of these extinctions?

Q9. HL **Define** the term *Anthropocene.*

Q10. HL **List** five human impacts that are having a planetary effect, which will be detectable in the geological record.

Q11. HL **To what extent** have human impacts on natural systems led to a new geological epoch, the Anthropocene?

HL end

3.2 Human impact on biodiversity

Guiding Question

What causes biodiversity loss, and how are ecological and societal systems impacted?

3.2.1. Biological diversity is being adversely affected by both direct and indirect influences.
3.2.2 Most ecosystems are subject to multiple human impacts.
3.2.3 Invasive alien species can reduce local biodiversity by competing for limited resources, predation and introduction of diseases or parasites.
3.2.4 The global conservation status of species is assessed by the International Union for the Conservation of Nature (IUCN) and is published as the IUCN Red List. Status is based on number of individuals, rate of increase or decrease of the population, breeding potential, geographic range and known threats.
3.2.5 Assigning a global conservation status publicizes the vulnerability of species and allows governments, non-governmental agencies and individual citizens to select appropriate conservation priorities and management strategies.
3.2.6 Investigate three different named species: a species that has become extinct due to human activity; a species that is critically endangered; and a species whose conservation status has been improved by intervention.
3.2.7 The tragedy of the commons describes possible outcomes of shared unrestricted use of a resource, with implications for sustainability and the impacts on biodiversity.
HL 3.2.8 Biodiversity hotspots are under threat from habitat destruction, which could lead to a significant loss of biological diversity, especially in tropical biomes.
HL 3.2.9 Key areas that should be prioritized for biodiversity conservation have been identified on the basis of the international importance of their species and habitats.
HL 3.2.10 In key biodiversity areas (KBAs), there is conflict between exploitation, sustainable development and conservation.
HL 3.2.11 Traditional indigenous approaches to land management can be seen as more sustainable but are facing challenges of population growth, economic development, climate change and a lack of governmental support and protection.
HL 3.2.12 Environmental justice must be considered when undertaking conservation efforts to address biodiversity loss.
HL 3.2.13 The planetary boundary 'loss of biosphere integrity' indicates that species extinctions have already crossed a critical threshold.

3.2.1 Adverse effects on biological diversity by direct and indirect threats

Human impacts are negatively affecting biological diversity. These effects can be either direct and have a direct effect on species, habitats and ecosystems, or indirect and cause changes to the environment, which in turn affect biodiversity.

4.4 Water pollution
5.2 Agriculture and food
6.2 Climate change – causes and impacts
6.4 Stratospheric ozone
7.2 Energy resources, use and management
8.4 Urban air pollution.

Why do people continue to damage the environment even when they know the effects on natural systems? Do people truly understand the consequences of their actions?

Direct threats

Direct threats to biological diversity include **overharvesting**, **poaching** and the illegal pet trade.

Overharvesting and hunting

Animals are hunted for food, medicines, souvenirs, fashion and to supply the exotic pet trade. Hunting up to a certain level is unlikely to be a threat, but the overharvesting of populations can significantly deplete numbers. Overharvesting of North Atlantic cod in the 1960s and 1970s, for example, led to a significant reduction in population size (Topic 1, Section 1.3.7).

Poaching

Poaching is the illegal hunting or capturing of wildlife. Some examples of poaching are well known, such as the hunting of elephants for their ivory tusks (Figure 3.41) and hunting of tigers for their skins and bones. Many other species are similarly exploited, from marine turtles to mountain gorillas. Between 1970 and 1992, 96% of the critically endangered black rhinoceros population was lost due to poaching. Some poaching is done for the bushmeat trade, where endangered animals are hunted for food. Pangolins are the most illegally trafficked mammals in the world and some species are on the brink of extinction (Figure 3.42).

Figure 3.41 Ivory tusks from poached elephants.

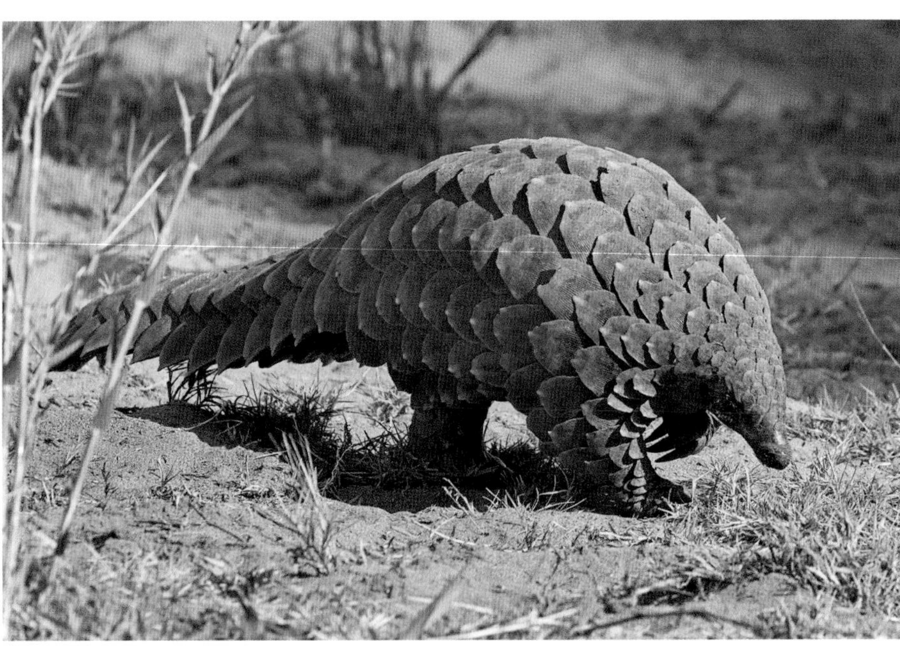

Figure 3.42 A pangolin.

Read more about poaching and the illegal wildlife trade on the Tusk and Zoological Society of London websites:

Illegal pet trade

The illegal pet trade involves the trade in species such as exotic birds, baby primates, baby alligators and crocodiles and big cat cubs, among many others. The illegal wildlife trade is the fourth biggest illegal activity worldwide, behind only arms, drugs and human trafficking. It is worth around US$ 23 billion a year and is threatening the ongoing existence of species. The Convention on International Trade in Endangered Species of Wild Fauna and Flora (**CITES**) acts to prevent the illegal trade in wildlife (this topic, Section 3.3.2).

Indirect threats

Indirect threats to biological diversity include habitat loss, climate change, pollution and the introduction of invasive alien species.

Pollution

Pollution damages habitats and kills animals and plants, leading to the loss of life and reduction in species' population numbers. It can be caused by build-up of waste products from human activities and examples include chemicals, litter, nets, plastic bags and oil spills, among many others. For example, the oceans can become polluted with waste plastic (Figure 3.43), which can then be eaten by the animals living in the ocean.

Figure 3.43 Ocean polluted with plastic garbage.

Habitat destruction

This includes habitat degradation, fragmentation and loss. Agricultural practices have led to the destruction of native habitats and the replacement of them with crops of only one species known as monocultures. Monocultures represent a large loss of diversity compared to the native ecosystems they replace. However, in certain countries, such as the UK, increased awareness of this has led to the re-establishment of hedgerows and undisturbed corridors in smaller-scale farming (rather than big New World prairies), that encourage more natural communities to return (Figure 3.44). Subsidies can be paid to encourage the establishment of such wildlife refuges.

HL a Environmental law
HL b Environmental economics
HL c Environmental ethics

Figure 3.44 Hedgerows (left of photo) provide habitats for native species. They also act as corridors for the movement of species from one area to another.

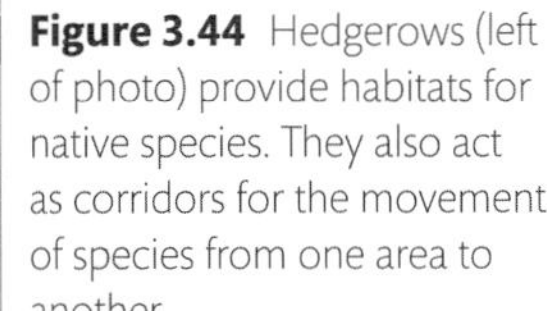

Non-specific pesticides used in agriculture can wipe out native as well as imported pest species, such as alien species that have been introduced into a country. This again leads to an overall loss of diversity.

Habitats can be lost through mining activities. Cell phones contain the element tantalum, which is obtained by mining coltan (a metallic ore that contains the elements niobium and tantalum). Coltan is found mainly in the eastern regions of the Democratic Republic of Congo and the mining activities in these areas have led to extensive habitat destruction of forests that contain gorillas and other endangered animals.

Natural habitats have also been cleared to make way for plantation crops. Sugar plantations have replaced tropical forest ecosystems, such as mangrove forests, in Australia, and palm oil plantations throughout South-East Asia have led to the widespread loss of tropical forests (this topic, Section 3.2.10).

Tropical biomes include some of the most globally biodiverse areas on Earth, such as tropical rainforests (Topic 2, Section 2.4.4) and coral reef (Topic 2, Section 2.1.20). Their unsustainable exploitation results in massive losses in biodiversity and their ability to perform globally important ecological services.

Threats to tropical biomes

Tropical biomes include some of the most diverse on Earth, such as tropical rainforests and coral reef. Mangrove is also a tropical biome (Figure 3.45). Coastal areas may have areas of mangrove forest that provide natural protection against the sea: mangroves provide a natural filter to sediment run-off from the land and stop erosion into the sea. Many tropical biomes are termed 'biodiversity hotspots' (this topic, Section 3.1.12) as they contain large numbers of species that are often endemic to the area (i.e. not found anywhere else).

Figure 3.45 Mangrove forest.

Should some knowledge not be sought on ethical grounds?

In order to establish which species live in an area, populations must be sampled. When sampling populations of abundant, small and poorly understood species such as insects, specimens are commonly returned to natural history museums for identification but the animals are killed in the process. Does this raise ethical issues or does the end justify the means?

Tropical rainforests are characterized by long wet seasons, tall trees and plants that grow year-round. These forests presently cover 5.9% of the Earth's land surface. In the tropics, the Sun's rays are the most concentrated and the areas are exposed to them for nearly the same number of hours every day of the year, making the climate warm and stable. About 33% of all rainforests are found in the Amazon Basin, 20% in Africa and a further 20% in Indonesia (Figure 2.98, Topic 2, Section 2.4.4). High levels of light and water make rainforests very productive. This explains why they can support such high biomass and wide diversity of life.

Some species, such as tree frogs, spend all their time in the rainforest canopy. As they never reach the forest floor they are not commonly seen. *Rhacophorus gadingensis* (Figure 3.46) was discovered in 2005 in a remote forest reserve in the centre of the island of Borneo.

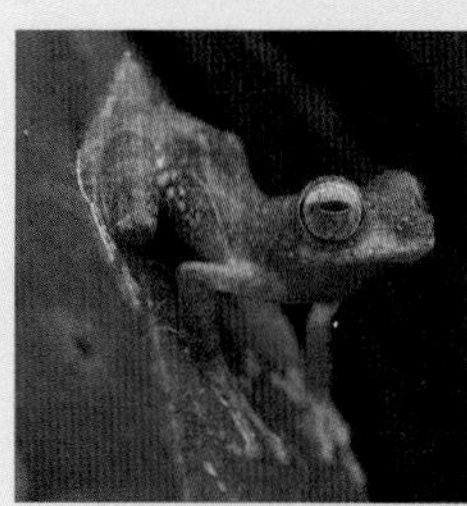

Figure 3.46 The rainforest tree frog, *Rhacophorus gadingensis*.

As seen in Topic 2, rainforests are complex ecosystems with many layers, including emergent trees, the canopy, the understorey and the ground (Topic 2, Section 2.4.4). The complex layered structure of rainforests enables them to support many different niches. Over 50% of the world's plant species and 42% of all terrestrial vertebrate species are endemic to 34 identified biodiversity hotspots (the majority of which are rainforests). In addition to their biodiversity value, tropical biomes such as rainforest provide many ecosystem functions. For example, they prevent soil erosion and nutrient loss, control the local water cycle (water evaporates from leaves in rainforest and falls locally as rain) and act as carbon sinks by locking the carbon up in trees and other vegetation and preventing its loss to the atmosphere. You will find out more about ecosystem services in this topic, Section 3.3.1, and Topic 7, Section 7.1.5.

The rate of loss of biodiversity may vary from country to country depending on the ecosystems present, protection policies and monitoring, environmental viewpoints and the stage of economic development.

3.2.2 Most ecosystems are subject to multiple human impacts

Impacts to ecosystems are increasing and their effects are amplified when combined. For example, threats such as invasive alien species have more impact than if they were acting alone when the impact of climate change has already reduced resilience.

1.2 Systems
6.2 Climate change – causes and impacts

Investigate the impact of human activity on biodiversity in an ecosystem by studying change in species diversity along a transect

See this page of your eBook for an activity related to this skill. Methods for sampling and analysing data are found in Topic 2, Section 2.1.6 and 2.1.7, Section 2.1.15, 2.1.16 and 2.1.17, Section 2.2.17 and Section 2.5.2.

3.2.3 Invasive alien species

Invasive alien species can reduce local biodiversity by competing for limited resources, predation and introduction of diseases or parasites.

Invasive alien species are those introduced into areas where they then compete with endemic (native) species. This can lead to the extinction of the native species. For example, the grey squirrel was introduced to the UK from North America. This species competes with the native UK red squirrel and has led to such a reduction in red squirrel numbers that the red squirrel is now rare. The red-clawed signal crayfish and the lionfish are also invasive alien species (see Examples).

2.1 Individuals and populations, communities and ecosystems

Example – North American red-clawed crayfish in the UK

The introduction to the UK of the larger more aggressive American, red-clawed signal crayfish (*Pacifastacus leniusculus*), has wiped out almost 95% of the native UK white-clawed species (*Austropotamobius pallipes*) since its introduction in the late 1970s. The white-clawed signal crayfish (Figure 3.47) is native to the UK but 70% of the population has been wiped out from the south west and it has been given priority status in the UK's Biodiversity Action Plan. The North American, red-clawed signal crayfish (Figure 3.48) was introduced in the 1970s for the fishery industry as a fashionable seafood and to supplement the North European crayfish (*Astacus astacus*) stocks, which were being damaged by crayfish plague. The red-clawed crayfish escaped the fisheries and quickly spread into rivers and streams. This aggressive species has now out-competed the white-clawed crayfish, decimating its population. The crayfish plague is carried by the red-clawed crayfish and can wipe out populations of white-clawed crayfish in a few weeks. The disease can be carried from stream to stream via boots, fishing equipment and recording equipment. In addition, habitat loss and declining water quality have restricted the number of sites in which the white-clawed crayfish can survive.

▲ **Figure 3.47** White-clawed signal crayfish (*Austropotamobius pallipes*).

The UK Southwest Crayfish Project

The UK Southwest Crayfish Project, working in association with the Bristol Conservation and Science Foundation, is attempting to preserve the white-clawed crayfish in a number of ways:

- increasing awareness about how crayfish plague can be transmitted and the problems facing native crayfish
- introducing a breeding programme and releasing white-clawed crayfish back into the wild
- moving 'at risk' populations to safe areas.

▲ **Figure 3.48** Red-clawed signal crayfish (*Pacifastacus leniusculus*).

Example – Lionfish in the Atlantic and Caribbean oceans

Figure 3.49 Invasive Lionfish on tropical Caribbean coral reef.

Lionfish (*Pterois volitans*) (Figure 3.49) are venomous and aggressive marine fish. They belong to the family Scorpaenidae and genus *Pterois*. This genus is characterized by red, white and black stripes (indicating toxicity and disguising body form), and by elaborate pectoral and dorsal fins. All members of the Scorpaenidae have venom glands in their dorsal, anal and pelvic spines. The main function of these spines is to defend against competitors and predators.

Lionfish are a benthic species – feeding at the bottom layers of the reef rather than in the water columns above (where pelagic fish feed). They suck small fish, crabs and other food off the surface of the reef and can use their pectoral (side) fins to trap food. The largest lionfish can grow to about 15 inches (0.4 metres) in length, but the average is closer to 1 foot (0.3 metres).

Lionfish are native to the Indo-Pacific ocean but have become increasingly abundant in the Atlantic and Caribbean oceans where they were not historically found. Lionfish overpopulate reef areas and force native species to move to areas where conditions may be less favourable for them. Lionfish therefore pose a major potential threat to reef ecological systems on the east coast of the USA and the Caribbean. Current distributions include the Atlantic coast of the USA, the Caribbean coasts of Central and South America, the Gulf of Mexico, the Greater Antilles and the Leeward Islands. Scientists believe that the fish escaped from aquaria in Florida into United States coastal waters where their numbers have expanded due to a lack of competition and predation, along with abundant food supplies.

Effects of the invasive species

Lionfish have become the second most abundant species of fish from the Bahamas to North Carolina. In the Bahamas they feed on more than 41 species of fish, including commercially valuable species like grouper and snapper as well as fish that keep the reefs clean of algae. *Pterois* could have a significant negative impact on prey populations by decreasing numbers, thereby directly affecting complex food web relationships and having knock-on effects for many food chains. Reef deterioration and the collapse of food chains could therefore be direct results of the lionfish invasion.

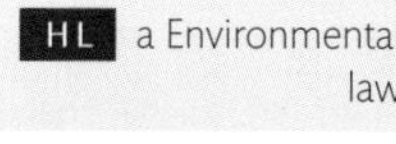

HL a Environmental law

Possible solutions

Thorough and repeated removal of lionfish from invaded waters will be necessary to control their numbers, which are currently growing exponentially. Conservation groups are organizing hunting expeditions for *Pterois*, and other scientists are training reef sharks to hunt and eliminate the lionfish.

Make sure you understand how alien species can arrive in an ecosystem and the factors that can result in their exponential increase.

Lionfish are used extensively in cooking – they are tasty and succulent with a similar texture to grouper. Many recipes for lionfish exist, including fried lionfish, lionfish ceviche, lionfish jerky and grilled lionfish. Human consumption of lionfish may prove to be one of the best ways to reduce population numbers and aim for total eradication from the invaded waters.

Activity

Find out about a local example of an alien species that has become invasive and the management strategy that has been used to reduce its impact.

Produce a fact sheet on the invasive species, outlining:

- the reasons for its introduction
- impacts on local communities and ecosystems
- management strategies to control it.

Activity

What other factors cause a loss of biodiversity?

1. If you live on the eastern seaboard of the USA, the Caribbean or other areas in its distribution zone, keep your eyes open for lionfish. Knowledge of the distribution of the species will be essential in planning ways of removing this unwanted invader.
2. If you live in an area where lionfish are commonly available, find a recipe and prepare a fish for family or friends. Promote this fish as an alternative to other edible species and help reduce population densities in areas where the fish are found outside their natural distribution.

The mnemonic 'A. H.I.P.P.O.' helps to recall the various threats that biodiversity faces, with each letter representing a different threat: **A**griculture, **H**abitat loss, **I**nvasive species, **P**ollution, **P**opulation (i.e. the effects of population growth) and **O**verhunting.

3.2.4 The IUCN Red List

For more than four decades, the IUCN has published documents called the *Red Data Books*. The books assess the **conservation status** of particular species in order to highlight plants and animals threatened with extinction, and to promote their conservation. Known informally as the **Red List**, the books are essentially an inventory of all threatened species. The genetic diversity represented by these plants and animals is an irreplaceable resource which the IUCN is aiming to conserve through increased awareness. These species also represent key building blocks of ecosystems, and information on their conservation status provides the basis for making informed decisions about conserving biodiversity from local to global levels.

The International Union for the Conservation of Nature (IUCN) publishes data in the **Red List** of Threatened Species in several categories.

The purposes of the Red List are to:

- identify species requiring some level of conservation
- identify species for which there is concern about their conservation status
- catalogue plants and animals facing a high risk of global extinction
- raise awareness of animals and plants that face a higher risk of global extinction than others and therefore require conservation efforts.

Precise criteria and data are used to assign status to a species and a sequence of conservation status ranks have been defined from Least Concern (LC) to Extinct (EX).

Factors used to determine the conservation status of a species include:
- population size
- degree of specialization
- distribution
- reproductive potential and behaviour
- geographic range and degree of fragmentation
- quality of habitat
- trophic level
- probability of extinction.

Figure 3.50 The European eel (*Anguilla anguilla*).

Figure 3.51 The peacock parachute tarantula (*Poecilotheria metallica*).

Factors used to determine a species' Red List conservation status

Various factors are used to determine the conservation status of a species and a sliding scale is used to represent the status from severe threat to low risk. The range of factors used to determine conservation status will now be described.

Number of individuals

Species with smaller populations are more likely to go extinct as they tend to have low genetic diversity and therefore an inability to adapt to changing conditions that can prove fatal. Many of the large cat species, such as cheetahs, snow leopards and tigers, are in this category.

Reduction in population size

A reduction in population size may indicate that a species is under threat. For example, numbers of European eel (*Anguilla anguilla*) (Figure 3.50) are at their lowest ever levels in most of its range and they continue to decline.

Geographic range

Species that occupy a restricted habitat are likely to be wiped out. For example, the slender-billed grackle (*Cassidix palustris*), a bird which once occupied a single marsh near Mexico City, was driven to extinction when a reduction in the water table drained the marsh.

Distribution

Species that live in a small area are under greater threat from extinction than those that are distributed more widely. Loss of the area they live in will lead to loss of the species. The peacock parachute tarantula (*Poecilotheria metallica*) (Figure 3.51) is known from a single location in the Eastern Ghats of Andhra Pradesh in India. Reasons for being on the Red List: restricted range and habitat loss caused by logging for firewood and timber.

Breeding potential

Animals that live a long time and have long gestation times, for example elephants and rhinos, have low rates of reproduction and can take many years to recover from any reduction in population number. This makes them vulnerable to extinction. If a change in habitat or the introduction of a predator occurs, the population decreases and there may be too few reproductive adults to support and maintain the population. Because they are slow to reproduce, any loss in numbers means a fast decline. The Steller's sea cow was heavily hunted and unable to replace its numbers quickly enough. Orangutans have one of the slowest reproductive rates of all mammal species as they give birth to a single offspring only once every 6 to 8 years. As they have such a low reproductive rate, even a small decrease in numbers could lead to their extinction.

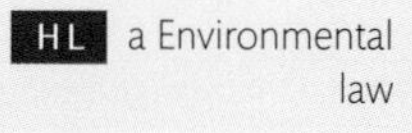

HL a Environmental law

Known threats

Degree of fragmentation

Fragmentation occurs when parts of a habitat are destroyed, leaving smaller unconnected areas. Species in fragmented habitats may not be able to maintain large enough population sizes. The Sumatran rhinoceros (*Dicerorhinus sumatrensis*) lives in tropical rainforest in South-East Asia. Fragmentation of the forest through deforestation and conversion to plantation forest has led to a reduction in habitat area for this species.

Quality of habitat

Species that live in poor-quality habitats are less likely to survive than species that live in higher quality habitats. For example, the fishing cat (*Prionailurus viverrinus*, see Figure 3.52) is found in South-East Asian wetland areas. The drainage of these wetland areas for agriculture has led to a reduction in habitat quality.

Figure 3.52 The South-East Asian fishing cat (*Prionailurus viverrinus*).

Publicizing global conservation status of species

Irrespective of human interference, any animal or plant that is rare, has a restricted distribution, a highly specialized habitat or niche, a low reproductive potential or is at the top of the food chain, will be at risk from extinction. Examples include:

After assessment by the IUCN, global conservation status of species is published as the IUCN Red List. Status is based on number of individuals, rate of increase or decrease of the population, breeding potential, geographic range and known threats.

- *Puya raimondii*, also known as 'Queen of the Andes' (Figure 3.53), is a spectacular Andean plant found at high altitude in Peru to Bolivia. Reasons for being on the Red List include isolated and very small population size, seeds only once in 80 years before dying, human impact including repeated fires to generate or maintain pastureland and usage as fuel or building material by local populations.

Figure 3.53 *Puya raimondii*, also known as 'Queen of the Andes.

- The European eel (*Anguilla anguilla*) (Figure 3.50) is at an historical low in most of its range and it continues to decline. Reasons for being on the Red List: low population numbers caused by over-fishing, the introduction of a parasitic nematode by humans that may affect the ability of eels to reach their spawning grounds, dam construction for hydropower has blocked migration routes.
- The Indri (*Indri indri*) (Figure 3.54) is a primate from Madagascar. Reasons for being on the Red List: loss of its rainforest habitat to supply fuel and timber and to make way for slash-and-burn agriculture, greatly reduced population numbers with an estimated 50% reduction over the last 36 years.

Figure 3.54 The Indri (*Indri indri*).

- The South-East Asian fishing cat (*Prionailurus viverrinus*) (Figure 3.52) is a skillful swimmer. Reasons for being on the Red List: loss of habitat due to human settlement, draining of wetlands for agriculture, pollution, excessive hunting and woodcutting; over-fishing leading to a reduction in fish stocks, which is likely to be a significant threat to this species as it relies heavily on fish for its survival.

Figure 3.55 A dodo.

Sometimes conservation actions come too late. Some of the more common reasons for extinction and examples of species that went extinct because of them are as follows.

- Small habitat area (not enough area for species to survive) – Holdridge's toad, St Helena olive, Percy Island flying fox.
- Narrow geographic area – golden toad (this topic, Section 3.2.6, Figure 3.60).
- Poor competitor – Holdridge's toad (deaf and mute), dodo (Figure 3.55) (cannot fly).
- Human intervention – dodo (introduction of rats), thylacine (introduction of non-native species such as dogs), desert rat kangaroo.
- Disease (the introduction of a non-native disease so no local immunity) – Darwin's Galápagos mouse.
- Hunting (over-hunting of species to extinction) – Bali tiger, passenger pigeon, thylacine, western black rhino, Queen of Sheba's gazelle, Madagascan pygmy hippo, Steller's sea cow.
- Shallow gene pool (little or no genetic variation so little chance to adapt to changing environment) – north elephant seal, saiga antelope.
- Co-extinction (loss of one species causes extinction of another) – the bird lice found on passenger pigeons went extinct when their hosts did.

Do some organisms have more of a right to conservation than others? How can this be justified?

Do pandas have a greater right to conservation than lichens?

Do 'pests' or pathogenic organisms have a right to be conserved?

To what extent are these arguments based on emotion and to what extent on reason? And how does this affect their validity?

3.2.5 Assigning a global conservation status

Assigning a global conservation status publicizes the vulnerability of species and allows governments, non-governmental agencies and individual citizens to select appropriate conservation priorities and management strategies.

1.1 Perspectives

There are differences between the *perspectives* of governments, agencies and individuals in conservation. These differences will affect their conservation priorities and management strategies.

Activity

What are the differences between the perspectives of governments, agencies and individuals in conservation?

Research each group and make a table showing their different perspectives and how these will affect their conservation priorities and management strategies.

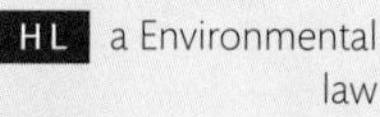

HL a Environmental law

HL c Environmental ethics

3.2.6 Extinct, critically endangered and back from the brink

Many factors can contribute to the decline of species, and conservation strategies can be employed to address these issues. The following examples discuss conservation strategies for three different species and whether they were successful or not. The examples examine the impacts of decline, disappearance or extinction on ecosystems and societies.

Example – Extinct: Falkland Islands wolf

Description

The Falkland Islands wolf (Figure 3.56) was the only native land mammal of the Falkland Islands. Europeans first sighted the islands in 1692. In 1833, Charles Darwin visited the islands and described the wolf as 'common and tame'.

The genus name, *Dusicyon*, means 'foolish dog' in Greek (dusi = foolish, cyon = dog).

Ecological role

The Falkland Islands wolf is said to have lived in burrows and its usual prey was rodents. As there were no native rodents on the islands, it is probable that its diet consisted of ground-nesting birds (such as geese and penguins), grubs, insects and carrion found from seashore scavenging.

Pressures

The many settlers of the Islands, mainly the Scottish inhabitants, along with the French and some English, considered the Falkland Islands wolf to be a threat to their sheep. A huge-scale operation of poisoning and shooting the wolf began with the aim of leading it to extinction. The operation was successful very rapidly, assisted by the lack of forests and the tameness of the animal. Due to the absence of predators, the animal trusted humans who would lure it with a piece of meat and then kill it. The wolf was also killed for its fur.

Consequences of disappearance

The Falkland Islands wolf was not particularly threatening nor was it a significant predator, although the removal of a top predator would have had an impact on the rest of the food chain as it would result in an increase in the prey population.

Figure 3.56 The Falkland Islands wolf.

Make sure you can discuss the examples of three different species: one that has become **extinct** due to human activity, another that is **critically endangered** and a third species whose conservation status has been **improved by intervention**. For three different named species, consider the factors that contributed to their decline and the impacts of their decline, disappearance or extinction on ecosystems and societies. Consider conservation strategies that either were or were not successfully employed.

Example – Critically endangered: Iberian lynx

Description

The Iberian lynx (*Lynx pardinus*) (Figure 3.57) is also known as the Spanish lynx and is native to the Iberian Peninsula. It has distinctive, leopard-like spots with a coat that is often light grey or various shades of light brownish-yellow. It is smaller than its northern relatives, such as the Eurasian lynx, and so typically hunts smaller animals that are usually no larger than hares. It also differs in habitat choice as it inhabits open scrub areas, whereas the Eurasian lynx inhabits forests. The Iberian lynx was listed as Critically Endangered on the IUCN Red List in 2002.

Ecological role

The Iberian lynx is a specialized feeder and rabbits account for 80–100% of its diet. Lynx often kill other carnivore species, including those regarded as pests by humans, such as feral cats and foxes, but do not eat them.

Pressures

The Iberian lynx's highly specialized diet makes it a naturally vulnerable species and the rapid decline in rabbit populations since the 1950s has had a direct impact on lynx numbers. The Iberian lynx occurs only in isolated locations of Spain and possibly Portugal (Figure 3.58). Habitat destruction, deterioration and alteration have impacted negatively on the lynx for centuries. The Iberian lynx was given

Figure 3.57 The Iberian lynx.

protection from hunting in the early 1970s. Since then, direct hunting has declined, but some lynxes are still shot and killed in traps and snares set for smaller predators, particularly on commercial hunting and shooting estates.

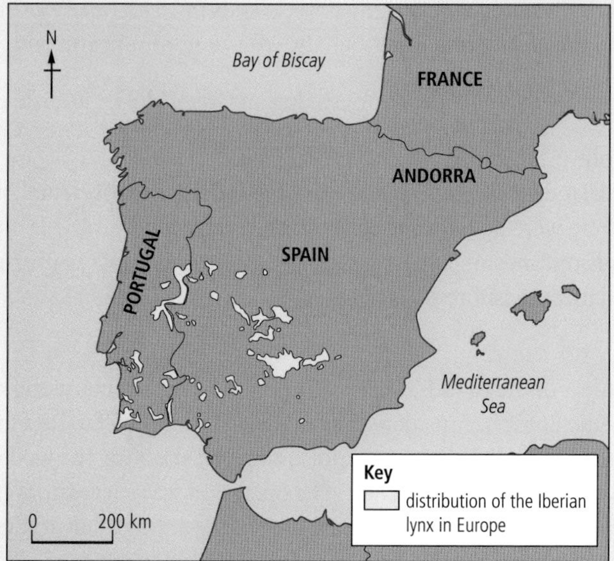

Figure 3.58 The present-day distribution of the Iberian lynx in Europe.

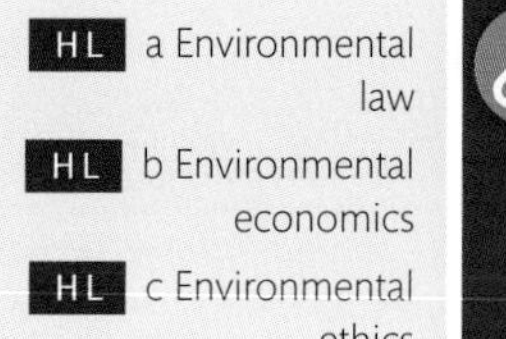

HL a Environmental law
HL b Environmental economics
HL c Environmental ethics

Methods of restoring population

The Iberian lynx is fully protected under national law in Spain and Portugal. Public awareness and education programmes have helped to change attitudes towards the animal, particularly among private landowners. International seminars have taken place to establish a coordinated strategy to save the Iberian lynx from extinction. A captive breeding programme has also been started in Spain. In Portugal, the National Action Plan foresees a reintroduction programme. The construction of facilities for breeding and reintroduction has been prepared. Further protection stems from the fact that one of the Iberian lynx's endemic areas has been turned into the Doñana National Park. In 2014, reintroduction projects began in four new areas, including eastern Sierra Morena (Castilla-La Mancha), Montes de Toledo (Castilla-La Mancha), Valle de Matachel (Extremadura) and Vale do Guadiana (Southern Portugal). In 2014, the positive trend in population number of the Iberian lynx led the IUCN to lower its threat category from Critically Endangered to Endangered. The latest census of Iberian lynx numbers in May 2023 showed its numbers have reached 1668.

Example – Improved by intervention: American bald eagle

Description

The American bald eagle (*Haliaeetus leucocephalus*) (Figure 3.59), also known as the American eagle, was officially declared the National Emblem of the United States in 1782. The Founding Fathers of the USA selected it because it is a species unique to North America. It has since become the living symbol of the USA's spirit and freedom.

Figure 3.59 The American bald eagle.

Bald eagles are one of the largest birds in North America with a wingspan of 6–8 feet (1.8–2.4 m). Females tend to be larger than males. They live for up to 40 years in the wild and longer in captivity. Bald eagles are monogamous and have one life partner.

Ecological role

American bald eagles live near large bodies of open water such as lakes, marshes, seacoasts and rivers. They nest and roost in tall trees. The eagles live in every US state except Hawaii. They use a specific territory for nesting, winter feeding or a year-round residence. Their natural domain is from Alaska to California and from Maine to Florida. American bald eagles that live in the northern USA and Canada migrate to the warmer southern areas during the winter to obtain easier access to food. Some American bald eagles that live in the southern states migrate slightly north during the hot summer months. They feed primarily on fish but also eat small animals such as ducks, coots, muskrats, turtles, rabbits, snakes and the occasional carrion.

Pressures

American bald eagle population numbers have been estimated at 300,000 to 500,000 birds in the early 1700s. Their population fell to fewer than 10,000 nesting pairs by the 1950s and to fewer than 500 pairs by the early 1960s. This population decline was caused by the mass shooting of eagles, the use of pesticides on crops, the destruction of habitat and the contamination of waterways and food sources by a wide range of poisons and pollutants. For many years, the use of DDT pesticide on crops (Topic 2, Section 2.2.18) caused thinning of eagle eggshells, which often broke during incubation.

Methods of restoring population

The use of DDT pesticide was outlawed in the USA in 1972 and in Canada in 1973. This action contributed greatly to the return of the American bald eagle.

The American bald eagle was listed as 'endangered' in most of the USA from 1967 to 1995. The number of nesting pairs of eagles in 48 of the states increased from fewer than 500 in the early 1960s to over 10,000 in 2007. That was enough to remove them from the list of threatened species on 28 June 2007.

Since de-listing, the primary law protecting American bald eagles has shifted from the Endangered Species Act to the Bald and Golden Eagle Act. Although American bald eagles have made an encouraging comeback throughout the USA since the early 1960s, they continue to face hazards that must be closely monitored and controlled. Even though it is illegal, American bald eagles are still harassed, injured and killed by guns, traps, power lines, windmills, poisons, contaminants and destruction of habitat.

Carefully planned strategies are needed to improve the conservation status of critically endangered species so that *sustainability* is ensured. These strategies need to address the ecological, sociopolitical or socio-economic pressures that are impacting on the species.

The golden toad (*Incilius periglenes*) (Figure 3.60) was a small, shiny, bright orange toad that was first discovered in 1966 and was recorded as extinct by the IUCN in 2004. The golden toad was once common in a small region of high-altitude, cloud-covered tropical forests, about 30 square kilometres in area, above the city of Monteverde in Costa Rica. The last recorded sighting of the toad was in 1989. Possible reasons for its extinction include a restricted range, global warming, airborne pollution, increase in ultraviolet radiation, fungal infection, parasitic infestation or lowered pH levels in the environment.

Figure 3.60 The golden toad.

Challenge yourself

Research and summarize the case histories of three other species. Find examples of species that are different to those used here and include one that is extinct, one that is critically endangered and a third whose conservation status has been improved by intervention.

For each species, list the ecological, sociopolitical and economic pressures that are involved, and outline the possible consequences of their disappearance on the ecosystem.

3.2.7 The tragedy of the commons

There are areas of land and water where no single person or society has overall control. These are known as the **'commons'**.

Garrett Hardin was an American ecologist best known for his 1968 paper titled *The Tragedy of the Commons* (Figure 3.61). In this paper he explained how the short-term interest of the individual can lead to overconsumption of common natural resources at the expense of the broader society.

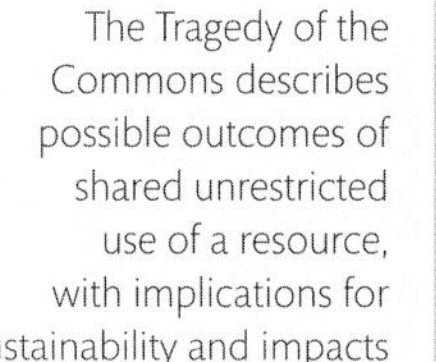
The Tragedy of the Commons describes possible outcomes of shared unrestricted use of a resource, with implications for sustainability and impacts on biodiversity.

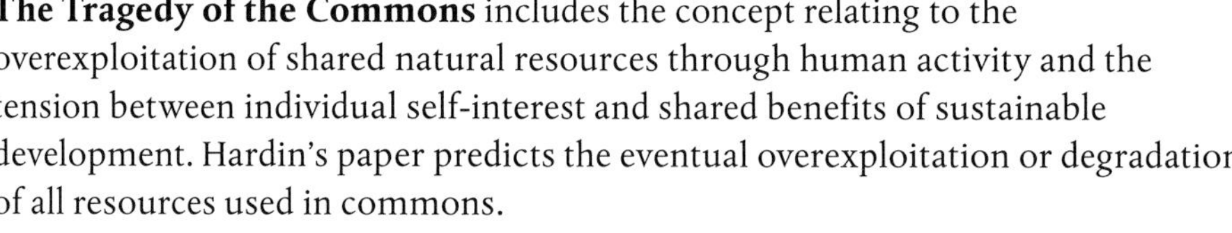
The Tragedy of the Commons includes the concept relating to the overexploitation of shared natural resources through human activity and the tension between individual self-interest and shared benefits of sustainable development. Hardin's paper predicts the eventual overexploitation or degradation of all resources used in commons.

Activity

Look at Figure 3.61. What does the photograph show? How does it exemplify the concept of the tragedy of the commons?

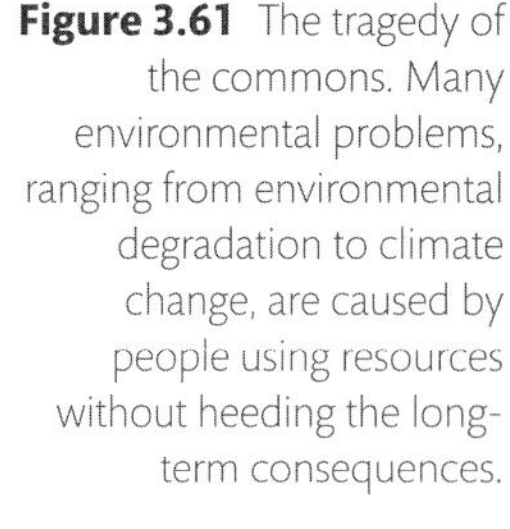
Figure 3.61 The tragedy of the commons. Many environmental problems, ranging from environmental degradation to climate change, are caused by people using resources without heeding the long-term consequences.

Activity

Read Garrett Hardin's original paper: Hardin, G. (1968), The Tragedy of the Commons. *Science*, New Series, Vol. 162, No. 3859 (Dec. 13, 1968), pp. 1243–1248.

Summarize, in fewer than 350 words, the discussion outlined in the paper. In what ways are the ideas still relevant today?

The Grand Banks

The overharvesting of fish stocks on the Grand Banks (Topic 1, Section 1.3.7) is an example of the tragedy of the commons. The concept can also be applied to areas where the environment is contaminated (see Example below – The Great Pacific Garbage Patch). Plastic pollution, for example, can have a negative effect on wildlife. Plastic garbage harms and kills approximately 100,000 sea turtles and other marine animals each year. Sea turtles mistake plastic bags for jelly fish, which is one of their favourite foods, and so attempt to eat them (Figure 3.62). The consequences of ingesting plastic can be fatal. For example, if the plastic debris gets lodged in the mouth, the turtle can have problems feeding, leading to eventual starvation.

Figure 3.62 Sea turtles cannot see the difference between jelly fish and plastic bags.

Garrett Hardin, who first wrote about the tragedy of the commons (see previous page), compared shared resources to a common grazing pasture. In this scenario, everyone in the local community who has rights to the pasture grazes as many animals as possible, acting in self-interest for the greatest short-term personal economic gain. Eventually, the herders use up all the grass in the pasture and so the shared resource is depleted and no longer useful. Each herder has a desire to put each succeeding cow he acquires onto the land, even if the carrying capacity of the common is exceeded and it is permanently damaged for all as a result. The individual herder receives all of the benefits from an additional cow, while the damage to the common is shared by all the herders involved. If all herders are free to make their own individual decisions about what is in their own best economic interests, the common will be over-exploited or perhaps eventually destroyed.

Example – The Great Pacific Garbage Patch

The Great Pacific Garbage Patch, also known as the Eastern Garbage Patch, is located between Hawaii and California and is known to be the largest accumulation of ocean plastic in the world (Figure 3.63). Plastic waste from countries surrounding and within the Pacific Ocean is carried by ocean currents to this area. Ocean currents that pull in debris are known as **gyres**. There are five gyres in total. These enormous gyres are another example of the tragedy of the commons, where individuals act in their own best interest, ignoring the impacts on the environment and global biodiversity, as well as the negative effect on other people.

Read more about the Great Pacific Garbage Patch on the Ocean Cleanup website:

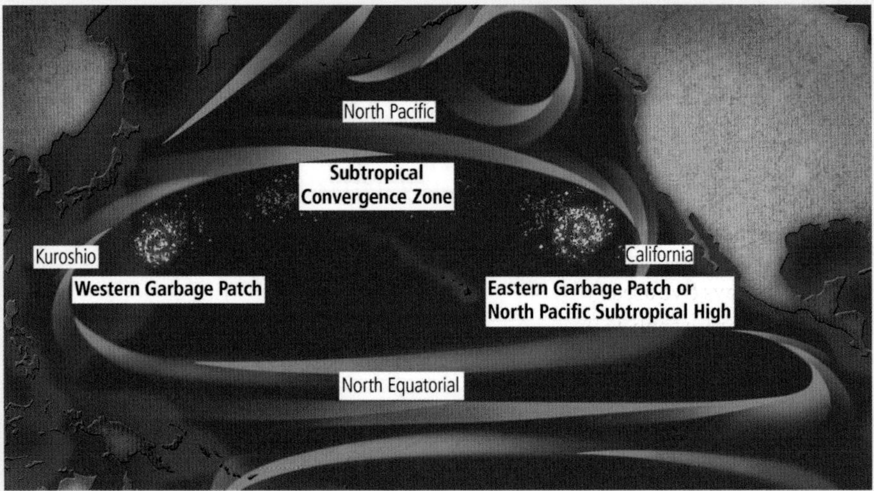

Figure 3.63 Great Pacific garbage patches. Large rotating ocean currents (gyres) contain marine debris particles and are characterized by exceptionally high concentrations of plastics, chemical sludge and other debris that have become trapped.

One research study found that microplastics were more prevalent than plankton in some South Pacific gyre sea surface samples. Any disturbances due to microplastics at such low levels of the food chain could have serious consequences, since plankton and small swimming organisms, such as fish larvae, support the transfer of energy to higher trophic levels.

Activity

Find out about the other ocean gyres.

- Where are they located?
- Which ocean currents draw the plastic to these locations?
- What are the impacts on local, regional and global biodiversity?

Produce a poster about the ocean gyres and how they are an example of the tragedy of the commons.

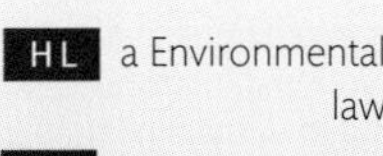
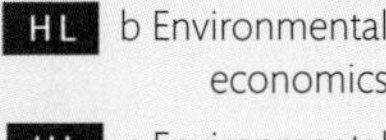

HL a Environmental law

HL b Environmental economics

HL c Environmental ethics

Activity

As the world's population increases and demands more access to resources, the issues associated with the commons become more severe. This may test the role of nation-states, leading to a redefinition of international governance.

Consider the role of government at the local, state, national and international levels in defining and managing shared resources.

Think about how governments can overcome the tragedy of the commons and share your ideas with someone else in your class. Do others agree with your ideas?

HL

3.2.8 Biodiversity hotspots under threat

HL

Biodiversity hotspots are under threat from habitat destruction, which could lead to a significant loss of biological diversity, especially in tropical biomes.

Figure 3.64 shows five areas where hotspots are under extreme threat, with each region having more than 1500 unique plant species but having lost 70% of its native vegetation.

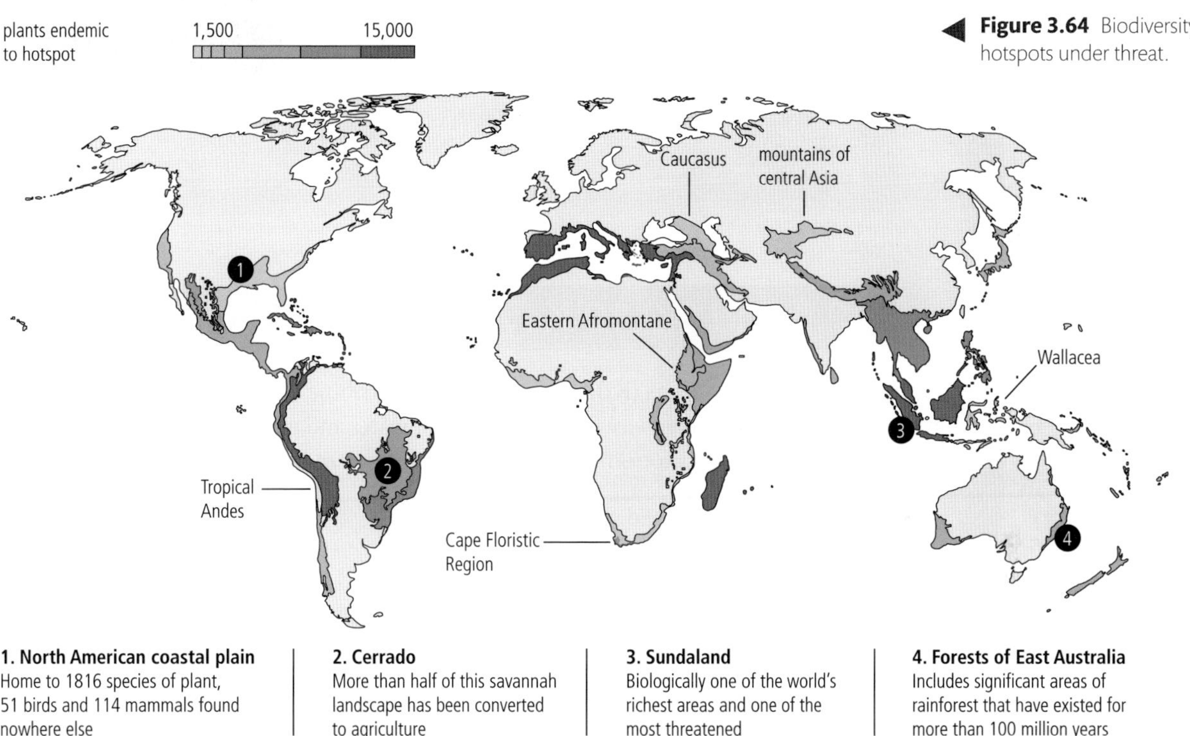
plants endemic to hotspot
1,500
15,000
Caucasus
mountains of central Asia
Eastern Afromontane
Wallacea
Tropical Andes
Cape Floristic Region
1
2
3
4
1. North American coastal plain
Home to 1816 species of plant, 51 birds and 114 mammals found nowhere else
2. Cerrado
More than half of this savannah landscape has been converted to agriculture
3. Sundaland
Biologically one of the world's richest areas and one of the most threatened
4. Forests of East Australia
Includes significant areas of rainforest that have existed for more than 100 million years

Figure 3.64 Biodiversity hotspots under threat.

Research indicates that animal populations have decreased rapidly by an average of 69% between 1970 and 2018. This decrease has been greatest in Latin America and the Caribbean (Figure 3.65). For further information, read the Guardian article *The biodiversity crisis in numbers - a visual guide.*

Figure 3.65 Decline in animal populations since 1970.

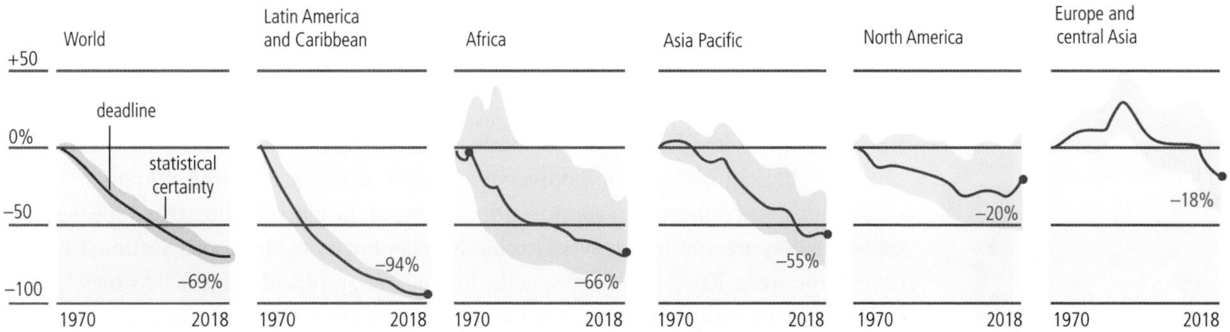

World: +50, 0%, −50, −100; deadline; statistical certainty; −69%; 1970, 2018
Latin America and Caribbean: −94%; 1970, 2018
Africa: −66%; 1970, 2018
Asia Pacific: −55%; 1970, 2018
North America: −20%; 1970, 2018
Europe and central Asia: −18%; 1970, 2018

Read more about how Kew Gardens in London, UK, is tackling threats to biodiversity hotspots, by searching for the threatened bioversity hotspots programme on its website:

Activity

What are the implications of biodiversity distribution for conservation? For example, because tropical biomes are frequently located in developing countries this can make effective conservation more challenging (this topic, Section 3.2.10).

Is biodiversity unevenly distributed in your country or local region? Has this caused difficulties in prioritizing and conserving key areas? What are the potential solutions to the problems? Produce a summary of your findings.

The map of biodiversity hotspots overlaps very well with the map of natural areas that most benefit people through the provision of ecosystem services such as clear water, aesthetic value and the production of food and medicines. *Why is this?* Hotspots are the most biodiverse and important ecosystems in the world and are also home to many vulnerable human societies who are directly dependent on nature to survive. One estimate suggests that despite comprising 2.5% of Earth's land surface, the forests, wetlands and other ecosystems in hotspots account for 35% of the ecosystem services (this topic, Section 3.3.1) that vulnerable human societies depend on.

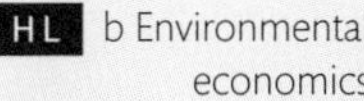

HL a Environmental law

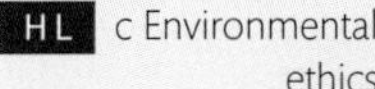

HL b Environmental economics

HL c Environmental ethics

HL

3.2.9 and 3.2.10 Key biodiversity areas (KBAs)

Key areas that should be prioritized for biodiversity conservation have been identified on the basis of the international importance of their species and habitats.

Key biodiversity areas (KBAs) are sites that contribute significantly to the global conservation of biodiversity in terrestrial, freshwater and marine environments. KBAs are identified using taxonomic and ecological criteria and thresholds, such as:

- presence of threatened species
- presence of threatened ecosystems
- geographically restricted species
- ecological integrity where the site remains ecologically intact, essentially unaffected by industrial human influence
- biological processes where the site holds a significant proportion of a species' population during one or more of its life stages, such as nesting, making it important for the continued survival of that species
- irreplaceability where the site has very high irreplaceability for the global persistence of biodiversity.

The concept of KBAs was developed at the World Conservation Congress in Bangkok in 2004. At the meeting, IUCN members recognized the need for a 'unifying framework' for conservation that could be applied across different taxonomic groups as well as ecosystems. The IUCN led a global consultation process to consolidate the criteria and methodology for identifying KBAs. In 2016, the global 'KBA Standard' was announced.

Key biodiversity areas (KBAs) have been used to identify sites that contribute significantly to the global persistence of biodiversity.

KBAs allow the identification of fine-scale priority areas for conservation. KBAs are sites of global significance for biodiversity conservation that are large enough or sufficiently interconnected to support populations of the globally threatened species for which they are important. Whereas biodiversity hotspots (this topic, Section 3.1.12) cover large areas, KBAs are more specific in their geographical range. KBAs may be fully within, partially within, or outside of protected areas (Figure 3.66).

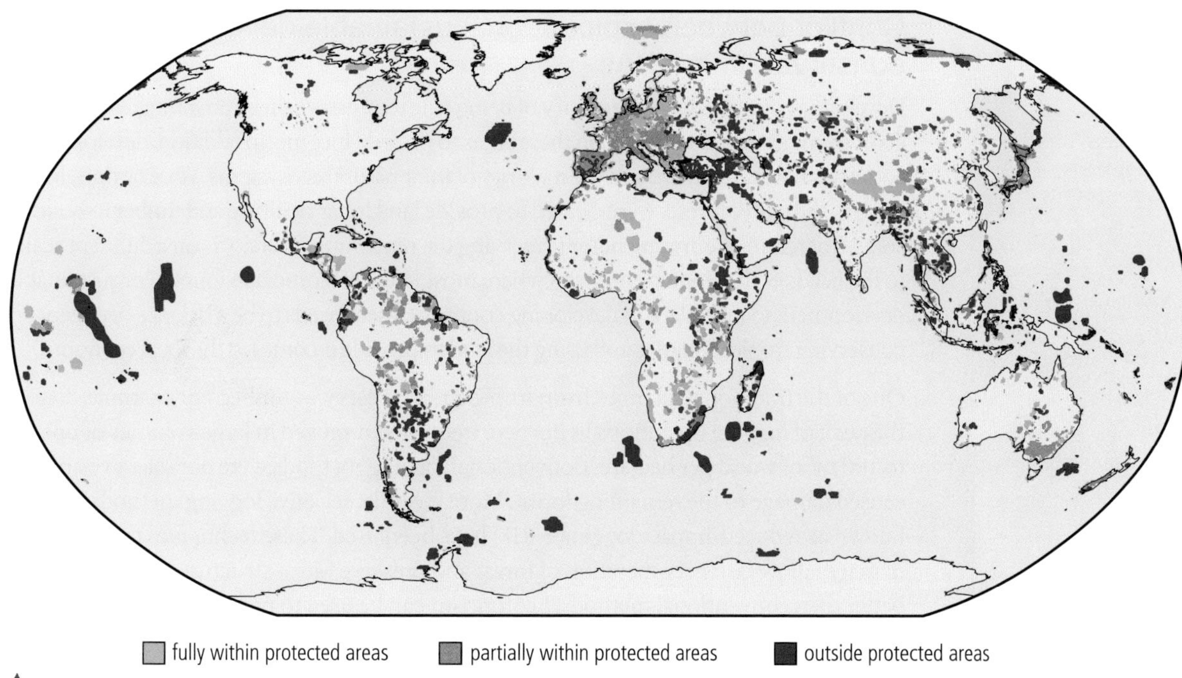

Figure 3.66 Key biodiversity areas around the globe. KBAs are coloured whether they are fully within (green), partially within (orange) or outside (red) protected areas on land and in the ocean.

Protected area coverage of KBAs is a formal indicator for targets under UN Sustainable Development Goals 14 and 15 as well as the Convention on Biological Diversity Aichi Target 11.

Activity

Find out about two areas that have been prioritized for conservation and have been designated as KBAs. The sites should hold species at risk of extinction or ecosystems at risk of collapse. Ideally, the two KBAs should include different habitats and ecosystems.

Produce a fact sheet for each KBA, that answers the following questions:

- What data supports their inclusion as KBAs?
- What is their importance for global biodiversity?
- What threatened species will be protected by the KBA?
- What geographically restricted species will be protected?
- How will the ecological integrity of the area be conserved?
- What are the similarities and differences between the two KBAs?

Use photos, figures and illustrations to make your fact sheet informative and visually interesting.

Search for 'explore the biodiversity hotspots' on the Critical Ecosystem Partnership Fund website:

Read more about KBAs on the Key Biodiversity Areas website:

Find further information by searching for 'what is a key biodiversity area' on the Critical Ecosystem Partnership Fund website:

Most tropical biomes occur in developing countries and therefore there is conflict between exploitation, sustainable development and conservation.

Conflict between exploitation, sustainable development and conservation in KBAs

Developed countries have the luxury of being able to preserve their remaining natural ecosystems as they do not rely on these areas to provide income. In addition, developed countries have already cleared the majority of their natural ecosystems. For example, in the UK, the native forests were cleared to provide land for agriculture and timber to build ships. Therefore, the argument for preserving the remaining diversity is on a different scale to the needs of developing countries where most tropical biomes are found. For sustainable development to take place in developing countries, there needs to be a balance between conserving tropical biomes and using the land to provide income for the local economy.

One of the traditional incomes from tropical rainforests was timber. For example, at the peak of logging operations in Borneo, trees were removed in large volumes of up to 100 m^3 of wood per hectare. Conventional logging methods were not selective and caused damage to the remaining forest. More recently, selective logging methods (also known as reduced-impact logging – RIL) have been used. These techniques cause less damage, allow faster regeneration of forest and preserve forest structure and biodiversity better than conventional methods. Ecotourism can be used to provide ongoing income without destroying natural capital (this topic, Section 3.3.14). Developing countries obviously wish to grow their economies and head towards developed country status, but the resulting conflict between exploitation, sustainable development and conservation can always be resolved providing there is local support and the political will to protect biodiversity before it is lost forever.

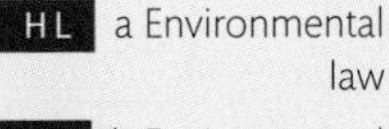 a Environmental law

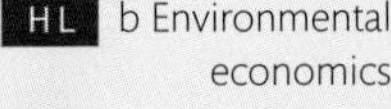 b Environmental economics

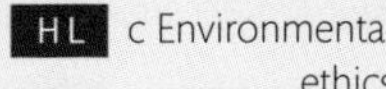 c Environmental ethics

An example of conflict between exploitation, sustainable development and conservation is outlined in the example below.

Example – CAMPFIRE in Zimbabwe

The Communal Areas Management Programme for Indigenous Resources (CAMPFIRE) is a Zimbabwean community-based management programme that assists rural development and conservation and helps people to manage their environment in a sustainable way.

Approximately 12% of the natural habitats of Zimbabwe are in **protected areas** and when these were set up, local people were relocated to surrounding areas. When wildlife, such as elephants, leave the parks and enter inhabited areas, conflicts can arise. CAMPFIRE encourages people to see their local wildlife as a resource rather than as a nuisance.

Five main activities help provide extra income to local communities.

- Trophy hunting where professional hunters and safari operators are allowed into the areas. This activity raises 90% of CAMPFIRE's income.
- Sale of wildlife where some areas with high wildlife populations 'sell' animals to National Parks or game reserves. For example, one district raised US$ 50,000 by selling 10 roan antelope.
- Harvesting natural resources where natural resources such as river sand and timber are harvested and sold.
- Tourism where the income from tourists is redirected to local communities. Some local people are employed as guides or run local facilities for tourists.
- Selling wildlife meat from some abundant species, such as impala. The National Parks Department supervise the killing of impala and the selling of their skins and meat.

Recent reports suggest, however, that communities have not been benefiting, despite the hunts being conducted in their areas.

Shereni, N.C. & Saarinen, J. (2021) Community perceptions on the benefits and challenges of community-based natural resources management in Zimbabwe. *Development Southern Africa*, Vol 38, Issue 6, pp. 879–895.

When the project began, communities looked forward to direct and indirect economic benefits as well as infrastructure development of schools and other buildings in their areas, but these benefits have not always been forthcoming. The current CAMPFIRE guidelines are not legally binding and there are no legal provisions for enforceability, accountability, monitoring or reporting. Some areas have not adhered to the CAMPFIRE guidelines, resulting in decreasing revenue to communities. In addition, areas not involved with the programme (non-CAMPFIRE wards) see CAMPFIRE as a divisive programme. These non-CAMPFIRE wards face the same losses arising from human wildlife conflicts which include death, injury and loss of crops and livestock. They have argued that although wildlife is not as abundant in their wards compared to CAMPFIRE wards, their wards provide refuges for wildlife when population pressures are high in CAMPFIRE areas. As such, communities in non-CAMPFIRE wards argue that revenue from the CAMPFIRE should be equally distributed.

Tropical biomes are under constant threat. Large areas of tropical rainforest with an average size of 1.5 hectares, the size of a football pitch, are lost every five seconds. Deforestation and forest degradation are driven by external demands for timber, beef, land for crops such as soya, palm oil and biofuels. Developing 'carbon markets' – which value ecosystems as stores of carbon (in vegetation) – could provide the means to give sufficient monetary value to rainforests to help protect them.

Human impacts, both direct and indirect, on the world's rainforest are having a major effect on species survival. Uncontrolled hunting (for bush meat and reasons such as the exotic pet trade) is removing large species and creating an 'empty forest syndrome' – the trees are there but the large species have disappeared. The replacement of natural tropical rainforest by palm oil plantations (Figure 3.67), in South-East Asia, is replacing a diverse ecosystem with a monoculture ecosystem.

Rainforests have thin, nutrient-poor soils (Topic 2, Section 2.4.4). Because there are few nutrients in the soil, it is difficult for rainforests to re-grow once they have been cleared. Studies in the Brazilian Atlantic forest have shown that parts of the forest can return surprisingly quickly – within 65 years – but for the landscape to truly regain its native identity takes a lot longer – up to 4000 years. Recovery depends on the level of disturbance – a large area of cleared land will take a lot longer to grow back, if it grows back at all, than small areas that have been subject to shifting cultivation (Topic 5, Section 5.2). Forest that has been selectively harvested for timber can grow back rapidly if only a few large trees have been removed. A larger amount of timber removal may mean that the forest never fully recovers. This is because fast-growing, light-loving species, such as vines and creepers, block out the light for slow growers, causing the forest to remain at a sub-climax level.

Example – The spread of palm oil plantations in South-East Asia and the consequences for biodiversity

Palm oil is the second most traded vegetable oil crop after soy. Over 90% of the world's palm oil exports are produced in Malaysia and Indonesia, in areas that were once covered by rainforest and peat forest. Palm oil is traditionally used in the manufacture of food products but is now increasingly used as an ingredient in biodiesel. It is also used as biofuel burned at power stations to produce electricity.

This new market has the potential to dramatically increase the global demand for palm oil. In the UK, the conversion of just one oil-fired power station to palm oil could double UK imports. The 6.5 million hectares of palm oil plantations across Sumatra and Borneo is estimated to have caused the destruction of 10 million hectares of rainforest – an increase in demand for palm oil as a biofuel would further increase the threat to natural ecosystems unless controls are put in place.

Figure 3.67 In 2020, Indonesia's palm oil plantations were projected to expand to 16.5 million hectares. Many conservationists believe that in Indonesia and other countries, this will lead directly and indirectly to the further clearance of a huge area of rainforest.

Land use in tropical areas is a contentious issue. The widespread clearance of natural ecosystems so that land can be made available for plantations leads to biodiversity loss. But the replacement plantations do provide valuable financial income, which is something that natural ecosystems on their own may not do. Diversification of the local economy into areas such as ecotourism can provide alternative sources of income and take pressure off local habitats, as can the development of conservation areas (this topic, Section 3.3.14, pages 322–324).

HL

3.2.11 Traditional indigenous approaches to land management

Indigenous peoples are distinct social and cultural groups that share collective ancestral ties to the lands and natural resources where they live. Traditional indigenous approaches to land management (Topic 5, Section 5.2.6) can be seen as more sustainable. But the Indigenous peoples are facing challenges including population growth, economic development, climate change and a lack of governmental support and protection.

Threats to the notions of the sustainability in traditional indigenous approaches often come from outside the community. However, as the society develops economically and hopes to follow the development model of the rest of the world, threats may then come from within the community.

Example – Flooding of river systems in the Ecuadorian Amazon

Indigenous societies in the Ecuadorian Amazon have traditionally used the flooding of river systems during rainy seasons to make the best or most effective use of their fishing practices. Now, due to climate change caused by fossil-fuel-based economic growth, flooding has increased in magnitude. This flooding has submerged the communities and their farms further upriver, and has affected crop growth, therefore increasing food insecurity among these societies.

Example – The effect of climate change on Aboriginal and Torres Strait Islander people, Australia

The Aboriginal and Torres Strait Islander people in Australia are being affected by rising water levels, tidal surges and coastal erosion due to climate change. These societies are disproportionally affected by the effects of climate change. For example, in floods outside Sydney in 2017, 6.2% of those affected were Aboriginal and Torres Strait Islander people, despite them only making up 3.3% of the total population. The Torres Strait Islands are being affected by high tides, strong winds and heavy rainfall. Land has been degraded, reducing the amount of food available from traditional fishing and farming. Fruit is an important part of the Islanders' traditional diet but on Masig Island, rising sea levels have led to saltwater entering the soil, killing fruit trees.

Activity

In Canada, between 2016 and 2021 the Indigenous population grew by 9.4%. The non-Indigenous population grew by 5.3% over the same period.

Read about the growth of Indigenous peoples in Canada by searching for 'Indigenous population continues to grow' on the Statistics Canada website:

- What factors are affecting the population growth of Indigenous peoples (First Nations people, Métis and Inuit) and why?
- What issues arise from increased population growth?
  For example, of the 1.8 million Indigenous people living in Canada in 2021, 18.8% lived in a low-income household, compared with 10.7% of the non-Indigenous population.

Summarize your findings as a fact sheet.

5.2 Agriculture and food

7.2 Energy resources, use and management

HL a Environmental law

HL b Environmental economics

HL c Environmental ethics

Make sure you consider threats to a named sustainable traditional indigenous land management practice.

3.2.12 Environmental justice and conservation

HL

The areas of the world that are expected to experience significant negative effects from both the loss of biodiversity and ecosystem functions are likely to be those with large concentrations of Indigenous people, such as rainforests (this topic, Section 3.2.10). These communities may have a low income and no access to legal support (see Example – Maasai in Serengeti).

Environmental justice must be considered when undertaking conservation efforts to address biodiversity loss.

Example – Maasai in Serengeti

The Maasai are an Indigenous group living semi-nomadically in Kenya and parts of Tanzania (Figure 3.68). They use a nomadic form of farming where their livestock are able to wander freely and are herded by their owners. The Maasai diet is traditionally meat, milk and blood supplied by their cattle. Virtually all social roles and status derive from the relationship of individuals to their cattle. This is an example of extensive subsistence farming (Topic 5, Section 5.2.5).

Nomadic herding is practiced by 2.7 billion people (44% of world population) and provides 20% of the world's food supply.

1.1 Perspectives

Figure 3.68 A Maasai man wearing traditional blankets overlooks the Serengeti in Tanzania.

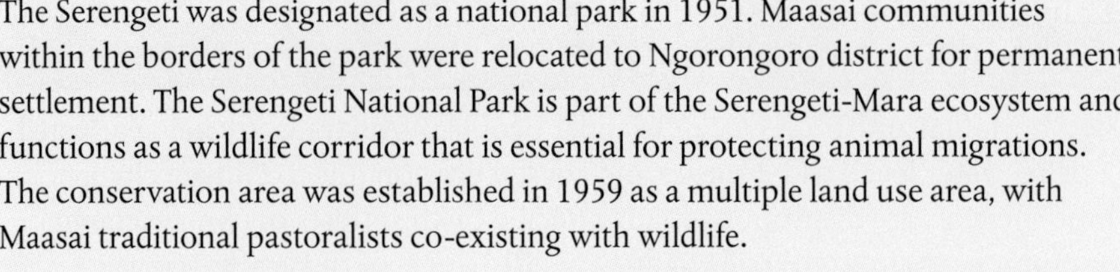

The Serengeti was designated as a national park in 1951. Maasai communities within the borders of the park were relocated to Ngorongoro district for permanent settlement. The Serengeti National Park is part of the Serengeti-Mara ecosystem and functions as a wildlife corridor that is essential for protecting animal migrations. The conservation area was established in 1959 as a multiple land use area, with Maasai traditional pastoralists co-existing with wildlife.

Maasai communities have continued to face resettlement, even from the regions where they were originally relocated to. New regulations have curtailed the rights of Maasai to graze cattle and cultivate subsistence gardens. The United Nations reports that 82,000 Maasai people are at risk of being removed from the Ngorongoro Conservation Area and Loliondo. The Tanzania tourism ministry plans to convert 1500 square kilometres around Ololosokwan from a 'game-controlled area', where Maasai are permitted to live, farm and graze livestock, to a 'game reserve' that would be used for safari tourism and the licensed hunting of wildlife.

Read more about the issues here:

Make sure that you consider one example of an Indigenous or marginalized community that has been forcefully relocated from their homeland due to conservation efforts or protected habitats.

HL a Environmental law

HL c Environmental ethics

HL

3.2.13 Species extinctions have crossed a critical threshold

The planetary boundary 'Loss of biosphere integrity' indicates that species extinctions have already crossed a critical threshold (Topic 1, Section 1.3.19).

Estimates of extinction rates are varied, but current extinction rates are thought to be between 100 and 10,000 times greater than background rates. Estimates range from 30,000 to 60,000 species a year.

In order to understand how many species are currently becoming extinct, existing species must be identified and named. Experts who study specific groups of organisms, such as moths, beetles and birds, are found in centres of excellence around the world and reference collections are often contained within natural history museums. For taxonomy to succeed, scientists from around the world must work together, and major surveys must be carried out using international teams of specialists.

We know that mass extinction events have happened in the past (this topic, Section 3.1.17, pages 362–364), but what do we know of current extinction rates? Throughout the history of Earth, diversity has never remained constant. There have been a number of natural periods of extinction and loss of diversity. More recently, humans have played an increasing role in diversity loss, especially in biodiverse ecosystems such as rainforest and coral reef.

The background (natural) level of extinction known from the fossil record is between 10 and 100 species per year. Human activities have resulted in an increase in this rate. Because the total number of classified species is a small fraction of the estimated total of species, estimates of extinction rates are also varied. Estimates from tropical rainforest suggest the Earth is losing 27,000 species per year from those habitats alone. The rate of extinction differs for different groups of organisms but examining the figures for one group (mammals) gives an indication of the extent of the problem. Mammal species have an average species lifespan, from origin to extinction, of about 1 million years. There are about 5000 known mammalian species alive at present. The **background extinction rate** for this group should be approximately one species lost every 200 years. Yet the past 400 years have seen 89 mammalian extinctions, almost 45 times the predicted rate. Another 169 mammal species are listed as critically endangered.

Many of the species found in Madagascar are endemic. Therefore, if these species become extinct in Madagascar, they will become extinct globally. Read more about the extinction risk to species in Madagascar in the article: Helmstetter, A.J. *et al.* (2021) The demographic history of Madagascan micro-endemics: have rare species always been rare? *Proceedings of the Royal Society B*, Vol 288, Issue 1959, 20210957, 29.09.2021.

A sixth mass extinction, caused by human activities, has become accepted (this topic, Section 3.1.17). According to the IUCN Red List, approximately 6% of described species have been assessed and 28% are threatened by extinction. Fewer than 135,000 species have been assessed and so there is very poor understanding of the extinction risk to many taxa, including those that are essential to human well-being. For example, only 54,000 plant species have IUCN assessments (approximately 13% of all plant species).

Activity

Consider the claim that species extinctions caused by human impacts could lead to a tipping point in the whole Earth system.

Discuss this claim within your class. Do you agree with the statement? What is the evidence that supports the claim?

1.3 Sustainability

HL end

Engagement

- Assess the tensions between exploitation, sustainable development and conservation in a local ecosystem or protected area. Promote the issues in your school or local community using posters or other visual stimulus material.
- Raise awareness of indigenous land rights through discussion groups or lectures (either in person or in virtual/online meetings), using a local or global example. Outline the issues and potential solutions in these meetings.
- Raise awareness of endangered species through leaflets handed out in your local community, and volunteer in a local non-governmental organization (NGO) for wildlife rehabilitation.

Exercise

Q12. List five factors that lead to the loss of diversity.

Q13. Describe how alien species become invasive.

Q14. Describe a species whose conservation status has been improved by intervention. Consider the factors that contributed to their decline, the impacts of their decline on ecosystems and societies, and conservation strategies that were successfully employed.

Q15. List five factors that are used to determine a species' Red List status.

Q16. Define the term *tragedy of the commons.*

HL

Q17. HL **Evaluate** the impact of human activity on the biodiversity of tropical biomes.

Q18. HL **Outline** how key biodiversity areas (KBAs) are identified and established.

Q19. HL **Describe,** using an example, the challenges facing traditional indigenous approaches to land management.

Q20. HL **Explain** why environmental justice must be considered when undertaking conservation efforts to address biodiversity loss.

Q21. HL **Evaluate** the claim that species extinctions caused by human impacts could lead to a tipping point in the whole Earth system.

HL end

3.3 Conservation and regeneration

Guiding Questions

How can different strategies for conserving and regenerating natural systems be compared?
How do worldviews affect the choices made in protecting natural systems?

3.3.1 Arguments for species and habitat preservation can be based on aesthetic, ecological, economic, ethical and social justifications.
3.3.2 Species-based conservation tends to involve *ex situ* strategies, and habitat-based conservation tends to involve *in situ* strategies.
3.3.3 Sometimes a mixed conservation approach is adopted, where both habitat and particular species are considered.
3.3.4 The Convention on Biological Diversity (CBD) is a UN treaty addressing both species-based and habitat-based conservation.
3.3.5 Habitat conservation strategies protect species by conservation of their natural environment. This may require protection of wild areas or active management.
3.3.6 Effective conservation of biodiversity in nature reserves and national parks depends on an understanding of the biology of target species and on the effect of the size and shape of conservation areas.
3.3.7 Natural processes in ecosystems can be regenerated by rewilding.
3.3.8 Conservation and regeneration measures can be used to reverse the decline in biodiversity to ensure a safe operating space for humanity within the biodiversity planetary boundary.
3.3.9 Environmental perspectives and value systems can impact the choice of conservation strategies selected by a society.
HL 3.3.10 Success in conserving and restoring biodiversity by international, governmental and non-governmental organizations depends on their use of media, speed of response, diplomatic constraints, financial resources and political influence.

HL 3.3.11 Positive feedback loops that enhance biodiversity and promote ecosystem equilibrium can be triggered by rewilding and habitat restoration efforts.
HL 3.3.12 Rewilding projects have both benefits and limitations.
HL 3.3.13 The success of conservation or regeneration measures needs to be assessed.
HL 3.3.14 Ecotourism can increase interdependence of local communities and increase biodiversity by generating income and providing funds for protecting areas, but there can also be negative societal and ecological impacts.

3.3.1 Arguments for species and habitat preservation

The value of biodiversity can be difficult to quantify. Goods harvested from an ecosystem are easier to evaluate than indirect values such as the aesthetic or cultural aspects of an ecosystem. There are many arguments for preserving species and habitats. These arguments can be divided into five groups.

- **Economic arguments** for preservation often focus on the value of ecotourism, genetic resource and commercial considerations of the natural capital. For example, it is easy to value rainforest in terms of the amount of timber present because this has direct monetary value. But intact rainforests also provide valuable ecosystem services for the local, national and global communities (Figure 3.69).

  Species and habitats provide financial income. Species should be preserved to maintain genetic diversity, so that genetic resources will be available in the future. For example, genetic diversity will allow crops to be improved in the future. Other reasons for preserving biodiversity are that commercial resources, such as new medicines, are still waiting to be discovered. The rosy periwinkle, a plant endemic to Madagascar, is used in cancer treatment. Ecotourism is successful when habitats high in biodiversity are preserved because they attract people to visit.

Economic arguments for preservation often involve valuation of ecotourism, the genetic resource and commercial considerations of the natural capital.

Arguments about species and habitat preservation can be based on aesthetic, ecological, economic, ethical and social justifications.

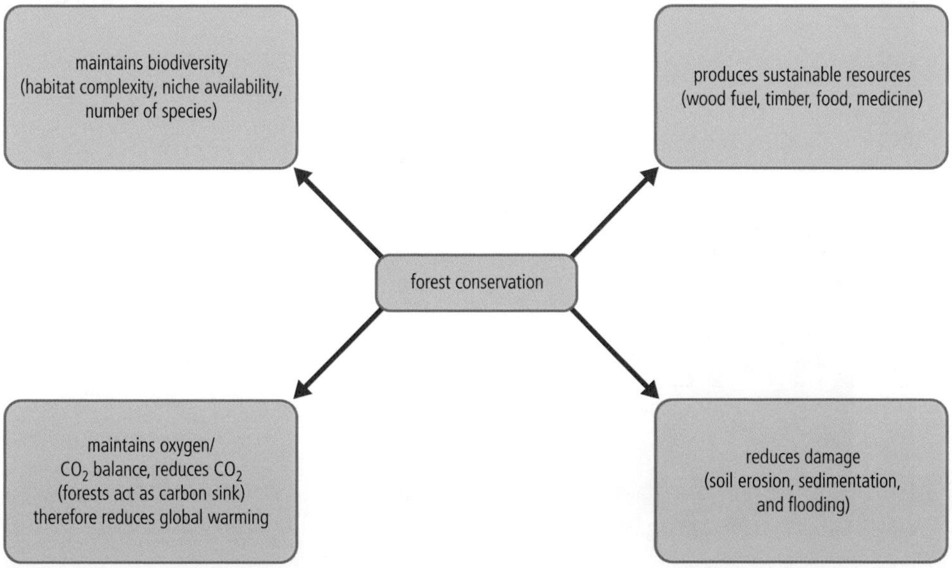

Figure 3.69 The biological significance of a forest.

Ecological arguments are concerned with ecosystems and their functioning.

- **Ecological arguments** may be related to the ecosystem services. Healthy ecosystems are more likely to provide ecosystem services such as pollination and flood prevention. Rainforests are vital to the hydrologic (water) cycle and they stabilize some of the world's most fragile soils by preventing soil erosion. Rainforests also are responsible for regulating temperature and weather patterns in the areas surrounding the forest, they sequester (isolate) and store huge amounts of carbon from the atmosphere, cool and clean the world's atmosphere, are a huge source of the world's biodiversity and provide fresh water. The Amazonian rainforest provides 20% of the world's fresh water.

  Rare habitats should be conserved as they may contain endemic species that require specific habitats. In addition, ecosystems with high levels of biodiversity are generally more stable and more likely to survive into the future. Species should be preserved because if they disappear, they could affect the rest of the food chain and ecosystem.

- **Aesthetic reasons** are that species and habitats are pleasant to look at and provide beauty and inspiration.
- **Ethical arguments** are very diverse and can include reference to the intrinsic or **instrumental value** of the species. Everyone has a responsibility to protect resources for future generations. Ethical reasons also include the idea that every species has a right to survive.
- **Social arguments** highlight the importance of goods and services for the well-being of humans. Many natural ecosystems around the world provide places to live for Indigenous peoples. Loss of these areas would mean loss of these peoples' homes, source of livelihood and culture. In addition, many areas of great biodiversity provide an income for local people, such as tourism and wildlife protection. These areas therefore support social cohesion and cultural services.

Ethical arguments are very broad and can include the intrinsic or the utilitarian value of the species.

Survival International is an organization that campaigns for the rights of Indigenous peoples and uncontacted peoples. Learn more about Survival International on their website:

Natural *systems* should be preserved for a variety of reasons:

- they have an economic value to humans that encourages their *sustainable* use
- they may contain food, medicines and materials for sustainable human use
- they have an **intrinsic value**
- they provide life-support functions that sustain life on Earth
- they may contain high biodiversity, which leads to stability in ecosystems
- they have aesthetic value
- the tourism function can bring income
- they may provide a home to Indigenous people
- they may provide spiritual, cultural or religious value to local communities
- the current human population has a duty to protect species and habitats for future generations.

Figure 3.70 An Iban man wearing a ceremonial headdress of feathers.

The Iban are the Indigenous people of Sarawak (Malaysia), Brunei and western Kalimantan (Indonesian Borneo) (Figure 3.70). Traditionally, they live in communal longhouses, hunting and fishing in rainforest areas, and growing crops using shifting cultivation. Pulp and paper companies have cleared Iban land and planted acacia trees, and other areas have been cleared for palm oil. The Iban have appealed against the loss of their traditional lands, although these rights have so far been denied as courts decided that landownership based on continuous occupation should 'not be extended to areas where the natives used to roam to forage for their food and building materials in accordance with their tradition'.

It is difficult to assign monetary value to most of these benefits as every person on the planet benefits from these services but none of us pay for them. Intact rainforests are aesthetically pleasing and this makes people want to visit them, which gives rainforest value from an ecotourism point of view. As rainforests contain such a high percentage of the existing global biodiversity, it could also be argued that we have an ethical responsibility to conserve them.

The value of ecosystems depends on cultural background as well as economic status. The value of a rainforest to someone who lives in it and relies on it for their livelihood is very different from its value to an outsider who does not have these concerns.

Forest people are found in rainforests in Brazil, Colombia, Ecuador, Paraguay, Canada, Peru, Argentina, Botswana, Kenya, Ethiopia, Sudan, Central Africa, Australia, Indonesia, the Philippines, India, Bangladesh, Russia, Malaysia and Sri Lanka. The majority of these people are under threat from logging and rainforest loss. For example, the territory of the Awá tribe in Brazil has been invaded and destroyed. Cattle ranchers illegally occupy Awá land and, in another part of their territory, groups of heavily armed loggers have destroyed much of the forest.

It is easier to give commercial value to resources such as timber, medicine and food. It is more difficult to give value to ecosystem services, cultural services and ethical and aesthetic factors, although this does not mean that these are not equally valid reasons for preserving biodiversity.

The Penan of Borneo are nomadic hunter-gatherers who have historically relied on the rainforests for their survival. They have a comprehensive knowledge of the forest and are highly skilled in surviving there. For example, they can use a poison-headed dart from a blowpipe to strike an animal 40 m above them in the upper canopy (Figure 3.71).

Figure 3.71 Nomadic Penan hunting with blowpipe.

Economically developed countries see the rainforest as an opportunity to exploit natural resources and use land for new settlements. Forest peoples' *perspectives* of rainforest differ from the *perspectives* of people from developed countries. The forest is the home of the forest people, from which they derive their livelihood and their cultural values. The loss of forest means losing not only their home, but also the loss of their food sources and the destruction of their culture, which has developed through generations of forest living.

To what extent is our perspective determined by our membership of a particular culture?

A species that has value to one culture may not have any value to another. For example, in South-East Asia, elephants are valued by tourists but not by the locals who see the elephants as pests that eat crops and destroy their forest plantations.

1.1 Perspectives

HL b Environmental economics
HL c Environmental ethics

3.3.2 Species-based conservation

Conservation means 'keeping what we have'. Conservation aims to protect habitats and ecosystems, and hence species, from human-made disturbances such as deforestation and pollution. Conservation activities aim to slow the rate of extinction caused by the knock-on effects of unsustainable exploitation of natural resources and to maintain biotic interactions between species.

Species-based conservation tends to involve *ex situ* strategies and habitat-based conservation tends to involve *in situ* strategies.

Conservation approaches include **habitat conservation**, **species-based conservation** or a combination of both approaches (a **mixed approach**).

***In situ* conservation** measures include use of national parks, reserves and sanctuaries.

***In situ* conservation** is the conservation of species in their natural habitat. For example, this enables endangered species to be conserved in their native habitat. Not only are the endangered animals protected, but also the habitat and ecosystem in which they live, leading to the preservation of many other species. *In situ* conservation works within the boundaries of conservation areas or nature reserves.

***Ex situ* conservation** measures include botanic gardens, zoos, CITES and seed banks.

***Ex situ* conservation** is the preservation of species outside their natural habitats. This usually takes place in botanic gardens and zoos, which carry out captive breeding and reintroduction programmes. The species-based approach to conservation is an approach that focuses on specific individual species (usually animals) that are vulnerable. The aim is to attract interest in their conservation and therefore funding and public pressure for conservation. *Ex situ* also includes preservation of plant biodiversity, in botanic gardens or seed banks.

Ex situ conservation

There are different strategies for conservation. *In situ* conservation preserves biodiversity in natural habitats within protected areas where *sustainability* is ensured. *Ex situ* conservation preserves biodiversity outside natural habitats in zoos or wildlife parks.

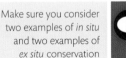

The Convention on International Trade in Endangered Species of Wild Fauna and Flora (CITES)

CITES was established in 1973 and celebrated its 50th anniversary on 3 March 2023, which is also the 10th anniversary of World Wildlife Day. CITES is an international agreement aimed at preventing trade in endangered species of both plants and animals. This trade is worth billions of dollars every year and involves hundreds of millions of plant and animal specimens.

Make sure you consider two examples of *in situ* and two examples of *ex situ* conservation measures.

Trade in animal and plant specimens, from whole organisms to parts and derivatives, as well as factors such as habitat loss, can seriously reduce their wild populations and bring some species close to extinction. The aim of CITES is to ensure that any international trade in specimens of wild animals and plants does not threaten the survival of the species in the wild. CITES gives varying degrees of protection to 35,000 species of animals and plants. Species under threat from extinction are protected under 'Appendix I' of the CITES agreement. Commercial trade in wild-caught specimens of these species is illegal (permitted only in exceptional licensed circumstances). Many wildlife species in trade are not endangered: these are listed under 'Appendix II'. CITES aims to ensure that trade of Appendix II species remains sustainable and does not endanger wild populations, so as to safeguard these species for the future. Countries who sign up agree to monitor the export and import trade of any threatened species and their products. Illegal imports and exports can result in seizures, fines and imprisonment, which aims to discourage illegal trade.

How CITES works

Membership of CITES is voluntary. Each member country agrees to adopt legislation to implement CITES at the national level. All import, export, re-export or introduction of specimens or parts and derivatives of any species covered by CITES has to be authorized through a licensing system and permits must be obtained.

The scheme has its limitations. It is voluntary and countries can 'enter reservations' on specific species when they join or when the Appendices are amended. Penalties may not necessarily match the seriousness of the crime or be sufficiently high to deter wildlife smugglers, particularly given the large amounts of money that can be earned by poachers. In addition, unlike other international agreements such as the Montreal Protocol (Topic 6, Section 6.4.9, and HL.a.8), CITES lacks its own financial mechanism for implementation at the national level and member states must contribute their own resources. However, taken overall, CITES has been responsible for ensuring that the international trade in wild animals and plants remains sustainable (Appendix II species) and for protecting species at risk of extinction (Appendix I).

CITES in numbers
Number of countries ('contracted parties') signed up to the agreement = 178.
Number of listed animals = 5500.
Number of listed plants = 29,500.
Number of listed species = 35,000.

Example – The effect of reclassifying African elephants from Appendix I to Appendix II

African elephants (Figure 3.72) provide an example of the effect of reclassification on wild populations.

Figure 3.72 An African elephant.

One of the biggest threats to elephant populations is the ivory trade, as the animals are poached for their ivory tusks. Other threats to wild elephants include habitat destruction and conflicts with local people.

African elephants were listed in Appendix I of CITES in 1990. Appendix I prohibits the trade of wild-caught specimens completely (so as to protect plants and animals under considerable threat of extinction), whereas under Appendix II specimens can be exported but with trade restricted by a tightly controlled permitting process. For example, the classification is extended to species that are not necessarily threatened but could easily become so.

As a result of the growth in elephant populations in Zimbabwe, Botswana and Namibia, in 1997 the classification of African elephants in these countries was downlisted to Appendix II. The down-listing of African elephants in these countries resulted in a single shipment of stockpiled ivory, estimated to be *c.* 50,000 kg, to Japan in 1999. African elephants were downlisted to Appendix II in South Africa in 2000. This delisting may have led to an increase in ivory poaching and a decline in many wild elephant populations.

Zoos, captive breeding and reintroduction programmes

Zoos have become increasingly focused on conservation and many now lead the way in the preservation of species threatened with extinction. In prioritizing species for conservation, zoos have to answer many crucial questions.

How to select what to conserve?

- What is the level of threat? It is better to conserve endangered animals than ones that are not endangered.
- What to focus on? Different zoos have different expertise and areas of influence; they focus on their particular strengths.
- Can the zoo afford to financially support the project in the long term?
- Should species that are threatened for natural reasons, such as natural ecology or natural predation, be conserved?
- What is the economic status of the country concerned? Zoos are more likely to support *in situ* conservation in developing countries than developed countries, who can help themselves.

***In situ* or *ex situ* conservation?**

- How big is the animal? Smaller ones are easier to keep in zoos.
- Species facing habitat loss need to be conserved *ex situ*. For example, 90% of the Livingstone fruit bat's habitat was lost due to cyclone damage.
- Animals threatened by diseases need to be kept *ex situ*. For example, many amphibian species are currently under threat globally from a fungus that is wiping them out in the wild and so individuals need to be kept in quarantine in zoos.
- Decisions on which projects to undertake will be influenced by staff expertise and whether the zoo vet has the knowledge to look after the species.
- If local people are willing to help, *in situ* conservation may be appropriate. If there are local political problems, *ex situ* may be preferred.
- Zoos often use species that are attractive to the public, such as lemurs and meerkats, to bring in visitors to provide funds for conservation. *Ex situ* conservation is therefore often used, even if the species is not especially threatened.

Is intervention helping?

Research to see if intervention is helping can be carried out by studying whether numbers are improving in the wild. Local expertise can assess whether the conservation effort is effective. For example, in February 2015 a giant panda census was carried out in China, indicating that populations had grown by 268 to a total of 1864 since the last survey in 2003. Panda censuses start every ten to fifteen years and last four to five years, and so the next one can be expected to end between 2025 and 2030.

The five freedoms were established in 1965 following an inquiry into the welfare of farm animals in the UK, and were important in establishing modern zoo standards.

How are zoo populations managed?

When keeping animals in zoos, the welfare of the species must be considered. Behavioural studies can indicate whether animals are under stress. These studies may look at male and female social interactions and how the animals use their enclosures. The zoo would also consider whether the 'five freedoms' are being met. The five freedoms are internationally accepted standards of care that assert every living being's right to humane treatment.

The five freedoms

1. Freedom from thirst, hunger and malnutrition through ready access to fresh water and a diet to maintain full health and vigour.
2. Freedom from thermal and physical discomfort by providing an appropriate shelter and a comfortable resting area.
3. Freedom from pain, injury and disease by prevention or rapid diagnosis and treatment.
4. Freedom to express normal behaviour by providing sufficient space, proper facilities and company of the animal's own kind.
5. Freedom from fear and distress by ensuring conditions and treatment avoid mental suffering.

Coordination of efforts between zoos helps in the effective conservation of species. The European Association for Zoos and Aquaria (EAZA) works out where specific zoos can help in specific areas. They have a number of Regional Collection Plans (RCPs), one of which has been produced for the Callitrichid group of monkeys. The golden lion tamarin (Figure 3.73) is a member of this group and has been brought back from the brink of extinction through captive breeding programmes.

Figure 3.73 The golden lion tamarin is one of the great success stories of zoo conservation. This small primate has been saved from extinction through captive breeding programmes.

How are breeding programmes managed?

For effective conservation and re-establishment of species in the wild, breeding programmes can be used. To be effective, details of the species' natural breeding behaviour must be known.

- Is it acceptable to choose a mate? Do you allow mate choice?
- The zoo may want to look at genes and the genetic compatibility of mates so as to avoid inbreeding. Leaving it to chance may lead to an animal choosing an unsuitable partner.
- Stud books can be used to establish genetic compatibility.
- Is artificial insemination a possibility? This will get round the problem of shipping in a mate.
- Birth control may be needed as the zoo may not want to have animals breeding (if zoo capacity is full).
- Keeper intervention may be needed – females sometimes reject young.
- The latest knowledge of reproductive biology and genetics is needed. Research such as DNA testing to establish parentage within a population.
- Correct enclosure design and enrichment schemes mean that a species is more likely to breed.

Strengths and limitations of zoos

The strengths of zoos include:

- Their role in educating the public about the need for conservation.
- They provide a way for people to empathize with wildlife.
- Although captivity is not the best solution, it acts as a good substitute and zoos can use breeding programmes to increase the population sizes of endangered animals, while ensuring genetic diversity through genetic monitoring.
- Well-managed zoos provide a proper diet and enough space, while keeping species in a controlled environment that protects individual organisms.
- They offer a temporary haven while efforts are made to preserve habitats, so that species can be reintroduced later.

TOK

How do we justify the species we choose to protect?

Is there a focus on animals we find attractive (the ones with fur and feathers) and is there a natural bias within the system? Do tigers have a greater right to exist than endangered and endemic species of rat?

The limitations of zoos include:

- Some animals may have problems re-adapting to the wild and captive animals released into the wild may become easy prey for predators.
- Not all species breed easily in captivity. For example, it has proved extremely difficult to breed giant pandas in zoos.
- People may get used to seeing species in zoos and assume it is normal.
- Habitats in zoos are very different from natural habitats, especially for animals that have complex interactions with their environment such as orangutans.
- There are ethical issues around caged animals and some people object to animals being kept in captivity for profit.
- The best solution for endangered animals lies in the protection of their habitats.

Example – The Asiatic lion – combining *ex situ* with *in situ* conservation

Figure 3.74 An Asiatic lion at the Cotswold Wildlife Park, UK.

Lions are not only found in Africa. One subspecies, known as the Asiatic lion (Figure 3.74), is found in Asia. Approximately 700 Asiatic lions live in the Gir Forest of Gujarat State, Western India, in their last remaining natural habitat. They are surrounded by human activity, with this small population surviving in a tiny patch of forest. One disease, epidemic or forest fire could wipe them out forever.

India is carrying out a captive breeding programme with the lions, in conjunction with zoos elsewhere, such as the Cotswold Wildlife Park in the UK. Asiatic lions have a life expectancy of around 16 years and those living at the Cotswold Wildlife Park are 11–12 years old.

Read more about Asiatic lions by searching on the One Earth website:

Activity

Some people think that zoos should not be used for *ex situ* conservation, saying that it is unethical to keep animals in captivity.

Divide your class into two groups. Using the Asiatic lion as an example, one group should argue for the continued use of zoos in *ex situ* conservation and the other group should argue against the use of zoos in conservation.

Summarize the arguments from both groups. Evaluate the evidence and write a conclusion that is supported by the evidence presented.

Example – The role of charismatic species in zoos

One question concerning *ex situ* conservation is, should only endangered or critically endangered animals be kept in zoos?

Zoos highlight their role in protecting animals that are very rare in the wild and in danger of extinction. Captive breeding programmes, with a view to reintroducing the animals to the wild, are a cornerstone of modern zoos. But is this always that case?

Zoos use animals, such as the meerkat (Figure 3.75), to attract people to the zoo and to raise money through the entry fee to support their activities. These animals are often not endangered and so are not subject to breeding and reintroduction programmes. Meerkats, for example, are classified as least concern on the IUCN's Red List.

As well as *ex situ* conservation, zoos play an important role in education. By learning more about the diverse array of animals that live on planet Earth, people are more likely to show an active interest in conservation.

The Northern bald ibis (*Geronticus eremita*) (Figure 3.76), also known as the Waldrapp ibis, has been classified as Critically Endangered since 1990. This species is not well known to the public but people will see it when they come to visit the more charismatic and widely known species, such as meerkats. Thus, public attention can be achieved, and funding can be raised to help support breeding programmes to increase the population of Northern bald ibis.

Figure 3.75 A meerkat at the Cotswold Wildlife Park, UK.

Figure 3.76 A Northern bald ibis at the Cotswold Wildlife Park, UK.

Example – The wild camel – the use of proxy species in zoos

Although the names 'Bactrian' and 'dromedary' are well known, the third camel species, the wild camel, is largely unknown. The wild camel (*Camelus ferus*) is only found in Mongolia and China. With an estimated population of around 1000 now remaining in the wild, it is the 8th most endangered large mammal on the planet. It is believed that approximately 600 survive in China and 450 in Mongolia. In 2002, the IUCN listed the wild camel as critically endangered.

Part of the reason for the wild camel's relative obscurity may be the lack of specimens in zoos around the world. The wild camel can only be kept in zoos in Mongolia and nowhere else.

Unable to house specimens of the wild camel, the Cotswold Wildlife Park in the UK keep a population of a more common, although still endangered, species instead, the Bactrian camel (*Camelus bactrianus*) (Figure 3.77). Bactrian camels are used here as a 'proxy species' and money from visitors is used to support conservation projects for the wild camel in Mongolia.

Proxy species are defined as 'charismatic but non-threatened species managed in zoos that could function as ambassadors for threatened and visually similar sister taxa not represented *ex situ*' (Kerr, 2020 – see reference below).

Read about wild camels by seaching for conservation of Mongolia's wild camels on the Zoological Society of London website:

Read more about proxy species and their role in conservation in this article: Kerr, K.C. (2020) Zoo animals as 'proxy species' for threatened sister taxa: Defining a novel form of species surrogacy. *Zoo Biology*, Vol 40, Issue 1, pp 65–75.

Figure 3.77 Bactrian camel (*Camelus bactrianus*) are used as a proxy species at the Cotswold Wildlife Park, UK.

Activity

Should proxy species be used in zoos to publicize the threats posed to their more endangered relatives?

Discuss this with someone in your class. Do you both have the same point of view? Now have a class discussion about the pros and cons of proxy species. Is there an agreed consensus? If not, why not?

In situ conservation

In situ conservation involves conserving species in their natural habitat. The use, design and operation of nature reserves and national parks are discussed in this topic, Sections 3.3.5 and 3.3.6.

Flagship species

Flagship species, including the giant panda, meerkats and gorillas, are 'charismatic' species selected to appeal to the public and thereby help to protect other species in an area. By focusing on these high-profile, iconic species there is a greater chance that conservation issues will catch the public attention, both nationally and internationally, and raise the necessary money for conservation initiatives. The advantages of this approach are twofold: money can be raised for the conservation of other species that may be equally endangered but are less appealing and, by preserving the habitat of the high-profile animal, other organisms in the habitat are also be preserved. One disadvantage of the approach is the favouring of charismatic species, including those that may not be endangered in the wild, at the expense of less attractive species, even though these may be more critically endangered. Another disadvantage is that while species are preserved in zoos, their native habitat may be destroyed, as is the case for the giant panda.

Comparing *ex situ* and *in situ* conservation

The main strengths of species-based conservation are that it attracts attention, and therefore funding for conservation, and successfully preserves vulnerable species in zoos, botanic gardens and seedbanks to preserve the genetic diversity for future restocking of habitats. The main limitation of this approach is that if the ecosystem is not treated as a holistic unit, and habitats are not directly preserved, it will be difficult to preserve species in, or return them to, their natural habitat.

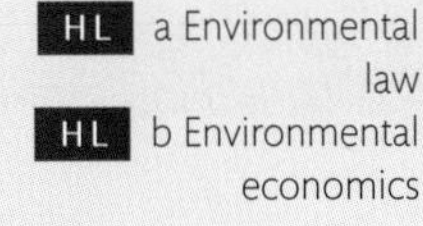

The main strength of protected areas is that they protect the whole ecosystem and the complex interrelationships that exist there, so the long-term survival of species is more likely. They also allow research to take place on intact ecosystems, greatly adding to our understanding of the factors that support biodiversity. Ecotourism raises awareness and profits are recycled back into biodiversity programmes. However, they do require considerable funding and protection to ensure the areas are not disturbed. Limitations may come from the fact they may become islands and may therefore lose biodiversity through their size, increased **edge effects** or reduced gene flow between populations.

3.3.3 A mixed approach to conservation

Sometimes a mixed conservation approach is adopted where both habitat and particular species are considered. Combining both *in situ* and *ex situ* methods can be the best solution for species conservation in many instances. A good example of this is giant panda conservation. Giant pandas can act as flagship species (this topic, Section 3.3.2) and were listed in Appendix I by CITES in March 1984. Other species-based approaches include breeding programmes in zoos. Chengdu Zoo began breeding giant pandas in 1953 and Beijing Zoo began breeding them in 1963. From 1963 to the present time, the giant panda has been bred in 53 zoos and nature reserves within China and internationally. Beijing Zoo has an impressive giant panda house and has established a successful breeding programme (Figure 3.78).

The mixed approach usually invokes flagship and/or keystone species (Topic 2, Section 2.1.23) to justify the need to conserve intact habitats and landscapes.

Figure 3.78 Billboard showing giant pandas at Beijing Zoo. Giant pandas enjoy a high profile within Chinese culture.

Raising giant pandas in captivity has three main difficulties. These are: getting the female to come into heat and become reproductively receptive; conducting artificial insemination, where the sperm is introduced into the female; and raising the cubs. In 1963, Beijing Zoo had its first success in artificially breeding giant pandas and in 1978 was the first zoo to successfully carry out artificial insemination. In 1992, Beijing Zoo also succeeded in raising a panda cub that had been artificially bred.

If asked to evaluate different conservation strategies, you need to examine the strengths and limitations of each strategy and then come to an overall conclusion.

In situ conservation of giant pandas has involved the establishment of protected areas. The first five nature reserves for giant pandas in China were established in 1963, four of which are located in Sichuan province. In 2021, China's Giant Panda National Park was established, spanning the Sichuan, Ningxia, and Shaanxi provinces. The national park is in development and will encompass the 67 existing panda reserves, with a total area of around 22,000 km^2. The national park is being set up through collaborative legislation between the three provinces, in an effort to unify criteria and standards.

HL a Environmental law

HL b Environmental economics

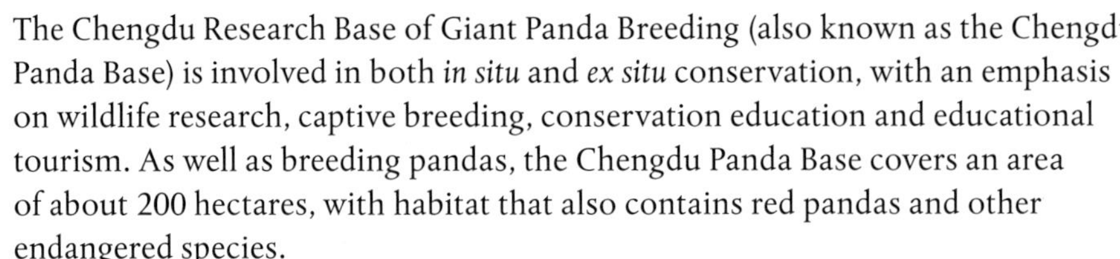

The Chengdu Research Base of Giant Panda Breeding (also known as the Chengdu Panda Base) is involved in both *in situ* and *ex situ* conservation, with an emphasis on wildlife research, captive breeding, conservation education and educational tourism. As well as breeding pandas, the Chengdu Panda Base covers an area of about 200 hectares, with habitat that also contains red pandas and other endangered species.

To learn more about the Chengdu Panda Base, go to the PandaHome website.

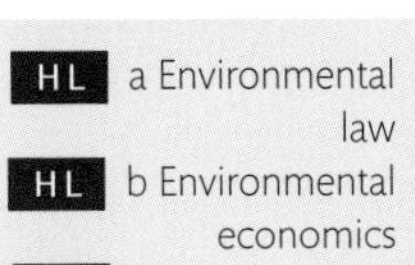

HL a Environmental law
HL b Environmental economics
HL c Environmental ethics

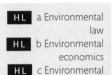

3.3.4 The Convention on Biological Diversity (CBD)

The Convention of Biological Diversity (CBD) is a UN treaty addressing both species-based and habitat-based conservation (Figure 3.79).

The objective of the CBD is to develop national strategies for the conservation and sustainable use of biological diversity. It also aims to identify protected marine areas outside of national jurisdictions.

The CBD includes the Nagoya Protocol, which promotes the fair and equitable sharing of genetic resources.

The CBD is discussed further in Topic 1, Section 1.1.10.

Figure 3.79 Logo for the Convention on Biological Diversity.

Read more about the CBD, and its Global Biodiversity Framework, using the worksheet in the eBook.

3.3.5 and 3.3.6 Habitat conservation strategies

Habitat conservation strategies protect species by conservation of their natural environment. This may require protection of wild areas or active management.

When protecting wild areas, use of surrounding land, and distance from urban centres, are important factors for consideration when designing the conservation area.

A detailed example of the design and implementation of a protected area (the Danum Valley Conservation Area) is outlined on the next page. Factors that need to be considered in the design of a protected area are covered later in this section.

Activity

Find out about two examples of *in situ* habitat conservation:

- one where active management has been required
- one where the establishment of an ecosanctuary used pest-exclusion fencing.

The examples can be local, regional or global.

Produce a fact sheet on each, explaining how the conservation strategies are protecting habitats and species.

You need to be able to evaluate the success of a named protected area. A specific example of a protected area and the success it has achieved should be studied.

Nature reserves and national parks

Effective conservation of biodiversity in nature reserves and national parks depends on an understanding of the biology of target species and on the effect of the size and shape of conservation areas.

Example – Danum Valley Conservation Area, Malaysian Borneo

The Danum Valley Conservation Area (DVCA) is a protected area located in the Malaysian state of Sabah on the island of Borneo, at a latitude of 5° North (Figure 3.80). The DVCA and surrounding areas model how effective conservation can be matched with local economic needs.

Granting protected status to a species or ecosystem is no guarantee of protection without community support, adequate funding and proper research. In north-eastern Borneo, the third largest island in the world, a large area of commercial forest is owned by the Sabah Foundation (also known as Yayasan Sabah). The Yayasan Sabah Forest Management Area (YSFMA) is an extensive area of commercial hardwood forest containing protected areas of undisturbed forest, areas that are being rehabilitated with 'enrichment planting' (adding seedlings to heavily disturbed logged forest) and areas of commercial softwood forestry.

Figure 3.80 Danum Valley Field Centre, Malaysia. Research at the centre focuses on local primary forest ecology as well as the effect of logging on rainforest structure and communities.

Research on the primary rainforest within the Danum Valley Conservation Area (DVCA) has established the biological importance of the native forest, and has acted as a focus for conservation in the region. The DVCA covers 43,800 hectares, comprising almost entirely lowland dipterocarp forest (dipterocarps are valuable hardwood trees). The DVCA is the largest expanse of pristine forest of this type remaining in Sabah (Figure 3.81).

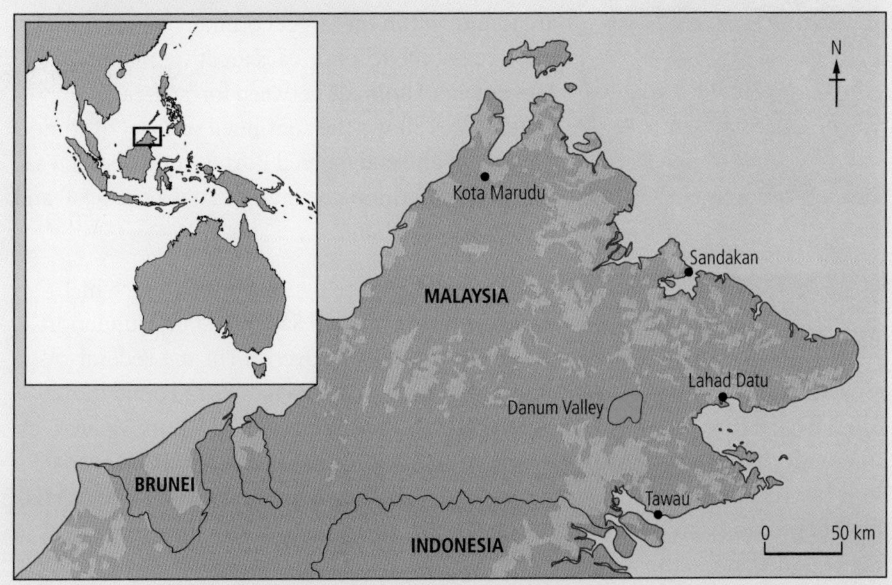

Figure 3.81 Location of the Danum Valley Conservation Area.

Until the late 1980s, the area was under threat from commercial logging. The establishment of a long-term research programme between Yayasan Sabah and the Royal Society in the UK, which is the oldest scientific body in the world, has created local awareness of the conservation value of the area and provided important scientific information about the forest and what happens to it when it is disturbed through logging. Danum Valley is controlled by a management committee representing all the relevant local institutions – wildlife, forestry and commercial sectors are all represented.

Two other conservation areas, the Maliau Basin and Imbak Canyon, are linked by commercial forest corridors. To the east of the DVCA is the 30,000-hectare Innoprise-FACE Foundation Rainforest Rehabilitation Project (INFAPRO), one of the largest forest rehabilitation projects in South-East Asia, which involves the replanting of areas of heavily disturbed logged forest. The Innoprise-IKEA project (INIKEA), to the west of the DVCA, is a similar rehabilitation project (Figure 3.82).

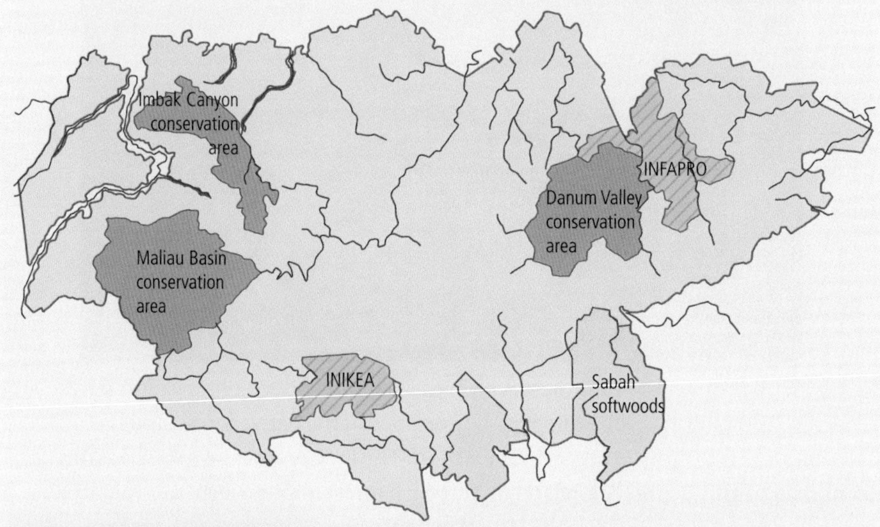

Figure 3.82 Location of conservation areas, rehabilitation projects and commercial softwood forestry within YSFMA. The combined network of different types of forest has enabled effective conservation of animals and plants important to the region.

Figure 3.83 Orangutans are found on the islands of Borneo and Sumatra. They are high-profile animals and are often used to promote the conservation of rainforest.

Because all areas of conservation and replantation are found within the larger commercial forest, the value of the whole area is greatly enhanced. Movement of animals between forest areas is enabled and allows the continued survival of some important and endangered Borneo animals such as the Sumatran rhino, the orangutan (Figure 3.83) and the Borneo elephant.

Such projects require significant funding, which has come from Yayasan Sabah (a state foundation funded by the Sabah Government and Federal Government of Malaysia) and companies including Malaysia's Petra Foundation, Shell, BP, the Royal Society and others. The establishment of the Danum Valley's international profile, along with the key research that has been completed over a long period of time (the programme is now the longest running in South-East Asia), have helped to establish the area as one of the most important conservation areas in the region, if not in the world.

Community support

The Danum Valley Field Centre is managed and maintained by a large staff of local people. Many are from the nearest town (Lahad Datu) or from east-coast kampongs (villages) such as Kampong Kinabatangan. The field centre and surrounding conservation area provides opportunities for employment, education and training. Support from the local community in running the various facilities, such as field centre offices, accommodation, research support and education centres, on site and in local towns, along with the interest from school nature groups, has been important to the success of the project.

As well as the strengths outlined previously, Danum Valley does have some limitations.

- Palm oil plantations are being grown near to the northern border of the DVCA. This could affect the ecotourism potential of Danum Valley as tourists do not want to see agricultural areas so close to a protected area. The presence of people so close to the conservation area may also lead to increased poaching activity or illegal logging activity.
- The funding that supports the DVCA has been raised by logging and by conversion of land that was once covered by rainforest to forest plantation. Some conservationists may see a conflict between the activities that have provided revenue for the DVCA and the aims of a protected area.
- The DVCA and surrounding area is currently designated a conservation area, but a change of leadership within the DVCA could see this designation changed. The establishment of the DVCA as a World Heritage Site would give international protection to the DVCA and ensure its long-term protection.

Overall, however, the impacts of the DVCA have been overwhelmingly positive. In June 2013, the Sabah State Assembly reclassified several forests as protected areas in the YSFMA, creating a continuous stretch of unbroken forest, including Maliau Basin, Imbak Canyon, and Danum Valley. This created the single largest protected area in Malaysia, covering nearly 500,000 hectares, which is about five times the size of Penang Island. This site has become known as The Danum-Maliau-Imbak Rainforest Complex or DaMaI. There have been proposals to nominate the site as a UNESCO World Heritage Site.

Search for DaMal progress report on the Global Conservation website:

Community support, adequate funding and proper research increases the chance of success for conservation efforts.

The DVCA contains more than 120 mammalian species including 10 species of primate. The DVCA and surrounding forest is an important reservation for the orangutan. These forests are also particularly rich in other large mammals including the Asian elephant, Malayan sun bear, clouded leopard, bearded pig and several species of deer. The area had also previously provided one of the last refuges in Borneo for the critically endangered Sumatran rhino (Figure 3.84), which is now extinct in the wild in Sabah. Over 340 species of bird have been recorded at Danum, including the argus pheasant, Bulwer's pheasant and seven species of pitta bird. Higher plants, such as mosses, ferns, conifers and flowering plants, make up more than 1300 species in 562 genera of 139 families and represent 15% of the species recorded in Sabah.

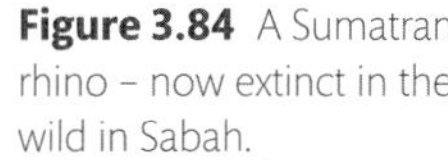

Figure 3.84 A Sumatran rhino – now extinct in the wild in Sabah.

The location of a conservation area in a country is a significant factor in the success of the conservation effort. Use of surrounding land and distance from urban centres are important factors for consideration in conservation area design.

2.1 Individuals, populations, communities and ecosystems

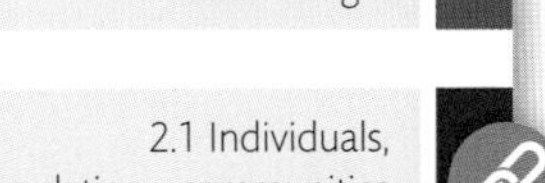

HL a Environmental law

Activity

UNESCO's Man and the Biosphere programme (MAB) started in 1970, creating a world network of international reserves that now has 480 reserves in over 100 countries.

Find out about UNESCO biosphere reserves using this website:

Research an example of a UNESCO biosphere reserve with high biodiversity and species of international conservation importance. Produce a fact sheet which answers the following questions:

- What are the management strategies used to conserve habitats and species in the reserve?
- Why has the reserve been designated as an appropriate area for conservation?
- Which species of international importance does the reserve contain?
- What are the potential human impacts on the reserve?

Designing protected areas

Make sure you can explain the criteria used to design and manage protected areas, including the effect of the size and shape of the area.

Most countries have large areas of land that have been cleared of native habitat for the development of residential areas such as cities. The remaining areas of native habitat can be made into protected areas. Protected areas can become isolated if they are surrounded by cleared/developed land. As a consequence, they may lose some of their diversity due to increased edge effects and localized extinctions.

'Island biogeography' theory was developed in the 1960s by the ecologist Robert MacArthur and the biologist Edward Wilson and was explored in their seminal text *The Theory of Island Biogeography*. The authors showed that smaller conservation areas contain comparatively fewer species and lower diversity than larger areas. Ever since, reserve designers have been using these ideas to ensure maximum preservation of species within conservation areas. Size, shape, edge effects and whether reserves are linked by corridors, are all considered when designing conservation areas (Figure 3.85).

Area

One of the great debates in reserve design is known as SLOSS (single large or several small). Is it better to have one large reserve of 10,000 ha or four smaller ones of 2500 ha each? Much depends on the location of the habitats – if the habitats to be preserved are not all found reasonably close together, then several small reserves may be necessary. Generally, larger areas contain a greater number of habitats and can therefore support a greater number of species than the smaller areas can. The best indicator of species survival and success of the reserve's size is the population size of individual species. In an ideal situation, several large reserves would allow the protected habitats to be replicated, thus guarding against the possible effects of fire or a disease that could lead to the extinction of species contained within the affected reserve.

Edge effects

At the edge of a protected area, there may be a change in abiotic factors, such as windier or warmer and less humid conditions compared to the interior of the reserve. Edge effects attract species that are not found deeper in the reserve and may also attract exotic species from outside the reserve, leading to competition with forest species and overall reduction in diversity.

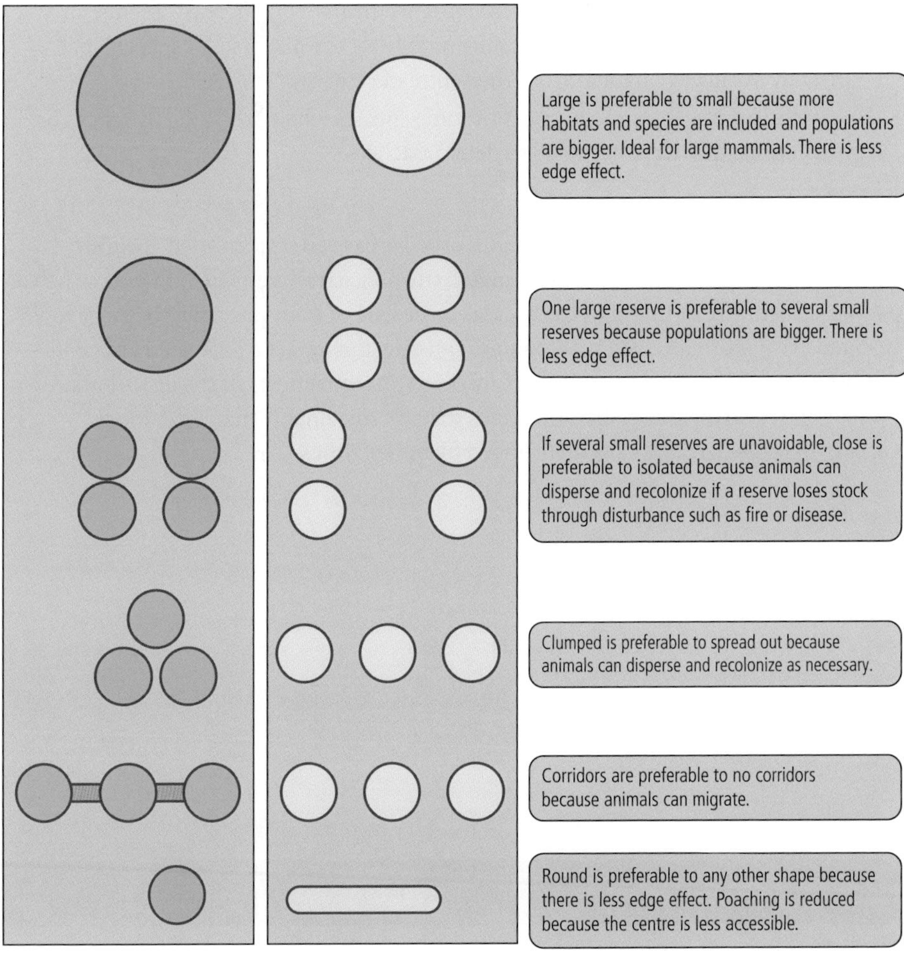

Large is preferable to small because more habitats and species are included and populations are bigger. Ideal for large mammals. There is less edge effect.
One large reserve is preferable to several small reserves because populations are bigger. There is less edge effect.
If several small reserves are unavoidable, close is preferable to isolated because animals can disperse and recolonize if a reserve loses stock through disturbance such as fire or disease.
Clumped is preferable to spread out because animals can disperse and recolonize as necessary.
Corridors are preferable to no corridors because animals can migrate.
Round is preferable to any other shape because there is less edge effect. Poaching is reduced because the centre is less accessible.

Figure 3.85 The shape, size and connectivity of reserves are important in the design of protected areas.

Shape

The best shape for a reserve is a circle because this has the fewest edge effects. Long thin reserves have large edge effects. In practice, the shape is determined by what is available and where the habitats to be conserved are located. Parks tend to have irregular shapes.

Corridors

The benefits of linking reserves by corridors include:

- allowing gene flow by immigration and/or emigration
- allowing seasonal movements
- reducing collisions between cars and animals
- having fewer or no roads that can act as a barrier to some species.

The disadvantages of linking reserves by corridors include:

- some species may breed outside the protected area rather than inside it, leading to a reduction in numbers; this effect is called 'outbreeding depression'
- potential invasion by exotic pests or disease from connected reserves
- poachers can easily move from one reserve to another

When designing a protected area, edge effects and the importance of wildlife corridors for connectivity need to be considered.

- corridors may be as narrow as 30–200 m; this means a big increase in edge conditions, rendering the corridors unsuitable for the dispersal of species that normally avoid edge habitat from the centre of reserves
- the corridors may become barriers to some species when protected by fences or obstructions that were designed to deter poachers.

Protected areas should have a pristine core, surrounded by **buffer zones** and outer transition zones that are sustainably managed.

Buffer zones

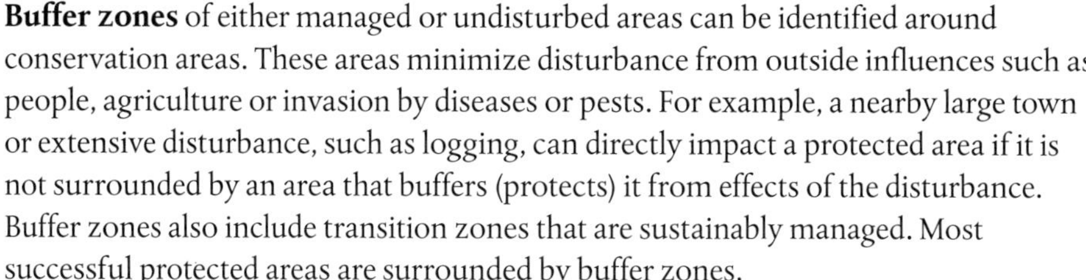

Buffer zones of either managed or undisturbed areas can be identified around conservation areas. These areas minimize disturbance from outside influences such as people, agriculture or invasion by diseases or pests. For example, a nearby large town or extensive disturbance, such as logging, can directly impact a protected area if it is not surrounded by an area that buffers (protects) it from effects of the disturbance. Buffer zones also include transition zones that are sustainably managed. Most successful protected areas are surrounded by buffer zones.

Criteria for consideration when designing protected areas include size, shape, edge effects, corridors and proximity to potential human influence. Well-designed protected areas should include the following considerations.

- They are large because this promotes large population sizes and high biodiversity, enables the protection of large vertebrates/top carnivores and reduces the perimeter relative to the area, so edge effects and disturbance are minimized.
- They are unfragmented and are connected to other reserves by corridors to allow the movement and migration of animals between reserves.
- They do not have roads that can act as barriers to migration and increase disturbance and edge effects.

Protected areas need to be designed following strategies that enable the maximum amount of biodiversity to be conserved and where *sustainability* is ensured.

3.3.7 Rewilding

Natural processes in ecosystems can be regenerated by **rewilding**.

Rewilding aims to restore ecosystems and reverse declines in biodiversity by returning an area to its natural processes and wildlife. Rewilding reintroduces lost animal species to natural environments, such as apex predators that have a significant effect on the food web and trophic levels in an ecosystem. Keystone species are also reintroduced, which are essential for the functioning of the ecosystem (Topic 2, Section 2.1.23). The establishment of corridors allows for movement of animals between fragments and gives larger animals the area they need to feed and breed. Agriculture and other resource harvesting are no longer allowed and natural ecosystems are allowed to recover through ecological management.

Example – The Hinewai restoration project

Figure 3.86 Northern area of the Hinewai Reserve, Banks Peninsula, New Zealand.

The Hinewai Reserve is an ecological restoration project on Banks Peninsula, New Zealand (Figure 3.86).

Human settlers cleared parts of the reserve. Clearance was started by Polynesian settlers from about 700 years ago and then European settlers, from around 1850 onwards, completed the clearance. The area covers 1500 hectares and is being managed to ensure the natural regeneration of native vegetation and wildlife. The ecological management involves minimal intervention and allows succession to occur, resulting in ecosystems (nearly all forest) similar to those that existed before forest clearance. Alien species, such as exotic trees and vines, are removed allowing the endemic flora and fauna to be re-established.

Rewilding methods include the reintroduction of apex predators and other keystone species, re-establishment of connectivity of habitats over large areas, cessation of agriculture and resource harvesting, and minimization of human influences including by ecological management.

Activity

Read more about the Hinewai Reserve in New Zealand on their website.

Using the example of the Hinewai Reserve in New Zealand, or any other appropriate rewilding project or a local example, produce a poster summarizing how communities and habitats are being restored. Use your knowledge of sustainability of ecosystems to include details about how the continuity of the ecosystem can be assured.

1.2 Systems

2.1 Individuals, populations, communities and ecosystems

2.2 Energy and biomass in ecosystems

HL a Environmental law

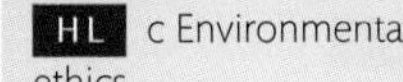

HL b Environmental economics

HL c Environmental ethics

3.3.8 Conservation and regeneration measures

Conservation and regeneration measures can be used to reverse the decline in biodiversity to ensure a safe operating space for humanity within the biodiversity planetary boundary (Topic 1, Section 1.3.19) and can be taken at individual, collective, national and international levels.

1.3 Sustainability

Use the QR code to access the website of the United Nations Environment Programme:

Activity

In pairs, discuss the role of individuals, local societies, governments and intergovernmental agencies in conserving and regenerating biodiversity. Use the following questions in your discussion.

- What impact can an individual have?
- Is the conservation and regeneration of biodiversity ultimately one for governments and intergovernmental organizations (such as the United Nations Environment Programme)?

Summarize the outcome of your discussion. Do others in your class agree with your points of view?

HL a Environmental law

3.3.9 Environmental perspectives and value systems impact the choice of conservation strategies

The success of conservation and regeneration measures depends on incorporating a diversity of approaches (see the example of Danum Valley, this topic, Section 3.3.5 and 3.3.6, pages 310–312), including:

- community support
- adequate funding
- education and awareness
- appropriate legislation
- scientific research.

1.1 Perspectives

Environmental perspectives and value systems can impact the choice of conservation strategies selected by a society. For example:

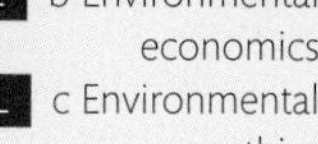

HL a Environmental law

HL b Environmental economics

HL c Environmental ethics

- more ecocentric perspectives may result in conservation for the intrinsic value of biodiversity and so focus on low intervention *in situ* strategies
- more anthropocentric or technocentric perspectives may be driven by the economic and societal value of biodiversity and thus embrace more scientific interventions involving zoos, gene banks and ecotourism.

Issues of environmental justice must be considered when choosing the most appropriate conservation strategy (this topic, Section 3.2.12).

HL

HL

3.3.10 International, governmental and non-governmental organizations

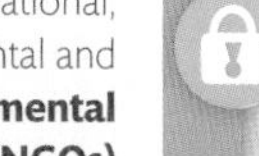

International, governmental and **non-governmental organizations (NGOs)** are involved in conserving and restoring ecosystems and biodiversity, with varying levels of effectiveness due to their use of media, speed of response, diplomatic constraints, financial resources and political influence.

It is often difficult to make your voice heard by those who influence global policies, such as national governments. Combined voices are more effective and conservation organizations that work at both local and global levels are good at campaigning on key environmental issues such as climate change and the preservation of biodiversity.

Non-governmental organizations (NGOs) are not run by, funded by or influenced by the governments of any country. Examples of NGOs include Greenpeace and the World Wide Fund for Nature (WWF).

Intergovernmental organizations (IGOs) are bodies established through international agreements to protect the environment and bring together governments to work together and carry out large surveys on an international scale. Examples of IGOs include the European Environment Agency (EEA), United Nations Environment Programme (UNEP) and IUCN.

Each type of organization has its own strengths and limitations. IGOs tend to be more conservative in that they have a more conventional approach to conservation and are not likely to be controversial. Whereas NGOs tend to be, and often have to be, more radical to get their message across and to be heard. NGOs also tend to be field-based, gathering information to back up their arguments, whereas IGOs tend to gather information from scientific research for which they pay.

Similarities

Both IGOs and NGOs are trying to promote conservation of habitats, ecosystems and biodiversity. Other similarities between the two organizations include the following.

- Use of media
  Both gather data from a variety of sources, provide environmental information to the public of global trends and publish official scientific documents and technical reports.

HL a Environmental law
HL b Environmental economics

- Public image
  Both lead and encourage partnership between nations and organizations to conserve and restore ecosystems and biodiversity.
- Legislation
  Both seek to ensure that laws are applied.

If you are asked to compare the roles of a named IGO and a named NGO, make sure you refer to specific examples. For example, UNEP is an IGO and WWF is an NGO. Answers should include similarities and differences between the two organizations.

- Agenda
  Both collaborate in global, transnational and national scientific research projects.
  Both provide forums for discussion.
- Geographical influence
  IGOs monitor regional and global trends. NGOs also monitor species and conservation areas at a variety of levels, from local to global.

Differences

Differences between the two organizations are shown in Table 3.3.

Table 3.3 Differences between IGOs and NGOs.

	IGO	NGO
Use of media	• work with media so communicate policies and decisions effectively to the public	• may gain media coverage through variety of protests • often run campaigns focused on large charismatic species such as whales/seals/pandas • sometimes access to mass media is hindered, especially in non-democratic countries • public protests put pressure on governments
Speed of response	• slow to respond – agreements require consensus from members • can be bureaucratic and take time to act • directed by governments, so sometimes may be against public opinion	• fast to respond – usually members already have reached consensus or they wouldn't have joined in the first place

Political pressures	• decisions can be politically and economically driven rather than by best conservation strategy	• can be idealistic and driven by best conservation strategy • focus on the environment • often hold the high moral ground over other organizations, although may be extreme in actions or views
Public image	• organized as businesses with concrete allocation of duties • cultivate a measured image based on a scientific and business-like approach	• can be confrontational and have a radical approach to an environmental issue like biodiversity
Legislation	• enforce decisions via laws, so may be authoritarian sometimes	• serve as watchdogs by suing government agencies or businesses who violate environmental law • rely on public pressure rather than legal power to influence governments as they have no power to enforce laws
Agenda	• provide guidelines and implement international treaties	• use public pressure to influence national governments • lobby governments over policies and legislation • buy and manage land to protect habitats and wildlife
Funding	• fund environmental projects by monies coming from national budget • usually manage publicly owned lands	• fund environmental projects by monies coming from private donations
Extent of geographical influence	• have influence both locally and globally	• focus more on local and/or national information, aiming at education – produce learning materials and opportunities for schools and for the public

HL

3.3.11 Positive feedback loops that enhance biodiversity

Positive feedback loops that enhance biodiversity and promote ecosystem equilibrium can be triggered by rewilding and habitat restoration efforts.

A positive feedback loop is a necessary condition for the emergence of alternative stable states on the community scale. This can lead to enhanced growth and biomass, reproduction and survival of species in food web interactions.

Rewilding looks to restore food webs in an ecosystem, by reintroducing either primary producer communities, including grasses and trees, or apex predators, such as the grey wolf in Yellowstone National Park (Topic 2, Section 2.5.9). By reintroducing such species, feeding relationships in food webs can be restored. This leads to increased reproduction and biomass of essential species, which in turn promotes ecosystem equilibrium. As populations increase, the number of reproducing individuals increases, which will further increase their population growth rate. This is an example of positive feedback. Increasing the biomass of species that are reintroduced has knock-on effects on other species in the food web. This is also considered to be positive feedback if the increase in biomass and reproduction of reintroduced species leads to the growth of biomass of interrelated species. These changes increase the survival of species in the food web and restore ecosystem equilibrium.

1.2 Systems

HL

3.3.12 Rewilding projects have both benefits and limitations

Example – Oostvaarderplassen rewilding reserve, the Netherlands

Oostvaardersplassen in the Netherlands is an example of an internationally famous rewilding reserve (Figure 3.87). When an inland sea was drained for two new cities in 1968, Oostvaardersplassen was created. During the 1970s, the area was left undeveloped. Dutch ecologist Frans Vera (Topic 2, Section 2.5.12) developed an innovative use for the area, using wild-living cattle and horses to mimic the grazing of extinct herbivores. A fenced-off area of 55 km^2 was created.

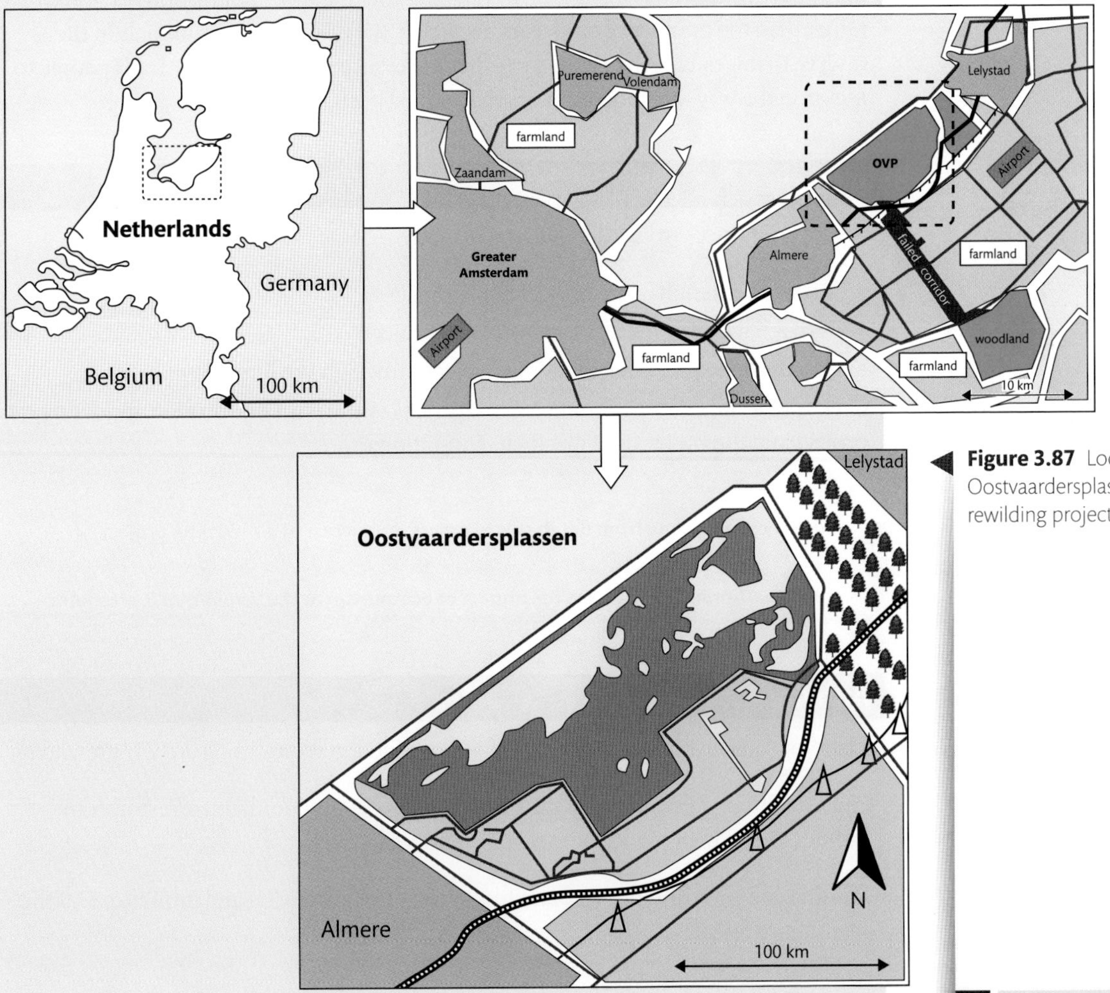

Figure 3.87 Location of the Oostvaardersplassen rewilding project.

In areas of the reserve that contained marshland and was therefore not used by herbivores, a sanctuary was created for rare birds, including bearded tits and sea eagles. By the end of 2017, following several mild winters, numbers of individuals of the three herbivore species – Konik horses, Heck cattle and red deer – rose to 5230 in the areas containing herbivores because of the plentiful supply of food and lack of predators. However, following a harsher winter, the carrying capacity of the land could no longer support the herbivore population numbers and the population fell

1.1 Perspectives

HL a Environmental law

HL b Environmental economics

HL c Environmental ethics

to 1850 (for more on carrying capacity and its effects, see Topic 2, Sections 2.1.10 to 2.1.12, pages 98–101). Unable to migrate, many animals starved. Around 90% of the animals that died were shot by the Dutch state forestry organization, which manages the reserve, before they could die of starvation. The project was criticized for allowing populations of large herbivores to rise unchecked. In 2018, it was decided to limit the number of grazing animals to 1100, which meant that many deer had to be destroyed. Horses were transported to other reserves in Belarus and Spain. Cattle are now fed hay in the winter, as required.

Frans Vera, no longer part of the decision-making team for the Oostvaardersplassen, has said that the experiment should have been allowed to continue to its natural conclusion. He claimed that mass starvation events are normal and that in areas such as the Serengeti in Africa it is food availability that regulates populations of grazers, rather than the number of predators. However, the inability of the animals in the reserve to migrate, as they would in other areas such as the Serengeti, leads people to question the way that Oostvaardersplassen had been managed.

Activity

Read about the Oostvaardersplassen project.

- To what extent has the project been a success?
- What have been the limitations of the project?
- Do the benefits of the rewilding project outweigh the limitations?

Carry out a class debate about Oostvaardersplassen, with one group supporting the project and the other highlighting its limitations.

The 'Data Sources' section of the Species Monitoring website is a useful source of secondary data.

Use secondary data from databases to assess the success of a rewilding project (see suggested weblink)

Use questionnaires to assess the impact of ecotourism or the values that it promotes (questionnaires are covered in Topic 1, Section 1.1.5, pages 5–7)

Activity

There are land-use issues concerning food production versus using areas for rewilding.

Find out about a rewilding project where land was used for habitat restoration rather than growing food for local populations.

Summarize your findings in a fact file, assessing the benefits and limitations of the rewilding project.

HL

3.3.13 Assessing the success of conservation or regeneration measures

Activity

Select a local example of a project to conserve or regenerate natural systems or use one of the following projects:

- Willie Smits rainforest restoration project in Kalimantan and Sulawesi
- Wangari Maathai's Kenyan Green Belt Movement
- Steve Elliot and FORRU-CMU's restoration of South-East Asian forests.

The success of the conservation strategy can be evaluated at three levels:

1. Did they succeed in the project as planned?
2. Was the project well received by the communities impacted?
3. Was this the best way to conserve nature?

Answer each of these questions in relation to the project you have chosen. Produce a poster that summarizes the outcomes of your research.

Make sure you can consider claims that conservation measures have successfully protected biodiversity and the impact of the measures on local communities.

HL a Environmental law
HL c Environmental ethics

3.3.14 Ecotourism

HL

Ex situ conservation provides the opportunity for people to see wildlife which they would not usually be able to experience (this topic, Section 3.3.2). Such nature tourism increases awareness of the value and need to preserve the natural world and raises revenues for the implementation of conservation strategies.

Figure 3.88 Tourist taking photo of a southern white rhinoceros.

Tourism has played an important role in conserving the southern white rhinoceros, by raising funds to help breed and protect the species. The southern white rhinoceros (*Ceratotherium simum simum*) (Figure 3.88) has been a conservation success story. In the early 1900s, only about 20 specimens remained after much of the population had been killed by hunters and farmers. This made them the rarest subspecies of any rhinoceros at that time. Excellent and sustained protection, along with the use of breeding programmes, has increased their population and they are now the most common of all the rhinoceros subspecies. There are now some 11,600 wild southern white

Read more about the southern white rhino by searching on the Cotswold Wildlife Park website:

rhinoceros, with 767 individuals in zoos. In contrast, the northern white rhinoceros is extinct in the wild due to poaching, with only two females remaining (at a sanctuary in East Africa).

Ecotourism is a form of tourism that focuses on travelling to natural areas that promote environmental conservation. Ecotourism experiences can either be *in situ* (such as a visit to a rainforest resort, see below) or *ex situ*, such as zoos (this topic, Section 3.3.2).

Ecotourism has the following characteristics:

- includes all nature-based forms of tourism, in which the main motivation of the tourists is the observation and appreciation of nature as well as the traditional cultures present in natural areas
- has an educational value
- is generally, but not exclusively, organized by specialized tour operators for small groups
- minimizes negative impacts upon the natural and sociocultural environment
- supports the maintenance of natural areas that are used as ecotourism attractions through education and fund-raising.

Ecotourism provides an alternative income for local communities and allows a variety of interesting wildlife to be seen. It also provides funds for protecting conservation areas and the organisms that live there. In addition, ecotourism encourages local people to value their natural wildlife, as they see how tourism increases when habitats are protected, which in turn generates a valuable income stream.

There are also negative and societal impacts of ecotourism.

- Increase in tourism leads to increased travel, resulting in greater use of transport that generates CO_2 (a greenhouse gas), along with nitrogen oxides (NOx) and volatile organic compounds (VOCs), which are precursors of tropospheric ozone (O_3) (Topic 8, Section 8.3.8).
- Growth of infrastructure, such as roads, can fragment habitats.
- Tourism can produce disturbance for local communities through pollution, such as sound pollution, which detracts from their daily lives.
- Noise from tourism can disrupt wildlife and alter animal behaviour.
- Increased tourism can lead to increased littering, including single-use plastics, which can degrade the environment and harm wildlife.
- Increase in tourism can increase demand of goods and services that cause the unsustainable use of resources such as the use of fossil fuels or deforestation.
- Increased tourism puts greater and unsustainable demand on limited supplies of freshwater.
- Greater access to wildlife areas can lead to increased poaching, illegal fishing or increased capture for the illegal pet trade.
- Wildlife used as a tourist attraction may be inappropriately or unethically treated.
- The focus on popular tourist sites may leave other sites with fewer conservation funds and other resources.

Ecotourism can increase interdependence of local communities and increase biodiversity by generating income and providing funds for protecting areas, but there can also be negative societal and ecological impacts.

Example – Ecotourism in Borneo

In the late 1990s, the Borneo Rainforest Lodge (Figure 3.89), was established on the north-eastern edge of the DVCA. Flourishing ecotourism has been established in the area, which has exposed the unique forest to a wider range of visitors than was previously possible. As well as raising revenue for the local area, the lodge has raised the international profile of the area as an important centre for conservation and research.

Figure 3.89 The Borneo Rainforest Lodge – an ecotourism destination at the edge of the DVCA.

For more information about the role of the DVCA in conservation, see this topic, Section 3.3.5.

Example – Ecotourism in Kenya

Figure 3.90 Ecotourism in Kenya – tourist taking photo of an African elephant.

Kenya is a major centre for ecotourism, with a number of national parks which attract visitors from around the world (Figure 3.90). For example, the Serengeti National Park (this topic, Section 3.2.12) which was established in 1951 and the Maasai Mara National Reserve (Topic 2, Section 2.5.9), which was first established in 1961. Overall, Kenya has six World Heritage Sites, six marine reserves, 23 National Parks and 28 National Reserves.

Kenya provides opportunities for a wide range of ecotourism activities, including cultural (Indigenous peoples), adventure (hot air balloon rides to observe the animals in their natural habitat) and environmental (hiking, guided walks and game drives). About 7.5% of the country is designated for wildlife conservation. There is a wide range of wildlife to be seen by tourists, including elephants, lions, leopards, rhinoceroses, zebra, Cape buffaloes and over 1070 bird species.

1.1 Perspectives
1.3 Sustainability

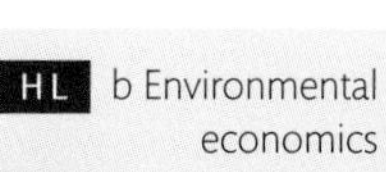

HL b Environmental economics
HL c Environmental ethics

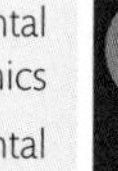

In 2022, a new strategy was launched by the Kenyan government, to reduce the country's dependence on game drives (safaris) and beach tourism. Kenya aims to develop more tourism that is based on health and medicine, community, business and conference, and heritage.

Many companies involved with ecotourism in Kenya employ local staff and source their goods and services from local suppliers. This helps to create jobs and preserve traditional cultures in these communities.

HL end

Engagement

- Investigate the role of an NGO in a conservation project. Find out if there are opportunities to participate in the project.
- Visit a rewilding project or protected area and raise awareness about the project in your local school or community. For example, you could make a presentation about the project and show this to your class. You could describe the techniques being used in the rewilding project and discuss any opportunities to volunteer in the project.
- Volunteer for a local conservation project, such as the removal of an invasive species or putting up bird boxes. This, along with the other activities listed here, can be used as a 'service' activity in your CAS programme.

Exercise

Q22. Outline arguments for species and habitat preservation.

Q23. Describe the criteria used to design protected areas. Your answer should address size, shape, edge effects, corridors and proximity to other reserves.

Q24. List five factors that are required to establish a successful protected area.

Q25. Evaluate the success of a named protected area.

Q26. Evaluate different approaches to protecting biodiversity.

Q27. Describe the mixed approach to conservation, using an example.

Q28. Outline how environmental perspectives and value systems can impact the choice of conservation strategies selected by a society.

HL

Q29. HL **Construct** a table contrasting governmental organizations and NGOs in terms of use of the media, speed of response, diplomatic constraints and political influence.

Q30. HL **Explain** how rewilding and habitat restoration can result in positive feedback loops that enhance biodiversity and promote ecosystem equilibrium.

Q31. HL **Evaluate** a rewilding project.

Q32. HL **Evaluate** the role of ecotourism in conservation.

HL end

Practice questions

1. **(a)** With reference to Figures 3.91 and 3.92, outline **one** relationship between the location of Hokkaido's national parks and their elevation. [1]

   (b) With reference to Figure 3.91, evaluate the design of Hokkaido's national parks as protected areas. [4]

(Total 5 marks)

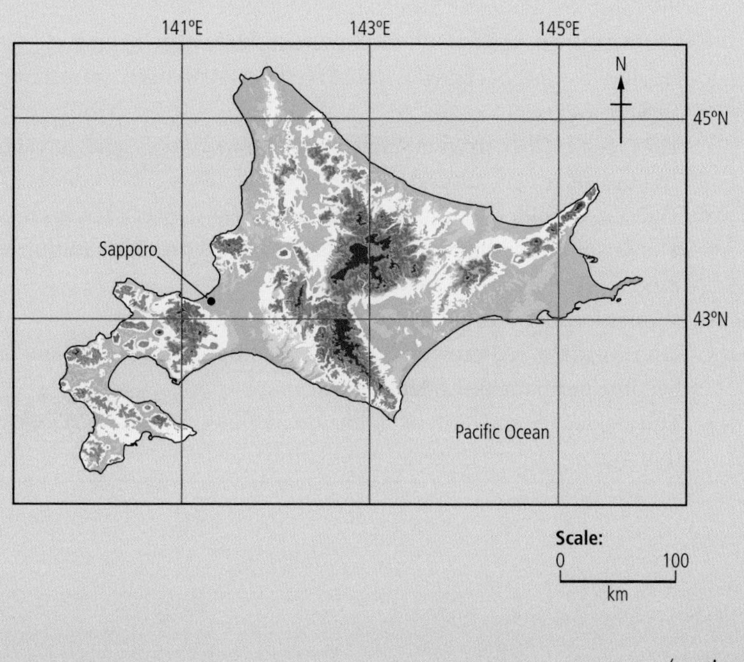

Figure 3.91 Elevation map of the island of Hokkaido.

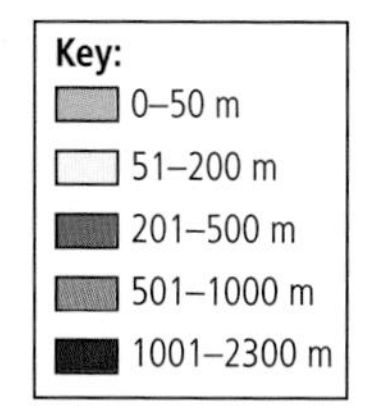

(continued)

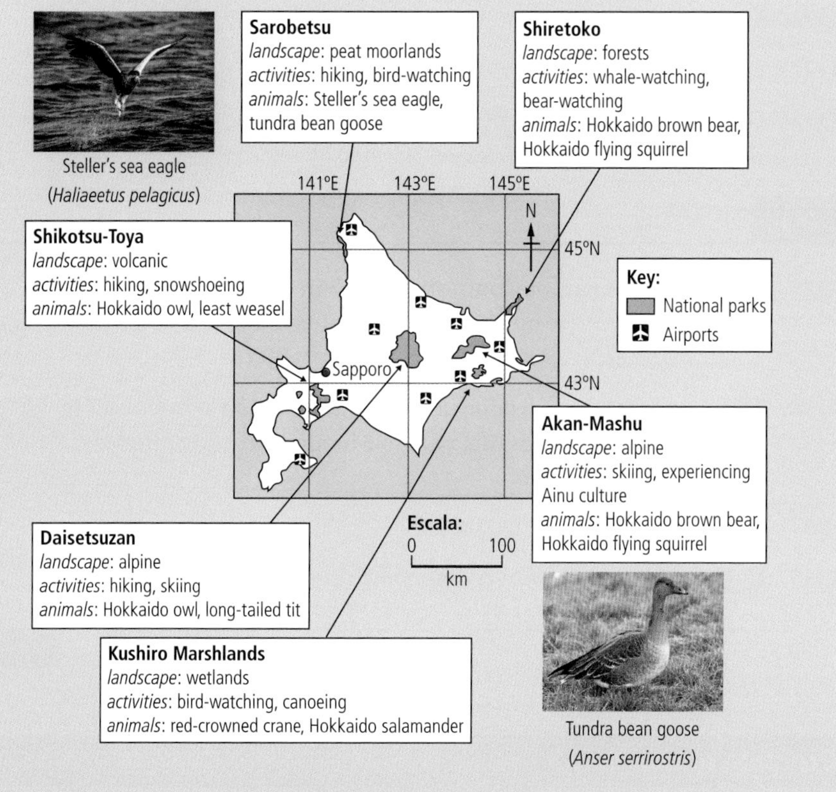

Figure 3.92 Map of Hokkaido's national parks.

2. Review Figures 3.93 and 3.94 before answering the questions.

Figure 3.93 Fact file on red-crowned cranes.

- In 2000, the IUCN listed red-crowned cranes as Endangered.
- In 2020, the IUCN made a recommendation to change their status from Endangered to Vulnerable.
- 50% of the world's population is found on Hokkaido.
- Breeding in captivity has been unsuccessful.
- They are protected from hunting across their entire habitat.
- Habitat loss has occurred because wetlands have been drained for agriculture.
- They feed on fish, frogs and salamanders in wetlands, and cereal crops and insects in agricultural areas.
- They are considered pests by some farmers as they eat cereal crops.
- The Kushiro Marshland National Park workers provide additional food in winter.
- Winter feeding stations in the park are overcrowded.
- On Hokkaido, red-crowned cranes have stopped migrating and have become permanent residents.
- The resident population of Hokkaido has lower genetic variability than the migratory Eurasian population.

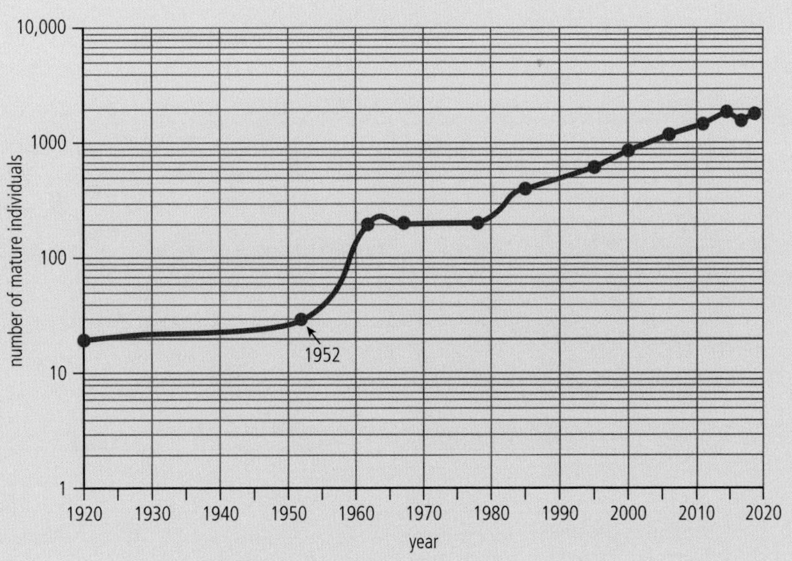

Figure 3.94 Population graph of mature, red-crowned cranes.

(a) **(i)** With reference to Figure 3.94, identify the number of mature, red-crowned cranes in 1952 and 2000. [1]

(ii) Calculate the average annual increase of mature, red-crowned cranes between 1952 and 2000. [1]

(b) With reference to the fact file in Figure 3.93, explain why some conservationists disagree with changing the status of the red-crowned crane from Endangered to Vulnerable. [3]

(c) The IUCN uses criteria to classify a species as Endangered. With reference to Figures 3.93 and 3.94, list **two** criteria that were met by the red-crowned cranes in 2000. [2]

(Total 7 marks)

3. Outline the mechanism of natural selection. [4]

(Total 4 marks)

4. Suggest reasons for the changes in the forested areas over the period shown in Table 3.4. [2]

(Total 2 marks)

Year	Percentage of forest cover / %
1940	76
1962	54
1987	22
1998	43
2010	53

Table 3.4 Variation in forest cover in Costa Rica between 1940 and 2010.

(continued)

5. Use Figure 3.95 to answer the questions below.

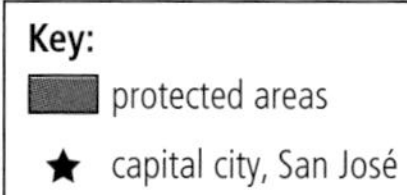

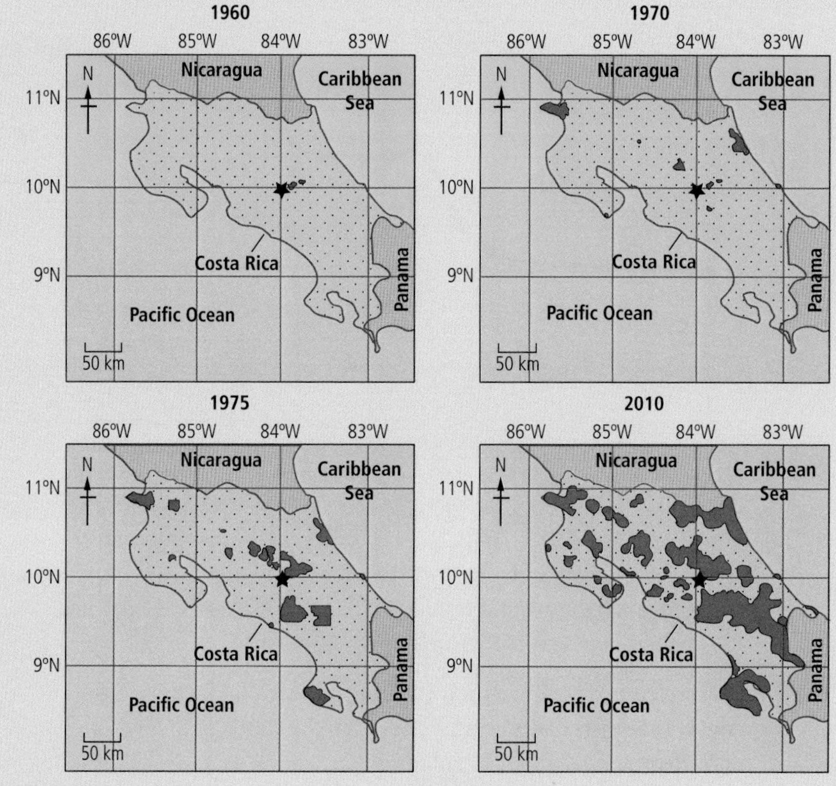

Figure 3.95 Development of protected areas in Costa Rica.

(a) Outline **one** reason it is difficult to determine the exact number of species in Costa Rica. [1]

(b) Explain **three** ways in which the development of protected areas shown in Figure 3.95 has improved the conservation of species. [3]

(Total 4 marks)

6. (a) State **one** criterion used to determine the IUCN Red List status of the jaguar shown in Figure 3.96. [1]

(b) Distinguish between the role of the jaguar as a keystone species and as a flagship species. [2]

(c) Identify **two** difficulties associated with establishing and maintaining wildlife corridors such as those shown in Figure 3.97. [2]

(Total 5 marks)

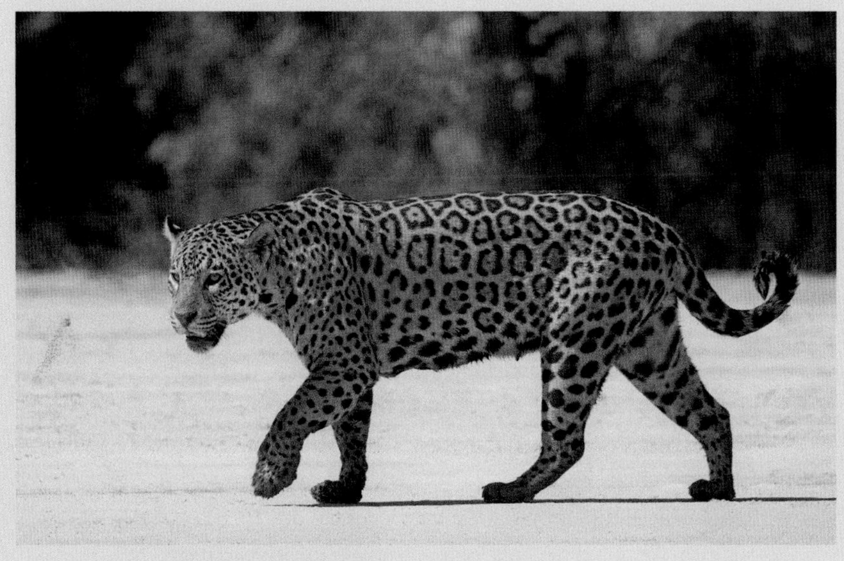

Figure 3.96 The jaguar (*Panthera onca*) is classified as 'near threatened' on the IUCN Red List of Threatened Species.

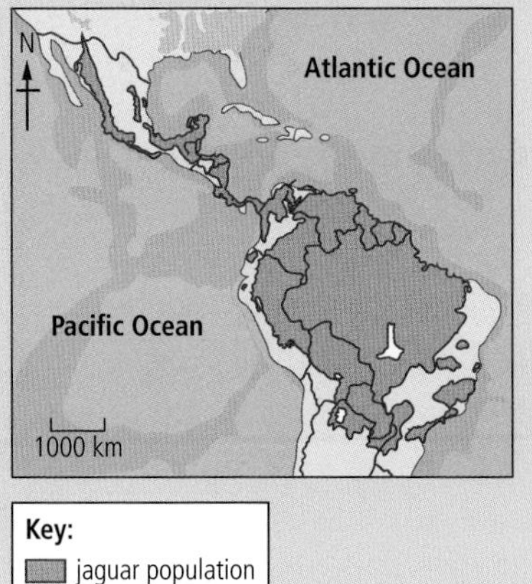

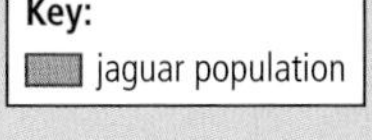

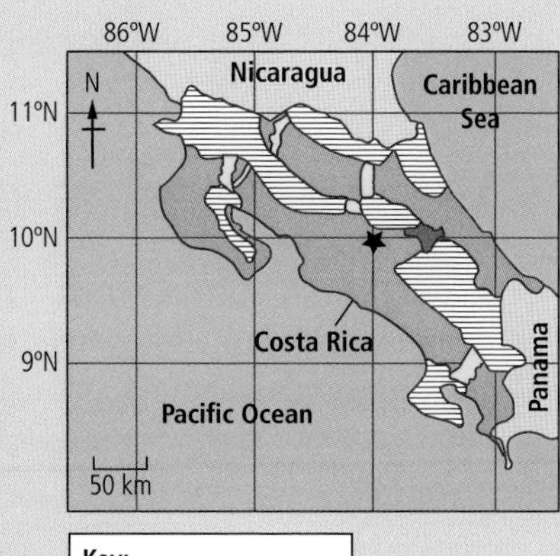

Key:
jaguar population
Barbilla Corridor
jaguar corridor
capital city, San José

Figure 3.97 The Barbilla Corridor within the larger international network connecting jaguar populations.

7. An area of temperate coniferous forest was deforested and allowed to regenerate. A survey of species numbers was conducted in three successional stages. The results of the survey are summarized in Table 3.5.

Table 3.5 The number of organisms found in each successional stage for selected species.

	Number of organisms in each successional stage		
Species	*Early*	*Intermediate*	*Late*
Red huckleberry (*Vaccinium parvifolium*)	100	80	70
Western hemlock (*Tsuga heterophylla*)	0	20	60
Douglas fir (*Pseudotsuga menziesii*)	50	132	90
Keen's mouse (*Peromyscus keeni*)	80	96	90
Douglas squirrel (*Tamiasciurus douglasii*)	5	30	40
American pine marten (*Martes americana*)	0	2	10
Total number of organisms	235	360	360
Simpson's reciprocal index (*D*)	2.94	3.80	---

(continued)

(a) Referring to the data in Table 3.5, calculate the Simpson's reciprocal index (*D*) of the late successional stage (show your working). [2]

$$D = \frac{N(N-1)}{\sum n(n-1)}$$

(b) Define the term *species diversity*. [1]

(Total 3 marks)

8. Review Figures 3.98, 3.99, 3.100 and 3.101 before answering the questions.

Figure 3.98 Fact file on the Siberian tiger (*Panthera tigris altaica*).

- Historically found in North and South Korea, Eastern China and Siberia but now mainly live within the Sikhote-Alin mountain range in Primorsky Krai and Khabarovsk Krai of Siberia.
- Female tigers reach sexual maturity after 4–5 years and give birth to 2–6 cubs once every two years.
- Reduction in tiger population has occurred due to:
  - loss of habitat because of logging and mining activity
  - poaching for fur and tiger parts used in traditional medicines (up to US$ 50,000 may be paid for a tiger)
  - loss of prey.
- Local communities have supported anti-poaching and environmental education campaigns.
- In the 1940s it was estimated that there were fewer than 50 individuals remaining in the wild and by 2010 this number had increased to about 500. During this period, the following conservation measures were introduced:

1947	Russia banned hunting of tigers.
1975	International trade in tigers and tiger parts banned through the Convention on International Trade of Endangered Species of Wild Fauna and Flora (CITES).
1992	The Siberian Tiger Project began attaching radio-collars to wild tigers to improve understanding of tiger ecology.
2007	Udege National Park and Zov Tigra National Park were created.
2010	Tiger protection was increased through policing and enforcement.

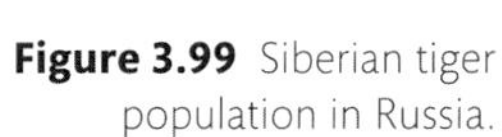

Figure 3.99 Siberian tiger population in Russia.

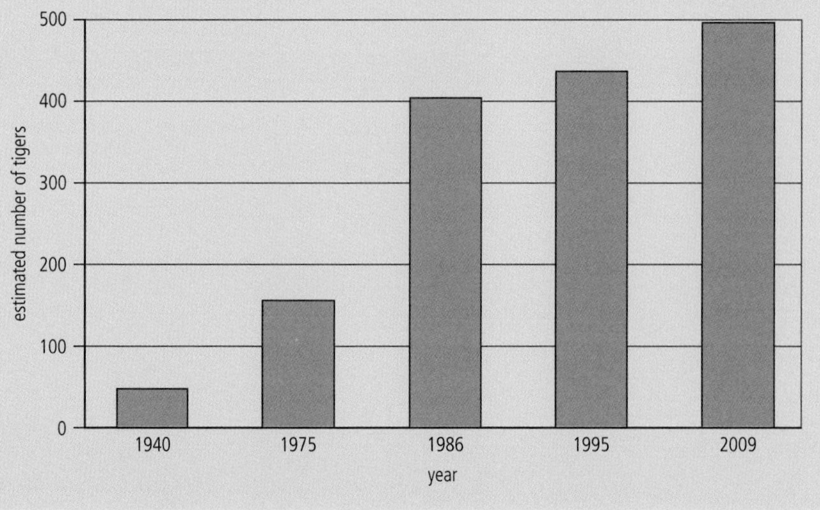

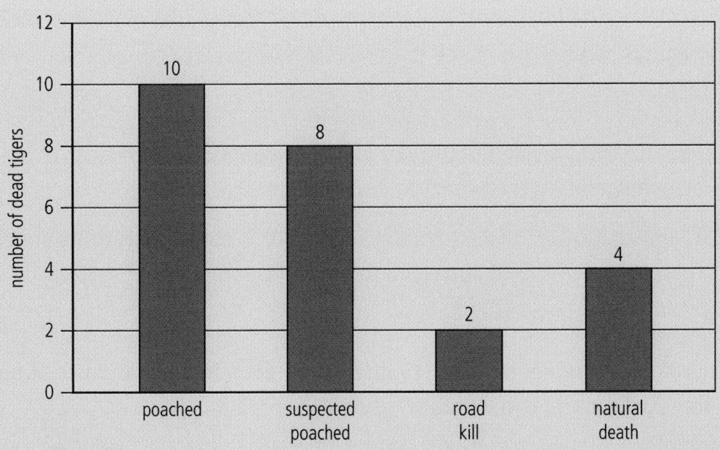

Figure 3.100 Causes of tiger mortality in and near Sikhote-Alin Biosphere Reserve, 1992–2005.

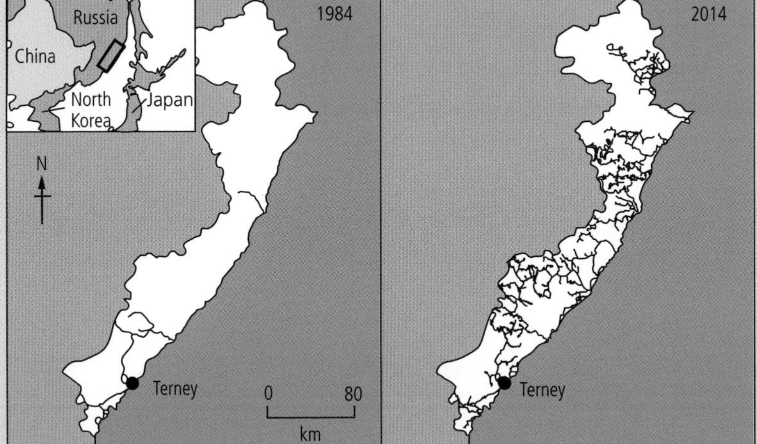

Figure 3.101 Increase of logging roads between 1984 (228 km) and 2014 (6278 km) in Primorsky Krai.

Conservation measures for the Siberian tiger between 1940–2010 involved tagging, setting up reserves, and bans on hunting and trade.

(a) With reference to Figures 3.98, 3.99 and 3.100, evaluate the relative success of these measures. [3]

In 2015, the logging company, the local authority, and an international NGO agreed to dismantle unused logging roads in the area.

(b) With reference to Figures 3.100 and 3.101, outline how the decision to remove logging roads in 2015 may benefit the tiger populations. [2]

(Total 5 marks)

9. **(a)** Outline the factors that contribute to total biodiversity of an ecosystem. [4]

(b) To what extent are strategies to promote the conservation of biodiversity successful? [9]

(Total 13 marks)

10. Identify **four** impacts on an ecosystem that may result from the introduction of an invasive species of herbivore. [4]

(Total 4 marks)

(continued)

11. Discuss the potential for designing a protected forest area that allows for the harvesting of natural resources while at the same time conserving its biodiversity. [9]

(Total 9 marks)

12. **(a)** Explain the causes, and the possible consequences, of the loss of a named critically endangered species. [7]

(b) Using examples, discuss whether habitat conservation is more successful than a species-based approach to protecting threatened species. [9]

(Total 16 marks)

13. With reference to Figure 3.102, evaluate the role of international zoos and wildlife parks in the conservation of aye-aye. [4]

(Total 4 marks)

Figure 3.102 Fact file on the aye-aye (*Daubentonia madagascariensis*).

- Aye-aye are a species of lemur.
- These nocturnal (active at night) primates live in trees.
- They feed on insects, fruits, nuts and fungi.
- In some areas they are killed because:
  - they are believed to be evil and bring bad luck
  - farmers consider them to be a pest, as they eat crops
  - they are a source of food.
- Aye-aye were considered to be extinct in 1933 but the population were rediscovered in 1957.
- They are classified as endangered on the IUCN Red List.

14. **(a)** Distinguish between the concept of a 'charismatic' (flagship) species and a keystone species using named examples. [4]

(b) Discuss the implications of environmental value systems in the protection of tropical biomes. [9]

(Total 13 marks)

15. **(a)** Identify **four** reasons why the genetic diversity of a population may change over time. [4]

(b) Environmental value systems differ in how they view the importance of biodiversity, and this could influence a community's approach to conservation.

Discuss how these different perspectives, including your own, may influence approaches to conservation. [9]

(Total 13 marks)

HL

16. HL **(a)** **(i)** With reference to Figure 3.103, identify when the diversity of species was lowest in the past 400 million years. [1]

(ii) Describe what may have caused the deviation from the trend line at point **X**. [2]

(b) (i) Identify the relationship between the number of continents and the diversity of species during the past 250 million years. [1]

(ii) Describe **two** reasons why there is a relationship between the number of continents and the diversity of species. [2]

(c) Outline the role of natural selection in increasing the diversity of species. [2]

(Total 8 marks)

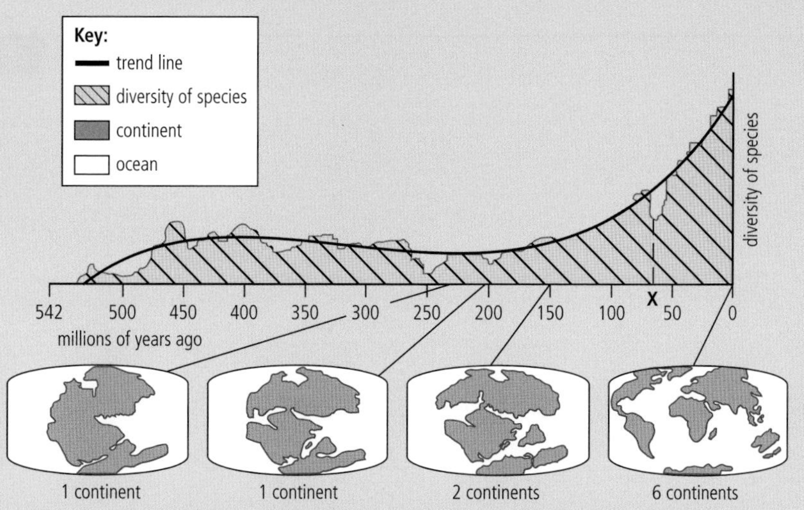

Figure 3.103 Distribution of continents and diversity of species over time.

17. HL **(a)** Outline **one** advantage of increased tourism on wildlife conservation. [1]

(b) Outline **one** disadvantage of increased tourism on wildlife conservation. [1]

(Total 2 marks)

18. HL Figure 3.104 shows past mass extinctions. Use Figure 3.104 to answer the questions.

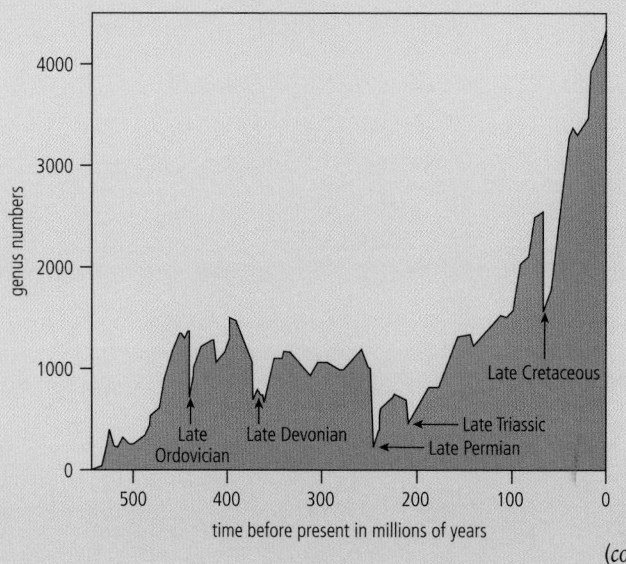

Figure 3.104 A graph showing past mass extinctions.

(continued)

(a) State **two** possible causes of these past mass extinctions. [2]

(b) Identify **two** ways in which the current extinction differs from mass extinctions in the past. [2]

(c) Explain **one** factor that may make a species less prone to extinction. [2]

(d) Outline how the process of natural selection is a mechanism for evolution. [2]

(Total 8 marks)

HL end

4 Water

4.1 Water systems

Guiding question

How do water systems support life on Earth, and how do they interact with other systems, such as the carbon cycle?

4.1.1 Movements of water in the hydrosphere are driven by solar radiation and gravity.
4.1.2 The global hydrological cycle operates as a system with stores and flows.
4.1.3 The main stores in the hydrological cycle are the oceans (96.5%), glaciers and ice caps (1.7%), groundwater (1.7%), surface freshwater (0.02%), atmosphere (0.001%), organisms (0.0001%).
4.1.4 Flows in the hydrological cycle include transpiration, sublimation, evaporation, condensation, advection, precipitation, melting, freezing, surface run-off, infiltration, percolation, streamflow and groundwater flow.
4.1.5 Human activities, such as agriculture, deforestation and urbanization, can alter these flows and stores.
4.1.6 The steady state of any water body can be demonstrated through flow diagrams of inputs and outputs.
HL 4.1.7 Water has unique physical and chemical properties that support and sustain life.
HL 4.1.8 The oceans act as a carbon sink by absorbing carbon dioxide from the atmosphere and sequestering it.
HL 4.1.9 Carbon sequestered in oceans over the short term as dissolved carbon dioxide causes ocean acidification; over the longer term, carbon is taken up into living organisms as biomass that accumulates on the seabed.
HL 4.1.10 The temperature of water varies with depth, with cold water below and warmer water above. Differences in density restrict mixing between the layers, leading to persistent stratification.
HL 4.1.11 Stratification occurs in deeper lakes, coastal areas, enclosed seas and open ocean, with a thermocline forming a transition layer between the warmer mixed layer at the surface and the cooler water below.
HL 4.1.12 Global warming and salinity changes have increased the intensity of ocean stratification.
HL 4.1.13 Upwellings in oceans and freshwater bodies can bring cold, nutrient-rich waters to the surface.
HL 4.1.14 Thermohaline circulation systems are driven by differences in temperature and salinity. The resulting differences in water density drive the ocean conveyor belt, which distributes heat around the world and thus affects climate.

4.1.1 Movements of water in the hydrosphere

1.2 Systems

Water can exist in three phases within the atmosphere:

- solid as tiny ice crystals
- liquid as water droplets
- gas as water vapour.

The hydrological cycle involves several processes.

- Solar radiation is needed for evaporation and evapotranspiration, which move water from the Earth's surface to the atmosphere.
- Heat is released when water condenses (Figure 4.1).
- Precipitation moves water from the atmosphere to the Earth's surface due to gravity.
- Air movements, including winds and weather systems, redistribute water from place to place.

Figure 4.1 Condensation on a window.

Solar radiation drives the hydrological cycle. Changes in temperature can cause changes in moisture from one phase to another, as shown in Figure 4.2. These changes are:

- liquid to solid by freezing
- solid to liquid by melting
- liquid to gas by evaporation
- gas to liquid by condensation
- solid to gas by sublimation
- gas to solid by deposition.

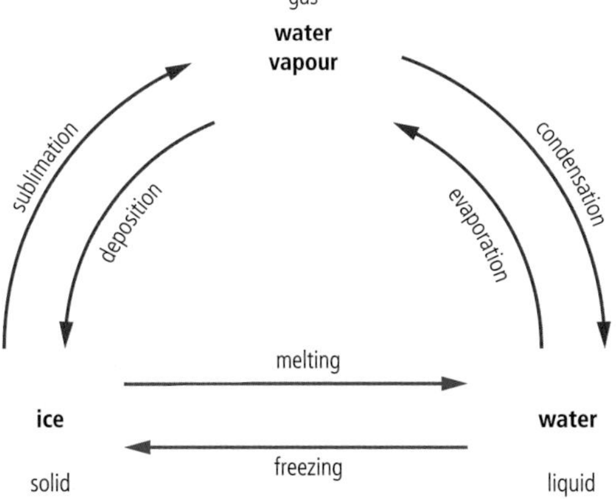

Figure 4.2 Phase changes of water.

4.1.2 Global hydrological cycle

1.2 Systems

The global hydrological cycle is complex. Several parts of the cycle cannot be observed. Therefore, to enable our understanding of how the cycle works, scientists use a systems model known as the drainage basin hydrological cycle (Figures 4.3 and 4.4). This is a simplified structuring of reality that shows just a few parts of the system. The drainage basin is studied, rather than the global system, as it is easier to observe and to measure. The basin cycle is an open system and the main input is precipitation, which is regulated by various means of storage.

In systems diagrams of the hydrological cycle, stores are shown as boxes and flows as arrows (see also Topic 1, Section 1.2.3, Figure 1.29), as in Figure 4.4, whereas Figure 4.3 shows the hydrological cycle as an image.

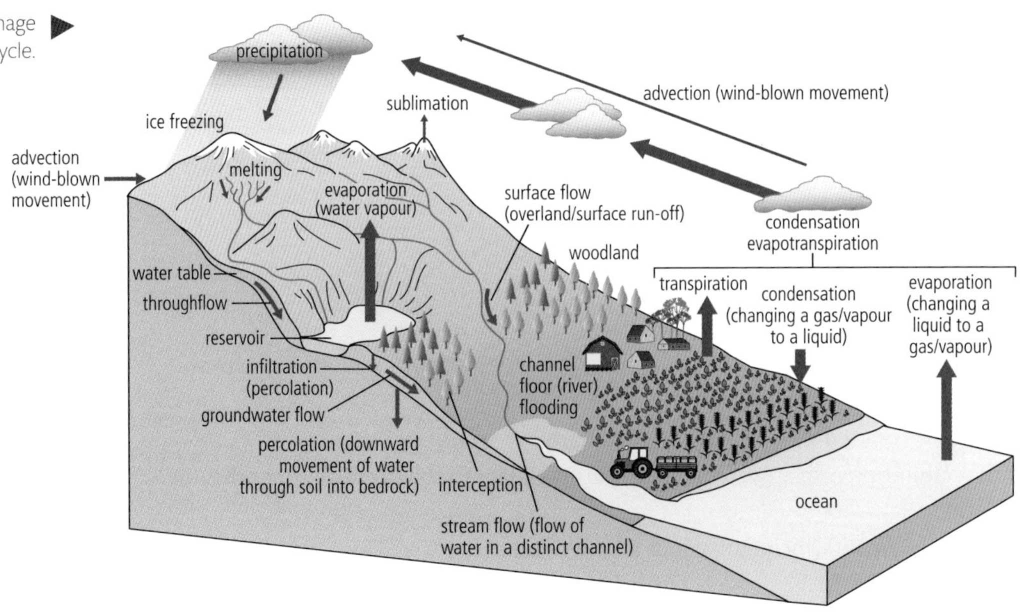

Figure 4.3 The drainage basin hydrological cycle.

How does the presentation of information influence the understanding of knowledge?

Compare Figures 4.3 and 4.4. Which do you find easier to understand? Which is the more detailed and accurate model of the water cycle?

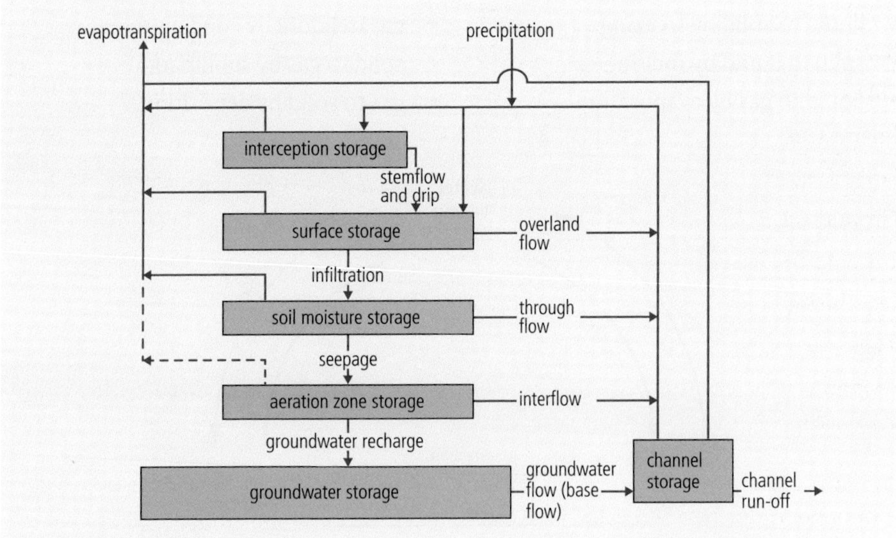

Figure 4.4 The drainage basin hydrological cycle as a system.

4.1.3 Stores in the hydrological cycle

The global hydrological cycle operates as a *system* with stores and flows.

Stores in the hydrological cycle can be divided into saltwater and freshwater stores. Oceans and seas make up the saltwater stores, whereas freshwater stores include glaciers and ice caps, rivers and lakes, soil water and ground water in aquifers (permeable rocks that can store water), the atmosphere and organisms (Figure 4.5).

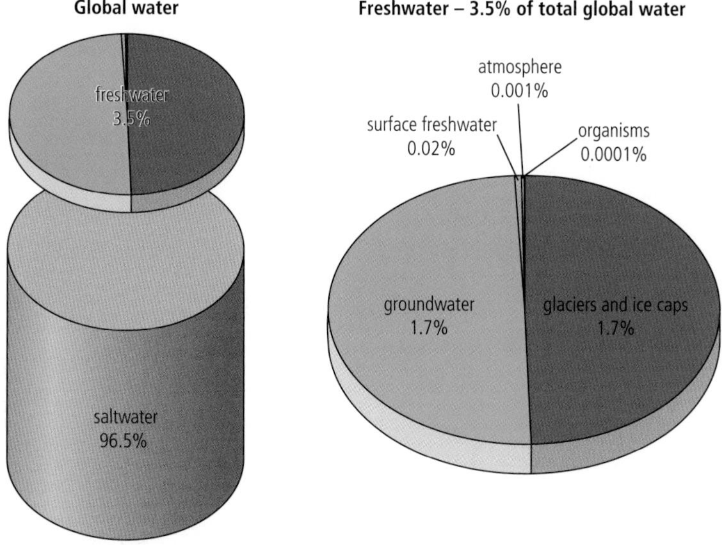

Figure 4.5 Stores in the global hydrological cycle.

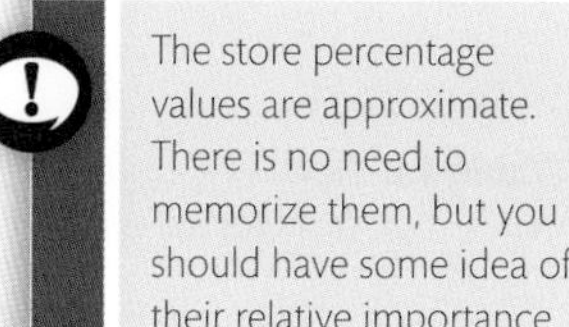

The store percentage values are approximate. There is no need to memorize them, but you should have some idea of their relative importance.

Table 4.1 Size of stores and residence time in the hydrological cycle.

Store	Best estimate / km³	Residence time
Oceans	1,350,000,000	2500 years
Atmosphere	13,000	8 days
Rivers	1700	16 days
Lakes	100,000	17 days
Inland seas	105,000	*
Soil moisture	50,000	1 year
Groundwater	8,200,000	1400 years
Glaciers and ice caps	27,500,000	**
Organisms	1100	hours

* Data not available

** Montane glaciers' residence time is 1600 years and polar ice caps' residence time is 9700 years

The oceans hold 96.5% of the water on the Earth and are therefore the largest component of the hydrological cycle. Ocean water is continually moving due to winds and tides and this movement has a significant impact on climates around the world. Ocean currents are also driven by changes in water density as the denser colder water sinks and less dense, warmer water rises.

According to Table 4.1, glaciers and ice sheets are the largest freshwater component of the world's freshwater. Ice currently covers about 10% of the Earth's terrestrial surface, mainly at high altitude and high latitude, although at the height of glacial advances during the Quaternary Ice Age, they covered about 30% of the terrestrial surface. Groundwater is the next most important freshwater store. Much groundwater lies deep beneath the surface (at a depth of more than 600 m) but some is closer to the surface and can be used by people and plants. Some groundwater is tens of thousands of years old, such as the groundwater beneath the Sahara and the Arabian deserts, and so is essentially a non-renewable resource. Rivers and lakes are the most accessible forms of freshwater to humans, although several sources are highly polluted.

1.2 Systems

4.1.4 Flows in the hydrological cycle

The hydrological cycle includes evaporation from oceans, water vapour, condensation, precipitation, run-off, groundwater and evapotranspiration (Table 4.2). If 100 units represent global precipitation (on average 860 mm per year), 77% falls over the oceans and 23% falls on land. About 84% enters the atmosphere by evaporation via the oceans, thus there is a horizontal transfer of 7% from the land to the sea. Of precipitation over the land, 16% is evaporated or transpired and 7% runs off to the oceans. There may be some time lag between precipitation and eventual run-off. About 96.5% of all free water on Earth is stored in the oceans.

Table 4.2 Flows in the global hydrological cycle.

Annual exchange		Thousands of km^3	
Evaporation		496.0	
of which	from oceans		425.0
	from land		71.0
Precipitation		496.0	
of which	from oceans		385.0
	from land		111.0
Run-off to oceans		41.5	
of which	from rivers		27.0
	from groundwater		12.0
	from glacial meltwater		2.5

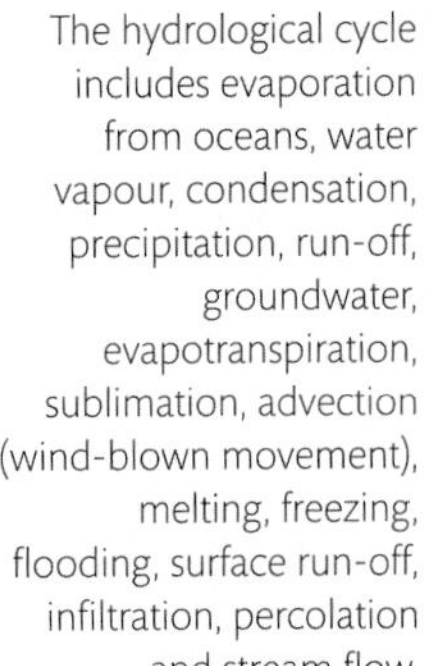

The hydrological cycle includes evaporation from oceans, water vapour, condensation, precipitation, run-off, groundwater, evapotranspiration, sublimation, advection (wind-blown movement), melting, freezing, flooding, surface run-off, infiltration, percolation and stream flow.

What role do models play in the acquisition of knowledge?

The hydrological cycle is represented as a systems model (e.g., Figure 4.4, Section 4.1.2). To what extent can systems diagrams effectively model reality, given that they are only based on limited observable features? Systems modelling provides a simplified version of reality, so how can modellers know which aspects of the system to include and which to ignore?

Precipitation is the conversion and transfer of moisture in the atmosphere to the land and includes all forms of rainfall, snow, frost, hail and dew.

Interception refers to the water that is caught and stored by vegetation.
Water not stored by plants may be lost through:

- interception loss, where the water is retained by plant surfaces and is later evaporated away
- throughfall, where the water either falls through gaps in the vegetation or drops from leaves, twigs or stems
- stemflow, where the water trickles along twig and branches and finally down the main trunk.

Evaporation is the process by which a liquid is changed into a gas. It is the conversion of liquid precipitation to water vapour in the atmosphere. It is most important when it happens to the water from oceans and seas. Factors affecting evaporation include meteorological factors such as temperature, humidity and windspeed. Of these, temperature is the most important factor. Evaporation increases under warm, dry and windy conditions, and decreases under cold, calm conditions. Other factors include the amount of water available, vegetation cover and colour of the surface (albedo or reflectivity of the surface, for example lighter-coloured surfaces such as ice are more reflective than darker surfaces such as bare soil). Evaporation losses will be greater in arid and semi-arid climates than they will be in polar regions.

Transpiration is the process by which water vapour escapes from living plants and enters the atmosphere. The combined effects of evaporation and transpiration are normally referred to as evapotranspiration. Evapotranspiration represents the most important aspect of water loss, accounting for the loss of nearly 100% of the annual precipitation in arid areas and 75% in humid areas. Purely evaporative losses only occur over ice and snow fields, bare rock surfaces, desert areas, water surfaces and bare soil.

Infiltration rates of 0–4 mm h^{-1} are common on clays, whereas 3–12 mm h^{-1} are common on sands. Vegetation also increases infiltration rate because it intercepts some rainfall and slows down the speed at which it arrives at the surface. For example, on bare soils where rain splash impact occurs, infiltration rates may reach 10 mm h^{-1}. On similar soils covered by vegetation, rates of 50–100 mm h^{-1} have been recorded. Infiltrated water is chemically rich as it picks up minerals and organic acids from vegetation and soils.

Infiltration is the process by which water soaks into, or is absorbed by, the soil. The infiltration capacity is the maximum rate at which rain can be absorbed by a soil in a given condition. Infiltration capacity decreases with time during a period of rainfall until a more or less constant value is reached.

Infiltration is inversely related to overland run-off and is influenced by a variety of factors such as duration of rainfall, antecedent (pre-existing) levels of soil moisture, soil porosity, vegetation cover, raindrop size and slope angle. In contrast, overland flow (surface run-off) is water that flows over the land's surface. It occurs when precipitation exceeds the infiltration rate and when the soil is saturated (all the pore spaces are filled with water).

In areas of high precipitation intensity and low infiltration capacity, overland run-off is common. This is clearly seen in semi-arid areas and in cultivated fields. By contrast, where precipitation intensity is low and infiltration is high, most overland flow occurs close to streams and river channels.

Condensation (Figure 4.1) is the process by which vapour passes into a liquid form. It occurs when air is cooled to its dew point or becomes saturated by evaporation into it. Further cooling leads to condensation on surfaces to form water droplets or frost.

▲
Figure 4.6 Frost on an azalea shrub.

Sublimation refers to the conversion of a solid into a vapour with no intermediate liquid state. Under conditions of low humidity, snow can be evaporated directly into water vapour without entering the liquid state. The reverse of sublimation, **deposition**, occurs when water vapour changes directly into ice, such as snowflakes and frost (Figure 4.6).

Advection is the movement of air and water in a horizontal direction, such as the transfer of heat and water vapour from low latitudes to high latitudes.

Percolation refers to the downward vertical movement of water within a soil into the underlying rocks. In contrast, the transfer of water within rocks is known as **groundwater flow**. Rocks that contain stores of water are called **aquifers**.

Stream flow refers to the run-off of surface water in a defined channel (rather than flood flow where the water spreads out over a wide area).

Create and use a systems diagram showing the transfers and transformations of the hydrological cycle

Use the data in Table 4.2 to create a flow diagram of the hydrological (water) cycle. Make the boxes and arrows proportional to the size of each store and transfer.

1.2 Systems 

4.1.5 Human activities

Human activities such as agriculture, deforestation and urbanization can alter stores and flows. Changes in land use, deforestation and urbanization often lead to reduced evapotranspiration and increased run-off leading to flash floods.

Agriculture

The type of agriculture being practiced can have varying impacts on drainage basin stores and flows.

Arable (crop) farming removes vegetation cover during the harvest and so leaves the land vulnerable to erosion.

In contrast, pastoral (livestock) farming may leave a grass cover throughout the year, but this may mean replacing a diverse, forested surface with a grass monoculture, leading to lower rates of interception, reduced storage and decreased infiltration.

Interception is determined by vegetation type and density. In farmland areas, cereals intercept less than broadleaf crops. Row crops leave a lot of bare soil exposed. Infiltration is up to five times greater under forests compared with grasslands. This is because the plants and trees in the forest channel water back into the ground.

Land-use practices influence infiltration (Table 4.3). Grazing leads to a decline in infiltration due to compaction of soil. Waterlogging and salinization are also common if there is poor drainage.

Table 4.3 Influence of ground cover on infiltration rates.

Ground cover	Infiltration rate/mm h^{-1}
Old permanent pasture	57
Permanent pasture: moderately grazed	19
Permanent pasture: heavily grazed	13
Strip-cropped	10
Weeds or grain	9
Clean-tilled	7
Bare, crusted ground	6

Deforestation

As Figure 4.7 shows, the presence of vegetation increases interception, reduces overland flow and increases evapotranspiration. When the vegetation cover is removed, for example in deforestation, the risk of more severe and more frequent flooding events increases. This is because deforestation reduces interception, increases overland flow and reduces evapotranspiration. Deforestation is also a cause of increased flood run-off and a decrease in channel capacity due to an increase in deposition within the channel.

The area experiencing deforestation is likely to be larger than the area experiencing urbanization. This is because deforestation may occur for land-use changes (for example, the conversion to agriculture), industrial development, to make way for tourist developments and to allow urbanization to occur. Hence it is likely to have a more widespread impact on hydrological processes, including:

- increased volume of sediment being transported by rivers
- increased overland flow leading to more frequent erosion
- reduced interception
- reduced infiltration
- reduced evapotranspiration.

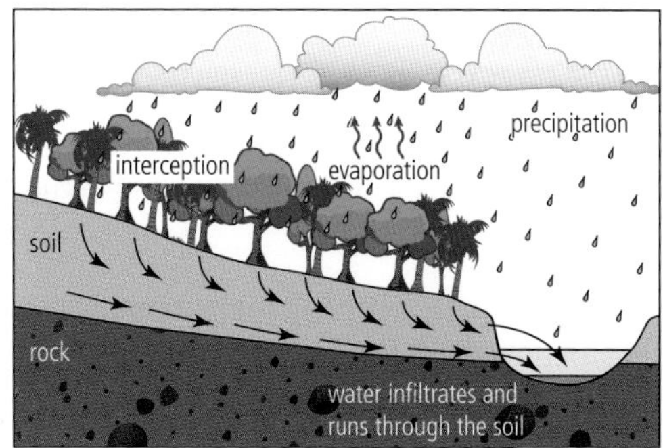

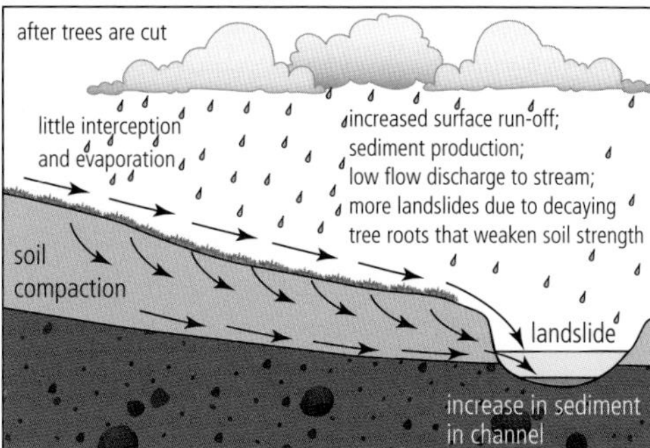

Figure 4.7 The influence of deforestation on drainage basin hydrology and flooding.

Activity

Working in pairs, examine the data in Table 4.4. One person should make a diagram or graph showing the relationship between (i) rainfall and annual run-off and (ii) rainfall and erosion. The second person should make a diagram or graph showing the relationship between (i) slope angle and annual run-off and (ii) slope angle and erosion. Compare your diagrams or graphs with your partner and discuss the similarities and differences.

Table 4.4 Changes in run-off and erosion following deforestation. A = forest or ungrazed thicket; B = crop; C = barren soil.

Locality	Average annual rainfall / mm	Slope / %	Annual run-off / %			Erosion / t ha^{-1} yr^{-1}		
			A	B	C	A	B	C
Ougadougou (Burkina Faso)	850	0.5	2.5	2–32	40–60	0.1	0.6–0.8	10–20
Sefa (Senegal)	1300	1.2	1.0	21.2	39.5	0.2	7.3	21.3
Bouake (Cote d'Ivoire)	1200	4.0	0.3	0.1–26	15–30	0.1	1–26	18–30
Abidjan (Cote d'Ivoire)	2100	7.0	0.4	0.5–20	38	0.03	0.1–90	108–170
Mbapwa (Tanzania)	*c.*570	6.0	0.4	26.0	50.4	0	78	146

Urbanization

Urbanization influences the hydrological cycle through the creation of highly impermeable surfaces such as roads, roofs and pavements, and smooth surfaces that are served with a dense network of drains, gutters and underground sewers to increase drainage density (Table 4.5).

Urbanization has a greater impact on processes in the lower part of a drainage basin than in the upper parts. This is because a greater number of urban areas are found in the lower, flatter parts of drainage basins than are found in higher altitude, steeper parts.

Urbanization can have conflicting impacts on hydrological processes, including:

- increased erosion due to an increase in the volume of water getting into rivers
- increased speed of flow and transport of materials in rivers due to enlarged channels
- less erosion due to riverbank protection schemes.

Table 4.5 Potential hydrological effects of urbanization.

Urbanizing influence	Potential hydrological response
Removal of trees and vegetation	Decreased evapotranspiration and interception Increased stream sedimentation
Initial construction of houses, streets and culverts	Decreased infiltration and lowered groundwater table Increased storm flows and decreased base flows during dry periods Sedimentation continues while bare ground is still exposed
Complete development of residential, commercial and industrial areas	Decreased porosity, reducing time of run-off concentration, thereby increasing peak discharges and compressing the time distribution of the flow Greatly increased volume of run-off and flood damage potential
Construction of storm drains and channel improvements	Local relief from flooding Concentration of floodwaters may aggravate flood problems downstream

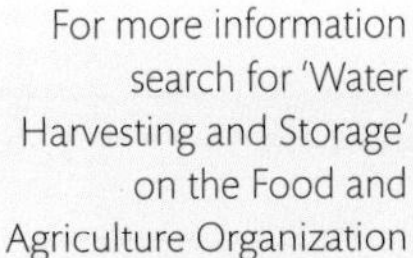

For more information search for 'Water Harvesting and Storage' on the Food and Agriculture Organization (FAO) website:

Find the 'Rainwater Harvesting Calculator' on the Knowledge tab of the FreeFlush website:

Activity

Study the area around your school/home. How and why does infiltration vary locally? Work with a partner to compare areas. Make a presentation to the class.

4.1.6 Steady state of water bodies

The steady state of any water body can be demonstrated using flow diagrams of inputs and outputs. These can be used to calculate sustainable rates of water-harvesting from lakes, aquifers and other water bodies.

The input of water into a drainage basin mostly occurs through precipitation. However, there could also be transfer from other drainage basins and from groundwater. Outputs include evaporation, transpiration, discharge out of the basin and groundwater flow into other drainage basins. Figure 4.8 shows the world's water balance, while Figure 4.9 shows the water balance for the Amazon rainforest.

Figure 4.8 The world's water balance.

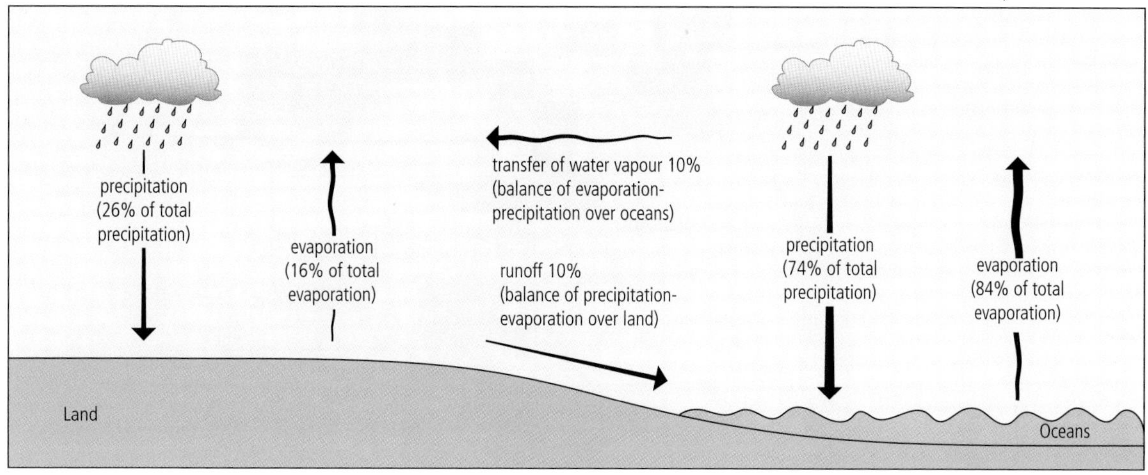

Figure 4.9 Water balance for the Amazon rainforest.

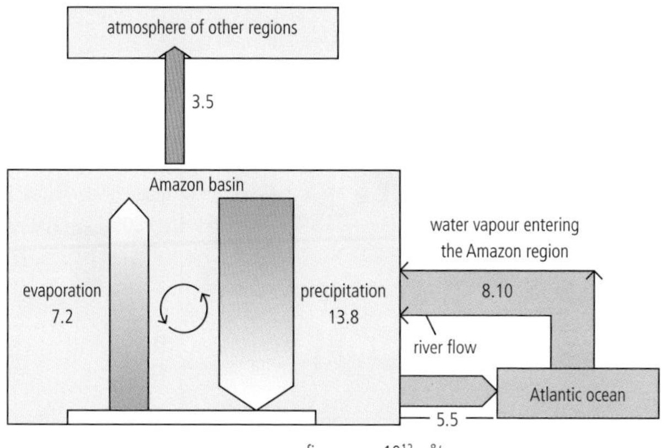

As the flow diagrams represent long-term water stores, rather than transfers, the moisture found in the soil and the bedrock may not be included.

Example – Water balance

For water use to be considered sustainable, the volume of water used needs to be lower than the volume of precipitation left after losses due to evapotranspiration. Any use of groundwater also needs to not exceed the annual recharge, as this would lead to a decline in groundwater resources.

Unfortunately, in many areas, the use of water for farming has depleted water resources beyond natural recharge. For example, the Ogallala Aquifer under the High Plains irrigates more than 20% of the USA's cropland. The aquifer is close to depletion in parts of Kansas because the water level has fallen so much (Figure 4.10).

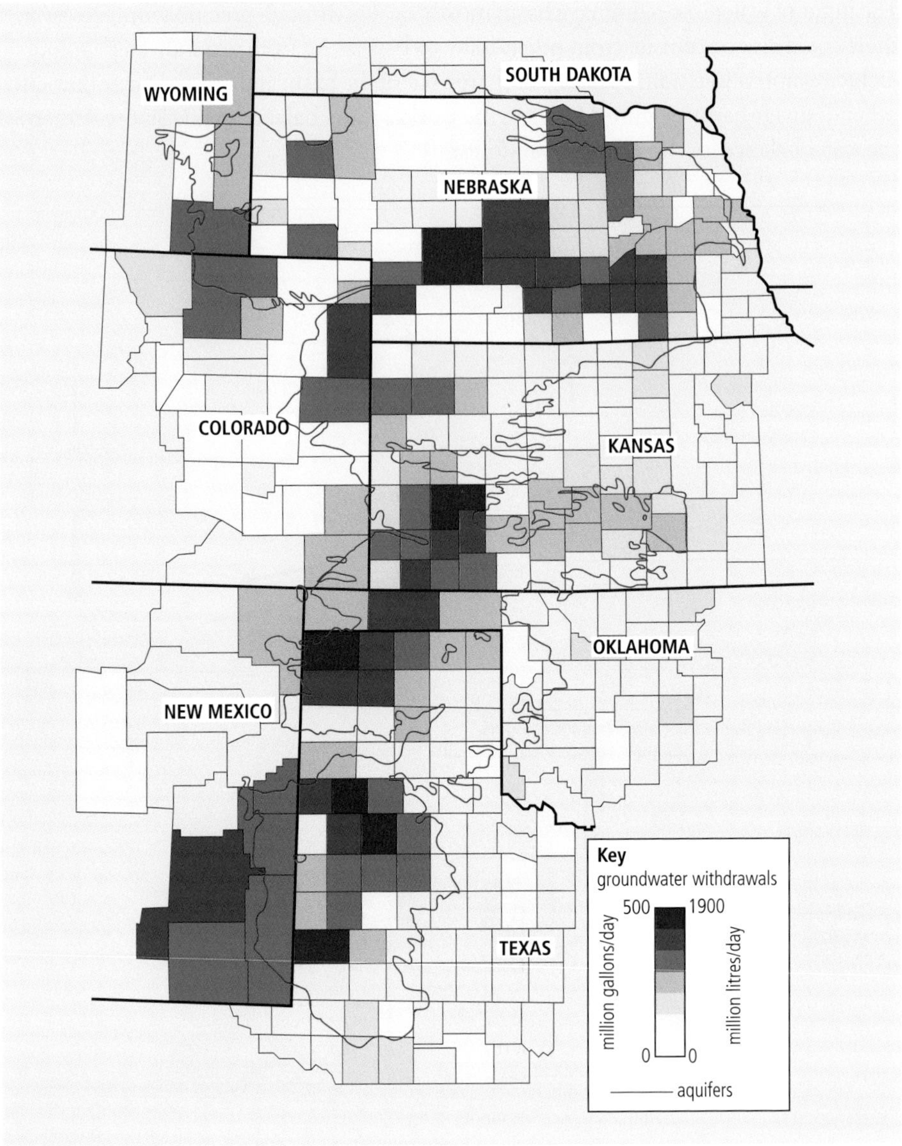

Figure 4.10 Impact of water use on the High Plains aquifer.

HL

4.1.7 Water properties

Water (H_2O) is an inorganic compound formed from hydrogen (H_2) and oxygen (O_2). It can exist as a solid, liquid or gas, and it covers over 70% of the Earth's surface as a liquid.

In a water molecule, the nucleus of the oxygen atom draws electrons (which are negatively charged) away from the hydrogen nuclei (which are positively charged). Although the water molecule is electrically neutral overall, there is a partial negative charge on the oxygen atom and a partial positive charge on the hydrogen atoms. This arrangement makes water a **polar molecule**. With water molecules, the partially positively charged hydrogen atoms of one molecule are attracted to the partially negatively charged oxygen atoms of nearby water molecules, causing attractive forces

HL

Specific heat capacity is the amount of heat energy needed to raise the temperature of 1 g of a substance by 1°C. Water has a higher specific heat capacity than land, i.e. it takes more heat energy to raise the temperature of water than of land.

called **hydrogen bonds**. Water molecules stay close together **(cohesion)** due to the hydrogen bonding between them. Hydrogen bonds are constantly breaking up and reforming.

Cohesion is the force by which individual molecules of the same type attract and associate (stick together). Attraction between water molecules is due to hydrogen bonding.

Land has a low specific heat capacity, which means that it heats up and cools down quickly. In contrast, water has a high specific heat capacity, which means that it takes a long time to heat up and cool down. This is because energy is needed to overcome the strong hydrogen bonds keeping the water molecules together. Hence, areas that are close to the sea have a more moderate climate, termed maritime, whereas those far from the sea have a more extreme climate, termed continental.

Water has a very high surface tension, caused by the strength of the hydrogen bonding between water molecules. This allows some insects to walk on the water's surface. Many gases are soluble in water. CO_2 is soluble in water and, increasingly, oceans are becoming more acidic.

Adhesion is the attraction between water and other substances, such as a surface.

Water also has high **adhesion** due to its polar nature. On clean glass, water may form a thin film because the forces between the glass and the water molecules are greater than the cohesive forces between the water molecules themselves.

Do not confuse the terms cohesion and adhesion. Cohesion ('co' means 'together') is attraction between water molecules. Adhesion ('ad' means 'toward') is attraction to a surface.

Water is also an excellent solvent, so many substances can dissolve in it. Substances that dissolve in water are termed hydrophilic ('water-loving') substances. An example of a hydrophilic substance is sodium chloride (NaCl), which dissolves in water producing separate sodium cations (Na^+) and chloride anions (Cl^-), both surrounded by water molecules. Substances that do not mix well with water are termed hydrophobic ('water-fearing') substances. An example of a hydrophobic substance is oil.

4.1.8 Oceans as carbon sinks

HL

Over the longer term, carbon is taken up into living organisms as biomass that accumulates on the seabed. Seabed sediments contain inorganic carbonates and carbon compounds in organic matter that is not fully decomposed. Over millions of years these sediments can become fossil fuels.

2.3 Biogeochemical cycles
6.2 Climate change – causes and impacts

Oceans are the largest carbon dioxide (CO_2) sink on Earth. Over geological time, more than 90% of the world's carbon has settled in the ocean. Biological processes, such as photosynthesis, convert the carbon from CO_2 into organic material. Gradually, organic carbon settles into the deep ocean. The deep ocean has a higher concentration of carbon than the upper ocean. Thus oceans have moderated the impact of increased atmospheric CO_2 by storing vast quantities in seawater and deep-sea sediments. If carbon on the ocean floor were lifted to the surface, the ocean would become a source of CO_2 rather than a sink.

Since the early 1800s, about half of the CO_2 released through the burning of fossil fuels has been absorbed by oceans. Absorbed CO_2 forms carbonic acid by dissolving into the water of the oceans. This raises the hydrogen ion (H^+) concentration in the ocean, making it more acidic and limiting organisms' access to carbonate ions that are needed to form shells.

Since 1900, the pH of surface seawater has fallen from 8.2 to 8.1 due to the quantity of CO_2 absorbed by oceans.

If the oceans continue to absorb CO_2 at the same rate, by 2100 the pH of surface seawater could have dropped to 7.8, representing an increase in acidity of about 150%.

The pH scale is logarithmic. Therefore, a difference in pH of 0.1 represents a change of 30% acidity.

During cold glacial phases atmospheric CO_2 levels may have decreased to around 180 parts per million by volume (ppmv) and it is thought that much of this was stored in the oceans (Topic 2, Section 2.3.9). By contrast, in the warm interglacial, CO_2 would have been released from the oceans and atmospheric CO_2 levels may have been around 280 ppmv. Current CO_2 levels are around 400 ppmv, indicating a substantial global warming.

The long-term trend in the ocean carbon sink since the 1960s has been driven by the uptake of anthropogenic CO_2. About 25–30% was absorbed by the oceans. However, the ocean carbon sink varies by as much as 20%. Some scientists suggest that oceanic uptake of carbon could be reduced in future as a result of reduced emissions of CO_2 due to climate change policies, reduced storage capacity due to increasing ocean acidification and ocean warming leading to an increase in the volume of CO_2 released from the oceans.

Activity

Use Figure 4.11 to calculate the amount of the world's carbon that is stored in the world's oceans and deep-sea sediments.

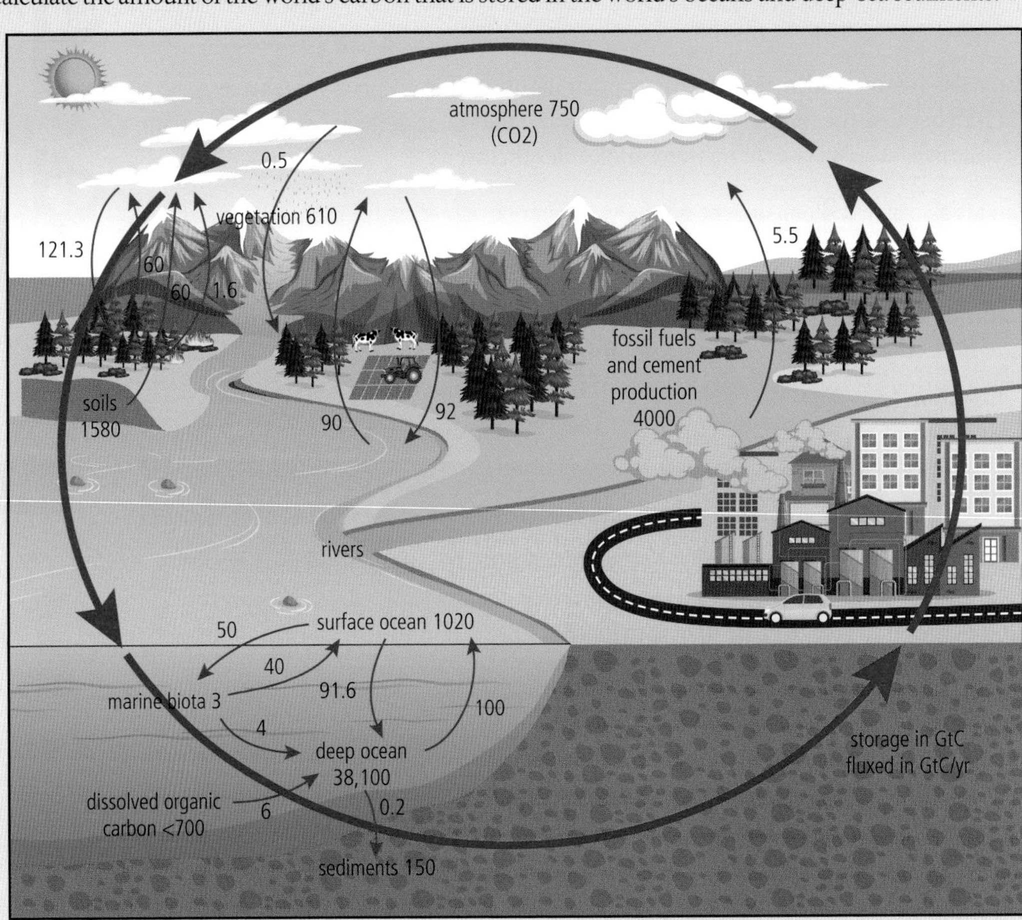

Figure 4.11 Oceans and the carbon cycle.

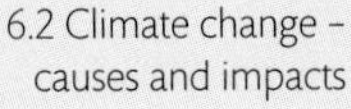

HL

4.1.9 Carbon sequestration and ocean acidification

2.3 Biogeochemical cycles
6.1 Introduction to the atmosphere
6.2 Climate change - causes and impacts

Carbon sequestered in oceans over the short term as dissolved CO_2 causes ocean acidification (Figure 4.12).

Over the long term, carbon is taken up into living organisms and when the organisms die, the biomass accumulates on the seabed. Seabed sediments contain inorganic carbonates and carbon compounds in organic matter that has not fully decomposed. Over millions of years these sediments can be compressed to become fossil fuels.

The cause of ocean acidification is believed to be anthropogenic sources – such as carbon emissions from industrial plants, power stations, cars and planes.

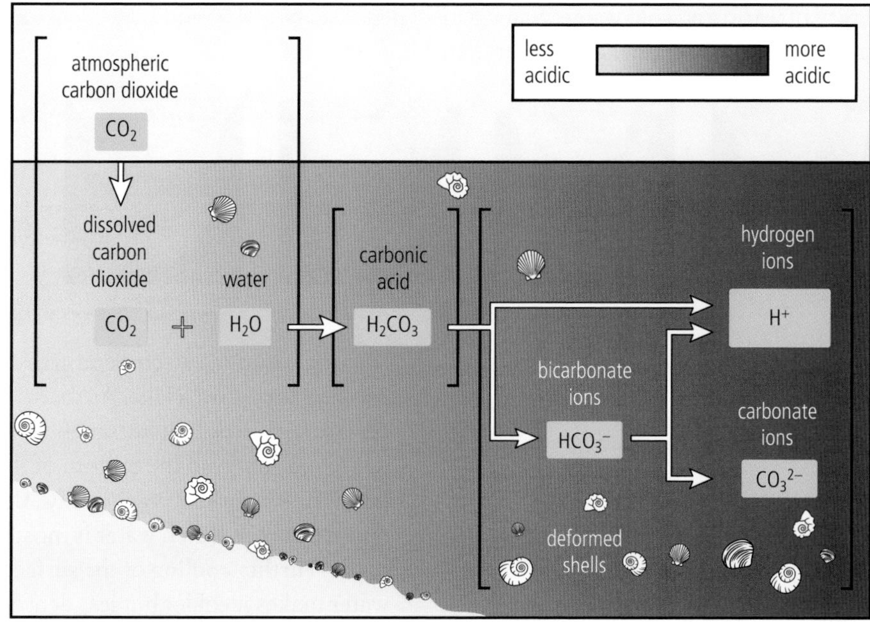

Figure 4.12 Ocean acidification.

1. Up to one half of the CO_2 released by burning fossil fuels over the past 200 years has been absorbed by the world's oceans.
2. Absorbed CO_2 in seawater (H_2O) forms carbonic acid (H_2CO_3), lowering the water's pH level and making it more acidic.
3. This raises the H^+ concentration in the water (making the water more acidic) and limits organisms' access to carbonate ions, which are needed to form hard parts.

Approximately 30% of CO_2 is absorbed by the oceans where it turns to carbonic acid. Scientists estimate that oceans absorb around a million tonnes of CO_2 every hour. Levels of oceanic acidity vary globally.

Increased acidity adversely affects levels of calcium carbonate, which forms the shells and skeletons of many sea creatures. This adversely affects coral reefs, shellfish beds and fish stocks causing slower growth and weaker skeletons and disrupting reproductive activity (Topic 2, Section 2.3.10). The growth rates of some corals species on the Great Barrier Reef have declined by 14% since 1990, either due to ocean acidification and/or to temperature stress.

Early warning signs of increased ocean acidity include:

- the decline of oyster- and shellfish-beds on the west coasts of the USA and Canada
- disintegration of coral reefs in several regions - by 2050 over 90% of coral may be affected by local and global threats, such as global warming
- a significant reduction in the number of pteropods (tiny shellfish that form the basis of food chains in high latitudes).

Activity

Find out about ocean acidification and coral reefs.

Make a poster to show the main causes and consequences of ocean acidification.

HL

4.1.10 Water stratification

Many lakes and reservoirs are deep enough to form layers of warmer, less dense, water and colder, denser, water. Thermal stratification develops due to the differences in density of warm and cold water. Water is most dense at about 4 °C and is less dense at temperatures both warmer and colder than 4 °C (Figure 4.13).

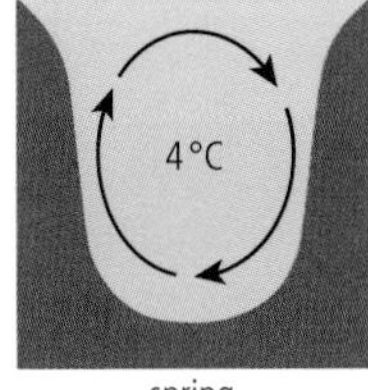

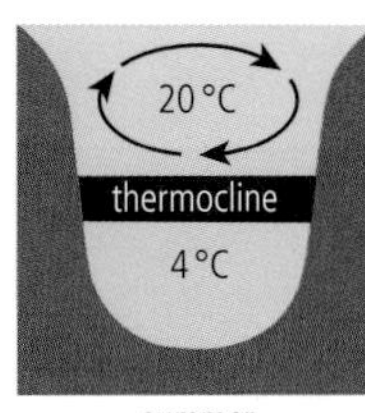

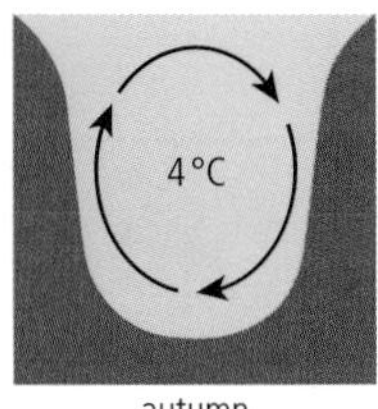

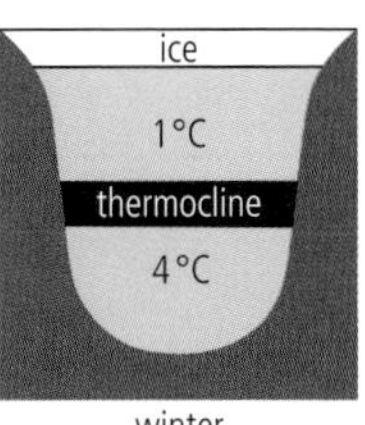

Figure 4.13 Variations in water temperature at depth and with seasons.

The temperature of freshwater varies with depth, with cold denser water below and warm less dense water above. Differences in density restrict mixing between the layers, leading to persistent stratification. Because water is most dense at 4 °C, colder water floats above it. This means a body of water freezes from the surface downwards, which allows freshwater ecosystems to survive beneath an insulating layer of ice. Salinity increases stratification as salty water becomes denser.

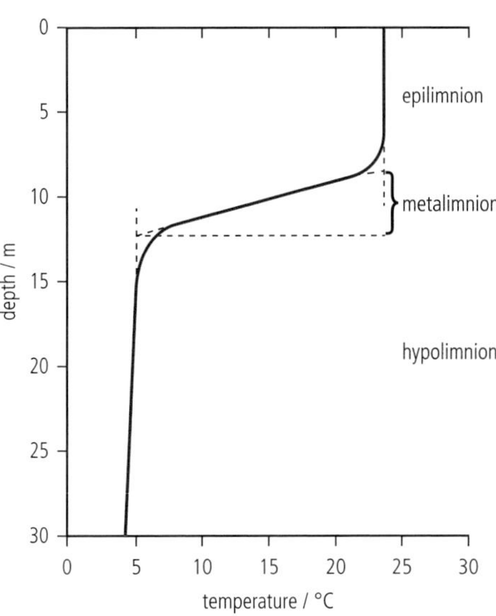

Figure 4.14 Features of lake stratification.

During Autumn, air temperatures cool the surface of a lake. As the surface water cools, it becomes denser and sinks to the bottom of the lake. The whole lake reaches 4 °C, the temperature at which water is most dense. Further cooling of the surface water makes it colder but less dense, so it 'floats' on top of the denser water at 4 °C. The surface water forms ice if the temperature reaches 0 °C. Water below the ice may remain at about 4 °C, allowing freshwater ecosystems to survive beneath the insulating layer of ice. The ice prevents the wind from mixing the different layers in the water. When conditions get warmer, the surface water begins to melt. The increasing density of the warming water causes the surface water to sink and mix with the deeper water.

In lakes where stratification occurs, the upper layer is a warm, well-mixed zone termed the epilimnion (Figure 4.14). The lowest zone is the colder, denser layer termed the hypolimnion and the transitional zone between them is metalimnion, where the temperature change may be rapid and large.

In lakes where stratification occurs, the upper layer is a warm, well-mixed zone (Figure 4.14). The lowest zone is the colder, denser layer. In the transitional zone between them the temperature change may be rapid and large.

The stability of a lake's stratification depends on the lake's depth, size and shape, as well as wind speed and water movements into and out of the lake. Lakes with a large amount of water flowing through them do not develop a persistent thermal stratification due to the short water-residence time.

In meromictic lakes, such as the crater lake, Lac Pavin, in France, there is a permanent stratification, that is, the waters do not mix. The top layer is called the mixolimnion, the middle layer is called the chemocline, and the bottom layer is called the monimolimnion. The monimolimnion is hypoxic (lacking in O_2) and saltier/denser than the other layers.

During summer stratification, the deepest layer may be rich in dissolved O_2 from spring mixing of the lake. However, it may be cut off from O_2 exchange with the atmosphere. In addition, deep lakes may be too dark for plants to produce O_2 by photosynthesis. In a **eutrophic** (nutrient-rich) lake, the deepest layer may become anaerobic as the summer progresses. This is because the O_2 that it contains will be consumed by bacteria and other bottom-dwelling organisms.
Under anaerobic conditions, phosphorus and nitrogen become more soluble and are released from sediments into the deep water. Occasionally, for example during a low-pressure system with high wind speeds, some of these nutrients may move to the surface and may lead to an algal bloom. Some metals and elements, such as iron, manganese and sulfides, become increasingly soluble and are released from sediments on the bottom of the lake. Low O_2 levels at depth may restrict the presence of fish there.

Example – Arctic ecosystem

Figure 4.15 shows the components of an ecosystem found below the sea ice.

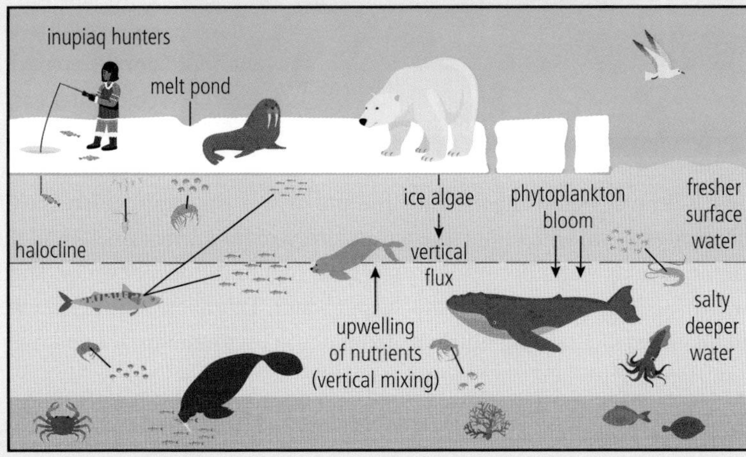

Figure 4.15 Arctic ecosystem below an ice cover.

Activity

1. Describe the main features of the ecosystem found below the sea ice, as shown in Figure 4.15.
2. Suggest the potential impact of a decline in sea ice on this ecosystem.

4.1.11 Stratification and thermoclines

Stratification occurs in deep freshwater lakes and marine areas. A **thermocline** forms a transition layer between the warmer mixed layer at the surface and the cooler water below. Warm water and cold water differ in their concentrations of dissolved O_2 and nutrients.

6.2 Climate change – causes and impacts

A thermocline is a layer within a large body of water (deep lake, coastal area, sea/open ocean) with a large variation in temperature with depth. It divides an upper mixed layer from an unmixed layer below. Thermoclines may be temporary or semi-permanent.

Most of the sunlight energy that falls on the oceans is absorbed in the top few centimetres of the ocean's surface. Waves mix the water near the surface and distribute heat within the top 100 m or so. Below this mixed layer, the temperature remains relatively stable during daytime and night-time.

The temperature of oceans declines gradually with depth (Figure 4.16). In addition, thermoclines vary with latitude. They are steepest in the tropics, variable in temperate areas and lowest in polar areas. There, sea ice may act as insulation for the water below.

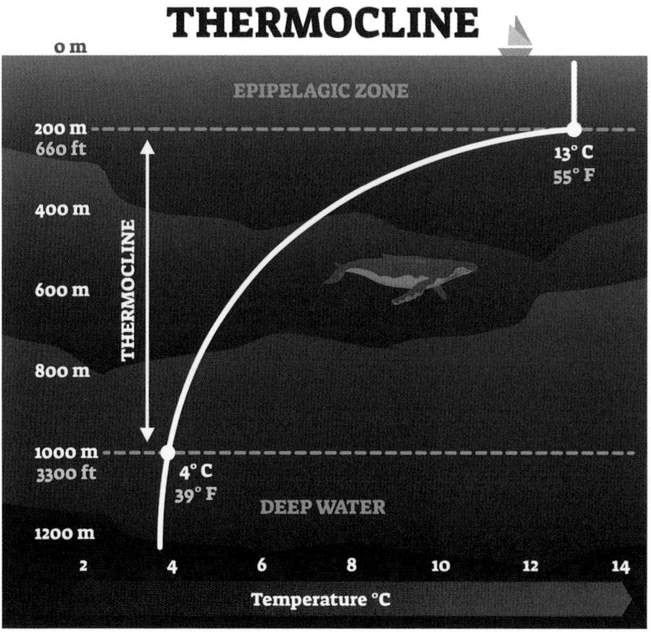

Figure 4.16 Stratification in water bodies.

Thermoclines also occur in lakes, leading to stratification. During the summer, water at the surface that has been heated becomes less dense and sits above the colder, denser water. The two layers are separated by a thermocline. Very little mixing occurs especially during calm, high pressure conditions. Although cold water can hold more dissolved oxygen than warm water, there is little O_2 below the thermocline and organisms there deplete the O_2 further. During autumn and winter, the temperature of the surface drops and the density of the cooling water becomes greater than that of the deeper water. Therefore, the denser surface water sinks below the deeper water. This allows the deeper water, lacking in dissolved O_2, to bring nutrients from depth up to the surface and may produce an algal/phytoplankton bloom.

As the temperature falls, the surface may freeze. The densest water sinks to the bottom of the lake, while less dense water (near 0 °C) may rise to the surface. This may remain until spring when the temperature rises above freezing and the ice melts.

HL

4.1.12 Global warming and salinity changes

6.2 Climate change – causes and impacts

Global warming and salinity changes have increased the intensity of ocean stratification. The changes to stratification are most pronounced in the upper 200 m of water.

If heat remains at the ocean surface and cannot be transported to the deeper parts of the ocean, global climate change and its impacts will increase. For example, there would likely be more frequent and more intense tropical cyclones.

Oceans have become more stratified over the past fifty years as global temperatures have increased as the temperature difference between warm-water and cold-water has increased. This has reduced the ability for heat, O_2 and CO_2 to be transported from the surface down to the ocean depths. The decrease in ocean mixing could, in turn, increase global warming due to warmer ocean surface temperatures. Oceans have absorbed much of the excess heat since the 1880s caused by human-induced climate change. Ocean stratification in the upper 200 m increased by about 7% between 1960 and 2018, and by 5.8% for the surface down to 2000 m. The largest increases have been in the Southern Ocean (9.6%) and the Pacific Ocean (5.9%).

Mixing between the ocean surface and deeper layers occurs due to the action of winds, currents and tides. However, as the difference in density between less dense warmer water and denser colder water increases, slower and less mixing will take place. The oceans become more stable. A warming climate makes the ocean surface less dense and increases ocean stability. Warming water expands as it is heated (the 'steric effect'). In addition, a warming climate melts ice, which adds freshwater to the oceans and decreases surface salinity.

The increase in stratification leads to increased global climate change. Warmer ocean surface water cannot absorb as much CO_2 from the atmosphere. The increased atmospheric CO_2 leads to increased atmospheric temperatures. This in turn raises the surface temperature of the oceans. Warmer waters can absorb less O_2 and there is limited mixing with the cooler ocean water at depth.

You need to be able to extract data from a database and analyse data on water temperatures with oxygen and salinity concentrations using an appropriate statistical test.

SKILLS

Extract data from a database and analyse data on water temperatures with oxygen and salinity concentrations using an appropriate statistical test

The data in Table 4.6a and Figure 4.17 are from the coastline of Oregon, USA. The example on the next page shows how the data in Table 4.6a and Figure 4.17 can be analysed to examine the relationship between water temperature and salinity (Table 4.6b).

Table 4.6a Water temperature, salinity and dissolved oxygen from the Oregon coastline.

Month	Temperature / °C	Salinity / PSU	Dissolved oxygen / mg l^{-1}
July	16	28	7.5
August	14	31	7.5
September	11	32	8.0
October	12	31	7.5
November	11	26	8.0
December	10	19	9.0
January	8	19	9.0
February	9	22	9.5
March	13	26	8.0
April	15	27	9.0
May	17	31	7.5
June	14	33	7.5

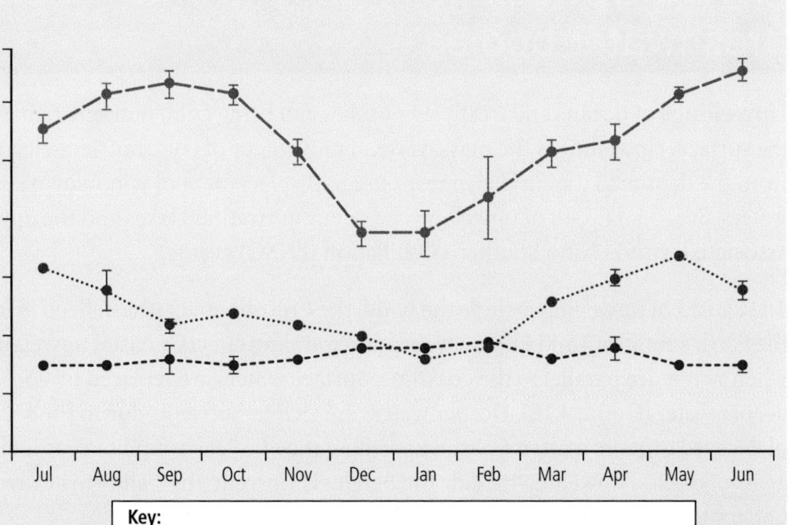

Figure 4.17 Annual variations in water temperature, salinity and dissolved oxygen.

Table 4.6b Analysing the relationship between water temperature and salinity.

Worked example of Spearman's rank correlation coefficient to test the relationship between water temperature and salinity

Temperature / °C	Salinity / PSU	Rank temperature	Rank salinity	Difference in ranks	Difference^2
16	28	2	6	4	16
14	31	4.5	4	0.5	0.25
11	32	8.5	2	6.5	42.25
12	31	7	4	3	9
11	26	8.5	8.5	0	0
10	19	10	11.5	1.5	2.25
8	19	12	11.5	0.5	0.25
9	22	11	10	1	1
13	26	6	8.5	2.5	6.25
15	27	3	7	4	16
17	31	1	4	3	9
14	33	4.5	1	3.5	12.25
					$\sum = 114.5$

d = difference in ranks; n = number of observations; $\sum$ = sum of

$$\text{Spearman's rank} = 1 - \frac{6\sum d^2}{n^3 - n}$$

$$= 1 - (6 \times 114.5)/12^3 - 12$$

$$= 1 - (687/1716)$$

$$= 1 - 0.4$$

$$= 0.6$$

For $n = 12$, the 95% level of significance is 0.51 and the 99% level of significance is 0.71. Therefore, we can conclude that at the 95% level of significance there is a statistically significant relationship between temperature and salinity, that is: as temperature increases, salinity increases.

Spearman's rank correlation coefficient is used when analysing the correlation between two variables.

HL

2.4 Climate and biomes

4.3 Aquatic food production systems

4.1.13 Upwellings in oceans and freshwater bodies

Upwellings in oceans and freshwater bodies can bring cold, nutrient-rich waters to the surface. Upwelling is the mass, vertical movement of cold, nutrient-rich waters from the depths to the surface in response to displacement of windblown surface waters. Seasonal cycles of upwelling can occur in stratified lakes and the upwelling is associated with El Niño Southern Oscillation (ENSO) events.

Upwelling in oceans results in colder, denser, nutrient-rich water moving from the depths towards the surface. This leads to the increased growth and reproduction of primary producers such as phytoplankton, providing excellent feeding grounds for fish.

The causes of upwelling include the wind, the Coriolis effect (the deflective force of the Earth's rotation) and Ekman transport (spiraling effect). Coastal upwelling occurs when winds are parallel to the coastline. Surface waters are replaced by cooler, denser, deeper water (Figure 4.18). Deeper waters are rich in nutrients due to the accumulation of decayed organic matter. Coastal upwelling may be year-round or seasonal. The main areas of coastal upwelling include the Benguela Current, the California Current, the Canary Current, the Humboldt Current and the Somali Current.

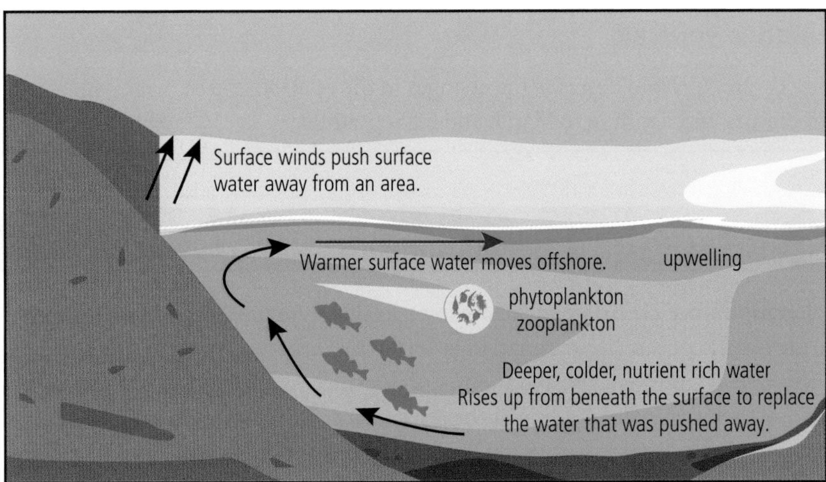

Figure 4.18 Upwelling in oceans.

Around 25% of global fish catches come from five upwellings, which accounts for just 5% of the ocean area.

ENSO – El Niño Southern Oscillation – a warm ocean current that occasionally replaces the cold Peru current off the coast of South America. ENSO usually occurs at intervals of two to seven years and leads to changes in the weather experienced e.g. drought in normally wet areas and rain and floods in areas that are normally dry.

During ENSO events, trade winds are weaker, leading to reduced upwelling in Equatorial regions. Coastal upwelling is reduced as the wind is reduced in strength. Hence, productivity is reduced as the upper waters are no longer receiving nutrient-rich upwelling water.

Example – Stratification in Lake Michigan

In large lakes such as Lake Michigan, USA, stratification may occur. For example, during calm days in summer, surface water temperatures may reach 20–25 °C, whereas water temperatures on the lake bed may decrease to as low as 5–10 °C (Figure 4.19). However, on days with strong winds, especially offshore winds (blowing away from the shoreline), cold water is brought to the surface. When there is a strong offshore wind, the warm water is pushed further away from the shore towards the middle of the lake.

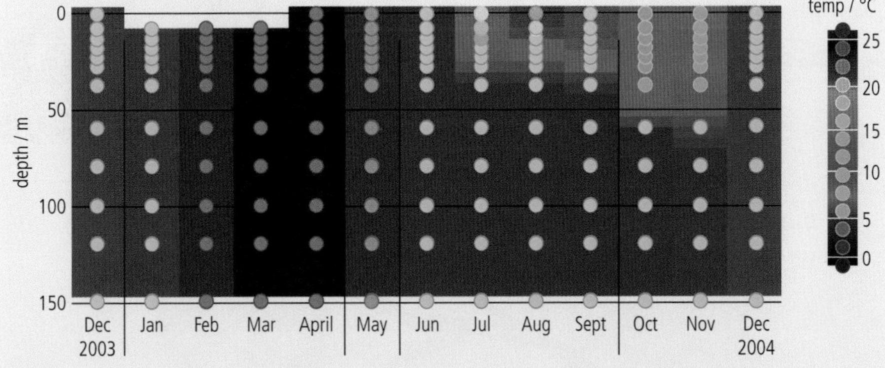

Figure 4.19 Temperature profile for Lake Michigan over a year.

Seasonal upwelling (and downwelling) occurs in many areas. Downwelling occurs when water builds up along a coastline. The surface water eventually sinks to the bottom. Seasonal upwelling and downwelling occur along the west coast of the USA. In winter, winds blow northerly and lead to downwelling. In contrast, in summer, winds blow southwards and water moves offshore, resulting in upwelling. This leads to cold coastal waters in the area around San Francisco and frequent summer fogs.

Challenge yourself

Study Figure 4.19 and describe the changes in the relationship between water temperature and depth in (i) March and (ii) September.

HL

4.1.14 Thermohaline circulation systems

6.2 Climate change – causes and impacts

The density of water is about 1 gram per cubic centimetre. Water is denser than ice, so ice floats on top of water. The density of seawater is greater than that of freshwater and depends on the salt content as well as the temperature of the water.

The **thermohaline circulation** (also known as the ocean conveyor belt) (Figure 4.20) is the part of the ocean circulation that is driven by variations in density and is caused by differences in temperature and salinity of seawater. Differences in temperature occur due to heating and cooling at the sea surface. Differences in salinity occur due to evaporation and sea ice formation (both increase salinity), as well as precipitation, run-off and melting ice (which all reduce salinity).

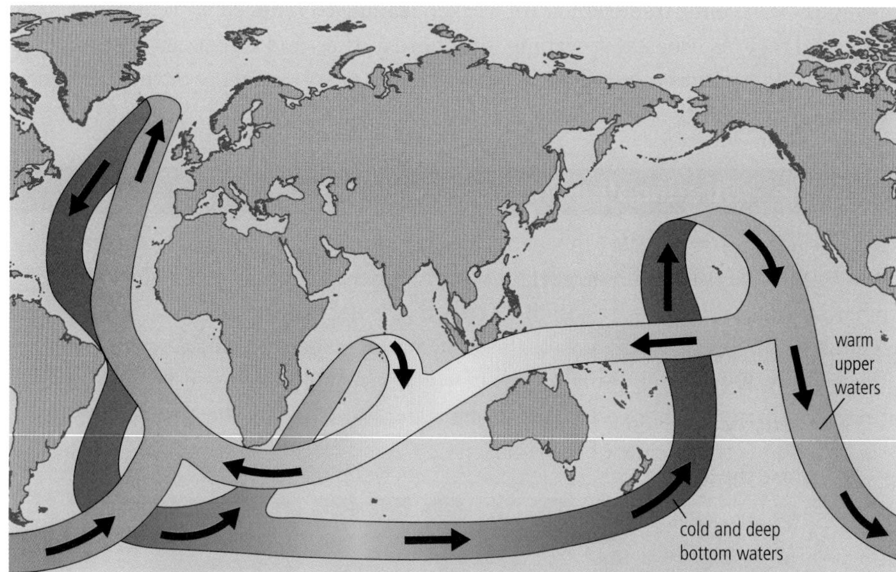

Figure 4.20 Thermohaline circulation.

The thermohaline circulation includes:

- deep formation (the sinking of water masses)
- spreading of deep water e.g. North Atlantic Deep Water
- upwelling of deep water
- near-surface currents – these complete the circulation.

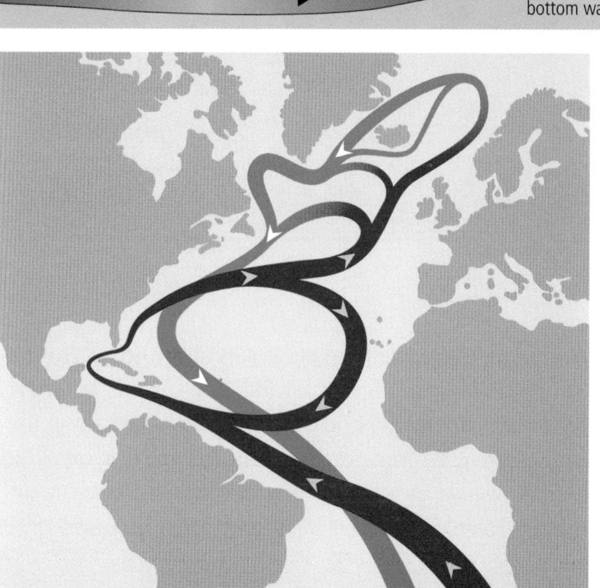

Figure 4.21 North Atlantic thermohaline circulation.

In polar regions, cold salty water sinks into the depths and makes its way towards the Equator. The densest water is found in the Antarctic area where seawater freezes to form ice at a temperature of around −2 °C. The ice is freshwater, and the seawater left behind is much saltier and therefore denser. This colder denser water sweeps round Antarctica and then spreads into the deep basins of the Atlantic, the Pacific and the Indian Oceans. Surface currents bring warm water to the North Atlantic from the Indian and Pacific Oceans. These waters give up their heat to cold winds which blow from Canada across the North Atlantic. This water then sinks and starts the reverse convection of the deep ocean current (Figure 4.21 and Topic 2, Section 2.4.6).

Because the thermohaline circulation operates in this way, the North Atlantic is warmer than the North Pacific, so there is proportionally more evaporation in the North Atlantic. The water left behind has higher salinity due to the evaporation and therefore it is much denser, which causes it to sink. Eventually the water is transported into the Pacific where it mixes with more water and its density is reduced.

Temperature, salinity and pressure affect the density of seawater. Large water masses of different densities are important in the layering of the ocean water (denser water sinks). As temperature increases, water becomes less dense. As salinity increases, water becomes denser. As pressure increases, water becomes denser. A colder, high salinity, deeper mass of water is very dense, whereas a warmer, lower salinity, surface water mass is less dense. When large water masses with different densities meet, the denser water mass slips under the less dense mass. Freshwater is less dense than seawater, so any run-off from land will flow over the saltwater.

Exercise

Q1. **Identify** the main inputs and outputs from the basin hydrological cycle.

Q2. **State** the approximate amount of the world's water that is freshwater.

Q3. **Identify** the largest store of the world's freshwater. Comment on its availability to people.

Q4. **Outline** the main impacts of urbanization on the hydrological cycle.

HL

Q5. HL **Explain** how the oceans have moderated the increases of atmospheric CO_2.

Q6. HL **Explain** why water has a higher specific heat capacity than land.

Q7. HL **Estimate** the amount of carbon that is stored in the world's oceans and deep-sea sediments.

Q8. HL **State** three impacts of more acidic seawater.

Q9. HL **Suggest** why warmer, surface water and colder, deeper water differ in concentrations of dissolved O_2 and mineral nutrients.

Q10. HL Briefly **explain** thermohaline circulation.

HL end

Engagement

- Record your own water use over a weekend. Create a table of your results and compare this to others in your class and to water use in other countries.
- Investigate the impact of human activities on the water cycle in your local area or region and summarize your findings in promotional material, such as a poster, for your school or college.
- Develop water-saving behaviour in your school by, for example, creating awareness posters and placing them in classrooms, common rooms and the dining hall.

4.2 Water access, use and security

Guiding questions

What issues of water equity exist, and how can they be addressed?
How do human populations affect the water cycle, and how does this impact water security?

4.2.1 Water security is having access to sufficient amounts of safe drinking water.
4.2.2 Social, cultural, economic and political factors all have an impact on the availability of, and equitable access to, the freshwater required for human well-being.
4.2.3 Human societies undergoing population growth or economic development must increase the supply of water or the efficiency of its utilization.
4.2.4 Water supplies can be increased by constructing dams, reservoirs, rainwater catchment systems, desalination plants and enhancement of natural wetlands.
4.2.5 Water scarcity refers to the limited availability of water to human societies.
4.2.6 Water conservation techniques can be applied at a domestic level.
4.2.7 Water conservation strategies can be applied at an industrial level in food production systems.
4.2.8 Mitigation strategies exist to address water scarcity.
HL 4.2.9 Freshwater use is a planetary boundary, with increasing demand for limited freshwater resources causing increased water stress and the risk of abrupt and irreversible changes to the hydrological system.
HL 4.2.10 Local and global governance is needed to maintain freshwater use at sustainable levels.
HL 4.2.11 Water footprints can serve as a measure of sustainable use by societies and can inform decision-making about water security.
HL 4.2.12 Citizen science is playing an increasing role in monitoring and managing water resources.

HL 4.2.13 'Water stress' like 'water scarcity' is another measure of the limitation of water supply; it not only takes into account the scarcity of availability but also the water quality, environmental flows and accessibility.
HL 4.2.14 Water stress is defined as a clean, accessible water supply of less than 1700 cubic metres per year per capita.
HL 4.2.15 The causes of increasing water stress may depend on the socioeconomic context.
HL 4.2.16 Water stress can arise from transboundary disputes when water sources cross regional boundaries.
HL 4.2.17 Water stress can be addressed at an industrial level.
HL 4.2.18 Industrial freshwater production has negative environmental impacts that can be minimized but not usually eliminated.
HL 4.2.19 Inequitable access to drinkable water and sanitation negatively impacts human health and sustainable development.

4.2.1 Water security

7.2 Energy resources, use and management

Water security is having access to sufficient amounts of safe drinking water. Water security is a significant component of sustainable societies.

Water security is the reliable availability of an acceptable quantity and quality of water for health, livelihood and production, coupled with an acceptable level of water-related risks.

Water security is the reliable availability of an acceptable quantity and quality of water for health, livelihood and production, coupled with an acceptable level of water-related risks. Water security depends on water availability, clean water, sufficient funding to develop water resources and political stability. Water security also suggests access to water, sanitation and hygiene (WASH) and integrated water resource management (IWRM).

In contrast, water insecurity refers to a lack of availability of a sufficient amount of good quality water for livelihood, health and the production of goods. Water insecurity (an absence of water security) can be caused by:

- water scarcity
- pollution
- climate change impacts
- natural disasters
- poverty
- political conflicts.

It can prove extremely difficult for countries or regions that lack water security to produce sufficient food for their population. Their economic growth can also be limited if they are unable to produce sufficient materials for production.

During the mid-2010s, over 25% of the world's population lived in water-scarce regions. This is projected to rise to over 40% by 2050.

Figure 4.22a Components of water security.

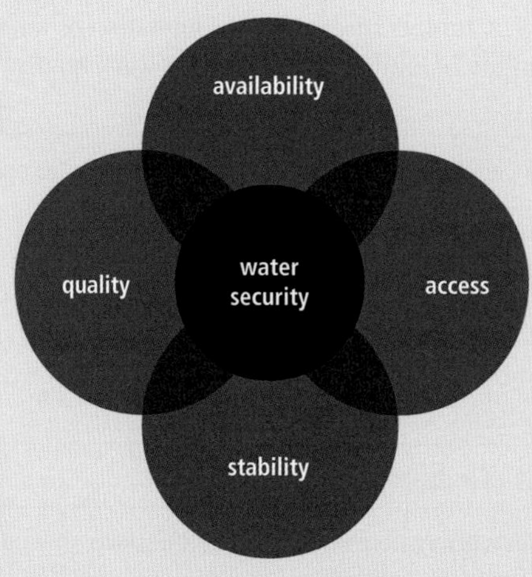

Several factors influence the sustainability of water security as shown in Figure 4.22a.

Firstly, the temporal and spatial variability of water resources are important. Areas with year-round rainfall and perennial river flows and groundwater flows are much more sustainable than areas in which there are seasonal (temporal) variations in water availability and spatial (locational) variations in water supply. In addition to the annual variations in water supply, there are long-term changes such as the megadrought experienced in western USA between 2000 and 2021.

Figure 4.22b shows variations in water security. The highest water security is found in high-income countries (HICs) in high latitudes such as Canada, Sweden and Finland. In contrast, the lowest water security is found in low-income countries (LICs) in relatively dry areas such as in the Sahel region south of the Sahara, and in northern India.

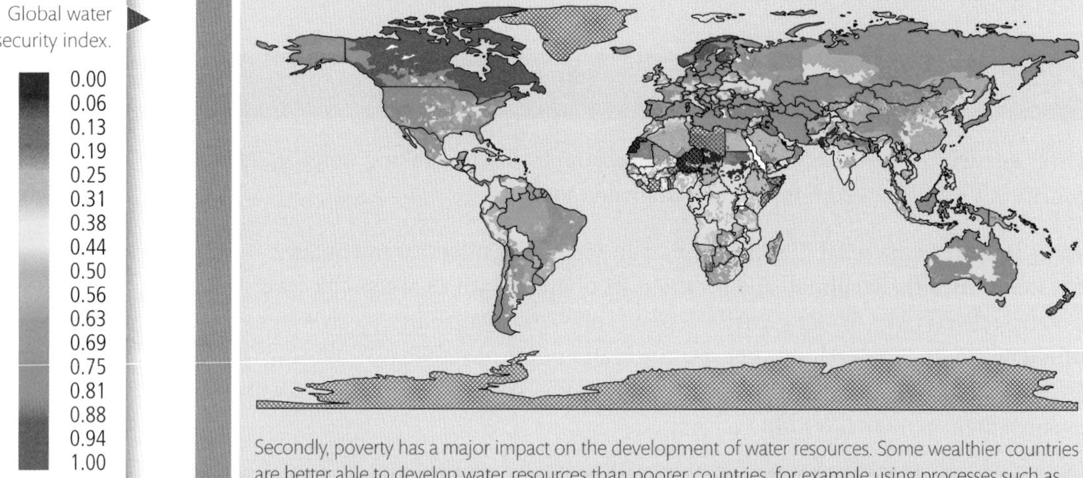

Figure 4.22b Global water security index.

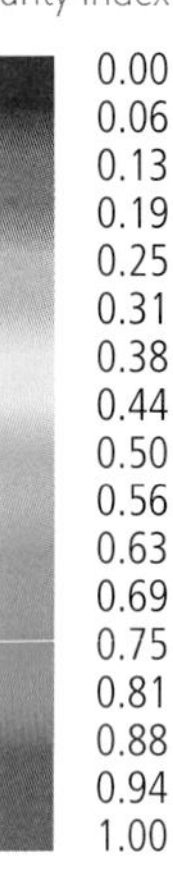

Secondly, poverty has a major impact on the development of water resources. Some wealthier countries are better able to develop water resources than poorer countries, for example using processes such as **desalination.** Desalination is the removal of salt from seawater to produce clean drinking water. It is an important process in countries with limited freshwater availability but with access to a coastline. There are two main types of desalination: reverse osmosis (RO) and thermal desalination. In reverse osmosis, seawater is forced through a membrane at high pressure, which allows water to pass through but prevents any salt from passing through. In thermal desalination, salt water is heated and the water is allowed to evaporate; the water vapour is collected, condensed and converted into freshwater (Figure 4.23). Moreover, some countries have a physical environment that may be more difficult to develop, for example mountainous areas, remote areas, areas underlain by permafrost and small islands.

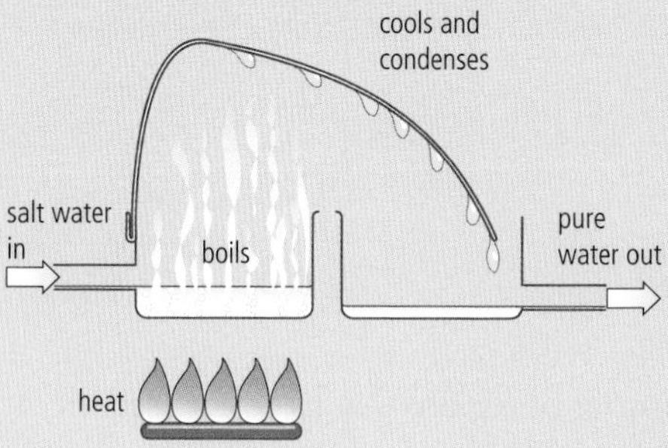

Figure 4.23 Simple thermal desalination apparatus.

Increasing global climate change is leading to heavier precipitation in some areas and drier conditions in others. It is also causing changes in the frequency and magnitude of floods, increased severity of droughts, increased hurricane activity and increased occurrence of wildfires. Accelerated melting of glaciers and permafrost lead to rising sea levels, which can contaminate freshwater supplies.

Other factors affecting water supply include population growth, increased standards of living, increased demand for water from farming, industry and increased pollution from farming, industry and transport.

4.2.2 Factors affecting availability and access to freshwater

1.1 Perspectives

HL a Environmental law
HL b Environmental economics
HL c Environmental ethics

Social, cultural, economic and political factors all impact the availability of, and equitable access to, the freshwater required for human well-being. These factors are discussed below.

Social factors

Social factors, especially population growth, affect access to water. As the world's population grows, and becomes increasingly middle-income, the demand for water increases. Education also influences water use. For example, greater awareness about WASH services increases the demand for clean water.

Economic factors

There is a clear contrast between water use per person in rich countries and those in poorer countries. Wealthier people use more water, not just for cooking and washing, but for recreation, watering gardens, washing cars and so on. Most of the world's water is used for agriculture, so in areas where farming is important, availability may decline. Access to freshwater also depends on cost. For those with piped water, the cost is often much lower than for those dependent on buying water from a vendor.

Cultural factors

Cultural factors can overlap with social and economic factors. The major cultural factor of our age is climate change. Greenhouse gas emissions have accelerated the rise in global temperatures (the enhanced greenhouse effect), and this has caused increased droughts and reduced access to water in many areas. Another example is the inequalities in gender access to freshwater (Figure 4.24). According to the UN, without access to safely managed WASH services, women and girls are more vulnerable to ill-health, abuse and attack. This affects their ability to study, work and live a proper life.

▲ **Figure 4.24** Although many women and girls collect water, they are less likely to have access to water than men.

Political factors

Some water resources are shared by different countries. This can lead to disputes over the allocation of water – see the examples below of the Middle East and of the Grand Ethiopian Renaissance Dam.

In 2020, some 2 billion people lived without safely managed drinking water (over 25% of the world's population). 80% of those who lack basic drinking water live in rural areas and about half of these live in LICs. Women and girls are disproportionately affected by poor water and sanitation. Marginalized groups, such as the Rohingyas in Myanmar, have less access to freshwater than Indigenous residents. In many shanty towns, poor people lack access to piped water and may have to buy water from vendors (sellers). For example, in Port au Prince, Haiti, surveys showed that households connected to the water system typically paid around US$ 1.00 per m^3 of water, whereas some unconnected to the mains water were paying between US$ 5.50 and US$ 16.50 per m^3 (Figure 4.25). In Lima, Peru, some poor families on the edge of town were paying twenty times more than families connected to the mains. In Jakarta, Indonesia, some residents were paying as much as 50 times that of those connected to the water mains.

▲ **Figure 4.25** Water shortages in Port au Prince.

Activity

In pairs, conduct research to find out why poorer people may be forced to pay more for their drinking water than wealthier people. How can this be justified? Present your findings to the rest of the class.

HL a Environmental law

Example – The Grand Ethiopian Renaissance Dam

Built on the Blue Nile, the Grand Ethiopian Renaissance Dam (GERD) is Africa's largest dam (Figure 4.26). It was completed in 2022 and should be filled with water between 2026 and 2029. It is designed to produce 6000 megawatts of electricity, more than double Ethiopia's current output. The Nile (the combination of the Blue Nile, the White Nile and the Atbara) provides nearly all of Egypt's water. Egypt claims two-thirds of the flow, based on a Treaty signed with Sudan in 1959. Ethiopia says that it will only use the dam for electricity generation, but water supply to Egypt will be reduced until the reservoir fills. The three countries all have growing populations and there is no longer sufficient water to satisfy all the needs of the people in the three countries.

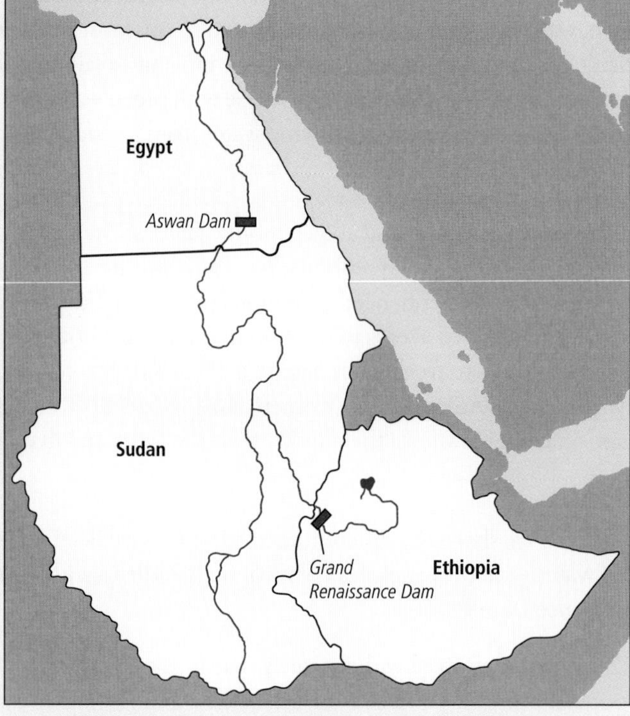

Figure 4.26 The location of the Grand Ethiopian Renaissance Dam.

Activity

Use the CIA World Factbook to find out the rate of population growth in Egypt, Sudan and Ethiopia. Outline the problems for resource development of population growth in these countries.

In the USA, some farmers have over-exploited freshwater resources because they did not have to pay for their use. This has led to several aquifers, such as the Ogallala aquifer, becoming depleted. Similarly, aquifers under the Sahara and Arabian deserts have been over-used to produce short-term economic benefits for farmers and the government. As a result, the amount of water available in many areas is falling. The negative impacts of this can vary depending on income and the country in which a person lives.

4.2.3 Human use of water

8.1 Human populations
8.2 Urban systems and urban planning
8.3 Urban air pollution

HL b Environmental economics

Human societies undergoing population growth or economic development must increase the supply of water or the efficiency of its utilization. Water is used for domestic purposes, for irrigation and raising livestock in agriculture, and for industry.

Access to an adequate supply of freshwater varies widely. For example, this could be due to population change, agricultural growth or global climate change.

Human populations require water for home use (drinking, washing and cooking), agriculture (irrigation and livestock), industry (manufacturing and mining) and hydroelectric power. Given the scarcity of freshwater resources, the pressure put on them is great and likely to increase in the future in some parts of the world (Figure 4.27). Without sustainable use it is likely that humans will face many problems. According to Oxfam, there are already over 2 billion people who live without clean drinking water at home and 2.3 billion who lack adequate sanitation.

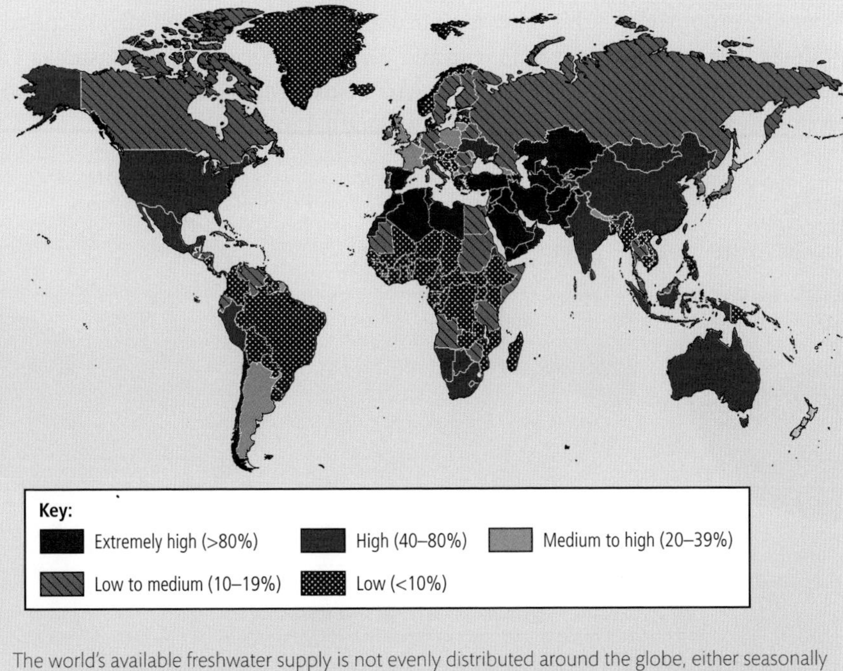

Figure 4.27 Projected water stress, 2040.

The world's available freshwater supply is not evenly distributed around the globe, either seasonally or from year to year. About three-quarters of annual rainfall occurs in areas containing less than one-third of the world's population, whereas two-thirds of the world's population live in the areas receiving only a quarter of the world's annual rainfall. For example, about 20% of the global annual run-off each year is accounted for by the Amazon Basin, a vast region with fewer than 10 million inhabitants. Similarly, less than 10% of Africa's population inhabit the Congo Basin but this region accounts for about 30% of Africa's annual run-off.

As Figure 4.27 suggests, the availability of freshwater is likely to become more stressed in the future. This may be, in part, the result of climate change, whereby rising temperatures lead to increased evaporation and water losses. There may be conflict between those who have abundant access to water supplies and those who do not.

Every year, more people die from drinking poor quality water than from all forms of violence, including war (Oxfam).

Climate change may disrupt rainfall patterns and further affect access to freshwater.

As population, irrigation and industrialization increase, the demand for water increases.

Unsustainable demands

The demand for water has continued to grow throughout the industrial period and is still expanding in HICs, middle-income countries (MICs) and LICs. Increased demand in MICs is due to expanding populations, rising standards of living, changing agricultural practices and expanding industries (Figure 4.28). In HICs, people require more water because they wash more frequently, water their gardens, wash their cars and so on. Overall, a general increase in water use per person increases the demand further. Water is a finite resource, and some countries are reaching their resource availability limits. Existing water resources therefore need to be managed and controlled more carefully and new water resources need to be found.

What counts as a good justification for a claim?

TOK

Countries at different stages of development place different sets of values on the natural environment. Many LICs wish to use their resources, such as freshwater, for economic development. They argue that they are only doing the same as HICs, albeit many decades later. Are they justified in this argument?

As world population and industrial output have increased, the use of water has accelerated, and this trend is projected to continue. By 2025, the global availability of freshwater may drop to an estimated 5100 m^3 per person, a decrease of 25% on the 2000 figure. Rapid urbanization results in increasing numbers of people living in urban shanty towns where it is extremely difficult to provide an adequate supply of clean water or sanitation.

Water availability is likely to decrease in many regions. For example, 300 million people in sub-Saharan Africa live in a water-scarce environment. Climate change can lead to water stress in many areas. Central and Southern Europe are predicted to get drier due to climate change.

HICs are tending to maintain or increase their consumption of water, although an increasing proportion of this water is embedded in agricultural and manufactured products. The average North American and Western European adult consumes 3 m^3 water per day, compared with an adult in Asia who consumes around 1.4 m^3 water per day and an adult in Africa who consumes around 1.1 m^3 water per day.

Figure 4.28 Water use in the two main income groups of countries and in the world.

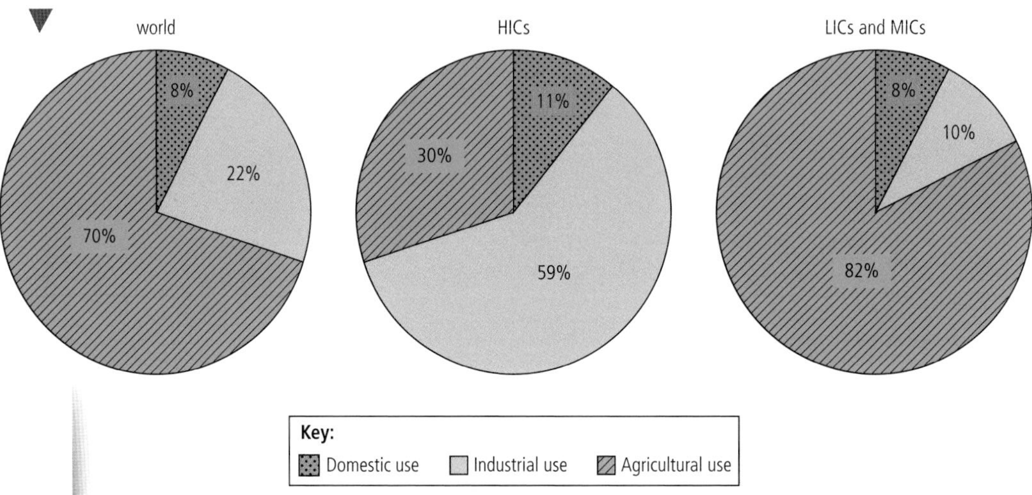

Global water requirement is increasing due to population growth, the increasing proportion of middle-income populations and changes in their diet, urbanization, climate change and a growth in tourism and recreation.

Challenge yourself

People in HICs obtain much of their food from LICs and MICs. Discuss in pairs the implications of this for the data shown in Figure 4.28.

4.2.4 Improving water supplies

1.3 Sustainability

Water supplies can be increased by constructing dams, reservoirs, rainwater catchment systems (Figure 4.29), desalination plants and enhancement of natural wetlands.

Figure 4.29 An improvised rainwater collection system on an allotment, England, UK.

HL a Environmental law

HL b Environmental economics

Desalination is the removal of salt and other minerals from water in order to obtain drinking water.

Dams and reservoirs

The construction of dams and reservoirs has several advantages, including flood and drought control, irrigation, hydroelectric power, improved navigation for year-round trading, recreation and tourism.

However, there are also several disadvantages to the construction of dams and reservoirs, including:

- water loss through evaporation
- salinization
- population displacement
- drowning of settlements
- increased earthquake activity
- channel erosion below the dam
- silting upstream of the dam
- reduced fertility downstream of the dam (because silt gets trapped behind the dam)
- increased potential for diseases such as malaria and schistosomiasis.

Rainwater catchment systems

Rainwater catchment systems refer to the systems used in the collection and storage of rainwater. These can vary in size, from large-scale dams to small-scale water butts. Water can be filtered to improve its quality. It can then be stored in tanks, wells and boreholes and/or used to recharge groundwater. The water may be used for drinking, cooking, washing, irrigation and cooling by households, schools, hospitals, farms and some industries (Figure 4.30).

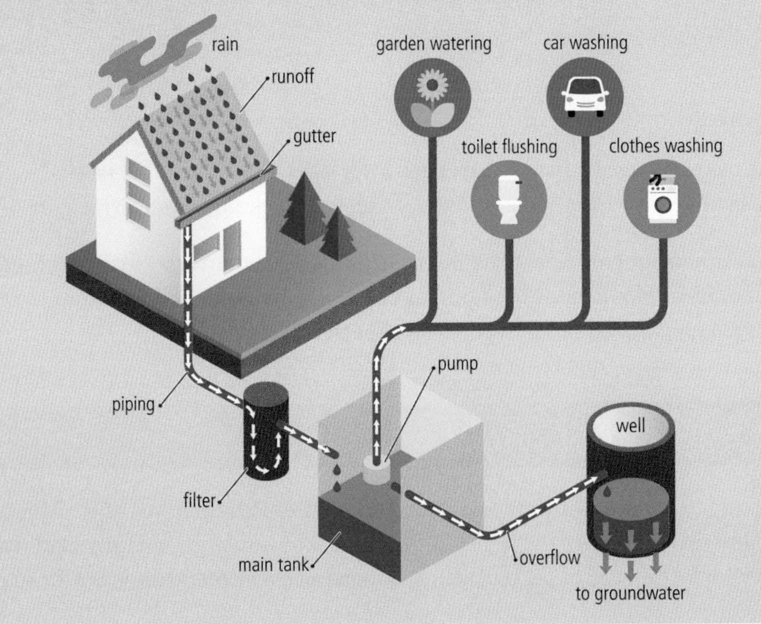

Figure 4.30 Rainwater catchment methods.

There are several advantages of rainwater catchment systems. They can be used to supplement the main water supply and provide water in areas where the supply of water is seasonal. They can also reduce pressure on the mains supply and reduce the cost of water by increasing supply.

For example, at Frankfurt Airport in Germany, the rainwater is collected from airport terminal roofs and stored in tanks in the basement. This water is then used for flushing toilets, cleaning air conditioning units and watering plants.

Rainwater catchment can also be used to reduce soil erosion by decreasing the amount of overland flow.

However, there are some drawbacks to these systems. Some types of rainwater catchment systems, notably large dams, are very expensive and can have negative ecological consequences. They depend on the amount of rain that falls. Rainwater collected from roofs may contain dust, pesticides and pollutants such as animal faeces. Filtering of the rainwater can improve the quality, although filters can be expensive.

In Thailand, about 40% of rural households rely on rainwater catchment systems. They are also widely used in parts of India, such as Tamil Nadu where they are compulsory, and Rajasthan. Rainwater catchment systems are also encouraged in new buildings in cities such as Mumbai and Bengaluru (Bangalore). Stored rainwater can become contaminated, saline and/or brackish over time.

Desalination and reverse osmosis

Desalination is the removal of salt and minerals from seawater and salt marshes to produce water that is fit for human consumption (potable water) and for irrigation.

Reverse osmosis is a method of desalination using a semi-permeable membrane.

Around 4% of the world's population depend on desalinated water to meet their daily needs. This is predicted to rise to around 14% by 2025.

In 2023, there were over 20,000 desalination plants in operation, producing around 100 million m^3 of water daily for some 300 million people.

Reverse osmosis technology requires a great deal of energy to force saltwater against membranes that contain pores that are small enough to let freshwater through, while holding salt ions back. Hence it is very costly.

Due to the high energy input, the costs of desalinating seawater are generally very high. However, new technology is bringing the cost of desalination down. The Sorek plant in Israel produces the cheapest water from saltwater at a cost of around US$ 0.60 per m^3. This compares with US$ 1.21 per m^3 in Japan and US$ 0.5–1.0 in the USA.

Another problem related to desalination is the disposal of the salt that has been removed. This often takes the form of a liquid known as brine (salted water) that, if added to local ecosystems, can have negative impacts.

Activity

Research the environmental impact of the disposal of salt/brine during the desalination process. Write a one-page summary and discuss your findings with the rest of the class.

Wetlands

In some places, rainwater may be harvested from lakes, rivers and other natural wetlands. These can be very variable in the amount of water available and its quality (Figure 4.31).

Figure 4.31 Natural wetland, Chalumna, Eastern Cape, South Africa.

Wetland enhancement refers to an increase/improvement in any particular function of a wetland. Examples include dredging or deepening to increase water storage, restoring indigenous species and removing invasive species.

HL b Environmental economics

4.2.5 Water scarcity

Water scarcity refers to the limited availability of water to human societies. Water availability may be limited by the actual abundance of water present (**physical water scarcity**) or by the storage and transport systems available (**economic water scarcity**).

The level of water scarcity in a country depends on several factors including:

- precipitation
- water availability
- population size
- affluence
- demand for water
- size of country
- level of technology available
- affordability of supplies and infrastructure.

Two types of water scarcity occur in different areas of the world. These are:

- Physical water scarcity, where water consumption exceeds 60% of the usable supply. Some countries, such as Israel and Saudi Arabia, have invested heavily in desalination plants and/or importing much of their food.
- Economic water scarcity, where a country has sufficient water to meet its needs but requires additional transport and storage facilities to get the water to where it is needed. Many Sub-Saharan countries experience economic water scarcity and need expensive water-development projects to store and transport water.

Water scarcity has increased due to increases in population, demand and global climate change.

Physical water scarcity occurs where water consumption exceeds 60% of the usable supply.

Economic water scarcity occurs where a country has sufficient water to meet its needs but requires additional transport and storage facilities to get the water to where it is needed.

See this page of your eBook for a worksheet on investigating variations in water use in different countries.

1.3 Sustainability

4.2.6 Domestic water conservation

There are many water conservation techniques that can be applied at a domestic level to conserve water in people's homes. These include:

- using a water meter to monitor water use
- rationing the amount of water used, for example taking shorter showers or only heating the volume of water that will be used when boiling a kettle
- recycling grey water (water that has been used in sinks, showers, baths, dishwashers and washing machines but does not contain faecal matter) to water lawns and gardens
- using a water butt to collect rainwater (Figure 4.32)
- using a low-flush toilet
- detecting and fixing leaks in pipes, tanks and fittings
- using pressure-reducing valves that lower the force and the volume of water flow
- using a shut-off nozzle on a hose pipe
- growing plants that require less water
- mulching (covering the soil around plants with compost or bark chippings) to hold water in the soil (Figure 4.33)
- using energy efficient appliances, especially washing machines
- only using the washing machine with a full load
- using a low-flow shower head
- taking showers (of less than five minutes) rather than a bath
- turning off the tap when brushing teeth or soaping hands
- using a brush to clean a footpath or driveway rather than a hosepipe

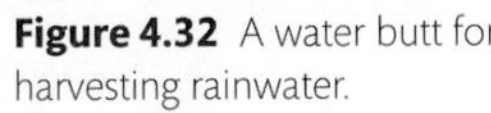

Figure 4.32 A water butt for harvesting rainwater.

Figure 4.33 Mulching around a plant to reduce water loss.

- water the garden, if necessary, either in the early morning or late evening, to reduce evaporation losses
- wash the car on the lawn without a hose.

Activity

Sort the water conservation methods into different groups e.g. kitchen, bathroom, other rooms and garden.

Which ones offer the greatest potential for water conservation? How important do you think domestic water conservation is compared with water conservation in other sectors e.g. agriculture, industry and/or water supply e.g. old, damaged pipes.

Challenge yourself

Arrange for your class to keep individual water use diaries for a week to estimate how much water you all use. Compare your results with those of others in the class at the end of the week and discuss the implications of your water use.

Challenge yourself

To what extent does the impact of domestic water conservation help reduce overall water usage when the dominant use of water is agricultural?

1.3 Sustainability

4.2.7 Industrial water conservation

HL a Environmental law
HL b Environmental economics
HL c Environmental ethics

Water conservation strategies can be applied at an industrial level in food production systems.

Greenhouses

Water recycling in greenhouses is relatively common, although this varies from small-scale greenhouses to very large-scale ones.

Example – Metrolina Greenhouses in Huntersville, North Carolina, USA

The Metrolina Greenhouses in Huntersville, North Carolina, USA recycle up to about 6 million litres of water daily. They have been harvesting rainwater and recycling it for around 50 years. They built their first retention pond for water storage in 1976 and now have three ponds which can hold up to about 950 million litres. Some 98% of the water is harvested rainwater and up to about 6 million litres of water is recycled every day.

The Metrolina Greenhouses site has around 80 hectares under glass and is the largest single-site heated greenhouse in the USA (Figure 4.34). Most of the greenhouses have 'flood floors', which are periodically flooded. This allows the plants to be watered at their roots, rather than on to the foliage, and allows the water to be collected and recycled.

Figure 4.34 Metrolina Greenhouses.

Aquaponics

Aquaponics is a food production system that combines **aquaculture** (raising aquatic animals such as fish or prawns in tanks) with **hydroponic farming** methods (cultivating plants in water). It enables farmers to increase yields by growing plants and farming fish in the same closed freshwater system.

Aquaponics as an integrated form of farming originated in Central America.

Bustan, Cairo was the first commercial aquaponics farm in Egypt. On this farm, the water circulates from tanks containing fish through hydroponic trays that grow vegetables including cucumber, basil, lettuce, kale, peppers and tomatoes. Each tank contains about a thousand tilapia fish, which are native to Egypt. Water from the pond is used to irrigate olive trees that produce high-quality olive oil. The fish tanks provide 90% of the nutrients that plants need to grow from fish waste.

Bustan uses 90% less water than traditional farming methods in Egypt. It produces 6–8 tonnes of fish per year and can potentially yield 45,000 heads of lettuce if it were to grow just a single type of vegetable. Hydroponic farming methods can make lettuce grow 20% faster than average using nutrients in the water rather than adding fertilizer to a soil.

However, it is quite costly, especially for those on a low income. Small hydroponic units could be established for rooftops, balconies and kitchens.

Drip irrigation

Drip irrigation systems are among the most efficient forms of irrigation and offer several advantages to farmers. These systems involve a series of plastic tubes, installed on or just below the surface, which deliver water to individual plants. The water, which can be enhanced with fertilizer, is delivered to the roots of the plant, so there is very little water lost to evaporation.

Drip irrigation systems can be up to 95% effective in water delivery compared with 50–70% for conventional flood irrigation systems.

In surveys conducted across the USA, Spain, Jordan, Israel and India, drip irrigation systems were shown to cut water use by 30–70% and to increase crop yields by 20–90%. Nevertheless, drip irrigation systems account for only a relatively small number of irrigation systems worldwide (less than 5%), largely due to the cost of implementing them.

Drought-resistant crops

Pastureland in the Eastern Cape, South Africa is especially fragile due to drought and overgrazing. During periods of prolonged drought, numbers of cattle, sheep and goats decrease significantly. However, trying to decrease herd size has proved unpopular and unsuccessful, as a large herd size is often seen as a sign of prestige. An alternative is to produce drought-resistant fodder crops such as the American aloe, prickly pear, saltbush and the indigenous gwanish.

▲ **Figure 4.35** The American aloe – a drought-resistant fodder crop.

The American aloe (Figure 4.35) has traditionally been used for fencing, for kraals (animal compounds) and to aid soil conservation but has also been used as a fodder in times of drought. The crop has a number of advantages, including:

- it raises milk production in cows
- it requires little moisture for growth (annual rainfall in this region is around 450 mm)

- it is not attacked by any insects
- it aids soil conservation
- after 10 years, it produces a pole that can be used for fencing or building
- it can act as a windbreak for other crops.

See also *Save Our Water: The Vegetarian Way* on the Vegetarian Resource Group (VRG) website:

Vegetarian food production

According to the Vegetarian Resource Group, livestock are one of the most significant contributors to the world's most serious environmental problems. Livestock are the largest users of freshwater, 15% of total use. Water is needed for drinking, cleaning and for the production of the food that they eat. In contrast, it takes much less water to grow grains, beans, legumes and fruit that make up much of a typical vegetarian diet.

1.3 Sustainability

4.2.8 Mitigating water scarcity

HL a Environmental law
HL b Environmental economics
HL c Environmental ethics

Mitigation strategies can address water scarcity.

Example – Managing water supply in Singapore

Singapore depends on four main sources of water, the 'four national taps', namely: rainfall collected in artificial reservoirs; imported water; reclaimed water (NEWater); and desalination. Demand for water is expected to double by around 2060 due to population growth and economic development. In addition, global climate change makes future water security uncertain. Although the majority of Singaporeans have access to clean mains water, there is potential for wastage. For example, up to 10,000 litres of water could be lost per year due to leaking taps. The Public Utility Board (PUB) is tasked with replacing ageing water pipes and fixing leaks.

The pricing of water is used to keep supply and demand in balance. Through long-term efforts at water conservation, the consumption of water per capita fell from 165 litres per day in 2013 to 158 litres per day in 2021. It is hoped that it will continue to fall, to 130 litres per day by 2030.

The Annual Water Conservation Awareness Programme sends volunteers to households with high water consumption to install water saving devices and give information about conservation.

Singapore imports some 1.1 million litres per day from Malaysia. The Malaysian government is treaty-bound to supply water to Singapore until 2061. However, Singapore has been developing its own water resources in a bid to reduce its dependency on Malaysia and to reduce water scarcity.

Although Singapore has high rainfall (about 2400 mm per year), it has limited room for storage. It has 17 reservoirs, such as the McRitchie Reservoir (Figure 4.36), and about 8000 km of drains for water supply. All major estuaries in Singapore have been dammed to create reservoirs. Due to Singapore's small size, pollution can be carried into the reservoirs following heavy rain. In recent years, weather patterns have become increasingly unpredictable and flash flooding can be a problem. These reservoirs are also used for recreation, which can cause some local contamination.

Figure 4.36 McRitchie Reservoir, central Singapore.

Nevertheless, Singapore's waterways are cleaned regularly, and booms and litter traps are used to prevent waste materials and litter from getting into the reservoirs.

It is estimated that Singapore's reservoirs provide between 825,000 litres per day and 1,375,000 litres per day depending on rainfall patterns.

NEWater is a brand name given to highly treated wastewater (Figure 4.37). Although the water is potable, most NEWater is used for non-drinking water, mainly by industries. The first NEWater plant was opened in 2000. There are currently five NEWater plants producing about 520,000 litres per day.

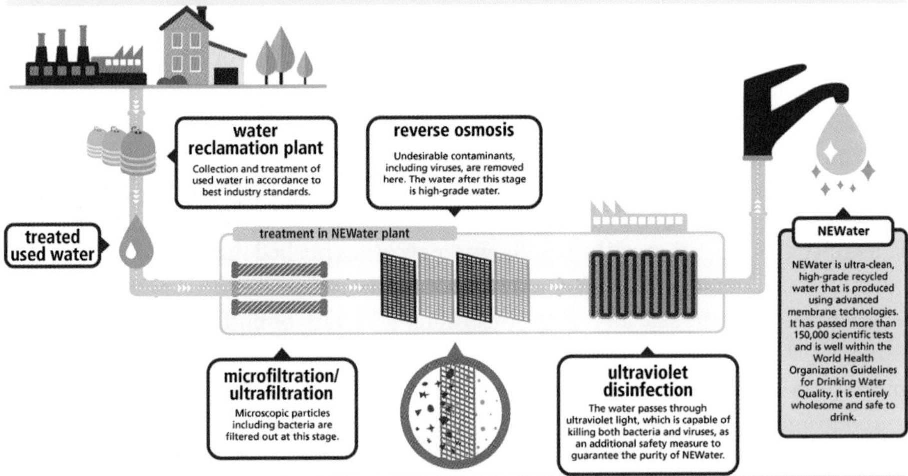

Figure 4.37 NEWater production.

Reverse osmosis desalination has been used to produce freshwater in Singapore since 2005. The method produces about 230,000 litres of safe water per day, which fulfils about 10% of the total demand. The costs of desalination are comparable with the costs of importing water from Malaysia and are becoming cheaper over time. Nevertheless, it is not a cheap source of water and there are also environmental issues. Desalination is predicted to be able to provide 30% of Singapore's future water demand by 2060.

Activity

Create a spider diagram to show how Singapore mitigates water scarcity.

HL

4.2.9 Freshwater use is a planetary boundary

HL

1.3 Sustainability

Freshwater use is a planetary boundary (Figure 1.71 in Topic 1, Section 1.3.19). Increasing demand for limited freshwater resources increases water stress and risks abrupt and irreversible changes to the hydrological system. This raises the questions: How can the planetary boundary be measured? What mitigation strategies are possible to avoid crossing the boundary?

Planetary boundaries for water use can be measured and assessed by comparing rates of consumption against sustainable water use or safe limits. If water availability per person is declining, then safe limits are likely to have been passed. Water consumption varies between places, by economic sector, by availability of water, by levels of wealth, and, increasingly, by the impacts of global climate change.

The original freshwater boundary focused on extraction of water from rivers, lakes and groundwater – 'blue water'. A newer assessment includes 'green water' – the water that is available to plants e.g. rainfall, evaporation and soil moisture.

There has been a widespread decline in soil moisture relative to pre-industrial levels. For example, the Amazon rainforest depends on soil moisture for its survival. However, due to deforestation and global climate change, more radiation is reaching the ground, and the Amazon is losing more soil moisture: there are fears that parts of the Amazon will be transformed into a savannah landscape. It is not just the Amazon. There is also evidence that boreal forests and farms around the world are experiencing declining soil moisture. Once soil moisture levels fall below a critical level, vegetation die-back increases, especially for trees that are not adapted to drought, such as rainforest species. Both the Amazon and the Congo rainforests are believed to be close to an environmental 'tipping point' due to deforestation and global warming.

The planetary boundaries framework, developed in 2009, illustrates a safe operating space for humanity. Water is one of the nine regulators of the Earth system. It is the sixth boundary to be passed. The planetary boundary for freshwater is 4000 km^3 per year.

Humanity's modification of the world's water cycle has pushed the world further beyond a safe operating space (Topic 1, Section 1.3.19). According to the Stockholm Resilience Centre, the safe level of the freshwater planetary boundary has been exceeded. Water availability per person is declining and demand is rising as a higher proportion of the Earth's population are now in middle- and high-income groups and are consuming more water.

Soil moisture is one of the key components for ecosystems and for agriculture. But, the Amazon rainforest, for example, is losing moisture due to climate change and deforestation. Many forests and farmland around the world are also losing soil moisture. When the amount of soil moisture is lower than the historical variability, the planetary boundary has been passed.

Mitigation strategies to avoid crossing the boundary – or indeed going back below the boundary – include:

- using indigenous (native) species in farming, rather than using ones that need irrigation
- fixing leaking water pipes and taps
- covering reservoirs, or filling them with sand and gravel, to reduce evaporation
- only using washing machines and dishwashers when the load is full
- taking showers rather than baths.

Example – Variations in water use

Some countries share water resources with other countries and so may be affected by processes/impacts that occur outside their national boundaries. Even though most countries operate within globally safe limits, for several countries, a large share of their water comes from watersheds that have reached unsafe water consumption levels. Many of these countries are located in the Middle East, North Africa, and Mediterranean regions. Water use in most arid and semi-arid regions tends to have a more detrimental environmental impact.

Livestock production has significant impacts on the environment, including the use of water. Livestock water use increased by about 1.4% per year between 1971 and 2012. Livestock drinking water accounts for about 10% of the total water use attributable to livestock production. In parts of northern India and the Middle East, excessive water withdrawals have reduced water flow in 7% of rivers to such an extent that they cannot sustain the aquatic environment.

4.2.10 Local and global governance

HL

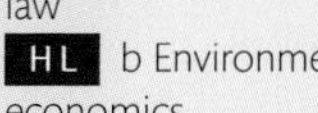

HL a Environmental law
HL b Environmental economics
HL c Environmental ethics

Example – Local governance: Cape Town's water crisis

The Cape Town water crisis peaked between mid-2017 and mid-2018. In late 2017, the concept of 'Day Zero' was mentioned, i.e. the point at which the water levels behind Cape Town's major dams would fall below 13.5% (the level that would define 'day zero'). Cape Town implemented various water restrictions and managed to decrease daily usage by over 50% to about 500 million litres per day in March 2018. Strong rains began again in June 2018, allowing the amount of water behind dams to recover.

Cape Town has a Mediterranean climate with hot summers and winter rainfall. The Western Cape Water Supply System relies on rainfall that is captured and stored in reservoirs behind six major dams in the nearby mountains. However, water levels in many of the reservoirs had fallen extremely low, such as that in the Theewaterskloof Reservoir (Figure 4.38).

Figure 4.38 Theewaterskloof Reservoir during the Cape Town drought.

Table 4.7 Water levels as a percentage of total dam capacity, 2014–2021.

Year	2014	2015	2016	2017	2018	2019	2020	2021
Water level as a percentage of total dam capacity	71.9	50.1	31.2	21.2	31.4	45.9	53.6	69.8

Cape Town began to experience drought in 2015, and an extreme drought continued for three years (Table 4.7). In May 2017, the amount of water stored behind the dams was less than 10% of capacity. Rainfall in 2017 was the lowest annual total since records began in 1933.

Cape Town's population increased from 2.4 million in 1995 to 4.1 million in 2015, an increase of 71% in just 20 years. Over the same time, dam water storage increased by 17%.

Responses to the crisis

The Cape Town authorities responded to the crisis in several ways:

- by buying an additional 2.5 million litres of water per day from the Molteno Reservoir in Oranjezicht and the Atlanta Reservoir
- commissioning three small, temporary desalination plants (two produced 7 megalitres of water per day and one produced 2 megalitres of water per day;
- recycling water.

The authorities also revised the limits for the personal use of water and increased tariffs for water. Many individuals and businesses installed water storage tanks to collect rainwater and/or drilled private boreholes to tap into groundwater reserves.

Activity

Write a paragraph describing the appearance of the Theewaterskloof Reservoir during the Cape Town drought, 2017–2018.

Example – Global governance: The Nile Basin

Transboundary waters are the lakes, aquifers and drainage basins that are shared by two or more countries. There is the potential for one country to disrupt the supplies of water to other countries.

Some 280 million people from 11 countries live in the Nile Basin. Over the last 50 years, six countries have built 25 dams on the Nile. Four more dams are under construction and there are four more proposals.

The new Grand Ethiopian Renaissance Dam (GERD) holds the promise of providing much-needed electricity for Ethiopia, but the possibility of reducing water supplies to Egypt. Some 40 million people live on the Nile Delta, accounting for about 50% of Egypt's agricultural production. However, since the building of the Aswan High Dam, the Delta has been shrinking due to sedimentation accumulating behind the dam.

In the past, a number of colonial treaties existed to allocate Nile water. In 1929, Egypt and Britain signed the Nile Waters Agreement (Britain signed as a representative of Uganda, Kenya, Tanganyika (now Tanzania) and Sudan). In 1959, Egypt and Sudan agreed a 66% and 22% share of the Nile for both countries, respectively. The other 12% was lost to evaporation. In 1999, the Nile Basin Initiative was agreed with the aims of developing cooperation, sharing benefits and promoting regional peace and security. For Egypt, the Nile is crucial as only 2% of its water originates within Egypt.

The construction of the GERD began in 2011 and filling of the reservoir should be complete by 2029. When complete, it and an auxiliary dam will store up to 75 billion m^3 of water and generate up to 6450 MW of electricity. In 2022, the GERD produced electricity for the first time. In contrast, the Aswan High Dam can store up to 162 billion m^3 of water and generate up to 2100 MW of electricity.

Ethiopia could generate US$ 580 million per year by selling its surplus energy to neighboring countries. Ethiopia wants to become Africa's largest energy exporter. There is conflict with Egypt as Ethiopia exports about 40 billion m^3 of water annually. With the GERD, more water may be held back to refill the reservoir to enable HEP throughout the year, and allowing Ethiopia to sell surplus energy to it neighbours. For Sudan, the GERD may reduce flooding but could also reduce the supply of silt that fertilizes farmers fields. For Egypt, the Nile provides 98% of its water needs and 95% of its population live in close proximity to the Nile. Egypt wants to keep its 55.5 billion m^3 share of the Nile and wants Ethiopia to fill the dam over a 21-year period and only during the wet season.

The options that Egypt could adopt to avoid a water crisis (for 21 years) include:

- using water from the Aswan Dam
- using non-renewable groundwater, however this is costly and unsustainable
- planting fewer water-intensive crops, such as cotton and rice
- recycling water/increasing desalination.

Challenge yourself

To what extent can the rivers of the Nile Basin be managed sustainably and equitably? Discuss with a partner and share your ideas with the class.

4.2.11 Water footprints

HL

A water footprint is a measure of the use of water by individual humans, or nations, or the amount needed to grow crops or livestock or manufacture textiles, steel or other products. Water footprints can serve as a measure of sustainable use by societies and can inform decision making about water security.

1.3 Sustainability

HL c Environmental ethics

A water footprint is a measure of the use of water by individual humans or nations, or the amount needed to grow crops or livestock or to manufacture textiles, steel or other products.

Water footprints relate the extent of water use to human consumption. It is the total volume of freshwater used to produce the goods and services consumed by individuals or communities, or produced by businesses. Previously, water use was only considered from the production side. However, products are not necessarily consumed in the country of production and so there is a flow of virtual water with the export of goods.

Water footprints, introduced in 2002, are based on the consumption of water. The water footprints show the amount of water consumed and where it is consumed (Figure 4.39).

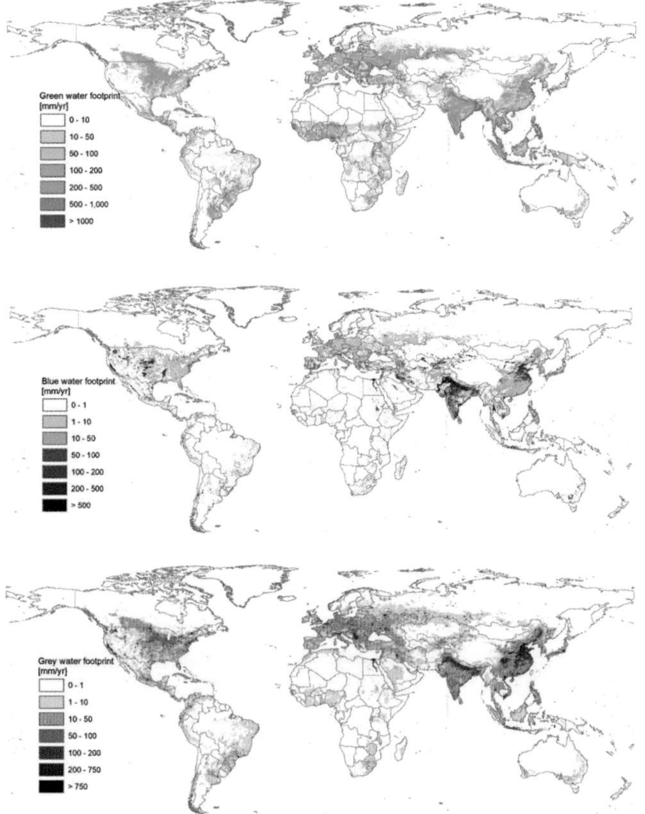

Figure 4.39 Green-water, blue-water and grey-water footprints.

Blue-water footprint refers to the water from groundwater, surface water and evaporation. Green-water footprint refers to the water from precipitation that is taken in by plants and may be stored in the root zone or lost by evapotranspiration. Grey-water footprint refers to the wastewater produced from homes and offices, which may come from showers, sinks, baths, dishwashers and washing machines but which does not include faecal material.

The average global water footprint of an individual is 1385 m^3 per year. However, there is great variation between individual countries. In absolute terms, India has the largest overall footprint with a total of 987 Gm^3 per year. In contrast, in relative terms, the USA has the largest footprint at 2842 m^3 per person per year.

Activity

Open the Water Footprint Assessment Tool (2020) and choose 'The World' option to explore the blue, green and grey water footprints for contrasting countries of your choice.

The internal water footprint refers to the amount of water that comes from domestic sources. In contrast, the external water footprint is the amount of water used in other countries to produce the goods and services that are imported and consumed in a different country.

Water footprints can be misleading in some cases. For example, the water used to produce cotton in a country may not be a drain on water resources if there is a plentiful water supply. But the same water footprint could be a drain on resources in a relatively dry area. High water footprints may give rise to over-consumption and may suggest environmental concerns because they can be unsustainable over long periods of time. However, moderate or even low water footprints may also be of concern in arid regions.

Water footprints can also consider the quality of the water, i.e., the presence or absence of pollution. An area needs an ample source of good quality water.

Activity

Suggest at least two reasons for global variations in grey water.

HL

4.2.12 Citizen science

1.3 Sustainability

Citizen science (Topic 1, Section 1.3.16), also known as community science or crowd-sourced science, involves research being carried out by members of the public with the aim of gathering scientific information for the purpose of aiding scientific projects. Anyone can take part in citizen science and all participants use the same methods. This means that the data is open access and high-quality data can be produced and shared. It has potential advantages, such as data collection at a scale not possible by professional researchers.

Citizen science is research carried out by members of the public with the aim of gathering scientific information for the purpose of aiding scientific projects.

Citizen science is playing an increasing role in monitoring and managing water resources. The availability of relatively inexpensive water quality monitoring field equipment suitable for citizen science enables great potential for field studies rather than laboratory testing.

Activity

Consider the benefits and limitations of citizen science in ensuring sustainable water use at a local level. For example, consider whether it is possible to crowdsource accurate water quality data.

Example – Citizen science investigating water quality, Killarney

A study including 26 citizen scientists from St. Brendan's College, Killarney, investigated water quality at various sites including the River Deenagh and the Folly Stream (Figure 4.40). The Folly Stream has experienced deteriorating water quality for a number of years whereas the River Deenagh has 'Good' ecological status.

Their study generated data that could be compared with results from a laboratory study. The United Nations Sustainable Development Goal (SDG) Indicator 6.3.2 refers to the 'proportion of waterbodies with good ambient water quality'.

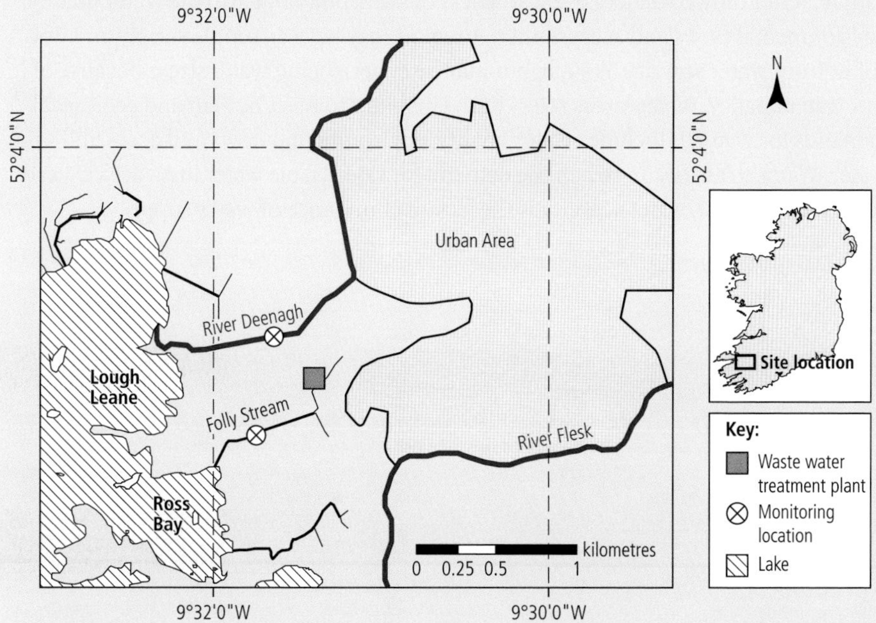

Figure 4.40 Location of study sites at Killarney, Ireland.

The UN has shown significant interest in the potential for citizen science to contribute to monitoring and improving ambient water quality. Water quality can be assessed in terms of the oxygen, salinity, nitrogen and phosphorus content and the amount of acidification present. These parameters can all be measured using simple and inexpensive field techniques that are available to citizen science networks.

The most significant barrier to the widespread use of citizen science is the perception of scientists who question the reliability, accuracy and quality of data collected by non-professionals. Is that justified?

Overall, the results of the Killarney water quality analysis indicated that citizen scientists were able to measure water quality with great accuracy for orthophosphates (dissolved phosphorus or part of dissolved organic matter) and nitrates, whereas biochemical oxygen demand (BOD) and pH had the least agreement with the laboratory results. Results were more reliable in the non-polluted river Deenagh and less reliable in the polluted Folly Stream. Results were considered more subjective/less reliable when using colour kits compared with digital data.

Numerous studies have shown that citizen scientists are capable of collecting data of equal quality to professional scientists provided they are given proper training and resources, and provided that the design of the study and data collection methods are appropriate.

Activity

With a partner, discuss what activities you could investigate for citizen science in your locality/region.

HL

4.2.13 Water stress and water scarcity

1.2 Systems
1.3 Sustainability

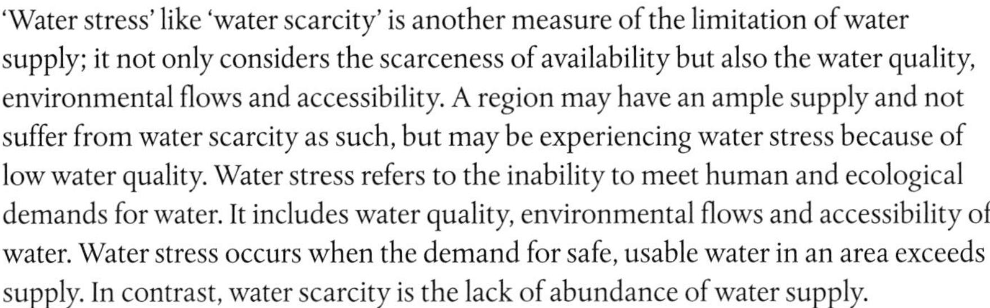

'Water stress' like 'water scarcity' is another measure of the limitation of water supply; it not only considers the scarceness of availability but also the water quality, environmental flows and accessibility. A region may have an ample supply and not suffer from water scarcity as such, but may be experiencing water stress because of low water quality. Water stress refers to the inability to meet human and ecological demands for water. It includes water quality, environmental flows and accessibility of water. Water stress occurs when the demand for safe, usable water in an area exceeds supply. In contrast, water scarcity is the lack of abundance of water supply.

Global climate change is likely to increase water stress. The UN predicts that for every 1 °C increase in global temperature, renewable water resources will decrease by 20%. Droughts will become more frequent and longer, and rainfall will become more intense.

The most water-stressed area includes the Middle East and North Africa (MENA). MENA receives low rainfall and experiences high temperatures and evaporation losses. It also has rapidly-growing, densely-populated urban areas – hence the demand for water is rising rapidly. Nevertheless, many countries there are wealthy and have found ways to meet their water needs; for example, the United Arab Emirates (UAE) imports most of its food and uses desalinated water.

The most water-stressed countries in 2040 are expected to be Bahrain, Kuwait, Qatar, San Marino, Singapore, UAE, Israel, Saudi Arabia, Oman and Lebanon. In addition, Botswana, Chile, Estonia and Namibia could experience a significant increase in water stress by 2040.

Singapore has the highest water stress ranking (5.0) (Figure 4.41). It is lacking in freshwater resources, is densely populated and has a demand for freshwater that greatly exceeds its natural supply (mainly rainfall). However, Singapore has invested heavily in technology, responsible management and international agreements to ensure that it is able to meet its freshwater needs (Table 4.8).

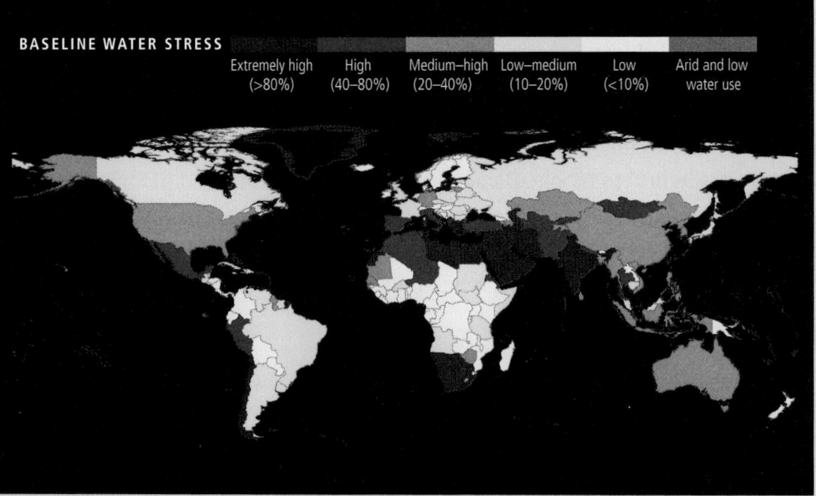

Figure 4.41 Global variations in water stress.

Advanced rainwater capture	20%
Imports from Malaysia	40%
Grey-water use	30%
Desalination	10%

Table 4.8 Freshwater supplies in Singapore.

Seventeen countries – about 25% of the world's population – experience extremely high levels of water stress (Figure 4.41) where water withdrawals exceed 80% of the supply. Over 40 countries – one-third of the world's population – experience 'high' levels of water stress where over 40% of the available water is withdrawn. Such a narrow gap between demand and supply makes countries vulnerable to fluctuations and/or rising demand.

There are possible solutions that could be used to make the situation better. For example, over 80% of MENA's wastewater is not re-used. Increased agricultural efficiency may lead to improved irrigation, precision watering and the use of seeds that require less water. Investment in grey-water and green infrastructure, such as wetlands and watershed management including afforestation and wetland restoration (this topic, Section 4.2.4), can improve quality and supply. The use of wastewater as a resource can lead to more water being available.

4.2.14 Water stress

HL

Water stress is defined as a supply of less than 1700 m^3 per year per capita of clean, accessible water.

1.3 Sustainability

HL b Environmental economics

HL c Environmental ethics

Water stress is defined as a supply of less than 1700 m^3 per year per capita of clean, accessible water.

Example – Water stress in Yemen

Yemen is the poorest country in the world and the most water-scarce country in the Middle East (Figure 4.42, Table 4.9). Its average water consumption is just 140 m^3 per year. Average annual water consumption for the Middle East as a whole is 1000 m^3.

Most of Yemen's water comes from groundwater, but water tables have been dropping for years and Yemen's groundwater is essentially a non-renewable resource. The water table at Sana, the capital city of Yemen, was 30 m below the surface in the 1970s but had dropped to 1200 m by 2012.

Agriculture accounts for about 90% of water use in Yemen but only accounts for 6% of GDP. Over half of the water used in agriculture is used to produce *khat*, a narcotic that is widely chewed in Yemen. Thus around 45% of the water used, is used for a drug that does not feed the Yemeni population.

Yemen has been in a civil war since 2015. Some water infrastructure has been targeted by war planes, including the desalination plant at Mokha. Moreover, global climate change and population growth have increased the pressure on Yemen's water resources.

Although running water is available in many parts of the country, rural areas are generally lacking in municipal water supplies. Approximately 70% of urban areas have access to water compared with less than half of rural areas. However, continuity of water supplies is poor, and some areas may have to wait weeks for water to be available.

Long-term rainfall levels have been falling from 240 mm (1932–1968) to 180 mm (1983–2000). Yemen's renewable water resources are just 125 m^3 per person per year. However, there are some 45,000–70,000 wells in Yemen, mostly private. In Sana, many wells are dug to a depth between 790 m and 1190 m.

One proposal to improve water supplies is to desalinate water from the Red Sea and transport it nearly 250 km, over mountains that rise to 2700 m, and on to Sana. However, the cost of such a project is huge and the transportation would be vulnerable to terrorist attack.

Figure 4.42 Location and precipitation in Yemen.

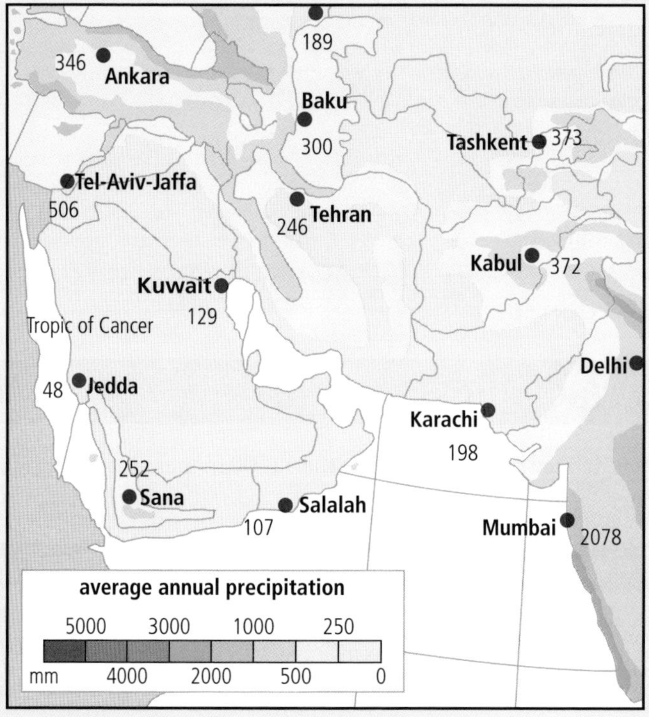

Table 4.9 Yemen fact file.

Population (million)	31.6
PPP* (US$)	2500
Growth rate (%)	1.83
Life expectancy (years)	67.8
Access to water – Urban (%)	99.6
Access to water – Rural (%)	84.2
Population below poverty line (%)	48.6

*PPP – Purchasing power parity – GDP in relation to local costs (i.e. local purchasing power)

Activity

Use Figure 4.42, Table 4.9 and the CIA World Factbook to find out more about Yemen.

Click on Countries to access the information. Using no more than one-side of A4, write a country profile for Yemen.

4.2.15 Causes of increasing water stress

HL

The causes of increasing water stress may depend on the socioeconomic context, e.g., the aim of increasing industrialization in an emerging economy and over-abstraction due to population pressure in a LIC.

1.1 Perspectives

HL b Environmental economics

Example – Water stress and the Indian textile industry

Of the world's 60 largest economies, 29 are ranked 'high to extremely high' for water stress, according to the World Resources Institute (WRI). Several water-intensive sectors have high concentrations in those 29 countries, including 88% of coal mining and 80% of textile production. The top four producers of textiles include China, India, the USA and Indonesia. The textile industry is worsening India's growing water crisis.

India overtook China as the world's largest population in 2023. India's population is increasing, whereas growth in China is falling.

Water stress in India is extremely high. Half of the country's population lack access to safe water and surface- and ground-water supplies are decreasing for the rest. The WRI ranks India 13th among the world's worst affected countries.

Part of the problem has been the growth of 'fast fashion'. This refers to retail brands that are bought and discarded in quick succession. This requires large volumes of clothing to be produced and sold. To keep production costs low, environmental protection and workers' rights may be ignored.

Indian cotton is among the cheapest in the world. This increases demand for it. However, cotton is very water-intensive and 22,500 litres of water is required to produce 1 kg of cotton, which is approximately the amount needed to produce one T-shirt and one pair of jeans.

In addition, there is competition with farmers for access to water. Population growth in India also increases demand for water. Moreover, as more Indians become middle-income, they too demand increased amounts of water. As a result, water stress is increasing.

A second water stress example is available on this page of your eBook.

4.2.16 Water stress and transboundary disputes

HL

HL a Environmental law

Water stress can arise from transboundary disputes when water sources cross regional boundaries e.g. the River Nile. Many current disputes have a historical or political context for the conflict.

Water shortages have caused major international disputes in many parts of the world (Table 4.10). Water management is particularly difficult when drainage basins cross many countries. Tension between countries competing for water is escalating, although full-scale war is unlikely. Water security depends not just on water availability but on wealth and adaptive capacity (Figure 4.43).

Table 4.10 International water disputes.

River or aquifer	Countries involved in the dispute	Subject of dispute
Nile	Egypt, Sudan, Ethiopia, Uganda, Kenya, DR Congo, Eritrea	Siltation, flooding, water flow/diversion
Euphrates, Tigris	Iraq, Syria, Turkey	Dams, reduced water flow, salinization, hydroelectricity
Brahmaputra, Ganges	Bangladesh, India	Siltation, flooding, water flow/diversion
Mekong	Cambodia, Laos, Thailand, Vietnam	Water flow, flooding, irrigation
Parana	Argentina, Brazil	Dam, land inundation
Lauca	Bolivia, Chile	Dam, salinization
Rio Grande, Colorado	Mexico, USA	Salinization, water flow, agrochemical pollution
Great Lakes	Canada, USA	Water diversion
Rhine	France, Netherlands, Switzerland, Germany	Industrial pollution
Danube	Austria, Slovakia, Hungary	Water diversion, hydroelectricity

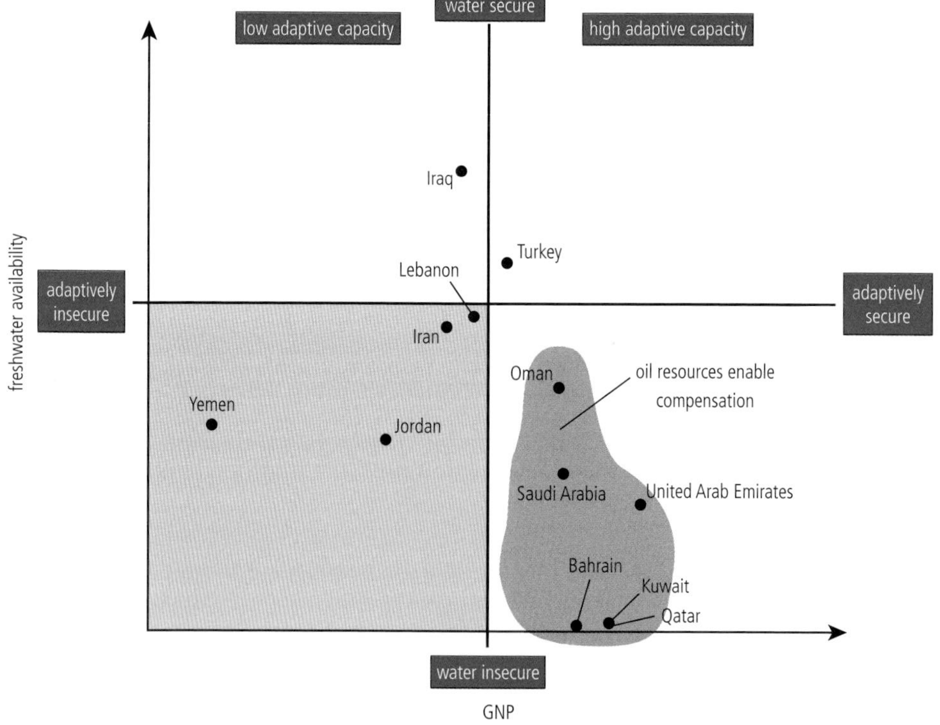

Figure 4.43 Water security in the Middle East in relation to freshwater availability, GNP and adaptive capacity.

Activity

Choose one of the international drainage basins listed in Table 4.10 and investigate its current status, as well as historical issues. Present your findings to the class.

There are many international water sharing or water division agreements in place. For example, agreements exist between India and Pakistan (Indus Water Treaty), India and Nepal (Mahakali Treaty) and the USA and Canada (International Boundary Waters Treaty Act). Nevertheless, there is potential for conflict. Future increases in water stress due to climate change could occur anywhere in the world but will be especially problematic in arid and semi-arid regions.

Example – International boundary disputes in the Middle East

The Middle East is an area of low precipitation (< 200 mm) and high evapotranspiration (> 2000 mm), making it an arid landscape. It contains a number of exotic rivers (those rising in a different environment – in this case mountains), including the Euphrates and Tigris (Figure 4.44). The limited water resources of the region have led to an international dispute over water supplies between Iraq, Syria and Turkey.

The Tigris and the Euphrates both rise in Turkey and flow southwards to Syria and Iraq. Turkey claims the right to control the water that rises within its borders, while Syria and Iraq both claim historic rights, having used the rivers for thousands of years for large-scale irrigation. In 1979, Syria cut off the flow of the Euphrates to Iraq in order to fill a reservoir. Iraq threatened to invade Syria, so Syria released the stored water. In 1990, Turkey stopped the flow of the Euphrates to fill the reservoir behind the Ataturk Dam.

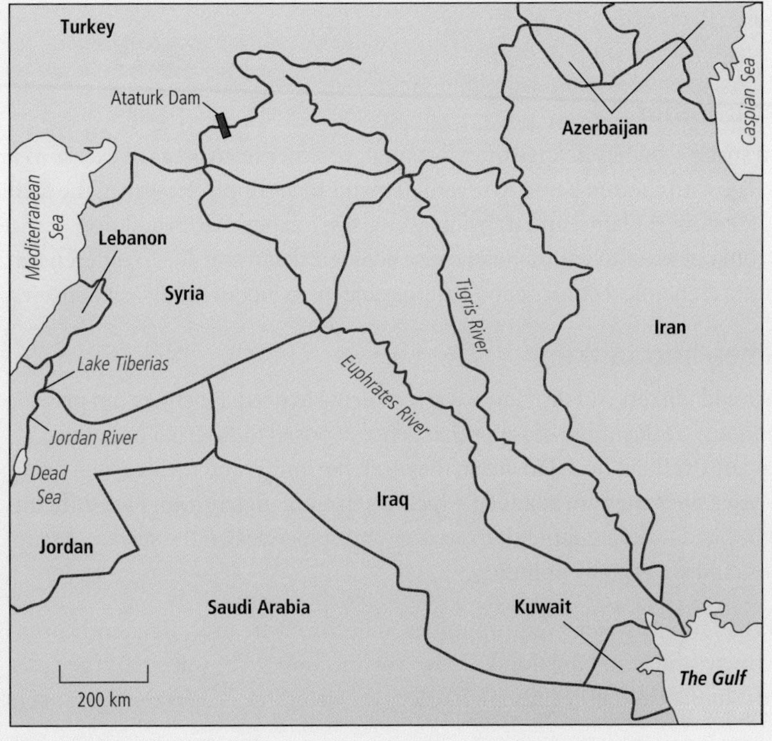

Figure 4.44 The location of Turkey, Syria and Iraq, and the Tigris and Euphrates rivers.

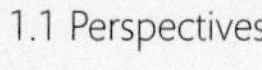

1.1 Perspectives

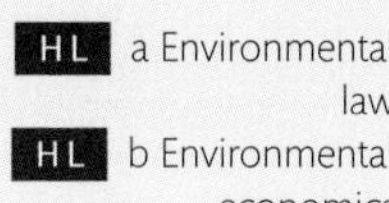

HL a Environmental law
HL b Environmental economics

4.2.17 Addressing water stress at an industrial level

Water stress can be addressed at an industrial level. There are several strategies including dams, water transfer, pipelines or tankers, estuary storage with barrages, rainmaking or cloud seeding, desalinization, solar distillation, dew harvesting, water treatment plants, aquifer storage and recovery (ASR) and artificial recharge of aquifers (AR). Each strategy has its advantages and disadvantages.

Dams

Dams are barriers placed across a river/valley to control the flow of water and enable it to be stored behind the dam in a reservoir. Dams can be of any scale and can be made from earth/clay or concrete and steel. Their benefits include the storage of water and its potential use for irrigation (Figure 4.45), fishing, hydroelectric power, transport, tourism and water sports.

Figure 4.45 Irrigated farmland next to the Yangtze River (Chang Jiang), upstream from the Three Gorges Dam, China.

However, dams also have disadvantages. Silt can be trapped behind the dam, leading to the spread of diseases such as malaria and schistosomiasis. Dams can also cause houses and farms to be flooded and may trigger earthquakes. They can also be very expensive.

Activity

Using the internet, investigate the advantages and disadvantages of the Grand Ethiopian Renaissance Dam.

Water transfer

Water transfer schemes involve the movement of water from areas of excess to areas of shortage with the aim being to match demand with supply. However, the facilities needed for storage (dams) and transfers (canals) are expensive. In addition, transferring water from one river to another can cause ecological damage due to differences in temperature, chemical content and the possible introduction of invasive species.

Pipelines and tankers

Pipelines and tankers can distribute water to areas in need. Pipelines can provide a continuous, clean supply of water that is not exposed to external pollutants, without any overland flow. However, they lack flexibility, and their capacity cannot be increased once they are installed. Pipelines that are underground are difficult to monitor and leaks are difficult to repair, while pipelines on the surface disrupt transport and are visually polluting.

Tankers can supply water to communities in need and are most frequently used in shanty towns and following floods. However, the amount of water that they can provide is limited and users face high prices for water that is delivered by tankers.

Estuary storage

Barrages across estuaries are built to harvest tidal energy as they can help build up water in an estuary rather than letting it flow out to the sea. Some of this water can then be transferred to the water network and made available to consumers. However, tidal barrages are extremely expensive and can reduce access to the estuary for boats in the area. There are relatively few sites where tidal barrages are built – this is mainly from the perspective of tidal energy, which needs a very large tidal range.

Cloud seeding

Cloud-seeding or rainmaking has been used to enhance rainfall through the use of tiny particles of silver iodide, ice and potassium iodide to increase condensation and cloud formation. There is little agreement on the success of cloud seeding. Some scientists suggest that it can increase rainfall by a small amount, but not necessarily in the area that it is needed or when it is needed. Others suggest that it might increase snowfall over a season by less than 5%. As a form of geoengineering, its success is limited.

Desalination

Desalination refers to the removal of salt and minerals from seawater to produce freshwater. It has been used in many parts of the world and can provide an almost unlimited supply of water for residents in the area. However, it is costly. There are also environmental impacts in dealing with the disposal of the salty brine that results from the process (this topic, Section 4.2.4).

Solar distillation refers to the removal of salt from seawater by using solar energy for water purification. The untreated water is heated slowly until reaching high temperatures. This causes the water to evaporate, cool and condense into vapour, thereby leaving the contaminants behind to be discarded. The water vapour can then be converted into liquid water. It is a relatively low-cost technique.

Dew harvesting

Dew- and mist-harvesting refer to attempts to catch dew, fog and mist on impermeable surfaces, such as heavy plastic sheets, and funnel the water into a collecting pot. This technique may collect enough water to support local agriculture and is relatively low cost. However, it can only be used in areas where there are frequent mists and fogs (e.g. in coastal areas where there are cold ocean currents).

Water treatment plants

Water treatment plants use several processes to provide clean water for consumers (Figure 4.46). First, water is collected from rainwater or groundwater. It may then be stored in reservoirs. Next, it is screened to remove large particles such as branches, twigs and leaves. Then smaller particles are removed in the process of flocculation, which allows particles to join together, making them heavier and easier to remove. Filtering is also used to remove even smaller particles of sand and silt. Finally, a small amount of chlorine is added to the water to get rid of any bacteria. At this point, the water is clean and can be transported to the consumers.

▲ **Figure 4.46** Water treatment plant.

Aquifers

Aquifer storage and recovery (ASR) refers to the direct implanting of water (drinking water, rainwater or river water) into an aquifer for future use. Much of the implanting is done using wells. Aquifer storage has been used in the USA and in Australia. In the latter, the city of Salisbury, northern Adelaide, injects storm water run-off in winter into underlying aquifers. This water is used in the summer for industry and for the irrigation of parks and school sports fields. A potential issue is the mixing of injected freshwater with saline waters in coastal aquifers.

Artificial recharge (AR) refers to increasing the amount of water in the groundwater zone (aquifer). In many places, groundwater has been over-extracted for many decades and the water table has dropped dramatically. By adding water to aquifers it is possible to help them recover. However, as over-extraction has taken place over decades, artificial recharge is a very time-consuming process. In addition, freshwater that is used to recharge aquifers cannot be used for other competing purposes.

Use secondary data sources to investigate the causes of water stress within a given society

Use information from the World Resources Institute to investigate water stress within a given society.

Make a presentation of your findings to your class.

HL

4.2.18 Environmental impacts of desalination

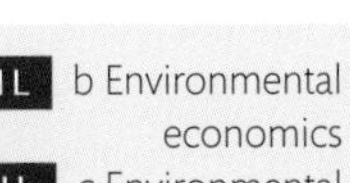

1.3 Sustainability
7.2 Energy resources, use and management

HL b Environmental economics
HL c Environmental ethics

Industrial freshwater production has negative environmental impacts, which can be minimized but not usually eliminated. Potential impacts of concentrated brine discharges from desalination plants include impacts on aquifers, such as saline intrusion. The combustion of fossil fuels to provide energy for the process can result in noise and air pollution.

Example – Desalination in the Middle East

Many Arab countries have very limited freshwater resources. Some 400 million people live in the region and desalination dependence is very high (Figure 4.47). Around 66% of the water produced by desalination depends on fossil fuel use although they can be run on renewable energy including solar power. Of the 18,000 commercial desalinations plants worldwide, 44% are located in the Middle East and North Africa and desalination in the region is expected to grow at a rate of 7–9% per annum. Between 2020 and 2040, desalinated water is expected to grow 14-fold in the Middle East. Desalination is energy intensive.

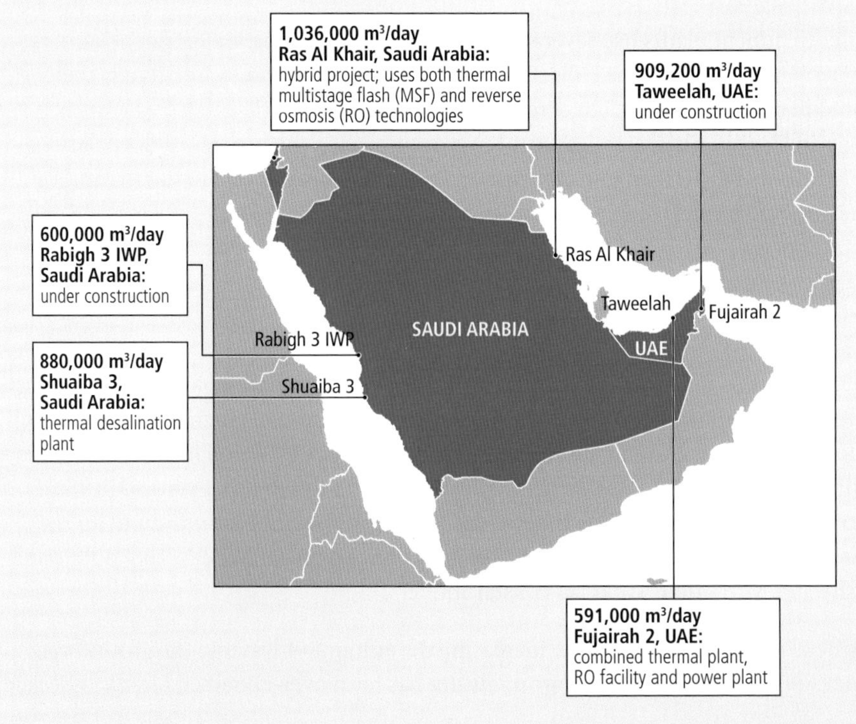

Figure 4.47 Distribution of large-scale desalination plants in the Middle East.

Desalination has many direct and indirect environmental impacts that are significant and always obvious (Figure 4.48). Increased salinity, discharged chemicals and increased temperature of seawater due to the discharge of waste materials, are among the impacts threatening marine ecosystems. Every day, around 22,000 kg of chlorine and 300 kg of copper enter the Arabian Gulf, from desalination plants for example. The materials come from the 120 or so desalination plants in the Middle East. Increased levels of chlorine reduce the photosynthetic efficiency of plankton, which is the basis of most marine food chains. Copper settles in marine sediments and is eventually consumed by organisms living on the sea floor, before becoming incorporated into marine food chains. Anti-scaling additives used in desalination plants have been linked with red tides in the region. In addition, the increased salinity of the Gulf is reducing the transfer of water between the Gulf and the Arabian Sea. Without mixing, the Gulf water is likely to accumulate very high levels of pollutants from desalination and industrial discharges.

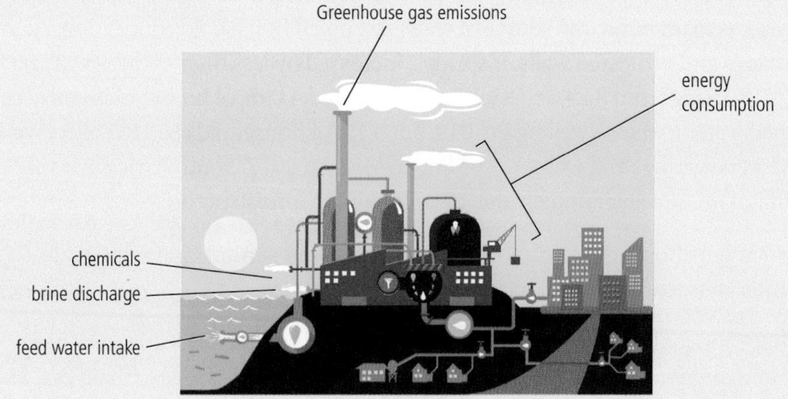

Figure 4.48 Environmental impacts of desalination.

The amount of pure groundwater in Abu Dhabi is limited to just over 10% of the country's groundwater reserves. Where pure groundwater occurs, it is usually surrounded by **brackish** water (a mix of freshwater and saltwater). As the water table drops, there is an increase in the amount of saline water from lower parts of the aquifer and surrounding areas. Mixing of saline water and freshwater reduces the quality of Abu Dhabi's groundwater. Aquifer quality is further reduced through the application of agricultural fertilizers, large numbers of livestock and localized dumping of brine and sewage effluent in desert areas.

Rising salinity in the Gulf is a major challenge because it impacts marine ecosystems and the efficiency of the desalination process. This increases the cost of production, and so increases the cost of water. Other strategies have been investigated, such as the transfer of lower salinity water from the Gulf of Oman, but this is only a temporary solution and even more expensive than desalination.

Abu Dhabi's power and desalination plants release about 13.5 million tonnes of greenhouse gases and particulates each year, about one-quarter of the country's emissions, contributing to global warming.

HL

4.2.19 Uneven access to water and sanitation

1.3 Sustainability

Inequitable access to drinkable water and sanitation negatively impacts human health and sustainable development. Marginalized groups could include Indigenous people or those from low-income households.

HL c Environmental ethics

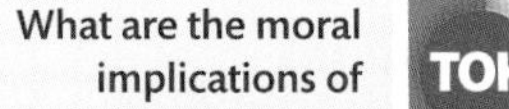

What are the moral implications of possessing knowledge?

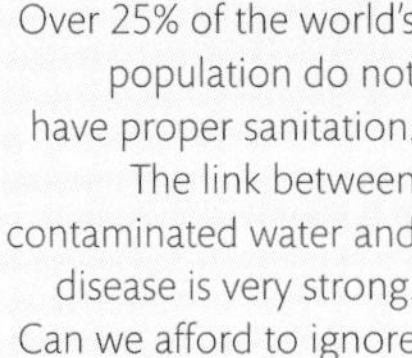

Over 25% of the world's population do not have proper sanitation. The link between contaminated water and disease is very strong. Can we afford to ignore solid domestic waste?

Example – Access to water and sanitation in South Africa

In 2020, on a global scale, 74% of the population (2 billion people) live without safely managed drinking water. 1.2 billion people lacked even a basic level of service. Between 2015 and 2020 the population with safely managed sanitation increased from 47% to 54%.

South Africa is a water-scarce country and faces a challenge in the delivery of water and sanitation services. This is caused by insufficient infrastructure maintenance and investment, recurring drought, unequal access and deteriorating water quality. According to the 2019 General Household Survey, the percentage of households with access to an improved source of water e.g. piped household connections, public standpipes and protected wells or springs, increased by less than 4% between 2002 and 2018, rising from 84.4% to 88.2%. An estimated 44.9% of households had access to piped water in their dwelling in 2019, but 3.1% of households had to collect water from rivers, springs and wells. According to Mission 2017, South Africa loses about 1.5 billion m^3 of water annually due to faulty piping infrastructure.

Over 13.5 million households (80%) had improved sanitation facilities, but 0.4 million households (2%) had no sanitation facilities.

The huge inequality in access to water supplies and sanitation is due to rising unemployment and the legacy of segregated services from the Apartheid era. Since the 1970s, large-scale rural to urban migration has resulted in fewer people living in rural areas. This means less revenue is collected to invest in WASH services.

The 1996 census showed that Black Africans accounted for 72% of the population. Only 27% of Black Africans had indoor taps, whereas 96% of the white population had indoor taps. More recent surveys do not produce data on different racial groups but the total number of households with indoor taps has remained at about 44%.

The Eastern Cape is the poorest province in South Africa. 76% of households there have an improved water source, the lowest percentage for any South African province. The Eastern Cape also had the highest proportion of households with no sanitation facilities, 6%, compared with all other provinces.

Exercise

Q11. **Distinguish between** water security and water scarcity.

Q12. **Explain** how political factors impact the availability of, and equitable access to, freshwater.

Q13. **Distinguish** between physical and economic water scarcity.

Q14. Look back at Figure 4.39 in Section 4.2.11. **Describe** the distribution of grey water shown in the figure.

Q15. **Outline** the advantages and disadvantages of large dams.

Q16. **Outline** contrasting reasons for water shortages in South Africa.

HL

Q17. HL **Explain** the advantages of drip irrigation.

Q18. HL Briefly **explain** why switching to vegetarian diets can help conserve water.

Q19. HL **Explain** the reasons for increasing water stress in contrasting places.

Q20. HL **Explain** two from of pollution caused by desalination.

HL end

Engagement

- Compare the water footprint for a variety of different food or clothing items (for example, a pair of denim jeans and a linen T shirt, a woolen jumper and a polyester fleece, or an avocado and an apple). Present your findings to your class.
- Select a charity that focuses on access to water such as WaterAid. Create a poster about where they work, what they do, who they influence and the main issues they deal with.
- Create a poster to show ways of reducing household and/or school water consumption in your locality. Discuss with the class the relative merits of different options.

TOK

In what ways can language be used to influence, persuade or manipulate people's emotions?

Aid agencies often use emotive advertisements around the water security issue. To what extent can emotion be used to manipulate knowledge and actions?

4.3 Aquatic food production systems

Guiding questions

How are our diets impacted by our values and perspectives?
To what extent are aquatic food systems sustainable?

4.3.1 Phytoplankton and macrophytes provide energy for freshwater and marine food webs.
4.3.2 Humans consume organisms from freshwater and marine environments.
4.3.3 Demand for foods from freshwater and marine environments is increasing due to the growth in human population and changes in dietary preferences.
4.3.4 The increasing global demand for seafood has encouraged use of unsustainable harvesting practices and overexploitation.
4.3.5 Overexploitation has led to the collapse of fisheries.
4.3.6 The maximum sustainable yield (MSY) is the highest possible annual catch that can be sustained over time, so it should be used to set caps on fishing quotas.
4.3.7 Climate change and ocean acidification are having impacts on ecosystems and may cause collapse of some populations in freshwater or marine ecosystems.

4.3.8 Unsustainable exploitation of freshwater and marine ecosystems can be mitigated through policy legislation addressing the fishing industry and changes in consumer behaviour.
4.3.9 Marine protected areas (MPAs) can be used to support aquatic food chains and maintain sustainable yields.
4.3.10 Aquaculture is the farming of aquatic organisms, including fish, molluscs, crustaceans and aquatic plants. The industry is expanding to increase food supplies and support economic development, but there are associated environmental impacts.
HL 4.3.11 Productivity, thermal stratification, nutrient mixing and nutrient loading are interconnected in water systems.
HL 4.3.12 Accurate assessment of fish stocks and monitoring of harvest rates are required for their conservation and sustainable use.
HL 4.3.13 There are risks in harvesting fish at the maximum sustainable yield (MSY) rate and these risks need to be managed carefully.
HL 4.3.14 Species that have been overexploited may recover with cooperation between governments, the fishing industry, consumers and other interest groups, including NGOs, wholesale fishery markets and local supermarkets.
HL 4.3.15 According to the UN Convention on the Law of the Sea (UNCLOS), coastal states have an exclusive economic zone stretching 370 km out to sea, within which the state's government can regulate fishing. Almost 60% of the ocean is the high seas outside these coastal zones, with limited intergovernmental regulation.
HL 4.3.16 Harvesting of seals, whales and dolphins raises ethical issues relating to the rights of animals and of Indigenous groups of humans.

2.2 Energy and biomass in ecosystems

4.3.1 Phytoplankton and macrophytes

Phytoplankton are microscopic aquatic organisms that photosynthesize and are found in marine and freshwater environments.

Macrophytes are aquatic plants adapted to living in freshwater and saltwater environments.

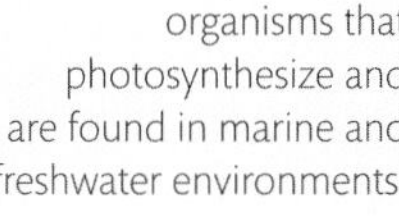

Phytoplankton

Phytoplankton are autotrophs (self-feeding). They obtain their energy through photosynthesis, using light from the Sun. They are found in the well-lit surface layers (euphotic zone) of oceans and lakes.

Phytoplankton form the base of marine and freshwater food webs. Phytoplankton are producers and create organic (carbon) compounds from dissolved CO_2 in the water. Although plankton only account for about 1% of global plant biomass, they account for about half of global photosynthesis activity and are responsible for at least half of the world's O_2 production. They are also a vital component of the Earth's carbon cycle.

Some plankton are heterotrophs and feed on other plankton or detritus. These are consumers and are known as zooplankton.

During photosynthesis, phytoplankton assimilate CO_2 and release O_2. If solar radiation is too high, phytoplankton may be photodegraded. Bacteria can also degrade them.

Phytoplankton cells depend on nutrients for growth, including macronutrients such as nitrate, phosphate and silicic acid. These nutrients are common where ocean water is upwelling. In contrast, in large areas of the oceans such as the Southern Ocean, phytoplankton are limited by the lack of the micronutrient, iron. Phytoplankton also depend on B vitamins for survival, thus oceanic areas lacking in B vitamins contain limited phytoplankton populations.

Figure 4.49 shows the factors that affect phytoplankton productivity. Each of these factors is expected to be affected by global changes such as oceanic temperature increase, changes in ocean stratification and circulation, and changes in cloud cover and sea ice resulting in an increased light supply to the ocean surface. Ocean acidification and warming will also reduce nutrient supply, due to increased stratification of the water column and reduced mixing of nutrients from the deep water to the surface.

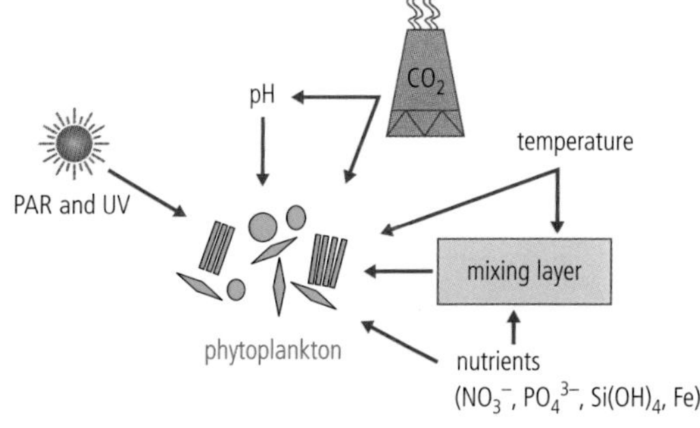

Figure 4.49 Factors affecting plankton productivity. PAR = photosynthetically active radiation (400–700 nm).

Phytoplankton has a significant impact on atmospheric gas composition, inorganic nutrients and trace element transfers as well as the transfer and cycling of organic matter via biological processes. Fixed carbon is rapidly recycled and reused in the surface ocean, while some biomass sinks to the deep ocean where it is remineralized.

Ocean acidification can have a negative impact on phytoplankton growth, particularly on coccolithophore phytoplankton. These have a calcium carbonate shell called a coccosphere that is vulnerable to ocean acidification. However, due to their short lifespans (or generation times) some phytoplankton may adapt to changes in pH over a short timescale (months to years).

In oligotrophic (nutrient-poor) oceanic regions, such as the Sargasso Sea, phytoplankton are characterized by small-sized cells, called nanoplankton and picoplankton (also referred to as picoflagellates) and nanoflagellates. Within more productive (eutrophic) ecosystems, such as those with upwelling currents or high terrestrial inputs, larger dinoflagellates are more frequent and form a larger portion of the biomass.

Aquaculture

Phytoplankton are a vital food supply in aquaculture and mariculture (marine farming). Both use phytoplankton as food for the animals being farmed. In mariculture, phytoplankton are naturally occurring, whereas in aquaculture, phytoplankton must be obtained and introduced directly. The phytoplankton can either be collected from a body of water or cultured.

Macrophytes

Aquatic plants (macrophytes) are those adapted to living in aquatic (freshwater and saltwater) environments. Macrophytes grow in or near the water and can be emergent, submergent or floating. Macrophytes are producers and therefore form the basis of the food chain for many organisms. They also slow down water velocity in rivers, increase sedimentation and may capture pollutants.

To survive in the water, either submerged or at the surface, plants have many adaptations including floating leaves, dissected leaves and/or lightweight cells. The main factors affecting the abundance and distribution of aquatic plants is the availability of water, nutrient availability, disturbance by waves, salinity and grazing.

Submerged plants have less access to CO_2 and light than terrestrial plants in general. Fully submerged plants have no requirement for woody biomass. Many submerged plants have finely dissected leaves to increase surface area for the exchange of minerals and gases and to reduce the impact of water flow in rivers. Some floating plants have developed leaves that only have stomata on the top surface of the leaf in order to capture atmospheric CO_2.

Emergent plants grow in water but are partially exposed to air. Leaves can photosynthesize more efficiently in air but the main reason for having part of the plant on the water's surface is reproduction, for example the flower may be on the surface in species of reeds and flowering rushes.

Submerged macrophytes grow under water and may or may not have roots attached to sediments at the water's base. Helophytes are partly submerged plants, such as

Figure 4.50 Water lilies at Kew Gardens, London, UK.

reeds and yellow flag, that grow in marshes from submerged buds. Floating-leaved macrophytes, such as water lilies (Figure 4.50) and pondweeds, have root systems attached to the riverbed or lakebed and leaves that float on the water's surface.

Some macrophytes, such as wild rice, watercress and Chinese water chestnut, are important food crops. Macrophytes can be important for wastewater treatment, especially in small-scale sewage works. A decline in macrophytes may suggest declining water quality caused by salination and/or the large-scale use of biocides. Some macrophytes have been introduced into new environments and can become locally dominant in many temperate areas, for example, water hyacinth in South Africa and New Zealand stone crop.

Macrophytes are important for pollution control and are widely used in the design of wetlands to remove dissolved nutrients such as nitrogen and phosphorus from polluted waters. Macrophytes may cause the deposition of suspended sediments by reducing the speed of water flow. Macrophytes also provide environmental services such as climate regulation and flood regulation, and provide recreational benefits to people.

2.2 Energy and biomass in ecosystems

Activity

Study Figure 4.50, which shows water lilies in a pond.

Discuss with a partner the environmental services provided by this ecosystem.

4.3.2 Human consumption of freshwater and marine organisms

Fauna

Humans consume organisms from freshwater and marine environments. According to the State of the World's Fisheries and Aquaculture, in 2020, finfish represented about 85% of total marine capture production, with anchoveta the top species harvested. However, only a small number of 'staple' species dominate aquaculture production, particularly grass carp for global inland aquaculture and Atlantic salmon for marine aquaculture (Figure 4.51).

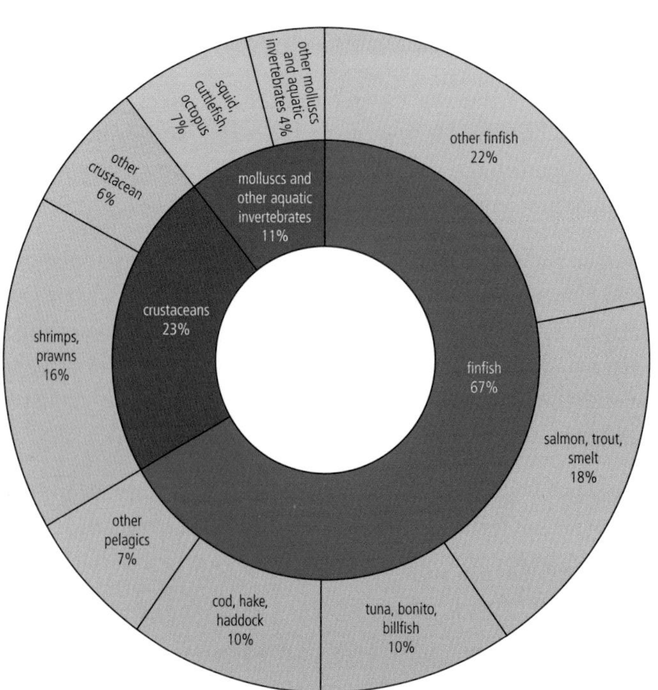

Figure 4.51 Share of main groups of species in exports of aquatic products by value, 2020.

In 2020, global exports of tuna, bonitos and billfish accounted for almost 10% of the value of exports of aquatic products and were worth over US$ 14 billion (Figure 4.52). This proportion has remained relatively steady for many decades, reflecting tuna's popularity with people worldwide (Figure 4.53). The trade in tuna can be divided into two main categories: (i) processed and preserved tuna and (ii) high-quality fresh tuna for the sushi and sashimi market. Bluefin and bigeye tuna are generally used for sushi and sashimi. Skipjack, yellowfin and albacore are used for processed products, which can be frozen and transported around the world.

Value by species (US$) in 2018 end

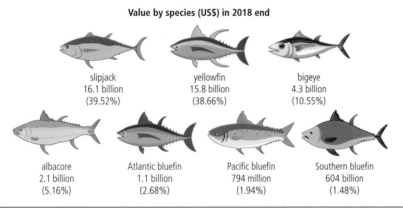

slipjack
16.1 billion
(39.52%)

yellowfin
15.8 billion
(38.66%)

bigeye
4.3 billion
(10.55%)

albacore
2.1 billion
(5.16%)

Atlantic bluefin
1.1 billion
(2.68%)

Pacific bluefin
794 million
(1.94%)

Southern bluefin
604 billion
(1.48%)

Figure 4.52 Global value of the trade in tuna.

Figure 4.53 Tuna on sale at a Tokyo fish market.

Challenge yourself

Outline the impact on the natural ecosystem of the fishing of top predators.

Thailand has a large tuna processing industry, which supplies the USA, while Ecuador supplies much of the tuna destined for the European Union. There are also smaller processing industries in Asia, Latin America and Africa, illustrating how important the tuna trade is globally.

Flora

Seaweed has many uses including as a food, as a flavouring, for thickening soups and broths, as a herbal tea, as a medication for sore throats, for use in baths to cleanse skin and as a soil fertilizer. The pepper dulse seaweed (*Osmundea pinnatifida*) (Figure 4.54) has been described as 'the smallest and most beautiful of all the Irish seaweeds'. It can be found in rock pools or on the base of rocks when the tide is out. It is also known as the 'truffle of the sea' due to its sweet-savory taste. Due to its size it is generally used as a garnish with mussels, clams and scallops. It has a shelf-life of just two days once harvested, so it tends to form part of local dishes in coastal areas. It can be dried and powdered, although the flavor of the dried version is not as strong as the fresh pepper dulse.

Figure 4.54 Pepper dulse seaweed.

4.3.3 Increasing demand for freshwater and marine organisms

1.3 Sustainability
8.1 Human populations

HL c Environmental ethics

Demand for foods from freshwater and marine environments is increasing due to the growth in human population and changes in dietary preferences.

According to the Food and Agriculture Organization (FAO), global fisheries and aquaculture production reached a record 214 million tonnes in 2020. This consisted of 178 million tonnes of aquatic animals and 36 million tonnes of algae. This was largely due to the growth of aquaculture, particularly in Asia (Figure 4.55). The amount destined for human consumption (excluding algae) was 20.2 kg per capita, more than double the average of 9.9 kg per capita in the 1960s.

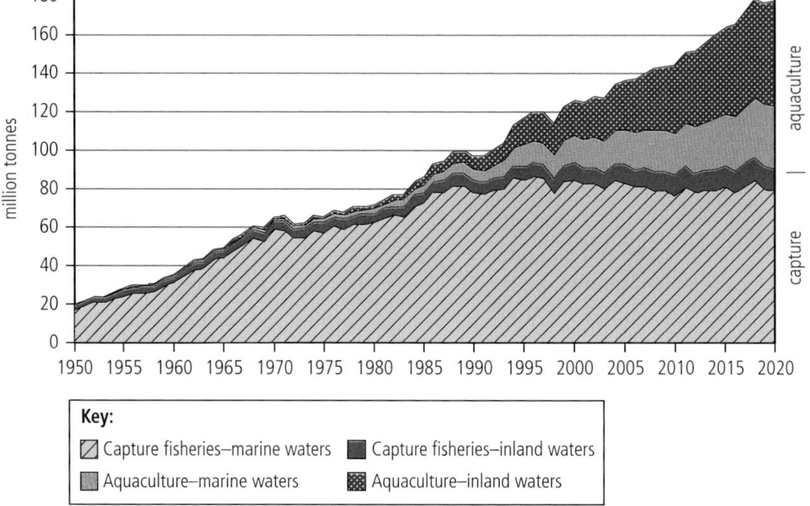

Figure 4.55 World capture fisheries and aquaculture, 1950–2020.

Global consumption of aquatic foods increased at an average annual rate of 3.0 % between 1961 and 2019, a rate almost twice that of annual world population growth (1.6 %) for the same period. Per capita consumption of aquatic animal foods grew by about 1.4 % per year, from 9.0 kg (live weight equivalent) in 1961 to 20.5 kg in 2019. Preliminary data for 2020 pointed to a slight decline to 20.2 kg. In the same year, aquaculture accounted for 56% of the amount of aquatic animal food production available for human consumption. During recent decades, per capita consumption of aquatic foods has been influenced most strongly by increased supplies, changing consumer preferences, advancements in technology and income growth.

Activity

Calculate the percentage change in total capture and total aquaculture during the period 1990s–2020, as shown in Table 4.11.

Table 4.11 World fisheries and aquaculture production, utilization and trade (Average per year, million tonnes – live weight equivalent).

	1990s	2000s	2010s	2020
Production				
Capture:				
Inland	7.1	9.3	11.3	11.5
Marine	81.9	81.6	79.8	78.8
Total capture	88.9	90.9	91.0	90.3
Aquaculture:				
Inland	12.6	25.6	44.7	54.4
Marine	9.2	17.9	26.8	33.1
Total aquaculture	21.8	43.4	71.5	87.5
Total world fisheries and aquaculture	110.7	134.3	162.6	177.8
Utilization				
Human consumption	81.6	109.3	143.2	157.4
Population (billions)	5.7	6.5	7.3	7.8
Per capita consumption (kg)	14.3	16.8	19.5	20.2

4.3.4 Unsustainable harvesting

1.3 Sustainability

HL a Environmental law
HL b Environmental economics
HL c Environmental ethics

The increasing global demand for seafood has encouraged use of unsustainable harvesting practices and overexploitation. Practices include bottom trawling, ghost fishing and the use of poisons and explosives as destructive methods of harvesting that are unsustainable.

Bottom trawling

Bottom trawling refers to trawling/dragging a net along the sea floor. Benthic trawling is along the seabed, whereas demersal trawling is just above the seabed. Bottom trawling accounts for about 30 million tonnes of fish captured annually. Bottom trawling has now been restricted in certain areas and at certain times because of the damage it does. Bottom trawling contributes 600–1500 million tonnes of CO_2 annually by disturbing carbon on the sea floor. Bottom trawling is also associated with the collapse of various species including barndoor skates, orange roughy and sharks.

Bottom trawling uses a plough-like action in digging up to 15 cm of the seabed. This creates a cloud of sediment, which scares the fish towards the open end of the net. Regulation of the net size has reduced the mortality of juvenile fish.

Bottom trawling operated for over a century in fishing grounds such as the North Sea and the Grand Banks. Some areas, such as Venezuela, have now banned bottom trawling and the USA's west coast Rockfish Conservation Area limits bottom trawling at depths of 140–270 m to protect the over-fished rockfish species. However, as the open ocean is free from national jurisdiction, bottom trawling is unregulated.

Ghost fishing

Ghost fishing or ghost gear is the fishing equipment that has been abandoned, lost or dumped at sea, including nets, long lines and fish traps. Fish that are caught in this equipment can suffer exhaustion, suffocation, starvation and finally death. In turn, they attract predators and scavengers that get caught in the same gear.

An estimated 25,000 nets are abandoned in the North Atlantic every year. Each net can weigh over 4500 kg. Ghost fishing can damage sensitive habitats such as coral reefs, enable invasive species to spread and can devastate shorelines and boats. Due to the durability of modern fishing gear, especially plastic, devastation may continue for decades.

Every year, some 640,000 tonnes of fishing gear is lost or discarded in oceans.
Over 136,000 seals and whales are trapped in lines, nets and traps every year.

Submarine drones (remote operated vehicles) can help to remove some of the materials from the sea floor, but the process is dangerous, difficult, expensive and time-consuming.

Poisons and explosives

Toxins have traditionally been used by some hunter-gatherers to stun fish, so that they can be easily collected by hand. For example, some of California's Native American populations use soaproot species, which contain saponin, as a poison. California buckeye is also used to produce aesculin, which is then applied to freshwater pools and small streams to stun fish. Olax is a fish poison used by the Gondi of India. The leaves of the plant are dried and powdered. When fish are stunned by the poison, they rise to the surface and can be easily collected by hand.

Blast fishing or dynamite fishing is an illegal practice that uses explosives to stun or kill large numbers of fish for easy collection. It is widespread in South-East Asia, coastal Africa and parts of the Aegean Sea. Underwater shock waves stun the fish, which may then rise to the surface. However, the explosions kill large numbers of fish and non-targeted species. Only about 20% of the fish killed float to the surface. In the Philippines, destructive fishing methods have degraded some 70% of coral reefs and were responsible for reduced fish production of about 175,000 tonnes. In some places, including Tanzania, Indonesia and the Philippines, sales of ammonium nitrate have been restricted or banned, making it more difficult to make explosives.

Challenge yourself

Carry out research to investigate whether it is possible to manage bottom trawling and ghost fishing.

4.3.5 Overexploitation

1.2 Systems
3.2 Human impact on biodiversity
7.2 Energy resources, use and management

 a Environmental law
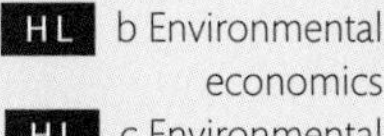 b Environmental economics
HL c Environmental ethics

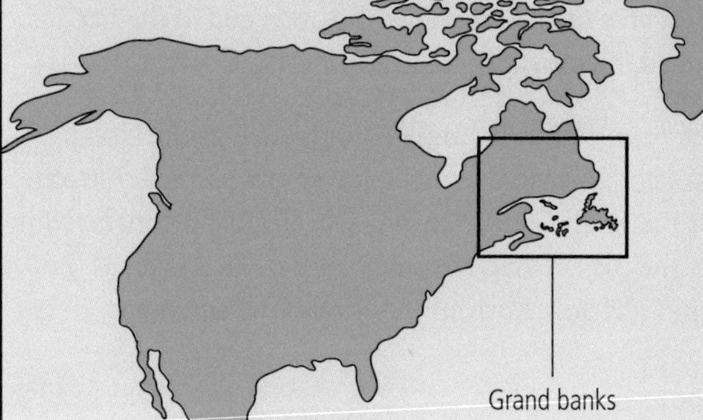

Figure 4.56 The location of the Grand Banks.

Overexploitation has led to the collapse of fisheries. There have been many 'fishery collapses' (dramatic and lasting decrease in stocks to a point where the commercial fish can no longer recover). One example happened to the cod fishery on the Grand Banks of Newfoundland, Canada (Figure 4.56 and Topic 1, Section 1.3.7).

Example – Overfishing and the Grand Banks of Newfoundland

In 1992, the northern cod population fell to 1% of historical levels due to over-fishing. A significant cause of the collapse was the introduction of equipment and technology that increased fish catches. The use of radar and sonar allowed trawlers to track fish. Canadian catches peaked around the late-1970s to early-1980s. Cod were being caught at rates that far exceeded the replenishment of the supplies. Countries fishing for cod in Newfoundland included France, Germany, Greenland, Portugal, Spain and the USA.

The large volumes of non-commercial fish and by-catch caught by trawlers were not commercially viable but were environmentally important. For example, capelin were caught as by-catch. As these fish are an important food-source for cod, the remaining cod population had a depleted food supply.

In 1968, the cod catch peaked at 810,000 tonnes (Topic 1, Section 1.3.7, Figure 1.62), which was around three times the maximum yearly catch before the super-trawlers. Between 1647 and 1770, around 8 million tonnes of cod were caught – factory trawlers took just 15 years to catch a similar amount. Improvements in sonar and radar allowed trawlers to track fish populations, meaning the larger vessels with refrigeration were able to store catches for many months while they remained at sea catching other fish.

In 1986, scientists warned that the total amount of cod fishing allowed needed to be reduced by 50%. By 1992, the cod industry had collapsed and a moratorium on cod fishing was introduced that year. The cod population had fallen by 99%. Some 37,000 fisherfolk lost their jobs. Newfoundland experienced out-migration and a re-structuring of their economy and society.

In 2000, the World Wildlife Fund for Nature (WWF) placed cod on the endangered list. Global cod catches had fallen by 70% in 30 years. By 2002, despite ten years of the moratorium, cod numbers were still low. Forage species, such as capelin, that used to provide food for cod, were now feeding on juvenile cod. Although a 2015 report suggested that cod numbers were on the increase, other reports suggested that cod numbers in the North Atlantic would remain low due to global climate change and warming of North Atlantic waters. It is hoped that the cod industry could return to pre-collapse levels by 2030.

Activity

Go online to watch a video about the collapse of the Grand Banks fishing industry.

Investigate the environmental, economic and social impacts of the collapse. Write a one-page report summarizing the main impacts of the collapse.

4.3.6 Maximum sustainable yield

1.3 Sustainability
2.2 Energy and biomass in ecosystems

HL a Environmental law
HL b Environmental economics

Maximum sustainable yield (MSY) is the highest possible annual catch that can be sustained over time.

Maximum sustainable yield (MSY) is the largest yield (or harvest) that can be taken from the stock of a species over an indefinite period (Topic 2, Section 2.2.26). MSY should be used to set caps on fishing quotas. Typically, harvesting at MSY levels requires much lower fishing rates than occurs in many fisheries.

Sustainable yield (SY) is calculated as the rate of increase in natural capital or natural income that can be exploited without depleting the original stock or its potential for replenishment. Exploitation must decrease long-term productivity. The annual sustainable yield for a given crop may be estimated as the annual gain in biomass or energy through growth and recruitment (in-migration of species).

SY is the amount of increase per unit time (i.e., the rate of increase)

where:

t = the time of the original nature capital

$t + 1$ = the time of the original capital plus yield

SY = (total biomass at $t + 1$) – (total energy at t)

or

SY = (total energy at $t + 1$) – (total energy at t)

The relationship can be simplified as:

SY = (annual growth and recruitment) – (annual death and emigration)

MSY aims to maintain the population size at the point of maximum growth rate by harvesting the number of individuals that would normally be added to the population, allowing the population to continue to be productive indefinitely. MSY is a measure of the point at which the highest rate of capture fisheries can occur (this is often difficult to determine). It is used extensively by fisheries management). Populations of cod have been particularly affected by over-fishing in the North Atlantic as discussed previously (Topic 1, Section 1.3.7, Figure 1.62).

Developments in fishing equipment and changes to fishing methods, coupled with over-capacity in fleets and inadequate management, lead to dwindling fish stocks and damage to habitats.

Most of the stocks of the top ten species, accounting for about 30% of world marine capture fisheries production, are fully exploited and therefore have no potential for increases in production. The stocks of anchoveta in the south-east Pacific, Alaska pollock in the north Pacific and blue whiting in the Atlantic are fully exploited. Among the seven principal tuna species, one-third are estimated to be over-exploited.

The declining global marine catch over the last few years, together with the increased percentage of over-exploited fish stocks and the decreased proportion of non-fully exploited species, suggests that the state of the world's marine fisheries is worsening and has had a negative impact of fishery production. Over-exploitation not only causes negative ecological consequences, but also reduces fish production, which further leads to negative social and economic consequences.

According to the UN SDG 14.4 there is a need to regulate harvesting and end overfishing, illegal, unreported and unregulated fishing, and destructive fishing practices, and implement science-based management plans, in order to restore fish stocks to achieve *sustainability*. The original intention was for this to have been achieved by 2020, but the SDGs extended this goal to 2030.

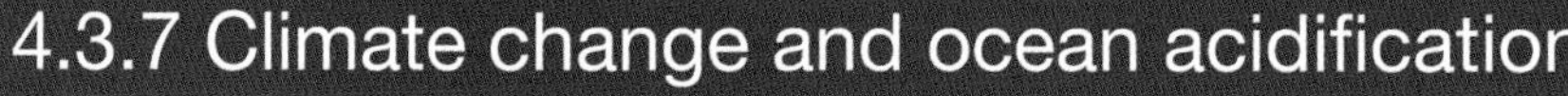

4.3.7 Climate change and ocean acidification

1.2 Systems
6.2 Climate change – causes and impacts

Climate change and ocean acidification are having impacts on ecosystems and may cause the collapse of some populations in freshwater or marine ecosystems.

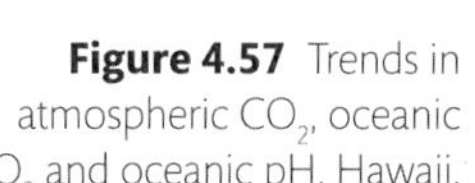

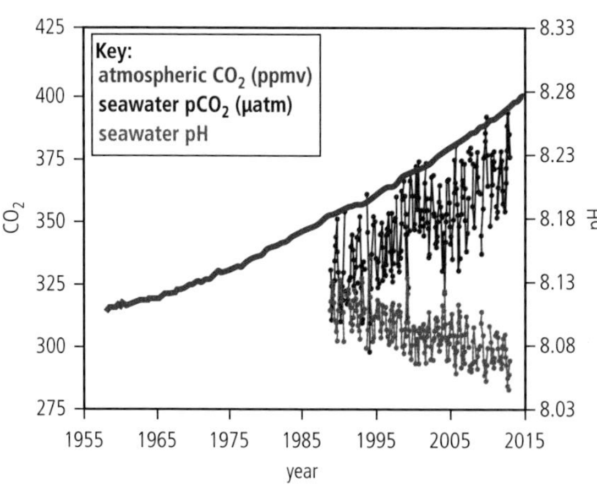

Figure 4.57 Trends in atmospheric CO_2, oceanic CO_2 and oceanic pH, Hawaii.

HL b Environmental economics

The partial pressure of carbon dioxide (pCO_2) is the gas phase pressure (i.e. in the air above a waterway) of CO_2 which would be in equilibrium with the dissolved CO_2.

Oceans naturally absorb CO_2 but since about 1850 they have absorbed around 33% of the carbon that humans have released into the atmosphere. This has increased ocean acidification by about 30%. If CO_2 emissions continue at the current rate, ocean surface pH could change from 8.1 to 7.7 over the next century. Between 1955 and 2015, atmospheric CO_2 increased steadily from about 315 ppmv to about 400 ppmv (Figure 4.57). The CO_2 content of oceans increased from about 325 µatm in 1990 to about 375 µatm in the 2010s. In contrast, the pH of seawater fell from about 8.13 to about 8.05 between 1990 and 2013.

Increasing CO_2 levels, mainly caused by the burning of fossil fuels, are driving ocean acidification. Ocean acidification makes it harder for some species to survive and affects ecosystems, food chains, food supply, the economy, tourism and recreation. The best way to prevent further ocean acidification is to reduce CO_2 emissions.

Seagrasses may grow more quickly if more dissolved CO_2 is available, but oyster numbers may be reduced because fewer larvae complete their life cycle due to the acidic conditions. Any life in the oceans is food for another species and change in the abundance of one species will have an impact on others. Humans are affected too, due to relying on the ocean for food and other resources. For example, some 500 million people depend on coral reefs for food, for coastal protection and for their income. Some reefs, such as Australia's Great Barrier Reef, are increasingly vulnerable to bleaching events caused by rising sea temperatures. In turn, acidification may make it harder for coral reefs to recover from bleaching.

Coral bleaching refers to the way in which coral reefs may turn white when they are stressed e.g. by changes in temperature, light or nutrients. They expel the symbiotic algae living in their tissues, causing the coral to turn completely white.

In Puget Sound, Washington, USA, the Suquamish people's economy and culture is related closely to shellfish and salmon. Ocean acidification reduces the number of shellfish and sea butterflies that are a key part of the diet of wild salmon. This is threatening the traditional way of life of the Suquamish.

Ocean acidification affects food chains. Populations of species that feed on calcifying organisms, such as baleen whales, may decrease. In turn, this can affect the populations of species that feed on baleen whales, such as killer whales. Marine life at risk includes oysters, mussels and squid. These species make up a high proportion of the seafood industry. In the USA, oysters, clams and scallops provide seafood valued at US$ 400 million per year.

In some coastal shorelines, acidification may also be caused by run-off from acidic soils and bedrock, such as gravels.

Plan an experiment to investigate the impact of acidification on shelled organisms

Access the link in the eBook for more details.

4.3.8 Mitigating unsustainable exploitation

1.3 Sustainability

HL a Environmental law
HL b Environmental economics
HL Environmental ethics

Unsustainable exploitation of freshwater and marine ecosystems can be mitigated through policy legislation that addresses the fishing industry and changes in consumer behaviour. Actions occur at international, national, local and individual level including instructions on permits, quotas, seasons, mesh size, zones and food labelling.

Many scientists argue that measures such as quotas, bans and the closing of fishing areas still fail to address the real problems of the fishing industry. Put simply, too many anglers are chasing too few fish and too many juvenile fish are being caught. For the fisheries to be protected, and for the industry to be competitive on a world scale, the number of boats and the number of people employed in fishing must be reduced. At the same time, the efficiencies that come from improved technology must be embraced.

The unsustainable exploitation of aquatic systems can be mitigated at a variety of levels (international, local and individual) through policy change, legislation and changes in consumer behaviour.

A World Bank and FAO report in 2008 showed that up to US$ 50 billion per year is lost in poor management, inefficiency and overfishing in world fisheries. The report puts the total loss over the last 30 years at US$ 2.2 trillion per year. The industry's fishing capacity continues to increase. The number of vessels is increasing slowly. However, each boat has greater capacity due to improved technology. Due to overcapacity, much of the investment in new technology is wasted. The number of fish caught at sea has barely changed over the last decade. Fish stocks are depleted so the effort to catch the ones remaining is higher than it needs to be.

Changing consumer behaviour

Consumer behaviour is changing in some societies. Awareness of bio rights and the problem of overfishing has led some people to demand that the fish they consume are taken from sustainable sources. The Marine Stewardship Council identifies and labels sustainable fisheries. Its website claims that by 'choosing MSC-labelled seafood, you reward fisheries that are committed to sustainable fishing practices'. MSC-labelled seafood is available in 149 countries around the world and the certified fisheries represent 10% of global wild-capture seafood. Researchers have identified nearly one thousand improvements made by MSC-certified fisheries, improving the sustainability of the fisheries to global best-practice levels of environmental performance. The Aquaculture Stewardship Council (ASC) sets standards for responsible aquaculture, i.e. farmed fish and seafood.

A number of publications and films have promoted sustainable fishing practices or highlighted unsustainable ones. These aim to further change consumer behaviour and to put pressure on governments and the fishing industry to stop unsustainable fishing.

Changing the fishing industry

Table 4.12 suggests some possible strategies to manage the fishing industry for the future, but there are clearly no simple solutions to the problems associated with such a politically, economically and environmentally sensitive industry.

Table 4.12 Possible strategies to manage the fishing industry in Europe.

Action	Type of measure	Objectives
Conservation of resources		
Technical measures	Small, meshed nets, minimum landing sizes, boxes	Protect juveniles and encourage breeding, discourage marketing of illegal catches
Restrict catches	Total allowable catches (TACs) and quotas	To match supply to demand, plan quota uptake throughout the season, protect sensitive stocks
Limit number of vessels	Fishing permits (which could be traded inter- or intra-nationally)	System applicable to EU vessels and other countries' vessels fishing in EU waters
Surveillance	To check landings by EU and third-country vessels (logbooks, computer/satellite surveillance)	To apply penalties to overfishing and illegal landings
Structural	Structural aid to the fleet	Finance investment in fleet modernization (although commissioning of new vessels must be closely controlled) while providing reimbursement for scrapping, transfer and conversion

Reduction in unemployment leading to an increase in productivity	Inclusion of zones dependent on fishing in Objectives 1, 2 and 5b of Structural Funds	To facilitate restructuring of the industry, to finance alternative local development initiatives to encourage voluntary/early retirement schemes
Action	**Type of measure**	**Objectives**
Markets		
Tariff policy	Minimum import prices, restrictions on imports	To ensure EU preference (although still bound under WTO)
Other measures		
Restrict number of vessels	Fishing licenses	Large license fees would discourage small, inefficient boats
Increase the accountability of anglers	Rights to fisheries	Where fish stay put (e.g. shellfish) sections of the seabed can be auctioned off; where a whole fishery is controlled, quotas could be traded which would allow some to cash in and leave the sea

Activity

Create a spider diagram to show the variety of ways in which it is possible to manage the fishing industry.

4.3.9 Marine protected areas

1.3 Sustainability

HL a Environmental law

Marine protected areas (MPAs) are areas of oceans, seas, estuaries and some lakes in which some human activities are restricted to conserve the area and its resources. MPAs can be used to support aquatic food chains and maintain sustainable yields. Protected areas can benefit wider areas of sea, for example by providing shelter or spawning grounds. MPAs include areas of oceans, seas, estuaries and some lakes in which some human activities are restricted to conserve the area and its resources. MPAs vary in scale, from large conservation areas off Antarctica and Greenland, to small reserves around small islands.

The International Union for the Conservation of Nature (IUCN) describes protected regions as distinct geographical areas that are acknowledged and maintained, either through legal provisions or other reliable methods, to ensure the enduring preservation of natural environments along with the ecosystem services and cultural significance they provide.

On what criteria could we decide whether activities are morally justifiable?

TOK

Many developed countries have polluted the environment in return for the economic benefits they gain (e.g., energy production). Many of the costs of this pollution, such as ocean acidification and marine pollution, are borne by other countries – is this moral?

There are many types of MPA:

- completely marine MPAs with no significant land masses
- MPAs including both marine and terrestrial areas
- MPAs that are mainly terrestrial/tidal, e.g. mangrove swamps.

There are many pressures on MPAs including global climate change, ocean acidification, marine pollution and extractive industries including fishing and oil/gas exploration and development. In many cases, MPAs will try to restrict unsustainable developments. For MPAs that are located entirely within one country's territorial waters, it is easier to enforce environmental legislation. Over 40% of Australia's MPAs are in its territorial waters. Some activities, notably fishing, may be restricted seasonally to protect spawning grounds. Some MPAs are multiple use and may have different levels of protections, such as a central preservation area surrounded by a buffer zone with lesser protection.

Example – The Queensland Coast, Australia

One of the main attractions for tourists in Australia is the Great Barrier Reef. The Reef extends for over 2000 km and covers an area of 343,800 km sq (Figure 4.58). It consists of over 2900 reefs and is the world's largest living structure. It is also the most used marine park in the world.

The Great Barrier Reef contains 1500 species of fish, 400 species of coral and 4000 species of mollusk. It is a major feeding ground for many endangered species and is a nesting ground for many species of turtle. It was placed on the World Heritage List in 1981.

The Reef is heavily managed but before it was managed it was used for tourism, agriculture and recreational and commercial fishing. Each year 77,000 tonnes of nitrogen, 11,000 tonnes of phosphorus and 15 million tonnes of sediment are washed into the coastal waters from Queensland, largely as a result of agricultural activity.

The Great Barrier Reef Marine Park Authority is responsible for the management and development of the reef and follows the Agenda 21 philosophy, namely that resources must be used and managed in such a way that they are not destroyed or devalued for future generations.

The main type of management is that of land use zoning (Figure 4.58). This means that some areas can be used for some activities, such as recreation or fishing, whereas others are used for other activities, such as conservation. The main aims of zoning are to:

- ensure permanent conservation of the area
- provide protection and shelter for selected species and ecosystems
- provide spawning grounds
- separate conflicting activities
- preserve some untouched areas
- allow human use of the reef as well as protecting the reef.

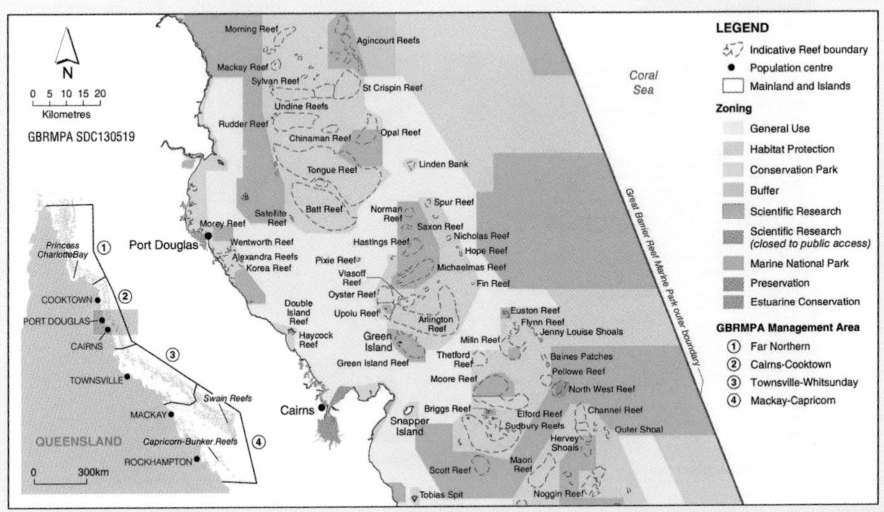

Figure 4.58 Land-use zoning along the Great Barrier Reef.

Activity

Visit the Great Barrier Reef Marine Park website and find out more about the issues and management concerning the Great Barrier Reef.

Discuss the issues with a partner and then make a presentation to the class.

4.3.10 Aquaculture

4.4 Water pollution

HL b Environmental economics
HL c Environmental ethics

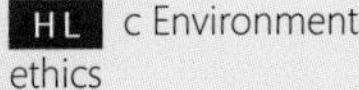

The aquaculture industry is expanding to increase food supplies and support economic development, but there are associated environmental impacts to be considered including the loss of habitat, pollution from feed, anti-fouling agents, antibiotics and other medicines used, spread of diseases and escapees that may be genetically modified. Management techniques can reduce the effect of negative impacts.

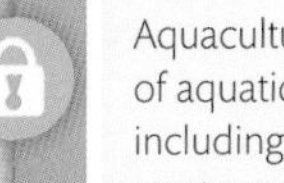

Aquaculture is the farming of aquatic organisms, including fish, mollusks, crustaceans and aquatic plants.

Aquaculture involves raising fish commercially, usually for food (Figure 4.59). In contrast, a fish hatchery releases juvenile fish into the wild for recreational fishing or to supplement a species' natural numbers. The most important fish species raised by fish farms are salmon, carp, tilapia, catfish and cod. Salmon makes up 85% of the total sale of Norwegian fish farming. Farming was introduced when populations of wild Atlantic salmon in the North Atlantic and Baltic seas crashed due to overfishing.

Figure 4.59 A Brunei fish farm.

Between 2010 and 2019, the world food fish production of aquaculture grew by, on average, 5.5% per annum (Table 4.13). World aquaculture production in 2020 was estimated at 122 million tonnes and worth over US$ 280 billion.

Table 4.13 Changes in global aquaculture by production and value, 2010–2019.

	2010	2011	2012	2013	2014	2015	2016	2017	2018	2019
Total/million tonnes	77.9	81.6	88.1	94.9	99.6	103.8	108.1	112.1	115.7	120.0
Value/US$ millions	140.0	163.8	180.6	203.3	222.1	217.2	235.2	251.0	262.1	274.3

Aquaculture production is vulnerable to adverse impacts of disease and environmental conditions. Disease outbreaks in recent years have affected farmed Atlantic salmon in Chile, oysters in Europe and marine shrimp farming in several countries in Asia, South America and Africa. However, growth in aquaculture has been seen in all regions except Africa. Most rapid growth has been in Chile, China and Norway.

Characteristics of aquaculture

Technological costs in aquaculture are high, including the use of drugs such as antibiotics to keep fish healthy and steroids to improve their growth. Breeding programmes are also expensive. But efficiency and outputs per hectare and per farmer are high.

Environmental effects can be damaging. Salmon are carnivores and are fed pellets made from other fish. It is possible that farmed salmon represent a net loss of protein in the global food supply because it takes 2–5 kg of wild fish to feed 1 kg of salmon. In contrast, most global aquaculture production (about 85%) uses non-carnivorous fish species, such as tilapia and catfish, for domestic markets. Fish like herring, mackerel, sardines and anchovy are used to produce the feed for farmed salmon and so the production of salmon leads to the depletion of other fish species on a global scale.

Other environmental costs include the sea lice and disease that spread from farmed salmon into wild stocks and pollution (created by uneaten food, faeces and chemicals used to treat the lice) contaminating the surrounding waters. Organic debris of this type, along with steroids and other chemical waste, can contaminate coastal waters. Marine aquaculture requires energy for service vessels, while freshwater aquaculture uses electricity for feed and water circulation.

The accidental escape of fish can affect local wild fish gene pools if they breed with individuals in the wild populations. This reduces genetic diversity and potentially introduces non-natural genetic variation. In some parts of the world, escapees of farmed fish threaten native wild fish because they are alien species. For example, the British Columbia salmon farming industry has inadvertently introduced a non-native species, Atlantic salmon, into the Pacific ocean.

The positive environmental benefits of not removing fish from wild stocks, but instead breeding them in farms, are great. Wild populations are allowed to breed and maintain stocks, while the farmed variety provides food.

Aquaculture produces a nutritious, healthy protein source, as well as vitamin D and omega-3 fatty acids. It can take place in a small area, unlike some large-scale farming systems. It also uses less water than conventional farming. Outputs/ha and efficiency are also high. However, it destroys natural habitats and technology costs are high, for example, the cost of antibiotics, steroids and drugs. Breeding programmes can be expensive, too. Aquaculture can lead to environmental damage, for example, the spread of disease from farmed fish to wild fish or the escape of farmed (genetically modified) fish, which can affect the local gene pool. It also takes a large amount of fish to produce the feed for farmed fish. Energy costs, for example for farmed salmon, can be high.

Strategies used to minimize the negative impacts of aquaculture include:

- moving the fish into deeper water
- only locating the farms in areas that are well-oxygenated
- reducing the size of fish stocks and fish density
- reducing food waste.

Activity

Using Table 4.13, calculate the percentage increase in size, in million tonnes, and value, in US$, in global aquaculture between 2010 and 2019.

HL

4.3.11 Productivity, thermal stratification, nutrient mixing and nutrient loading

1.2 Systems
2.3 Biogeochemical cycles

Rates of productivity are higher in shallow areas, where sunlight can penetrate to the seabed, and in areas where there are more nutrients, such as estuaries and where there are upwelling currents. Some coastal areas may also benefit from nutrients carried offshore by rivers and overland flow. Variations in productivity can also be seen in some lake systems.

The highest productivity tends to occur near coastlines or in shallow seas, where upwellings and nutrient enrichment of surface waters occurs.

Ocean productivity largely refers to the production of organic matter by phytoplankton. Phytoplankton are photoautotrophs, converting sunlit energy into food energy (Topic 2, Section 2.2.22).

Sunlight is the main energy resource for almost all life on Earth, including that found in the deep ocean. However, in the ocean, light is absorbed and scattered, so very little of it penetrates below a depth of about 80 m. Penetration can occur at depths of up to about 150 m in the least productive subtropical regions and as shallow as 10 m in highly productive coastal regions (Figure 4.60). Hence, photosynthesis is largely restricted to the upper light-penetrated layer of the ocean (the photic zone).

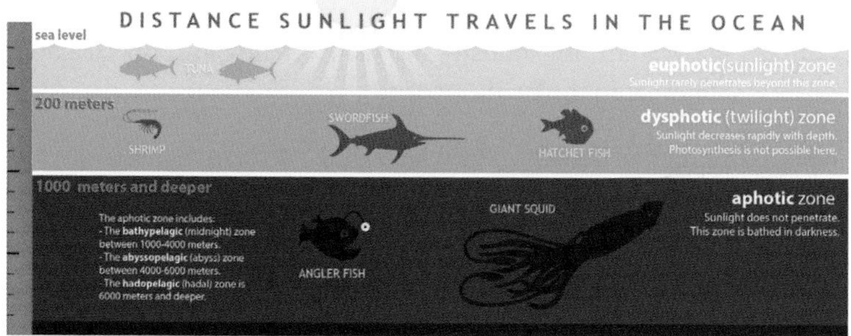

Figure 4.60 Variation in temperature, nutrient availability, chlorophyll and organic carbon with depth.

In low- and mid-latitude oceans, the absorption of sunlight causes surface water to be much warmer and less dense than water in the deep ocean. Warm water is more buoyant than cold, which causes the upper sunlit layer to float on the denser deeper ocean water. The transition between the two is known as the thermocline (this topic, Sections 4.1.13 and 4.1.14). Winds may mix water across the thermocline, thus some water from the photic zone may transfer some nutrients to the deep ocean. This combined effect of light on photosynthesis and seawater density is critical for the success of ocean phytoplankton.

The deep chlorophyll maximum (DCM) occurs where there is adequate light for photosynthesis and significant nutrient supply from below (Figure 4.60).

The existence of a thin buoyant surface leads to nutrient limitation on ocean productivity. Dead organic matter sinks to the ocean floor taking with it surface nutrients, causing the nutrients to accumulate in deep waters where there is no light available for photosynthesis. Due to differences in the density between surface water and the deep seawater, dissolved nutrients can only be returned to the surface very slowly or where there are upwelling currents. By driving nutrients out of the sunlit, buoyant surface waters, ocean productivity limits itself.

Geographic and seasonal variations in productivity

Satellites can record the colour of the ocean surface to track the concentration of chlorophyll used in photosynthesis (Figure 4.61). Higher chlorophyll concentrations and higher productivity are found towards the Equator, near coastlines. This is especially true in the eastern margins where the wind pushes aside the buoyant, warm surface water and allows nutrient-rich deeper water to be upwelled and in the high latitude oceans. The main causes of higher productivity are upwelling currents and/or mixing of high nutrient subsurface water into the euphotic zone.

In the unproductive low- and mid-latitude ocean, warm and sunlit surface water is separated from denser, cold, nutrient-rich water due to the strong difference in density that limits mixing of water and so reduces nutrient supply. This limits the potential for productivity in surface waters. In the high latitude ocean, surface water is cold and therefore sinks, causing vertical mixing of water to depths much greater than the euphotic zone. This means that the nutrient supply is greater than the phytoplankton can consume, given the available light.

Seasonality in productivity is greatest at high latitudes, driven by the availability of light (Figure 4.61). The areal intensity (intensity of sunlight over a given area) and daily duration of sunlight are much greater in summer, allowing for increased photosynthesis.

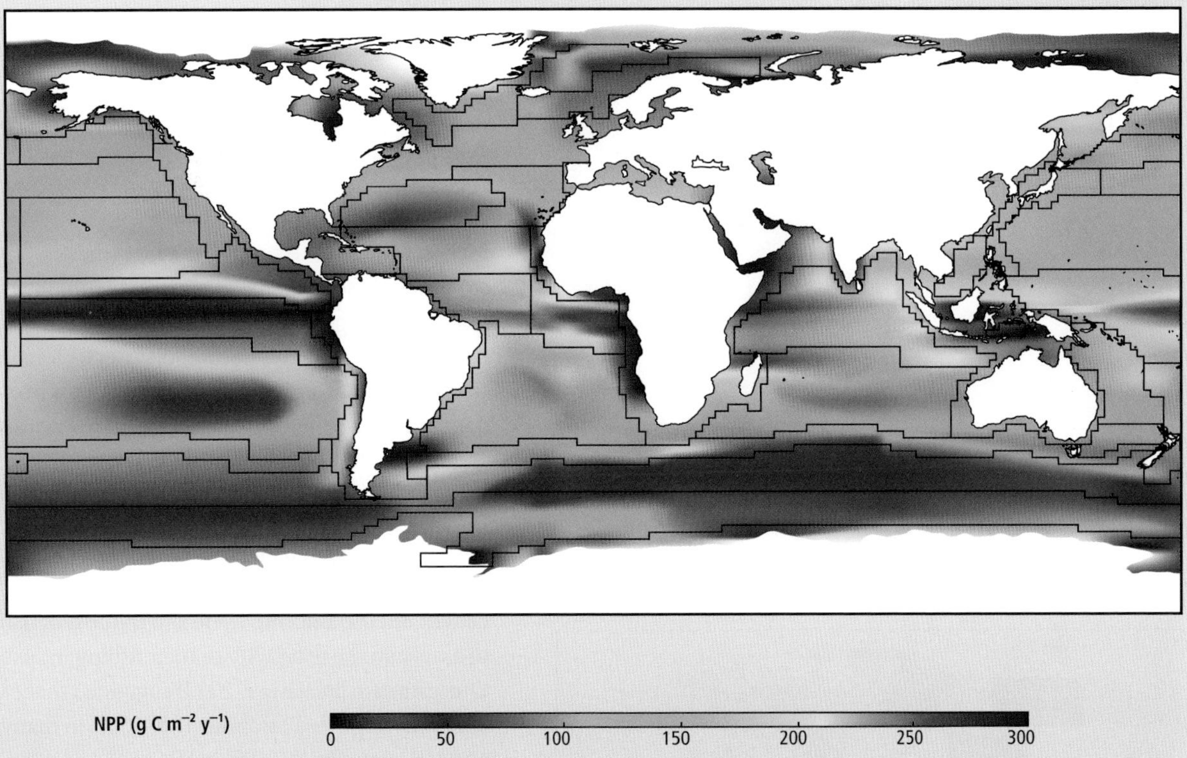

Figure 4.61 Geographic variations in Net Primary Production (NPP).

4.3.12 Assessment of fish stocks and monitoring of harvest rates

Accurate assessment of fish stocks and monitoring of harvest rates are required for their conservation and sustainable use.

2.2 Energy and biomass in ecosystems

HL b Environmental economics
HL c Environmental ethics

Scientists collect several types of data to estimate the size and health of fish populations being exploited including:

- The age and size of the fish populations being caught. Catch data is one of the most widely used methods and includes the weight and species caught by commercial and recreational fisherfolk, which can then be used to estimate the size and distribution of the fish population.
- The results of scientific surveys carried out from research vessels.
- Information from tag and recapture surveys.

Harvest rates can be monitored through the study of fish logbooks. Logbooks have data on the size of the catch, the species caught, the equipment used and area where the fish were caught. Data from UK vessels has to be handed in within 48 hours of landing at a port. This allows government officials to monitor harvest rates over time. However, it does not monitor illegal fishing.

In 1996, the FAO introduced the 'stock status plot' (Figure 4.62). For about 400 well-studied fisheries, researchers analysed long-term trends in catches and assigned different terms, such as 'developing' where catches were increasing and 'senescent' (ageing) where

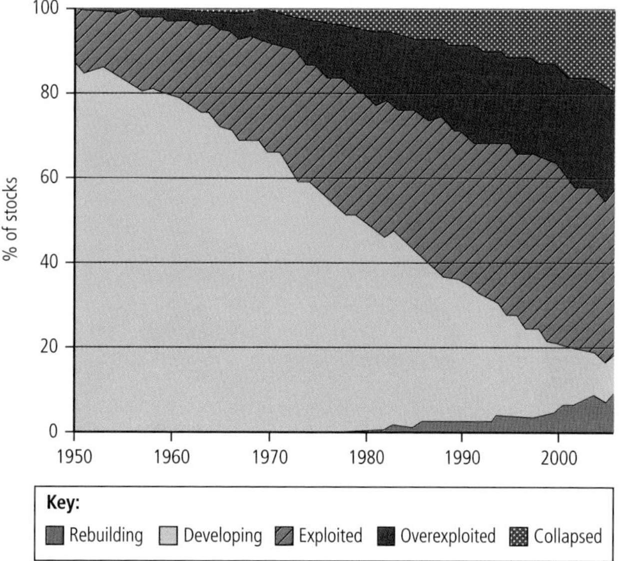

Figure 4.62 The FAO's stock status plot.

the catch had collapsed. The FAO found that the number of collapsed stocks had steadily increased over time and by the mid-1990s, 20% of the stocks exploited in the 1950s had collapsed.

It is very difficult to predict the future size of fish stocks because many factors affect fishing, such as changes in government policy, rising energy costs, market crashes, natural disasters, global warming, ocean acidification and changes in demand. Nevertheless, catch data are important for estimating the size and health of fish stocks.

However, expert stock assessments can be very costly, especially if using research vessels. National governments could collect data on the number of fish caught, their economic value and the cost of fishing to ascertain the feasibility of their fishing industry. One estimate (in Nature, 2013) suggested that catches are under-reported by about 100–500% in many LICs and MICs, and by 30–50% in HICs.

On the other hand, the number of fish caught does not necessarily reflect the number of fish in the ocean. By the mid-2000s, 14% of the 166 stocks analysed had collapsed (Figure 4.63 Canary rockfish). In many cases, when fishing restrictions were introduced, stocks began to stabilize or even rebuild (Figure 4.66 Rougheye rockfish). Along the east coast of the USA, the abundance of haddock and redfish increased more than five-fold between 1995 and 2007 due to stricter fishing regulations.

Smaller catches compared to previous larger catches does not necessarily mean that there are fewer fish. For example, 34 fish stocks on the west coast of the USA would appear to have collapsed based on falling catches, whereas only three had actually collapsed (anchovies, candlefish and abalone). Instead, catches fell due to changes in markets and new fishing regulations. Catches of sharks may appear to have fallen, partly because the sharks have been reclassified into new groups.

Catch data can also be affected by changes in the size of exclusive economic zones, disasters such as oil spills, increased fuel costs and low fish prices. Most countries only monitor their largest or most economically important fisheries.

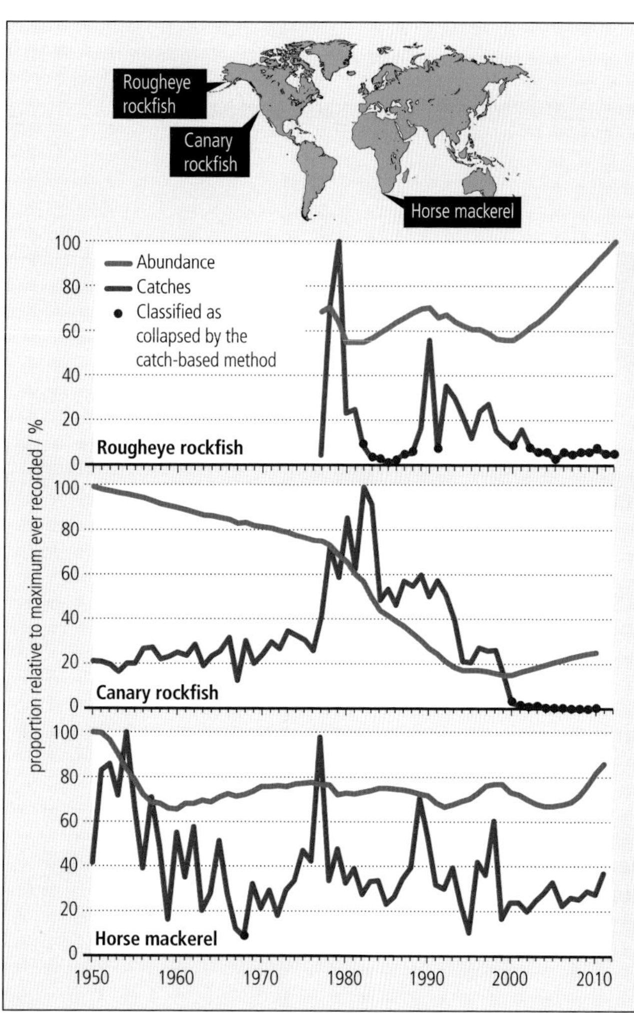

Figure 4.63 Changes in fish catches and abundance.

Activity

Visit the Pew Trust website and use the search function to investigate issues and examples related to fishing.

With a partner, design and create a leaflet about the issues, and make a presentation to the class.

4.3.13 Risks of fishing at the MSY

1.3 Sustainability

2.2 Energy and biomass in ecosystems

HL b Environmental economics

HL c Environmental ethics

There are risks in harvesting fish at MSY levels and these risks need to be managed carefully. MSY is only an estimated value and attempting to harvest at exactly that rate will inevitably be inaccurate. Exceeding the rate may lead to reduction in reproductive potential and positive feedback causing rapid decline in fish stocks.

MSY is the largest annual harvest that a fish stock can produce on a long-term scale (Figure 4.64). It is a harvesting model that can be used to calculate how much fish can be taken from a stock without depleting it. However, it is very difficult to calculate MSY because it is affected by several factors. At best, it should be seen as an estimate.

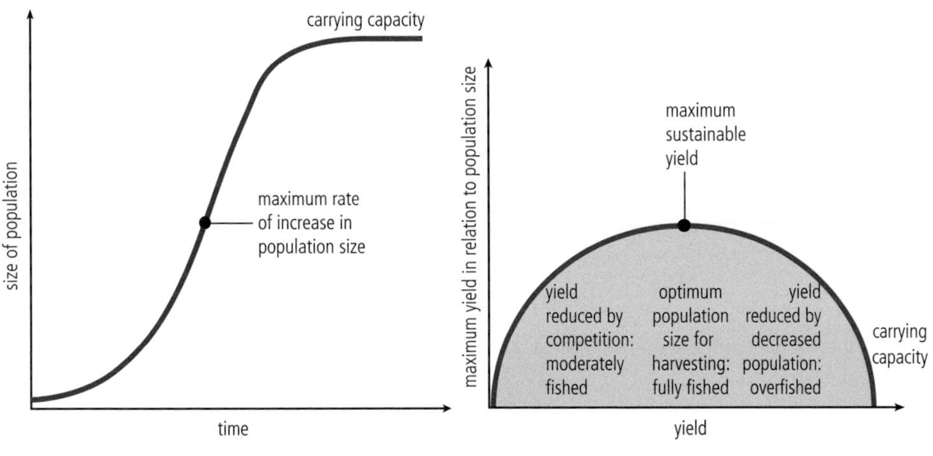

Figure 4.64 Maximum sustainable yield.

Biomass refers to the total weight of a stock. It varies with growth, reproduction and mortality. Some species, such as cod, grow quickly whereas others, such as herring, grow slowly. Some species, such as cod and herring, produce many offspring each year, whereas others, such as sharks, do not. Some species, such as sand eels, are short-lived and highly reproductive, while others, such as cod, have a more stable stock size. For fished populations, the number of fish that are caught (or killed by fishing activities) affects the size of the total biomass of the stock. As large numbers of fish are removed from the population, the reproductive potential decreases and eventually the population decreases in size.

The calculation of MSY for a single fish stock must consider many factors:

- how quickly the fish grow
- when the fish reproduce
- the death rate of the fish
- changes in abiotic factors such as water temperature, salinity, oxygen or acidification
- changes in biotic factors such as predator-prey relationships and parasites
- the method of fishing used.

According to Peter Larkin (1977) in *An epitaph for the concept of maximum sustainable yield*, MSY puts populations at risk because it:

- does not consider spatial variations in productivity
- does not consider non-target species
- only considers the benefits of fishing and ignores the costs
- is open to political manipulation.

In addition, MSY tends to assume that all individuals in a population are identical.

Calculations of MSY involve the assumption that the annual harvest will be the same year after year. However, this is not always the case as harvests are dynamic and experience natural fluctuations and changes due to anthropogenic activities. Consequently, some scientists interpret MSY as a maximum average yield that can also show fluctuations.

An example of the misunderstanding of fish stocks involves the Orange roughy fishery in New Zealand. It was believed that Orange roughy had a short lifespan but bred quickly and so it was fished widely. It was later found that Orange roughys lived lengthy lives (about 30 years) and bred slowly. The stocks were largely depleted.

In many parts of the world, such as the northwest Atlantic, the North Sea and in Peru's anchovy industry and whale fisheries, overfishing has devastated large fish stocks. As fishing depletes the oceans of large, long-lived predators, such as cod and tuna, fishing fleets move down the food chain to fish for smaller, shorter-lived species that are of less economic value.

Critics argue that fishing according to the principles of MSY is difficult in practice. Estimates of MSY may be based on unreliable data. For example, biologists may have insufficient data to accurately estimate population size and/or growth rates

4.3.14 Recovery of overexploited fish species

1.3 Sustainability

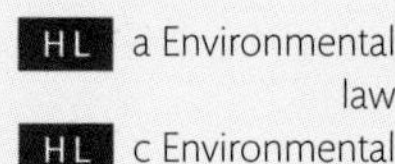

a Environmental law

c Environmental ethics

There are many stakeholders in the fishing industry including governments, consumers, non-governmental organizations (NGOs) and retailers such as fish markets and supermarkets.

Governments are generally keen to keep people employed in the fishing industry, as it makes money for the country, may provide tax revenues and keeps people employed. Therefore, maintaining a healthy and sizeable fish population is in their best interests. Similarly, the fishing industry would prefer a large fish population.

However, many in the industry are out to make a profit and so will try to maximize their catch sizes. If the catch size goes down, they will often move to other fishing grounds, including overseas.

Consumers generally want fish to be available in the shops and markets at affordable prices. This will encourage large-scale fishing as this can keep prices low. It may also encourage aquaculture, especially species such as salmon.

NGOs, especially environmental NGOs, are more likely to want to protect fish stocks and to keep fishing to within sustainable limits. They may also call for bans on certain fishing practices such as the fishing of young fish or endangered species.

Retailers require a secure and sufficient supply of fish so they can continue to sell them throughout the year. They also want fish to be available at affordable prices.

Differences are generally managed, if at all, through discussions and negotiations. There can also be bans on certain species being fished and on when fishing can take place. Certain areas may be closed to fishing vessels either seasonally or permanently. Fines can be given to vessels that break the law.

Species that have been overexploited may recover with cooperation between governments, the fishing industry, consumers and other interest groups, including NGOs, wholesale fishery markets and local supermarkets. Measures that help to restore stocks include temporary fishing bans, limits to fishing licenses, prevention of by-catch and information being provided to help consumers choose species that are not being harvested unsustainably.

In many areas around the world, fish species are overexploited and their numbers are in decline. When a fish stock becomes overfished, some agency must develop a plan to rebuild the stock to a sustainable level. Interested organizations can include national governments, the fishing industry, researchers (scientists), retailers, consumers, environmental organizations and individuals. Many of these have differing interests such as increasing employment, making a profit from fishing, providing a food supply, having access to a varied and healthy diet, and maintaining a healthy ecosystem.

Typically, the process of fish stock rebuilding requires a reduction in fishing so that populations can reach their target level or MSY. When the numbers have first increased to the overfished level, the fish is removed from the overfished list. However, it remains on the rebuilding list until it has reached its target population. In 2021 in the USA there were 45 fish stocks with rebuilding plans, but only six were no longer overfished.

Example – Skagerrak lobster reserves

In Skagerrak, south-east Norway, in the early 2000s, numbers of the European lobster reached an all-time low at about 10% of the historical maximum. Skagerrak was once characterized by very productive fish and shellfish stocks, but these had become depleted. In 2006, Norway's first lobster reserves were created, with the aim of restoring the population through a ban on fixed gear. Before and after surveys of the lobster population were carried out to investigate the impacts of protection on the depleted population. The capture-release-recapture method was used to measure changes in the size of lobsters and to track their movements. Additional surveys were carried out to see the effects of the lobster reserves, and of the ban on fixed gear, on other fish species such as cod, trout and wrasse.

The results showed an increase in population density, abundance, body size and emigration into surrounding fisheries. The survival rate of large lobsters was noted, and there was a re-building of the age- and size-structure of the lobster population. Body-size increased by about 13% in the protected areas compared with control sites (Figure 4.65). There was also a significant rebuilding of the size-structure of the cod population within the protected areas. After the initial six years of protection, about 5% of lobsters had migrated from protected sites into surrounding areas. Increasingly, cod populations were emigrating from protected areas. After 16 years of protection, the reduced harvest pressure had had a number of positive effects on many fish populations.

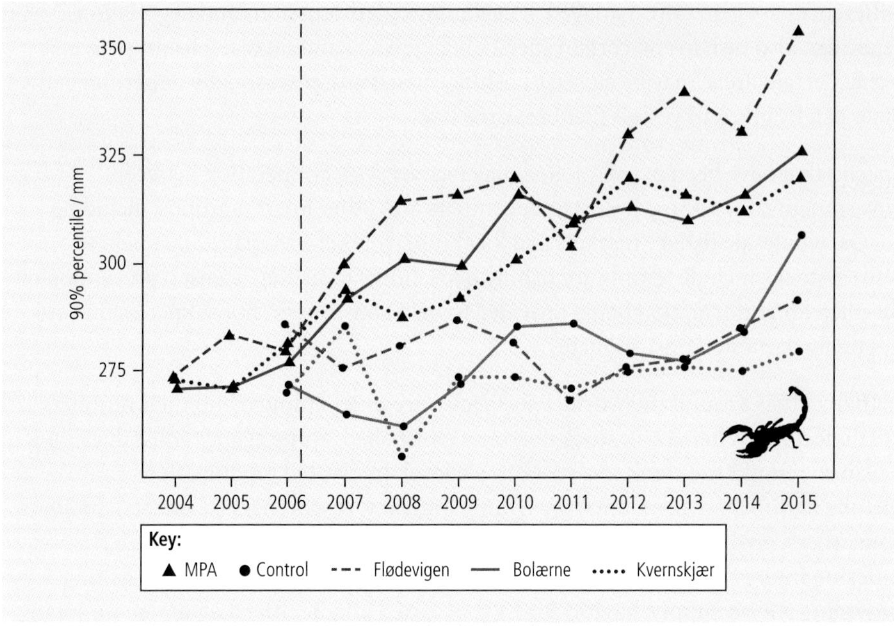

Figure 4.65 Changes in the size-structure of European lobsters (*Homarus gammarus*) in three reserves in Norway.

4.3.15 Exclusive economic zones

HL a Environmental law
HL c Environmental ethics

According to the UN Convention on the Law of the Sea (UNCLOS), coastal states have an exclusive economic zone stretching 370 km out to sea, within which the state's government can regulate fishing. Almost 60% of the ocean is the high seas outside these coastal zones, with limited inter-governmental regulation. There is an equity and justice issue when countries sell access to their fishing zones rather than managing it for local people. The UN is attempting to develop an international treaty to protect the high seas.

Sovereign country – a country/nation whose government has authority over its population and territory.

An exclusive economic zone (EEZ) is an area of the sea in which a sovereign country has special rights for exploration and the use of marine resources, such as fish, minerals and energy resources. It stretches from the outer limit of territorial waters at 12 nautical miles (NM) (roughly 22.2 km) to 200 NM (roughly 370 km) from the coast baseline (Figure 4.66).

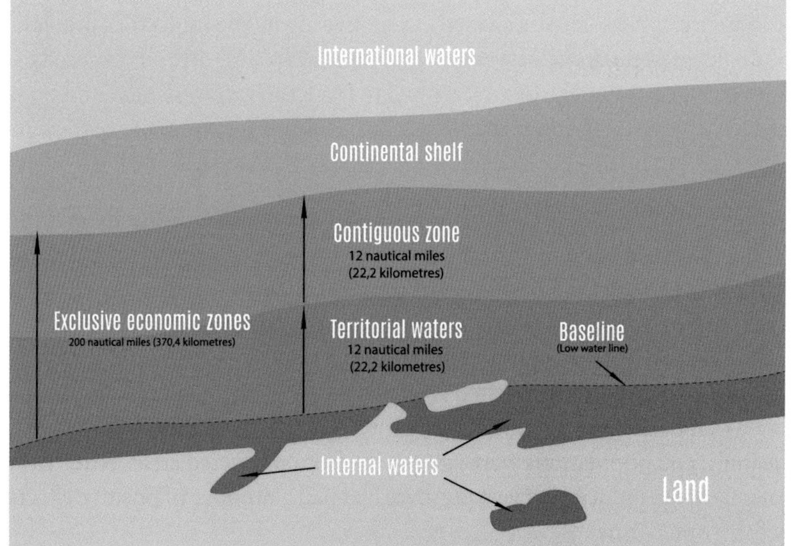

Figure 4.66 Exclusive economic zone.

In the territorial sea, a country has full sovereign rights over the waters. In an exclusive economic zone, the country has rights below the ocean surface. Where there are overlapping claims on the ocean, any point in the overlapping zone should be within the EEZ of the nearest country. The contiguous zone forms the outer edge of the territorial waters, i.e., between 12 NM and 24 NM from the coastline. In contrast, the open oceans or high seas fall outside of sovereignty issues and, as a common resource, can be overexploited without much regulation.

TOK

As knowers, do we have a moral duty to examine our own assumptions and biases?

How can the unregulated exploitation of a common resource, such as the open ocean, be just and/or equal?

Initially EEZs only extended for 3 NM but in 1982 the UN Convention on the Law of the Sea declared that EEZs should extend for 200 NM.

There have been a number of disputes, both past and present, over access to resources in what are now EEZs. For example, in 1952 Iceland extended its fishing zone to 3–4 NM, in 1958 to 12 NM and in 1976 to 200 NM. Other countries needed Iceland's permission to fish in its waters. There were conflicts known as the 'cod wars' between Iceland and the UK over the fishing rights in 1958–1961, 1972–1973 and 1975–1976. In each case, Iceland won the dispute. An agreement in Iceland's favour was finally reached in 1976.

As of 2023, current disputes include a section of the Beaufort Sea, which is disputed by Canada and USA. The area potentially has large reserves of oil.

A survey of fishing practices in EEZs found that fleet sizes were only quantified and regulated in 20% of the world's EEZs. Controls on fleet size were more common among high-income than low-income EEZs. Access to foreign fishing is granted in over 50% of all EEZs and is more frequent in low-income than in high-income EEZs. The survey suggested that in 33% of the EEZs that are classified as low income (mostly in Africa and Oceania), most fishing is carried out by foreign fleets from either the European Union, South Korea, Japan, China or the USA.

4.3.16 Animal rights and Indigenous hunters

HL

The harvesting of some species, such as seals, sharks and whales, is controversial. There are ethical issues regarding bio rights – the rights of an endangered species, a unique species, or a landscape to remain unmolested. The rights of Indigenous culture and international conservation legislation should also be considered.

1.1 Perspectives
1.3 Sustainability

HL c Environmental ethics

The harvesting of some species, such as seals, sharks and whales, is controversial. Ethical issues arise over bio rights, rights of Indigenous cultures and international conservation legislation.

In the late 1930s, more than 50,000 whales were killed annually. The International Whaling Commission (IWC) was set up to decide on hunting quotas based on the findings of its Scientific Committee. In 1982, the IWC voted to establish a ban on commercial whaling, which took effect in 1986. Japan wants to lift the ban on stocks that have recovered. However, anti-whaling countries and environmental groups believe that whale species remain vulnerable, and that whaling is both immoral and unsustainable.

According to the IWC, Indigenous subsistence whaling occurs in Greenland (involving the fin, bowhead, humpback and minke whales), in Siberia, (involving the grey and bowhead whales), St Vincent and The Grenadines (involving the humpback whales) and North America (involving the bowhead and grey whales).

Example – Inuit whaling

Narwhal hunting

Around 120,000 narwhals are found in Arctic waters, mostly around Greenland and Canada.

To what extent is our perspective determined by our membership of a particular culture?

TOK

The Inuit people have an historical tradition of whaling. To what extent does our culture determine or shape our ethical judgments? Can the practices of one culture be judged with any validity by applying the moral values of another culture?

Narwhals provide cultural and nutritional importance to communities on the east coast. Narwhal meat remains a vital source of nutrients and income and can fetch over US$ 70 per kilo.

In 2004, Greenland's government introduced quotas for hunting narwhal and banned the export of their tusks. However, despite these hunting restrictions, populations are plummeting. In east Greenland there were about 1900 narwhals in 2008, but in 2016 this number decreased to 400. The Greenland Institute of Natural Resources has warned that narwhals are at considerable risk of extinction in east Greenland and has advised a ban on hunting.

The government implemented a gradual reduction in quotas – from 50 narwhals a year in 2020 to 20 in 2023. Some scientists claim that without a ban on hunting, there is a 30% risk that narwhals will become extinct in east Greenland by 2025, rising to 74% risk by 2028.

Bowheads

The Inuit hunt a variety of animals for meat – including caribou, walrus seal and geese – depending on the season and the migratory movements of the species.

North American whaling is carried out by small numbers of the Inuit population. The only species hunted is the bowhead whale. Whaling is a central part of Inuit culture and provides a vital source of protein in their diet. The 10,000 Inuit in Alaska are allowed to kill a total of up to 40–70 bowhead whales annually. This represents about half of the meat in the Inuit diet. Scientific research suggests that the bowhead whales are not an endangered species and hunting them is sustainable. But conservationists take a very different view and state that whales have bio rights and should not be killed, especially in such a way that causes them great pain and suffering.

Another whaling example is available on this page of your eBook.

In Greenland, Inuit whalers catch around 175 whales per year, making them the third largest whale hunters in the world after Japan and Norway, which annually averaged around 730 and 590 whales, respectively, from 1998 to 2007. The IWC allows the more densely populated west coast to take over 90% of the catch. In a typical year, around 150 minke and 10 fin whales are taken from west coast waters and around 10 minke whales are taken from east coast waters.

In some places, whale hunting has been replaced by whale watching.

Example – Faroe Islanders capturing whales and dolphins

The Faroe Islanders hunt up to about 800 long-finned pilot whales annually, which they catch mainly in summer. Other fish and mammals, notably dolphins, may also get caught up as by-catch. For the Islanders, whaling is part of their tradition and culture but animal rights groups believe it to be barbaric.

Whole groups of dolphins, including entire families, are herded to the shore and killed in a bloody, painful and lengthy death process (Figure 4.67). The annual hunt, called 'grindadrap', was initially a subsistence form of hunting but recently some of the dolphin and whale meat has been sold commercially.

Ironically, eating whale and dolphin meat is a health hazard due to the large amount of mercury and persistent organic compounds in their meat and blubber.

Figure 4.67 Part of the annual slaughter of dolphins.

Activity

Visit the Islands and the Whales website to find out more about the lifestyle of the Faroe Islanders.

Produce a report about the Faroe Islanders' lifestyle and present this to your class.

Exercise

Q21. Outline the reasons why phytoplankton are important.

Q22. Describe how the type of plankton varies with levels of nutrients.

Q23. Describe the changes in the production of fishing and aquaculture between 1990 and 2020.

Q24. Suggest reasons for the decline in the Grand Banks cod population.

Q25. Distinguish between territorial waters and EEZs.

HL

Q26. HL **Explain** how the use of quotas and total allowable catches can be used to make fisheries more sustainable.

Q27. HL **Suggest** why the maximum sustainable yield may have limitations.

Q28. HL **Suggest** reasons why many fishing fleets from HICs fish in the EEZs of LICs.

Q29. HL **Define** the meaning of the term *bio rights*.

Q30. HL Should Indigenous populations be allowed to hunt the number of whales they do annually? To what extent are the modern versions of 'grindadrap' to be considered just and equitable?

HL end

Engagement

- Explore the role of marine protected areas in conserving ocean biodiversity and the approaches taken by a regional or national government. Produce a one-page summary of what you find.
- Raise awareness about the loss of access to local fishing due to the international sale of fishing rights. Make a poster illustrating the issue. Raise awareness at a school assembly or in another way of your choice.
- Host a film show highlighting the tensions around the consumption of fish.
- Raise awareness around marine certification programs for fish consumption. You could, for example, place leaflets in the school dining halls, or on a classroom wall/noticeboard.
- Choose an NGO that has an interest in fishing. Using their website, find the contact details for the NGO and write an email to call for changes that could alleviate environmental challenges around aquaculture.

4.4 Water pollution

Guiding questions

How does pollution affect the sustainability of environmental systems?
How do different perspectives affect how pollution is managed?

4.4.1 Water pollution has multiple sources and major impacts on marine and freshwater systems.
4.4.2 Plastic debris is accumulating in marine environments. Management is needed to remove plastics from the supply chain and to clear up existing pollution.
4.4.3 Water quality is the measurement of chemical, physical and biological characteristics of water. Water quality is variable and is often measured using a water quality index. Monitoring water quality can inform management strategies for reducing water pollution.
4.4.4 Biochemical oxygen demand (BOD) is a measure of the amount of dissolved oxygen required by microorganisms to decompose organic material in water.
4.4.5 Eutrophication occurs when lakes, estuaries and coastal waters receive inputs of mineral nutrients, especially nitrates and phosphates, often causing excessive growth of phytoplankton.
4.4.6 Eutrophication leads to a sequence of impacts and changes to the aquatic system.
4.4.7 Eutrophication can substantially impact ecosystem services.
4.4.8 Eutrophication can be addressed at three different levels of management.
HL 4.4.9 There is a wide range of pollutants that can be found in water.
HL 4.4.10 Algal blooms may produce toxins that threaten the health of humans and other animals.
HL 4.4.11 The frequency of anoxic/hypoxic waters is likely to increase due to the combined effects of global warming, freshwater stratification, sewage disposal and eutrophication.
HL 4.4.12 Sewage is treated to allow safe release of effluent by primary, secondary and tertiary water treatment stages.
HL 4.4.13 Some species are sensitive to pollutants or are adapted to polluted waters, so these can be used as indicator species.
HL 4.4.14 A biotic index can provide an indirect measure of water quality based on the tolerance to pollution, relative abundance and diversity of species in the community.
HL 4.4.15 Overall water quality can be assessed by calculating a water quality index (WQI).
HL 4.4.16 Drinking water quality guidelines have been set by the World Health Organization (WHO), and local governments can set statutory standards.
HL 4.4.17 Action by individuals or groups of citizens can help to reduce water pollution.

4.4.1 Water pollution

Water pollution has multiple sources including sewage, agricultural run-off, industrial effluent, urban run-off, solid waste disposal and oil spills. These can all have major impacts on marine and freshwater systems (Figure 4.68).

Figure 4.68 A polluted stream.

Freshwater and marine pollution sources include run-off, sewage, industrial discharge, solid domestic waste, transport, waste from recreation and tourism, and energy waste. Sources of marine pollution also include rivers, pipelines, atmosphere, oil spills, deliberate and accidental discharges from ships, sewage from cruise ships, aquaculture farms, power stations and industry.

Storm water that washes off roads and roofs can be a more significant source of pollutants than sewage. Such water may contain high levels of heavy metals, volatile solids and organic chemicals. Studies of water quality during floods of the Silk Stream in London recorded that between 20–40% of storm water sediments were organic and mostly biodegradable. Highway run-off has a concentration of heavy metals that is five to six times that of roof run-off. Annual run-off from 1 km of a single carriageway of the M1 (a highway in the UK) included 1.5 tonnes of suspended sediment, 4 kg of lead, 126 kg of oil and 18 g of hazardous polynuclear aromatic hydrocarbons.

HL a Environmental law
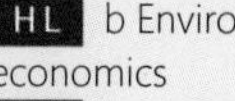
HL b Environmental economics
HL c Environmental ethics

There are a variety of freshwater and marine pollution sources including sewage, agricultural run-off, industrial effluent, urban run-off, solid waste disposal and oil spills.

Types of aquatic pollutant include floating debris, organic material, inorganic plant nutrients (nitrates and phosphates), toxic metals, synthetic compounds, suspended solids, hot water, oil, radioactive pollution, pathogens, light, noise and biological entities (invasive species).

Example – Water pollution in the Flint River, Flint, Michigan, USA

The Flint River flows through the center of the town of Flint in Michigan, USA. For over a century, the Flint River has been used as an unofficial waste disposal site for refuse from local industries, car factories, meat packaging firms and paper mills. The river also received waste from agricultural run-off, raw sewage from the city's water treatment plant, toxins from leaching landfills and urban run-off. There are also claims that it caught fire on two occasions.

As the industries boomed, so did Flint. Home to car manufacturer General Motors, Flint's population reached about 200,000. However, in the 1980s, rising oil prices and the financial crisis led to massive decreases in the working population. Flint's population crashed to 100,000 inhabitants, with about 45% of the population living in poverty. About one in six homes were abandoned.

In 2011, Flint was in a desperate state economically, with debts of over US$ 25 million. City governors made the decision to stop piping treated water from Detroit and to use a cheaper alternative, namely water from the Flint River. The water from the Flint River was highly corrosive and contained lead that had leached out of ageing pipes in thousands of homes (Figure 4.69). The change of water supply occurred in 2014 and residents complained of foul-smelling, discoloured and poorly tasting water. This went on for 18 months. Later studies revealed that contaminated water was contributing to raised levels of lead in the blood of about 9000 children. Samples from over 250 homes found that about 17% of the samples had levels of over 15 parts per billion (ppb) lead (the state 'action level') and that over 40% were above 5 ppb, indicating a 'very serious problem'. The highest level recorded by a Virginia Tech study found 158 ppb.

Figure 4.69 The pipes providing water to the city contained various types of corrosion and rust.

In early 2016, a number of citizens and groups sued the city and state officials in order to secure safe drinking water. Among their demands were the proper testing of the water and its treatment for lead, the replacement of all the city's lead pipes and the provision of bottled water to vulnerable populations (those unable to get to free water distribution sites).

In 2016, a federal judge ruled in favour of the Flint resident and pressure group and door-to-door deliveries of bottled water were ordered for all those without properly installed and maintained tap filters. The following year, it was announced that the city would have to replace all of the city's lead pipes. However, progress has been slow, and many residents continue to use lead pipes. According to the EPA, there is no safe level of lead in water.

Activity

Research water pollution in your own region/county.

Create a poster or a leaflet to identify the causes, consequences and potential solutions to the problem. Present your findings to the class.

4.4.2 Plastic pollution in oceans

2.2 Energy and biomass in ecosystems

HL a Environmental law

HL c Environmental ethics

Plastic debris is accumulating in marine environments. Management is needed to remove plastics from the supply chain and to clear up existing pollution. Oceanic plastic pollution threatens ocean health, the health of marine species, food safety and quality, human health and coastal tourism and can influence climate change.

Over 14 million tonnes of plastic end up in the oceans every year. The main sources are land-based coming from urban and stormwater run-off, sewer overflows, poor waste disposal and management, tyre-abrasion, construction, industrial activities and illegal dumping of plastic waste. Due to solar radiation and wind currents, plastic breaks down into small particles – microplastics (< 5 nm) and nanoplastics (< 100 nm). Being so small, these particles are easily ingested by marine organisms.

Figure 4.70 Dead albatross with plastic debris in its stomach.

The most visible impact is the death of organisms caused by the ingestion of plastics (Figure 4.70). Microplastics have been found in tap water, salt and beer and are present in all the world's oceans. Several chemicals used in the production of plastics are carcinogenic. The burning of plastic waste releases CO_2 and methane (CH_4) and so contributes to global warming. Plastic waste may reduce the aesthetic value of tourist destinations and so lead to decreased tourist revenue. In addition, it may be costly to clean up polluted areas.

Efforts are needed to reduce the amount of plastic that is in use and to promote circular economies (recycle, reuse and reduce). One of the more successful campaigns has been the introduction of fees being charged in supermarkets for the use of plastic bags. This has led to a major decrease in their use in some countries. In Ireland, for example, plastic pollution accounted for 5% of pollution in 2001 but just 0.13% of pollution in 2015, following the introduction of a levy on plastic bags.

Example – The Great Pacific Garbage Patch

The Great Pacific Garbage Patch (Topic 3, Section 3.2.7) is an area of marine debris, approximately 135° to 155° W and 35° to 42° N (Topic 3, Section 3.2.7, Figure 3.63). It shifts its exact position every year but remains within the North Pacific Gyre (a system of circular ocean currents) because it is confined by ocean currents.

In 2006, the UN Environment Programme reckoned that every km^2 of sea held nearly 18,000 pieces of floating plastic. Much of it was, and still is, in the central Pacific, where scientists believe as much as 100 million tonnes of plastic waste are suspended in two separate gyres (large rotating ocean currents) of garbage in the Great Pacific Garbage Patch. Estimates of its size vary from 700,000 km^2 to more than 15,000,000 km^2 – between 0.41% and 8.1% of the size of the Pacific Ocean.

Plastics never biodegrade so they do not break down into natural substances. Instead they go through a photodegradation process, splitting into smaller and smaller particles that are still plastic.

Problems caused by plastic

- Plastic fouls beaches throughout the world and reduces potential income from tourism and recreation.
- Plastic entangles marine animals, strangles them, makes them immobile and drowns them.
- Plastic garbage, when washed ashore, destroys habitats.
- Plastic gets inside ship propellers and keels making ship maintenance more expensive.
- Microplastics (Topic 2, Section 2.2.18) can accumulate in the food chain.
- Plastic does not degrade.
- Plastic makes an ideal medium for the transfer of invasive species.

Hence, on account of its sheer size and the small nature of some of its content, it is nearly impossible to clean up the Great Pacific Garbage Patch. Plastic garbage can be collected when washed up on beaches – but there are relatively few beaches in the region of the Great Pacific Garbage Patch. Some scientists have suggested putting booms around the Patch and hauling in the plastic. However the size of the Patch makes this an impractical option. Others have suggested 'hoovering' up the plastic – again the sheer scale of this makes its success unlikely. Ultimately, it would be far easier to control the pollution at the source by reducing waste and increasing recycling and reuse.

Activity

Research plastic pollution in a coastal area/freshwater area in your home country or a country of your choice.

Create a poster to raise awareness of the issues caused and the potential management strategies that could be used to reduce the pollution.

1.3 Sustainability

4.4.3 Monitoring water quality

A wide range of parameters can be used to directly test the quality of aquatic systems, including pH, temperature, total suspended solids (turbidity) and the concentrations of metals, nitrates and phosphates.

Water quality in freshwater aquatic systems is assessed by monitoring dissolved O_2, pH, temperature, turbidity, and concentrations of nitrates, phosphates, specific metals and total suspended solids. Data can be used to inform management strategies for reducing pollution.

Standard water quality tests on drinking water, rivers and other sites can be performed with portable equipment that enables detection of nitrate and nitrite ions, free chlorine, chloride and fluoride ions, hardness and traces of heavy metals such as lead. Water-quality tests on rivers include biochemical oxygen demand (BOD), turbidity, ammonia and dissolved oxygen.

There are two main ways of measuring water quality. These are known as direct and indirect measures.

Direct measures take samples of the water and measure the concentrations of different chemicals that it contains. If the chemicals are dangerous or the concentrations are too high, the water is polluted. Measurements like this are known as chemical indicators of water quality (Table 4.14).

Table 4.14 Chemical indicators of water quality.

Indicator	Method	What the results show
Dissolved oxygen	• test kit, meter or sensor • oxygen is usually measured as percentage saturation • follow instructions to measure oxygen saturation	• 75% oxygen saturation = healthy, clean water • 10–50% oxygen saturation = polluted water • <10% oxygen saturation = raw sewage
pH	• indicator paper dipped in sample and compared to a colour chart • record the pH number (e.g., pH 8)	• pH 1–6 = water is acidic • pH 7 = water is neutral • pH 8–14 = water is alkaline
Phosphate	• test kit • follow instructions to measure phosphate concentration • phosphate is measured in mg dm^{-3}	• < 5 mg dm^{-3} = clean water • 15–20 mg dm^{-3} = polluted water
Nitrate	• test kit • follow instructions to measure nitrate concentration • nitrate concentration is measured in mg dm^{-3}	• 4–5 mg dm^{-3} = clean water • 6–15 mg dm^{-3} = polluted water
Salt (as chloride)	• test kit, meter or sensor • follow instructions to measure salinity the amount of chloride (salinity) is measured in mg dm^{-3}	• 20,000 mg dm^{-3} = seawater • 100–20,000 mg dm^{-3} = tidal or brackish water
Ammonia	• test kit • follow instructions to measure ammonia concentration • ammonia concentration is measured in mg dm^{-3}	• 0.05–1.00 mg dm^{-3} = clean water • >1–10 mg dm^{-3} = polluted water • 40 mg dm^{-3} = raw sewage

Indirect methods involve examining the fish, insects and other invertebrates that live in the water. If many different types of creatures can live in a river, the water quality is likely to be very good. If the river supports no fish life at all, the quality is obviously much poorer. Measurements like this are called biological indicators of water quality.

Turbidity

Turbidity is a measure of the amount of suspended sediment present in a water sample. A large amount of suspended sediment will give the water a turbid (dirty) appearance and this may indicate large amounts of organic pollutants in the water. To assess turbidity, use either a Secchi disc or a turbidity tube (Figure 4.71, and Topic 2, Section 2.1.6). The Secchi disc is lowered into the water and the depth at which the markings can no longer be seen is recorded.

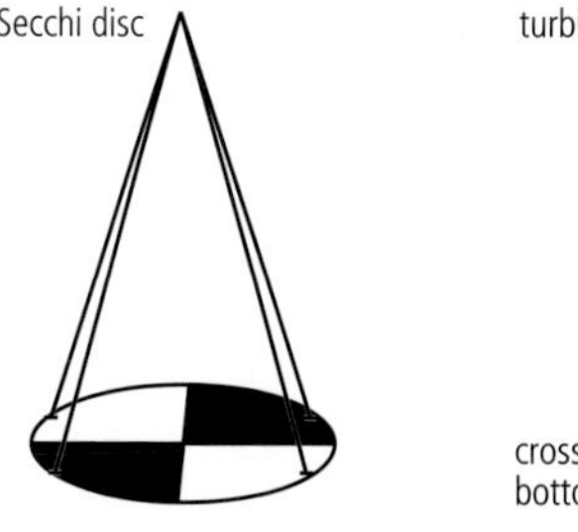

Figure 4.71 Secchi disc and turbidity tube.

Temperature

Temperature partly limits stream O_2 levels. The lower the temperature, the more O_2 that can be dissolved in the stream. Temperature can easily be measured using a waterproof thermometer.

Figure 4.72 Students measuring water quality.

Chemical tests

Dissolved oxygen

Bacteria use oxygen to break down organic pollutants, therefore streams with low O_2 concentrations may be experiencing pollution, for example, from raw sewage. Low O_2 concentrations have an impact on societies. Fish are unable to survive in streams with low levels of O_2, so a potential food supply is affected. O_2 levels can be assessed with a meter and probe, or through the use of a specialized chemical testing kit (Figure 4.72).

Nitrate and ammonia levels

Nitrates are essential for plant growth, but levels of 50 ppm are the recognized limits for safe drinking water. High levels of nitrates may originate from agricultural fertilizers or manure and are associated with eutrophication. Test strips are available for the assessment of nitrate levels and ammonia levels.

TOK

To what extent is certainty attainable?

A wide range of parameters are used to test the quality of water and judgments are made about causes and effects of water quality. How can we effectively identify cause–effect relationships, given that we can only ever observe correlation?

pH

Changes in stream pH are quite complex and may not necessarily be related to a particular source. The acidification of watercourses can be investigated, although it normally occurs over a very long time period. To measure pH, a pH probe, pH meter or test strips can be used.

SKILLS

Use methods for measuring key abiotic factors in aquatic systems

Investigate water quality in a local stream. Make sure that your chosen location is safe: ensure that the stream is a safe depth, that the speed of the current is safe, and that the test site is not located downstream of industrial or other effluent.

You could choose two sites (e.g. upstream and downstream of a tributary or a specific infrastructure such as a housing estate).

Analyse changes in abiotic factors including dissolved oxygen, temperature, turbidity and concentrations of nitrates, phosphates and total suspended solids. Possible methods may include the use of oxygen and pH probes, a thermometer, a Secchi disc and nitrate/phosphate tests.

4.4.4 Biochemical oxygen demand

BOD is a measure of the amount of dissolved oxygen required by microorganisms to decompose organic material in water.

BOD is a measure of the amount of dissolved O_2 required to break down the organic material in a given volume of water through aerobic biological activity. BOD is used to indirectly measure the amount of organic matter in a sample. BOD is usually measured as milligrams of O_2 per litre of water (mg O_2 l^{-1}).

Aerobic organisms use O_2 in cellular respiration. The higher the number of organisms at a particular site, such as a river, and the faster their rate of respiration, the more O_2 they will use. So, the BOD at any particular point in the river is determined by the number of aerobic organisms at that point and their rate of respiration.

BOD can indicate whether a particular part of a river is polluted with organic matter such as sewage or silage. This is because the presence of an organic pollutant stimulates an increase in the population of organisms that feed on and break down the pollutant. In doing so, they respire and use up a lot of O_2. This could eventually lead to a lack of O_2 and subsequent anaerobic decomposition, which then leads to the formation of toxic gases such as CH_4, hydrogen sulfide (H_2S) and ammonia (NH_3).

BOD is measured using the following method:

1. Take a sample of water of measured volume. If this is not a litre, a calculation will be needed to give the usual unit of mg O_2 dm^{-1}.
2. Measure the O_2 level.
3. Place the sample in a dark place at 20 °C in an air-tight container for 5 days. The lack of light prevents photosynthesis, which would otherwise release O_2 and give an artificially low BOD.
4. After 5 days, re-measure the O_2 level.
5. The BOD is the difference between the two measurements of the O_2 level.

The symbol used for the units milligrams per decimetre cubed is mg dm^{-3}. This is also milligrams per litre as 1 dm^3 is the same as 1 litre.

4.4.5 Eutrophication

1.2 Systems

Eutrophication occurs when streams, lakes, estuaries and coastal waters receive inputs of mineral nutrients, especially nitrates and phosphates, often causing excessive growth of phytoplankton (Figure 4.73). Algal blooms only occur if phytoplankton growth had previously been limited by lower concentrations of phosphate and/or nitrate. Humans cause eutrophication when releasing detergents, sewage or agricultural fertilizers into water bodies. It can cause algal blooms, oxygen starvation and, eventually, the decline of biodiversity in aquatic ecosystems.

Eutrophication refers to the nutrient enrichment of streams, ponds and groundwater due to increased levels of nitrates and/or phosphates.

(a)

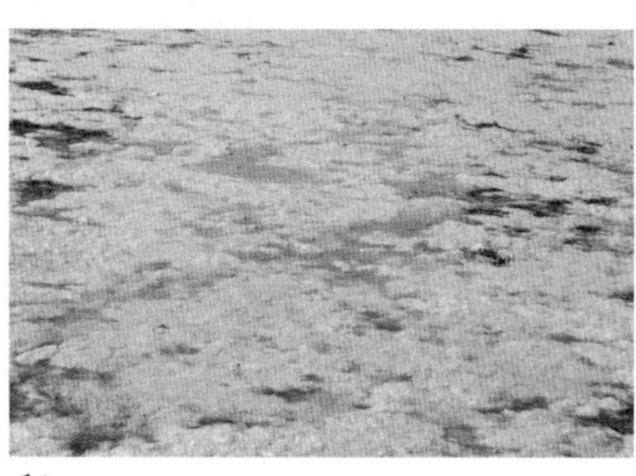

(b)

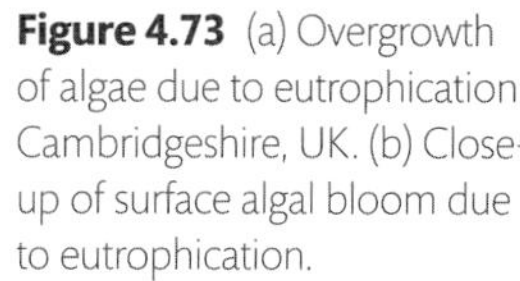

Figure 4.73 (a) Overgrowth of algae due to eutrophication, Cambridgeshire, UK. (b) Close-up of surface algal bloom due to eutrophication.

In eutrophication, increased amounts of nitrogen and/or phosphorus are carried in streams, lakes and groundwater causing nutrient enrichment. This leads to an increase in algal blooms as plants respond to the increased nutrient availability. As the algae die back and decompose, further nutrients are released into the water. This is an example of positive feedback. However, the increase in algae and plankton shades the water below, cutting off the light supply for submerged plants. The prolific growth of algae and cyanobacteria (formerly known as blue-green algae), especially in autumn as a result of increased levels of nutrients in the water and higher temperatures, results in **anoxia** (oxygen starvation in the water). The increased plant biomass and decomposition lead to a build-up of dead organic matter and to changes in species composition.

Some of these changes are the direct result of eutrophication, for example the stimulation of algal growth in water bodies, while others are indirect, for example changes in the diversity of fish species due to reduced O_2 concentration. Eutrophication produces a dynamic system – as levels of nitrates and phosphorus in streams and groundwater change, there is a corresponding change in species composition.

Anthropogenic eutrophication

Human activities worldwide have caused the nitrogen and phosphorus content of many rivers to double and, in some countries, local increases of up to 50 times have been recorded.

Phosphorus

Phosphorus is a rare element in the Earth's crust. Unlike nitrogen, there is no reservoir of gaseous phosphorus compounds available in the atmosphere. In tropical systems, phosphorus is more likely to be a growth-limiting nutrient than nitrogen, whereas in temperate regions, nitrogen is the main limiting factor.

Domestic detergents are a major source of phosphates in sewage effluents. Estimates of the relative contribution of domestic detergents to phosphorus build-up in Britain's watercourses vary between 20% and 60%. As phosphorus increases in a freshwater ecosystem, the number of plankton increases, and the number of freshwater plants decreases.

Nitrogen

Nearly 80% of the atmosphere is nitrogen. In addition, air pollution has increased rates of nitrogen deposition. The main anthropogenic source is a mix of nitrogen oxides (NOx), mainly nitrogen monoxide (NO), released during the combustion of fossil fuels in vehicles and power plants. Despite its abundance, nitrogen is more likely to be the limiting nutrient in terrestrial ecosystems (as opposed to aquatic ones), as soils can typically retain phosphorus while nitrogen is leached away.

Nutrients applied to farmland through fertilizers may spread to the wider environment by:

- drainage water percolating through the soil, leaching soluble plant nutrients
- washing of excreta, applied to the land as fertilizer, into watercourses
- erosion of surface soils or the movement of soil particles into subsoil drainage systems.

In Europe and the USA, for example Chesapeake Bay, large quantities of slurry from intensively reared and housed livestock are spread on the fields. Animal excreta is very rich in both nitrogen and phosphorus and, therefore, its application to land can contribute to problems from polluted run-off.

Activity

Using the internet, investigate the levels of eutrophication in your home region or a region of your choice.

Find out how the levels have changed over recent decades. Write a one-page report with statistics to back up your findings.

1.2 Systems

4.4.6 Impacts of eutrophication

Excessive growth of phytoplankton is typically followed by their death, high rates of decomposition, rapid consumption of dissolved O_2 which causes **hypoxia** (low oxygen) and anoxia (lack of oxygen) in the water, and the deaths of aquatic organisms that depend on dissolved O_2 (Figure 4.74).

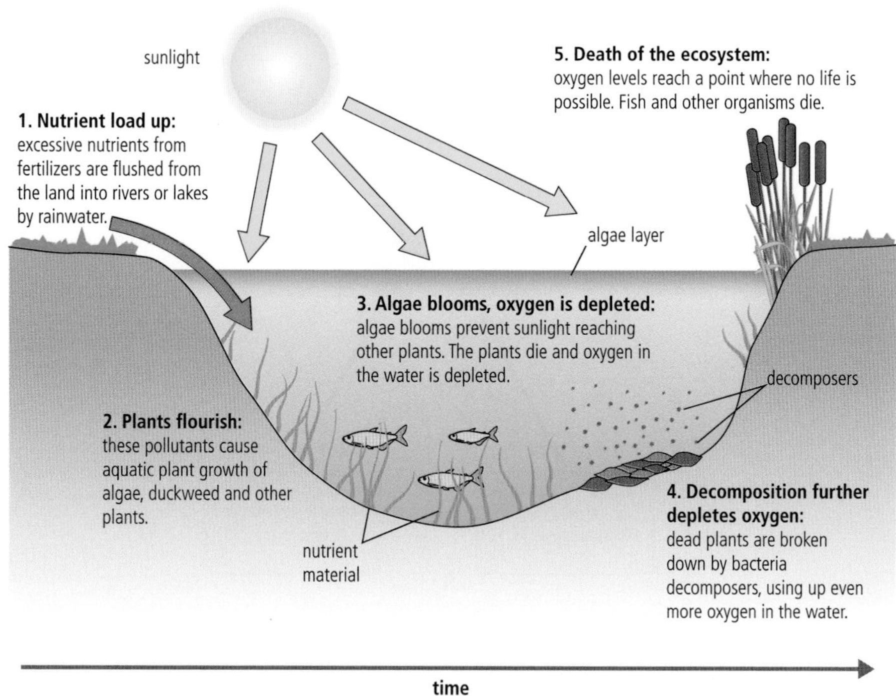

Figure 4.74 The process of eutrophication.

A number of changes may occur as a result of eutrophication:

- Turbidity (murkiness) increases and reduces the amount of light reaching submerged plants.
- Rate of deposition of sediment increases because of increased vegetation cover. This reduces the speed of water flow and decreases the lifespan of lakes.
- Net primary productivity is usually higher compared with unpolluted water and may be seen by extensive algal or bacterial blooms.
- Dissolved O_2 in water decreases, as organisms decomposing the increased biomass respire and consume O_2.
- Diversity of primary producers changes and finally decreases, and the dominant species change. Initially, the number of primary producers increases and may become more diverse. However, as eutrophication proceeds, early algal blooms give way to cyanobacteria.
- Fish populations are adversely affected by reduced oxygen availability and the fish community becomes dominated by surface-dwelling coarse fish, such as pike and perch, as happened in the Wabigoon River, Ontario, Canada. Other species migrate away from the area if they can. In freshwater aquatic systems, a major effect of eutrophication is the loss of the submerged macrophytes (aquatic plants). Macrophytes are thought to disappear because they lose their energy supply as there is a reduction in sunlight penetrating the water. Sunlight is intercepted by the increased biomass of phytoplankton exploiting the high nutrient conditions. In principle, the submerged macrophytes could also benefit from increased nutrient availability, but they have no opportunity to do so because the free-floating microscopic organisms shade them.

Create a systems model to show the impacts and changes eutrophication produces in an aquatic system

For example, Figure 4.75 shows a systems model that shows the positive feedback that can occur during eutrophication, where an increase in nutrients leads to an increase in death of organisms. This can cause an increase in decomposition, which in turn leads to an increase in nutrients.

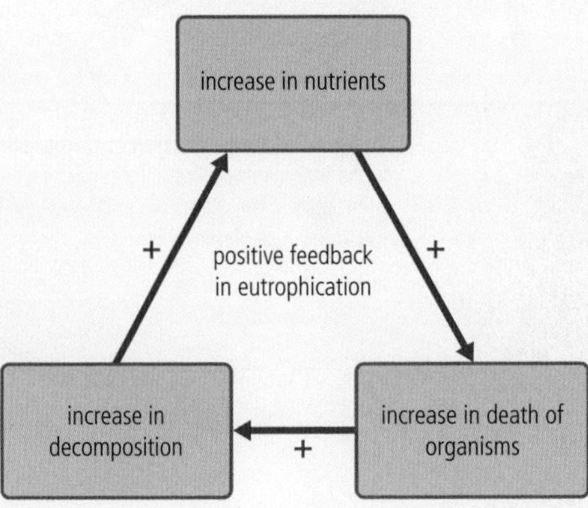

Figure 4.75 Eutrophication and positive feedback.

Activity

Create your own model of positive feedback in eutrophication.

Example – Eutrophication of Lake Erie

Natural eutrophication normally takes thousands of years to progress. In contrast, anthropogenic or cultural eutrophication is very rapid. During the 1960s, Lake Erie (on the USA–Canada border) was experiencing rapid anthropogenic eutrophication and was the subject of much concern and research. Eutrophication of Lake Erie produced algal and cyanobacterial blooms, which caused changes in water quality. The increase in cyanobacteria at the expense of water plants led to a decline in biodiversity. With fewer types of primary producer, there were fewer types of consumers, and so the overall ecosystem biodiversity decreased. Cyanobacteria are not eaten by zooplankton, thus their expansion proceeds rapidly. The cyanobacterial blooms led to O_2 depletion and the death of fish. In addition, algal and bacterial species can cause the death of fish by clogging their gills and causing asphyxiation. Many indigenous fish disappeared and were replaced by species that could tolerate the eutrophic conditions. Low O_2 levels caused by the respiration of the increased lake phytomass killed invertebrates and fish. The death of macrophytes on the lake floor increased the build-up of dead organic matter in the thickening lake sediments. Rotting bacterial masses covered beaches and shorelines.

Researchers at the University of Manitoba set up the Experimental Lakes Area (ELA) in 1968 to investigate the causes and impacts of eutrophication in Lake Erie and between June 1969 and May 1976, it was the main focus of experimental studies at the ELA.

Over a number of years, seven different lakes (ELA lakes 227, 304, 302, 261, 226, 303 and 230) were treated in different ways. Lakes 227 (Figure 4.76) and 226 were especially important in showing the effect of phosphorus in eutrophication. Studies of gas exchange and internal mixing in lake 227 during the early 1970s clearly demonstrated that algae in lakes were able to obtain sufficient CO_2, via diffusion from the atmosphere to the lake water, to support eutrophic blooms. The cyanobacteria were found to be able to fix nitrogen that had diffused naturally into the lake from the air, making nitrogen available for supporting growth.

Figure 4.76 Aerial view of lake 227 in 1994. The green colour is caused by cyanobacteria stimulated by the experimental addition of phosphorus for the 26th consecutive year. Lake 305 in the background is unpolluted.

ELA lake 226 was the site of a very successful experiment. The lake was divided into two relatively equal parts using a plastic divider curtain (Figure 4.77). Carbon and nitrogen were added to one half of the lake, while carbon, nitrogen and phosphorus were added to the other half of the lake. For 8 years, the side receiving phosphorus developed eutrophic cyanobacterial blooms, while the side receiving only carbon and nitrogen did not. The experiment suggested that in this case phosphorus was the key nutrient. A multi-billion-dollar phosphate control programme was soon instituted within the St Lawrence Great Lakes Basin. Legislation to control phosphates in sewage, and to remove phosphates from laundry detergents, was part of this programme. By the mid-1970s, North American interest in eutrophication had declined. Nevertheless, the nutrient pollution problem remains the number one water-quality problem worldwide.

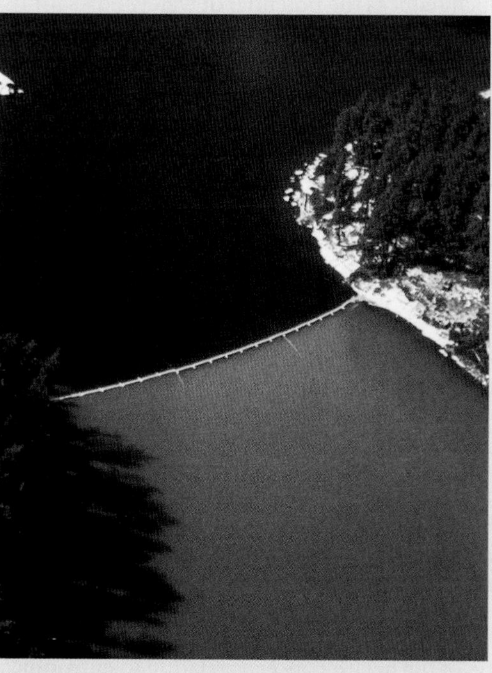

Figure 4.77 Aerial view of lake 226 in August 1973. The green colour is due to cyanobacteria growing on phosphorus added to the lake on the nearside of the dividing curtain.

Algae may be a nuisance, but they do not produce substances toxic to humans or animals. Cyanobacteria, on the other hand, produce substances that are extremely toxic causing serious illness and death if ingested. This is why cyanobacteria are a very worrying problem in water sources or reservoirs used for leisure facilities.

4.4.7 Eutrophication and ecosystem services

1.1 Perspectives

HL b Environmental economics

Eutrophication can substantially impact ecosystem services, including fisheries, recreation, aesthetics and health.

Effects on fishing

In certain areas, an increase in nitrates/phosphorus in water bodies can lead to an increase in productivity and an increase in the fish stock. Eutrophication can also affect the fish species that can survive in waters (Figure 4.78). Eutrophic waters tend to have dominant species such as carp, which many people find to be less desirable than species such as salmon or trout. Carp may also disturb the sediments at the base of water bodies, which can lead to a decline in water clarity. In North America, some eutrophic waterbodies produce large populations of stunted panfish. These populations grow in size as predators are unable to see them due to increased turbidity from planktonic algae and suspended sediments. The increase in algae in the upper part of the water not only stops light from reaching down to the water's depth but also causes O_2 depletion, thereby affecting the quality and quantity of fish that can survive.

Oceanic waters are generally nutrient poor and fisheries are limited by the primary production that occurs there. However, there are some cases where marine water nutrients washed into coastal waters can lead to algal blooms or 'red tide' organisms, such as dinoflagellates.

▲ **Figure 4.78** Fish swimming in eutrophic water.

Effects on recreation

The growth of large populations of macrophytes can reduce access to waterways, which reduces the potential of waterbodies for fishing, sailing, paddle-boarding and swimming. The presence and smell of scum may make some waterbodies unpleasant to view and smell. Large numbers of species, such as water hyacinths and Nile cabbage, may cover large areas and move into open water, preventing light from reaching submerged plants. The presence of large quantities of dead organic matter in waterbodies results in low O_2 concentrations and emissions of CH_4 and H_2S, making it unpleasant for recreational users.

Aesthetics

Aesthetics refers to the appreciation of beauty. Many natural environments are very beautiful, but many have been degraded. Eutrophication has a range of negative environmental impacts, including:

- reducing the visual appeal of streams and lakes
- making water unsafe for swimming
- altering the biodiversity, making the area less attractive for environmentalists
- making areas less attractive for walkers due to the smell.

Health concerns

One of the health concerns relating to eutrophication is increased rates of stomach cancer, which can be caused by nitrates in the digestive tract.

Critics argue that the case against nitrates is not clear as stomach cancer could also be caused by a variety of other factors. However, in some parts of Nigeria where nitrate concentrations have exceeded 90 mg dm^{-3}, the death rate from gastric cancer is abnormally high.

Another health concern is blue baby syndrome (methemoglobinemia), which is caused by insufficient O_2 in the mother's blood for the developing baby. Critics argue that the number of cases of blue baby syndrome is statistically small. However, according to the Department of Health in Minnesota, USA, when nitrates in well water exceed 10 mg/l, this can trigger methemoglobinemia in infants under six months of age.

Activity

With a partner, investigate the impacts of eutrophication on ecosystem services, for your home region or a region of your choice.

4.4.8 Managing eutrophication

1.1 Perspectives
1.3 Sustainability

HL a Environmental law
HL b Environmental economics
HL c Environmental ethics

Water pollution management strategies

Eutrophication can be addressed at three different levels of management (Figures 4.79 and 4.80). These are:

- reduction of human activities that produce pollutants (for example, using alternatives to current fertilizers and detergents)
- reduction of the release of pollution into the environment (for example, treatment of wastewater to remove nitrates and phosphates)
- removal of pollutants from the environment and restoring ecosystems (for example, removal of mud from eutrophic lakes and reintroduction of plant and fish species).

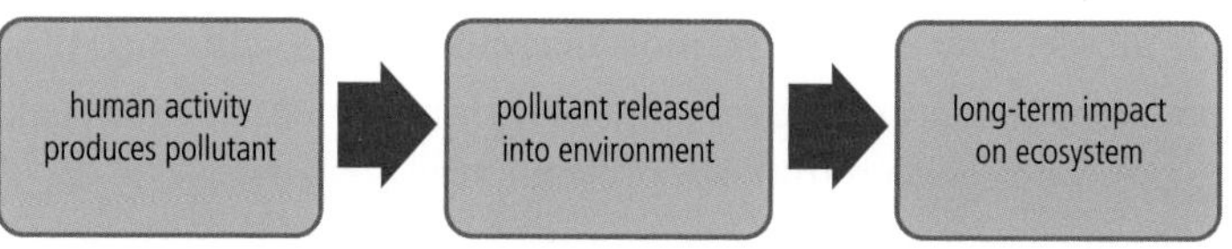

Figure 4.79 Model demonstrating the stages leading to pollutants having an impact on the environment.

Altering human activities

Public campaigns in Australia have encouraged people to reduce eutrophication by:

- using zero- or low-phosphate detergents
- washing only full loads in washing machines
- washing vehicles on porous surfaces away from drains or gutters
- reducing the use of fertilizers on lawns and gardens
- composting garden and food waste
- collecting and burying pet faeces.

Figure 4.80 Pollution management targeted at three different levels.

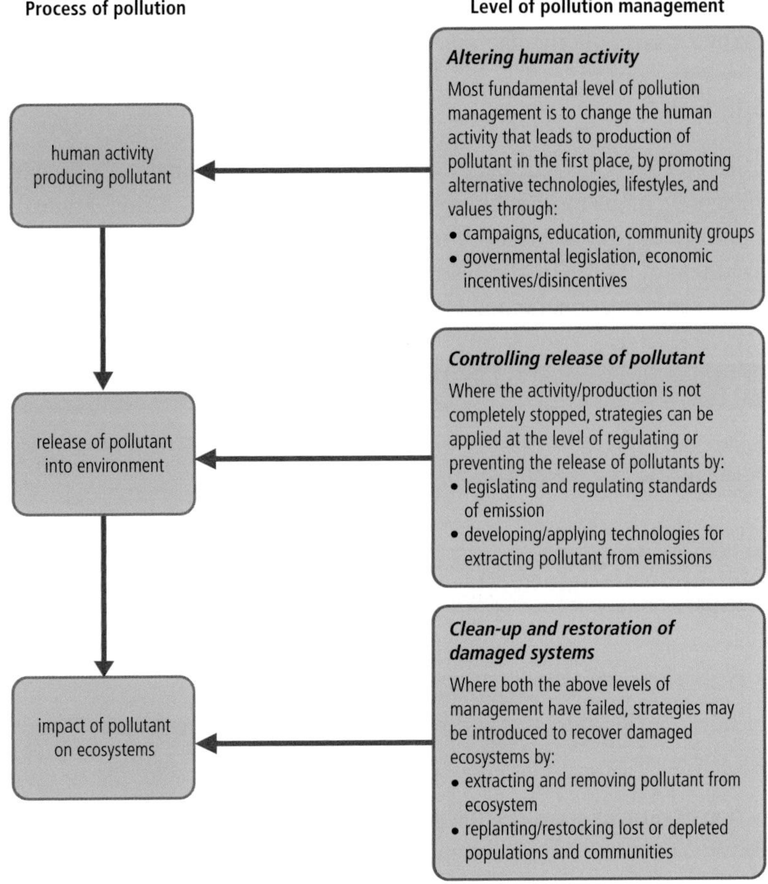

Process of pollution
Level of pollution management
human activity producing pollutant
release of pollutant into environment
impact of pollutant on ecosystems
Altering human activity
Most fundamental level of pollution management is to change the human activity that leads to production of pollutant in the first place, by promoting alternative technologies, lifestyles, and values through:
• campaigns, education, community groups
• governmental legislation, economic incentives/disincentives
Controlling release of pollutant
Where the activity/production is not completely stopped, strategies can be applied at the level of regulating or preventing the release of pollutants by:
• legislating and regulating standards of emission
• developing/applying technologies for extracting pollutant from emissions
Clean-up and restoration of damaged systems
Where both the above levels of management have failed, strategies may be introduced to recover damaged ecosystems by:
• extracting and removing pollutant from ecosystem
• replanting/restocking lost or depleted populations and communities

Possible measures to reduce nitrate loss

Measures used on the mid-latitude northern hemisphere include the following:

Up to 45% of total phosphate loading to freshwater in the UK comes from sewage works. This input can be reduced by 90% or more by carrying out phosphate stripping. The effluent is run into a tank and dosed with a precipitant, which combines with phosphate in solution to create a solid. The solid then settles out and can be removed.

- avoiding the use of nitrogen fertilizers during the wet season when soils are wet and when the fertilizer is therefore most likely to be washed through the soil.
- giving preference to autumn-sown crops as their roots conserve nitrogen in the soil and use up the nitrogen left from the previous year
- sowing autumn-sown crops as early as possible and maintaining crop cover through autumn and winter to conserve nitrogen
- avoiding the application of nitrogen-based fertilizers when the field is by a stream or lake
- avoiding the application of nitrogen-based fertilizers just before heavy rain is forecast (assuming that forecasts are accurate)
- using less nitrogen if the previous year was dry because less will have been, although, this is difficult to assess precisely.

Regulating and reducing the nutrient source

Prevention of eutrophication at source has the following advantages, compared with treating its effects or reversing the process:

- technical feasibility – in some situations, prevention at source may be achieved by diverting a polluted watercourse away from the sensitive ecosystem; the removal of nutrients from a system by techniques such as mud-pumping is more of a technical challenge

- cost – nutrient stripping at source using a precipitant is relatively cheap and simple to implement; biomass stripping of affected water is labor-intensive and therefore expensive
- products – restored wetlands may be managed to provide economic products such as fuel, compost or thatching material more easily than trying to use the biomass stripped from a less managed system.

Clean-up strategies

Once nutrients are in an ecosystem, it is much harder and more expensive to remove them than it would have been to tackle the eutrophication at source. The main clean-up methods available are:

- precipitation (e.g., treatment with a solution of aluminium or ferrous salt to precipitate phosphates)
- removal of nutrient-enriched sediments by, for example, mud pumping
- removal of biomass, for example. The harvesting of common reed, and using it for thatching or fuel.

Temporary removal of fish can allow primary consumer species to recover and control algal growth. Once water quality has improved, fish can be re-introduced.

Mechanical removal of plants from aquatic systems is a common method for mitigating the effects of eutrophication. Efforts may be focused on removal of unwanted aquatic plants, such as water hyacinth, that tend to colonize eutrophic water. Each 1000 kg of wet biomass harvested removes about 3 kg of nitrogen and 0.2 kg of phosphorus from the system. Alternatively, plants may be introduced deliberately to mop-up excess nutrients.

How can we decide between the judgments of experts if they disagree with each other?

Experts sometimes disagree about pollution management strategies. Given access to the same facts, how is it possible that there can be disagreement between experts? On what basis might we decide between the judgments of the experts when they disagree?

In some circumstances, it may be possible to divert sewage effluent away from a water body. This was achieved at Lake Washington, near Seattle, USA. In 1955, cyanobacteria affected Lake Washington. The lake was receiving sewage effluent from about 70,000 people. The sewerage system was redesigned to divert effluent away from the lake to the nearby sea inlet of Puget Sound..

Activity

Investigate how eutrophication is being managed in an area of your choice. Discuss your findings with a partner.

Make a presentation to your class.

HL

4.4.9 Pollutants in water

HL

Pollutants in water include organic matter, dissolved substances, persistent chemicals that get biomagnified (Topic 2, Section 2.2.18), plastics and heat energy.

Example – Water pollution in the Ganges

The Ganges is the longest river in India and provides water for about 500 million people.

It is said to be the most polluted river in the world (Figure 4.81) and is heavily polluted with human waste, as well as agricultural and industrial discharge. It flows through a number of industrial cities, such as Varanasi and Patna, which have large numbers of factories, chemical plants, distilleries, textile mills, tanneries, slaughterhouses and some coal-based power stations. The burning of coal produces fly ash, which contains heavy metals such as lead and copper.

Figure 4.81 Water pollution on the Ganges, India.

Water pollution includes sewage (this topic, Section 4.4.12), dissolved substances, persistent chemicals, plastics and heat energy. Tributyltin (TBT) is an example of a dissolved substance in water. TBT was, for many decades, used as a biocide, to prevent the attachment of organisms to ship hulls. The TBT slowly leaks into the marine environment where it can have a major impact on non-target species. Through bioaccumulation and biomagnification, TBT can make its way up the food chain. TBT can lead to immunosuppression in dolphins and sea otters and can cause hearing loss in toothed whales. Humans exposed to TBT may experience fatigue, respiratory problems and headaches. Long-term exposure may impact the kidneys and the liver.

PCBs (polychlorinated biphenyls) are human-made persistent chemicals, such as pyranol, that are used in air conditioning units. They were produced in large quantities for use in transformers, paints, sealants and machinery. Plastics may also contain PCBs. PCBs can accumulate in fatty tissues, and, through bioaccumulation and biomagnification (Topic 2, Section 2.2.18), they can be harmful to top predators such as seals, tuna, polar bears and humans. In humans they have been linked with increased risk of cancer, suppression of the immune system, failure of the reproductive system and interference with hormone systems.

Heat energy is also a form of pollution in water. Heat energy may come from industrial waste or from cooling towers in power stations. It might also occur due to vegetation removal along the sides of lakes and riverbanks. This may allow more solar energy to reach the water. Changes in water temperature can have a significant impact on water chemistry and the ecosystem. Impacts include:

- reduction in the amount of dissolved O_2
- increase in the amount of toxins present
- loss of biodiversity
- changes in ecology
- migration of species
- increased metabolic rate within organisms.

Activity

With a partner, investigate the causes and consequences of water pollution in one named urban area and one named rural area.

Present your findings to the class.

4.4.10 Harmful algal blooms

HL

2.1 Systems

4.3 Aquatic food production systems

Harmful algal blooms (HABs) contain a variety of organisms including cyanobacteria, protists, algae and dinoflagellates. A small number of these organisms produce potentially fatal toxins. In freshwater, cyanotoxins are the most common toxins. Within the HABs that occur along coastlines, dinoflagellates produce different toxins including neurotoxins. Other algae may be non-toxic but can use up all the O_2 in a body of water. Protists are a set of organisms that are not classed as animal, plant, bacteria or fungi. Examples of protists include amoeba, brown algae and red algae.

Example – Harmful algal blooms in the USA

Every coastal state in the USA and the Great Lakes states experiences HABs. These have an effect on the health of the ecosystem and the health of the economy, through their impact on fishing, recreation and tourism. The frequency of HABs may be increasing and they may be affecting a wider area due to climate change and increasing discharges of nitrates and phosphorus.

Some of the impacts of HABs on areas of the USA and the Great Lakes include:

- in Texas in 2011, tides of harmful algae known as red tides caused a loss of over US$ 10 million due to reduced oyster catches
- in Ohio, in 2014, 500,000 people were without clean drinking water for three days due to HABs near a water treatment plant
- in the Gulf of Mexico, HABs of toxins carried by the algal species *Karenia brevis* regularly become airborne and mix with airborne sea spray
- in 2015, HABs led to the closure of the Pacific Northwest Quinault fisheries, resulting in a loss of income of US$ 2.4 million
- in 2015, the closure of Washington's recreational razor clam harvest led to a loss of up to US$ 40 million from tourism spending.

Freshwater

In freshwater, cyanobacteria produce cyanotoxins. People can come in contact with these through recreational water activities, drinking contaminated water, breathing in contaminated air droplets and eating contaminated shellfish and fish. Symptoms include irritation of the skin, eyes, throat, lungs and/or nose.

Marine waters

Along coastlines, dinoflagellates are a major component of HABs. Many dinoflagellates produce neurotoxins, many of which are extremely dangerous. Consumption of seafood contaminated with algal toxins could lead to:

- paralytic shellfish poisoning (PSP)
- neurotoxic shellfish poisoning (NSP)
- amnesic shellfish poisoning (ASP)
- diarrheal shellfish poisoning (DSP).

In many cases, toxic dinoflagellates are present in low concentrations with no environmental or human impact. However, when present in high density and ingested by shellfish, zooplankton and herbivorous fish, toxins bioaccumulate and biomagnify up the food chain.

Activity

Research the impact of harmful algal blooms in one LIC or MIC.

HL

4.4.11 Anoxic and hypoxic water

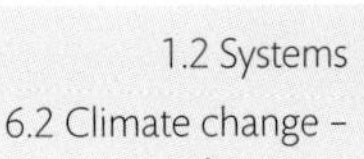

Hypoxia (low O_2) and anoxia (lack of O_2) in water result from several causes and can create aquatic dead zones. The frequency of anoxic/hypoxic waters is likely to increase due to the combined effects of global warming, freshwater stratification, sewage disposal and eutrophication. Hypoxia and anoxia are very common in stagnant water.

Many conditions can lead to hypoxic waters.

- Warm water, which could be due to factory discharges, shallow water or summer heating, holds less O_2 than cold water.
- Acute incidents may be caused by excessive use of nutrients on farms, discharge from sewage plants and from bird or animal waste. The over-loading of nutrients results in an algal bloom, which deprives submerged plants of sunlight. When the algal bloom dies and sinks to the bottom of the waterbody, it decomposes, taking O_2 out of the water.
- Sheltered bays with low wind speeds and/or gentle currents may allow water to stratify, forming a layer of low-O_2 water near the surface.

Anoxic and hypoxic water have, for example, limited dissolved O_2 but large amounts of phosphorus and nitrogen, and experience phytoplanktonic blooms (Figure 4.82).

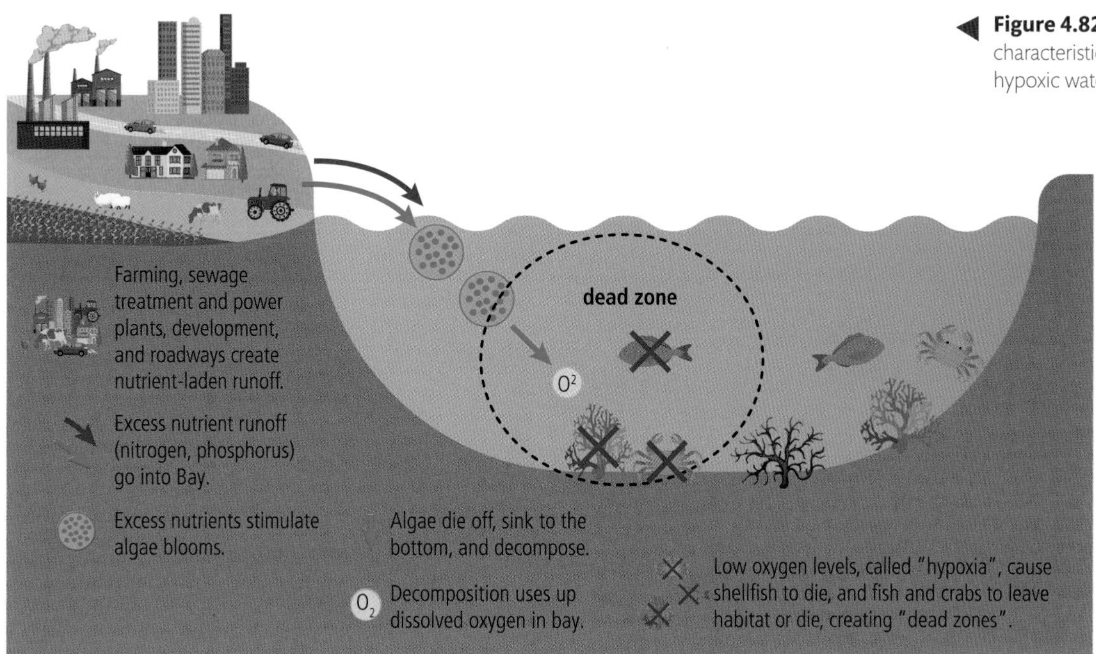
dead zone
O^2
Farming, sewage treatment and power plants, development, and roadways create nutrient-laden runoff.
Excess nutrient runoff (nitrogen, phosphorus) go into Bay.
Excess nutrients stimulate algae blooms.
Algae die off, sink to the bottom, and decompose.
Decomposition uses up dissolved oxygen in bay.
Low oxygen levels, called "hypoxia", cause shellfish to die, and fish and crabs to leave habitat or die, creating "dead zones".

Figure 4.82 The characteristics of anoxic and hypoxic water.

Example – The development of hypoxia in Narragansett Bay, Rhode Island, USA

Narragansett Bay is a temperate estuary that experiences low O_2 (hypoxic) events most summers. These events generally persist for a few days to a week, several times each summer. Prior to the late-1990s, the bay was considered to have low vulnerability to hypoxia, despite high levels of nitrogen. However, as nutrient loading continued, hypoxia increased in frequency, as did the length of each event. In 2003, low O_2 levels in the water led to the death of some 1 million fish. This was followed in 2004 by increased mortality among clams.

As a result, Rhode Island passed a bill in 2004 that set the nitrogen limits for the area's largest wastewater treatment facilities. By 2006, the summer levels of nutrients were reduced by over one-third compared to the levels between 1995 and 1996. They continued to reduce and have since been reduced to half compared to the levels from 1995–1996.

Activity

With a partner, research examples of hypoxia and anoxia in water bodies. Find examples in contrasting areas e.g., urban/rural and/or HIC versus LIC/MIC. Present your findings to the class.

4.4.12 Sewage treatment

HL

1.3 Sustainability

Sewage is treated biologically and chemically to allow the safe release of effluent by primary, secondary and tertiary water treatment stages. There are major variations in access to sewage treatment around the world.

Sewage treatment aims to remove contaminants from sewage to produce a clean, safe effluent that can be discharged into the surrounding environment or used again for another purpose. Sewage treatment involves at least two stages – primary and secondary treatment – and advanced treatment has a tertiary stage with disinfection and even a fourth stage to remove micropollutants (Figure 4.83).

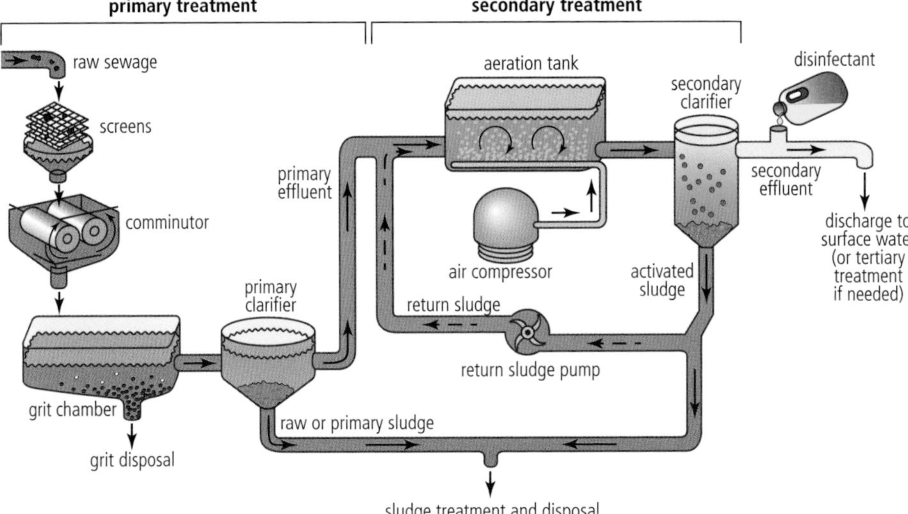

Figure 4.83 Sewage treatment in a septic tank.

Types of sewage treatment can be divided into high technology, expensive, intensive treatments and low cost, low technology, extensive or natural treatments.

Primary stage

Primary sewage treatment refers to the removal of some of the suspended solids and organic matter from the sewage. The sewage is allowed to pass slowly through a primary sedimentation tank (basin) in which heavy solids sink to the bottom. Lighter solids, oil and grease rise to the surface and can be skimmed off. About 50–70% of suspended solids are removed in the primary sedimentation tanks.

Secondary stage

Secondary sewage treatment uses biological processes to digest and remove organic material. Microorganisms that feed on organic matter grow and multiply, reducing even more of the organic matter. This can be done aerobically or anaerobically.

Tertiary stage

Tertiary sewage treatment, or advanced treatment, provides a final stage to improve effluent quality before it is discharged. More than one tertiary treatment may be used. If disinfection is used this becomes the final stage. This is also known as effluent polishing and can also involve biological nutrient removal.

In some situations, treated sewage may be stored in large-scale ponds or lagoons. Macrophytes, such as reeds, may help to filter out some of the treated sewage. Disinfection may also be used in order to kill any microorganisms that could be carrying diseases. Chlorination is the most widely used form of disinfection owing to its effectiveness and low cost, although iodine and other chemicals can also be used. The use of ultraviolet (UV) light as a form of disinfection is becoming widespread in many countries owing to concerns about the side-effects of chlorine.

Treatment differences in HICs and LICs

In 2021, it was estimated that 52% of sewage is treated globally. However, for many parts of the world, there is little data available.

In HICs, 74% of sewage was treated, but in LICs only just over 4% of sewage was treated.

In urban areas of HICs, sewers take waste products to a sewage treatment plant, whereas in many LICs, the bulk of wastewater is discharged directly into rivers and the ocean without any treatment.

HICs treat about 70% of the wastewater they produce, whereas only about 8% of wastewater produced in LICs is treated.

There are wide variations in the amount of domestic water that is treated safely (Figure 4.84). Many HICs, such as the USA and Japan, have very high levels of safely treated waters whereas a number of LIC and MICs have much lower levels of safely treated domestic water, including Algeria, Libya and Niger.

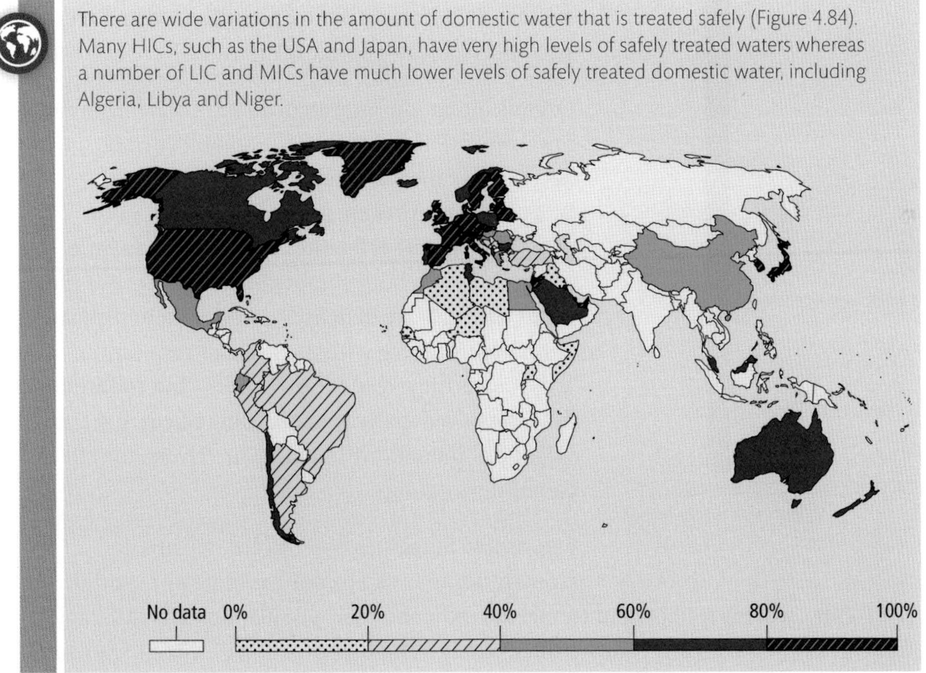

Figure 4.84 Global variations in domestic water that is safely treated.

Activity

With a partner, find out about sewage treatment in your home area. Are there any equity issues related to sewage treatment in your country?

Make a poster to show your findings and present it to the class.

HL

3.1 Biodiversity and evolution

HL a Environmental law
HL b Environmental economics
HL c Environmental ethics

4.4.13 Water pollution and indicator species

Indicator species

An **indicator species** is one whose presence, absence or abundance can be used as an indicator of pollution. It does not have to be water pollution – some species can be used to indicate air pollution, soil nutrient levels and abiotic water characteristics. For example:

- lichen (*Usnea alliculata*) indicates very low levels of sulfur dioxide (SO_2) in air
- nettles (*Ullica dioica*) indicate high phosphate levels in soil
- red algae (*Corauina officinalis*) indicate saline rock pools (as opposed to brackish ones).

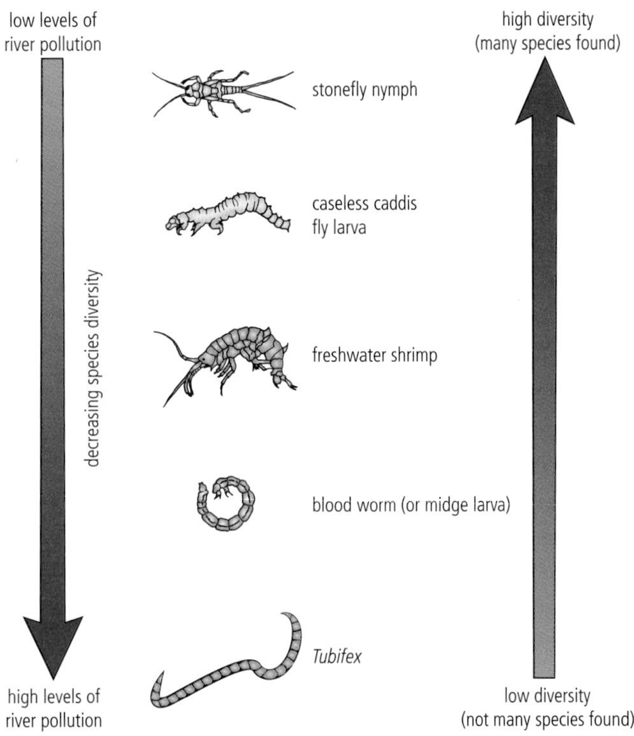

Figure 4.85 Indicator species.

Certain species are tolerant of organic pollution and the low O_2 levels associated with it. They are found in high population densities where an organic pollution incident occurs. Other species cannot tolerate low O_2 levels and, if organic pollution enters the river where they live, they move away or die. These groups can be used as indicators of organic pollution and are known as indicator species (Figure 4.85).

Organic pollutants in water can be more dangerous in summer. This is because the solubility of O_2 decreases as the water temperature increases. So on warm days there is less available O_2 in the water. Aquatic invertebrates and fish can do little to regulate their body temperature, therefore as the water temperature increases, so does their internal temperature, along with their rate of respiration. This means they need more oxygen – but the amount of O_2 dissolved in the water is going down. If warm organic pollutants are released into rivers, the effect can be devastating.

Figure 4.86 illustrates how Tubifex worms and stonefly nymphs can be used as indicator species. The Tubifex worms feed on and tunnel into effluent; their populations increase rapidly immediately downstream of any effluent entry. A high population of these organisms in any river could indicate that organic pollution has recently occurred. In contrast, the population of stonefly nymphs crashes as soon as effluent enters their habitat. They need clean water and, at the point of effluent entry, either die or move away. Thus, the absence of stonefly nymphs in a particular river might indicate organic pollution has occurred and large populations might indicate clean, unpolluted water.

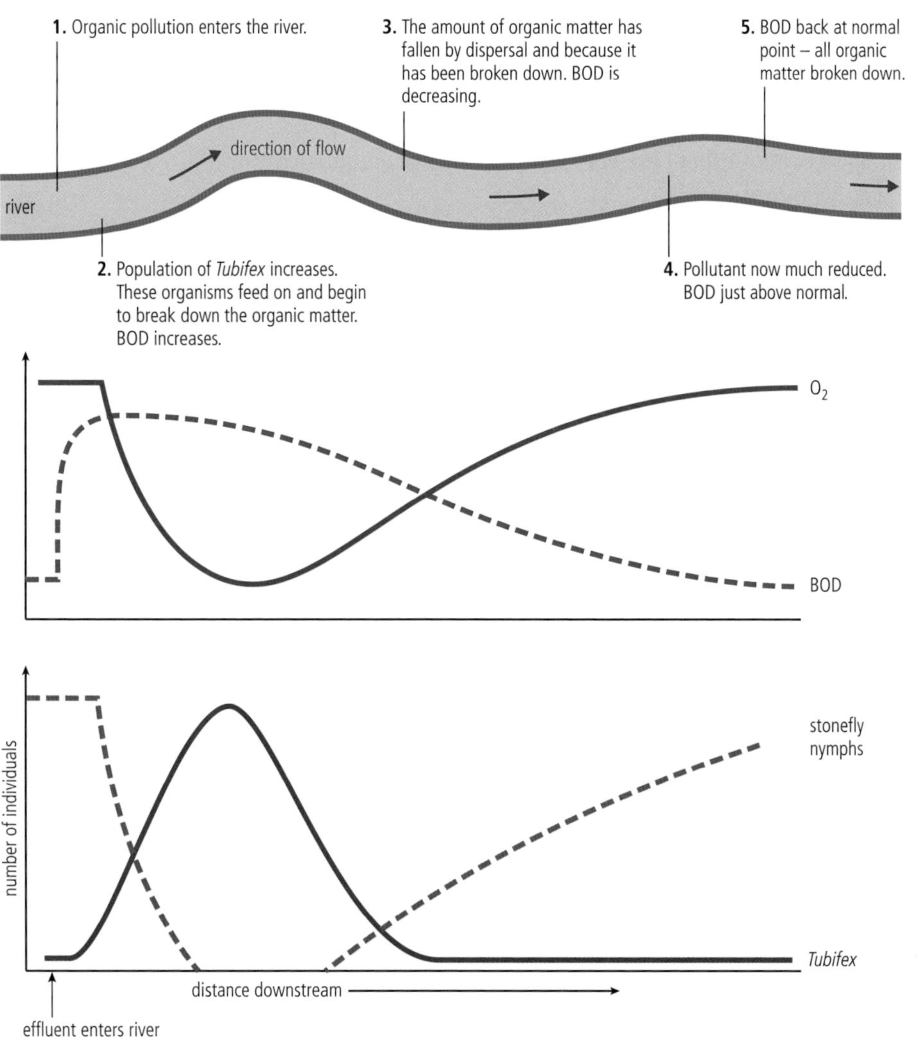
1. Organic pollution enters the river.
3. The amount of organic matter has fallen by dispersal and because it has been broken down. BOD is decreasing.
5. BOD back at normal point – all organic matter broken down.
direction of flow
river
2. Population of Tubifex increases. These organisms feed on and begin to break down the organic matter. BOD increases.
4. Pollutant now much reduced. BOD just above normal.
O_2
BOD
number of individuals
stonefly nymphs
Tubifex
distance downstream
effluent enters river

Figure 4.86 Using indicator species to estimate river pollution.

It is often faster and cheaper to measure the populations of indicator species organisms such as Tubifex or stonefly nymphs than it is to measure the concentration of specific pollutants – this is one of the advantages of using indicator species. Table 4.15 shows how the types of fauna present in a waterway relate to levels of BOD (this topic, Section 4.4.4).

Table 4.15 BOD and the type of fauna present.

Class of water	Fauna present	BOD / mg O_2 per dm^3 of water at 20 °C in 5 days	Water suitable for
I	salmon, trout, grayling, stonefly and mayfly nymphs, caddis larvae, Gammarus	0–3	• domestic supply
II	trout rarely dominant; chub, dace, caddis larvae, Gammarus	4–10 (increases in summer in times of low flow)	• agriculture • industrial processes
III	roach, gudgeon, Asellus, mayfly nymphs and caddis larvae rarely	11–15	• irrigation
IV	red chironomid larvae (bloodworms), Tubifex	16–30 (completely deoxygenated from time to time)	• unsuitable for amenity use
V	barren/sewage fungus and small Tubifex	>30	• none

Generally, waterbodies that are in healthy biological condition are able to support a wide variety and high number of macroinvertebrate taxa, including many that are intolerant of pollution, such as freshwater shrimps, stone fly, caddis fly and mayfly larvae. Samples yielding only pollution-tolerant species, such as blood worms and sludge worms, or that have very little diversity or abundance may indicate a less healthy body of water.

Otters and wetland quality

Otters live in freshwater, brackish water and seawater. These carnivores feed mainly on fish, amphibians and crustaceans and, to a lesser extent, on waterfowls, mammals and reptiles. However, otter numbers have fallen in many parts of Western and Central Europe. They face several threats including habitat destruction, wetland drainage, river regulation and, increasingly, water pollution. Contamination of fish prey with pesticides and PCBs (this topic, Section 4.4.9) is a major cause of the decline. Due to their sensitivity to environmental stresses, otters are considered to be a good biological indicator for the quality of a wetland habitat. Thus, the disappearance of otters in many parts of Europe reflects the environmental damage to wetlands.

Indicator species are certain species of fauna whose presence can be indicative of the level of pollution. Make sure you evaluate the uses of indicator species and biotic indices in measuring aquatic pollution.

Activity

Find out about indicator species in a waterbody in your home area/country.

Identify the indicator species and give a brief description of what they tell you about the water quality.

4.4.14 Biotic index

3.1 Biodiversity and evolution

Trent Biotic Index

The Trent Biotic Index is based on the disappearance of indicator species as the level of organic pollution increases in a river. This occurs because the species are unable to tolerate changes in their environment such as decreases in O_2 levels or light levels. Those species that are best able to tolerate the existing conditions become abundant, which can lead to a change in diversity. In extreme environments, such as highly polluted rivers, diversity is low. However, the numbers of individuals from pollution-tolerant species may be high. Diversity decreases as pollution increases.

A biotic index indirectly measures pollution by assaying the impact on species within the community according to their tolerance, diversity and relative abundance.

SKILLS

Apply protocols for assessing biological oxygen demand and a named biotic index (HL only)

1. The Trent Biotic Index has a maximum value of 10. The indices are allocated in the form of marks out of 10 and provide a sensitive assessment of pollution level. A score of 10 indicates clean water and a score of 0 indicates highly polluted water.

The method used is shown below:

- Sort your sample, separating the animals according to group by taxonomic order.
- Count the number of groups.
- Note which indicator species are present, starting from the top of the list in Table 4.16.
- Take the highest indicator species on the list and read across the row, stopping at the column with the appropriate number of groups for your sample.

So, for example, if your highest indicator animal belongs to the order Trichoptera, and you have more than one species and a total of 7 groups, then the Trent Biotic Index for your sample is 6.

		Total number of groups present				
		0-1	2-5	6-10	11-15	16+
Indicator present	**Number of species**	**Trent Biotic Index**				
stonefly nymphs (Plecoptera)	>1	-	7	8	9	10
	1	-	6	7	8	9
mayfly nymphs (Ephemeroptera)	>1	-	6	7	8	9
	1	-	5	6	7	8
cassias fly larvae (Trichoptera)	>1	-	5	6	7	8
	1	4	4	5	6	7
Gammarus	all above absent	3	4	5	6	7
shrimps, crustaceans (*Asellus*)	all above absent	2	3	4	5	6
Tubifex / chironomid larvae	all above absent	1	2	3	4	-
all above absent	organisms not requiring dissolved oxygen may be present	0	1	2	-	-

Table 4.16 Indicator species for the Trent Biotic Index.

2. With a partner, measure levels of BOD (this topic, Section 4.4.4) along a stretch of a small river or stream. Make sure that the water is not too deep and that you wear protective clothing. Use the Trent Biotic Index to measure the water quality in a waterbody near your home/school. Find out if there are other species that you could use for your local area.

4.4.15 Water quality index

HL

1.3 Sustainability

The water quality index (WQI) was developed in the 1960s and has become a popular tool among water scientists. There are four main stages in the WQI model:

1. selection of water quality parameters
2. generation of sub-indices for each parameter
3. allocation of weighting values
4. addition of all sub-values to find the overall WQI.

A water quality index is a single weighted average, combining the results of several water quality parameters for a given waterbody.

Water is crucial for life, but it is widely known that water quality has been in decline in many areas for a long time. Some of this could be natural, due to tropical cyclones or El Niño events, but much of it is anthropogenic, due to human activities such as intensive farming, mining and waste disposal.

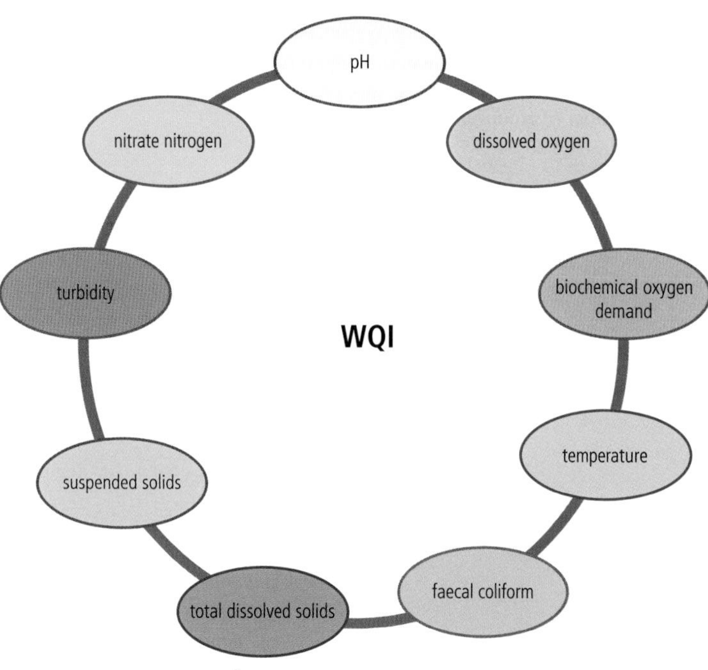

Figure 4.87 Most frequently used water quality parameters.

Poor water quality is a problem wherever it occurs, in HICs and LICs alike. It is likely to increase due to population growth, rising living standards and global climate change.

There are many local variations in the parameters used in the WQI, considering local conditions. There are at least 35 variations of the WQI. Most WQIs have been designed to assess river quality but some have been used for lakes, reservoirs, estuaries and groundwater.

The number of parameters used in WQIs varies from 4 to 26. The most common parameters used include temperature, turbidity, dissolved oxygen (DO), suspended solids (SS), total dissolved solids (TSD), faecal coliforms (FC), BOD and nitrate nitrogen (Figure 4.87). However, a number of WQI models do not include suspended solids, microbiological contamination and toxic compounds due to the high cost and lack of modern laboratory facilities.

Activity

Use the parameter from the Water Quality Index that is most relevant for your school/home area to investigate the water quality of a chosen body of water.

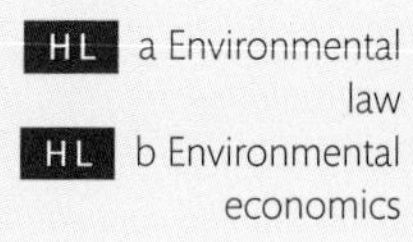

HL a Environmental law

HL b Environmental economics

4.4.16 Drinking water standards

There are no universally accepted national standards for drinking water. Drinking water guidelines have been suggested by the WHO and local governments can set their own standards.

However, where drinking water standards do occur, they are generally guidelines and targets for the levels of fluoride, lead, nitrates and selenium (Table 4.17). Very few have any legal enforcement apart from the European Drinking Water Directive and the Safe Drinking Water Act in the USA.

Table 4.17 Variations in drinking water standards.

Parameter	WHO	European Union	USA	Canada	India
Fluoride	1.5 mg/l	1.5 mg/l	4 mg/l	No standard	1.0 mg/l
Lead	No standard	10 µg/l	15 µg/l	10 µg/l	0.5 µg/l
Nitrate	50 mg/l	50 mg/l	10 mg/l	No standard	45 mg/l
Selenium	40 µg/l	10 µg/l	50 µg/l	10 µg/l	0.01 µg/l

Example – Access to drinking water in Monterrey, Mexico

An example of the conflict between international companies and local residents over access to water can be seen in Monterrey, Mexico. The drought since 2020 has seen water in the Cerro Prieto reservoir fall to just 0.5% of its capacity. Drink manufacturing companies such as Coca-Cola® and Heineken® have continued to extract water from reservoirs. These companies use up to 90 billion litres of water each year, of which over 50% comes from public reservoirs and the rest comes from private wells and groundwater. Many homes in Monterrey had no running water during the summer of 2022. That summer, the price of bottled water in shops tripled.

The Mexican president called on the companies to stop production. In response, Heineken said it would allocate 20% of its water for public use, while Coca-Cola stated that people could collect water for free from one of its mineral water factories, although this was too far to travel for most residents. Moreover, while some drinks companies pledged to give up to 28% of their water during the drought, they did not lower the price of water.

A pressure group, the Alliance of Users of Public Services, called for the removal of Monterrey's director of water and drainage because his family founded the company of one of the bottle suppliers for Coca-Cola.

Even without the actions of the water bottling companies, there was still uneven access to water in Monterrey. Wealthier areas were given higher water quotas than poorer areas and had access to tap water for up to 12 hours per day during the drought.

In order to improve Monterrey's water supply, the Mexican President and the Governor of Neuvo Leon and ten Monterrey companies developed the Cuchillo II Aqueduct and dam to improve water storage and transfer. The dam and aqueduct will provide up to 5000 l/second when fully operational. Nevertheless, there remains uncertainty about future demand and supply for water services in Monterrey.

Activity

With a partner, investigate the global bottled water market.

Search 'bottled water market' on the Mordor Intelligence website to read a useful industry report.

Make a poster to illustrate your key findings and make a presentation to the class.

4.4.17 Reducing water pollution

There are several actions that individuals and groups of citizens can take to reduce water pollution. These include changes in consumption and waste disposal, protesting, data collection, lobbying politicians and forming legal teams.

1.3 Sustainability

There are many ways that people can reduce water consumption and pollution. These include:

HL a Environmental law
HL c Environmental ethics

- not pouring fat from cooking or any type of oil or grease down the sink
- not pouring household chemicals or cleaning agents down the sink or toilet
- not flushing any pills or medication down the toilet
- installing a water-efficient toilet
- only running the dishwasher/washing machine with a full load

- using the minimum amount of detergent when washing clothes
- minimizing the use of herbicides, pesticides and/or fertilizers
- turning off taps when running water is not necessary.

Activity

Find out about water pollution prevention at the City of Dubuque website:

With a partner, discuss ways in which water in your school/college could be conserved and how water pollution could be minimized. Share your findings with the rest of the class.

Exercise

Q31. Briefly **explain** why lead pollution became an environmental problem in Flint.

Q32. **Explain** the meaning of the term *photodegradation*.

Q33. **Outline** one problem in using a test kit to measure water pH.

Q34. **Give** an example of positive feedback in eutrophication.

Q35. **Outline** the options for altering human activities in the management of eutrophication.

Q36. **Explain** how BOD can be used to measure pollution.

HL

Q37. HL **Outline** the meaning of the term *indicator species*.

Q38. HL **Explain** why the release of nitrates and phosphates into the environment can cause algal blooms.

Q39. HL **Explain** why some algal blooms are harmful.

Q40. HL **Distinguish between** hypoxia and anoxia.

HL end

Engagement

- Investigate the effects of pollution on aquatic systems in your local area or region. Health and safety, and ethical issues, should be considered. Suggest mitigation schemes to reduce the pollution and its effects. Make a poster to show your findings.
- Produce an information film about water quality in your local area. Make sure you look at the positive aspects, negatives aspects, issues and potential management options.
- Engage in plastic pollution clean-ups. Start with a small-scale environment, such as your school and/or home area, and evaluate the success of the clean-up.
- Work with your teacher to organize a visit to a water-treatment or wastewater-treatment plant. Take notes and photos from the visit and then make a display to put up on a noticeboard at school.

Practice questions

1. The table shows the results of a survey of a stream above and below an outlet from a sewage works.

Site	Cross-sectional area / m²	Velocity / m sec⁻¹	Temp / °C	Oxygen / %	pH	Number of caddis flies	Number of bloodworms
1	2.1	0.2	18	0.1	6.0	12	0
2	2.3	0.2	17	0.2	6.0	15	0
3	2.2	0.3	18	0.1	7.0	11	0
4	3.8	0.3	23	0.3	6.5	0	16
5	3.9	0.6	22	1.8	7.0	0	1
6	4.1	0.8	22	1.7	7.5	1	0
7	3.9	0.7	22	1.6	6.5	2	0
8	4.0	0.7	20	1.5	7.0	7	0

Figure 4.88 shows a sketch map of the stream and the outlet.

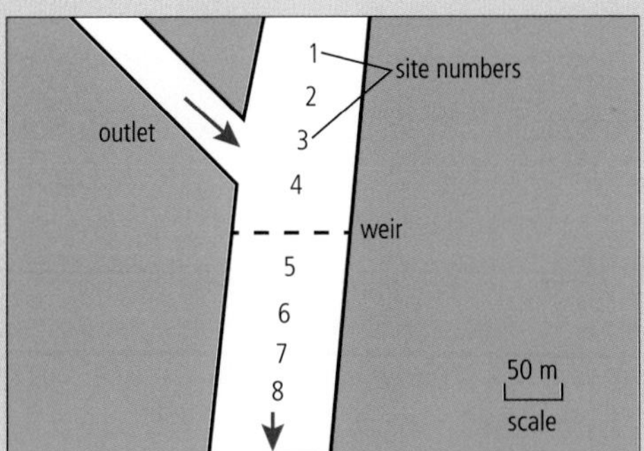

Figure 4.88 Sketch map of the stream and the outlet.

(a) Define the terms *water quality, pollution,* and *discharge.* [3]

(b) **(i)** Plot the results for variations in oxygen content along the course of the stream. [3]

(ii) State how the oxygen content changes between sites 4 and 5. [1]

(iii) Suggest reasons why the change in (ii) occurs. [4]

(c) **(i)** Describe the variations in the number of caddis flies and bloodworms between sites 1 and 8. [4]

(ii) Explain why the changes in the numbers of caddis flies and bloodworms occurs along the stream. [3]

(Total 18 marks)

(continued)

2. Study Figure 4.89, which shows sources of cultural eutrophication.

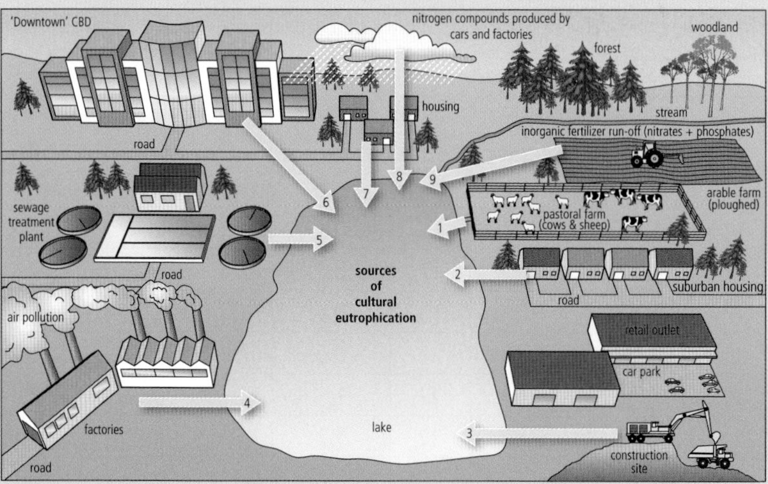

Figure 4.89 Sources of cultural eutrophication.

(a) Explain what is meant by the term *cultural eutrophication.* [1]
(b) Suggest two ways in which urban areas may contribute to eutrophication. [2]
(c) Identify the natural sources of nutrients as suggested by Figure 4.92. [1]
(d) Briefly explain the process of eutrophication. [5]

(Total 9 marks)

3. (a) Outline the impacts of the excessive growth of phytoplankton. [4]
(b) Discuss the impacts of increasing demand for seafood on marine ecosystems. [7]
(c) Examine the advantages and disadvantages of aquaculture. [9]

(Total 20 marks)

4. (a) Using examples, explain how urbanization can affect stores and flows in the hydrological cycle. [4]
(b) Examine the causes and consequences of water stress. [9]

(Total 13 marks)

5. Evaluate water conservation techniques at a domestic level. [9]

(Total 9 marks)

HL

6. HL Explain the importance of stratification in oceans. [9]

(Total 9 marks)

7. HL Discuss the impact of inequitable access to drinking water and sanitation on human health and sustainable development. [9]

(Total 9 marks)

8. HL Examine how the harvesting of seals, whales and dolphins raises ethical issues relating to the rights of animals and of Indigenous peoples. [9]

(Total 9 marks)

9. HL Evaluate methods for determining water quality. Consider the different methods for aspects of water quality e.g. water temperature, pH, chemical content and indicator species. [9]

(Total 9 marks)

HL end

5 Land

5.1 Soil

Guiding questions

How do soils play a role in sustaining natural systems?

How are human activities affecting the stability of soil systems?

5.1.1 Soil is a dynamic system within the larger ecosystem that has its own inputs, outputs, storages and flows.
5.1.2 Soil is made up of inorganic and organic components, water and air.
5.1.3 Soils develop a stable, layered structure known as a profile made up of several horizons, produced by interactions within the system over long periods of time.
5.1.4 Soil system inputs include those from dead organic matter and inorganic minerals.
5.1.5 Soil system outputs include losses of dead organic matter due to decomposition, losses of mineral components and loss of energy due to heat loss.
5.1.6 Transfers occur across soil horizons, into and out of soils.
5.1.7 Transformations within soils can change the components or the whole soil system.
5.1.8 Systems flow diagrams show flows into, out of and within the soil ecosystem.
5.1.9 Soils provide the foundation of terrestrial ecosystems as a medium for plant growth (a seed bank, a store of water and almost all essential plant nutrients). Carbon is an exception; it is obtained by plants from the atmosphere.
5.1.10 Soils contribute to biodiversity by providing a habitat and a niche for many species.
5.1.11 Soils have an important role in the recycling of elements as a part of biogeochemical cycles.
5.1.12 Soil texture defines the physical makeup of the mineral soil. It depends on the relative proportions of sand, silt, clay and humus.
5.1.13 Soil texture affects primary productivity through the differing influences of sand, silt, clay and dead organic matter, including humus.
5.1.14 Soils can act as carbon sinks, stores or sources, depending on the relative rates of input of dead organic matter and decomposition.
HL 5.1.15 Soils are classified and mapped by appearance of the whole soil profile.
HL 5.1.16 Horizons are horizontal strata that are distinctive to the soil type. The key horizons are organic layer, mixed layer, mineral soil and parent rock (O, A, B and C horizons).
HL 5.1.17 The A horizon is the layer of soil just beneath the uppermost organic humus layer, where present. It is rich in organic matter and is also known as the mixed layer or topsoil. This is the most valuable for plant growth but, along with the O horizon, is also the most vulnerable to erosion and degradation, with implications for sustainable management of soil.
HL 5.1.18 Factors that influence soil formation include climate, organisms, geomorphology (landscape), geology (parent material) and time.
HL 5.1.19 Differences between soils rich in sand, silt or clay include particle size and chemical properties.
HL 5.1.20 Soil properties can be determined from analysing the sand, silt and clay percentages, percentage organic matter, percentage water, infiltration, bulk density, colour and pH.
HL 5.1.21 Carbon is released from soils as methane or carbon dioxide.

5.1.1 Soil systems

1.2 Systems

Soil forms the outermost layer of the Earth's surface and consists of weathered rock, organic matter, air and water.

Soil is a good example of an open system as it has inputs, processes and outputs of energy and matter (Topic 1, Section 1.2.5). Soil is also closely linked to other environmental systems, notably the climate, and vegetative and lithospheric (rock) systems (Figure 5.1). If there is a change in one or more of the inputs, e.g. climate change, there will also be a change in the soil's characteristics.

Figure 5.1 Soil as an open system.

Soil is a dynamic *system* that has its own inputs, outputs, storages and flows.

A **soil profile** shows the vertical changes of layers in a soil from the surface to the bedrock.
A **pedon** is a three-dimensional sample of a soil that is large enough to show its characteristics.

Soil inputs include solar energy and heat, nutrients from weathered bedrock, sediment from upslope, moisture and organic matter (Figure 5.2). Although most diagrams of soils show them as a two-dimensional **soil profile**, they are, in fact, three dimensional features and are sometimes referred to as **pedons**.

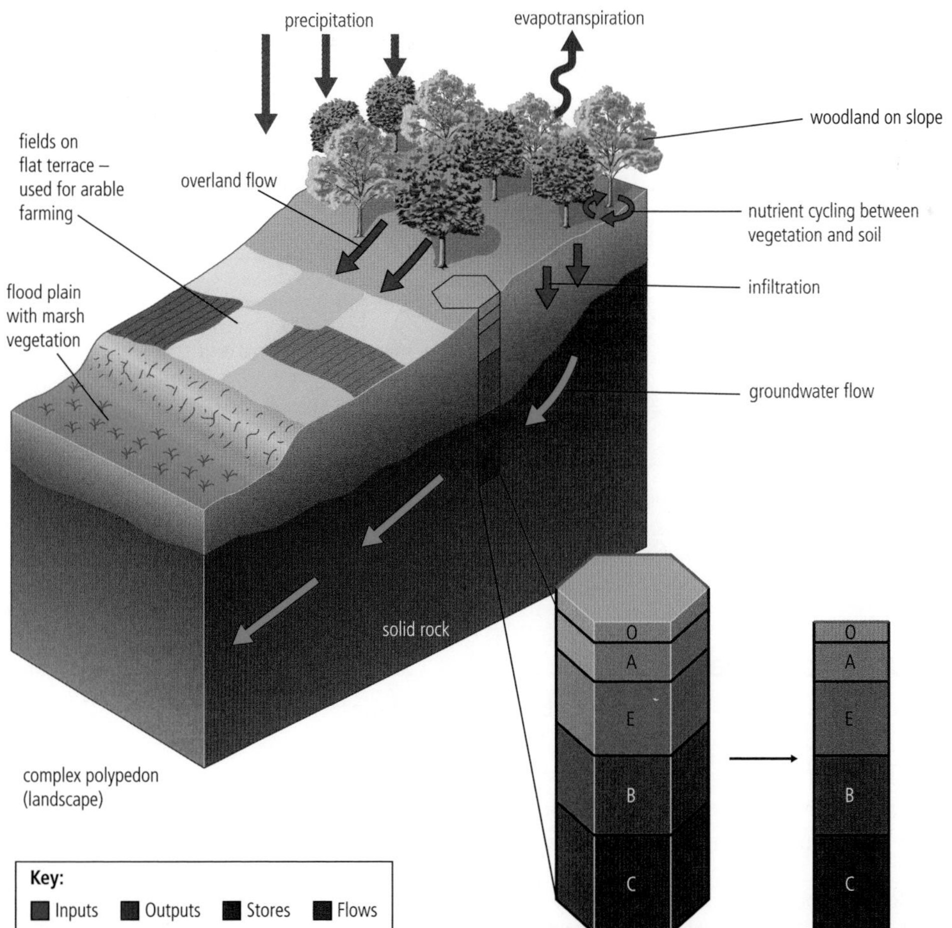

Figure 5.2 Soil systems in the environment.

O organic horizon
A mineral horizon
E eluvial (leached horizon)
B illuvial (deposited horizon)
C weathered bedrock

There are stores of weathered materials, organic matter, air and moisture in the soil.

Soil outputs include sediment, organic matter, nutrients, air and moisture.

What shapes my perspective as a knower? TOK

Fertile soil can be considered as a non-renewable resource because, once depleted, it can take significant time to restore the fertility. How does our perception of time influence our understanding of change?

Soils are vital resources for humans, but they can take a long time to develop. Fertile soil may be considered as a non-renewable resource due to the amount of time needed for soil development, which is much longer than a human lifetime. Soils are very dynamic as there are physical, chemical and biological activities continually taking place within them.

Soils have several properties that make them useful. These include:

- providing water, nutrients and anchorage for vegetation in ecosystems and agriculture landscapes
- providing a habitat for decomposers (organisms that break down dead plant and animal matter and release energy and nutrients into the soil), which have an essential role in the cycling of carbon and mineral nutrients
- being able to act as a buffer for temperature change and for the flow of water between the atmosphere and groundwater
- their ion exchange properties, which allow them to act as a pH buffer and be able to retain nutrients and other elements against loss by leaching and volatilization. Volatilization is the loss of applied nitrogen, especially from fertilizers applied in farming, to the atmosphere as ammonia gas (NH_3).

5.1.2 Soil composition

Soil forms the outermost layer of the Earth's surface. It contains weathered bedrock (**regolith**), organic matter (both living and dead), air and water (Figure 5.3).

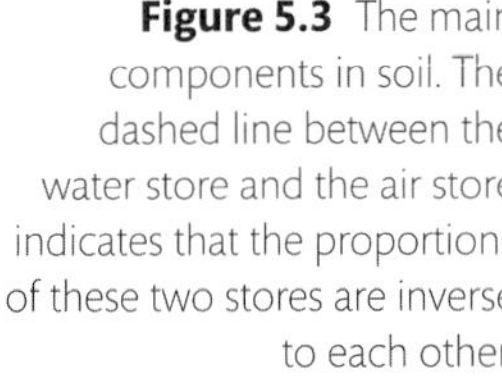

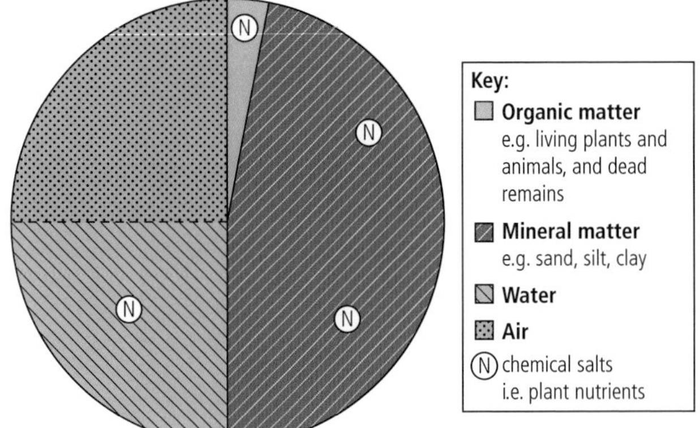

Figure 5.3 The main components in soil. The dashed line between the water store and the air store indicates that the proportions of these two stores are inverse to each other.

Organic matter

Soil organic matter can be divided into three categories:

- decomposing plant and animal matter called litter
- resistant organic matter called humus
- living organisms such as earthworms, springtails, bacteria and plant roots.

Soil microorganisms progressively decompose the plant and animal matter to produce litter, which is resistant to further decomposition. As the organic matter is broken down, nutrients are released, especially nitrogen, phosphorus and sulfur. In soil science, this process is known as **mineralization**.

The average amount of organic matter in the soil is generally low at 2–6%, but ranges from about 0.5% in semi-arid locations to around 90% in peatlands.

Soil organic matter is important because it:

- is the main food for several soil organisms
- binds mineral particles together and reduces the risk of soil erosion
- improves water holding capacity
- improves porosity and aeration and aids the growth of plants
- is a major source of nutrients
- improves soil fertility.

Soil pores are spaces in the soil that may be filled with air and/or water, **Macropores** are large pore spaces whereas **micropores** are small spaces. Micropores are often filled with water whereas macropores may contain both air and water.

2.3.4 Carbon cycle

Air and water

The **pore** spaces in soil may be filled with a mixture of air and water. As the amount of water in the pores increases, the amount of air in the same pores decreases.

Soil water

Water is essential for soils as it enables the weathering of bedrock, the horizon development due to upward and downward movement of water in the soil (this topic, Section 5.1.3) and the survival of plants and animals.

As soil water contains dissolved organic and inorganic substances, it is scientifically known as a soil solution. Soil solutions supply important **ions** known as cations and anions that plants need for growth and development (Figure 5.3). Soil solution also carries matter through translocation to the sub-surface soil.

An **ion** is an electrically charged particle that is produced when an atom gains or loses an electron. Salt compounds that dissolve into the soil solution contain negative anions and positive cations, which separate once they enter the solution.

For example, the salt sodium chloride (NaCl) contains positively charged sodium cations (Na^+) and negatively charged chloride anions (Cl^-).

There are three main states of water in soils, namely **gravitational water**, **capillary water** and **hygroscopic water** (Figure 5.4).

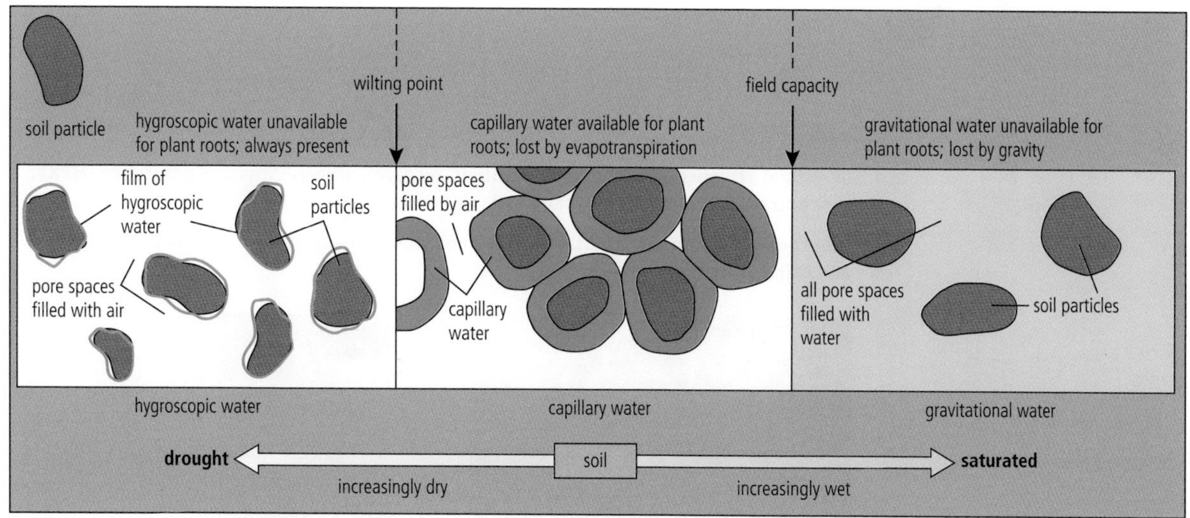

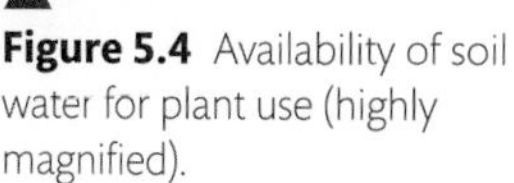

Figure 5.4 Availability of soil water for plant use (highly magnified).

Gravitational water refers to water movement down through the soil due to gravity. The higher the permeability of the soil, the faster the gravitational water flows through the soil. **Field capacity** occurs when all the smaller pores are filled with water and the larger pores are filled with air.

Capillary water refers to the water held by surface tension on small particles in the pore space. Capillary water can move upwards or downwards in the soil. In warm, dry areas capillary water may be drawn up to an evaporating surface to provide water for plants and/or evaporating from the soil. Thus, capillary water moves from wetter to drier locations.

Hygroscopic water refers to water that is held in a very thin layer around each individual soil particle. It is not very accessible to plants. The **permanent wilting point** occurs when plants are unable to withdraw any water tightly held by the soil.

Soils with more small particles, such as clay, will hold more water than ones with larger particles, such as sand (see figure accessed from this page of your eBook).

Clay has many small pores **(micropores)**, which reduce the rate at which water passes through but may also reduce infiltration.

In contrast, sand has much larger pores **(macropores)**, which allow water to pass through quickly but reduces the amount of water available for plant use.

A loam soil has both micropores and macropores. It provides water in the micropores and air in the macropores.

5.1.3 Soil profiles

2.5 Zonation, succession and change in ecosystems

Soil formation is a slow process, sometimes taking place over thousands of years.

Soil horizons develop as a result of the transfer processes (translocation, transformations, addition and removal) that occur in the open system of the soil.

In most soils there is a transition where the organic compounds in the upper surface layer transform into more inorganic compounds in the lower horizons.

SKILLS

Sample two soils from the subsoil (B horizon): one from a local garden or field, and one from a natural ecosystem

Examine samples of soil from your local area/school/college. Make sure that you compare (where possible) two or more contrasting soils. Examples you could use may include soils from below grass, below shrubs, below a deciduous tree, below a coniferous tree or soil that is close to water. Figure 5.5a shows urban soil taken from close to a building and Figure 5.5b shows soil taken from a garden.

Soil texture – the proportion of different sized materials in a soil – usually sand, silt and clay.

Investigate texture, organic matter content, nitrogen, phosphorus and potassium (NPK) concentrations, aeration, drainage and water retention

Determine the amount of carbon in a dry soil sample by burning off the organic matter and calculating the change in mass

Figure 5.5a A soil located on land at the edge of an urban area.

Figure 5.5b A garden soil sample.

You could use a table such as Table 5.1 to record your observations.

Observed soil characteristic	Soil 1 (e.g. below grass)	Soil 2 (e.g. below a flower bed)
Texture		
Organic matter		
NPK concentration		
Aeration		
Drainage		
Water retention		
Carbon content		

Table 5.1 A comparison of two soils.

Finger assessment of soil

Collect a sample of soil, about the size of a golf ball. Moisten the sample so that it is damp and work it between your thumb and forefinger. Work through the statements in the worksheet 'Soil testing by feel' on this page of your eBook to identify the type of soil texture.

You can work out the proportions of sand, silt and clay in a soil by feel, sieving (Figures 5.6a and 5.6b) and/or sedimentation (Figure 5.7). First, compare the three methods, identify their relative strengths and weaknesses and provide an overall evaluation of the three methods.

There are also keys published online that can be used to classify each of the soils studied.

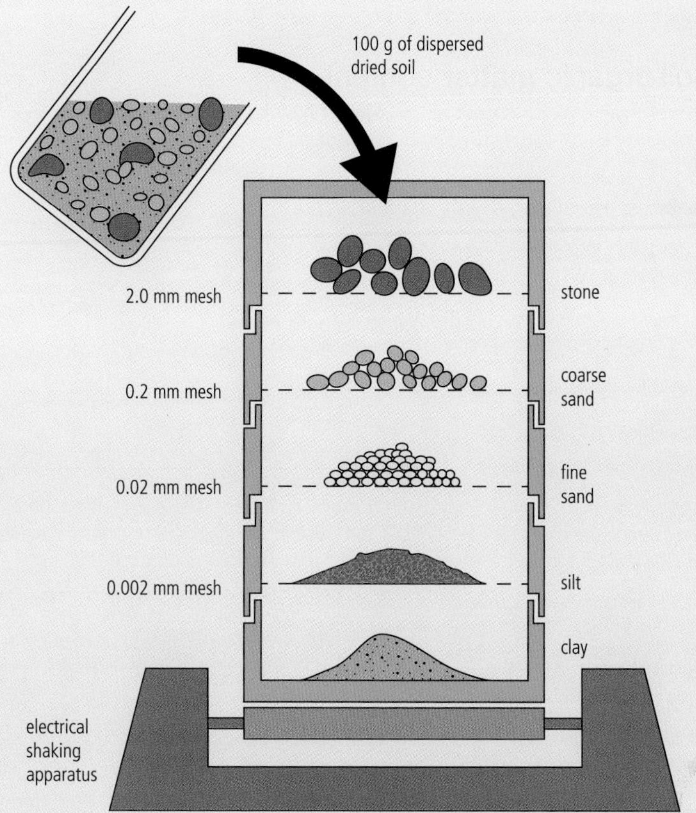

Figure 5.6a and b Soil sieves for calculating soil texture.

Sieving

Sieving involves the use of sieves with different sized meshes (Figures 5.6a and 5.6b). A mesh of 2 mm will trap stones but will allow smaller materials to pass through. A mesh of 0.2 mm will trap coarse sand but will allow finer materials to pass through. When all the material has been sieved, the percentage of each type of soil can be measured and expressed as a percentage of the total soil sample.

This value can then be compared with a soil textural triangle to determine the soil's texture (Figures 5.29a and 5.29b, this topic, Section 5.1.20).

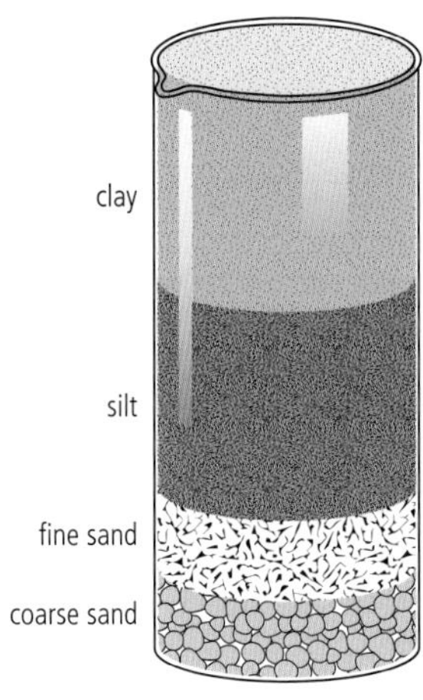

Figure 5.7 Soil sedimentation analysis.

Sedimentation

In this method, a sample of soil is first placed into a cylinder of water. The cylinder's contents are shaken vigorously and then allowed to settle.

According to Stoke's law, the larger particles will settle first forming a bottom layer. Then progressively finer materials settle to form additional layers, until the finest clay settles last to form the top layer (Figure 5.7). The height of each sediment layer in the cylinder can be measured and compared to the total height so that the percentage of each can be calculated and the results compared to a soil texture triangle (Figures 5.29a and 5.29b).

Soil moisture content

The soil moisture content can be measured by heating a sample of the soil twice and measuring the difference in the mass (Topic 2, Section 2.1.6 and 2.1.7).

1. Collect a sample of soil and measure its mass (S1).
2. Place the sample into an oven and heat it at 105 °C for 24 hours.
3. Remove the sample from the oven and measure its mass again (S2).

To work out the moisture content of the sample, use the formula:

$$\text{soil moisture content} = \frac{(S1 - S2)}{S1} \times 100\%$$

For example, a sample of soil with a mass of 34 g is baked. After 24 hours the mass of the soil was found to be 26 g.

The soil moisture content is calculated as: $\frac{(34 - 26)}{34} \times 100\% = 24\%$

Soil organic matter content

The soil organic matter content can be measured using a sample of the dry soil collected from the previous experiment. The dry soil should be ground up into finer particles so that it will fit into a crucible.

1. Record the initial mass of the crucible.
2. Add the dry soil sample and record the combined mass of soil and crucible.
3. Burn the soil sample in the crucible over a Bunsen burner for 30 minutes.
4. Allow the crucible to cool down, then measure the new combined mass of the crucible and the burned soil.
5. Subtract the initial mass of the crucible from both masses recorded in steps 2 and 4.

To determine the percentage of soil organic matter use the formula:

$$\text{soil organic matter content} = \frac{(\text{mass of soil before burning} - \text{mass of soil after burning})}{\text{mass of soil before burning}} \times 100\%$$

For example, the combined mass of the crucible and dry soil before the soil was burned was 47 g. After burning the combined mass of soil and crucible was 45 g. The crucible had a mass of 25 g so the soil's mass before burning was 22 g and the soil's mass after burning was 20 g.

The soil organic matter content is calculated as: $\frac{(22 - 20)}{22} \times 100\% = 9\%$.

To measure the nitrogen, phosphorus and potassium content of the soil you can use NPK test strips or an NPK meter. Both of these are generally available in gardening shops. The strips can be quite subjective, whereas the meter is usually more accurate.

Ask for permission to use a science laboratory and, under supervision, work out the moisture content for two soils from contrasting parts of your school grounds or your local environment.

Measuring aeration – soil bulk density

Soil bulk density (SBD) is influenced by three main factors: the proportions of mineral matter and organic matter, the soil texture, and the compaction of the ground.

Mineral matter is generally much denser (*c.* 2.5 g/cm^3) than organic matter (*c.* 0.5 g/cm^3).

SBD values increase with soil depth due to compaction and the presence of smaller quantities of organic material. This means that SBD values can be affected by land-use practices such as ploughing, tilling and the use of heavy machinery.

SBD is expressed in g/cm^3 and can be measured by dividing the mass of a dry soil sample in a cylinder by its volume.

The volume of the soil in the cylinder is calculated using the formula: $V = \pi r^2 h$, where V = volume, r = radius of the cylinder and h = height of the soil sample.

For example, a soil sample with a mass of 900 g was placed into a cylinder. The cylinder has a radius of 5 cm and the height of the soil in the cylinder was 10 cm.

The volume of the soil sample is calculated as $\pi \times 5^2 \times 10 = 785$ cm^3.

The SBD of the soil sample is calculated as: 900 g/785 cm^3 = 1.15 g/cm^3.

The average SBD for mineral soils is around 1.25 g/cm^3, whereas for peat soils the average SBD is 0.5 g/cm^3.

Drainage – measuring infiltration

Infiltration (water retention) can be measured fairly easily and cheaply (Figure 5.8). Sink a bottomless container, which has a diameter of 20 cm and a height of at least 30 cm, with marks at 5 cm intervals, 10 cm into the ground. Then fill the container with water until the water level reaches a height of 15 cm above the ground. Record the time it takes for the water level to drop by 5 cm. (This can be changed to 1 cm for slow-draining soils.) Keep topping up the water and recording the time until the times recorded are roughly constant for at least three successive repeats. The results can be expressed in terms of cm/second by dividing the difference in levels (5 cm) by the time taken (seconds).

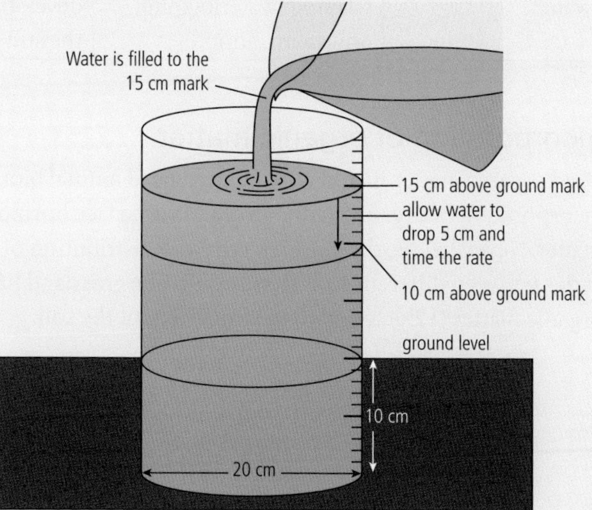

Figure 5.8 Measuring infiltration.

Consider the environmental impacts of your investigations e.g. soil compaction, removal of living soil and organisms from an environment, disturbance of an environment and potential impacts on vegetation. You should also consider the ethical considerations, for example, working out the soil organic content requires the burning of the organic matter. Is this justifiable? Do the benefits of increased knowledge and understanding outweigh the environmental destruction? Is the destruction so small-scale that it does not matter?

Risks in the lab may include burning soil in an oven for over 24 hours. Is it safe to leave an oven unattended overnight for such an experiment? What could go wrong? What measures have you taken to reduce risk? What are the risks when using Bunsen burners? How can you reduce these risks? Is there a responsible person in charge of you during the experiment?

5.1.4 Soil system inputs

1.2 Systems
2.5 Zonation, succession and change in ecosystems

Soils are open systems as there are flows of energy and matter across soil boundaries (Figure 5.1). In these systems, there are inputs, outputs (losses), transfers and transformations, resulting in the formation of soil. Inputs include heat, water and oxygen (O_2) from the atmosphere, organic matter from plant and animal remains, particulates from weathering and materials deposited from wind and water.

The development of soil is largely the result of three sets of processes: decomposition of organic matter, weathering and movement of water in the soil (Table 5.2).

Table 5.2 Soil processes divided into general and specific types and the resulting soil effects.

Primary or general process	Secondary or specific process	Role in soil formation
Incorporation of organic matter	Formation of humus Soil aggregation	Main agents responsible for development of horizons within the soil
Weathering	Oxidation Hydration	Accumulation of parent material
Movement of water	Leaching Gleying (waterlogging) Soil salinization	Main agents responsible for development of horizons within the soil

Incorporation of organic matter

Dead organic matter includes plant litter, dead animal biomass and manure. The incorporation of organic matter produces a surface horizon that is rich in organic matter. Nevertheless, the amount, type and distribution of incorporated organic matter varies between different soils (Figure 5.9). The grassland has the highest proportion of organic matter (12%) found in the top 60 cm of the soil.

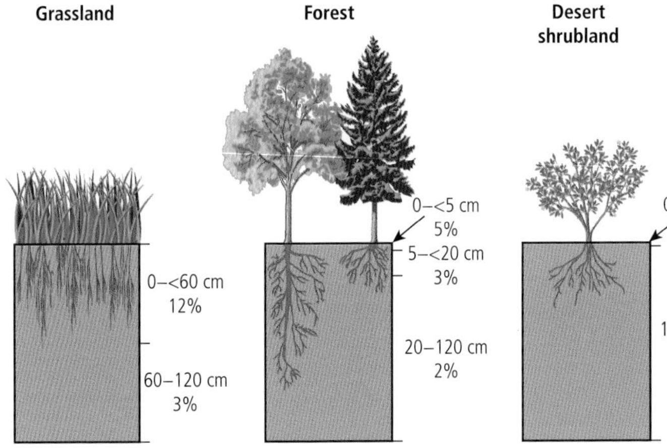

Figure 5.9 Differences in the content and distribution of soil organic matter in the upper 1.2 m of soils from a grassland, forest and desert.

Grassland: 0–<60 cm 12%; 60–120 cm 3%
Forest: 0–<5 cm 5%; 5–<20 cm 3%; 20–120 cm 2%
Desert shrubland: 0–<1 cm 1%; 1–120 cm trace

Some soils, such as those in tropical rainforests, deserts and young soils have low organic matter content due to rapid decay and breakdown or due to limited inputs. In contrast, in cool, wet climates, where waterlogging is present, organic decay is slowed resulting in thick layers of peat/humus in the upper layers of the soil.

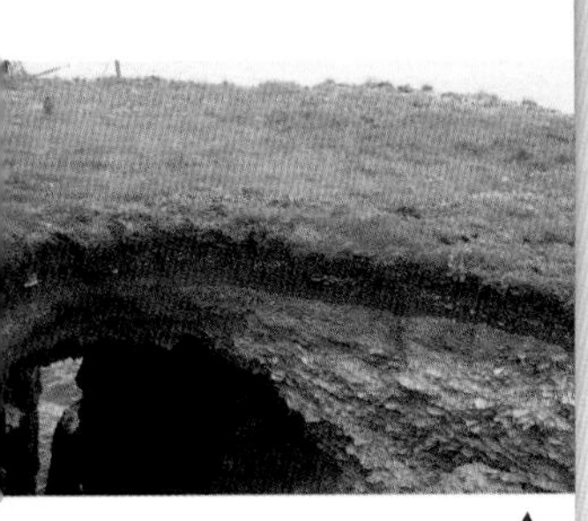

Figure 5.10 The dark organic horizon at the top of a soil can be clearly seen.

Dead organic matter is largely found on the uppermost layer of the soil having got there by leaf-fall or litter fall. Some matter is added into the upper zone of the soil through the decay of plant roots. Millions of soil organisms, such as earthworms, insects, fungi and other microscopic bacteria, are decomposers and break down this dead organic matter. These organisms mix the decayed organic matter with the mineral soil. The top horizon in soil is generally rich in organic matter and therefore darker in colour than the lower layers (Figure 5.10).

Activity

Make a sketch of Figure 5.11 and label the vegetation, organic horizon and bedrock.

The type of organic matter varies with region. In temperate regions associated with deciduous forests, the organic remains are fully broken down and humified most years. Earthworms and other soil organisms mix organic matter with the minerals, forming a mull humus. In areas of heathlands and coniferous forests, where conditions are more acidic, the soil organisms are much less active. This means that there is less mixing and the organic layers within the soil are more distinct, forming an acidic mor humus.

Figure 5.11 shows the three distinct layers representing the different stages of decomposition in a **podzol** (leached under acidic conditions). At the surface, the fresh litter (L) contains recognizable plant remains. Below this is the partly degraded fermentation layer (F) where decay is active, and the plant remains are difficult to recognize. Below is the humus layer (H) where all the plant material has been degraded. As the plant material is converted to humus, any inorganic or mineral materials, such as carbon and nitrogen, are released. Beneath the humus, the mineral-organic layer (A horizon) is found.

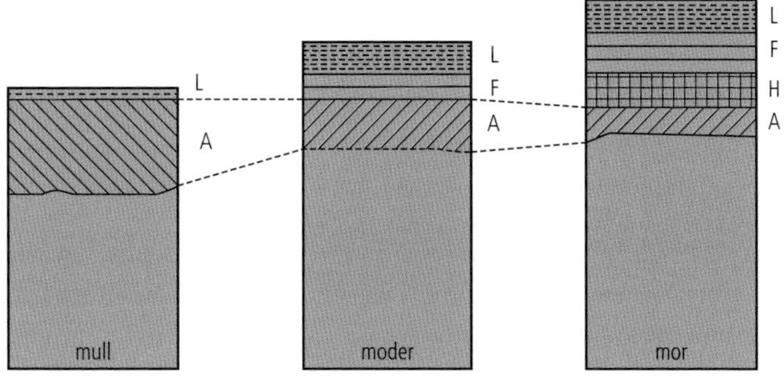

Figure 5.11 Organic matter accumulation in soils.

Weathering

In soil science, the term weathering can be defined as the breakdown of rocks *in situ* (without movement). The weathering of bedrock provides mineral particles (Table 5.3) in the lower horizon.

Primary minerals	Minerals from the bedrock that are resistant to weathering, such as mica and feldspar. They are mainly present in the sand and silt factions.
Secondary minerals	The products of chemical weathering are present in the clay faction. They include aluminosilicates and hydrated oxides of iron, aluminium and manganese, which are collectively referred to as clay minerals.

Table 5.3 Mineral components in soils.

Mull humus has a slightly acidic pH of 5.5–6.5 and is associated with well-drained deciduous woodlands in lowland areas. Mor humus has a pH of 3.5–4.5 and is associated with coniferous forests and/or upland heathlands. Acidic soils often have a thin litter layer at the surface because less mixing of organic material and mineral matter occurs due to the lack of earthworms in acidic conditions. An intermediate form, moder humus, is found in areas with a pH of 4.5–5.5.

Figure 5.12 Mechanical weathering producing a mass of angular rocks in a soil.

Figure 5.13 Chemical weathering of granite resulting in kaolinite (china clay).

There are two types of weathering. Mechanical (physical) weathering leads to the development of smaller particles of the same rock, such as scree or pebbles/stones (Figure 5.12). In chemical weathering, a rock substance is transformed into a different and new material. An example of chemical weathering is the transformation of granite into kaolinite (china clay) (Figure 5.13).

The process of weathering is important in the early development of a soil, as it provides several nutrients. The weathering of calcareous rocks tends to produce basic soils, whereas soils developed on non-calcareous rocks tend to produce acidic soils that are liable to **podzolization.** Podzolization is a form of leaching under acidic conditions in which iron and aluminium are leached from the upper horizons and deposited in the lower horizons.

Weathering also influences soil texture (the size of individual soil particles). The weathering of sandstones and gritstones produces coarse-grained, free-draining soils. In contrast, the weathering of shales produces much finer clay-rich soils that are less well-drained.

Materials can also be carried onto the soil by deposition from rivers. This mainly occurs on flood plains when the sediment that was being carried by the water is deposited because the river's velocity reduced when it bursts its banks.

Some materials, especially fine-grained sediments, may be deposited by winds. This mainly occurs when the exposed ground is dry and in areas with limited vegetation where the wind speed can remain relatively high (no slowing down by vegetation). This type of deposition favours arid and semi-arid areas.

Precipitation

Precipitation may include several solutes such as calcium, nitrates, chlorine, potassium, sulfates, bicarbonates of sodium and magnesium, and dissolved gases. However, there are many more minerals that are also held in minute quantities. The soil solution (soil moisture) is important for the transfer of nutrients to plants, as well as for the transfer of elements to the groundwater and the atmosphere. Some solutes are very soluble, such as sulfur dioxide. Some solutes are moderately soluble, such as carbon dioxide (CO_2) and nitrous oxide (N_2O). Others, such as O_2 and methane (CH_4), have low solubilities.

In soils with a pH above 5, the most common ions present include calcium, magnesium, potassium, sodium, nitrates, chlorides and sulfates. In acidic soils, aluminium, aluminium hydroxides and manganese may be present, while in anaerobic (O_2 deficient) conditions manganese and iron are normally present.

Soil temperature and the movement of heat

Soil temperature has an important impact on soil organism activity, germination of seeds, plant growth, root growth, rock weathering, soil formation and the evaporation of water.

Soil temperature can differ from air temperature for several reasons, including:

- incoming solar radiation and albedo
- heat loss by radiation, convection, conduction and latent heat of vaporization
- thermal conductivity of soil
- heat capacity of soil.

Albedo is a measure of how reflective a surface is.

Part of the incoming solar radiation is reflected by the surface. The remaining part of the solar radiation is absorbed at the soil's surface and transferred to heat energy that is radiated back out. This warms the soil and the air immediately above the soil and can vaporize water.

Diurnal and seasonal variations in soil temperature are reduced because vegetation intercepts part of the incoming solar radiation and part of the outgoing heat radiation from the soil. Air within the plant canopy is a poor conductor of heat, so this decreases temperature fluctuations in the soil beneath.

A layer of dead organic matter (litter) and/or a layer of snow has a similar effect. For example, the temperature of soil under a mulch is much lower during a sunny day but much higher at night than that of bare soil.

Anthropogenic inputs

Composting

The use of compost can improve the physical, chemical and biological characteristics of soil, soil organic matter and nutrient status. Mature composts increase soil organic matter better than fresh, immature composts do, due to their higher content of stable carbon.

Some of the benefits of adding compost rather than synthetic fertilizers to soil include:

- The addition of organic matter improves water retention. For example, compost helps sandy soils to retain water that would otherwise drain away and so protects the soil against drought.
- The aiding of porosity in clay soils, making the soil drain more easily so it is less likely to become waterlogged.

Compost has an equalizing effect on the annual/seasonal variations of water, soil and air heat balance and the availability of plant nutrients, which are released slowly.

Compost can off-set a decline in soil fertility and improve the conditions for plant germination due to better aeration and moisture retention.

Compost lowers SBD due to the addition of low-density organic matter into the soil. Lower bulk density matter has an increased pore space, especially containing macropores.

Compost contains several valuable plant nutrients including nitrogen, phosphorus, potassium, calcium, magnesium and sulfur. Thus, compost is a multi-nutrient fertilizer. Soils treated with compost show an improvement in their nutrient exchange capacity.

Fertilizers

Synthetic fertilizers are human-made products that are used to increase the level of nutrients in the soil and enhance plant growth. The main nutrients involved are nitrogen, phosphorus and potassium (NPK). Although several synthetic fertilizers increase plant growth, there are serious disadvantages to their use.

Sometimes synthetic fertilizers are referred to as 'chemical fertilizers' or 'inorganic fertilizers'.

Some synthetic fertilizers are highly soluble. As plants can only absorb a certain proportion of the fertilizer, the rest is open to leaching and/or overland flow.

Sulfuric acid is used to extract phosphorus from phosphate rocks. Sulfuric acid may dissolve soil crumbs, such as clay particles, which are combined with humus/ organic matter. These crumbs improve soil drainage and soil aeration. The use of fertilizers containing these acids can result in a compacted soil that has poor aeration and poor drainage. Synthetic fertilizers can also change soil pH and can kill some microorganisms that, if present, would benefit soil health. These microorganisms include bacteria (such as nitrogen-fixing bacteria), mycorrhizal fungi and other types of fungi. For example, the treatment of citrus trees with nitrogen fertilizer decreases their vitamin C yield.

Most of the phosphorus from fertilizers is absorbed by clay particles, iron oxides and aluminium oxides. The results of studies from European countries (notably Ireland,

Figure 5.14 Applying synthetic fertilizer to soil.

the UK, the Netherlands and Denmark)[1] suggest that sometimes phosphorus inputs from fertilizers and manure exceed phosphorus outputs from crop and livestock production. In the UK, the surplus is *c.* 15 kg h^{-1} yr^{-1}. Thus, the total amount of phosphorus in the soil may increase over time and the soil can become 'over-loaded' with respect to phosphorus.

Synthetic fertilizers can reduce trace elements in soils, which can increase the incidence of fungal bacterial diseasc in those soils. Some synthetic fertilizers contain heavy metals, such as cadmium and copper, which remain in the soil for a long time (Figure 5.14).

Agro-chemicals (pesticides, herbicides and insecticides)

Organic compounds such as pesticides, oil, tars, chlorinated hydrocarbons and dioxins are widely used in agriculture. Modern agriculture depends on pesticides (fungicides, herbicides and insecticides) for crop protection and disease control. These pesticides can be applied directly through direct spraying or atmospheric deposition, or indirectly through contamination from wastewater and waste-disposal. During direct spraying, only a small amount of the toxic chemicals reaches the target pest, diseases and weeds. The rest contaminates the surrounding soil, water and air.

Some bacteria can 'fix' nitrogen, releasing nitrate ions (NO_3^-) and making the soil fertile. However, agrochemical spills over plants can be detrimental to bacteria and therefore affect the levels of nitrogen and other minerals in the soil.

The impact of pesticide use depends on several factors including chemical properties of the soil and pesticide, climate and soil type, especially soil texture. Many older pesticides affect a broad range of organisms including some 'non-target' species. Pesticides can affect soil by adsorption onto clays and organic matter, by affecting soil microorganisms and plant growth, or by moving through the soil to surface water and groundwater.

Some pesticides, such as DDT, can build up in soils and in the tissues of living organisms, becoming toxic. As a result, they can also harm or kill species other than those that they were intended to kill.

The large-scale use of agrochemicals (Figure 5.15) reduces biodiversity in soil, as microorganisms are killed, their reproductive success is reduced and there is less growth. These microorganisms are essential for maintaining soil structure and mineralization of organic matter making nutrients available for plants.

Figure 5.15 Agrochemicals on sale in a garden centre.

The use of copper-based fungicides has led to a long-term reduction in earthworm populations. Earthworms enhance soil fertility by decomposing organic matter and releasing nutrients into the soil. They also create channels for the movement of air and water through the soil, thus improving aeration and drainage.

Organophosphate insecticides have had a negative impact on bacterial and fungal populations in soil. Pesticide toxicity has more than doubled since 2005 and pesticides can linger in the soil for decades.

Pesticides, such as persistent organic pollutants (POPs), are very persistent in soils and break down very slowly. Pesticides can enter the soil via spray drift during treatment and through the run-off from treated vegetation and treated seeds in the soil. Agrochemicals and fertilizers contain impurities e.g. heavy metals such as lead, zinc and arsenic, and trace elements such as cobalt and molybdenum, which can build up to toxic levels in the soil.

Research conducted in the USA showed that pesticides harmed beneficial soil-dwelling invertebrates in over 70% of cases reviewed (Centre for Biological Diversity, 2021).

[1]Withers, P.J.A., Forber, K.G., Lyon, C. et al. Towards resolving the phosphorus chaos created by food systems. Ambio 49, 1076–1089 (2020). https://doi.org/10.1007/s13280-019-01255-1

Irrigation and soil salinization

Irrigation refers to the additional input of water into agricultural systems to encourage plant growth. It is one of the oldest techniques used by people to improve food supplies. Worldwide, it is estimated that about 18% of cultivated land is irrigated, but this land accounts for 40% of crop production.

A major problem with irrigation in areas of low rainfall is the accumulation of salts, especially sodium salts, which can make the soil infertile and toxic. The sources of the salts include the irrigation water and saline ground water, which rises to the surface when excess water is applied (Figure 5.16).

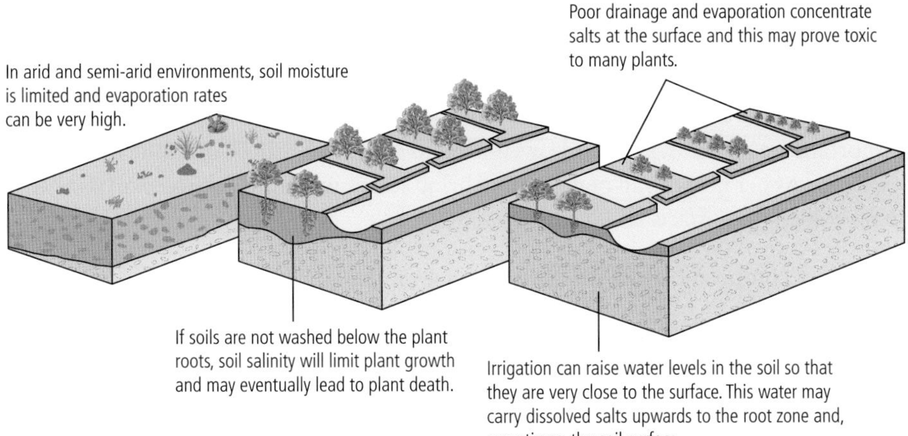

Poor drainage and evaporation concentrate salts at the surface and this may prove toxic to many plants.
In arid and semi-arid environments, soil moisture is limited and evaporation rates can be very high.
If soils are not washed below the plant roots, soil salinity will limit plant growth and may eventually lead to plant death.
Irrigation can raise water levels in the soil so that they are very close to the surface. This water may carry dissolved salts upwards to the root zone and, sometimes, the soil surface.

Figure 5.16 The process of soil salinization.

To prevent the accumulation of excess salts, it is necessary to add excess water, which washes the salts into the subsoil and into rivers via throughflow. **Sodicity** is the presence of large amounts of sodium ions in relation to other cations. As sodium salts are leached out of the soil, some sodium ions remain bound to clay products. Sodicity weakens the bonds between soil particles. It also reduces water flow through soils, which can therefore allow salts to accumulate over time.

The most common types of salinity are those caused by chlorides and sulfates of sodium and calcium. Arid soils differ from humid soils in that sodium makes up a higher proportion of the total cation exchange capacity (CEC). Hydrogen cations are rare in arid soils.

Natural inputs

Natural inputs can originate from within the ecosystem, e.g. from the weathering of bedrock and litter from vegetation and decomposition. The weathering of rock allows soil development to take place. Some rocks can be weathered to a great depth. For example, in humid tropical areas the depth of weathering can be up to 90 m. Weathering controls whether soils are deep or shallow. Litter from above ground vegetation may be decomposed, with minerals and elements being released back into the soil. Materials may be transferred from other ecosystems, for example through windblown and waterborne deposition. Nutrients may also be transferred into an ecosystem by the feeding patterns of animals. For example, birds such as gannets (Figure 5.17) can deposit guano onto islands resulting in a transfer of nutrients from oceans to terrestrial ecosystems.

Figure 5.17 Gannets, guano and an island.

5.1.5 Soil system outputs

Soil system outputs can cause the loss or modification of soil components and are different from total loss of soil by erosion. However, they can also lead to the degradation of productive soil.

1.2 Systems

Decomposition

Decomposition is the process whereby complex organic materials in dead plant and animal tissue are broken down into their original inorganic materials such as CO_2, water, minerals and elements.

The most important group of decomposers are the microorganisms – bacteria and fungi. Certain species of bacteria are responsible for the oxidation of sulfur compounds (from which they obtain their energy), the fixation of atmospheric nitrogen (N_2) and the release of inorganic nitrogen (nitrification) from organic compounds. The amount and variety of soil animals can vary depending on the amount and quality of the dead organic matter available, soil temperature, soil moisture and soil acidity.

In general, there is a correlation between the rate of biological productivity and the rate of decomposition. However, optimum temperatures for decomposition (30–35 °C) are higher than those for productivity (20–25 °C). Decay rates decrease 25-fold between the tropical rainforest and boreal forests, whereas productivity falls by a factor of 2.5 times. The result is a thick layer of dissolved organic matter in boreal forests. Decomposition also decreases as the age of the dissolved organic matter increases. Therefore, nutrient availability for microbial decomposers also declines.

The most important group of macroanimals decomposers in temperate environments are earthworms and in tropical humid (wet) and arid (dry) environments the most important are termites. In a fertile, well-aerated soil, there may be over one million earthworms per hectare, all of which can bring soil upwards from lower horizons and deposit it on the surface.

Organic decomposition involves three processes:

- rapid leaching of soluble chemical products
- mechanical breakdown of dead organic matter through wetting and drying cycles, freezing and thawing
- biological degradation involving the feeding on dissolved organic matter by animals and oxidation by microbial respiration, producing water and CO_2.

The rate of decomposition depends on several factors, including the chemical composition and age of the dissolved organic matter and the local environmental conditions. Decomposition is at a maximum when optimal temperature and moisture conditions occur in a well-aerated soil.

Erosion

Water erosion

Water causes soil erosion through raindrop impact, overland flow and flow in channels. Water can also cause landslides on steep slopes. When raindrops hit the soil surface, they may displace sand and silt grains that then can block pore spaces. As a result, infiltration is reduced and overflow occurs, causing increased soil erosion. Soils that have been eroded become shallower and lose much of their nutrient content.

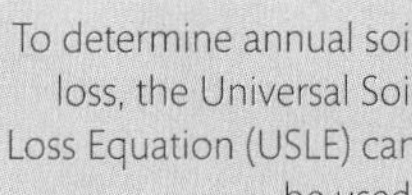

To determine annual soil loss, the Universal Soil Loss Equation (USLE) can be used.

The equation is:
$A = RKLSCP$
where:

A = annual soil loss, R = erosivity of the rain, K = soil erodibility, L = length of soil slope, S = slope angle, C = crop management and P = soil conservation methods.

There are several effects of soil erosion by water including:

- loss of soil to support the growth of vegetation and crops
- silting of dams and reservoirs
- deposition of sediment loads causing rivers to change course
- variable seasonal flow of rivers and flooding
- water pollution – the erosion of 1 tonne of soil containing 0.2% nitrogen and 0.05% phosphorus will transfer 2 kg of nitrogen and 0.5 kg of phosphorus to rivers and lakes.

The amount of soil lost depends on several factors.

The erodibility of soil increases if there are particles that are easily detached through raindrop impact. Dry clay, silt and fine sand are easily eroded on account of their size, but wet clay is very cohesive and may resist erosion. The volume of soil erosion increases with slope angle and the length of the slope, while vegetation forms a protective cover against raindrop impact. However, although the root systems of agricultural crops on hills protect the soil while they are growing, once harvested, their level of protection drops. Conservation methods, such as terraces (Figure 5.18) may reduce erosion.

Figure 5.18 Terraces of a steep slope reducing the amount of overland flow and soil erosion.

Wind erosion

Wind erosion occurs on dry, bare soil. The main factors that influence wind erosion are wind speed and particle size. Soil particles may be transported in different ways.

In soil creep, particles sized 0.5– 2 mm are rolled or dragged along the soil surface. In saltation, particles sized 0.05–0.5 mm are 'bounced' along the surface. In suspension, fine particles that are less than 0.05 mm in size may be carried aloft over long distances.

The removal of fine materials leaves the surface dominated by large particles, such as coarse sands, gravels and stones.

i

The formula used to determine the amount of soil lost through wind erosion is:

$A = f(I, K, C, L, V)$

where:

f = function of, A = soil loss, I = soil erodibility based on soil texture/laboratory testing,
K = soil surface roughness,
C = climate including wind speed, rainfall and evapotranspiration,
L = length of unsheltered land downwind and
V = vegetation cover.

Activity

Make a table with three columns. In the first column, write down the factors that influence both water erosion and wind erosion. In the second column, write down the factors that influence water erosion only. In the third column write down the factors that influence wind erosion only.

Water and mineral absorption by roots

Water is removed from the soil by plants. Water is transferred up the plant through small vessels known as xylem, and eventually lost from plants to the atmosphere by evaporation (a process known in plants as transpiration).

The elements that plants require are shown in Table 5.4. Nitrogen and potassium are the two elements that are generally taken up in the largest amounts, which can be up to 100 kg ha^{-1} year^{-1}.

Table 5.4 Elements required by plants.

Elements from the atmosphere and water		carbon hydrogen oxygen
Elements from the soil	Macronutrients	nitrogen phosphorus potassium calcium magnesium sulfur
	Micronutrients	iron manganese copper zinc boron molybdenum chlorine nickel
	Beneficial elements	cobalt sodium silicon

These elements are often found in compounds and ions in the soil solution.

For example, nitrogen can be found in ammonium (NH_4^+) and nitrate (NO_3^-) ions; phosphorus in dihydrogen phosphorus and monohydrogen phosphorus, sulfur in sulfate ions and metals in the form of metal cations such as calcium cations and magnesium cations.

The plant takes these compounds and ions up from the soil solution through its roots into the plant where they undergo chemical reactions to liberate the elements.

Leaching

Rainwater is naturally acidic. As it moves down through the soil, it reacts with and removes basic cations from the soil solution and those adsorbed to the clay and humus particles. Acidic rainwater removes basic calcium ions from clay particles and replaces them with acidic hydrogen ions. When this occurs over a long period, the soil becomes more acidic.

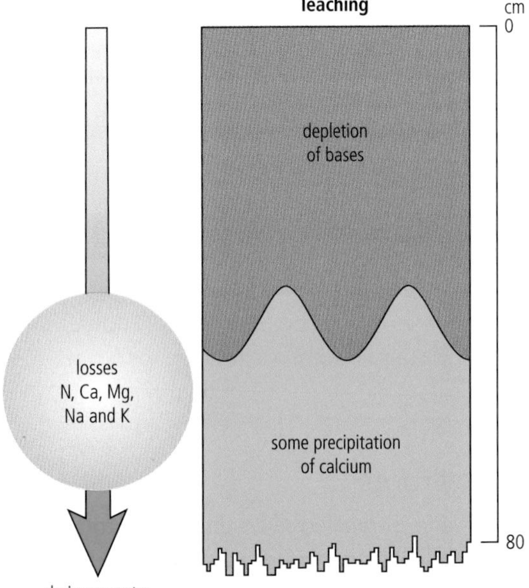

Figure 5.19 Leaching.

Basic elements that are typically leached out of soils in this way include calcium, magnesium, sodium, nitrogen, potassium and phosphorus (Figure 5.19). The water contains dissolved O_2, CO_2 and acids from decaying plants. In areas of tropical rainforest, deforestation leads to reduced interception and increased rainfall passing down through the soil. Nutrients are leached from the soil owing to the large amount of water moving down through the soil.

In temperate areas, where precipitation (PPT) > potential evapotranspiration (pEVT) there is a downward movement of water through the soil.

Leaching can transfer NO_3^- ions and phosphate ions into groundwater. These chemicals may also react with the clay to form a hardened layer, known as a hard pan, within the soil (Figure 5.20).

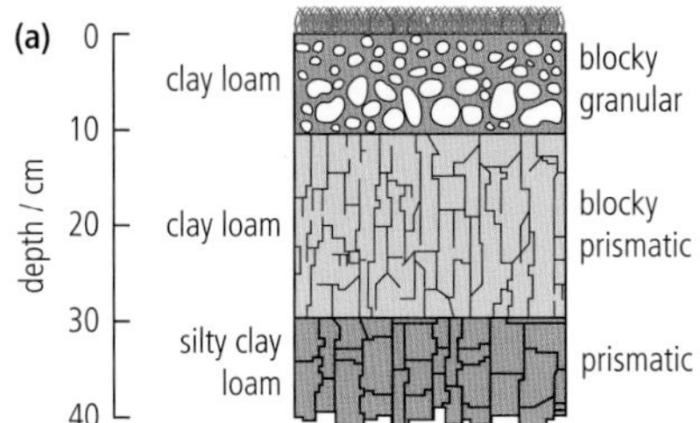

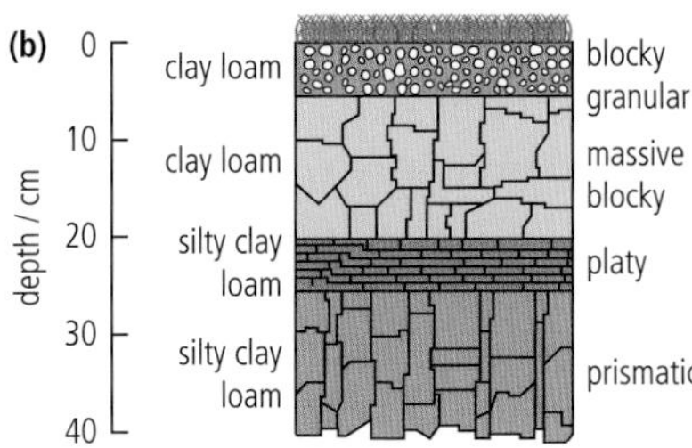

Figure 5.20 A soil pan showing the compaction of the silty, clay loam.

Diffusion of gas

Diffusion occurs when there is a greater concentration of molecules or ions at one point compared to another. In diffusion there is a net movement of molecules or ions from the point with the greater concentration to the point with lower concentration, until the concentration at both points becomes equal.

Soil air is different to atmospheric air in that it has a higher concentration of CO_2 and water vapour, but a lower concentration of O_2. CO_2 and water vapour therefore move out of the soil into the air, whereas O_2 moves into the soil.

Diffusion occurs more slowly in liquids than in gases. If the total pore space is completely occupied by water, i.e. saturated, O_2 will diffuse very slowly through the water, which is insufficient for most plants. However, with unimpeded diffusion, nutrients can reach the root surface. Thus, the best situation for plants is when there is air in the soil, rather than it being completely saturated with water.

Evaporation of water and heat loss

Evaporation is the diffusion of water from exposed water surfaces such as those in lakes, rivers, soils and plant surfaces. The rate of evaporation is greatly affected by solar radiation, which provides the energy needed to convert liquid water into water vapour. Other factors that affect the rate of evaporation include wind speed, the initial humidity of the air and the type of soil/rock surface. Bare soils and rocks have high rates of evaporation compared with surfaces that have a protective tilth where rates are low. The humidity of the air above an evaporating surface will continue to increase.

Heat loss from soils occurs in the form of out-going long-wave radiation. Heat loss is greatest at night and in those areas where there is limited cloud cover and/or vegetation cover. On a cloudless night there is very little return of long-wave radiation from the atmosphere due to the lack of clouds. Hence, there is a net loss of heat from the soil surface. In contrast, on a cloudy night the clouds return some long-wave radiation to the surface, hence the overall loss of energy is reduced. However, the heat transferred to the soil and bedrock during the day may be released back to the surface by night. This may partly offset the night-time cooling at the surface.

5.1.6 Transfers across horizons within the soil

1.2 Systems 

Transfers occur across soil horizons and include infiltration, percolation, groundwater flow, biological mixing, aeration, erosion and leaching.

Infiltration

Infiltration is the process by which water soaks into or is absorbed by the soil. It is distinguished from percolation, which is the downward flow of water through the zone of aeration towards the water table, although the two are closely related. The **infiltration capacity** is the maximum rate at which rain can be absorbed by soil in any given condition.

How different vegetation cover and types of vegetation affect infiltration

Infiltration capacity decreases with time through a period of rainfall until a constant value is reached (Figure 5.21). The main factors affecting infiltration are soil surface, surface cover and flow conditions. Infiltration rates of 0–4 mm/hour are common in clays, whereas 3–12 mm/hour are common in sands. Vegetation also increases infiltration. On bare soils where rain splash impact occurs, infiltration rates may reach 10 mm/hour. On similar soils covered by vegetation, rates of between 50 and 100 mm/hour have been recorded. Infiltrated water is chemically rich as it picks up minerals and organic acids from vegetation and soil.

Figure 5.21 Variations in infiltration with vegetation and time.

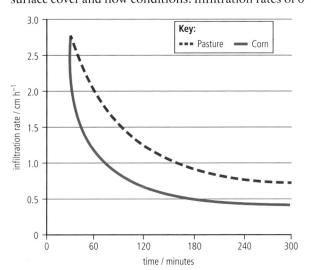

Source: *Advanced Geography: Concepts & Cases* by P. Guinness & G. Nagle (Hodder Education, 1999), p. 247

Infiltration is inversely related to overland runoff and is influenced by a variety of factors such as duration of rainfall, antecedent soil moisture (pre-existing levels of soil moisture), soil porosity, vegetation cover (Figure 5.22), raindrop size and slope angle.

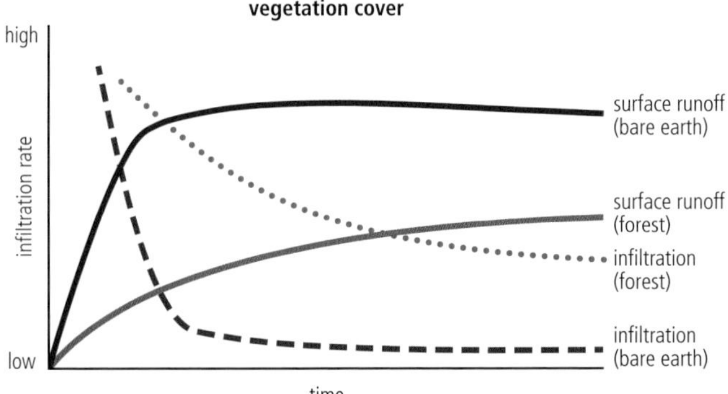

Figure 5.22 Infiltration rates and vegetation cover.

Figure 5.22 shows that infiltration on bare earth is initially high but decreases rapidly as the soil becomes saturated. The opposite is true for surface runoff on bare earth. In contrast, where there is a forest cover over the soil, infiltration is lower because more of the water is intercepted by the trees and less reaches the ground.

Activity

1. Using the data in Figure 5.21, describe how infiltration varies with vegetation and over time.
2. Explain why infiltration and surface runoff differ on bare ground and in forest (Figure 5.22).

Percolation

Water moves slowly downwards from the soil into the bedrock. This is known as percolation. Depending on the permeability of the rock, this may occur very slowly or quite quickly locally, as is the case in rocks such as carboniferous limestone and chalk.

Groundwater

Groundwater occurs in the sub-surface/underground in the pores of soils and rock (Figure 5.23).

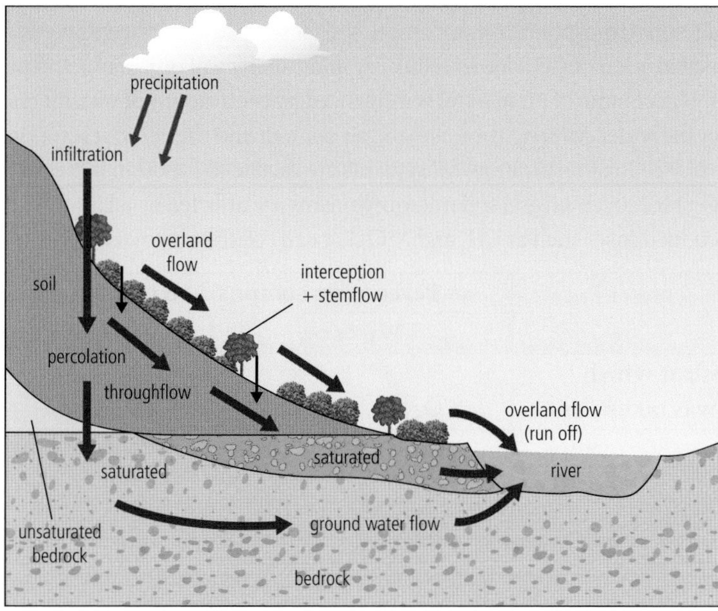

Figure 5.23 Groundwater flows.

The upper layer of the permanently saturated zone (where nearly all the pore spaces are filled with water) is known as the water table. The water table varies seasonally. It is higher following increased levels of precipitation.

The zone that is seasonally wetted and seasonally dries out is known as the aeration zone. Most ground water is found within a few hundred metres of the surface, but it has been found at depths of up to 4 km beneath the surface.

Aquifers (rocks which contain significant quantities of water) provide a great reservoir of water. Aquifers are permeable rocks such as sandstones and limestones. Water in aquifers moves very slowly and acts as a natural regulator in the hydrological cycle by absorbing rainfall that otherwise would reach streams rapidly. In addition, aquifers

Groundwater is important as it accounts for 96.5% of all freshwater on the earth. However, while some soil water may be recycled by evaporation into atmospheric moisture within a matter of days or weeks, groundwater may not be recycled for as long as 20,000 years. So, in some places, where recharging is not taking place, groundwater is considered a non-renewable resource.

Figure 5.24 A brown earth has a relatively uniform appearance due to the mixing of horizons by biological activity, notably by earthworms.

maintain stream flow during long dry periods. A rock that will not hold water is known as an aquiclude or aquifuge. These are impermeable rocks that prevent the large-scale storage and transmission of water.

The groundwater balance is the difference between discharge (use) from groundwater and recharge to groundwater. The reasons groundwater recharge occurs include:

- infiltration of part of the total precipitation at the ground surface
- seepage through the banks and beds of surface water bodies such as ditches, rivers, lakes and oceans
- groundwater leakage and inflow from adjacent aquicludes and aquifers
- artificial recharge from irrigation and reservoirs.

Biological mixing

Biological mixing can mix the layers of a soil. The soil in Figure 5.24 is brown earth. This type of soil has a very mildly acidic pH and contains many earthworms that ingest the soil, carry it up to the surface and deposit it. As a result of this movement, the soil has a much more uniform character than podzols, for example, that are formed under acidic conditions and rendzinas that are formed on chalk and limestones.

Aeration

Compared to the atmosphere above the soil, soil air has a lower concentration of O_2 but a higher concentration of CO_2 due to cellular respiration by soil organisms and plant roots (Table 5.5). The volume of air in a soil is influenced by the amount of water it contains. The greater the water content, the lower the air content and the easier it is for the O_2 to be depleted by cellular respiration. Most plants are unable to function if they do not have access to O_2. Moreover, several soil microorganisms are affected by a lack of O_2, causing them to produce gases such as CH_4 and N_2O that can contribute to global climate change.

Table 5.5 Composition of the air in a poorly drained silty loam soil.

	Percentage composition of extracted air			
	Winter		Summer	
Soil depth at which sample was taken / cm	CO_2	O_2	CO_2	O_2
30	1.2	19.4	2.0	19.8
61	2.4	11.6	3.1	19.1
91	6.6	3.5	5.2	17.5
122	9.6	0.7	9.1	14.5
152	10.4	2.4	11.7	12.4

Erosion and leaching

Erosion can remove material from one soil and transport it to a soil in another area. Overland flow removes topsoil, while rivers can erode soils on their riverbanks. This eroded material can be deposited later on the surface of other soils, thereby changing their characteristics. Some soils, notably those in floodplains, are formed due to the impacts of repeated deposition following floods. These soils are often nutrient-rich, as it is the mineral soil that generally gets eroded. Erosion can also carry soil materials in rivers out to the oceans. Wind erosion can also remove topsoil and deposit it on the surface of other soils or carry it to oceans. Erosion can remove fine-grained materials, such as clays from the upper parts of the soil profile to the lower parts (this topic, Section 5.1.5). Leaching can transfer soluble soil material down through the soil.

5.1.7 Transformations within soils

1.2 Systems

Transformations within soils can change the components of the whole soil system. Types of soil transformations include decomposition, weathering, nutrient cycling and soil salinization.

Decomposition

During the process of decomposition, organic matter that has been added to the soil is transformed into humus and mineral elements.

Decomposition returns nutrients that were taken up by plants, and potentially consumed by animals, to the soil. Most of the nutrients are found in the top layer of the soil and, under mildly acidic conditions, this gets thoroughly mixed by earthworm activity. Without the presence of decaying organic matter, the topsoil would not be able to support plant life. Dead organic matter helps the topsoil hold water and O_2 – humus can hold more water than clay. During organic decay and the formation of humus, chemical salts are released that provide soil nutrients. Humus can also bind individual minerals into larger structures (called aggregates).

Weathering

Weathering is central to soil development and provides the soil with many of its nutrients. It also breaks down rock and enables erosion and transport. These processes can lead to changes in the whole soil system, either directly or indirectly. Several features of weathering can be recognized:

- Weathering causes changes in volume, density, grain size, surface area, permeability consolidation and strength. These factors can affect soil drainage, aeration and fertility.
- Weathering forms new minerals and solutions, which can affect soil fertility.
- Some minerals, such as quartz, may resist weathering. This can affect soil drainage, temperature, aeration and fertility.
- Weathering prepares rocks for subsequent mass movement. For example, steep slopes may be made more vulnerable to landslides.

Example – Earthworm populations

UK earthworm populations may have fallen by between 33% and 41% in 1997–2022. Such a decline could sit alongside 'insectageddon' and the global destruction of wildlife. However, there has been no long-term monitoring of soil invertebrates. The decline of earthworms would not only have an impact on species that feed on them but would also affect soil processing, nutrient cycling and the whole functioning of ecosystems. Causes of this decline include extensive land drainage, pesticide use and the application of synthetic fertilizers. The decline in earthworm populations in deciduous forests is likely to be due to climate change.

Nutrient cycling

Nutrients are circulated and re-used frequently. All natural elements are capable of being absorbed by plants, either in gases or in soluble salts. Nutrients are taken in by plants and built into new organic matter. When animals eat the plants, they take up these nutrients.

Nutrient cycles can be shown by means of a simplified diagram, known as Gersmehl's model of nutrient cycling. This model includes representations of the nutrient stores, as well as the transfers that occur between them. The most important factors that determine these stores and transfers are the availability of moisture, heat, fire (in grasslands), density of vegetation, competition and the length of the growing season.

The nutrients eventually return to the soil when the plants and animals die and are broken down by the decomposers. All nutrient cycles involve an interaction between the soil and the atmosphere and involve several food chains. Nevertheless, there is great variety between the cycles. Nutrient cycles can be sedimentary-based, in which the source of the nutrient is from rocks, or they can be atmospheric-based, as in the case of the nitrogen cycle. Generally, atmospheric-based cycles are more complete than sedimentary-based ones as the latter are more susceptible to disturbance, especially that caused by human activity.

Challenge yourself

Consider how Gersmehl's model can be considered a system.

Explaining the differences between nutrient cycles in different ecosystems involves consideration of several processes.

Soil salinization

Figure 5.25 Soil salinization.

Irrigation can lead to an increase in the amount of salt in the soil. This may occur in hot areas when groundwater levels are close to the surface (Figure 5.25). In clay soils this may occur within 3 m of the surface, whereas in sandy and silty soils this may occur closer to the surface. Capillary forces bring water to the surface where it may evaporate leaving behind any soluble salts that it is carrying. This process is known as soil salinization. Some irrigation, especially that occurring in rice paddy fields, requires huge amounts of water. As water evaporates in the radiated heat from the Sun, the salinity levels of the remaining water increase. The development of a saline crust can be toxic for plants and soil microorganisms and the soil structure may be changed accordingly.

Example – Saltwater intrusion

Some areas affected by saltwater intrusion. Saltwater intrusion is a widespread problem and has been identified in a range of places including California, the United Arab Emirates (UAE), London, Japan and the east coast of the USA. The construction of the Aswan Dam in Egypt led to a fall in groundwater levels in the Nile Valley and Delta. In addition, the population increase has led to an increased use of groundwater. Consequently, there has been a decline in groundwater levels on the delta and salt-water intrusion has contaminated parts of it. Soil salinization can occur from below the soil (due to rising water tables) as well as on the surface of the soil.

1.2 Systems

5.1.8 Systems flow diagrams

Systems flow diagrams show flows into, out of and within the soil ecosystem. A system is a simplified structuring of reality (Topic 1, Section 1.2).

Systems are used because natural systems such as soils are complex. To understand them, we need to break them down into:

- factors that affect the system
- processes that operate within the system
- the results of those processes and the changes they bring about.

This can, in turn, affect how the system operates. Figure 5.26 shows a systems flow diagram for a soil environment. Soil systems are essential for water-, carbon- and nitrogen-cycles.

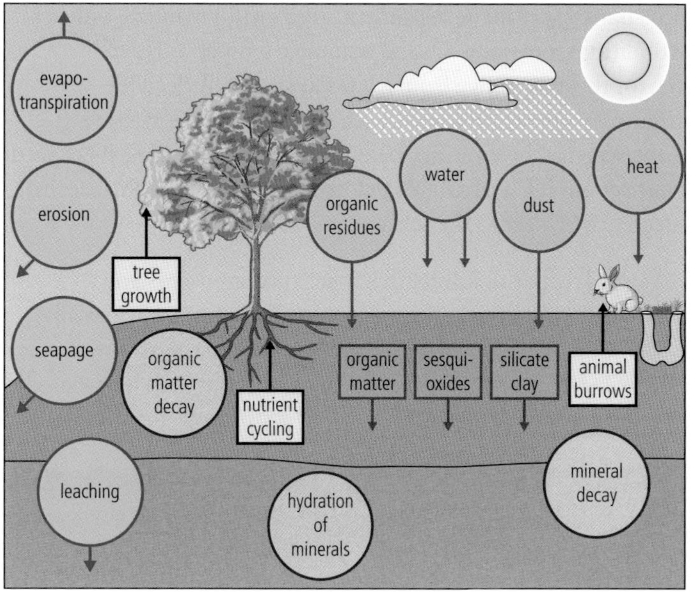

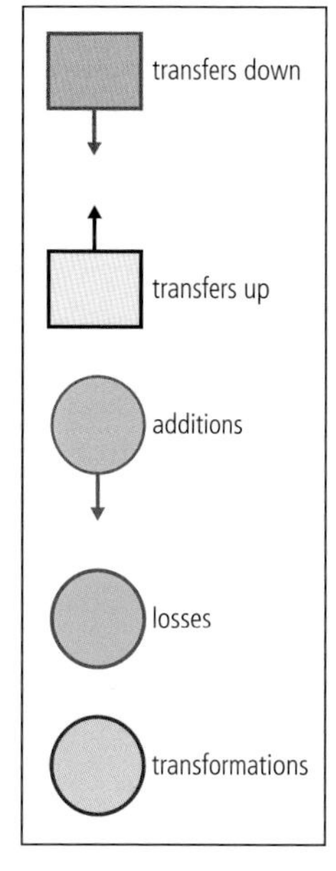

Figure 5.26 A systems flow diagram for a soil environment.

Create a systems flow diagram representing the soil system

Figure 5.26 shows an example of a systems flow diagram for a soil environment.

5.1.9 Soils provide a medium for plant growth

2.3 Biogeochemical cycles

Soils provide plants with anchorage for roots, a supply of water and air (especially O_2), key nutrients such as nitrogen, phosphorus and potassium and some protection against changes in temperature and pH.

However, soils rarely provide ideal conditions for plant growth. Therefore, in farming, inputs including water and fertilizer may be added to improve soil conditions for plant growth.

The depth of the soil can have a major impact on plant growth. A plant with a deep root system has access to more water than a plant with a shallow root system but most of the nutrients in the soil are found in a shallow zone near the surface. Nevertheless, there are several soil characteristics that may restrict root growth, as shown in Table 5.6.

Table 5.6 Restrictions to root growth.

Physical	Chemical
• mechanical impedance may prevent roots from growing downwards or sideways • absence of cracks may reduce the amount of water and/or O_2 entering the soil • shortage of O_2 due to waterlogging may reduce root growth • temperature too high or too low may damage plants	• high aluminium concentrations, usually associated with low pH, may be toxic for some plants • low nutrient supply may reduce plant growth • phytotoxic chemicals are substances that are toxic to plants • anaerobic soils reduce leaf growth and shoot growth and cause wilting

Soils provide a major seed bank for plant development. Seeds will germinate only when the appropriate conditions, i.e. water, O_2 and a suitable temperature, are available. The time taken for this may range from a few days to many decades depending on the environment. Once again, soil depth may be crucial – if the seed is too close to the surface the soil may become dry before germination occurs. If the seed is too deep, it may not have enough food reserves before it emerges at the surface. In general, smaller seeds need to be closer to the surface.

See this page of your eBook for a table of nutrients needed by plants.

Once the seedling has emerged from the soil surface, it will take nutrients and moisture from the soil and use sunlight to make its own food. The soil provides all the nutrients for plants, except for carbon which plants obtain from the atmosphere. The soil, therefore, is a basis for terrestrial ecosystems, since without soils land-based plants would not survive and grow.

5.1.10 Soils contribute to biodiversity by providing habitats and niches

2.1 Individuals, populations, communities and ecosystems

Soil communities have a large biodiversity, including microorganisms, animals and fungi, that still includes many unclassified species (Table 5.7).

Earthworms can be found in soils with a pH of between 4.0 and 7.0 and they can tunnel down to soil depths of about 2 m. They are more abundant in neutral soil (pH 7.0) and are absent from very acidic soils (pH below 4). The channels that the earthworms dig allow air and water to be transmitted down through the soil.

Table 5.7 Groups of organisms present in soils.

Microorganisms in fertile soil	Millions / g^{-1}
Bacteria	1–100
Actinomycetes	0.1 – 1
Fungi	0.1–1
Algae	0.01–0.1
Protozoa	0.01–0.1

Animals in mull soil under beech trees	Millions / ha^{-1}	% of total animal mass (total was 286 kg)
Earthworms	1.8	75.1
Enchytraeid worms	5.3	1.5
Gastropods	1.0	7.0
Millipedes	1.8	10.6
Centipedes	0.8	1.8
Mites and springtails	44.1	0.4
Others	7.2	3.6

Soil animals can be classified in terms of body length as micro (less than 0.1 mm), meso (0.1–10 mm) and macro (more than 10 mm). Earthworms are an example of macroanimals and are present in large numbers in many soils. For example, their populations can reach up to 1.8 million per hectare in soil under beech trees. Their mass can reach about 2 tonnes/hectare, which is about the same as that of the herbivore population above ground.

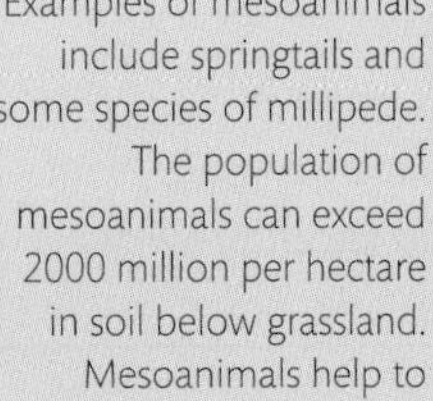

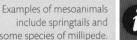

Examples of mesoanimals include springtails and some species of millipede. The population of mesoanimals can exceed 2000 million per hectare in soil below grassland. Mesoanimals help to decompose litter.

All microorganisms require nutrients, like plants. There are five groups of microorganisms. Some are heterotrophs and feed on other organisms. Some are autotrophs and convert sunlight energy into food energy.

- There is a great variety of bacteria, although most are heterotrophs and feed on the remains of plants and animals.

- Actinomycetes are a group of bacteria that feed on dead plant tissue. These occur mainly in warm soils and in aerobic conditions.
- Fungi are heterotrophs and mostly saprophytic (living on dead tissue) and can decompose all components of plant tissue. These microorganisms tend to be the dominant decomposer in acidic soils. Some fungi have a symbiotic relationship with plant roots, known as a mycorrhiza relationship.
- Algae are autotrophs and can photosynthesize. They are found near the soil surface. They are important colonizers of mineral debris and produce organic material for other microorganisms. On dry surfaces, such as rocks or trees, the algae are protected from drying-out (desiccation) through their association with a fungus, forming a lichen (Figure 5.27). Blue-green algae (cyanobacteria) can fix N_2 (see The nitrogen cycle, Topic 2, Section 2.3.17–2.3.21) and can also photosynthesize, making them important members of ecosystems.
- Protozoa are single-celled animals. Some feed selectively on fungi and bacteria, whereas others are autotrophs. Their main function in ecosystems appears to be the control of bacterial and fungal populations.

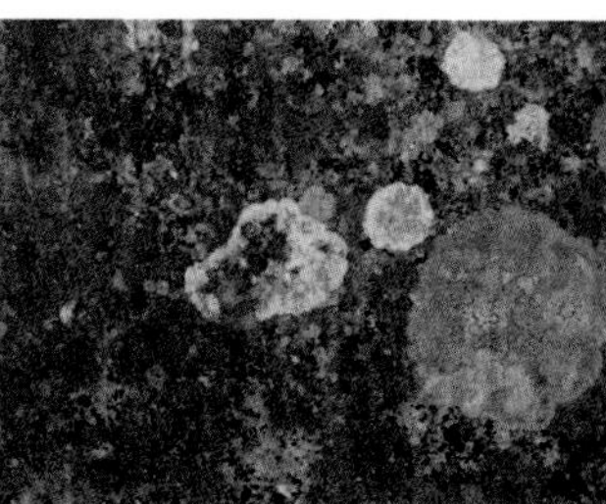

Figure 5.27 Lichen – a symbiotic relationship between an alga and a fungus.

HL Soil communities have a very large biodiversity including soil microorganisms, animals and fungi. Soils provide a range of habitats and niches for many species. However, the study of soil microorganisms, their interactions and impacts on higher plants has not been thoroughly investigated and there are many unknown species to be identified. Much work needs to be carried out.

5.1.11 Soils and recycling

Soils have an important role in nutrient cycling as they store and regulate nutrients. Organic compounds, such as leaves, are broken down into simple compounds before they can be re-used by plants. Some bacteria convert N_2 into NO_3^-, which are essential for plant growth. Bacteria and fungi decompose plant and animal remains and release the nutrients back to the soil. These nutrients are then taken up from the soil by other plants and used to make new organic material.

2.3 Biogeochemical cycles

Decomposition liberates nutrients from organic material, putting them back into circulation for use by other organisms. Decomposition can also break down materials that would be pollutants if they entered the ground or surface water.

HL The soil plays a very important role in the nitrogen cycle (Topic 2, Sections 2.3.17 to 2.3.21). Nitrogen-fixing bacteria in the soil transform N_2 from the atmosphere into NH_4^+ ions. Nitrifying bacteria in the soil then transform these NH_4^+ ions into nitrite ions (NO_2^-) and then into NO_3^-. Denitrifying bacteria transform NO_3^- into N_2. Decomposers break down organic nitrogen (protein) into NH_3 (deamination).

Decomposition is a step-by-step process. Macroorganisms, such as earthworms, digest the decaying material and excrete it, mixing it with soils. Fungi may break down complex compounds into simple components. Bacteria then attack these components. Generally, compounds become simpler after each step. The cycling of nutrients conserves them against leaching and volatilization (conversion of chemical substances from a liquid/solid state to a gaseous state). The portion of plant/animal remains that is not broken down forms humic substances that can persist for decades in the soil.

The carbon cycle and soil

More carbon is stored in the soil than in the atmosphere and above ground biomass combined. During photosynthesis, plants convert atmospheric CO_2 into plant matter consisting of carbohydrates, proteins and fibres. After death, plant and animal remains are left to decay on or in the soil. Soil organisms begin to consume organic matter, extracting energy and nutrients, and releasing water, heat and CO_2 back to the atmosphere. If plant matter is added to the soil faster than soil organisms can convert it to CO_2, carbon will be removed from the atmosphere and stored in the soil (Figure 5.28).

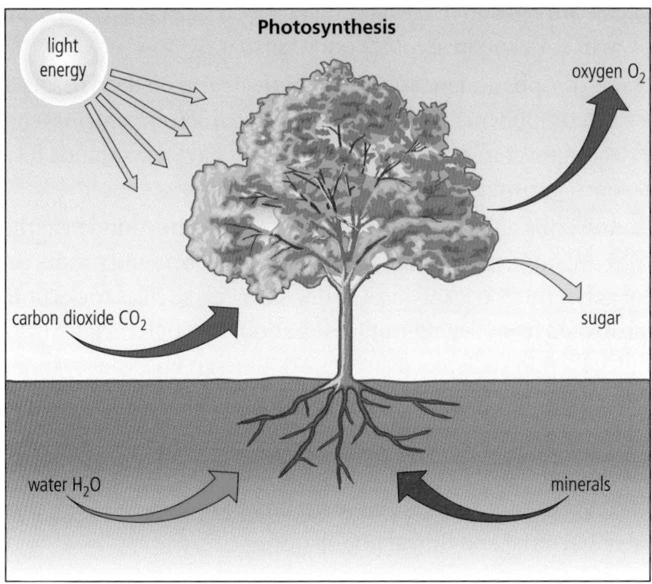

Figure 5.28 Soil and the carbon cycle.

5.1.12 Soil texture

The ideal soil for cultivation is a loam in which there is a balance between water-holding ability and freely draining, aerated conditions. These properties are influenced by several factors, especially soil texture. Soil texture refers to the proportion of differently sized materials, usually sand, silt and clay, present in a soil.

A soil texture triangle illustrates the differences in the composition of different types of soils (Figure 5.29a).

Triangular graphs are used to show data that can be divided into three parts, such as sand, silt and clay, for soil (Figure 5.29b). The data must be in the form

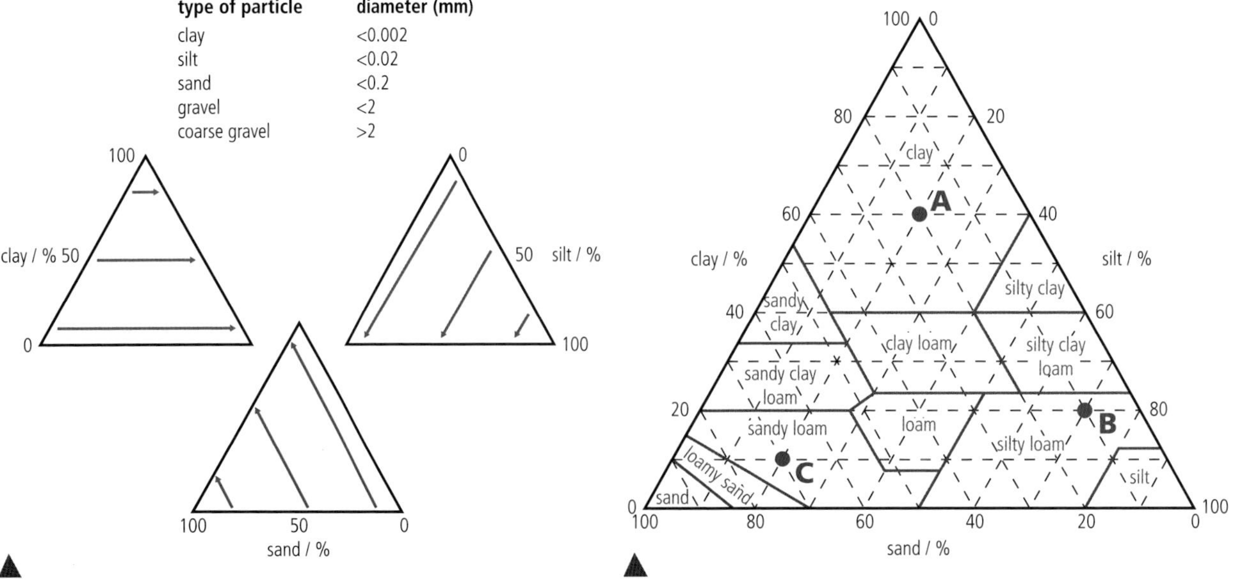

type of particle	diameter (mm)
clay	<0.002
silt	<0.02
sand	<0.2
gravel	<2
coarse gravel	>2

Figure 5.29a Measuring the proportions of sand, silt and clay.

Figure 5.29b Triangular graph showing soil textural groups.

of a percentage and the percentage must add up to 100%. The main advantage of triangular graphs are that:

- a large amount of data can be shown on the same graph
- groupings are easily recognizable, e.g. loams
- dominant characteristics can be shown
- classifications can be drawn up.

Soil texture triangles can be difficult to interpret, so it can be easy to get confused.

Your three percentages for sand, silt and clay must add up to 100%. If they don't, you have made a mistake!

5.1.13 Soil texture and primary productivity

The primary productivity (Topic 2, Section 2.2.23) of a soil depends on its:

- mineral content
- drainage
- water-holding capacity
- air spaces
- biota
- potential to hold organic matter.

Different soils have different levels of primary productivity (Topic 2, Section 2.2.23–2.2.25). This can be summarized as follows:

- sandy soil – low primary productivity due to poor water-holding capacity and low nutrient status
- clay soil – quite low primary productivity due to poor aeration and poor water infiltration
- loam soil – high primary productivity due to medium infiltration rate, water-holding capacity, nutrient status, aeration and ease of working.

In the film *Wallace and Gromit and the Curse of the Were-rabbit*, the van's windscreen wipers have three settings – light rain, heavy rain and heavy loam. The wipers were turned to heavy loam as it was dragged underground.

For optimum structure, a variety of pore sizes is required to allow root penetration, good aeration, free drainage and water storage. This is because pore spaces of over 0.1 mm allow root growth, oxygen diffusion and water movement, whereas pore spaces below 0.05 mm allow water storage.

Humus is a dark brown or black substance with a loose, crumbly texture formed by the partial decay of dead plant material. Humus contributes significantly to the texture of soils by improving mineral nutrient retention, water retention and aeration, all of which aid primary productivity.

In the past, and in many traditional societies, the main sources of additional nutrients have been organic forms such as compost, crop residue, animal dung and, in coastal areas, seaweed. The decay of organic matter releases N_2. Humus, like clay, can act as a negatively charged material to attract and hold (i.e. adsorb) positively charged cations and thereby counteract acidification.

Organic matter also keeps the soil in good structural condition. Soil structure refers to the way in which soil particles are combined to form larger soil aggregates.

The agricultural potential of a soil depends on the porosity and permeability of the soil and the surface area of the soil particles.

The structure and properties of sand, clay and loam soils differ in many ways, including their mineral and nutrient content, drainage, water-holding capacity, air spaces, biota and potential to hold organic matter. Each of these variables is linked to the ability of the soil to promote primary productivity.

Workability of a soil refers to the ease or difficulty of ploughing a soil.

The pore spaces determine the rate at which water drains through soil. The surface area determines the amount of water and nutrients in solution that can be retained against the force of gravity. For example, heavy clay soil can hold twice as much water as light soil. The terms 'light', 'medium' and 'heavy' refer to the **workability of a soil**. Light soils (over 80% sand) are coarse-textured and are easily drained of water and nutrients. They do, however, warm up more quickly than heavy clay soils and so allow early growth, e.g. the expansion of root crops such as potatoes, in spring. Heavy soils contain more than 25% clay and are fine-textured. Many of their pores are <0.001 mm and their large chemically active surface area means that these soils are water- and nutrient-retentive. Clay absorbs water, so that the soil swells when wet and shrinks when dry. Silt, in contrast, is coarser grained than clay and finer grained than sand. Hence it drains better than clay but drains less well than sand. Silt does not retain water or chemicals well, so its potential for farming is reduced. The soil structural condition can also be measured by its porosity – this determines its air capacity and water availability (Table 5.8). A loam is a well-balanced soil with significant proportions of sand, silt and clay. Soils that enable greater primary productivity tend to have a greater air capacity and availability of water.

Table 5.8 Influence of soil texture on properties and behaviour of soils.

Property/behaviour	Sand	Silt	Clay
Water holding capacity	Low	Medium	High
Aeration	Good	Medium	Poor
Infiltration and drainage rate	High	Slow to medium	Slow
Organic matter decomposition	Rapid	Medium	Slow
Compaction	Resists	Easily compacted	Easily compacted
Susceptibility to water erosion	Low	High	Low
Ability to hold nutrients	Poor	Medium to high	High
Leaching of pollutants	Allows	Moderately retards	Retards
Ease of working	Good	Medium	Poor

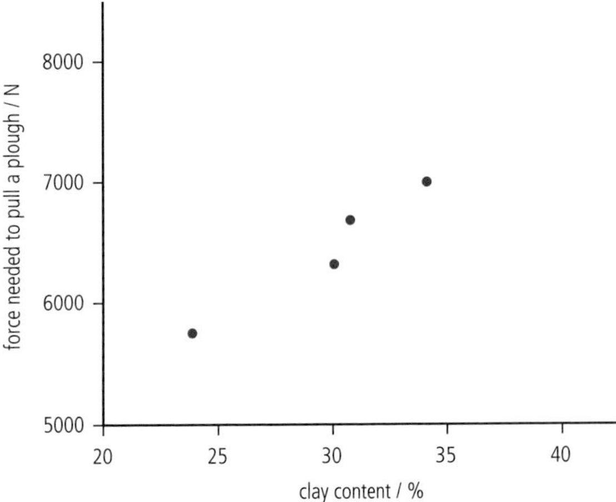

Figure 5.30 The force needed to plough soils with different clay content.

The main limiting factor for light soils is drought during the growing season because these soils have a poor nutrient-holding capacity.

The workability of a soil depends on the amount of clay present. As Figure 5.30 shows, the force needed to pull a plough increases with the percentage clay content.

Heavy soils in which the clay content is over 28% are the most difficult for arable cultivation. They are highly water retentive and have low permeability. This means that field drainage and drying out are slow. Heavy soils can become waterlogged when wet, or hard when too dry. The number of days over which they can be ploughed is low in comparison with other soils.

5.1.14 Soils can act as carbon sinks, stores or sources

2.3 Biogeochemical cycles
6.2 Climate change causes and impacts

The amount of carbon stored in soils can vary greatly. There are small amounts of carbon stored in tropical forest soils and relatively large amounts stored under tundra, wetlands and temperate grasslands.

Carbon is one of the most important elements on Earth. The carbon cycle transfers carbon between living organisms and the environment (Topic 2, Section 2.3.3 and 2.3.4). The largest carbon store is found in the continental crust and the upper mantle (Figure 5.31). In contrast, the atmosphere is a relatively minor store, although it is vital for global climate change.

Soils store approximately 1325 gigatonnes of carbon (GtC) in the topsoil and as much as 2300 GtC when soils and vegetation are included (Figure 5.31). In addition, 1600 GtC of carbon in permafrost (ground that is frozen for a minimum of two years) has been protected from decomposition, although this changes as global temperatures rise (Topic 6, Section 6.2).

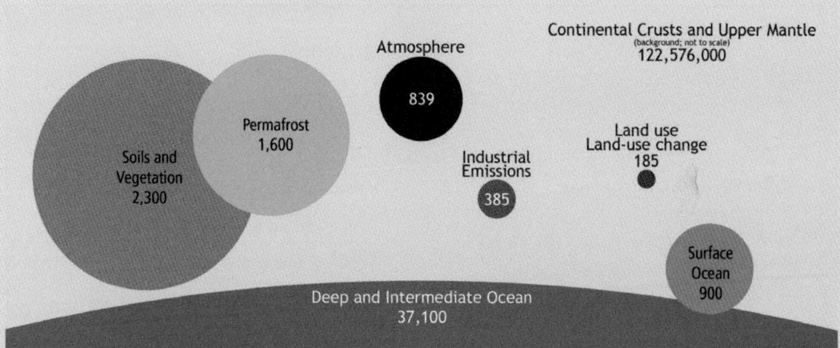

Figure 5.31 Global stores in the carbon cycle shown in gigatonnes.

Forests account for about 90% of terrestrial biomass, storing about 400 GtC. Different ecosystems store different amounts of carbon in different locations (Figure 5.32). For example, low latitude tropical rainforests, e.g. the Amazon and the DR Congo rainforests, store greater amounts of carbon in above-ground components, whereas cooler regions, such as the tundra of Siberia and northern Canada and the temperate grasslands such as the North American prairies, have very large amounts of carbon stored in below-ground components (Topic 2, Section 2.4.2–2.4.4, Figures 2.95, 2.98, 2.101, 2.103 and 2.105). This is due to the low temperature and low rainfall reducing the amount of leaching and bacterial activity. In contrast, in tropical rainforests, although the input of dead organic matter may be high, decomposition is high under hot, humid conditions.

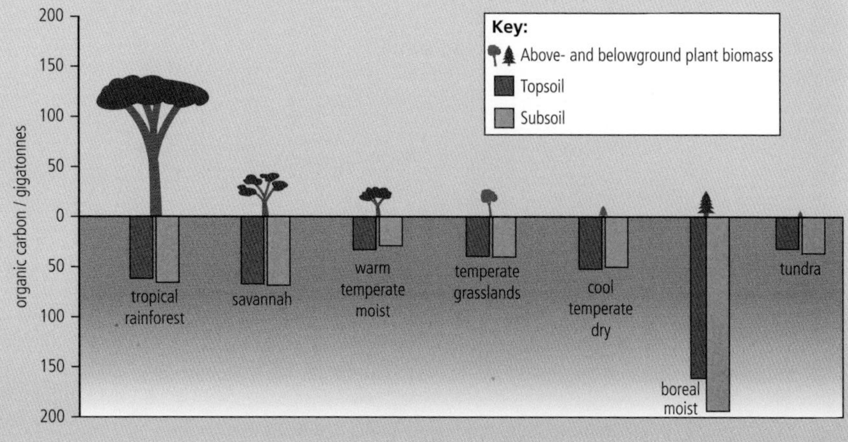

Figure 5.32 Carbon stored in topsoil, subsoil and plant biomass by ecosystem.

According to NASA, Central Park in New York city is 4 km long and 0.8 km wide. A gigatonne of carbon placed there would be 341 m high.

HL

HL

5.1.15 Soil profiles

2.4 Climate and biomes

Soil profiles can show transfers and transformations.

One of the most widely used soil classification systems is the US Department of Agriculture (USDA) soil taxonomy system, which is based on observed soil properties rather than genetic considerations.

The primary soil orders in the system are not associated with any particular climatic or geographic environments and so avoid some of the weaknesses of the zonal system.

See this page of your eBook for a table showing the major orders of the USDA soil taxonomy system.

SKILLS

Use soil profile diagrams to classify examples of soils that can be linked to the biomes studied, for example, brown earths to temperate deciduous forests, or oxisols to rainforests

A brown earth (Figure 5.33) is a leached soil associated with warm temperate climates. Rainfall exceeds potential evapotranspiration, so there is a net downward movement of water through the soil. The soil is only mildly acidic, so soil animals, especially earthworms, help to mix the soil horizons. At the surface, the annual shedding of leaves helps to conserve nutrients. The A horizon is dark brown due to the presence of organic matter, whereas the B horizon is lighter brown due to the removal of clay, humus, iron and aluminium.

The characteristic soil of a tropical rainforest is an oxisol (Figure 5.34). It too is a leached soil, often intensely so. Rainforests were unaffected by glaciations, and some have existed for millions of years. Hence, they have been weathered over a very long period and their soils may be quite deep (metres) and very infertile as they lack nutrients. This is unusual given the richness of the vegetation they support. The soils may have accumulations of insoluble minerals containing iron, aluminium and manganese. In the hot, wet conditions of the rainforest, the rates of chemical weathering and rates of decomposition of organic matter are high. Nutrients are passed directly from the litter to the trees by fungi that live on the tree roots. This by-passes the soil storage stage where there is a high chance that the nutrients would be completely lost from the nutrient cycle.

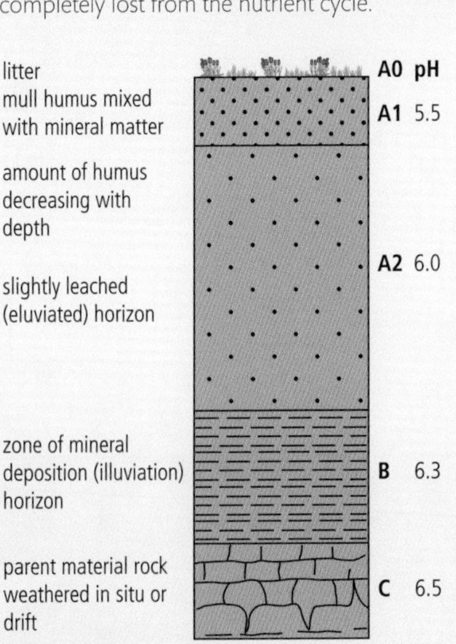

Figure 5.33 Characteristics of a brown earth.

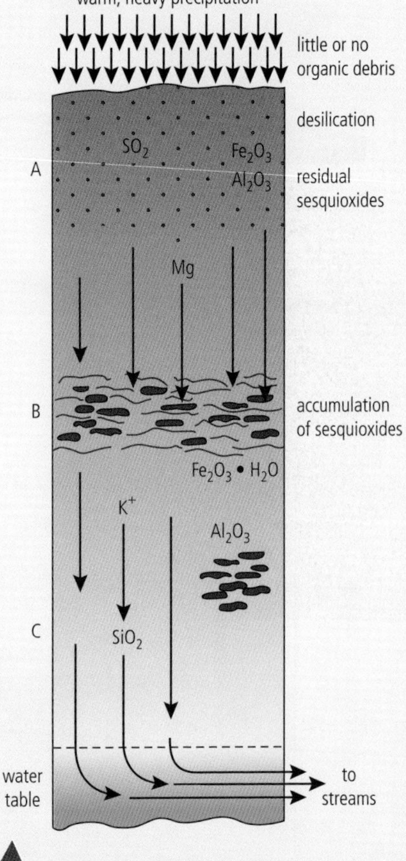

Figure 5.34 Formation of an oxisol.

5.1.16 Soil horizons

HL

Natural soil systems with several horizons can be contrasted against intensive agricultural systems that have only one or two horizons.

Soil horizons are the horizontal layers present in a soil, which each possess distinct physical and chemical characteristics (Figure 5.35). The top layer is the organic horizon (O), consisting of undecomposed litter, partly decomposed litter and well-decomposed litter. Below that is the mixed mineral-organic horizon (A), consisting largely of humus. This layer generally has a dark colour due to the presence of organic matter. Leaching takes place in some soils, producing an eluvial horizon (E). This layer removes minerals from upper horizons leaving a horizon that is lighter in colour. The next layer down is the illuvial or deposited horizon (B), which contains some of the material removed from the E horizon, such as iron (Fe) humus (h) and clay (t). At the base of the soil is the bedrock/parent material known as the C horizon.

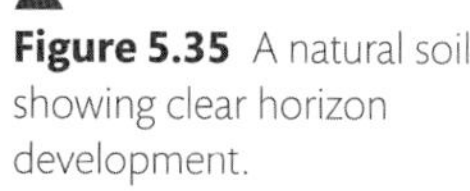

Figure 5.35 A natural soil showing clear horizon development.

In contrast, intensively farmed agricultural soils (Figure 5.36) are much simpler. Agriculture can involve many processes including ploughing, sowing (planting), drainage and/or irrigation, fertilization, weed removal and harvesting. These processes can have several impacts on soil characteristics, including soil horizon development.

Figure 5.36 An agricultural soil.

Tillage (ploughing) is the initial stage in cultivation. It aims to create conditions that will favour seed germination, seedling emergence and root development, destroy competitive species (weeds, pests and pathogens) and allow crops to be harvested. To achieve these conditions, the upper portion of the soil is disturbed and turned over. This mixes the upper horizons. Evidence suggests that the ploughing of soils has been done since as far back as the Egyptian times, i.e. for at least 5000 years.

The plough was the most widely used tool for breaking up soils and burying weeds until the 18th century. Ploughing for the purpose of weed control became unnecessary after the introduction of herbicides. Today, the main use of ploughing is the provision of optimum growing conditions for the next crop. Traditional ploughing in temperate areas generally turns soil to a depth of about 20 cm. However, the depth of turning can vary with type of soil, soil moisture and slope angle. The increasing size of modern tractors has resulted in an increase in the amount of land that is ploughed and the ease and speed with which the land can be ploughed.

The impact of farming can change the nature of soil horizons (Table 5.9) and compact them to form a compressed plough pan (Figure 5.20).

Table 5.9 The impact of intensive farming on selected soil characteristics.

Soil characteristic	Natural state	Intensive agriculture
Organic content	A horizon – high (7%) B horizon – low (0%)	Uniform (3–5%) in ploughed horizon
Carbonates	A horizon – low/zero B/C maximum	Uniform if limed and tilled
Nitrogen	Medium/low	High (nitrate fertilizers)
Biological activity	High	Medium
Exchangeable cation balance	Ca 80% K 5% P 3% H 7%	Ca 70% K 10% P 12% H 4%

HL

5.1.17 The A horizon

5.2 Agriculture and food

The A horizon is the layer of soil just beneath the uppermost organic humus layer. It is rich in organic matter and is known as the mixed layer or topsoil. This is the most valuable layer for plant growth but, along with the O horizon, is also the most vulnerable to erosion and degradation.

Topsoil has more O_2, organic matter, microorganisms and nutrient recycling than lower soil horizons, therefore this is where there is most root growth and other biological activity. Intensive farming leads to the removal of trees, leading to soil erosion. Monocropping can lead to soil exhaustion and the need for fertilizers to maintain productivity.

Usually topsoil is *c.* 12–25 cm deep. It has a high concentration of roots and a large population of soil animals and microorganisms. Topsoil contains both carbon and nitrogen. Carbon provides energy for plant growth, while nitrogen is a component of amino acids used for building plant cells/tissues and for making chlorophyll. Typical carbon to nitrogen ratios in topsoil are <20 : 1.

Example – Topsoil erosion

The world uses topsoil to grow 95% of the food produced globally (excluding capture fisheries where the food is caught rather than produced). Worldwide, up to half of the world's topsoil has disappeared over the last 150 years.

In temperate areas it can take up to 1000 years to form topsoil with a depth of 2.5 cm and yet it can be destroyed in several years. Topsoil is vulnerable to wind and water erosion e.g. in Australia (Figure 5.37) and South Africa, so it is important to preserve existing topsoil.

The decline of many civilizations – both large and small, such as those of the Egyptian Empire and Easter Island – has been linked to a decline in soil quality/soil erosion (and vegetation cover).

Figure 5.37 Soil erosion caused by agriculture in western Australia.

In the USA, the cost of soil erosion exceeds US$ 45 billion annually and soil is being used up at 10 times the rate at which it is being replaced! Topsoil is not only important for food production, but also as a carbon store and a water store and filter. The combination of synthetic fertilizers, pesticides and insecticides, intensive tilling and lack of cover crops have combined to reduce the amount of minerals, nutrients and soil organic matter contained in agricultural soils. On the other hand, there is evidence that practices are changing. In the USA, the use of no-till farming rose from c. 21% of the cropland area in 2017[1] to c. 30% of the cropland area by 2023[2]. Cover crops increased by 50%, especially in the corn belt.

Monocropping, the practice of growing the same crop on the same piece of land year after year, can lead to soil exhaustion, i.e. the depletion of selected minerals. Even using a two-crop rotation, such as soybeans and corn, can have a similar impact. To maintain the fertility of the A horizon, a more complex rotation such as a 3– or 4–year crop rotation should be used instead. Ideally in combination with a leguminous crop (e.g. peas, beans or lentils) to fix nitrogen into the soil (Topic 2, Section 2.3.17–2.3.21

---

[1]Creech, E. *Saving Money, Time and Soil: The Economics of No-Till Farming*. US Department of Agriculture (30 November 2017). https://www.usda.gov/media/blog/2017/11/30/saving-money-time-and-soil-economics-no-till-farming

[2]Edwards, R. *Ohio State Professor Rattan Lal Aims to Eliminate Hunger While Helping the Environment*. Columbus Monthly (November 2023). https://eu.columbusmonthly.com/story/lifestyle/features/2023/11/28/ohio-state-university-professor-rattan-lal-research-to-produce-more-food-and-solve-climate-crisis/71729285007/

and this topic, Section 5.1.16). Monocropping often results in the need for the use of synthetic fertilizers to replace the missing nutrients.

Pesticides are also used to reduce pests, such as fungi and insects. However, the use of these can lead to a reduction in soil organic matter and the ecosystem functions that they provide. Some types of nitrogen fertilizer have also been linked with soil acidification.

Pesticides are used to control weeds (herbicides), fungi (fungicides) and insects (insecticides). Some pesticides may be broken down by microbes in the soils, but others may remain in the soil and pass up through the food chain by bioaccumulation and biomagnification. Pesticides, such as glyphosate, can have an adverse effect on earthworms. Soil fumigants are designed to kill all organisms in the soil before the farmer starts planting.

Large amounts of animal waste (slurry) from factory farms may contain antibiotics, steroids and other pharmaceutical waste, which can lead to antibiotic-resistant bacteria in the soil. Antibiotics can remain in the soil for months. Slurry can also contain heavy metals, such as copper, lead and zinc, which were used in feeds.

The use of heavy farm machinery, such as tractors and combine harvesters, can lead to soil compaction and soil erosion. Compaction is an increasing problem as the size of machinery has increased (for economic efficiency) and ploughing is sometimes done when the soil is wet. Compaction leads to poor aeration, reduced water movement and retarded root growth.

Example – Impacts of farming on soils in Iowa, USA

Erosion of topsoil is a major problem as this is generally the layer with most organic matter and natural nutrients. A study of soils in Iowa, USA showed the effects on soil quality and agricultural yields. Loss of surface soils, and therefore organic matter, led to a decline in soil productivity and crop yield. Conversely, adding 150–300 mm of topsoil led to increased yields of corn and oats. Yields were lower on upper slopes where topsoil had been eroded and higher on lower slopes where the topsoil had been deposited. Moisture moving from the upper slopes to the lower slopes was transporting organic-matter enriched topsoil to the lower slopes. Downslope movement was encouraged by tillage as the land was left bare and erosion increased. However, continued cultivation led to losses in carbon, magnesium, nitrogen, organic phosphorus and sulfur. Concentrations of these minerals decreased as length of cultivation increased. Overall, yield losses of 25–40% suggested that erosion on an undulating surface is having a major impact on the quality of the topsoil and to rectify it additional costs of fertilizers and/or organic matter are required.

The requirements for the sustainable management of soil include:

- complex crop rotation
- greater use of organic matter (compost)
- green manure (the use of fast-growing plants to cover bare soil – sown late in summer/autumn to take up nutrients, store them over winter and return to the soil the following spring)
- cover-cropping and mulching
- adding animal manure onto pasture and onto cropland
- no-till or low-till techniques
- wind breaks and check dams (Figure 5.38) to reduce wind and water erosion.

Figure 5.38 Check dam, Eastern Cape, South Africa.

For example, organic farming relies on biological processes for the production of crops and livestock and their protection from pests and diseases. It avoids the use of pesticides and synthetic fertilizers. To provide nitrogen, organic farmers use leguminous crops. Crop rotation helps reduce weeds, disease and insect pests. Animal manure and composted plant residue help maintain soil organic matter. Soil fertility may be maintained through crop rotation, the use of farmyard manure, using legumes and keeping some fields fallow. In tropical areas, agroforestry has been used to help maintain soil fertility, by growing trees and shrubs alongside crops and pasture.

5.1.18 Factors influencing soil formation

HL

The formation of soil is a function of climate, geomorphology, parent material (geology), biota and time (this topic, Section 5.1.3).

2.4 Climate and biomes

Geomorphology (landscape)

Slope angle is of great importance in soil erosion as susceptibility to soil erosion increases with gradient. Steeper slopes are associated with thinner soils.

Situation is also important. On a flat hilltop, material is exposed to erosional processes, whereas on a flat lowland, material is likely to be buried by deposition. Soils on hillsides tend to be better drained, whereas those in valley bottoms are subject to waterlogging (gleying). Aspect, the direction in which a slope faces, has an important bearing on soil formation as it affects the local climate or microclimate, including the temperature and evaporation rates. Figure 5.39 shows how climate, drainage, slope and bedrock influence soil development.

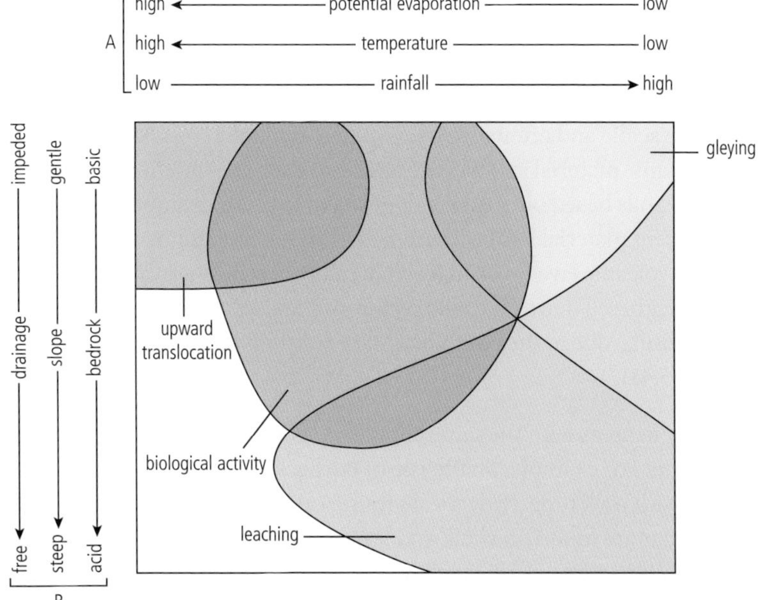

Figure 5.39 A model of climate, topography and soils.

The term 'soil catena' refers to the sequence of different soils, which varies with relief and drainage, though derived from the same bedrock (Figure 5.40). Such a sequence can be found when following a transect from a mountain or hilltop to the valley bottom, reflecting changes in microclimate (temperature, wind, PPT, pEVT), drainage and the position of the water table.

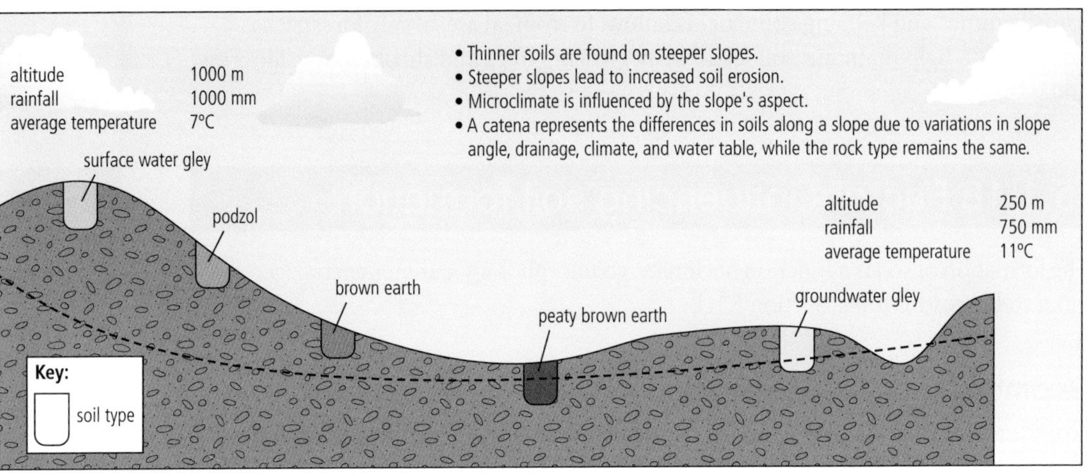

Figure 5.40 Variations in soils and topography.

Geology

There is a widespread misunderstanding that geology (bedrock) determines soil composition. In general, it is only the C horizon that is related to geology and the main global soil groups relate more to climate than geology. Rock type has a lasting effect through texture, structure and fertility. Sandstones and gritstones produce free draining, coarse textured soils, whereas clays and shales give much finer soils. Soils also vary in terms of fertility, which is a function of the initial nutrients and bases provided by the weathering of the bedrock. These may be removed, or added to, at a later stage by various geomorphological processes.

The distinction between calcareous and non-calcareous rocks is very important. Calcareous rocks are rich in bases (positively charged nutrients), whereas non-calcareous rocks tend to be acidic and often give rise to acidic podzolic soils. Similarly, soils that develop on volcanic material can be very fertile, as they are enriched with magnesium and potassium. Soils based on volcanic deposits in Java, for example, may be very fertile as the parent material has been deeply weathered under hot, wet conditions. In contrast, the volcanic lava flows in Iceland, many of which are over 10,000 years old, have not weathered due to the cold conditions and in many places, such as the Reykjanes Peninsula, due to the combination of resistant lava flows and low biological activity (Figure 5.41).

Figure 5.41 The lack of soils on lava flows on the Reykjanes Peninsula is due to the cold conditions and low rates of bacterial activity over the last 11,000 years. Ironically, in some volcanically active areas, such as Heimaey, soils have not developed because the ground is too hot: ~300 °C at 1 m depth.

On a local scale, in areas with the same climate, rock type may lead to differences in soils that occur. For example, on the Isle of Purbeck in the south of England, soils generally vary with rock type. Podzols are found on heathland (acidic sands and gravels), rendzinas are found on chalk and limestone, and brown earth is found on clays and gley soils in wetter, low lying areas.

Organisms

Organic matter is a fundamental component of soil although the influences of biotic factors range from microscopic creatures to humans. Some influences may be somewhat external, such as interception of PPT by vegetation and the reduction of PPT via pEVT. Other influences are more internal to the soil, such as the release of humic acids by decaying vegetation or the return of nutrients to the soil via litter decay. There is also a relationship between the type of vegetation and the type of soil found. This is partly because certain types of vegetation require specific nutrients. For example, grass tends to be found in areas where calcium and magnesium are dominant. Animals too influence soils. In the top 30 cm of one hectare of soil, there can be on average 25 tonnes of soil organisms, approximately 10 tonnes of bacteria, 10 tonnes of fungi, 4 tonnes of earthworms and 1 tonne of other soil organisms such as springtails, mites, isopods, spiders, snails, mice and so on (this topic, Section 5.1.10). Earthworms alone can represent 50–70% of the total weight of animals in arable soils. In one hectare of soil, 18–40 tonnes is ingested each day by earthworms and passed on to the surface, this produces a layer that can be up to 5 mm deep. Humans have obvious effects, ranging from liming, fertilizer application and mulching, to mining, deforestation, agricultural practices and extraction for gardening purposes.

TOK

To what extent do the names and labels that we use help or hinder the acquisition of knowledge?

Soils are continually undergoing changes due to changes in weather, extreme events, natural hazards and human impacts, so should all soils be considered 'azonal'? Is it true that the precision of the language used in the natural sciences successfully eliminates all ambiguity?

Time

Time is not a causative factor. It does not cause soils to change but allows processes to operate to a greater extent, therefore allowing soils to evolve. The amount of time required for soil formation varies from soil to soil. Coarse sandstones develop soils more quickly than granites or basalts. On glacial outwash, a few hundred years may be enough time for a soil to evolve. Thin soils are not necessarily young soils, nor are deep ones 'mature'. Phases of erosion and deposition keep some soils in a permanent state of evolution. Most mid-latitude soils are referred to as polycyclic, i.e. they undergo frequent changes as the major soil forming processes change in relation to changing inputs. Immature soils that have not fully developed are referred to as 'azonal' soils.

Activity

Draw a spider diagram to identify the factors that influence soil formation.

5.1.19 Differences between soils rich in sand, silt or clay

HL

Sand and silt have a low cation-exchange capacity, whereas clays have a much greater cation-exchange capacity.

Soil **colloids** are the smallest particles of the soil. Soil colloids range in diameter from 0.01–10 μm (e.g. clays to fine silt). They include clay and humus and are often referred to as the **clay-humus complex**. Soil colloids are of great significance because they are the main areas of chemical exchange. Clay has a complicated structure and a vast surface area in relation to its weight. Being negatively charged, nutrients are given up by the clay to plants in a process known as **base exchange** (Figure 5.42). Bases (cations) are the positively charged ions, such as calcium, magnesium and potassium. In return, the plants release acidic hydrogen ions, which tends to make the soil more acidic over time. These bases or nutrients may be returned to the soil through litter decay, release through weathering or else added as fertilizers. Soft calcareous (lime-rich) rocks are generally quite fertile because the rate of weathering and release of calcium into the soil is sufficient to make up for the loss of nutrients to plants or through leaching. These rocks, such as chalk, are often referred to as **base-rich** rocks. Sandy and silty soils are derived from quartz and have no charge so have a much lower ability to retain cations than clay soils do. Thus sandy soils are much less fertile than soils containing clay or humus. Cations can also be removed through leaching.

Figure 5.42 Base exchange.

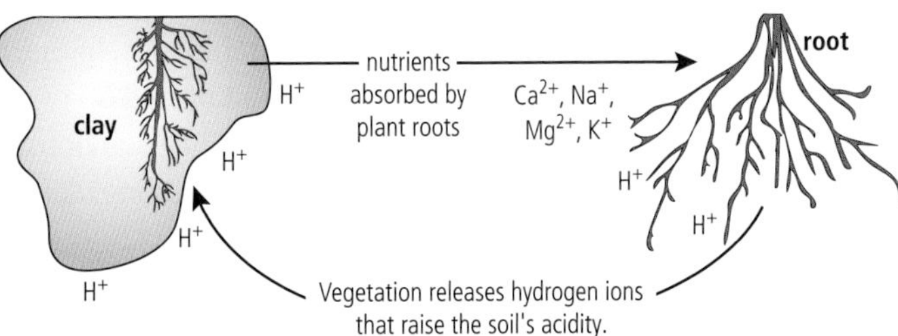

Some bases or nutrients are required in large doses. These are the **macronutrients**, which include carbon (C), hydrogen (H) and calcium (Ca). Others, by contrast, are only needed in small quantities. These are **trace elements**, which include iron (Fe), copper (Cu), magnesium (Mg) and sodium (Na).

Cation exchange capacity (CEC) is the capacity of a soil to hold exchangeable ions. The ability to hold on to ions reduces the likelihood of soil acidification. Soils with a higher proportion of clay and/or humus have a higher CEC. The clay mineral content and organic matter components are negatively charged, and they attract and hold positively charged ions. In general, soils with more negatively charged ions will attract more cations and so are more fertile. Sand has a low CEC, so sandy soils rely on their organic content to retain cations.

The main ions associated with CEC in soils are the base cations, including calcium, magnesium, sodium and potassium. However, as soils become more acidic these base cations are replaced by acidic ions including hydrogen, aluminium and manganese. Soils with a low CEC are more likely to develop deficiencies in nutrient cations, whereas soils with a high CEC are less likely to experience leaching of these bases. The addition of organic matter to soils with a low CEC will increase the retention of nutrients but this may take many years to achieve. Figure 5.43 shows how CEC can change with depth. The soil in this figure is a sandy duplex soil, so there is a distinct boundary between sand at a soil depth of 0–40 cm and clay at a soil depth below 40 cm. There is also a high organic content in the top 10 cm of soil.

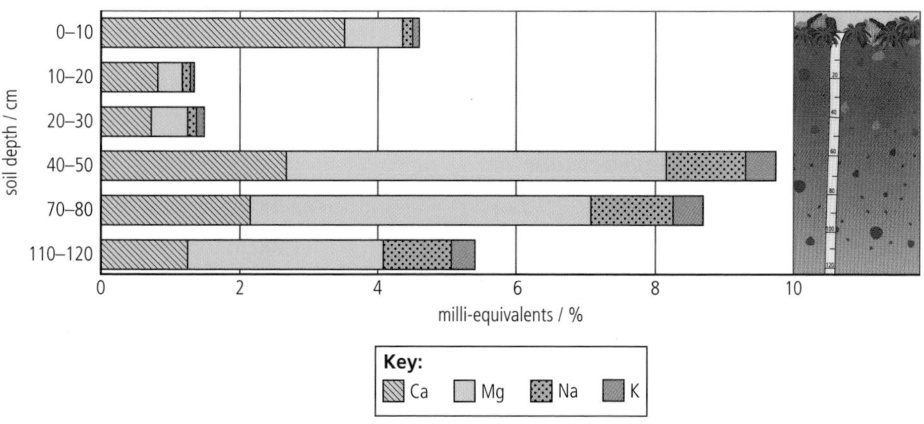

Figure 5.43 CEC in a sandy duplex soil; CEC can change with depth.

5.1.20 Determining soil properties

HL

Analyzing the percentage of sand silt and clay in a soil can be done by feel (see the worksheet 5.1.3 'Soil testing by feel' in your eBook) 'Soil testing by feel' in your eBook), by sieving and by sedimentation. Soils can be classified based on the relative proportions of sand, silt and clay they contain (Figure 5.29b).

Soil colour may give some indication of the processes of formation, or of the minerals present. For example, black soils contain a large amount of humus, whereas red soils contain a large amount of iron. A white crust on the soil indicates soil salinization. Grey or blue speckles in a soil suggest reduced iron compounds, poor drainage and the occurrence of gleying (waterlogging).

The calculation of soil organic and moisture content, bulk density and infiltration are described in this topic, Section 5.1.3. See worksheet 5.1.20 in your eBook for an activity.

5.1.21 Carbon is released from soils as methane or carbon dioxide

HL

2.3 Biogeochemical cycles
6.2 Climate change – causes and impacts

Soil organic matter contains *c.* 60% carbon and is an important part of the carbon cycle as it regulates the atmospheric content of two important greenhouse gases:

- CO_2
- CH_4.

Scientists estimate that the sequestration of atmospheric CO_2 in soil organic matter could absorb an amount of CO_2 that is roughly equal to the total amount of CO_2 emitted from agriculture, industry and the burning of fossil fuels.

CO_2 is removed from the atmosphere by plants through the process of photosynthesis. It is returned to the atmosphere by the process of cellular respiration by plants, animals and soil microbes, the decomposition of soil organic matter and by fires that oxidize living and dead organic matter. On a global scale, the amount of carbon in terrestrial, biomass and soils is more than three times greater than the amount of carbon in the atmosphere (Table 5.10).

Table 5.10 Major sinks or stores of carbon on Earth.

Carbon pool	Size / gigatonnes of carbon
Atmosphere	839
Ocean	38,000
Continental crust/upper mantle	122,000,000
Living biomass	2300
Soil	1500
Peat	250
Coal	3510
Oil	230
Natural gas	140

Global warming is increasing the release of carbon. As atmospheric CO_2 increases, microbial respiration by microbes also increases due to increased temperatures and plant remains. This varies spatially (from place to place). Some carbon-rich soils, such as those found in the tundra and boreal forests, may remain as sinks under higher temperatures. Other more vulnerable and fragile soils, such as those in semi-arid and tropical environments, are likely to become carbon sources.

The cultivation of soils has generally led to large losses of soil organic matter and has added to atmospheric CO_2. The most important impact on the carbon content of soils has come from mechanical cultivation. The cultivation of soil at greater depths causes more disturbance, which allows for greater oxidation of soil horizons and faster metabolism of aerobic microorganisms, which then release greater quantities of CO_2 as a result of increased respiration. The highest losses of soil organic matter generally occur in the first year of ploughing (of permanent pasture such as grassland). If cultivation continues over the next 25 years, between 25% and 40% of the original soil carbon may be lost. Ploughing also removes weeds from the soil surface and buries them underground. These weeds were active stores of carbon when growing, but once dead and buried they will decompose and so add to the levels of carbon being released. In addition, the tractors used to do the work will burn large amounts of fuel while ploughing and produce CO_2 gas, thus contributing further to carbon emissions.

According to Ramsar (The Convention on Wetlands and its mission), the drainage of peat bogs is estimated to produce emissions equal to 10% of all fossil fuel emissions.

Peat soils and soils with very high levels of soil organic matter present a particular challenge. As global warming proceeds, they may dry out, or be drained for agriculture, as the warming temperatures will allow more pastoral farming or crop cultivation. Cultivation or drainage of wetlands can release four times the amount of greenhouse gas emissions as an 'average' soil with just 5% organic matter, i.e. 12 tonnes of carbon/hectare/year compared with 3 tonnes of carbon/hectare/year.

Wetlands account for about 10% of the planet's surface but store over one-third of terrestrial carbon. Drainage of wetlands is taking place for many reasons including the creation of new farmland, reduction of the risk of disease (e.g. malaria), the building of new homes, the creation of new industries (e.g. Disney World in Florida, USA) and due to climate change, among others. It is estimated that over the last 100 years, 60% of wetlands in the USA have been drained to provide land for agriculture.

Changes in atmospheric carbon levels could lead to a tipping point. Tipping points can be incremental small-scale changes that, over time, lead to large-scale irreversible change. The increase in global temperatures and the breakdown of methane clathrates (hydrates) in sub-surface geological structures is one such tipping point. Methane clathrate is a large amount of CH_4 trapped within an ice-like structure. It is estimated that globally there are between 1000 and 5000 gigatonnes of methane clathrates. In contrast, global wetlands contain between 350 and 535 gigatonnes of carbon.

Example – Methane clathrates

Methane clathrates are generally found in shallow marine sediments, with depths of less than 2000 m, in polar regions and in deep ocean sediments where water temperatures are around 2°C. Some methane clathrates may be as old as 800,000 years. The global warming potential of CH_4 is much greater than that of CO_2 – up to 30 times more potent over a century. However, most of the deposits of methane clathrates are too deep to respond to surface temperature and oceanic temperature changes, although deposits in the Arctic Ocean are at a much shallower depth than in other oceans so could respond to temperature change.

Methane clathrate is released as CH_4 gas into the surrounding water/soil as temperatures rise. Two large-scale deposits that are worrying scientists include one below the Beaufort Sea, off the coast of Canada, and one below the East Siberian Arctic Shelf (Figure 5.44), an area of over 2 million km^2 in size with an average depth of 45 m. One estimate suggests over 14,000 gigatonnes of carbon is locked up as CH_4 and methane hydrates under the Arctic submarine permafrost. A release of just 50 gigatonnes of methane hydrate would increase the Earth's CH_4 content twelve-fold. This would have the same effect as an increase of *c.* 385 ppm CO_2. The potential methane clathrate destabilization has been identified as one of the most serious problems for global climate change.

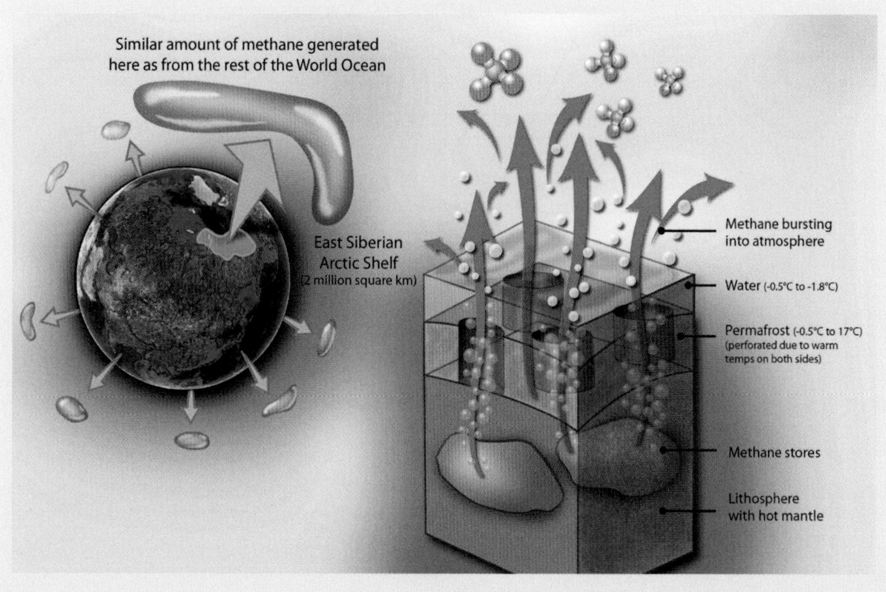

Figure 5.44 CH_4 release from the East Siberian Arctic Shelf.

Engagement

- Research how local farms in your area (including urban farms/allotments, schools with vegetable gardens and/or community groups) manage and value soil in relation to agriculture, climate change, biodiversity and overall sustainability. Present your findings to the class.
- Host a documentary film festival about soil and food and display your findings.
- If there is space around your school, you could start an organic vegetable garden, applying good soil care.

Exercise

Q1. Explain why soil can be considered as an 'open system'.

Q2. Outline the main components in soil.

Q3. Distinguish between transfers and transformations in soil horizons.

Q4. Briefly outline the process of soil salinization.

Q5. Explain one advantage and one disadvantage of using fertilizers for soil.

Q6. Calculate the percentage of sand, silt and clay in soils A, B and C in Figure 5.45.

Figure 5.45 Soil textural triangle.

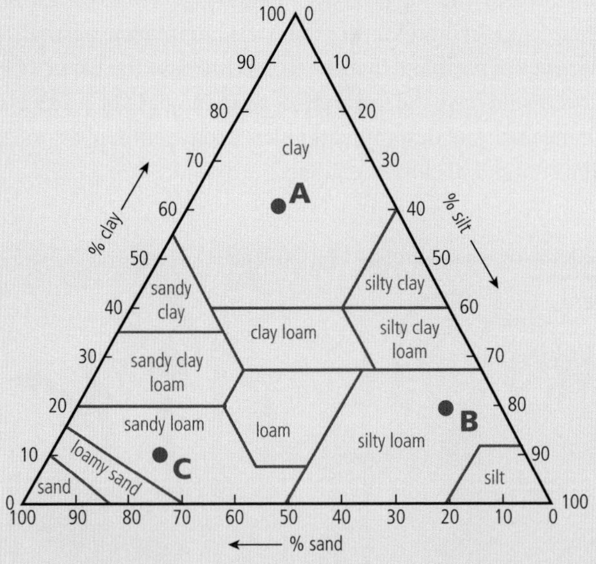

Q7. On a copy of Figure 5.45, plot the points that identify each of the following soils:

D clay 40%, sand 50%, silt 10%

E clay 30%, sand 40%, silt 30%

F clay 30%, sand 10%, silt 60%.

Q8. Describe the main features of Gersmehl's model of nutrient cycling.

Q9. Study Figure 5.46.

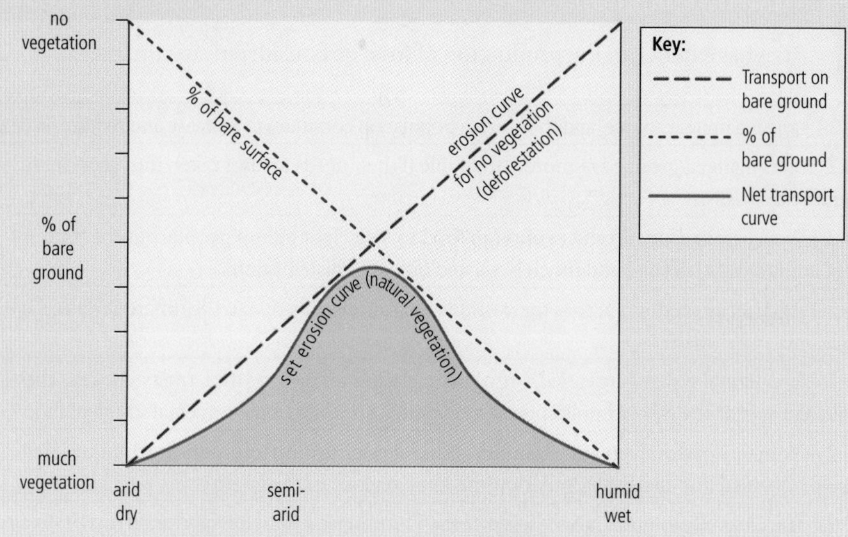

Figure 5.46 The effects of vegetation and rainfall on soil erosion.

Use Figure 5.46 to outline the reasons why rates of erosion are highest in semi-arid areas and lowest in arid and humid areas.

Q10. Study Figure 5.47.

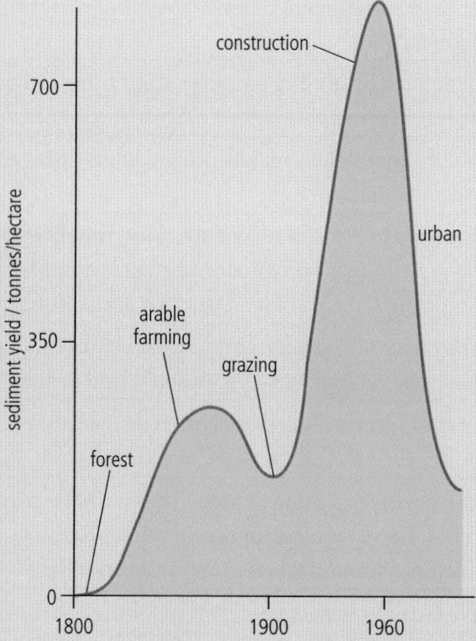

Figure 5.47 The effect of land use on soil erosion and sediment yield in North America.

Use the information provided in Figure 5.47 to describe how rates of soil erosion vary with land-use in North America from 1800 onwards.

5.2 Agriculture and food

Guiding question

To what extent can the production of food be considered sustainable?

5.2.1 Land is a finite resource, and the human population continues to increase and require feeding.
5.2.2 Marginalized groups are more vulnerable if their needs are not taken into account in land-use decisions.
5.2.3 World agriculture produces enough food to feed eight billion people, but the food is not equitably distributed and much is wasted or lost in distribution.
5.2.4 Agriculture systems across the world vary considerably due to the different nature of the soils and climates.
5.2.5 Agricultural systems are varied, with different factors influencing the farmers' choices. These differences and factors have implications for economic, social and environmental sustainability.
5.2.6 Nomadic pastoralism and slash-and-burn agriculture are traditional techniques that have sustained low-density populations in some regions of the world.
5.2.7 The Green Revolution (also known as the Third Agricultural Revolution in the 1950s and 1960s) used breeding of high-yielding crop plants – combined with increased and improved irrigation systems, synthetic fertilizer and application of pesticides – to increase food security. It has been criticized for its sociocultural, economic and environmental consequences.
5.2.8 Synthetic fertilizers are needed in many intensive systems to maintain high commercial productivity at the expense of sustainability. In sustainable agriculture, there are other methods for improving soil fertility.
5.2.9 A variety of techniques can be used to conserve soil, with widespread environmental, economic and sociocultural benefits.
5.2.10 Humans are omnivorous and diets include fungi, plants, meat and fish. Diets lower in trophic levels are more sustainable.
5.2.11 Current global strategies to achieve sustainable food supply include reducing demand and food waste, reducing greenhouse gas emissions from food production and increasing productivity without increasing the area of land used for agriculture.
5.2.12 Food security is the physical and economic availability of food, allowing all individuals to get the balanced diet they need for an active and healthy life.
HL 5.2.13 Contrasting agricultural choices will often be the result of differences in the local soils and climate.
HL 5.2.14 Numerous alternative farming approaches have been developed in relation to the current ecological crisis. These include approaches that promote soil regeneration, rewilding, permaculture, non-commercial cropping and zero tillage.
HL 5.2.15 Regenerative farming systems and permaculture use mixed farming techniques to improve and diversify productivity. Techniques include the use of animals like pigs or chickens to clear vegetation and plough the land, or mob grazing to improve soil.
HL 5.2.16 Technological improvements can lead to very high levels of productivity, as seen in the modern high-tech greenhouse and vertical farming techniques that are increasingly important for supplying food to urban areas.
HL 5.2.17 The sustainability of different diets varies. Supply chain efficiency, the distance food travels, the type of farming and farming techniques, and societal diet changes can all impact sustainability.
HL 5.2.18 Harvesting wild species from ecosystems by traditional methods may be more sustainable than land conversion and cultivation.

HL 5.2.19 Claims that low productivity indigenous, traditional or alternative food systems are sustainable should be evaluated against the need to produce enough food to feed the wider global population.
HL 5.2.20 Food distribution patterns and food quality variations reflect functioning of the global food supply industry and can lead to all forms of malnutrition (diseases of undernourishment and overnourishment).

5.2.1 Land is a finite resource and is used to provide food for humans

8.1 Human populations

About 70% of ice-free land is used for agriculture and forestry. Not all soils or lands are suitable for arable crops. Some land is too steep, and some soils are too nutrient poor. These areas are often used for livestock production instead.

Middle-income countries (MICs) are those where the average annual income is between US$ 1025 and US$ 12,475. These can be split into lower middle income (US$ 1025 – US$ 4035) and upper middle income (US$ 4036 – US$ 12,475).

Less than one-third of the earth's surface is land and less than half of this is used for agriculture (Figure 5.48). Of the world's agricultural land, just over three-quarters is used for livestock and just under one-quarter is used for growing crops. The more fertile land is used for growing crops, whereas drier, less fertile land, may be used for livestock. It is also possible to modify/create new agricultural landscapes through, for example, terracing, drainage, irrigation and land reclamation.

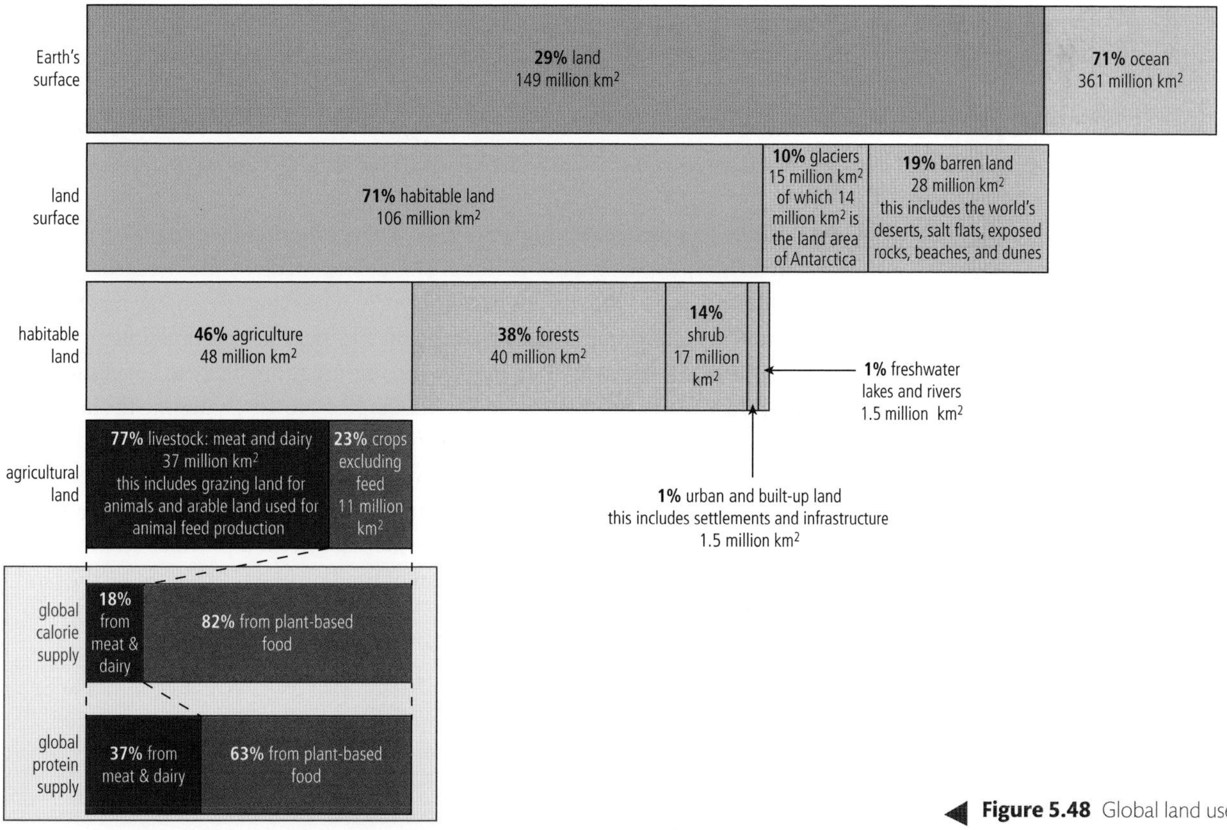

Figure 5.48 Global land use.

Figure 5.48 shows that, of the Earth's surface:

- land covers 29% and the oceans 71%
- of the land surface, 71% is habitable
- of the habitable land, 46% is used for agriculture, approximately one-third of which is used for crops and two-thirds for livestock.

The global population increased from about 3 billion in 1961 to 8 billion in 2022. As a result, the amount of agricultural land per person has declined in all regions of the world (Figure 5.49). However, it is not just the size of the population that is important, it is also its characteristics, such as the increase in the number of people on a middle income.

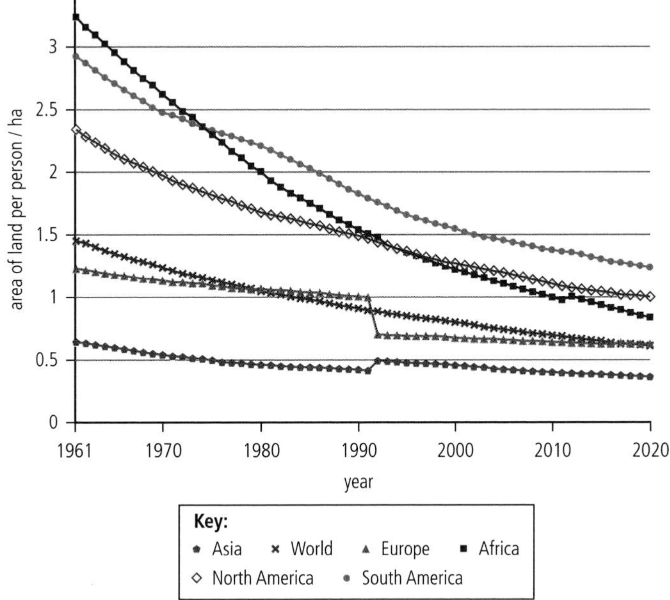

Figure 5.49 Agricultural land per person, 1960–2020.

People on middle incomes have a higher disposable income and tend to have a different diet compared with people on a low income. This change in diet with increasing income (up to a point) is known as the nutrition transition, in which people on low incomes tend to consume a higher proportion of staples such as rice, cassava and flour, whereas those that have made the transition to middle-income are more likely to consume meat, vegetable and dairy products as well as the staples. However, despite the large growth in population and the expansion of the middle class, the world has not, overall, experienced major food shortages because of over-population. Nor has there been a major increase in the amount of land cultivated in recent years – most of the best land has been cultivated for over a century. The increase in food production in recent decades has occurred due to the intensification of food production, i.e. using the land to produce more food.

i

'Globally, the size of the middle class could increase from 1.8 billion people to 3.2 billion by 2020 and to 4.9 billion by 2030. Almost all of this growth (85 per cent) comes from Asia. The size of the middle class in North America is expected to remain roughly constant in absolute terms. This is because as many people graduate out of the middle class and become rich as move into the middle class from being poor. Europe enjoys some early growth in the numbers of the middle class, but then sees a fall as populations decline in Russia and elsewhere.' OECD Development Centre, 2010

5.2.2 Marginalized groups are more vulnerable

1.1 Perspectives
1.3 Sustainability

HL a Environmental law
HL b Environmental economics
HL c Environmental ethics

Marginalized people and Indigenous cultures have a low socio-economic status and examples include low caste or women farmers or people in low-income countries (LICs). Many marginalized people are deprived of sufficient land rights to support their needs.

Example – A marginalized population in South Africa

South Africa has a history in which racial segregation was enshrined in law during the Apartheid era (1948–1994). During that period there was segregation of schools, health care, employment opportunities and where people were allowed to live. Despite the ending of the Apartheid era in 1994, there is still evidence of racial inequalities in South Africa.

Subsistence farming refers to farming in which the produce is mainly for (the) household consumption whereas commercial farming is mainly to sell and make a profit.

South Africa currently has just over 40,000 predominantly white commercial farmers and about two million, largely subsistence (unpaid), black farmers. Despite the large number of black farmers, they account for a small proportion of output (Figure 5.50).

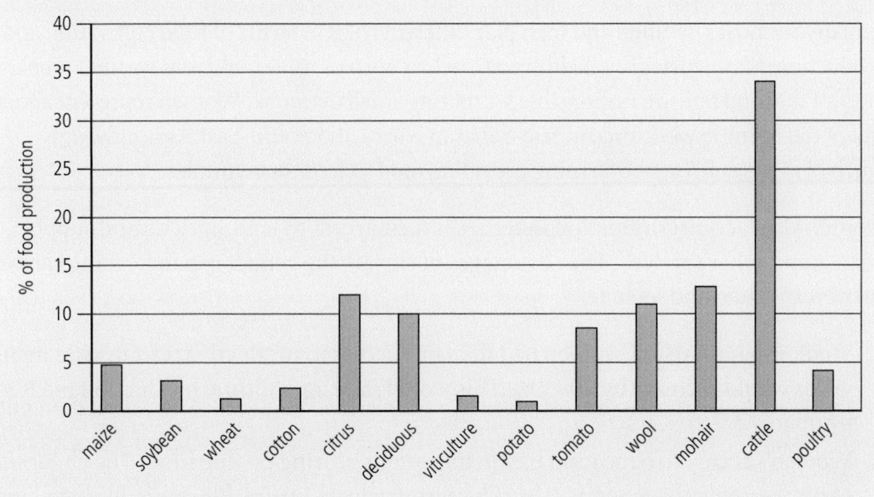

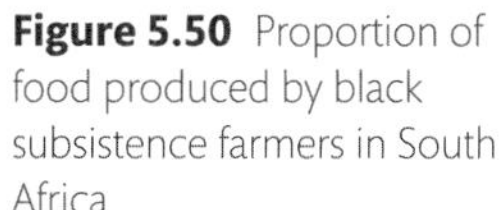

Figure 5.50 Proportion of food produced by black subsistence farmers in South Africa.

Figure 5.51 shows that there is a strong relationship between GDP (gross domestic product – a measure of wealth) and the daily supply of calories. The graph shows a positive relationship between wealth and calorie intake – as wealth increases, calorie intake also increases. At the lower end of the graph, this is very much a good thing and may help reduce hunger and malnutrition in poor communities. However, at the top end, excessive calorie intake may lead to obesity and to diseases caused by over-consumption. As Figure 5.51 has shown, there is an increasing proportion of the world's population that are middle-income and this is helping reduce hunger and malnutrition.

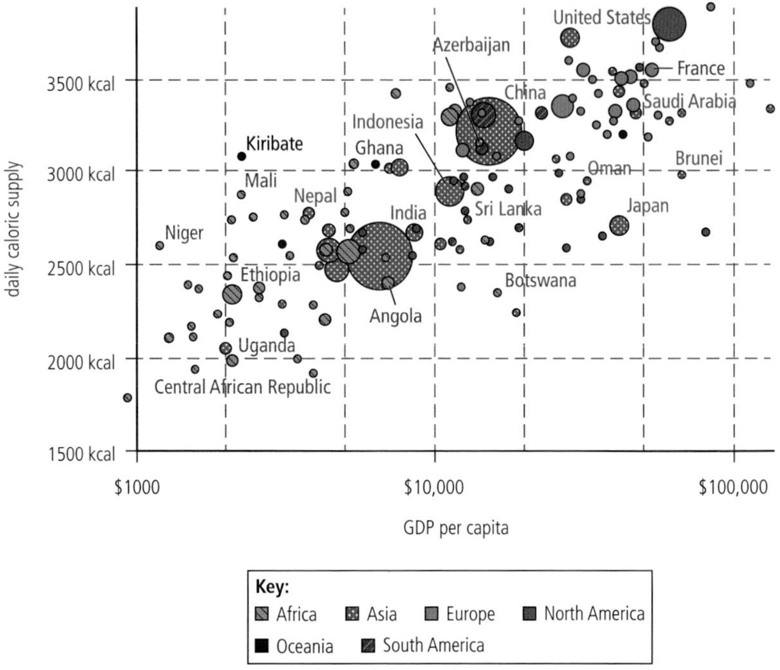

Figure 5.51 Daily supply of calories in relation to GDP.

In many countries, women and men play different roles in terms of food cultivation and production. Many men grow field crops, such as corn or millet, whereas women prepare most of the food and are responsible for rearing small livestock. Women represent about half of the farming workforce in Sub-Saharan Africa and South-East Asia, although much of this is subsistence farming providing food to feed their families.

Women also face discrimination in terms of their access to land, agricultural support, finance and other services. The advantages of closing the gender gap in farming cannot be overestimated and include:

- Studies suggest that if women had the same access to productive resources as men, yields would increase by 20–30%. This would raise agricultural production in LICs by up to 4%.
- Women's access to education has an important bearing on nutrition. The children of mothers who have spent at least 5 years in education are 40% more likely to live beyond the age of 5 years.
- People on low incomes are more likely to live in conditions of poor hygiene and sanitation. Improvements in hygiene and sanitation will lead to an increase in household health.
- Women have limited access to land ownership. Therefore, many are marginalized onto small holdings that they use for subsistence farming.
- Much of women's time is spent collecting water, cooking and looking after children and the elderly. Therefore, they have less time to grow and prepare food.
- Access to most financial services and credit is limited for many women in rural areas. This limits farming innovation in these areas.
- Women may have limited market-access due to poor access (limited transport) and a lack of time.

5.2.3 World agriculture, food distribution and food waste

1.3 Sustainability

HL b Environmental economics
HL c Environmental ethics

World agriculture produces enough food to feed everyone on Earth, but the food produced is not equitably distributed and at least one third of food produced is wasted either post-harvest, during storage, or in distribution. Goal 12.3 of the Sustainable Development Goals aims to halve food waste by 2030.

By 2050 there are likely be at least 9 billion people on Earth, compared with 6 billion in 2000 and 8 billion in 2022. The idea that an expanding population would place limits on the world's ability to feed the population was first published in 1798 by Thomas Malthus in *An essay on the principles of population growth*. While the human population has grown more than six-fold since then, the world's production of food has grown even more rapidly and, in fact, food availability per person has increased. This growth has been made possible using science and technology, as well as social and economic change.

However, despite the increase, there is an unequal distribution of global food resources. More than half (425 million) of undernourished people in the world in 2021 lived in Asia and over one-third (278 million) lived in Africa (Figure 5.52). Approximately one in six people has a diet lacking in sufficient nutrients/calories and one in six people consume too much food in relation to their needs. Although the solution would seem simple – move excess food from areas of surplus to areas of deficit – there are arguments against this: it could create dependency and it could weaken the desire for self-sufficiency by countries that are in need.

Activity

Consider the pros and cons of moving food from areas of surplus to areas of deficit.

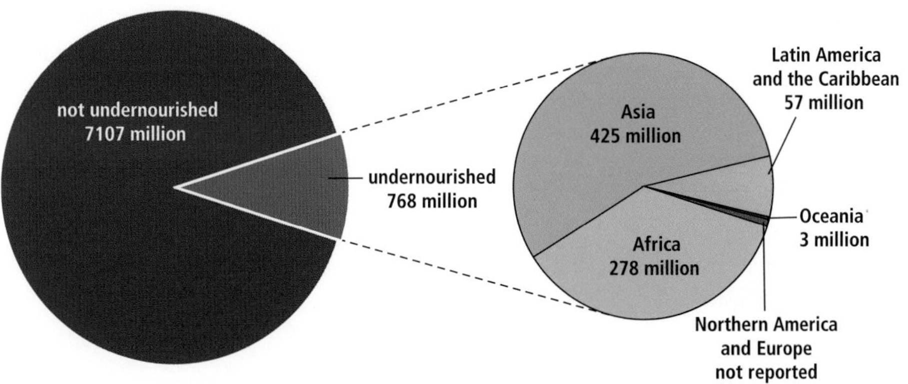

Figure 5.52 Inequalities in the distribution of the world's undernourished population, 2022.

Food waste

Food waste (Figure 5.53) occurs in both LICs and HICs, but for different reasons.

The UN Sustainable Development Goal 12.3 calls for food waste to be halved and food losses worldwide to be reduced by 2030. According to the UN, the COVID-19 pandemic increased the food loss and waste challenge at every stage of the food value chain. However, it also reported positive gains made. For example, several companies such as Tesco® and Arla® Foods achieved food loss and waste reductions of more than 30%, largely in Europe.

Figure 5.53 Food waste.

A report by the UK's Institution of Mechanical Engineers, *Global Food: Waste Not, Want Not* (2013), claimed that as much as half of all the food produced in the world – equivalent to 2 billion tonnes – ends up as waste every year. The report lists the reasons for the food waste as:

- poor agricultural practices
- inadequate infrastructure for transporting food
- poor storage facilities
- strict sell-by dates on supermarket food
- buy-one-get-one free promotions on food in supermarkets
- Western consumer demand for food that appears perfect (i.e. free from deformities).

Access this page of your eBook for a food waste fact file.

The report found that 30–50% of the total amount of food produced around the world each year (about 4 billion tonnes) never makes it on to a plate. This amounts to 1.2–2 billion tonnes of food wasted every year.

The nature of waste

Low-income countries

In LICs, such as those of Sub-Saharan Africa and South-East Asia, wastage tends to occur primarily at the farmer-producer end of the supply chain. Inefficient harvesting, inadequate local transportation and poor infrastructure mean that produce is frequently handled inappropriately and stored under unsuitable farm site conditions.

As a result, mould and pests (e.g. rodents) destroy or at least degrade large quantities of food material. Substantial amounts of foodstuffs simply spill from badly maintained vehicles or are bruised as vehicles travel over poorly maintained roads.

As the development level of a country increases, the food-loss problem generally moves further up the supply chain with deficiencies in regional and national infrastructure having the largest impact. In South-East Asian countries, for example, losses of rice range from 37% to 80% of the entire production, depending on development stage. The total is about 180 million tonnes annually. In China, a country experiencing rapid development, the loss is about 45%. In less-developed Vietnam, rice losses amount to 80% of production.

In HICs, approximately 25% of all the food bought is discarded as waste, despite there often being nothing wrong with it. Most of the waste is generated at the consumer stage. Estimates show that the value of the food that goes to waste and is thrown away amounts to approximately US$ 250 billion globally.

Saving water by reducing food waste, increasing productivity, plant breeding and wastewater recycling are critical to everyone. Over 25% of all the water we use worldwide is taken to grow over one billion tonnes of food that nobody eats.

High-income countries

In high-income countries (HICs), consumerism, excess wealth and mass marketing lead to wastage. More efficient farming practices and better transport, storage and processing facilities ensure that a larger proportion of the food produced reaches markets and consumers. However, produce is often wasted through retail and customer behaviour. Major supermarkets, in meeting consumer expectations, often reject entire crops of perfectly edible fruit and vegetables at the farm because they do not meet exacting marketing standards for their physical characteristics, such as size and appearance. Globally, retailers generate 1.6 million tonnes of food waste annually in this way.

Overall, wastage rates for vegetables and fruit are considerably higher than for grains. The UK Food Security Report (2021) showed that 46% of the potato crop is not delivered to the retail market. The details revealed that 6% is lost in the field, 12% is discarded on initial sorting, 5% is lost in storage,

1% is lost in post-storage inspection and 22% is lost due to rejection after washing. The *Global Food: Waste Not, Want Not* (2013) report showed that at least 40% of all fruit and vegetables in India are lost between grower and consumer due to lack of refrigerated transport, poor roads and poor weather.

Of the produce that does appear in the supermarket, commonly used sales promotions frequently encourage customers to purchase excessive quantities which, in the case of perishable foodstuffs such as vegetable and fruit, inevitably generates wastage in the home. Overall, *c*. 25% of the produce bought in HICs is thrown away by the purchaser.

Controlling and reducing the level of wastage is frequently beyond the capability of the individual farmer, distributor or consumer, since it depends on market philosophies, security of energy supply, quality of roads and the presence of transport networks.

Challenge yourself

Find out about food waste (a) in your school, (b) in your home and (c) in your local area. Present your findings to the class.

Activity

Think about ways in which you can reduce food waste. Discuss ideas within your class. Ideas for cutting food waste could include the following:

- Make meals from leftover food. For example, use refried vegetables or make soup from a chicken carcass.
- Think before you shop. Look in the fridge and have an idea of meals or recipe needs before you go shopping.
- Use teabags and leftovers to produce compost for your garden and recycle nutrients.
- Look for local recipes for using excess bread, potatoes and other staples.
- Use your freezer. If you know you are not going to use something, freeze it so it will stay fresh for another day. A full freezer retains cold better than an empty one.
- Store food carefully. Get into the habit of putting cereal, biscuits and fresh nuts into tins or airtight containers.
- Remember that best before dates may be over cautious. Often with non-meat or dairy products, you can use your common sense to check if they're still safe to eat.

5.2.4 Agriculture systems across the world

Agriculture systems around the world vary considerably due to the nature of the soils and climates. Soils in different biomes have very different potentials for crop types and productivity.

2.4 Climate and biomes
5.1 Soil

Among the physical factors that can influence agriculture systems, soils and climate are of great importance.

There are four broad soil types that influence farming patterns. Soils formed under temperate grasslands have become extremely important for food production. Since the development of steel ploughs that were sufficiently strong to break up the prairies soils, these soils became the breadbaskets of the world, especially in the North American Great Plains, the South American Pampas and the steppes of Russia.

On a smaller scale, the soil developed on volcanic ash supported high population densities in places such as Ecuador, Rwanda and parts of Japan.

Some soils of medium-high fertility, which attracted people to occupy them, have become degraded and no longer support high population densities. Other soils such as brown earths and chernozems (black earths) are relatively fertile and have great potential for agriculture.

Soils in the tropical rainforest are leached, acidic and lacking in nutrients. Hence, they have much less potential for farming. Indeed, it is a paradox that some of the world's most luxuriant vegetation is found on some of the world's least fertile soils.

Soils in temperate grasslands are generally fertile due to the large amount of organic matter found in the soil. The grasses have deep roots and when the grasses decompose, they release organic matter deep into the soil. The warm, summer temperatures and summer rainfall in these grasslands also help with plant productivity.

In contrast, in areas of coniferous woodland, the low temperatures and short growing season limit plant productivity and the potential for agriculture. This may change with global climate change patterns.

5.2.5 Agricultural systems are varied with different factors influencing the farmers' choices

1.3 Sustainability

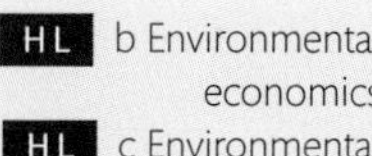

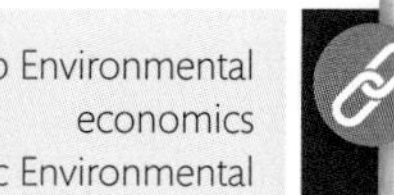

HL b Environmental economics
HL c Environmental ethics

There are several differences in farming including intensive or extensive, arable, pastoral or market gardening, mixed or livestock based, subsistence or commercial, organic or inorganic, monocultures or diverse farms, family or corporate ownership, irrigated or rain fed, soil-based or hydroponic. These differences have implications for economic, social and environmental sustainability.

Types of farming vary in terms of outputs such as arable (crops), pastoral (livestock), mixed (arable and pastoral), non-food (e.g. cotton and tobacco), monoculture (farming of a single product) and diverse (farming of many products). Reasons for farming can be divided into commercial (aiming to sell products and make a profit) and subsistence (aiming to provide food products for the household). However, many farms are a mix of both commercial and subsistence. Most modern farms are sedentary, meaning that the farmer farms the same area each year, but some farming involves movement such as **shifting cultivation** and **nomadic pastoralism**.

Intensive farming maximizes the productivity from a given unit of land with relatively high number of inputs per hectare, whereas extensive farming has low levels of inputs of fertilizers, pesticides, machinery and labour per hectare. However, the total amount of inputs can still be large or expensive, for example the use of combine harvesters to harvest. Some farms rely on natural rainfall whereas others, in relatively dry areas, use irrigation water. Most farming is soil-based but there have been modern developments that include growing crops in water (hydroponics), which may be done in combination with fish cultivation (aquaculture). Other forms of farming include organic, which attempts to be a natural form of farming, and inorganic, which may use synthetic fertilizers and pesticides.

Classifying agriculture

The following categories and explanations are not exclusive but provide an indication of a scale along which all farming types can be placed.

Arable farming: a type of farming involving the cultivation of crops. For example, wheat farming in the Great Plains of the USA.

Commercial farming: a type of farming where the products are sold to make a profit. For example, market gardening in the Netherlands.

Corporate farms: large-scale farms that are owned by companies and their shareholders and the work is mainly done though a farm-manager and hired labour.

Diverse farming: the rearing/cultivation of a variety of crops and/or livestock.

Extensive farming: a type of farming producing low inputs or yields per unit area. For example, free range chicken production or nomadic pastoralism as used by the Pokot people of Kenya.

Family farms: farms that are owned and run by families. These are generally small-scale and are becoming less common in HICs, especially in North America and Europe, as large-scale agribusinesses account for an increasing proportion of food production. They remain common in many LICs and newly-industrialized countries (NICs), such as India and South Africa.

Hydroponic farming: a type of farming in which crops are grown (and fish are reared) in water. For example, farming in Busan, Cairo.

Inorganic farming: a type of farming that uses synthetic fertilizers, pesticides, insecticides and/or herbicides. Many modern types of farming in HICs are forms of inorganic farming. For example, cereal farming and livestock farming in the North American prairies.

Intensive farming: a type of farming producing high inputs or yields per unit area. For example, battery hen production and rice cultivation in the Ganges Valley, India.

Battery hens are egg-laying hens that are kept in battery cages. These cages are connected and arranged in rows and columns.

Irrigated farming: a type of farming in which extra water, taken from rivers, groundwater and/or reservoirs, is provided for crop growth.

Market gardening/horticulture: a type of farming involving the intensive production of high value food and flowers in gardens and greenhouses. For example, the production of tomatoes, lettuces, fruit and flowers for a largely urban market.

Mixed farming: a type of farming that involves both crops and livestock, not necessarily in equal amounts.

Monoculture farming: a type of farming involving the production of only one type of crop. For example, the wheat belt of Canada or rice cultivation in South-East Asia. Monoculture encourages specialization in one product but can lead to soil exhaustion (depletion of one or more specific minerals) and/or low prices due to over-production.

Nomadic farmers: farmers that move seasonally with their herds. For example, the Pokot pastoralists in Kenya (this topic, section 5.2.6).

Organic farming: a type of farming that does not use synthetic fertilizers, pesticides, insecticides and/or herbicides. It instead favours animal and plant manure/waste. This farming system requires a high input of labour per unit area. Organic farming attempts to produce food in a 'natural way'. Typically, their yields are much lower than intensive farming (about 40% lower), thus, to produce the same amount of food, organic farmers must use more land. This requires the ploughing of more non-agricultural land, which releases more carbon into the atmosphere. An alternative may be to farm some land more intensively and rest the other areas of land.

Pastoral farming: a type of farming involving the rearing of animals. For example, sheep farming in New Zealand.

Rain-fed farming: a type of farming that relies on natural rainfall for crop germination and growth.

Sedentary farmers: farmers that remain in the same place throughout the year. For example, dairy farmers in Devon and Cornwall, UK.

Soil-based farming: a type of farming in which crops are grown in soil in fields.

Subsistence farming: a type of farming in which the products are not sold and are instead consumed by the cultivators. For example, the case of shifting cultivation by Kayapo in the Amazonian rainforest.

Make sure you know how to make a detailed study of a pair of named contrasting systems.

Example – Intensive chicken farming in Denmark

The inputs, processes and outputs of intensive chicken farming can be seen in Figure 5.54.

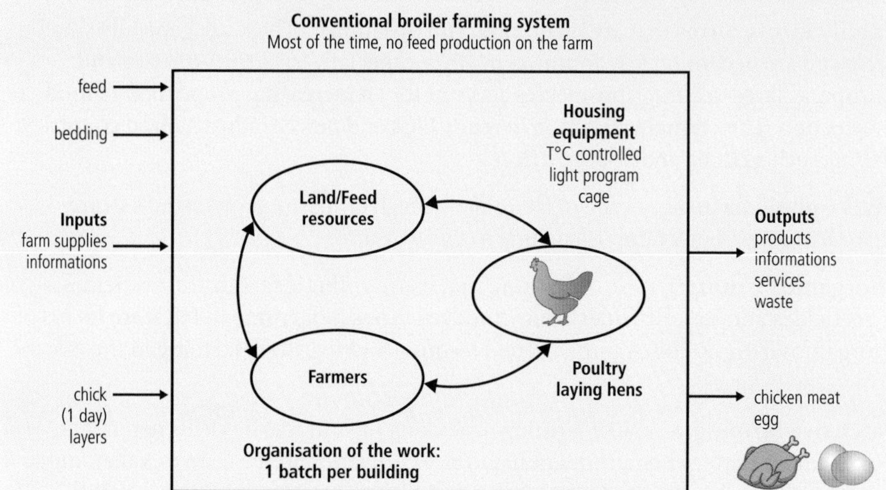

Figure 5.54 A farming system with inputs, processes and outputs.

Example – Small farms in Cockpit Country, Jamaica

The farms in Cockpit Country, Jamaica are generally small, with most of them being less than 1 ha in size (Figures 5.55 and 5.56). Most farms are broken up into several fragments with at least two or three parcels of land, although some have as many as ten. Being fragmented has its advantages. For example, it allows farmers to farm in different environments and to spread their risk among many different types of crops. For instance, the forested areas (cockpits) contain rich, fertile soils and are moister and cooler than the rocky slopes and high ground. On the other hand, some farmers can spend up to two hours cycling to one piece of land, representing a considerable waste of the farmer's time.

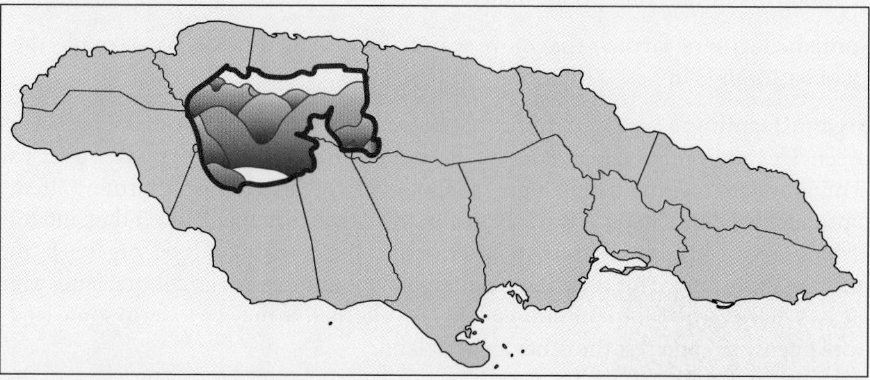

Figure 5.55 The location of Cockpit Country, Jamaica.

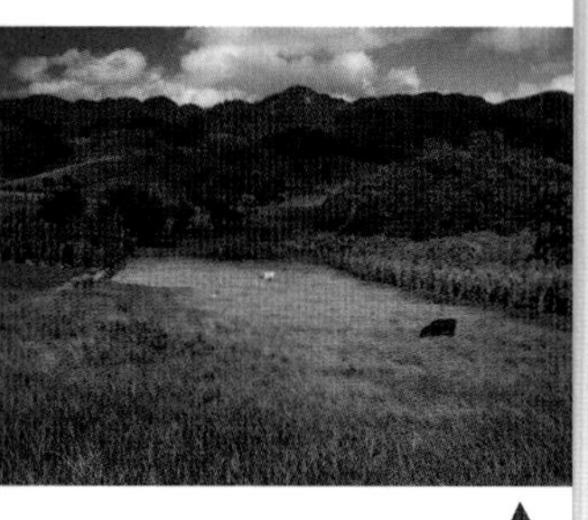

Figure 5.56 Farming in Cockpit Country, Jamaica.

Small farm production is characterized by a variety of crops. Sugar cane is the most important cash crop. Other important cash crops include coffee and bananas. Other crops are used for a mix of subsistence needs and for sale at the market some 16 km away. Field crops include yams, dasheen, maize, sweet potatoes and cabbage, while tree crops include breadfruit, coconuts and avocado pears. On some of the rocky slopes, farmers grow 'creeping crops' that can spread over the bare rock. These include pumpkin, cucumbers and yams. Many farmers also keep livestock – cattle and goats are the most important in the region.

To sustain their farming, most farmers use a variety of measures such as intercropping, crop rotation and fallow. The main problem is an economic one – that of being able to market the farm products. The area is relatively isolated and there are few good roads to the nearby towns. The future for these small-scale farmers appears bleak. Farmers need more land to farm effectively, but there are competing claims for the land from mining companies, environmentalists and forestry companies. In particular, bauxite mining is a major threat to farmers in the area, as it removes much of the topsoil in order to extract the minerals below.

Most of the farmers in this area are elderly. Surveys have shown that over 60% of the farmers in this area are aged over 50 years and that 43% are aged over 60. In contrast, the proportion of young farmers is very low – less than 3% of the farmers are younger than 25 years of age.

Extensive farming in Canada – the case of wheat

Farming on the Canadian Prairies is relatively recent – much more recent than in the Caribbean. However, it now accounts for a high proportion of the world's share in the production of wheat.

The Canadian Prairies is a very large area (almost 180 m ha), is relatively flat and undulating, and has deep, well-drained fertile soils (Figure 5.57). The region is characterized by very cold winters and long, hot summers. The cold winters break up the soil and kill off weeds and other plants. The long hot summer days, with an average daily temperature exceeding 20 °C, allow the crops to ripen. Although the region is relatively dry – it only receives between 250 mm and 500 mm of rain – much of the rain falls in the early summer when the crops need it most. Traditionally, wheat requires 375 mm of rain and 120 days of frost-free sunshine to mature.

Figure 5.57 Wheat farming in the Canadian Prairies.

The highly commercialized and large-scale farming that occurs in this region is known as **agribusiness.** Many of the farms include large rectangular fields with an area of land greater than 500 ha, which allows the use of large machinery such as SMART seeders (high tech machines that monitor soil conditions while seeding, Figure 5.58). There is little use of human labour in the Prairies and most of the work is done by machines. There is a high input of capital, in the form of money and machines, in relation to the size of the labour force. Much of the workforce is made up of seasonal and hired contract labourers. Given the very large size of the farms, the input of capital and labour per hectare is quite low, so the land is farmed **extensively** (that is, with low inputs and outputs per unit of land, although the total cost of the inputs can be very high).

Figure 5.58 SMART seeders allow farmers to achieve optimum seed and fertilizer productivity.

Compared with Cockpit Country, there is a good communications infrastructure in the region. Buildings include large grain elevators or silos, in which the harvested wheat is stored. These are frequently built next to railway lines so that the wheat can be exported by rail.

The main crop grown in the Prairies is spring wheat. This is sown (planted) in the spring when the snows have melted. Fertilizers, pesticides and herbicides are used to increase wheat yields. Many of these inputs are applied by machines, sometimes aircraft.

Many of the farms are extremely large. As some of the smaller farmers have left farming, their farms have been bought and taken over by the larger farms, thereby increasing their size. Thus some farmers own many different farms. This leads to **farm fragmentation**. This means that a farmer owns many different plots of land rather than just a single piece. (Fragmentation also occurs in the Caribbean although it is often the very small holdings that are fragmented.) Many of these large farmers choose to live in the towns and commute to their farms for work. Such farmers are called 'sidewalk' farmers.

To deal with the extra labour needed to harvest the crops during harvest time, teams of contract labourers are employed. These workers, who bring their own combine harvesters with them, begin their year much further south, in Texas, USA. They work their way northwards with the ripening crops. They generally reach the Canadian Prairies by mid-August/early September. These labourers, who live in mobile homes, are known as 'suitcase' farmers.

High-yielding varieties of wheat have been produced. Some varieties, such as Saunders wheat, only require 90 days of frost-free sunshine and 300 mm of rain to mature. This selective use of crops, in combination with fertilizers and pesticides, enables a high proportion of the world's wheat to be produced in the region. Nevertheless, there are environmental problems associated with wheat farming, particularly soil erosion. Various measures have been tried to combat this problem, such as crushing and powdering the soil to retain moisture, laying straw on the surface and contour ploughing on undulating ground.

The wheat crop is still vulnerable to several natural hazards. A late frost in spring or an early frost in autumn may damage the crop. Heavy convectional (thunder) storms in summer may destroy the crop in the field, as may a hailstorm. Even hot conditions are not without risk – warm weather may lead to infestations of insects, such as grasshoppers. In future, global warming may make some parts of Canada wetter and some parts drier. Predictions for the Prairies are that summer temperatures are likely to rise. This may lead to an increase in the number of summer droughts, which would have a negative impact on the growth of wheat in most areas apart from those that are irrigated.

Canada continues to supply a large amount of the world's wheat and an even higher proportion of its exports. Wheat remains a good crop to grow because there is a great demand for it, it can be transported easily and cheaply, and it can be stored for long periods without losing quality.

Make a detailed study of one example of a pair of named contrasting systems

This skill is covered by the Activity on the next page.

Activity

The data in Table 5.11 provides a comparison between small-scale farming in Jamaica and large-scale farming in Canada.

1. Using this data, construct a systems diagram (like Figure 5.54) to show the main features of farming in Cockpit Country and of wheat farming in Canada.

Table 5.11 A comparison between small-scale farming in Jamaica and large-scale farming in Canada.

Location	Cockpit Country, Jamaica	Canadian Prairies
Physical factors		
Physical features	Tropical karst – rocky slopes and forested lowlands	Large areas of flat and undulating land
Relief	Varied – a mix of flat land and steep land close together	Land relief changes gradually rather than quickly
Soil	Fertile on flatter areas, thin on rocky slopes	Generally fertile black earths
Farm size	Generally less than 1 ha; very fragmented	Generally over 300 ha but also fragmented
Temperature	Warm throughout the year (over 25 °C)	Cold winters (below 5 °C) Hot summers (above 25 °C)
Rainfall	High – maximum in May and September (over 1300 mm)	Maximum in summer (relatively low: less than 500 mm)
Water supply	Relatively good	Variable – irrigation needed in the south and south-east
Crops/livestock	Cash crops: mainly sugar, bananas and coffee	Mainly wheat, some oilseed rape
Economic factors		
Tenure	Mix of family land, ownership and rental	Mainly ownership and rental
Research and development	Limited – mainly traditional knowledge	Large-scale use of research and development in crop manipulation, fertilizers, pesticides and so on
Processes		
Type of farming	Intensive	Extensive
Land preparation	Much human labour	Mechanized labour
Cropping	Intercropping; varied species	Mainly monoculture
Soil conservation	Limited	Varied – contour ploughing, mulching, crushing and powdering soil
Marketing	Limited – remote and isolated region	Organized by large wheat boards
Outputs	Small yields overall	Large yields overall (low yield per ha)
Volume of production	Low	High

2. Using Figures 5.56 to 5.58, describe the nature of the terrain (landscape) and vegetation in Cockpit Country and the Canadian prairies. Suggest how these factors may affect the type of farming that is practiced in each location.

1.1 Perspectives
1.3 Sustainability

5.2.6 Nomadic pastoralism and slash-and-burn agriculture

Nomadic pastoralism and shifting cultivation are traditional, sustainable forms of agriculture that supported Indigenous populations at low densities. However, as Indigenous populations modernize and exist in higher population densities or fixed locations, these practices become less sustainable.

Nomadic pastoralism is a form of agriculture with a large degree of mobility or wandering as a way of life. It is synonymous with livestock herding and generally occurs in semi-arid or mountainous environments. Other seasonal movements include **transhumance** in the Alps (seasonal movements up to higher slopes in summer and down to lower slopes during winter) and 'suitcase farming' in the USA.

Full, or true, nomads have no permanent dwellings and do not practice cultivation. Instead, they graze their livestock on natural vegetation. They do, however, engage in trading/exchange to acquire food and goods that they need.

Pastoralism involves the breeding and rearing of animals to produce food, clothing and shelter. Nomadic pastoralism is generally subsistence in nature. The variety of animals used in pastoralism is limited – camels, cattle, sheep and goats in particular. Camels are well-adapted to drought and are therefore the most important type of livestock for pastoralism. It was necessary to move around due to shortages of water. The more reliable the water supply, and consequent vegetation, the less need for movement. In less extreme environments, sheep, cattle and goats may be farmed.

In several places, partial nomadism and sedentary farming are replacing nomadism. For example, the Pokot of Kenya have been affected by government policies, climate change and bush encroachment, and there has been a movement away from nomadic pastoralism of cattle to sedentary herding of small herds (mainly goats) for commercial purposes, as well as new sources of income such as tourism. In other areas, such as the UAE, many former nomadic pastoralists have entered the tourism sector as it provides a better income (Figure 5.59).

Figure 5.59 Many former nomadic pastoralists in the UAE are now engaged in the tourist industry.

Shifting cultivation (slash-and-burn)

Shifting cultivation is an agricultural system characterized by the rotation of fields (area farmed) rather than crops. Periods of fallow are generally longer than the periods of cropping. Fields are created by cutting down areas of forest (Figure 5.60) and burning the vegetation to increase the levels of nutrients in the soil. There may be up to 250 million shifting cultivators in the world, with as many as 100 million in South-East Asia.

Figure 5.60 An area of tropical rainforest in Malaysia that has been destroyed to make way for cultivation.

Shifting cultivation is an extensive form of agriculture in many areas of tropical rainforest but is threatened by population growth and expanding agricultural development, such as commercial agriculture in the Amazonian rainforest. Nutrient ash provides a nutrient-rich seedbed in which a diverse and complete cover crop can be established quickly, reducing the threat of leaching and soil erosion.

The loss of nutrients during burning and cultivation can be rapid. Losses of nitrogen, phosphorus and exchangeable bases are high. Soil organic matter can decline by 30–40% during the first year of cultivation. After 2–3 years the yields and soil fertility decline dramatically, and the plot is abandoned (Figure 5.61). The re-establishment of primary rainforest can take a very long time, up to 500 years or so.

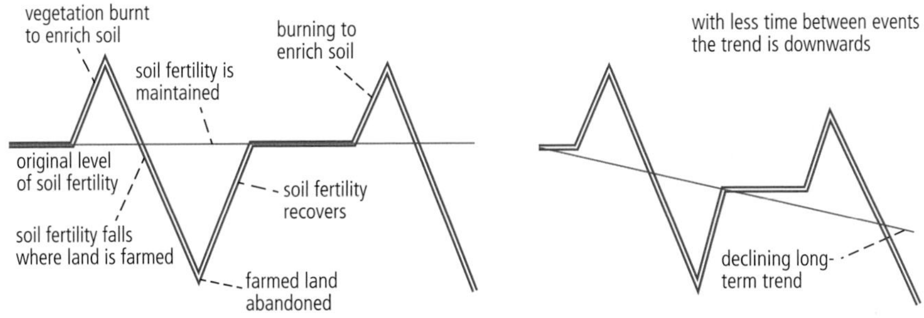

Figure 5.61 The impact of shifting cultivation on soil quality.

Activity

Find out about other types of seasonal variations in farming including transhumance and 'suitcase farming'.

Summarise your findings in a fact sheet.

5.2.7 The Green Revolution

1.1 Perspectives
1.3 Sustainability
2.3 Biogeochemical cycles
6.2 Climate change – causes and impacts

See this page in your eBook for more on the Green Revolution.

The Green Revolution involved the application of science and technology to increase crop productivity. It included a variety of techniques such as genetic engineering to produce higher yielding varieties (HYVs) of crops and animals, mechanization, pesticides, herbicides, synthetic fertilizers and irrigation water. HYVs are the flagship of the Green Revolution. During the period 1967–1968, India adopted Mexican Rice IR8, which yielded twice as much grain as the traditional crop varieties. However, Mexican Rice IR8 also required large amounts of water and fertilizer. Up to 55% of India's crops and 85% of the Philippines' crops are HYVs. In contrast, only 13% of Thailand's crops are HYVs.

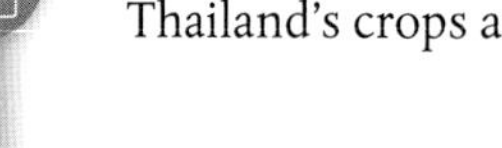

The consequences

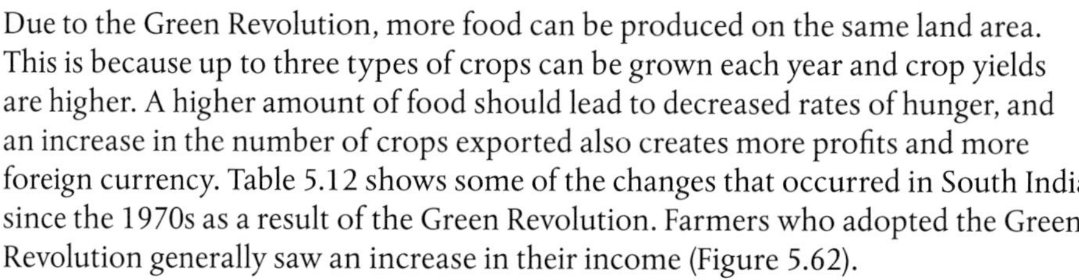

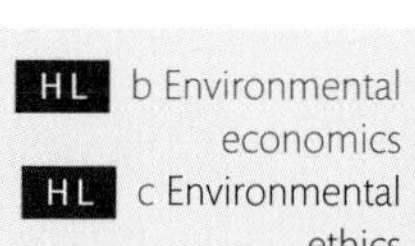

HL b Environmental economics
HL c Environmental ethics

Due to the Green Revolution, more food can be produced on the same land area. This is because up to three types of crops can be grown each year and crop yields are higher. A higher amount of food should lead to decreased rates of hunger, and an increase in the number of crops exported also creates more profits and more foreign currency. Table 5.12 shows some of the changes that occurred in South India since the 1970s as a result of the Green Revolution. Farmers who adopted the Green Revolution generally saw an increase in their income (Figure 5.62).

However, the Green Revolution has been criticized because it led to increased inequalities between farmers i.e. between those who adopted the new techniques and those who did not (Figure 5.63).

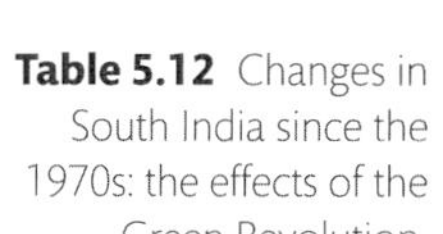

Table 5.12 Changes in South India since the 1970s: the effects of the Green Revolution.

Use of fertilizer	+138%
Human labour	+111%
Paddy rice	+ 91%
Sugar cane	+ 41%
Income	+ 20%
Subsistence food	–90%
Energy efficiency	–25%
Casual employment	–66%

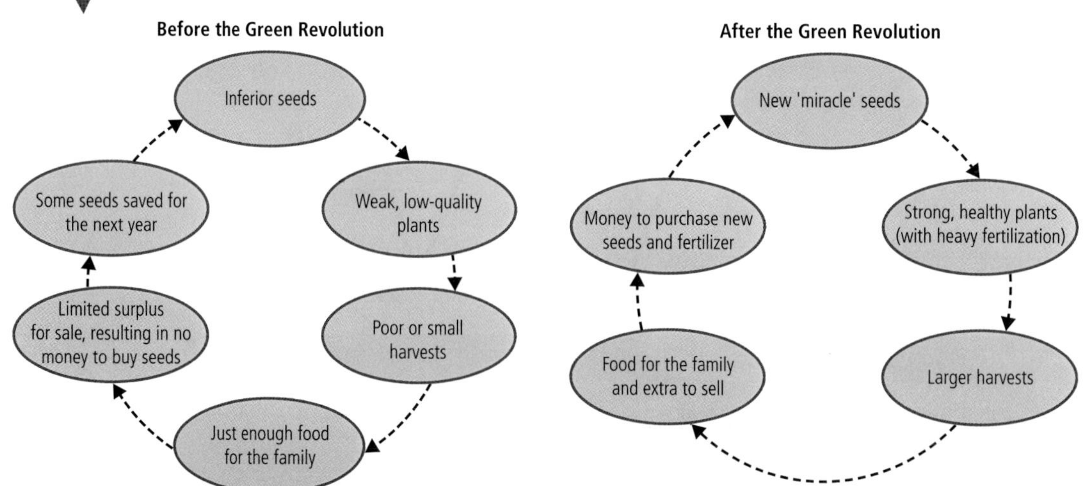

Figure 5.62 The impact of the Green Revolution on household economies.

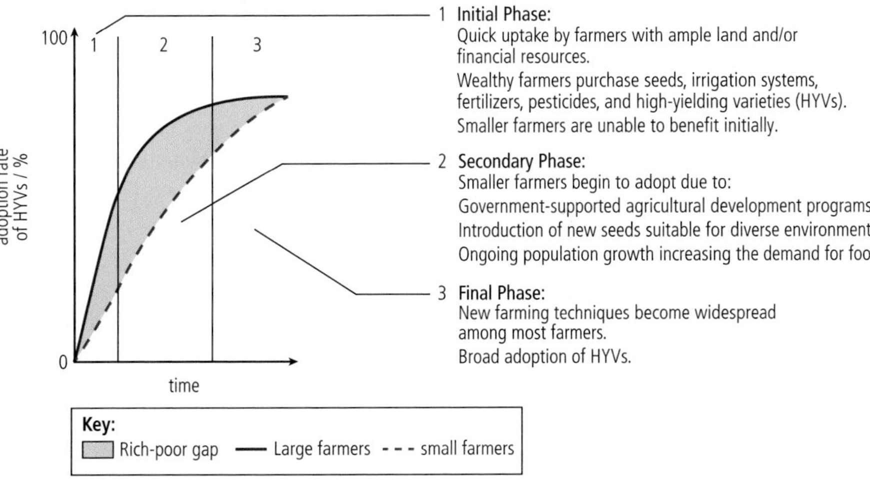

100
0
1
2
3
adoption rate of HYVs / %
time
1 Initial Phase:
Quick uptake by farmers with ample land and/or financial resources.
Wealthy farmers purchase seeds, irrigation systems, fertilizers, pesticides, and high-yielding varieties (HYVs).
Smaller farmers are unable to benefit initially.
2 Secondary Phase:
Smaller farmers begin to adopt due to:
Government-supported agricultural development programs
Introduction of new seeds suitable for diverse environments
Ongoing population growth increasing the demand for food
3 Final Phase:
New farming techniques become widespread among most farmers.
Broad adoption of HYVs.
Key:
Rich-poor gap
Large farmers
small farmers

Figure 5.63 The spread of HYVs and inequalities.

There are also several problems with reliance on HYVs, including:

- Not all farmers adopt HYVs as some cannot afford the cost.
- As the cost rises, indebtedness increases.
- Rural unemployment has increased due to mechanization.
- Irrigation has led to soil salinization – 20% of Pakistan and 25% of central Asia's irrigated land is affected by salt.
- Soil fertility is declining as HYVs use up all the nutrients. These nutrients can be replaced by fertilizers, but this is expensive and uses fossil fuels to produce synthetic fertilizers.
- LICs are dependent on many HICs for the inputs.

Activity

Draw two spider diagrams – one showing the potential advantages of the Green Revolution and the other showing the potential disadvantages of the Green Revolution.

5.2.8 Synthetic fertilizers and alternative measures for improving soil fertility

2.3 Biogeochemical cycles
4.4 Water pollution

HL b Environmental economics
HL c Environmental ethics

Synthetic fertilizers are used in many intensive farming systems, but they can lead to problems such as eutrophication and dependence on fossil fuels. However, there are alternative techniques that can be used to improve/restore natural productivity such as fallowing, using organic fertilizers, using herbal mixed leys, using mycorrhizae, using continuous cover crops and agroforestry.

Fallowing

Fallowing is a technique used in arable farming in which certain fields are left without crops for a season/year. The aims are to allow the soil to regain some of its fertility, to increase the store of soil organic matter and to retain soil moisture. Fallowing is sometimes included as a feature of crop-rotation systems in which different crops are grown in different fields and are changed around annually. Usually, one field is left fallow to allow it to restore its natural productivity.

The length of fallow can vary with soil potential. Better soils are farmed intensively and the fallow periods may be quite short, whereas poorer quality soils may require longer fallow periods. The length of fallow is also determined by population density. As population has increased there has been a decline in the amount of fallow land and length of fallow period. Between 1960 and 1990, the length of fallow in the Gambia declined from 30 years to 3 years.

One potential problem of leaving land fallow is weed infestation. Weeds may invade an area and proliferate. On the other hand, weeds may recycle nutrients from depth, protect the soil from direct insolation and help reduce erosion.

Organic fertilizers

Organic fertilizers are fertilizers that are derived from animal matter, human excreta and/or vegetation matter (compost). Compost is generally made by decomposing biodegradable wastes. Organic fertilizers contribute to improving soil fertility. In contrast, synthetic (inorganic) fertilizers bring short-term benefits but long-term side-effects such as soil toxicity, soil compaction, decreased soil fertility and erosion. Organic fertilizers improve soil structure, texture, aeration and water retention, and help root growth. There are many sources of organic fertilizers such as minerals, animals, farmyard manure (FYM) and plant materials, such as straw that was used for animal bedding.

Many tropical soils are acidic, contain excessive aluminium ions and limited organic matter and have a strong phosphate fixation (i.e. making phosphorus unavailable to plants). Such soils may need large doses of phosphate-rich fertilizers to encourage plant growth. However, in Ethiopia since 1998, conservation tillage and compost (organic fertilizer) have been used to reverse land degradation. Results suggest that this combination can result in yields that are comparable to those obtained by farms that use synthetic fertilizers. The use of organic fertilizers relies on local, or farm, resources and so is relatively cheap. Organic fertilizers generally release nutrients more slowly than inorganic fertilizers as they decompose naturally. Organic fertilizers reduce acidity in the soil and do not cause leaching. They do not kill soil microorganisms and they improve the circulation of air in the soil.

Herbal mixed leys

Figure 5.64 Herbal mixed ley.

Herbal leys (meadows) are fields/meadows used mainly in temperate climates and made up of a mix of grasses, herbs and legumes (Figure 5.64). They can be used in crop rotations and have several advantages, including:

- the variety of vegetation produces many flowers that attract pollinators
- they improve soil structure and increase soil organic matter
- the legumes add nitrogen to the soil, so increase soil fertility
- carbon is captured from the atmosphere and transferred to the soil as organic matter
- they reduce overland flow by intercepting rainfall.

Mycorrhizal fungi

Mycorrhizal fungi associated with plant roots increase the absorption of minerals, especially phosphorus, and this improves the growth of plants, crops and trees. Mycorrhiza occur in about 90% of plants including most of the world's agricultural species. Currently, mycorrhizal fungi are used in fumigated soil (soils which have been treated to control the amount of soil organisms), greenhouse crops and in the reclamation of disturbed sites.

Continuous cover crops

Continuous cover crops are used to maintain a vegetation cover over the soil and to reduce the potential for wind and water erosion. In addition, covering crops such as legumes (peas, beans, lentils) can trap and add nitrates to the soil, improving its fertility.

Forestry/silviculture

The establishment and management of forests and woodlands meets a variety of needs such as conservation and environmental services including flood control, a carbon sink, timber, habitats and recreation space, as well as some gathering of food.

For example, farmers in Niger use Gao trees for farming and to help tackle desertification. Since the 1990s, some 200 million Gao trees have grown naturally on 5 million ha of land. The trees have an extensive root system that draws in nitrogen from the air, fertilizing the soil. The tree also drops its leaves in the rainy season allowing more sunlight to reach the crops on the ground. When Gao trees are used along with fertilizer, the crop yields double. The trees also allow the soil to hold more water, which in turn allows a better crop to be produced in dry years.

Agroforestry

Agroforestry refers to the combination of agriculture and forestry. Two main types exist:

- silvo-pastoral agroforestry, involving the grazing of animals under trees
- silvo-arable agroforestry, involving the growing of crops under trees.

Tree roots reach deep into the ground releasing carbon into the soil. They also recycle nutrients and help bind the soil together. Agroforestry boosts productivity. Diverse ecosystems are more productive than monocultures. Tree roots reach further down than crop roots, allowing farmers to increase production from the same soil. Although trees take out some nutrients from the soil, under natural conditions they return them through leaf fall.

5.2.9 Soil conservation and its benefits

There are many methods of soil conservation such as cover crops, application of mulching, compost or other soil conditioners, wind reduction techniques, cultivation techniques such as terracing and contour ploughing, stone lines, reduced tillage systems, crop rotation, tree planting, agroforestry and selective harvesting (Figure 5.65).

HL b Environmental economics
HL c Environmental ethics

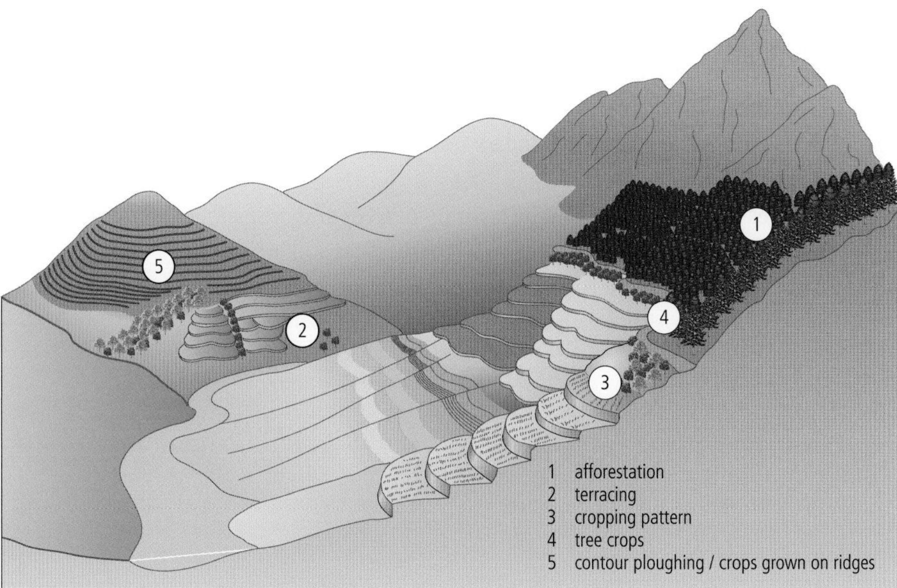

Figure 5.65 Soil conservation methods.

There are many types of soil conservation methods that can be used. Examples include soil conditioners (e.g. organic materials and lime), wind reduction techniques (e.g. wind breaks, shelter belts), cultivation techniques (e.g. terracing, contour ploughing, strip cultivation) and avoiding the use of **marginal lands** (land that is of little agricultural or developmental value).

Soil conservation methods

Table 5.13 summarizes several soil conservation methods that can be used to reduce or prevent the erosion of topsoil.

Table 5.13 Methods of soil conservation.

Method of soil conservation	Action involves
Conservation from wind or water erosion	
a. wind	• deliberate planting of trees/cover crops and/or hedges • suppression of fire and grazing to allow regeneration • use of cover crops, especially at critical times of the year • planting tree/hedge windbreaks
b. water	• construction of weirs, dams and gabions • use of terracing to reduce slope angle and runoff • use of retaining walls (bunds) to capture runoff and sediment • use of drainage systems that keep water in the soil and reduce overland flow • use of cover crops to intercept rainfall, reduce overland flow and bind the soils through their roots
Conservation of soil fertility with soil conditioners	• use of lime (crushed limestone) to decrease the acidity of soils • use of compost to increase soil organic matter
Cultivation techniques	• avoiding marginal land as it is fragile and vulnerable to soil erosion and degradation • avoiding overgrazing as it can reduce vegetation cover and encourage wind- and water-erosion • avoiding overcultivation as it depletes the soil of important soil nutrients and can lead to declining soil fertility/soil exhaustion • use of strip cropping: leaving a strip of soil between rows of crops that acts as a break in the movement of wind and water thereby reducing erosion • use of mixed cropping to decrease the uptake of individual nutrients and reduce wind and water erosion • use of crop rotation to reduce the uptake of individual nutrients and replace nutrients, e.g. from legumes • use of reduced tillage, which results in less soil being exposed to wind erosion and rain splash compaction and erosion • use of agroforestry, which refers to the farming of trees and crops together – trees intercept rainfall and reduce wind speeds so there is less soil erosion • reduced use of heavy machinery results in less soil compaction, which encourages overland runoff and erosion by water

Strategies for combating accelerated soil degradation are lacking in many areas. To reduce the risk, farmers are encouraged towards the use of more extensive management practices such as organic farming, afforestation, pasture extension and benign crop production. Nevertheless, there is a need for policy makers and the public to combat the pressures and risks to the soil resource.

Methods to reduce or prevent erosion can be mechanical (e.g. physical barriers such as embankments and wind breaks) or they may focus on vegetation cover and soil husbandry. Overland flow can be reduced by increasing infiltration.

Mechanical methods used to reduce water flow include bunding, terracing and contour ploughing. The key is to prevent or slow down the movement of rainwater down slopes. Contour ploughing takes advantage of the ridges formed at right angles to the slope to prevent or slow the downward accumulation of soil and water. Stone lines (diguettes) and check dams and low bunds (Figure 5.66) help to reduce overland flow and so trap water. On steep slopes, and those with heavy rainfall (such as the monsoon in South-East Asia), contour ploughing is insufficient and terracing is undertaken. The slope is broken up into a series of flat steps (terraces) with bunds (raised levées) at the edge. The use of terracing allows areas to be cultivated that would not otherwise be suitable for cultivation. The land around gullies and ravines can be fenced off and planted with small trees and grass. Check dams can be built across gullies to reduce the flow of water and trap soil. Cropping and soil husbandry methods to protect against water and wind damage focus on maintaining a crop cover for as long as possible, keeping the stubble and root structure of the crop in place after harvesting and planting a grass crop.

▲ **Figure 5.66** Low bund (wall) Eastern Cape, South Africa.

A grass crop maintains the action of the roots in binding the soil and minimizes the action of wind and rain on the soil surface. Green composts are materials rich in nitrogen and protein. They help soil microorganisms in the compost to grow and multiply quickly and so break down the compost. Increased organic content allows the soil to hold more water, thus reducing mass movement and erosion and stabilizing the soil structure. Soil organic matter is a vital component of productive and stable soils. It is an important source of plant nutrients, improves water retention and soil structure and is important in terms of the soil's buffering capacity against many of the threats. In addition, to prevent damage to the soil structure, care should be taken to reduce the use of heavy machinery on wet soils and to minimize ploughing on soils sensitive to erosion. Ground lime can be added to acidic soil to make it more alkaline.

TOK

How can we know when we have made progress in the search for knowledge?

Our understanding of soil conservation has progressed in recent years. What constitutes progress in different areas of knowledge?

In areas where wind erosion is a problem, shelterbelts of trees or hedgerows are used. The trees act as a barrier to the wind and disturb its flow. Wind speeds are reduced, which in turn reduces the wind's ability to disturb the topsoil and erode particles.

Multicropping is also useful if it maintains a cover crop throughout the year. On the steepest slopes, cultivation is not recommended and the land should be forested or vegetated to maintain soil cover and reduce runoff.

Table 5.14 summarizes some comments on soil conservation measures that can be used to reduce or prevent erosion by wind.

Table 5.14 Comments on some measures to curb wind erosion.

Measure	Comment
Measures that minimize actual risk (short-term effect)	
autumn-sown varieties	need to be sown before the end of October (in the Northern hemisphere) to develop a sufficient cover
mixed cropping	after the main crop is harvested, second crop remains on the field
nursing or cover crop	more herbicides needed
straw planting	unsuitable on light sandy soils
organic protection layer (e.g. liquid manure; sewage sludge; sugar beet factory lime)	depends on availability and regulations on the use of these products
synthetic stabilizers	unsuitable on peat soils
time of cultivation	depends on availability of labour and equipment
cultivation practice (e.g. minimum tillage; plough and press)	not suitable for all crop or soil types
Measures that lower the potential risk (long-term effect)	
smaller fields	increase in operational time and costs
change of arable land to permanent pasture or woodland	loss of agricultural production and farm income
marling (increasing the clay content to 8–10%)	suitable material should be available close by
wind barriers	high investment cost and loss of productive land takes several years before providing full protection; level of protection reduces with distance from the shelter

5.2.10 Humans are omnivores, diets lower in trophic levels are more sustainable

1.3 Sustainability
2.2 Energy and biomass in ecosystems

HL c Environmental ethics

The yield of food per unit of land area is greater in quantity and lower in cost for crops rather than livestock. Thus, a dietary shift by humans towards eating more foods from lower trophic layers may be more sustainable.

The nutrition transition

As income increases in LICs, there is an increase and a change in food consumption patterns. People in LICs generally derive their food energy mainly from carbohydrates, while the contribution of fats, dairy products and meat is small. In Bangladesh, for example, people derive up to 80% of their nutritional energy from carbohydrates and 11% from fats. In contrast, people in HICs generally derive most of their food energy from carbohydrates and fat, with a substantial contribution from meat and dairy. For example, the average consumer in France and Denmark derives 45–50% of their food energy from carbohydrates and 40% from fats.

Studies of human nutrition have shown that, globally, a nutrition transition is occurring, in which people are moving towards a pattern of more affluent food consumption. The nutrition challenge in HICs began about 300 years ago and coincided with a period of economic growth. For LICs, a small increase in wealth may lead to a large increase in calorie intake, whereas for HICs any further increase in income is unlikely to lead to an increase in calorie intake.

Food consumption per capita, both in terms of energy and protein, has increased substantially since the 1960s. Population growth rates have been higher in LICs compared with HICs, although consumption in HICs is still significantly higher. The transition is caused by higher incomes – but other factors such as food prices, the development of refrigeration and cultural preferences are also important.

Diet in LICs has diversified. Intakes of meat, dairy and fish are increasing, whereas sugar intake is stabilizing. It appears that diets in LICs and MICs are becoming more like those in HICs.

TOK

Is it possible to discover laws of human behaviour in the same way that the natural sciences discover laws of nature?

Consumer behaviour plays an important role in food production systems. Are there general laws that can describe human behaviour?

Figure 5.67 shows that it takes a lot less land to produce 1 kg of vegetable matter than it does to produce 1 kg of meat, especially lamb and mutton. This suggests a plant-based diet could support many more people than a diet that is based on meat. In agricultural systems, food is harvested at low trophic levels, i.e. the primary producers (plants) and herbivores (secondary producers). Farming systems that are based on crops are therefore more energy efficient than those that produce livestock. Owing to energy losses between trophic layers, less than 10% of the energy that is made available to plants is available to herbivores. Plants also provide a number of nutrients (Table 5.15). Thus, plant-based farming systems are more sustainable than animal-based ones and potentially could support more people.

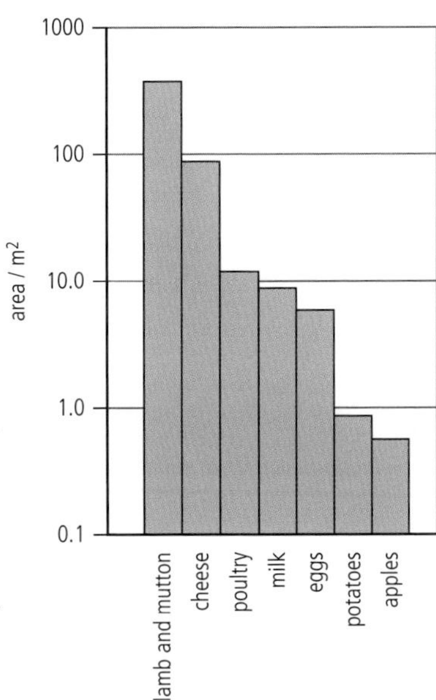

Figure 5.67 Semi-log graph to show the area of land needed (m^2) to produce 1 kg of selected food types.

A vegetarian diet is associated with a lower risk of death from ischemic heart disease. Vegetarians also have lower low-density lipoprotein cholesterol levels, lower blood pressure, lower rates of hypertension and lower rates of type 2 diabetes than meat eaters. They also generally have a lower risk of chronic disease.

i

Pescatarians - eat shellfish, fish and vegetables.

Pesco-pollo-vegetarians - eat fish, shellfish, chicken and vegetables.

Flexitarians - eat mainly plants, with occasional small amounts of meat.

Advantages of food from a higher trophic level

Meat, poultry and fish contain several nutrients needed for optimal health e.g. proteins, vitamin B, iron and zinc. In contrast, plants contain smaller amounts and fewer of these important nutrients. In addition, iron and zinc are more easily absorbed from animal sources compared with plant sources. Although a vegetarian diet can make it easier to reduce cardiovascular disease risk and reduces agricultural carbon emissions, it is harder to consume enough protein (Table 5.15).

Protein	tofu, lentils, beans, soybeans
Calcium	beans, nuts, seeds, dark leafy greens
Omega-3 oil	fats, flax seeds, hemp seeds, walnuts, dark leafy greens
Iodine	kelp, asparagus, dark leafy greens, iodized salt
Iron	beans, lentils, dark leafy greens, seeds, nuts

Table 5.15 Some plant sources of nutrients.

Challenge yourself

Outline the negative effects of a plant-based diet.

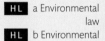

5.2.11 Global strategies to achieve sustainable food supply

1.3 Sustainability
2.3 Biogeochemical cycles
3.1 Biodiversity and evolution
6.3 Climate change – mitigation and adaptation

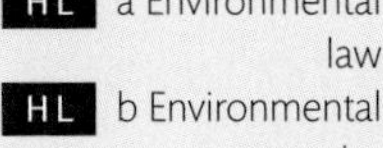

HL a Environmental law
HL b Environmental economics
HL c Environmental ethics

Current global strategies to achieve sustainable food supply include reducing demand and food waste, reducing greenhouse gas emissions and increasing intensification. These strategies include producing plant-based meat substitutes, reducing nitrogen loss to the atmosphere, growing low methane rice, reducing the amount of CH_4 released by animals, having a longer shelf life for food, genetic modification to increase crops yields and using solar powered fertilizers. To what extent can reducing demand for food, decreasing food waste, reducing greenhouse gas emissions and increasing intensification of farming lead to increased food sustainability?

According to the IPCC's Sixth Assessment Report (2021–2023), changing consumer behaviour could possibly result in a reduction of greenhouse gas emissions of 40–70% by 2050. Today, about 17% of all food produced in the world is wasted and that is predicted to double by 2050 (Figure 5.68). In addition, the decomposition of this food waste results in high emissions of CH_4, a potent greenhouse gas.

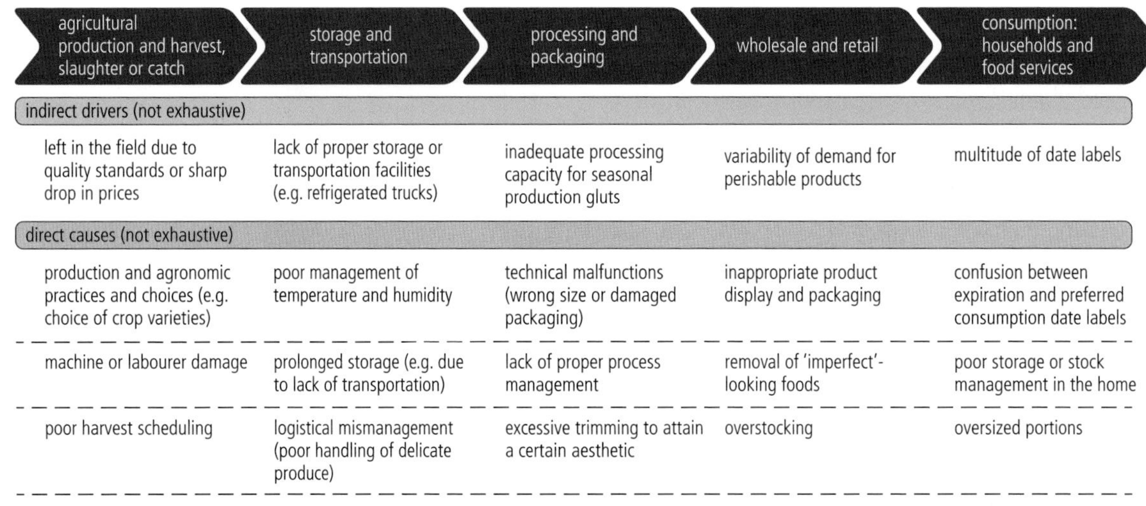

agricultural production and harvest, slaughter or catch
storage and transportation
processing and packaging
wholesale and retail
consumption: households and food services
indirect drivers (not exhaustive)
left in the field due to quality standards or sharp drop in prices
lack of proper storage or transportation facilities (e.g. refrigerated trucks)
inadequate processing capacity for seasonal production gluts
variability of demand for perishable products
multitude of date labels
direct causes (not exhaustive)
production and agronomic practices and choices (e.g. choice of crop varieties)
poor management of temperature and humidity
technical malfunctions (wrong size or damaged packaging)
inappropriate product display and packaging
confusion between expiration and preferred consumption date labels
machine or labourer damage
prolonged storage (e.g. due to lack of transportation)
lack of proper process management
removal of 'imperfect'-looking foods
poor storage or stock management in the home
poor harvest scheduling
logistical mismanagement (poor handling of delicate produce)
excessive trimming to attain a certain aesthetic
overstocking
oversized portions

Figure 5.68 Potential direct causes and indirect drivers of food loss and waste.

Demand for certain food types can fluctuate in the short term and the long term. It can range in scale from individuals and households to the national and even international scale. Demand may decrease, for example, if there are worries about the safety of food, worries about the way it is produced (e.g. battery farms), if there is an increase in food prices and if changes in household income occur.

Food loss and waste could be reduced by electrification e.g. more fridges in poorer households, more recycling of food, more use of waste food e.g. composting, improvements in food safety and durability (extending shelf life) and a decrease in offers, such as buy-one-get-one-free, which encourage people to buy more but may lead to more food waste.

Plant-based meat substitutes

Plant-based meat substitutes are prepared from plants and may be like conventional meat in terms of taste and appearance (Figure 5.69). They are made from plants such as wheat, lentils, soybeans, tofu, nuts, fungi and microbial protein. These plant-based products can be transformed into any shape, such as nuggets.

Figure 5.69 Plant-based meat substitutes at a supermarket in London.

The growth in demand for plant-based meat substitutes includes increased awareness of the benefits of a vegetarian diet and changes in opinions about animal rights. The global plant-based meat substitute market was worth over US$ 10 billion in 2022 and is growing at a rate of *c.* 18% per year. However, the high price of the products, compared with conventional meat products, is a major drawback. In 2021, Asia-Pacific was the largest market in the plant-based meat substitute market, followed by Western Europe.

Activity

Find out which (if any) plant-based meat substitutes are available in your nearest supermarket. How do they differ in cost compared with conventional meat?

Nitrogen loss to the atmosphere

Nitrogen applied to the soil is susceptible to loss. Loss may occur as it is converted to a gas and escapes into the atmosphere. Volatilization is the loss of nitrogen into the atmosphere as NH_3. The greatest loss occurs from the application of fertilizers containing NH_4^+ ions to the soil. Large losses of nitrogen in manure occur through emissions of NH_3 and N_2O to the atmosphere.

Low methane rice

Rice is a nutritious staple crop that feeds about half the world's population. However, rice production releases CH_4. The CH_4 produced from rice farming contributes *c.* 1.5% of total greenhouse gas emissions.

Rice is grown in different types of paddy fields. The water prevents O_2 from getting into the soil, thereby creating ideal conditions for bacteria that emit CH_4. The longer the flood season lasts, the higher the number of bacteria.

In some countries, notably China and Japan, farmers drain their paddy fields in the middle of the growing season as it increases yields. In contrast, during intense monsoon rains, some farmers find it difficult to drain fields regularly. However, farmers receive no rewards for reducing CH_4 emissions and no penalties for increasing them. Thus, there is little incentive to reduce CH_4 emissions overall (Figure 5.70).

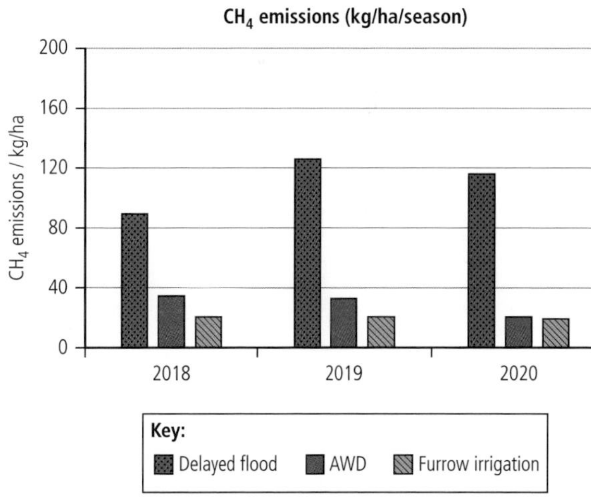

Figure 5.70 CH_4 emissions (kg/ha/season) from conventional delayed flood, alternate wetting and drying (AWD), and furrow irrigation (row rice) cultural management practices.

The addition of a single gene, barley SUSIBA2, has resulted in an increase in the biomass and starch content of seeds and stems and a reduction in CH_4 emissions. SUSIBA2 offers a sustainable means of increasing food production, while reducing greenhouse gas emissions from rice cultivation.

Ways to reduce CH_4 emissions from cattle

CH_4 emissions from agriculture account for about 5% of the UK's total greenhouse gas emissions. Livestock accounts for 14.5% of anthropogenic greenhouse gas emissions, 65% of these come from cattle. Livestock contribute to global climate change directly through the emission of CH_4 and indirectly from feed production, conversion of forest to pasture and the transport of feed and food products. There are several ways in which CH_4 emissions from cattle could be reduced.

In January 2023, the UK government launched an appeal to look for new types of animal feeds that could reduce greenhouse gas emissions. The balance of the feed given to cattle could be adjusted. An example could be the addition of greater amounts of corn. Grass contains many fibres and hydrogen (H_2) gas is produced as the grass is broken down. Microorganisms in the cow's gut convert the H_2 into CH_4. Adding corn to cattle feed can reduce greenhouse gas emissions by 10%. However, growing corn may require pastureland to be ploughed, thereby releasing stored carbon to the atmosphere. High quality forage, such as young plants and maize silage, can reduce CH_4 production because they contain a higher percentage of easily fermentable carbohydrates compared to older plants and/or grass silage.

Supplements that slow down the production of CH_4 could be added to the diet of cattle (Figure 5.71). Experiments on artificial cow rumens (stomachs) where red algae was added to cattle feed, showed that CH_4 emissions were reduced by over 90%. 3-NOP (3-nitrooxypropanol) is an example of a supplement that can lead to a 20–30% decrease in CH_4 emissions. However, it needs to be given frequently for long-term reductions in greenhouse gas emissions. The addition of fat supplements to the diet can also lower CH_4 emissions.

Figure 5.71 CH_4 reduction from feed additives.

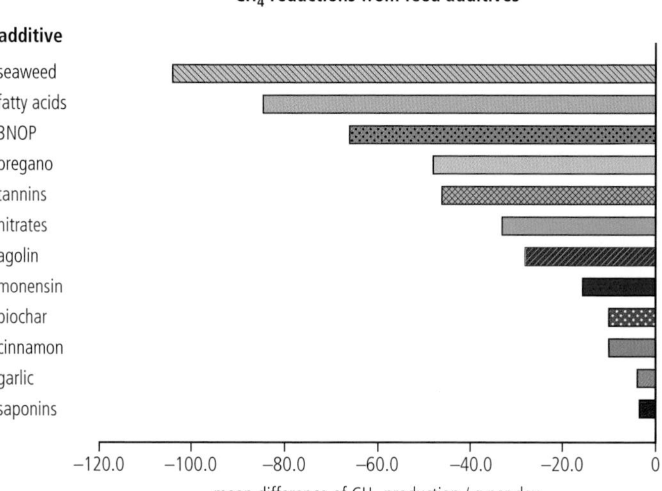

Climate friendly cows could be bred that have lower CH_4 emissions. Cattle vary in their rates of CH_4 emissions, so it should, in theory, be possible to breed cattle with lower rates of methane CH_4 emissions – just as it is possible to breed more productive cattle. Breeding climate-friendly cattle could lead to a decline of CH_4 emissions of 1% per year.

It is possible to capture CH_4 from cattle in stables, and this CH_4 could be used as an energy resource. However, this will only be feasible when cattle are inside stables for long periods of time.

The reduction of livestock numbers should reduce greenhouse gas emissions. However, as long as demand for meat and dairy products remains high (and it is increasing), the demand for livestock will continue to stay high and therefore CH_4 emissions are likely to stay high.

Shelf life of foods

'Use by' dates are a safety issue – foods that are highly perishable have a risk of causing food poisoning once they exceed their 'use by' date. 'Best before' dates are a quality issue – food can be expected to keep at its optimal condition until the end of the 'best before' date.

The use of antioxidants and biopreservatives can help to extend the food's shelf life in a natural way. Tocopherol (vitamin E), mixed tocopherol (natural vitamin E) and ascorbic acid (vitamin C) are all antioxidants that can reduce or slow down the spoiling of food and thereby extend its shelf life. The use of biopreservatives, such as lactic acid bacteria, is also a sustainable way to extend the shelf life of certain foods.

Several supermarkets in the UK have dropped such 'use by' and 'best before' dates from fresh fruit and vegetables as part of a strategy to reduce food waste.

Solar fertilizers

The use of synthetic fertilizers has been central to the improvements in crop yields. However, the production of synthetic fertilizers is energy- and carbon-intensive and is highly centralized, leading to an uneven distribution of fertilizers around the world (Figure 5.72).

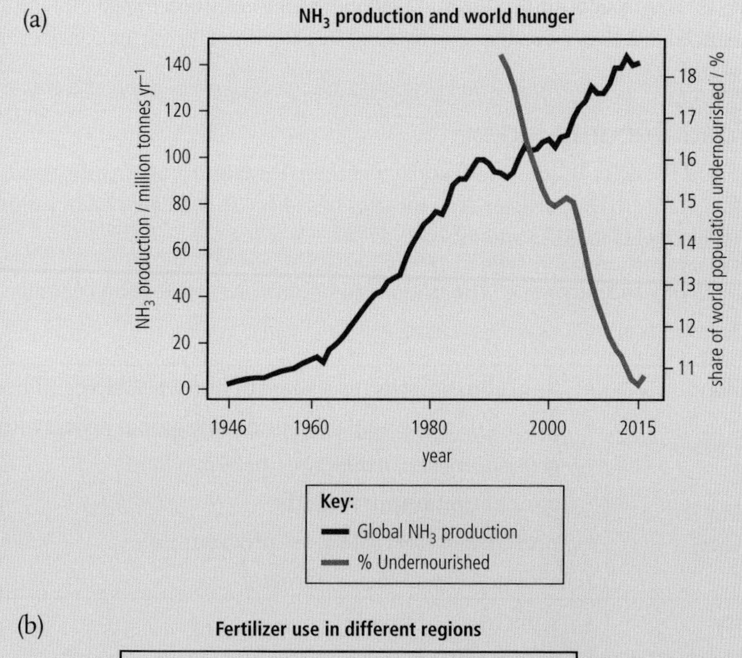

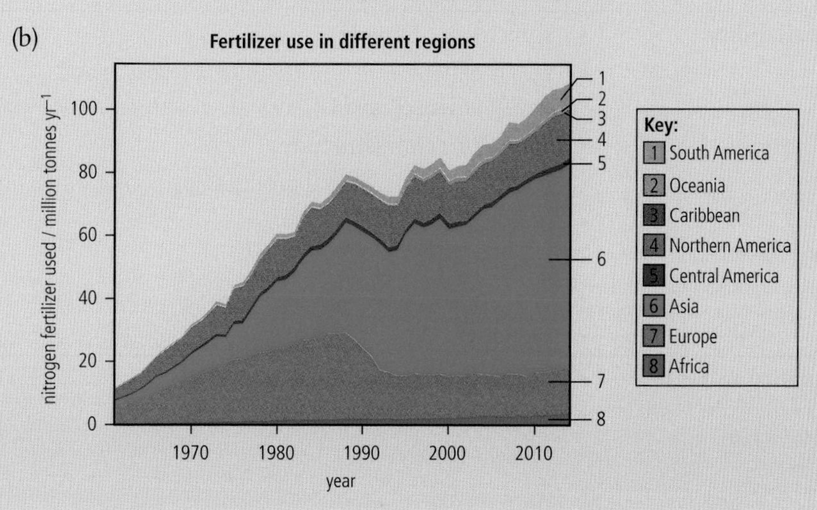

Figure 5.72 Global NH_3 consumption.
(a) The worldwide NH_3 production each year since 1946 and the percentage of individuals who are undernourished globally.
(b) The use of nitrogen fertilizer over time by region.

Figure 5.72b shows a compound line graph or stacked line graph. To work out the contribution for each region, you must measure the thickness of their colour. For example, for Asia in 1990, the area in green starts at *c.* 20 mt/year and stops at *c.* 60 mt/year, thus the use of fertilizer in Asia in 1990 was *c.* 40 mt/year.

Solar fertilizers, in contrast, attempt to combine solar energy with nitrogen, O_2 and water to produce nitrogen-based nutrients for plants, as this is often the most limiting nutrient in agricultural production. Using solar fertilizers in LICs can improve access to fertilizers in remote rural areas and help to achieve goal 2 of the United Nations Sustainable Development Goals, which is ending hunger and ensuring access to safe, nutritious and sufficient food for all people.

The economic advantages of using solar fertilizers include inexpensive raw materials, the elimination of long-distance transport and the reduction of greenhouse gas emissions. Social benefits include improved access to fertilizers for farmers in LICs and increased availability of food. Solar fertilizer production facilities need to be set up with one facility per hectare – that could be difficult to achieve.

Challenge yourself

To what extent can global strategies to achieve sustainable food supply be achieved through reducing demand and food waste, reducing greenhouse gas emissions and increasing intensification?

5.2.12 Food security

1.3 Sustainability
7.2 Energy resources, use and management

According to the World Bank, food security is achieved when all people, at all times, have physical and economic access to sufficient safe and nutritious food that meets their dietary needs and food preferences for an active and healthy life.

Food security is the physical and economic availability of food, allowing all individuals to get the balanced diet they need for an active and healthy life. This varies considerably around the world.

Global Food Security Index

The Global Food Security Index (GFSI) considers the affordability, availability and quality of food across 109 countries. The index is based on 28 indicators that influence food security across LICs, MICs and HICs.

The GFSI looks beyond hunger to the underlying components of food security (Table 5.16).

Table 5.16 The components of food security.

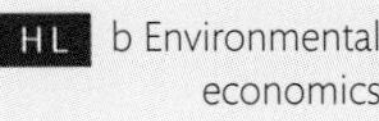

HL b Environmental economics

Affordability	• food consumption as a share of household expenditure • proportion of population under the global poverty line • gross domestic product per person (GDPP) • agricultural **import tariffs** • presence of food safety net programme • access to financing for farmers
Availability	• sufficiency of supply • public expenditure on agricultural research and development (R and D) • agricultural infrastructure • volatility of agricultural production • political stability risk • corruption • urban absorbtion capacity • food loss
Quality and safety	• diet diversification • micronutrient availability • protein quality • food safety

In 2022, food security improved across most regions of the world. HICs still dominate the top of the rankings, but LICs and MICs made the biggest gains. The Middle East and North Africa (MENA) made the largest strides in food security. Food security is lowest in Sub-Saharan Africa. Europe is the only region that has worsened in food security, but it still has a high level of food security overall. Diet diversification and access to high-quality protein are increasing rapidly in LICs. Nutritional standards have improved substantially across almost every region.

Activity

Click on the QR code or search online for the Global Food Security Index to access The Economist article. Scroll down to the map and click on the options to show variations in affordability, availability, quality and safety. Choose a range of countries. Hover the computer mouse over the proportional circles to access the data on individual countries.

Use the 'Interactive' tool to explore food security in countries of your choice. Click on a country to find out about its strengths and challenges in terms of food security, affordability, availability, quality and safety.

HL

5.2.13 Contrasting agriculture in a single biome

HL

In this section, contrasting examples of farming from one biome, namely the temperate grasslands of North America, are examined.

2.4 Climate and biomes
5.1 Soil

Example – Cereals and ranching in the prairies of North America

The Prairies are a temperate grassland biome, largely located in the interior of the USA. They have a continental climate with hot summers (up to 30 °C) and cold winters, with temperatures below freezing. Rainfall is low 250–750 mm) with convectional rain (thunderstorms) in summer and snow in winter. Rainfall generally decreases from east to west. Evaporation rates are high in summer.

Mollisols

Mollisols (chernozems, black earths, prairie soils) are fertile, productive and cover over 900 million hectares, which is equivalent to *c.* 7% of the world's ice-free land. They are found in mid-latitude areas such as the Great Plains of the USA. In North America, they account for *c.* 300 million hectares, of which *c.* 200 million hectares are in the USA (Figure 5.73).

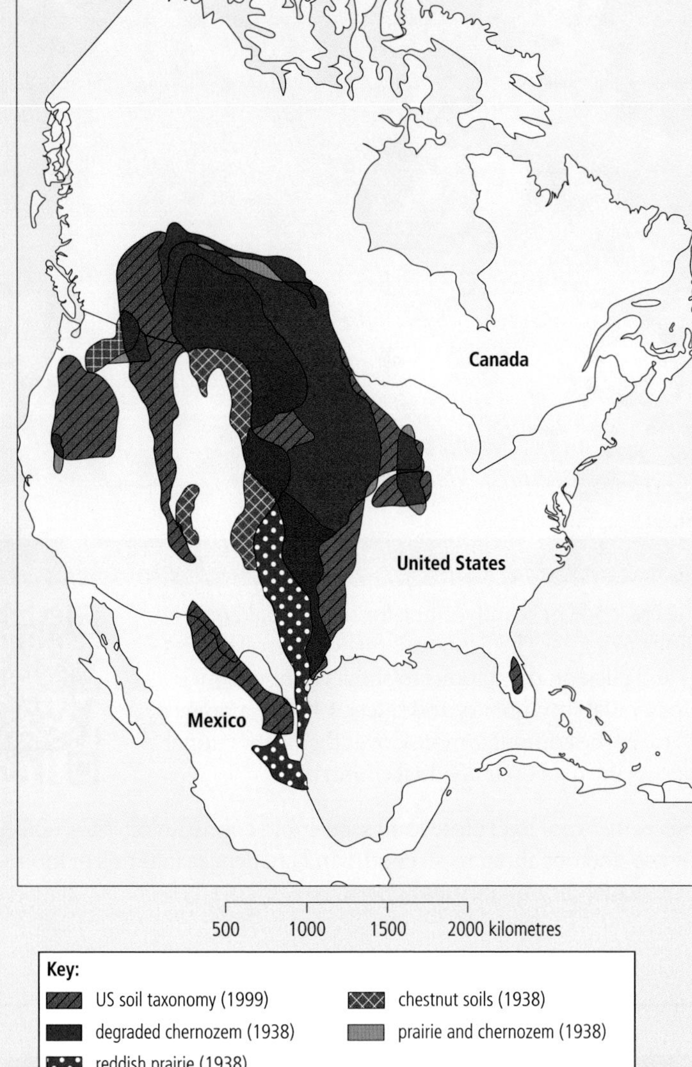

Figure 5.73 Distribution of mollisols in North America.

Mollisols can be farmed intensively in wetter areas and extensively in drier areas, but are vulnerable to soil erosion, loss of soil organic matter and acidification.

However, due to the long period of farming needed, the land used previously for mollisols is increasingly being given over to crops.

Soil scientists recommend using minimum/zero tillage, adding organic matter/manure to soils to reduce soil erosion and adding crushed limestone to replenish soil calcium reserves and reduce acidity.

Chestnut soils

In the drier parts of the prairies, there is slower growth. Grasses are shorter, occur in tussocky clumps and provide less organic matter to soils. With less organic matter, the A horizon is chestnut-brown colour rather than black. The depth of soil also decreases with aridity, while the level of calcium-carbonate accumulation is relatively thicker. These soils can be cultivated with the use of irrigation, but they are mostly used for livestock ranching.

Mollisols and agriculture

Mollisols in North America have been used for agriculture since the 19th century, both for intensive arable and livestock farming. The four most common crops are maize, soybean, wheat and sorghum. Maize and soybeans are grown in areas with more than 1000 mm of precipitation, whereas wheat is grown in sub-humid and semi-arid areas. Irrigation is used to grow maize and rice. Across all areas of North American mollisols, livestock is produced. In drier areas that cannot support annual cropping, livestock grazing predominates. However, the prairies have a relatively short growing season and experience hail, droughts and tornadoes, which can damage crops and pasture.

Mollisols in the USA are among the most intensively farmed soils in the world and are increasingly used for arable farming. Fertilizer use has more than doubled since the 1960s. Long-term use of nitrogen fertilizers has resulted in soil acidification. Areas that are intensively cropped also experience extensive erosion and sedimentation.

Crops

Spring wheat is produced in the far north of the North American prairies, (Figure 5.74). This is planted in spring and is harvested after a growing season of around 90 days. In contrast, further south, winter wheat is planted in winter and harvested in the following autumn (Figure 5.75).

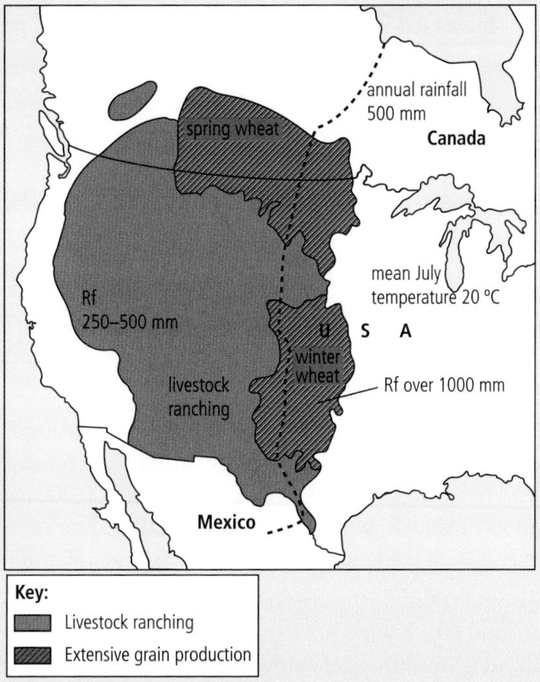

spring wheat
annual rainfall 500 mm
Canada
mean July temperature 20 °C
Rf 250–500 mm
U S A
winter wheat
livestock ranching
Rf over 1000 mm
Mexico

Key:
Livestock ranching
Extensive grain production

Figure 5.74 The North American Prairies.

Figure 5.75 Wheat farming on the Great Plains.

The prairies have several advantages that make them suitable for growing wheat, including:

- the mollisols (chernozems and/or black earths) are fertile and deep
- the growing season is long enough for wheat to grow
- the summers are warm, with temperatures more than 15 °C, with long hours of daylight
- most precipitation falls during the growing season
- the land is relatively flat, favouring the use of machinery
- winter frosts help break up the soil.

On the other hand, there are several disadvantages including drought, tornadoes in summer, thunderstorms in summer and, if the vegetation is removed, the soil becomes vulnerable to soil erosion.

Farming in the wheat belt is generally capital intensive and productivity per worker is high. Farming methods are adapted to the amount of moisture present. In drier parts, the land might only be farmed in alternate years. Increasingly, stubble is left in the soil to collect the moisture from melting snow.

Over the last fifty years or so, farms sizes have increased as smaller farms have amalgamated. Nevertheless, there are pros and cons to large-scale and small-scale farming (Tables 5.17 and 5.18). High yielding varieties of wheat are used, which may be drought-, frost- and disease- resistant and mature faster. The use of strip-farming (ploughing at right angles to the wind) with alternate strips of vegetation reduces soil erosion and is used by many farmers. The use of irrigation has increased in some areas, in places depleting aquifers. Greater use of fertilizers and pesticides may benefit wheat production for farmers and consumers, but it can have a negative impact on soil organisms, wildlife and ultimately the soil.

Table 5.17 The pros and cons of large-scale farming.

Pros	Cons
• increased food production • lower cost of food for consumer • encourages technological development and innovation • increased food availability	• negatively impacts small farmers • negative environmental impacts e.g. greater use of large machinery releases greenhouse gases and use of synthetic fertilizers can cause eutrophication • risks of poor animal welfare

Table 5.18 The pros and cons of small-scale farming.

Pros	Cons
• stimulates local economy • employs many people • increased biodiversity through field and farm boundaries • more environmentally sustainable	• lack of resources to compete with larger farms • boundaries reduce the amount of land farmed • lower yields • less profitability • lacks economy of scale

Livestock ranching

Livestock ranching is a form of commercial, pastoral and extensive farming. It earns some of the lowest profits per unit area of any type of commercial farming, but farms tend to be large. In the USA there are over 700,000 cattle farms, ranches and feedlots (plots of land on which livestock are fattened for market). Livestock ranching takes up over 25% of the land area in the USA (about 250 million hectares).

About 80% of farms are family-operated, with fewer than 1000 head of cattle, with around 60% having been in the same family for three or more generations. There are about 93 million beef cattle in the USA, compared with about 326 million people.

Cattle feedlots

Figure 5.76 A cattle feedlot.

In intensive beef production, the cattle are housed all year round and fed a diet of rolled barley mixed with a protein concentrate (often beans, soy, or rapeseed meal), fortified with vitamins and minerals. In the USA, cattle are put into pens containing up to 100,000 individuals. They are fed corn for the last few weeks of their lives, which can double their biomass before slaughter. These pens are known as cattle feedlots (Figure 5.76).

The movement of the cattle within the pens is restricted. Intensive beef production is an energy inefficient form of farming, with the amount of energy provided by the yield being only one tenth of the energy input. In terms of costs, however, it is very efficient and significantly increases yield per acre, per person and per input, relative to extensive farming. There is not much space for the animals to move about, so they use less energy. This means less food is required, which leads to a cheaper product. On the other hand, the animals are fed continuously for maximum growth and selective breeding has been used to produce cows that produce high yield and good quality meat, both of which add to the overall costs. Inputs are therefore high (technology, heating, food) but so are the outputs (cost-effective production), although there may also be hidden costs, such as transportation of the cattle. The environmental impact is also high as the energy usage releases greenhouse gases and cows emit CH_4 gas as waste. Restricting the movement of the animals in this way also has ethical implications.

5.2.14 Alternative farming approaches

HL

1.3 Sustainability

HL b Environmental economics
HL c Environmental ethics

Alternative farming approaches have been developed to respond to soil crises. Approaches to restore and conserve soils include approaches promoting soil regeneration, rewilding, permaculture, non-commercial cropping and zero tillage (this topic, Section 5.2.9).

Soil regeneration

There are several ways to regenerate soils and improve soil quality, including **agroecology** (the application of ecological concepts and principles to farming), cover cropping, crop rotation, mulching (adding compost), reducing soil disturbance through ploughing, and nutrient management. Soil regeneration leads to the retention of a greater amount of carbon than is lost, an increase in biodiversity and the maintenance of water and nutrient recycling.

Rewilding

Rewilding refers to conservation efforts to restore and protect wilderness areas and natural processes (Topic 3, Section 3.3.7). There are many types of rewilding projects that exist, such as Pleistocene megafauna replacements, release of captive-bred animals, the removal of dams and bridges, connection of different natural areas or reintroduction of keystone species (Topic 2, Section 2.1.23). Rewilding can mitigate climate change by increasing the number of trees. However, the increased popularity of rewilding, especially some large-scale projects, has led to criticism.

Pleistocene rewilding refers to the reintroduction of extinct Pleistocene megafauna, or their close ecological equivalents such as elephants, to the Cerrado of Brazil. In 1988, Pleistocene Park was opened in north-east Siberia with the introduction of reindeer, European and Plains bison, domestic yak, moose and Bactrian camels. There are also plans to reintroduce the Siberian tiger to Pleistocene Park. In the USA, bison have been reintroduced to private land in the Great Plains. In 1997, the Edwards Dam in Maine was removed so that salmon and sturgeon could reach their spawning grounds.

Critics have argued that rewilding may lead to productive farmland being abandoned, which could lead to a decline in the protection of rare species in small reserves. The lack of predators at the Oostvaardersplassen rewilding project (Topic 3, Section 3.3.12) led to the mass starvation of large herbivores.

Activity

Find out about rewilding in your home country. Create a poster to summarize your findings.

Permaculture

Permaculture attempts to make agricultural systems resemble natural ecosystems as closely as possible. It includes several practices, such as the rotation of crops, which aim to restore nitrogen to soils and maintain the quality of the soil so that it can be continuously used for agriculture. It is an attempt to work with nature rather than against it. It views modern forms of agriculture as being dependent on fossil-fuels, polluting land and water, reducing biodiversity and eroding valuable topsoil from previously fertile land.

Permaculture is a type of soil management that attempts to increase the carbon content of soils by using natural processes such as capturing rainfall, planting nitrogen-fixing plants such as legumes close to nitrogen-demanding plants and using indigenous (native) plants. In addition, monitoring and changing the pH of the soil, adding nutrients, encouraging soil organisms and adding materials such as wood ash and ground limestone can benefit soils. Mulching reduces soil erosion and regulates soil temperature. Adding compost increases the moisture and nutrient contents of the soil and promotes the growth of soil organisms. Composted animal waste and human waste can also be added to increase nutrient content.

Hugelkultur refers to the burying of wood to improve soil moisture-holding capacity. The decomposing wood acts like an underground sponge and holds in the water. Vermicomposting refers to the practice of using earthworms to break down green and brown waste to produce worm castings that can be used to fertilize soils. Rainwater harvesting can be done using bunds (large bins) that collect rainwater before it becomes overland runoff or infiltrates the soil. Mulching is a protective cover of organic matter, leaves and woodchips that is placed on the soil surface to absorb rainfall, reduce evaporation, provide nutrients and increase soil organic matter.

Non-commercial cropping

Non-commercial cropping refers to any crops that may be produced but not sold commercially. This includes subsistence production, production for fodder crops, crops that are grown for foraging and the production of crops that are not suited for storage or transport.

Non-commercial cropping (and other forms of non-commercial farming) are generally small-scale and use allotments (Figure 5.77), although some estates can be very large.

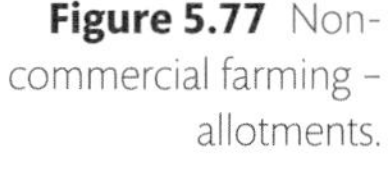

Figure 5.77 Non-commercial farming – allotments.

One study involving nearly 400 non-commercial farmers identified several different types of non-commercial farms. Most had a mix of commercial and non-commercial interests. They included:

- specialist smallholdings, which specialize in pigs, poultry and other livestock
- agricultural residences, which do not engage in crop or animal production
- horsiculture holdings, which have horses on a commercial or recreational basis and may also have small-scale cattle, sheep, pigs and poultry
- mixed smallholdings, which have cattle and sheep on a commercial or recreational basis
- amenity livestock farms, which have cattle and sheep on a commercial basis
- large farms/estates, which are over 200 ha in size and have cattle/sheep on a commercial scale.

The degree of how 'non-commercial' the farmers were varied considerably!

No-till farming

This is also known as zero tillage or direct drilling and is a technique for growing crops or pasture without disturbing the soil through ploughing. There are three main methods of no-till farming defined as:

- direct seeding, where the seeds are sown through the remains of previous crops
- surface seeding, where the crops are left on the surface of the soil
- sod seeding, where the seeds are sown into the soil using machinery, and herbicides are applied to cover the crops.

In Australia, about 80% of the 20 million ha of cropland is not ploughed. In contrast, Brazil has about 50% of no-till farming and the USA just over 20% of cultivated cropland. No-till farming may reduce the costs of labour, machinery and energy. In some cases, because of irrigation, it may prove possible to have a second crop in the same year thereby raising profitability. No-till farming can produce problems as it may require more herbicides compared to conventional tilling, for the control of weeds. However, no-till farming sometimes uses cover crops to control weeds, increasing soil organic matter in the soil and thus increasing soil sequestration. The use of legumes can also increase soil fertility.

No-till farming is also known as zero tillage or direct drilling farming. This is a technique used for growing crops or pasture without disturbing the soil through ploughing.

5.2.15 Regenerative farming systems and permaculture

HL

1.3 Sustainability

HL c Environmental ethics

In addition to soil regeneration, regenerative farming uses a variety of sustainable agricultural techniques to conserve and rehabilitate food and farming systems. It focuses on maintaining the topsoil, maintaining crops in the soil all year round, minimizing the disturbance of soils, integrating livestock and increasing biodiversity.

Regenerative farming can improve soil quality and so can be sustainable. Permaculture may protect the soil from erosion and add nutrients to the soil.

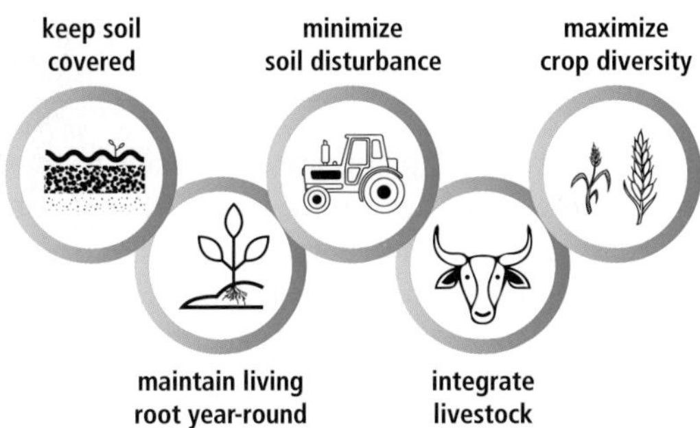

Figure 5.78 The principles of regenerative farming.

There are several principles of regenerative farming as shown in Figure 5.78. These include:

- keeping the soil covered to reduce the risk of wind- and water-erosion
- maintaining living roots in the soil to help bind it together and also reduce the risk of erosion
- minimizing soil disturbance e.g. by using no-till farming to reduce compaction of soil by machinery
- integrating livestock to provide a source of manure and can also provide a separate income
- maximizing crop diversity e.g. by polyculture, to reduce the risk of disease spreading.

Regenerative farming and permaculture include crop rotation, rotational grazing, cover-cropping, low- and no-till farming, agroforestry, agroecology, **polyculture** (the practice of cultivating multiple types of crops in the same field/greenhouse), permaculture and restoration ecology. Practices are very varied and include reducing farm waste, adding composted material and silvopasture. Indeed, practices that restore organic matter to the soil may increase the amount of nutrients in the soil. Regenerative farming may increase species diversity and decrease the density of pests (Table 5.19).

Regenerative farming in south-west Britain has led to an increase in the numbers of cattle egrets (an African bird species), wagtails, barn owls and hares. Livestock trample the ground with their hooves, which exposes invertebrates and forces insects into the air where they are then fed upon by the cattle egrets and other predators.

Domesticated animals may contribute to regenerative agriculture. Animals such as chickens, geese, turkeys and rabbits may scratch the topsoil during foraging and help break it down. This helps to circulate nutrients, remove weeds, spread seeds and control pests. Nutrients are transformed from less digestible forms (such as grass and leaves) into nutrient-dense manure.

The key to regenerative farming is that it should not harm the environment and should also regenerate, restore and revitalize the soil and the environment. For example, regenerative farming in ranching aims to: be more sustainable, produce more food, decrease greenhouse emissions, reverse climate change, improve crop yields, create drought-resistant soils, revitalize local economies, preserve traditional knowledge, nurture biodiversity and improve nutrition.

Table 5.19 The pros and cons of regenerative farming.

Pros	Cons
• improves soil health • reduces carbon emissions • increases water infiltration • reduces reliance on chemicals	• time-consuming • difficult to do on a large scale • requires careful planning and organization

Mob grazing is characterized by grazing by a high density of stock for a short duration, coupled with a long recovery period. Mob grazing copies nature. This can be seen in temperate and tropical grasslands where thousands of bison and wildebeest travel over vast areas over the course of a year. They eat the fresh grass, return some faeces and nutrients to the soil, all the while trampling the soil and moving on without returning to the same area for months or years. Mob grazing is also called 'tall grass grazing', as the grass can grow very tall in the time between periods of grazing. The benefit of mob grazing is the recovery or 'rest' period for the grass and soil.

In contrast, in continuous grazing, the plants are continually having to move nutrients upwards through the plant towards the leaves where photosynthesis occurs. Photosynthesis is needed to give the plant energy to grow new leaves. However, in continuous grazing, the leaves are eaten at the early stages of their life and the plant cannot grow. Thus, tastier (palatable) plants get weaker with less root structure, whereas the less palatable plants and weeds get stronger.

With mob grazing, fields are given more time to rest. This allows livestock farmers the opportunity to improve soil health without having to drastically alter their systems. The extended nature of mob grazing allows grass leys more time to recover. This improves leaf growth, allows root development and improves soil health, as well as increasing grassland productivity.

Activity

Visit the Farm Wilder website to see how farming can be made more natural and more sustainable. Select a local farm and write some recommendations for how they could be more sustainable.

5.2.16 Greenhouse and vertical farming

HL

1.3 Sustainability

 b Environmental economics

HL c Environmental ethics

There are many technological developments in farming that are leading to very high levels of productivity. These include modern high-tech greenhouse farming, vertical farming, precision agriculture and hydroponics. Although improvements to agriculture in the 21st century can greatly improve productivity and food supply to urban areas, they are not always sustainable because the technology and equipment needed may be dependent on fossil fuels.

Greenhouse farming is a form of protected crop production. The crops are grown under glass or plastic, so the climate can be controlled, the application of water and fertilizers can be closely monitored and insects can be isolated. The sustainability of greenhouse production depends on the minimal use of fossil fuels, water, fertilizers and pesticides. However, some greenhouse production has been criticized for contaminating water resources. Greenhouse cultivation can also be a heavy consumer of energy resources, depending on the season and the location. Greenhouse production in Iceland (Figure 5.79a) is largely fueled by geothermal heat, while production in Mediterranean areas in the summer has a large amount of solar radiation provided, allowing mass production of crops.

Figure 5.79a Greenhouse cultivation in Fridheimar, southern Iceland.

Greenhouse horticulture is situated in some of the most arid parts of Europe, such as Almeria, Spain. With a sufficient supply of water, crop yields can be much higher than those produced in fields. The use of drip irrigation minimizes water use (Figure 5.79b). However, this method also involves the excessive use of chemical treatments such as fertilizers and pesticides. In addition, some pests, such as the tomato leaf miner (*Tuta absoluta*), have developed resistance against insecticides, leading to major losses in production.

Figure 5.79b Pipe network for climate control in the greenhouse.

Vertical farming refers to growing crops in stacked layers or training them upwards (Figure 5.80). This method can incorporate controlled environmental conditions and can be practiced in buildings, shipping containers and underground areas. Vertical farming is often soil-free, making use of artificial LED lighting, irrigation water, fertilizers and climate control. Globally, vertical farming was worth just over US$ 5 billion in 2022 and its worth is projected to rise to over US$ 12 billion in 2026. The trends driving vertical farming include the environmental impact of food production, the demand for safe and healthy food, population growth and urbanization and the scarcity of natural resources. Japan increased its production of food from vertical farms following the Fukushima-Daiichi nuclear explosion that had affected much of the region's farmland with radiation. It is now the world's leading producer of vertically farmed crops.

Figure 5.80 Large-scale vertical farming.

In-vitro meat, also known as cultured meat or synthetic meat, is grown in a lab. In 2013, the world's first lab-grown burger was produced at a cost of US$ 266,000. Cultured meat has fewer environmental impacts than naturally reared meat; although the cost is currently excessive, it should decrease as the technology becomes more widespread.

Example – Bustan, Cairo, Egypt

Bustan (Arabic for 'orchard') is a commercial aquaponics farm in Cairo, Egypt. It produces tilapia fish in tanks and re-uses water carefully to grow vegetables in hydroponic trays and to irrigate olive oil-producing olive trees. It is labour-intensive and uses sustainable pest-control methods, such as ladybirds, to kill aphids and so reduces chemical inputs. It also uses 90% less water than traditional methods. Outputs include 6–8 tonnes of fish per annum and the farm is Egypt's largest producer of bay leaf salad. The farm also grows several herbs including basil, rosemary, thyme and mint.

Precision farming is a type of farming that uses high-tech IT equipment to observe, measure and identify small-scale variations in environmental conditions, for example moisture content, temperature, nutrient availability and pH, within and between fields on a farm. It then uses the data to identify areas where treatment methods such as irrigation, fertilizers and pesticides need to be applied. Initially, precision farming was limited to rich farmers who could afford the technology, but the development of mobile apps, drones and cloud computing are making precision farming increasingly accessible to a greater number of farmers. However, there is a problem because it often provides so much information that it can be difficult to take it all into account. Cost also remains a problem for many small farmers.

HL

5.2.17 The sustainability of different diets varies

1.3 Sustainability

HL b Environmental economics

HL c Environmental ethics

Different diets have varied environmental impacts. Reduced meat diets, vegetarian diets or vegan diets and shorter supply chains (social, economic and physical distance) are generally more sustainable in terms of carrying capacity. According to the Planetary Health Diet Report 2019, people around the world should have a plant-dominant diet where whole grains, fruits, vegetables, nuts and legumes comprise a greater proportion of foods consumed, with less consumption of meat and dairy (Figure 5.81). Vegetarian, vegan and reduced-meat diets have lower environmental impacts than a diet that is high in red meat. These impacts can be shown in terms of food miles and/or the planetary health diet.

Figure 5.81 The planetary health diet.

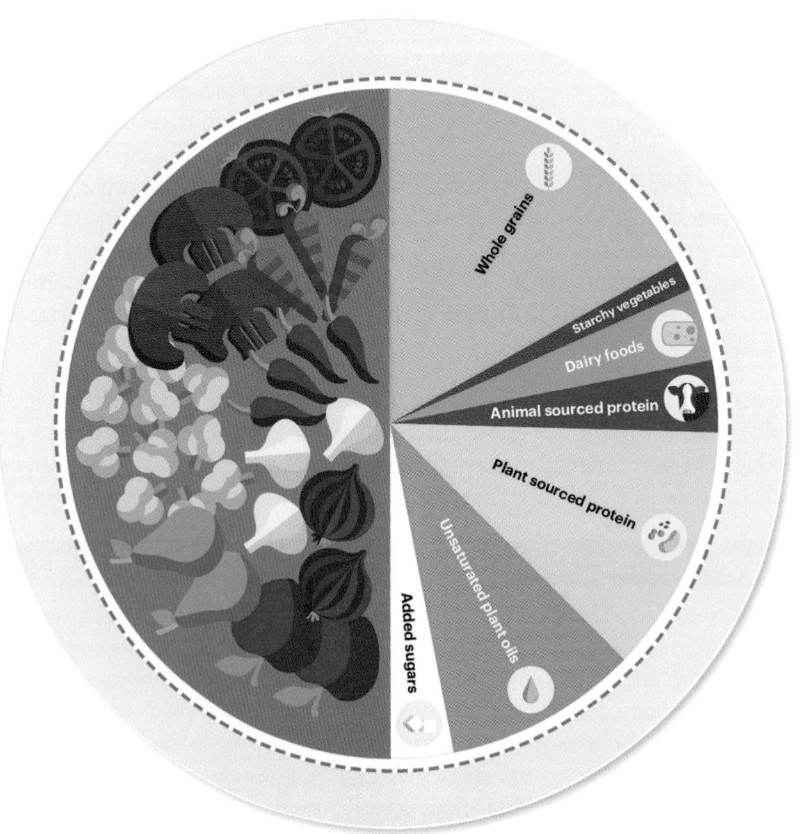

'Food miles' refers to the distance that food travels from where it is produced to where it is consumed. The global food industry has a major impact on transport and greenhouse gas emissions. Food distribution accounts for about 33–40% of UK road freight. The food system has become very dependent on crude oil, making it vulnerable, inefficient and unsustainable. An example of unsustainability is the wastefulness of a Christmas dinner. A report in 2004, called Eating Oil, suggested that, in a UK supermarket, the ingredients for Christmas dinner (potatoes, sprouts, carrots, poultry, runner beans and mange tout) could have been transported some 38,000 km to get them to warehouses and supermarkets, because possibly only the sprouts might be sourced in the UK.

Figure 5.82 shows the CO_2-equivalent kilograms of greenhouse gas emissions that it takes to produce each kilogram of some different food products.

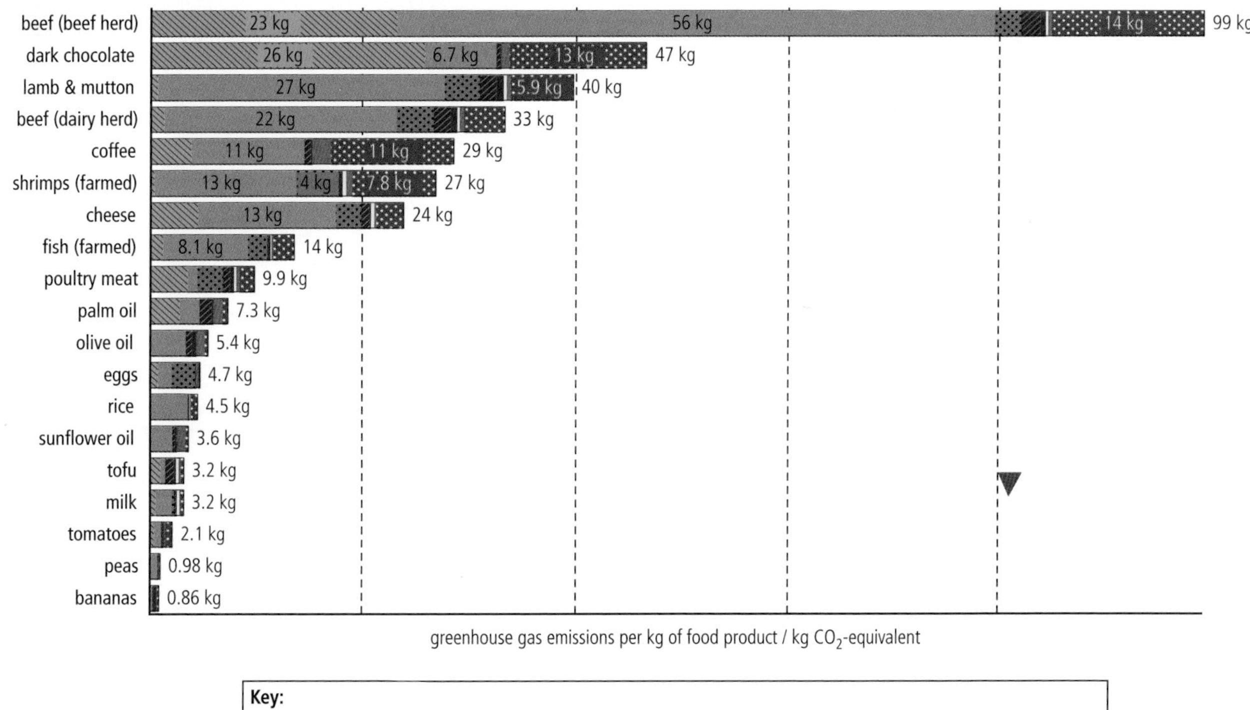

Figure 5.82 Food: greenhouse gases across the supply chain.

The main findings that can be taken from the information shown in Figure 5.82 are that:

- CH_4 production from cows, and from land conversion for grazing and animal feed, means beef from dedicated beef herds has a very high carbon footprint
- dairy products means beef from dairy herds has a lower carbon footprint than dedicated beef herds
- flooded rice fields produce CH_4
- CO_2 emissions from plant-based products are as much as 10–50 times lower than most animal-based products
- poultry are non-ruminants so do not produce CH_4 and have significantly lower emissions than cattle
- the costs of other factors such as transport distance, retailing, packaging or specific farming methods, may be less significant than the importance of the food type.

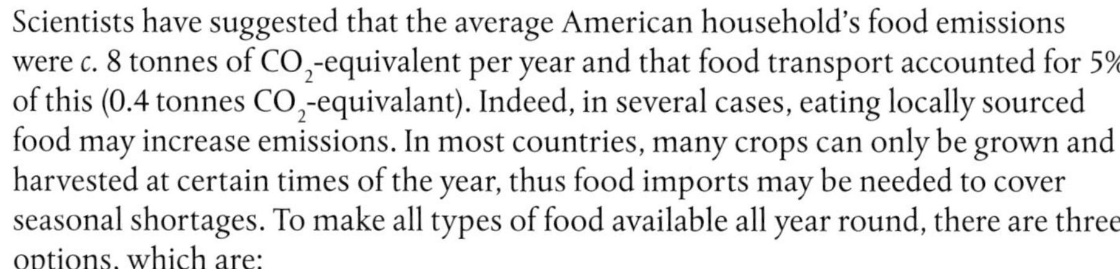

Eating locally-produced goods might not lead to a significant decrease in greenhouse gas emissions, as these make up a very small amount of the emissions from food. Of far more importance is what people eat, rather than where it came from. Animal-based foods tend to have a higher carbon-footprint than plant-based foods. For example, producing a kg of beef emits 99 kg CO_2-equivalent per kg of food, lamb emits 40 kg CO_2-equivalent per kg of food produced, poultry emit almost 10 kg per kg CO_2-equivalent per kg of food produced and peas emit *c.* 1 kg CO_2-equivalent per kg of food produced (Figure 5.82). Transport accounts for less than 1% of beef's greenhouse emissions.

Scientists have suggested that the average American household's food emissions were *c.* 8 tonnes of CO_2-equivalent per year and that food transport accounted for 5% of this (0.4 tonnes CO_2-equivalant). Indeed, in several cases, eating locally sourced food may increase emissions. In most countries, many crops can only be grown and harvested at certain times of the year, thus food imports may be needed to cover seasonal shortages. To make all types of food available all year round, there are three options, which are:

- import goods from countries where the food is in-season
- use energy-intensive greenhouses to allow year-round production
- use energy-intensive refrigeration to store food all year round.

The production of tomatoes in greenhouses in Sweden uses 10 times as much energy as importing them from southern Europe when they are in-season. However, the impact of transport can be very large when food is transported by air as foods such as avocados, almonds and other foods that have a very short shelf life have to travel long distances and may not stay fresh.

SKILLS

Create a survey to investigate food preferences and the worldviews of various groups

There are a number of different categories of worldview shown below. Which worldview best describes your views?

Localised – the desire to fix problems and address social issues
Orthodox – preserve the status quo
Pragmatist – protective/self-interested
Reward – work hard to obtain a desired goal
Survivor – fatalist; distrust in others and the need to obtain a desired goal

Food survey
Which is your favourite type of food?
Do you follow any type of diet e.g. vegan, vegetarian?
How often do you eat out in a week/get a take-out (take-away)?
Do you eat locally-produced food?
What do you do with your food waste?
Do you check sell-by dates or best-before dates?
Do you limit your consumption of red meat and/or dairy products?
How often does your family shop in
(a) a large supermarket
(b) a small local shop?

Explain how two different worldviews may influence food preferences.

HL

5.2.18 Sustainability of harvesting wild species

1.1 Perspectives
1.3 Sustainability

HL c Environmental ethics

Harvesting wild species from ecosystems by traditional methods may be more sustainable than land conversion and cultivation (Figure 5.83).

According to the Intergovernmental Science-Policy Platform on Biodiversity and Ecosystem Services (IPBES):

- one in five people rely on wild species for income and food
- more than 10,000 wild species are harvested for human food
- 2.4 billion people (one in three) depend on wood as fuel for cooking.

Billions of people benefit daily from wild species for food, materials, energy, medicine and recreation. The accelerating biodiversity crisis threatens these uses. The sustainable

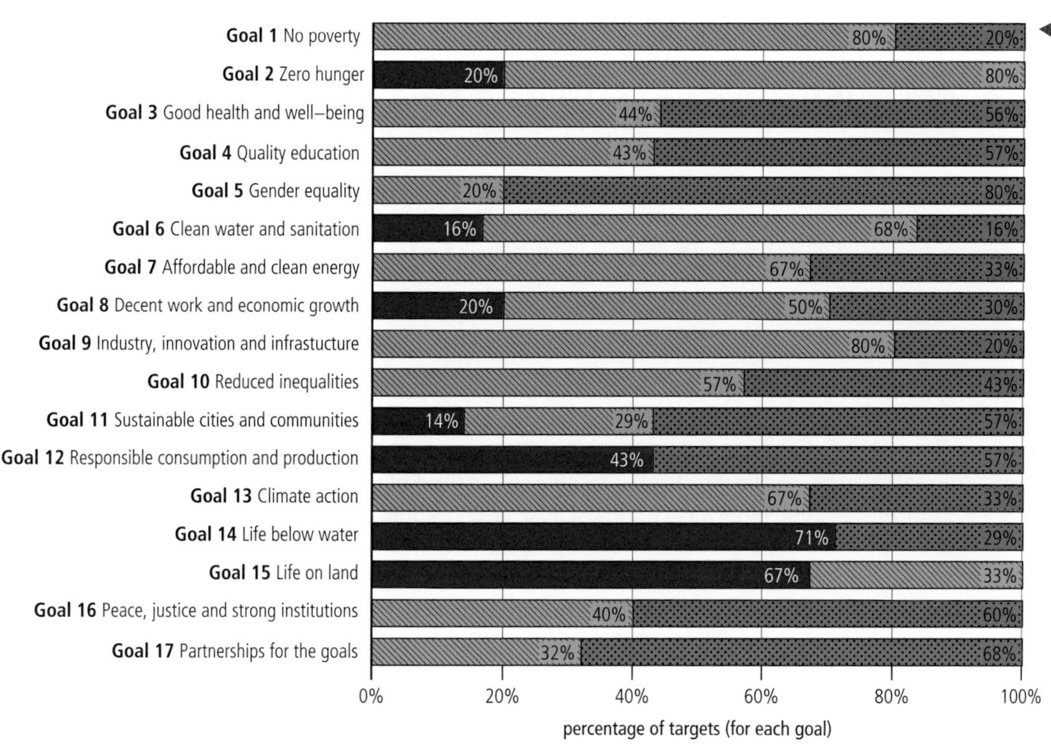

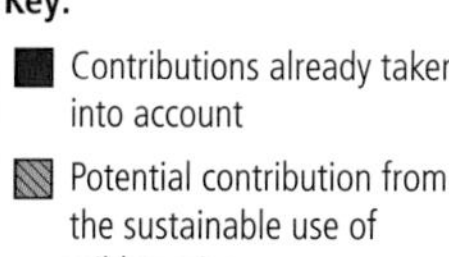

Figure 5.83 Sustainable use of wild species has unacknowledged potential to contribute to the achievement of several UN Sustainable Development Goals.

use of wild species occurs only if biodiversity and ecosystem functioning is maintained. Approximately 70% of the world's poor directly depend on wild species. Some 20% of people rely on wild plants, algae and fungi for their food and income. About 90% of the 120 million people working in capture fisheries are supported by small-scale fishing. A report by IPBES (2022)[1] on the sustainable use of wild species identified five main categories in the use of wild species: fishing, gathering plants, nuts and berries, logging, terrestrial animal harvesting (including hunting) and non-extractive purposes, such as observing.

IPBES estimate that the survival of *c.* 12% of wild tree species is threatened by unsustainable logging and that unsustainable gathering is threatening several plant groups notably cacti, cycads and orchids. Unsustainable hunting threatens over 1300 species of mammals and there have been significant declines in the populations of large species with low reproduction rates linked to hunting. The main drivers of these changes include land-use changes, changes to the marine environment, climate change, pollution and invasive species. In addition, the global trade in wild species has increased in volume, value and trading networks over the last 40 years. IPBES estimates that illegal trade in wild species is worth about US$ 200 billion, and that timber and fish make up the largest volumes and value of this trade.

The use of wild species by Indigenous peoples can be sustainable. Indigenous populations sustainably manage fishing, gathering, hunting and other uses of wild species in about 40% of conservation areas of terrestrial regions – about 38 million km^2.

Brazil nuts

Non-timber food products, such as Brazil nuts, are harvested sustainably by the Trio Indigenous community in south-west Suriname. Brazil nut harvesting offers an opportunity to generate a sustainable income. The growing of Brazil nuts is a

[1] IPBES (2022). Thematic Assessment Report on the Sustainable Use of Wild Species of the Intergovernmental Science-Policy Platform on Biodiversity and Ecosystem Services. Fromentin, J.M., Emery, M.R., Donaldson, J., Danner, M.C., Hallosserie, A., and Kieling, D. (eds). IPBES secretariat, Bonn, Germany.

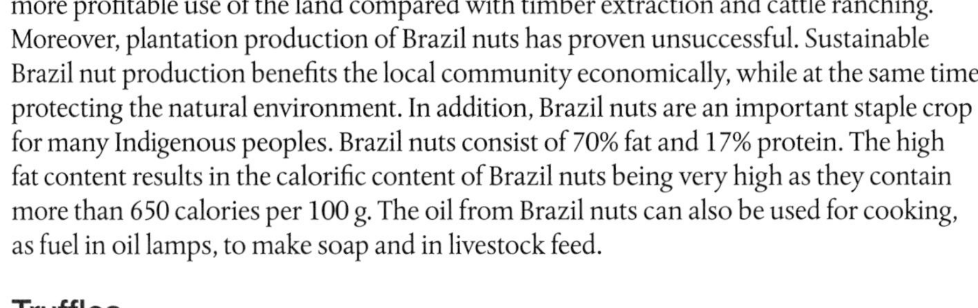
more profitable use of the land compared with timber extraction and cattle ranching. Moreover, plantation production of Brazil nuts has proven unsuccessful. Sustainable Brazil nut production benefits the local community economically, while at the same time protecting the natural environment. In addition, Brazil nuts are an important staple crop for many Indigenous peoples. Brazil nuts consist of 70% fat and 17% protein. The high fat content results in the calorific content of Brazil nuts being very high as they contain more than 650 calories per 100 g. The oil from Brazil nuts can also be used for cooking, as fuel in oil lamps, to make soap and in livestock feed.

Truffles

Figure 5.84 Truffles have a strong flavour so are only used in small amounts.

Truffles are the fruiting part of an underground fungus that grows on plant roots (Figure 5.84). Truffles have a limited shelf life (3–5 days) although they can be preserved in oil. Truffles have traditionally been harvested using dogs or female pigs that can smell them despite the truffles being located underground. Globally, there is over 2 million km^2 of suitable truffle terrain. The traditional method of truffle farming can support local and regional biodiversity and small-scale economic development, and has many environmental benefits. Truffle plantations have been developed since the mid-2000s. Truffle farms grow trees from seeds. They ensure that the soil, which is kept in bags, has the right chemical composition. Mushroom spawns are then added to the soil mix in a process known as inoculation. When the seedlings have grown into small plants, they are transplanted into larger pots and continue to grow for a further 10 years. The process is a long-term type of farming and success is not guaranteed. Global climate change is one of the main threats to the quality and quantity of truffle production. In addition, low truffle prices during the COVID-19 pandemic, as well as a reduction in the demand for truffles, made truffle production economically precarious.

Bamboo

Figure 5.85 Bamboo has a number of uses.

Bamboo is a very fast-growing grass that requires no fertilizer and limited water (Figure 5.85). It has a variety of uses including flooring, roofing, house building, furniture, cloth, paper and fuel, and its shoots can be used as food. There is a very high demand for bamboo products in China. Farmers may cut down natural forests and replace them with bamboo plantations. Bamboo has environmental advantages – it produces 35% more O_2 than equivalent-sized trees and can absorb 12 tonnes CO_2/ha/year, so is excellent for carbon sequestration. However, it is a form of monoculture and bamboo plantations lead to a large decline in biodiversity. Most of the world's bamboo is grown in China and there are shipping costs and carbon costs associated with the transfer of bamboo. An alternative would be to use locally sourced goods instead of using bamboo.

Honey

When bees are farmed for honey, they are stripped of the resource they most need. The honey they produce is used for human consumption and the bees may be fed a sub-standard syrup to keep them alive. In addition, queen bees may have their wings clipped and may only live for 2 years rather than the usual 7 years for non-farmed bees. The advantages of farming bees include: they live as close to nature as possible, they eat the diet that nature intended, they are roaming and there are no water or fertilizer requirements for the farmer to meet. In contrast, commercial bees are over-worked, under-compensated and are prevented from natural swarming and breeding behaviours. Honey is removed from hives in autumn rather than being left for the bees to use as their food source through the winter months.

Insects

Insects are harvested as human and animal feed. However, over-exploitation, habitat change and environmental contamination have reduced this. Several caterpillar species in Sub-Saharan Africa and South America have disappeared due to habitat change. In Australia, honey ants and wood grubs were used by Indigenous peoples for many generations. However, increased exploitation for restaurants, ecotourism and by Indigenous people has threatened their availability. Some insects are considered to be pests in agro-ecosystems and so are eliminated. Insect-farming can be done on a small scale or on a large scale. The advantages of insect farming include the small amount of land needed, limited greenhouse gas emissions, the high food conversion efficiency of insects and the fact that insects can be used as a source of food for humans and for fish meal.

Hunting of controversial and endangered species

Many species have been threatened by hunting for human consumption (Figure 5.86). Pangolins have been over-hunted and are now at risk of extinction. They were hunted in their millions for the supposed healing properties of the scales. Thus, pangolins are more valued dead than alive. For some poachers, trading in pangolins was the only way to earn enough money to feed their families. Pangolin meat is considered a delicacy in some parts of the world and, moreover, their skin is used to make leather products such as boots, bags and belts. Although pangolins are protected under national and international law, there is a huge trade in pangolins, with over one million being trafficked over a 10-year period.

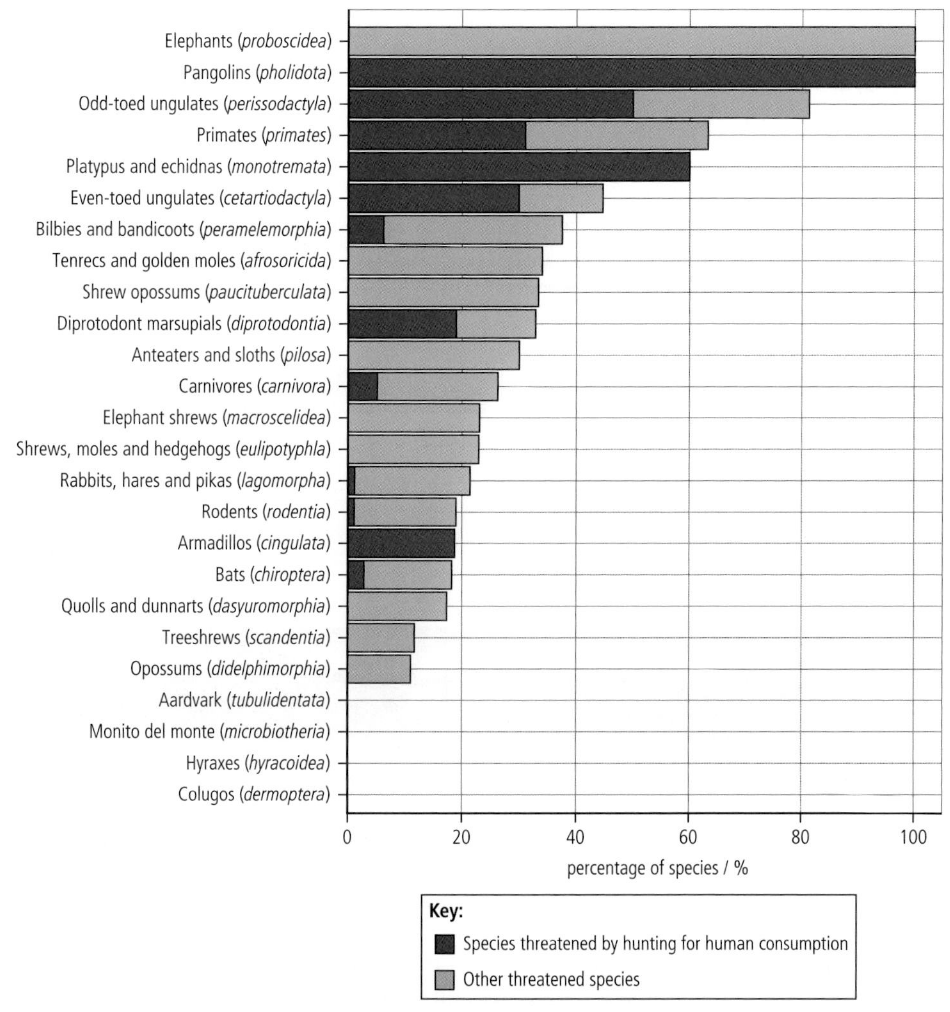

Figure 5.86 The percentage of species threatened by hunting for human consumption and other threatened species in each mammalian order.

Bushmeat

Bushmeat hunting refers to the harvesting of locally available wild animals and is widespread in parts of Africa, South America and Asia. The demand for bushmeat is increasing, partly due to larger population size and partly due to improved hunting technology. In Cameroon, the bushmeat sector employs over 500,000 people, produces more than 87,000 tonnes/year and has sales that are worth *c.* US$ 50 million. Up to 75% of bushmeat hunting in the Serengeti National park is done for subsistence use. In Sub-Saharan Africa, the poorest rural households rely on bushmeat, but in urban areas it is consumed as a luxury product. Around 5 million tonnes of bushmeat are harvested each year in Sub-Saharan Africa. It is estimated that some 250 tonnes of bushmeat are imported into Europe each year.

Hunting of bears

Bears have traditionally been hunted for their meat and fur and for use of products in cooking oils and medicines by some North American tribes. According to the International Union for Conservation of Nature (2015), six of the eight species of bear are either endangered or vulnerable. Hunting methods include guns, bear spears, snaring, hunting dogs and the use of poison. In North America, 50,000 bears are legally hunted each year. According to Bear Attack Statistics (2022) there are around 40 bear attacks on humans each year (664 occurred between 2000 and 2015). Bears are an important keystone species and are of significance to the whole ecosystem. In the past in North America, Indigenous people, frontiersmen and settlers ate bear meat. However, today hunters are not allowed to sell bears they have killed. Hence, there is a very limited supply of bear meat.

Search online for the New Jersey Black Bear Recipe Guide.

Challenge yourself

Can the hunting of controversial and endangered species and the hunting of bears ever be justified? Explain your reasons.

Are some things unknowable?

To what extent is it possible to assess the environmental impact of food production? Are the costs of food miles higher than the cost of fertilizer use or habitat destruction?

Activity

Visit the IPBES website and look at their assessment on the sustainable use of wild species at investigate trends and issues, such as illegal use and illegal trade in wild species. Present your findings to the class.

5.2.19 Sustainability of low-productivity food systems

1.1 Perspectives
1.3 Sustainability

HL b Environmental economics
HL c Environmental ethics

Although low productivity Indigenous, traditional or alternative food systems are sustainable they do not produce enough food to feed the wider global population.

Modern farming systems are largely unsustainable. They account for about 33% of the world's greenhouse gas emissions and are responsible for *c.* 60% of global biodiversity loss. Modern food systems are very unequal with much power and wealth concentrated in a few multinational corporations. Despite raised yields and production, over 820 million people are hungry, and some two million people are food insecure.

In contrast, the food systems of the world's 476 million Indigenous people are equitable, sustainable and highly productive (Table 5.20). They are climate resilient, preserve biodiversity, produce a wide range of food and have low carbon emissions.

Pros	Cons
Harvesting of forest products: • occurs naturally • can be sustainable • products are healthy as they are unprocessed foodstuffs • products can provide food and medicines • wild species provide sustenance for 70% of the world's population	• threatened by deforestation/declining biodiversity • over-harvesting could reduce supplies • may reduce size of breeding stock • can lead to extinction • increased demand leads to a decline in local population and reduced population sizes • may disrupt the ecological balance of ecosystems
Harvesting of endangered species: • is a part of cultural heritage • provides food for some Indigenous populations • can provide a sustainable income • provides bushmeat • is free	

Table 5.20 The pros and cons of sustainable production methods.

Indigenous populations account for 6% of the world's population but inhabit 28% of the world's surface. Their farming systems are adapted to extreme environments and changeable ones. For example, the terracing of steep slopes in mountainous areas and floating gardens to make use of flooded fields are well-suited for the changes that climate change may bring.

In addition, Indigenous populations conserve and restore forests and natural vegetation and are very highly connected with nature. Most have a varied diet. Whereas modern farming is based on a few key crops and animals, Indigenous peoples use a wide range of shrubs, herbs, grains, fruits, animal and fish. Moreover, they cultivate indigenous crops that are adapted to the local environment and ones that may be adapted to drought, altitude, flooding or other extremes.

Example – Contrasting farming methods in Mexico

The Popoluca Indians of Santa Rosa, Mexico practice a form of agriculture that resembles shifting cultivation, known as the traditional milpa system (Figure 5.87). This is a labour-intensive form of agriculture that uses fallow. It is a diverse form of polyculture with over 200 species cultivated, including maize, beans, cucurbits, papaya, squash, watermelon, tomatoes, oregano, coffee and chili. The Popoluca have developed this system into a fine art that mimics the natural rainforest.

Figure 5.87 Popoluca settlement near Catemaco, Mexico.

The variety of natural rainforest is repeated by the variety of shifting cultivation. For example, lemon trees, pepper vine and spearmint are light-seeking heliophytes and prefer open conditions rather than shade. Coffee, by contrast, is a sciophyte and prefers shade. The mango tree requires damp conditions.

The close associations that are found in natural conditions are also seen in the Popoluca's farming system. For example, maize and beans can be grown well together, as maize extracts nutrients from the soil, whereas beans return them. Tree trunks and small trees are left because they are useful for many purposes such as returning nutrients to the soil and preventing soil erosion. They are also used as a source of material for housing, hunting spears and for medicines.

As in a rainforest, the crops are multi-layered containing tree, shrub and herb layers. This layering increases the net primary production per unit area because photosynthesis is taking place on at least three levels and soil erosion is reduced, as no soil or space is left bare. Most plants are self-seeded, which reduces the cost of inputs. The Popoluca show a huge amount of ecological knowledge and management. Overall, 244 species of plant are used in the farming system. Animals include chickens, pigs and turkeys. These are used as a source of food, for bartering, sold in exchange for money and their waste is used as manure. Rivers and lakes are used for fishing and catching turtles. Thus, it is not entirely a subsistence lifestyle since wood, fruit, turtles and other animals are traded for some seeds, mainly maize.

Pressures on the Popoluca

About 90% of Mexico's rainforest has been cut down in recent decades, largely for new forms of agriculture. This is partly a response to Mexico's huge international debt, with the government strongly encouraging a change in the mode of farming so as to increase agricultural exports and reduce its imports. The main new forms of farming are cattle ranching for export and plantations or cash crops, such as tobacco.

However, these new methods are not necessarily suited to the physical and economic environment (Table 5.21). Tobacco needs protection from excess sunlight and excess moisture and the soil needs to be very fertile. However, the cleared rainforest is frequently left bare and this leads to soil erosion. Unlike the milpa system, the new systems are very labour-intensive. Pineapple, sugar cane and tobacco plantations require large inputs of fertilizers and pesticides. Inputs are expensive and the costs are rising rapidly.

Ranching prevents the natural succession of vegetation because of a lack of seed from nearby forests and the grazing effects of cattle. Grasses and a few legumes become dominant. One hectare of rainforest supports about 200 species of trees and up to 10,000 individual plants. By contrast, one hectare of pastoral land supports just one cow and one or two types of grass. But it is profitable in the short-term because land is available and it is supported by the Mexican government. Extensive monoculture is increasingly mechanized and uses large inputs of fertilizers, pesticides and insecticides. However, it is very costly and there are problems of soil deterioration and microclimatic change. Yet there is little pressure to improve efficiency because it is easy to clear new forest.

The Mexican rainforest can be described as a 'desert covered by trees'. Under natural conditions it is very dynamic, but its resilience depends on the level of disturbance. Sustainable development of the rainforest requires the management and use of the natural structure and diversity, namely local species, local knowledge and skills, rather than using a type of farming that has been developed elsewhere and imported.

Table 5.21 A comparison between the milpa system and the new forms of agriculture.

Factor	Milpa system	Plantation or ranching
Net primary production	High, stable	Declining
Number of people employed	High	Higher and increasing
Inputs (clearing and seeding)	Few	Very high 2.5–3 tonnes fertilizer/ha/pa
Crops	Polyculture (244 species used)	Monoculture (risk of disease, poor yield, loss of demand and/or overproduction)
Yield (compared to inputs)	200%	140% (if lucky)
Reliability of farming system	Quite stable	High risk operation
Economic organisation	Mainly subsistence	Commercial
Income	None/little	More
Carrying capacity (livestock)	Several families/4 ha	More than one family on a plantation (200 ha) Ranching: 1 ha of good land with one cow or 20 ha of poor land with one cow

5.2.20 Food distribution patterns and food quality variations

HL

1.1 Perspectives
1.3 Sustainability

HL b Environmental economics
HL c Environmental ethics

Uneven distribution of food and variations in food quality cause health issues.

According to the World Bank (2023) over 9% of the world's population faced hunger in 2022, compared with less than 8% in 2019. In addition, moderate or severe food insecurity affected nearly 30% of the global population (2.4 billion people) in 2022, with 11.3% being severely food insecure. On average, enough food is produced around the world to supply its population but there is an imbalance in the food supply. Many people in LICs are suffering from under-nourishment (their food intake does not contain enough energy) or malnutrition (their food intake lacks essential nutrients such as protein and minerals).

There has been an increased demand for food production in many societies around the world. Reduced death rates due to better medical care have led to increases in population growth. The increased wealth in HICs and NICs enables people to consume more – in many cases, more than they need. In Europe, the economics of food-production systems means that food production is a business, and the Common Agricultural Policy subsidizes farmers.

There are concerns in HICs about food availability, stability of supply and access to supplies. The result is that these countries often take protectionist measures to protect supplies. Import tariffs imposed by HICs make the importing of food more expensive, which can have knock-on effects for exporting countries. In LICs, food production is used to generate foreign currency, especially from cash crops such as sugar cane, so there is often an emphasis on export in these countries.

Huge domestic support and **export subsidies** provided by HICs to their farmers make farm products from LICs uncompetitive. For example, rice subsidies for farmers in the USA have affected rice farmers in the Asia–Pacific region (Thailand, Vietnam and India). Corn subsidies have also driven prices down, affecting farmers in the Philippines and China.

TOK

Why do facts sometimes not change our minds?

Some reports estimate that for people in developing countries to enjoy the same level of meat and dairy consumption as people in developed countries, the latter will have to halve their meat and dairy intake. Is this something developed countries are morally expected to do? Should legal agreements be put in place to force developed countries to adopt this strategy? Can we all expect to continue to eat as much meat if it puts global food production at risk? Why, given our knowledge of the impact of meat consumption on environmental systems, do we not change our own patterns of consumption?

The rapid increases in food prices in the early 21st century were due, in part, to increased demands to use land for biofuel, leaving less land available for food crops. High meat consumption in HICs, as well as increased meat and dairy consumption in NICs, has meant a higher proportion of corn crops going to feed cattle than to feed human populations directly. This has also resulted in higher corn prices. Increased oil prices have also contributed to higher food prices due to increased fertilizer costs and increased transport costs. Despite these increases in prices, the overall cost of food in HICs is relatively inexpensive. Seasonal foods have generally disappeared as imports fill gaps. Modern technology and transport ensure that foodstuffs can be imported from all round the globe.

In some LICs, however, many populations struggle to produce enough food and generally food prices remain high. Political, economic and environmental issues may all limit food production. The export-driven economies of many LICs may lead to crops being generated for cash (cash crops) rather than to feed the local population. For example, in Kenya, vegetable crops often end up in HIC supermarkets rather than being used to feed the local population, many of whom remain hungry. More recently, increased demands for biofuel by HICs means that LICs are increasingly allocating fertile land for the growth of biofuel crops, because they get an income from the biofuel, rather than using this land to grow food for their Indigenous population. In India, for example, the *Jatropha* plant is grown as a biofuel because the plant produces seeds that are up to 40% oil. The plant is grown on land that was once used for growing crops, pushing up the cost of food as land for edible crops becomes more limited.

Climate change has had more impact on LICs than on HICs. For example, in some LICs the increased incidence of drought has reduced the amount of growing land. Global warming could lead to tropical and subtropical countries like India facing short periods of super-high temperatures – with temperatures approaching 50 °C. These temperatures could completely destroy the harvest if they coincide with the flowering period.

As the amount of land used for settlement and industry increases, there is an increasing need to intensify production on existing farmland. In HICs, food production is a complex process, involving high levels of technology, low labour costs and high fuel costs. Fertilizers and pesticides are factory produced and the product's processing and packaging is done on a large scale. In HICs, the advent of technological approaches has enabled yield to be maximized. During the 19th century and early in the 20th century, agricultural production in Europe and the USA involved large numbers of labourers. As tractor use increased in the 20th century, farm labour decreased and agriculture became more mechanized and intensive, with many small fields being combined into smaller numbers of larger fields. Pesticide use (to protect crops and livestock), along with the use of high-yielding crop species, have increased crop yields. More recently the introduction of genetically modified (GM) crops have increased yields further. Overall in HICs, agriculture has become more technocentric.

Much agriculture in LICs, in contrast, suffers from low levels of technology and a lack of capital, and uses high levels of labour. The countries are poor and cannot afford the high tech, and so rely on human capital instead. Rice farming is typical of tropical wet LICs, where rice is often the staple crop. There is a dependence on working animals rather than machinery, making it a labour-intensive process, with the labour often coming from within families. While HICs have large monocultures, mixed cropping on a small scale is common in LICs.

A lack of food at a household level could be caused by a lack of food production or a lack of entitlement to food. Food availability decline refers to the situation when not enough food is produced. This could occur during famines or long-term drought. Food entitlement decline occurs when a person's entitlement to food decreases. For example, they might lose their job and so have no income, or the cost of food may rise steeply, and they cannot afford to buy enough food.

Calorie intake is the amount of food (measured in calories) per person per day. Figure 5.88 shows the global daily calorie intake per person. The global average calorie intake is about 2780 kcal/person per day and the minimum recommended amount is around 1800 kcal/person/day. However, this varies with age, gender, type of work, amount of physical activity and climate. Countries with the highest daily intake include Austria and the USA with 3800 and 3750 kcal/person/day, respectively. In general, HICs have a calorie intake of around 3400 kcal/person/day. In contrast, people in LICs have a calorie intake of around 2600 kcal/person/day. However, in Sub-Saharan Africa the intake is down to 2240 kcal/person/day and in Central Africa it is just 1820 kcal/person/day. In Burundi and Eritrea, daily calorie intakes are as low as 1680 and 1590 kcal/person/day, respectively.

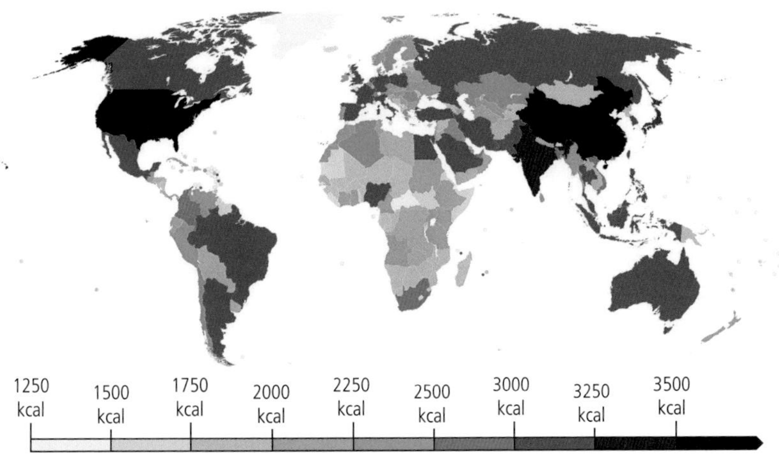

Figure 5.88 Global daily calorie intake per person, 2018.

Malnutrition

Malnutrition refers to a diet that is lacking (or has too much) in quantity or quality of foods. There are many types of malnutrition, including:

- deficiency diseases, referring to a lack of specific vitamins or minerals
- kwashiorkor, which is caused by a lack of protein
- marasmus, which is a lack of calories/energy
- obesity, which occurs when there is too much energy/protein in the foods eaten
- starvation, which refers to a limited/non-existent intake of food
- temporary hunger, which is a short-term decline in the availability of food to a population in an area
- famine, which occurs when there is a long-term decline in the availability of food in a region.

Malnourished people

According to the Global Hunger Index (2022), the Central African Republic and Yemen had over 40% of their population classified as malnourished, while in Chad and DR

Congo it was over 35%. The countries with the lowest proportion of malnourished people were generally from Europe, South America or the Middle East.

Stunted growth/stunting

Stunted growth or stunting refers to long-term malnutrition and is usually defined as a child who has a low height for their age. Figure 5.89 shows the global variations in stunting rates. Very high rates of stunting (over 50%) are found in Timor-Leste, Burundi and Eritrea. There are also very high rates of stunting in several Sub-Saharan African countries and South Asian countries. Rates for stunting tend to be much higher than rates for wasting (chronic or short-term malnutrition). In contrast, the lowest rates of stunting, below 5%, were found in parts of the Middle East, Latin America and southern and eastern Europe. An exception is Fiji, which had a stunting prevalence of 3.7%.

Figure 5.89 Global variations in stunting.

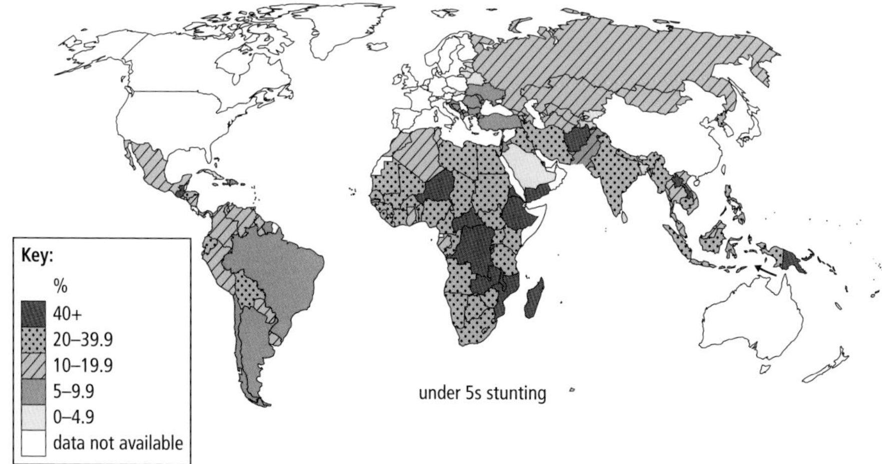

Wasting

Wasting is classified as acute and short-term malnutrition and can be defined by a child who has a low weight for their age. Figure 5.90 shows the global variations in wasting rates. Very high rates of wasting (over 20%) were found in South Sudan, Djibouti and Sri Lanka. There are also high rates of wasting in several countries throughout South Asia and Sub-Saharan Africa. The lowest rates of wasting, of less than 2%, are generally found in HICs (not shown on the map) and much of Latin America and South America. There are several anomalies such as Pakistan and Mongolia (both less than 1%) and Swaziland (2%).

Figure 5.90 Global variations in wasting rates.

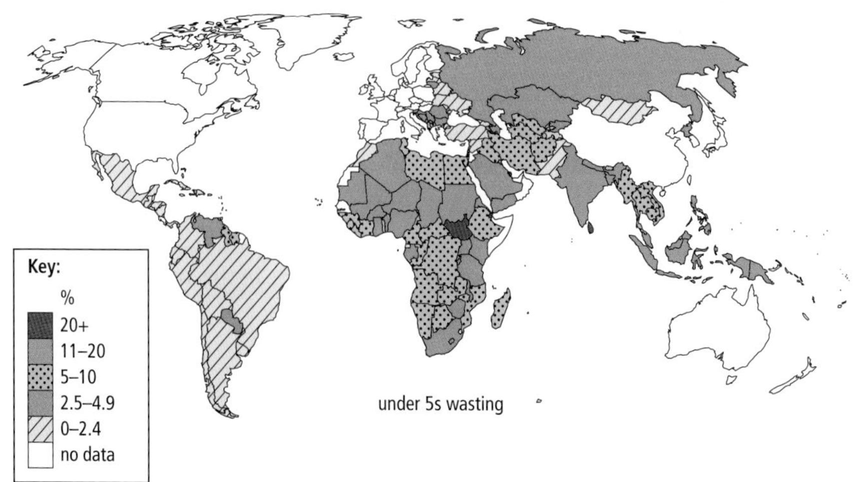

Famine

Famine refers to the long-term decline in the availability of food in a region. There are several factors affecting the severity of a famine including:

- the length and severity of a drought: the longer and more severe the drought, the greater the impact of famine
- governance: where there is poor governance, populations are not protected and the risk of food scarcity increases
- access to land and production of food: households that lose access to the land are at increased risk of food shortages
- unemployment and entitlement to food: people who are unable to pay for food are just as vulnerable as those who cannot grow it
- population growth: rapid population growth, especially of refugees and internally displaced people, increases the impact of famine in an area
- women and children make up a high proportion of the population affected by famine (Figure 5.91)
- civil unrest, including war: this disrupts food production and distribution and decreases the number of young workers, thereby increasing the impacts of famine
- access to international aid: this needs to be directed to those who need it most.

Figure 5.91 Internal displaced refugees of civil war queue up prior to a food distribution carried out by the United Nations World Food Programme (WFP) in Kitgum, Uganda.

HL

Engagement

- Conduct a survey in your school or college to investigate food preferences, such as meat, dairy, fruit, vegetables, grain and protein. Ask whether people should continue to consume large amounts of meat and dairy or whether they should consume more nuts, legumes, fruit and vegetables. Summarise the results of your survey. Did you find anything surprising?
- Volunteer with an organization that helps support access to food by those that need it, for example a soup kitchen or food bank.
- Plan a meat-free weekly lunch menu for your school.
- Look for recipes for vegetarian or vegan meals. How does the carbon footprint of these meals compare to meals that contain animal products?
- Find out about named, local examples of regenerative farming in your country or an area of your choice. Create a poster for your classroom summarizing your findings.

Exercise

Q11. **(a)** Define the term *system*.

(b) Explain how farming can be considered as a system.

Q12. Outline the causes of famine.

Q13. Explain why the Green Revolution initially led to an increase in the inequalities of incomes.

Q14. Explain how soil erosion can be reduced using cover crops, stone lines and contour ploughing.

Q15. Outline the benefits of the no-till farming method.

Q16. Examine how waste varies between LICs and HICs.

HL

Q17. HL Explain the term *rewilding*.

Q18. HL Outline the principles of regenerative farming.

Q19. HL Explain the term *mob grazing*.

Q20. HL Explain how vertical farming can lead to increased food supply in urban areas.

HL end

Practice questions

1. Figure 5.92 shows a model of the nutrient cycle from a tropical rainforest.

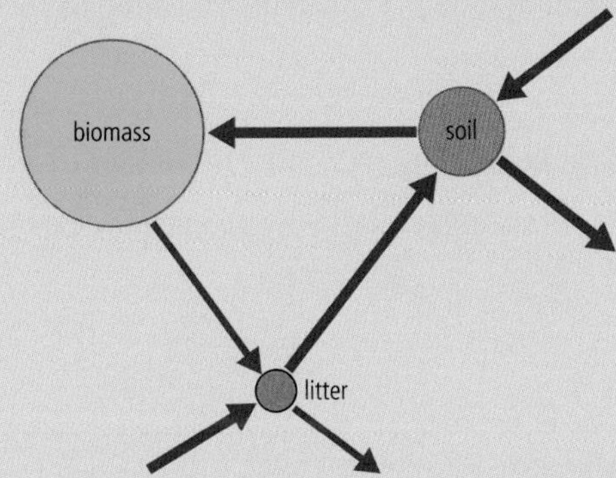

Figure 5.92 A model of a nutrient cycle.

(a) Identify two inputs and two outputs from the nutrient cycle. [2]

(b) Explain why the three stores of nutrients vary in size. [6]

(c) Explain the likely impact of commercial farming on the nutrient cycle of the tropical rainforest. [6]

(Total 14 marks)

2. Figure 5.93 shows the global daily intake of calories per person.

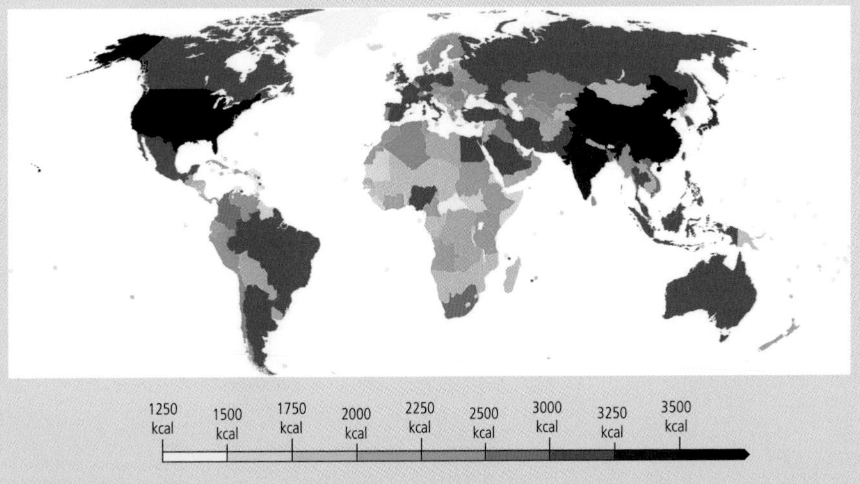

Figure 5.93 Global variations in daily calorie intake.

(a) Describe the global variations in calorie intake per person. [3]

(b) Outline potential problems related to:

(i) a very low calorie intake [2]

(ii) a very high calorie intake. [2]

(c) Suggest ways in which food supply in LICs could be increased. [6]

(Total 13 marks)

3. Outline the importance of soil texture in different types of soils. [2]

(Total 2 marks)

(continued)

4. Describe the impact of shifting cultivation on soil fertility. [3]

(Total 3 marks)

5. For any chosen farming system, explain how farming has been influenced by soil and climate. [2]

(Total 2 marks)

6. **(a)** Define the term *food security*. [1]

   (b) Explain two contrasting reasons why people may experience food security. [1]

(Total 2 marks)

HL

7. HL Discuss the principles of regenerative farming. [2]

(Total 2 marks)

8. HL Analyze the advantages and disadvantages of greenhouse farming. [2]

(Total 2 marks)

9. HL Explain the factors that may influence soil formation. [2]

(Total 2 marks)

10. HL Evaluate current global strategies used to achieve sustainable food supply. [2]

(Total 2 marks)

HL end

6 Atmosphere and climate change

6.1 Introduction to the atmosphere

Guiding question

How do atmospheric systems contribute to the stability of life on Earth?

6.1.1 The atmosphere forms the boundary between Earth and space. It is the outer limit of the biosphere and its composition and processes support life on Earth.
6.1.2 Differential heating of the atmosphere creates the tricellular model of atmospheric circulation that redistributes the heat from the equator to the poles.
6.1.3 Greenhouse gases (GHGs) and aerosols in the atmosphere absorb and re-emit some of the infrared (long-wave) radiation emitted from the Earth's surface, preventing it from being radiated out into space. They include water vapour, carbon dioxide, methane, nitrous oxide (GHGs) and black carbon (aerosol).
6.1.4 The greenhouse effect keeps the Earth warmer than it otherwise would be due to the broad spectrum of the Sun's radiation reaching the Earth's surface and infrared radiation emitted by the warmed surface then being trapped and re-radiated by greenhouse gases.
HL 6.1.5 The atmosphere is a dynamic system, and the components and layers are the result of continuous physical and chemical processes.
HL 6.1.6 Molecules in the atmosphere are pulled towards the Earth's surface by gravity. Because gravitational force is inversely proportional to distance, the atmosphere thins as altitude increases.
HL 6.1.7 Milankovitch cycles affect how much solar radiation reaches the Earth and lead to cycles in the Earth's climate over tens to hundreds of thousands of years.
HL 6.1.8 Global warming is moving the Earth away from the glacial-interglacial cycle that has characterized the Quaternary period, toward new, hotter climatic conditions.
HL 6.1.9 The evolution of life on Earth changed the composition of the atmosphere, which in turn influences the evolution of life on Earth.

1.2 Systems

6.1.1 The atmosphere

The Earth's atmosphere is the outer limit of the biosphere and its composition and processes support life on Earth (Topic 2, Section 2.1.1). The atmosphere is a mixture of solids, liquids and gases that are held to the Earth by gravitational force (Figure 6.1). These gases are redistributed around the world through physical processes, such as wind. The atmosphere extends upwards from the Earth. Up to a height of about 80 km, the composition of the atmosphere is fairly constant, with 78% nitrogen gas (N_2), 21% oxygen gas (O_2), 0.9% argon gas and a variety of other trace gases such as water vapour, carbon dioxide (CO_2), helium and ozone (O_3). In addition, there are solids such as dust, ash and soot.

Figure 6.1 The Earth's atmosphere.

Air moves from areas of high pressure to areas of low pressure – this is known as the pressure gradient force. The strength of the wind varies with the differences in pressure. Where there is a large difference, for example, in a tropical cyclone (hurricane), wind speeds tend to be very high, often exceeding 119 km/hour.

There is no outer limit for the atmosphere, but most *weather* occurs in the lower 16–17 km of the atmosphere, in the layer known as the **troposphere**. In the troposphere, temperatures fall with height above the Earth's surface (on average 6.5 °C per km). Certain gases are concentrated at particular heights of the atmosphere (Figure 6.2). Ozone occurs mostly around 25–30 km above the surface and is important for the filtering of harmful ultraviolet (UV) radiation.

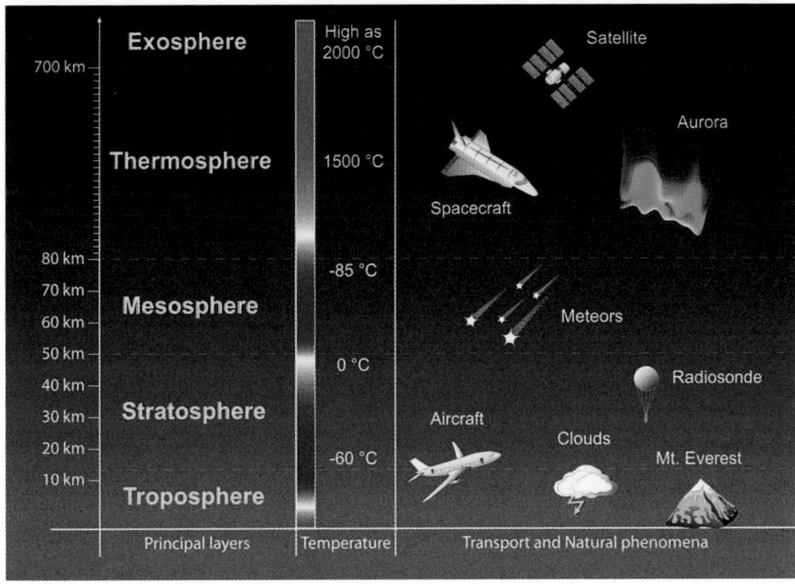

Figure 6.2 Vertical structure of the Earth's atmosphere.

6.1.2 Differential heating and the tricellular model

1.2 Systems
2.4 Climate and biomes

The Earth's energy is mostly derived from the Sun. Incoming solar radiation is referred to as insolation. In some places, there may also be important local sources of energy, such as **heat islands** in urban areas and **geothermal** heat in **tectonic regions** (areas of the Earth that are close to **tectonic plate** boundaries or where the plate is thin enough to allow geothermal heat to rise to the surface).

Geothermal heat is thermal energy in the Earth's crust.

The fundamental factor causing atmospheric circulation is the unequal heating with **latitude**. Between 38°S and 38°N there is an excess of energy, whereas polewards there is a deficit of energy. Energy is transferred from low latitude to high latitude to balance this unequal heating.

Latitude is the position of a place on Earth relative to the equator e.g. north or south.

Air moves in towards centres of low pressure (convergence), rises, and then spreads out when it reaches the tropopause (divergence). When air converges at high altitude, it sinks and forms high pressure at ground level. From there, it moves outwards (diverges) at ground level (Figure 6.3).

The global pattern of winds is thus determined by the location of pressure systems. However, there are also seasonal differences due to the position of the Sun.

At the equator, warm air rises forming an area of low pressure. It then moves towards the North and South Poles. In subtropical areas, 20–30° N and S, high-pressure areas are formed when this air sinks because it has become cold and dense.

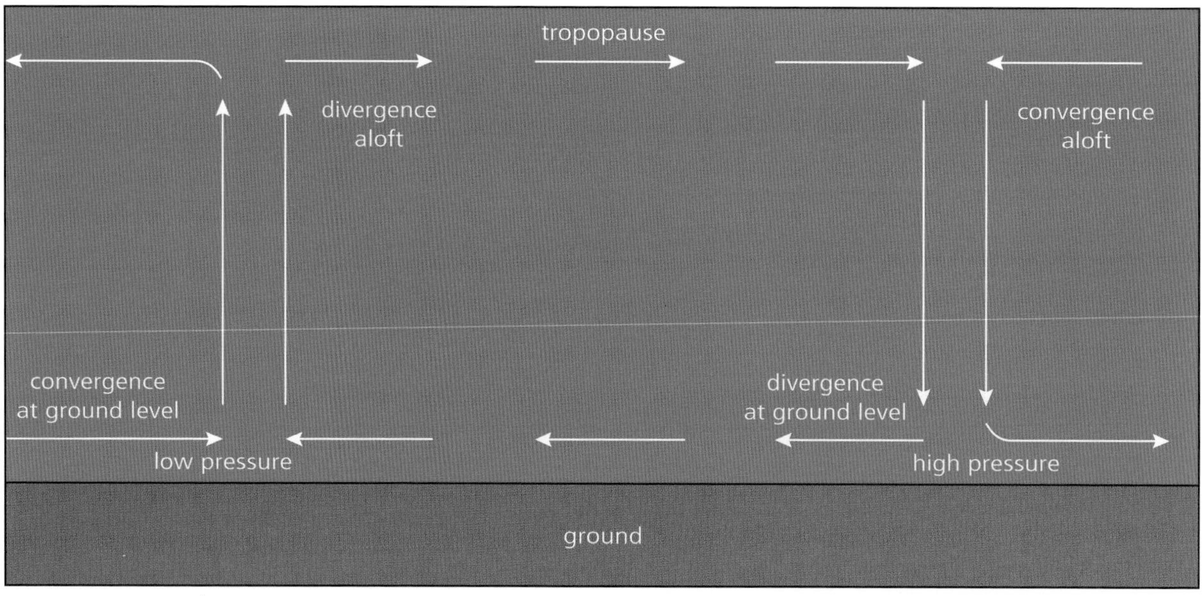

Figure 6.3 Air rises in low pressure systems and sinks in high pressure systems.

Some of this air moves from the subtropical areas back to the equator to replace the rising air. This convectional cell is known as the Hadley cell.

At each pole a second cell, known as the Polar cell, has cold dense air sinking (polar high pressure) and moving outwards to the mid-latitudes. Between each Polar cell and Hadley cell is a third cell, known as the Ferrel cell, which is driven by the movements in the Polar and Hadley cells (Topic 2, Section 2.4.5). The action of the three cells together forms a model of atmospheric circulation known as the tricellular model (Figure 6.4).

Figure 6.4 The tricellular model of atmospheric circulation.

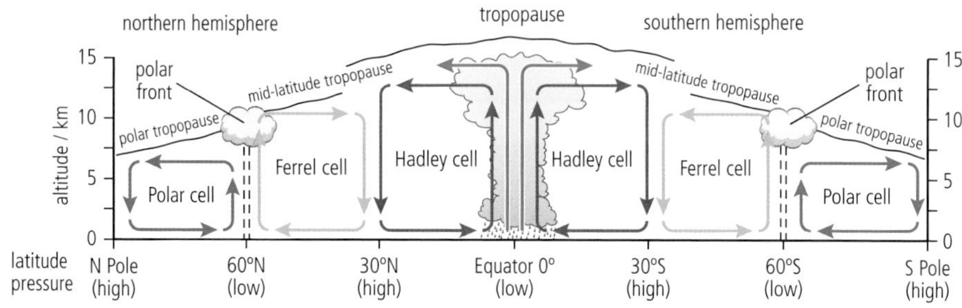

Create system diagrams to represent the atmospheric system

Create a system diagram to represent the atmospheric circulation system. Make sure you use boxes to represent stores and arrows to represent processes.

Consider the factors which influence atmospheric circulation and the processes of circulation.

6.1.3 The effect of greenhouse gases and aerosols

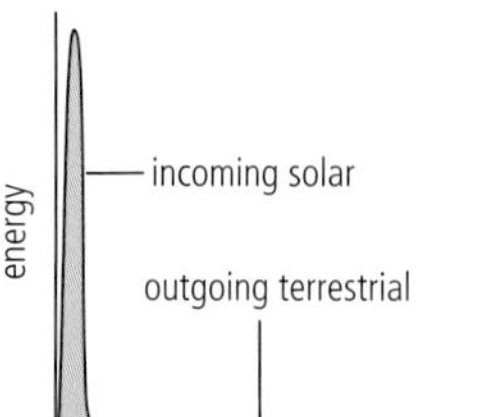

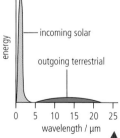

Figure 6.5 Incoming solar radiation and outgoing long-wave radiation – a comparison of wavelengths.

Greenhouse gases (GHGs) found in the atmosphere include water vapour, CO_2, tropospheric O_3, methane (CH_4) and nitrous oxide (N_2O). Black carbon is also found in the atmosphere as an aerosol. Greenhouse gases permit incoming short-wave radiation from the Sun to pass through but can absorb long-wave radiation since incoming solar radiation and outgoing long-wave radiation operate at different wavelengths (Figure 6.5).

Most greenhouse gases lead to a warming effect, but there can also be a cooling effect (Figure 6.7 and Figure 6.8). This can occur due to the amount of aerosols in the atmosphere. Many of these aerosols, such as sulfur emissions, are produced by humans. The aerosols can have a direct effect on the proportion of solar radiation reaching the Earth's surface. Aerosols can have a local or regional effect on temperature. For example, many industrial areas have not warmed as much as expected with an increase in greenhouse gases. This *global dimming* or *regional dimming* can be caused by the increase in cloud cover, caused in part by aerosol loading and in part by increased water vapour, which may reflect large quantities of solar radiation away from the Earth's surface.

Black carbon (aerosol)

Black carbon (aerosol) (Figure 6.6) is formed from the incomplete combustion of fossil fuels, biofuels and biomass.

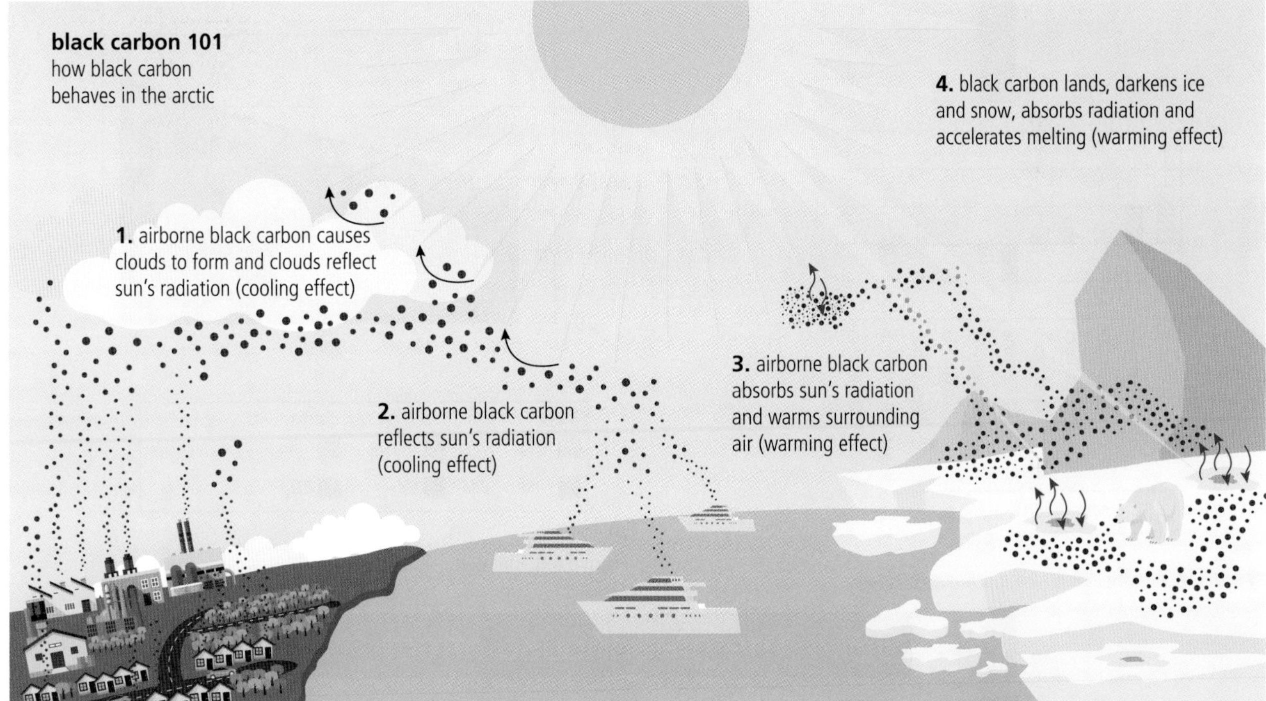

Figure 6.6 The impact of black carbon.

Approximately 20% of black carbon is emitted from burning biofuels, 40% from fossil fuels and 40% from open biomass such as savannah and rainforest. Black carbon is very fine particulate matter of diameter less than 2.5 μm. However, black carbon only stays in the atmosphere for days or weeks before being removed by rain or snow.

The impacts of black carbon on the climate include:

- direct effects: when suspended in the atmosphere, black carbon absorbs sunlight and reduces albedo
- semi-direct effects: black carbon absorbs insolation and affects cloud cover
- snow and ice albedo effects: when deposited on snow or ice, black carbon reduces the albedo; this can lead to a positive feedback effect where the decreased albedo leads to increased surface temperatures, which in turn decreases ice cover and reduces the surface albedo
- indirect effects: black carbon can cause indirect changes in absorption or reflection of solar radiation through changes in cloud cover.

Hydrochlorofluorocarbons (HCFCs) are compounds that contain only carbon, hydrogen, chlorine and fluorine. These are 'temporary' alternatives to chlorofluorocarbons (CFCs), have shorter atmospheric lifetime, and release less reactive chlorine to the stratosphere.

Hydrofluorocarbons (HFCs) are synthetic gases mainly used for cooling and refrigeration. They are powerful and short-lived but do not contain chlorine, so do not destroy stratospheric ozone.

According to the Intergovernmental Panel on Climate Change (IPCC), the combined direct and indirect snow-albedo effects make black carbon the third largest contributor to radiative forcing (see below) since pre-industrial times. Black carbon is also a significant contributor to Arctic ice-melt. The IPCC estimates that the *soot on snow* change in albedo could be responsible for up to 25% of global warming.[1]

Radiative forcing

Radiative forcing is a measure of the balance between incoming solar radiation and outgoing long-wave radiation. A positive radiative forcing means that the Earth is receiving more incoming energy than it is radiating back out to space. Radiative forcing varies with insolation, albedo and the concentration of greenhouse gases (Figures 6.7 and 6.8).

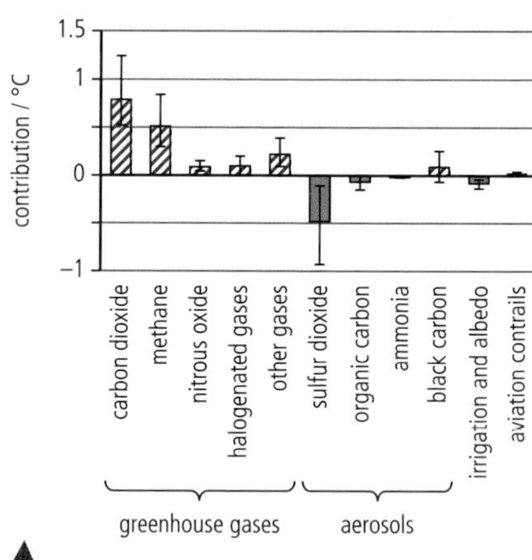

Figure 6.7 Principal drivers of climate change.

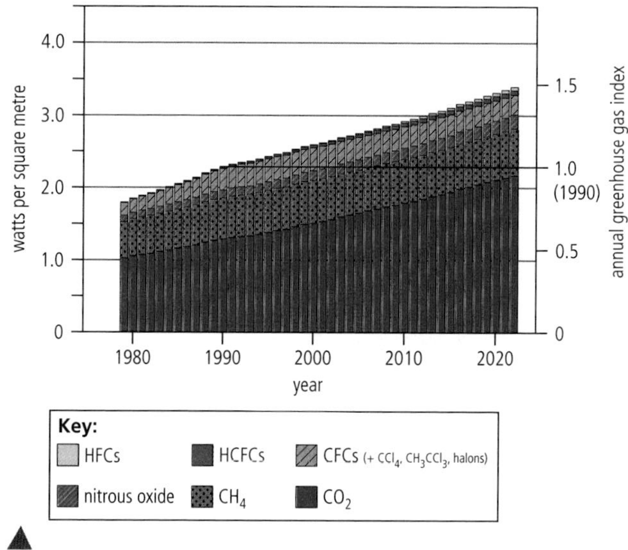

Figure 6.8 The contribution of greenhouse gases to radiative forcing.

1.2 Systems

6.1.4 The greenhouse effect

The greenhouse effect is the natural process in which greenhouse gases and aerosols trap a proportion of outgoing long-wave radiation, which keeps the Earth warm enough to support life.

The enhanced greenhouse effect is the increase in greenhouse gases in the atmosphere, largely due to human activities, which trap increasing amounts of outgoing long-wave radiation, thereby leading to global warming.

The **greenhouse effect** is the natural process by which greenhouse gases and aerosols in the atmosphere absorb and re-emit long-wave infrared (IR) radiation that has been reflected from the Earth's surface back to Earth, thereby warming the atmosphere.

The greenhouse effect makes the Earth warmer than it otherwise would be and makes life possible. Without the greenhouse effect, the Earth would be too cold for most lifeforms to survive.

Although the gases O_2 and N_2 make up the bulk of the atmosphere, they do not absorb or emit long-wave radiation. In contrast, water vapour and some other minor gases absorb some of the long-wave radiation emitted by the Earth's surface and act as a type of blanket. These are the greenhouse gases, without which the average temperature on Earth would be about −18 °C rather than 15 °C, as it actually is. This blanketing effect is

[1]IPCC Fourth Assessment Report: Climate Change 2007: Working Group I: The Physical Science Basis: 2.5.4 Radiative Forcing by Anthropogenic Surface Albedo Change: Black Carbon in Snow and Ice.

known as the natural greenhouse effect, which is a normal part of the Earth's climate and has existed for nearly the whole of the atmosphere's history.

The **enhanced greenhouse effect** refers to the increase in greenhouse gases, such as CO_2 and CH_4, due to human activity. This leads to temperatures on Earth being greater than they should be, causing the effects known as global warming/climate change/climate crisis/global heating (Figure 6.9).

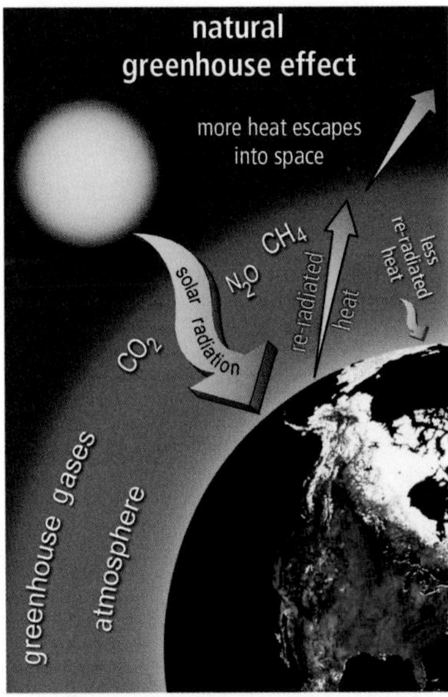

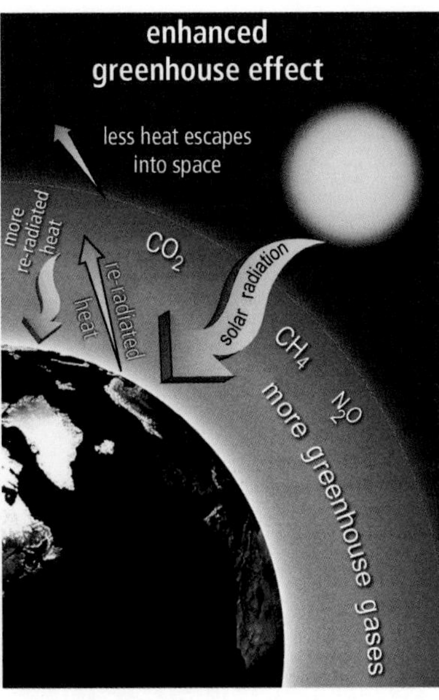

Figure 6.9 The natural and enhanced greenhouse effects. CO_2, CH_4 and water vapour in the atmosphere limit the amount of heat escaping from the Earth's surface.

Although CO_2 is the most important greenhouse gas, other gases, such as CH_4, N_2O and tropospheric O_3 (Topic 8, Section 8.3.3) also contribute to the enhanced greenhouse effect and global warming. The combined impact of these minor greenhouse gases adds a warming equivalent of about 60% of CO_2.

Nitrous oxide (N_2O) is a direct greenhouse gas. There are other oxides of nitrogen, NOx (nitrogen oxides), which include NO and NO_2: the role of these pollutant gases in the greenhouse effect is complex, and they are described as 'indirect' greenhouse gases.

HL

6.1.5 The atmosphere is a dynamic system

HL

1.2 Systems

The atmosphere is a dynamic system, and the components and layers are the result of continuous physical and chemical processes including global warming and the production of O_3 from O_2 gas.

The atmosphere is a complex, open system with inputs of solar radiation, water, aerosols such as dust and salt and, over geological time, comets and meteors. Even if we consider the Earth as a closed system, the atmosphere is influenced by many factors including:

- Milankovitch cycles (this topic, Section 6.1.7)
- latitude
- altitude
- proximity to the sea
- winds and pressure
- ocean currents
- ice sheets and glaciers
- aspect
- tectonics (geothermal energy)
- natural hazards
- vegetation changes
- human impacts.

The stratosphere is a layer of the atmosphere that extends from the troposphere (the lowest layer) to *c.* 50 km above the Earth's surface. The stratosphere is very dry and lacks clouds. The stratosphere contains the ozone layer, which absorbs some of the high energy UV radiation emitted by the Sun.

Physical processes

Physical processes include air movements and the greenhouse effect (this topic, Sections 6.1.4 and 6.1.5). Pressure differentials are the basic cause of air motion.

In addition to the pressure gradient force, winds (this topic, Section 6.1.1) and ocean currents are affected by the Coriolis force, which is a deflecting force caused by the Earth's rotation. The strength of the force increases with distance from the equator. It causes winds to be diverted to the right of their path in the Northern Hemisphere and to the left of their path in the Southern Hemisphere.

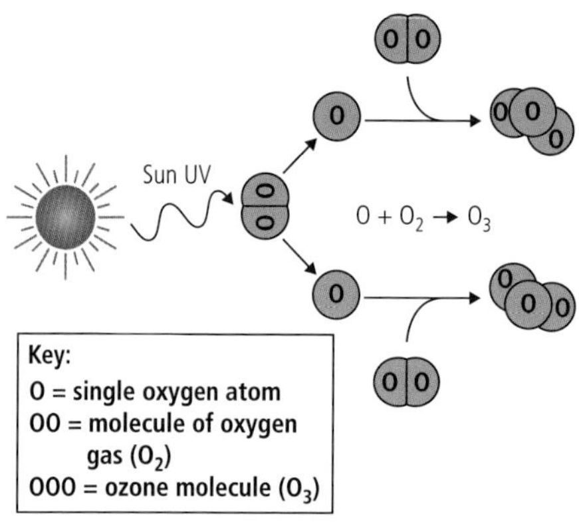

Figure 6.10 The formation of O_3 in the stratosphere.

Chemical processes

In the stratosphere, high-energy UV radiation strikes O_2 molecules and splits them into two single oxygen atoms. One of these freed oxygen atoms can then combine with an O_2 molecule to form a molecule of O_3 (Figure 6.10). This is also known as the ozone-oxygen cycle. Stratospheric ozone absorbs some of the high energy UV radiation emitted by the Sun.

HL

6.1.6 Atmosphere and altitude

Molecules in the atmosphere are pulled towards the Earth's surface by gravity. Because gravitational force is inversely proportional to distance, i.e. as distance increases gravitational force decreases, the atmosphere becomes thinner with distance from the Earth's surface (Figure 6.11).

Figure 6.11 Mountain climbers require O_2 tanks at high altitude due to the thinning of the atmosphere.

Air motion is dependent on pressure systems. In areas of high pressure, air is generally descending, whereas in low pressure systems, rising air cools as it expands and increases the vertical temperature gradient.

The overall vertical change in temperature over time is known as the **lapse rate**. The average lapse rate for the Earth is 6.5 °C per km (slightly less than 1 °C for about every 100 m). However, lapse rates vary with the level of moisture present in the air. The temperature of dry air may decrease at a rate of 10 °C per km, whereas saturated air may decrease more slowly at rates of between 4 °C and 9 °C per km. Winter rates are generally lower, and in continental areas may even be negative, caused by excessive cooling over snow surfaces.

HL

6.1.7 Milankovitch cycles

Milankovitch cycles affect how much solar radiation reaches the Earth and lead to cycles in the Earth's climate that last between tens and hundreds of thousands of years.

There are three types of Milankovitch cycles, relating to the shape of Earth's orbit, angle of tilt, and axis of rotation.

Milankovitch cycles are very long cycles in the Earth's orbit around the Sun, the tilt of its axis and the *wobble* of the Earth in space. They do not account for the more recent changes associated with global warming.

Milankovitch cycles can lead to positive feedback changes (Topic 1, Section 1.2.10) such as decreasing concentrations of atmospheric carbon dioxide with cooling and glaciations, or increasing concentrations of atmospheric carbon dioxide with warming and interglacial conditions.

1.2 Systems

The 96,000-year stretch

The Earth's orbit around the Sun varies from being more circular to more elliptical over a cycle of about 96,000 years (Figure 6.12a).

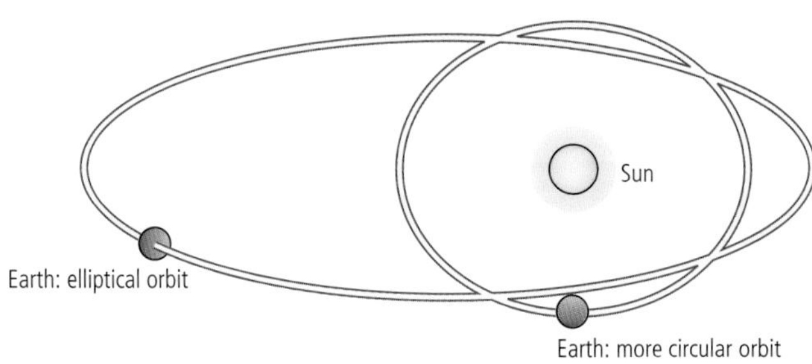

Figure 6.12a The 96,000-year stretch.

Glacials are phases in the Earth's climate when glaciers and ice caps increase in extent. During the last glacial phase, glaciers and ice caps covered 30% of the Earth's surface, now they cover 10%.

Interglacials are warm phases during an ice age when ice covers less of the Earth's surface. As ice currently covers only about 10% of the Earth's surface, we are in an interglacial phase.

The 42,000-year tilt

The Earth's axis is currently tilted at 23.5°, so the Tropics of Cancer and Capricorn are found at 23.5° N and S, respectively. However, the tilt can vary between 21.5° and 24.5° (Figure 6.12b). When the tilt increases, summers become hotter and winters are colder, favouring interglacials (warm phases).

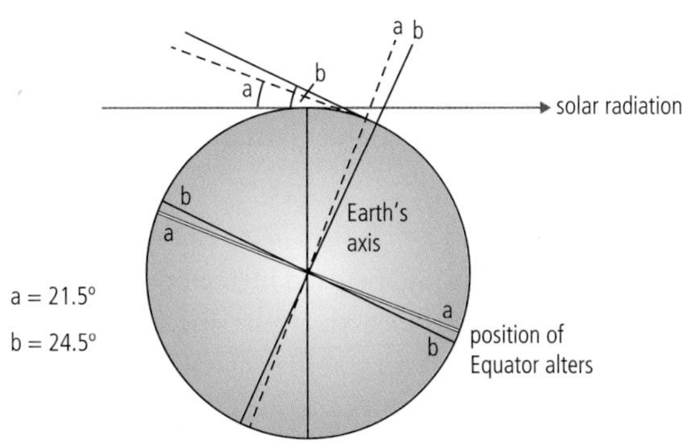

Figure 6.12b The 42,000-year tilt.

Lines of latitude are parallel lines indicating how far north or south of the equator a place is.

The Tropic of Cancer is a line of latitude located at 23.5° north of the equator.

The Tropic of Capricorn is a line of latitude located at 23.5° south of the equator.

The 21,000-year wobble

As the Earth slowly wobbles in space, its axis moves in the shape of a circle every 21,000 years. At present, the orbit makes the Earth closest to the Sun in the Northern Hemisphere's winter and furthest away in summer (Figure 6.12c). These conditions favour the growth of glaciers. In contrast, when the Earth is closest to the Sun during the Northern Hemisphere summer and furthest away during the winter, conditions are warmer. This helps explain, in part, the present warm interglacial that the Earth is experiencing.

Figure 6.12c The 21,000-year wobble.

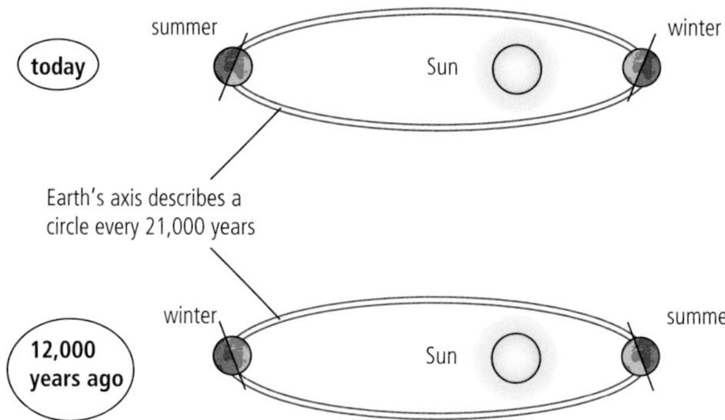

The greenhouse effect is misunderstood by many people. It is a natural process which is vital for life on Earth. In contrast, the enhanced greenhouse effect has a negative impact and can lead to global warming.

HL

3.1 Biodiversity and evolution

The Anthropocene is the period of time during which human activities have impacted the natural environment to such an extent as to form a new geological era.

Figure 6.13 The Earth may have experienced many episodes of *Hothouse Earth* in the past.

What are the roles and limitations of models in the acquisition of knowledge?

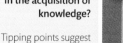

Tipping points suggest changes which are irreversible e.g. melting of Arctic permafrost.

However, how do we know how much CO_2 and CH_4 will be released, and therefore, how can we predict future changes?

6.1.8 Hothouse Earth

Albedo refers to the reflectivity of a surface. Light-coloured materials, such as snow and ice, are highly reflective and have a high albedo, sometimes 75–90%. Dark wet soil has an albedo of 5–15% and so may absorb much of the incoming solar radiation. The ice-albedo feedback is a positive feedback mechanism whereby a decrease in temperature may lead to an increase in the area covered by light-coloured materials and so increase the albedo. This means it reflects more of the incoming solar radiation and so the area gets cooler. This can be very important for regional, and global, climate change. On the other hand, if warming occurs, snow- and ice-cover could be reduced, meaning light-coloured surfaces would be replaced with the darker surfaces of bare ground and soil. The albedo would decrease, and more solar energy would be absorbed, leading to further increases in warming.

The Quaternary period is the geological era that started about 2.58 million years ago. Climate change has occurred naturally during the Quaternary, but the recent anthropogenic (human-induced) changes have occurred more rapidly than any natural changes that have happened.

In a report entitled *Trajectories of the Earth System in the Anthropocene*, Steffen et al. (2018)[1] argue that the term *global heating* should be used instead of global warming. The report states that there is a risk that the Earth is entering a new climate phase – called *Hothouse Earth* – in which the climate will stabilize at a much higher temperature than desired by scientists (Figure 6.13). It suggests, as does the UK Met Office, that temperatures could be as much as 4–5 °C higher than pre-industrial levels (since *c.* 1800) and warns that sea levels could be up to 1 m higher than today. This would be much greater than anything over the last 1.2 million years. Such a change may be considered part of the new geological era known as the Anthropocene (Topic 3, Section 3.1.18), in which human activities play a major part in physical processes on Earth (Topic 3, Sections 3.1.18 and 3.1.19).

The Earth's climate may change so much that it will be taken out of the glacial–interglacial cycles that have characterized the Holocene. In the words of the report, the *Earth system has likely departed from the glacial–interglacial cycle of the Late Quaternary* and *it would take in the order of 100,000 years for conditions to return to their pre-perturbation levels.*

[1]Steffen, W., et al., 2018, Trajectories of the Earth System in the Anthropocene, *Earth, Atmospheric, and Planetary Sciences*, 115 (33) 8252–8259. https://doi.org/10.1073/pnas.1810141115

Activity

Figure 6.14 shows the difference in sea ice cover between 1979 and 2023.

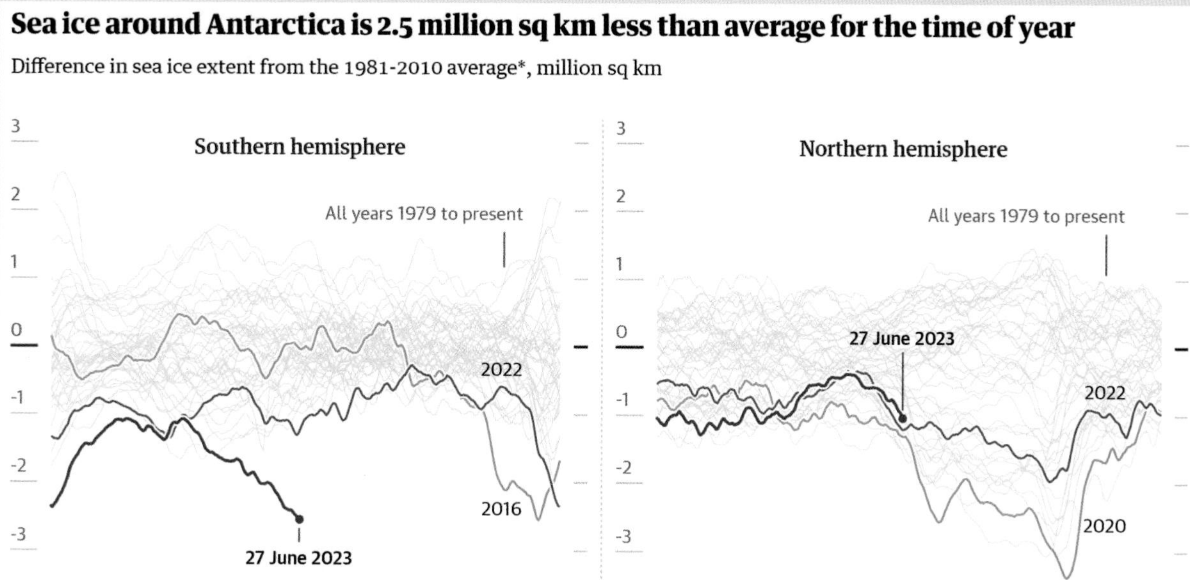

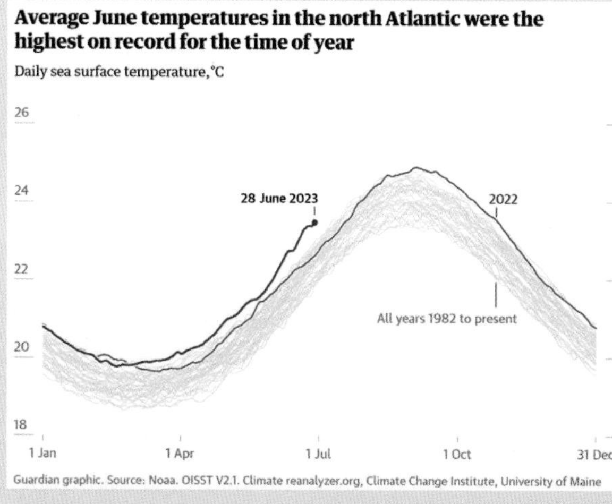

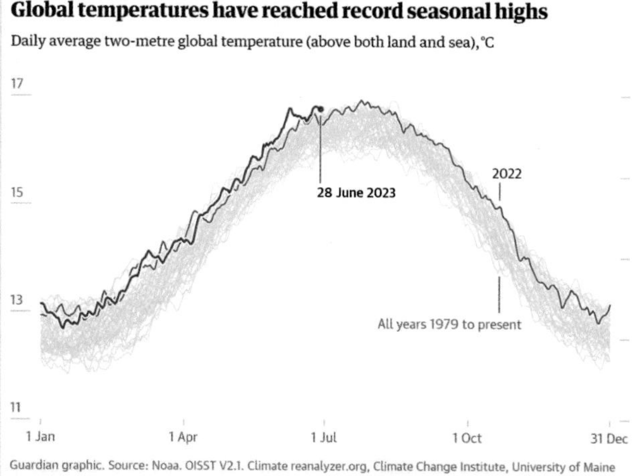

▲ **Figure 6.14** State of sea ice cover and temperature changes, 2023.

1. Draw two positive feedback diagrams to show the effect of:
   (a) warming in high-latitude areas and
   (b) cooling in high-latitude areas.
2. Study the diagrams of sea ice cover in Antarctica. Suggest how they relate to global temperatures.
3. Outline the relationship between sea ice cover in the Northern Hemisphere and average daily sea surface temperatures in the North Atlantic.

In wetlands, soil minerals are forced to metabolize under anaerobic conditions. This leads to CH_4 production. Warming causes wetland soils to warm and/or flood, releasing CH_4 into the atmosphere.

Flooding in rice fields cuts off the O_2 supply from the atmosphere to the soil, resulting in anaerobic fermentation of soil organic matter. CH_4 is the end product of anaerobic fermentation.

Tipping points

The Hothouse Earth report suggests that even an increase of just 2 °C could be enough to trigger a series of positive feedback mechanisms, called tipping points (Topic 1, Section 1.2.12 and Topic 2, Section 2.1.22), in places such as the Arctic and around Antarctica, which could throw the Earth out of stability. However, there are uncertainties about these suggestions. For example, increased atmospheric CO_2 has led to increased plant growth and therefore a greater carbon sink. On the other hand, rising temperatures make the plants' leaves hotter, which makes enzymes lose their quality (they are *denatured*), reducing photosynthesis. Furthermore, atmospheric warming raises soil temperatures, increasing microbial respiration and thereby releasing CO_2 back into the atmosphere. Increased temperatures will cause permafrost melting and the release of some CH_4 frozen within peat. However, the scientists do not agree on how much CO_2 and CH_4 will be released as this will depend partly on the size of the temperature increase. The Earth has entered very uncertain times (Systems (Topic 1, Sections 1.2.11–12), Ecology (Topic 2, Section 2.1.22) and Biodiversity (Topic 3, Sections 3.1.18–19)).

Investigate the impact of albedo or different GHGs on the temperature of a closed system

Find some small boxes and cover them with different coloured paper, including some light colours and some dark colours. Attach a maximum-minimum thermometer to each box and leave in an open area for 24 hours. At the end of that time, record the maximum and minimum temperature for each box. How do the maximum temperatures vary with colour? Is there any impact on minimum temperature? How do you explain the differences that you found?

Alternatively, find some plastic containers. Fill one with water, one with CO_2 (ask your teacher for help) and one with a liquid that is not a known greenhouse gas e.g. tea or coffee. Attach a maximum-minimum thermometer to each container and leave in an open area for 24 hours. At the end of that time, record the maximum and minimum temperature for each container. How do the maximum temperatures vary with colour? Is there any impact on minimum temperature? How do you explain the differences that you found?

3.1 Biodiversity and evolution

HL

6.1.9 Evolution of life and the development of the atmosphere

Although you need to know how the evolution of life changed the atmosphere, you do not need to remember the timings of oxygenation.

The evolution of life has changed the Earth's atmosphere. The Earth's first atmosphere was formed by emissions of gases trapped in the Earth's interior. This still occurs today in volcanic eruptions but on a much smaller scale. The earliest atmosphere developed about 3.5–4 billion years ago. It was almost certainly developed as the Earth's interior melted to form a core, mantle and crust. This early atmosphere probably had large amounts of N_2, CO_2, CH_4 and ammonia (NH_3), but virtually no O_2. The earliest O_2 was released by geological and biological processes. For example, prokaryotic organisms produced O_2 as a by-product of photosynthesis.

When the mineral olivine comes in contact with water, it starts chemical reactions that can use and lock up O_2. However, as the Earth's continental crust evolved into one similar to that of today, olivine virtually disappeared. Without olivine to react with water, O_2 was allowed to accumulate, first in the oceans and then in the atmosphere.

Iron ore formation began about 1.8 million years ago when iron was dissolved in seawater. Photosynthetic organisms take in CO_2 and produce O_2. However, initially this O_2 did not build up in the atmosphere but instead was taken up in rocks as a result of chemical reactions. As these organisms evolved, the CO_2 content of the atmosphere reduced and increasing amounts of O_2 were released into seawater where it combined with dissolved iron to form iron oxides, such as hematite and magnetite, in **banded iron formations** and **continental red beds**. Indeed, most of the O_2 produced over geological time is trapped inside rocks.

The composition of the present atmosphere needed the formation of O_2. The atmosphere was marked by a decrease in atmospheric CO_2 and an increase in O_2 due to life processes. There are two basic processes that produce O_2 gas in abundance:

- the breakdown of water (H_2O) into hydrogen gas (H_2) and O_2 in the presence of UV radiation
- plant photosynthesis using solar energy, CO_2 and H_2O to produce carbohydrates and O_2 as a by-product.

Photosynthesis led to high O_2 levels in the current atmosphere. As levels of O_2 increased in the atmosphere, organisms evolved to use O_2 in aerobic respiration: this change allowed the evolution of very complex, multicellular lifeforms. For example, once O_2 built up to 1–2% of its present levels, photosynthetic prokaryotes (single-celled organisms without a nucleus) were replaced by more efficient eukaryotes (organisms whose cells had a nucleus). Once efficient photosynthetic organisms evolved, they had a major impact on the atmosphere, reducing CO_2 levels and further increasing the amount of O_2 available.

The release of O_2 by cyanobacteria was responsible for changes in the Earth's atmosphere and for evolution. Cells that could access O_2 had a notable metabolic benefit. Most life on Earth needs O_2 to produce usable chemical energy in the cell, necessary for growth and reproduction. As O_2 levels increased, the evolution of life progressed.

Exercise

Q1. **Identify** the two lowest layers of the atmosphere and **state** the altitudes at which they occur.

Q2. **Describe** the relationship between latitude and seasonality of insolation.

Q3. **Distinguish between** the natural greenhouse effect and the enhanced (anthropogenic) greenhouse effect.

Q4. **Identify** the greenhouse gas that has the greatest global warming potential.

Q5. **Explain** how air movements are affected by:

(a) the pressure gradient

(b) the Coriolis force.

Q6. **Describe** the changes in radiative forcing between 1979 and 2022.

Q7. **Outline** the state of the sea ice around Antarctica and **explain** the changes that have occurred.

Q8. HL **Identify** the three Milankovitch cycles and **state** what they cause.

Q9. HL **Explain** the meaning of the term *Hothouse Earth*.

Q10. HL Briefly **explain** how, and why, the Earth's early atmosphere differed from the present atmosphere.

Engagement

- Citizen science (Topic 1, Section 1.3.16) and voluntary agencies offer opportunities for you to participate in gathering knowledge of the atmosphere and the impacts of air pollution. You could find out from your local government what the state of air pollution is in your home region and how it is being managed.

6.2 Climate change – causes and impacts

Guiding questions

To what extent has climate change occurred due to anthropogenic causes?
How do differing perspectives play a role in responding to the challenges of climate change?

6.2.1 Climate describes the typical conditions that result from physical processes in the atmosphere.
6.2.2 Anthropogenic carbon dioxide emissions have caused concentrations of atmospheric carbon dioxide to rise significantly. The global rate of emission has accelerated, particularly since 1950.
6.2.3 Analysis of ice cores, tree rings and deposited sediments provide data that indicates a positive correlation between the concentration of carbon dioxide in the atmosphere and global temperatures.
6.2.4 The greenhouse effect has been enhanced by anthropogenic emissions of greenhouse gases. This has led to global warming and, therefore, climate change.
6.2.5 Climate change impacts ecosystems at a variety of scales, from local to global and affects the resilience of ecosystems and leads to biome shifts.
6.2.6 Climate change has an impact on (human) societies at a variety of scales and socioeconomic conditions. This impacts the resilience of societies.
6.2.7 Systems diagrams and models can be used to represent cause and effect of climate change with feedback loops, either positive or negative, and changes in the global energy balance.
6.2.8 Evidence suggests that the Earth has already passed the planetary boundary for climate change.
6.2.9 Perspectives on climate change for both individuals and societies are influenced by many factors.
HL 6.2.10 Data collected over time by weather stations, observatories, radar and satellites provides opportunity for the study of climate change and land-use change. Long-term data sets include the recording of temperature and greenhouse gas concentrations. Measurements can be both indirect (proxies) and direct. Indirect measurements include isotope measurements taken from ice cores, dendrochronology and pollen taken from peat cores.
HL 6.2.11 Global climate models manipulate inputs to climate systems to predict possible outputs or outcomes using equations to represent the processes and interactions that drive the Earth's climate. The validity of the models can be tested via a process known as hindcasting.
HL 6.2.12 Climate models use different scenarios to predict possible impacts of climate change.
HL 6.2.13 Climate models show the Earth may approach a critical threshold with changes to a new equilibrium. Local systems also have thresholds or tipping points.
HL 6.2.14 Individual tipping points of the climate system may interact to create tipping cascades.

HL 6.2.15 Countries vary in their responsibility for climate change and also in vulnerability, with the least responsible often being the most vulnerable. There are political and economic implications and issues of equity.

6.2.1 Climate

2.4 Climate and biomes

The main factors impacting climate in an area are seasonal variations in temperature and precipitation (Figure 6.15). *Weather* is the specific conditions being experienced at a particular time or over a short period, including temperature, humidity, air pressure and wind speed (Topic 2, Section 2.4.7).

Figure 6.15 Changes in vegetation in a deciduous woodland caused by seasonal changes in temperature and precipitation.

The term *climate* refers to the state of the atmosphere over a period of 30 years or longer. It includes variables such as temperature, rainfall, winds, humidity, cloud cover and pressure. This is the total experience of weather at a place over a specific length of time and refers not just to the averages of these variables but also to the extremes. The data obtained over a period of 30 years are considered adequate, so many climate statistics are based on the periods 1931–60 or 1961–90. However, there are a number of arguments against using a 30-year set of data. For example:

- the database may be too short
- the years 1931–60 and 1961–90 may not be representative
- it is impossible to create a 50-year maximum or a 100-year event using only 30 years of records.

Climate is the typical conditions that result from physical processes in the atmosphere.

In contrast to climate, weather refers to the state of the atmosphere at any particular moment in time. However, we usually look at the weather over a period of between a few days and a week.

Using climate data

The use of climate data has some weaknesses. For example, planners have extensively used the assumption of climatic consistency. This assumes that using 30 years of statistics is sufficient to provide data for modelling any future climate. But now we know that climates change, so 30 years of records from a cold or wet period will not provide much guidance as the climate warms or dries.

To what extent is certainty attainable?

Climate is defined as the average and extreme of weather over a period of not less than thirty years. Climate graphs show us that annual weather patterns have been changing since the 1880s, so how can we describe the climate of a place with any certainty?

Evidence from the early 20th century shows a gradual warming until the 1950s, then a gradual cooling, followed by an intensification of warming accompanied by extreme events. For example, the years 1931–60 were among the warmest and wettest years of the 20th century until 1960. However, extreme events were less common. Winters in Europe were generally quite warm and annual variability of temperature decreased over this period. Rainfall increased in drier areas and the monsoon became more regular. So, even in this period of less obvious climate change, the climate was changing.

6.2.2 Anthropogenic CO_2 emissions

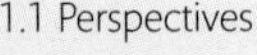

1.1 Perspectives

Anthropogenic emissions have caused atmospheric CO_2 concentrations to rise significantly. The global rate of emissions has accelerated, particularly since 1950. Increases can be traced back to the start of the Industrial Revolution in late 18th-century Europe, with the main acceleration occurring through the 20th century due to the spread of industrialization and human population increase.

In the pre-industrial era, levels of atmospheric CO_2 were around 280 ppm (Figure 6.16) and were fairly constant for about 6000 years. By the late 1950s, atmospheric CO_2 had risen to around 315–316 ppm. However, by the 2020s, atmospheric CO_2 had reached 420 ppm, an increase of 50% compared with the pre-industrial levels.

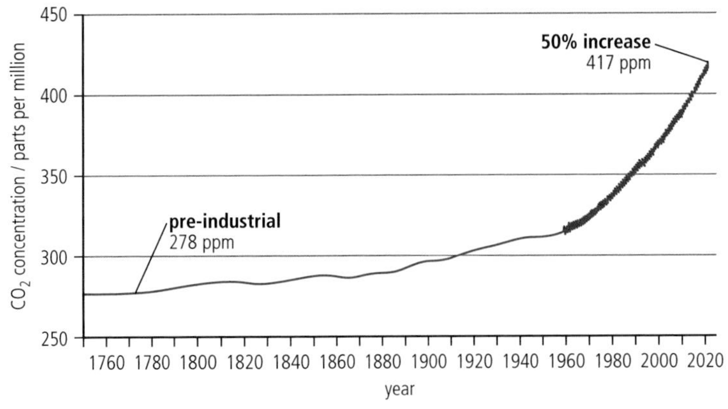

Figure 6.16 CO_2 levels 1750–2020s.

The Keeling Curve was developed by Charles (Dave) Keeling in 1953. The levels of CO_2 in the atmosphere at that time were *c.* 310 ppm.

6.2.3 Ice cores, tree rings and deposited sediments

Analysis of ice cores, tree rings and deposited sediments provides data that indicate a positive correlation between the concentration of CO_2 in the atmosphere and global temperatures (Figure 6.17).

Every year, billions of tonnes of dead organisms, dust and sediment settle to the ocean floor on top of sediment from previous years. About 55 million years ago, a huge amount of CO_2 entered the atmosphere over a period of about 1000 years, causing the temperature to rise steeply. Although the cause for this is unknown, the quantity is thought to be similar to the amount that humans will put into the atmosphere over the next century.

Cores from Antarctica and Greenland show an 800,000-year record of CO_2, CH_4 and temperature. The ice cores contain tiny bubbles from ancient atmospheres that contain CO_2, enabling scientists to show how temperature has varied over time.

- CO_2 and CH_4 levels are higher today than for the previous 800,000 years.
- There are strong correlations between CO_2, CH_4 and temperature over the last 800,000 years.
- The long-term cyclical changes in temperature, CH_4 and CO_2 are consistent with Milankovitch cycles over the last 800,000 years.

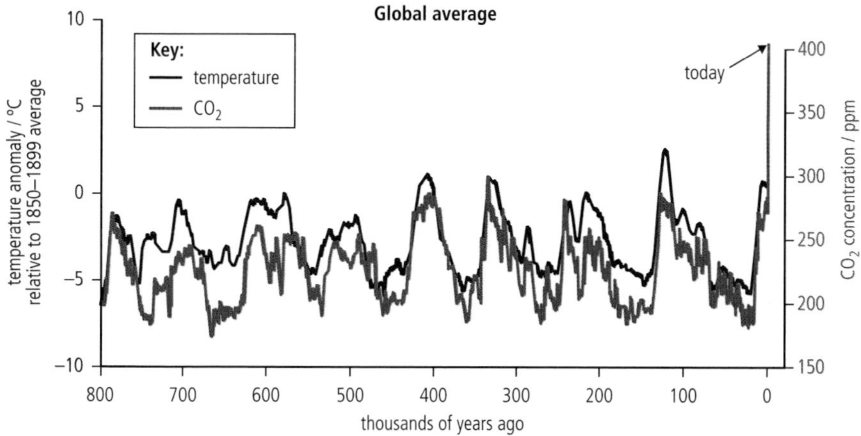

Figure 6.17 Global average CO_2 and temperature changes over the last 800,000 years.

Studies of cores taken from ice packs in Antarctica and Greenland show that the concentration of CO_2 remained stable at about 270 ppm from around 10,000 years ago until the mid-19th century. By 1957, the concentration of CO_2 in the atmosphere was 315 ppm and it has since risen to about 400 ppm in 2014. Most of the extra CO_2 has come from burning fossil fuels, especially coal, although some of the increase may be due to the deforestation of the rainforests. Much of the evidence for the greenhouse effect comes from ice cores dating back 160,000 years. These show that the Earth's temperature closely parallels the amounts of CO_2 and CH_4 in the atmosphere. For every 1 tonne of carbon burned, 4 tonnes of CO_2 are released. By the early 1980s, 5 gigatonnes (Gt) of fuel were burned every year. Roughly half the CO_2 produced is absorbed by natural sinks, such as vegetation and plankton.

1 Gt is 1000 million tonnes.

Climate has always changed, year by year, decade by decade and over longer terms involving glacials and interglacials. However, the recent changes in atmospheric CO_2 have led to levels unprecedented in hundreds of thousands of years.

The ice cores show a very strong correlation between temperature and greenhouse gas levels through the ice age cycles. In previous warm periods, it was not changes in greenhouse gases that caused the temperature to change but small and predictable *wobbles* in the Earth's rotation around the Sun. Although these changes were small, CO_2 amplified their effects.

For example, as the Earth began to cool, more CO_2 dissolved into the oceans, reducing the greenhouse effects and causing increased cooling. As the planet warmed, the water from the oceans evaporated and CO_2 was released from the oceans to the atmosphere, causing more warming to occur. At present, human activities are adding huge amounts of CO_2 to the atmosphere, rapidly. At the end of cold, glacial phases, CO_2 levels increased by about 35 ppm over 1000 years. Humans have emitted the same amount of CO_2 in just 17 years.

Before the Industrial Revolution, atmospheric CO_2 was about 280 ppm. During the ice ages, CO_2 levels were about 180 ppm. In 2023, atmospheric CO_2 was about 417 ppm. At the current rates of CO_2 increase, temperatures at the end of the 21st century could be more than 4 °C higher than pre-industrial levels.

Tree rings, CO_2 and climate change

Tree rings (Figure 6.18) have been used to reconstruct past climates. Wide rings indicate good growth from warmer, wetter years, whereas narrower rings indicate limited growth due to drought and/or colder temperatures. Tree rings can also be used to assess the effects of recent climate change on tree growth.

A number of tree-ring studies from temperature-sensitive species suggest recent warming. Tree-ring evidence exists for warming in Alaska, the Urals, the Arctic and Mongolia, of between 0.5 °C and 1.0 °C since 1900. Some of the evidence is contradictory. For example, a 1000-year-long tree-ring temperature record from Siberia shows recent warming compared to the long-term trend, whereas a millennium-long record from Fennoscandia suggests that it was warmer in the Medieval warm period compared with today. Some studies in the USA found unusual growth of bristlecone and lumber pines in the 20th century. However, this could be due to less CO_2 being available to higher-elevation plants than to plants at lower elevations.

Deposited sediments may also indicate changing climates. Pollen from oak and cedar has been found in parts of the Sahara, indicating that the area was once much more moist. Former lake terraces indicate that some areas were also much wetter, while fossil sand dunes indicate areas that were drier but now contain vegetation. Analysis of carbon and oxygen isotopes in the shells of microorganisms from sediment cores retrieved from the ocean floor also provides details of climate change.

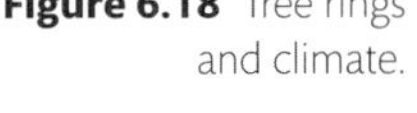

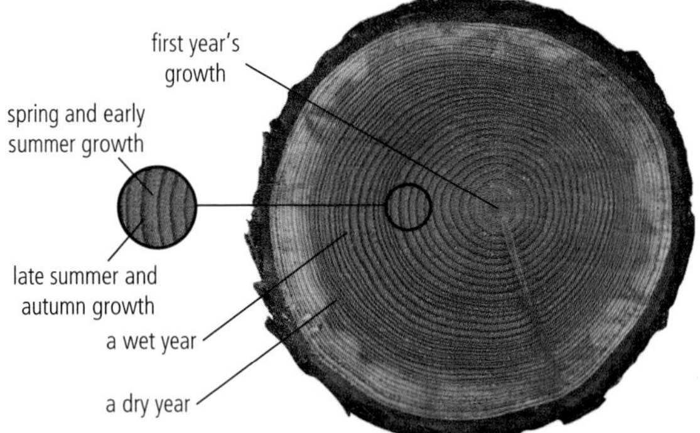

Figure 6.18 Tree rings and climate.

SKILLS

Investigate graphs of data for the past 800,000 years and show how these variables have changed during the glacial cycles

Using a search engine, find examples of graphs that show changes in temperature and CO_2 over the last 800,000 years.

Figure 6.17 is one such graph. Annotate the graph to show when there were

(a) highs of temperature (b) lows of temperature (c) highs of CO_2 and (d) lows of CO_2.
Are there any correlations between highs of temperature and CO_2 and between lows of temperature and CO_2?

Estimate the length of time between the highs and between the lows. Is there any evidence of cycles on the scale that Milankovitch suggested?

6.2.4 The enhanced greenhouse effect

2.3 Biogeochemical cycles

The concern about global warming is the build-up of greenhouse gases (Figure 6.19). These vary in their concentration, rate of increase, lifetime and global warming potential. CO_2 levels have risen from about 315 ppm in 1950 to about 420 ppm currently. The high estimate is that they could reach 500 ppm by 2030. The increase in CO_2 levels is largely due to human activities such as the burning of fossil fuels, including coal, oil and natural gas, and the deforestation of rainforests. The burning of fossil fuels releases CO_2 into the atmosphere. Deforestation removes the trees that would otherwise be able to reduce CO_2 levels by converting CO_2 to O_2 during the process of photosynthesis.

Parts per million (ppm) and parts per billion (ppb) tell us how many units of a substance e.g. CO_2 there are, for every million (or billion) units of atmosphere.

CH_4 is the second largest contributor to global warming and levels in the atmosphere are increasing at a rate of 0.6–0.75% per annum (Table 6.1). It is estimated that cattle convert up to 10% of the food they eat into CH_4 and emit 100 million tonnes of CH_4 into the atmosphere each year. Natural wetland and paddy fields are two other important sources, with paddy fields alone emitting up to 150 million tonnes of CH_4 annually. As air temperatures increase, bogs trapped in permafrost will melt and release vast quantities of CH_4.

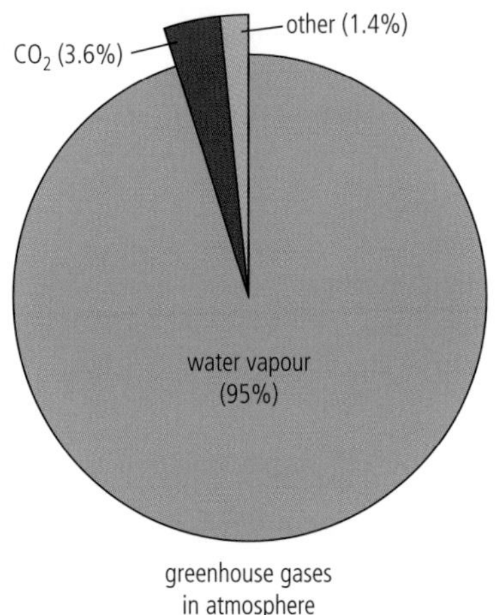

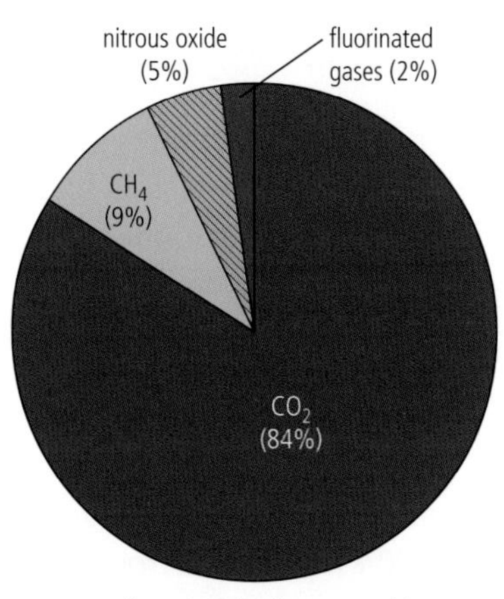

Figure 6.19 Sources of greenhouse gases – natural and anthropogenic.

Water vapour is the most significant greenhouse gas by volume. However, it is generally excluded from climate models as its abundance varies with global warming. It cannot be mitigated against since it is essential for life.

Table 6.1 Properties of key greenhouse gases.

Greenhouse gas	Pre-industrial level	Average atmospheric concentration (2018)	Rate of change per annum (%)	Direct global warming potential	Lifetime (years)
CO_2	278 ppmv	407 ppmv (> 45% increase)	0.5	1	120
CH_4	700 ppbv	1859 ppbv (250% increase)	0.6–0.75	96	12.4
N_2O	275 ppbv	331 ppbv (> 20% increase)	0.2–0.3	264	121
CFCs	Not naturally occurring	508 ppbv	4	508	100

The natural greenhouse effect has been intensified by anthropogenic emissions of greenhouse gases. This has led to global warming and climate change. The quantity of greenhouse gases emitted by any individual country depends on its economy, level

Global warming is the long-term heating of the Earth's surface since pre-industrial times (1850–1900) due to human activities, especially the burning of fossil fuels.

of development and societal expectations. Figure 6.20 shows that greenhouse gas emissions in the USA are dominated by CO_2.

This reflects the high energy demands of the USA. Transport, a lifestyle with expectations of air-conditioning, and other high-level energy demands at home and work, all lead to the high fuel economy seen there. On the other hand, emissions such as CH_4 are relatively lower, due to an absence of rice growing, again reflecting the culture and environment of the USA.

ppbv = parts per billion per volume in the atmosphere

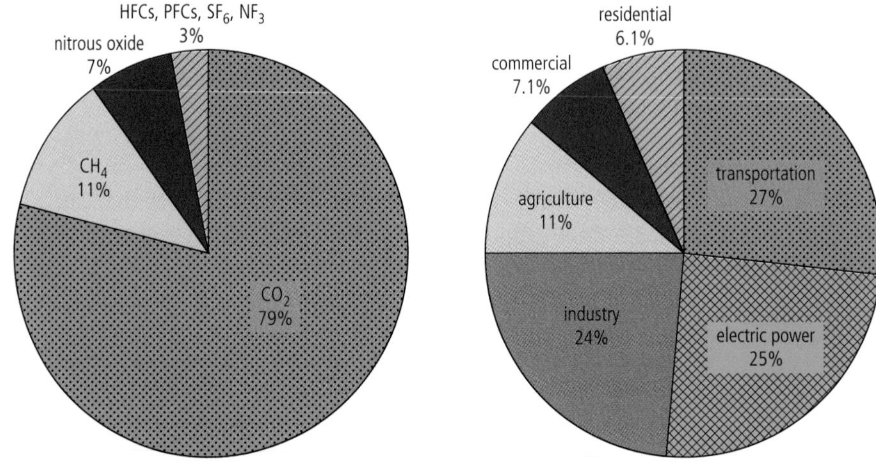

Figure 6.20 Greenhouse emissions in the USA, 2020, by gas and sector.

Annual global production of greenhouse gases (in carbon equivalent) is approximately 55 billion tonnes, of which 35 billion tonnes CO_2 is produced by the burning of fossil fuels. Some 3.5 billion tonnes comes from land-use changes, such as deforestation and clearing land for pasture.

Do not confuse nitrous oxide (N_2O) with nitrogen oxides (NOx). N_2O is not classified as NOx. Nitrous oxide is a direct greenhouse gas, whereas NOx are 'indirect' greenhouse gases. Nitrogen oxides are involved in urban air pollution (Section 8.3.1)

In the 18th century, global carbon emissions were about 3–7 million tonnes per year. By the early 19th century, these had risen to over 50 million tonnes per year. In the 2020s, this value is in the region of 8000 million tonnes per year.

Estimates of CH_4 emissions suggest a value of about 570 million tonnes per year. Of this, 40% is produced from natural sources such as peat bogs and 60% is from anthropogenic emissions (Figure 6.21).

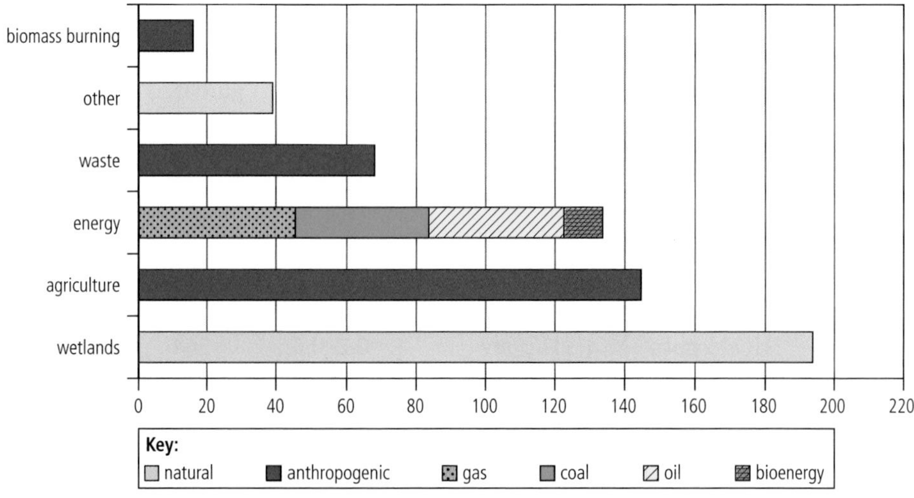

Figure 6.21 Global annual CH_4 emissions (million tonnes).

In addition, there are around 17 million metric tonnes of N_2O emitted each year, 40% of which is related to human activities. Emissions of other greenhouse gases are much lower.

6.2.5 Climate change impacts on ecosystems

1.2 Systems
2.2 Energy and biomass in ecosystems
2.4 Climate and biomes

The potential impacts of climate change may vary from one location to another and may be perceived as either adverse or beneficial (Table 6.2). These impacts may include:

- changes in water availability
- distribution of biomes (a naturally occurring community of plants and animals e.g. savannah, tropical rainforest) and crop-growing areas
- loss of biodiversity and ecosystem services
- coastal flooding and sea level rise
- ocean acidification (a reduction in the pH of seawater) (Topic 4, Section 4.1.9)
- damage to human health.

Environmental feature	Effect or impact
ice and snow	melting of polar ice caps and glaciers
coastlines	increase in sea level causing coastal flooding
water cycle	increased flooding and more rapid circulation
ecosystems	change in biome distribution and species composition (e.g. poleward and altitudinal migration)

Table 6.2 The impact of temperature increase on aspects of the environment.

Biome shifting

Climate change may cause biomes to move with changes in global temperature in the future (Topic 2, Section 2.4.7).

During the most recent globally warm period, 50–60 million years ago, the Arctic was free of ice and subtropical forests extended northwards to Greenland. During the **Pleistocene glaciations** (18,000 years ago) these areas were covered by ice sheets. During the last 18,000 years, temperatures have increased, and tundra and temperate forest biomes have shifted north. With further increases, all biomes are likely to move further towards the poles, with the probable disappearance of tundra and boreal forests.

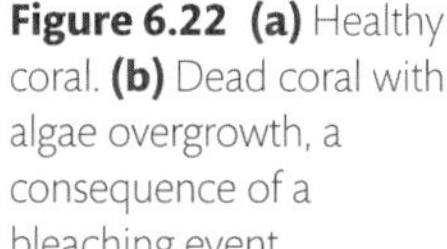

Figure 6.22 **(a)** Healthy coral. **(b)** Dead coral with algae overgrowth, a consequence of a bleaching event.

The effects of global warming

Coral bleaching

Coral bleaching is an example of a local impact, although it is becoming an increasing threat to many of the world's coral reefs (Figure 6.22). Corals become bleached when the symbiotic algae that they support are lost. The algae can re-enter the coral if conditions improve and the bleached reefs have recovered. However, if the algae are absent for prolonged periods, the coral dies. The extent of bleaching varies with depth – the shallower the water, the worse the bleaching. There are believed to be a number of factors that can lead to coral bleaching, including:

- stress brought on by unusually warm water
- changes in salinity
- excessive exposure to UV radiation
- extreme climate change.

Most coral thrive at temperatures between 25 °C and 29 °C and the algae may die at temperatures above 29 °C.

Figure 6.23 Desertification.

Desertification

Desertification is the spread of desert-like conditions in semi-arid and humid areas due to human impact, including climate change (Figure 6.23). It is generally a local impact, although it is affecting many parts of the world. Determining the cause of desertification can be difficult as it may be short-term drought periods of high magnitude or long-term climate change towards aridity.

Desertification can occur via anthropogenic climate change, or it may be due to ecosystem degradation in dry and semi-arid environments. More often it is caused by a combination of human activities and a series of dry years. Reduction of vegetation cover due to overgrazing, overcultivation and fuelwood collection leads to wind and water erosion, both of which reduce the ability of the land to support an ever-increasing number of people.

Ocean circulation

Climate change is having a global impact on ocean circulation. The two main types of ocean current are surface currents and vertical currents. Surface currents mainly occur as a result of wind pushing on the surface of the water. Vertical currents are created by differences in the density of water, as denser water sinks and less dense water rises.

The vertical circulation is known as the thermohaline circulation and is caused by differences in temperature and salinity. Thermohaline circulation (Topic 4, Section 4.1.14) moves warm surface water from the equator towards the poles, where the water becomes colder and denser, and therefore sinks. As the world warms due to increased levels of greenhouse gases in the atmosphere, changes in ocean and atmospheric circulation will affect regional climates and ecosystems around the world. For example, the Gulf Stream and the North Atlantic Drift bring heat from the Gulf of Mexico towards north-west Europe, making it much warmer than other areas at similar latitudes. However, some scientists predict that this current may become weaker due to increased melting of ice from Greenland and Iceland flowing into the North Atlantic and keeping the North Atlantic Drift much further south. If this were to happen, the regional climate of north-west Europe could become much colder, despite global warming.

Sea level rise

Climate change is also having a global impact on sea level rise (Figure 6.24).

Figure 6.24 Global mean sea level rise, 1993–2015.

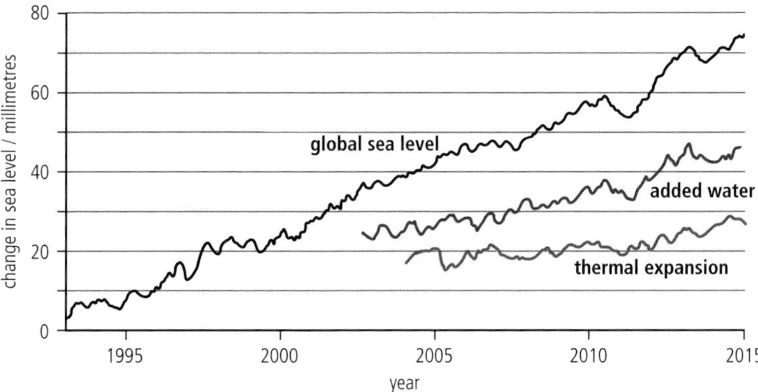

The sea level changes every day and month between low tide and high tide, and between spring low tide and spring high tide. How do we measure sea level changes if it is always changing?

Figure 6.25 shows relative changes in global average temperature, CO_2 levels and sea level over the last 420,000 years. It shows four major glacial advances on a cycle of about 100,000 years. The last glacial peak was around 20,000 years ago. At that time, the sea level was around 120 m below the present level. In contrast, sea levels were about 8 m higher during the previous interglacial (warm phase), around 120,000 years ago, than they are today. The present warming is taking place much more quickly compared with natural climate change in the past. Figure 6.25 shows a clear correlation between CO_2 and temperature. Global CO_2 levels are now around 400 ppm. The last time they were at this level was about 55 million years ago, when there were no polar ice sheets, and the sea level was about 75 m higher than it is today.

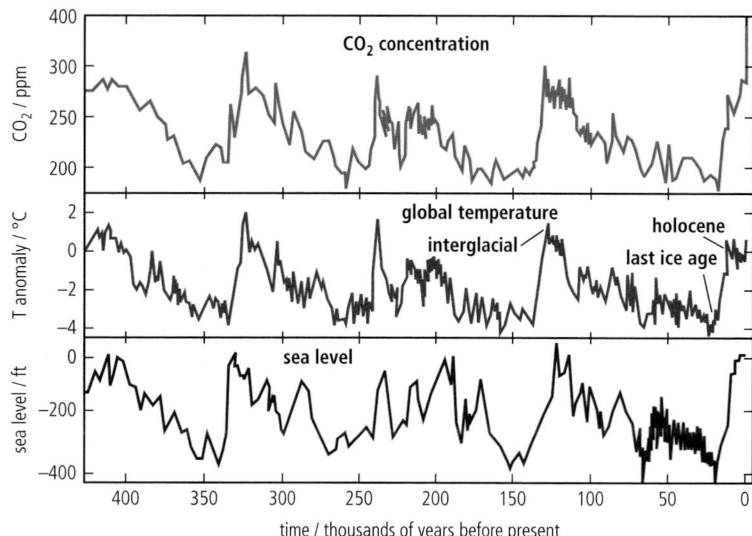

Figure 6.25 Long-term changes in CO_2 level, global temperature and sea level.

Sea levels rise due to an increased amount of water in oceans and due to the expansion of seawater as it becomes warmer (the *steric effect*). Much of the extra water in the oceans is due to human activities that have contributed to global warming, causing glaciers and ice sheets to melt.

However, there are other factors that cause sea levels to rise and fall, although these occur on a very long-term scale. These include tectonic activity causing land to be uplifted or sink. Glaciations can depress the land deeper into the mantle, which causes the land to sink relative to the oceans. When the ice melts, the weight pushing down the continental crust is released, and the continent may begin to rise through isostatic rebound or recovery.

Other long-term changes may include changes in the Earth's spin, tilt and orbit around the Sun and the movement of tectonic plates causing continents to collide and to form new mountain ranges and volcanic islands.

Human activities may also cause land to subside. For example, in Los Angeles the pumping of groundwater, oil and gas has caused subsidence and damaged many buildings and much of the city's infrastructure. Shanghai is built on marshy soil and is believed to be sinking by 2–4 cm/year due to the weight of many tall skyscrapers on the soft ground material.

Resilience

The resilience of a system is the ability to endure and recover from disturbance (Topic 1, Section 1.2.16).

Diversity, species richness and the size of storages within systems can contribute to their resilience and affect the speed of response to change. Large storages, or high diversity/species richness, will mean that a system is less likely to reach a tipping point and move to a new equilibrium. Humans can affect the resilience of systems through reducing these storages and diversity.

Tropical rainforests, for example, have high diversity as there are large numbers and proportions of species present. However, catastrophic disturbance through logging (i.e. rapid removal of tree biomass storages) or fires can lower resilience and can mean the rainforest takes a long time to recover.

Natural grasslands, in contrast, have low diversity but are very resilient. This is because a lot of nutrients are stored below ground in root systems, so after fires the grasslands can recover quickly.

Complex ecosystems such as rainforests have complex food webs that provide animals and plants with many different ways to respond to disturbance of the ecosystem and therefore maintain stability. Rainforests also contain long-lived species and dormant seeds and seedlings that promote steady-state equilibrium. Rainforests have thin, low-nutrient soils and although storage of biomass in trees is high, nutrient storage in soils is low. Nutrients are locked up in decomposing plant matter on the surface and in rapidly growing plants within the forest. This means that when the forest is disturbed, nutrients are quickly lost. For example, leaf layer and topsoil can be washed away, along with the nutrients they contain. Ecosystems with higher resilience have nutrient-rich soils, which can promote new growth.

Example – Impact of temperature change on a specific ecosystem: global climate change and deciduous forests in England

The south of England is predicted to have an increase in winter rainfall of 10–20% and a reduction in summer rainfall of 10–20% by 2050. Summer and winter mean temperatures are predicted to rise by 2–3 °C by 2050.

What are the implications of this for deciduous forests and how can they be managed?

Southern, central and eastern England will have drier, warmer summers, resulting in severe moisture deficits that will reduce forest growth. Drought-tolerant species such as oak and ash will need to be introduced on sites vulnerable to drought. Warmer growing seasons and rising CO_2 levels will stimulate productivity where soil water and nutrients are plentiful. The increase and severity of tree diseases and pest outbreaks will also increase.

Example – Impacts of climate change in high latitudes

Declining duration of Arctic sea ice leads to a decline in the abundance of ice algae. The algae are consumed by zooplankton, which in turn are eaten by cod. Cod is an important food source for seals, which in turn are eaten by polar bears. Hence, rising temperatures causing a decline in sea ice can lead to a decline in polar bears.

As temperatures have risen, some tundra areas in North America are being invaded by boreal forests. This has reduced the habitat for some unique species that depend on the tundra such as caribou, arctic foxes and snowy owls.

The Adelie and Chinstrap penguins in Antarctica depend on different habitats for survival. The Chinstrap penguins remain close to water over winter whereas the Adelie penguins inhabit winter pack ice. Over the last 50 years, the mid-winter temperatures over the Western Antarctica peninsula have increased by as much as 5 °C, leading to a loss of sea ice. Since the 1980s, the Adelie penguin population has fallen by over 20% whereas the Chinstrap penguin population has increased by over 400%.

Climate change and plant productivity

Rising CO_2 levels can increase plant productivity – this is known as the carbon fertilization effect. Between 1982 and 2020, atmospheric levels of CO_2 increased by 17% while plant productivity increased by 12%. However, climate change is affecting temperature, nutrient availability and water availability. Researchers found that between 1980 and 2017 most unfertilized terrestrial ecosystems became more deficient in nutrients, especially N_2. If N_2 is limited, the extra productivity from CO_2 may be short-lived. Trees currently absorb about one-third of human-caused CO_2 emissions but their ability to continue to do this depends on the amount of N_2 available to them. If N_2 is limited, the benefits of increased CO_2, such as increased productivity, will be limited too.

Moreover, the increase in temperature speeds up plant life cycles giving less time for photosynthesis and so they produce lower crop yields.

Rising temperatures are making growing seasons longer and warmer. Plants may grow more and for longer periods but their need for water will increase. Soils may become drier and dry soils increase the amount of plant-stress. This could cause the plants to absorb less CO_2 which would limit photosynthesis. Warmer winters and longer growing seasons help pests, pathogens and invasive species. Rising temperatures allow a higher number of insects to move into new areas.

Higher temperatures and increased moisture make crops vulnerable. Weeds, many of which thrive in warm and wet conditions, already cause about one-third of crop losses. For corn and soya beans, every additional increase of 1 °C can cause a decline in yields of 3–7%. The combination of heat and dry conditions has caused maize yields to fall by up to 20% in parts of the USA and up to 40% in Eastern Europe and South-East Asia. With increased atmospheric CO_2 levels, protein concentrations in wheat, rice, barley and potatoes have fallen by 10–15%.

Overall, more plants will be more stressed and less productive in future, although there are many uncertainties.

These impacts can lead, indirectly, to social problems such as hunger and conflict, which may have implications for levels of economic development (Figure 6.26).

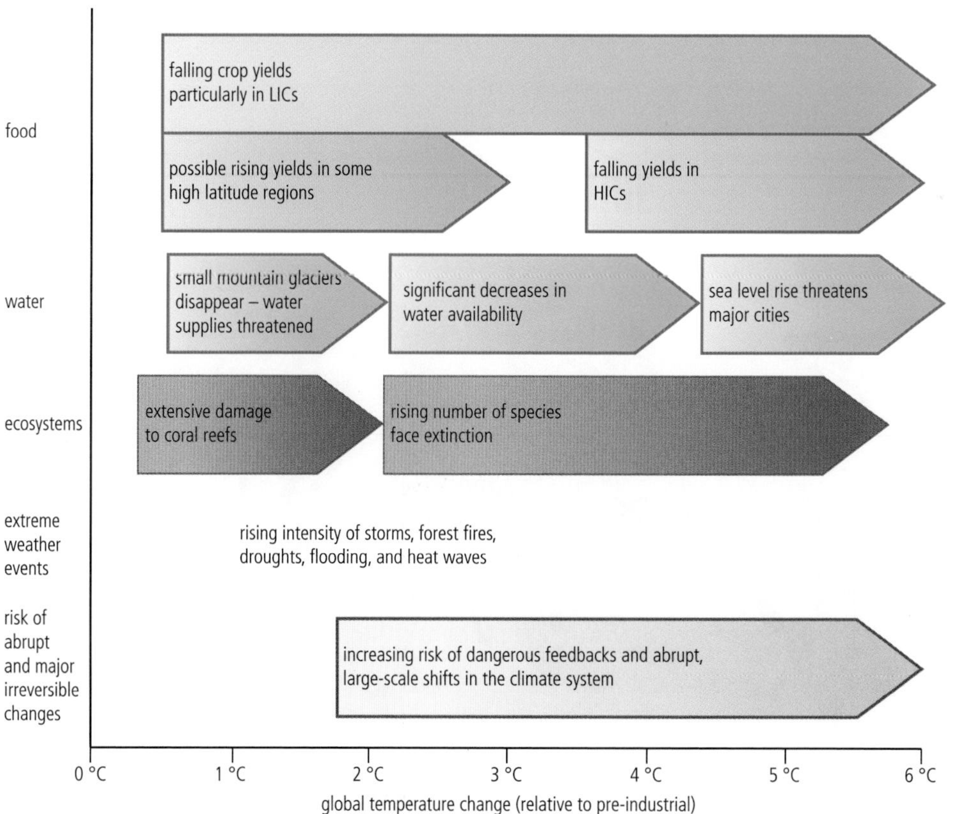

Figure 6.26 The projected impacts of climate change.

Biodiversity

Climate change may lead to a reduction in biodiversity as species change their distribution in response to changes in climate. Some species, especially high altitude and high latitude species, have fewer options for migration and so may become endangered (Topic 2, Section 2.5.1).

Ecosystem services

Climate change may also lead to a loss in ecosystem services. Ecosystems provide a range of services, such as primary productivity, pollination, flood control, climate regulation and provision of timber products, and these may be placed at risk if there are significant changes to climate (Topic 3, Section 3.3.1).

Ocean acidification

Ocean acidification is another problem (Topic 4, Sections 4.1.9 and 4.3.7). The ongoing decrease in ocean pH is caused by CO_2 emissions from burning fossil fuels. The oceans currently absorb about half of the CO_2 produced by burning fossil fuels. When CO_2 dissolves in seawater, it forms carbonic acid, which causes the seawater to become acidic. This can reduce the growth of organisms with shells or exoskeletons, such as shellfish, crabs and lobsters, therefore altering marine food chains and food supply to humans. It could also reduce tourism and recreational opportunities, for example through a decrease in demand to use areas for fishing and snorkeling, and lead to increased algal blooms.

Investigate climate graphs for different global locations
Use databases to explore the impact of temperature change on a specific ecosystem

1. Choose two or more contrasting locations from Figure 6.27 (e.g. high and low latitudes, continental-interior versus coastal) and compare their climates. Make sure you analyse maximum and minimum temperatures, temperature range and seasonality. Make sure you also analyse rainfall totals (approximate) and seasonal distribution. Is snow likely to feature? Is drought likely?

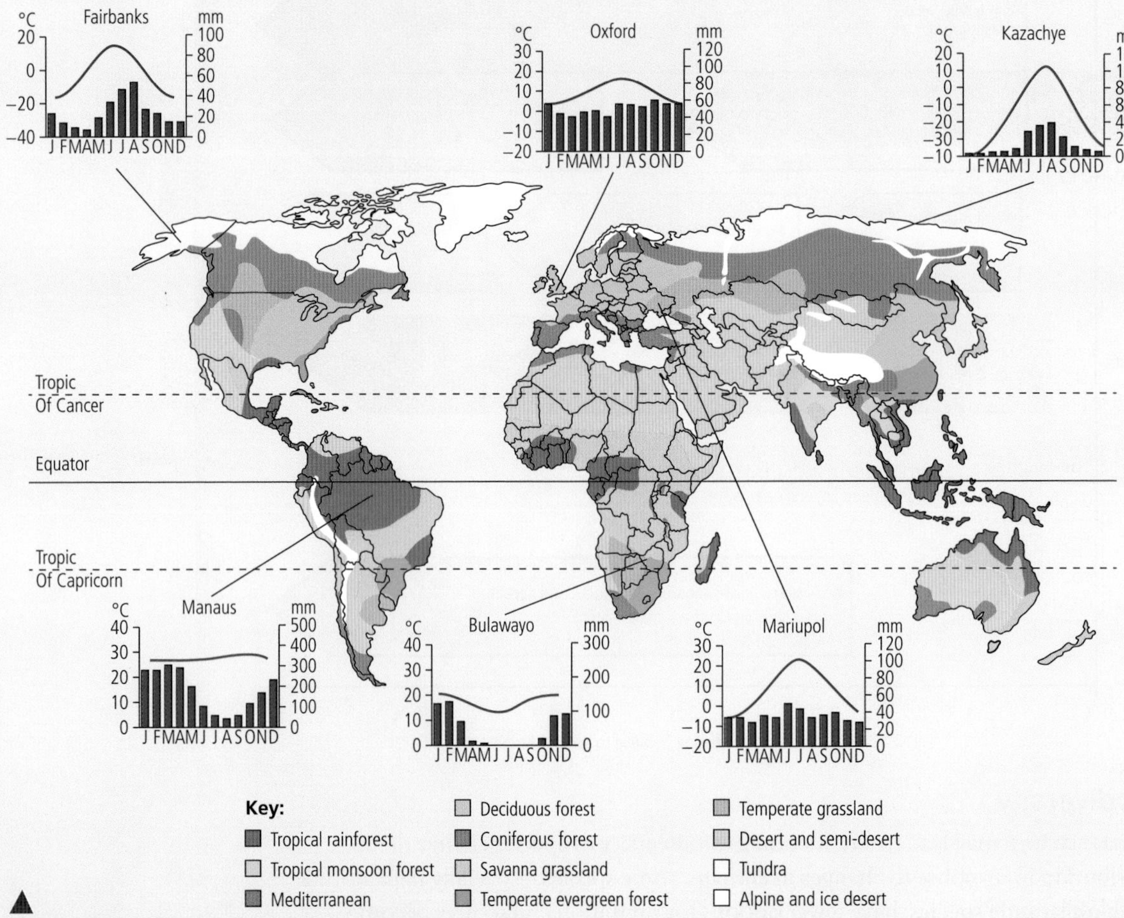

Fairbanks
Oxford
Kazachye
Tropic Of Cancer
Equator
Tropic Of Capricorn
Manaus
Bulawayo
Mariupol

Key:
- Tropical rainforest
- Tropical monsoon forest
- Mediterranean
- Deciduous forest
- Coniferous forest
- Savanna grassland
- Temperate evergreen forest
- Temperate grassland
- Desert and semi-desert
- Tundra
- Alpine and ice desert

▲ **Figure 6.27** Climate graphs for different global locations (local scale).

2. Atmospheric and oceanic CO_2 levels in long term graphs provide evidence for anthropogenic global warming and ocean acidification.

   Study Figure 6.28. To what extent does the graph provide evidence for anthropogenic global warming and ocean acidification? Justify your answer.

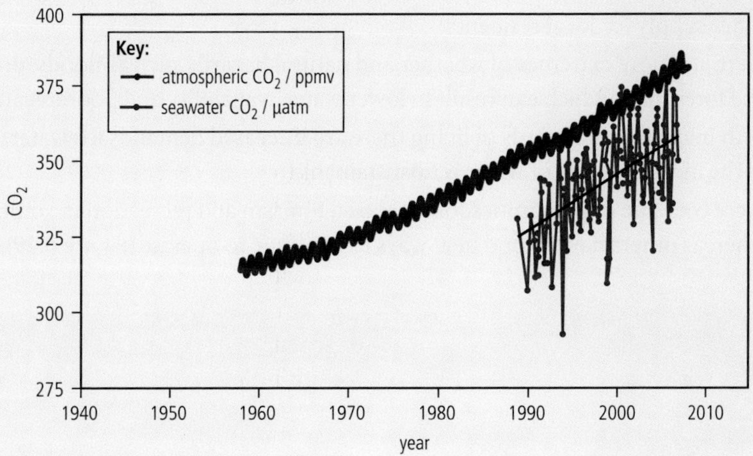

Figure 6.28 Changes in (global scale) atmospheric CO_2 and ocean CO_2.

3. Use databases to explore the impact of temperature change on a specific ecosystem, e.g. coral reefs or forests. Make sure you find out about the size of the population, size of individuals in the population, variety of species present, changes in abundance over time, extinction rates, and changes in temperature over time. Make a presentation to show your findings. Explain how climate change is impacting the ecosystems in your chosen area.

6.2.6 Impacts on societies

1.3 Sustainability
4.2 Water access, use and security
5.2 Agriculture and food
8.2 Urban systems and urban planning
8.3 Urban air pollution

HL b Environmental economics

Climate change affects societies on many scales and in many ways. This can affect the resilience of communities and societies.

The potential impacts of climate change may vary from one location to another and may be perceived as either adverse or beneficial. These impacts may include changes in water availability, distribution of biomes and crop-growing areas, loss of biodiversity and ecosystem services, coastal inundation, ocean acidification and damage to human health (Table 6.3).

Societal features	Effect or impact
water sources	severe water shortages and possibly wars over supply
agriculture	may shift towards poles (away from drought areas)
coastal residential locations	relocation due to flooding and storms
human health	increased disease (e.g. risk of malaria)

Table 6.3 The impact of temperature increase on aspects of society.

Water supply

Climate change is already disrupting the water supply in many societies. Global temperatures have already risen by 1.1 °C since pre-industrial levels and they are predicted to rise further. Thus the impact on water supply is likely to intensify. Several changes have already been observed, including:

- droughts have become more widespread and occur over longer periods in places such as USA, South Africa and Australia
- with increased temperature there are more evaporation losses
- many glaciers in mountainous areas are melting, potentially removing a long-term water supply for local residents
- there are more extremes of weather and natural hazards such as floods, droughts and forest fires, which can result in lower water availability and poorer water quality
- with increasing standards of living there are increased demands for water – much of the increasing use of water is unsustainable
- there could be opportunities for increased tourism and recreation in some areas, whereas others have to find new ways to continue to operate (Figure 6.29).

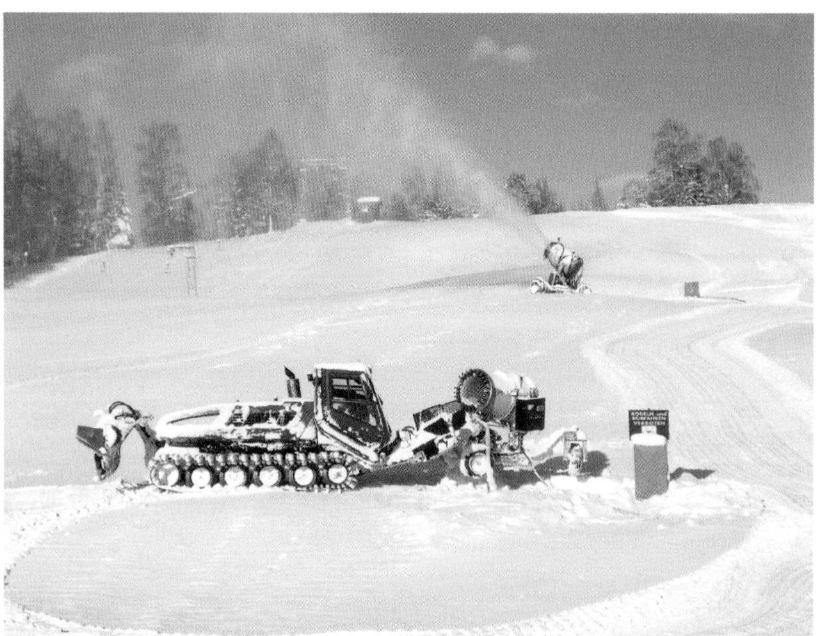

Figure 6.29 Ski cannon making up for the lack of snowfall.

Agriculture

As global temperatures rise, changes in agricultural patterns are likely. If temperatures rise by 3 °C, there will be a 35% drop in crop yields across Africa and the Middle East, and up to 550 million people could be exposed to hunger.

Changes in the location of crop-growing areas can be expected, with movements polewards. For example, viticulture (grapes), corn and wheat will move northwards in the Northern Hemisphere. Many wheat growing areas in the USA will decline, but they may increase in Canada. This will have a serious impact on the US economy. Wheat yields in the north of the UK are predicted to increase by 30%, whereas those in the south could decrease by 30%.

Since drought reduces crop yield, the reduction in water sources will make it increasingly difficult for farmers in many areas to irrigate their fields. Crop types may need to change and changes in water sources could limit or expand crop production in different areas.

Climate change and labour productivity

Climate change also affects human labour productivity. Warming can affect the number of working hours and it can also reduce performance (productivity). Workers under heat stress slow down and take more breaks to rehydrate and cool down. Excessive body heat can cause workers to make more mistakes, which potentially leads to an increased number of accidents. It has been estimated that climate change could reduce labour by over 25% in Africa, by almost 20% in Asia and by over 10% in the Americas.

Natural resources

Natural resource bases will change, which will drive economic, social and cultural change. These issues are more likely to affect low-income countries (LICs) than high-income countries (HICs) because LICs are technologically and economically less able to cope. Moreover, a greater percentage of the population in LICs and lower-middle-income countries (MICs) is already vulnerable to the effects of climate change. For example, in Bangladesh 20% of GDP and 65% of the labour force is involved in agriculture, which would be threatened by floods in low-lying areas. Coastal flooding, caused by melting of the polar ice caps and thermal expansion of the oceans, will affect countries that have land at or below sea level (e.g. the Netherlands). This may lead to economic and social stress due to the loss of land and resources. LICs and lower-MICs are also more likely to have weak infrastructure, communications and emergency services, which will make them less able to respond to the effects of climate change.

Human health

There is also likely to be an impact on human health. Diseases such as malaria are likely to spread, as temperatures rise and allow mosquitoes to breed in areas that are currently too cool for them (Figure 6.30). Hunger and malnutrition are predicted to increase due to warmer temperatures and a decrease in water availability. Heat stress is also more likely during extremes of weather such as heatwaves.

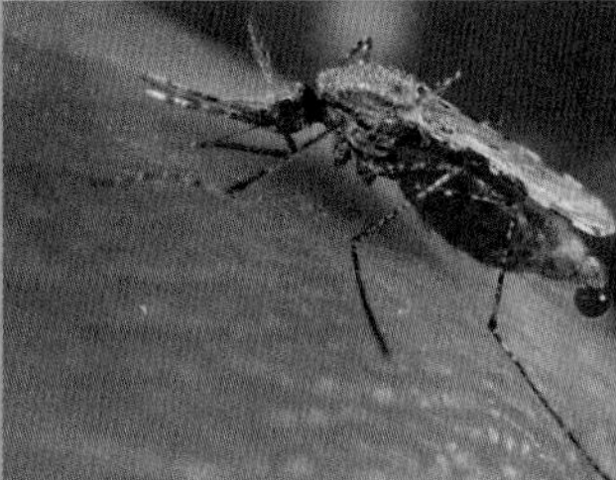

▲ **Figure 6.30** As a result of global warming, mosquitoes will be able to survive in some areas that are currently too cold for them.

Infrastructure

Climate is having a major impact on infrastructure, and this is likely to increase. For example, extreme heat can cause roads to buckle and bend and pavements to crack. Large holes in the ground known as sinkholes may also develop in areas of limestone.

Flooding of metro systems can also occur. For example, the metro systems in New York and New Jersey were flooded in 2012 following Hurricane Sandy.

Airports are also vulnerable. Many of them are built at altitudes just above sea level and so are vulnerable to sea level rises. As airports are generally built in areas with favourable wind conditions, any extreme weather events, such as hurricanes, could cause airports to remain closed for increasingly long periods of time.

Intense rainfall can trigger landslides. Railway lines that are cut into steep ground are at increased risk of landslides covering their tracks.

Tourism

Tourism and recreation are also likely to change as global warming changes weather patterns. Summer seasons may be extended and coastal resorts offering *sun, sea and sand* may develop further north. Winter sports holidays may be stopped by lack of snow and ice but may be more comfortable (Figure 6.31). Reduced precipitation in some areas may make some currently popular resorts uneconomic due to lack of water sources.

▲ **Figure 6.31** Tourism and recreation in cold environments may be changing.

Up to 4 billion people could be affected by water shortages if temperatures increase by 2 °C.

TOK

Does all knowledge impose ethical obligations on those who know it?

The poor are more vulnerable to global warming than the rich. However, on average, people in rich countries produce a larger amount of greenhouse gases per person than people in poor countries. Is this morally just?

1.2 Systems

In summary

The effects of global warming are very varied. Much depends on the scale of the changes, but impacts could include the following.

- A rise in sea levels, causing flooding in low-lying areas such as Tuvalu, Netherlands, Egypt and Bangladesh. Up to 200 million people could be displaced.
- Four million square kilometres of land, home to a twentieth of the world's population, is threatened by floods from melting glaciers.
- A decrease in water supply and energy as glaciers disappear.
- An increase in storm activity, such as more frequent and intense hurricanes, is likely, due to an increase in atmospheric energy.
- Reduced rainfall over the USA, southern Europe and the Commonwealth of Independent States (CIS) is likely.
- Changes in agricultural patterns may occur. For example, a decline in the USA's grain belt but an increase in the length of Canada's growing season.
- A 35% drop in crop yields across Africa and the Middle East is expected if temperatures rise by 3 °C.
- An estimated 200 million more people could be exposed to hunger if world temperatures rise by 2 °C. This figure could increase to 550 million if temperatures rise by 3 °C.
- Around 60 million more people in Africa could be exposed to malaria if world temperatures rise by 2 °C.
- Extinction of up to 40% of species of wildlife is expected if temperatures rise by 2 °C.

6.2.7 Systems diagrams and feedback loops

Systems diagrams and models are used to show the cause and effect of climate change (Figure 6.32).

Negative feedback results in a return to the original status, whereas positive feedback moves the system away from equilibrium (Topic 1, Section 1.2.11). Some feedbacks may involve a small number of stages, whereas other feedbacks are much longer. The same factors may sometimes cause positive feedback, and at other times result in negative feedback.

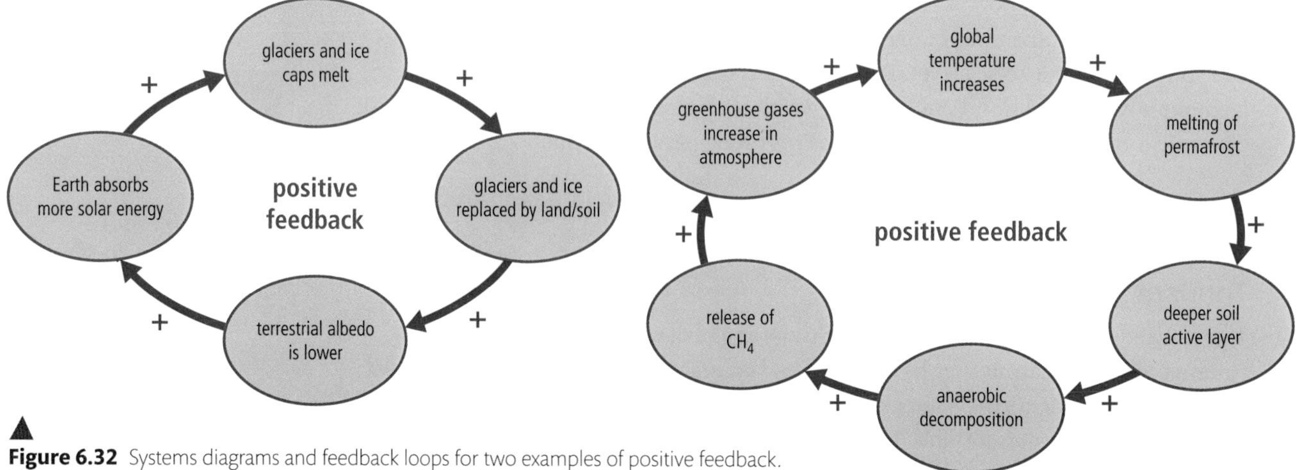

Figure 6.32 Systems diagrams and feedback loops for two examples of positive feedback.

Activity

Construct a systems diagram to show how solar radiation can produce a negative feedback loop.

Negative feedback is a self-regulating method leading to a steady state.

Positive feedback occurs when a change in the state of a system leads to additional and increased change, i.e. deviation away from its original state.

6.2.8 Planetary boundary for climate change exceeded

Published evidence suggests that the Earth has already passed the planetary boundary for climate change.

In 2023, the United Nations (UN) Secretary General, Antonio Guterres, announced that the world was in an era of global boiling. He said *Climate change is here. It is terrifying. And it is just the beginning*. The UN, through Conference of the Parties (COP) agreements, has adopted a target to keep global heating to between 1.5–2.0 °C above pre-industrial levels. This is extremely dangerous as people are already badly affected by extremes of droughts, heatwaves and floods, and temperatures are only 1.1 °C above pre-industrial levels. A safer target would have been 1.0 °C but that is unlikely to materialize.

Likely climate tipping points (Figure 6.33) include:

- the collapse of the North Atlantic oceanic circulation
- dieback of the Amazon rainforest
- thawing of boreal permafrost
- the collapse of the Greenland ice sheet.

1.3 Sustainability

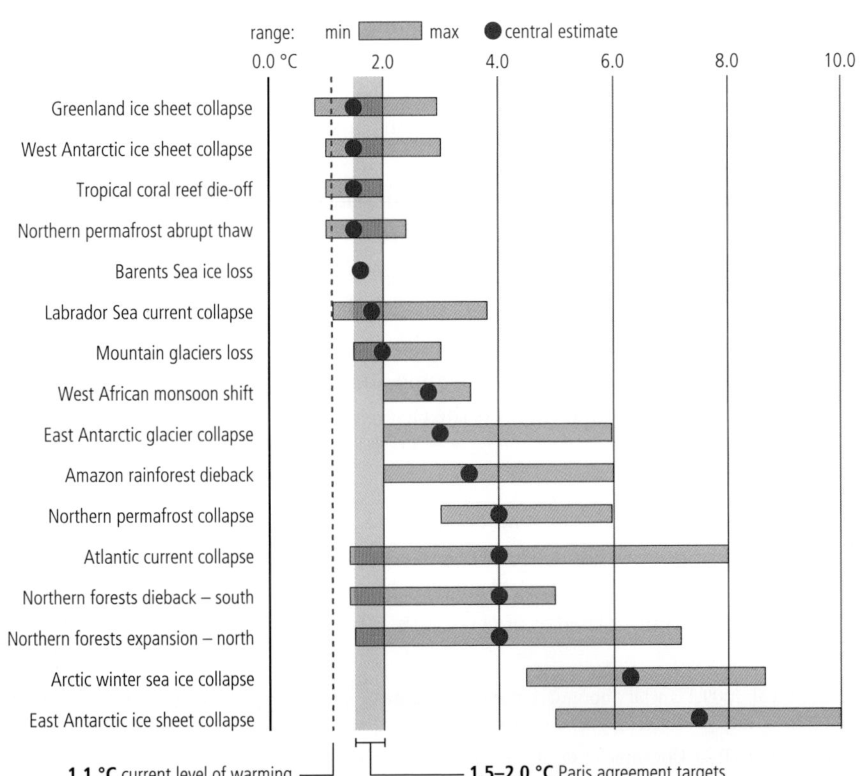

Figure 6.33 The risk of climate tipping points.

The greater the increase in global temperatures, the more damage will be caused. An increase of 1.5 °C could expose over 200 million people – disproportionately those already vulnerable, poor and marginalized – to extreme temperatures. At the same time, around 500 million people would be exposed to sea level rise.

Climate tipping points

In 2009, the authors of *Planetary Boundaries*[1] suggested that the maximum concentration of CO_2 in the atmosphere should not exceed 350 ppm. It is now over 400 ppm. Betts and McNeall[2], writing in *Nature Climate Change*, stated that if atmospheric CO_2 reaches 507 ppm, average temperatures will have increased by 1.5 °C and at 618 ppm temperatures will have risen by 2 °C. According to UN Climate Change, the climate change planetary boundary has been crossed. This shows that there has been concern for a long time, but this concern has not led to a reduction in CO_2.

1.1 Perspectives

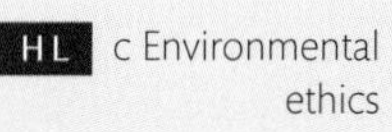

HL c Environmental ethics

6.2.9 Perspectives on climate change

There are many different perspectives among individuals, communities and societies about climate change (Topic 1, Section 1.1.8). These perspectives are influenced by many factors including experience of climate change, occupation, level of wealth, place of residence, education, age and access to media.

People who are farmers or who live in coastal areas and/or areas subject to flooding may be more aware of recent climate changes. For example, farmers may be more aware of variations in crop yields caused by year-on-year changes in weather patterns and extremes.

Perspectives in the USA

In a study by the Pew Research Centre (2023) of over 10,000 adults in the USA:

- nearly half of US adults said that climate change is due to human activity and about the same number said that it is due to natural causes or that there is no evidence for climate change
- around 40% of US adults expected harmful impacts from climate change on weather patterns, coastal erosion and wildlife
- over half of US adults believed that restrictions on power plants and international agreements could have a major impact on global climate change
- there was a variation in the views of members of different political parties – 79% of Democrats believed the Earth is warming due to human activities whereas only 15% of Republicans felt that this was the case.

Bjorn Lomborg

In his 2001 book, *The Skeptical Environmentalist*, Bjorn Lomborg argues that many global problems, such as aspects of global warming, overpopulation, biodiversity loss and water shortages, are unsupported by statistical analysis. He argues that many of the problems are localized and are generally related to poverty, rather than being of global proportions.

---

[1]Rockström et al, 2009. Planetary boundaries: exploring the safe operating space for humanity. *Ecology and Society* 14(2): 32. http://www.ecologyandsociety.org/vol14/iss2/art32/

[2]Betts, R.A., McNeall, D. How much CO_2 at 1.5 °C and 2 °C? *Nature Climate Change* 8(7), 546–548 (2018). https://www.nature.com/articles/s41558-018-0199-5

Regarding global warming, Lomborg accepts that human activity has added to global temperature increases. However, he outlines a number of uncertainties (e.g. the simulation of future climate trends) and some weaknesses in the collection of data worldwide. Nevertheless, he finds issues relating to the politics and policy responses to global warming. For example, he concludes that the cost of combating global warming will be disproportionately borne by poor countries. He also believes that the Kyoto Protocol and various carbon taxes are among the least efficient ways of dealing with global warming. Instead he argues that a global cost–benefit analysis should be carried out before deciding on how to deal with global warming.

Greta Thunberg

Greta Thunberg (born 2003) is a Swedish environmental activist who, from the age of 15, challenged the Swedish parliament for stronger action on climate change (Topic 1, Section 1.1.10). She attracted attention due to her age and the blunt language that she used. She addressed the UN Climate Change Conference in 2018 when she said that the world leaders present were *not mature enough to tell it like it is* (Figure 6.34).

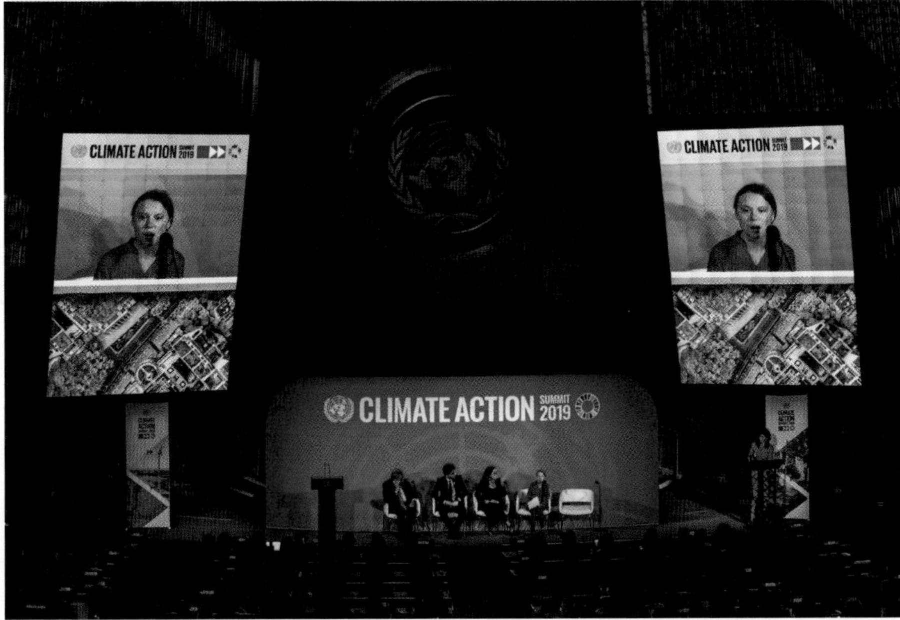

Figure 6.34 Greta Thunberg addressing the UN Climate Action Summit.

In 2019, Thunberg attended the Climate Action Summit in New York. She sailed in a yacht to North America to avoid carbon-intensive flying. In her own words, she said, *I was diagnosed with Asperger's syndrome, OCD and selective mutism. That basically means I only speak when I think it's necessary. Now is one of those moments.* At the Climate Action Summit she stated, *You have stolen my dreams and my childhood with your empty words. And yet I'm one of the lucky ones. People are suffering. People are dying. Entire ecosystems are collapsing. We are in the beginning of a mass extinction and all you can talk about is money, and fairy tales of eternal economic growth. How dare you!*

Thunberg believes humanity is facing an existential crisis due to global warming and that climate change will have a disproportionate effect on young people, whose futures will be profoundly affected. She believes that global leaders have taken too little action to reduce global emissions and that commitments made at the 2015 Paris Agreement are insufficient to limit global warming to 1.5 °C. Political leaders set targets for decades ahead but do little in the present.

Thunberg has received numerous awards and has been included in the *Times* list of the 100 most influential people. She was the youngest *Times* Person of the Year and was included in the *Forbes* list of the 100 most powerful women. She was also nominated for the Nobel Peace Prize every year between 2019 and 2022.

Extinction Rebellion

Figure 6.35 Extinction Rebellion climate change activists lie on the floor to symbolize a *mass die* at the Gendarmenmarkt square in Berlin.

Extinction Rebellion (XR) is a global environmental movement based in the UK. Its aim is to use non-violent protests to force governments to avoid tipping points in climate change, biodiversity loss and social and environmental decline (Figure 6.35). It aims to create a *sense of urgency* to prevent further environmental damage, such as climate change. XR uses mass arrests as a tactic to attract attention to their cause by disrupting the public and wasting police time. Off-shoots include Doctors for XR, who have warned about the effects of climate change on human health, and XR Youth who focus on issues regarding the Global South, Indigenous people and climate justice. XR has been criticized for alienating potential supporters due to the protests and disruption that has been created. It has also been criticized for being largely middle-class white privilege.

Climate change denial

Climate change deniers may believe that attempts to adapt to climate change may make them less competitive compared with countries that do not adapt to climate change. Some people may believe that it damages their way of life, or makes everyday life harder e.g. not driving as much/taking public transport.

There are people who deny climate change. For example, former US president Donald Trump has made many comments about climate change, including:

- *we must reject the perennial prophets of doom and their predictions of the apocalypse*
- suggesting that climate change is *mythical, non-existent* and *an expensive hoax.*

Intergovernmental Panel on Climate Change (IPCC)

The IPCC was established in 1998 by the United Nations Environmental Panel (UNEP) and the World Meteorological Organization, to deal with concerns regarding global warming. The IPCC assesses the state of knowledge about the scientific, environmental and socioeconomic impacts of climate change, and potential strategies to deal with it. The IPCC does not undertake independent research but gathers together the findings from key research that has been published.

The IPCC is recognized as the most authoritative scientific and technical voice on climate change and its assessments have had a major influence on the United Nations Framework Convention on Climate Change (UNFCCC). The IPCC has three working groups:

- Group I, which assesses the scientific aspects of climate change
- Group II, which examines vulnerability of human and natural systems to climate change and options for adapting to climate change
- Group III, which assesses options for limiting greenhouse gas emissions and mitigating climate change.

The IPCC provides governments with information relevant to evaluating risks and developing a response to climate change. Around 500 experts from 120 countries were involved in writing the 2021 IPCC report. (See also Section 6.3.1 on global action to deal with climate change.)

Activity

Working with a partner, outline your perspectives on climate change. There are several questions that you can ask each other, such as:

- How do you justify your views?
- Are there any victims of global climate change? Who are they and where are they?
- If there are no victims of global climate change, why not?
- What can be done to manage global climate change?
- Why is not enough being done to manage climate change despite all the natural disasters that are happening?

HL

6.2.10 Direct and indirect measurements of weather

HL

1.2 Systems

The weather can be recorded by taking direct measurements of temperature, rainfall and other key meteorological features. The weather of the past, sometimes dating back hundreds of thousands of years, can be inferred from ice cores, tree rings and pollen-types from peat bogs.

Direct measurements

Most weather stations record the following weather elements:

- air temperature at 1.25 m above the ground and over the surface (concrete or grass/ artificial equivalent)
- soil temperature at 0.1 m, 0.3 m and 1.0 m below ground level
- relative humidity
- amount of rainfall
- mean wind speed, mean wind direction and maximum gust at 10 m above the ground
- atmospheric pressure at the station level and at mean sea level
- visibility
- amount and type of cloud and height of cloud base.

Individuals can make observations as regards the current state of the local environment. On a larger scale, satellites can be used to monitor cloud formations, rainfall and temperatures. Tropical cyclones are tracked by satellites (Figure 6.36). For example, small-scale depressions that form over West Africa and travel over the Atlantic towards the Americas can only be tracked effectively by satellites. The use of radars in weather forecasting is useful for flood prediction, changes in humidity and monitoring of high wind speeds, such as in tropical cyclones and tornadoes.

Figure 6.36 Satellite image of Hurricane Irma (2017).

Activity

Use the data in the table found on this page of your eBook. The table shows long-term data for CO_2 and temperature in Boston, USA between 1973 and 2022.

1. Produce line graphs to show the changes in CO_2 and temperature over time. Describe the results and identify any trend.
2. Make a scatter graph of CO_2 and temperature. Is there any correlation? If so, is it positive or negative? Give reasons to explain the results you have described.

Indirect measurements

There are a number of indirect measures of climate change including oxygen isotopes from ice cores, study of tree rings (dendrochronology) and pollen analysis from peat cores. It is also possible to use written records, journals and old photographs or paintings of glaciers.

Ice sheets and glaciers develop from the build-up of snow over time. The weight of the snow on top compresses the snow below and may convert it into layers of ice. Ice cores are long cylinders of ice removed from a glacier or ice sheet. Most are collected from ice sheets in Greenland and Antarctica. The longest ice core in Greenland dates back to 130,000 years, while in Antarctica an ice core dating back 2.7 million years was drilled in 2017. The youngest ice is at the top of the core and the oldest is at the base. Ice cores contain air bubbles which contain gases such as O_2 and CO_2, along with some solid particles such as soot, ash and dust.

Oxygen can be used to show changes in global temperatures. Oxygen exists as two naturally occurring isotopes, the more common ^{16}O and the less common ^{18}O, which has two additional neutrons in its nucleus. Water molecules that contain ^{18}O are heavier than usual and do not evaporate as easily as water containing ^{16}O. However, when the climate is warmer, more of the water molecules containing ^{18}O are able to evaporate and later fall as snow on glaciers and ice sheets. Hence, ice formed in glaciers in warmer conditions contains higher concentrations of ^{18}O than the ice formed in colder conditions.

In the sample taken in Vostok (Figure 6.37), ^{18}O levels were mainly between 55% and 60%, and therefore ^{16}O levels would have been between 40% and 45%.

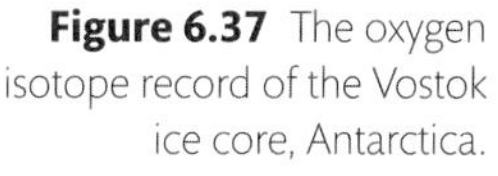

Figure 6.37 The oxygen isotope record of the Vostok ice core, Antarctica.

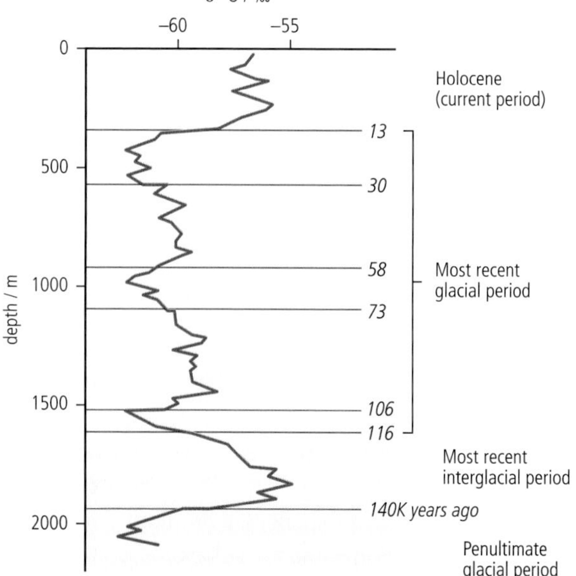

Tree rings

Temperature and precipitation affect the rate of growth of trees. Hence, the thickness of the annual growth rings seen in tree trunks is a proxy indicator of climate (Figure 6.38). Most trees only indicate climate change over a few hundred years, although some trees can date back thousands of years. During the preboreal oscillation stage, where there was increased humidity, we see increased tree ring width. And during cold/arid periods, like the younger dryas, we notice diminished tree ring widths.

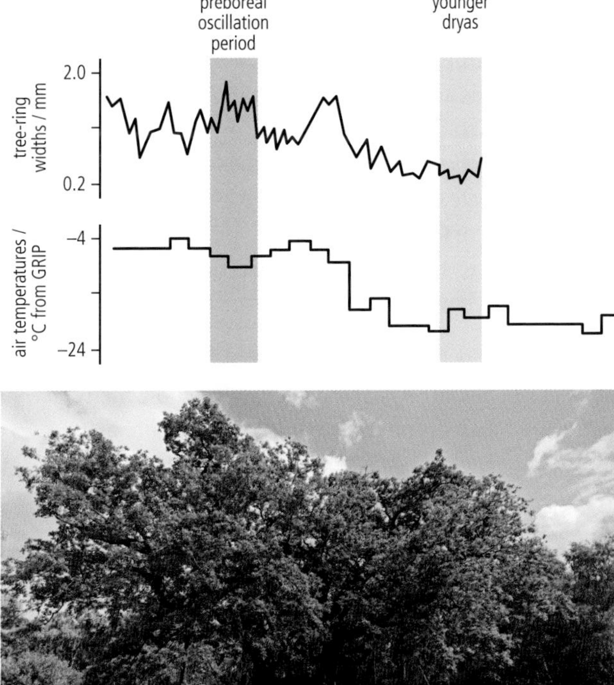

Figure 6.38 A comparison of air temperature and tree widths.

It is also possible to study tree rings from fossilized trees e.g. find out about the Florissant Fossil Beds National Monument, USA.

The Major Oak in Sherwood Forest, UK is estimated to be between 800-1100 years old.

Pollen analysis from peat cores

Pollen analysis has been used as an analytical tool since the early 1900s and is widely used in reconstructing past environments. Pollen is produced by higher plants such as trees, shrubs and herbs, while spores are produced by lower plants such as mosses and ferns. Both pollen and spores are released into the atmosphere and eventually settle on land or water. Most are degraded but those deposited in peat bogs and lakes may be well-preserved in the waterlogged environment. Peat and lake sediments can be sampled using coring techniques. The length of the core represents a temporal sequence, with the lower layers representing the oldest environments and the upper layers the most recent (Figure 6.39).

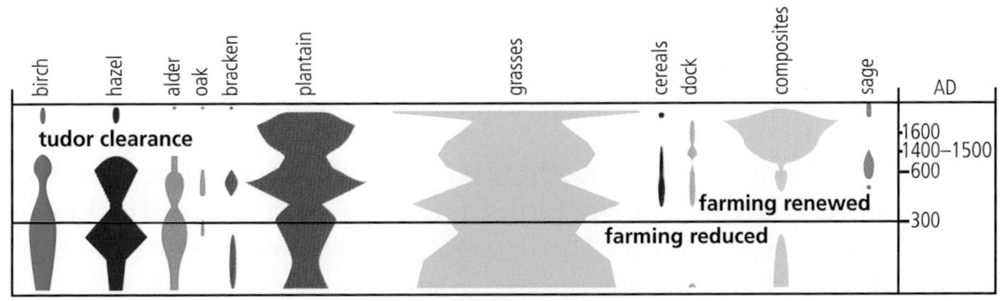

Figure 6.39 Pollen from blanket bog at Goodland, County Antrim, Ireland showing changes in land use on the drier soils in the vicinity of a wetland area.

HL

6.2.11 Global climate models

1.2 Systems

Global climate models manipulate inputs to climate systems to predict possible outputs or outcomes (Topic 1, Sections 1.2.13 and 1.2.14). There is often uncertainty about the inputs (for example, the use of proxy data) and hence over the outputs from the systems, leading to a range of possible future outcomes.

Models are essential tools for understanding the Earth's climate. They take many forms e.g. global, regional, local and/or different parts of the physical environment. Climate modelling is similar to weather forecasting but is done over a much longer timescale. Increasingly, climate models are very complex, often requiring supercomputers to run them, and using equations to represent processes and interactions that drive the Earth's climate. For example, models use fundamental physical principles, such as the first law of thermodynamics that states that in a closed system energy cannot be created or lost, only changed from one form to another. Another principle is the Stefan-Boltzmann law, which scientists have used to show that the natural greenhouse effect keeps the Earth's surface 33 °C warmer than it would be without greenhouse gases.

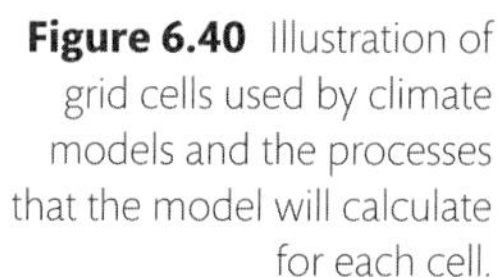

Make sure you know the main features of climate models e.g. the differences between energy balance models and coupled models, but you do not need detailed figures or statistics about their predictions.

Due to the complexity of the Earth's climate system and the scale involved, climate models cannot calculate all of the processes for every cubic metre of the Earth. Instead, the Earth is divided up into a number of cells or grids (Figure 6.40).

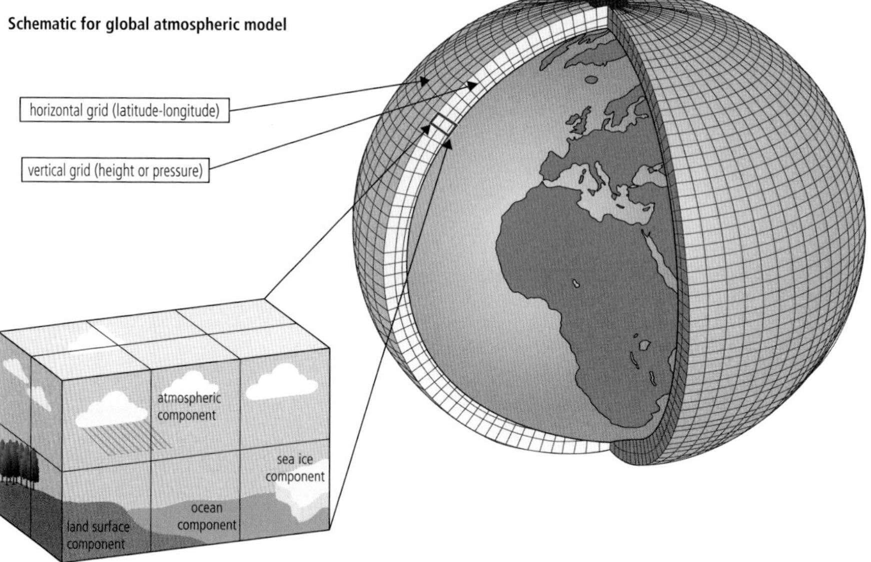

Figure 6.40 Illustration of grid cells used by climate models and the processes that the model will calculate for each cell.

The size of each cell is known as the *spatial resolution*. In the mid-latitudes, cells are typically 100 km in latitude and longitude. Smaller cells have higher resolution and more detailed results can be produced. However, this takes longer because more calculations need to be carried out. Increasing the spatial resolution twofold requires around ten times the computing power. Earth climate models use *leapfrogging*, i.e. they take past and recent climate information to project into the future.

The earliest and simplest climate models are energy balance models. These relate the balance between energy entering the Earth's atmosphere and heat released back to space. A more detailed type of model is the radiative convective model that looks at the transfer of energy through the atmosphere, e.g. by convection, as warm air rises. These models can be used to calculate the temperature and humidity of different altitudes. General circulation models (GCMs) show the flows of air and water in the atmosphere and oceans, as well as the transfer of heat around the Earth.

More detailed *coupled* models (Figure 6.41) link multiple models to provide a detailed representation of the Earth's climate. These can show, for example, the transfer of heat and water between land, ocean and atmosphere.

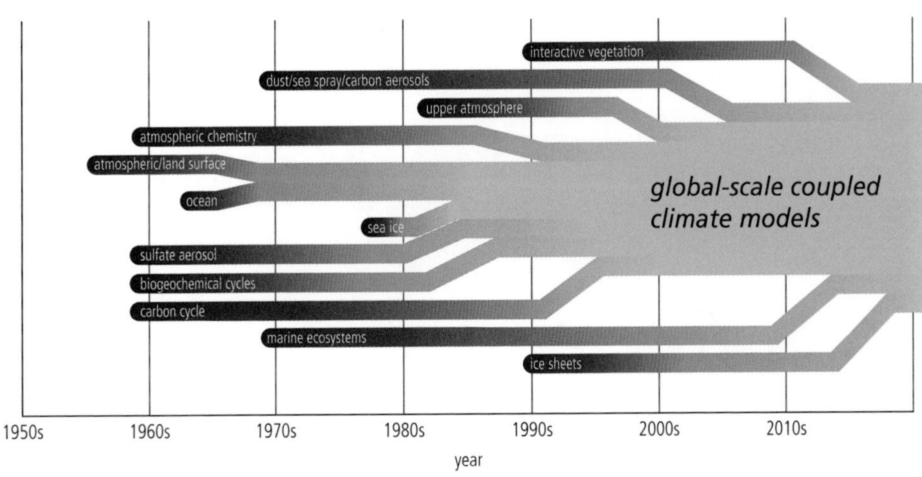

Figure 6.41 A *coupled* climate model linking many separate components.

Over time, scientists have added more aspects of the Earth's system to GCMs. Recent GCMs include biogeochemical cycles, i.e. the transfers of chemicals between organisms and the environment and their interaction with climate systems. These *Earth system models* can include carbon and nitrogen cycles, changes in vegetation and land use, ocean ecology, atmospheric chemistry, and human impacts such as emissions of greenhouse gases.

Integrated assessment models focus on how human impacts (for example, population growth, economic development and energy use) affect climate. Scientists can alter the size of the variables to project likely impacts on future climate change.

Inputs

The main inputs into climate models are the external factors that influence the amount of solar energy absorbed by the Earth or trapped in the atmosphere. These external factors (*forcings*) include changes in solar output, the amount of greenhouse gases in the atmosphere, aerosols, volcanic eruptions and forest fires. Models are used to estimate past conditions as well as potential future scenarios. Past forcings may show the operation of Milankovitch cycles and long-term climate change (for example, glacial advances and retreats).

Outputs

Outputs essentially show the state of the atmosphere and include temperature, humidity, salinity, acidity, snow cover, extent of glaciers and sea ice. Climate models can produce an estimate of *climate sensitivity*. This means how sensitive the Earth is to changes in, for example, greenhouse gases and to various feedback mechanisms such as changes in albedo as ice recedes.

Climate models can be used to examine changes in the past and to work out how much is due to human impact. Scientists can compare model predictions with past records/observations in **hindcasting** or backtesting (see below). If the models can successfully hindcast past climate variables, it gives scientists more confidence for future modelling.

Although climate models have become more complex, detailed and accurate, the problem of climate change remains and is affected by many factors (Figure 6.42), with human impacts having an increasing impact on climate, both directly and indirectly. Moreover, most models use a grid pattern that assumes the same physical characteristics over the whole grid or cell. This is very unlikely to be the case because it does not consider human activities.

Figure 6.42 Some factors used in climate models.

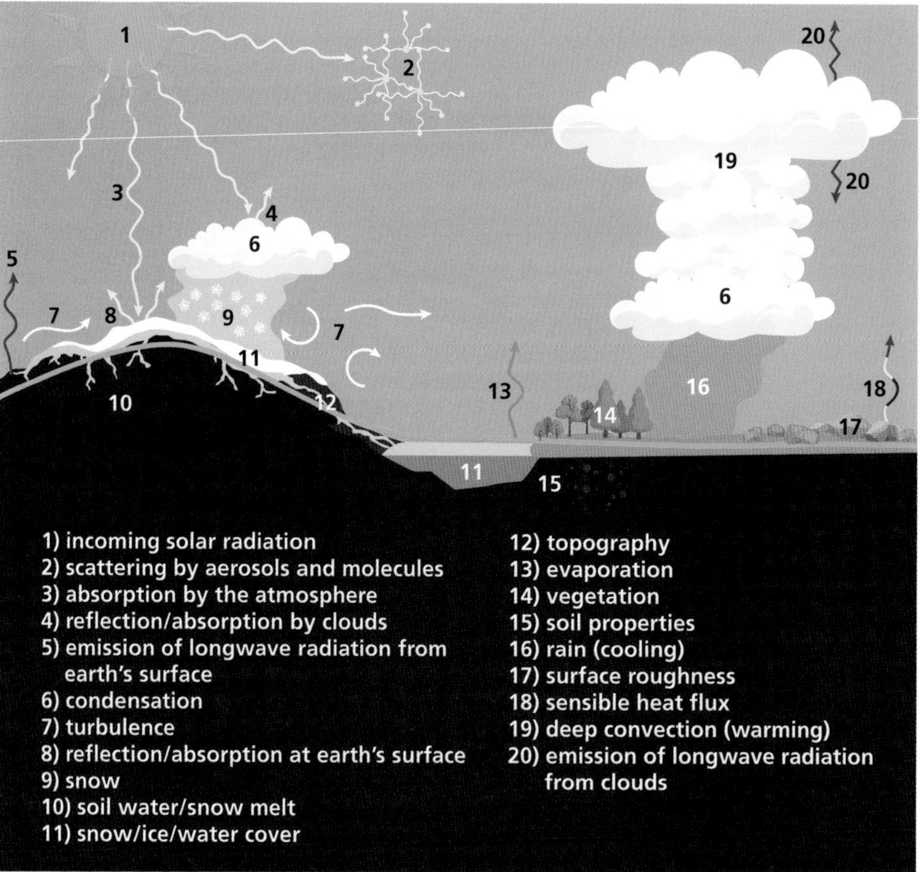

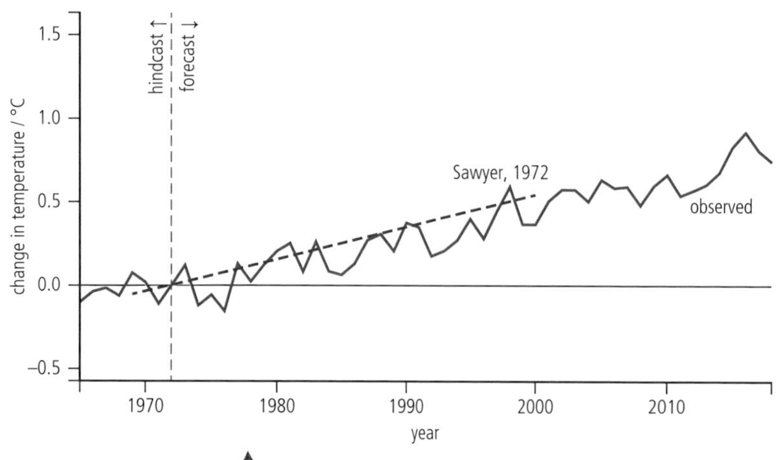

Figure 6.43 Hindcasting as predicted by Sawyer.

Hindcasting

Hindcasting runs models backwards from the present time to test their validity. An early example was that of Sawyer (1972)[1] in which he examined the impact of CO_2 in the atmosphere and oceans and how this feeds back into other Earth systems processes. The only greenhouse gases Sawyer accounted for were CO_2 and water vapour. However, he acknowledged that several other factors are important and make it difficult to predict the warming effect. Nevertheless, his predictions for changing temperatures offer a good approximation (Figure 6.43).

[1]Sawyer, J. Man-made Carbon Dioxide and the 'Greenhouse' Effect. *Nature* 239, 23–26 (1972). https://www.nature.com/articles/239023a0

A later model by Hansen et al. (1988)[1] was much more detailed and considered the interaction of land, ocean and cloud simulation. This model was able to predict how climate change would affect different parts of the world (Figure 6.44). Nevertheless, the ocean was a major source of uncertainty for their model.

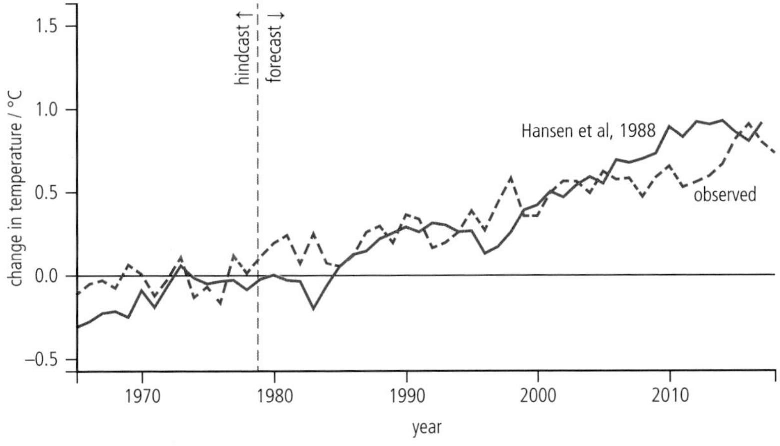

Figure 6.44 Climate model hindcasting – Hansen et al, 1988.

6.2.12 Climate change models

HL

1.2 Systems

Climate models use different scenarios to predict possible impacts of climate change.

Sea level change

Past climate changes have been accompanied by very large changes in sea levels. Some 20,000 years ago, at the peak of the Ice Age, sea levels were 120 m lower than today, yet global temperatures were, on average, only about 4–7 °C cooler than today. During the Pliocene, three million years ago, temperatures were just 2–3 °C warmer than today but sea levels were 25–35 m higher.

Sea levels can rise and fall for several reasons:

- the steric effect, i.e. the expansion of seawater as it becomes warmer
- an increase in the volume of water due to the melting of ice sheets and ice caps
- isostatic changes, i.e. changes in the relative position of land and sea due to the removal of large weights such as ice caps and ice sheets.

It is also possible to model thermal expansion. The critical factor is the depth to which heat penetrates into the ocean and how quickly it does so. Scientists suggest this could cause a 20 cm rise in sea levels by 2100.

Modelling mountain glacier melt is difficult owing to the large number and variety of glaciers (differing in, for example, altitude, size, thickness, latitude and aspect). Predictions about the changes in the Greenland and Antarctic ice sheets are even more uncertain due to the limited extent of research and understanding of all aspects of both ice sheets.

Predictions for the size of the rise in sea levels by 2100 range from about 60 cm to almost 200 cm with an average just over 100 cm (Figure 6.45). The rise by 2100 is only a small start to a much larger, multi-century response of ocean and ice sheets to global climate change.

[1]Hansen, J., et al. 1988, Global climate changes as forecast by Goddard Institute for Space Studies Three-Dimensional Model, *J. Geophysical Research*, Vol. 93, pp. 9341–9364.

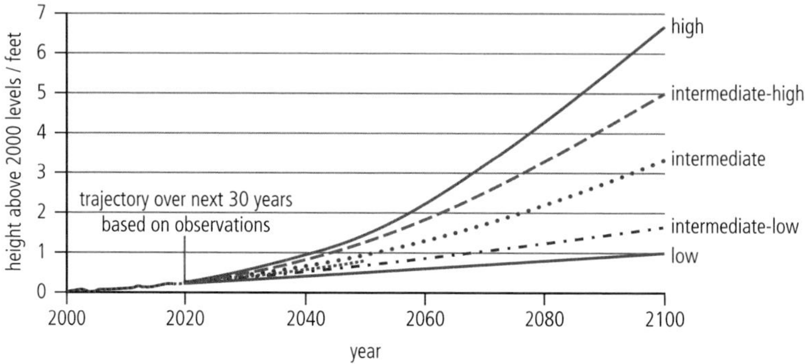

Figure 6.45 Projected sea level rise 2020–2100.

Sea level changes are not constant around the world but vary for several reasons:

- ocean water is moved by winds and currents
- natural oscillations, such as El Niño, and anthropogenic changes, such as global climate change, may lead to a change in ocean circulation, e.g. a weakening of the North Atlantic circulation
- vertical land movements due to tectonic processes, isostatic adjustment and subsidence caused by extraction of groundwater and/or oil.

Temperature change

The Earth's temperature has risen by an average of 0.08 °C per decade since 1880, but the rate of warming has been more than twice as fast since 1981 (0.18 °C per decade).

Most land areas have warmed faster than most ocean areas and the Arctic is warming faster than most other regions. (Figure 6.46). Only a few areas, mostly in the Southern Hemisphere oceans, have cooled.

The year 2022 was the sixth warmest year since global records began in 1880 and was 0.86 °C above the 20th century average of 13.9 °C. The ten warmest years have all occurred since 2010.

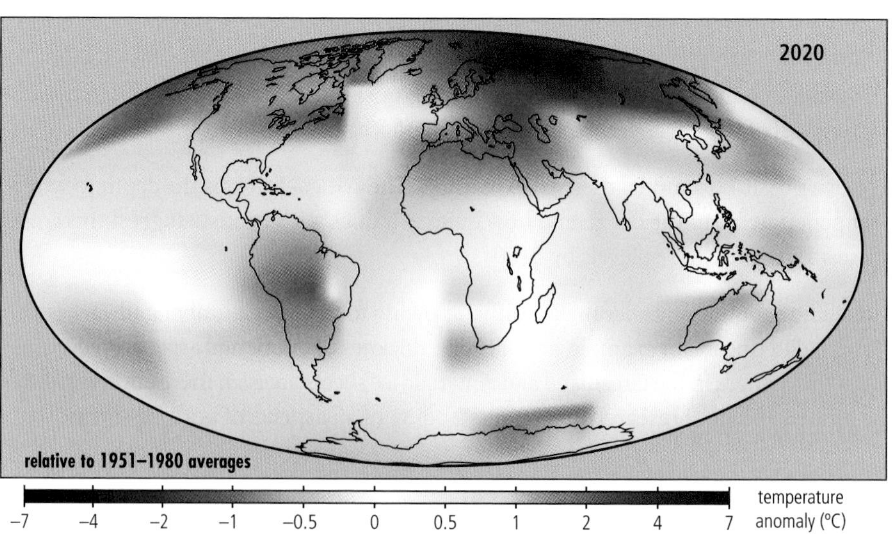

Figure 6.46 Trends in global surface temperature 2020 compared to the 1951–1980 long-term average.

Precipitation change

Scientists are less confident about predicting changes in rainfall. In theory, with higher temperatures, there should be a greater amount of evaporation and surface drying. There could be a greater volume of rainfall, as warm air can hold more moisture, or there may be an increase in the intensity and duration of droughts.

In general, warming is expected to make dry areas drier and wet areas wetter, especially in mid and high latitudes. Most models suggest there will also be large increases in precipitation near the equator, especially over the Pacific Ocean. Many areas with a Mediterranean-type climate, such as the Mediterranean, southern Africa, Australia and Chile, are projected to be 10–20% drier. As well as changes to annual rainfall, there are also likely to be changes in the intensity of rain, with much of the world projected to experience a 16–24% increase in precipitation intensity by 2100 (Figure 6.47).

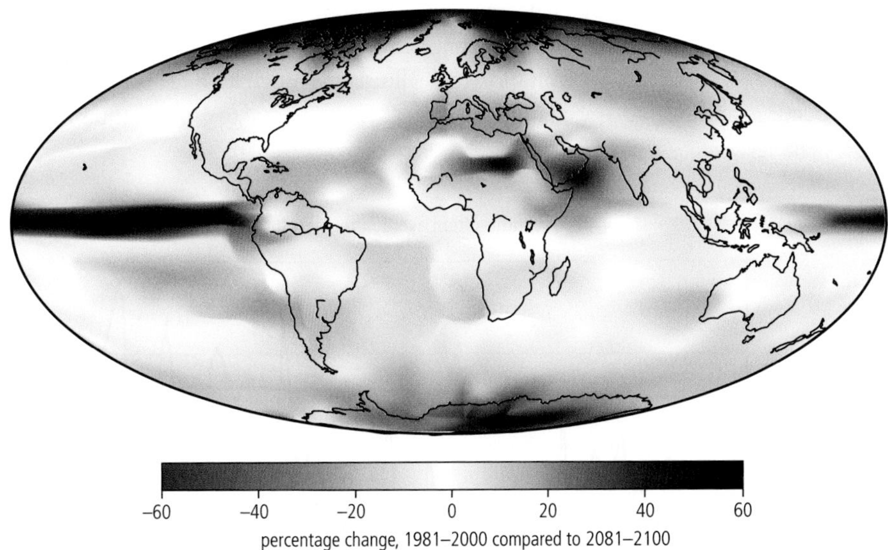

Figure 6.47 Potential changes in precipitation between 2081 and 2100 compared with the period between 1981 and 2000.

6.2.13 Climate tipping points

HL

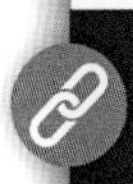

1.2 Systems
2.2 Energy and biomass in ecosystems
2.4 Climate and biomes

According to the UN Secretary General Antonio Guterres, irreversible climate tipping points lie alarmingly close. Tipping points are the point at which small changes become significant enough to cause large-scale changes that can cause abrupt, irreversible cascading effects (Figure 1.40 and Sections 1.2.12 and 2.1.22). The Earth's climate may change so much that it will be taken out of the glacial-interglacial cycles that have characterized the Holocene.

The idea of climate tipping points was introduced over 20 years ago. Back then it was believed that tipping points would only occur if global warming temperature increase reached 5 °C. Now it is believed that could occur if global warming caused a temperature increase between 1 and 2 °C.

In the world's polar regions, data shows that Greenland's glaciers are melting at an accelerating rate. Between 2002 and 2016, Greenland lost 280 billion tonnes of ice per year, enough to raise global sea levels by 0.75 mm annually. Antarctica is losing 219 billion tonnes of ice annually, which could lead to a rise in sea level of 25 cm by 2070.

Positive feedback mechanisms tend to drive systems towards a tipping point. Positive feedback occurs when a disturbance leads to an amplification of that disturbance, destabilizing the system and driving it away from equilibrium.

According to modelling by scientists at the University of Copenhagen, the Gulf Stream systems of warm ocean currents in the North Atlantic could collapse as early as 2025, or as late as 2095, with an average estimate of 2050. The Gulf Stream and North Atlantic Drift are currently believed to be at their weakest for about 1600 years. As global temperatures increase, freshwater is pouring into the North Atlantic. This could lead to changes to the Atlantic thermohaline circulation, which could lead to reduced temperatures in Europe, 10–15 °C lower in some places. In addition, sea levels in the eastern USA could rise. The last time the North Atlantic circulation stopped and was restructured was during the glacial period between 115,000 years ago and about 12,000 years ago.

It has been suggested that if deforestation reaches 40%, the Amazon rainforest could pass a tipping point whereby it changes irreversibly into a savannah landscape. The replacement of forest with pasture is likely to have caused a widespread increase in temperature (Figure 6.48) and a decrease in evapotranspiration. Complete deforestation could lead to an increase in temperatures in the eastern Amazonian rainforest of 3 °C and cause precipitation to decline by as much as 40%. These changes would occur in addition to any changes in the local climate due to global human-made climate change.

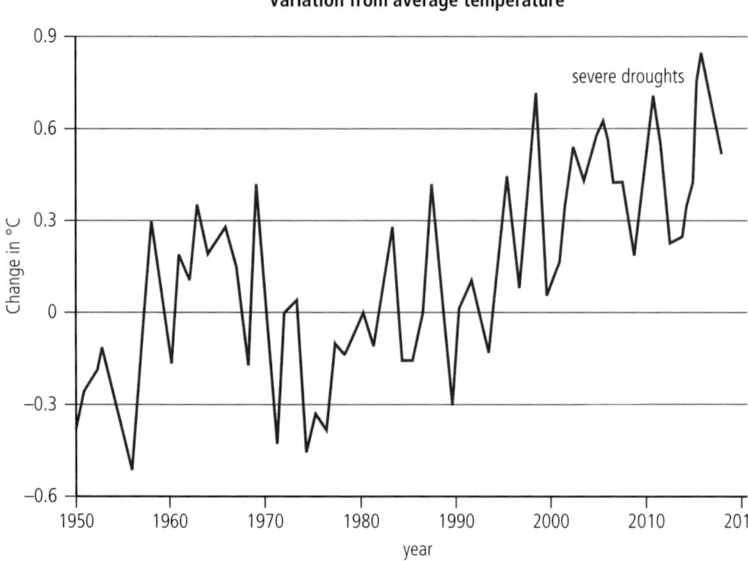

Figure 6.48 Changing air temperature over the Amazon compared with the 1961–90 average.

Figure 6.49 Amazon forest fire and die-back.

Both deforestation and extreme drought may increase tree mortality and disrupt the stability of the rainforest biome. Larger trees are especially vulnerable as they are exposed to solar radiation and require more moisture. Mortality of taller trees may then reduce shading of lower trees and lead to increased temperatures at ground level, more dryness and potential for drought and fire. Rainforest species are not adapted to fire, whereas savannah species are (Figure 6.49).

6.2.14 Tipping cascades

HL

1.2 Systems
2.2 Energy and biomass in ecosystems
2.4 Climate and biomes

Individual tipping points of the climate system may interact to create **tipping cascades**, i.e. a number of tipping points acting together. This makes predictions about the scale and pace of climate change very uncertain.

Tipping point interactions

A recent study titled *Interacting tipping elements increase risk of climate domino effects under global warming* (European Geosciences Union 2021) showed that the West Antarctic ice sheet, the Greenland ice sheet, Atlantic Meridional Overturning Circulation (AMOC) and the Amazonian rainforest tipping points could interact with one another before temperature increase reaches 2 °C (Figure 6.50). This interaction could allow climate tipping to occur at lower temperatures than previously expected.

For example, when freshwater is released into the North Atlantic from the Greenland ice sheet, the AMOC could slow. This might result in less heat being transported northwards. As the North Atlantic cooled, it could help stabilize the Greenland ice sheet. However, it would also lead to warmer water in the Southern Ocean that could lead to drought in some parts of the Amazon and higher rainfall in other parts.

These changes would occur over long timescales and scientists say that it is difficult to predict detailed interactions.

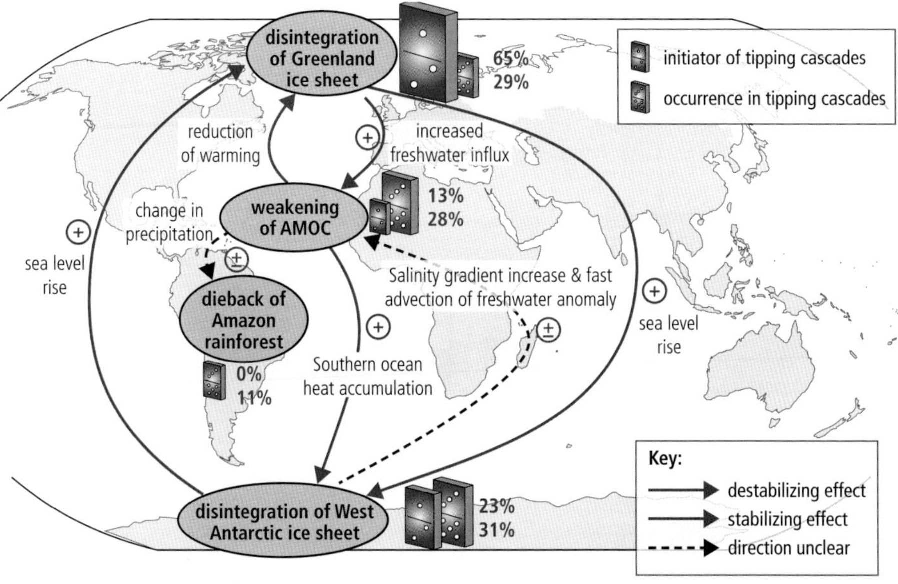

Figure 6.50 Interactions between climate tipping elements and their roles in tipping cascades.

Individual tipping points can be biotic (living), abiotic (non-living, physical) or a combination of both biotic and abiotic factors. Biotic factors include plants, animals and other forms of life, whereas abiotic factors include soil, water, air, and climate.

As well as physical tipping points, there are also social tipping points. These are the points when some people change their behaviour. Some of these changes could help stabilize climate change, including:

- removing subsidies for fossil fuels
- building carbon-neutral cities
- expanding climate change education
- greater use of public transport.

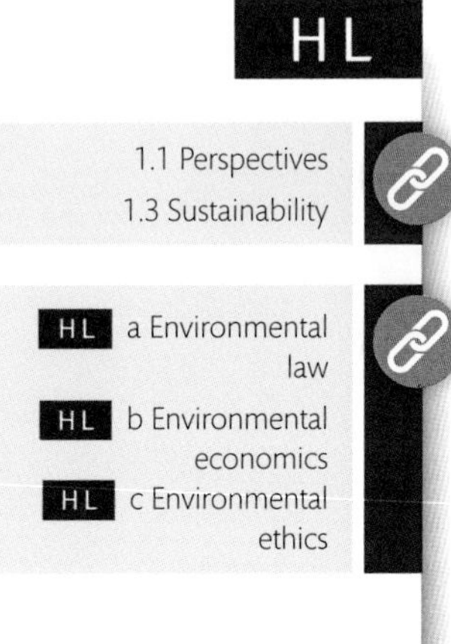

HL
1.1 Perspectives
1.3 Sustainability
HL a Environmental law
HL b Environmental economics
HL c Environmental ethics

6.2.15 Variations in countries' responsibility and vulnerability to climate change

Current CO_2 emissions by country

Different countries emit widely different amounts of CO_2. The highest overall emissions come from countries with large populations, industrialized countries and countries with large oil and gas deposits. However, when looking at CO_2 emissions per person by country, the pattern is different. Those countries with the highest emissions per person are small countries, mainly oil-rich countries, wealthy countries and some countries where tourism is an important economic sector.

Figure 6.51 shows the CO_2 emissions per capita by country, as well as the total national emissions. The area of each bar shows the total CO_2 emissions for each country. For example, the Middle East gulf states have the highest CO_2 emissions per capita at 20.7 tonnes per year, but India has one of the largest national emissions due to its population size (shown by the size of its bar).

Figure 6.51 CO_2 emissions per capita by country.

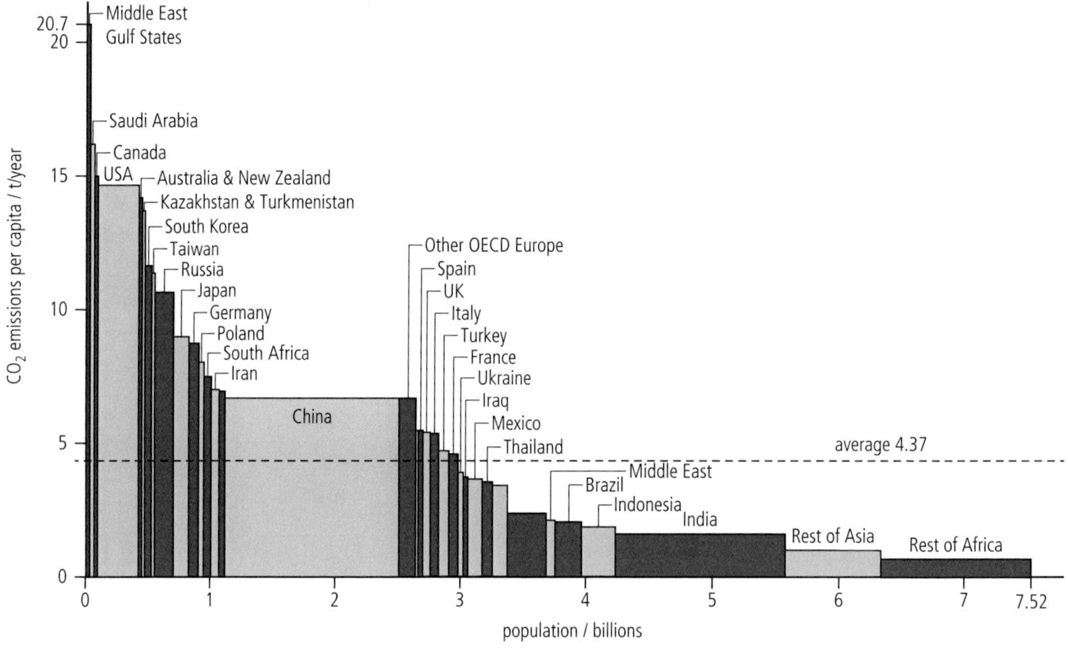

Cumulative emissions

Since 1850, the USA and India have accounted for about 23% of global CO_2 emissions. By 1990 the USA had emitted 250 Gt of CO_2 since the industrial revolution whereas India had emitted just over 11 Gt CO_2. However, by 2021 the USA had emitted over 400 billion metric tonnes of CO_2 and India's emissions had increased to about 57 Gt CO_2, mainly on account of its rapid industrial growth.

What criteria can we use to decide between contrasting knowledge claims?

Who should bear responsibility for greenhouse gas emissions – the countries producing the goods (e.g. USA and Brazil) or those consuming the products (e.g. Germany and Middle Eastern countries)?

Countries most vulnerable to global climate change

The countries that contribute most to global climate change are rich, industrialized and/or oil rich. Those that are most vulnerable to the impacts of climate change are poor and low-lying countries, including many island nations. According to the International Rescue Committee, the most vulnerable nations include Somalia, Syria, DR Congo, Afghanistan, Yemen, Chad, South Sudan, Central African Republic, Nigeria and Ethiopia. On the other hand, it can be argued that all countries are vulnerable to global climate change, directly and indirectly, for example through the increase in extreme weather events and the impacts of food supply, water supply and employment.

Activity

Search for '10 countries at risk of climate disaster' on the International Rescue Committee website to find out which countries are most at risk of climate change and the reasons why they are at risk. To what extent are physical factors the main cause of the increased risk of climate change?

Exercise

Q11. **Distinguish between** the greenhouse effect and global warming.

Q12. Using examples, **explain** positive and negative feedback in climate systems.

Q13. **Outline** the main anthropogenic sources of greenhouse gas emissions.

Q14. **Explain** the importance of planetary boundaries.

Q15. **Outline** the evidence for long-term climate change.

Q16. **Explain** the term *hindcasting*.

Q17. **Suggest** reasons why perspectives on climate change can vary for individuals and societies.

Q18. HL **Outline** the importance of models in our understanding of climate systems.

Q19. HL With the use of examples, **explain** the importance of tipping points in global climate change.

Q20. HL Using examples, **explain** why some countries are more likely to contribute to global climate change, whereas others are more vulnerable to its impacts.

Engagement

- Create a presentation or display for your school to raise awareness about the issue of climate change.
- Look for and participate in local and virtual climate action events.
- Join a citizen action group or youth parliament to create policies around climate change.
- Search online for the University of Reading, UK's *climate stripes*, which were developed by Professor Ed Hawkins in 2018. Analyse the climate stripes for your home region/country. Shades of blue represent cold years and shades of red, warm years. The darker the colour, the greater the variation from the average temperature.

6.3 Climate change—mitigation and adaptation

Guiding question

How can human societies address the causes and consequences of climate change?

6.3.1 To avoid the risk of catastrophic climate change, global action is required, rather than measures adopted only by certain states.
6.3.2 Decarbonization of the economy means reducing or ending the use of energy sources that result in CO_2 emissions and their replacement with renewable energy sources.
6.3.3 A variety of mitigation strategies aim to address climate change.
6.3.4 Adaptation strategies aim to reduce adverse effects of climate change and maximize any positive consequences.
6.3.5 Individuals and societies on a range of scales are developing adaptation plans, such as National Adaptation Programmes of Action (NAPAs), and resilience and adaptation plans.
HL 6.3.6 Responses to climate change may be led by governments or a range of non-governmental stakeholders. Responses may include economic measures, legislation, goal setting commitments and personal life changes.
HL 6.3.7 The United Nations has played a key role in formulating global strategies to address climate change.
HL 6.3.8 The IPCC has proposed a range of emissions scenarios with targets to reduce the risk of catastrophic climate change.
HL 6.3.9 Technology is being developed and implemented to aid in the mitigation of climate change.
HL 6.3.10 There are challenges to overcome in implementing climate management and intervention strategies.
HL 6.3.11 Geoengineering is a mitigation strategy for climate change, treating the symptom not the cause.
HL 6.3.12 A range of stakeholders play an important role in changing perspectives on climate change.
HL 6.3.13 Perspectives on the necessity, practicality and urgency of action on climate change will vary between individuals and between societies.
HL 6.3.14 The concept of the tragedy of the commons suggests that catastrophic climate change is likely unless there is international cooperation on an unprecedented scale.

6.3.1 Global action for climate change

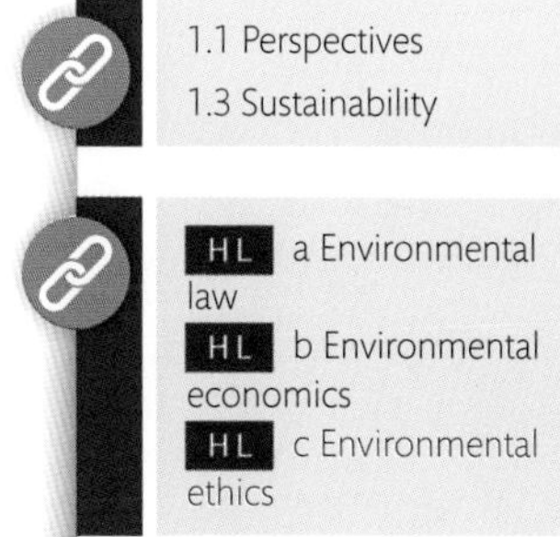

1.1 Perspectives
1.3 Sustainability
HL a Environmental law
HL b Environmental economics
HL c Environmental ethics

To avoid the risk of catastrophic climate change, global action is required, rather than measures adopted only by certain states. There is a need for international cooperation through negotiation, protocols, conventions and treaties. There have been many UN treaties and protocols addressing climate change. It is possible to introduce sanctions such as cross-border carbon taxes.

The solution for the climate change problem is to reduce greenhouse gas emissions. At the Paris climate conference in 2015, world leaders agreed that global temperature rises should be kept to a maximum of 2 °C and preferably 1.5 °C. However, despite this agreement, global carbon emissions have continued to rise every year.

The UNFCCC was created at the Rio Earth Summit in 1992 (Topic 1, Section 1.1.10) to negotiate a global agreement for reducing greenhouse gases and limiting the impact of global climate change. The UNFCCC has 198 parties (countries). The general principle is that every country must reduce its emissions and that countries should aim for net zero emissions (Figure 6.52). For most countries, net zero is planned for 2050.

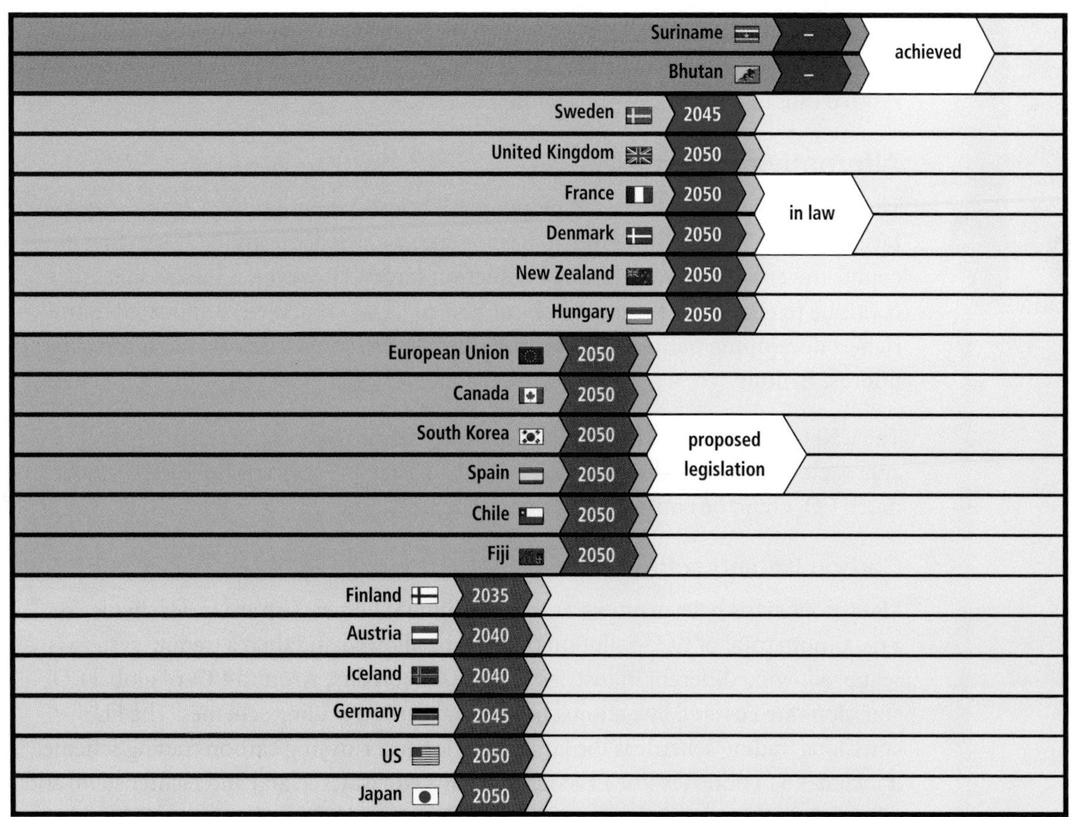

Figure 6.52 The time line for net zero emissions, as proposed in 2021.

Activity

Use the Energy & Climate Net Zero Scorecard website to access the 2023 tracker for all nations. With a partner, explore the tracker for five contrasting countries. Prepare a presentation to give to your class.

Since the UNFCCC was established, the countries involved have met most years at the COP. In 1997 the Kyoto Protocol was agreed. This called for developed nations to cut their greenhouse gas emissions by 5.2% of their 1990 levels by 2008–12. The Kyoto Agreement became a legal treaty in 2001. However, the USA withdrew from the treaty. This was a major blow as the USA was responsible for producing about 25% of the world's CO_2. In addition, the treaty did not include any LICs.

At the Copenhagen Summit in 2009, the scientific case for keeping temperature rise to below 2 °C was recognized, but no commitments were made towards achieving that target. Earlier proposals to reduce greenhouse gas emissions by 80% by 2050 were dropped. It took nearly 5 years for UNFCCC negotiations to get back on track. Negotiations in Paris 2015 were considered to be a success. The Paris Agreement stated that parties were required to keep temperature rises to *well below 2 °C above pre-industrial levels and to pursue efforts to limit the temperature increase to 1.5 °C above pre-industrial levels.* A number of LICs came together as the Climate Vulnerable Forum and managed to push the 1.5 °C target further up the agenda. In 2023, COP 28 was held in the UAE, under the leadership of Sultan Al Jaber, the head of the country's national oil company, Adnoc.

Overall, it has been argued that the UNFCCC does not go far enough. Despite 25 years of negotiations, no lasting agreement has been made. In addition, there is no enforcement. This is the main problem with international agreements and treaties. Many scientists and politicians claim that climate negotiations are a form of *green colonialism*, i.e. HICs are dictating to LICs how and when they should develop. Countries such as India have resisted calls to reduce emissions for many years.

In 2017, the Paris Agreement suffered a major setback when US President Trump stated he was taking the USA out of the agreement as he believed it was unfair and biased towards LICs. However, in 2020, after the election of President Biden, the USA re-engaged with the Paris Agreement.

Alternative schemes

There are alternative schemes to reduce greenhouse gas emissions. Clean Development Mechanisms (CDMs) allow HICs to pay for emissions reductions in LICs so that it counts towards their own national reduction target. However, it means that HICs continue to emit CO_2. Moreover, about 80% of CDM credits were allocated to the richest developing nations such as India and Brazil, so the funding did not reach the poorest nations.

The UNFCCC approach is based on individual nation-states rather than a global approach. In addition, the approach could be based on economic sectors, e.g. how much CO_2 could be emitted per tonne of concrete used.

Carbon trading schemes

Many politicians have promoted carbon trading schemes. *Cap and trade* schemes set a maximum total of CO_2 pollution that can be allowed and then a trading system is set up, allowing different industries to trade CO_2 credits. Around 13% of global CO_2 emissions are covered by national or regional carbon trading schemes. The EU's emissions trading scheme is the largest and longest running carbon trading scheme. It includes 31 countries (the EU countries plus Norway, Iceland and Lichtenstein) and 50% of their CO_2 emissions. The scheme has resulted in the reduction of CO_2 emissions by over 1 billion tonnes between 2008 and 2016.

Carbon tax

In addition, the EU has proposed placing a tax on carbon-intensive products, such as steel and concrete. This has proved controversial with many of their trading partners. It could become a form of protectionism, shielding local producers from foreign competition, or it could be seen as an attempt to reduce the amount of carbon used to produce goods. EU importers would have to buy a *carbon certificate* corresponding to the carbon-price that would have been paid in the EU, had the goods been produced there. Some other countries are concerned over the plans. They have several alternative options:

- reduce imports from the EU
- create their own carbon tax
- negotiate an exemption with the EU
- challenge the EU's plans at the World Trade Organization.

Activity

Is the lack of enforcement the main problem with international agreements and treaties? Discuss this question with a partner.

6.3.2 Decarbonization

1.3 Sustainability

HL b Environmental economics

Decarbonization means any attempt to reduce or end the use of energy sources that result in CO_2 emissions, and to replace them with renewable energy sources, which are essential for *sustainable* development.

Decarbonization of the economy means reducing or ending the use of energy sources that result in CO_2 emission and replacing them with renewable energy sources. Many states are attempting to achieve carbon neutrality.

Decarbonization refers to the lowering of the amount of greenhouse gas emissions produced from the burning of fossil fuels. It involves increasing the amount of renewable energy sources used such as wind power, solar power and hydroelectric power (although carbon is used in the construction of the power plants). Decarbonization was outlined in the Paris Agreement. Rapid decarbonization is becoming more possible due to the electrification of the transport sector, increasing the demand for electric power at the expense of fossil fuels such as diesel and petrol. The use of greater energy efficiency and less-carbon-intense energy sources are vital to achieve decarbonization.

Energy production and consumption accounts for about 75% of global greenhouse gas emissions, hence it is a major focus of attempts to achieve decarbonization (Table 6.4). To achieve decarbonization, countries need to:

- optimize: reduce energy use through improved efficiency
- electrify: increase the demand for electricity and reduce the demand for fossil fuels
- decarbonize: move towards zero-carbon technology.

Table 6.4 Systems and their contributions to greenhouse gas emissions.

System	Examples	Percentage of all CO_2 emissions (%)	Percentage of all CH_4 emissions (%)	Percentage of all N_2O emissions (%)
power	electricity and heat generation	30	0	3
industry	various industrial processes, including production of steel, cement and chemicals, and extraction and refining of oil, gas and coal	30	33	8
mobility	road, aviation, rail, maritime and other forms of transportation	19	0	2
buildings	heating and cooking	6	0	0
agriculture	direct on-farm energy use and emissions from agricultural practices and fishing	1	38	79
forestry and other land use	primarily land cover change	14	5	5
waste	solid waste disposal and treatment, incineration and wastewater treatment	0	23	3

Countries are decarbonizing their energy systems in several ways.

- Improvements in energy efficiency: China, Denmark, Ethiopia and the UK have decreased their energy intensity by over 4% per year, compared with the global average of 2.3%.
- Use of hydroelectric power (HEP): Costa Rica and Ethiopia get most of their energy from clean sources including Ethiopia's Grand Renaissance Dam.
- Increase in non-HEP renewables: many countries are developing wind, solar and geothermal energy. Costa Rica, Denmark and the UK all increased their share of non-hydro renewables from virtually zero in 1990 to over 20% by 2017.
- Increased wealth and economic development results in electrification of the energy sector. China now gets about 25% of its energy from electricity compared with just 6% in 1990. However, coal is still being used to generate over 60% of China's electricity.
- Electrification in buildings has been significant but in transport systems it has lagged behind. Electricity increased its market share in residential and services buildings globally from 19% in 1990 to 31% in 2017. In contrast, transportation is less than 1% electrified in most countries. China is the exception, increasing from 1.6% to 3.4% between 1990 and 2017.
- Increasing government commitments to clean, efficient energy and decarbonization: Costa Rica, Denmark and the UK have all set net-zero targets for 2050.

Carbon neutrality occurs when CO_2 emissions (or all greenhouse gas emissions) are balanced by the amount of CO_2 absorbed via carbon sinks (Figure 6.53).

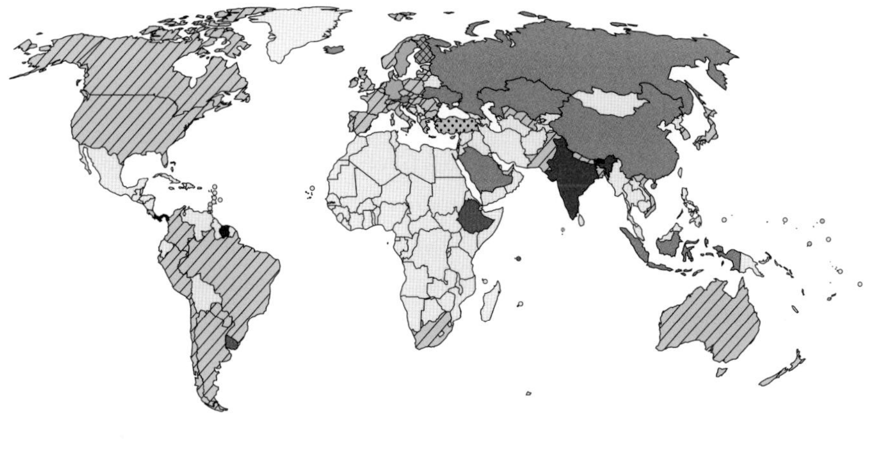

Figure 6.53 Countries by year of intended carbon-neutrality.

Key:
Countries and nations by intended year of climate neutrality
- Carbon neutral or negative
- 2030
- 2035
- 2040
- 2045
- 2050
- 2053
- 2060
- 2070
- Unknown or undeclared

6.3.3 Mitigation strategies

1.1 Perspectives
1.3 Sustainability
5.2 Agriculture and food

HL a Environmental law
HL b Environmental economics
HL c Environmental ethics

A variety of **mitigation strategies** aim to address climate change. There are three main categories of mitigation strategies:

- **Reducing the process of global warming**, for example from household choices to geoengineering.
- **Reducing production of greenhouse gases**, for example energy efficiency measures, replacing fossil fuels with renewable energy, food choice changes, agriculture changes, carbon tax.
- **Removing CO_2 from the atmosphere**, for example through carbon sinks, rewilding, afforestation, carbon capture and storage.

Mitigation involves reduction and/or stabilization of greenhouse gas emissions and their removal from the atmosphere.

Mitigation strategies aim to reduce the quantity of GHGs in the atmosphere, avoiding further development of the enhanced greenhouse effect.

Reducing the process of global warming

One of the main ways to reduce emissions of greenhouse gases is to consume less energy. This can be done in a variety of ways, including increased use of public transport, carpooling, use of alternatives to fossil fuels (Figure 6.54) and energy conservation.

Figure 6.54 Wind turbines and solar panels provide alternatives to fossil fuels.

Household choices

Table 6.5 shows some potential mitigation strategies that can be used on an international, national and domestic scale to help reduce global warming.

Mitigation refers to any attempt to prevent global climate change whereas **adaptation** refers to efforts to learn to live with aspects of global climate change.

Table 6.5 Some mitigation strategies for global warming.

National and international methods to prevent further increases in mean global temperature	Ways in which individuals can contribute to the reduction of greenhouse gas emissions
• controlling and reducing the amount of atmospheric pollution • stopping forest clearance • increasing forest cover • developing alternative renewable energy sources • improving public transport • setting national limits on carbon emissions • developing CO_2 capture methods • recycling programmes	• grow your own food • eat locally produced foods • use energy-efficient products rather than traditional ones • reduce your heating needs by insulating your home • unplug standby appliances when not in use • turn off lights • reduce the use of air conditioning and refrigerants • use a manual lawnmower rather than an electric or diesel one • turn off taps • take a shower rather than a bath • walk more • ride a bike • use public transport • use biofuels • eat food from further down the food chain, e.g. vegetables rather than meat • buy organic food • get involved in local political action

Geoengineering

Many large-scale geoengineering interventions allow households to reduce the process of global warming (Figure 6.55).

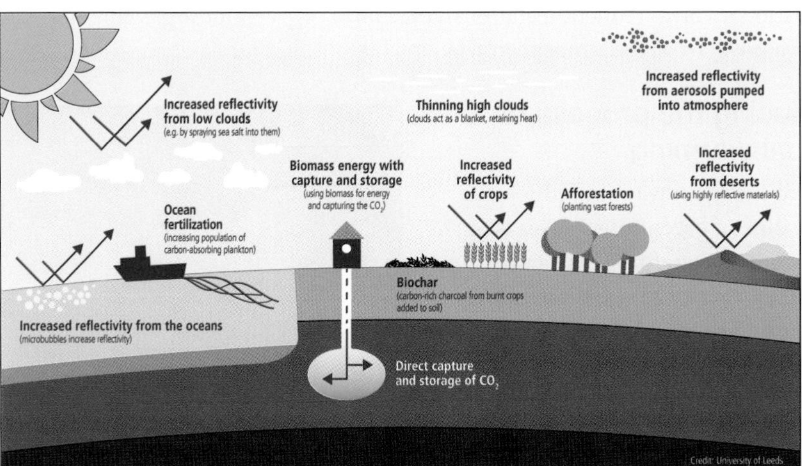

Figure 6.55 Some forms of geoengineering.

Some scientists have suggested the use of sulfate aerosol particles in the air in order to dim the incoming sunlight, and thereby cool the planet, in order to offset the warming effects of CO_2. Another idea is to place giant mirrors in space in order to deflect some incoming solar radiation. These ideas are fairly radical and perhaps unworkable. However, there are some small-scale ideas that are workable, such as painting roofs white in order to reflect more solar energy.

Reducing production of greenhouse gases

There are many approaches to producing low carbon energy, such as the use of photovoltaic (PV) cells to convert light energy into electrical energy. However, these cells rely on the ability to produce larger storage/batteries, which are currently not very environmentally friendly. There is great potential to expand wind power in the mid-west of the USA and the north-east desert regions of North Africa, northern Europe, and parts of central and western China. However, some of the areas that have the highest potential for renewable energy are very distant from centres of population and their source of energy is intermittent. Hence, large-scale renewable energy will require the construction of new transmission lines. For example, the DESERTEC project (Figure 6.56) was designed to link North Africa, the Middle East and Europe in a single grid. This system would tap the strong solar and wind potential of North Africa and the Arabian Peninsula both to supply energy for these economies and to export the surplus energy to Europe. The idea is potentially a key solution to Europe's unsolved challenge of deep decarbonization and could provide an enormous boost to the economies of North Africa and the Middle East. But the large-scale project stalled, as it was believed that Europe could produce all its energy needs, and so the DESERTEC project would be uneconomical. However, there are several smaller-scale solar projects going ahead in Tunisia, Morocco and Algeria.

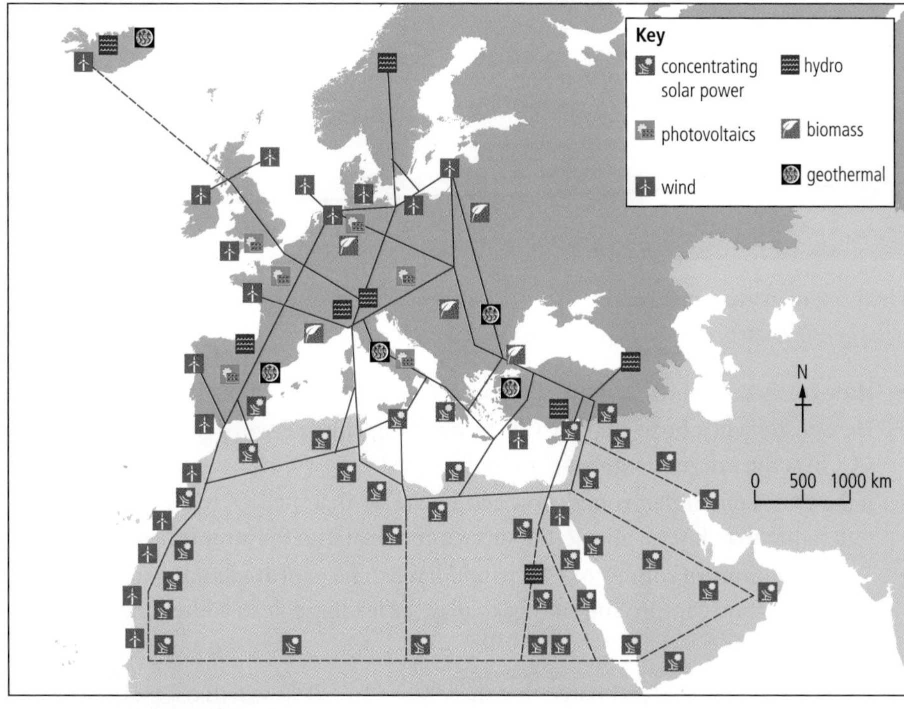

Figure 6.56 The proposed DESERTEC project linking North Africa, the Middle East and Europe.

Other ways of reducing greenhouse gas production include:

- the use of increased energy efficiency measures for household appliances and vehicles
- food choice changes such as eating less red meat and eating food from further down the food chain
- agricultural changes such as producing more grains and vegetables and local crops rather than non-native ones
- increasing carbon taxes (this topic, Section 6.3.1).

Removing CO_2 from the atmosphere

Carbon capture and storage (CSS)

Currently, when fossil fuels are burned, CO_2 is released into the atmosphere, where it may reside for decades or even centuries. A potential solution is to capture the CO_2 at the source instead of allowing it to accumulate in the atmosphere. Two main ways to do this have been proposed.

- The first way is to capture the gas at the site where it is produced, e.g. the power plant, and then store it underground in a geologic deposit such as an abandoned oil reservoir (Figure 6.57).
- The second way is to allow the gas to enter the atmosphere but then to remove it directly from the atmosphere using specially designed removal processes such as collecting the CO_2 with special chemical sorbents that attract it. This approach is called direct air capture of CO_2.

Figure 6.57 Carbon capture and storage.

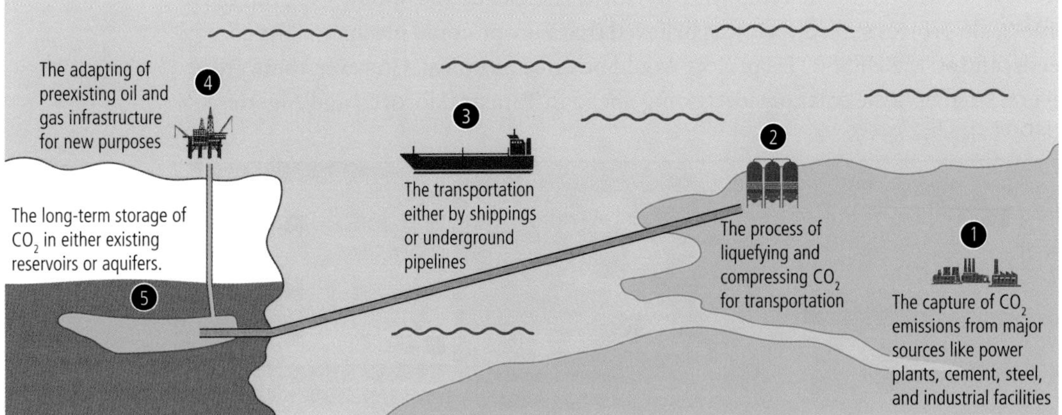
Understanding carbon capture and storage (CCS)
4
The adapting of preexisting oil and gas infrastructure for new purposes
3
The transportation either by shippings or underground pipelines
2
The process of liquefying and compressing CO2 for transportation
1
The capture of CO2 emissions from major sources like power plants, cement, steel, and industrial facilities
5
The long-term storage of CO2 in either existing reservoirs or aquifers.

There are many technical and policy issues about the feasibility and cost-effectiveness of large-scale carbon capture and storage technologies.

- How costly will it be to capture CO_2 on a large scale?
- How costly will it be to ship the CO_2 by a new pipeline network and then store the CO_2 in some safe, underground geologic deposit?
- If the CO_2 is put underground, how certain are we that the CO_2 will stay where it is put, rather than it returning to the surface and then into the atmosphere?
- Tens of billions of tonnes of CO_2 would have to be captured and stored each year for carbon capture and storage to play the leading role in addressing CO_2 emissions.

Nevertheless, it has been estimated that the UK has 16–20 Gt worth of storage capacity in abandoned hydrocarbon fields and 19–716 Gt worth of storage capacity in saline aquifers. This is enough to store over 500 years of the UK's annual emissions. Opened in 2010, the Century Plant carbon capture facility in Texas, USA, is the largest facility in North America. It can capture up to 8.4 million tonnes of carbon each year.

Enhancing CO_2 absorption

CO_2 absorption in oceans can be increased by fertilizing the ocean with compounds of iron, nitrogen and phosphorus. This introduces nutrients to the upper layer of the oceans, increases marine food production and removes CO_2 from the atmosphere. In some cases it may trigger an algal bloom. The algae remove CO_2 from the upper layers of the oceans as they absorb the gas from the water and sink to the ocean floor, taking the CO_2 with them.

Sperm whales transport iron from the deep ocean to the surface during prey consumption and defaecation. Increasing the number of sperm whales in the Southern Ocean could help remove carbon from the atmosphere. In the Southern Ocean, 12,000 sperm whales are responsible for the transfer of about 36 tonnes of iron to surface waters each year.

In some locations, such as off the coast of Peru, upwelling currents bring nutrients to the surface. These currents support large-scale fisheries and also help to lock up carbon. Artificial upwelling can be produced by devices that help pump water to the surface. Ocean wind turbines can also cause upwellings. These can then support plankton blooms, which help lock up CO_2. However, these turbines are costly to build and run.

There are certain issues regarding ocean fertilization. The 2007 London Convention on marine dumping stated that there were concerns over *the potential for large scale iron fertilization to have negative impacts on the marine environment and human health*. In 2022 proposals to remove sewage sludge from the list of permitted materials for dumping were announced.

Even if mitigation strategies drastically reduce future emissions of greenhouse gases, past emissions will continue to have an effect for some time.

Carbon sinks

Carbon sinks include anything that accumulates and stores carbon compounds, thereby removing CO_2 from the atmosphere. Figure 6.58 shows how the atmosphere has become an increasingly important sink for carbon and that the amount of carbon it stores has increased by almost 44% since 1850.

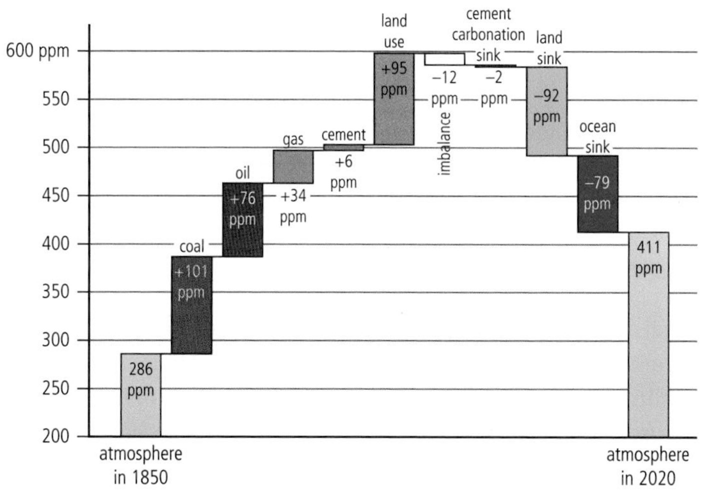

Figure 6.58 Carbon sources and sinks.

Afforestation is when new trees are planted in an area where there were no trees before, creating a new forest.

Reforestation is when new trees are planted in a forest where the number of trees has been decreasing.

Rewilding is allowing an environment to return to its natural state.

Afforestation and rewilding

Afforestation and rewilding are important ways for taking CO_2 out of the atmosphere. Since the beginning of farming, humans are believed to have cut down half of the trees on Earth. However, in many areas the processes of afforestation and rewilding are increasing the amount of land covered by trees. For example, in Spain the amount of land covered by trees increased from 8% in 1900 to 25% today.

Planting trees reduces soil erosion and adds moisture to the soil and atmosphere.

In 2019, researchers claimed that planting 1 trillion trees on 900 million ha of land (about the size of continental USA) could store over 200 billion tonnes of CO_2, which is about two-thirds of the amount that people have put into the atmosphere. Other research suggests new trees could store about 55 billion tonnes by 2100. It takes between 70 and 125 years for a tree to maximize its carbon storage potential.

Research the potential of a trillion trees at the Trillion Tree Campaign website.

As humanity puts 11 billion tonnes into the atmosphere each year, this would only tackle five years' worth of pollution. Hence afforestation and rewilding are not alternatives to large-scale cuts in fossil fuel emissions.

6.3.4 Adaptation strategies

1.3 Sustainability

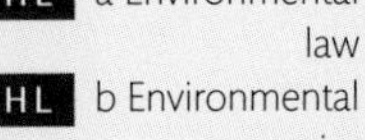

HL a Environmental law
HL b Environmental economics
HL c Environmental ethics

Adaptation strategies aim to reduce the adverse effects of climate change and maximize any positive consequences of global warming. There are two main categories of adaptation strategies:

- structural adaptations, for example flood defenses, desalination plants and moving infrastructure
- non-structural changes, for example, adapting agricultural practices like drought resistant crops, vaccination for new diseases, land zoning and building code changes.

Adaptation strategies can be used to reduce adverse effects and maximize any positive effects of global warming. Examples of adaptations include flood defenses, vaccination programmes, desalinization plants and planting of genetically modified crops in previously unsuitable climates.

It is possible to reduce human emissions of greenhouse gases substantially. The technologies are within reach and measures such as energy efficiency, low-carbon electricity and fuel switching (e.g. the electrification of buildings and vehicles) are all possible. Nevertheless, even with the use of these measures, CO_2 levels will continue to rise for a number of decades. By the time that the oceans warm, they are likely to add a further 0.6 °C to global temperatures. Thus, as well as trying to *mitigate* climate change, humanity needs to *adapt* to climate change as well.

Structural changes include protection against rising ocean levels and greater likelihood of storm surges and flooding, especially in low-lying coastal cities. To cope with changes in the supply of, and demand for, water, more desalinization plants will be required. However, these plants are expensive, and some LICs may struggle to meet the demand for fresh water.

Non-structural changes in agriculture include growing genetically modified crop varieties that are more resilient to higher temperatures and increases in the occurrence of floods and droughts. To cope with an increased risk of the spread of diseases such as malaria, more widespread vaccination programmes will be needed. The geographic range of some diseases, such as malaria, will spread as temperatures rise.

TOK

What constraints are there on the pursuit of knowledge?

There is a degree of uncertainty in the extent and effect of climate change - how can we be confident of the ethical responsibilities that may arise from knowledge when that knowledge is often provisional or incomplete?

The IPCC gives six reasons why humanity must adapt to climate change:

- climate change impacts cannot be avoided even if greenhouse gas emissions fall to zero
- adaptation is more effective and less costly than responding to emergencies in future
- climate change may accelerate and there are likely to be more extreme events e.g. cyclones, flooding, and wildfires such as in Hawaii in 2023
- immediate benefits would occur due to better adaptation
- there are immediate benefits from disallowing poor building practices such as building on flood plains
- there are opportunities, as well as threats, from climate change.

Figure 6.59 shows how countries could adapt to rising sea levels.

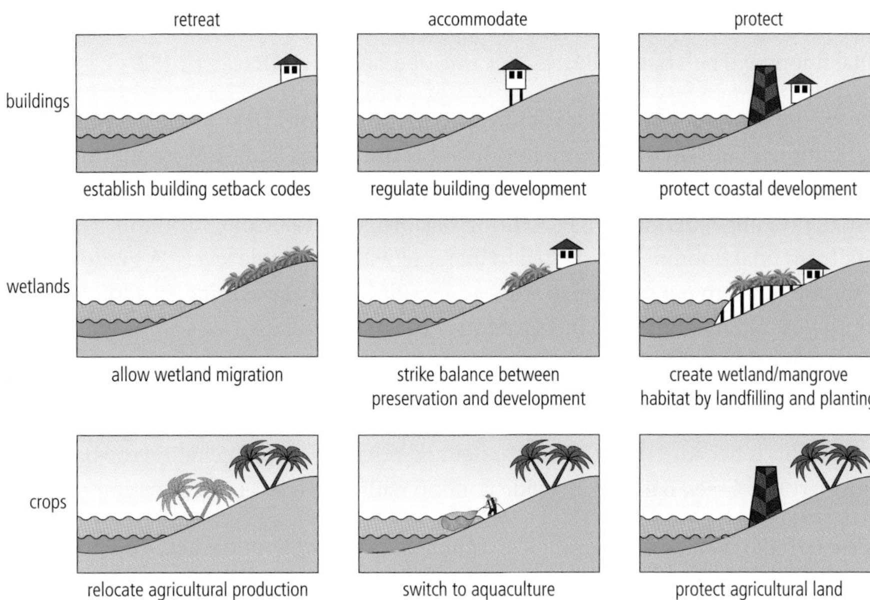

Figure 6.59 Model response strategies for rising sea levels.

One of the major threats from climate change is its unpredictability. Climate change will produce more extreme events, which will also be more unpredictable in scale and timing. Physical adaptations can take many decades to plan, develop and build (Figure 6.60).

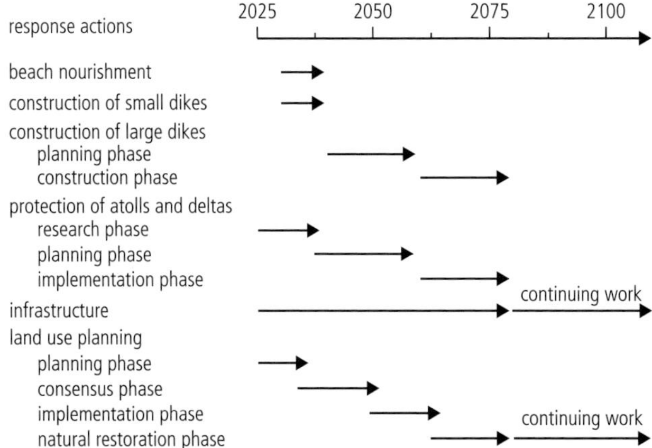

Figure 6.60 Lead times for response strategies to sea level rise due to climate change.

Social adaptations are also important. For countries where food and water security are likely to be affected by climate change, there need to be policies and actions that ensure continued access to food and water following climate change.

Nevertheless, there are limits to adaptation. For example, continued rises in sea levels will force some low-lying islands and regions to be abandoned. In 2019, the Indonesian president announced that the capital would move from Java to East Kalimantan as parts of Jakarta were sinking at 25 cm/year due to sea level rise and subsidence caused by extraction of groundwater from shallow aquifers.

Adaptation is costly. Many countries cannot afford it and many people do not want to pay for a future development. Moreover, most politicians are elected for periods of less than five years, so they tend to focus on short-term issues rather than long-term ones. For example, they will call for extra funds following a disaster rather than plan to protect against something that may happen sometime in the future.

Example – The Thames Barrier, London

Figure 6.61 The Thames Barrier.

The Thames Barrier (Figure 6.61) protects London from the most severe form of tidal flooding. The Thames Barrier became operational in October 1982.

Before the construction of the Thames Barrier, an area of 116 km^2 was at risk. Much of London is built on the natural floodplain of the River Thames. Without flood defenses, 420,000 homes on the Thames tidal floodplain would have a 0.1% annual risk of flooding. This amounts to a flood risk property value of £80 billion. The risk from tidal flooding is expected to increase with rising tide levels. A gradual sea level rise of 4 mm per year is expected as a result of global warming. In addition, the south-east of England is sinking. London is 30 cm lower than it was at the end of the Second World War.

The risk of tidal flooding from the River Thames is significant, but the probability is low. This is because the Thames Barrier and other defenses, including the Barking and Dartford Creek Barriers, provide London with a high level of protection.

Although the risk remains small, it is estimated that it will double between now and 2030. From 2030, the protection offered by the barrier will continue to decline unless improvements are made. On average, the barrier is closed three times per year. But during the winter of 2000/01 there were 24 closures.

By 2030, it is forecast that the barrier will have to close about 30 times per year to maintain the standards of tidal defense in the Thames Estuary. Closures of this kind of frequency would severely disrupt shipping. This has serious implications for London's ambitions to revitalize the use of the River Thames for freight and passenger transport. Similarly, the damage caused by Superstorm Sandy in New York in 2012, estimated at a cost of US$ 19 billion, highlighted the need for improvements in storm barriers, which could cost as much as US$ 22 billion. The potential risk from more intense storms is driving up the size and the cost of protective barriers.

Create surveys to investigate attitudes to a proposed solution in the school or community to mitigate climate change

Table 6.5 on page 600 shows a number of mitigation schemes for climate change.

1. Conduct a survey in your school/local community to investigate attitudes towards climate mitigation. If using your school, choose three groups – younger students, older students and teachers/adults. If you are using your local community, select young people aged under 25 years, adults aged 25–59 and older people aged 60 years and over.
2. Explain the term *climate mitigation* to at least 12 people in each age group and show them a copy of Table 6.5. Then ask the following questions:
   - Are you aware of any of these strategies taking place in this location? If so, which ones?
   - Which two climate mitigation strategies do you think offer the best hope for this location? Justify your choices.
   - Which two climate mitigation strategies do you think offer the least hope for this location? Justify your choices.
3. Analyse your results to see whether the different age groups have different attitudes to proposed solutions for global climate change in your location.

6.3.5 National Adaptation Programmes of Action (NAPAs)

1.1 Perspectives
1.3 Sustainability

HL a Environmental law
HL b Environmental economics
HL c Environmental ethics

Individuals and societies on a range of scales are developing adaptation plans such as National Adaptation Programmes of Action (NAPAs) and resilience and adaptation plans. The United Nations Development Programme provides a process whereby developing countries can obtain assistance to develop local priority activities to address the imminent consequences of climate change.

The main content of NAPAs is a list of ranked priority adaptation activities and projects. NAPAs focus on urgent and immediate needs – those for which any further delay could increase vulnerability or lead to increased costs at a later stage. NAPAs use existing information, are action oriented and country driven. The steps for the preparation of NAPAs include:

National Adaptation Programmes of Action (NAPAs) are plans of action whereby LICs identify priority actions that require immediate and urgent attention so as to reduce their vulnerability to global climate change.

- synthesis of available information
- assessment of vulnerability to current climate and extreme events
- identification of key adaptation measures as well as criteria for prioritizing activities
- selection of a prioritized short list of activities.

There is an example of a NAPA on this page of your eBook.

By 2017, the UNFCCC had received NAPAs from 51 LICs.

HL

6.3.6 Responses to climate change – governments and non-government stakeholders

HL

1.1 Perspectives

HL a Environmental law
HL b Environmental economics
HL c Environmental ethics

Responses to climate change may be led by governments or a range of non-government stakeholders. Measures include economic measures, legislation, goal setting commitments and personal life changes.

Economic measures

Economic measures include putting a price on carbon, emission trading and the use of subsidies and tariffs. Carbon taxes attempt to reduce emissions by requiring the largest greenhouse gas producers to pay for the damage they cause. By attaching fees to emissions, carbon taxes encourage governments, businesses and individuals to decrease their emissions. Sweden introduced a carbon tax in 1991 and successfully lowered its greenhouse gas emissions by almost 30%. Over 40 countries have national carbon taxes including Argentina, Canada, Japan and Singapore.

Legislation

Legislation includes country-specific legislation to reduce carbon emissions. Cap and trade systems are government programmes implemented to limit (cap) greenhouse gas emissions. Governments allocate or sell a number of permits, which allow companies to emit a specified amount of greenhouse gases. If a company needs additional permits to produce its products, it has to trade with another company to buy them. California introduced the USA's first cap and trade system in 2013. As a result, carbon emissions fell by 10% between 2013 and 2018.

Clean energy standards are a form of legislation designed to reduce the production of greenhouse gases. They encourage utility companies to generate a percentage of their energy from low-emission energy sources such as solar and wind. In 1999, Texas introduced a clean energy standard. Today, about 25% of its electricity is derived from renewable energy sources.

Goal setting

Goal setting includes mechanisms such as B Corp branding and company goals to reduce carbon emissions and change to renewable energy sources.

Across and within stakeholders there are different views on the need and urgency for climate action. For example, older people are more skeptical of climate change than younger people and men more skeptical than women (UK, ONS Census 2021).

Most climate analysts agree that governments play a crucial role in the attempt to manage global climate change. However, there is little agreement on which methods are the most effective.

Example – IKEA: corporate response to climate change

IKEA™ is a multinational brand that sells ready-to-assemble furniture. IKEA's sustainability report shows three main areas of focus.

- Healthy sustainable living. This involves inspiring over one billion people to live a better everyday life and helping people to live sustainably at home through methods including saving energy, saving water, using LED lighting and using second-hand furniture.
- IKEA plans to play a role in contributing to a fair and equal society, by respecting and promoting human rights across the value-chain and contributing to resilient societies.
- Being circular and climate positive. This includes making products that can be maintained, repaired and passed on to others. Some 60% of IKEA products are based on renewable materials and 10% of their products contain recycled materials. According to IKEA's website, *waste is no longer waste if it is given a second life.*

IKEA has three climate goals:

- to drastically reduce greenhouse gas emissions to 50% by 2030 and achieve net-zero by 2050
- to remove and store carbon through forestry, agriculture and products
- to extend responsibility to its customers, suppliers and sourcing.

Find out more about the B Corp movement on the Resources page of the bcorporation website:

B Corp branding

B Corp brands are sustainable companies that put sustainable practices first. There are more than 2500 certified B Corps in over five countries, including companies such as Ben and Jerry's and Innocent.

Example – Egypt: government response to climate change

Due to climate change, Egypt is increasingly vulnerable to sea level rise, saline intrusion, soil salinization, water shortages and desertification. Saline intrusions, for example, affect 15% of the Nile Delta's most fertile land. Climate challenges have intensified for reasons beyond Egypt's control including COVID-19, which reduced food security, and the conflict between Russia and Ukraine, which caused a supply crisis. According to the 2022 Climate Change Performance Index, Egypt was ranked 21st out of 60 countries for climate protection, 8th for greenhouse gas emissions, 12th for energy use, 56th for use of renewable energy and 29th for climate policy.

The Egyptian government has a number of plans and schemes to deal with these threats. In 2022 it produced its National Climate Change Strategy. This shows that Egypt plans, by 2050, to reduce greenhouse gas emissions from electricity by 33%, from oil and gas by 65% and from transport by 7% compared with current rates.

Three sectors that the government is focusing on are agriculture, transport and energy. In agriculture, the government is encouraging farmers to use heat-tolerant plants, use solar power for harvesting equipment, farm hydroponically and to use water-efficient forms of irrigation, especially drip irrigation. Whether farmers can afford these is an issue.

There are also plans to decarbonize transport across Egypt. The Egyptian government is keen to accelerate the electrification of transport and to shift away from the use of private cars to public transport. They also plan to improve the road network through the quality of roads and improve the underground metro system through expansion.

The Egyptian government initially had an ambitious plan to produce 20% of energy through renewable energy sources by 2022 and 42% by 2035. However, the increase in demand for energy, due to population growth, is largely met by an increased use of fossil fuels. For example, a new gas-field was opened at Zohr, which enabled Egypt to become self-sufficient in natural gas.

To deal with sea level rises Egypt is building a number of sand dikes, which are planted with reeds and local vegetation to stabilize them. The current project is due to be finished in 2026. Some critics argue that by protecting Cairo and selected parts of the Nile Delta, they will simply push the problem elsewhere, resulting in the flooding of farms and other cities.

Investigate mitigation and adaptation policies of the regional or national government

4. Use the internet to investigate mitigation and adaptation strategies of the regional or national government for an area of your choice.
5. Identify policies that have been adopted by a regional or national government.
6. Which mitigation and adaptation policies have been used? Outline their aims and evaluate their success.

6.3.7 Global strategies for climate change

The United Nations has played a key role in developing global strategies to address climate change. These strategies have been led by the UNFCCC, the IPCC and COP summits.

1.1 Perspectives

HL a Environmental law

There are many technological, economic and political obstacles to achieving a low-carbon world. Political obstacles are found nationally and internationally. The fossil fuel industry is the most powerful lobby group in the USA, where coal, oil and gas interests have managed to veto climate control regulations. The main obstacle to a global agreement on climate change remains the bargaining power of the major fossil fuel countries such as the USA, Canada, China, Russia and countries in the Middle East.

Greenhouse emissions are influenced by many factors including population size, the amount of energy used per person and the amount of energy used by economic sectors, transport and buildings. As the world's population increases in size and becomes wealthier, and economies grow, the amount of greenhouse gas emissions also increases. These emissions need to be managed.

There are international efforts and conferences to address mitigation and adaptation strategies for NAPAs (this topic, Section 6.3.5) and the UNFCCC.

The Kigali Amendment was used to control the use of hydrochlorofluorocarbons (HCFCs), which were allowed by the Montreal Protocol, but which subsequently proved to be greenhouse gases.

See also this topic, Section 6.3.1 on the role of the United Nations and Sections 6.4.8–9 and 6.4.12 on the Montreal Protocol and the Kigali Amendment.

COP 27 Sharm El Sheikh

The COP 27 meeting in Sharm El Sheikh, Egypt 2022 recognized that climate change is a common concern for all humankind. It issued a number of statements, including:

- plans to implement ambitious, just, equitable and inclusive transitions to low-emissions and climate-resilient development
- emphasizing the need for immediate, deep, rapid and sustained reductions in global greenhouse gas emissions
- realizing that limiting global climate change to 1.5 °C required a cut in global greenhouse gas emissions of 43% by 2030 compared with 2019 levels
- highlighting that about US$ 4 trillion would need to be invested in renewable energy up until 2030 to be able to reach net zero emissions by 2050.

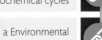

6.3.8 The IPCC range of emissions scenarios

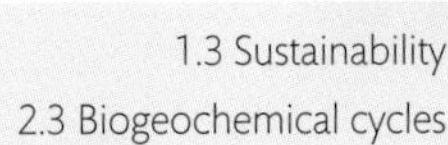

1.3 Sustainability
2.3 Biogeochemical cycles

HL a Environmental law

The IPCC has proposed five emission scenarios with targets to reduce the risk of catastrophic climate change. These scenarios address future greenhouse gas emissions (Figure 6.62 and Table 6.6). Because there is a range of uncertainty in how emissions by countries may change, there are five scenarios in the IPCC model.

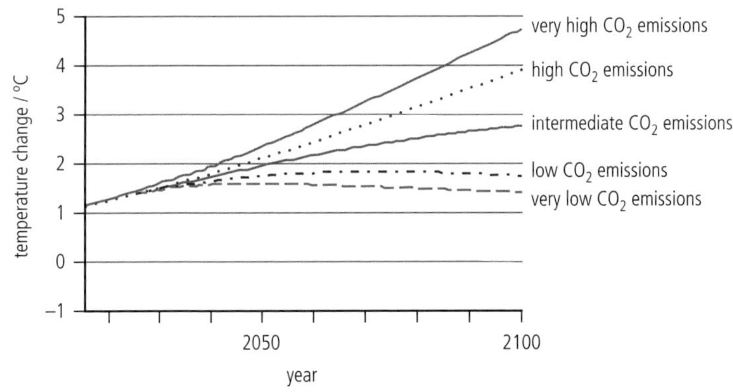

Figure 6.62 The IPCC's five emissions scenarios.

Scenario	Estimated warming (2041–2060) / °C
very high: CO_2 emissions triple by 2075	2.4 °C
high: CO_2 emissions double by 2100	2.1 °C
intermediate: CO_2 emissions around current levels until 2050, then falling but not reaching net zero by 2100	2.0 °C
low: CO_2 emissions cut to net zero around 2075	1.7 °C
very low: CO_2 emissions cut to net zero around 2050	1.5 °C

Table 6.6 Estimated warming for the IPCC's five emissions scenarios.

Many of the changes occurring in the world's climate today are unprecedented in light of the past thousands or hundreds of thousands of years. Some of the changes, such as sea level changes, will be irreversible over hundreds to thousands of years. Unless there are immediate rapid, large-scale reductions in greenhouse gas emissions, limiting warming to 1.5 °C or less will be extremely unlikely. Within 20 years, the IPCC is expecting that the temperature increases caused by global warming will reach or exceed 1.5 °C.

Figure 6.63 Possible changes in temperature due to different carbon emissions.

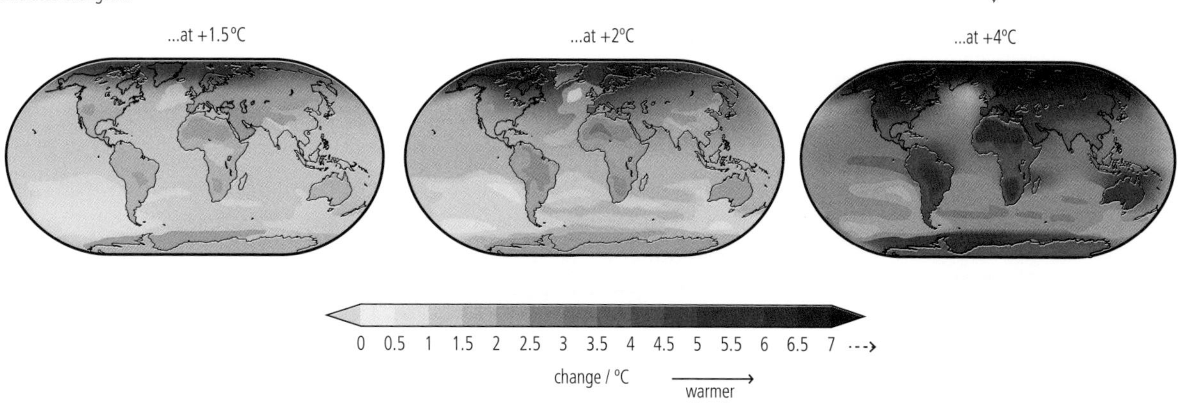

The low and very low scenarios suggest a rise in average temperature of around 1.5–1.8 °C by 2100. However, not all areas would experience the same degree of heating (Figure 6.63). The greatest rises in temperatures would occur at high latitudes and over land rather than over oceans. Moreover, it is not just about temperature but also includes rainfall, snow, aridity and sea level rises. According to the IPCC (*Climate Change 2021: The Physical Science Basis*), changes include:

- intensification of the water cycle, namely more intense rainfall associated with flooding and more extreme droughts
- rainfall is likely to increase in high latitudes but decrease over large parts of the subtropics
- coastal areas will experience continuous sea level rises causing more frequent and severe coastal flooding in low-lying areas and coastal erosion – events that once occurred once a century (a 100-year event) could occur every year by 2100
- warming will increase the rate of thawing of permafrost, the loss of seasonal snow cover, melting of glaciers and ice sheets and loss of summer Arctic sea ice
- changes to oceans will include warming, more frequent marine heatwaves, ocean acidification and reduced O_2 levels

Since 1880, global average temperatures have risen by 1.1 °C. According to the IPCC, global temperatures are predicted to increase by 1.5 °C by 2050 and by 2 °C by 2100.

According to NOAA's 2021 Annual Climate Report, the combined land and ocean temperature increased at an average rate of 0.08 °C per decade from 1880, but since 1981 it has increased by 0.18 °C per decade.

- cities will have increased urban heat islands, flooding from intense rainfall and sea level rise in coastal cities.

The higher the rise in global temperature, the worse the impacts and these will continue beyond 2100.

Investigate graphs of the IPCC scenarios and their implications

7. Use the IPCC's interactive atlas of climate change to investigate changes in temperature and rainfall in your home area at four different possible global warming levels.
8. Use the Figures section of the IPCC website to investigate graphs of the IPCC's scenarios and their implications.

The IPCC also published a list of five different shared socioeconomic pathways (SSPs) to show the full range of possible climate futures until 2100 (Table 6.7).

- In SSP1, the world shifts gradually but continually towards a more sustainable path, with environmentally aware economic development and social inclusion.
- In SSP2, social, economic and technological trends do not change dramatically from historic conditions. Development and income growth is uneven, with some countries making good progress and others less so.
- In SSP3, there is a resurgence of nationalism and concerns about energy security. Countries focus increasingly on domestic or regional issues. Countries focus on achieving energy- and food-security and government policies are orientated to national and regional security.
- In SSP4, investment is highly unequal and there are rising inequalities in economic development and political power, leading to increased inequalities within and between countries.
- In SSP5, the world turns towards innovation, technological developments, competitive markets and human ingenuity to find a solution for sustainable development.

Table 6.7 SSPs from the IPCC's Sixth Assessment Report.

	Near term, 2021-2040		Mid term, 2041-2060		Long term, 2081-2100	
Scenario	**Best estimate (°C)**	***Very likely* range (°C)**	**Best estimate (°C)**	***Very likely* range (°C)**	**Best estimate (°C)**	***Very likely* range (°C)**
SSP1-1.9	1.5	1.2 to 1.7	1.6	1.2 to 2.0	1.4	1.0 to 1.8
SSP1-2.6	1.5	1.2 to 1.8	1.7	1.3 to 2.2	1.8	1.3 to 2.4
SSP2-4.5	1.5	1.2 to 1.8	2.0	1.6 to 2.5	2.7	2.1 to 3.5
SSP3-7.0	1.5	1.2 to 1.8	2.1	1.7 to 2.6	3.6	2.8 to 4.6
SSP5-8.5	1.6	1.3 to 1.9	2.4	1.9 to 3.0	4.4	3.3 to 5.7

Commentary on the SSPs suggests that SSP1 and SSP5 are highly unlikely but that SSP3 is likely. It is most likely that by 2041–60, estimated warming will be 2.0 °C. By 2081–2100, the estimated warming will be 2.7 °C and the very likely warming range will be 2.1–3.5 °C.

6.3.9 Technology and climate mitigation

HL

1.1 Perspectives
1.3 Sustainability

HL b Environmental economics

Technology is helping in the mitigation of climate change.

Over half of the world's population live in urban areas and this is expected to reach nearly 70% by 2050. Cities are responsible for most of the world's economic activity, energy consumption and greenhouse gas emissions. Smart cities are technologically modern urban areas that use electronic methods and sensors to collect data and manage resources and services efficiently, including mitigating global warming. Smart cities are closely linked to the *Internet of Things*, which includes items that can communicate with other devices electronically. There are a number of potential applications for climate mitigation using smart city applications (Figure 6.64).

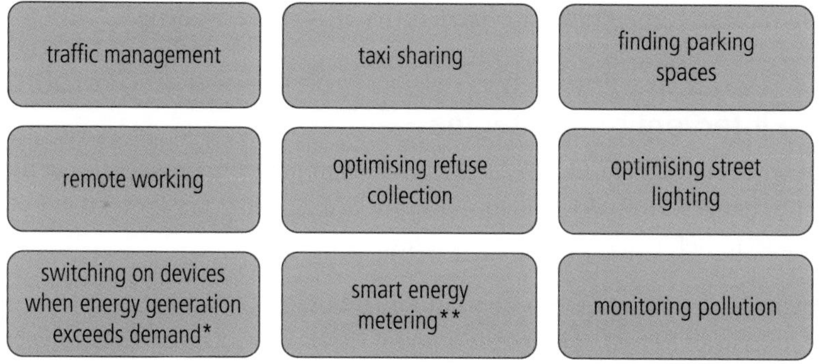

*Examples include charging electric cars and switching on washing machines. This will be useful because energy generation from renewable sources, such as wind and solar, is intermittent.

**Users may reduce consumption if they are more aware of how much energy they are using.

Figure 6.64 Potential smart city applications.

Singapore first trialled Beeline, an application for crowd-sourced bus services, in 2015. It works by the government sharing data with private bus operators to show where there is greater demand for public transport. This led to more efficient public transport and helped to reduce private car use.

There have been a number of collaborations between universities and industries for the removal of carbon and reduction of emissions. One such international collaboration occurred between:

- the universities of Cambridge (UK), Stanford (USA) and Melbourne (Australia)
- CO_2 CRC, a world leader in carbon capture, utilization and storage research
- BHP, one of the world's largest mining companies.

This collaboration investigated the possibility of carbon storage at Otway, south-west Victoria, Australia.

Activity

1. Investigate the following recycling apps: iRecycle, RecycleNation, Recycle Coach, and Recyclebank.

   Which of them do you think offers the best prospects for recycling? Which of them could you use in your school? Are there any costs involved in any of them? Make a presentation of your results to the class.

2. Outline the advantages of recycling.

HL

1.1 Perspectives
1.3 Sustainability

HL a Environmental law

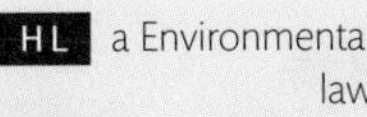

HL b Environmental economics

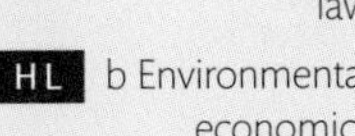

HL c Environmental ethics

Climate change deniers are people who believe that either climate has not changed or that it is entirely natural and that it is not caused by any human activities.

6.3.10 Challenges to overcome

There are many challenges to overcome when implementing climate management and intervention strategies, including:

- lack of belief that climate change is a serious problem
- lack of financial resources or planning strategies from national governments
- lack of leadership from a range of stakeholders e.g. individuals, NGOs, political leaders and transnational companies
- international inequalities e.g. economies that profit from fossil fuels and those that do not, LIC versus HIC societies
- differences in perspective between younger and older, coastal/low-lying and inland/upland communities are barriers that may cause challenges.

Lack of belief in climate change is a challenge to overcoming climate intervention strategies

Some people believe that CO_2 responds to global temperature changes rather than causes the changes. However, evidence over the last 20,000 years shows that CO_2 increases occur before temperature increases.

Other people believe that CO_2 concentrations (about 0.04% of the atmosphere) are too low to have an impact. It is not the amount that is important but the potency – although greenhouse gases are important for the greenhouse effect, they are increasing in volume and global temperatures are responding.

Some deniers also believe that recent changes in temperature are caused by variations in solar radiation. There is evidence of an 11-year solar cycle, but the solar output only varies by about 0.1%. Between 1880 and about 1960, solar radiation increased, but since the 1960s it has been decreasing, whereas temperatures have increased dramatically.

Other people state that as different models give different results, they cannot be correct. However, the models all predict the same trend, i.e. temperatures and sea levels will continue to rise until 2100 and beyond. This gives scientists confidence in their models. Moreover, the number of climate models has increased from 7 in 2001, to 40 in 2013 and over 100 in 2021.

Some people argue that clouds cause negative feedback and that this will reduce the impact of climate change. Clouds can absorb and reflect radiation, so can warm and cool the Earth's surface.

Other people believe climate change is a natural process and it is natural variability causing the changes. However, scientists include the natural variables in their climate models, including the ones that cool the planet.

Lack of financial resources

Some national governments lack the financial resources to deal with climate change. This makes them less likely to have a planning strategy to deal with the changes. According to the UN, US$ 100 billion has been pledged annually by HICs to LICs towards tackling the climate crisis. In 2020, US$ 83 billion was provided, 25% of it going to Africa. The UN also called for funding to be doubled. However, much of the financial aid is in the form of loans and so many poor countries become more indebted over time.

Lack of leadership

A lack of leadership – or having the wrong leader – may make it difficult for countries to implement strategies to mitigate climate change policies or practices that lead to climate change. For example, the former Brazilian President Jair Bolsonaro encouraged deforestation of the Amazonian rainforest for economic development. When he was replaced by Luiz Inácio Lula da Silva in 2003, the new president vowed to stop the illegal destruction of the rainforest and set a target of zero-deforestation by 2030. Some transnational companies (TNCs), especially the energy producing TNCs such as ExxonMobil, Shell and BP, continue to have a major negative impact on the environment. As long as they continue to produce energy from fossil fuels, global climate change will continue (Figure 6.65). Moreover, as the Arctic warms, it will become less inhospitable, and the likelihood of further energy developments will increase.

▲

Figure 6.65 A natural gas field near Nowy Urengi, Russia.

Non-governmental organizations (NGOs)

Most NGOs are in favour of managing climate change. For example, the UNEP states that they tackle climate change in several ways:

- encouraging the transition to low- and zero-carbon emissions in key sectors including energy, industry and transport
- working with stakeholders to improve air quality and reduce emissions of pollutants
- protecting and restoring natural ecosystems while combating the sources of degradation
- empowering communities to adapt to changing conditions by building resilient ecological foundations
- supporting public engagement and behaviour change through global campaigns and education programmes.

However, for many NGOs there may be a lack of funding and skilled personnel, donor-fatigue, a lack of acceptability from the targeted community, communications problems and the scale of the problem may be too great for them to deal effectively with.

International inequalities

Climate management is also made more difficult in that some economies continue to profit from fossil fuels e.g. many countries in the Middle East, Brunei and Russia before the conflict between Russia and Ukraine. In 2022, the UK Prime Minister Rishi Sunak announced plans to build the UK's first new coal mine in 30 years, much to the dismay of environmentalists. In general, HICs profit from past and present use of fossil fuels, whereas the poorest LICs experience energy-insecurity.

Different personal perspectives

There are also different perspectives from different population groups. Research has shown that a higher proportion of younger people worry about the potential impacts of climate change compared with older people. This would also vary by location of residence. For example, people in coastal areas and low-lying areas are more likely to feel vulnerable than those living in inland areas and upland areas. However, many people living in upland areas might be worried about changes in water availability (e.g. less snow in winter), changes to the economy (e.g. decline of ski industry) and an increase in extreme weather events.

HL

1.1 Perspectives
1.3 Sustainability

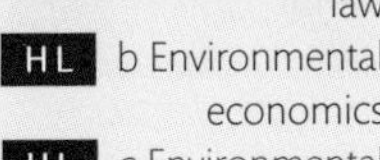

HL a Environmental law
HL b Environmental economics
HL c Environmental ethics

6.3.11 Geoengineering

Geoengineering is a mitigation strategy for climate change, treating the symptoms not the cause. However, it has potential high costs, uncertainty of impacts, political hesitancy, lack of convincing trials and the potential for geopolitical conflict.

Geoengineering is a deliberate large-scale intervention in the Earth's natural systems used to counteract climate change (Figure 6.66).

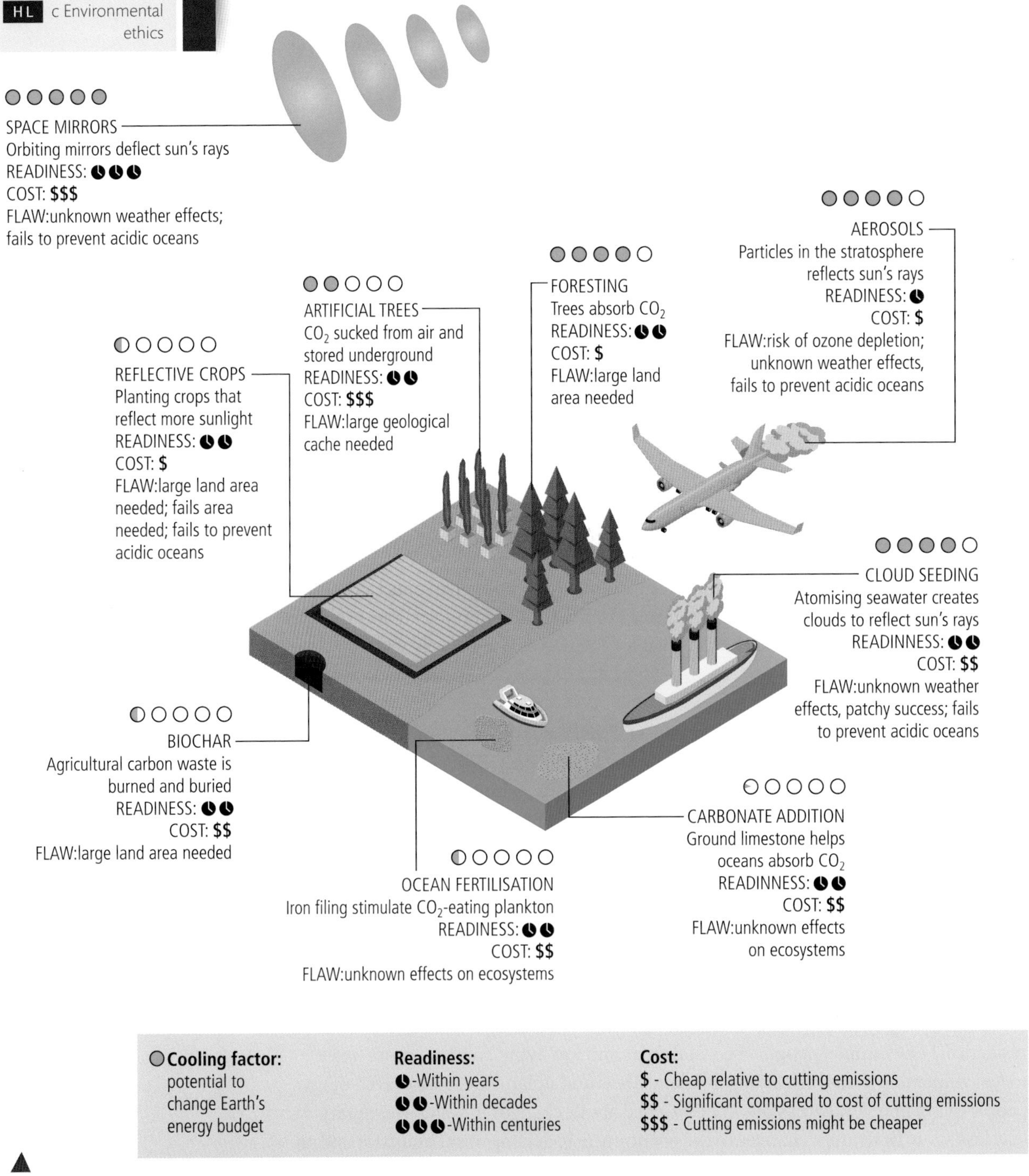

●●●●●
SPACE MIRRORS
Orbiting mirrors deflect sun's rays
READINESS: ◔◔◔
COST: **$$$**
FLAW:unknown weather effects; fails to prevent acidic oceans

●●●●○
AEROSOLS
Particles in the stratosphere reflects sun's rays
READINESS: ◔
COST: **$**
FLAW:risk of ozone depletion; unknown weather effects, fails to prevent acidic oceans

●●●●○
FORESTING
Trees absorb CO_2
READINESS: ◔◔
COST: **$**
FLAW:large land area needed

●●○○○
ARTIFICIAL TREES
CO_2 sucked from air and stored underground
READINESS: ◔◔
COST: **$$$**
FLAW:large geological cache needed

◐○○○○
REFLECTIVE CROPS
Planting crops that reflect more sunlight
READINESS: ◔◔
COST: **$**
FLAW:large land area needed; fails area needed; fails to prevent acidic oceans

●●●●○
CLOUD SEEDING
Atomising seawater creates clouds to reflect sun's rays
READINNESS: ◔◔
COST: **$$**
FLAW:unknown weather effects, patchy success; fails to prevent acidic oceans

◐○○○○
BIOCHAR
Agricultural carbon waste is burned and buried
READINESS: ◔◔
COST: **$$**
FLAW:large land area needed

◔○○○○
CARBONATE ADDITION
Ground limestone helps oceans absorb CO_2
READINNESS: ◔◔
COST: **$$**
FLAW:unknown effects on ecosystems

◐○○○○
OCEAN FERTILISATION
Iron filing stimulate CO_2-eating plankton
READINESS: ◔◔
COST: **$$**
FLAW:unknown effects on ecosystems

○ **Cooling factor:** potential to change Earth's energy budget	**Readiness:** ◔-Within years ◔◔-Within decades ◔◔◔-Within centuries	**Cost:** $ - Cheap relative to cutting emissions $$ - Significant compared to cost of cutting emissions $$$ - Cutting emissions might be cheaper

Figure 6.66 Some of the main forms of geoengineering.

There are two main types of geoengineering: solar radiation management or solar geoengineering and greenhouse gas removal (GGR) or carbon geoengineering.

Solar radiation management

This aims to reflect a small proportion of the Sun's energy back to space. There are three main techniques:

- albedo enhancement – which increases the reflectivity of the clouds or land surface; the impact from marine cloud brightening would last just 10 days
- space reflectors – using mirrors in space to block and reflect a small proportion of sunlight before it reaches the Earth
- stratospheric aerosols – putting small, reflective particles into the upper atmosphere to reflect sunlight before it reaches the Earth; it is estimated that the cooling effect from stratospheric aerosols would cease 1–3 years after the last injection of aerosols.

Greenhouse gas removal

Greenhouse gas removal (GGR) aims to remove CO_2 and other greenhouse gases from the atmosphere and bury/store them in geological, terrestrial or submarine reservoirs.

GGR methods include:

- afforestation
- reforestation
- wetland restoration
- ocean fertilization
- ocean alkalinity
- biochar
- direct air capture when combined with storage.

GGR techniques would need to be carried out on a global scale to have an impact on atmospheric greenhouse gas levels. There are several different methods, outlined below.

- Afforestation would need to be done on a vast scale where one trillion trees would need to grow to remove the equivalent of 200 gigatonnes of carbon.
- Reforestation and wetland restoration are favoured by some environmental organizations, including Greenpeace and Friends of the Earth. These nature-based projects would need to be carried out on a huge scale to have a global impact, which means they are very unlikely to happen, due to competing demands for land use for settlements, food production, industry and infrastructure developments.
- Ocean alkalinity (liming) refers to the enrichment of the oceans with lime. The alkaline lime helps neutralize the acid in the ocean, reducing ocean acidity, which reduces the pressure on marine life, such as lobsters and crabs. It raises oceanic pH and increases the ocean's ability to store carbon.
- Iron fertilization introduces iron to parts of the ocean where iron is lacking. Iron is a trace element necessary for photosynthesis. The addition of iron increases phytoplankton growth and productivity. Large-scale algal blooms can occur, and these absorb CO_2 from the atmosphere. When the algae die, they carry the CO_2 down to the seabed and so remove the CO_2 from the surface of the ocean.
- Biochar refers to *charring* (partially burning) biomass and burying it so that the carbon is locked in the soil. In contrast, bioenergy with carbon capture and sequestration refers to growing biomass, burning it for energy, but capturing and sequestering (removing) the CO_2 from the atmosphere.
- Ambient air capture involves building large machines that can remove CO_2 directly from the ambient (surrounding) air and store it elsewhere.

The equation showing how oceans become acidic is:

$$CO_2 + H_2O \rightleftharpoons \underset{\text{carbonic acid}}{H_2CO_3} \rightleftharpoons H^+ + \underset{\text{bicarbonate}}{HCO_3^-}$$

There are issues with geoengineering. Some of the ideas, such as placing giant mirrors in space and adding aerosols to the stratosphere, are fairly radical and expensive and are perhaps unworkable. Indeed, geoengineering may reduce people's perception of the urgency for reducing carbon emissions. Technology could become an excuse not to address the causes of climate change. Most efforts, other than reducing greenhouse gas emissions, have temporary impacts and would lead to a rapid rebound if they were abandoned.

HL

6.3.12 Stakeholders

1.1 Perspectives

HL c Environmental ethics

In theory, everyone is a stakeholder of climate change because everyone is affected by weather and climate on a daily basis. A range of stakeholders play an important role in changing perspectives on climate change. Stakeholders can influence an individual perspective held on climate change. Admittedly, some people are more affected than others and some people depend on climate for their livelihood.

Government bodies have legally binding powers to make and enforce decisions on many issues including climate change. Historically, modern governments have prioritized economic development, often to the detriment of health, environment quality and social equality e.g. the use of subsidies for the fossil fuel industry in Saudi Arabia.

Civil society includes a mix of private citizens, NGOs, informal groups, charities and universities, who can make their voices heard and help sway public opinion. Environmental activists have managed to have nuclear testing in the Pacific declared illegal and establish a ban on the international trade in ivory.

Companies and the private sector are generally responsible for creating economic value in nations. The influence of companies has increased as the power of the nobility has largely declined in many countries. Companies are trying to create wealth for their shareholders. Nevertheless, the question as to who is more responsible for climate change, the consumer or the producer, has not yet been answered.

Stakeholders hold varying viewpoints. For example, a farmer in India has a different view on water allowances compared with the CEO of Coca-Cola®.

Individuals may also be stakeholders and the choices they make are influenced by many factors including wealth, access to resources, place of residence, occupation and level of education.

Some stakeholders are charismatic and can influence people in a positive or negative way. The impacts of people such as Bolsonaro and Trump have been mentioned previously. An example of a positive stakeholder is Sir David Attenborough, the environmentalist and broadcaster. His television series have gone a long way to influencing people and educating the public about the wonders of nature and also the causes and dangers of climate change.

Programmes like Attenborough's are so compelling and impactful because they combine high-definition visuals, the latest scientific discoveries, and engaging, accessible storytelling.

6.3.13 Contrasts in perspectives

HL

1.1 Perspectives
1.3 Sustainability

HL b Environmental economics
HL c Environmental ethics

Perspectives on the necessity, practicality and urgency of action on climate change vary between individuals and between societies (Topic 1, Section 1.1.2). Differences in perspectives exist between age groups, developed and developing societies, coastal and inland communities, and economies that profit from fossil fuels and those that do not.

Perceptions and perspectives on climate change differ widely between individuals and societies on the basis of demographic factors, residence, levels of wealth and energy availability.

- Younger populations increasingly see climate change as a serious issue, whereas older people (especially retirees in HICs) may feel that it will not adversely affect them in their lifetime.
- Certain occupations, notably agriculture, fishing, the ski industry and tourism, may be more aware of short- and long-term climate changes compared with office workers or those who spend most of their time indoors.
- People who live in low-lying coastal areas may be more aware of rising sea levels and the frequency of coastal flooding than those who live in higher altitude areas. People living in coastal, tropical and sub-tropical areas may also be more aware of changes in the frequency and intensity of tropical cyclones and hurricanes. People in Alpine areas, on the other hand, may be more aware of changes in snowfall and glacial retreat caused by climate change, compared with people living in large urban areas which are mostly located in lowland areas.
- Governments and people in oil-rich countries may feel that fossil fuels bring many benefits such as cheap fuel and consumer goods. Those who live in countries that import fossil fuels do not benefit and may want greater access to renewable energy sources.

However, another important aspect is the worldview of the individual. There are many different types of worldview. Some are based on economic factors such as agricultural, industrial or post-industrial, while others have an environmental outlook such as ecocentric, anthropocentric and technocentric, and others are based on personality such as optimists, pragmatists or pessimists. Table 6.8 looks at different worldviews and how they view climate change.

Table 6.8 Three worldviews and how they view climate change.

Worldview	How climate change works	Solutions	Possible themes
Traditional (Agricultural)	Seen as local weather causing personal effects (*my well is dry, I can't plant beans on time*) that are caused by forces beyond control, such as fate or God.	Change local behaviours – for example, to improve drainage so increased rains do not destroy crops. Prefer to do what makes their lives better.	God has sent these drastic weather changes to test our faith and responsibility in caring for and stewarding His creation.
Modern (Industrial)	The result of interrelated cause-and-effect chains such as pollution, poorly applied technologies (fossil fuels, intensive agriculture), inept government policies and market failures.	New technologies (renewable energies, sustainable forestry, LEED-certified buildings) and ways of operating institutionally (government incentives) and individually (retraining). Prefer quantitative evidence of problems and solutions.	Climate change is a logical consequence of rapid human sociotechnological advancement since the Industrial Revolution and it can be solved through technical innovation, ingenuity and geoengineering.
Post-modern (Post-industrial)	Caused by inappropriate human values (i.e. modernist) driving place-based, poor decisions that create global problems. These problems are also tied to environmental and social injustices which must be addressed for an equitable solution.	Redefine humanity's relationship to nature and change systems and ways people think in a complex economic, environmental, social system. Prefer qualitative changes of heart and well-being.	Human-induced climate change reflects the imbalance between those privileged few and the rest of humanity and nature. Problems are caused by capitalism, greed, injustice and environmental disregard.

Activity

Which worldview above do you hold? How do you think it compares to that of your grandparents? Discuss with a partner.

HL

6.3.14 The tragedy of the commons and climate change

1.1 Perspectives
1.3 Sustainability

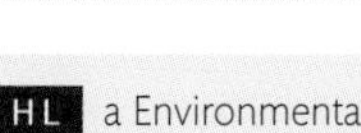

HL a Environmental law
HL b Environmental economics
HL c Environmental ethics

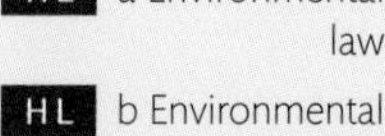

Figure 6.67 The tragedy of the commons – atmospheric pollution.

The tragedy of the commons suggests that catastrophic climate change is likely unless there is international cooperation (Topic 3, Section 3.2.7 and HL.b.6). The atmosphere is a common resource to all humanity, but when one nation harms the atmosphere, the costs are shared by all nations (Figure 6.67).

The USA, India, Russia and Japan are the largest emitters of CO_2, although Singapore, Qatar, Trinidad and Tobago, the UAE and Bahrain emit more CO_2 per person. Who should pay? Who will pay?

Although Garrett Hardin is credited with introducing the concept of the tragedy of the commons, Aristotle wrote in 350 BCE *that which is common to the greatest number gets the least amount of care* (Politics, Book II, Chapter 3).

Exercise

Q21. Using examples, **explain** the term *decarbonization.*

Q22. **Evaluate** methods of climate change mitigation.

Q23. **Outline** ways in which individuals and societies have adapted to global climate change.

Q24. **Examine** the advantages and disadvantages of NAPAs.

Q25. **Outline** the mitigation and adaptation policies of one regional or national government.

Q26. **Explain** why there is uncertainty regarding future emissions of greenhouse gases.

Q27. HL **Examine** the role of the UN in formulating global strategies to address climate change.

Q28. HL **Evaluate** geoengineering strategies for climate change.

Q29. HL **Explain** the term *tragedy of the commons* and **outline** how it relates to global climate change.

Q30. HL **Identify** the main stakeholders in global climate change.

Engagement

- Create information posters for your school about personal behaviours that can be taken to mitigate climate change.
- Form a student council on climate change.
- Engage with the doughnut economics groups around the world, e.g. Doughnut Türkiye Community and Donut Latam (Latin America), and implement a plan for your school.
- Create a social media channel to inform others about behaviour change to act on climate change.
- Work with your teacher to organise a visit to a local power production site or carbon offsetting project.

6.4 Stratospheric ozone

Guiding questions

How does the ozone layer maintain equilibrium?

How does human activity change this equilibrium?

6.4.1 The Sun emits electromagnetic radiation in a range of wavelengths, from low frequency radio waves to high frequency gamma radiation.
6.4.2 Shorter wavelengths of radiation (namely, UV radiation) have higher frequencies and, therefore, more energy, so pose an increased danger to life.
6.4.3 Stratospheric ozone absorbs UV radiation from the Sun, reducing the amount that reaches the Earth's surface and, therefore, protecting living organisms from its harmful effects.
6.4.4 UV radiation reduces photosynthesis in phytoplankton and damages DNA by causing mutations and cancer. In humans, it causes sunburn, premature ageing of the skin and cataracts.
6.4.5 The relative concentration of ozone molecules has stayed constant over long periods of time due to a steady state of equilibrium between the concurrent processes of ozone formation and destruction.
6.4.6 Ozone-depleting substances (ODSs) destroy ozone molecules, augmenting the natural ozone breakdown process.
6.4.7 Ozone depletion allows increasing amounts of UVB radiation to reach the Earth's surface, which impacts ecosystems and human health.
6.4.8 The Montreal Protocol is an international treaty that regulates the production, trade and use of CFCs and other ODSs. It is regarded as the most successful example yet of international cooperation in management and intervention to resolve a significant environmental issue.
6.4.9 Actions taken in response to the Montreal Protocol have prevented the planetary boundary for stratospheric ozone depletion being crossed.
HL 6.4.10 ODSs release halogens such as chlorine and fluorine into the stratosphere, which break down ozone.
HL 6.4.11 Polar stratospheric ozone depletion occurs in the spring due to the unique chemical and atmospheric conditions in the polar stratosphere.
HL 6.4.12 Hydrofluorocarbons (HFCs) were developed to replace CFCs as they can be used in similar ways and cause much less ozone depletion, but they are potent greenhouse gases. They have since been controlled by the Kigali Amendment to the Montreal Protocol.
HL 6.4.13 Air conditioning units are energy-intensive, contribute to greenhouse gas emissions and traditionally have contained ODSs.

6.4.1 Solar radiation

The Sun emits electromagnetic (EM) radiation in a range of wavelengths, from low-frequency radio waves to high-frequency gamma radiation (Figure 6.68). The EM spectrum includes IR radiation, visible light and UV radiation, which all have different roles in relation to the biosphere.

Almost all the energy available at the Earth's surface comes from the Sun. EM waves are characterized by wavelength and frequency. Wavelength is inversely proportional to frequency e.g. shorter wavelengths have a higher frequency and longer wavelengths have a lower frequency. Frequency is expressed in hertz (Hz) and refers to the number of wavelengths that pass a fixed point per second.

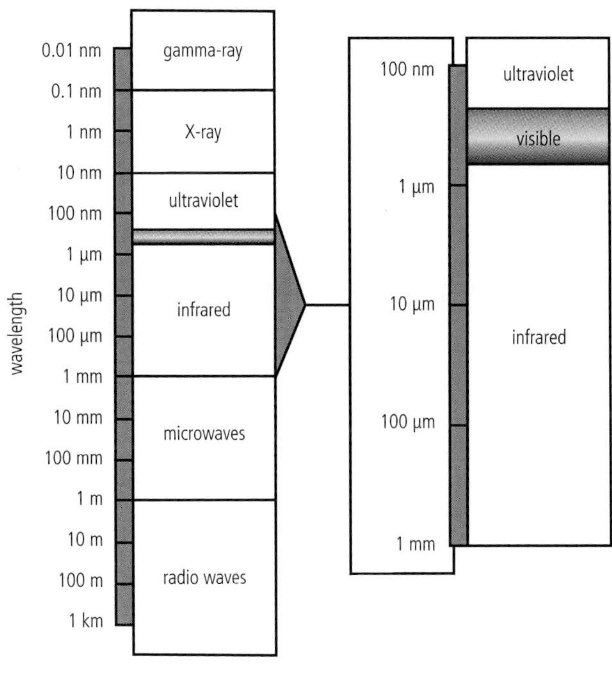

Figure 6.68 EM spectrum range.

- Radio waves are long-wavelength low-frequency waves that are used for communications e.g. TV, radio and satellites. They travel easily through the air and do not damage humans.
- IR radiation is the portion of the EM spectrum with longer wavelengths than the visible spectrum, i.e. between 700 nm–1 mm.
- Visible light is the portion of the EM spectrum that is visible to the human eye with a wavelength range of 400–700 nm. Visible light supports photosynthesis so is vital for life on Earth.
- UV radiation is the portion of the EM spectrum with shorter wavelengths than the visible spectrum, i.e. from 10 nm to 400 nm. UVA (315–400 nm) helps produce Vitamin D, but can cause sunburn and cataracts. UVB (280–315 nm) can cause damage to DNA. UVC (100 to 280 nm) is absorbed by atmospheric O_3.
- Gamma radiation has the shortest wavelength on the EM spectrum and is caused by radioactive decay of atomic nuclei.

6.4.2 UV radiation

UV radiation has shorter wavelengths, higher frequencies and more energy than other types of radiation, so posing increased danger to life.

UVA, UVB and UVC radiation damages organisms.

UVA radiation is immunosuppressive and mutagenic in humans and carcinogenic in animals. Research suggests radiation with a wavelength between 360 and 380 nm suppresses immunity in humans, but radiation of wavelengths between 320 and 350 nm does not. UVA has also been linked with skin cancer.

Research has shown that members of the same species react differently to UVB radiation. Stress to organisms and ecosystems from increased exposure to UVB radiation may be modified by other stresses such as a lack of water or nutrients.

Stratospheric ozone protects the Earth by absorbing all incident UVC (which has the shortest wavelength) and most UVB rays. However, there are ozone holes over Antarctica and the Arctic so not all UV radiation is absorbed (this topic, Section 6.4.7).

6.4.3 Stratospheric ozone

Ozone (O_3) is formed by the reaction of one free oxygen atom (O) with oxygen (O_2).

O_3 is a highly reactive and unstable triatomic form of molecular oxygen formed through the action of solar energy on O_2 (this topic, Section 6.4.6).

Stratospheric ozone absorbs UV radiation from the Sun, reducing the amount that reaches the Earth's surface and therefore protecting living organisms from its harmful effects. UV radiation is damaging because it is high-energy, especially at the shortest wavelengths.

O_3 formation occurs in the stratosphere when an oxygen molecule (O_2) is broken into two single O atoms by solar (UV) radiation. Next, each atom (O) combines with an O_2 molecule to produce an O_3 molecule (this topic, Section 6.1.5, Figure 6.10).

O_3 is constantly being created and destroyed through natural processes in the atmosphere that have been taking place for millions of years. Because of this, the thickness of the ozone layer at any particular time can vary greatly.

Figure 6.69 The role of ozone.

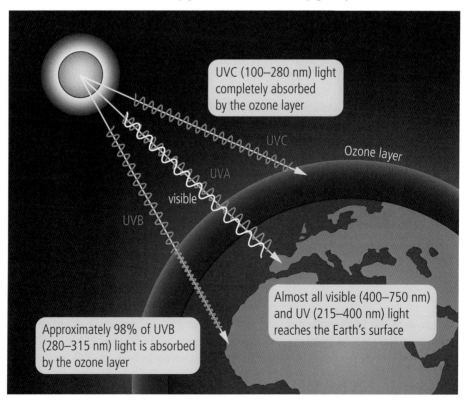

UVC (100–280 nm) light completely absorbed by the ozone layer
UVC
Ozone layer
UVA
visible
UVB
Almost all visible (400–750 nm) and UV (215–400 nm) light reaches the Earth's surface
Approximately 98% of UVB (280–315 nm) light is absorbed by the ozone layer

The amount of O_3 in the atmosphere is small but it is vital (Figure 6.69). It occurs because O_2 rising up from the top of the troposphere reacts under the influence of sunlight to form O_3. Most of this O_3 is created over the equator and the Tropics because this is where solar radiation is strongest. However, winds within the stratosphere transport the O_3 towards the polar regions where it tends to concentrate.

Stratospheric ozone is *good* ozone and protects the Earth from harmful UV radiation. In contrast, tropospheric ozone is *bad* ozone and can lead to respiratory illnesses.

O_3 is essential for sustaining life. The highest concentrations of O_3 occur between 16 and 35 km (in particular between 16 and 25 km) above the Earth's surface and this shields the Earth from harmful radiation that would otherwise destroy most life on the planet.

O_3 has the vital role of absorbing UV radiation (wavelength 100–400 nm). It also absorbs some outgoing terrestrial radiation (wavelength 10 000–12 000 nm) – so it is a greenhouse gas. O_3 is constantly being produced and destroyed in the stratosphere in a natural balance i.e. as well as being produced by sunlight it is also being destroyed by N_2O.

6.4.4 Impacts of UV radiation

2.2 Energy and biomass in ecosystems

UV radiation reduces photosynthesis in phytoplankton and damages DNA by causing mutations and cancer. In humans it causes sunburn, premature ageing of the skin and cataracts.

Exposure to UVB can have effects on human health, crops, terrestrial ecosystems, aquatic ecosystems and biogeochemical cycles. UVB has been linked to cancer. It can also cause cataracts and snow blindness. UVB decreases photosynthesis and reduces the size and productivity of crops including corn, rice, soya beans, winter wheat and cotton. It has also been linked to reduced plankton productivity. This is especially important around Antarctica, due to the ozone hole there, which allows a greater amount of UV radiation to pass through the Earth's atmosphere. There has been a decline in plankton productivity here of 6–12%.

High UV radiation decreases photosynthetic efficiency and reduces growth in some plants. With a decrease in stratospheric ozone in some regions, there has been an increase in UV radiation reaching the Earth's surface. UVB levels have increased 6–14% compared with pre-1980 levels. Springtime levels for 2010–2020 compared with 1979–92 had increased by 14% in parts of the Northern Hemisphere and by 40% in the Southern Hemisphere. Levels of stratospheric ozone have fallen by 3% in the Northern Hemisphere and by 6% in the Southern Hemisphere. A 30% increase in UVB levels could seriously affect crop production around the world. Studies by Schneider et al (2022)[1] showed that growth of red alga (*Gracilaria cornea*) was reduced by increased levels of UVB reaching the Earth's surface.

Skin cancers are mainly caused by exposure to UV radiation, either from the Sun or from artificial sources such as sunbeds. In 2020, over 1.5 million new cases of skin cancer were diagnosed globally and over 120,000 deaths occurred. UV radiation also causes people to age prematurely. It is believed that 15 million people worldwide are blind due to cataracts and up to 10% of these may be due to exposure to UV radiation. Excessive exposure to the Sun in children can cause skin cancer later in life. UV radiation can also lead to suppression of the immune system. Children and adolescents are more at risk from UV radiation due to their less-developed skin and eye structure.

UVC radiation can impact DNA. Some scientists studying microorganisms in deserts and high-altitude environments have found high levels of resistance to UVC radiation.

[1]Schneider, G., et al., 2022, Effects of UV–visible radiation on growth, photosynthesis, pigment accumulation and UV-absorbing compounds in the red macroalga Gracilaria cornea (Gracilariales, Rhodophyta), Algal research, https://doi.org/10.1016/j.algal.2022.102702

1.2 Systems
2.2 Energy and biomass in ecosystems

6.4.5 Ozone equilibrium

The relative concentration of O_3 molecules has stayed constant over long periods of time due to a steady state of equilibrium between the concurrent processes of O_3 formation and destruction. However, there are global variations in levels of O_3 and seasonal variations, too (Figure 6.70).

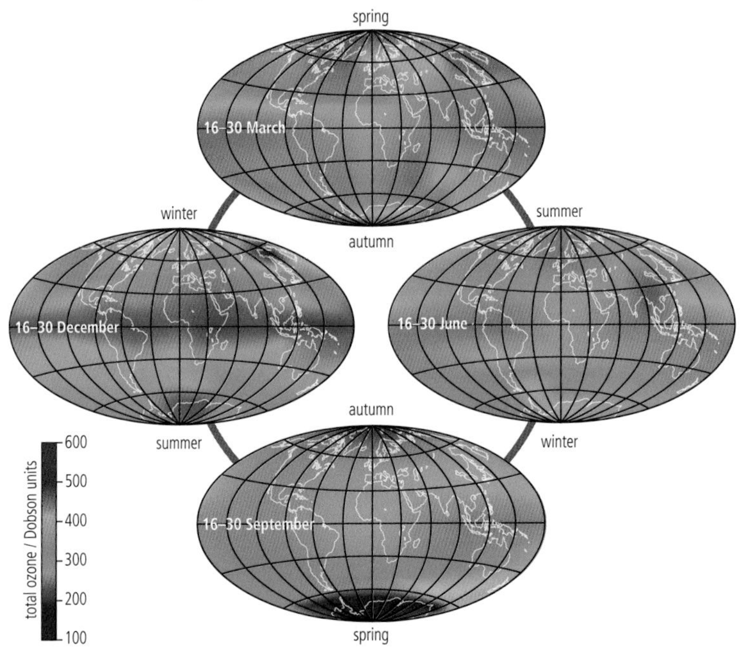

Figure 6.70 The global and seasonal distribution of stratospheric ozone, 2021.

The destruction of ozone involves two separate chemical reactions. The net or overall reaction is that of atomic oxygen (O) with ozone (O_3), forming two oxygen molecules ($2O_2$). The cycle begins with either chlorine monoxide (ClO) or chlorine (Cl). ClO reacts with O to form Cl. Then, Cl reacts with O_3 and re-forms ClO, destroying O_3 in the process. The cycle then begins again with another reaction of ClO with O. Cl is considered a catalyst for O_3 destruction because Cl and ClO are re-formed each time the reaction cycle is completed, and O_3 is simply removed. Atomic oxygen (O) is formed when solar UV radiation (sunlight) reacts with O_3 and O_2. This cycle is most important in the stratosphere at tropical and middle latitudes, where solar ultraviolet radiation is most intense.

$Cl + O_3 \longrightarrow ClO + O_2$

$ClO + O \longrightarrow Cl + O_2$

Net: $O + O_3 \longrightarrow 2O_2$

Some UV radiation from the Sun is absorbed by stratospheric ozone causing O_3 molecules to break apart. Under normal conditions, the O_3 molecules reform. This O_3 destruction and reformation is an example of a dynamic equilibrium.

6.4.6 Ozone-depleting substances (ODSs)

Chlorofluorocarbons (CFCs) are synthetic chemicals that can act as greenhouse gases by absorbing long-wave radiation but are also responsible for the destruction of O_3 in the **stratosphere**. CFCs are increasing at a rate of 4% per annum from unknown sources (Western et al, 2023)[1] and are more than 500 times more efficient at trapping heat than CO_2. Thus, with the loss of O_3 from the stratosphere and higher volumes of CFCs in the stratosphere, a higher amount of long-wave radiation is absorbed.

Increasing quantities of CFCs in the atmosphere correlate with declining O_3 levels. Ozone-depleting substances (ODSs) destroy O_3 molecules, augmenting the natural O_3 breakdown process. When rates of O_3 formation and depletion are unequal, the equilibrium will tip to increase formation or destruction. O_3 depletion is not a cause of global warming.

Some UV radiation from the Sun is absorbed by stratospheric ozone causing the O_3 molecule to break apart. Under normal conditions, the O_3 molecule will reform. This O_3 destruction and reformation is an example of a dynamic equilibrium. ODSs (including halogenated organic gases such as CFCs) are used in aerosols, gas-blown plastics, pesticides, flame retardants and refrigerants. When halogen atoms, such as chlorine and bromine, from these pollutants come into contact with O_3 molecules in the stratosphere they break the O_3 down to O_2 in a repetitive cycle so allowing more UV radiation to reach the Earth. One chlorine atom can destroy 100,000 O_3 molecules before it is removed from the atmosphere. Molecules of O_3 can be destroyed more quickly than they are naturally formed.

---

[1]Western, L.M., Vollmer, M.K., Krummel, P.B. et al. Global increase of ozone-depleting chlorofluorocarbons from 2010 to 2020. *Nat. Geosci.* 16, 309–313 (2023). https://doi.org/10.1038/s41561-023-01147-w

Ozone depletion by CFCs

CFCs were used in aerosols, refrigerants and plastics due to their low reactivity in the troposphere. However, in the stratosphere, higher energy UV radiation breaks these CFCs down, releasing chlorine radicals.

CFC molecules are made up of chlorine, fluorine, hydrogen and carbon atoms and are very stable. This stability allows CFCs to slowly make their way into the stratosphere and reach high altitudes where photons are more active. When the CFCs come in contact with high energy photons, the bond between the carbon and chlorine atoms is broken, which releases chlorine radicals.

1.2 Systems

Radicals are atoms, molecules or ions that have one unpaired valence electron and so are highly chemically reactive.

Photons, or light quantums, are minute packets of EM radiation.

6.4.7 The impacts of ozone depletion

2.2 Energy and biomass in ecosystems

O_3 depletion allows increasing amounts of UVB radiation to reach the Earth's surface, which impacts ecosystems and human health. O_3 depletion has affected the stratosphere over the whole Earth. At the poles, *ozone holes* with greater depletion appear every spring due to the effects of ODSs and seasonal atmospheric weather patterns.

O_3 depletion allows increased levels of UV radiation to reach the Earth's surface. This can have many negative impacts including:

- damaging plant tissue and causing the death of primary producers
- damaging marine phytoplankton which are among the main primary producers of the biosphere
- increased risk of skin cancer, cataracts and ageing of the skin in humans
- genetic mutations in DNA.

The ozone hole is an area of reduced concentration of O_3 in the stratosphere, which varies from place to place and over the course of a year. There is a very clear seasonal pattern – each springtime in Antarctica (between September and October) there is a huge reduction in the amount of O_3 in the stratosphere (Figure 6.71).

In 2002 there was a major change in the size of the ozone hole over Antarctica caused by unusual weather in the stratosphere.

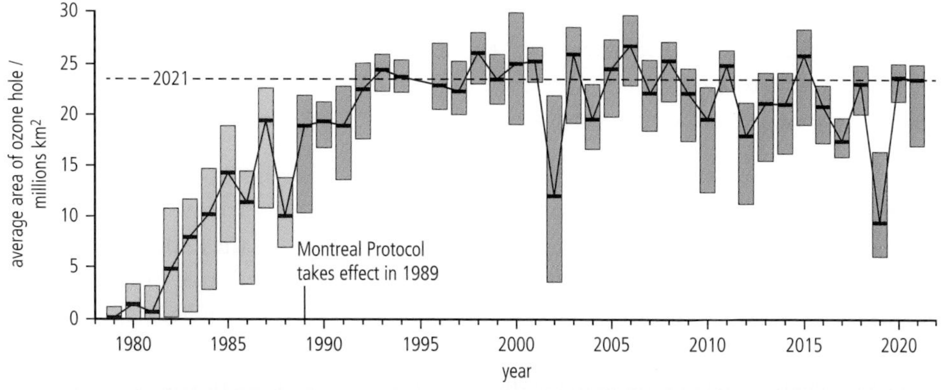

Figure 6.71 Average ozone hole over Antarctica, between 7 September and 13 October 1980–2022.

Activity

1. Use the NASA Ozone Watch tool to access up-to-date maps of the ozone layer (Figure 6.72).
2. Search online for the NASA Earth Observatory Antarctic Ozone Hole animation. It shows changes in the ozone hole over Antarctica during 1979–2019.

   How has the ozone hole changed during that time?

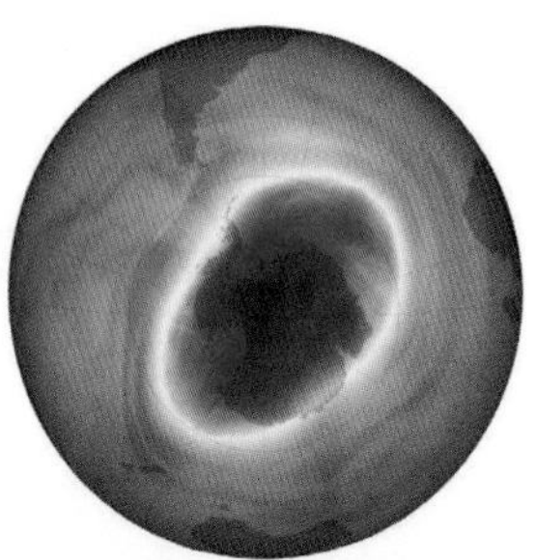

Figure 6.72 The ozone hole over Antarctica, October 5, 2022 (its largest size for that year).

The size of the ozone hole is variable but always relatively large. As early as 1987, it covered an area the size of continental USA and was as deep as Mount Everest. The maximum size of the ozone hole was 29.9 million km^2 in 2000. By 2014 it was down to 24.1 million km^2 and has remained around 24–25 million km^2 since then. This is likely to be related to the success of the Montreal Protocol.

According to NOAA, the ozone hole over Antarctica is continuing to decrease in size. In 2022 it was over 23 million km^2 smaller than its maximum in 2000. This is largely due to the success of the Montreal Protocol, and the ban on the use of ODSs.

Although there are natural sources of chlorine that affect the ozone layer (e.g. small amounts are released in volcanic eruptions), the increases recorded are probably too large to be entirely natural. There are now ozone holes at both poles, the one over Antarctica stretching as far as Argentina. The balance of formation and destruction of stratospheric ozone is seriously affected by ODSs, notably those containing the halogens chlorine, fluorine and bromine. Most ODSs do not occur naturally but are industrial products or byproducts and include CFCs, HCFCs, halons and methyl bromide (bromomethane). These are usually very stable compounds – they persist in the atmosphere for decades as they travel upwards to the stratosphere – but once in the stratosphere and under the influence of UV radiation, they break down and release halogens. The halogen atoms act as catalysts for the reactions that destroy O_3 molecules. Thus, ODSs greatly accelerate the rate of O_3 destruction.

HL a Environmental law

6.4.8 The Montreal Protocol

The Montreal Protocol (Section HL.a.8) is an international treaty that regulates the production, trade and use of CFCs and other ODSs and is regarded as the most successful example yet of international cooperation in management and intervention to resolve a significant environmental issue.

The *Montreal Protocol on Substances that Deplete the Ozone Layer* (1987), and subsequent updates, is an international agreement for the reduction of use of ODSs signed under the direction of UNEP. National governments complying with the agreement made national laws and regulations to decrease the consumption and production of halogenated organic gases such as CFCs.

In 1987, UNEP brought together 24 countries to sign the initial Montreal Protocol on Substances that Deplete the Ozone Layer. Now, 197 countries have signed the Protocol. In 1987, production of ODSs exceeded 1.8 million tonnes annually. By 2010, it had fallen to 45,000 tonnes. Nevertheless, the work of the Montreal Protocol is not finished. UNEP is working towards finally ending production of HCFCs by 2040.

The Montreal Protocol is considered to be a success because the production and consumption of ODSs has reduced by more than 95% compared to 1986. However, illegal trade in ODSs has developed. It is believed that India and the Republic of Korea account for approximately 70% of the total global production of CFCs. Countries in the region with a high consumption of CFCs include India, Malaysia, Pakistan and the Philippines. In many LICs, there is still a significant demand for CFCs as reliance on equipment using these chemicals remains high. The problem is made worse by the imports of used refrigeration and air-conditioning equipment.

The Parties to the protocol have amended it to enable the control of new chemicals and create a financial mechanism to enable LICs to comply. These amendments include:

- the London Amendment (1990) to phase out CFCs, halons and carbon tetrachloride by 2000 in HICs and by 2010 in LICs
- the Copenhagen Amendment (1992), which accelerated the phaseout of ODSs

- the Beijing Amendment (1999), which tightened controls on the production and trade of HCFCs
- the Kigali Amendment (2016), which called for a phasedown in the production and consumption of hydrofluorocarbons (HFCs) because they are potent greenhouse gases.

6.4.9 Ozone and planetary boundaries

1.3 Sustainability

HL a Environmental law

Actions taken in response to the Montreal Protocol have helped keep the planetary boundary for stratospheric ozone depletion from being crossed (Section HL.a.8).

International cooperation between governments on the reduction of ODSs has been successful. Much of this has been organized by the UNEP. In 1985, the UNEP implemented the Vienna Convention for the Protection of the Ozone Layer. This aimed to protect human health and the environment against adverse effects resulting from human activities which modified or were likely to modify the ozone layer.

There is a figure showing a time line of the history and action related to stratospheric ozone on this page of your eBook.

As a result of the 1987 Montreal Protocol on Substances that Deplete the Ozone Layer, the hole in the ozone layer has been decreasing in size. By the end of 2002, industrialized countries had reduced their ODS consumption by more than 99% and developing countries had reduced their consumption by slightly more than 50%. A total phasing out worldwide is due by 2040. A total phaseout in Europe had occurred by 2000. Nevertheless, CFCs are persistent in the atmosphere and long-lasting, so their impact will continue for many decades. Production and consumption of CFCs, halons and other ODSs have been almost completely phased out in industrialized countries and the timetable for banning the use of methyl bromide, a pesticide, has been agreed.

Activity

Work through the activity *Changes in the ozone hole* in your eBook.

HL

6.4.10 ODSs release halogens into the stratosphere, which break down ozone

HL

HL a Environmental law

ODSs include CFCs and carbon compounds that release highly reactive fluorine and chlorine.

National governments complying with the Montreal Protocol made national laws and regulations to decrease the consumption and production of halogenated organic gases such as CFCs.

The sources of the chlorine atoms are CFCs and include materials used in fridges, air cooling systems, foamed plastics and aerosols. CFCs are particularly dangerous because they are very long-lived – over 100 years – and they spread throughout the atmosphere. In the case of Antarctica, the build-up of chlorine appears to have had little impact until it reached a critical threshold. Once that was reached, a small increase in chlorine led to a large change in the ozone hole.

The following series of equations shows how Cl radicals, for example, can destroy O_3 in the presence of UV radiation:

Stage 1: $Cl\bullet + O_3 \rightarrow ClO\bullet + O_2$

Stage 2 $ClO\bullet + O_3 \rightarrow Cl\bullet + 2O_2$

Overall reaction $2O_3 \rightarrow 3O_2$

The chlorine radical initiates the breakdown of O_3 to create an O_2 molecule and a chlorate radical. The chlorate radical can then combine with another O_3 molecule to produce another chlorine radical and two O_2 molecules.

As long as there are chlorine radicals present, the O_3 molecules will be continually broken down through this cycle of reactions. The chlorine radicals are not used up in these reactions, therefore one chlorine radical can cause the destruction of thousands of O_3 molecules.

Freons are a series of stable, non-flammable, low toxicity halocarbons that have been used as aerosol propellants and refrigerants. For example, the CFC Freon reacts in the presence of UV radiation as follows:

$$CCl_2F_2(g) \xrightarrow{\text{UV radiation}} CClF_2\bullet(g) + Cl\bullet(g)$$

The weaker C–Cl bond breaks in preference to the C–F bond, and the resultant chlorine radicals catalyse the decomposition of O_3.

$$Cl\bullet(g) + O_3(g) \rightarrow O_2(g) + ClO\bullet(g)$$

$$ClO\bullet(g) + O\bullet(g) \rightarrow O_2(g) + Cl\bullet(g)$$

Here $Cl\bullet(g)$ has acted as a catalyst and the net reaction is again:

$$O_3(g) + O\bullet(g) \rightarrow 2O_2(g)$$

HL

6.4.11 Seasonal pattern of ozone depletion

1.2 Systems

O_3 depletion occurs in the spring due to the atmospheric and chemical conditions in the polar stratosphere.

What causes the springtime depletion in O_3? During winter in the Southern Hemisphere, the air over Antarctica is cut off from the rest of the atmosphere by circumpolar winds – these winds block warm air from entering Antarctica. Therefore, the temperature over Antarctica becomes very cold, often down as far as –90 °C in the stratosphere. This allows the formation of clouds of ice particles. The ice particles provide surfaces on which chemical reactions can take place, involving chlorine compounds present in the stratosphere as a result of human activities. The reactions release chlorine atoms. In the presence of UV radiation in the spring, the chlorine atoms destroy O_3 in a series of chemical reactions as described previously. Hence the hole in the ozone layer enlarges very rapidly in the spring.

By summer, the ice clouds have evaporated, and the chlorine is converted to other compounds such as chlorine nitrate. As the summer progresses, the concentration of O_3 recovers. Thus, the ozone hole diminishes, although it returns the following spring.

In 2023 the ozone hole over Antarctica began to form early. Normally it begins forming around the end of September/early October but in 2023 it began forming in early August. Scientists feared that it could lead to warming of the Southern Ocean because the amount of Antarctic sea ice was at a record low.

The ozone hole is normally smaller in El Niño years. 2023 was an El Niño year but it was likely to have been larger due to long-lasting atmospheric changes caused by the eruptions of the Hunga Tonga-Hunga Ha'apai volcano emitting a huge amount of water vapour into the stratosphere in January 2022. This led to more ice clouds forming in the stratosphere than usual, which allowed ozone-destroying molecules to collect on ice particles.

The risk was that the more UV radiation that reached Antarctica and the Southern Ocean, the more energy would be available to melt ice and sea ice. Already much of the sea ice has been replaced by ocean water, thereby reducing the albedo (reflectivity) of the surface and increasing warming.

6.4.12 Hydrofluorocarbons and chlorofluorocarbons

HL

HL a Environmental law

HFCs were developed to replace CFCs because they can be used in similar ways and cause much less O_3 depletion, but they are still potent greenhouse gases. HFCs have since been controlled by the Kigali Amendment to the Montreal Protocol (Section HL.a.8). CFCs and HFCs have been used in aerosols and as coolants in refrigerators and air-conditioning systems. This means they need to be carefully collected from redundant appliances, so they do not leak into the atmosphere.

The most widely used ODSs (CFC-11 and CFC-12) have often been replaced with HFCs. Although HFCs are still greenhouse gases, their global warming potential (GWP) is lower than that of CFCs. However, even greater GWP reductions can be achieved by replacing CFCs with substances such as hydrocarbons, CO_2, water and air. These substances contribute only minimally (or not at all) to GWP.

Example – Australia

Australia's obligations under the Montreal Protocol have been implemented at the national level. State legislation for O_3 protection has been replaced by national legislation. For example, the New South Wales Ozone Protection Regulation 1997 was repealed in 2006.

The manufacture, import and export of all major ODSs has been completely phased out in Australia. National regulations allow for limited categories of essential or critical use for halons, CFCs and methyl bromide where no alternatives are available, for example, methyl bromide is used for quarantine and feedstock purposes.

Transition substances, such as HFCs, are strong greenhouse gases and contribute to climate change. Their concentrations are rising rapidly in the atmosphere, albeit from currently low concentrations. Australia was the first country to implement integrated control measures to manage both ODSs and their synthetic replacements that can also act as greenhouse gases. This is largely because they were one of the first countries to suffer the consequences of O_3 depletion.

Future directions

Australia's response to phasing out the use of ODSs under the Montreal Protocol has been swift and effective. However, Australia accounts for less than 1% of these global emissions. To assist the phasing out process, Australia participates in the Multilateral Fund for the Implementation of the Montreal Protocol (London, 1990), which provides funds to help developing countries phase out their usage of ODSs.

The Montreal Protocol now covers all CFCs, carbon tetrachloride and most halons. Consumption of these compounds is banned in HICs. There is, however, still some use of CFCs and halons in LICs. A small volume of these chemicals is therefore manufactured for essential uses and LICs. Because they are highly stable, ODSs will persist in the atmosphere for decades to come despite action to reduce their usage. There is, therefore, a lag between action addressing ODSs and recovery of the ozone layer. Based on projections of future levels of ODSs in the stratosphere, the recovery of the ozone layer over much of Australia is likely by 2049 and over Antarctica by 2065.

New chemicals depleting ozone

TOK

What are the limitations of knowledge?

To what extent is it possible to manage O_3 depletion when new chemicals, such as CFC 113a, which destroy O_3, are still being made?

In 2014, it was reported that scientists had identified and measured four previously unknown compounds in the atmosphere – three CFCs and one HCFC – and warned of the existence of many more. The level of one of the compounds had doubled in just 2 years. Over 74,000 tonnes of the new gases have been released in the past 40 years (Figure 6.73). CFC-113a and the HCFC are accumulating rapidly. Until 2014, a total of 13 CFCs and HCFCs were known to destroy O_3 but were controlled by the Montreal Protocol. Despite the production of all CFCs having been banned since 2010, the concentration of CFC-113a is rising at an accelerating rate. The source of the chemical is a mystery, although it may be being used in the production of agricultural crop and soil pesticides.

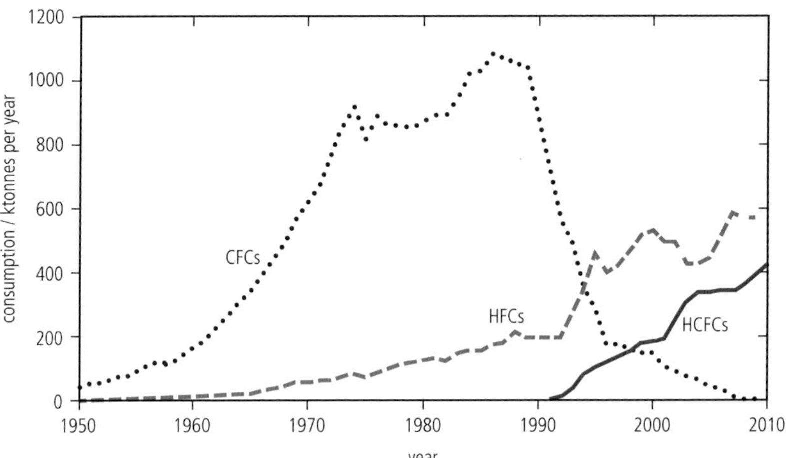

Figure 6.73 The usage of CFCs, HCFCs and HFCs, 1950–2010.

However, the solution to one problem leads to the creation of another. HFCs were designed specifically to replace ODSs, but they too are potent greenhouse gases. HFCs are made of carbon, fluorine and hydrogen – they are completely human-made, having no known natural sources. The GWP of HFCs ranges from 1370 to 4180.
A number of alternatives are being considered including hydrofluoroolefins (HFOs), which only remain in the atmosphere for a short time but can produce toxic chemicals when they break down. Hydrocarbons, such as butane, have also been suggested. However, these are highly flammable and can have impacts on air quality. NH_3 has been used as a refrigerant for a long time but is highly toxic.

The Kigali Amendment

The Kigali Amendment to the Montreal Protocol aims to reduce the production and consumption of HFCs by over 80% by 2050 (Section HL.a.8). As well as protecting the ozone hole, the reduction could avoid up to 0.5 °C of global warming by 2100. The Amendment came into force 1 January 2019. HFCs are organic compounds frequently used as refrigerants in air conditioners and other devices as alternatives to ODSs. Implementation of the targets will be done in three phases – a group of HICs will phase down from 2019, most LICs will stop HFC consumption from 2024 and a few other LICs will freeze consumption in 2028. It is hoped that the Northern Hemisphere and mid-latitude ozone should heal by the 2030s, the Southern Hemisphere by the 2050s and polar regions by 2060.

6.4.13 Air conditioning units

HL

1.1 Perspectives
6.2 Climate change – causes and impacts
8.3 Urban air pollution

HL b Environmental economics

Air conditioning (AC) units are energy intensive, contribute to greenhouse gas emissions and traditionally have contained ODSs. However, alternative refrigerants have been developed and improved building design, greening and rewilding of cities can reduce the need for air conditioning.

SkyCool is a company using an innovative technique that exploits radiative cooling even during the daytime. A film on the panels (Figure 6.74) reflects the sunlight, preventing the panels from heating up during the day and emitting infrared heat to the cold sky, keeping the panels and any fluid flowing in them cool. SkyCool believe this can reduce temperatures by 5 °C below the ambient temperature and could reduce energy consumption in small- and medium-sized offices by 30–50%.

Figure 6.74 SkyCool's cooling panels on a southern California grocery store roof.

With record-breaking heatwaves across the world in 2023, the demand for air-conditioning is likely to soar and, although AC units save lives, they are damaging the environment. Oppressive heatwaves have become more frequent and more severe as a result of the climate crisis.

To cope with the heat many people are using AC units. The number of AC units could increase by nearly 250% by 2050. In the USA, extreme heat is the single deadliest form of extreme weather and demand for AC is likely to rise by about 60%. However, there are billions of people who do not have access to AC units and the energy costs of running the units are great. A 2019 study found that between 1.8 and 4.1 billion people in LICs and MICs, who are regularly affected by extreme high temperatures, lack access to cooling technology.

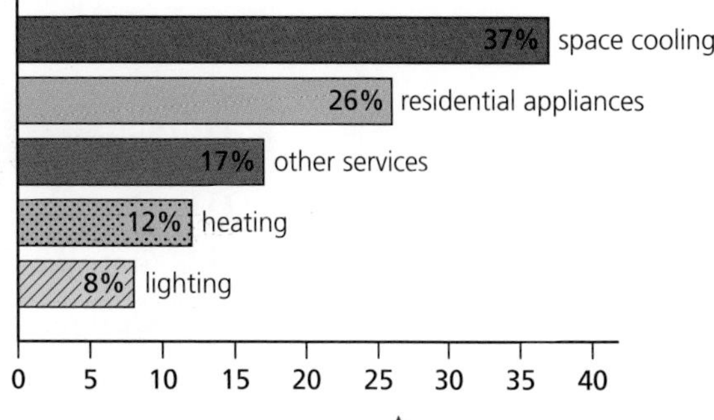

Figure 6.75 Cooling is projected to take up over one-third of new electricity demands related to buildings from 2018 to 2050.

In addition to the inequality of access to AC units, the units actually warm the Earth. AC units are energy intensive, so improving their efficiency is important. The least efficient models are often found in low-income households and require more power to run them, making them expensive as well as climate-warming. According to the Intergovernmental Energy Agency, between now and 2050, cooling technology, including AC units, is projected to be one of the largest contributors to growing energy demand (Figure 6.75). Most of the energy used for this comes from fossil fuels. The most commonly used refrigerants in AC units are HFCs, potent greenhouse gases. Some air conditioners use hydrofluoroolefins although these can also cause environmental damage. Other alternatives include NH_3, butane (C_4H_{10}) and propane (C_3H_8), which can be harmful to people if they leak.

Review the alternatives to air conditioning units

Use databases to collect data on the use of air conditioning units in different societies and present this data graphically, considering the reasons for the differences per capita

There are many other strategies that can be used to lower temperatures in houses. Fans, for example, are much cheaper and use less energy. Swamp coolers are fans which circulate air across a cool, wet surface and then direct the dampened, cool air into houses. Buildings can also be designed to reduce temperatures. Insulating or sealing up cracks can reduce the amount of heat entering a building. Homes that are constructed with steel or aluminium are very vulnerable to extreme heat. These include metal roofs, which are common in some shanty towns in LICs, as well as in mobile homes in the USA. Brick and stone can absorb and release heat far more slowly – improving the availability and affordability of these materials could help reduce heat stress and save lives.

Roofs, or indeed whole houses, that are painted white will reflect more solar energy and lower indoor temperatures. Buildings can be designed to improve ventilation – wind towers can help draw cool breezes inside. Shade also helps. Neighbourhoods with trees can be as much as 9 °C cooler than those without trees. Vegetation on rooftops can insulate buildings from hot air. These are especially important in urban areas.

Table 6.9 Percentage of households with air conditioning.

Country	Percentage of households with air conditioning (%)
Japan	91
USA	90
South Korea	86
China	60
Mexico	16
Brazil	16
Indonesia	9
South Africa	6
India	5

1. Plot the data for the percentage of households with air conditioning shown in Table 6.9.
2. Using the CIA World Factbook, find data for the average income per person for these countries (Look under Countries, Economy and then Real GDP per person).
3. Make a spreadsheet with the data for the percentage of households with air conditioning and real GDP per head. Construct a scatter graph to see if there is any relation between the two data sets. Suggest reasons for your findings.
4. Suggest other reasons why there may be a variation in the use of air conditioning units per person by country.

Exercise

Q31. Describe the role of O_3 in the absorption of UV radiation.

Q32. State the effects of UV radiation on living tissues and biological productivity.

Q33. Outline the potential health impacts of increased levels of UVB radiation.

Q34. Describe the changes in the ozone hole over Antarctica between 1979 and 2022.

Q35. Describe three methods of reducing the manufacture and release of ODSs.

Q36. Describe and **evaluate** the role of national and international organizations in reducing the emissions of ODSs.

Q37. **Identify** the international treaty that led to a decline in the production of CFCs.

Q38. **Outline** the difficulties in implementing and enforcing international agreements.

Q39. HL **Explain** the interaction between O_3 and halogenated organic gases.

Q40. HL **Examine** the changes in demand for electricity in new buildings between 2018 and 2050.

Engagement

- With a partner, discuss the extent to which the Montreal Protocol sets a precedent for how environmental issues can be addressed on a global scale. Make sure you identify one or more global environmental issues, analyse the causes of the problems, consider potential solutions, investigate why the Montreal Protocol was considered to be successful and evaluate the lessons that can be learnt from the Montreal Protocol and how they can be used to help manage other environmental issues.
- Present findings on alternatives to air conditioning to the school management.
- Produce a digital resource or social media campaign containing information about protection against UV radiation during the highest-risk periods of the year.

Practice questions

1. Figure 6.76 shows the rise in atmospheric CO_2 between 1960 and 2020.

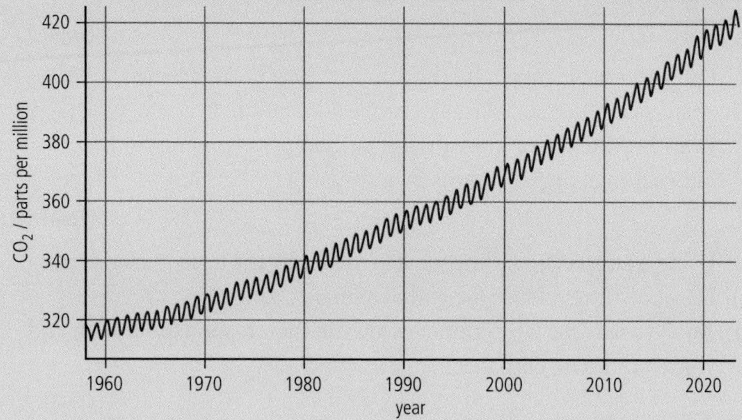

Figure 6.76 The rise in atmospheric CO_2 between 1960 and 2020.

(a) State the concentration of atmospheric CO_2 in 2020. [1]

(b) Calculate the increase in atmospheric CO_2 between 1960 and 2020. [2]

(c) Briefly explain two reasons for the growth of atmospheric CO_2. [2]

(d) Identify one greenhouse gas, other than CO_2. [1]

(e) Distinguish between the natural greenhouse effect and the enhanced (anthropogenic) greenhouse effect. [2]

(f) Outline two ways in which the enhanced greenhouse effect is causing a rise in sea levels. [2]

(Total 10 marks)

(continued)

2. Figure 6.77 shows the maximum extent of the ozone hole over Antarctica in 2022.

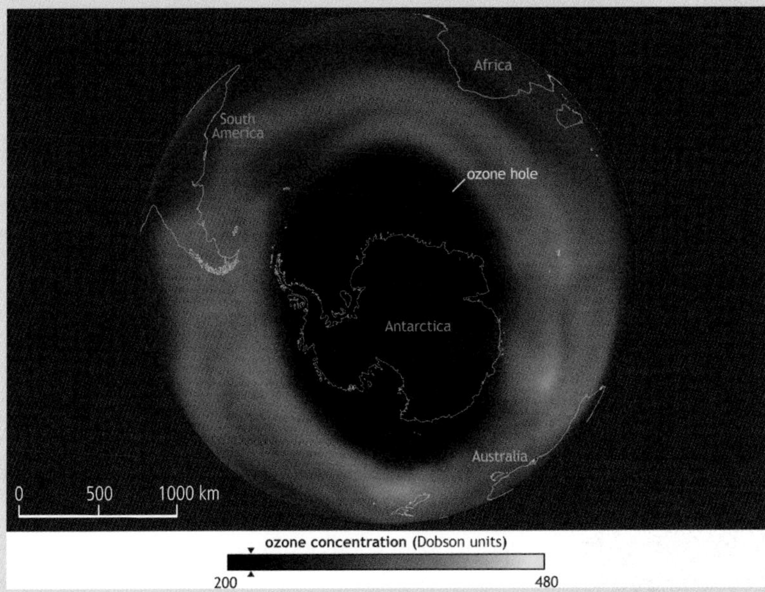

Figure 6.77 The Antarctic ozone hole.

(a) Describe the maximum size of the ozone hole over Antarctica in 2022. [2]
(b) Identify the variations in the concentration of O_3 over Antarctica when the hole was at its maximum extent. [2]
(c) Explain how ozone-depleting substances destroy O_3 molecules. [2]
(d) Outline two impacts of O_3 depletion. [2]
(e) Explain how the ozone hole problem has been managed. [3]

(Total 11 marks)

3. **(a)** Outline what is meant by the phrase *tragedy of the commons.* [4]
(b) Analyse methods of climate change adaptation. [7]
(c) Examine the role of individuals, national governments and international organizations in addressing global climate change. [9]

(Total 20 marks)

4. **(a)** Using example(s), outline what is meant by the term *tipping points.* [4]
(b) Examine the evidence for global climate change. [7]
(c) Analyse reasons why countries vary in their responsibility for, and vulnerability to, climate change. [9]

(Total 20 marks)

5. HL Analyse how Milankovitch cycles affect the amount of radiation reaching the Earth and the impact this has on the Earth's climate. [4]

(Total 4 marks)

6. HL Examine the view that countries that are most vulnerable to global climate change are the least responsible for it. [6]

(Total 6 marks)

7. HL To what extent is geoengineering a successful mitigation strategy for global climate change? [9]

(Total 9 marks)

8. HL Analyse the impact of air conditioning units on greenhouse gas emissions and ozone depletion. [9]

(Total 9 marks)

7 Natural resources

7.1 Natural resources–uses and management

Guiding questions

How does the renewability of natural capital have implications for its sustainable use?

How might societies reconcile competing perspectives on natural resource use?

To what extent can human societies use natural resources sustainably?

7.1.1 Natural resources are the raw materials and sources of energy used and consumed by society.
7.1.2 Natural capital is the stock of natural resources available on Earth.
7.1.3 Natural capital provides natural income in terms of goods and services.
7.1.4 The terms 'natural capital' and 'natural income' imply a particular perspective on nature.
7.1.5 Ecosystems provide life-supporting ecosystem services.
7.1.6 All resources are finite. Resources can be classified as either renewable or non-renewable.
7.1.7 Natural capital has aesthetic, cultural, economic, environmental, health, intrinsic, social, spiritual and technological value. The value of natural capital is influenced by these factors.
7.1.8 The value of natural capital is dynamic in that it can change over time.
7.1.9 The use of natural capital needs to be managed in order to ensure sustainability.
7.1.10 Resource security depends on the ability of societies to ensure the long-term availability of sufficient natural resources to meet demand.
7.1.11 The choices a society makes in using given natural resources are affected by many factors and reflect diverse perspectives.
HL 7.1.12 A range of different management and intervention strategies can be used to directly influence society's use of natural capital.
HL 7.1.13 The UN Sustainable Development Goals (SDGs) provide a framework for action by all countries in global partnership for natural resources use and management.
HL 7.1.14 Sustainable resource management in development projects is addressed in an environmental impact assessment (EIA).
HL 7.1.15 Countries and regions have different guidance on the use of EIAs.
HL 7.1.16 Making EIAs public allows for local citizens to have a role as stakeholders in decision-making.

HL 7.1.17 While a given resource may be renewable, the associated means of extracting, harvesting, transporting and processing it may be unsustainable.
HL 7.1.18 Economic interests often favour short-term responses in production and consumption which undermine long-term sustainability.
HL 7.1.19 Natural resource insecurity hinders socio-economic development and can lead to environmental degradation and geopolitical tensions and conflicts.
HL 7.1.20 Resource security can be brought about by reductions in demand, increases in supply or changing technologies.
HL 7.1.21 Economic globalization can increase supply, making countries increasingly interdependent, but it may reduce national resource security.

7.1.1 Natural resources

Natural resources are the raw materials and sources of energy that are used and consumed by societies (Figure 7.1). They include sunlight, air, water, land, soil, minerals, fossil fuels and ecosystems.

Renewable natural capital can be generated and/or replaced as fast as it is being used. It includes living species and ecosystems that use solar energy and photosynthesis. It also includes non-living items, such as groundwater, and the ozone layer.

A resource is only a resource when it becomes useful to people – uranium only became a resource in the 20th century despite it having already existed for millions of years. The Earth contains many resources that support its natural systems including the core and crust of the planet; the biosphere (the living part) containing forests, grassland, deserts, tundra and other biomes and the upper layers of the atmosphere. Soil and soil microorganisms are vital for our food supply, while glaciers provide drinking water for millions of people.

Humans tend to have an anthropocentric (human-centred) view of these resources as they are all extensively used by humans to provide food, water, shelter and life-support systems.

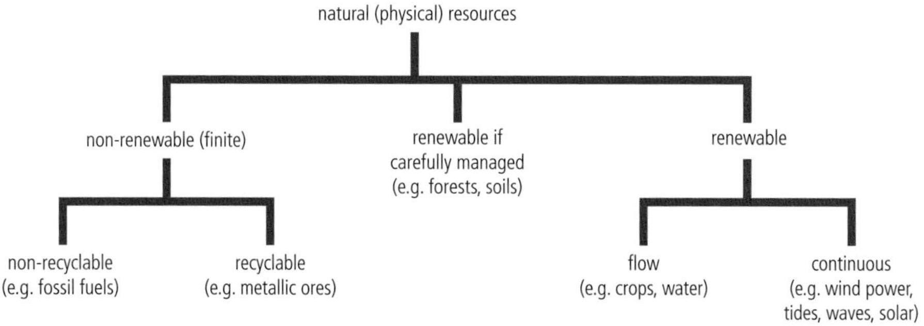

Figure 7.1 Natural resources.

Natural resources may exist as a natural entity, such as the air, freshwater or the oceans. They may also be transformed into products that can be used by humans. For example, humans can use fossil fuels to produce electricity, diesel and petrol. Exploitation of natural resources can lead to conflicts within and between countries. It can also lead to environmental degradation and the abuse of human rights. An example of this situation arose for the Ogoni population in the Niger Delta over the exploitation of oil.

Figure 7.2 Urban areas contain many different forms of natural resources. This image shows a city centre park in Hong Kong.

Natural resources can be classified in a number of ways:

- biotic, such as flora and fauna, or abiotic, such as freshwater and minerals, as shown in Figure 7.2
- renewable, such as solar power and wind power, or non-renewable, such as fossil fuels
- stage of development, for example reserves (resources that can be used), or stocks (resources that cannot be used due to lack of technology such as hydrogen vehicles)
- ownership being individual, community, national or international.

Activity

Create a spider diagram to identify the natural resources in your home area.

1.3 Sustainability

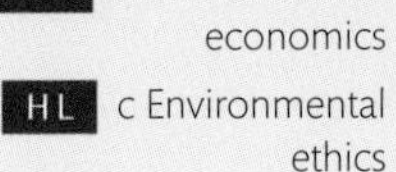

HL b Environmental economics

HL c Environmental ethics

7.1.2 Natural capital

Natural capital is the stock of natural resources available on Earth. It includes natural resources, environmental assets, ecosystem services, ecosystems, biodiversity and natural resources (Figure 7.3). According to the Organization for Economic Co-operation and Development, natural capital is defined as 'natural assets in their role of providing natural resource inputs and services for economic production'. Natural capital includes water, fresh air, soil, minerals, vegetation (including timber) and animals. Ecologically minded economists describe resources as natural capital. This is equivalent to the store of the planet, or stock, which is the present accumulated quantity of natural capital. It is possible, and somewhat controversial, to put a value on natural capital. Many ecosystem services are essential for life and therefore are priceless. Nevertheless, some researchers have valued the Canadian coniferous forest at approximately US$ 3.7 trillion and the annual value of the ecosystem services it provides at US$ 93 million.

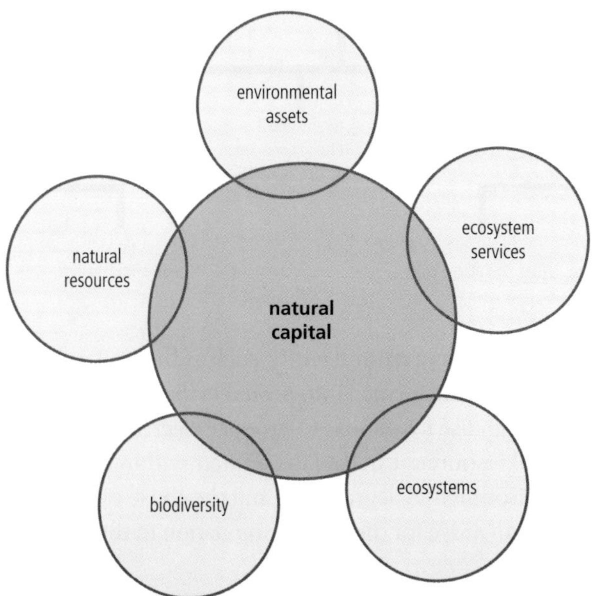

Figure 7.3 Natural capital.

TOK

What constraints are there on the pursuit of knowledge?

As resources become scarce, we have to make decisions about how to use them. To what extent should potential damage to the environment limit our pursuit of knowledge?

According to NatureScot, natural capital in Scotland is worth almost £200 billion and supports approximately 240,000 jobs. Scotland's beaches and salt marshes protect £13 billion worth of coastal buildings and infrastructure, compared to £5 billion protected by engineered sea walls. Insect pollination services in Scotland are valued at an estimated £43 million per year.

Some forms of natural capital provide people with free goods and services, such as fresh air, whereas other forms may require some investment through the mining of rocks or harvesting of food or timber (Figure 7.4). Natural capital also provides essential services such as climate regulation, flood control and pollination.

Figure 7.4 Natural capital from mudflows, Paradise River, Montserrat, Caribbean.

7.1.3 Natural capital and natural income

1.1 Perspectives
1.3 Sustainability

HL a Environmental law
HL b Environmental economics
HL c Environmental ethics

The Earth contains many resources that support its natural systems: the core and crust of the planet; the biosphere (the living part) containing forests, grassland, deserts, tundra, and other biomes; and the upper layers of the atmosphere. Renewable resources can be used over and over again. If properly managed, renewable resources are forms of wealth that can produce natural income indefinitely in the form of valuable goods and services (Figure 7.5).

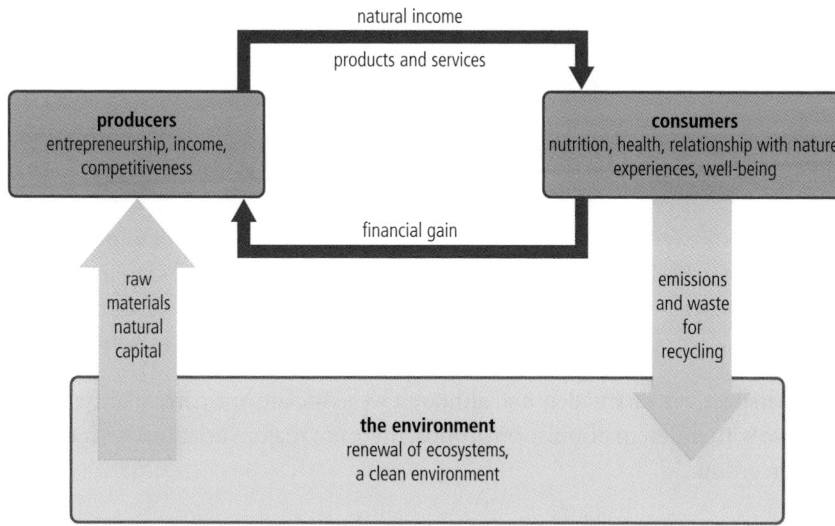

Figure 7.5 Natural capital and natural income.

Natural income is the yield obtained from resources. Goods such as fish or timber may provide natural income. Natural income services include climate regulation and flood prevention.
Natural capital is a term used for resources that can produce a sustainable natural income of goods or services.

Natural capital includes the raw materials from the environment that are harvested and used by producers to generate products and services (Figure 7.6).

Natural income relates to the products and services that are then used by consumers.

A renewable resource is a natural resource that the environment continues to supply or replace as it is used and whose emissions and waste are recycled in a sustainable way.

In order to provide income indefinitely, the products and services used should not reduce the original resource or capital. For example, if a forest is to provide ongoing income in the form of timber, the amount of original capital, in the form of the forest, must remain the same while income is generated from new growth. This is the same as living on the interest from a bank account – the original money is not used and only the interest is removed and spent.

Figure 7.6 Nodding donkey in Brunei. The oil industry is unsustainable because the mining of oil exceeds the rate at which oil is being renewed.

Natural capital can be lost. For example, in 2023 it was reported that over just six years, 800 million trees had been cut down in the Amazon rainforest to make way for cattle ranching, destroying 1.7 million ha of rainforest. Much of the beef was said to be destined for the EU, UK and China. However, the EU adopted a new law in 2020 to prevent the importing of beef from any cattle raised on land that had been deforested after 2020. The supermarkets Lidl® and Aldi® stopped selling Brazilian beef in 2021 and 2022, respectively.

Natural capital and natural income

Types of natural capital such as land, water, minerals, air and biodiversity provide benefits for people, as well as providing processes and functions within ecosystems such as productivity and nutrient recycling. However, in many cases, natural capital has been undervalued or has been considered as being free. Putting a monetary value on nature can be difficult and controversial as it is difficult to measure and is, arguably, priceless. Nevertheless, there are parts that can be valued, such as the amount of pollution a wetland can absorb or the amount of carbon a forest can store. According to the *Climate Change Business Journal*, the value of the Earth's natural capital is approximately US$ 38 quadrillion, although this falls to US$ 33 quadrillion due to degradation caused by humans.

Natural income is the yield obtained from natural resources, which is the value of natural capital that humans consume. For natural income to be sustainable, the natural capital must be able to renew itself. For example, over-fishing is unsustainable if a greater number of fish are removed than can be replenished annually. Deforestation may also be unsustainable if the rate of forest removal, that is the natural income, is greater than the rate of forest growth and renewal. However, if the rate of forest removal is lower than the rate of forest annual growth, then the deforestation can be considered to be sustainable.

Activity

Discuss with a partner the forms of natural capital and natural income that are found in your home region.

1.1 Perspectives
1.2 Systems
1.3 Sustainability

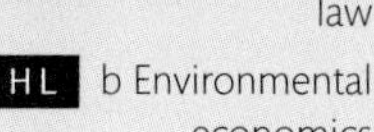

HL a Environmental law
HL b Environmental economics

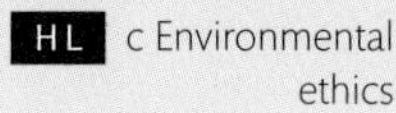

HL c Environmental ethics

The terms 'natural capital' and 'natural income' imply a particular *perspective* on nature.

7.1.4 Perspectives on nature

One view of nature is that it is made up of capital, natural services and resources. This perception in itself might be associated with the contentious, and extremely anthropocentric, view that nature is there for human exploitation. However, nature may also be seen to serve very effectively as a model for the sustainable use of resources.

People's perspectives vary widely and although we associate one particular type of perspective with different population groups, there are major variations within each population group.

Thus, an ecocentric approach in relation to natural resources might suggest that the Indigenous people, such as the Dobe !Kung in southern Africa, use resources as hunter gatherers who take only what they need as any over-exploitation of the resources would ultimately lead to their own demise.

The technocentric view argues that resources are there to be used by societies and that if shortages occur, society (or individuals) would produce new ideas to make more resources or new resources. Examples of this view can be seen through the Green Revolution in farming and the use of GM crops.

The anthropocentric view is a human-centred view that suggests rules and regulations may allow for increased exploitation of the Earth's resources. Agricultural and fishing policies may be adopted to govern the production or exploitation of resources. Such governance suggests that policies are good, as they have been debated and accepted, and so nature can be exploited for the benefit of society.

Example – World Bank *The Changing Wealth of Nations, 2021*

The Changing Wealth of Nations, 2021 examines the wealth of 146 countries between 1995 and 2018 by measuring the economic value of:

- renewable natural capital, including forests, cropland, seas and ocean resources
- non-renewable natural capital, including minerals and fossil fuels
- human capital, as earnings over a lifetime
- produced capital, including infrastructure and buildings.

From the findings of the report it was concluded that global wealth had grown significantly overall but had done so at the expense of future prosperity and while exacerbating inequalities.

They found that medium-income countries (MICs) were catching up with high-income countries (HICs). They also found that a growth in prosperity was accompanied by a decline in natural resources. Low-income countries (LICs) and MICs experienced an 8% decrease in forest wealth per capita and an 83% decrease in marine fish stocks.

Globally, the share of total wealth in renewable natural capital is decreasing, but this is also threatened further by global climate change. This is due in part to population growth and the unsustainable rate of the use of natural resources. Moreover, renewable natural capital is becoming more valuable because it provides crucial ecosystem services (this topic, Section 7.1.7). For example, the value of mangrove forests for coastal protection was approximately US$ 550 billion by 2018.

7.1.5 Ecosystem services

1.2 Systems
1.3 Sustainability

HL a Environmental law
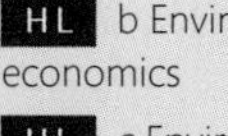
HL b Environmental economics
HL c Environmental ethics

All ecosystems provide life-supporting ecosystem services. These ecosystem services support all living things, including humans.

Ecosystems provide many life-supporting services such as water supply replenishment, protection from floods and erosion, control of pollution, carbon sequestration and the provision of goods for human use such as timber, fish stocks and agricultural crops.

The income from natural capital from ecosystems may come from:

- goods in the form of marketable commodities such as timber and grain
- services such as flood and erosion protection, climate stabilization and maintenance of soil fertility (Table 7.1).

Types of ecosystem service

Ecosystems provide four types of services for living organisms. These are supporting, regulating, provisioning and cultural.

Supporting services

These services are essential for life and include primary productivity, soil formation and the cycling of nutrients. All other ecosystem services depend on these. Supporting services are essential for the health of ecosystems but do not yield direct benefits to humans.

Ecosystem	Service provided										
	freshwater	food	timber and fibre	new products	regulate diversity	cycle nutrients	air quality and climate regulation	human health	detox	regulate hazards	cultural
cultivated		✔	✔	✔	✔	✔	✔				✔
dry land		✔		✔	✔	✔	✔	✔	✔		✔
forest	✔	✔	✔	✔	✔	✔	✔	✔	✔	✔	✔
urban		✔			✔		✔	✔	✔		✔
lakes and rivers	✔	✔		✔	✔	✔	✔	✔	✔	✔	✔
coastal	✔	✔	✔		✔	✔	✔	✔	✔	✔	✔
marine		✔		✔	✔	✔	✔		✔		✔
polar	✔	✔			✔		✔				✔
mountain	✔	✔			✔		✔			✔	✔
island		✔			✔		✔				✔

▲
Table 7.1 Ecosystem types and the services they provide.

Regulating services

These are a diverse set of services and include pollination, regulation of pests and diseases and the production of goods, such as food, fibre and wood. Other regulating services include climate and hazard regulation and water quality regulation.

By having a **complete vegetation cover**, the impact of raindrops on soils is reduced and there is an increase of infiltration. Some of the water can percolate into the underlying rocks thereby replenishing water supplies. In addition, having a complete vegetation cover can help reduce the risk of flooding and provide erosion protection. Plants intercept rainfall and reduce raindrop impact on the ground by reducing the velocity of the falling raindrops. Once vegetation has been removed, the rates of erosion increase.

Reedbeds can help with pollution mitigation. An example of this was observed when a new reedbed was created in a redundant part of the River Cole, UK. The aim of the project was to create a small buffer zone to help intercept silts contaminated with agricultural pollutants and increase the habitat diversity of the river.

Carbon sequestration is the process of removing carbon from the atmosphere and storing it. Around 45% of the carbon dioxide (CO_2), emitted by humans remains in the atmosphere, contributing to global warming. Carbon sequestration can occur biologically or geologically. Biological carbon sequestration occurs when carbon is stored in the natural environment in 'carbon sinks' such as oceans, water bodies, forests, grasslands and soil. Forests provide one of the best forms of carbon sequestration as the trees and plants undergo photosynthesis. Geological sequestration occurs when carbon is stored underground in rocks through carbon capture and storage. This can be rapid if using human intervention but can take millennia if left to nature.

Provisioning services

These are the services that allow people to obtain goods such as food, fibre and fuel (peat, wood and non-woody biomass) from forests and cultivated lands, and water from aquifers, rivers and lakes. The production of such goods can come from heavily managed ecosystems, such as intensive farms and fish farms, or from semi-natural ones in the forms of hunting and fishing.

Cultural services

These services are derived from places where people enjoy cultural goods and benefits while also being able to interact with nature. Open spaces such as gardens, parks, rivers, forests, lakes, the seashore and wilderness, provide opportunities for outdoor recreation, education, spiritual well-being and improvements to human health.

Figure 7.7 shows how these services can be provided in a marine ecosystem.

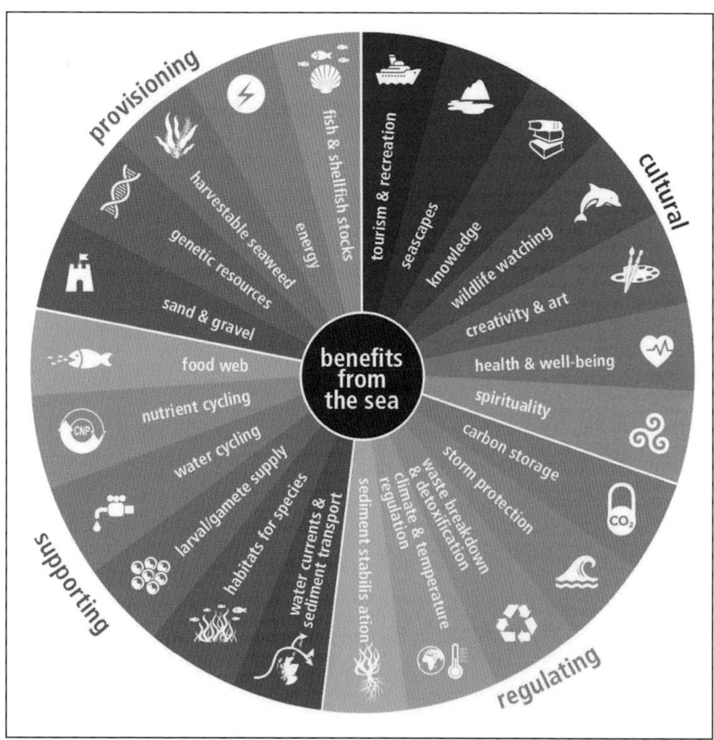

Figure 7.7 Marine ecosystem services.

7.1.6 All resources are finite

1.1 Perspectives
1.3 Sustainability

HL a Environmental law
HL b Environmental economics
HL c Environmental ethics

All resources are finite. Resources can be classified as either renewable or non-renewable.

Renewable resources are those that do not get depleted as they can be regenerated and/or replaced as quickly as they are being used. This can occur either through natural growth or reproduction for resources such as food, crops or timber or through natural processes for resources such as freshwater or ozone.

The Sun is the ultimate renewable energy source for most living organisms on Earth. Plants use solar energy to make their own food through photosynthesis. Water is another renewable resource although it can be contaminated through pollution or lost from an area through evaporation. Hydroelectric power (HEP) can be a renewable source of

Non-renewable natural capital, such as fossil fuels, soil and minerals, is either irreplaceable or can only be replaced over expansive geological timescales.

energy. Any surplus energy can be used at night to pump water back up to a reservoir, which means that it can flow back down and generate more energy the next day.

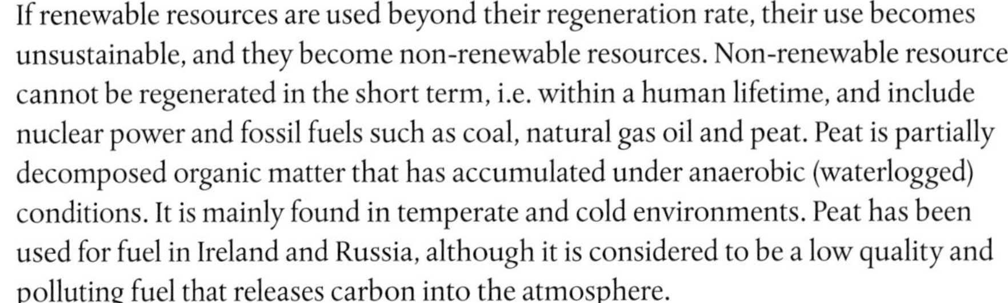

If renewable resources are used beyond their regeneration rate, their use becomes unsustainable, and they become non-renewable resources. Non-renewable resources cannot be regenerated in the short term, i.e. within a human lifetime, and include nuclear power and fossil fuels such as coal, natural gas oil and peat. Peat is partially decomposed organic matter that has accumulated under anaerobic (waterlogged) conditions. It is mainly found in temperate and cold environments. Peat has been used for fuel in Ireland and Russia, although it is considered to be a low quality and polluting fuel that releases carbon into the atmosphere.

Renewable natural capital can be used sustainably or unsustainably. If renewable natural capital is used beyond its natural income, this use becomes unsustainable.

Nuclear power is also often classified as an alternative energy (along with renewable sources such as solar and wind) because greenhouse gases are not emitted during the production of energy. However, a large amount of greenhouse gases are emitted during the construction and deconstruction of nuclear power stations.

7.1.7 The value of natural capital

1.1 Perspectives

Natural capital has many values including aesthetic, cultural, economic, environmental, health, intrinsic, social, spiritual and technological.

HL b Environmental economics

HL c Environmental ethics

Aesthetic value

Aesthetic values refer to the appreciation of a landscape, such as a forest or waterfall, for its visual attractiveness. These values can bring money to the area through tourism.

Cultural value

Natural capital has aesthetic, cultural, economic, environmental, health, intrinsic, social, spiritual and technological value. The value of natural capital is influenced by these factors.

Some natural features may have an important cultural significance for a population. Examples include Uluru, which has significance for Australia's Indigenous population, Mount Fuji in Jalan and Thingvellir in Iceland, which is the site of the country's first parliament.

Economic value

Economic value can be determined from the market price of the goods and services provided by a resource. Examples include the value of wood produced and the value of fish caught.

Environmental value

Although environmental values have no formal market price, they are nevertheless essential for humanity. Soil erosion control, nitrogen fixation and photosynthesis are all essential processes for human existence but none of them have direct monetary value. Environmental and aesthetic values do not provide easily identifiable commodities, so it is difficult to assess the economic contributions of these values using traditional methods of accounting.

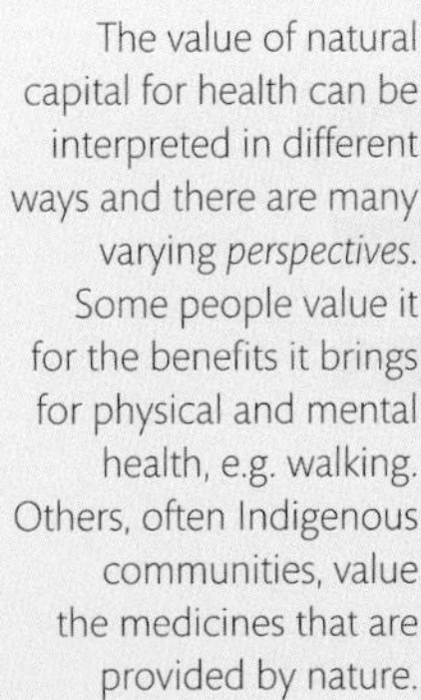

The value of natural capital for health can be interpreted in different ways and there are many varying *perspectives*. Some people value it for the benefits it brings for physical and mental health, e.g. walking. Others, often Indigenous communities, value the medicines that are provided by nature.

Health values

There are several health benefits derived from people's interactions with natural capital. For example, activities such as walking, jogging, open-water swimming and hiking not only benefit physical health but can also improve mental health.

Intrinsic values

Ethical, spiritual, and philosophical perspectives tend to prescribe intrinsic values to organisms and ecosystems. For example, the rights of organisms such as badgers or foxes in an ecosystem such as a deciduous forest are values in their own right, irrespective of economic value and regardless of their potential use to humans.

Social values

Social values refer to the well-being of individuals and communities. These include the health aspects mentioned previously. Social values also consider the state of the environment. For example, urban areas that are heavily polluted reduce the well-being of those living there. Poor water quality also impacts those who derive their water from rivers and lakes.

Spiritual values

Many environments have spiritual values for people. The Mountain Institute provides programmes to support the cultural and spiritual significance of nature in the Andes, the Himalayas and the USA.

Technological values

Natural capital has significant technological values. It provides the raw material for the fossil fuels industry, food industry, timber industry and so on. For example, in 2019, the value of UK natural capital was valued at approximately £1.2 trillion.

The evaluation of natural capital therefore requires many diverse perspectives that lie outside the remit of conventional economics.

Direct use values are ecosystem goods and services that are directly used by humans, most often by people visiting or residing in the ecosystem. Consumptive use includes harvesting food products, timber for fuel or housing, medicinal products and hunting animals for food and clothing. Non-consumptive use includes recreational and cultural activities that do not require harvesting of products (Figure 7.8).

Figure 7.8 Wytham Woods, Oxford, UK, gives an example of non-consumptive use. Woodlands and other natural environments can provide spiritual, health and aesthetic ecosystem services.

Indirect use values are derived from ecosystem services that provide benefits outside the ecosystem itself. For example, the use of natural water filtration, which may benefit people downstream. Optional values are derived from potential future use of ecosystem goods and services not currently used.

Create a survey to investigate the value that members of the school community place on different ecosystem services

1. Arrange a survey in your school to investigate the value placed on different ecosystem services by members of your school community. You should use three different population groups – students, teachers and support staff (non-teaching staff) – and include at least ten people in each of the population groups.

   Introduce the concept by telling the participants 'Environmental services are the benefits that people receive from nature'.

   Ask participants to rank the four services below in order of importance, with 1 being the most important and 4 being the least important.

   Create a different table for students, teachers and support staff.

Ecosystem services	**(Rank 1–4 where 1 is highest and 4 is lowest)**
Provisioning e.g. food resources, energy sources	
Supporting e.g. nutrient cycling, provision of water	
Regulating e.g. climate regulation, flood control	
Cultural e.g. tourism and recreation, creativity and art	

There is a resource explaining the different statistical tests and when they are used on this page of your eBook.

2. Add up the scores allocated for each of the ecosystem services by each of the population groups. Are there any differences in the way in which ecosystem services are valued by the three different population groups?
3. Using a Chi-squared (χ_2) test, investigate whether there is a statistically significant difference in the environmental values of the three population groups.

Worked example

To investigate whether there is any variation in the importance of four values of natural capital, a survey was conducted of 50 people.

We will use Chi-squared (χ^2) = Σ (o – e)^2/e (where (o) are the observed frequencies and (e) is the expected frequency) to test the null hypothesis that there is no statistically significant difference value of natural capital.

Value of natural capital	Number of responses
Economic	25
Environmental	12
Social	8
Spiritual	5

The 'number of responses' in the table are our four observed figures (o). If there is no statistically significant difference in their value, they should all be roughly the same, i.e. close to the mean, in this case 12.5. This mean is our expected value (e).

Soil	Observed value (o)	Expected value (e)	(o – e)	(o – e)^2	(o – e)^2/e
Economic	25	12.5	12.5	156.25	12.5
Environmental	12	12.5	–0.5	0.25	0.02
Social	8	12.5	–4.5	20.25	1.62
Spiritual	5	12.5	–7.5	56.25	4.5
					Σ 18.64

To use the statistical tables, use (n – 1) degrees of freedom (DF). As there were four categories, we use 3 DF. At the 95% level of significance, the critical value is 7.82. Our computed value (18.64) is higher than the critical value, so we reject the null hypothesis. Therefore, in this case there is a significant difference in the perception of the value of natural capital.

1.1 Perspectives
1.3 Sustainability

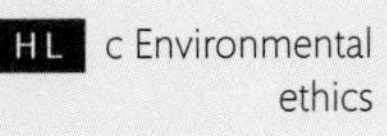

HL b Environmental economics
HL c Environmental ethics

7.1.8 Natural capital is dynamic

The value of natural capital should be seen as dynamic, in that it can increase and decrease over time for several reasons. Examples of dynamic natural capital include coal, uranium, lithium, cobalt, whale oil and cork.

As humans advance culturally and technologically, and our resource base changes, the importance of a resource may be transformed. Resources become more valuable as new technologies need them. For example, Stone Age tools were made from a variety of stones such as flint (Figure 7.9). Stones were shaped by chipping to provide a sharp edge. The tools could be attached to arrows or held by hand to skin animals and cut meat. Although flint was once an important resource as a hand tool, it is now redundant as it has been superseded by technological progress in the development of metal extraction from ores.

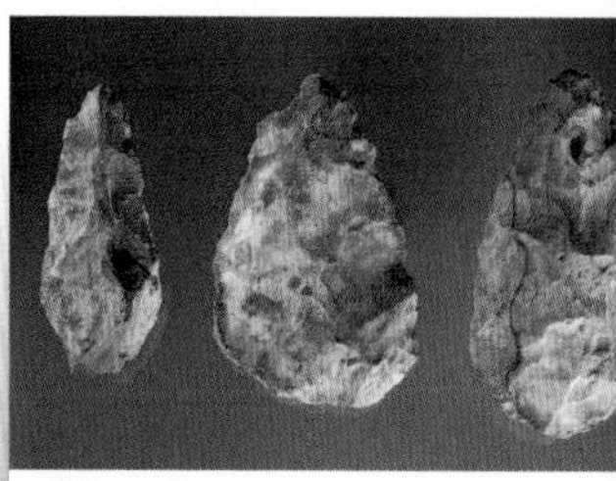

Figure 7.9 Stone age tools made from flint.

Uranium, in contrast, was of little value before the advent of the nuclear age. Nuclear fission involves the bombardment of uranium atoms with neutrons. A neutron splits a uranium atom, releasing a great amount of energy as heat and radiation. A different process, nuclear fusion, powers the Sun. In nuclear fusion, the nuclei of atoms fuse together, causing a much greater release of energy than in nuclear fission. If we ever learn to generate power by harnessing the energy from nuclear fusion, uranium, like flint before it, may lose its value. Attempts to harness nuclear fusion are continuing. For example, nuclear fusion facilities are to be built at the University of New South Wales, Sydney, Australia. They hope to have a working device by 2026. In 2023, the US President, Joe Biden, said that there were hopes to create a commercial nuclear fusion facility within 10 years in America, and in August 2023 US scientists were successful in achieving net energy gain for the second time through nuclear fusion reactions.

7.1.9 The use of natural capital needs to be managed

1.1 Perspectives
1.2 Systems
1.3 Sustainability

HL a Environmental law
HL b Environmental economics
HL c Environmental ethics

The use of natural capital needs to be managed in order to ensure sustainability. The long-term well-being of ecosystems and humans depends on resources not being used more rapidly than they can be regenerated and on waste products not being released more rapidly than they can be transformed.

These issues can be highlighted with regard to plastic. Most plastic is made from the fossil fuel crude oil. Plastics are a valuable resource and provide many benefits to society, including comfort, hygiene and safety. However, the single-use nature and disposal of plastics outweigh the benefits of their use in many places.

In 1950, global plastic production was just 1.5 million tonnes. In 2019, the global production of plastic reached 370 million tonnes, but less than 10% of it was recycled. There are predictions that global production of plastic could rise to 12 billion tonnes by 2050.

The irresponsible and unethical disposal of plastic waste causes major problems in all of the world's ecosystems due to fly tipping, inappropriate disposal at landfill and poor recycling management. According to the United Nations Environment Programme (UNEP), the use of single-use plastics, such as plastic bottles, caps, cigarette butts, grocery bags, straws and food wrappers, are evidence of poor waste management systems and societies' attitudes towards natural systems.

Plastics can be transported from land to oceans by rivers. In water, plastics create major challenges for aquatic organisms and may be incorporated into food chains. Larger plastics may be degraded into smaller plastic particles, such as microplastics (between 1 mm and 0.1µm in size) and nanoplastics (less than 0.1 µm in size). The presence of microplastics can be found in terrestrial, aquatic and atmospheric ecosystems (Figure 2.69 in Topic 2, Sections 2.2.18 and 2.2.19).

The presence of microplastics and nanoplastics in terrestrial ecosystems reduces their ability to sequester carbon, which is one of the main ecosystem services provided by soil. Microplastics are also entering marine ecosystems at unprecedented levels of up to 12.7 metric tonnes each year. Microplastics are believed to reduce ecosystem services in oceans by as much as 5%, which amounts to a value of approximately US$ 2.5 trillion.

Microplastics and nanoplastics in the atmosphere obstruct and reduce pollination, pose a major threat to plant diversity in tropical rainforests and can cause serious health problems in humans including lung congestion, ulcers, cancers, nasal infections and olfactory (smell) disorders.

At the end of their lifetime, some plastics are incinerated or recycled but most end up being disposed of in landfills because they are degraded and/or contaminated and are not fit for recycling. Globally, only approximately 10% of plastics are recycled.

1.2 Systems
1.3 Sustainability
4.2 Water access, use and security
5.2 Agriculture and food
7.2 Energy sources, use and management
8.2 Urban systems and urban planning
8.3 Urban air pollution

7.1.10 Resource security

Resource security depends on the ability of societies to ensure the long-term availability of sufficient natural resources to meet demand. This can easily be demonstrated in relation to food or water security.

Food security refers to having sufficient quantity of good quality food so that people can remain healthy and be productive. According to the Economist Global Food Security Index, global food security has been declining in recent years due to a combination of COVID-19, high commodity prices, global climate change and the conflict between Russia and Ukraine.

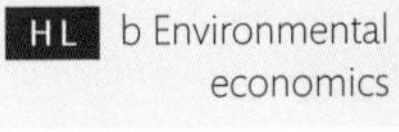

HL b Environmental economics

Table 7.2 shows the global food security ratings for the top five and bottom five countries in 2022.

Table 7.2 Global Food Security Index, 2022.

Top five countries	Bottom five countries
Finland 83.7	Madagascar 40.6
Ireland 81.7	Sierra Leone 40.5
Norway 80.5	Yemen 40.1
France 80.2	Haiti 38.5
Netherlands 80.1	Syria 36.3

You need to consider the extent to which resource security in two contrasting named societies has been achieved for food or water.

Ireland's wealth per capita is US$ 102,500 (5th in the world) whereas that of Haiti is US$ 2900 (197th in the world).

Ireland has a high food security index. The country has a temperate climate with mild summers and plenty of rainfall. It is a major livestock producer, especially of dairy products, beef and lamb, but also produces crops such as barley, wheat, potatoes and oats.

In contrast, Haiti is a 'hunger hotspot' with approximately 1.8 million people facing an emergency level of food insecurity and nearly 4.9 million people (approximately half the country's population) not having enough food to eat. The reasons for such a high level of food insecurity are complex and historical (Figure 7.10). Haiti has experienced widespread economic pressure since it claimed its independence. It has also experienced a devastating earthquake in 2010, has numerous tropical cyclones, widespread deforestation and soil erosion and, most recently, has an increase in the rate of gang violence. Some 40% of the population live in rural areas with limited access to resources needed for food production including land, fertile soil, water, money and so on. The highest level of food insecurity is found in the Cité Soleil commune in Port au Prince, where intergang violence severely affects the access of households to markets and essential services.

Over 99% of Ireland's rural and urban populations have access to piped water, whereas in Haiti 91.9% of the urban population (approximately 6.4 million out of approximately 7 million people) and only 56.1% of the rural population (approximately 2.6 million out of approximately 4.6 million people) have access to piped water.

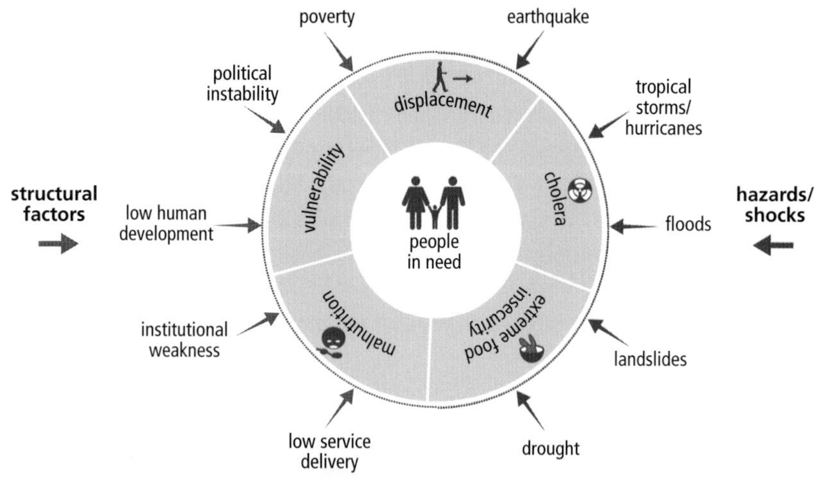

Figure 7.10 Causes of food insecurity in Haiti.

4.2 Water access, use and security

Activity

1. Choose another one of the countries in the 'bottom five' shown in Table 7.2 and carry out research to investigate why its food security is so low.

7.1.11 Choices are affected by many factors and different perspectives

1.1 Perspectives

1.2 Systems

HL a Environmental law

HL b Environmental economics

HL c Environmental ethics

The choices a society makes in using given natural resources are affected by many factors and reflect diverse perspectives. Factors affecting such choices may include economic, sociocultural, political, environmental, geographical, technological and historical factors. International agreements on cutting greenhouse gas emissions to aim for net zero emissions change the priority of these choices. The following two examples show very different choices.

Example – Costa Rica

Costa Rica has a population of 5 million, population growth of 0.9% per year, and GDP/head of US$ 21,200.

Costa Rica is one of the most sustainable countries in the world. Costa Rica has embraced sustainability and, in doing so, is meeting the needs of the present society without compromising the needs of future generations. Although there are different interpretations of sustainability depending on a person's values and viewpoint, there are three core principles:

- inter-generational equity so that future generations are not disadvantaged
- intra-generational equity so that all people have an equal share of the available resources
- eradicating poverty by combating hunger, malnutrition, gender inequality and illiteracy.

The choices a society makes in using given natural resources are affected by many factors and reflect diverse *perspectives*.

Costa Rica has a number of sustainable practices, showing that it is possible to have a high standard of living and to live sustainably. The government has banned single-use plastics and established protected areas, such as Tortuguero National Park, to help preserve natural resources. It offers incentives for sustainability initiatives such as rainwater harvesting and desalination of local water supplies. It has one of the highest standards of living in Central America.

Costa Rica has a number of cloud forests and many of these now have important tourist functions, as well as conservation functions. The Monteverde Cloud Forest Reserve was established in 1972 and covers over 14,200 ha. The Santa Elena Cloud Forest Reserve was established in 1989 and is managed by the Santa Elena community. It was one of the first reserves in Costa Rica to be community-run rather than being run by a government agency. Similarly, the Bosque Eterno de los Niños ('Children's Eternal Rainforest') is maintained by the Monteverde |Conservation League. Initially, this area was purchased with money raised by Swedish school children to protect threatened wilderness areas. The Bosque Eterno de los Niños is partnered with organizations from over 40 different countries.

Example – Carmichael mine, Australia

In contrast, the Carmichael coal mine in Queensland, Australia, shows how new developments can have negative impacts on the environment and local communities. The Carmichael coal mine in Queensland, Australia, is an open cast mine covering an area of approximately 280 km^2, and is located in the Galilee Basin not far from the Great Barrier Reef (Figure 7.11). Construction of the mine began in 2019 and the first batch of coal was mined and shipped out in December 2021. A 200 km extension railway line was also built to link the mine with an existing narrow gauge railway line.

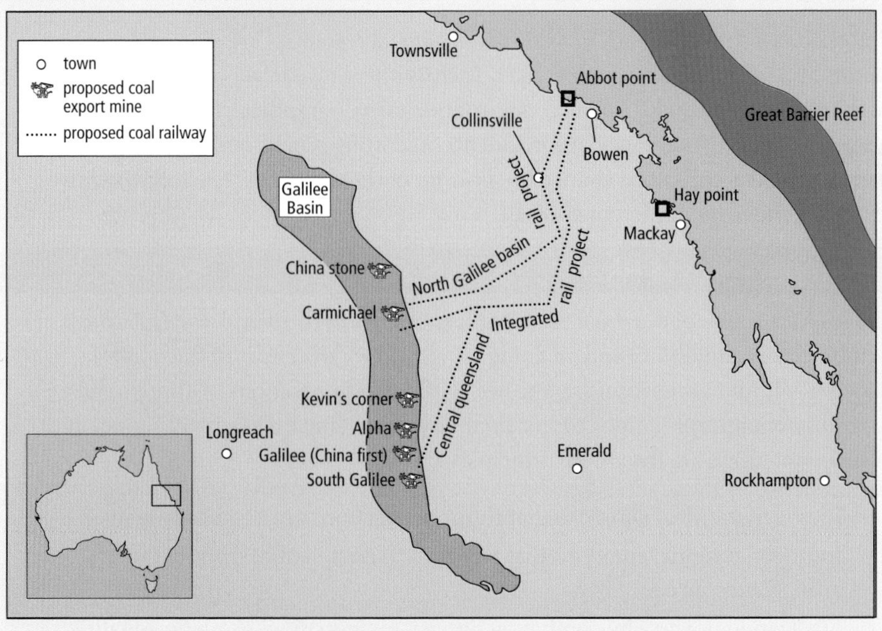

Figure 7.11 The location of the Carmichael Mine, Galilee Basin and the Great Barrier Reef.

The initial plan was to mine 60 million tonnes of coal per year, but this was scaled down to 10 million tonnes. According to the Environmental Impact Statement, the mine was expected to produce 200 million tonnes of CO_2 over 60 years. Adani, an Indian Company who developed the mine, had originally planned to use 12,500 megalitres of water per week from the Belyando River. This would cause water tables to drop in height by between 20 m and 50 m.

The mine site is home to a number of species, including the largest known community of black-throated finches (Figure 7.12). Adani Australia produced a management plan for the finches that involved clearing land around the mine and forcing the finches to move away. In November 2020, Adani changed the name of its Australian subsidiary from Adani planning to Bravus mining and resources.

Figure 7.12 A black-throated finch. Their habitat is threatened by the development of the Carmichael coal mine.

A number of major international banks publicly ruled out financing the coal mine, railway line and shipping terminal. In addition, three of the big four Australian mines pulled out of funding the project.

There has been much criticism over the potential impacts of the mine on the Great Barrier Reef, along with the mine's water usage, carbon emissions, economic benefits and impacts on Indigenous people.

Indigenous landholders launched a case against the granting of Adani's mining lease, but the court ruled against them. Members of the Wangan and Jagalingou peoples continue to occupy a cultural site close to the mine.

Environmentalists claim that dredging coral reefs to create shipping routes is damaging the coral and the animals that feed on these, such as dugongs (a type of manatee). The use of coal also contributes to global warming. Those in favour of the mine suggest that it will create 15,000 construction jobs in Queensland and that it will provide cheap energy across Asia. In this example, it would appear that international agreements on cutting greenhouse gas emissions aiming for net zero emissions did not change the priority of these choices.

Activity

1. Research the environmental impacts of the Carmichael Mine using the following weblink:
2. Write a one-page report about your findings to present to your class.

HL

HL

7.1.12 Management and intervention strategies to influence society's use of natural capital

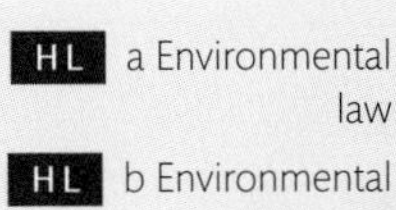

A range of different management and intervention strategies can be used to directly influence society's use of natural capital. Government management strategies can include national action plans for sustainable development goals. Government intervention strategies include the use of taxes, fines, subsidies, legislation, publicity campaigns and education. For example, research is conducted by the government and industry on ways to improve sustainability. NGOs, local communities and social movements can influence society through campaigns, social media or actions, such as recycling.

Concrete industry and CO_2

The concrete and cement industry accounts for 7% of global CO_2 emissions. With the increase in population growth and urbanization, the usage of concrete will increase. The low-carbon transition in the concrete industry requires innovative techniques. One development has been the use of carbon capture and storage. This is a safe and sustainable solution to reduce the amount of CO_2 transferred to the atmosphere. In carbon capture and storage methods, the CO_2 collected is reacted with a naturally alkaline mineral, such as fly ash, to create a type of mineral called a carbonate. Carbonates can be stored in concrete as an aggregate so the CO_2 will never get into the atmosphere.

Recycling and reusing wind turbines

Most of the elements of a wind turbine can be recycled, apart from the blades used in early turbines. Increasingly, engineers are using biodegradable thermoplastics to make the turbine blades. The fiberglass used in the early turbines is made of very fine plastic and glass and is therefore non-biodegradable and not at all recyclable. However, fiberglass can be used in the production of cement. Moreover, the blades can be used for other functions. For example, the blades have been used as bicycle sheds in Denmark, noise barriers in the USA and used to make a pedestrian footbridge in Ireland.

Biological production of ammonia replacing the Haber process

The most commonly used method to produce ammonia (NH_3) is the Haber–Bosch process (Topic 2, Section 2.3.23). However, this process produces significant greenhouse gas emissions and uses large amounts of energy. Biological nitrogen fixation is a natural process that converts atmospheric nitrogen (N_2) to NH_3. Nitrogen-fixing organisms produce NH_3 at ambient temperatures. The main microorganisms that carry out N_2 fixation include *Rhizobia*, which colonize the roots of legumes, along with *Azotobacter* and *Klebsiella*.

Government intervention

Sweden is a country in which government intervention to achieve sustainable resource use has been clearly demonstrated. The Swedish government have been climate policy pioneers. Sweden's first carbon tax was introduced in 1991 and in 2008, the government proposed a strategy and timescale for the reduction of greenhouse gas emissions. The government was keen to reduce pollution without harming the economy. A number of questions were posed by the Swedish government:

- Should emissions be reduced at home or in other countries?
- By how much could carbon taxes within Sweden be increased?
- How would the economy respond to emission reduction targets of 25, 30 or 40%?

A key concern was the impact on the export industry because Sweden depends to a large extent on exports.

An increase in the carbon tax was introduced in 2009. By 2021, emissions had fallen to 40 million metric tonnes, which is 40% lower compared with 1990 levels. Overall, Sweden has the lowest greenhouse gas emissions in the European Union (EU).

Sweden had data on CO_2 emissions for all sectors since 1993. The researchers believed that CO_2 emissions could be reduced by approximately 50%. The new policy is expected to save over 700,000 tonnes of carbon annually, while costing the economy 25% less than the original policy. Researchers believe this will save Sweden over US$ 1 billion per year.

Upcycling

Upcycling is the modification or creation of new products from used materials. Upcycling products can vary but examples include clothing made into new products such as soft furnishings, pieces of jewelry made from used metal and plastics, fibres and souvenirs made from old drink cans (Figure 7.13). The upcycling movement allows for a decrease in the amount of new raw materials used by extending the lifetime of used materials and products. It also reduces energy consumption and reduces the amount of waste.

Figure 7.13 Upcycling old cans into souvenir goods for tourists, Cuba. (a) Cars (b) Cameras

Missed opportunities

However, not all goods are upcycled or even recycled as much as they could be. Take, for example, cell phones.

In North America, Western Europe and Japan, most people change their phone every two years. Generally, cell phones are light (less than 160 g), but their materials and components have considerable economic value because they contain many valuable resources such as gold, silver and rare earth elements (REEs). In the EU, some 160 million cell phones are discarded annually, representing a loss of materials worth US$ 500 million a year.

Only approximately 15% of phones are currently collected and recycled. Increasing collection rates to 50% would make a huge difference as second-hand sales of phones would be profitable even after collection, processing and remarketing. Collecting reusable components and remanufacturing could be made easier if the design of certain parts of a phone were standardized. The main parts that could be remanufactured include the charger, battery, camera and screen.

Recycling of phones would generally occur close to the market and result in reduced imports of phones, which are mainly produced outside the EU.

HL

7.1.13 SDGs, resource use and management

1.1 Perspectives
1.2 Systems
1.3 Sustainability

HL a Environmental law
HL b Environmental economics
HL c Environmental ethics

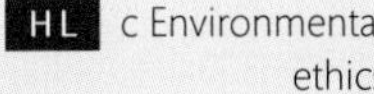

The SDGs continue – and extend – the efforts to end poverty, reduce inequalities and tackle environmental degradation, including climate change. The Goals are wide ranging and include 169 targets. Although the SDGs are not legally binding, governments are expected to develop systems in order to achieve them.

Some countries, including Japan and the UK, have reservations about the SDGs and believe that there should be fewer of them. There are also doubts about how the funding will be made available within all countries to achieve these goals.

The UN Sustainable Development Goals (SDGs) are a set of social and environmental goals and targets to guide action on sustainability and environmental justice (Topic 1, Section 1.3.18). The SDGs provide a framework for sustainable development, including action by all countries in global partnership for natural resources use and management. For example, Goal 12 of the SDGs (Ensure responsible consumption and production patterns) aims to ensure sustainable production and consumption patterns. It was considered by the UN as essential for sustainable development, along with poverty eradication and management of natural resources.

SDG 12 Ensure responsible consumption and production

- Between 2000 and 2019, total domestic material consumption rose by more than 65% globally and reached a total of 95.1 billion metric tonnes in 2019. During this period, East and South-East Asia showed the steepest rise in domestic material consumption, from 31% in 2000 to 43% in 2019.
- In 2020, an estimated 13.3% of the world's food was lost after harvesting and before reaching retail markets (Topic 5, Section 5.2.3).
- An estimated 17% of total food available to consumers (931 million metric tonnes) is wasted at household, food service and retail levels.
- The collection and recycling/reuse of electronic waste are relatively high in HICs but are much lower in LICs and MICs – only 1.6% in sub-Saharan Africa and 1.2% in Latin America and the Caribbean.

Activity

Table 7.3 shows progress by region towards reducing domestic material consumption and rationalizing inefficient fossil fuel subsidies.

Table 7.3 Progress towards SDG 12: Ensure sustainable consumption and production patterns.

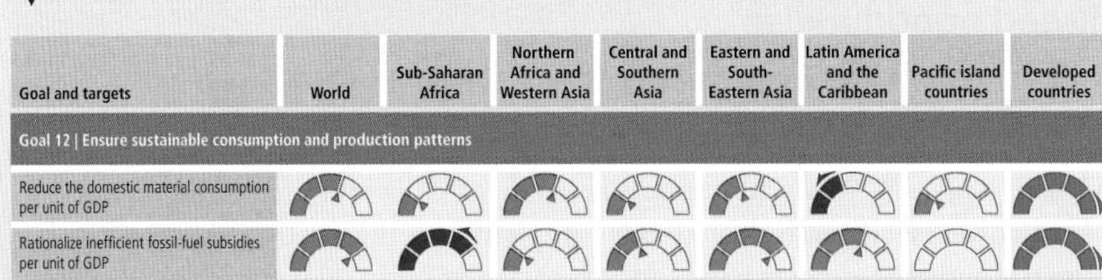

Goal and targets	World	Sub-Saharan Africa	Northern Africa and Western Asia	Central and Southern Asia	Eastern and South-Eastern Asia	Latin America and the Caribbean	Pacific island countries	Developed countries
Goal 12 | Ensure sustainable consumption and production patterns								
Reduce the domestic material consumption per unit of GDP								
Rationalize inefficient fossil-fuel subsidies per unit of GDP								

1. Find the Goal 12 targets on the United Nations Sustainable Development Goals website and investigate the targets for responsible production and consumption.
2. Write a one-page report summarizing your findings and present it to the class.

Activity

Find the *Bringing Data to Life* flipbook on the United Nations Sustainable Development Goals website.

1. Go to page 26 to find out about plastic recycling in the Gambia.
2. Go to page 27 to find out about the 'Women waste warriors'.
3. Make a poster about either plastic recycling in the Gambia or 'Women waste warriors'.

7.1.14 Environmental Impact Assessment

HL

An **environmental impact assessment (EIA)** is a detailed survey that takes place before a major development occurs, with the purpose of assessing the potential impact of the development on the environment.

1.1 Perspectives
1.2 Systems
1.3 Sustainability

The EIA predicts possible impacts on habitats, species and ecosystems and helps decision-makers to decide whether the development should go ahead. Figure 7.14 shows an example of the assessment of the potential environmental impacts of developing a dam.

HL a Environmental law

HL b Environmental economics

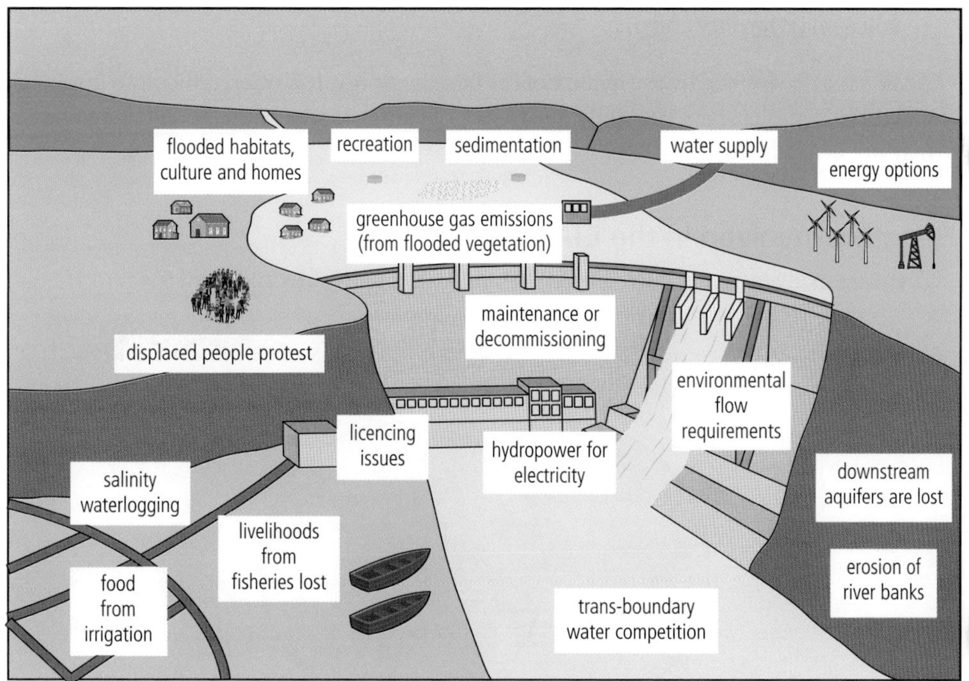

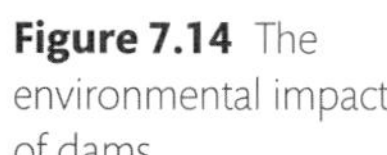

Figure 7.14 The environmental impact of dams.

An EIA assesses the environmental, social and economic impacts and *sustainability* of a development project through independent, detailed surveys, followed by audits and continued monitoring after project completion.

An EIA also addresses the mitigation of potential environmental impacts associated with the development. The report should provide a non-technical summary at the conclusion so that lay-people and the media can understand the implications of the study.

TOK

What counts as good evidence for a claim?

The impact of dams can be weighed up by using cost-benefit analysis. To what extent do the advantages of large dams outweigh the disadvantages of large dams? How do we interpret the validity of different conclusions when there is conflict between them?

Some countries incorporate EIAs within their legal framework, with penalties and measures that can be taken if the conditions of the EIA are not fulfilled. Other countries may simply use the assessment to inform policy decisions. In some countries, the information and suggestions of the EIA are often ignored or take second place to economic concerns.

The first stage of an EIA is to carry out a baseline study. This study is undertaken because it is important to know what the physical and biological environment is like before the project starts so that it can be monitored during and after the development. Variables measured as part of a baseline study should include assessment of:

- the habitat types and abundance, with the total area of each habitat type being recorded
- species, with the number of faunal and floral species present being recorded
- species diversity, including an estimate of the abundance of each species and a calculation of the diversity of the community
- the presence of any endangered species
- land use type and coverage
- hydrological conditions in terms of volume, discharge, flows and water quality
- presence of any human populations
- soil quality, fertility and pH.

An EIA may be limited by the quality of the baseline study. It is often difficult to put together a complete baseline study due to lack of data, so some of the potential impacts may not be identified.

Factors involved in the EIA process

There are many factors involved in the EIA process (Figure 7.15 and Table 7.4).

Figure 7.15 Some factors involved in the EIA process.

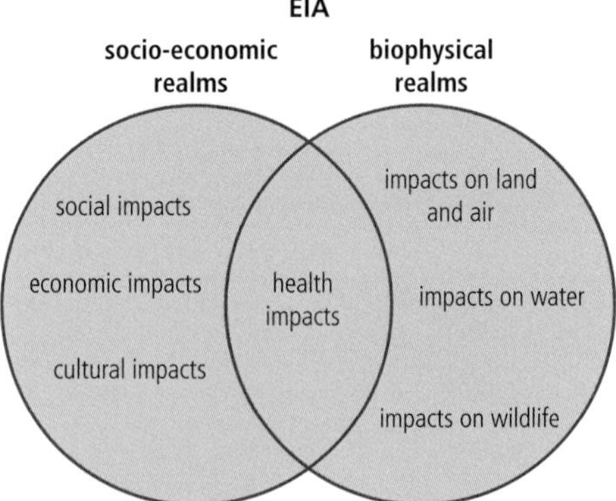

The objectives of EIAs include identifying and evaluating the environmental, economic and social impacts of planned developments and, where possible, suggesting alternative schemes.

Process stage	Details
Screening	identification of projects that need a full/partial assessment
Scoping	• identification of impacts to be assessed • alternative solutions/designs to reduce negative impacts
Assessment and evaluation of impacts and development of alternatives	environmental impacts are analyzed and alternatives are considered
EIA report (Environmental Impact Statement)	environmental management plan (EMP) and non-technical summary for the general public are produced
Decision making	decisions as to whether project should go ahead are taken
Monitoring, compliance, enforcement and environmental auditing	monitoring of the predicted impacts and mitigation efforts

Table 7.4 The EIA process.

7.1.15 Countries and regions have different EIAs

HL

1.3 Sustainability

HL a Environmental law

HL b Environmental economics

HL c Environmental ethics

Countries and regions have different guidance on the use of EIAs. Baseline studies are generally used to predict and evaluate possible impacts of a project and suggest mitigation strategies to alleviate or avoid environmental harm.

EIAs were introduced in the late 1960s by the USA. The guidelines were formalized between the late 1970s and early 1980s and were adopted by a number of developing countries including Colombia in 1974 and the Philippines in 1978. By 1990 the World Bank was using EIAs in European countries including Latvia and Estonia.

The use of EIAs in India began during the period 1976–77. The government introduced the Air (Prevention and Control of Pollution) Act (1981) and Environment (Protection) Act 1986, which made EIAs compulsory. The government also introduced a start-rating system for EIAs to improve efficiency and accountability. However, the government still allows long-distance transport of coal to India from Australia's Carmichael mine.

Activity

Visit the Summary EIA for the Assam Inland Water Transport Project:

With a partner, produce a summary report on one side of A4 paper.

The Swedish International Development Cooperation Agency (Sida) produced guidelines for simplified EIAs:

- **Could the programme/project offer opportunities** for positive contributions to an environmentally sustainable development? What are these opportunities? Which of them are most relevant to address? Has the programme/project been adjusted to enhance these opportunities?
- **Could the programme/project have any negative impacts on the environment**, including the climate, or increase vulnerability to disasters? What are the potential negative impacts? Which of these are most relevant to address? Has the programme/project been designed to avoid, or reduce and manage, these impacts?
- **What are the current and projected impacts of climate change and other environmental degradation** in the area where the programme is operating? Are they likely to impact the sustainability of the contribution? How can such risks be avoided, or reduced and managed?
- **Are environmental concerns and opportunities addressed in management plans** for the programme's/project's implementation, monitoring and evaluation?
- **Does the partner organization have capacity** for environmental management, in terms of staff capacity, policies, guidelines and environmental management system? Are there opportunities to improve the capacity?

HL

7.1.16 Local citizens as stakeholders

1.1 Perspectives
1.3 Sustainability

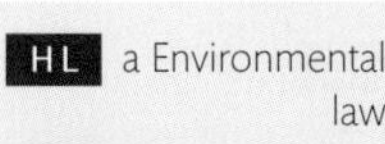

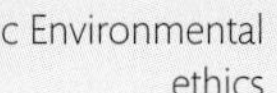

HL a Environmental law
HL c Environmental ethics

Giving the public access to EIAs allows local citizens to have a role as stakeholders in decision-making, which is a vital component for effective environmental assessment.

For example, evidence from Tanzania showed that EIAs that included a broad range of stakeholders – including local stakeholders – tended to lead to greater social and environmental benefits.

However, it may not be possible to consult all stakeholders due to time, cost, literacy levels, education, cultural differences, gender and physical remoteness.

A lack of stakeholder consultation can lead to even greater costs. For example, during the development of a commercial mine development in northern Tanzania, local artisanal miners were not consulted about the design and benefit-sharing. This led to years of conflict with neighbouring miners and high costs for security.

Some benefits of stakeholder involvement include:

- helping the EIA to address relevant issues
- harnessing local knowledge
- giving a greater sense of ownership
- providing a better response to user's needs.

The potential costs of insufficient public involvement include:

- conflicts between government and local people
- failure to generate local support

- marginalization of the local community
- a lack of accountability
- failure to match the project outcomes to the needs of the local community.

Table 7.5 shows examples of key stakeholders involved in a typical EIA.

Organizations	Public and community stakeholder groups
• **Co-ordination**: planning commissions and departments, government agencies at national, regional, district and village level. • **Advisory**: research institutes, universities, colleges. • **Regulatory**: government authorities at national, regional, district and village level. • **Implementation**: relevant ministries/departments at national, regional and district levels, training organizations, private companies, NGOs. • **Funding**: development assistance agencies, banks, entrepreneurs, taxpayers. • **Conservation**: environment departments, museums, zoos, botanical gardens.	• **Political**: members of Parliament (MPs), local councilors, party functionaries, lobbying groups. • **Cultural**: community and religious leaders, community service groups, community organizations/NGOs, traditional leaders. • **Business**: business leaders, Chambers of Commerce, trade unions, resource owners and those with tenure rights, common property resource users. • **Environment**: community interest groups, international and local environmental NGOs, local experts.

Table 7.5 Examples of key stakeholders in a typical EIA.

Stakeholder interest can vary at different scales. For example, on a local level, people may be concerned about access to land, food and water. On a national level, governments may be interested in policies related to international trade and energy policies. On an international scale, multi-government organizations may be interested in global climate change, the loss of biodiversity and deforestation.

7.1.17 Unsustainable use of renewable resources

While a given resource may be renewable, the process through which it is extracted, harvested, transported and processed may be unsustainable.

1.2 Perspectives
1.3 Sustainability

HL b Environmental economics

According to a number of scientists, many large-scale HEP projects in the USA and EU have had a major negative impact on the environment. Large numbers of dams are being decommissioned (over 50/year) and many are uneconomic and/or dangerous. In contrast, thousands of new dams are being built/planned for Africa and Asia (Topic 4, Section 4.2).

HEP accounts for over 70% of renewable energy throughout the world. However, dam building in the USA and Europe peaked in the 1960s and has been in decline ever since. HEP provides approximately 6% of electricity supplied throughout the USA.

Over 90% of the dams built since 1930 went over-budget during building. In addition, they have damaged river ecosystems, displaced millions of people and contributed to global climate change either in the concrete used for building them, or in the decomposition of vegetation covered by the reservoirs.

Two dams built on the Madeira River in Brazil in 2013 are now expected to produce much less HEP than was anticipated. This is largely due to the rapid sedimentation behind the dam. In LICs and MICs around 3700 dams are currently being built. On the Congo River, for example, the Grand Inga project is predicted to produce 40,000 MW of electricity. However, over 90% of the energy will be exported to South Africa, for use in its mining industry.

Large dams on major rivers destroy food sources both on land and in water. Up to 60 million people who live off fisheries from the Mekong River will have their food supplies reduced as more dams are built. Brazil relies on its dams for approximately two-thirds of its electricity supply. As the water-holding capacity of the dams is reduced, the population of Brazil will have either less access to electricity or they will have to diversify their electricity production or build more dams.

Other examples of unsustainable use could include overfishing (Topic 4, Section 4.3.5) or the unsustainable use of water in agriculture.

7.1.18 Excessive consumption

1.2 Systems
1.3 Sustainability

HL b Environmental economics

Economic interests often favour short-term responses in production and consumption, which undermine long-term sustainability. Resources can be depleted by excessive consumption.

SDG 12 is about ensuring sustainable consumption and production. Unsustainable consumption and production can lead to climate change, pollution and loss of biodiversity. Countries around the world need to find ways to manage finite resources while meeting the needs of a growing and increasingly middle-income population. According to UNEP, sustainable consumption and production is an integrated approach to minimizing the negative impacts of consumption and production, while promoting quality of life for all.

The two main principles of sustainable consumption and production are:

- improving quality of life without increasing environmental degradation and without compromising the needs of future generations
- reducing material and energy use while reducing emissions and waste.

Resources depleted by excessive consumption

The global production of fish and seafood has quadrupled in the last fifty years. In that time, the world's population has doubled, and the average person consumes twice as much seafood as they did 50 years ago.

In 2017, over one-third of the global fish stocks were over-fished (Figure 7.16). Two-thirds of the world's fisheries are sustainable (60% maximally fished and 6% underfished). Sustainable fisheries account for approximately 80% of the fish caught. In 1974 just 10% of fisheries were overfished but in 2008 that had increased to 32%.

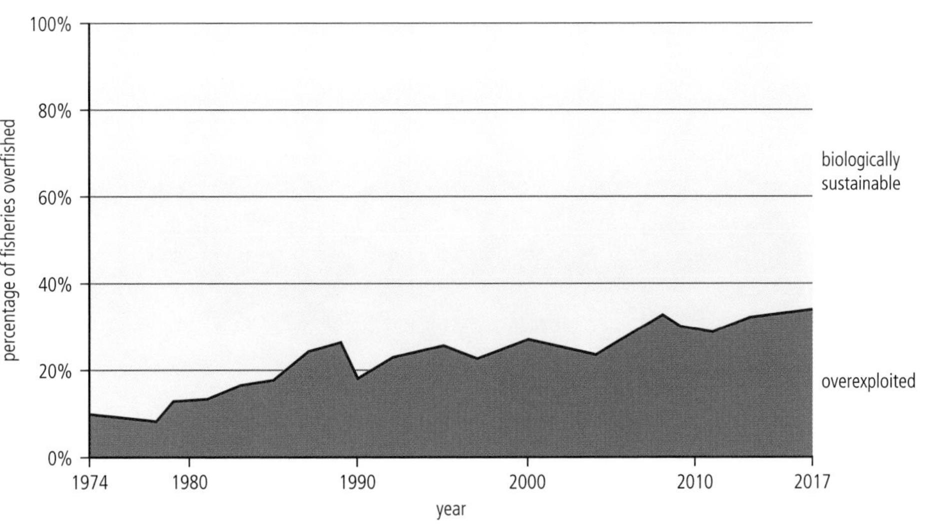

Figure 7.16 State of the world's fish stocks.

The *Seaspiracy* documentary in 2006 (updated in 2021) claimed that if current fishing trends continued, the oceans would be empty of fish by the year 2048.

Activity

Go online and search for 'Empty oceans by 2048'. Discuss your findings with a partner.

The 'collapse' of fisheries is defined as the point at which fish catch falls to below 10% of its historical maximum. There are fish stocks that are of major concern (Topic 4, Section 4.3.5). However, in the majority of regions where there is high quality data, mainly in the oceans off HICs, the fish stocks are stable. This may be because fishing is instead being done in other waters or international waters. The reduction in the size of fish catches in the UK is due to the decrease in the availability of fish. In parts of Asia, Africa and South America, fish stocks are believed to be low. In countries such as India and Indonesia, bottom-trawling is common and monitoring is limited. It is likely that fish stocks are not in a healthy state in those areas.

The 'collapse' of fisheries is defined as the point at which fish catch falls to below 10% of its historical maximum.

7.1.19 Resource insecurity and geopolitical tensions

HL

1.2 Systems

1.3 Sustainability

HL b Environmental economics

HL c Environmental ethics

Natural resource insecurity hinders socio-economic development and can lead to environmental degradation and geopolitical tensions and conflicts. Geopolitical power dynamics change if resource use changes.

Example – Resource insecurity in the Sahel

The Sahel is the region to the south of the Sahara Desert in Africa (Figure 7.17). The food sector accounts for approximately 27% of the Sahel's GDP and up to 80% of its workforce in some countries.

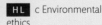

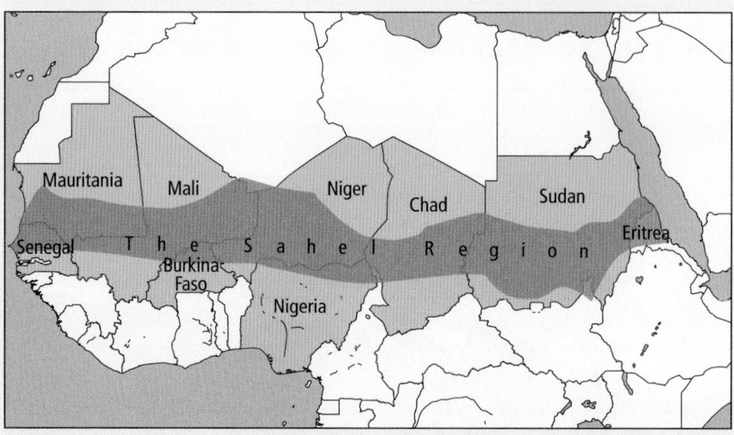

Figure 7.17 The location of the Sahel, Africa.

Farming depends on the availability of land, water and biomass resources. Water is especially scarce in the Sahel. Around 60% of the Sahel is arid and a further 10% is semi-arid or sparsely vegetated. Access to water is a key determinant of land prices. Biomass is another scarce resource. Forest cover is virtually non-existent and most of the land is either savannah, semi-desert or desert.

Artisanal and small-scale mining is also important in Mali, Niger and Burkina Faso and accounts for up to 50% of total gold output and 10% of the workforce. However, due to variations in global market prices, annual incomes vary.

The Sahel is fragile and land degradation is widespread. There are several reasons that help explain this (Figure 7.18):

- environmental fragility – over 40% of the population live in areas of high flood risk
- economic fragility – ineffective governance of land and water
- political fragility – unclear natural resource regulation fuels corruption and impede government effectiveness
- security fragility – in 2021 over 80% of fatalities from violent deaths occurred in regions where over 75% of the population work in agriculture and over 30% have no access to improved water sources.

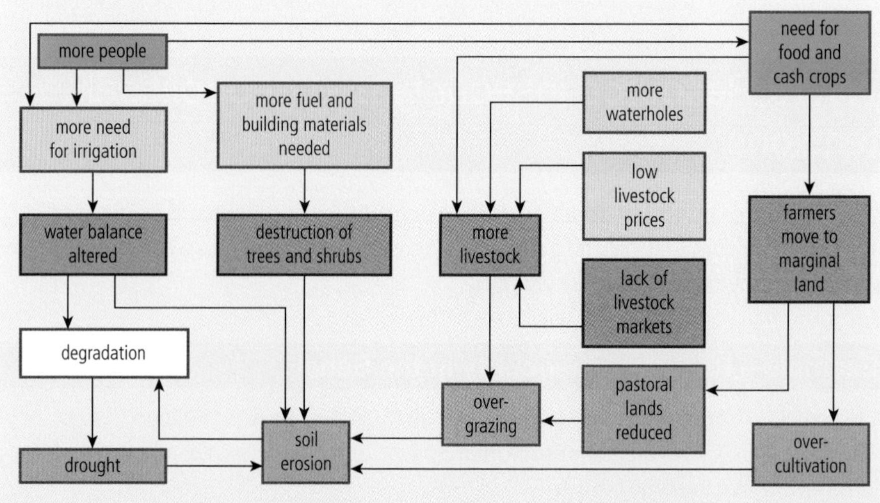

Figure 7.18 A model of land degradation in the Sahel, Africa.

TOK

To what extent do models represent reality?

Models are simplified constructions of reality. In the construction of a model, how can we know which aspects of the world to include and which to ignore?

All Sahelian countries rank in the bottom 40% worldwide in at least two of the three indicators of political fragility, clientelism (the exchange of goods and services for political support) and lack of government effectiveness. Natural resource governance failures widen the gap between population and the state.

7.1.20 Resource security

HL

1.2 Systems
1.3 Sustainability

HL b Environmental economics

Resource security for food, water and energy can be brought about by reductions in demand, increases in supply or changing technologies. Reduced demand can occur through increased efficiency of use or conservation measures. Reduced reliance on imported resources can be brought about by technological shifts.

Food security

Food security is defined as having a diet that provides a sufficient amount of good food that is necessary for a healthy life (Figure 7.19) (Topic 5, Section 5.2.12). There are several ways in which food security can be improved. These include:

- reducing food waste and food loss
- improving infrastructure, including storage and transport
- promoting fair trade practices
- diversifying farming and avoiding monoculture
- increasing crop yields through crop rotation and increasing the use of fertilizer, irrigation and improved seeds
- combatting climate change though agro-forestry rather than livestock ranching
- intensification of farming
- use of urban farming and vertical farming
- use of *in-vitro* farming, GM crops and GM livestock.

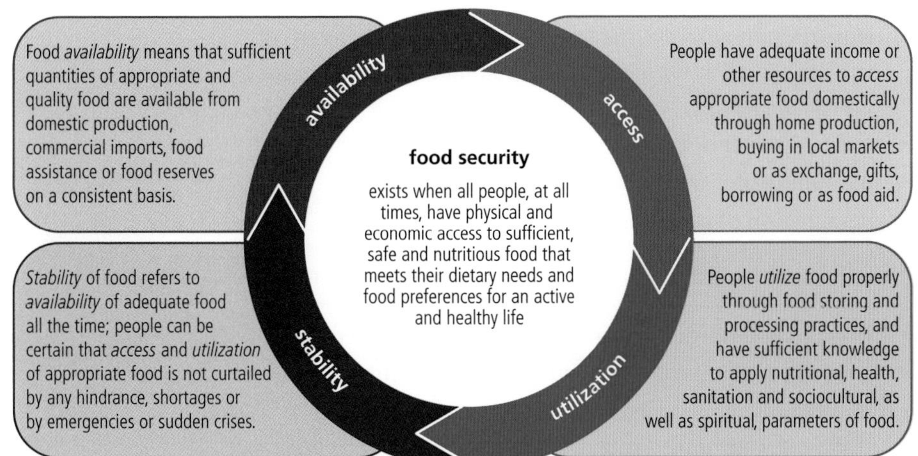

Figure 7.19 Food security.

The combined effects of the COVID-19 pandemic and the conflict between Russia and Ukraine in the early 2020s have shown how fragile supply chains can be, including those needed for food security. In addition, the introduction of national policies to restrict trade and increase domestic production will make the situation worse. Food security needs more global cooperation for open markets and resilient food chains.

Water security

Water security is having reliable access to sufficient amounts of safe drinking water (Topic 4, Section 4.2.1). Water supply depends on many factors including rainfall, temperature, vegetation, presence of rivers, groundwater, soil moisture, glaciers, climate change and the use/misuse through human activities. Demand for water also varies in relation to standards of living, availability, cost, ownership, type of economy (e.g. agricultural, industrial, tourist) and political disputes, including water boundary disputes (Topic 4, Section 4.2.16).

Water resources can be managed sustainably if individuals and communities make changes locally and if these changes are supported by national government. Water usage needs to be coordinated within natural processes and management strategies should ensure that non-renewable sources of freshwater, such as aquifers, are not used at an unsustainable rate. Water use can be reduced by self-imposed restraint. Examples include using water only when it is essential, not causing waste, and reusing supplies such as bath water. Education campaigns can increase local awareness of issues and encourage water conservation.

There are many ways in which freshwater supplies can be increased, including:

- retaining water in reservoirs for use in dry seasons
- redistributing water from wetter areas to drier areas, for example redistributing water from southern China to northern China
- desalination of seawater – although this is expensive
- water conservation through recycling grey-water (water that has already been used so is not fit for drinking but could be used for other purposes).

Water harvesting refers to making use of available water before it drains away or evaporates. Water can be harvested using several high technology or low technology methods. The main methods used are:

- extraction from rivers and lakes – e.g. by primitive forms of irrigation such as the shaduf and Archimedes screw – aided by gravity
- trapping water behind dams and banks (bunds)
- pumping water from aquifers (water-bearing rocks)
- desalination of saltwater to produce freshwater.

The efficient use or storage of water can also be achieved in many ways, including:

- irrigation of individual plants rather than of whole fields
- covering expanses of water with plastic or chemicals to reduce evaporation
- storage of water underground in gravel-filled reservoirs (to reduce evaporation losses).

The sustainable use of water in cities and populated areas could be achieved by:

- making new buildings more water-efficient by recycling rainwater for sanitation and showers

- offsetting new demand by fitting homes and other buildings with more water-efficient devices and appliances such as dishwashers and toilets
- increasing the use of water meters to encourage households to use water more efficiently.

Irrigation uses up large volumes of freshwater, much of which is then wasted through evaporation. Irrigation can also cause soil degradation leading to further water loss.

In rural areas, solutions for sustainable water use could also include selecting drought-resistant crops to reduce the need for irrigation.

The contamination of water supplies through fertilizers and pesticides can be addressed by instead making use of organic fertilizers, which cause less pollution, and biocontrol methods where natural predators of pests can be used to reduce crop pests. Industries can also be forced to remove pollutants from their wastewater through legislation.

The response of individuals and governments to make their use of freshwater more sustainable depends on the level of development of their country. Competing demands for freshwater vary between countries. Domestic water consumption is the minority water use in all countries, so the biggest impacts in terms of sustainable water use would be seen within the agricultural sector in LICs and within the industrial sector in HICs (Figure 7.20).

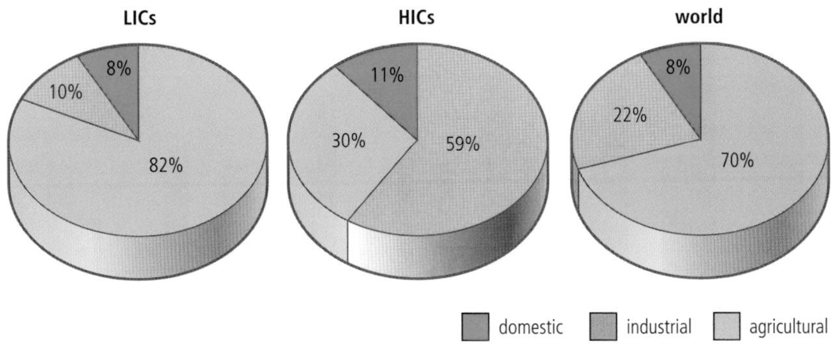

Figure 7.20 Water use in LICs and HICs.

Energy security

Increasing **energy security** (this topic, Section 7.2.7) can be achieved by increasing the amount of energy produced/imported and reducing the amount of energy used. Producing more energy depends on the energy sources available to a country and whether the country is able to develop them. Most oil-rich and coal-rich countries have developed their energy sources, but for some the sources are running low. There are opportunities to develop renewable forms of energy but again the right conditions are needed. For example, Nepal could develop more HEP stations, but this poses risks from landslides and floods that could affect human populations.

Domestic energy security can be improved by reducing the use of energy through:

- energy conservation methods such as loft and wall insulation in buildings
- turning central heating temperatures down by 1–2 °C
- wearing extra clothing rather than using central heating
- switching off appliances when not in use
- using public transport rather than private cars
- using energy efficient appliances such as fridges and LED light bulbs.

7.1.21 Globalization impacts on food, water and energy

1.2 Systems
1.3 Sustainability

HL b Environmental economics

Economic globalization can increase supplies, making countries increasingly interdependent, but this may also reduce national resource security.

Food

Globalization of food production includes the production and trade of food, foreign direct investment in food processing and retailing, and global advertising. In theory, globalization can increase the availability of different types of food throughout the world as it affects food supply, food availability (see the Skills box on the next page), cost and desirability/demand for food.

Figure 7.21 shows the top ten countries involved in food trade. The USA and China are the largest combined importers and exporters of food, followed by Germany and the Netherlands.

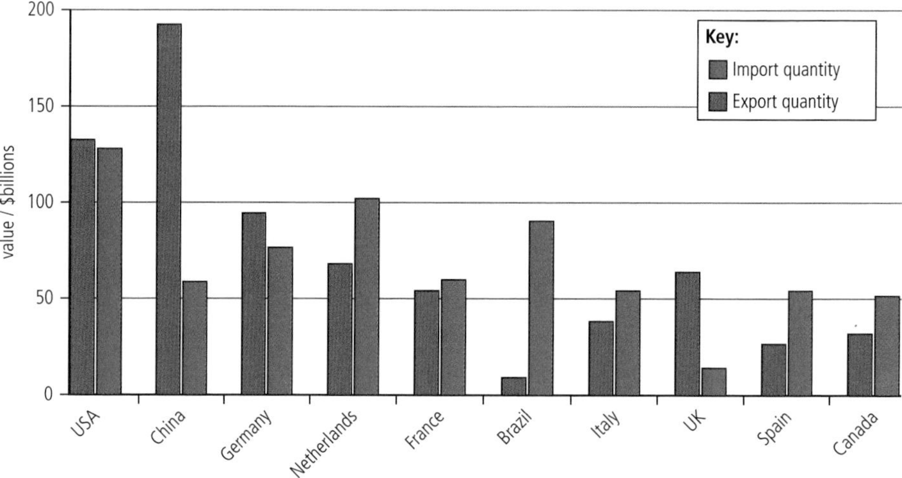

Figure 7.21 The main food trading countries, 2020.

Globalization has led to a convergence in consumption habits in HICs and in MICs, such as 'coca-colonization'. However, the alternative view sees the globalization of food as having led to increased obesity and diet-related chronic diseases worldwide. Globalization has placed power in the hands of a small number of food-commodity companies and seed companies. These companies have great wealth and power, and their main aim is to increase profits rather than increasing global food security.

Water

Water scarcity is an unprecedented challenge to human security. Much of the world's population is likely to be directly or indirectly affected by water scarcity caused by global climate change and water marketization. Water resources are increasingly viewed as an economic resource to be managed through privatization and marketization. International trade moves water from areas of abundant supply to areas of high demand either directly or through trade, i.e. virtual or embedded water.

Water marketization means that it is no longer supplied as a free or nominally priced good, but instead it follows market rules. As supply decreases, e.g. due to drought, prices increase. This was observed during Cape Town's Day Zero, which peaked between mid-2017 and mid-2018. Users of greater volumes of water were charged higher prices in an attempt to discourage excessive use.

Impacts of climate change and globalization overlap in relation to water resources. For example, in parts of India, farmers are expanding irrigation schemes for water-intensive crops for export. This is increasing the general demand for water. At the same time, climate change and variability are reducing water availability.

Activity

Investigate the development of 'sponge cities' around the world. Produce a table outlining the advantages and disadvantages of sponge cities.

Use secondary data sources to investigate the use of a named resource

Table 7.6 shows the use of inorganic fertilizer in India and the USA (kg/ha), 1961–2021.

	India	USA
1961	2.2	16.19
1971	16.6	38.50
1981	37.3	53.75
1991	78.0	55.05
2001	108.2	60.37
2011	180.7	76.90
2021	193.2	72.44

Table 7.6

There is a resource explaining the different statistical tests and when they are used on this page of your eBook.

Figure 7.22 is a semi-log graph showing changes in the use of nitrogen fertilizer in the USA between 1961 and 2021.

Use the Mann-Whitney U-test to test for a significant difference between the medians of the two data sets.

Null hypothesis: There is no significant statistical difference in the usage of nitrogen fertilizer in India and the USA.

Alternative hypothesis: There is a significant statistical difference in the usage of nitrogen fertilizer in India and the USA.

Calculating the Mann-Whitney U-test:

$$U_1 = n_1n_2 + \frac{n_1(n_1+1)}{2} - R_1$$

$$U_2 = n_1n_2 + \frac{n_2(n_2+1)}{2} - R_2$$

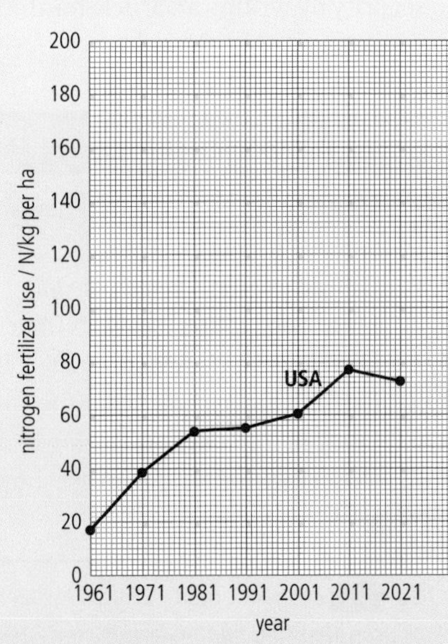

Figure 7.22

The graph is a semi-log or log-normal graph. This is because one axis (usually the vertical) is logarithmic and increases to the power of 10. Three cycles are shown on this graph – the first goes up in 1s (10^0) from 1 to 10, the second goes up in tens (10^1) from 10 to 100 and the third goes up in hundreds (10^2) from 100 to 1000. This allows us to plot very small values such as 9 and 16 on the same graph as values such as 109 and 190 and, at the same time, it avoids clustering lots of relatively small values as they would appear on a normal graph.

Activity

Using the data for India from Table 7.6, plot a line graph to show its growth of inorganic fertilizer, between 1961 and 2021.

Energy

The energy sector is a good example of globalization. Countries have become interdependent, up to a point. Many countries depend on the Middle East for oil and gas supplies. As countries develop, their demand for energy increases, which in turn increases competition for energy supplies. This may cause countries to develop their own sources of energy, especially clean, renewable forms.

However, the world has experienced a global energy crisis as a result of the conflict between Russia and Ukraine. This has had far-reaching implications for households, businesses and entire economies. The crisis has led to the number of people without access to modern energy falling. However, it may also offer a significant opportunity for developments in renewable energy.

Engagement

- HL Study an example of an EIA, such as the story of Nauru and resource depletion. Make a poster and present your findings to the class.
- With a partner, investigate and promote the ecological services provided by local or regional ecosystems, such as water provision and soil stability.
- Investigate the sustainability of food production in your local area. Make a poster and report your findings to the class.
- Find an opportunity to participate in citizen science (Topic 1, Section 1.3.16) such as those available on Zooniverse, Project Noah or Scistarter. Present what you did/what you learned to the class.
- With a partner, select an SDG and investigate potential solutions related to this SDG. Choose your own way to show examples of the potential solutions and present these to the class.
- Promote renewable energy production for your school to increase energy security by writing an article for the school magazine and/or to put up on the department notice board.

Exercise

Q1. **Identify** two sources of renewable energy and two sources of non-renewable energy.

Q2. **Define** the term *natural capital*.

Q3. **State** two cultural services obtained from the sea.

Q4. **Distinguish between** renewable and non-renewable resources.

Q5. **Explain** what is meant by the 'intrinsic' value of natural capital.

Q6. **Outline** the benefit of having local people involved in development projects.

Q7. **Describe** the trend in overfishing between 1974 and 2017.

HL

Q8. HL *Economic interests often favour short-term responses in production and consumption that undermine long-term sustainability.* **Discuss** this statement with reference to **one** named natural resource.

Q9. HL **Analyze** how economic globalization can reduce natural resource security.

Q10. HL Using examples, **discuss** the extent to which human societies can use natural resources sustainably.

HL end

7.2 Energy sources–uses and management

Guiding questions

To what extent can energy consumption be equitable across the world?

How can energy production be sustainable?

7.2.1 Energy sources are both renewable and non-renewable.
7.2.2 Global energy consumption is rising with increasing population and with per capita demand.
7.2.3 The sustainability of energy sources varies significantly.
7.2.4 A variety of factors will affect the energy choices that a country makes.
7.2.5 Intermittent energy production from some renewable sources creates the need for energy storage systems.
7.2.6 Energy conservation and energy efficiency may allow a country to be less dependent on importing a resource.
HL 7.2.7 Energy security for a country means access to affordable and reliable sources of energy.
HL 7.2.8 The global economy mostly depends on finite reserves of fossil fuels as energy sources; these include coal, oil and natural gas.
HL 7.2.9 Nuclear power is a non-renewable, low-carbon means of electricity production.
HL 7.2.10 Battery storage is required on a large scale to meet global requirements for reduction of carbon emissions, but it requires mining, transporting, processing and construction, all of which produce emissions and pollution, and cause sociopolitical tensions.

7.2.1 Energy sources

Energy can be generated from both non-renewable (this topic, Section 7.1.6) and renewable sources.

Renewable energy sources include wind, solar, tidal, wood, HEP, geothermal and biomass. Renewable energy sources are sustainable because there is no depletion of natural capital. They can be large-scale such as country-wide schemes of energy generation, or microgeneration on a small-scale for use within houses or communities.

There is a worksheet explaining the different energy sources on this page of your eBook.

The majority of the world's fuel comes from non-renewable sources, and this is unlikely to change much by 2030. Fossil fuels have been popular on account of their availability, reliability and the amount of energy they produce compared with alternatives such as solar or wind.

Fossil fuels

From the industrial revolution onward, transport and energy generation have been founded on fossil fuel technology. Easily mined sources of coal led to early forms of transport based on this fuel. Processing of fossil fuels to produce petroleum led to the invention of the combustion engine and this technology has continued to dominate until the present day. The growth of fossil fuel technology has been accompanied by a general unawareness of the effects on the environment. Pollution and global warming were not factors that were considered when fossil fuels were adopted as the primary source of energy generation. Recently, our growing awareness of environmental problems linked to fossil fuel use has put more emphasis on renewable energy sources.

Energy consumption is much higher in HICs than in LICs. The economies of HICs have been based on energy generation built on fossil fuel use (Figure 7.23), whereas energy demands in LICs have traditionally been much lower due to less available technology and reliance on natural resources such as wood burning or other biomass sources.

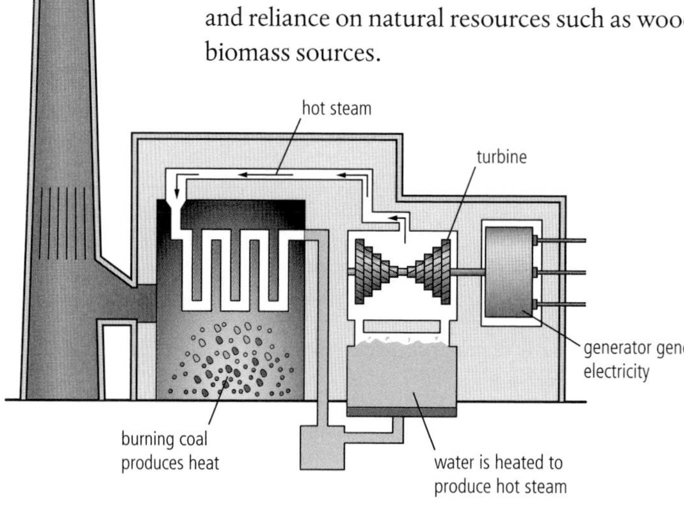

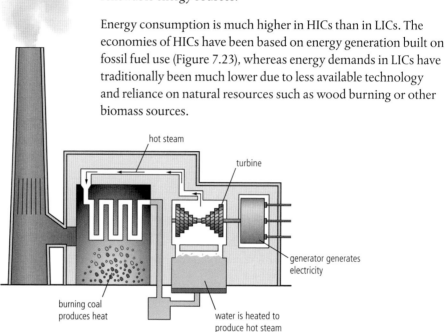

Figure 7.23 Coal is used in the production of electricity.

Much of the energy from fossil fuels is converted to electricity (Figure 7.24).

Figure 7.24 Coal-fired power stations turn chemical energy in the coal into, approximately, 40% electricity and 60% waste heat. The clouds emitted from their cooling chimneys are formed by condensed water vapour created by this method of energy generation.

Renewable fuels

Renewable sources of energy have been slow to grow globally. There are several reasons for this. Non-renewable sources of energy such as gas are generally cheaper than renewables. Gas is cheap because it is relatively plentiful, can be burned directly without the need for refining and the technology is already in place to access the gas and burn it in existing gas-fired power stations. Renewable sources such as wind power often require high set-up costs, for example the cost of the installation of new wind turbines, and may still be unreliable. In addition, there is a need to store the energy produced so that it can be used when needed and the cost of storage methods, such as batteries, is high. Some energy sources, such as biomass, may be widely used but only provide relatively low amounts of energy.

In future, the cost of non-renewable energy is likely to be much higher (a possible exception is shale gas). This is because stocks will become depleted and the easiest and most accessible resources will have already been mined. Only resources that are difficult to access, and therefore more costly to reach, will remain. The increasing scarcity of non-renewable sources will push costs up, and environmental taxes to compensate for global warming will also make fossil fuels more expensive. Therefore, in the future, renewable sources of energy will become more attractive and increased use is likely. Adoption of sustainable energy sources will have significant benefits for the planet.

7.2.2 Global energy consumption

1.2 Systems
1.3 Sustainability

HL b Environmental economics
HL c Environmental ethics

Over hundreds, if not thousands, of years there have been many changes in the types of energy sources used by humans (Table 7.7). These have sometimes been referred to as energy eras. Nevertheless, some people around the world make use of different types of energy sources depending on the environment and resources available.

Society	Energy source/type	Energy quality	Carrying capacity
Hunter-gatherer	Biomass	Improving ↓	Increasing ↓
Agriculturalist	Biomass, wind and water (mills)		
Pre-Industrial societies	Wood, wind and water (mills)		
Industrial societies	Fossil fuels (mainly coal) and wood		
Modern, service-based economies	Fossil fuels (oil, gas, coal) nuclear, and, increasingly, renewables		

Table 7.7 Changes in energy forms with different societies (energy eras).

Generally, global energy consumption appears to be increasing with increasing population and increasing per capita demand. However, it is not that straightforward.

Globally, most energy is supplied by fossil fuels although the amount supplied from renewable energy sources is increasing. The role of fossil fuels in supporting the steel, concrete and synthetic fertilizer industries suggests dependence on them is likely to continue for some time in the future. The world currently produces approximately 4.5 billion tonnes of cement, 1.8 billion tonnes of steel, 400 million tonnes of plastic and 180 million tonnes of NH_3, which is the basis of nitrogen fertilizers. The world's current use of cement every year is equal to all that was used between 1900 and 1950.

The demand for cement, plastics and steel is likely to increase in the future due to increases in population size and urbanization. The mass-production of these goods relies heavily on fossil fuels. No other material is as suitable for building strong infrastructure as concrete, which may be reinforced with steel. The transition to renewable energy sources will require large volumes of steel, concrete and plastics. Take wind turbines, for example. They frequently have concrete reinforced foundations, their towers and rotors are made of steel and their blades are made from strengthened plastics. Transportation of the turbine parts to their sites requires articulated lorries or ships. The turbines are then erected using cranes made of steel and their gearboxes need to be lubricated with oil.

The ability of energy supplies to meet the ever-growing demand is a challenge that has to be addressed by changing energy production sources and reducing energy consumption. The reasons for global and local changes in energy production and consumption include:

- sustainability of energy sources
- increasing proportion of middle-income households with increased demand for energy
- competition between economic sectors
- impacts of global climate change
- geopolitical conflict between two or more countries.

The rapid growth in global energy consumption has been relatively recent. Figure 7.25 shows that global energy consumption expanded exponentially from the 1950s but has slowed down from the 2000s. It is predicted to peak around 2030, mainly caused by an increase of renewables in the energy mix. The demand for energy could also slow due to the shift from heavy industries to services, improved energy efficiency and the rise of electrification.

Figure 7.25 Global energy demand between 1850 and 2050.

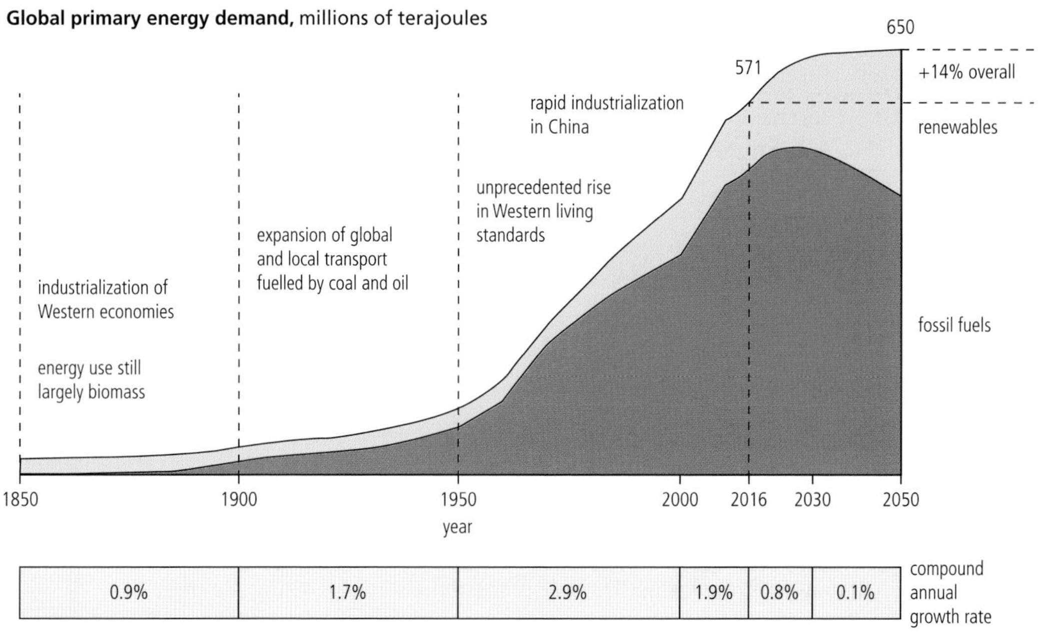

1 terajoule (TJ) = 1×10^{12} joules

Figure 7.26 is a compound line graph. This means that the values for each energy resource are placed on top of the previous resource. Thus to work out the amount of natural gas used in 2030, you measure from the bottom of the orange zone (approximately 390 TJ) to the top of the orange zone (approximately 570 TJ), so the amount of natural gas that will be consumed in 2030 is estimated to be approximately 180 TJ. Alternatively, you could use a ruler and measure against the scale on the vertical axis.

Figure 7.26 shows the world's fuel sources between 1970 and 2030. Total energy consumption is expected to increase from c. 230 TJ to c. 700 TJ, an increase of about 300%. The majority of the world's energy comes from non-renewable sources such as oil, coal and gas. The use of oil is predicted to nearly double between 1970 and 2030, while the use of coal could increase three-fold and of gas could increase five-fold.

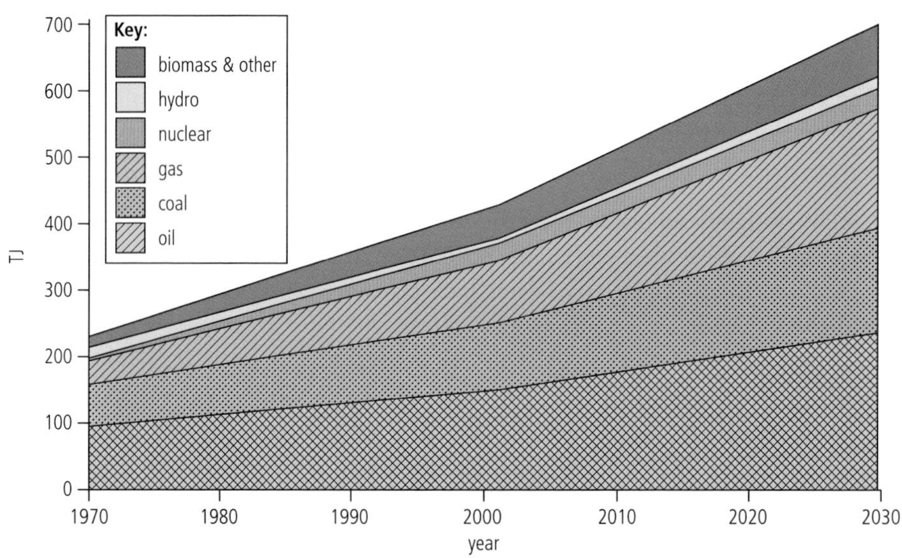

Figure 7.26 The world's fuel sources, 1970–2030.

Figure 7.27 shows that as GDP/head increases, there is generally an increase in energy use/head. The graph shows that above US$ 10,000 per head, energy use increases more rapidly and above US$ 50,000 it increases much more rapidly.

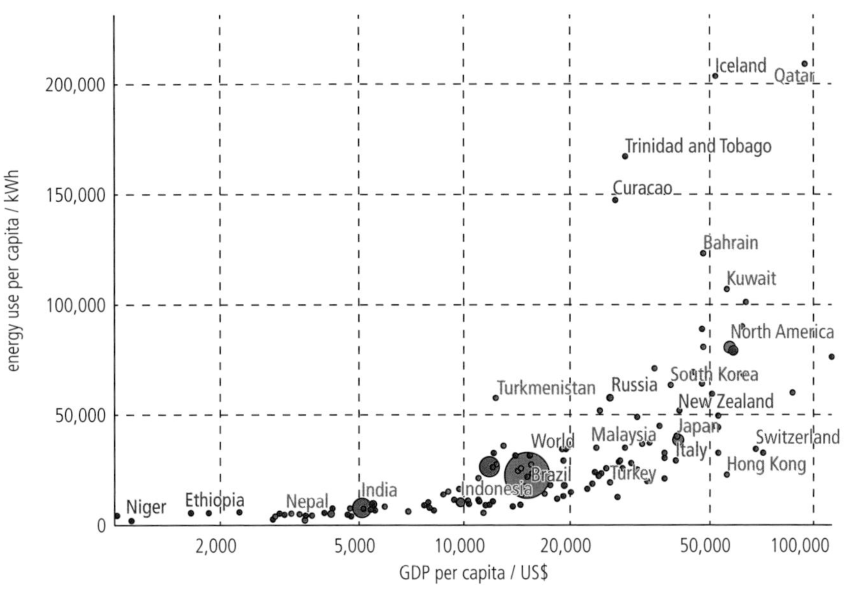

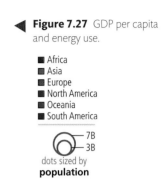

Figure 7.27 GDP per capita and energy use.

Some research suggests that energy efficiency increases in densely populated cities due to the concentration of people and buildings. Other research suggests that in ageing societies, many households will downsize, leading to less energy usage. In addition, many older people may cut back on energy usage due to reduced incomes once they retire, despite tending to need warmer homes. These are examples of local changes.

7.2.3 The sustainability of energy sources varies

1.2 Systems
1.3 Sustainability

HL b Environmental economics

The sustainability of energy sources varies significantly. Both non-renewable and renewable energy sources have environmental costs that include environmental restoration. For non-renewable sources, the extraction of fossil fuels, refining of crude oil, liquefaction of natural gas and mining of uranium all have negative impacts on the environment. Renewable energy sources, too, can have impacts on the environment resulting from construction, transport and recycling.

The assumption that fossil fuels are 'bad' and that renewables are 'good' is simplistic. New technologies such as carbon capture and storage, and managing emissions of methane (CH_4) may help meet CO_2 reduction targets. Batteries required to store renewable energy require non-renewable REEs such as lithium. The need to reduce emissions does not preclude the use of fossil fuels, but the 'business as usual' attitude must change. Energy efficiency and renewable energy sources are currently insufficient to meet global energy needs.

Fossil fuels

The petroleum industry has an extensive environmental impact and, as such, it is unsustainable. Large volumes of toxic and non-toxic waste are generated during the extraction, processing and transport of fossil fuels. The use of oil and gas emit greenhouse gases, and these have contributed, in large part, to global climate change, ocean acidification and sea level rises.

There are many hidden costs related to fossil fuels. Extraction can cause air and water pollution, degradation of the land surface and habitat loss. Transportation of the fuels can cause air pollution, accidents and spillages.

The stages involved in the process of mining have many potential environmental impacts as shown in Table 7.8.

Table 7.8 The potential environmental impacts of mining.

Extraction and ore removal	Ore concentration	smelting/refining
Potential environmental impacts of extraction and ore removal: • habitat destruction • land subsidence • increased erosion and silting of lakes and streams • generation of waste • acid drainage and mineral contamination of groundwater, lakes and streams.	Potential environmental impacts of ore concentration: • generation of waste • organic chemical contamination • acid drainage and metal contamination of groundwater, lakes and streams.	Potential environmental impacts of smelting/ refining; • air pollution • generation of waste • high energy use.

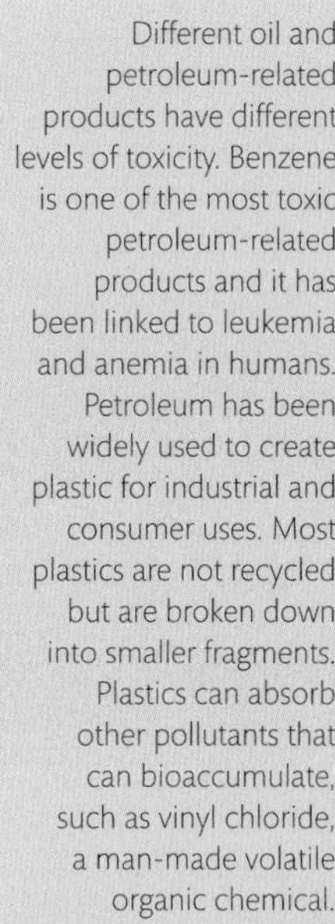

Different oil and petroleum-related products have different levels of toxicity. Benzene is one of the most toxic petroleum-related products and it has been linked to leukemia and anemia in humans. Petroleum has been widely used to create plastic for industrial and consumer uses. Most plastics are not recycled but are broken down into smaller fragments. Plastics can absorb other pollutants that can bioaccumulate, such as vinyl chloride, a man-made volatile organic chemical.

Underground mining can affect the health and safety of miners. In the USA, black lung disease (pneumoconiosis) was responsible for the deaths of 10,000 former miners between 1990 and 2000 at a rate of approximately 1% per year. Mines can collapse and/ or cause subsidence.

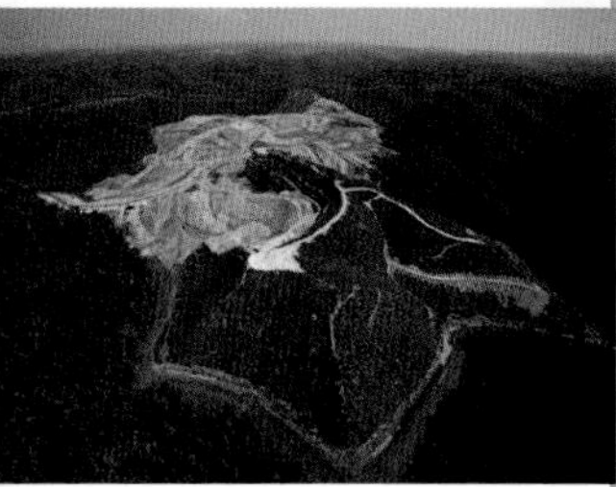

Figure 7.28 Mountaintop removal.

Mountaintop removal (Figure 7.28) and open-cast mining are particularly destructive forms of surface mining, removing all of the ecosystems from mountain tops/peaks. In the Appalachian region of the USA, some 500 mountaintop removal sites have been affected, equating to approximately 570,000 ha. The excess or 'waste' rock and soil are dumped in adjacent valleys, disrupting river flows and destroying ecosystems.

The transport of fossil fuels generates its own pollution, including nitrous oxides (NOx), coal dust and soot. Leaks of natural gas may result from transport, transmission and distribution pipelines. Oil spills and leaks continue to be a major risk of pollution.

Example – Deepwater Horizon oil spill

The Deepwater Horizon oil spill is the largest oil spill in US history. In April 2010, an explosion ripped through the Deepwater Horizon oil rig in the Gulf of Mexico, 80 km from the coast. Two days later the rig sank, and oil poured into the sea at a rate of up to 62,000 barrels a day. It took 3 months to completely cap the well. The oil spill threatened wildlife along the US coast, as well as the livelihoods of those people who were dependent on tourism and fishing. Over 160 km of coastline were affected, including oyster beds and shrimp farms.

The extent of the environmental impact was severe and lasted a long time. A state of emergency was declared in Louisiana. The cost to BP, who operated the rig, was almost US$ 9 billion, with over US$ 7 billion being used for restoration work starting in 2017 and continuing to date with the aim of completion being 2032. BP's attempts to plug the oil leak were eventually successful. Dispersants were used to break up the oil slick, but BP was ordered by the US government to limit their use, as they could cause even more damage to marine life in the Gulf of Mexico. By the time the well was capped, in July 2010, approximately 4.9 million barrels of crude oil had been released into the sea.

Rare earth elements (REEs)

The use of electric vehicles, along with electricity generation using wind turbines, are important parts of the global drive toward reducing carbon emissions. However, both of these require the use of rare earth elements (REEs) and the extraction of these elements is energy intensive and polluting (Figure 7.29).

Figure 7.29 REE mining in DR Congo.

The first REE mine opened in 1952 in California, USA. Now, most of the production of REEs is in China, approximately 95% of the total. In 2010 an embargo was placed on the sale of REEs to Japan. Countries around the world were alerted to the risk of having only one country in control of the supply and distribution of REEs. However, there has still been only limited growth in the production of REEs throughout Australia, Brazil and the USA.

In 2021, the demand for REEs was approximately 200,000 tonnes and it is predicted that demand will reach 450,000 tonnes by 2035. As the development and use of wind turbines and electric vehicles increases, so too will the demand for REEs.

The environmental impacts of REEs are widespread. Mines can have a detrimental effect on local ecosystems (Figure 7.30). Site preparation and access routes cause destruction of the local environment, while pollution from the mining process and waste, otherwise known as tailings, can lead to widespread chemical contamination. REE tailings contain chemicals, salts and radioactive materials. For every ton of REE produced, 2000 tonnes of waste are produced including up to 1.4 tonnes of radioactive waste. Tailings are often stored in tailing ponds. Poor construction of these ponds can lead to seepage of waste into groundwater and/or overflowing into surface water.

Figure 7.30 Environmental destruction caused by REE mining.

Dust from cutting, drilling and blasting rocks can accumulate in surrounding areas and lead to respiratory problems and contamination of food, as plants absorb airborne pollutants.

In future, it may be possible to recycles REEs from wind turbines and electric vehicles but this will only account for a small proportion of the total demand.

The mining of REEs is currently unsustainable and is causing great harm to the environment and to people.

Nuclear power

Nuclear power is very efficient, especially in comparison to fossil fuels. The amount of energy that can be generated from 1 kg uranium is 20,000 times greater than the amount that can be generated from 1 kg coal. There is currently believed to be up to 60 years' worth of uranium remaining globally (this topic, Section 7.2.9).

Nuclear energy is a zero-carbon, clean energy source. It produces more energy per unit of land than any other energy source, and it produces minimal waste. For example, the amount of nuclear waste produced by the USA over the last sixty years would fill one football pitch to a depth of 10 m. In theory, the waste could be reprocessed and recycled, although the USA does not currently do so. It can also be used to desalinate seawater.

Solar panels

The production of solar panels requires the mining of raw materials especially quartz, aluminium, copper and silver. The extraction, transport and processing of the raw materials, along with the manufacturing of the solar panels, may use large amounts of fossil fuels and thus produce high emissions of CO_2 and other greenhouse gases. There may also be unfair and unsafe working conditions.

The issue of how to dispose of old solar panels has become an increasing problem. Solar panels are a relatively new invention and have a life span of approximately 25 years. In 2016 there was just 250,000 tonnes of solar panel waste. It is estimated that this will have increased to 25 million tonnes by 2050.

TOK

How does the way that we organize or classify knowledge affect what we know?

The term 'renewable' suggests a more sustainable and environmentally friendly solution to energy generation than 'non-renewable'. But do the names and labels we use help or hinder the acquisition of knowledge? For example, to what extent are renewable forms of energy dangerous to the environment?

The chemicals used in each panel are varied but generally include copper. If panels are not disposed of correctly, chemicals will seep into the ground, contaminating soil and water. Although solar panels can be recycled, only European manufacturers are legally required to collect and recycle solar waste.

Wind

Wind is a renewable energy source. For wind energy to be effective, there need to be consistently high wind speeds. If there is no wind, no energy can be produced. If the wind speed is too great, the turbines can be overloaded and damaged. Wind speeds in excess of 90 km/hour may cause damage to turbines, so they are generally switched off during very stormy conditions. Compared with other energy sources, the CO_2 emissions from wind power are relatively low (Table 7.9).

Table 7.9 Emissions CO_2 emissions of different energy sources.

Energy source	CO_2 emissions / g per kWh
Wind turbines	11
Solar	44
Natural gas	450
Coal	1000
Nuclear	9

7.2.4 Factors affecting energy choices

Several factors affect the energy choices of a country.

There are many important factors to consider in the choice of energy sources used by societies. These include:

- **Availability and reliability of supply** Certain climates allow for the use of certain types of energy sources such as solar or wind power. For example, the UK used to use only coal, then oil and natural gas became available. The UK has plentiful wind energy potential but limited potential for solar or geothermal energy. In contrast, countries in the Middle East have plentiful potential for solar energy, whereas New Zealand has good potential for geothermal energy.
- **Sustainability of supply** The global supplies of oil and coal are currently estimated to last 50 years and 150 years respectively, but this may vary depending on changes in the reliance on fossil fuels. However, the supplies of solar and geothermal energy have no time limitation and so are sustainable.
- **Pollution** Some energy sources, notably fossil fuels, can be very polluting, as they release CO_2, which contributes to global climate change. The use of coal releases sulfur dioxide (SO_2), which can contribute to acid rain.
- **Energy efficiency** Energy forms such as peat and wood are very energy inefficient. Nuclear power provides a very large amount of energy for each unit of uranium and is therefore very energy efficient, but is also costly.
- **Economic factors** such as cost of production, distribution and use mean that nuclear power or tidal energy may be too expensive for many countries.
- **Energy security issues** Energy security depends on the availability and supply of energy sources. Energy sources can be depleted over time, e.g. the UK's supply of North Sea oil. Energy supplies may be disrupted during times of conflict, e.g. gas supplies to Europe were reduced following the conflict between Russia and Ukraine.

1.1 Perspectives
1.2 Systems
1.3 Sustainability

HL b Environmental economics

HL c Environmental ethics

The energy choices adopted by a society may be influenced by factors including sustainability, economic cost, pollution, energy efficiency, availability and energy security issues.

Energy choices may be made for economic or political reasons e.g. the cost, or the need for a government to provide employment, rather than on the basis of what is environmentally or socially *sustainable*.

Table 7.10 shows the advantages and disadvantages of different energy sources.

Table 7.10 Advantages and disadvantages of different energy sources.

Energy source	Advantages	Disadvantages
Oil and gas	• very efficient energy sources • can be used as fuels and to produce electricity • relatively cheap	• come from crude oil, which is a finite source and will run out • burning these energy sources releases the greenhouse gas CO_2 • risk of oil spills causing damage ecosystems
Coal	• large reserves are still available • can be used for domestic heating and in power stations • is important in the iron and steel industry	• relatively inefficient fuel • very polluting as it releases greenhouse gases and SO_2 • burning of coal is linked to acidification of seas and the atmosphere
Nuclear power	• reliable source of energy • once operating, costs are relatively low • there is up to 60 years' worth of uranium available	• can produce radioactive waste which can cause explosions, for example Chernobyl, 1986 • start-up costs and decommissioning costs are very high • safety issues over the disposal of used nuclear reactor fuel

HEP	• renewable source of energy • can be a multi-purpose scheme, for example reservoirs can be used for fishing, recreation and transport • once built, HEP schemes can be cheap to run	• reservoirs flood habitats and displace people • dams act as barriers for species to move up and down the river • large dams are associated with an increase in earthquake activity
Wind power	• renewable form of energy • wind turbines can be placed in areas with high wind speeds • no greenhouse gases released when the turbines operate	• dependent on wind speed • turbines are often located in remote areas • turbines can affect local wildlife
Solar power	• clean, renewable form of energy • solar panels can be placed on individual buildings and have low maintenance costs • solar panels can be used in any climate	• not a very efficient form of energy • the disposal of used solar panels can cause environmental issues • cost of installation is relatively high

The choice of energy sources adopted by different countries often has an historical basis. Large reserves of oil, coal and gas in certain countries, such as the UK, made fossil fuels an obvious choice for exploitation in those countries. Energy generation may also depend on economic, cultural, environmental and technological factors.

Oil use in HICs is almost 50% greater than in LICs. Fossil fuels in HICs account for 85% of energy use as opposed to 58% in LICs (Figure 7.31).

Figure 7.31 Regional consumption patterns, 2021 (%).

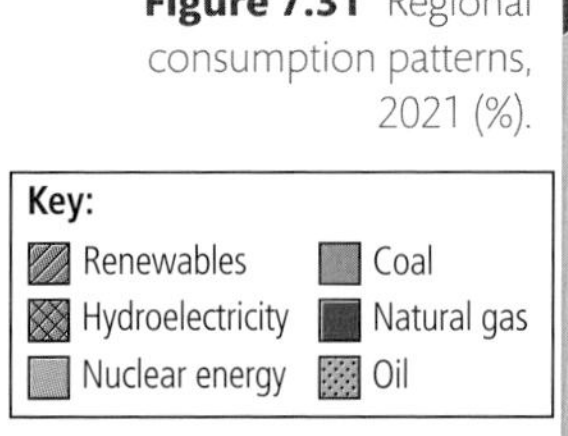

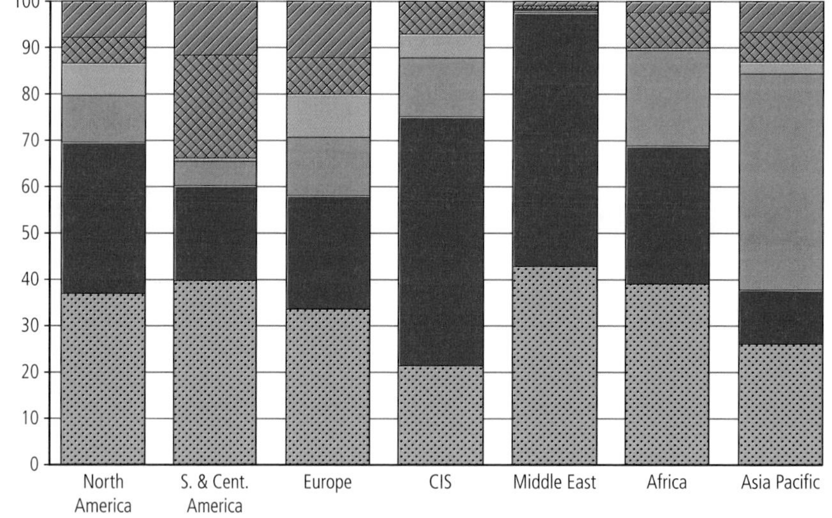

There are various explanations for these observed patterns. Oil is used extensively to produce petroleum products. The difference in oil use between LICs and HICs can be explained by the more prevalent use of cars in HICs. Biomass is very important in LICs as fuel for cooking, whereas HICs use gas or electricity generated from fossil fuels. The relatively small contribution from nuclear power may be due to the problems caused by the disposal of nuclear fuel, along with the cost of nuclear technology. The relatively small proportion of nuclear power generation in HICs may also be affected by the general distrust of the industry and cultural fears, based on perception of nuclear accidents and waste, which have made this a politically unpopular choice in many countries.

The various factors that are currently restricting the use of renewable energy sources include:

- fossil fuel resources are still economically cheaper to exploit
- the technology to harness renewable sources is currently not available on a large scale
- culture and tradition mean that non-renewable sources are favoured; for example, in the Middle East during the 20th century, much development has been funded through the exploitation of fossil fuels
- the locations for renewable energy sources are often limited by local political issues and available sites, e.g. HEP generally requires a mountain site and a high-discharge river (this topic, Section 7.3.7).

The low uptake of renewable energy globally means that renewables are not able to meet current demand. However, recession can change things.

Changes in methods of energy generation employed can result from changing costs of production and from changes in social perspectives on established fuel supplies, which in turn may lead to shifts in environmental philosophy. In countries that rely on fossil fuels, the costs of exploitation have increased as the most easily accessible reserves have been used up, thus alternative sources have been sought. The increasing cost of fossil fuels will change peoples' views of them.

At the same time, increasing awareness of the environmental implications of fossil fuel exploitation, including global warming, has led to a shift in attitude towards renewable energy sources such as wind power. This is despite the aesthetic and environmental implications and increased demand for renewable, non-polluting sources. This has led to greater investment and research into alternative energy sources such as wind and tidal power.

Example – Energy policy in Switzerland

Switzerland is trying to reduce its dependency on fossil fuels, become more sustainable in terms of energy sources and reduce its dependence on other countries for energy imports (Figure 7.32). Switzerland has very few natural energy sources, so it imports approximately 70% of the energy it consumes, mainly in the form of oil, gas, coal and nuclear energy. It aims to ensure a secure supply of affordable and environmentally friendly energy.

Since the Fukushima nuclear disaster in Japan in 2011, Switzerland has undergone an energy transition involving:

- increasing the share of renewable energy produced
- phasing out nuclear power
- improving energy efficiency of buildings, machinery and transport.

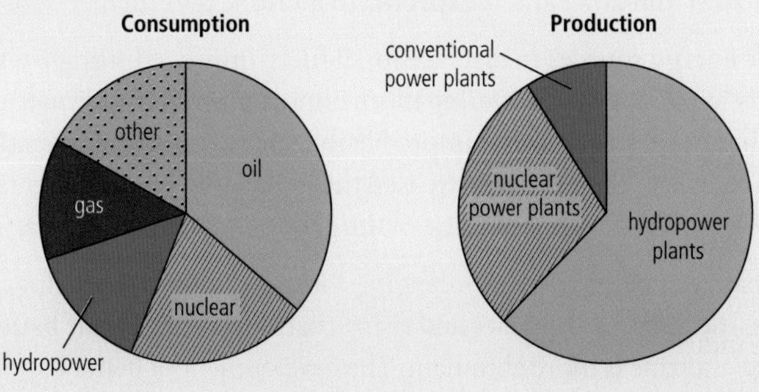

Figure 7.32 Energy consumption and production in Switzerland.

Example – Energy sources in Nepal

Nepal's main energy sources are biomass (75%) and petroleum products (22%) (Figure 7.33). Renewable sources account for around 3%. Nepal has no major oil or coal reserves. The country is remote, land-locked and mountainous, making imports difficult and expensive. Energy consumption per head is only approximately 20% of the world average. However, Nepal has the potential for the development of renewable energy sources.

Biomass, including fuelwood, agricultural waste and dung, is the main form of energy in Nepal. Burning biomass leads to the emission of greenhouse gases and also may contribute to indoor air pollution when it is burnt indoors.

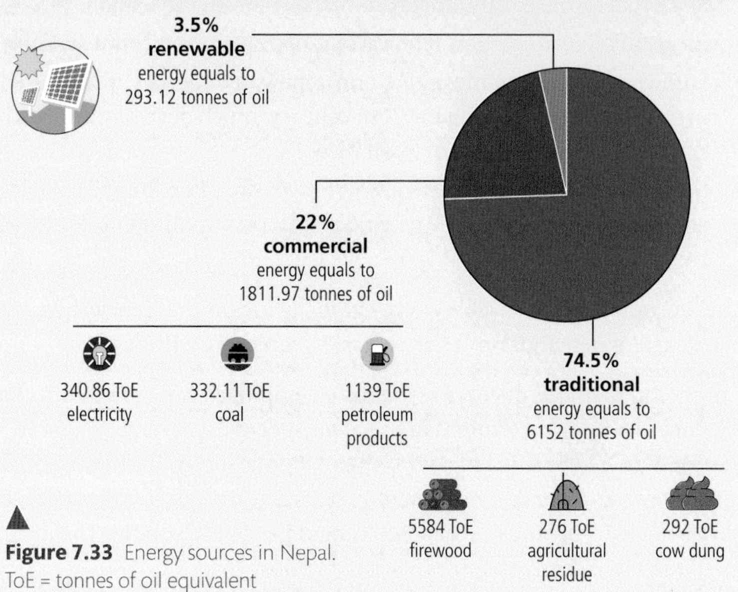

Figure 7.33 Energy sources in Nepal. ToE = tonnes of oil equivalent

There is a large potential for the development of biogas as a source of energy in Nepal, although the start-up costs are high. The isolation of many villages makes installation of biogas projects difficult.

Nepal also has considerable potential for HEP. There are over 120 HEP plants currently in use in Nepal and there are plans for around 250 more. However, the Nepal earthquake of 2015 destroyed at least 14 HEP plants, affecting 30% of Nepal's generating capacity. This prompted the government to diversify Nepal's energy mix. There are currently plans to develop solar energy further.

1.2 Systems
1.3 Sustainability

Intermittent energy production from some renewable sources creates the need for energy storage systems

7.2.5 Intermittent energy production and energy storage systems

Renewable energy sources such as wind power, solar power and tidal power are intermittent, resulting in variations in the supply of energy that are not always able to meet demand. In order to ensure that supply is able to meet demand at all times, including peak times, distribution grids have to rely on energy storage and other energy sources including batteries, pumped storage in HEP, fuel cells and thermal storage.

Advances in energy storage include new battery types and longer-duration batteries. Battery development is a vital area of research to maximize the potential for the use of renewable energy sources. The global battery energy storage system market increased by approximately 30% between 2021 and 2022 and is expected to increase by a further 50% by 2026.

For renewable energy sources to displace fossil fuels, improved storage will be vital. Improvements in storage are becoming more important because climate change is making weather more extreme and unpredictable. In addition, the reduction of gas exports from Russia to the EU has increased the need for EU governments to find alternatives to gas. This illustrates some of the geopolitical limits on sharing energy.

The types of batteries being used are changing. Lithium batteries are being replaced due to safety issues, declining availability and rising costs. In contrast, zinc batteries give greater storage and zinc is more abundant. The development of better batteries is vital for high-quality, long-duration storage. Most energy storage currently has a short duration.

Pumped energy such as HEP is the dominant form of long-duration energy storage, but many stations are of limited size and use.

HEP is a renewable form of energy that harnesses fast-flowing water with a sufficient 'head' of water (Figure 7.34). The location of HEP station sites depends on factors such as:

- local valley shape, which ideally should be narrow and deep
- local geology, which ideally should be impermeable and strong
- lake potential, which is given by the presence of a large head of water
- local land-use, which should be non-residential
- local planning with a lack of restrictions.

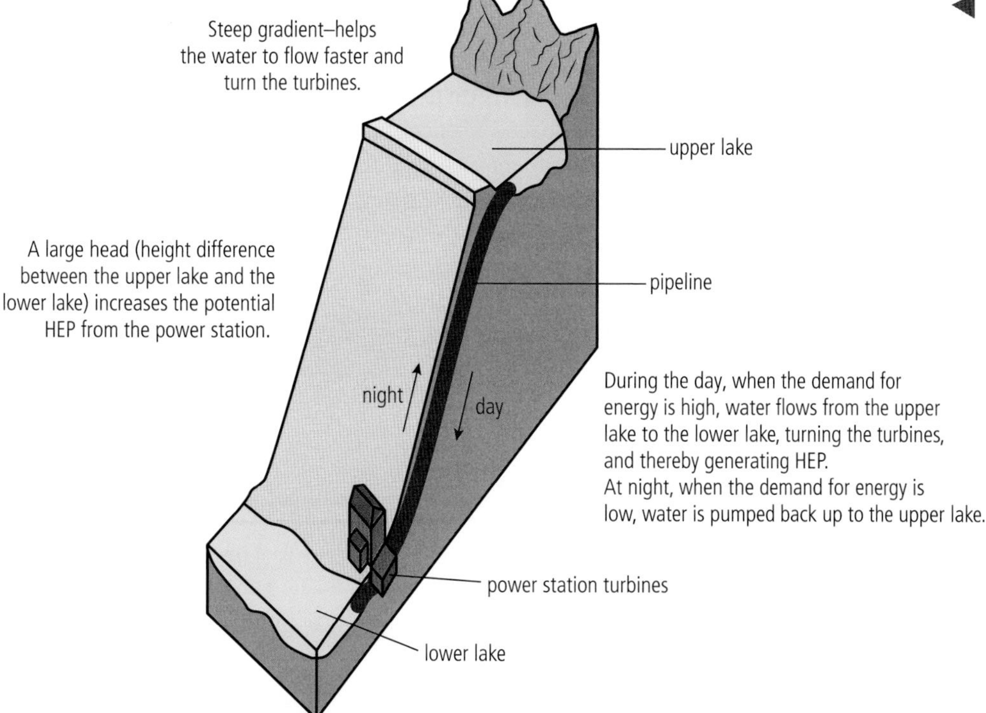
Steep gradient–helps the water to flow faster and turn the turbines.
upper lake
A large head (height difference between the upper lake and the lower lake) increases the potential HEP from the power station.
pipeline
night
day
During the day, when the demand for energy is high, water flows from the upper lake to the lower lake, turning the turbines, and thereby generating HEP.
At night, when the demand for energy is low, water is pumped back up to the upper lake.
power station turbines
lower lake

Figure 7.34 Site conditions for a HEP station.

However, HEP plants are expensive to build and only a small number of locations have a sufficiently large head of water. Markets are critical. HEP plants are often sited close to aluminium smelters because of the large amount of electricity the plants can produce.

7.2.6 Energy conservation and efficiency

1.2 Systems

Improvements in energy efficiencies and energy conservation can limit growth in energy demand and contribute to energy security.

Energy conservation and energy efficiency may allow a country to be less dependent on importing energy and energy sources and extend the lifetime of their existing reserves.

There are a number of possibilities for greater energy conservation. These include greater efficiency and the use of alternatives. Greater efficiency could be achieved through the use of smart meters and enhanced environmental standards.

Improved building design strategies could include:

- reduced energy use and emissions of CO_2
- use of solar panels rather than reliance of fossil fuels
- reduction of waste

- improved thermal efficiency of walls and windows
- reduction of heat loss between inner and outer walls
- energy-efficient domestic appliances
- improved daylighting by larger windows.

Energy saving is the quickest, most effective and most cost-effective way of reducing greenhouse gas emissions. It also reduces the use of scarce resources.

Example – Beddington Zero Energy Development

Figure 7.35 BedZED, Wallington, London, UK.

Beddington Zero Energy Development (BedZED) is an environmentally friendly housing development near Wallington, in the London Borough of Sutton (Figure 7.35). Between 2000 and 2002, there were 99 homes and 1405 m^2 of workspace built on the development.

Because of BedZED's low energy-emission targets, cars are discouraged. Instead, the project has limited parking space and encourages the use of public transport, cycling and walking. The development is close to the tramline that runs between Croydon and Wimbledon. Monitoring found that BedZED had achieved the following in comparison to UK averages:

- 88% decrease in heating requirements
- 57% decrease in hot water consumption
- 25% decrease in electric power usage, with 11% of the power used being produced by solar panels
- 65% decrease in the car mileage of residents.

BedZED has achieved these reductions through a combination of:

- a zero-energy import policy where renewable energy is generated on site by 777 m^2 of solar panels and tree waste
- energy efficiency from houses facing south, having triple glazing and having high thermal insulation
- water efficiency as most of the rainwater falling on the site is collected and reused
- low-impact building materials that were selected from renewable or recycled sources within 35 miles of the site, to minimize the energy required for transportation
- waste recycling
- encouraging eco-friendly transport, public transport, car-sharing and cycling.

Example – Sharjah sustainable city, UAE

The UAE's Vision 2021 aims to secure a sustainable environment and infrastructure for future generations. Methods of energy conservation and efficiency used in Sharjah sustainable city include:

- modern technology such as smart thermometers and energy-efficient appliances
- proper insulation of buildings, which can reduce cooling costs by 30%
- installation of solar panels, which can offset energy usage by up to 50%
- keeping air conditioners at a temperature of 24 °C as energy consumption increases by 9% for every degree under 24 °C
- use of LED lights, which use 75% less energy than traditional light bulbs.

Activity

In groups, research energy efficiency/net zero homes and give a presentation on each to the rest of your class.

HL

7.2.7 Energy security

HL

1.2 Systems
1.3 Sustainability

HL b Environmental economics

Energy security depends on an adequate, dependable and affordable supply of energy that provides a degree of independence.

Energy security for a country means having access to affordable and reliable sources of energy. A country can improve its energy security through energy efficiency measures, decreasing reliance on imported energy supplies and developing energy sources within its own boundaries.

Energy security refers to a country's ability to secure all its energy needs, whereas energy insecurity refers to a lack of security over energy sources. Inequitable availability and uneven distribution of energy sources may lead to conflict. According to the analyst Chris Ruppel (2006)[1], the period from 1985 to 2003 was an era of energy security based on fossil fuel dependence and since 2004 there has been an era of energy insecurity. He claims that following the energy crisis of 1973 and the Iraq War (1990–91), there was a period of low oil prices and energy security. However, insecurity has since increased due to a number of reasons, including:

- increased demand, especially by newly industrialized countries (NICs), notably China and India
- decreased reserves as supplies are used up
- geopolitical development where countries such as Iran and Russia have used their oil resources with respect to the decreasing resources in the Middle East and North Sea
- global warming and natural disasters such as Hurricane Ida in 2021, which have increased awareness about the misuse of fossil fuels
- terrorist activity in countries such as Nigeria and Iraq
- the use of long-distance pipelines that cross geopolitical/national boundaries such as the one from Kazakhstan to China and Europe
- the conflict between Russia and Ukraine, which began in 2022.

How is current knowledge shaped by its historical development?

How are the energy choices of today shaped by decisions of the past? What effect do these choices have on energy security? In the face of increasing energy insecurity, why do facts sometimes not change peoples' minds?

Energy insecurity can cause, and be the result of, geopolitical tension. For most consumers, the use of a diversified energy source mix is the best policy, rather than depending on a single supplier.

Example – Changes in energy use: USA and Norway

Approximately 80% of the USA's energy sources are fossil fuels with petroleum and natural gas being the two dominant sources (Figure 7.36). Norway has huge oil and gas reserves but derives most of its energy from renewable sources (Figure 7.37).

[1]The G forces of energy insecurity, Chris Ruppel, 10 June 2006 https://www.resilience.org/stories/2006-06-10/g-forces-energy-insecurity/

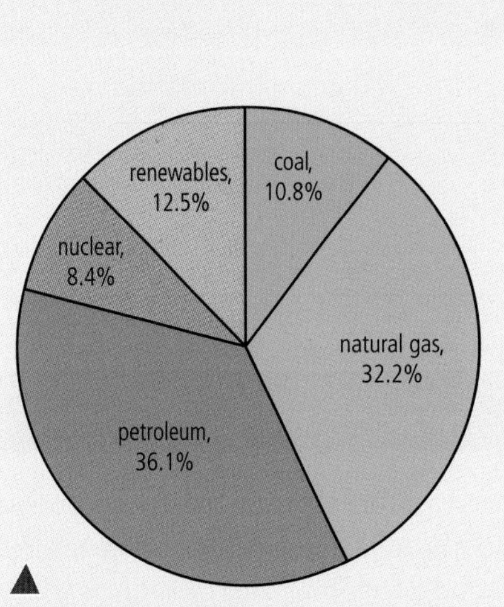

thermal power 1.6%

wind power 10.1%

HEP 88.2%

Figure 7.36 Energy consumption by source in the USA in 2021.

Figure 7.37 Norway's energy consumption, 2022.

TWh - one trillion watt hours. A kilowatt hour is 3.6 million joules (3.6 megajoules).

The USA's fuel consumption increased steadily in the 1950s and 1960s, then slowed slightly in the 1980s and 1990s (Figure 7.38). It has remained relatively steady since 2000 but year on year variations have been seen. Since 1965, Norway's energy consumption has more than doubled (Figure 7.39). Use of fossil fuels has been relatively stable, whereas the main growth has been in HEP, which has tripled from over 100 TWh to over 350 TWh.

British thermal unit (Btu) is a measure of the heat content of fuels/energy sources. One Btu is the amount of heat required to raise the temperature of one pound of liquid water by 1° Fahrenheit (F)

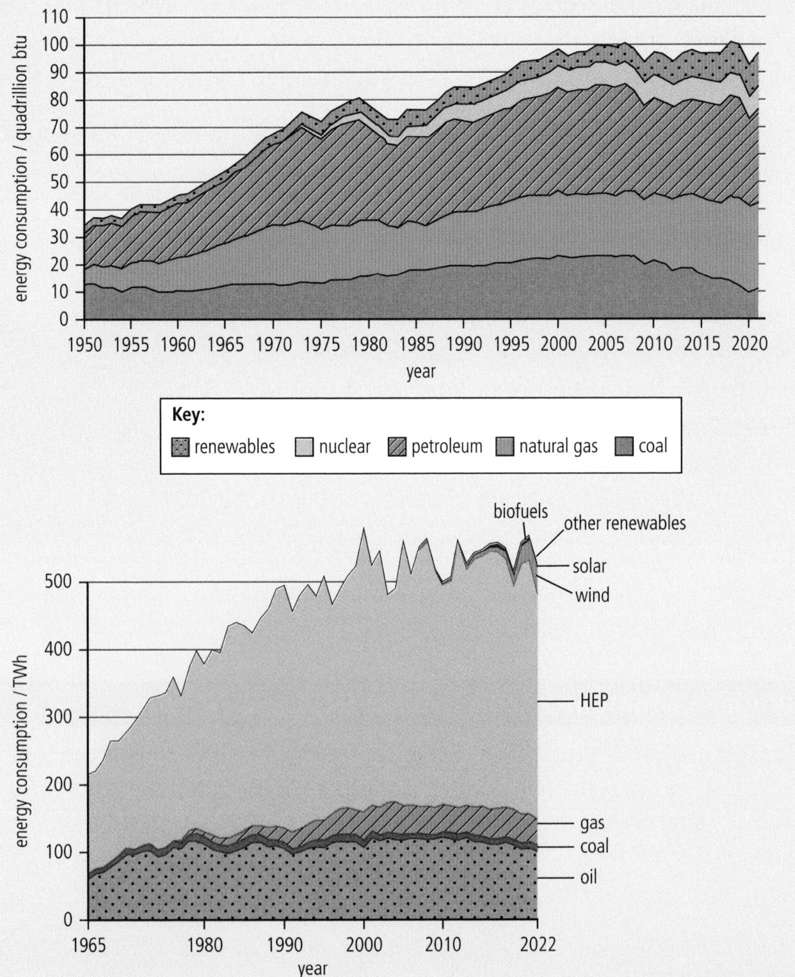

Figure 7.38 Changes in energy consumption in the USA, 1959–2021.

Figure 7.39 Changes in energy consumption by source, Norway.

Construct graphs (scatter graph) to demonstrate relevant correlations in the data

Select and use appropriate statistical tests (Spearman's rank correlation coefficient)

Table 7.11 shows data for level of wealth (US$/head) and energy consumption (million btu/person)

Country	Level of wealth (US$/year)	Energy consumption (million btu)
Singapore	106,000	638.9
Denmark	58,000	124.1
UK	45,000	119.9
Spain	37,900	122.7
Panama	29,000	98.9
Belarus	19,800	102.5
Botswana	14,800	34.1
St. Lucia	13,000	50.8
Jamaica	9600	49.7
Tonga	6100	22.8
DR Congo	3200	16.1
Zimbabwe	2100	11.5
Malawi	1500	1.8
Burundi	700	1.1

Table 7.11 Level of wealth (US$/head) and energy consumption (million btu/person).

The data can be plotted using a scatter graph as shown in Figure 7.40. However, due to the large variations in sizes (both of wealth and energy consumption) a double log scale is used. This means that both the level of wealth and the level of energy consumption can be clearly shown. The use of the double log scale also allows us to show both very large values and very small values on the same graph.

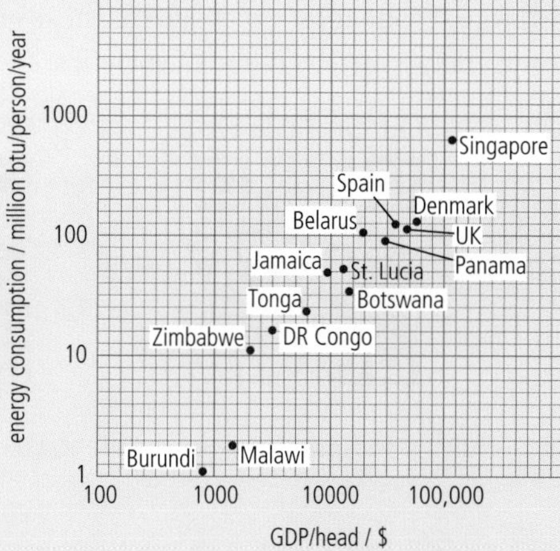

Figure 7.40 Scatter graph to show the relationship between level of wealth and energy consumption.

To test for statistical significance, we can use Spearman's Rank correlation coefficient (Topic 4, Section 4.1.12), where d is the difference in ranks and n is the number of observations.

$$\text{Spearman's rank} = 1 - \frac{6\sum d^2}{n^3 - n}$$

The answer must lie between −1 and +1. Table 7.12 shows the Spearman's rankings for the level of wealth and energy consumption data.

There is a resource explaining the different statistical tests and when they are used on this page of your eBook.

Table 7.12 Spearman's Rank Correlation Coefficient – worked example.

Country	Level of wealth (US$/year)	Energy consumption (million btu)	Rank wealth	Rank consumption	Difference in ranks (d)	d^2
Singapore	106,000	638.9	1	1	0	0
Denmark	58,000	124.1	2	2	0	0
UK	45,000	119.9	3	4	1	1
Spain	37,900	122.7	4	3	1	1
Panama	29,000	98.9	5	6	1	1
Belarus	19,800	102.5	6	5	1	1
Botswana	14,800	34.1	7	9	2	4
St. Lucia	13,000	50.8	8	7	1	1
Jamaica	9600	49.7	9	8	1	1
Tonga	6100	22.8	10	10	0	0
DR Congo	3200	16.1	11	11	0	0
Zimbabwe	2100	11.5	12	12	0	0
Malawi	1500	1.8	13	13	0	0
Burundi	700	1.1	14	14	0	0
						$\sum = 10$

Thus, $Rs = 1 - (60/14^3 - 14) = 1 - 60/2744 = 1 - 0.02 = 0.98$

Thus, there is a positive correlation showing that an increase in the level of wealth leads to an increase in the consumption of energy.

With 14 sets of data, the significance level for 95% is 0.46 and for 99% is 0.65. So, we have more than 99% confidence that there is a relationship between the two sets of data.

Activity

With a partner, investigate secondary sources such as those given below, to compare the amount of energy used by different societies.

Gapminder:

Our World in Data:

The World Bank:

Make a poster of your findings and present your results to the class.

1.2 Systems
1.3 Sustainability

HL b Environmental economics

HL

7.2.8 Fossil fuel reserves

Figure 7.41 Fossil fuel reserves.

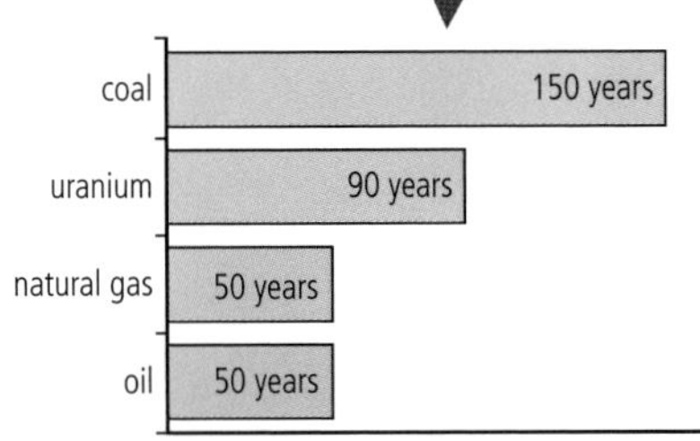

The global economy mostly depends on fossil fuels, such as coal, oil and natural gas as energy sources. The reserves of oil and natural gas should last another 50 years (Figure 7.41). The reserves of coal may last for 150 years, however, most of the coal is found deep underground rather than at the surface. The length of time these reserves last for depends on factors such as rate of consumption, discovery of new deposits, developments in technology for extraction and increased use of renewable energy sources or nuclear.

Most of the more accessible resources have already been extracted so the remaining ones tend to be less accessible, and many of them are in extreme environments.

7.2.9 Nuclear power

HL

1.2 Systems
1.3 Sustainability

HL c Environmental ethics

The equations of Albert Einstein first alerted scientists to the possibility of generating huge amounts of energy from fission reactions. Fission technology was first developed in 1945. It was used in atomic bombs at the end of the Second World War and was then used in generating nuclear energy.

Nuclear power is a non-renewable, low carbon means of electricity production. Most nuclear power stations obtain energy by fission reactions involving uranium or plutonium.

When enough fissionable material (e.g. uranium or plutonium) is brought together, and the process is initiated, a chain reaction occurs that splits atoms releasing a tremendous amount of energy.

Nuclear fission refers to the splitting of a heavy unstable nucleus into two lighter nuclei. In contrast, nuclear fusion refers to the combining of two light nuclei, which releases a vast amount of energy. Nuclear energy at present depends on fission, but there is research and development into nuclear fusion. In addition, research has shown that uranium can be extracted from oceans as well as mined on land. The amount of uranium in oceans is about 3.3 parts per billion, which amounts to a total of some 4.5 billion tonnes of uranium. Potentially, nuclear power could be sustainable and renewable.

When a fission reaction takes place, a large amount of heat is given off. This heats water around the nuclear core and turns it to steam. The steam passes over the turbine causing it to spin. This in turn causes a large generator to rotate, which generates electricity. The steam is then cooled by cold water travelling from the cooling tower through the condenser below the turbine. The drop in temperature condenses the steam back into water, which is pumped back to the reactor to be reheated and the process continues (Figure 7.42).

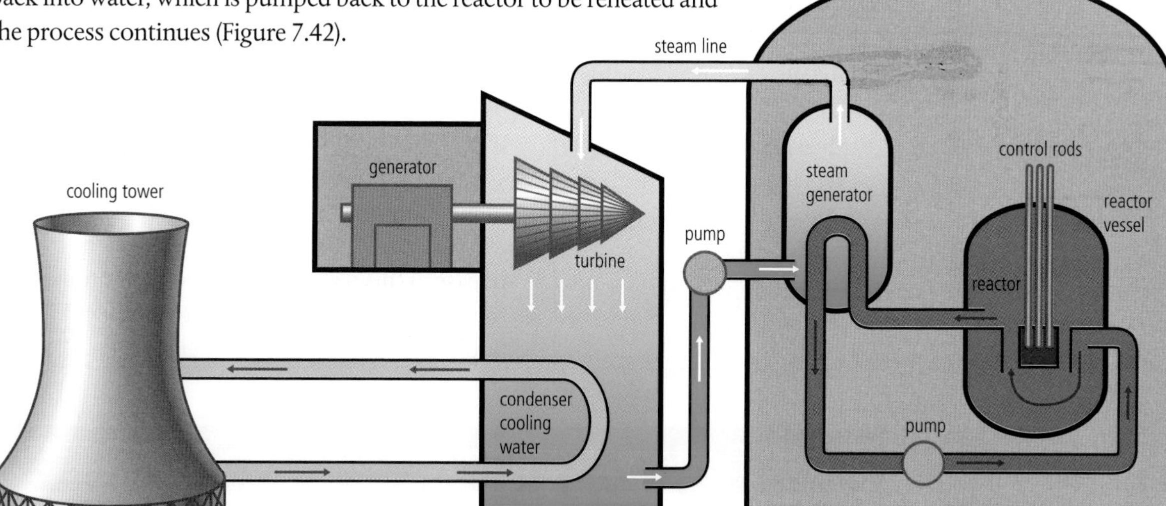

Figure 7.42 Nuclear fission.

Although construction costs are high, once constructed, nuclear power stations produce low-cost, constant, zero-carbon energy. Mining for uranium has negative effects. Thermal pollution from power stations changes water chemistry and there is the risk of nuclear accidents. Radioactive waste is also produced but this is stored indefinitely in containers that shield the environment from radiation.

Nuclear power plants produce radioactive waste that can remain dangerous for tens of thousands of years. Radioactivity is the result of nuclear changes in which unstable (radioactive) isotopes emit particles and energy continuously until the original isotope is changed into a stable one. When people are exposed to such radiation, the DNA in their cells can be damaged by mutation. Mutations of the DNA in body cells can result in cancer, miscarriages and burns. If the mutation occurs in the reproductive egg and sperm cells, genetic defects can appear in subsequent generations.

Advantages	**Disadvantages**
The advantages of nuclear power generation include: • It does not emit CO_2 and so does not contribute to global warming. • The technology is readily available. • A large amount of electrical energy is generated in a single plant. • It is very efficient, especially in comparison to fossil fuels. For example, 1 kg uranium produces 20,000 times more energy than 1 kg coal. • The energy resource for nuclear power is uranium, which is a non-renewable source. It is estimated that supplies of uranium will last for the next 200 years depending on actual demand.	The disadvantages of nuclear power generation include: • The waste from nuclear power stations is extremely dangerous and remains so for thousands of years. The best long-term way of disposing of this waste has not yet been determined but in the short-term, waste is stored in containers to shield the environment from radiation. • The associated risks are high. It is impossible to build a plant with 100% reliability and there will always be a small probability of failure, such as those that happened in the Chernobyl and Fukushima-Daiichi disasters. The greater the number of nuclear power plants and nuclear waste storage shelters built, the higher the probability of a disastrous failure somewhere in the world. The potential for nuclear power plants to become targets for terrorist attack has been pointed out by opponents of this type of energy generation. • The timeframe needed to plan and build a new nuclear power plant is 20–30 years. It will therefore take time for the uptake of nuclear power between planning and being ready. • Thermal pollution. The water used for cooling in nuclear power stations may be at higher temperatures than local water bodies. The release of this water from the power stations can therefore increase the temperature of local water bodies, affecting local ecosystems.

HL

7.2.10 Battery storage

Battery storage is required on a large scale to meet global requirements for reduction of carbon emissions.

Battery development is a vital area of research if the potential for renewable energy sources is to be maximized. Battery storage is required on a large scale to meet the global requirements for carbon emission reductions, but it requires mining, transporting, processing and construction, all of which produce emissions and pollution, and cause sociopolitical tensions. The sources needed to produce effective batteries are lithium, cobalt and REEs. However, the mining and processing of these elements create toxins and pollution. Lithium is produced in Australia and Chile, while the DR Congo and Russia produce cobalt.

Lithium-ion batteries are currently the dominant storage technology and are widely used in electric vehicles and cell phones. The UK government estimates that battery storage systems could save the UK's energy network up to US$ 48 billion by 2050. The UK has the world's largest offshore wind capacity, and the ability to capture, store and distribute energy would be a massive boost to the nation.

Storage of renewable energy requires low-cost technology that is safe, dependable and has a long life. Although lithium batteries are the most common, there are others. REEs, and also, notably lithium and cobalt, are used in the manufacture of most electric vehicle batteries. There are several issues regarding the sustainability of sources (this topic, Section 7.2.3). Lithium is relatively scarce and mostly refined in China. Most cobalt is found in the DR Congo (see Example below). However, a number of companies are now making batteries based on sodium. Sodium's chemical properties are similar to those of lithium and it makes good, but heavier, batteries. Sodium is found in salt in seawater, so is very abundant. It is also cheaper to produce. Lithium batteries use cobalt and nickel in their electrodes, whereas sodium batteries use iron and manganese in their electrodes, and these elements are plentiful.

Battery storage requires mining, transporting, processing and construction, all of which produce emissions and pollution, and cause sociopolitical tensions.

Battery storage power stations often make use of disused power stations and may make use of their grid connections. Batteries may occasionally explode or catch fire and release harmful gases such as hydrogen fluoride.

Example – Cobalt mining

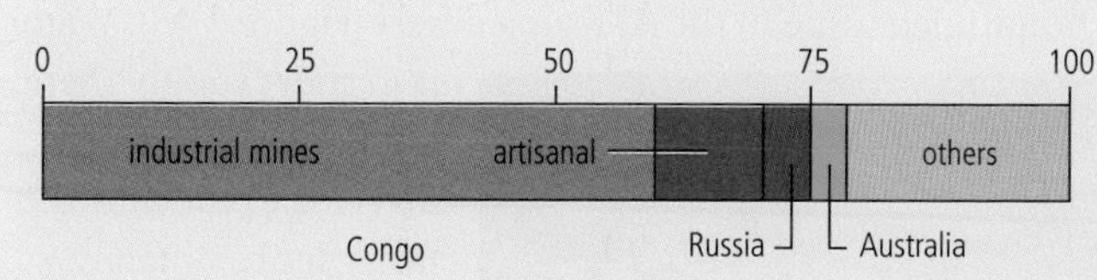

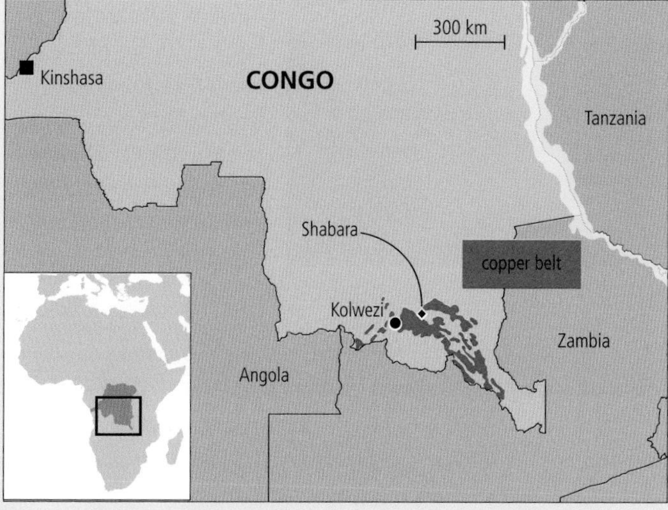

Figure 7.43 The location of the Shabara mine, near Kolwezi, DR Congo.

The DR Congo possesses over half of the world's cobalt and accounts for 70% of global production (Figure 7.43). In 2021 alone, the market grew by over 20%. However, the environmental and health impacts of cobalt mining are increasing (Figure 7.44). A study of Lake Tshangalele in 2016 found that its water and fish were contaminated with cobalt, and this had spread to humans, either through eating the fish and/or through drinking the lake water. In addition, the air surrounding the mines was heavily polluted with dust and particulates. Miners worked in very over-crowded conditions with minimal (if any) health and safety precautions. People who worked in cobalt mines had increased risks of birth defects in their children, including limb abnormalities and spina bifida.

Figure 7.44 Shabara mine near Kolwezi. Some 20,000 people work at Shabara, in shifts of 5000 at a time.

(The Economist, 2023)

Activity

Ask your school librarian to order a copy of Siddharth Kara's book *Congo Red: How the Blood of the Congo Powers our Lives*. It details the impacts of cobalt mining on the DR Congo, its environment and its people.

Make a presentation to the class about the impacts.

Lithium mining

Lithium has been described as 'white gold' and the 'next oil'. Lithium has a combination of high energy and power density, making it ideal for portable electronics, power tools and hybrid/electric vehicles. The global lithium market is worth US$ 8 billion, and in 2019, Australia's exports of lithium were valued at US$ 1.6 billion. Demand for lithium is predicted to rise to 3–4 million tonnes by 2030, up from 500,000 in 2021. As electric vehicle sales increased by 50% in 2020, and doubled in 2021 to seven million units, the demand for lithium escalated, as did its price. The Global Management Company, McKinsey, suggest that lithium batteries will grow at an annual compound growth of approximately 30% by 2030. In 2015, less than 30% of lithium was used for batteries but by 2030 this could rise to 95%. Almost all lithium mining occurs in Australia and South America. The 'lithium triangle' occurs near where the borders of Chile, Argentina and Bolivia meet. One of the largest mines is the Soquimich mine in the Atacama desert (Figure 7.45). Water is in short supply there, but large volumes are diverted to the mine. It takes approximately 2.2 million litres of water to produce one ton of lithium. In addition to the large volumes of water used, lithium mining leads to an increase in the release of CO_2, changes to the hydrological cycle and an increase in air pollution.

Figure 7.45 Separation ponds at the Soquimich lithium mine, Atacama desert, Chile.

Engagement

- Evaluate individual, school and community use of energy and consider whether it should be reduced and how reduction can be achieved. Make a list of potential solutions.
- Carry out a survey or questionnaire to see if energy use can be reduced in your school. You could ask students and teachers to justify three ways in which energy use in the school could be improved or in which energy wastage could be reduced.
- Arrange a class debate on the opportunities and dangers of nuclear power.

Exercise

HL

Q11. HL **Describe** the changes in global energy demand, as shown in Figure 7.46.

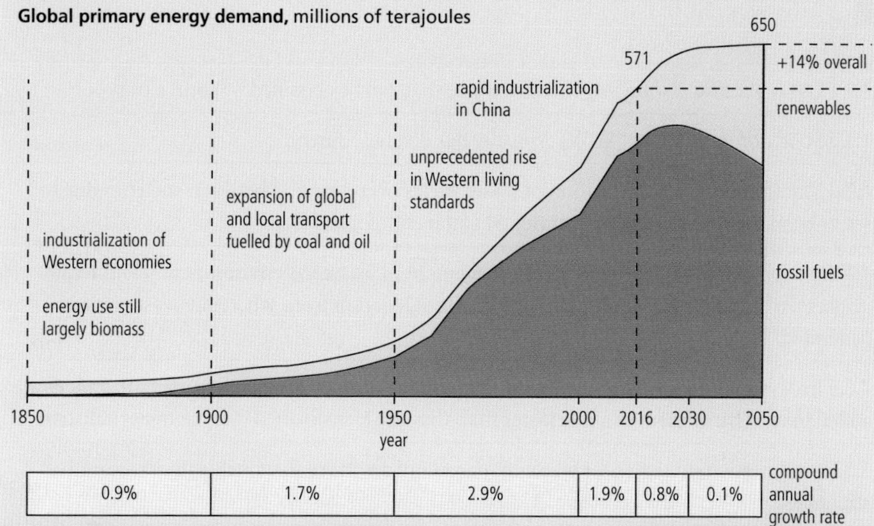

Figure 7.46 Global energy demand between 1850 and 2050.

Q12. HL **Calculate** the change in the amount of renewable energy (hydro, biomass, nuclear) between 1970 and 2020 as shown in Figure 7.47.

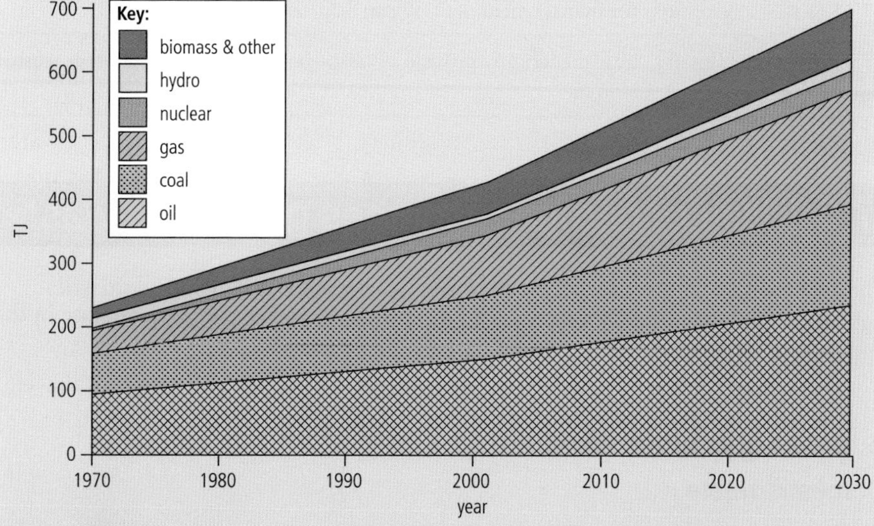

Figure 7.47 The world's fuel sources, 1970–2030.

Q13. HL **Examine** how energy security varies between countries.

Q14. HL **Describe** the relationship between income and energy use.

Q15. HL **Describe** the impact of mountaintop removal.

Q16. HL **Explain** why the demand for REEs is increasing.

Q17. HL **Outline** the health problems related to the mining of REEs.

Q18. HL **Compare** the trends in the consumption of coal in the USA and Norway.

Q19. HL **Analyze** the advantages and disadvantages of nuclear power.

Q20. HL **Discuss** the extent to which battery storage is a sustainable form of energy development.

HL end

7.3 Solid waste

Guiding question

How can societies sustainably manage waste?

7.3.1 Use of natural resources generates waste that can be classified by source or type.
7.3.2 Solid domestic waste (SDW) typically has diverse content.
7.3.3 The volume and composition of waste varies over time and between societies due to socio-economic, political, environmental and technological factors.
7.3.4 The production, treatment and management of waste has environmental and social impacts, which may be experienced in a different location from where the waste was generated.
7.3.5 Ecosystems can absorb some waste, but pollution occurs when harmful substances are added to an environment at a rate faster than they are transformed into harmless substances.
7.3.6 Preventative strategies for waste management are more sustainable than restorative strategies.
7.3.7 Different waste disposal options have different advantages and disadvantages in terms of their impact on societies and ecosystems.
7.3.8 Sustainable options for management of SDW can be promoted in societies.
7.3.9 The principles of a circular economy provide a holistic perspective on sustainable waste management.

7.3.1 Use of natural resources generates waste

Use of natural resources generates waste that can be classified by source or type.

The use of natural resources can create waste. Sources of waste include domestic, industrial and agricultural, while types of waste include electronic waste, food and biohazardous materials.

Sources and types of waste

Domestic waste

Domestic or household waste includes any waste materials generated from day-to-day activities in the home. It includes organic waste such as foods and flowers, recyclable waste such as bottles and papers, toxic waste such as batteries and paint and other waste such as nappies and animal waste. Some of this waste, such as food waste, can be composted whereas other waste, such as plastic and glass bottles, can be recycled.

Industrial waste

Industrial waste includes all waste produced by industrial activities such as scrap metals, chemicals, concrete, masonry, textiles and even food from restaurants. It can be solid, liquid or gaseous, and it can be hazardous or non-hazardous. This waste can also pollute nearby soils, water and habitats.

Many traditional heavy industries are located close to rivers with access to water for cooling, as an energy supply and for discharging waste materials. Iron and steel plants, chemical industries, food processing plants and paper mills are all examples of large-scale water users. Water that has been used for cooling may be discharged back into rivers at higher temperatures. This can affect water oxygen levels and impact the food chain.

Agricultural waste

Agricultural waste refers to any substance or object that is generated by farming activities but is not used for food or as an industrial raw material. It includes crop residues, such as branches, roots and leaves and animal waste, such as manure and slurry. It also includes old tractors, combine harvesters, milking machines, tyres, pesticide containers, bags from fertilizers and so on. In urban areas, garden waste is often referred to as 'green waste'.

Electronic waste

Electronic waste (e-waste) refers to all items with electronic components such as televisions, computers, cell phones and household appliances, such as fridges and freezers. Many electrical goods are dumped in landfill and potentially dangerous substances such as mercury and lead can leach into soil and water. Globally, some 50 million tonnes of e-waste is generated each year, and this could rise to 75 million tonnes by 2030.

Food waste

Food waste refers to any food not consumed by humans or animals that is not composted or recycled. Over one-third of all food produced is lost or wasted each year. This is approximately 2.5 million tonnes of food valued at around US$ 2390 billion. The loss of food results in approximately one-quarter of all food calories being lost. According to US EPA, the USA wastes around 60 million tonnes of food each year.

Biohazardous waste

Biohazardous waste includes biological substances that threaten human or animal health, including pathogens, viruses, toxins, spores and fungi. It also includes infectious waste such as animal waste including body parts, carcasses or bedding infected with microorganisms, used syringes and needles that can cut/puncture the skin, discarded vaccines and pathological waste.

7.3.2 Solid domestic waste

Solid domestic waste (SDW) is very diverse and includes paper, glass, metal, plastics, organic/green waste (kitchen or garden), plastic and cardboard packaging, construction debris and clothing (Figure 7.48). Globally, approximately 35% of SDW is dumped in some form of landfill.

The amount of waste produced by the global population is steadily increasing. The world faces an ongoing problem of how and where to dispose of this waste. Household waste includes a wide variety of materials including plastics, cardboard, paper, food and glass.

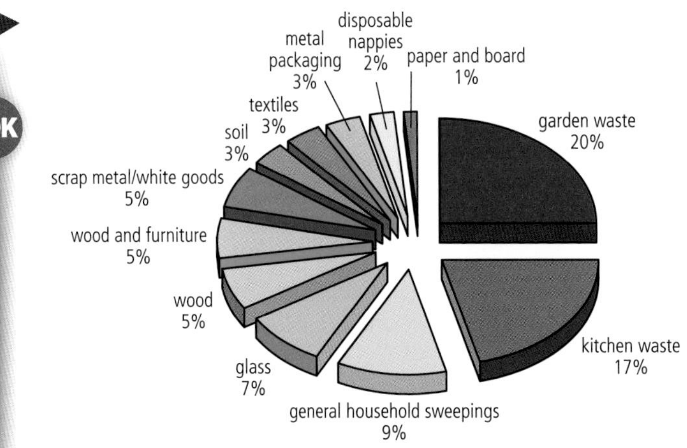

Figure 7.48 Composition of SDW.

TOK

In what ways do values affect our representations of the world, for example, in language, maps or visual images?

Figure 7.49 is a choropleth map. How realistic is it to suggest that all parts of Australia, for example, generate the same amount of waste? How could this map be improved?

The volume of waste varies by society and over time. HICs generate more waste than LICs (Figure 7.49). There is now more non-biodegradable waste (e-waste and plastics). It increases as countries become more developed. It also increases when there are festivities such as Christmas, Easter, Ramadan, Diwali, birthdays and so on.

The world's waste

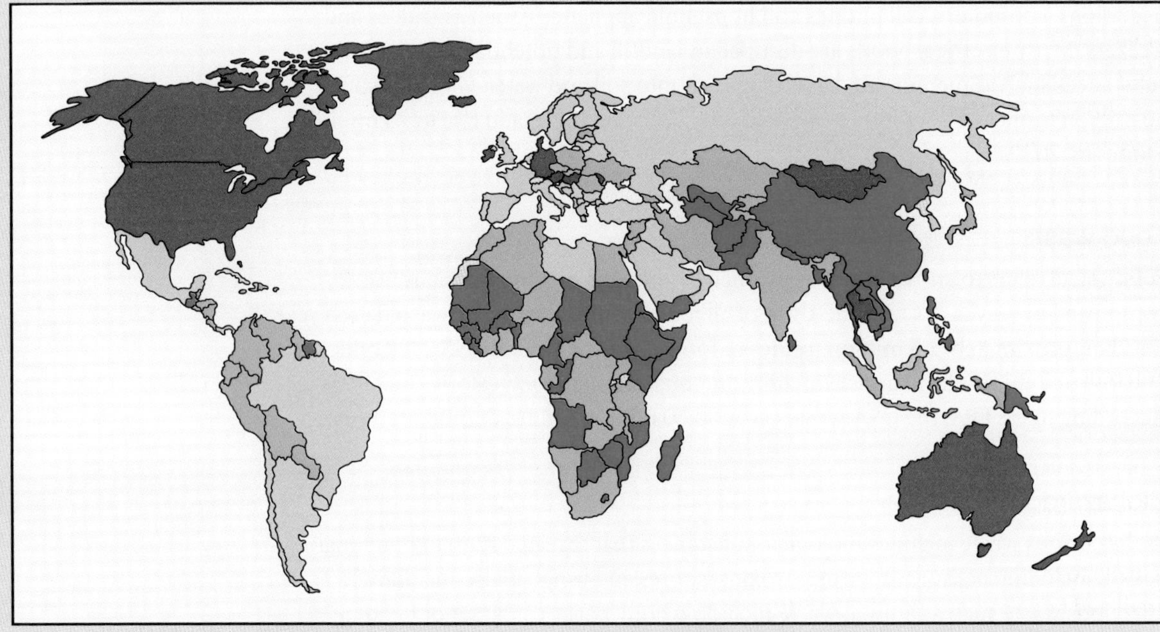

Figure 7.49 The world's waste, kg per person, 2018. Note: kg = kilogram.

Much of the world's waste is generated by city-dwellers. According to the World Bank, the potential costs of dealing with increasing rubbish are high. The world's cities currently generate around 1.3 billion tonnes of SDW a year, or 1.2 kg per city-dweller per day. Almost half of this waste comes from HICs. The World Bank predicts that by 2050 daily per capita waste in HICs will increase by 19%, whereas in LICs and MICs it will increase by 40%. The total quantity of waste generation in LICs is expected to increase by over threefold by 2050.

SDW in the UK

Some facts about SDW in the UK.

- The UK population produces approximately 28 million tonnes of SDW per year.
- This is almost 500 kg per person per year.
- The figure is growing by approximately 3% per year.
- The disposal of this waste has local, natural and global consequences for the environment.

Up to half of the world's population lacks access to the most basic methods of waste collection and safe disposal. Almost 40% of the world's waste ends up in huge landfill sites, mostly found near urban populations in LICs, posing a serious threat to human health and the environment. The Mbeubeuss waste dump in Senegal covers some 175 ha. The dump used to receive a few thousand tonnes of rubbish a year in the 1960s. Now it takes in 475,000 tonnes of rubbish a year, increasingly made up of e-waste from computers, televisions and cell phones.

The world's largest landfill sites are increasingly polluting rivers, groundwater, air and soil and are having an adverse impact on those who live and work nearby or on the site. Waste pickers often have no protective clothing. The most common human health problems are gastro-intestinal disorders, skin disorders, respiratory disorders and genetic disorders.

Figure 7.50 Plastic waste in the River Thames, London, UK.

Example – Plastic waste in the River Thames

Scientists from London collected rubbish over a three-month period from seven locations along the Thames estuary. They collected over 8400 items including plastic cups, food wrapping and cigarette packaging (Figure 7.50). The two most contaminated sites were close to sewage treatment works, which could suggest that plants were not filtering out larger waste or were letting sewage overflow when heavy rains created extra waste. However, the scientists were unable to estimate the volume of litter that was actually entering the North Sea. The potential impacts this could have for wildlife are far-reaching. For example, not only are the species that live in and around rivers affected, but also those in the seas that rivers feed.

7.3.3 Volume and composition of waste

1.2 Systems
1.3 Sustainability

The volume and composition of waste varies over time and between societies due to differences in socio-economic, political, environmental and technological factors.

The world generates over 2 billion tonnes of solid municipal waste. The amount generated varies considerably. HICs account for 16% of the world's population but generate approximately 34% of the world's waste, which is over 680 million tonnes. Global waste is expected to reach 3.4 billion tonnes by 2050. The growth in waste is likely to be twice that of population growth over the same period. Daily waste is predicted to rise by almost 20% in HICs but by over 40% in LICs and MICs. As Figure 7.51 shows, the percentage of waste collected is highest in HICs and lowest in LICs. Nevertheless, there will be variations in LICs just as there are variations in HICs. For example, more waste in urban areas is collected than in rural areas. More waste in rural areas may be incinerated and there is probably more reuse and recycling in densely populated shanty towns and in poor communities (Figure 7.52).

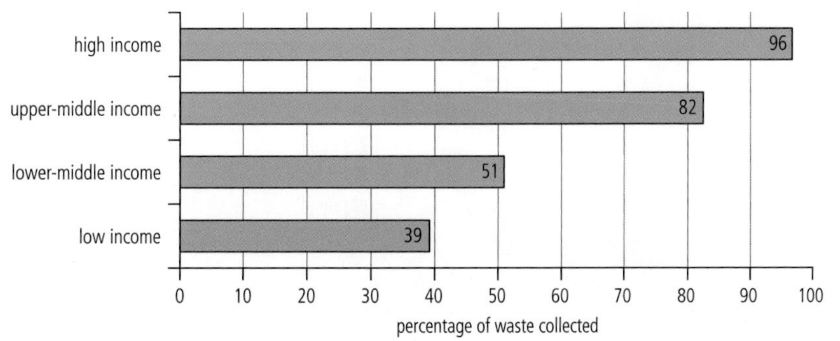

Figure 7.51 Waste collection by type of country.

Figure 7.52 A resident sifting through waste, Zwelitsha, South Africa.

Waste collection is widespread in HICs and upper-MICs. In LICs, just below 50% of the waste in cities is collected and just over 25% in rural areas.

According to Statista, there are over 4 m tons of plastic waste exports and 5 m tons of electronic waste annually. The main exporters of plastic waste include Germany, the Netherlands and Japan. The main destinations for EU waste include Turkey, India and Vietnam. In Vietnam, most of this waste goes to landfill but only 20% of landfill sites there meet sanitary requirements. According to National Geographic, around 32% of exported waste gets recycled but most ends up in landfill.

Several factors influence the volume and composition of waste. HICs and MICs generally produce more waste than LICs, and a higher proportion of that waste includes plastics and electrical/electronic goods (see Figure 7.54). In contrast, LICs produce less waste (although this is predicted to rise rapidly as countries develop) and more of it is low-value household goods such as waste food. Studies by the World Bank suggested that organic waste in LICs accounted for nearly two-thirds of all waste compared with about one-quarter of waste in HICs. Paper accounted for the major share of HIC waste (over 30%) compared with just 5% in LICs.

Waste generation varies regionally. The least amount of waste is generated in the Middle East and North Africa, whereas most waste is generated in East Asia and the Pacific (Figure 7.53). There may be many reasons for these differences. For example, population densities may be lower in some desert-regions and dry areas, such as large parts of the Middle East and North Africa. The relatively low rates in parts of Sub-Saharan Africa could be due to large areas being rural/agricultural economies and/or relative poverty. Where farming is mainly subsistence, especially among nomadic pastoralists, possessions may be limited, and little waste is generated. Among rapidly industrializing regions there may be rapid urban-rural migration as people seek out better paid jobs. Increased incomes generally lead to increased consumer spending and an increase in waste generation. Looking towards 2030 and 2050, with greater development, increased urbanization and rising incomes, it is likely that waste generation will increase in all regions. The type of waste will also change with an increase in electrical waste from portable digital devices.

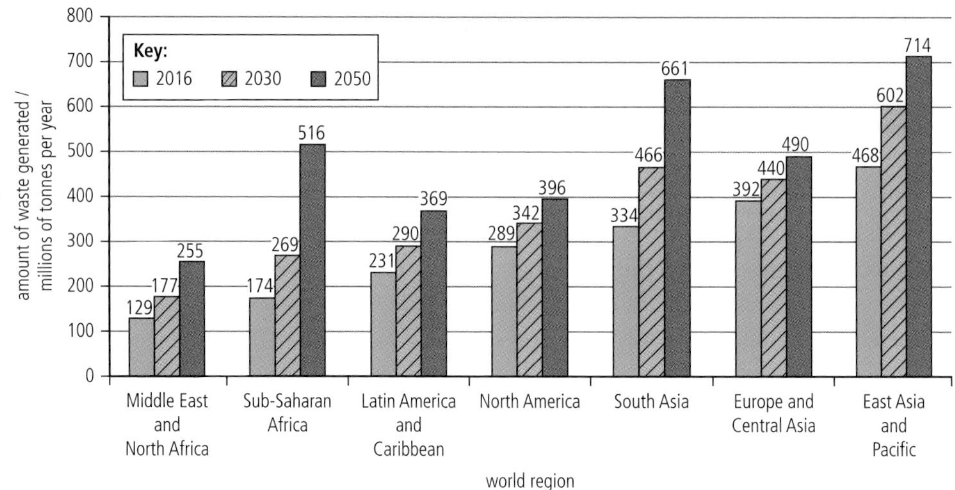

Figure 7.53 Waste generation in the world's regions 2016–50.

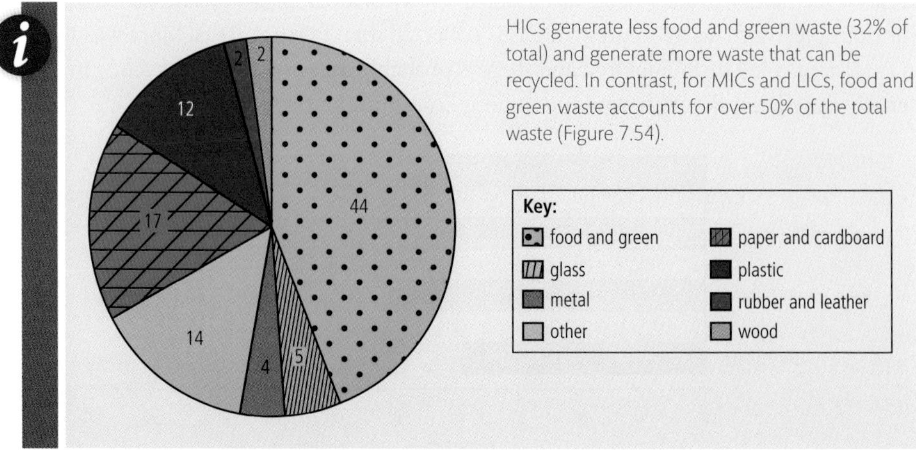

Figure 7.54 Global waste composition (%).

Activity

Download a copy of *What a waste 2.0: A global snapshot of solid waste management to 2050* from the World Bank website.

With a partner, write a one-page summary outlining the opportunities and problems for global waste management in 2050.

7.3.4 Environmental and social impacts of waste management

1.3 Sustainability

The production, treatment and management of waste has environmental and social impacts. Many of these may be experienced in a different location than that from which the waste was generated. Some waste is transported long distances, usually from HICs to LICs.

Globally, around 37% of waste ends up in landfills (Figure 7.55). Open dumping accounts for 33% of waste, while approximately 19% is recycled and composted and just over 11% is incinerated. 93% of open dumping occurs in LICs compared with 2% in HICs. Landfills are more common in upper-MICs (over 50%), falling to 39% in HICs. Incineration is mainly used in HICs and countries with a lack of space.

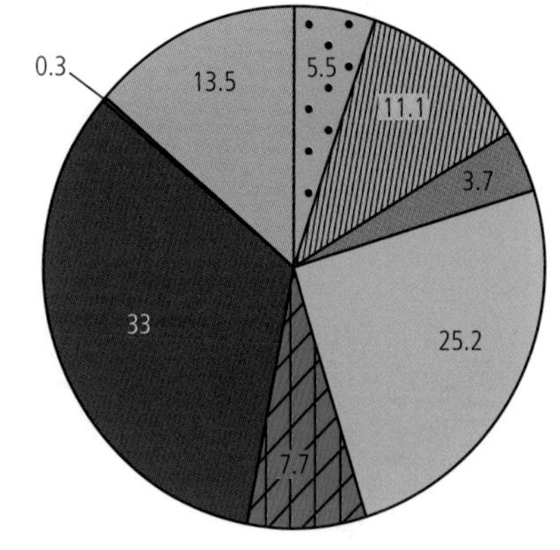

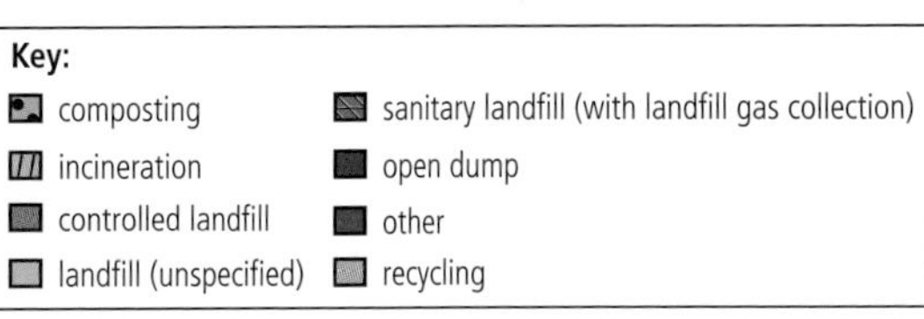

Figure 7.55 Global disposal of waste.

In most countries, solid waste management is a local responsibility rather than a national one. Financing solid waste management is a challenge. In most HICs, operating costs for integrated management, including collection, transport, treatment and disposal, generally exceed US$ 100/tonne of waste. In LICs less is spent on waste management, approximately US$ 35 per tonne. Waste management is labour intensive and transport costs are often US$ 20–50 per tonne.

Waste is often disposed of in areas further away from where it was generated. For example, landfills are often located at some distance from urban areas due to health/pollution concerns and a desire from local residents not to have such facilities located close to their residences, even if the waste was generated in urban areas. There are examples from HICs and LICs where individuals have dumped their waste illegally, known as fly-tipping, rather than pay the costs associated with legal waste disposal. A number of HICs send their waste to LICs and MICs. For example, the UK sends some of its waste, including milk cartons, unread newspapers and corrugated sheets used for wrapping electronic gadgets, to Indian factories where they are pulped and recycled to make fresh paper to meet India's growing demand for it. British wastepaper imports to India increased by nearly three times in four years, from 2016 to 2019, and increased in value from £35.5 million in 2016 to £102 million in 2019. In contrast, due to the polluting effects of burning plastics and landfilling, in 2018 China restricted the import of imported mixed wastepaper. Other countries, including India and Turkey, took over the recycling of wastepaper from HICs.

Example – E-waste including cell phones

In 2022, it was believed that 16 billion cell phones existed in the world and that 5.3 billion cell phones were discarded. Every year approximately 50 million tonnes of electronic waste (e-waste) is generated worldwide, equating to some 7 kg for every person on the planet. The global volume of e-waste is predicted to reach 75 million tonnes by 2030. Just 17% of the world's e-waste is recycled. These goods are made up of hundreds of different materials and contain toxic substances such as lead, mercury, cadmium, arsenic and flame retardants.

Once in landfill, these toxic materials seep out into the environment, contaminating land, water and the air. Those who work at these sites suffer frequent bouts of illness. The increase in e-waste is happening because there is so much technical innovation. TVs and portable digital devices are all being replaced increasingly quickly. The lifetime of products is shortening.

In 2019, China generated 11.1 million tonnes of e-waste, followed by the USA with 7 million tonnes. However, per capita figures were reversed. On average, each American generated 29.5 kg of e-waste, compared to less than 5 kg per person in China. In Europe, Germany as a nation discards the most e-waste in total, whereas Norway and Liechtenstein discard a higher amount per person. The European Environment Agency estimates that between 250,000 tonnes and 1.3 million tonnes of used electrical products are shipped out of the EU every year, mostly to west Africa and Asia.

Most cell phones contain precious metals. The circuit board can contain copper, gold, zinc, beryllium and tantalum. The coatings are typically made of lead and cell phone manufacturers are now increasingly using lithium batteries. Yet less than 10% of cell phones are dismantled and reused. Part of the problem is that computers, cell phones and other devices are becoming increasingly complex and made of smaller and smaller components. The failure to recycle is also leading to shortages of REEs to make future generations of electronic equipment.

Figure 7.56 Disposing of e-waste, Agbogbloshie, Ghana.

Agbogbloshie in Ghana has been described as the e-waste capital of the world (Figure 7.56). Up to 40,000 people live in the area and work on recycling electrical equipment. Half a sack of copper or aluminium can be sold for US$ 4–6. The population has elevated rates of chest pains and respiratory problems, nausea and headaches. By sending e-waste to Agbogbloshie, EU countries are believed to save between US$ 165 million and US$ 658 million annually on the cost of dealing with their own e-waste at home.

1.2 Systems

7.3.5 Ecosystems and pollution

Ecosystems can absorb some waste, but pollution occurs when harmful substances are added to an environment at a rate faster than they are transformed into harmless substances. Different substances biodegrade at different rates and their half-lives vary.

Some ecosystems are good at absorbing waste. Reeds, for example, absorb CO_2 in the air through photosynthesis, but they also absorb nitrogen and phosphorus during growth and development and so they can be used for pollution management. Research at Baiyangdian Lake in Hebei, China, suggests that planting 100 m^2 of reeds can create carbon sinks of 290 kg. In addition, 1 m^2 of reeds can absorb nearly 19 g of nitrogen and 1.25 g of phosphorus. Thus, planting reeds can increase carbon sequestration and absorb nitrogen and phosphorus, thereby improving water quality. Higher content of nitrogen and phosphorus encourages the growth of reeds which in turn increases the absorption of nitrogen and phosphorus through positive feedback.

Reeds have also been used to stop pollution entering the River Cain in Llanfyllin, Wales. Reeds were planted to purify drain water from a local car park before it entered the river. The car park contained a range of pollutants including oil, sediments and hydrocarbons produced by the combustion of fossil fuels. In addition to reducing the risk of pollution, the reeds slowed down surface run-off and reduced the risk of flooding.

Wetlands, both natural and constructed, improve water quality and reduce the risk of flooding. They are also easy to design and construct and can be very cost-effective.

Nevertheless, in some cases levels of pollution are rising and ecosystems and crop yields are suffering e.g. eutrophication at Slapton Ley, UK (Figure 7.57), and reduced wheat yields in Europe due to high levels of ground level ozone. For example, as levels of CO_2 in the atmosphere increase, over 85% of terrestrial ecosystems are becoming less efficient at absorbing it. CO_2 is vital for plant growth, so increased atmospheric CO_2 should increase plant growth – up to a point. The carbon fertilization effect refers to the increase in plant growth due to increased CO_2. However, since 1982 the average carbon fertilization effect has decreased from 21% to 12% per 100 ppm of CO_2 in the atmosphere. In addition to CO_2, plants require moisture and nutrients such as nitrogen and phosphorus. Plant growth in the tropics may be limited by a lack of nutrients, while at higher latitudes plant growth may be limited by a lack of soil moisture.

Figure 7.57 Eutrophication at Slapton Ley, Devon, UK.

Biodegradation is the breakdown of organic matter by living organisms such as bacteria and fungi. The time this takes depends on the conditions. For example, leaves in a tropical rainforest may be biodegraded in approximately 6–8 weeks once they have fallen to the ground. In contrast, leaves that fall to the ground in a temperate deciduous woodland may take much longer to biodegrade because bacterial activity is not as rapid in a cooler climate.

Half-life refers to the length of time it takes for a quantity of a substance to be reduced to half of its original amount. The radioactive half-life is the length of time it takes for half of the radioactive atoms of a specific radionuclide to decay. For example, the radioactive isotope cobalt-60, which is used for radiotherapy, has a half-life of 5.26 years. If a sample of 10 g were used in radiotherapy, 5.26 years later, there would be just 5 g remaining and after another 5.26 years there would only be 2.5 g remaining. This process would continue with the amount of the isotope remaining halving after every 5.26 years.

Biodegradability

Some waste takes a very long time to break down (Tables 7.13 and 7.14). Biodegradation varies with light, temperature, water and oxygen.

Table 7.13 Approximate timescale for materials to biodegrade in a marine environment.

Product	Time to biodegrade
Paper	2–4 weeks
Newspaper	6 weeks
Apple core	2 months
Cardboard box	2 months
Cotton	1–5 months
Wool gloves	1 year
Painted wooden sticks	13 years
Plastic bag	10–20 years
Tin cans	50 years
Aluminium cans	200 years

Table 7.14 Approximate timescale for materials to biodegrade in a terrestrial environment.

Product	Time to biodegrade
Vegetables	5 days – 1 month
Paper	2–5 months
Cotton	6 months
Orange peel	6 months
Plastic carton	5 years
Leather shoes	25–40 years
Tin cans	50–100 years
Aluminium cans	80–100 years
Glass bottles	1 million years

1.1 Perspectives
1.2 Systems
1.3 Sustainability

7.3.6 Preventative strategies for waste management

Preventative strategies for waste management are more sustainable than restorative strategies.

There are a number of preventative strategies for managing waste. These include:

- altering human activity, for example by reducing consumption rates and composting food waste
- controlling release of pollutants: governments can create legislation to encourage recycling and reuse initiatives, impose tax for SDW collection and impose taxes on disposable items
- reclaiming landfills, using SDW for trash-to-energy programmes and implementing initiatives to remove plastics from the Great Pacific Garbage Patch (Topic 3, Section 3.2.7 Example) through clean-up and restoration.

Preventative strategies for waste management are more *sustainable* than restorative strategies. Why is this?

These strategies can be influenced by cultural factors (e.g. is it acceptable?), economic factors (e.g. is it affordable?), technological factors (e.g. can it be achieved?) and political factors (e.g. is there support for the strategy?). Table 7.15 summarizes waste management options for SDW.

Restorative strategies are varied and include restoration, rehabilitation and remediation. Restoration refers to restoring the natural environment, e.g. rivers, to their original quality, i.e. before human activities damaged them. It may not be possible to fully restore rivers, such as those in urban areas, so rehabilitation may take place. This leads to an improvement in the natural environment/habitat but it does not reach the same quality as the original environment. It is a pragmatic way of 'fixing'/ improving certain parts of an environment. Remediation occurs when an environment has changed so much that it cannot be returned to one that resembles the original. Instead, a new 'natural' environment may be created.

Table 7.15 Waste management options.

Waste management options	How it works
Prevent waste	Alters human behaviour to reduce consumption or control the release of pollutants. For example, excessive plastic packaging for computer accessories (ink, memory sticks) can be replaced, and customers can use reusable bags rather than using plastic bags from supermarkets and other stores.
Reduce the amount of waste	Producers think more about the lifespan of goods and reduce packaging and consumers consider packaging and lifespan when buying goods. For example, re-use goods, buy second-hand goods, purchase wisely and avoid 'buy two-for-one' type offers.

Reuse goods to extend their lifespan	Bring-back schemes where containers, such as milk bottles, are refilled. Refurbish/recondition goods to extend their useful life, for example the upcycling of electrical goods. Put used goods to another use rather than throwing them away. For example, re-use plastic bags as bin liners, the use of old car tyres to stabilize slopes/reduce soil erosion or use old clothes as cleaning cloths. Charity shops pass on goods to new owners.
Recover value	Recycle goods such as glass bottles and paper. Compost biodegradable waste for use as fertilizer. Incinerate waste to produce heat energy and generate electricity.
Dispose of waste in landfill sites	Put waste into a hole, either a natural hole or one that has been created as the result of quarrying, or use it to make artificial hills. For example, modern landfill sites can be eco-friendly through the use of impermeable layers to prevent the contamination of soil and groundwater.
Clean-up	There are various groups around the world who are attempting to clean up waste from the environment. One of these is The Ocean Cleanup – see the Example.
Restore damaged ecosystems	River restoration schemes, for example, involve the rehabilitation and restoration of rivers that have been polluted. The river is returned to its original quality e.g. the rivers Cole and Skerne in the UK, the Brede in Denmark and the Kissimmee in the USA. However, the process is expensive and time-consuming.
Reduce consumption	The best form of waste management is to reduce the amount of waste. This is best achieved through the removal of demand for a product. Denmark has had a tax on plastic bags since 1993, while Croatia banned the use of plastic bags in 2022 and Cyprus banned their use in 2023.

Example – The Ocean Cleanup

The Ocean Cleanup is perhaps the most ambitious plan to tackle ocean plastic pollution–their goal is to remove 90% of floating plastic pollution in the ocean. They are attempting to clean up and restore ocean garbage patches, such as the Great Pacific Garbage Patch.

For over a decade, The Ocean Cleanup has been researching and cleaning plastic pollution in oceans and rivers. Trillions of pieces of plastic are polluting the oceans, and the problem is intensifying. Plastic can persist for centuries and have a detrimental effect on ocean food chains. The Ocean Cleanup aims to remove 90% of floating ocean plastic. However, in order to prevent the build up of ocean plastic, they need to clean rivers and prevent the plastics from reaching the oceans.

TOK

Are there ethical responsibilities that necessarily come with knowing something or knowing how to do something?

Development organizations frequently provide aid for conservation, clean water and housing developments. Rarely do they provide funding for SDW projects. Assuming that these organizations understand the cause and effects of SDW, should they have a moral responsibility to include funding for its treatment in the development process? Why is it that they may not be doing this?

Critics claim that the ships used to tow barriers to clean up the plastic emit 660 tonnes of carbon per month of clean-up. As most plastic in the oceans has entered from rivers, it tends to be located within 160 km of the coastline. This means that some of the plastic waste will be washed up on beaches. Beach clean-ups may be an effective way of reducing ocean plastics and microplastics but ultimately it would be far easier to control the pollution at the source with less waste, more recycling and reuse or substitution of plastic materials with compostable materials and so on.

1.3 Sustainability

7.3.7 Waste disposal options

The various waste disposal options have different advantages and disadvantages in terms of their impact on societies and ecosystems. Landfill, incineration, waste to energy, exporting waste, recycling and composting have different merits and demerits.

Figure 7.58 Worker incinerates electronic waste at Agbogbloshie, Accra, Ghana.

Landfill

Landfill may be cheap, but it is not always healthy (Figure 7.58), and the space will eventually run out. Recent research and surveys show that living near landfill sites increases the risk of health problems, including heart problems and birth defects (this topic, Section 7.3.4). Landfills need to be located relatively close to the source of waste to be economical, so they tend to be found near areas of high population density. Landfills can emit polluting gases such as CH_4, which may contaminate water supplies. However, landfills are generally designed to prevent leaching by having an impermeable clay lining. Many landfills are sited in old quarries, which could otherwise be turned into lakes or nature reserves.

Up to 60% of household waste in the USA is recyclable or compostable. But Americans only compost about 8% of their waste. Surveys suggest that the main reason Americans don't compost is because they think that it is a complicated process. In contrast, the Zabbaleen, who are responsible for much of the waste collection in Cairo, Egypt, recycle as much as 80% of the waste collected.

Currently, much domestic waste ends up in landfill sites. However, the reliance on landfill is unsustainable for a number of reasons.

- There are already areas struggling to find suitable new landfill sites. This shortage of space will become more acute as the amount of waste continues to grow.
- When biodegradable waste, such as food, decomposes anaerobically it releases CH_4, which, as a greenhouse gas, contributes to global warming. It is also explosive.
- Chemicals and heavy metals can pollute the soil and groundwater. Leachate, produced from organic waste, breaks down causing the same problem.
- Communities are often violently opposed to the creation of any new sites (the not-in-my-back-yard (NIMBY) principle).

Unfortunately, the measures used to try to reduce the escape of gases and leachates (liner systems, waste compaction and capping) also stop oxygen entering and this increases the generation of CH_4, which is 21 times more powerful as a greenhouse gas than CO_2.

Activity

Create a graphic to illustrate the problems with landfill.

Incineration

Incineration means burning. The process converts the waste into ash and gas particulates. The heat generated through incineration can be used to generate electricity. Incinerators can reduce the volume of the original waste by as much as 80–90%. Thus, the technology could significantly reduce the volume of waste for which landfill disposal is necessary. Incineration is particularly useful for the safe disposal of clinical and hazardous waste.

The main environmental problems associated with incineration are:

- Air pollution – CO_2, SO_2, NOx, chlorine, dioxins and particulates are all produced by incineration. In turn, these pollutants lead to other environmental problems such as acid rain, smog and lung disease.
- The volume of traffic generated is increased due to the need to get the waste to the incinerators. This leads to greater air pollution, noise, vibration and risk of accidents.
- The ash that is produced, usually equal to 10–20% of the mass of the original waste, is often toxic and still needs to be disposed of in landfill. Building incinerators represents a high initial capital cost.

Example – Incineration in Singapore

Singapore incinerates approximately 8200 tonnes of waste every day, reducing its volume by approximately 90%. The incineration plants produce over 2500 MWh of energy daily, enough to support 900 homes daily.

Waste to energy

Energy-from-waste is a form of energy recovery. As the waste is burned, heat is created that is used to convert water to steam. Steam turns a turbine and electricity is generated. In contrast, early incinerators only burned the waste and did not attempt to recover energy. Many municipal incinerators are trying to produce energy from waste through energy from waste or waste to energy programmes. However, in many places, communities prefer these facilities to be located 'somewhere else'. The USA has some 1900 municipal landfill sites. The largest is Puente Hills landfill in Los Angeles. The dump is over 160 m high. With 60 years' worth of decomposing rubbish, Puente Hills collects and uses enough CH_4 to generate electricity to 70,000 homes.

Exporting waste

Some countries (usually HICs) export their waste to be dealt with in other countries (usually LICs). The country exporting the waste benefits from not having to deal with the materials while the importing country benefits from job creation and payments for taking in the waste. However, there are costs involved in the transport of the material and the poor working conditions.

Example – Exporting waste – China

Until recently, China used to import more than 3 million tonnes of plastic waste and 15 million tonnes of paper and cardboard each year. Containers arrived in HICs with goods produced in China and were then loaded up with waste products for the journey back. One-third of the UK's plastic and paper (200,000 tonnes of plastic rubbish and 500,000 tonnes of paper) was exported to China annually. Low wages and a large workforce meant that the waste could be sorted more cheaply in China, despite the distance it had been transported. China has since restricted imports of waste.

Recycling and composting

The recycling of paper, glass and some metals saves scarce raw materials and helps reduce pollution. In Europe, for example, there are high rates of recycling in Austria, Germany, the Netherlands and Switzerland (Figure 7.59).

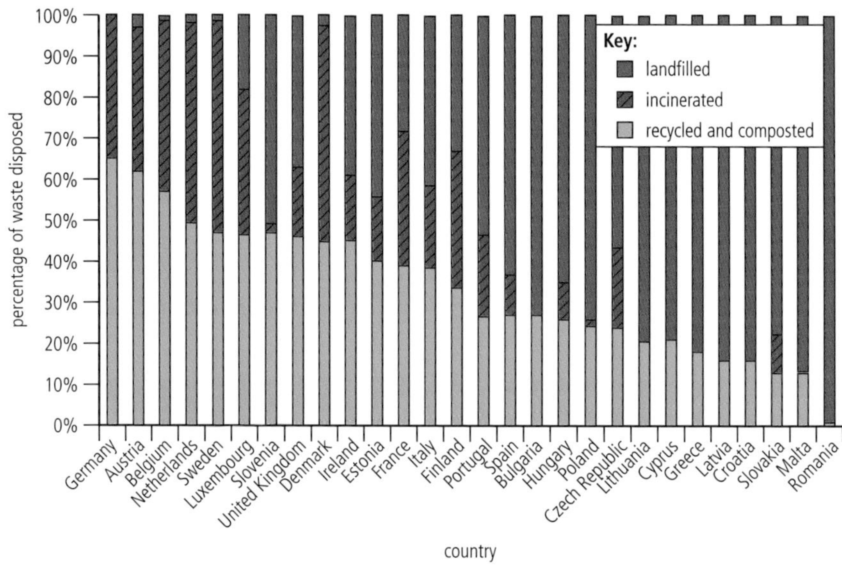

Figure 7.59 Waste disposal methods in Europe.

'Recycle, reuse and reduce' keeps materials out of landfills. Reuse may include donating to charity organizations and charity shops. Many items, such as bottles and tyres, can be reused, rather than disposed of (Figure 7.60). They can be used for other purposes than they were originally intended for.

Figure 7.60 Use of (a) tyres and (b) used plastic bottles for growing food.

1.3 Sustainability

HL a Environmental law
HL b Environmental economics
HL c Environmental ethics

7.3.8 Sustainable options

Sustainable options for management of SDW can be promoted in societies. Strategies for promoting more sustainable management include taxes, incentives, social policies, legislation, education, campaigns and improved access to disposal facilities.

There are a number of options to manage SDW in different countries.

Example – Plastic bag tax in Ireland

In 2002 the Irish government introduced a tax on plastic bags. Instead of being issued free of charge, customers were forced to pay a tax of 0.15 euros (this has since been increased). This led to a 94% drop in the use of plastic bags, customers choosing mainly to use reusable cloth bags instead.

Most incentives work by making people better off in some way. For example, in the Veneto region of Italy, people who compost their food and garden waste get a 30% reduction on their waste bill. In Catalonia, Spain, there are charges for using landfill and incineration to make these options more expensive than recycling. The tax and fees collected are then reinvested and used for improving biowaste collection and recycling.

Social policies that could be adopted as incentives include:

- charging a deposit for bottled drinks, with the deposit being paid back on the return of the bottle
- encouraging people to borrow books from a library or use an e-book reader rather than buying many books (although there are significant costs in the manufacture and running of e-book readers)
- encouraging people to donate materials to charity shops and libraries rather than disposing of them in a waste bin.

Legislation can be very effective. When the EU imposed a ban on the use of landfills for hazardous waste, it encouraged member states to use incineration instead and generate electricity using the heat produced. Thus, the taxation on landfill increased the economic cost of using landfill and made the alternatives more attractive.

Waste management could become part of the school curriculum. This may be even more important in HICs and MICs compared with LICs.

Education programmes can inform people about the advantages of recycling and reuse, and create a positive attitude towards waste management. In general, waste disposal has a high cost. Once organizations know how to compost, recycle and practice zero waste initiatives, waste management programs run themselves. This means that the time and money spent on thorough education quickly pays for itself.

Activity

Find out about the Stem Discovery Campaign waste management blog.

Write your own blog post about the Stem Discovery Campaign.

There have been a number of campaigns used to increase public awareness about the needs and advantages of waste management. Phrases such as 'There is no planet B' and 'Recycle your trash or trash your Earth' create an awareness about the importance of waste management. In many places, especially in urban areas and HICs/MICs, improved access to recycling facilities occurs at supermarkets (Figure 7.61), town centres and petrol stations. This makes it easier for people to recycle goods, especially if they do not have regular collections of SDW.

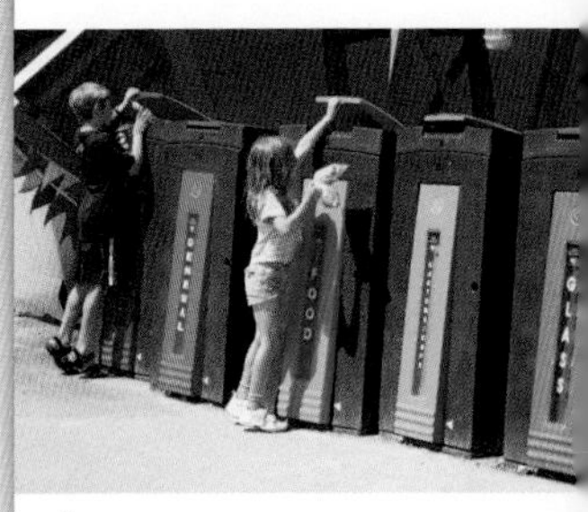

Figure 7.61 Young people recycling – sometimes younger generations are more environmentally switched on than older generations.

Activity

Visit the European Environmental Bureau website and research ways in which waste management in European countries is being tackled.

Make a poster showing some of the strategies that are being used.

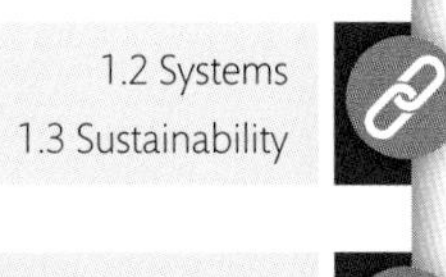

1.2 Systems
1.3 Sustainability

HL b Environmental economics

7.3.9 The circular economy and SDW

The principles of a circular economy provide a holistic perspective on sustainable waste management (Topic 1, Section 1.3.21). In the circular economy, waste is minimized by the use of biological materials, artificial materials are designed for repeated use, and systems are run on renewable energy.

Example – The textile industry and the circular economy

Figure 7.62 shows the textile industry and the circular economy.

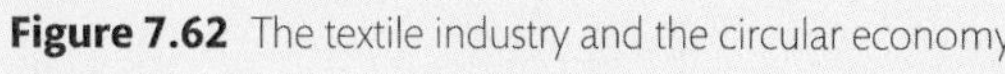

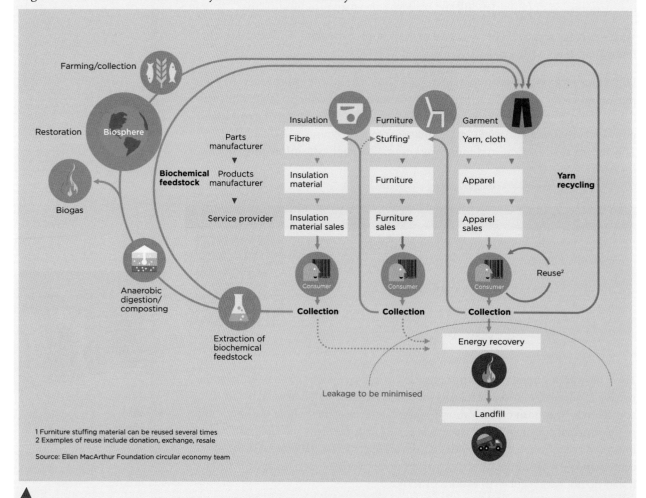

Figure 7.62 The textile industry and the circular economy.

Jute is grown, harvested and manufactured for use in the textile industry for products including insulation material, furniture and clothing.

There are a several ways in which the textile industry can be considered sustainable or 'circular'. Leakage is reduced through reuse and recycling, e.g. some of the clothing can be re-used and yarn is recycled. Used insulation material can also be re-used. There is extraction of biochemicals and some used materials are composted or used for biogas. Energy is also recovered from textiles that are being sent to landfill, and some clothing is used for alternative uses e.g. as cleaning cloths or second-hand clothing.

TOK

What role do paradigm shifts play in the progression of knowledge?

The circular economy can be seen as a paradigm shift. Does knowledge develop through paradigm shifts in all areas of knowledge?

For more details on the textile industry and the circular economy search the Wageningen University & Research Library website for the *Circular Economy in the Textile Industry* eBook:

Engagement

- Work with your teacher to arrange a trip to a local recycling centre to learn about how waste is handled locally. Create a poster to promote recycling in your local area.
- Work with a partner to find out what happens to waste in your society – how much is recycled, reused, remade, goes to landfill or incineration or is shipped to another country. Create a fact sheet to show your results.
- Create a questionnaire to assess the perception of waste management in your school. Give this questionnaire to staff and students. Include some questions asking what they consider the best ways of reducing or reusing waste to be in your school.
- Raise awareness of circular economy options in the community by producing a poster and placing copies in the classrooms, department notice boards and in the dining hall.
- Set up and/or promote initiatives such as a Repair café or a Library of Things in your school.

Exercise

Q21. **Describe** the global variations in the world's waste.

Q22. Study Figure 7.63, which shows waste generation in the world's regions.

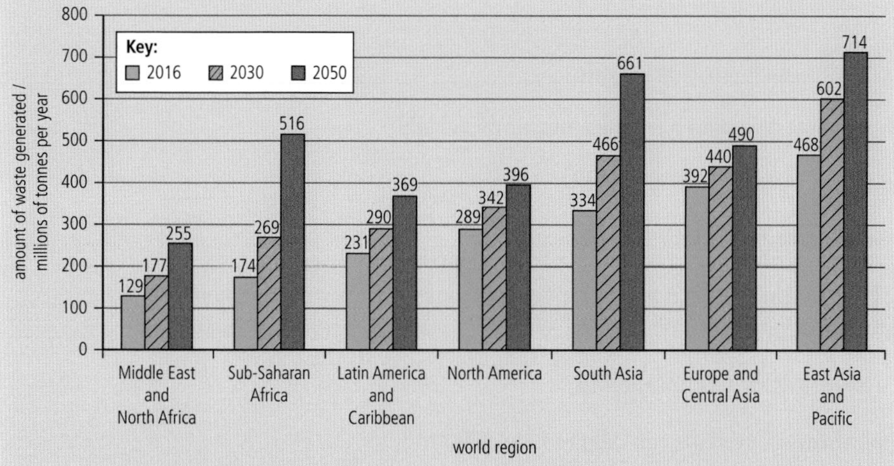

Figure 7.63 Waste generation in the world's regions 2016–50 (million tonnes/year).

(a) **Calculate** the growth rate from 2016–30 for Sub-Saharan Africa, South Asia and North America.

(b) **Calculate** the growth rate from 2016–50 for Sub-Saharan Africa, South Asia and North America.

Q23. Study Figure 7.64 on the textile industry and the circular economy.

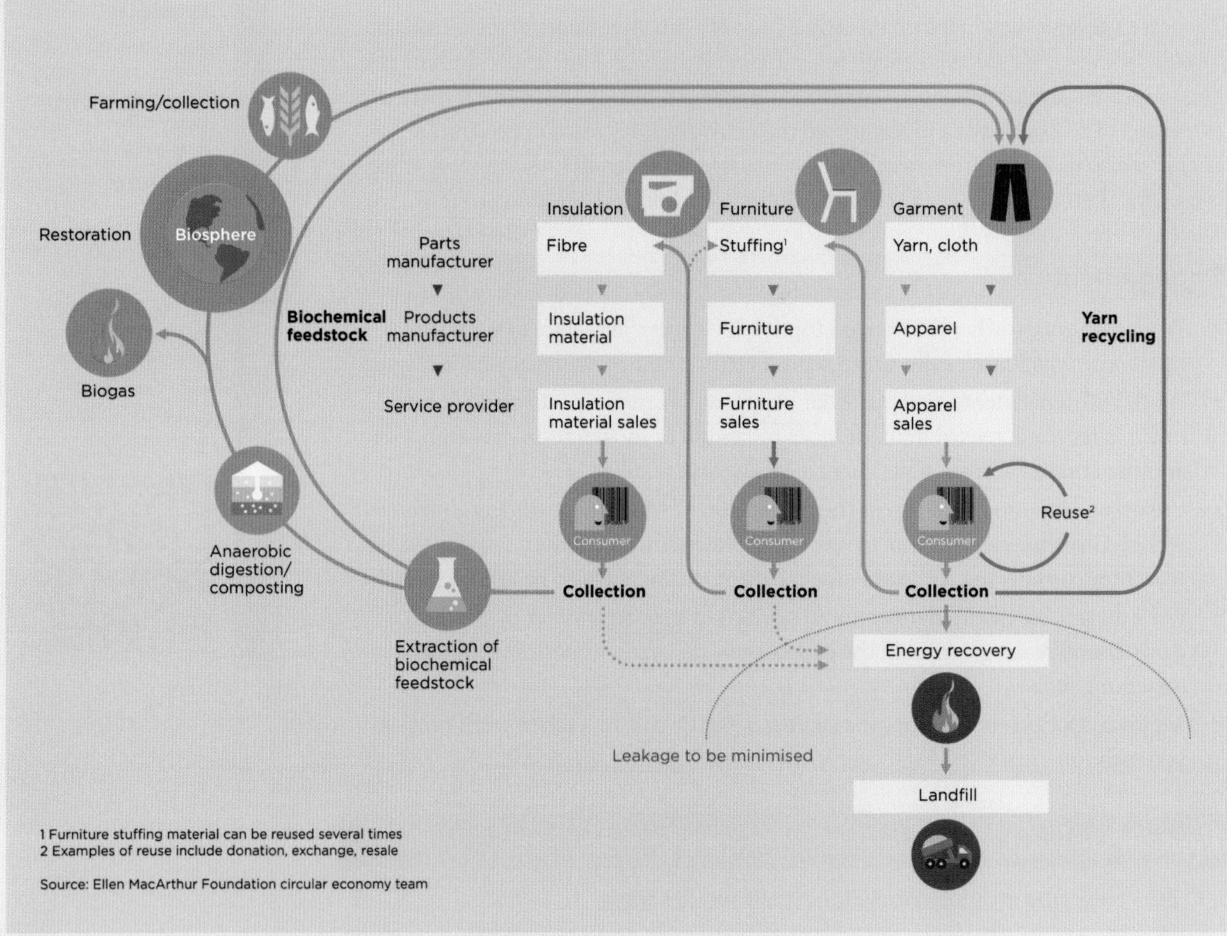

Figure 7.64 The textile industry and the circular economy.

(a) **Identify** three products that are made from textiles.

(b) **Outline** two ways in which textiles can be reused and/or recycled.

(c) **Suggest** two ways in which leakage is minimized.

(d) **Explain** how textiles can contribute to the energy sector.

Q24. Using examples, **analyze** the extent to which preventative strategies for waste management are more sustainable than restorative strategies.

Q25. **Explain** why some HICs export waste to LICs and MICs.

Q26. **Explain**, using an example, how ecosystems can help reduce pollution.

Q27. **Explain** how waste can be used to produce energy.

Q28. **Compare and contrast** the advantages and disadvantages of waste to energy and recycling.

Q29. **Examine** how a circular economy contributes to sustainable waste management.

Q30. State and justify which of the options for waste management in Table 7.16 is the best.

Waste management options	How it works
Prevent waste	alters human behaviour to reduce consumption or control the release of pollutants
Reduce the amount of waste	producers think more about the lifespan of goods and reduce packaging and consumers consider packaging and lifespan when buying goods
Reuse goods to extend their lifespan	bring-back schemes where containers, such as milk bottles, are refilled refurbish/recondition goods to extend their useful life, for example the upcycling of electrical goods used goods put to another use rather than being thrown out, for example reusing plastic bags as bin liners, the use of old car tyres to stabilize slopes/reduce soil erosion or using old clothes as cleaning cloths charity shops pass on goods to new owners
Recover value	recycle goods such as glass bottles and paper compost biodegradable waste for use as fertilizer incinerate waste to produce heat energy and generate electricity
Dispose of waste in landfill sites	put waste into a hole, either a natural hole or one that has been created as the result of quarrying, or use it to make artificial hills
Clean-up	There are various groups around the world who are attempting to clean up waste frmo the environment. One of these is The Ocean Cleanup - see the Example.
Restore damaged ecosystems	River restoration schemes, for example, involve the rehabilitation and restoration of rivers that have been polluted. The river is returned to its original quality e.g. the rivers Cole and Skerne in the UK, the Brede in Denmark and the Kissimmee in the USA. However, the process is expensive and time-consuming.
Reduce consumption	The best form of waste management is to reduce the amount of waste. This is best achieved through the removal of demand for a product. Denmark has had a tax on plastic bags since 1993, while Croatia banned the use of plastic bags in 2022 and Cyprus banned their use in 2023.

Table 7.16 Waste management options.

Practice questions

1. Figure 7.65 shows ecosystem services.

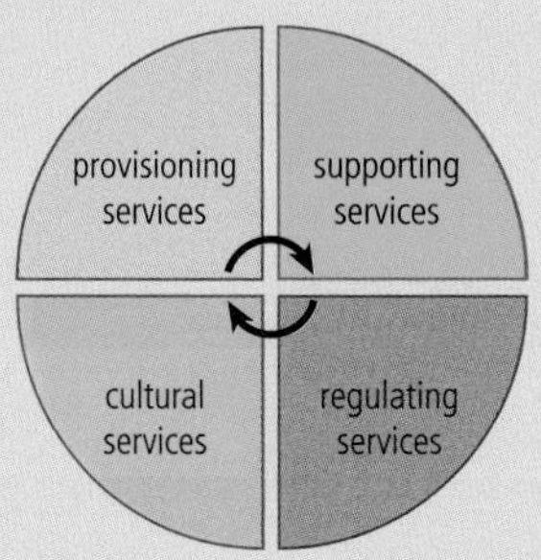

Figure 7.65 Ecosystem services.

(a) Define the term *ecosystem services.* [2]

(b) Explain how ecosystems can provide cultural services. [2]

(c) Identify two forms of supporting services. [2]

(d) Distinguish between ecosystem goods and services. [2]

(e) Outline one regulating service provided by forests. [1]

(Total 9 marks)

2. Study Figure 7.66, which shows energy consumption in North America and the Middle East.

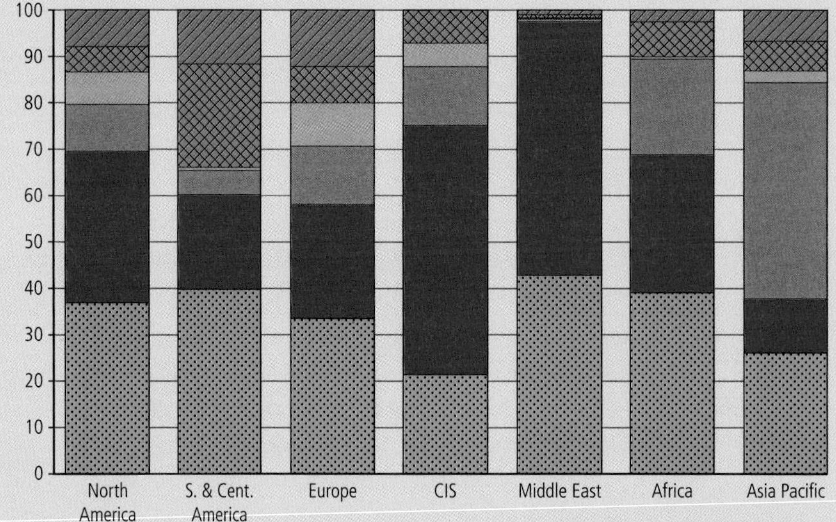

Figure 7.66 Energy consumption in North America and the Middle East.

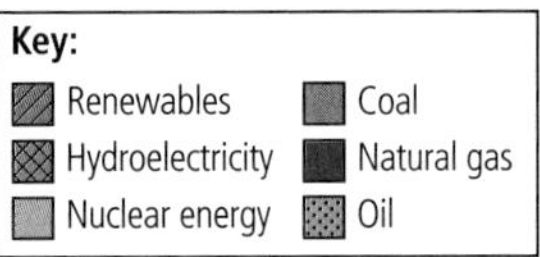

(a) Calculate the amount of gas consumed in North America in 2021. [2]

(b) Suggest two reasons why the Middle East produces a very limited amount of HEP. [2]

(c) Calculate the amount of renewable energy in North America in 2021. [2]

(d) Suggest two reasons why the energy mix in the Middle East is unsustainable. [2]

(Total 8 marks)

3. **(a)** Identify the type of country that produces the most waste. [1]

(b) Suggest two reasons why the amount of waste is likely to increase by 2050. [2]

(c) Explain how waste has become an international problem. [2]

(d) Identify one form of electronic waste (e-waste) that can cause problems for human health. [1]

(e) **(i)** Define the term 'green waste'. [3]

(ii) Outline how the amount of green waste varies between HICs and LICs. Suggest reasons to explain the difference(s). [2]

(Total 11 marks)

4. **(a)** Explain the concept of resource security. [4]

(b) Analyze the causes of water insecurity. [7]

(c) Discuss ways in which natural capital can be managed to ensure sustainability. [9]

(Total 20 marks)

5. **(a)** Using examples, distinguish between renewable and non-renewable energy sources. [4]

(b) Examine the factors that affect energy choices. [7]

(c) Examine how energy conservation and energy efficiency can reduce energy imports into a country. [9]

(Total 20 marks)

6. **(a)** Outline the sources and types of waste. [4]

(b) Explain how ecosystems can absorb some waste but can also be negatively affected by pollution. [7]

(c) Evaluate strategies for waste management. [9]

(Total 20 marks)

HL

7. HL Examine how natural resource insecurity can lead to environmental degradation and geopolitical tensions and conflicts. [9]

(Total 9 marks)

8. HL Analyse the environmental and geopolitical consequences of large-scale battery storage. [9]

(Total 9 marks)

9. HL To what extent can the management of solid domestic waste be made more sustainable? [9]

(Total 9 marks)

HL end

8 Human populations and urban systems

8.1 Human populations

Guiding questions

How can the dynamics of human populations be measured and compared?

To what extent can the future growth of the human population be accurately predicted?

8.1.1 Births and immigration are inputs to a human population.
8.1.2 Deaths and emigration are outputs from a human population.
8.1.3 Population dynamics can be quantified and analysed by calculating total fertility rate, life expectancy, doubling time and natural increase.
8.1.4 The global human population has followed a rapid growth curve. Models are used to predict the growth of the future global human population.
8.1.5 Population and migration policies can be employed to directly manage growth rates of human populations.
8.1.6 Human population growth can also be managed indirectly through economic, social, health, development and other policies that have an impact on births, deaths or migration.
8.1.7 The composition of human populations can be modelled and compared using age–sex pyramids.
8.1.8 The demographic transition model (DTM) describes the changing levels of births and deaths in a human population through different stages of development over time.
HL 8.1.9 Rapid human population growth has increased stress on the Earth's systems.
HL 8.1.10 Age–sex pyramids can be used to determine dependency ratio and population momentum.
HL 8.1.11 The reasons for patterns and trends in population structure and growth can be understood using examples of two countries in different stages of the DTM.
HL 8.1.12 Environmental issues such as climate change, drought and land degradation are causing environmental migration.

8.1.1 Births and immigration are inputs to a human population

Demography is the study of population, hence the term demographic means related to population. Countries need to know basic demographic indicators, such as birth t-rates and death rates, so that they can plan for future needs of their population.

The crude birth rate (number of live births per 1000 people in a population per year) and immigration rate (number of immigrants per 1000 population per year) are the quantitative measures of population input. The rates can be used at a variety of scales from small urban areas like a town, to a country or a region or to the global population.

2.1 Individuals, populations, communities and ecosystems

Demographic tools for quantifying human population include crude birth rate (CBR), crude death rate (CDR), total fertility rate (TFR), doubling time (DT) and natural increase rate (NIR).

Birth rates

Demography is the scientific study of populations. People who study demography (demographers) want to understand population dynamics. Changes in human populations can be studied by investigating three demographic processes: birth, migration, and death.

The crude birth rate (CBR) refers to the number of live births per 1000 (‰) people per year in a country or area. It is crude because it does not consider the age-structure of a country. Table 8.1 shows the countries with the highest CBRs and some of the countries with the lowest CBRs. Those countries with the highest CBRs have a youthful population, whereas those with the lowest CBRs are wealthy countries with ageing populations.

The birth rate is calculated by dividing the total number of births in a country in a year by the total population and then multiplying by 1000. This gives a birth rate per thousand population.

In the USA in 2019, there were 3.7 million births out of a total population of 328 million, which gives a CBR of 8.7‰ per year.

In Mauritius in 2022, there were 11,940 births out of a population of 1,262,523, which gives a CBR of 9.5‰ per year. Globally, there are major variations in the CBR, with the highest rates in poorer countries and lower rates in richer countries (Figure 8.1 and Table 8.1).

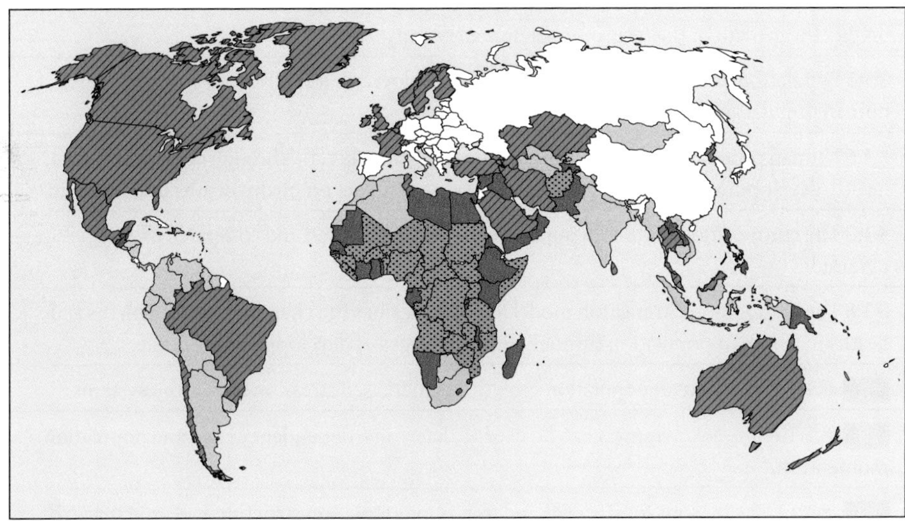

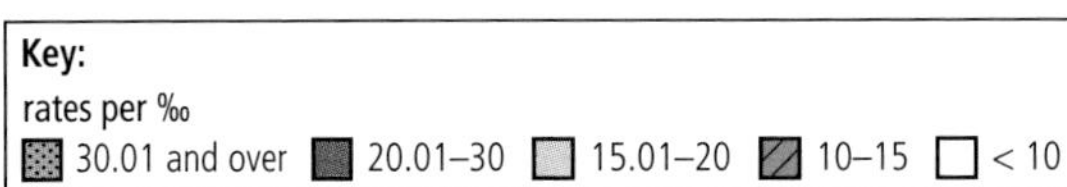

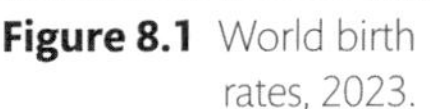

Figure 8.1 World birth rates, 2023.

Crude birth rates and crude death rates are given in rates per thousand (‰) whereas natural increase is expressed in percentage terms (%).

Table 8.1 Countries with high birth rates and low birth rates, 2023.

Country	Crude birth rate (‰)	Country	Crude birth rate (‰)
Niger	47.08	Spain	7.13
Angola	41.80	Italy	6.95
Benin	41.15	Japan	6.95
Mali	41.07	South Korea	6.92
Uganda	40.94	Monaco	6.66

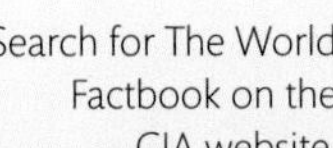

Search for The World Factbook on the CIA website.

Choose any country, then go to 'People and society' and find and record the CBRs for three contrasting countries (e.g. look for a LIC, a MIC and a HIC).

CBR is easy to calculate using readily available data.
The formula is:

$$\text{CBR} = \frac{\text{total number of births}}{\text{total population}} \times 1000$$

Immigration

Populations can also grow due to immigration (Figure 8.2 and Table 8.2). In some countries, immigration is an important factor in population growth. For many high-income countries (HICs), international migration (net inflow) exceeds the excess of births over deaths. In contrast, for low-income countries (LICs) and middle-income countries (MICs), the main driver of population growth tends to be the excess of births over deaths. According to the UN, between 2010 and 2021, some 40 countries experienced a net inflow of over 200,000 immigrants and in 17 of these, the number of immigrants exceeded 1 million. Many of the immigrants were refugees, especially from Syria. The USA has been the main destination for migrants since 1970. The number of foreign-born residents quadrupled from 12 million in 1970 to over 50 million in 2019. The number of foreign-born residents in Germany increased from 8.9 million in 2000 to nearly 16 million in 2020.

Visit the International Organization for Migration, UN World Migration Report.

Go to the interactive page and click on the map to find out the number of migrants in three contrasting countries (e.g. look for a LIC, a MIC and a HIC).

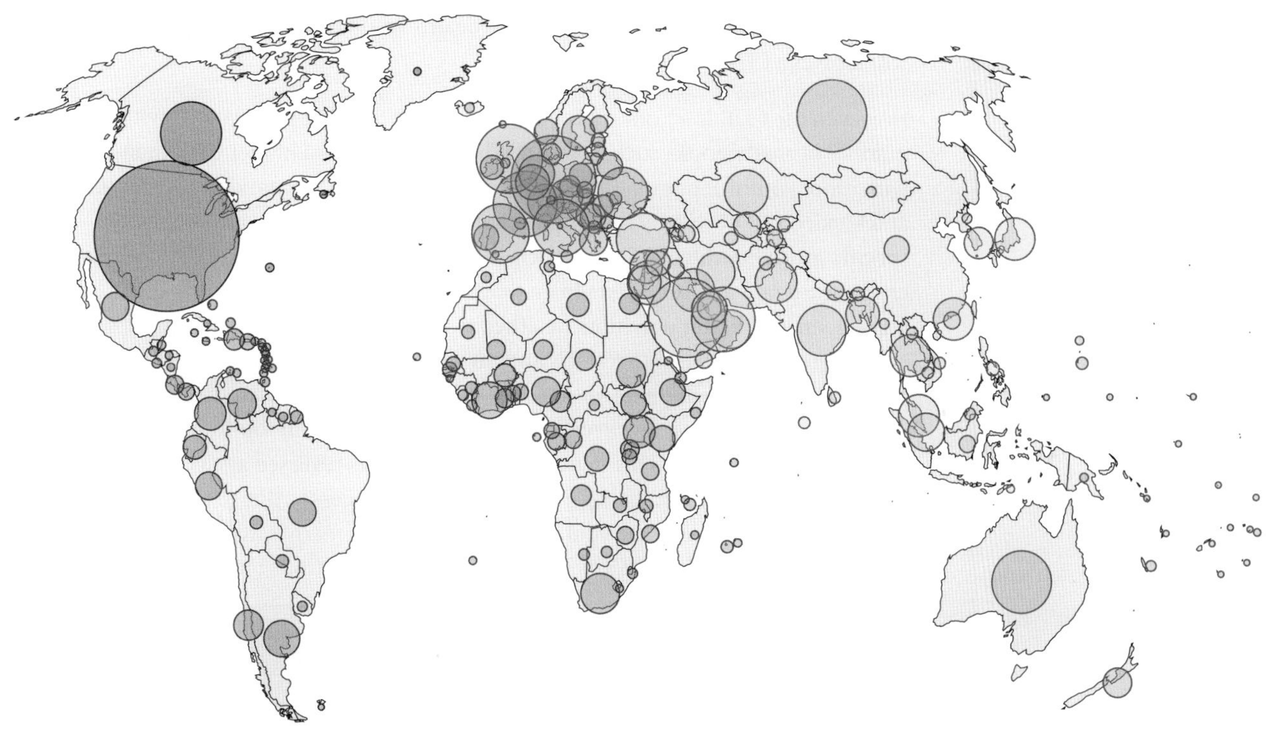

Key: pink: the Americas; orange: Africa; blue: Europe incl. Russia; yellow: Asia; olive: Australia/NZ

Figure 8.2 The total number of international migrants within each country.

Table 8.2 Countries with the highest rates of migrants (‰).

Country	Rate of migrants(‰)
Syria	40.58
Sudan	20.97
Equatorial Guinea	13.96
Venezuela	13.88
Luxembourg	12.01

2.1 Individuals, populations, communities and ecosystems

8.1.2 Deaths and emigration are outputs from a human population

The death rate and emigration (out-migration) represent the losses (the outputs) from a population. **Emigration** refers to the movement of people away from an area. **Immigration** refers to the movement of people into an area.

Crude death rate (CDR) is the number of deaths in a population per year (‰). The emigration rate is the number of emigrants per year (‰). These are both quantitative measures of population input. The rates can be used on a variety of scales, from small urban areas like a town, to a country, to a region or to the global population.

CDR is calculated using the formula: $\frac{\text{number of deaths per year}}{\text{total population}} \times 1000 = \text{CDR‰}$

In China in 2022, there were 10.41 million deaths among a population of 1.4118 billion, which gives a CDR of 7.3‰.

However, the CDR is a poor indicator of mortality trends – populations with a large number of aged people, such as those in most HICs, have a higher CDR than countries with more youthful populations. For example, in 2022, Denmark's CDR was 9.52‰ and Mexico's CDR was 7.7‰. To compare mortality rates more accurately, age-specific mortality rates (ASMRs), such as the infant mortality rate (IMR), are used. The crude death rate in HICs differs from that in LICs and MICs (Figure 8.3). In HICs, as a consequence of better nutrition, healthcare and environmental conditions, the death rate fell steadily between the 1850s and the 1950s to a level of about 12–16‰. In many very poor countries, high death rates are still common. However, the CDR had shown a decrease over the past few decades due to improvements in food supply, water, sanitation and housing. This trend, unfortunately, was reversed as a consequence of AIDS, particularly in sub-Saharan Africa and more recently, due to the COVID-19 pandemic. Nevertheless, the youthful age-structure of many MICs produces a lower death rate than in many HICs, which have ageing populations (Table 8.3).

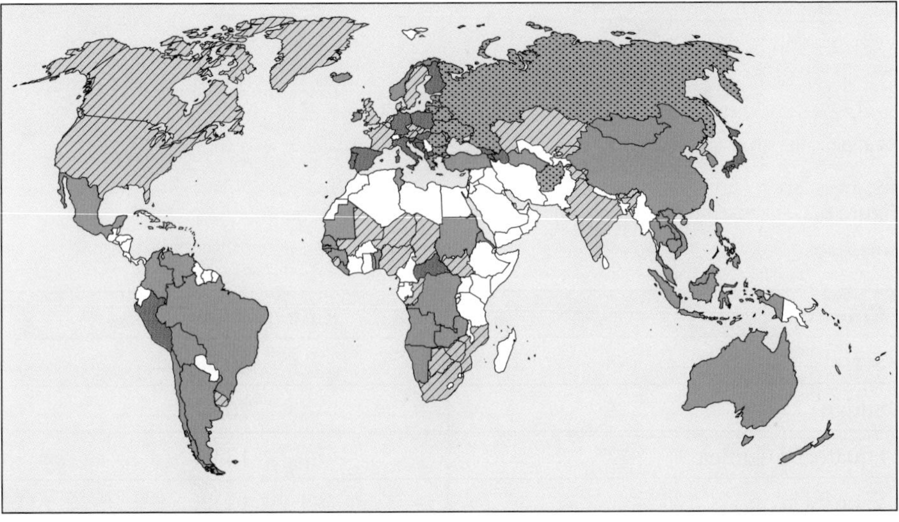

Figure 8.3 Global crude death rates, 2023.

Key:
rates per ‰
12 and over | 10–11.99 | 8–9.99 | 6–7.99 | less than 6

Country	Crude death rate (‰)	Country	Crude death rate (‰)
Serbia	16.39	Saudi Arabia	3.42
Romania	15.26	Oman	3.23
Lithuania	15.12	Kuwait	2.25
Latvia	14.65	United Arab Emirates	1.56
Bulgaria	14.41	Qatar	1.42

Table 8.3 The world's highest and (some of the) lowest death rates.

Important variations also occur within countries and even within cities. Figure 8.4 shows the death rates among homeless people, those living in hostels (often short-term accommodation) and people living in their own homes in Oxford, UK.

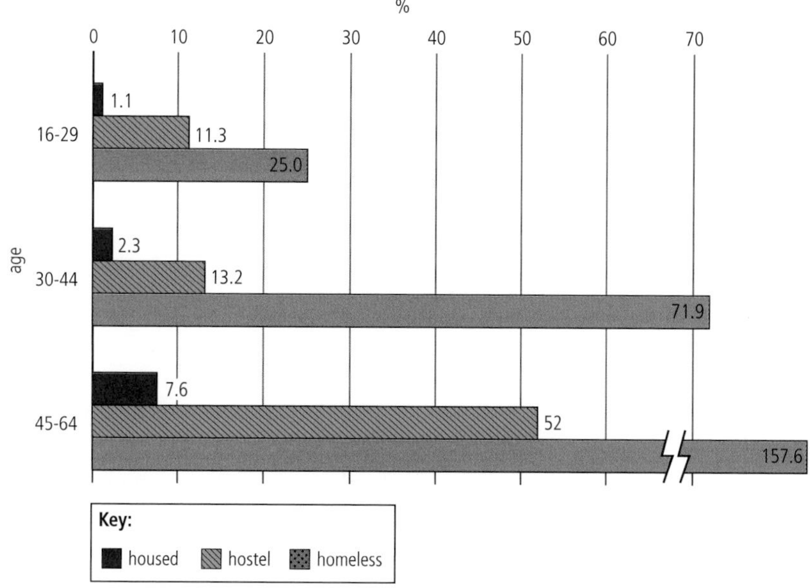

Figure 8.4 Death rates in Oxford, UK.

Emigration

Countries with high levels of emigration include poor countries, small island developing nations (Table 8.4), countries that experience repeated natural hazards, including global climate change, and countries experiencing war and social tensions. Most migrants tend to be young adults who can afford to make the journey, so it is not the poorest who emigrate. Most migrants move to find a job and/or have a better quality of life.

Country	Rate of emigration (‰)
American Samoa	29.80
Cook Islands	27.31
Tonga	18.01
Jordan	11.08
Eritrea	10.11

Table 8.4 Countries with some of the highest rates of emigration (migrants ‰).

1.2 Systems
1.3 Sustainability

8.1.3 Population dynamics can be quantified and analysed

Make sure that you know examples of demographic data for contrasting countries.

Total fertility rate (TFR) is the average number of births per woman of childbearing age. Life expectancy is the average number of years that a person can be expected to live, usually from birth, if demographic factors remain unchanged. Doubling time is the number of years it would take for a population to double its size at its current growth rate and can be calculated as 70 divided by the natural increase as a percentage. Natural increase is birth rate minus death rate, expressed as a number per 1000, or as a percentage where the birth rate – minus death rate per thousand is divided by 10. You can read more about natural increase later in this section.

In general, the highest fertility rates are found among the poorest countries, especially in sub-Saharan Africa, and very few LICs have made the transition from high birth rates to low birth rates (Table 8.5 and Figure 8.5). The birth rates and TFRs have decreased in most HICs. Although individual TFR values vary, all European countries have a relatively low TFR, with an average fertility rate of 1.5. Changes in fertility are caused through a combination of sociocultural and socio-economic factors. While there may be strong correlations between these sets of factors and changes in fertility, it is impossible to prove the linkages or to prove that one set of factors is more important than the other.

Table 8.5 World's highest and lowest fertility.

Country	Highest in 2022	Country	Lowest in 2022
Niger	6.82	Italy	1.22
Angola	5.83	Macau (SAR)	1.22
DR Congo	5.63	Singapore	1.16
Mali	5.54	South Korea	1.10

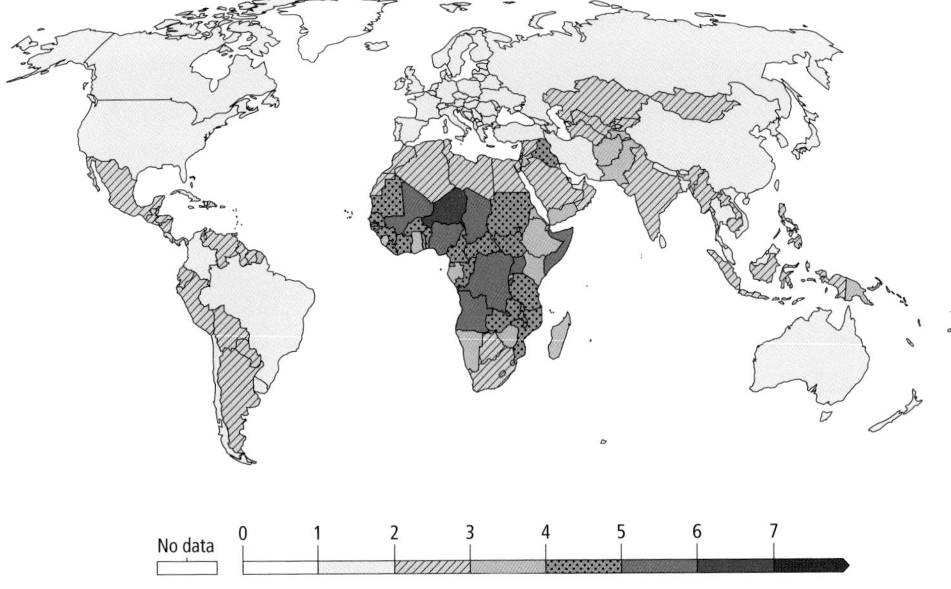

Figure 8.5 Total fertility rates globally, 2022.

Life expectancy

Life expectancy at birth compares the average number of years to be lived by a group of people born in the same year, if mortality at each age remains constant in the future.

Life expectancy is much higher for people who live in HICs and lower for those who live in LICs (Table 8.6 and Figure 8.6). Life expectancy can also vary within small areas such as cities. In 2023, it was reported that wealthy people in north Oxford, UK lived an average of 12 years longer than residents in poorer parts of the city.

High life expectancy does not necessarily mean a higher quality of life. Many of the very elderly have long-term health problems.

Country	Highest in 2022	Country	Lowest in 2022
Monaco	89.52	Sierra Leone	58.76
Singapore	86.35	Mozambique	57.10
Macau (SAR)	84.98	Somalia	55.72
Japan	84.83	Central African Republic	55.52
San Marino	83.86	Afghanistan	53.65

Table 8.6 Highest and lowest life expectancies (years), 2023.

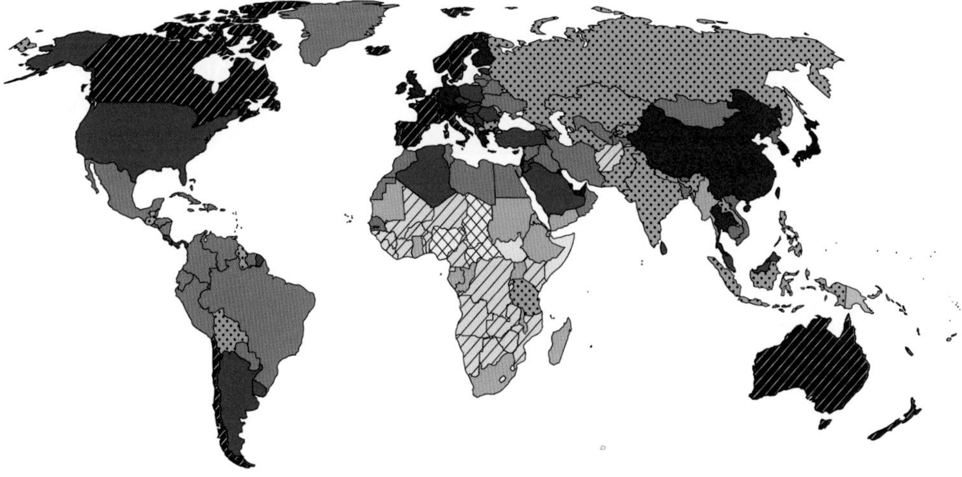

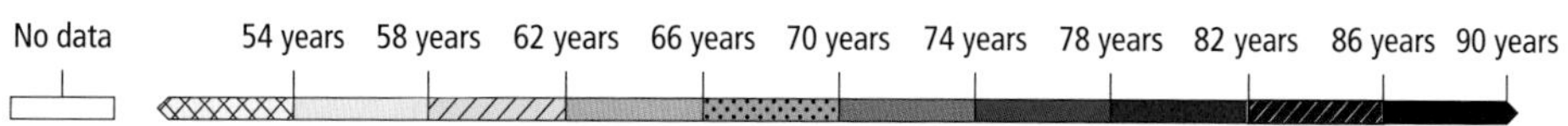

Figure 8.6 Life expectancy, 2021.

Natural increase rate

Natural increase rate (NIR) is usually expressed as a percentage and is calculated by subtracting the CDR from the CBR. If the NIR is expressed per thousand rather than as a percentage the total would need to be divided by 10.

$$\text{NIR (‰)} = \frac{(\text{CBR} - \text{CDR})}{10} \text{ (‰)}$$

Doubling time (DT) is the number of years needed for a population to double in size, assuming the natural growth rate remains constant. It is expressed in years and is found by dividing 70 (years) by the rate of natural increase (%) using the formula:

$$\text{Doubling time (years)} = \frac{70}{\text{NIR}} \text{ (years)}$$

For example, Ethiopia, with a population of 113.7 million in 2023, had a birth rate of 30.49‰ and a death rate of 5.70‰, giving it a natural increase rate of 24.79‰ or 2.48%. Ethiopia's doubling time can be worked out using 70/2.49 (years) = 28.1 years. This means that by 2051, the population of Ethiopia would be 227.4 million if the rate of natural increase stays the same.

SKILLS

Work out natural increase rates from given data

Complete Table 8.7 to work out natural increase and projected population size for different countries.

Table 8.7 Natural increases and projected population sizes.

	Afghanistan	China	Malaysia	Mexico	Niger	South Africa	USA
CBR (‰)	35.46	9.93	14.55	13.55	47.08	18.56	12.28
CDR (‰)	12.33	7.90	5.69	7.71	9.87	9.26	8.38
NIR (‰)							
Doubling time (years)							
Year by which the 2023 population will have doubled							
Population in 2023 (millions)	38.3	1410	33.8	129.1	24.5	57.5	337.3
Population if it doubles (million)							

2.1 Individuals, populations, communities and ecosystems

8.1.4 Global human population has followed a rapid growth curve

Human population has grown rapidly over the last 300 years and most of this growth has happened relatively recently. The world's population doubled from 1 billion to 2 billion between 1804 and 1922, and then doubled again to 4 billion between 1922 and 1974. It is projected to double yet again to 8 billion by 2028. These numbers show that it is taking less and less time for the population to double, although growth has slowed down since 1999. Up to 95% of population growth is taking place in LICs and MICs. However, the world's population is expected to stabilize at about 8.5 billion following a peak at 11 billion (Figure 8.7)

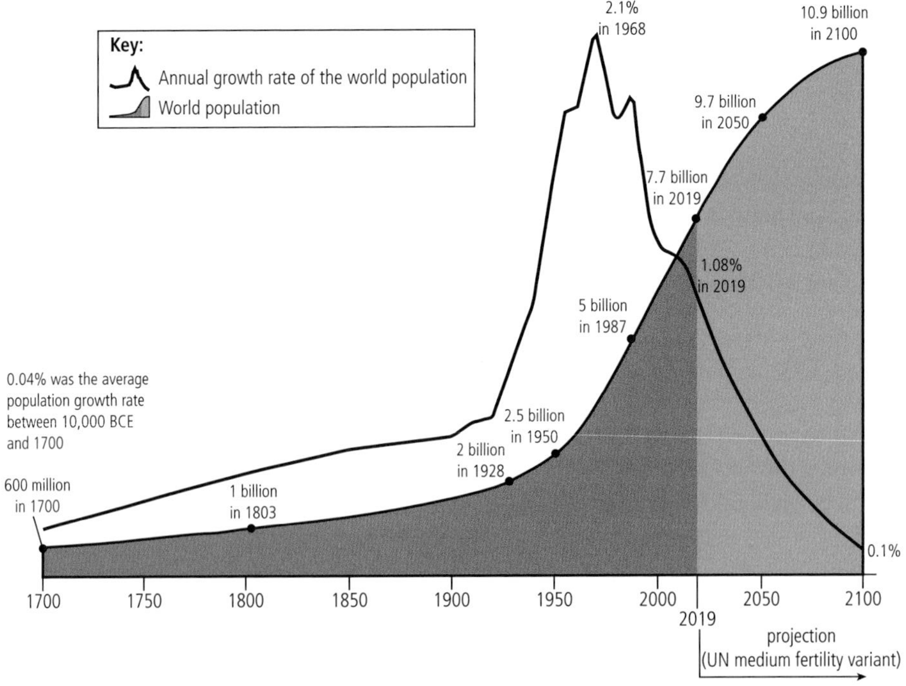

Figure 8.7 World population growth, 1700–2100.

In 1990, the world's women were, on average, giving birth to 3.3 children over their lifetime. By 2002, the number had dropped to 2.6 children and by 2020 it was 2.42 – slightly above the level needed to ensure replacement of the population. If these trends continue, the level of fertility for the world as a whole will drop below replacement levels before 2050. The projections also suggest that AIDS, which has killed more than 40 million people over the past 40 years, has lowered the average life expectancy at birth in some countries. AIDS continues to have its greatest impact in the developing countries of Asia, Latin America and, especially, sub-Saharan Africa. Botswana and South Africa are among the countries that may see population decline because of deaths related to AIDS. Global deaths from COVID-19 are estimated to be about 7 million. Figure 8.7 shows that global population growth is beginning to slow down.

For the population of a country to remain at the same level over time, the total fertility rate needs to be 2.1. This means that, on average, every woman needs to have 2.1 children over her reproductive lifetime. This is known as the replacement level and considers the number of children that will die and/or will not have children themselves.

Long-range population projection models are highly uncertain, especially for high-fertility countries. Figure 8.8 was produced by the United Nations, Institute of Health Metrics and Evaluation and Joint Research Center of the European Commission and shows the comparisons of long-term global population projections between 2022 and 2100 resulting from various scenarios. The figure shows that there is a probability of 95% that the size of the global population will lie between 9.4 and 10.0 billion in 2050 and between 8.9 and 12.4 billion in 2100 (Figure 8.8). Thus, the size of the world's population is almost certain to rise over the next several decades, as is the degree of uncertainty associated with these projections. Increasing uncertainty about dates farther into the future is reflected in a widening band of prediction intervals for projections of the number of births and of the total population size.

The UN population projection models up to 2100 vary by about 7 billion, from a high of *c.* 14 billion to a low of *c.* 7 billion, with a medium projection of *c.* 10 billion.

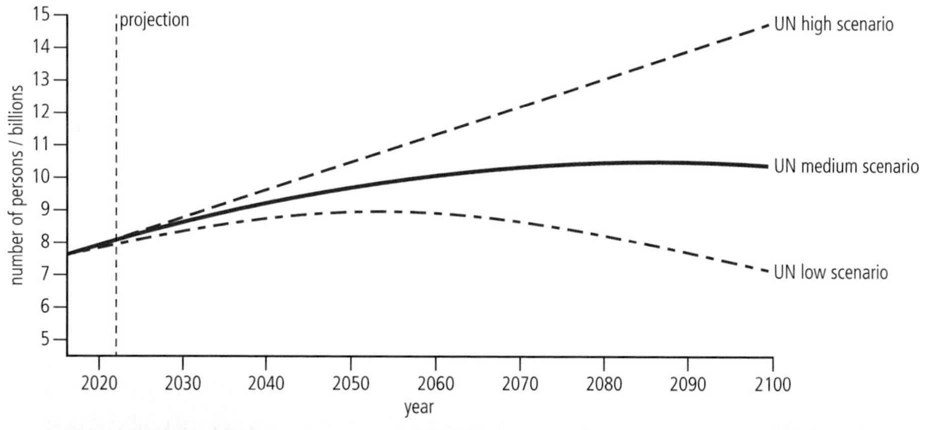

Figure 8.8 Comparisons of long-term global population projections under various scenarios.

8.1.5 Policies can be employed to directly manage growth rates of human populations

1.3 Sustainability

HL a Environmental law
HL b Environmental economics
HL c Environmental ethics

Population and migration policies can be used to directly manage human population growth rates. These may be anti-natalist or pro-natalist, directly addressing birth rates, or they may address immigration and/or emigration. They may use a variety of cultural, religious, economic, social and political factors to achieve their aims. Population and migration policies may be necessary for reasons such as growing the size of the labour force or reducing population growth.

National population policies

Population policies refer to official government actions that can be used to control the population in some way. Pro-natalist policies act in favour of increasing the birth rate. Anti-natalist policies attempt to limit the birth rate.

Example – Russia's pro-natalist policy

Russia has had low fertility for many decades. The reasons include an ageing population structure, women choosing to have fewer children, problems with reproductive healthcare services, high divorce rates and infertility.

The Soviet Union and the Russian Federation have a long history of pro-natalist policies. This started in 1936, when families were rewarded for having a third or fourth child and then later rewarded for having a second child. The government also imposed a tax on childless people between 1941 and 1990.

In the 1970s, fertility rates were slightly below the replacement level, which led to renewed pro-natalist policies in 1981. However, analysis of the 1981 policy suggests that it reduced the childbearing age rather than increasing the number of children born.

By 2006, fertility had dropped to less than 1.3 births per woman. President Putin announced further measures to increase the birth rate, including:

- an increase in pregnancy, birth and child benefits based on the number of children a family had
- increased parental leave following the birth of a child
- increased payments to mothers of second and third children (increased to US$ 12,500 in 2012).

The Russian government also considered introducing another tax on childlessness.

As a result, between 2006 and 2011, fertility increased by 21%. Births of second and third children increased by 40% and 60%, respectively. However, these values increased from what was a very low starting point and proved less successful than the 1981 reforms. Further analysis of the results suggests that the effects of the policies wore off year by year. After five years of the policy, women's intentions to have another child had hardly changed. As they had under the 1981 policy, families had children earlier but did not have significantly more.

In May 2012, President Putin announced that he wanted Russia to have a TFR of 1.75 by 2018. In 2022, Russia's TFR was 1.6. Demographers believe that Russia will have to double the state's financial support if the TFR is to be improved further. Others believe that Russia will need to increase the immigrant population if it is to increase the fertility rate, but many Russians are strongly opposed to immigration.

Russia's population decline is therefore likely to continue. Their TFR is likely to remain lower than the replacement level (2.1) for the next 20 years. As the population continues to age, the number of people entering childbearing age is likely to be 20% less than those currently at childbearing age.

On what grounds might an individual believe that they know what is right for others?

To what extent should national governments be allowed to manage population growth rather than the population managing it themselves?

It is possible that Russia's population in 2100 will be similar to that of 1950 and will be around 100 million. As the population ages, the workforce is predicted to decline by about 15% by 2024. This could be reduced by increasing the retirement age. In 2020, Putin announced a series of plans to increase average fertility to 1.7 by 2024. He promised larger tax breaks for bigger families. The 'maternity capital' had previously only been paid to families with at least two children. However, it is unlikely to have much impact because the pattern of falling fertility is happening in all industrialized nations, including wealthier ones.

Political factors and family planning

Most governments in LICs and MICs, such as the Gambia, have introduced some programmes aimed at reducing birth rates. The effectiveness of these programmes is dependent on:

- a focus on general family planning not specifically birth control
- investing sufficient finance in the schemes
- working in consultation with the local population.

Where birth controls have been imposed by government, they are less successful. In the HICs, financial and social support for children is often available to encourage a pro-natalist approach. However, in countries where there are fears of negative population growth, more active and direct measures are being taken by the government to increase birth rates.

Migration policies to manage the growth of population

Since it is not easy to manage populations using pro/anti-natalist policies, migration policies can also be used. The number of international migrants – people living in countries other than where they were born – was almost 260 million in 2017. This was an increase of 85 million, or 49%, compared to 2000. Economic and social factors such as the search for employment, better pay, better healthcare and education facilities, are the main reasons for people to migrate but political instability and conflict are becoming increasingly important.

Make sure you know about pro-natalist and anti-natalist population policies.

According to the UN SDGs (Topic 1, Section 1.3.18), Target 10.7 calls on countries to facilitate orderly, safe, regular and responsible migration and mobility of people through planned and well-managed migration policies. According to the UN, when supported by appropriate policies, migration can contribute to inclusive and sustainable economic growth and development. The overall impact of migration is positive for both the country of origin and the country of destination. As migrants tend to be of working age, they can reduce the level of old-age dependency in host countries. Globally, most countries seek to maintain current levels of migration. Europe has the highest proportion of countries seeking to raise immigration levels at 32%, followed by Asia at 10%. In contrast, Asia also has the highest proportion of countries trying to reduce levels of immigration at 23%, followed by Africa at 13%. Globally, over two-thirds of governments state that meeting labour demands in certain sectors is the main reason for their migration policy (Figure 8.9).

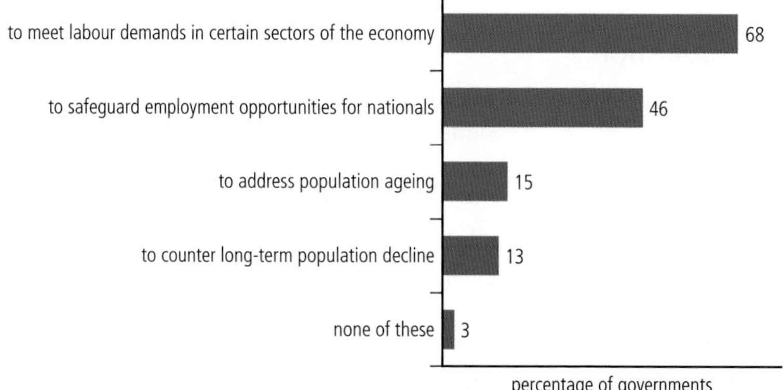

Figure 8.9 The advantages to host countries of having migrant workers.

Some countries, such as the UAE and Saudi Arabia, rely heavily on migrant workers who often work in sectors such as farm labour, which are unappealing to many of the host country's residents.

Many migrants send remittances (part of, very often most of, their earnings) back home to their family. As shown in Table 8.8, for some countries these remittances form a major part of their GDP.

Table 8.8 Countries with the highest share of remittances as a percentage of GDP.

Rank	Country	Remittances as a percentage of GDP (%)
1	Nepal	31.2
2	Kyrgyzstan	30.4
3	Haiti	29.4
4	Tajikistan	26.9
5	Liberia	26.1
6	Moldova	21.7
7	Gambia	21.5
8	Comoros	21.2
9	Tonga	20.3
10	Honduras	18.0

1.1 Perspectives
1.2 Systems
1.3 Sustainability

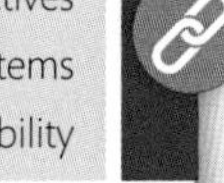

8.1.6 Human population growth can also be managed indirectly

HL a Environmental law
HL b Environmental economics
HL c Environmental ethics

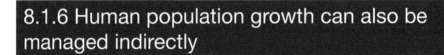

Human population growth can also be managed indirectly through economic, social, health, development and other policies. Many development policies address gender equality, education, improvements in public health and welfare, and will indirectly affect births, deaths and migration.

Gender equality

Gender equality has a significant impact on reducing the birth and fertility rates. In countries where women play an important role in the workforce, fertility rates are low. This is also true at a state level. For example, in India, the state of Kerala has the highest levels of gender equality in the country and its fertility rates are among the lowest in India. By contrast, in countries where there are fewer women in the workforce, fertility rates remain high. Where women have choice over the number of children they have, birth rates tend to be lower.

Level of education

In societies where girls have equality in education, for example Norway, Sweden and Germany, fertility rates are low. In contrast, in countries where girls do not have the same access to education, for example Afghanistan, fertility rates remain high. In general, the higher the level of parental education, the fewer the children. Poor people with limited resources often have large families. Affluent people can afford large families but often choose not to. Middle-income families with high aspirations but limited means tend to have the smallest families. They wish to improve their standard of living and limit their family size to achieve this. In addition, people with higher education qualifications often have better paid jobs and may choose a more materialistic lifestyle rather than having large families.

The correlation between economic prosperity and birth rate is not complete, but there are links. As gross national product (GNP) per capita increases, the birth rate tends to decrease (Figure 8.10).

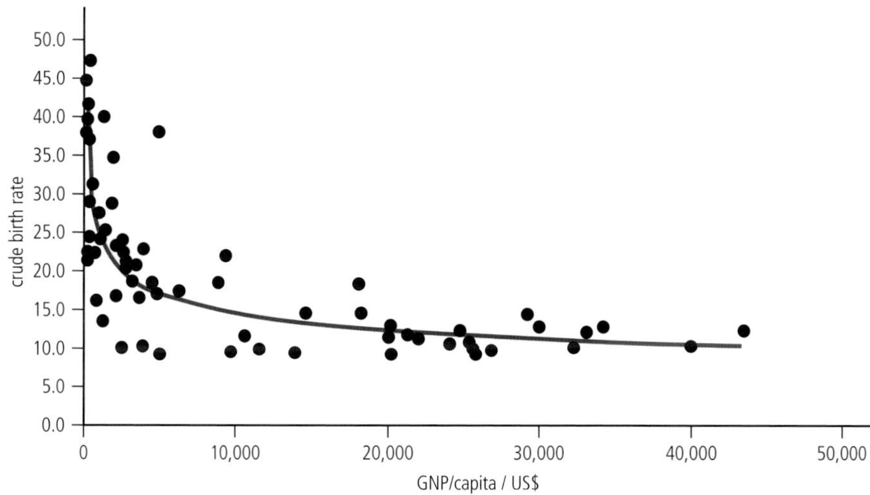

Figure 8.10 GNP per capita and crude birth rate.

Economic factors

Economic prosperity favours an increase in the birth rate, while increasing costs lead to a decline in the birth rate. Recession and unemployment are also linked with a decline in the birth rate as it is related to the cost of bringing up children. Surveys have shown that the cost of bringing up children in the USA can be over US$ 240,000, partly through lost earnings on the mother's part. Some governments, e.g. France and Russia, offer payments to families to support their children. Whether the cost is real or perceived (imagined) does not matter. If parents believe they cannot afford to bring up children, or that having more children will reduce their standard of living, they are less likely to have children. On a global scale, a strong link exists between fertility and the level of economic development. The UN and many NGOs believe that a reduction in the high birth rates in LICs and MICs can only be achieved by improving the standard of living in those countries.

Social factors – the need for children

In some agricultural societies, parents have larger families to provide labour for the farm and as security for the parents in old age. It is much less important in MICs as fewer families are engaged in farming although many adults look after their elderly parents. Urbanization also has a major impact on the birth rate. In 1960, one-third of the world's population lived in urban areas, now the figure has reached over 50%. Whereas many children on a farm may be a benefit by providing more hands to do the work, in urban areas, many children mean many mouths to feed. In urban areas, women are more likely to have an education, a career and greater access to contraceptives, resulting in lower births rates. In very poor countries, high infant mortality rates may increase the pressure on women to have more children. Such births offset the high mortality losses and are termed replacement births or compensatory births.

The impact of disease

As countries develop, there is a decreasing risk of death from infectious diseases, such as measles, cholera and tuberculosis. This is largely due to improvements in public health and welfare, such as greater access to clean water and sanitation, better quality housing and improvements in diet. However, as risk of death from infectious disease decreases, the risk of death from non-communicable diseases e.g. heart disease, cancer and strokes, increases. This is because, in part, people are not dying from contagious, infectious diseases but are living longer and contracting degenerative (non-communicable) diseases.

In many countries, COVID-19 has reduced population growth by causing a decline in the birth rate and migration rates. Most children that are born are planned, especially in HICs. Deciding to have a child depends on being optimistic about the future. Optimism was difficult to find during the COVID-19 pandemic. The Brookings Institute estimate that in the USA there were 300,000 fewer babies born during the COVID-19 pandemic as a result of economic insecurity. Migration rates were also affected by the pandemic. In 2020, Australia experienced its first population decline since the First World War, due to stricter COVID-border controls. In 2020, Canada granted permanent resident status to 180,000 people compared with its target of 381,000. In the USA, the death toll from COVID-19 led to a reduction of life-expectancy by two years for African Americans and three years for Latin Americans. Moreover, the global number of deaths due to the COVID-19 pandemic was estimated at 6–7 million people in February 2024, although the data may be inaccurate due to the accuracy of reporting.

1.2 Systems

8.1.7 The composition of human populations can be modelled and compared using age–sex pyramids

Age–sex pyramids

Population structure or composition refers to any measurable characteristic of the population. It includes the age, sex, ethnicity, language, religion and occupation of the population. These are usually shown by age–sex (or population) pyramids. The shape of an age–sex pyramid can provide a great deal of information about the age and sex structure of a population (Figure 8.11). For example:

Age–sex pyramids are measured in absolute numbers or as a percentage of the total population and show the proportion of the population of either sex in each age group.

- a wide base indicates a high birth rate (Figure 8.11b, 2000)
- a narrowing base (i.e. where the number or proportion of 0–4 year olds is less than the number or proportion of 5–9 year-olds) suggests falling birth rate (Figure 8.11a and b, 2025)
- straight or near vertical sides indicate a low death rate (Figure 8.11a, 2025)
- concave slopes characterize a high death rate (Figure 8.11b, 2000)
- 'bulges' in the slope suggest baby booms or high rates of immigration or in-migration (e.g. a high number of males aged 20–35 years will be economic migrants looking for work, a high number of elderly, usually female, will inundate retirement resorts)
- 'slices' in the slope indicate emigration or out-migration or age-specific or gender-specific deaths during epidemics or times of conflict
- the total population or percentage of the total population in each age-group (cohort) is shown at the side of each bar.

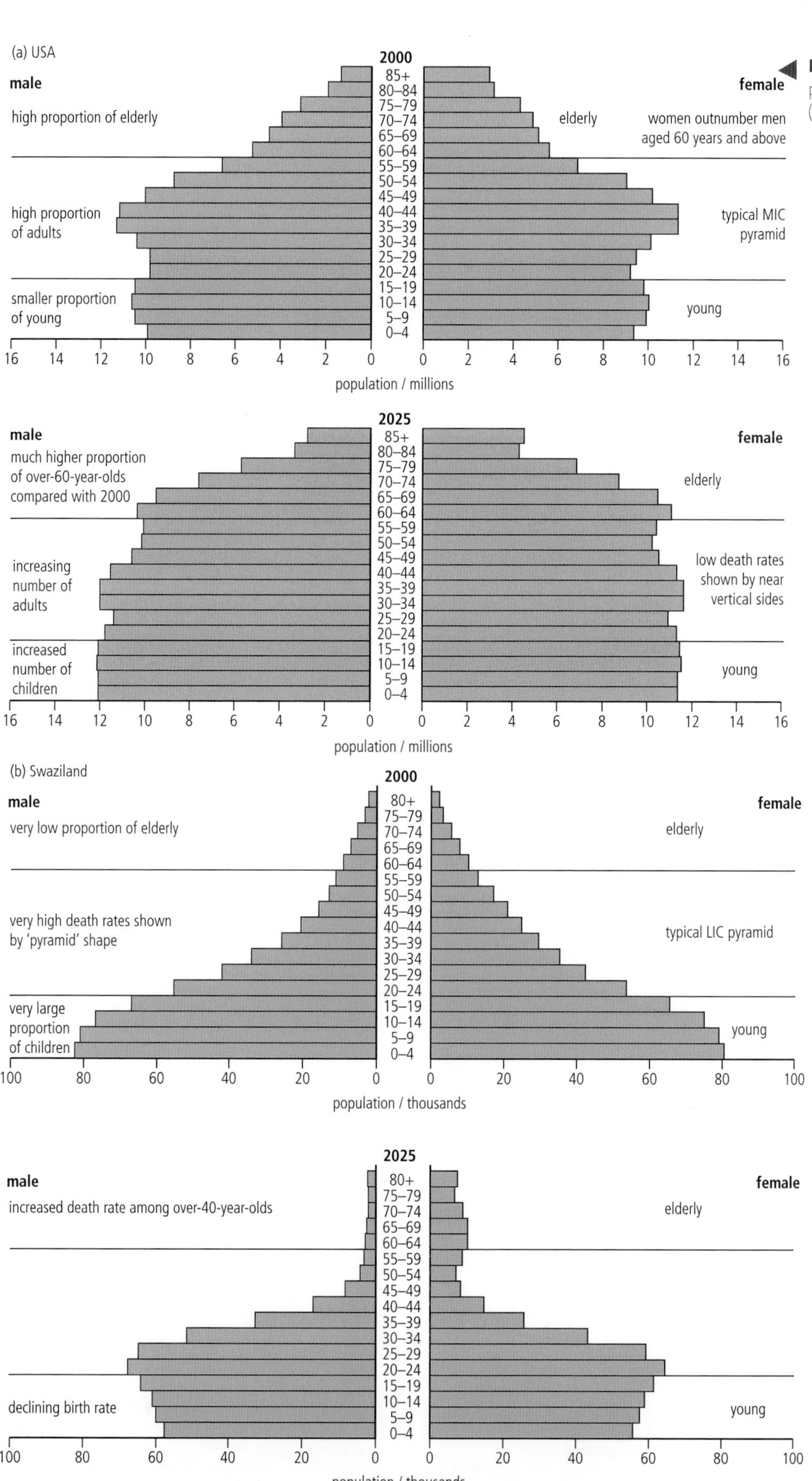
(a) USA
2000
male
female
high proportion of elderly
elderly
women outnumber men aged 60 years and above
high proportion of adults
typical MIC pyramid
smaller proportion of young
young
85+
80–84
75–79
70–74
65–69
60–64
55–59
50–54
45–49
40–44
35–39
30–34
25–29
20–24
15–19
10–14
5–9
0–4
16 14 12 10 8 6 4 2 0
0 2 4 6 8 10 12 14 16
population / millions
2025
male
female
much higher proportion of over-60-year-olds compared with 2000
elderly
increasing number of adults
low death rates shown by near vertical sides
increased number of children
young
population / millions
(b) Swaziland
2000
male
female
very low proportion of elderly
elderly
very high death rates shown by 'pyramid' shape
typical LIC pyramid
very large proportion of children
young
80+
100 80 60 40 20 0
0 20 40 60 80 100
population / thousands
2025
male
female
increased death rate among over-40-year-olds
elderly
declining birth rate
young
population / thousands

Figure 8.11 Age-sex pyramids for (a) the USA and (b) Swaziland, 2000 and 2025.

1.2 Systems

8.1.8 The Demographic Transition Model (DTM)

The general demographic transition model (DTM) shows the change in population structure from high birth rates and death rates to low birth rates and death rates. This change largely occurs as a country changes from being a LIC to becoming a HIC (Figure 8.12). The DTM suggests that death rates fall before birth rates and that the total population expands. There are five stages of the DTM showing exponential increase, stabilization and possible decline in population.

Age-sex pyramids and the demographic transition model (DTM) can be useful in the prediction of human population growth. The DTM shows how a population transitions from a pre-industrial stage with high CBR and CDR to an economically advanced stage with low or declining CBR and low CDR.

Figure 8.12 The general demographic transition model.

Stage 1
High and variable:
- birth rates and death rates are high and variable
- population growth fluctuates
- no countries, only some indigenous (primitive) tribes still at this stage
- UK at this stage until about 1750

High birth and death rates
Parents want children:
- for labour
- to look after them in old age
- to continue the family name
- prestige
- to replace other children who have died

People die from:
- lack of clean water
- lack of food
- poor hygiene and sanitation
- overcrowding
- contagious diseases
- poverty

Stage 2
Early expanding:
- birth rate remains high but the death rate comes down rapidly
- population growth is rapid
- Afghanistan and Sudan are at this stage
- UK passed through this stage by 1850

Stage 3
Late expanding:
- birth rate drops and the death rate remains low
- population growth continues but at a smaller rate
- Brazil and Argentina are at this stage
- UK passed through this stage in about 1950

Stage 4
Low and variable:
- birth rates and death rates are low and variable
- population growth fluctuates
- UK and most developed countries are at this stage

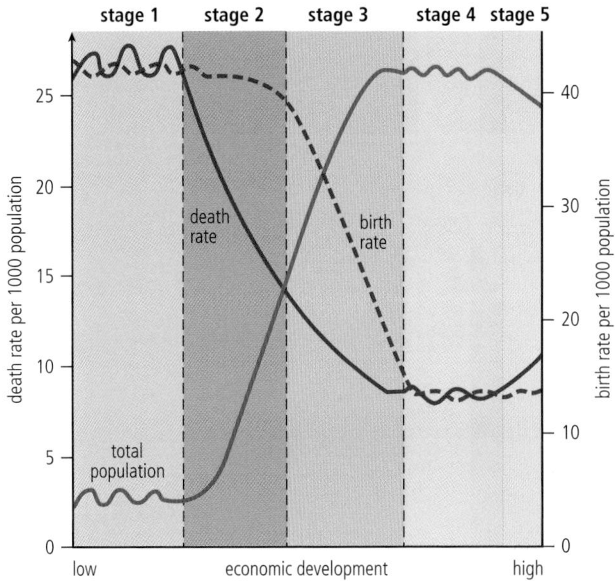

Stage 5
Low declining:
- the birth rate is lower than the death rate
- the population declines
- Japan and Sweden are in this stage

Low birth and death rates
Birth rates decline because:
- children are very costly
- the government looks after people through pensions and health services
- more women want their own career
- there is more widespread use of family planning
- as the infant mortality rate comes down there is less need for replacement children

Death rates decline because:
- clean water
- reliable food supply
- good hygiene and sanitation
- lower population densities
- better vacations and healthcare
- rising standards of living

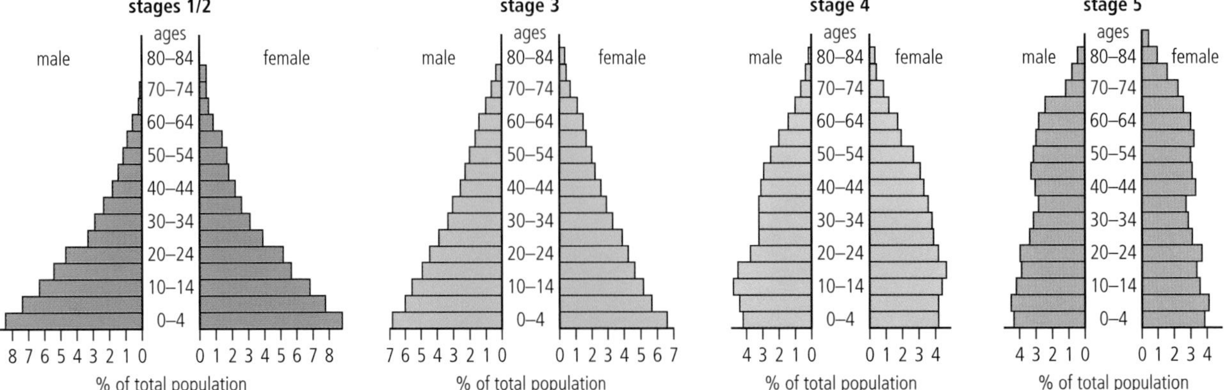

However, the DTM is based on the data from just three countries – England, Wales and Sweden – because the timescale for the DTM in these countries is longer than that of many LICs.

Stage 1	Birth rates and death rates are high and variable, so population growth fluctuates. There are no countries at this stage, but some populations of Indigenous peoples are.
Stage 2	The population is increasing. Birth rates remain high, but the death rates fall, and population growth is rapid. Some countries such as Benin, Niger and Afghanistan are in the later part of stage 2.
Stage 3	The population is still increasing. Birth rates and death rates are both low. Many LICs are in this stage.
Stage 4	Birth rates and death rates are low and variable. Population growth fluctuates. Most HICs, including Australia and the USA, are in this stage.
Stage 5	Some countries have moved into stage 5. This occurs when the death rate is higher than the birth rate, due to an ageing population. Total population begins to decline. Japan and Sweden are in stage 5.

The reasons why people may have children can vary and include:

- for labour
- so the children can look after them in old age
- high child mortality rates
- social pressures to have children
- religious reasons (pro-large families).

There are many reasons for low birth rates including:

- raising children is very costly
- some governments look after the elderly through pensions and health services
- more women want their own career
- greater use of family planning
- as infant mortality rate decreases there is less need for replacement children.

High death rates can be caused by:

- a lack of clean water
- poor diet in terms of quantity and/or quality
- poor hygiene and sanitation
- overcrowding
- infectious disease
- poverty.

The reasons why death rates may decrease include:

- availability of clean and safe water
- reliable food supplies
- good hygiene and sanitation
- better vaccinations and healthcare
- improvement in living standards.

TOK

To what extent are the methods used to gain knowledge in the human sciences 'scientific'?

Statistics are used to study population dynamics, indicating a scientific basis for demographic studies. A variety of models and indicators are employed to quantify human population dynamics - can these methods be termed 'scientific'? Is it true to say that there is a single 'scientific method'?

There are other types of DTM. For example, Ireland's DTM was based on falling birth rates and rising death rates as a result of emigration following the 1845–49 famine. The DTM in Japan shows a period of population expansion before the Second World War, followed by population contraction once the country's expansionist plans could not be fulfilled. Other nations, for example France, have experienced a similar drop in birth rates and death rates.

HL

HL

8.1.9 Rapid human population growth has increased stress on the Earth's systems

1.2 Systems
1.3 Sustainability

The increased stress on Earth's systems from rapid human population growth is related to biocapacity disparity and to the crossing of social foundation and planetary boundaries in the doughnut economy model (Topic 1, Sections 1.3.19 and 1.3.20).

The drivers of population growth include changes in fertility, mortality and migration. The global human population reached 8 billion in 2022 and the UN predicts that it will level out by 2100 at between 10 and 11 billion (see Figure 8.8 on page 723). However, the population may not rise that high since fertility decreases as education and level of wealth increase. Decreased fertility rate may also occur due to other improvements brought about, in part, by the UN SDGs, e.g. better access to clean water and improvements in food production (because the need for replacement children to replace those expected to die decreases). Some organizations believe that peak global population may occur by 2060. For example, The Lancet[1] believes that peak population will occur around 2065 at 9.7 billion. Many people believe that most of the growth will take place in Africa (Table 8.9). In 1992, the UN produced a long-range world population projection, which stated that the high estimate was 23 billion, the medium estimate 11 billion and the low estimate just 5 billion! This is very different from current predictions and suggests that fertility would remain very high in LICs. As a result of falling fertility, the numbers predicted in current population projection models are much lower than they were in 1992. It is clear that the further into the future the projections are made, the less precise they become.

Table 8.9 UN 2019 World Population Prospects – median scenario.

	World population in 2000 (billions)	World population in 2050 (billions)	Growth (%)	% change/year
Asia	3.74	5.29	+ 41	+ 0.7
Africa	0.81	2.49	+ 207	+ 2.3
Europe	0.73	0.71	– 3	– 0.1
South/Central America and Caribbean	0.52	0.76	+ 46	+ 0.8
North America	0.31	0.43	+ 39	+ 0.7
Oceania	0.03	0.06	+ 100	+ 1.4
World	6.14	9.74	+ 60	+ 0.9

Population growth, and the increase in the number of middle-income households, along with high-income households, is putting great pressure on many environmental systems (see Topic 1, Section 1.3.20). Rapid population growth places great stress on the Earth's systems. Increasing affluence intensifies these stresses. For example, there

[1]https://www.healthdata.org/news-events/newsroom/news-releases/lancet-world-population-likely-shrink-after-mid-century

is increased demand for freshwater and for meat and dairy products, which use more land than arable farming. Resources, such as fossil fuels, are used in great quantities. Forests arc cut down for timber, fuel and to make way for farming. In addition, human activity pollutes many environments.

Biocapacity or biological capacity refers to the goods and services that an ecosystem (or the Earth) provides. It includes goods such as food, water and timber, as well as services such as climate-regulation and flood control. An increase in population leads to a decrease in biocapacity (Topic 1, Section 1.3.19).

8.1.10 Age–sex pyramids can be used to determine dependency ratios and population momentum

HL

1.2 Systems
1.3 Sustainability

The **dependency ratio** compares the number of dependents, i.e. non-workers, commonly those aged under 15 years and over 64 years, to the economically productive people, aged 15–64 years, in a population.

It is often shown as a formula: $$\frac{\text{Dependent population (\%)}}{\text{Workers (\%)}} \times 100\%$$

Or alternatively:

$$\frac{\text{Young people (\% aged 0–14 years) and Elderly (\% aged 65 years and over)}}{\text{Adults (\% aged 15–64 years)}} \times 100\%$$

The dependency ratio tends to be high in populations with either a very high or a very low fertility rate.

Activity

1. Visit the Population Pyramid website.
2. Use the interactive pyramid to work out :
   (a) the dependency ratio for Japan in 2100.
   (b) the dependency ratio for Japan in 2025.

Population momentum

Population momentum explains why a population will continue to grow even if the fertility rate declines. Population momentum occurs because it is not only the number of children per woman that determine population growth, but also the number of women of reproductive age.

Population momentum occurs if there is a significant bulge in the youthful population yet to enter their reproductive years. For example, during China's one-child policy (1980–2016), China's population continued to grow and is expected to peak in the 2030s, despite decades with a TFR below the replacement level of 2.1. At the start of the one-child policy, one-third of China's population was below the age of 15 years. Negative population momentum occurs when, despite a rise in the TRF, the number of people in reproductive cohorts has shrunk, and so there are fewer people having children. Figure 8.13 shows the age–sex pyramid for Japan in 2021. For Japan (2021) there are relatively few women of reproductive age, so the population momentum is decreasing. In contrast, the age–sex pyramids for Swaziland (Figure 8.11b) show that population momentum will continue to occur for a few years there but will start to decline after 2025.

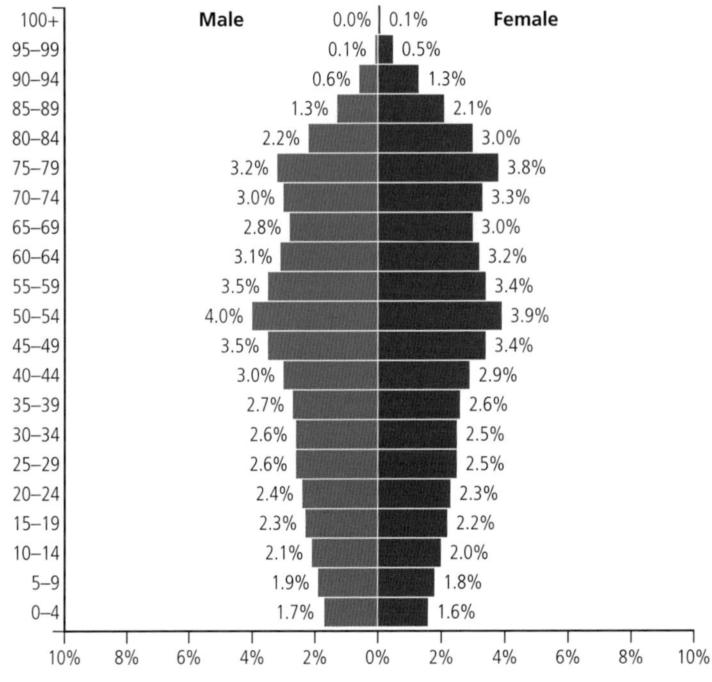

Figure 8.13 Age–sex pyramid for Japan, 2021, when the population was 121,960,407.

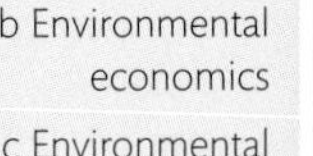

HL

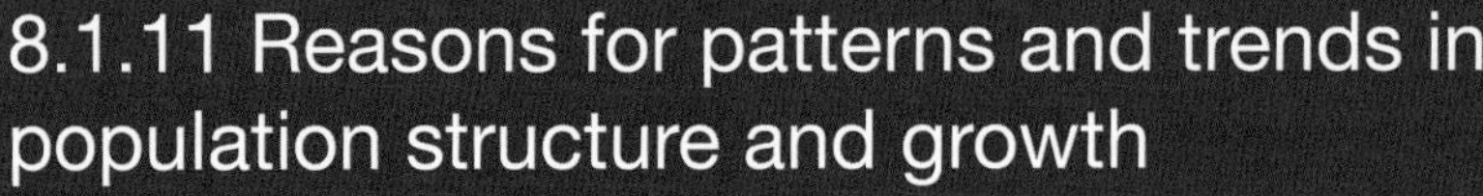

8.1.11 Reasons for patterns and trends in population structure and growth

1.1 Perspectives
1.2 Systems
1.3 Sustainability

HL a Environmental law
HL b Environmental economics
HL c Environmental ethics

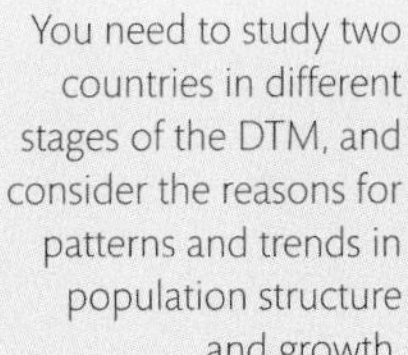

You need to study two countries in different stages of the DTM, and consider the reasons for patterns and trends in population structure and growth.

Different countries have contrasting patterns and trends in population structure and growth for historical, cultural, religious, economic, social and political reasons. For example, Ethiopia and the USA have very different patterns.

Example – Comparing Ethiopia and the USA

Ethiopia and the USA are countries at different stages of the DTM. Ethiopia is in stage 3, having a high CBR (30.5‰) and a low death rate (5.7‰) as shown in Table 8.10. The USA is in stage 4 of the DTM as its CBR and CDR are both quite low (CBR 12.28‰ and CDR 8.38‰). Ethiopia's population has grown from 38 million in 1983 to 113 million in 2023, despite over 1 million people dying in the famine of 1984. Ethiopia's population is predicted to reach 214 million in 2053. In contrast, the population of the USA rose from 233 million in 1983 to 337 million in 2023 and is projected to reach 377 million in 2053.

Table 8.10 Selected population data for Ethiopia and the USA.

	Ethiopia	USA
Population (millions)	113	337
Population growth (%)	2.46	0.69
CBR (‰)	30.5	12.28
CDR (‰)	5.7	8.38
IMR (‰)	33.5	5.17
Life expectancy (years)	68	80
TFR	3.99	1.84
Population with access to contraceptives (%)	38	74
Urban population (%)	23	83
Age-structure (%)		
0–14 years	40	18
15–64 years	57	65
65 and over	3	17
GNP/head (US$)	2300	63,700
Population in employment (%)		
Agriculture/primary industries	72.7	1
Industry	7.4	20
Services	19.9	79

There are many reasons for these differences. First, Ethiopia has a very youthful age-structure (Figure 8.14) as over 40% of the Ethiopian population is under 15 years of age and only about 3% is aged over 64 years. Such a youthful age-structure will help produce a high birth rate.

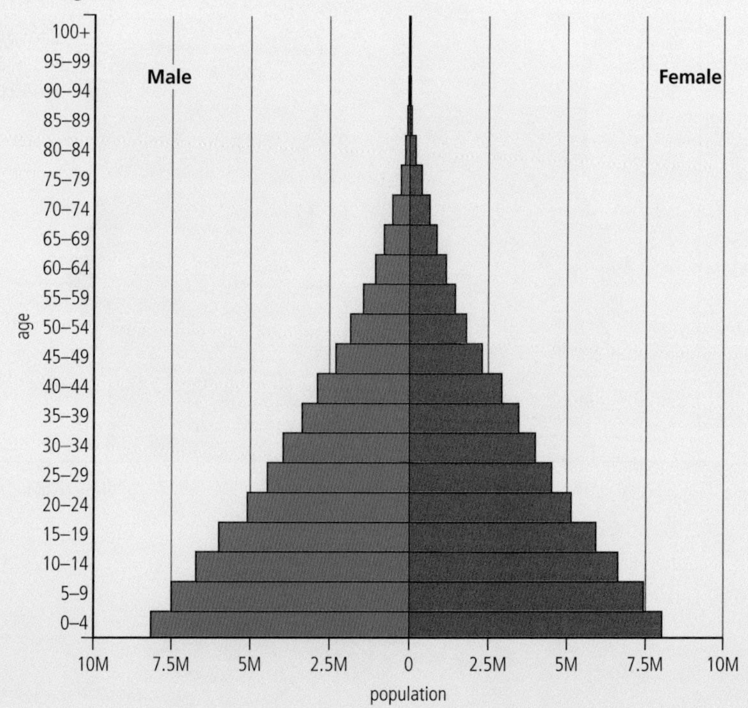

Figure 8.14 Age-sex pyramid for Ethiopia, 2023.

The TFR in Ethiopia is 3.99, which is more than double that the USA's rate of 1.84. In addition, over 70% of Ethiopians are employed in farming. Having children can be a benefit to farmers for the extra labour they provide. Ethiopia also has a relatively high IMR. Some families will decide to have more children to compensate for the high IMR. Most Ethiopians follow one of the three major religions – Ethiopian Orthodox (44%), Muslim (31%) and Protestant (23%). Most religions are in favour of large families (pro-natal), and many are anti-contraception. The contraceptive prevalence rate in Ethiopia is 38%.

In contrast, in the USA, only 14% of its population is under 15 years old, and there is a clear decline in the birth rate. This is shown in Figure 8.15 by the inward-sloping cohorts under the age of 34 years (with the exception of 0–4-year-olds). There are a greater number of elderly people in the USA compared to Ethiopia. In the USA, 17% of the population are aged over 64 years. Only around 1% of the workforce is employed in farming, so there is no need for children to work on farms. In addition, the IMR in the USA is low, so there is no need for compensatory births. In the USA, around 83% of people live in urban areas, compared with just 23% of Ethiopia's population. The main religions in the USA are Protestantism (46%) and Roman Catholic (21%), with 23% of the population not being affiliated to any religion. Contraceptive prevalence in the USA is 74% so is much higher than in Ethiopia. Thus in the USA, there is a smaller reproductive group and greater use of contraceptives (family planning).

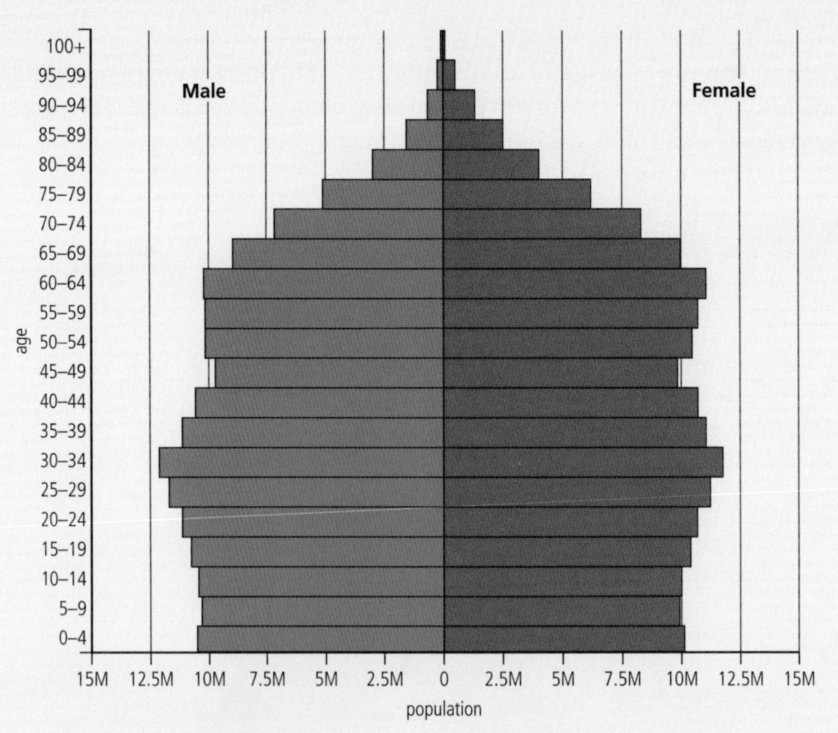

Figure 8.15 Age-sex pyramid for the USA, 2023.

Activity

The CIA World Factbook is an excellent source of data for all countries around the world.

1. Find out about levels of education in Ethiopia and USA and also about access to contraceptives. How might these affect population growth rates in both locations?
2. With a partner, go to the CIA World Factbook website and investigate two contrasting countries in terms of factors that affect population growth.
3. Compute the relative population growth for
   (a) Ethiopia from (i) 1983–2023 and (ii) 2023–53, and for
   (b) the USA from (i) 1983–2023 and (ii) 2023–53.
4. Suggest reasons why the birth rate and fertility rate are higher in Ethiopia than in the USA.

When studying countries in different stages of the DTM, you need to consider the patterns and trends from the past (at least 30 years or more ago), the present, and into the future (at least 30 years). You should also consider reasons (e.g., historical, cultural, religious, economic, social and political factors) for the countries selected.

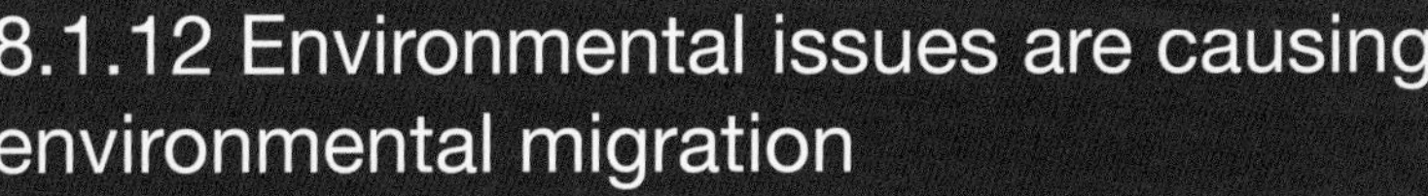

8.1.12 Environmental issues are causing environmental migration

HL

Environmental migration may occur as a result of climate change and sudden onset events such as flooding, droughts, forest fires or intensified storms. However, it is also increasingly occurring as a result of slow onset events such as desertification, sea-level rises and saltwater inundation. An example that demonstrates the occurrence of migration due to an environmental issue is the emigration from Mozambique occurring due to repeated cyclones that have caused local devastation. Another example is the increased migration from Tuvalu to New Zealand due to the impacts of climate change on the islands. See examples below.

1.2 Systems
1.3 Sustainability
6.2 Climate change – causes and impacts

HL a Environmental law
HL c Environmental ethics

Example – Climate change and the impact on Tuvalu and Kiribati

Tuvalu is an island group and Kiribati is an atoll in the South Pacific ocean. Tuvalu and Kiribati are among the countries most at risk from global climate change despite not having contributed much to it. The land in Tuvalu has an average height less than 2 m above sea level. Sea levels are rising at a rate of about 3.9 mm per year around Tuvalu, which is approximately twice the global average, and have risen about 30 cm over the last century. Table 8.11 shows some of the main population characteristics of Tuvalu and Kiribati.

	Tuvalu	Kiribati
Population size	11,639	115,372
Growth rate (%)	0.81	1.02
GDP per person (US$)	4900	1900
Employment structure (%)	Agriculture and fishing 24.5 Industry 5.5 Services (incl. tourism) 70	Agriculture and fishing 23 Industry 7 Services (incl. tourism) 70

Table 8.11 Characteristics of Tuvalu and Kiribati (2023).

As global climate change increases, the number of climate change migrants will increase.

Both countries have limited access to New Zealand for migration, with just 75 spaces available each year. Applicants are selected by ballot (which costs US$ 150 for the first try and US$ 50 for every try thereafter). This, along with the cost of travel to New Zealand and the limited opportunities for low-skilled workers to migrate to Australia and New Zealand, limits the number of emigrants.

Kiribati has relatively low levels of emigration and a very small disparate population in Australia and New Zealand. The migrant population of Kiribati is about 4% of the population compared with 19% in Tuvalu (Figure 8.16).

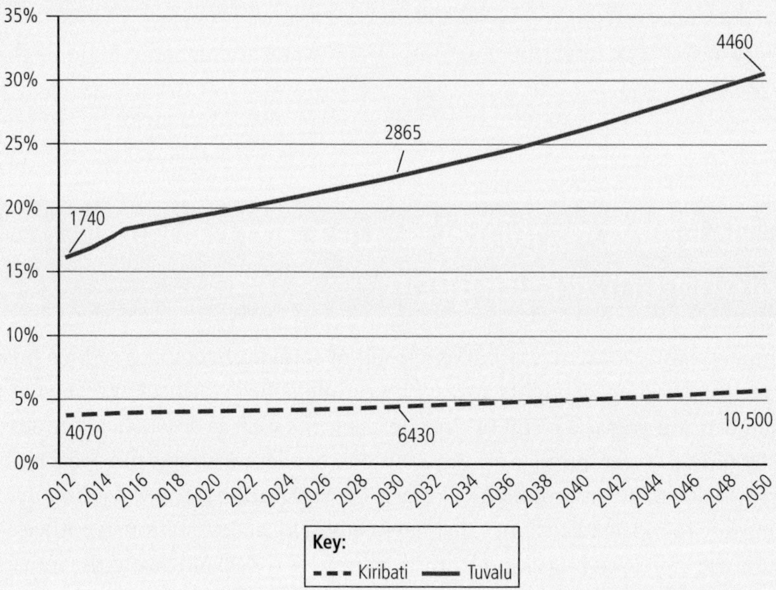

Figure 8.16 Projected migrant population as a percentage of resident population, 2012–50.

Migration strategies are important for dealing with climate change as rising sea levels, coastal flooding and seawater intrusion threaten lives and livelihoods. However, climate change is not the only factors influencing migration from these countries. Increasing population density and the limited amount of arable land are also putting a stress on the ability of the land to support the people. The human-carrying capacity of small islands is estimated to be 100 people/km^2. However, in Tuvalu the population is approximately 367/km^2 and in Kiribati the population is 251/km^2. Population pressure in Kiribati is increasing due to the limited availability of land, as more land is eroded, and saltwater intrusion affects water quality (Figure 8.17). Approximately 15% of Kiribati's population have left over the last decade.

Figure 8.17 Seawater seeps inland in Funafuti atoll, the capital of Tuvalu.

The problems being experienced in the Pacific Islands should act as a warning to the rest of the world – 70% of the world's major cities, including Kolkata, Shanghai, Bangkok and New York, lie within 1 km of the coast and global sea level rise could lead to a huge increase in environmental refugees. According to the Internal Displacement Monitoring Centre (IDMC) more than 250 million people were internally displaced between 2008 and 2019 due to climate disasters worldwide. In 2019, around 24 million people from 140 countries were displaced due to climate disasters.

The 1951 Geneva Convention does not cover climate-induced migrants, only those affected by war. Thus, climate-vulnerable populations cannot easily migrate to overseas countries.

Tropical cyclones are becoming stronger and more frequent. Other problems affecting the water supply in Kiribati include saltwater intrusion, storm surges and drought. Some 70% of households in Kiribati and Tuvalu, along with 35% of households in Nauru, wish to migrate due to global climate change, but only 25% can afford to do so. Between 2005 and 2015, 10% of Nauru's population and 15% of Tuvalu's population emigrated. By 2055, it is predicted that international migration from Kiribati will increase by 35% and from Tuvalu by 100%. To make migration easier, the UN has suggested that training people to become nurses, teachers and police will improve the chances of gaining employment.

Example – Repeated cyclones in Mozambique

In March 2019, Cyclone Idai devasted large parts of central Mozambique. Some 3 million people were affected and 200,000 people were displaced. Around 1 million ha of crops were destroyed. Idai was the second deadliest cyclone in the Southern Hemisphere. It may have killed more than 1000 people and caused damages that cost in excess of US$ 2 billion. It also produced a storm surge of over 4 m in height that completely or partially destroyed up to 80% of areas in Macomia, Mozambique.

Just five weeks later, Cyclone Kenneth hit northern Mozambique and affected a further 300,000 people. Over 30,000 homes and thousands of ha of crops were destroyed. A further 20,000 people were displaced. Cyclone Kenneth was classified as a Category 4 tropical cyclone. It struck at the peak of the harvest season, causing a potential 6-month period with limited food supplies.

This was the first time that two major tropical cyclones had hit Mozambique in the same year. The impacts were especially severe in the remote areas of central Mozambique and in the north of the country. Overall, between 5 and 10% of Mozambique's population was displaced. The majority were unable to return to their lands as the government believed the risk of future cyclones made it unsafe and uninhabitable.

By July 2019, the appeal for aid for Mozambique following Cyclone Idai had reached only 46% of its target and for Cyclone Kenneth only 20% of its target was reached. The 200,000 people displaced were forced to live in tents, while those able to return to their homes found that many of their possessions had been lost and their homes had been partially or totally destroyed.

Use secondary data to test a hypothesis about the relationship between a socio-economic indicator and a demographic factor using a suitable statistical tool

Using the data in Table 8.12, carry out a Spearman's rank correlation test to see whether there is a statistically significant relationship between gross national income (GNI) per person and CBR.

Country	GNI (US$)	CBR (per thousand)
Monaco	115,700	6.61
Austria	54,100	9.39
Kuwait	43,900	17.65
Poland	34,900	8.31
Argentina	21,500	15.38
Gabon	13,800	25.89
Ecuador	10,700	16.19
India	6600	16.53
Senegal	3500	30.84
Niger	1200	46.86

Table 8.12 GNI per person and CBR data for different countries.

There is a resource explaining the different statistical tests and when they are used on this page of your eBook.

Engagement

- In your class, assess and debate issues regarding population change in your local or regional area.
- Investigate the main migration routes that exist into and out of your home country, the threats to migrants using these routes and the solutions involved into making these routes safer (if necessary).
- With the help of your teacher, find out if there is a refugee/immigration centre in your home area and volunteer or raise funds for the centre.
- Find out if there are any local NGOs supporting seasonal or Indigenous communities and volunteer to help them.
- With your teacher, find out how you can help with the work of the United Nations High Commissioner for Refugees (UNHCR).

Exercise

Q1. **Investigate** rates of migration for a country of your choice.

(a) At a national level, do more people enter the country or leave it? Where are they mainly coming from and going to?

(b) At a local level, what type of settlements are migrants moving to and coming from?

Q2. **Describe** the global pattern of birth rates.

Q3. **Suggest** reasons for the high rates of migration to the USA and Saudi Arabia.

Q4. **Calculate** the doubling time of a population that has a natural increase of **(a)** 1% **(b)** 2% **(c)** 3%.

Q5. **Describe** the changes in the annual growth rate of the world's population, 1700-2100.

Q6. **(a)** **Define** the terms *pro-natalist* and *anti-natalist.*

(b) **State** one example of a country with a pro-natalist programme and one with an anti-natalist policy.

Q7. Describe the changes in Russia's population between 1990 and 2020, as shown in the age–sex pyramids in Figures 8.18a and 8.18b.

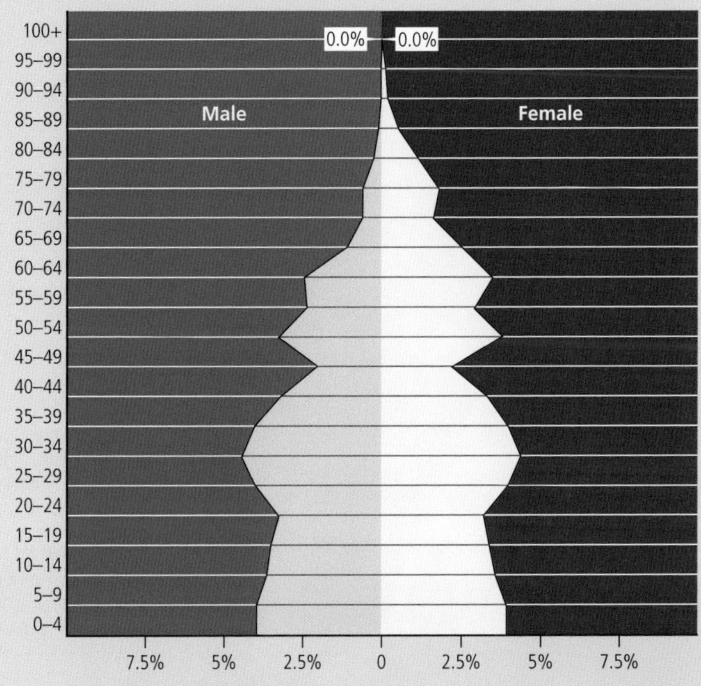

Figure 8.18a Russia's population in 1990 (largest population 147 million).

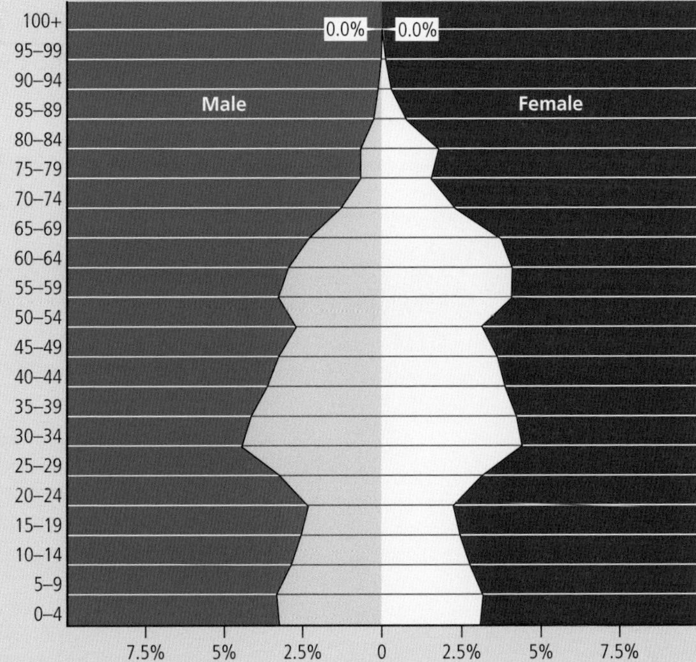

Figure 8.18b Russia's population in 2020 (143 million)

Q8. Describe the global pattern of death rates.

Q9. Describe the main characteristics of the world's age–sex pyramid in 1950 and the projected pyramid for 2100, as shown in Figure 8.19.

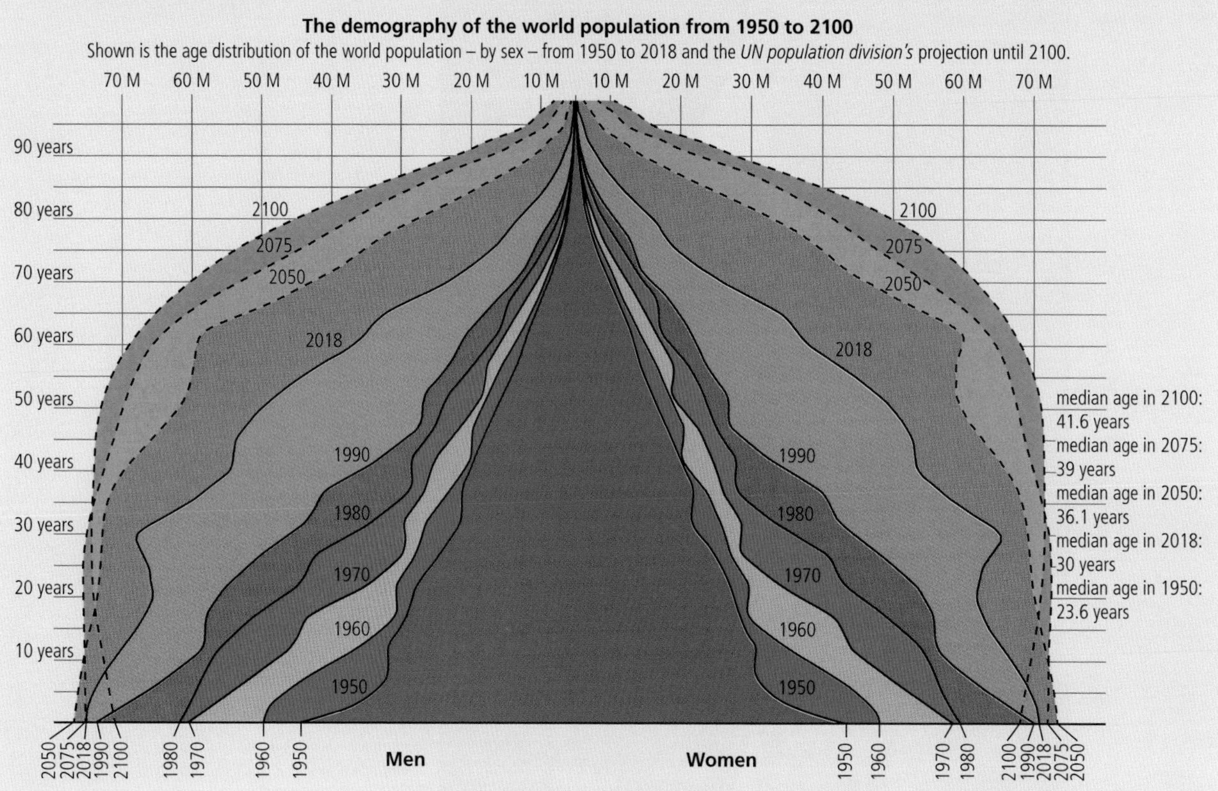

Figure 8.19 The global population pyramid: How global demography has changed and what we can expect for the 21st century - Our World in Data.

Q10. In which stage(s) of the DTM does exponential growth occur?

Describe what happens to the total population in stage 5 of the DTM.

Q11. Explain why population growth decreases in stage 5 of the DTM.

8.2 Urban systems and urban planning

Guiding questions

To what extent are urban systems similar to natural ecosystems?
How can reimagining urban systems create a more sustainable future?

8.2.1 Urban areas contain urban ecosystems.
8.2.2 An urban area is a built-up area with a high population density, buildings and infrastructure.
8.2.3 An urban area works as a system.
8.2.4 Urbanization is the population shift from rural to urban areas.
8.2.5 Due to rural-urban migration, a greater proportion of the human population now live in urban rather than rural systems, and this proportion is increasing.
8.2.6 Suburbanization is due to the movement of people from dense central urban areas to lower-density peripheral areas.
8.2.7 The expansion of urban and suburban systems results in changes to the environment.
8.2.8 Urban planning helps decide on the best way to use land and buildings.
8.2.9 Modern urban planning may involve considering the sustainability of the urban system.
8.2.10 Ecological urban planning is a more holistic approach that treats the urban system as an ecosystem, understanding the complex relationships between its biotic and abiotic components.
HL 8.2.11 Ecological urban planning will follow principles of urban compactness, mixed land use and social mix practice.
HL 8.2.12 Societies are developing systems that address urban sustainability by using models such as a circular economy or doughnut economics to promote sustainability within the urban system.
HL 8.2.13 Green architecture minimizes harmful effects of construction projects on human health and the environment, and aims to safeguard air, water and earth by choosing environmentally friendly building materials and construction practices.

8.2.1 Urban areas contain urban ecosystems

1.2 Systems

Urban ecosystems, like all ecosystems, are composed of biotic components (plants, animals and other forms of life) and abiotic components (soil, water, air, climate and topography).

An ecosystem is a community and the physical environment with which it interacts (Topic 1, Section 1.2.20). Ecosystems are open systems in which energy and matter are exchanged (Topic 2, Section 2.2.1). They contain a variety of habitats to which different species are adapted.

Urban habitats are very diverse, with a large variety of **microhabitats** that include both biotic and abiotic elements. Urban ecosystems vary in terms of size and diversity. There are at least ten types of urban ecosystem:

- residential gardens
- industrial sites
- inner city derelict land
- green areas and open spaces
- cemeteries
- traffic corridors
- waste disposal areas
- forests
- fields
- water bodies.

To what extent do the names and labels that we use help or hinder the acquisition of knowledge?

To what extent are 'waste land' and 'derelict land' misnomers (poor labels)? These areas can become important habitats in urban areas and can have many environmental benefits and provide many environmental goods and services.

Some older cities have well-established ecosystems and habitats and may have similarities with rural ecosystems, whereas other developing cities have rapidly changing ecosystems. In addition, some urban habitats are very unstable owing to severe human impact and disturbance. Most of the plant and animal species in urban areas have been recently introduced. There are relatively few **indigenous** (native) species. Urban areas are attractive for immigrant species on account of the variety of microhabitats, reduced competition and the creation of new habitats. A large proportion of animals are scavengers and opportunistic generalists. Omnivorous, surface feeding, nocturnal and crepuscular (twilight) animals have an advantage over others. Urban species diversity is increased by hybridization and deliberate introductions. Urban areas may also have distinct microclimates.

The city centre

For many organisms, the city centre is a severe and stressful ecosystem because it includes:

- hard and impermeable surfaces
- high steep cliffs such as tower blocks and skyscrapers
- very little soil material
- extreme variations in temperature, shade and shelter.

Open spaces may be very rare, although some city centres, along with other parts of the city, have tree-lined avenues and large parks. Examples include Central Park in New York and La Rambla in Barcelona. However, there are many habitats that are very small. These include roof top gardens, window boxes, trees on pavements and areas where sufficient dust and debris can accumulate to form a soil.

For some species, however, city centres offer an ideal habitat. Species that live on cliffs are ideally suited. Birds such as gulls, pigeons, sparrows and kestrels have expanded their numbers as they have adapted to urban environments. This has often included a change in diet to include garbage, small birds and insects.

Most mammals find it less easy to adapt to urban environments. There are notable exceptions such as rats, mice and grey squirrels. Grey squirrels are mainly found in areas where there are trees, whereas rats and mice can be found in many buildings.

Residential suburbs

There are a variety of planted and managed ecosystems in residential areas. These might include domestic gardens (Figure 8.20), school grounds, allotments, sports fields and cemeteries. The advantages of these ecosystems over those found in the city centre, include:

Figure 8.20 A suburban garden.

- a greater range of habitats
- a larger food supply
- increased plant cover
- greater soil development.

Consequently, there is a larger range of animal life in residential areas. As well as more breeding birds, there are mammals such as foxes, hedgehogs and squirrels.

Waste land

There is a large amount of unused waste land and derelict land in urban areas. The ground in these areas may have:

- important variations in microrelief
- a hard, impermeable surface
- a mixed substrata including building rubble
- increased chemical loads.

These areas are the first to be colonized by plants from the surrounding area. These plants, known as **ruderal** species, are those that can tolerate waste land, rubbish and debris. Plant succession is usually very rapid. Rapidly growing annual plants are replaced by **perennial** grasses. In the UK, over time, this leads to the development of dense thickets of bramble, hawthorn and elder.

Urban areas are a good place to look for evidence of succession (see also Topic 2). Derelict land, abandoned works, railway cuttings, parks and open spaces can be found in many places. If parts become derelict, weeds, such as dandelions, would become common within a year. This would start the process of urban succession. Grass and clover would cover level areas within about five years. Within a decade, soil would build up and deeper-rooted trees and shrubs would take hold. Flooding would become more common as flood control would not be maintained. This would allow marshes and ponds to develop. Within thirty years, birch woodland would fill open spaces between buildings. Animal diversity would increase rapidly. However, some species would not survive. Sewer rats, for example, would not have people to provide for them.

8.2.2 The characteristics of an urban area

No two urban areas are the same. Make sure that you have supporting evidence for the points you make in an answer by referring to a named urban area.

Urban areas are characterized by large densities of buildings (Figure 8.21a) and people, located together for residential, cultural, productive, trade and social purposes. Cities, towns and suburbs are classified as urban areas. Rural areas have low population densities and dispersed settlements. Figures 8.21a–c show parts of central and suburban Seoul in South Korea. Table 8.13 and Figure 8.22 show land use in Seoul.

Figure 8.21a The central part of Seoul, South Korea.

Figure 8.21b Part of Seoul's suburban area – the grounds of the Academy of Korean Studies, Seoul.

Figure 8.21c Candle Fountain at Cheongye Plaza, one of central Seoul's main attractions.

Table 8.13 Land use in Seoul (%).

Urbanized areas	Land use (%)
Residential	18.9
Commercial and business	5.9
Mixed residential and business	13.0
Industrial	5.1
Public facilities	1.2
Transport	10.5
Urban infrastructure	1.1
Derelict	1.8
Total	57.5
Forest and open space	**Land use (%)**
Rivers and lakes	8.1
Forest	31.9
Inaccessible (steep slopes)	2.5
Total	42.5

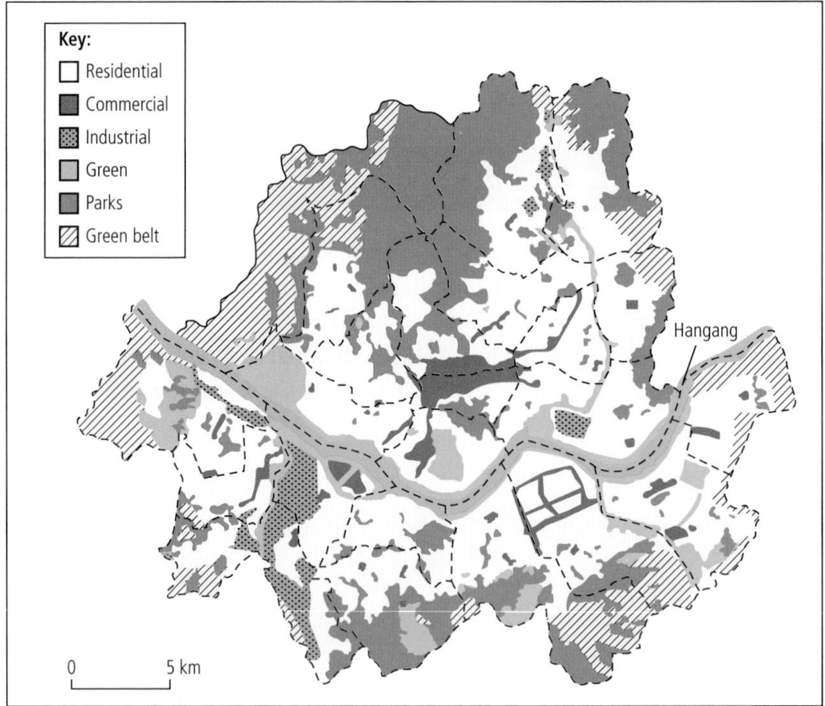

Figure 8.22 Land use in Seoul.

1.2 Systems

8.2.3 An urban area works as a system

An urban system is the interconnected system of buildings, microclimate, transport, goods and services, power/energy, water/sewage supply, humans, plants and animals.

If urban areas are to be successful, they need to provide employment, housing, access to clean water, sanitation, waste disposal, transport facilities and telecommunications networks. Without these, the ability to attract new economic activity is limited. It is important to have green spaces for the wellbeing of people. More recently, it has been recognized that it is important to encourage businesses to make their buildings as environmentally friendly as possible.

For many rapidly growing cities, traffic jams, air pollution, unclean water and inadequate telecommunications reflect a failure to match population growth with infrastructure growth. The Example on Shanghai below examines the growth of population and infrastructure as the city consolidates its position as one of the world's great cities.

A *system* is a simplified way of looking at complex features. Urban areas are complex but we can look at them in terms of inputs (factors that influence their growth), processes (what functions occur in urban areas) and products (what urban areas produce, e.g. energy, work, waste, goods etc).

Example – Shanghai

Shanghai (Figure 8.23) covers an area of over 6300 km². Its population is about 23 million, giving it an average population density of over 3500 people per km². The Shanghai urban system consists of the city itself and its surrounding area (hinterland), which provides many supporting features including labour, goods, capital (money), manufactured goods, services, water supplies and sites for refuse disposal (Figure 8.24).

Figure 8.23 Shanghai skyline.

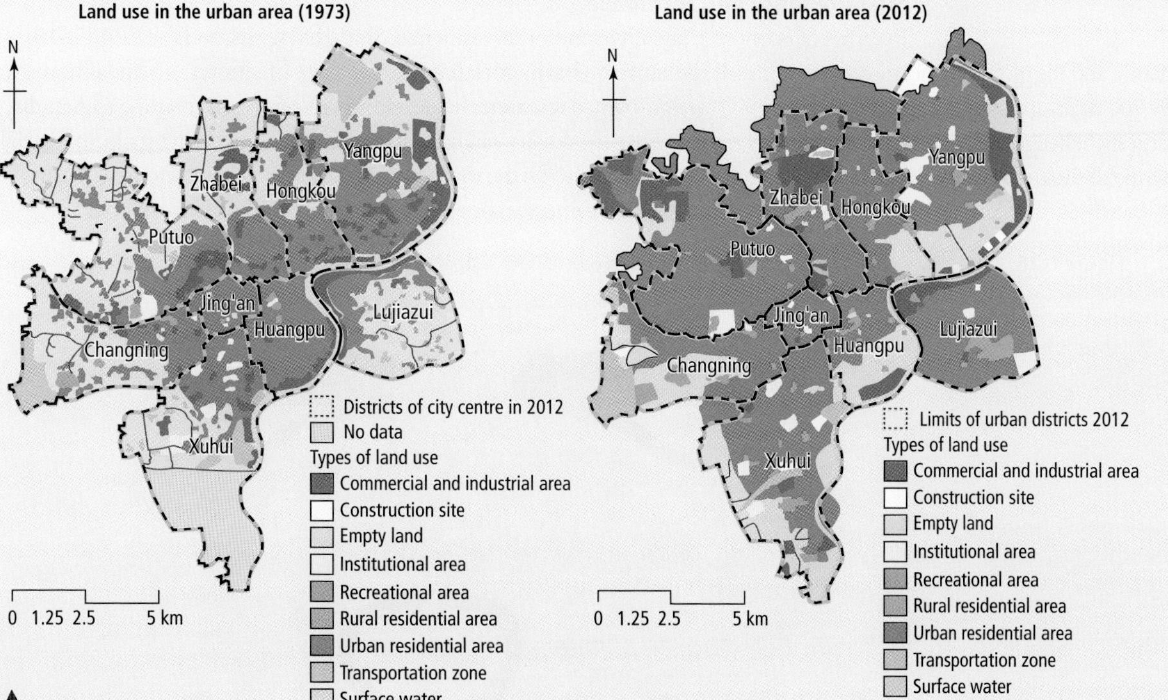

Figure 8.24 Changes in Shanghai, 1973–2012.

Transport

Rail transport is the key feature of Shanghai's public transport. The urban rail network, which is powered by electricity and oil, was developed in less than 20 years. It is over 400 km long and has 13 metro lines, which together carry over 5 million passengers daily. Approximately 25% of the city centre is covered by railway stations, serving 40% of the city centre's population. The Metro began in 1995 and is projected to include 33 lines by 2030. In addition, there are over 1000 bus lines and 17,000 buses. Shanghai has over 12,000 km of roads, including nearly 800 km of expressways. The target for planners has been referred to as '15, 30 and 60', that is, motorists in suburban areas should be able to reach an expressway within 15 minutes, then travel to the city centre in 30 minutes and travel between any two suburban areas in less than 60 minutes.

Water and sanitation

In urban areas throughout China, the proportion of the population with access to piped water rose from 40% in 1990 to nearly 95% in 2007. Nearly 95% of Shanghai's wastewater is treated. Over 70% of households have access to sewerage services. Although water is abundant in Shanghai, there are high levels of water stress due to increasing demand, pollution and saltwater intrusion.

Waste treatment

In the past, most of Shanghai's rubbish ended up in landfill sites or in unregulated heaps on the edge of the city. Increasingly, Shanghai is turning to incineration and generating electricity at 'waste to energy' plants, such as the one at Rat Hangzhou. A waste collection scheme was introduced in 2019 with separate collections for residual, kitchen, recyclable and hazardous waste, to be sent to incineration sites, landfill, recycling centres and areas for hazardous waste disposal.

Figure 8.25 A green wedge in Shanghai.

Environmental protection

Zhangjiabang is the first of Shanghai's 'green wedges' and is the city's largest park (Figure 8.25). The park created woodlands and wetlands that provide a habitat for plants and animals. It also provides beneficial environmental services for people including recreation, walking and positive mental health effects, as well as benefiting Shanghai's urban microclimate through lower temperatures. A series of habitat gardens were also created in the Changning District.

Sustainability and resilience

In terms of economic and environmental resilience, Shanghai withstood the COVID-19 pandemic and the global economic uncertainties. It remains a global financial centre and a city of innovations and is home to nearly 900 multi-national companies and over 500 foreign-owned research and development centres. According to Arcadia, the largest challenge to Shanghai's sustainability is to improve the quality of life for its residents and to clean up old, industrial (brownfield) sites and rivers. Nevertheless, Shanghai is considered to be the most sustainable city in China (Figure 8.26). In 2020, nearly 50% of Shanghai's energy came from renewable energy sources, while over 30% came from coal.

Figure 8.26 A very simplified flow diagram for sustainable cities – the Rogers Model.

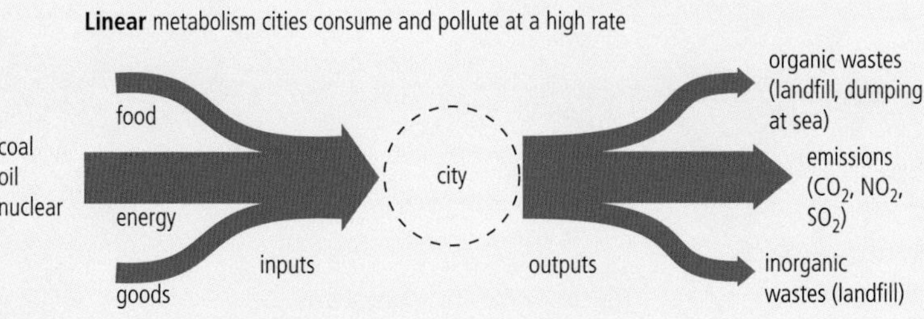

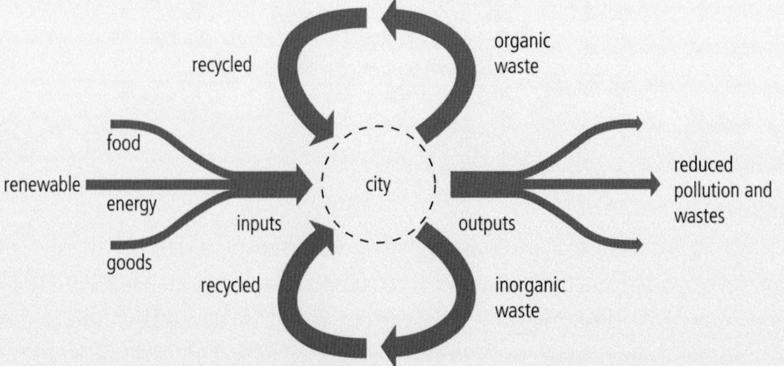

Create a systems flow diagram representing an urban system

Create a flow diagram to represent an urban system. You could use Shanghai or an urban area near where you live. Your diagram should contain boxes for stores and arrows for flows (inputs and outputs).

8.2.4 Urbanization: the population shift from rural to urban areas

Urbanization is the population shift from rural to urban areas and includes the process of land becoming more built-up, industrialized and dominated by dense and continuous human settlement and infrastructures.

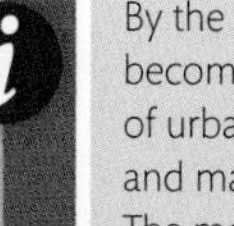

By the time countries have become HICs, the rates of urbanization level off and may go into decline. The movement of people from large urban areas to smaller urban areas and rural areas is known as **counter-urbanization**.

Urbanization is the process by which an increasing percentage of a country's population comes to live in towns and cities (Figure 8.27). The process may involve rural–urban migration, natural increase and the reclassification of rural settlements as they are engulfed into an expanding city. Initially, rates of urbanization in LICs are low, but as countries begin to industrialize and develop, urbanization increases rapidly.

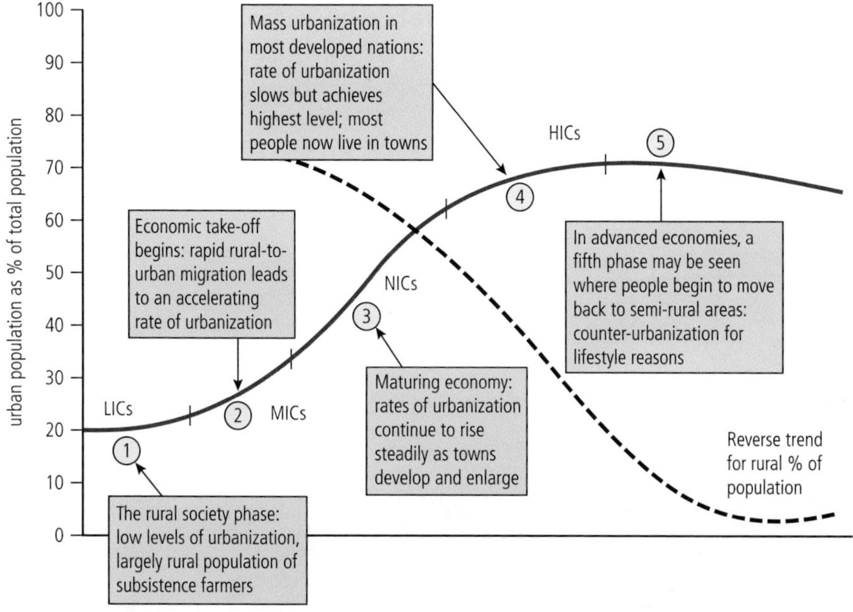

Figure 8.27 The process of urbanization (NICs = newly-industrialized countries).

Figure 8.28 shows that as urbanization proceeds, land use changes from farming to industry, services and residential uses. Building density increases, buildings get taller and there is more infrastructure.

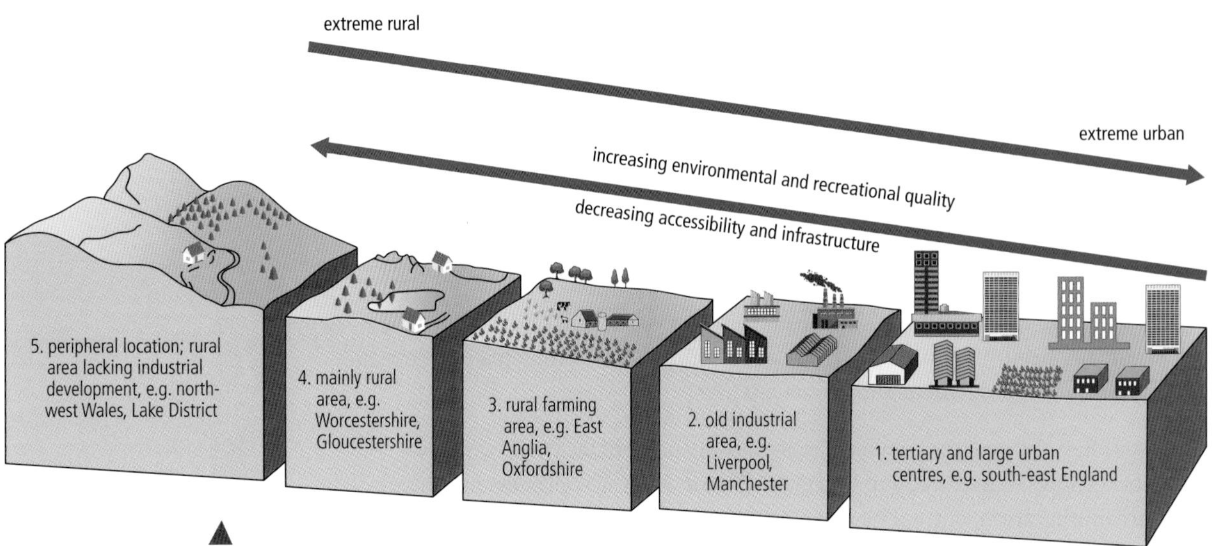

Figure 8.28 The rural–urban continuum.

The rural–urban continuum is the range of settlement types from remote (extreme) rural (Figure 8.29), through accessible rural, rural–urban fringe (Figure 8.30), suburbs, inner city and the commercial core of a city known as the **central business district (CBD)**. According to sociologists, in HICs it is increasingly difficult to distinguish between urban and rural. Although extremes exist, it is better to think of a rural–urban continuum.

Figure 8.29 New small village development, Oxfordshire, UK.

Figure 8.30 Farming on the rural–urban fringe.

1.2 Systems
1.3 Sustainability

8.2.5 Rural–urban migration

Due to rural–urban migration, a greater proportion of the human population now live in urban rather than rural systems (Figure 8.31). The proportion of populations living in rural areas is decreasing. Reasons for rural–urban migration include push–pull factors, including the perceived advantages of urban settlements. Most rural–urban migration is an internal migration.

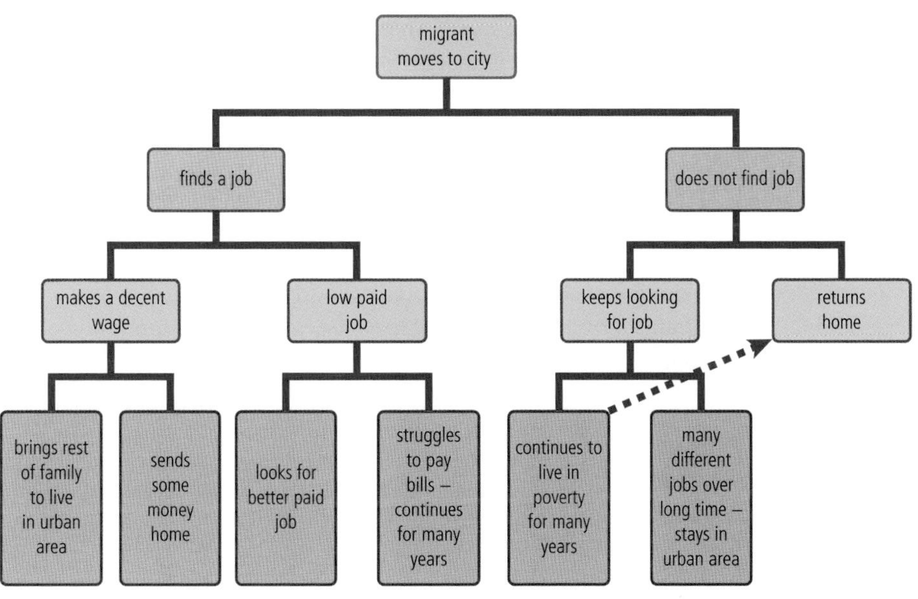

Figure 8.31 A flow chart to show potential outcome of migration to urban areas.

There are widespread differences in the level of urbanization around the world (Figure 8.32) and urbanization continues to increase in most regions, especially in newly industrializing/emerging economies. Rural–urban migration has fueled

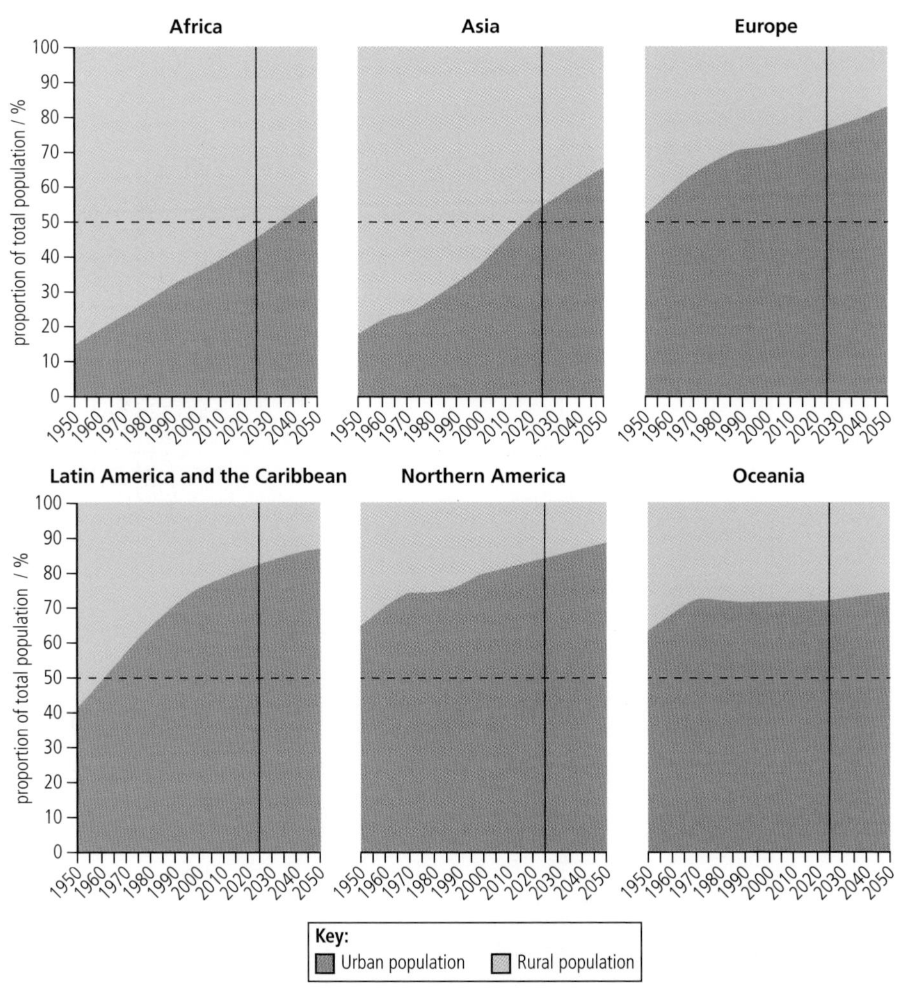

Figure 8.32 Global variations in the level of urbanization over time.

the growth of Shenzhen, China from a small fishing village in 1979 to a city with a population of over 16 million in 2022. Dubai in the UAE has increased in size since 2010 also by migration, although many of the migrants are overseas migrants. Many industries move to urban areas as have important marketplaces as well as sources of labour. Many people move to urban areas because there are more jobs in those areas than there are in rural areas. In contrast, urban growth in HICs seems to level out when the urban population has reached around 80–85%.

Most rural–urban migration occurs within a country and so it is a form of internal migration. Rural migrants move for a variety of reasons (Figure 8.33) commonly known as push and pull factors.

Push factors are the negative aspects of the area in which the migrant lives, including unemployment, low wages in rural areas, lack of housing, intolerance and so on. For many migrants, the true nature of life at the destination, including the availability of jobs, how well they pay and what the living conditions are like, are unknown until the migrants arrives there – hence the advantages are 'perceived'.

Pull factors are the perceived benefits of the location that the migrants want to move to. This is mainly seen to be employment opportunities in urban areas but can also include social factors, such as education and political factors, such as freedom from oppression, war and so on.

Figure 8.33 Push and pull factors.

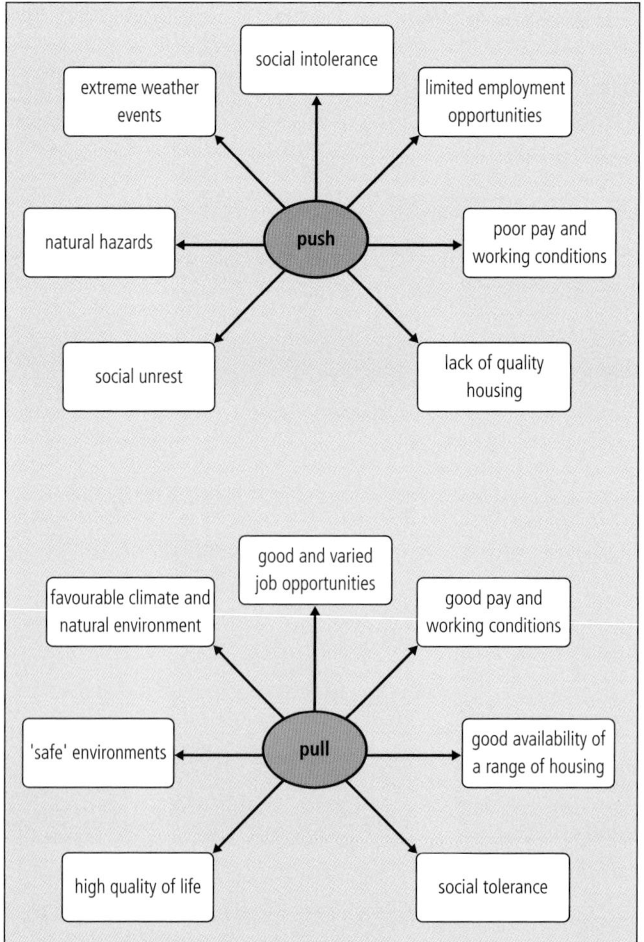

In many HICs, rural–urban migration is changing as many urban residents desire the perceived peace and higher quality of life that may be found in smaller settlements compared with larger urban areas. This trend accelerated during the COVID-19 pandemic as large urban areas were considered less safe than smaller settlements. This reverse migration to smaller settlements and rural areas is known as counter-urbanization or de-urbanization.

8.2.6 Suburbanization

Suburbanization refers to the growth of urban areas at their edges (suburbs). It is the movement of people from inner areas to the suburbs, as well as the movement of people from outside of the city from other cities and rural areas. Suburbanization is sometimes referred to as urban sprawl because lower density settlements require larger areas of land (Figure 8.34).

▲ **Figure 8.34** Suburban development, south Oxford, UK.

Suburbanization takes place due to several reasons. At the start of the 20th century, many cities in HICs had widespread poverty, slum conditions and the health of the population was poor. Governments and industrialists were keen to improve the living standards and productivity of workers. Governments provided subsidies for new housing to be built. At the same time, improvements in transport allowed workers to live further away from their place of work. Land was available on the edges of cities rather than in the centres. The increase in global trade meant that some farmland could be used for housing developments rather than for food production. The result was a rapid expansion of suburban housing which provided better quality housing, with water, sewers, electricity, gardens and more living space.

In some places, such as Phoenix in Arizona, USA, the expansion of the suburbs led to uncontrolled urban sprawl and environmental impacts including reduced biodiversity, lack of green space, changes in land use, increased impermeable surfaces, an increase in flooding, increase in transport and congestion costs and impacts on farming.

Suburban development did not benefit everyone. In the HICs, especially North American and European countries, the poorest people experienced increased mortgage costs and increased transport costs, which increased their level of debt. Suburban areas were also criticized for their lack of community compared with inner city areas. There were also fears that some cities were growing too much, and that urban sprawl was destroying the landscape. Consequently, attempts were made to stop the spread of suburbs/urban sprawl by introducing green belts (areas of restricted development), the development of new cities and new towns, redevelopment and regeneration of inner cities and infilling of green spaces (undeveloped land) and redevelopment of brownfield (derelict) sites.

Suburbanization is caused by several factors. For example, the expansion in the USA and Australia was largely caused by increased private car ownership. In contrast, suburbanization in Europe in the first half of the 20th century was largely aided by improvements in public transport.

8.2.7 The expansion of urban and suburban systems results in changes to the environment

4.4 Water pollution
8.3 Urban air pollution

The expansion of urban and suburban systems results in changes to the environment including loss of agricultural land, forests or other natural ecosystems, changes to water quality and river flows and air pollution.

Figure 8.35 Urban sprawl, Phoenix, Arizona, USA.

Globally, cities occupy 2–3% of the land area and account for over 50% of the population but consume around 75% of the world's resources. The footprint of major urban and suburban areas has increased due to urban sprawl (Figure 8.35) with low density development spiraling outwards from urban centres leading to habitat fragmentation, water and air pollution, increased infrastructure costs (e.g. more roads) and social homogeneity.

Characteristics of urban sprawl

There are a number of characteristics of urban sprawl including:

- low-density, single-family dwellings
- vehicle dependency, even for short journeys
- cul-de-sac street plans producing a lack of connectivity
- linear development along major road links
- undefined edges between rural and urban areas.

Causes of urban sprawl

Lower land values on the rural–urban fringe are the main drivers of urban sprawl. Population growth requires more houses. Increased incomes allow a greater number of households to afford new homes. Decreased commuting time also allows a greater number of people to live in the rural–urban fringe. Many of the households that are moving away from inner cities are younger and are looking for more space for their children. In the USA, race has been another issue as seen with the 'white flight' from cities such as Los Angeles and Detroit. In Chicago, USA the population increased by 40% between 1950 and 1995, while the population in built-up areas increased by 165%.

The consequences of urban sprawl include increased use of cars leading to air pollution, water pollution from impermeable surfaces and a reduction in natural sites such as wetlands and wildlife corridors. Gardens and public spaces create habitats for nature, help urban cooling and slow down the rate of water flow.

Urban areas contain many 'natural' areas such as grassland, parks, allotments and public gardens. The benefits of urban natural capital include:

- removal of air pollution
- mitigation of noise
- health benefits from nature
- support of biodiversity
- absorption and storage of carbon
- reduction of the heat island effect with urban ecosystems
- reduction of flood risk.

As an increased number of people live in greater densities in urban areas, the benefits of natural capital are received by a greater number of people compared with rural areas.

Within many urban areas, habitats are fragmented and/or degraded.

Urban waters

Pollution in water includes hydrocarbons, nutrients, garbage, metals, heat and sewage. It is estimated that around 68,000 tonnes of microplastics are generated annually from tyres in the UK and around 19,000 tonnes of this waste ends up in surface waters. In 2020, around 18% of water bodies in England were classified as damaged by pollution from urban areas and transport.

The main sources of water pollution in urban areas include:

- run-off from roads, pavements, car parks, industrial areas and contaminated areas
- broken pipes from toilets and kitchen appliances
- inappropriate disposal of fats, sanitary products and wet wipes
- discharge from sewage treatment works.

Urban air quality

Air pollution is the single largest environmental threat to health in many cities, including Delhi, London and Tehran, shortening lives by many years. Urban areas have a concentration of vehicles, industries, offices, businesses and residential areas releasing greenhouse gases and particulate material. Some of the trends are contradictory – there has been a downward trend in air pollution due to improvements in vehicle emissions and the phasing out of coal, and according to NASA, there was a decline in air pollution during the COVID-19 pandemic. However, since the pandemic, many people have avoided using public transport due to the risk of COVID-19.

Resource waste

Most of the food consumed in urban areas is produced elsewhere, often overseas.

The volume of water consumed in urban areas is often large due to high population densities, although agriculture is the largest user overall.

Urban areas often have lower recycling rates, especially in high density areas and deprived areas, due to a lack of space, mobile populations and a lack of household engagement.

Energy consumption

Urban areas use large amounts of energy to power domestic, service and industrial activities. The total greenhouse gas emissions of urban areas are derived from:

- those produced by activities such as residential, commercial, industrial and transport within the urban area
- those embedded in resources, energy and water used to produce the goods imported and consumed within the city.

Activity

1. Read the Guardian article *Revealed: almost everyone in Europe is breathing toxic air.*
2. Find out why the problem is so bad, and why poorer countries, and poorer people in all countries, are most affected by poor air quality.

1.2 Systems

Urban planning is as old as towns and cities themselves. For example, there is evidence of planning in Greek and Roman cities with their grid patterns. In the UK, company towns such as Bourneville and Port Sunlight were developed in the 19th century by wealthy philanthropists, while in Germany, the engineering company Krupp developed company towns in the Ruhr region. These towns benefited residents with higher quality, lower density housing than in the city slums, and benefited employers with a healthy and loyal workforce, higher productivity and lower absenteeism.

8.2.8 Urban planning

Urban planning aims to meet all the needs of all stakeholders in the community. Planning should aim to ensure that the use of land, resources, facilities and services benefits the urban and rural communities. Many stakeholders are involved in urban planning including public employees, local and national governments, professional planners, residents, neighbourhood groups, community development organizations, environmentalists, housing developers and investors. Any planning decision requires debate, trade-offs and compromises.

In the UK, the Garden City movement of Ebenezer Howard (1902) was an attempt to incorporate the best aspects of urban and rural living and to create a sense of belonging (Figure 8.36). Garden cities became associated with neighbourhoods, trees and green spaces, houses clustered around greens and cul-de-sacs.

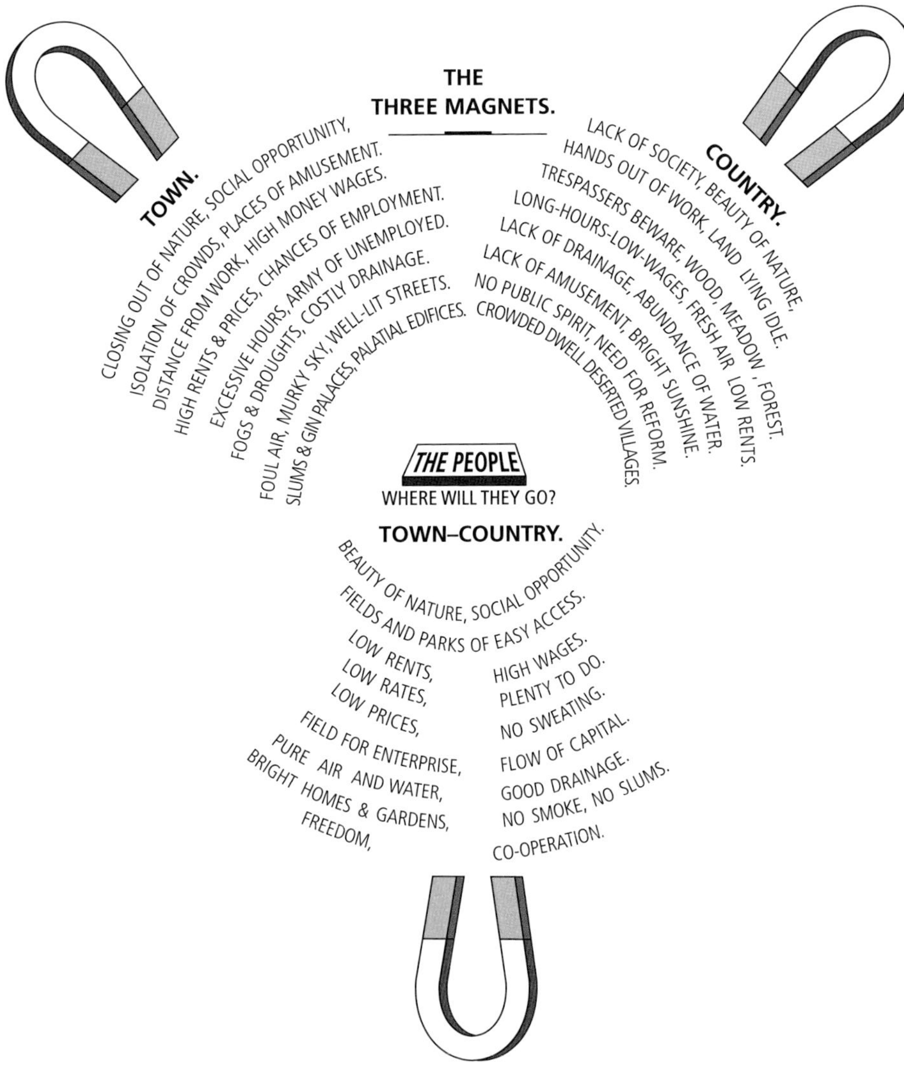

Figure 8.36 Howard's three magnets.

In contrast, most cities were characterized by a very dense network of narrow roads, overcrowding, a lack of open spaces and poor sanitation.

Garden suburbs (also called garden villages), such as Hampstead Garden Suburb and Mitcham Garden Village, combined the ideas of company towns and garden cities but applied them on a smaller scale.

In the 1920s, the Swiss planner Le Corbusier revealed his plans for the Radiant City (Ville Radieuse), a series of skyscrapers and high-rise blocks. His plans did not prove popular, although decades later high-rise blocks have been used in many locations for housing large numbers of people (Figure 8.37).

Figure 8.37 La Cité Radieuse in Marseille, France was designed by Le Corbusier.

Table 8.14 shows a comparison of Howard's plan with Le Corbusier's plan.

Table 8.14 A comparison of Howard and Le Corbusier.

Ebenezer Howard – The Garden City	Le Corbusier – The Radiant City
• based on neighbourhoods • community • small-scale • a mix of the best of rural and urban	• high rise tower blocks • a linear city

Challenge yourself

Suggest how your life would be different if you lived in a garden village or in a high-rise block.

From the late 1940s, New Towns were developed in countries such as Germany, Egypt, Hong Kong, France, Italy and Sweden. Many of these countries experienced large-scale damage during the Second World War, so much of early post-war planning was about the provision of new housing. New Towns were also introduced as an attempt to reduce the unequal distribution of population in some countries. However, many of the early New Towns, such as Stevenage and Basildon in the UK, were too small and lacked sufficient employment opportunities to be self-sufficient. Later New Towns, such as Milton Keynes, UK, were larger, further away from existing cities and more successful.

In the 1960s and 1970s, more attention was given to social and economic problems such as unemployment, racial integration and environmental issues including inner city renewal and urban regeneration. In the 1980s 'new urbanism' developed, which focused on environmentally friendly habitats in small-scale neighbourhoods containing a wide range of jobs and housing, building a sense of community. According to the Charter of the New Urbanism: 'neighbourhoods should be diverse in use and population. Communities should be designed for the pedestrian and transit as well as the car. Cities and towns should be shaped by physically defined and universally accessible public spaces and community institutions. Urban places should be framed by architecture and landscape design that celebrate local history, climate, ecology and building practice.'

Activity

1. Find out about Chandigarh, India, which was the only city ever planned by Le Corbusier. Make a presentation to your class.
2. Find out about the problems associated with the early New Towns and compare them with the later New Towns..
3. With a partner, research the development of New Towns in one or more of Germany, Egypt, Hong Kong, France, Italy and Sweden.

1.3 Sustainability
6.3 Climate change – mitigation and adaptation

8.2.9 Modern urban planning

Modern urban planning has evolved since the 1850s. Different planners have focused on different elements of planning such as quality and affordability of housing, integrated public transport systems, green spaces, security, education and employment, use of renewable resources, reuse and recycling of waste, energy efficiency, involvement of the community and green buildings.

One of the early urban planners was the 19th century Spaniard Ildefons Cerda, who designed the 'extension of Barcelona' called *Eixample*, in the 1860s. Cerda focused on key needs such as light, ventilation, greenery and waste disposal. However, the *Eixample* was, and is today, largely inhabited by wealthy people rather than having a broad social mix.

The population density of Paris in the 1850s exceeded 5300 people/km^2 and cholera epidemics were frequent. Between 1853 and 1870, Georges-Eugene Haussmann oversaw the demolition of a number of medieval neighbourhoods, which were considered to be overcrowded and unhealthy. These neighbourhoods were replaced with wide avenues, parks and squares, and new aqueducts, sewers and fountains were constructed. Prior to Haussmann's development, Paris had just four parks. Haussmann gave Paris air and open spaces through four large parks, twenty-four new squares and the addition of 2000 ha of parks and open space including a network of wide, tree-lined boulevards and parks in all neighbourhoods, which is how central Paris appears today. Haussmann was responsible for the planting of around 6000 trees.

Copenhagen has managed to reduce private car ownership and favours cycling and walking rather than the use of cars. It introduced a sales tax of 180% on new cars that has greatly reduced ownership of cars.

San Francisco has been called the 'electronic charging' capital of the USA, with over 900 electronic charging stations in the city. It aims to reach 100% electrification of all vehicles in the city by 2040.

In the 1950s, Brasilia became Brazil's capital city and this was created as an ideal city. The city was built inland on an empty plateau as a city of the future. It was designed like an airplane and was built on the assumption that cars would be used for transport. The city was carved up into different zones including the administrative, hotel, banking and embassy sectors. It was originally intended that the city should have a population of 500,000, but the city now has a population of over 2.5 million residents. The scale of the city is very large, and it is not pedestrian friendly – the vehicle was a symbol of modernity. The city is the wealthiest in Latin America, having the highest GDP/head. The poor tend to reside in satellite cities outside of Brasilia. Although the original plan was to avoid segregation and the development of slum areas (favelas), tower blocks (superquadra) were built, and this led to segregation of the poor.

Urban planning that uses vegetation and water leads to improvements in the micro-climate, as well as being visually attractive.

A less than successful project was Forest City in Johor, Malaysia. This city was built on a mangrove swamp inhabited by local farmers and fisherfolk in Kampung, Tanjung. Kupang Forest City is a residential development of around 1370 ha, which was opened in 2016. It targeted wealthy residents, mainly from China. However, partly due to the COVID-19 pandemic and partly due to the economic downturn, the development has not been a success and has been described as a 'ghost town'. It has caused large-scale environmental degradation of environmentally sensitive areas, including intertidal seagrass meadows and mangrove forest reserves. Building of the city began in 2014 and local fisherfolk complained about falling fish catches. By 2019, only 15,000 out of a target of 700,000 housing units had been sold and only 500 people actually lived there.

Figure 8.38 Green spaces in Dubai.

In Dubai, there are plans to have over 40% of the country's energy coming from renewable resources by 2050, for an overall 40% reduction in energy consumption. One development on the outskirts of Dubai has been called the Sustainable City. The development is a testing ground for new technologies and aims to use as little energy and water as possible. All the buildings and parking spaces have solar panels that feed into the energy grid. Residential areas are designed to avoid direct exposure to the Sun, as far as possible. A grey-water system has been set up to recycle water from showers and washing machines to use for irrigation. However, the city also uses water from desalination plants. The UAE plans that, by 2030, all new buildings will produce no more emissions than they can absorb and that all buildings will achieve this goal by 2050. Other plans include an increase in green spaces (Figure 8.38) and improved landscaping of infrastructure (Figure 8.39).

▲ **Figure 8.39** Artificial trees under the bridge on Palm Jumeirah, Dubai – each of the tree trunks has a concrete pillar inside, helping support the monorail.

SKILLS

Investigate maps that show the urban development of a city over time

Cairo is the capital city of Egypt (Figure 8.40). It is a cultural centre, an important tourist location and an important university city.

1. Describe the changes in the growth of Cairo between 1984 and 2014.
2. Using an atlas, or the Internet, find out about Egypt's land and climate.
3. Outline the problems that are created by the increased growth of Cairo.

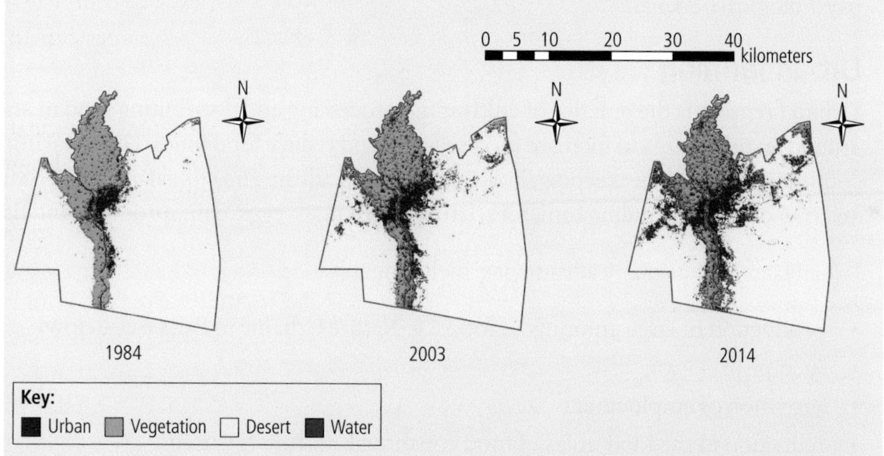

◀ **Figure 8.40** The growth of Cairo, 1984–2014.

Watch the London Evolution Animation showing the growth of London from Roman times.

8.2.10 Ecological urban planning

Ecological urban planning is a more holistic approach that views the urban system as an ecosystem, understanding the complex relationships between its biotic and abiotic components. This contrasts with some of the earlier forms of urban planning that did not consider human or environmental wellbeing.

1.2 Systems
2.1 Individuals, populations, communities and ecosystems
6.3 Climate change – mitigation and adaptation

Ecological planning includes:

- urban ecology considerations such as green spaces and habitats for wildlife
- urban farming including beekeeping, horticulture, aquaculture and city farms

In 2023, vandals cut down the world-famous sycamore tree (Figure 8.41) that featured in the film *Robin Hood Prince of Thieves*. Many people were saddened by this action, as they lost mental and spiritual benefits. The local community were shocked by this event. The tree had become a symbol of the local community, was the name of a local public house, and even had a local beer named after it. The place was popular for wedding and engagement photographs and some people had their ashes deposited there. The benefits of this tree were indeed varied.

Figure 8.41 The world-famous sycamore tree in the Sycamore Gap that was felled by vandals.

- biophilic design including living green walls and roofs, water features and natural light
- resilience planning including vertical farming in cities, building on stilts in flood-prone areas and fail-safe grids
- regenerative architecture including building skins that scrub the air clean, capturing rainwater that replenishes aquifers and solar panels/wind turbines/biodigesters that export energy.

Urban ecology

Urban ecology is the scientific study of the relationships of living organisms with their surroundings in areas dominated by high density residential and commercial developments and by paved or otherwise sealed areas. At a very basic level, it is the study of green spaces and water bodies in urban areas such as gardens, parks, sports pitches, cemeteries, ponds and nature reserves and so on. Urban ecology has a 'natural' aspect as well as a human dimension.

The human dimension accelerated with the industrial revolution. As urban areas grew, their impact on natural ecology intensified.

Urban ecosystems provide many key services to urban residents including urban cooling, air quality, food production, water supply, disease control and recreational/psychological benefits.

Urban farming

Urban farming is the practice of cultivating, processing and distributing food in and around an urban area to increase food security and reduce food miles. Urban farming commonly includes beekeeping, horticulture, aquaculture and city farms, and produces an array of foods including tomatoes, lettuces, potatoes, eggs, dairy products and fish.

Urban farming has many advantages, including:

- production of large amounts of food e.g. Nature Urbaine in Paris (see below)
- income provision
- provision of employment
- reduction in the food miles of food consumed, and energy used
- positive effect on people's mental and physical wellbeing
- makes use of unused land
- increases food security
- may improve the quality of the urban environment through greening.

Nevertheless, there are certain problems involved with urban agriculture, including:

- the soil may be contaminated with chemicals from industry/vehicles
- air quality may be poor
- urban greening may make an area attractive and can cause property prices to rise.

Urban beekeeping

Urban beekeeping is increasing and occurring in gardens, rooftops and abandoned land. For example, in Birmingham, UK there are 50,000 urban bees on the rooftop of the Custard Factory building. Some of the first plants to colonize areas where buildings have been demolished include rosebay willowherb, brambles and buddleia, which are favoured by bees. In addition, the area is unlikely to be treated with pesticides. Beekeeping allows people to reconnect to nature. However, there is a safety aspect with the possibility of people being stung by bees. This can largely be avoided by having hedges or fences around the hives forcing the bees to fly above head height.

Activity

1. Find out more about urban beekeeping at the Urban Bees website.
2. Watch the Ted Talk, Urban Buzz, on YouTube.
3. Make a presentation to your class about the importance of urban beekeeping.

Horticulture

Urban horticulture refers to the growing of crops in urban locations. Production varies in scale from herbs and tomatoes grown in small pots and growbags to large-scale urban rooftop farms, such as the Nature Urbaine, in Paris, which covers 14,000 m^2 and produces 200 kg of fruit and vegetables daily. According to the Food and Agriculture Organization, (FAO), market gardening is the most important source of locally grown fresh food in over one-third of African countries. Nevertheless, much of the market gardening in Africa is informal or illegal, with little government support or regulation. Most farmers do not own the land they farm and so they have no security of tenure, meaning they could lose the use of the land without warning. To increase crop yields farmers may resort to using pesticides and wastewater for irrigation.

Aquaculture

Urban aquaculture can involve any type of aquatic organisms (plants and animals) in rivers, ponds, lakes and canals in urban areas. There are many advantages of urban aquaculture including increased food supply for less wealthy residents, increased food security, increased employment and reduced food miles. However, there are limits to urban aquaculture caused by competing land uses, theft, water pollution, disease, high costs of fish food and contamination of fish food. In South Africa, annual aquaculture increased from about 3000 tonnes in 2000 to about 10,000 tonnes in 2020. The Fish Farm in Philippi, Cape Town is an aquaculture project in a shipping container, located in an under-privileged community. It produces 4 tonnes of fish per container annually, mostly tilapia in summer and trout in winter. The project is profitable, affordable, repeatable, transportable, lockable and stackable. In addition to the fish produced, water from the tanks and waste from the fish (broken down by nitrogen-fixing bacteria) provides nitrates and nitrites that help grow cucumbers, lettuces, onions and spinach.

Activity

1. Visit the Fish Farm's website and watch the video *Taking fish farming to new heights*.
2. Download the Fabulous Fish Farm brochure from the Siemens-Stiftung website.
3. Produce a one-page summary on the advantages of urban aquaculture.

Aquaponics is a food production system that couples aquaculture (raising aquatic animals such as fish in tanks) with hydroponics (cultivating plants in water).

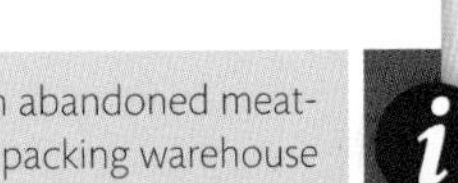

An abandoned meat-packing warehouse built in New York in 1925 for Peer Foods is being converted into an aquaponics farm that will produce vegetables, fish, tea and beer.

City farms

There are many untapped areas in cities that could be used for farming. In New York, Square Roots have transformed shipping containers into farm spaces. They are able to grow herbs, leafy greens, aubergine, turnips, strawberries and tomatoes. Square Roots sells to retail outlets within 8 km of where the food is produced, delivered by battery-powered tricycles with a cold-storage unit on the front of the bike. However, ultra-intensive multi-storey indoor farms rely heavily on LED-lighting and are major consumers of energy.

Example – Urban farming in Detroit, USA

The city of Detroit in the USA has experienced a major decline in population and in industry. Since the 1950s, the population of Detroit has fallen from around 2 million to around 700,000 residents. Since the year 2000 there has been a large increase in the amount of vacant land and number of derelict buildings and a significant increase in the number of urban farms (Figure 8.42). The Michigan Urban Farming Unit is using urban farming to promote education and social justice and empower local communities. Hantz Woodlands (Hantz Farms) is an urban forest project, which involved clearing over 2000 vacant lots and demolishing derelict homes to produce a 56-ha forest containing over 25,000 trees. The project has made the area more attractive and house prices have increased by nearly 500%. Critics argue that the project might sell off property for development at higher prices. The Greening of Detroit (Figure 8.43) is another project with over 130,000 trees planted. The project team also manages Lafayette Greens, a green space in central Detroit which grows chemical-free fruits, vegetables, herbs and flowers.

Figure 8.42 Derelict Detroit.

Figure 8.43 The Greening of Detroit project.

Biophilic design

Not all human impacts are negative. In recent years, urban planning has been considering factors that will reduce environmental impact and improve human wellbeing. **Biophilic design** is an attempt to increase connections to the natural world through the direct and indirect use of nature, space and place. According to Stephen Kellert, one of the pioneers of biophilic design, people derive benefits from their experience of nature through light, air, water, plants, animals, weather and landscapes.

Green walls

A green wall is a vertical built structure covered by vegetation. Green walls provide many beneficial impacts including:

- deflecting water away from walls during heavy rain
- providing the building with an extra layer of insulation
- helping to keep homes cool in summer
- contributing to improvement of urban air quality
- providing habitats for insects
- contributing to reduced noise pollution
- offering great aesthetic benefits.

However, there are negative aspects to the use of green walls including:

- they may need lots of maintenance
- the plants may need much irrigation
- some plants, such as ivy, can weather the rock that they are growing on
- some of the plants used may be invasive or they may contain invasive insects.

Water features

Similarly, water features such as fountains, ponds and streams provide habitats for many organisms, offer aesthetic benefits and have an impact on human health. They offer recreational activities as well as offering environmental services such as water storage and mitigation of urban heat island effects.

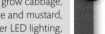

Aeroponic farming is a method of farming without soil. Plants are suspended in the air and their roots are wetted with a fine spray of nutrient-enriched water. As the roots are exposed, they receive more oxygen and so they grow faster. No run-off occurs as the water is recycled, so there are fewer environmental impacts. However, the system relies on energy to run the misting process, so the roots could quickly dry out if there is an energy shortage.

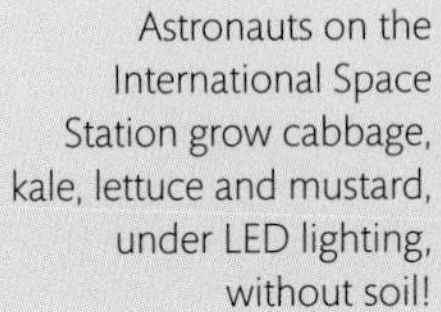

Astronauts on the International Space Station grow cabbage, kale, lettuce and mustard, under LED lighting, without soil!

Resilience planning

Vertical farming

Resilience planning allows farmers to use areas that could not traditionally be farmed. **Vertical farming**, for example, refers to the production of crops in vertical layers, usually in trays stacked within a building. Vertical farms need to supply lighting, water, nutrients and sometimes, pollinators and pest control. Some vertical farms grow crops in water (hydroponics) or in the air (aeroponics) with water or air enriched with nutrients flowing around the root system. Although technology exists, and shows great promise, the cost in terms of money and energy are high. Hence, leafy salads and smaller vegetables, including fast-growing high-value crops such as strawberries and tomatoes, are mainly produced. Vertical farming does not require much land and so can take place in urban areas. The biggest barrier to vertical farming is the large amount of energy and infrastructure needed. Some vertical farms rely on fossil fuels which makes them vulnerable to changes in oil prices. In many places, the electricity used for vertical farms comes from fossil fuels.

In 2021, a punnet of Japanese Omakase strawberries that had been grown by vertical farming in New Jersey sold for US$ 50 in a high-end New York supermarket. This shows that vertical farming has the ability to produce high quality foods.

Building on stilts

A number of settlements (and parts of settlements) are built on stilts (Figure 8.44). Traditionally, these buildings were used in areas that were vulnerable to river flooding, such as areas of tropical rainforest and monsoonal areas. Coastal areas are increasingly at risk from tidal flooding caused by global climate change. One solution will be to build settlements in these coastal areas including buildings on stilts. This is already being done in some areas such as the Netherlands where houses are being developed on raiseable stilts.

Figure 8.44 Housing on stilts to protect it from flooding.

In Lake Tadane, West Ghana, the village of Nzulezo is built on stilts. The village has a population of over 500 people and has two churches, a guesthouse and primary school. It was nominated in 2000 for inclusion as a UNESCO World Heritage Site.

Fail-safe grids

As global climate change increases, the possibility and frequency of greater magnitude weather events will also increase. This means that infrastructure designed to cope with specific sized events may no longer protect people. Protection schemes may no longer be fail-safe (i.e. designed not to fail), but instead become safe-to-fail, meaning they may be more likely to fail but are designed to do so in a safer way.

An example of a safe-to-fail grid (or system) can be seen in the Indian Bend Wash in Scottsdale, Arizona, USA. Alongside the river are numerous green spaces, a cycle path and recreational areas. The vegetation provides many ecosystem services such as climate regulation, carbon capture and production of oxygen. After rainfall events, the wash fills with water. If the rain is very heavy or intense, the cycle path and green areas may flood temporarily, but any repairs are easily made. Thus, the Indian Bend Wash can be considered to be a resilient safe-to-fail infrastructure.

In contrast, following floods in the 1880s of the Los Angeles River, attempts were made to control flooding. In the 1930s the river was finally altered from a meandering natural channel to a straightened, concreted and controlled channel. Although the new channel has helped reduce flooding, it has removed the ecosystem services that were once provided. In addition, were the new channel to be affected by an earthquake, the city could experience major problems. The 2020 Los Angeles River strategy has a revised plan that includes, among others, plans to revitalize parts of the river and re-establish environmental goods and services. Thus, there is a recognition that fail-safe infrastructure, such as the Los Angeles river channel, does not offer the same level of multifunctional resilience as a safe-to-fail system.

Natural flood plains are often developed because they are flat and relatively easy to build on. However, flood plains get flooded regularly. Sometimes they are favoured by poor communities as the land is relatively cheap. However, building on a flood plain requires protective measures such as stilts, raised floor levels and openings to let water drain through.

Regenerative architecture

Regenerative architecture is the practice of designing and operating buildings to have a positive impact on the natural environment and reverse ecological damage. It also aims to produce a more resilient environment that can resist challenges such as global climate change. Whereas sustainability limits the use of resources, regeneration replenishes their supplies. Regeneration sees buildings as a part of a large system containing the place, microclimate, site and ecosystem. Interventions may include air-cleansing building skins (e.g. types of paint, filters and building materials that can take pollutants out of the atmosphere), water-purification schemes and carbon-capturing buildings.

Special grades of titanium dioxide (TiO_2) can remove ('scrub') nitrogen oxides (NOx) from the air through the process of 'photocatalysis' and convert them into harmless nitrate salts, which then cover the building but can be removed from a building by rainfall. Research in London showed that NOx levels were reduced by between 15% and 38% on London streets where the buildings used titanium dioxide. In Mexico City, the Torre de Especialidades hospital has a coating of TiO_2 tiles covering the outside of the building. It is estimated that this coating can neutralize the NOx emissions of up to 8750 cars daily. The Eindhoven University of Technology applied TiO_2 to pavements and found that smog levels fell by between 19% and 45%.

A number of other initiatives exist including the use of large-scale water butts to capture urban or hillside run-off and to replenish aquifers, and the use of solar panels and wind turbines to generate and export renewable energy.

The use of **biodigesters** is another useful initiative. Biodigesters convert manure into biogas. The biogas can be used as a clean cooking fuel and waste from the biodigesters can be used to fertilize kitchen gardens or fields, saving money.

HL

HL

8.2.11 Principles of ecological urban planning

1.3 Sustainability
6.3 Climate change – mitigation and adaptation
7.1 Natural resources, uses and management

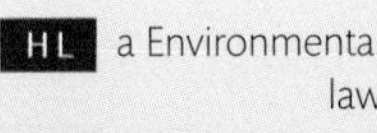

HL a Environmental law

HL c Environmental ethics

Ecological urban planning follows the principles of urban compactness, mixed land use and social mix practice. The sustainable advantages of these practices include reduced urban sprawl, less car dependency, reduced energy consumption, better public transport, increased accessibility and social equality. Avoiding social inequality in access to green areas is a matter of environmental justice.

Urbanization is one of the defining features of the modern age, but urban development has had a major negative impact on the natural environment, reducing biodiversity and threatening human wellbeing. In contrast, ecologically based urban planning considers the impacts on the natural environment, including impacts on ecosystem services, socio-ecological systems, resilience, biodiversity, landscape and green infrastructure, and therefore will have a more positive overall effect on the natural environment.

Reducing urban sprawl

Urban sprawl mainly occurs in HICs and MICs. Reducing urban sprawl can be achieved through the use of green belts and green wedges, new towns and expanded towns. Green belts (and wedges) are areas of land surrounding or penetrating a city, where development of the natural environment is largely controlled. Some low-density developments may be allowed such as parks, hospitals and cemeteries, but large-scale residential developments are not generally permitted. Housing developments are generally diverted to other existing towns (expanded towns), or new developments are built elsewhere to form new towns. Urban sprawl has largely occurred due to the increase in private car ownership and the construction of low-density suburbs. To prevent any further expansion in urban sprawl, housing in urban areas will need to be built at higher densities and there will need to be improvement and investment in public transport.

Reducing car dependency

There are several options for reducing the use of cars including the use of public transport, walking, cycling or micromobility involving the use of electric bikes and scooters. The aim is not to ban cars altogether but instead to channel them to places where options for other forms of transport are reduced such as remote or peripheral areas. Increases in vehicle tax, along with the introduction of congestion charges and low emission zones all help reduce the number of vehicles entering urban areas. In London, the revenue from the congestion charges is used to fund public transport. Reallocating road space from car use to use by bicycles and buses could also reduce the number of cars on the road. Similarly, a reduction in car parking spaces and an increase in the cost of car parking may make the use of cars less desirable. For example, in Waltham Forest, a suburb in north-east London, a series of road closures were introduced to reduce non-local traffic. These closures resulted in a decline in the daily flow of vehicles from around 8500 to around 4800, a 22% reduction in the number of vehicles and a reduction in the average speed of vehicles. Some 74% of residents supported the scheme.

Elsewhere, a variety of schemes have been used. In Singapore, residents need a permit to own a car and are charged for using selected roads. Charges vary by vehicle size, the day of the week and the time of driving. In Mexico City, the pedestrianization of Madero Street led to a 30% increase of commercial activity and a 96% fall in reported crime. In Auckland, New Zealand there are plans to increase residential density both vertically and horizontally and to increase the usage of public transport and electric vehicles. Greater use of public transport could reduce carbon dioxide (CO_2) emissions by 40% and the use of electric vehicles could reduce emissions by 30%.

Net zero is achieved when any greenhouse gas emissions are balanced by schemes to offset an equivalent amount of greenhouse gases from the atmosphere, such as planting trees or using geoengineering schemes such as carbon capture and storage.

Reduced energy consumption

Cities use about 66% of the world's energy and create about 75% of the world's greenhouse gases. Energy problems in urban areas include increasing demand, ageing infrastructure, volatile energy markets (e.g. as a result of the conflict between Russia and Ukraine) and climate change. Energy supplies need to be secure, affordable and have a net zero status.

Helsinki in Finland can be used as an example of a city where the provision of energy has been a success, despite rising demand. Helsinki is part of the Decarbon-Home Project, which has the dual aims of reducing the need for energy production and switching to renewable energy resources. The goal is to achieve a status of net zero by 2040. Since 1990, greenhouse gas emissions have decreased by 33%, economic growth has increased by 65% and per capita emissions have decreased by 50%. The total energy usage in Helsinki has remained unchanged despite the increase in population (Figure 8.45). In addition, renewable energy now accounts for around 25% of energy production. The project also targets vulnerable groups such as the elderly and immigrants, adapting their housing to be more energy efficient.

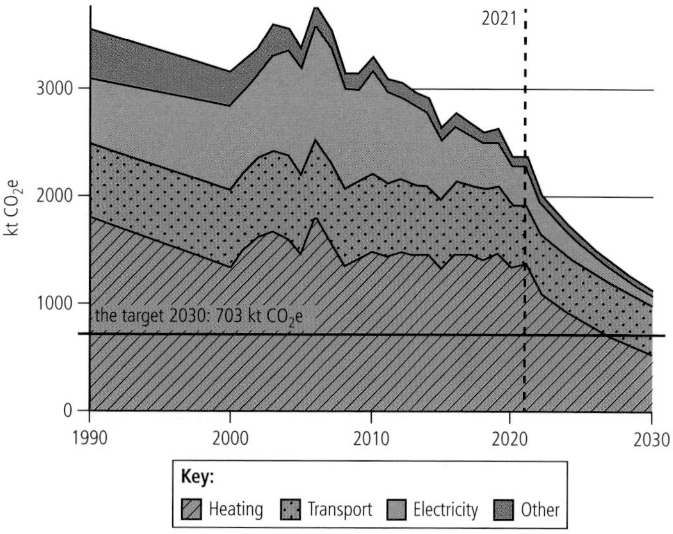

Figure 8.45 Energy emissions in Helsinki, 1990–2030, by sector.

Better public transport

Curitiba, a city in south-west Brazil, is an excellent model for better public transport (Figure 8.46). Curitiba experienced rapid population growth from the 1950s and now has a population of almost 2 million, making it Brazil's eight largest city. Nevertheless, it has managed to avoid all the problems normally associated with rapid urban growth. This success was largely due to innovative planning:

- public transport is preferred over the use of private cars
- the environment is used rather than changed
- cheap, low technology solutions are used rather than high technology ones
- development occurs through the participation of citizens (bottom-up development) rather than top-down development (centralized planning).

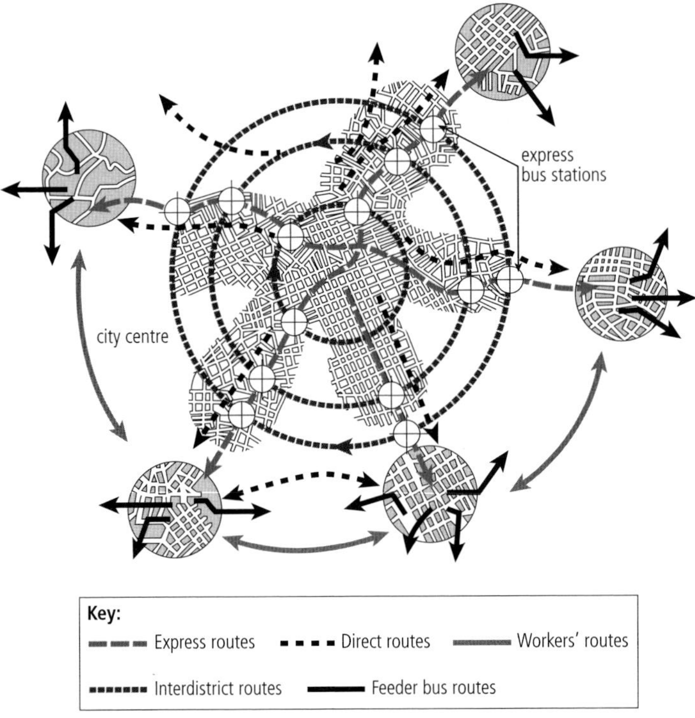

Figure 8.46 Transport network in Curitiba, Brazil.

The approach to transport in Curitiba is very different. The road network and public transport system have structural axes. These allow the city to expand but keep shops, workplaces and homes closely linked. Curitiba's mass transport system is based on the use of buses. Interdistrict and feeder bus routes complement the express bus lanes along the structural axes. The improvements are geared towards the speed of journey and convenience of passengers and include:

- a single fare being charged that allows transfer from express routes to interdistrict and local buses
- extra wide doors allow passengers to crowd on quickly
- double and triple length buses that allow for rush hour loads
- bus routes and bicycle paths that integrate the parks into the urban life of the city.

The rationale for the bus system was economic as well as sustainability. A subway would have cost US$ 70–80 million per km but the express busways only cost US$ 200,000 per km. The bus companies are paid by the kilometres of road they serve rather than the number of passengers they carry. This ensures that all areas of the city are served.

Increased accessibility

Increased accessibility allows people to reach a greater number of locations and activities in a shorter amount of time. It creates more opportunities for employment, social interactions, healthcare, retail and so on. Improved accessibility may therefore bring about improvements in the quality of life. Accessibility may be measured in the amount of time it takes to get to a place or the amount it costs to get to a place.

Social equality

Social equality suggests that all population groups are equal in terms of their rights and status. However, this is often not the case. Certain groups may be disadvantaged or deprived in several ways, including low incomes, a lack of employment opportunities, ill health, poor educational achievement, limited access to housing and services, high rates of crime and a poor living environment. For example, the city of Barcelona has a population of about 1.6 million people – and around 5 million in the wider metropolitan area. The greatest level of deprivation is seen in two main areas – the inner-city district of El Ravel, associated with poor-quality housing built during the industrial era, and the edge-of-town locations of Can Peguara and La Mina, where social housing was built to accommodate migrants to the city during the 1960s. During the 1970s and 1980s Barcelona deindustrialized rapidly. In the 1980s, unemployment in the city was 20% and many locations became derelict. Barcelona still has a large population that are disadvantaged. According to the 2017–27 Strategy for Inclusion and Reducing Social Inequality in Barcelona, the five aspects of social inequality with the most impact on social inclusion/exclusion processes are:

- inequality in income
- inequality in education
- inequalities in access to community assets or networks between people
- the stigmatization and social segregation of people according to income, education, culture or the area they live in
- territorial inequalities.

Avoiding social inequality in access to green areas

Open spaces are important for physical and mental wellbeing, but the amount of open space in urban areas varies enormously. For example, London has 50 m² of open space per resident, whereas Mumbai has less than 2 m² of open space per resident. India's national building code recommends at least 4 acres of open space per 1000 residents, but Mumbai has just 0.3 acres of open space per 1000 residents. Mumbai now has the second-highest childhood obesity rate in India and some 68% of the city's children are said to have sedentary lifestyles.

It is not just green spaces that are important. In the 1960s in Bengaluru (Bangalore), there were over 280 lakes but now there are fewer than 70 and many of these are biologically dead. The government turned many of these spaces into vehicle parking spaces, a bus station and a sports stadium, while others have been surrounded by slums. In addition, between 2010 and 2014, over 50,000 trees in Bengaluru were cut down to make way for road widening schemes. Some critics have suggested that compensatory afforestation projects should be set up to counter the loss of trees. However, the creation of forests elsewhere will not affect the lives of citizens in Bengaluru (Bangalore), who are affected by air and noise pollution.

Activity

1. Visit the Our Cities page on the Carbon Neutral Cities Alliance website and investigate methods to make cities more sustainable.

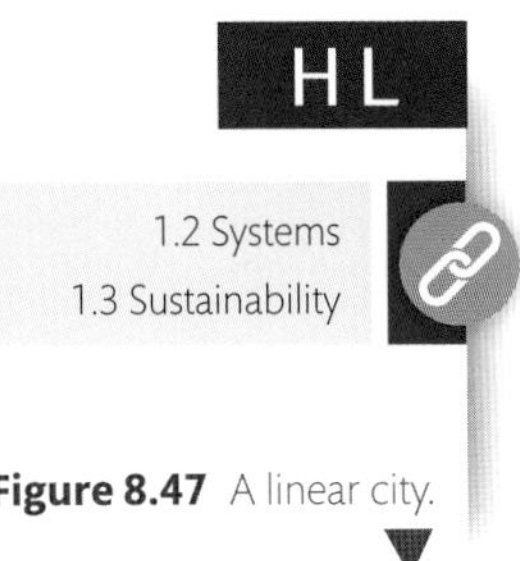
HL
1.2 Systems
1.3 Sustainability

8.2.12 Societies are developing systems that address urban sustainability

The linear model of urban systems can be summarized as 'take, make and waste' (Figure 8.47). Cities consume about 75% of the world's natural resources and generate about 50% of the world's waste (Topic 1, Section 1.3.20).

Figure 8.47 A linear city.

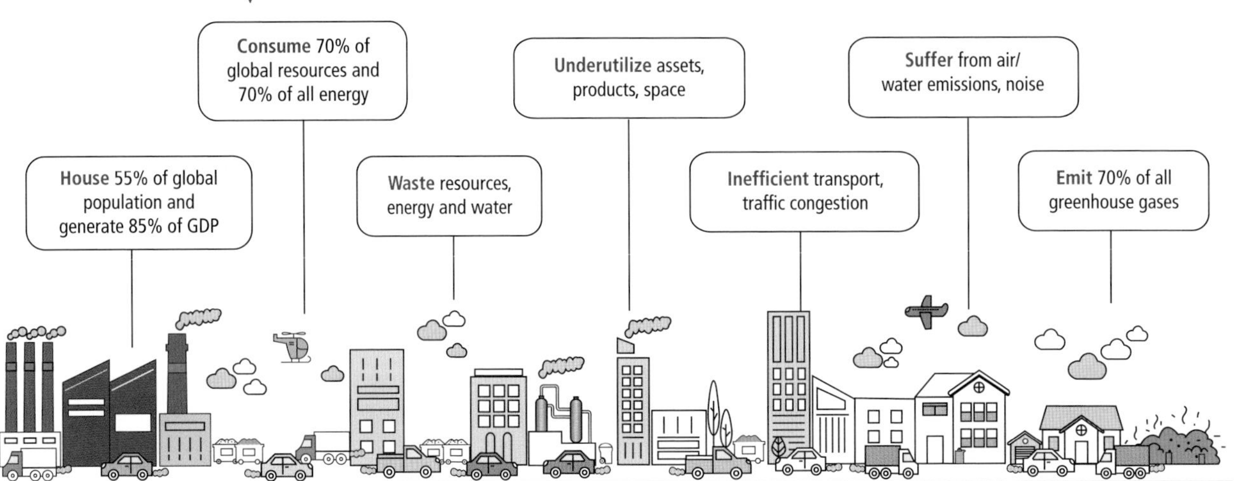
Consume 70% of global resources and 70% of all energy
Underutilize assets, products, space
Suffer from air/ water emissions, noise
House 55% of global population and generate 85% of GDP
Waste resources, energy and water
Inefficient transport, traffic congestion
Emit 70% of all greenhouse gases

The circular economy model (Topic 1, Section 1.3.20) can lead to cities that are:

- thriving – increased economic growth occurs due to reduced congestion, waste and costs
- liveable – improved air quality and reduced pollution
- resilient – because of reduced reliance on raw materials and keeping products in use (Figure 8.48).

Figure 8.48 A circular city.

Assets/products are *shared/leased* with end-of-life *recovery*
Urban bio-economy with organic by-product/waste recovery and urban farms
Reverse logistics to facilitate re-use, repair and remanufacturing
Digital tools facilitate sharing/recovery applications
Mobility systems are clean and shared
Production with local value loops and industrial symbiosis
Energy production is renewable and local
Buildings are modular, shared, and designed for disassembly

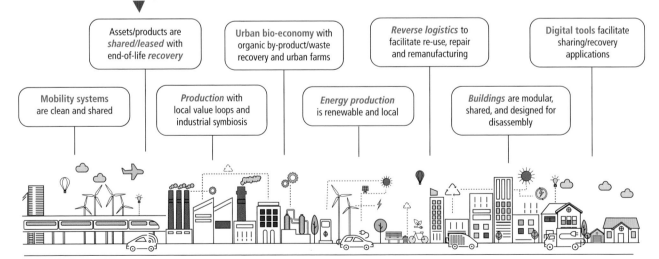

HL b Environmental economics

Traditional economic theory suggests that there is a circular flow of goods and money. However, it does not consider the negative environmental externalities such as raw material and energy use or the production of waste (HL.b.3 and HL.b.4). Moreover, it does not consider the fact that not all work is paid for, including child-rearing, fuelwood collection and water collection.

- According to Oxfam (2023) *Survival of the richest*, the richest 1% of the world's population received 63% of the new wealth (worth about US$ 42 trillion) since 2020. Doughnut economics offers a route for humanity in the 21st century (see Figure 1.72, Topic 1). The centre of the doughnut is the 'social foundations', including the basic human needs of water, food, energy and health. The outer part of the doughnut is the 'ecological ceiling', which is the planetary boundaries including climate change, ozone layer depletion and ocean acidification.

Whereas traditional models of economic growth may suggest that an increase in GDP per head illustrates economic growth, the doughnut economics model suggests that development is a balance between an increase in the quality of life and the avoidance of depleting the Earth's resources.

Currently, about 12% of the world's population experience severe food insecurity and about 13% do not have access to electricity. Five of the nine planetary boundaries have been exceeded including climate change, biodiversity loss and biogeochemical flows. Arguably, these boundaries have been exceeded as the result of linear economic flows, for example due to a lack of recycling, re-use and reduction.

Amsterdam has identified a number of issues in relation to becoming a sustainable city and, in some cases, has set targets for how to resolve the issues. For example, the city aims to have a 50% decrease in the use of primary raw materials in industry and for buildings by 2030 and to have a fully circular economy by 2050. In 2018, the Amsterdam Metropolitan Area processed around 8.5 million tonnes of industrial and commercial waste and 1.1 million tonnes of household waste. Amsterdam's target for healthcare is that all people should have an equal chance of a healthy lifestyle. However, 40% of the population are overweight and 49% have a moderate or high risk of anxiety or depression. In addition, the city aims to be an inclusive city with equality in diversity. However, 15% of residents reported discrimination in 2017, with 39% of incidents being related to ethnicity or skin colour and 29% being related to nationality. One area of success for the city is mobility. The city aims to be accessible to everyone via public transport in a safe and sustainable way. There are about 665,000 bike journeys made daily, and the routes taken by trains, buses and trams are integrated to allow people to reach most of the city and its suburbs using a simple fare structure.

Singapore has adopted a compact, biodiversity-rich approach to urban planning. Despite having a population density of over 7000 people per km^2, the city has managed to expand its green areas from 36% of the island in 1970 to 47% in 2020. The city has 72 ha of rooftop gardens (Figure 8.49) and this figure is expected to triple by 2030. The city has over 4000 ha of green space, which provides several ecological services such as climate regulation, flood regulation, space for recreation and increased biodiversity. Singapore is believed to be home to between 23,000 and 28,000 terrestrial species.

Figure 8.49 Green roof in Singapore.

In Sao Paulo, Brazil, the organization Connect the Dots is creating a circular economy that tackles social inequality and supports regenerative farming. The project buys food from local farmers at 30% above the market price and provides food for vulnerable people. They have also helped local farmers to improve soil quality, promote biodiversity, reduce use of chemical fertilizers and pesticides and help to tackle global climate change.

1.3 Systems
6.3 Climate change – mitigation and adaptation

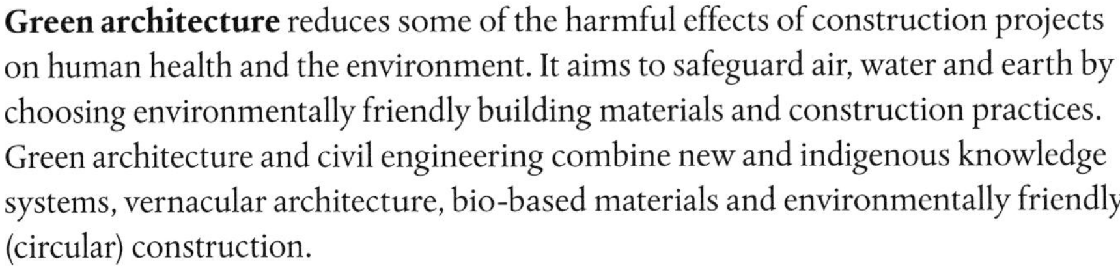

8.2.13 Green architecture

Green architecture is a philosophy focused on designing buildings with the lowest possible negative impact on the surrounding environment by using sustainable materials and energy sources in construction.

Green architecture reduces some of the harmful effects of construction projects on human health and the environment. It aims to safeguard air, water and earth by choosing environmentally friendly building materials and construction practices. Green architecture and civil engineering combine new and indigenous knowledge systems, vernacular architecture, bio-based materials and environmentally friendly (circular) construction.

Green architecture

Green architecture (also called 'sustainable architecture and/or 'green building') refers to buildings that are designed and constructed with environmentally friendly principles. Green architecture uses sustainable energy resources, reduces energy use and updates existing buildings with new technology. It helps reduce pollution, conserve natural resources and prevent environmental degradation. Economically, green architecture reduces the amount of money spent on water and energy. Socially, green architecture places limited strain on local infrastructure. Environmentally, green architecture is resource efficient as it uses traditional design and is built with local materials. Green building materials are generally composed of renewable resources and/or plentiful resources. For example, clay and sand mixed with water and fibres, such as straw, form adobe (clay blocks). Some advantages of green architecture are shown in Table 8.15.

Table 8.15 Advantages of green architecture.

Energy	Natural resources	Pollution
Energy consumption is minimized by using: • ventilation systems with efficient heating and cooling • energy efficient appliances and lighting • renewable energy resources e.g. solar and wind	Natural resources are conserved by: • water-saving features • designing landscape to maximize solar energy • re-use of older buildings • efficient use of space • use of responsibly harvested wood	Pollution is reduced by • more vegetation present, especially trees, so more pollution is filtered out of the atmosphere • reduced carbon emissions through use of renewable energy sources • less use of concrete as a building material and greater use of clay, vegetation and adobe rather than the use of concrete • use of sustainably harvested wood • reduced harm to the natural environment

Individual buildings do not have to have all of these features but will have at least some of them.

The disadvantages of green architecture include limited availability of materials and high cost due to expensive materials and technology.

Bale construction

Bale construction uses bales of straw and other materials to create housing and/or roofing (Figure 8.50). Many traditional homes in rural areas had straw bales in their construction or for insulation. Construction with straw bales has become more popular in places such as Australia, the USA and Europe, partly for environmental reasons (straw is renewable) and partly for cost. Straw bales have also been used to create earthquake-resistant housing in Pakistan, where the compressed bales are held together by nylon netting and sandwiched between layers of plaster.

Figure 8.50 Use of straw for roofing, South Africa.

The use of straw bales can pose problems related to moisture, mould and vermin but some of the bales can be replaced with newer ones if they have deteriorated over time.

Construction using plastic bottles

Bottles made from PET (polyethylene terephthalate) are clear, strong, lightweight plastic bottles that are 100% recyclable and may be able to last for up to 300 years.

Constructing buildings from plastic bottles has several advantages including:

- low cost
- materials are re-usable
- easy to build
- less construction material needed.

3D-printed houses

In 2021, 2.2 million 3D printers were shipped worldwide, and this is predicted to rise to 21.5 million by 2030. The global market was valued at around US$ 14 billion and is expected to grow annually by about 20% until 2030. Materials used for 3D printing include plastics, resins, concrete, mortar and polylactic acid (PLA), which is a bioplastic made from renewable plant-based materials including corn, sugarcane and cassava. 3D-printed houses provide design flexibility, increased productivity and efficiency compared with traditionally built houses, reduced transport costs, and can save time and eliminate waste. Traditional forms of building have faced skilled-labour shortages, housing shortages and impacts from hazards/climate change. There are several examples of 3D-printed houses. 'House zero' is a 186 m^2 3D-printed three-bedroomed house in Austin, Texas, USA. The walls, reinforced with steel, were printed in just three days. 'Project Milestone' is a 94 m^2 boulder-shaped single-storey home and is part of a five-home 3D-printing project in Eindhoven, The Netherlands. 'House 1.0' is a 37 m^2 3D-printed house in Holstebro, Denmark and is more affordable than most conventional housing. 'Kamp C' was printed in one piece using Europe's largest 3D printer and was the world's first two-storey home, built at Westerlo in Belgium.

Vernacular housing

Traditionally, the design of a building is closely related to the local climate. By understanding the potential impacts of local climate on buildings, architects can create safe, efficient, comfortable and sustainable building-types. For example, in many hot, humid areas such as in the Caribbean and southern Asia where flooding was either a seasonal or permanent problem, houses were built on stilts (Figure 8.51).

Figure 8.51 Housing built on stilts, Kampong Ayer, Bandar Seri Begawan, Brunei.

In contrast, nomadic and semi-nomadic peoples needed to create housing that could be moved around the landscape e.g. the Nenet nomadic reindeer herders of the Yamal Peninsula, Siberia with their chums (tents) (Figure 8.52).

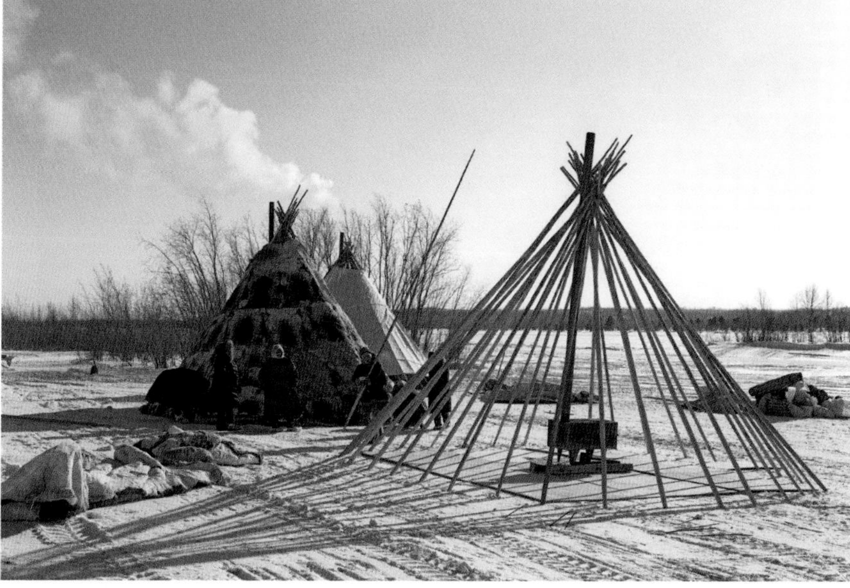

Figure 8.52 Nenet's chums.

Climate change has certain easily-observed effects on architectural forms e.g. the relative size of window area to wall area becomes lower as you move to countries that are closer to the equator. In hot environments, people limit the glare and heat of the Sun, by limiting the size of the windows. In addition, projecting balconies and overhangs cast long shadows on walls. Glazing uses materials in walls, windows or roofs to let in natural light while reducing the effect of sunlight. Lattices may fill large openings to reduce glare, while permitting breezes to pass through. Gabled roofs decrease in pitch as the rate of precipitation decreases. For example, in areas that receive heavy snow, gables are steep, while in hot environments, the pitch steadily decreases. In hot, dry countries, roofs become quite flat, even providing a comfortable place to sleep! In contrast, in areas of tropical rainfall, the roofs are again steep to provide protection from the torrential downpours.

In hot, dry areas a major focus of building design is minimizing heat penetration into the house. Walls are commonly painted white to reflect solar radiation and to limit heat absorption. Shady areas are designed for comfort and openings, such as windows, are often very narrow and have shutters that let light but not heat in and are able to withstand strong winds.

In hot, humid climates the impacts of extremely high temperatures can drastically affect the design of a structure. Cool roofs are specially designed to be reflective, thereby lowering temperatures inside the building and reducing the amount of energy needed to keep it cool. Shades, such as awnings, overhangs and trellises, block sunlight from entering a space. An example of adaptation to a hot and humid environment is seen in the Palace of Justice in Klungkung, Bali, Indonesia (Figure 8.53). Built in 1710, the pavilion is surrounded by a moat filled with water. Evaporation from the moat allows moist air to circulate round the pavilion producing a cooling effect. Rooms on the first floor are completely open to the outdoors to allow maximum ventilation. The ceiling is shaped like a tent so that heat accumulates and forms an insulating layer that protects the inside of the building from the sun's heat. The roof has an overhang that protects the base of the walls from rain.

Figure 8.53 Palace of Justice in Klungkung, Bali, Indonesia.

Figure 8.54 Wind tower house, Dubai.

Arabic wind tower houses

Arabic wind tower houses (or windcatchers) are a traditional form of housing that creates cross-ventilation and cooling in buildings. They are common in North Africa and West Asia and have been used for over 3000 years (Figure 8.54). Their popularity has increased in the 21st century as a method to increase ventilation and reduce the use of costly air-conditioning units. There are a number of designs, but the principle of each is the same – catch the wind and transfer it into buildings where it can have a cooling effect (Figure 8.55). Some air filtering may be needed to reduce the amount of dust or insects carried by the wind. Within buildings, warm air rises and escapes through the top of the wind tower whereas denser, colder air sinks to the ground. Wind towers are used in other environments too, for example they are used in the Bluewater shopping centre in Dartford in the UK.

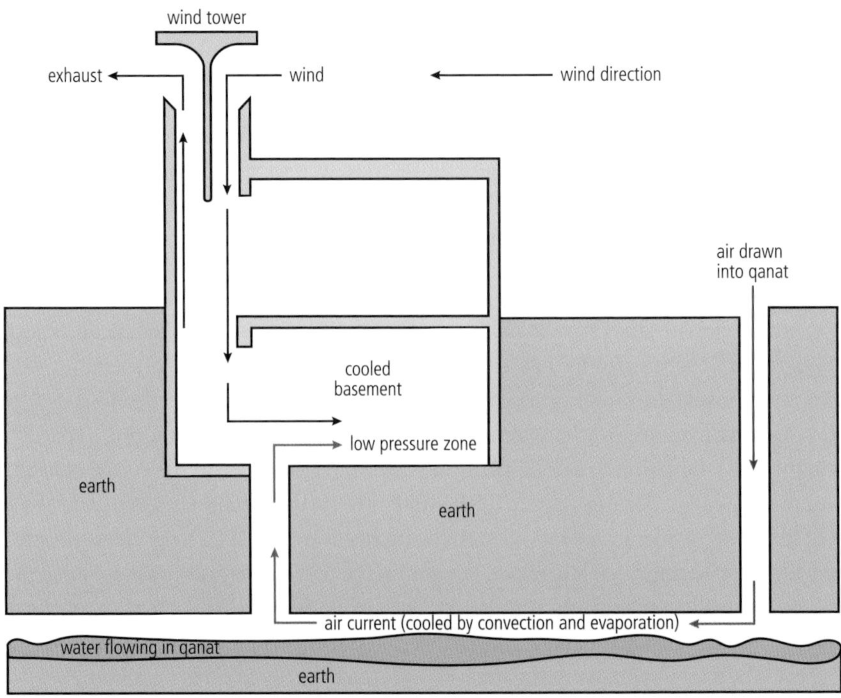

Figure 8.55 The principles of an Arabic wind tower.

Engagement

- Investigate population change in your own country or the country you live in. Have a class discussion on the impacts on society and options for population management.
- Volunteer with a local organization that works to support those people who may have suffered from social and environmental inequity.
- Evaluate the extent to which an urban environment local to your school is sustainable. Write some recommendations to improve the sustainability of a local urban area.
- Investigate what actions and activities to achieve Sustainable Cities and Communities occur in your local area.
- Make a poster including proposals for smart city functionality for your school community. Put copies of the poster in busy places around your school.

Exercise

Q12. Using Figure 8.56 **estimate** the proportion of the population that were urban in 2025 in **(a)** Africa **(b)** Asia and **(c)** Latin America.

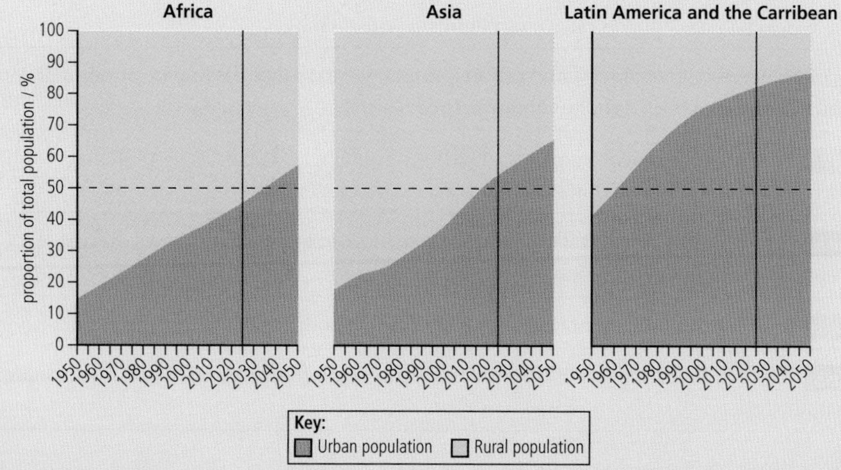

Figure 8.56 Variations in the level of urbanization over time.

Q13. **Distinguish** between push and pull factors.

Q14. **Outline** the advantages of the Garden City as seen by Ebenezer Howard.

Q15. **Describe** an example of urban ecology.

Q16. **Describe** one example of urban farming.

Q17. **Describe** the main characteristics of urban ecosystems.

Q18. **Explain** how urban areas work as systems.

Q19. **Outline** the main characteristics of suburban areas.

HL

Q20. HL **Describe** the main characteristics of an unsustainable (linear) city and a sustainable (circular) city as shown by the Rogers Model.

Q21. HL **Outline** the advantages of green architecture.

HL end

8.3 Urban air pollution

Guiding question

How can urban air pollution be effectively managed?

8.3.1 Urban air pollution is caused by inputs from human activities to atmospheric systems, including nitrogen oxides (NOx), sulfur dioxide, carbon monoxide and particulate matter.
8.3.2 Sources of primary pollutants are both natural and anthropogenic.
8.3.3 Most common air pollutants in the urban environment are either derived directly or indirectly from combustion of fossil fuels.
8.3.4 A range of different management and intervention strategies can be used to reduce urban air pollution.
8.3.5 NOx and sulfur dioxide react with water and oxygen in the air to produce nitric and sulfuric acid, resulting in acid rain.
8.3.6 Acid rain has impacts on ecology, humans and buildings.
8.3.7 Management and intervention strategies are used to reduce the impact of sulfur dioxide and NOx on ecosystems and to minimize their effects.
HL 8.3.8 Photochemical smog is formed when sunlight acts on primary pollutants causing their chemical transformation into secondary pollutants.
HL 8.3.9 Meteorological and topographical factors can intensify processes that cause photochemical smog formation.
HL 8.3.10 Direct impacts of tropospheric ozone are both biological and physical.
HL 8.3.11 Indirect impacts of tropospheric ozone include societal costs and lost economic output.

8.3.1 Causes of urban air pollution

1.2 Systems
6.1 Introduction to the atmosphere

Urban air pollution is caused by inputs from human activities to atmospheric systems. The main urban air pollutants are nitrogen oxides (NOx), sulfur dioxide (SO_2), carbon monoxide (CO) and **particulate matter**. NOx and SO_2 can be carried downwind and may combine with rain to produce acid rain. Particulate matter is categorized according to size of particle, with $PM_{2.5}$ being fine particulate matter with a diameter of 2.5 microns or less and PM_{10} being larger particulate matter with a diameter of 10 microns. Figure 8.57 shows Los Angeles with good air quality whereas Figure 8.58 shows the same location with poor air quality.

One micron (or one micrometre) is one-thousandth of a millimetre.

Figure 8.57 Los Angeles with good air quality.

Figure 8.58 Los Angeles with poor air quality.

Nitrogen oxides

Nitrogen monoxide (NO) and nitrogen dioxide (NO_2) are collectively known as nitrogen oxides (NOx) and are gases that are formed when nitrogen gas (N_2) and oxygen gas (O_2) from the air combine in the high temperature of vehicle engines during combustion processes. High concentrations of NOx usually occur in winter, when an increased number of vehicles are being used, particularly in calm cold weather when the pollutants are trapped close to the ground by temperature inversions. Overall, approximately 50% of NOx come from vehicles, 25% from industry/domestic resources and 25% from power stations.

The effects of NOx are varied but high concentrations in the atmosphere can reduce plant growth and cause visible damage to sensitive crops, cause acid rain and play a part in the formation of ground level ozone. The gases can also cause coughs and sore throats and can cause breathing difficulties in people with asthma or bronchitis.

Sulfur dioxide

Sulfur dioxide (SO_2) is released by the combustion of sulfur-containing fuels including coal, smokeless fuel and oil. Oil and natural gas emit very small amounts of SO_2, and diesel emits greater amounts. Increasingly, sulfur emissions are falling due to the increasing use of sulfur-free fuels such as natural gas, lower industrial energy demand and energy conservation, particularly in urban areas. SO_2 can form smog (tropospheric ozone), cause respiratory problems, aggravate heart conditions and damage plants.

Carbon monoxide

CO is formed from the incomplete combustion of fuels such as petrol and diesel in inefficient car engines as well as incomplete combustion in fires and faulty boilers. The increase in vehicle ownership may not be to blame for the increase in CO emissions as vehicles are checked through emissions testing (via MOT testing in the UK) and if the CO levels are excessive the vehicle fails the test. If CO is produced in the vehicle engine and comes out of the exhaust into the atmosphere it also creates additional CO_2.

Carbon monoxide is toxic and very high levels may be found at busy road junctions, especially at rush hour. The highest levels occur in underground car parks, enclosed bus stations and tunnels. CO reduces the absorption of oxygen by hemoglobin in the red blood cells, which in turn increases heart stress and affects the nervous system.

Particulate matter

Black smoke is produced from the incomplete combustion of fossil fuels and consists of fine particles (mainly carbon) known as particulate matter. PM_{10} are particulate matter with a diameter of less than 10 microns while $PM_{2.5}$ have a diameter of less than 2.5 microns (Figure 8.59). The main sources of particulate matter are vehicle emissions, but some is formed by the incomplete combustion of solid and liquid fuels, for power generation and domestic heating.

Figure 8.59 PM_{10} and $PM_{2.5}$.

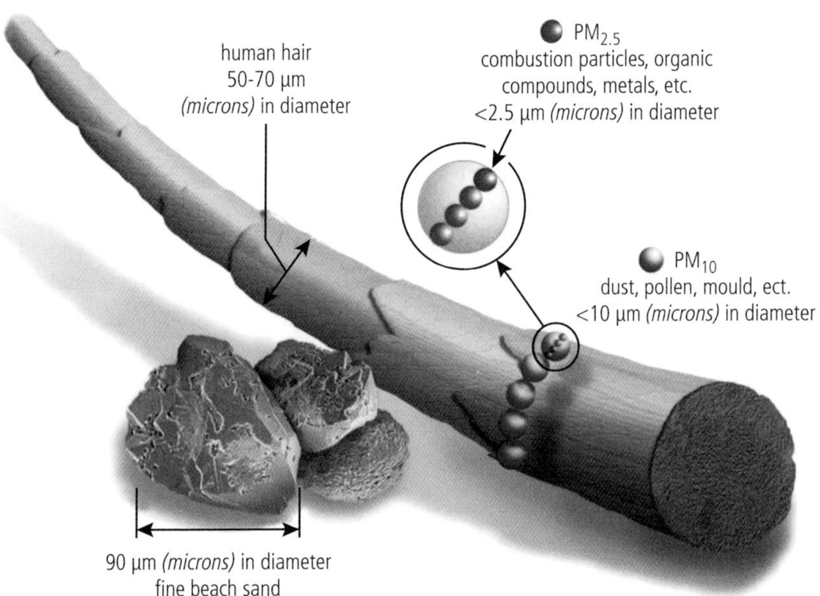

Increased levels of particulates, including PM_{10}, are associated with higher levels of morbidity (illness) and mortality (death). Even quite low concentrations lead to decreased lung capacity and increased heart and respiratory diseases, including asthma. Levels of PM_{10} pollution may cause 60,000 deaths each year in the USA and 10,000 in the UK, mostly among the elderly and those with respiratory diseases. There is no safe limit and even if a small proportion of PM_{10} pass through the alveoli they can reduce lung function. $PM_{2.5}$ may pass into the alveoli and are even more potent than PM_{10} as a cause of death. The levels of particulate matter are increasing because of the increased use of diesel due to it being a more efficient and economical fuel. Diesel emits fine particulates that can penetrate the lungs. Very fine particulates that are less than 10 microns in size are small enough to penetrate deep within the lung.

Example – India and England

India

Air pollution in India contributes to the deaths of over 1.6 million people per year. Some 35% of India's population live in areas of poor air quality, putting them at risk of heart attacks, strokes and lung cancer. Air pollution also causes a decline in happiness and an increase in depression. Economic impacts include absenteeism and reduced productivity. Exposure to high levels of pollutants during academic examinations has been linked with reduced performance. People living in areas with excessive amounts of $PM_{2.5}$ also have an increased risk of dementia.

England

According to Public Health England (PHE), there could be up to 2.5 million new cases of coronary heart disease, lung cancer, childhood asthma, low birth weight, dementia and diabetes by 2035, mainly in cities and industrial areas, if existing air pollution levels continue. However, a reduction of $PM_{2.5}$ by 1 μm/m³ compared with 2015 levels in Lambeth (London) could lead to a reduction of over 150 new cases of disease per 100,000 people. Similarly, a reduction of 1 μm/m³ in NO_2 over a year could lead to nearly 30 fewer cases per 100,000 people there.

What constitutes a 'good reason' for us to accept a claim?

To what extent does correlation mean causation? Is there a correlation between global climate change and population growth in India? Yes, there is, but does it mean they are related?

8.3.2 Sources of primary pollutants

6.2 Climate change – causes and impacts

There are natural and **anthropogenic** sources of **primary pollutants.**

Anthropogenic means as a result of human activities.

Primary pollutants are those that are active at the point of emission (Figure 8.60). For example, forest fires used to clear trees release CO_2, CO and particulate matter into the atmosphere. This, in turn, leads to less oxygen being produced due to less photosynthesis, increased surface and air temperatures and reduced humidity, partly due to increased temperatures and partly to increased run-off. An increase in particulates in the atmosphere may lead to a gradual reduction in the amount and quality of solar radiation reaching the Earth's surface. This results in less light reaching the green plants and so the potential for photosynthesis to occur is reduced.

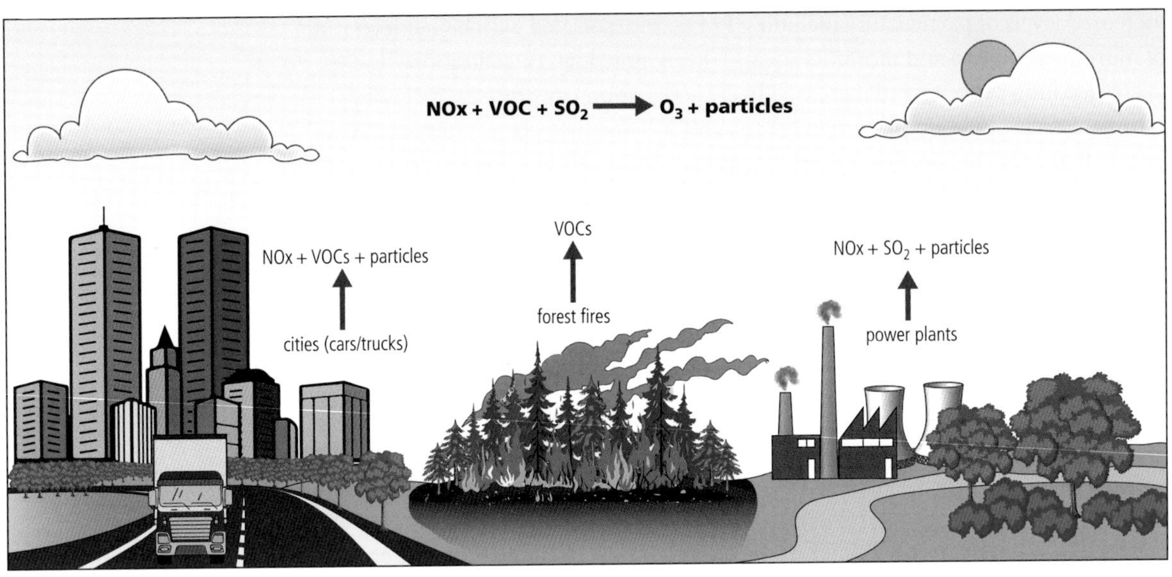

Figure 8.60 Sources of primary pollutants in urban areas.

Dust, soil, fine sand and particulate matter are common air pollutants. Natural sources of these types of pollutant include the erosion and transport of fine sands from dust storms or sandstorms, while in urban areas they can occur from any unvegetated surface such as building sites, road surfaces, power stations and from industrial waste. Some cities may also experience fallout from volcanic eruptions, such as Plymouth on the Island of Montserrat (Figure 8.61). Large-scale volcanic eruptions, such as Mount St Helens in 1980, can eject material high into the atmosphere and can have global implications.

Not all pollution is man-made. Volcanic eruptions create poor air quality but are entirely natural.

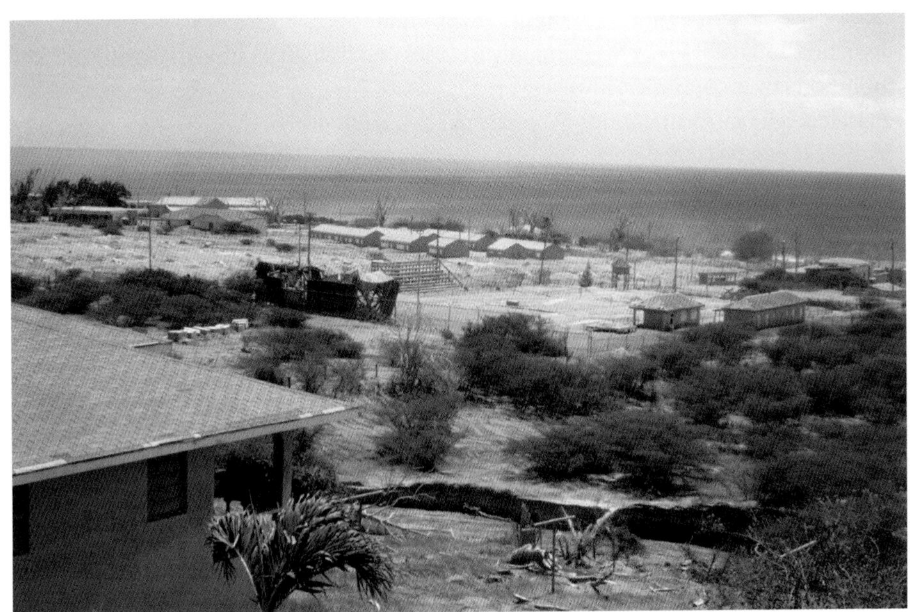

Figure 8.61 Plymouth, Montserrat covered in volcanic dust.

TOK

What challenges are raised by the dissemination and/or communication of knowledge?

Are natural sources of pollution really 'pollution' or are they just short-term variations in the natural environment?

Anthropogenic sources of primary pollutants include the clearance of land for urban development, and the burning of fossil fuels and biomass for energy production.

Indicator species

An indicator species is an organism that is used to assess a specific environmental condition (see also Topic 4, Section 4.4.13). For example, nettles are found in soils with high levels of phosphorus and most lichen are associated with low levels of SO_2.

A lichen is a symbiosis formed between an alga and a fungus. Lichen are found in all parts of the world, including extreme environments such as hot deserts and the tundra. In many parts of the developed world, and increasingly in developing countries, the use of coal led to higher levels of SO_2 in the atmosphere and many lichen species became extinct locally. However, as a result of declining coal consumption in many countries, there has been a reduction in the proportion of SO_2 in the atmosphere and many species of lichen have expanded their range. Thus, in these locations, lichens can be used as an indicator of clean air with respect to SO_2. There are three main types of lichen:

- shrubby or fruticose lichens, which are very sensitive to pollution and will only grow in clean air
- leafy or foliose lichens, which can tolerate only small amounts of pollution
- crusty or crustose lichens (Figure 8.62), which can survive in higher amounts of pollution.

Figure 8.62 Crusty lichen growing on a gravestone.

SKILLS

Plan an experiment to use an indicator species as a correlate for pollution in the local environment

Most studies of lichens involve a transect (linear sample) from an area of higher pollution, such as a city centre or industrial area, to an area of lower pollution, such as a residential area.

Use a lichen key to record the percentage cover of lichen species at each sample site. Make sure that the samples are taken at the same height. You could use a bar chart/compound bar chart to show the changes in percentage cover and composition of lichen between the starting point and the finish.

An alternative activity would be to look at the percentage cover of lichen in terrestrial environments such as walls, trees and gravestones. Most gravestones face east-west and many are dated, so it could be possible to work out whether there is a relationship between the age of the gravestone and the amount of lichen cover and/or to see whether there is a difference in the percentage cover of lichen with aspect, for example west-facing as opposed to east-facing, as there may be important differences in the microclimate. For example, west-facing may be warmer and wetter than east-facing.

Watch the video *Studying Lichens* on YouTube to find out how to measure lichens and how fast they grow.

8.3.3 Urban air pollutants are derived from combustion of fossil fuels

1.3 Sustainability

Most common air pollutants in the urban environment are derived either directly or indirectly from combustion of fossil fuels.

Tropospheric ozone - ozone in the lower atmosphere, the troposphere - produces smog and is bad for human health.

Stratospheric ozone - ozone in the upper atmosphere, the stratosphere-is good as it prevents ultraviolet radiation from reaching the Earth's surface.

Particulate matter

$PM_{2.5}$ are very fine particles that are 2.5 microns or less in diameter. Domestic combustion and industrial combustion are the major source of $PM_{2.5}$ emissions. Burning wood in stoves and open fires accounts for about three-quarters of domestic emissions worldwide. Annual emissions of $PM_{2.5}$ and PM_{10} fell by around 80% between 1970 and 2021 in the UK due to lower amounts of coal being used and improved emissions standards for transport and industry, although domestic wood burning has increased (Figure 8.63). Globally, trends in PM emissions have been downwards, largely driven by improvements in air quality in China, but there have been increases in the Middle East and Africa.

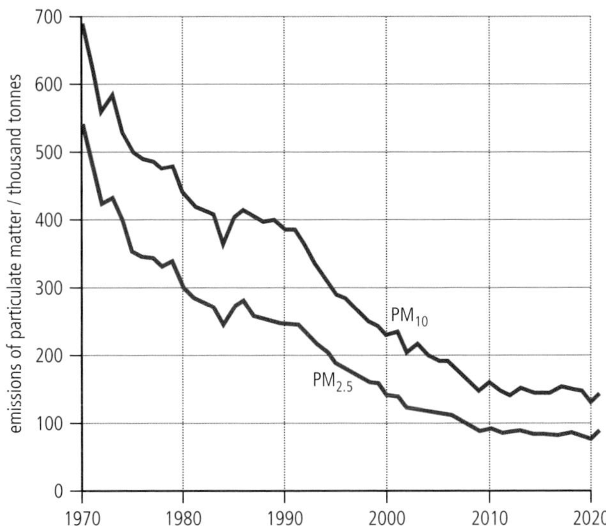

Figure 8.63 Trends in emissions of $PM_{2.5}$ and PM_{10} in the UK.

Primary pollutants are pollutants that are active on emission including gases such as $PM_{2.5}$, PM_{10}, SO_2 and CO_2 that are released from burning coal and other fossil fuels. Secondary pollutants are pollutants that require a physical or chemical change. For example, the chemical reactions between NOx and volatile organic compounds from vehicle exhausts in the presence of sunlight to form tropospheric (ground level) ozone.

Carbon monoxide

Most of the CO emitted into the atmosphere comes from motor vehicles. In the USA, vehicles account for *c.* 55% of CO emissions, with non-road vehicles (including boats and construction equipment) accounting for a further 20%. However, in many urban areas, with road congestion, road traffic accounts for between 85% and 95% of CO emissions. CO levels are highest in winter when people are in their cars for longer, there is an increase in traffic congestion and more time is spent in traffic queues. Other sources include industries such as metal processing and chemical manufacturing, both largely located in urban areas. Wood stoves and open fires are indoor sources of CO, as is smoking.

Sulfur dioxide

Sulfur dioxide (SO_2) is released by the combustion of fuels such as coal, oil and ores that contain lead, aluminium and iron sulfides. The highest emissions of SO_2 occur around power stations and major industrial areas. In the past, SO_2 was a major cause of poor air quality in many cities in HICs, but the increasing use of sulfur-free fuels such as natural gas, lower industrial energy demand and energy conservation have contributed to a decline in SO_2 levels, particularly in urban areas. In such places, poor air quality may exist, but is now more likely to be caused by the increase in the volume of vehicles (Figure 8.64). In cities that burn large amounts of coal, sulfur dioxide emissions continue to cause issues.

Tropospheric ozone

In the presence of sunlight, secondary pollutants are formed when primary pollutants undergo a variety of reactions with other chemicals already present in the atmosphere. Tropospheric ozone is a secondary pollutant, formed when oxygen molocules react with oxygen atoms that are released from nitrogen dioxide in the presence of sunlight.

A 'peasouper' is a thick fog that is often yellow, green or black in colour caused by air pollution that contains particles of soot and SO_2 gas, which is poisonous to humans.

Ozone, O_3, is made up of three oxygen atoms. Tropospheric ozone is a secondary pollutant formed through the interaction of sunlight and other pollutants.

Figure 8.64 Changing causes of poor air quality in London, 1950s and 1990s.

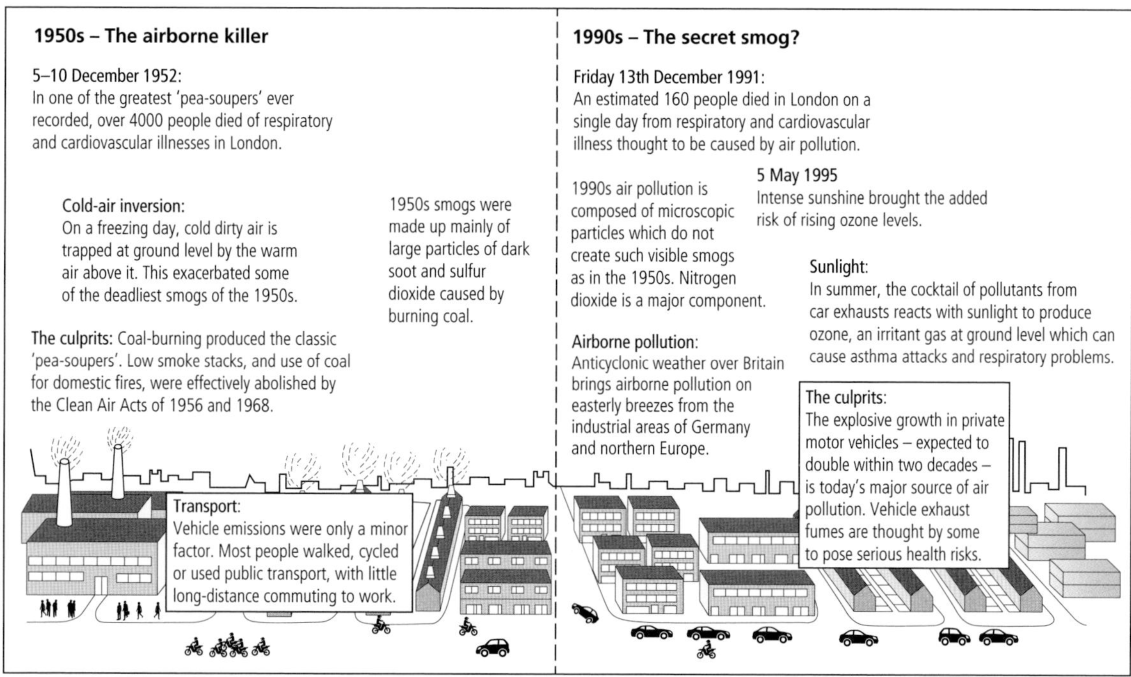

8.3.4 Strategies to reduce urban air pollution

1.3 Sustainability
8.3 Urban air pollution

A range of different management and intervention strategies can be used to reduce urban air pollution. Some examples are given here.

The most common management and intervention strategies relate to the transport sector, removing industry from urban areas and changing energy resources. Most policies fall into three sectors:

1. incentives, such as cheap public transport to reduce the use of private cars
2. supportive policies, such as subsidies to change household fuels
3. punitive policies, such as tolls for cars to enter congestion charge areas.

In addition, greater use of renewable energy, clean fuels and lower-/non-polluting vehicles are important for reducing urban air pollution.

Improved public transport

Improved public transport, and increased use of public transport, reduces emissions from private vehicles. Some places have made parts of the public transport network completely free. For example, in Miami, USA, a free train system (metro mover)

According to the World Health Organization there were up to 7 million premature deaths due to air pollution in 2022, and these mainly occurred in urban areas.

In 1306, King Edward I of England issued a proclamation banning the use of sea coal due to the pollution it caused.

In 1852, Charles Dickens opened *Bleak House* with 'smoke lowering down the chimney pots, making a soft black drizzle, with flakes of soot in it, as big as full-grown snowflakes . . . fog everywhere . . . in the eyes. . . in the throat. . . cruelly pinching the toes and fingers.'

provides some 17,000 free rides daily and in Detroit, the Detroit People Mover provides a free service for a 5 km loop in the downtown area. Bangkok offers some free seats in third class on some buses and trains. Benefits of free public transport include reduced numbers of vehicles on the road, decreased energy usage, fewer emissions, clearer skies and healthier communities.

Congestion is one of the most important concerns as it causes delays, increased fuel consumption and poor air quality. The establishment of metro systems as a means of mass public transport has a major impact on the improvement of air quality. For example, since 2005 (ahead of the 2008 Olympic Games), Beijing has achieved rapid growth in its metro system and vastly improved air quality. In Oslo, Norway, increases in parking fees were considered the most effective measure to control air pollution.

Sea coal may be washed up on shorelines after being eroded from coastal areas or submarine deposits.

Infrastructure for cycling

Cycling can be encouraged by the introduction of cycle lanes. Copenhagen is described as the best capital city for cycling. Its population of around 600,000 residents cycle around 1.5 million km each day and almost half of all trips to school and work are made on bicycles. The cycling infrastructure includes cycle lanes, traffic calming measures and separated routes for bicycles and vehicles. On quieter roads that are shared by bikes and cars, cars are restricted to a maximum speed of 30 km/hour. The use of narrow lanes, tight corners and textured surfaces also helps to reduce car speeds. Along busier streets, cycle lanes are separated from car lanes by painted stripes.

A number of countries, including France, Italy, Belgium, UK, Ireland and New Zealand, encourage people to cycle to work and help people to buy bikes and equipment. The benefits are not just for people's health but also for the environment.

Growing trees as natural screens

Trees and other vegetation screens can improve urban air quality by removing some particulate pollution from the air. For example, there was widespread planting of London plane trees during the 18th and 19th centuries (Figure 8.65 and Table 8.16).

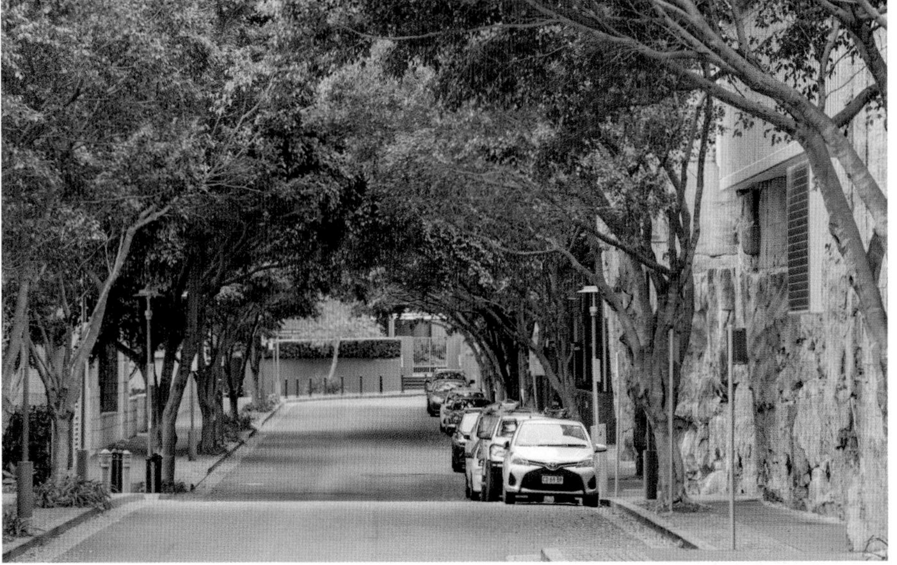

Figure 8.65 A Sydney road, in Australia, with London plane trees.

Advantages	Disadvantages
• Very tolerant of air pollution. The hairs on young shoots and leaves help to trap pollutants. • Rarely affected by disease and pests, although some shoots are killed each year by fungal infection. • Very tolerant of poor soil conditions including compacted soil, although some stunting of growth is caused by road salt. • Grows vigorously and tolerates pruning. • Trees rarely blow over or shed branches. • Open canopy provides light shade. Will intercept some rain, especially when in leaf. • Provide valuable nesting sites for birds. • Sufficient light beneath canopy to allow significant plant growth.	• Leaves, fruit and bark need clearing from streets and pavements. • Its large size makes it unsuitable for some locations. • Due to their water uptake, roots can cause problems in the foundations of buildings on clay soils. • Fine hairs on shoots, leaves and fruit may cause irritation and allergies in some people.

Table 8.16 Advantages and disadvantages of managing air pollution using London plane trees.

Green walls

Research has suggested that in certain locations, green walls could reduce urban air pollution by as much as 30%. Urban air pollution cannot easily escape from narrow roads with tall buildings (urban canyons). However, green walls of climbing ivy, grass and other vegetation (Figure 8.66) can clean the air moving into canyons and take some pollution, notably NOx and PM, out of the atmosphere. In contrast, larger street trees may cause some pollution to be trapped at street level. Trees can absorb harmful gases such as CO, SO_2, NOx and PM. However, when it rains, these particles can be washed down to the ground. Problems for urban trees include drought, heat stress and vandalism. In addition, green walls can have high maintenance costs (e.g. irrigation) and a need for fertilizers.

Figure 8.66 An example of a green wall.

Catalytic converters

Catalytic converters reduce emissions of carbon monoxide (CO), hydrocarbons (HC) and oxides of nitrogen (NOx). Since 1993, all new cars in the European Union have been fitted with catalytic converters.

As the vehicle exhaust gas passes through the catalytic converter, the pollutant gases CO and NOx are converted to the less harmful gases nitrogen and CO_2. Some catalytic convertors can be up to 90% efficient but these need temperatures of 150 °C to be effective and some need temperatures of 200 °C. However, catalytic convertors in cars in urban areas rarely reach these temperatures and may be only 50% efficient. New research is taking place to replace platinum group metals as a catalyst with synthetic materials or nano-based catalysts in order to improve the efficiency of catalytic converters.

Limited car use

Traffic restriction in city centres (Figure 8.67), low emission zones (LEZs) in city centres and congested areas and the introduction of tolls in different parts of cities help to reduce vehicle numbers. For example, the introduction of LEZs in Rome led to a reduction of NO_2 emissions by 23% and the reduction of PM_{10} emissions by 10%. A number of cities, such as Mexico City, Athens and Singapore, limit the cars that can enter a city to odd or even number plates. This can backfire by encouraging people to have two cars with odd and even number plates. Often the second car is an older, more polluting car.

Figure 8.67 Traffic restrictions in city centres, such as reducing access for private cars, Oxford, UK.

Car use can also be reduced through car-sharing or pooling. Emissions can also be reduced by driving at lower speeds and not having the engine on when stationary (idling).

Pedestrianized town centres

A number of towns and city centres have changed from being vehicle-focused to being pedestrianized (Figure 8.68). As well as reduced vehicle access at selected times, pavements have been widened to make walking more convenient. In many cities in developed countries, pedestrianized malls became commonplace during the 1970s and 1980s. There are several advantages of pedestrianized town centres including better air quality, reduced levels of noise, easier and safer to walk and cycle, more outdoor dining and increased footfall for shops. However, some critics claim that pedestrianization makes it more difficult for some people to reach the town centre, that bus services are re-routed (some pedestrianized centres allow public transport to continue) and that traffic will get diverted into surrounding areas.

Figure 8.68 Pedestrianized city centre, Stroge Street, Copenhagen.

8.3.5 Acid rain

Rainfall is naturally acidic, with a pH of between 5.0 and 5.5. When we talk about 'acid rain' we are talking about rainfall with an enhanced acidity, that is, rain with a pH lower than 5.0. Each unit on the pH scale represents a tenfold increase in acidity, so a pH of 4.5 is ten times more acidic than a pH of 5.5.

In cold environments acid snow can fall and dry deposition can occur, which is the deposition of acid particulates that generally occurs close to the point of emission but can be as far as 30 km away.

NOx and sulfur dioxide pollutants in the air react with water and oxygen in the air to produce nitric and sulfuric acids. These acids then dissolve into the water in the atmosphere to create acid rain with a pH between 4 and 5.

Nitrogen monoxide (NO) reacts with oxygen (O_2) to form nitrogen dioxide (NO_2). The equation representing this reaction is:

$$2NO + O_2 \longrightarrow 2NO_2$$

The nitrogen dioxide then reacts with water and oxygen in the air to produce nitric acid (HNO_3). The equation representing this reaction is:

$$4NO_2 + O_2 + 2H_2O \longrightarrow 4HNO_3$$

Sulfur dioxide (SO_2) dissolves in rainwater to produce sulfurous acid (H_2SO_3). The equation representing this reaction is:

$$SO_2 + H_2O \longrightarrow H_2SO_3$$

The sulfurous acid is then oxidized by oxygen in the air to produce sulfuric acid (H_2SO_4). The equation representing this reaction is:

$$2H_2SO_3 + O_2 \longrightarrow 2H_2SO_4$$

Natural emissions of sulfur dioxide come from volcanoes, forest fires and the decay of organic matter. Anthropogenic emissions of sulfur dioxide come from the burning of fossil fuels (Figure 8.69).

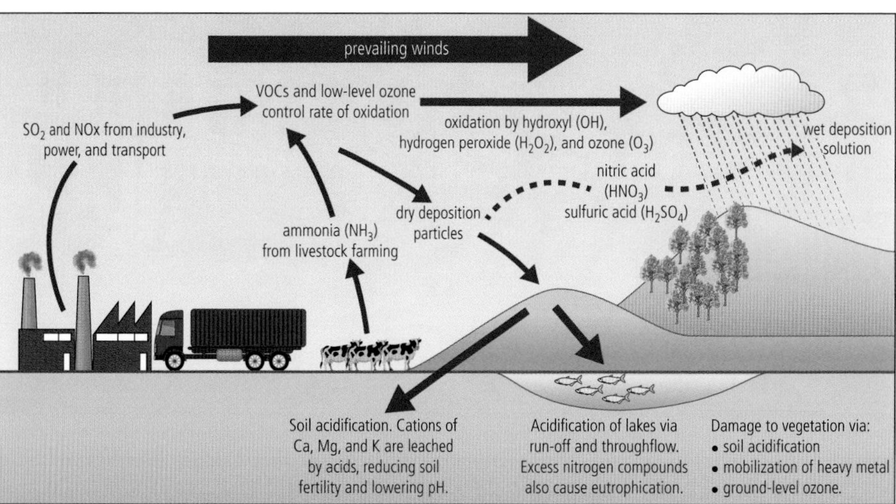

Figure 8.69 Wet and dry acid deposition.

2.2 Energy and biomass in ecosystems

8.3.6 Acid rain has impacts on ecology, humans and buildings

The observed effects of acid rain can vary. Leaching, toxification of the soil and foliage damage can be seen in terrestrial habitats. In freshwater habitats, increased toxicity due to aluminium solubilization can be seen, along with the impacts on fish gills and invertebrate exoskeletons. Corrosion marble, limestone, steel, paint and other construction materials can be seen on buildings. The effects on human health can include detrimental effects on breathing from nitrate and sulfate particles (components of $PM_{2.5}$ and dry acid deposition).

An increase in the acidity of soils and water produces an increased solubility of certain metal ions. Iron and aluminium ions have increased mobilization when the pH is 4.5 or lower. High levels of aluminium ions in freshwater have a toxic effect on fish. In particular, aluminium ions affect fish gills making respiration more difficult. Exposure to aluminium ions can also lead to reproductive failure, reduced growth and skeletal deformities in fish. Acidification of seawater has a major impact on animals with shells or exoskeletons made from calcium carbonate, including crabs, lobsters and sea snails. The acid in the water dissolves the calcium carbonate shells and the more acidic the water, the faster the shells dissolve.

One of the most important impacts of acidic water occurs as a result of its ability to flush trace metal ions from soil and pipes, including lead. The water of some wells in Sweden contains aluminium ion levels of up to 1.7 mg dm^{-3}. The World Health Organization safe limit for aluminium ion levels is 0.2 mg dm^{-3}. Eating fish that contain high accumulated levels of mercury can result in serious health problems including neurological and behavioural disorders such as tremors, insomnia, memory loss and headaches.

Figure 8.70 shows the effect of soil acidification on nutrient availability in soils. Changes in pH affect the solubility of different nutrients. With increasing acidity, many nutrients such as nitrogen and phosphorus become unavailable to plants, but copper becomes more available in acidic soils. Calcium, magnesium, iron and aluminium can all be leached from acidic soils.

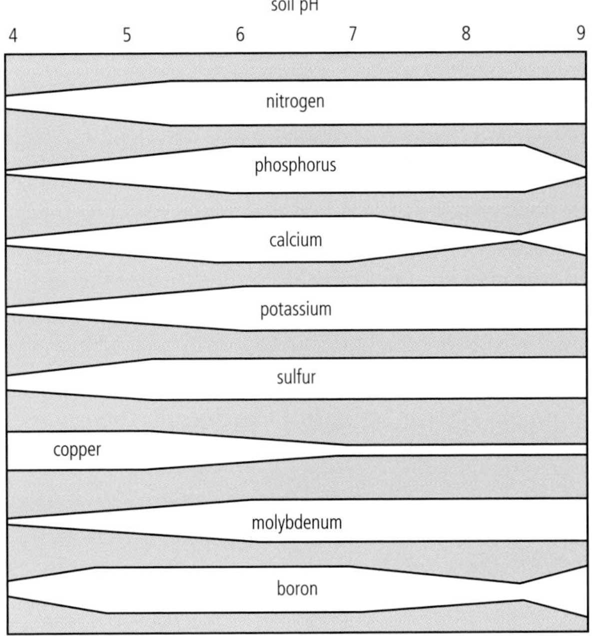

Figure 8.70 The effect of soil acidification on nutrient availability (the thickness of the bar represents relative availability).

Acidified lakes are characterized by:

- a less varied species structure
- clearer water with visibility several times greater than normal
- white moss spreading across the bottom of the lake
- increased levels of dissolved metals such as cadmium, copper, aluminium, zinc and lead (so these metals become more easily taken in by plants and animals).

One of the most obvious environmental effects of acid rain has been the loss of fish in acidified lakes. Many species of fish are not able to survive in acidic water (Figure 8.71). Very often organisms are exposed to extremely low pHs during the most sensitive part of their life cycle (for fish this might be the fry stage). These periods coincide with snowmelt and the accompanying acid surge. At these times, the water also has a high metal ion content. Earthworms, for example, cannot tolerate very acidic soils. More acidic pH values, e.g. below pH 5, cause most damage to plants and animals.

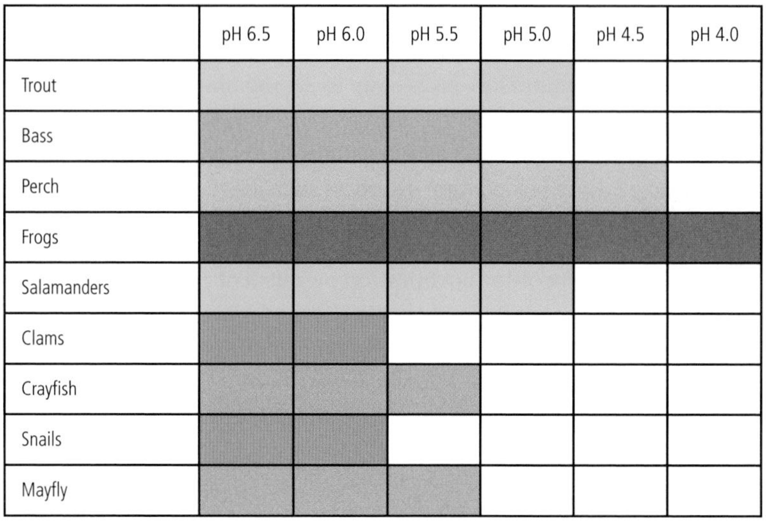

Figure 8.71 pH tolerance levels for selected aquatic organisms.

	pH 6.5	pH 6.0	pH 5.5	pH 5.0	pH 4.5	pH 4.0
Trout						
Bass						
Perch						
Frogs						
Salamanders						
Clams						
Crayfish						
Snails						
Mayfly						

Acid rain severely affects trees and forests (Figures 8.72 and 8.73) as it breaks down fats in the foliage and damages membranes, which can lead to plant death. Sulfur dioxide interferes with the process of photosynthesis by increasing the amount of particulates in the atmosphere and reducing the amount of sunlight reaching the Earth's surface. Coniferous trees seem to be most at risk from acid rain. These trees do not shed their needles at the end of every year. On a healthy conifer, the needles can be up to 7 years old, but the oldest needles on trees affected by acid rain are between 2 and 3 years of age. This means that the tree has far fewer needles than normal. If a conifer loses over 65% of its needles, it will probably die. Acid rain also decreases the soil pH below 4.2, meaning that aluminium ions can be leached into the soil. These ions damage root systems and decrease tree growth, as well as increasing development of abnormal cells and premature loss of needles from the tree.

Figure 8.72 The effects of acidification on trees.

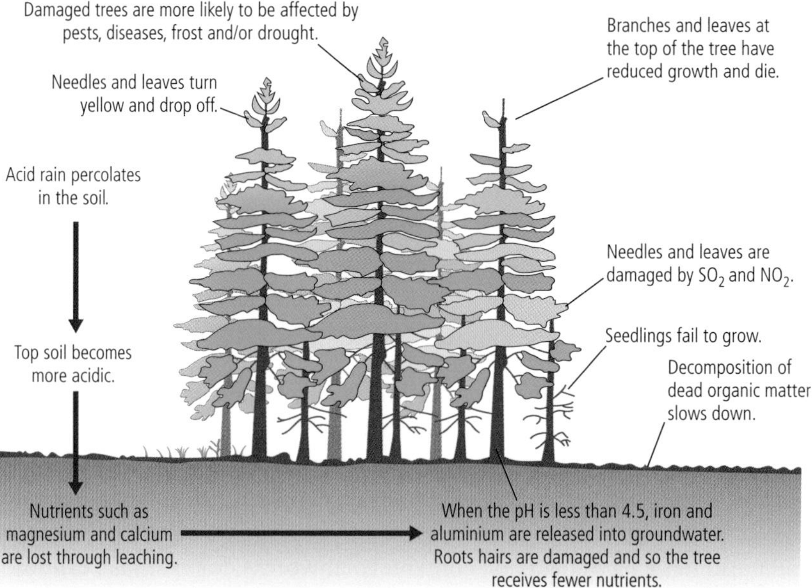
Damaged trees are more likely to be affected by pests, diseases, frost and/or drought.
Branches and leaves at the top of the tree have reduced growth and die.
Needles and leaves turn yellow and drop off.
Acid rain percolates in the soil.
Needles and leaves are damaged by SO_2 and NO_2.
Seedlings fail to grow.
Top soil becomes more acidic.
Decomposition of dead organic matter slows down.
Nutrients such as magnesium and calcium are lost through leaching.
When the pH is less than 4.5, iron and aluminium are released into groundwater. Roots hairs are damaged and so the tree receives fewer nutrients.

Figure 8.73 Trees damaged from acidification, Chance's Peak, Montserrat.

Damaged conifers are easily recognizable. The extremities of the tree die, especially the crown, which is most exposed. Needles drop, so the tree looks very thin. Branches on some trees droop. In most cases, acid rain does not kill the tree directly, but is an added pressure on the tree which is then more likely to suffer damage from insects, fungi, frost, wind and drought. Although deciduous trees generally do not suffer so much, research shows that their growth is also affected.

Young trees in soil affected by acid rain often show abnormally rapid growth. This is because the nitrogen ions from the acid rain get released and can act as fertilizer. However, the strength of the root systems does not develop as much as the stems and the trees are more easily blown over. As they are also deprived of other vital nutrients from the soil the wood is likely to be very soft, making the trees more prone to attacks from insects.

The low pH of soils and the presence of metals may cause damage to root hairs (used by the tree to absorb nutrients). The tree loses vitality, growth is retarded, there is an inability to cope with stress (such as frost, drought and pests) and the tree becomes susceptible to injury. Needles and leaves turn brown, fall off, and finally whole branches snap away. In parts of Germany, more than 50% of newly planted spruce trees died or were damaged within a year.

Acid rain can also weather rocks such as limestone, which is made from calcium carbonate (Figure 8.74).

Figure 8.74 The weathering of limestone rock by acid rainfall.

Marble is also made from calcium carbonate and, along with other building materials such as steel, copper, bronze, brass and construction materials including cement and concrete, can also react with, and be weathered by, acid rain. Human health can also be affected by PM and acid rain. Acid deposition, which is the dry deposition of tiny particulates, can cause respiratory problems such as asthma and chronic bronchitis. It can also make existing conditions worse. Particles of nitrates and sulfates at ground level can help form ground level ozone and can also cause pneumonia and bronchitis, sometimes leading to permanent lung damage.

1.3 Sustainability 

8.3.7 Strategies to reduce the impact of SO_2 and NOx on ecosystems

As with other forms of pollution, SO_2 and NOx can be managed by altering human activity.

Management and intervention strategies

Given that the predominant causes of acid rain are industrial and transport emissions it is not easy to target all potential polluters. But it is equally expensive and time-consuming to treat extensive areas already affected by acid deposition.

As prevention is better than cure, there are several options that could help to manage pollutant levels (Figure 8.75).

Figure 8.75 Pollution management targeted at three different levels.

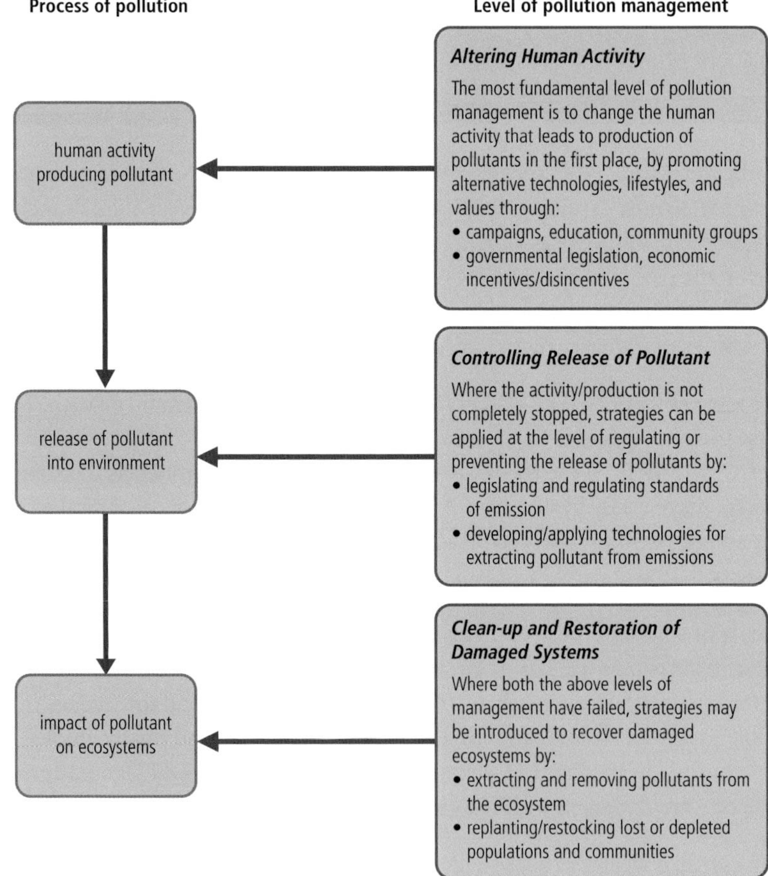

Process of pollution
Level of pollution management
human activity producing pollutant
release of pollutant into environment
impact of pollutant on ecosystems
Altering Human Activity
The most fundamental level of pollution management is to change the human activity that leads to production of pollutants in the first place, by promoting alternative technologies, lifestyles, and values through:
• campaigns, education, community groups
• governmental legislation, economic incentives/disincentives
Controlling Release of Pollutant
Where the activity/production is not completely stopped, strategies can be applied at the level of regulating or preventing the release of pollutants by:
• legislating and regulating standards of emission
• developing/applying technologies for extracting pollutant from emissions
Clean-up and Restoration of Damaged Systems
Where both the above levels of management have failed, strategies may be introduced to recover damaged ecosystems by:
• extracting and removing pollutants from the ecosystem
• replanting/restocking lost or depleted populations and communities

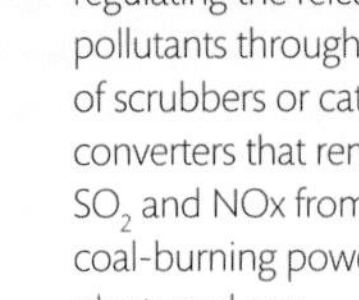

Pollution management strategies for acid deposition could include

- altering human activities, for example reducing the use of fossil fuels or using alternative renewable resources or the introduction of international or national agreements by governments
- regulating the release of pollutants through use of scrubbers or catalytic converters that remove SO_2 and NOx from coal-burning power plants and cars.

Methods to reduce pollution:

1 Reduce the use of fossil fuels

- Reduce use of fossil fuels on an industrial and domestic scale, although this requires a government initiative in order to switch to large-scale energy generation from alternative resources such as nuclear or hydroelectric power.
- Reduce the number of private cars and large vehicles on the road by increasing the number of people using public transport or park-and-ride schemes.
- Transfer the transportation of goods from road to railways, rivers or canals.
- Switch to low-sulfur fuels such as oil, gas and high-grade coal.

2 Regulate the release of pollutants

- Remove sulfur from fuels before combustion, although this is expensive for coal and cheaper for oil.
- Reduce SO_2 and NOx released on combustion using fluidized bed technology (FBT), which is done by burning coal in the presence of crushed limestone.
- Remove SO_2 from waste gases after combustion using flue-gas desulfurization (FGD).

Both FBT and FGD are well developed and effective methods, but they are also very expensive. FBT brings the flue gases into contact with a SO_2-absorbing chemical, such as limestone, which can capture up to 95% of the SO_2 produced in power stations. FGD removes SO_2 from exhaust flue gases in power stations. There are three types of FGD used:

- wet scrubbing, which uses alkaline scrubbers such as limestone to absorb the SO_2
- spray dry scrubbing, which uses hydrated lime to form a mix of calcium sulfate/sulfite
- scrubbing with a sodium sulfite solution.

In the UK, 46% of NOx comes from power stations and 28% comes from vehicle exhausts. Emissions from power stations can be reduced through special industrial boilers which reduce the amount of air present at combustion. Car exhaust emissions can be reduced by different types of engines or exhausts, lower speed limits and greater use of public transport.

Global impact

As acid rain is often a transboundary issue, meaning the source of the pollution is from a different country to where the impacts occur, legislation has to be agreed on by many countries. The 1979 Convention on Long-Range Transboundary Air Pollution was crucial in the clean-up of acidification in Europe as it brought together polluter and polluted countries, set clear targets for pollution reduction and made polluters recognize their international environmental responsibilities.

The 1999 Gothenburg Protocol to abate acidification, eutrophication and ground-level ozone commits countries to reduce their emissions of SO_2 and NOx.

Clean up and restoration

Adding crushed limestone can limit the impact of acidification at least in the short-term. This process, called liming, has been used extensively in lakes in Norway and Sweden but has not been used much in the USA. It is an expensive process and has to be done repeatedly. It allows fish to remain in a lake and enables aquatic ecosystems to function. However, it is a short-term solution. As long as energy power plants, vehicles and industries continue to emit NOx and SO_2, the problem will remain.

Clean-up and restoration measures may include spreading ground limestone in acidified lakes or recolonization of damaged systems, but the scope of these measures is limited.

HL

8.3.8 Photochemical smog formation

HL

6.1 Introduction to the atmosphere

Primary pollutants are those that are emitted directly from source e.g. sulfur dioxide, carbon monoxide. Secondary pollutants are that undergo a transformation e.g. tropospheric ozone, in which ozone interacts with sunlight

Smog is a mix of primary and secondary pollutants, of which the main pollutant is tropospheric ozone (O_3).

Photochemical smog is formed when sunlight acts on primary pollutants causing their chemical transformation into **secondary pollutants**.

O_3 occurs naturally in the upper atmosphere layer known as the stratosphere at a height of between 15 and 30 km and is beneficial to humanity because it provides protection against some of the most harmful types of ultraviolet radiation from the Sun.

Unlike other pollutants, tropospheric O_3 is not directly emitted from human activities in large quantities. The lower atmosphere, known as the troposphere, extends up to a height of about 10–15 km. Tropospheric ozone (O_3) is considered to be a pollutant in this layer and is formed here as the result of chemical reactions between volatile organic compounds (VOCs), CO, PM, unburned hydrocarbons, NOx, SO_2 and sunlight to produce photochemical smog (Figure 8.76).

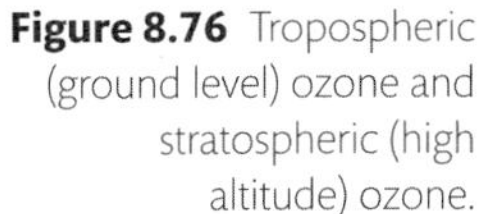

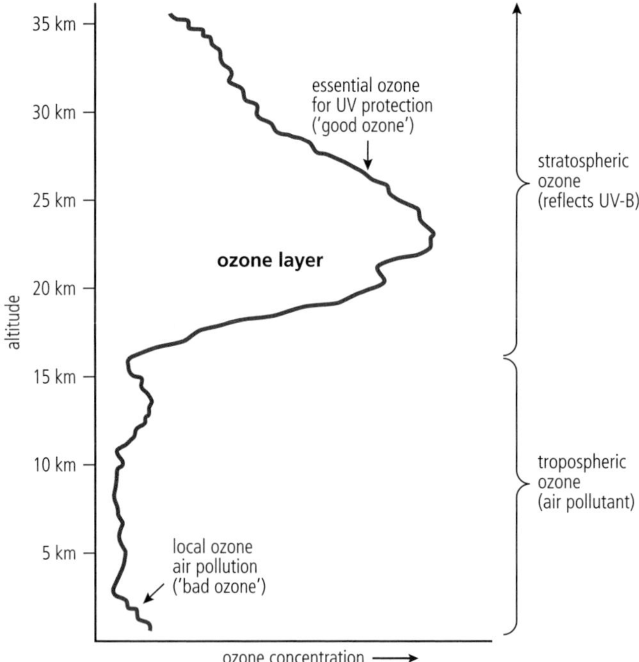

Figure 8.76 Tropospheric (ground level) ozone and stratospheric (high altitude) ozone.

VOCs are organic compounds that are able to evaporate and take part in photochemical reactions. There are many different VOCs including methane, ethane and alcohol.

The main sources of VOCs and NOx are road transport, solvent release from drying paints, glues, or inks and petrol handling and distribution. Nitrogen is present in fuels and in the air. In the high temperature of the internal combustion engine, nitrogen is oxidized to NO. Once the exhaust gases leave the engine, NO reacts with oxygen to form NO_2, a brown gas that contributes to urban haze and smog and causes acid rain.

Hydrocarbons (from unburned fuel) and NO gas are given off when fossil fuels are burned.

Peroxyacyl nitrates (PANs) are another component of photochemical smog and are produced when oxidized VOCs combine with NO_2. Other sources of PANs include motor vehicles, burning of fossil fuels and tobacco smoke.

Sunlight and primary pollutants

Nitrogen dioxide can absorb sunlight and break up to release oxygen atoms that combine with oxygen in the air to form ozone (Figure 8.77).

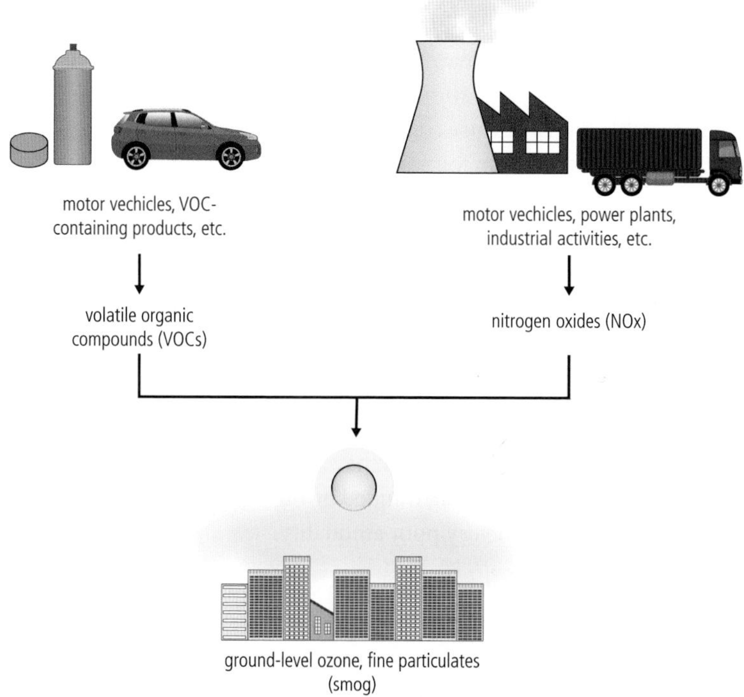

Figure 8.77 The causes of tropospheric ozone.

In the presence of sunlight, secondary pollutants are formed when primary pollutants undergo a variety of reactions with other chemicals already present in the atmosphere. Tropospheric ozone is an example of a secondary pollutant.

It may take hours or days for the photochemical reactions between the NOx and VOCs to produce ozone. Because the reactions occur in sunlight, the ozone concentrations are greatest during the day, especially during warm, sunny and stable conditions. Above temperatures of 20 °C, these reactions are accelerated.

As ozone formation may take a number of hours, the polluted air drifts away from the source into surrounding suburban and rural areas. Hence, ozone pollution may be greater outside the city centre.

HL

8.3.9 Meteorological and topographical factors can intensify processes that cause photochemical smog formation

2.4 Climate and biomes
6.1 Introduction to the atmosphere

The frequency and severity of smog in an area depends on local topography, climate, population density and fossil fuel use.

Meteorological factors refer to weather conditions, such as sunshine, wind and temperature, while topological factors include the main physical features of the landscape such as altitude, relief and gradient.

High levels of O_3 are more common in low-lying areas and depressions, where polluted air tends to collect. Places such as Mexico City and Athens, which are surrounded by high ground, tend to have poor air quality because cold, denser air sinks from the higher ground, preventing the dispersion of pollutants.

Photochemical smog is associated with certain climates – in particular, high air pressure systems with high levels of sunlight. This is because winds in a high-pressure system are usually weak. Hence pollutants remain in the area and are not dispersed. Poor air quality often persists for many days because stable high-pressure conditions generally prevail for a few days. In some climates, notably Mediterranean ones and desert climates, stable high-pressure conditions prevail for a whole season or annually, hence poor air quality can remain for months. In monsoonal areas, such as South-East Asia, smog only occurs in the dry season.

Tropospheric O_3 is also associated with large populations. In general, the larger the population, the greater the number of vehicles. As vehicles are one of the main sources of NOx, it follows that in larger cities there is greater potential for the production of tropospheric O_3. In societies that continue to use fossil fuels, the chances of tropospheric O_3 being produced remain high. In contrast, in cities where there is a greater reliance on sustainable forms of transport, such as Curitiba in Brazil, the risk of tropospheric O_3 is reduced. Places which have high air pressure, a large population, continue to use fossil fuels and are surrounded by high ground, such as Mexico City and Athens, are associated with very poor air quality.

Background levels of ground-level O_3 have risen substantially over the last century. There is evidence that the pre-industrial near ground-level concentrations of O_3 were typically 10–15 ppb. The current annual mean concentrations are approximately 30 ppb over the UK, for example. The number of hours of high O_3 concentrations tends to increase from north to the south across the UK. Concentrations can rise substantially above background levels in summer heat waves when there are periods of bright sunlight with temperatures above 20 °C and light winds. Once formed, O_3 can persist for several days and can be transported over long distances. Summer heatwaves have become an increasing health problem for the UK since 2000.

Thermal (temperature) inversions occur due to a lack of air movement when a layer of dense, cool air is trapped below a layer of less dense, warm air. This causes concentrations of air pollutants to build up near the ground instead of being dispersed by 'normal' air movements.

Thermal inversions

Smog is associated with temperature inversions (Figure 8.78). These may be more common in winter because of high levels of SO_2 and other pollutants resulting from increased heating of homes, offices and industries. Under cold conditions, vehicles operate less efficiently (until they have warmed up). This inefficient operation releases larger amounts of CO and hydrocarbons. Urban areas surrounded by high ground are especially at risk from winter smog. This is because cold air sinks in from the surrounding hills, reinforcing the inversion.

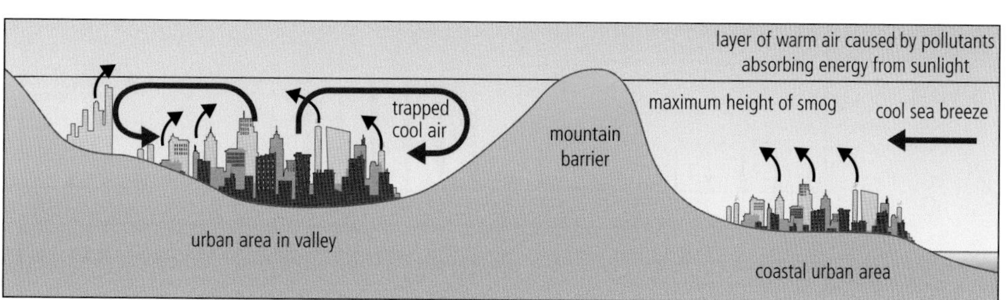

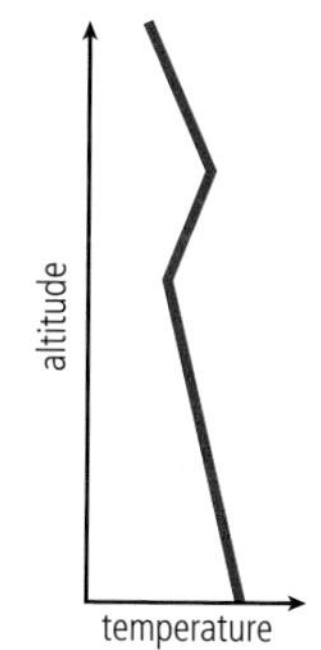

Figure 8.78 A temperature inversion and smog.

SKILLS

Use graphs showing diurnal changes in urban air pollution
Use secondary databases to show change over time in local air quality

In Mexico City, the average visibility has decreased from about 100 km in the 1940s to about 10 km in the 2020s.

The average altitude of Mexico City is 2240 m above sea level. Consequently, average atmospheric pressure in the city is roughly 25% lower than it is at sea level. The lowered partial pressure of oxygen (pO_2) has a significant effect on transport – fuel combustion in vehicle engines is incomplete and results in higher emissions of CO and other compounds such as hydrocarbons and VOCs. The dry season is from November to April and the wet season is from May to October.

The most important air pollutants in Mexico City include O_3, PM_{10} and $PM_{2.5}$, (Figure 8.79). Intense sunlight turns these into photochemical smog (Figure 8.80). In turn, the smog prevents the Sun from heating the atmosphere enough to penetrate the inversion layer blanketing the city.

The combined activity of vehicles and industry uses over 45 million litres of petroleum fuel every day, generating thousands of tonnes of pollutants. These emissions, along with the climatic and topographic nature of the region, lead to the production of tropospheric ozone and particulate matter.

Dry season

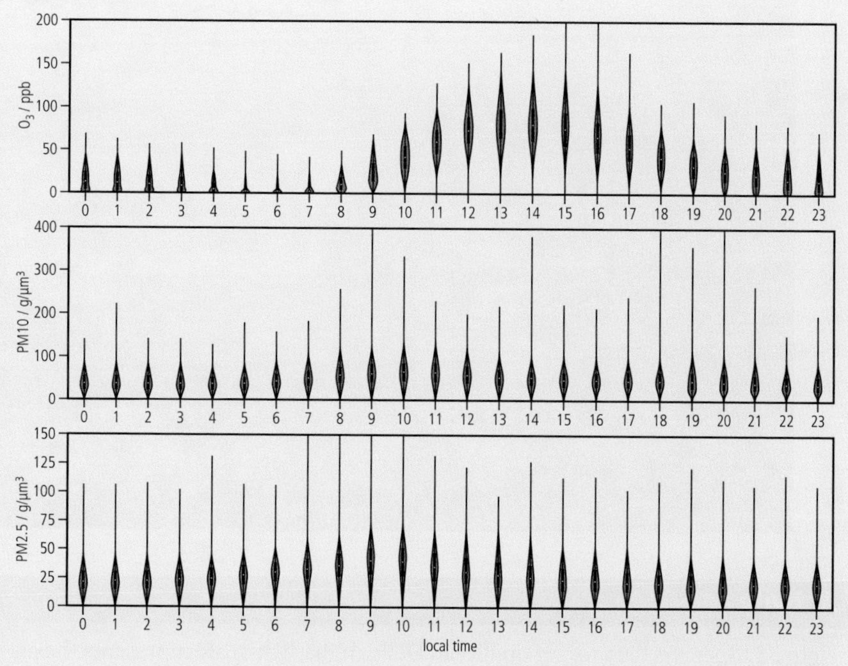

Figure 8.79 Diurnal changes in air quality in Mexico City.

When describing graphs, look for the maximum, minimum, trends and exceptions, using the data provided.

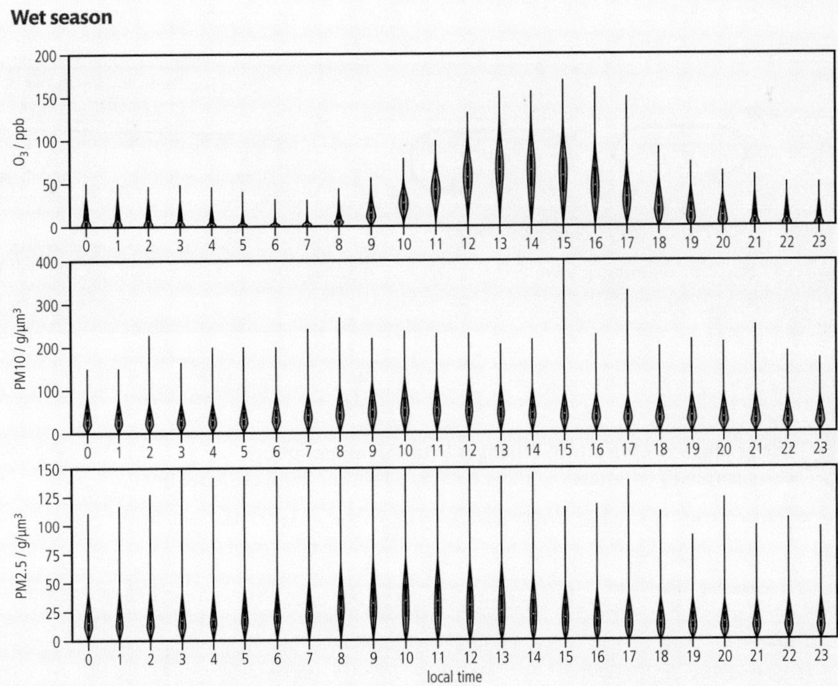

The levels of O_3 show a clear peak during the afternoon for both dry and wet seasons, while PM_{10} are predominantly found in the late evening, especially in the dry season. $PM_{2.5}$ pollution peaks in the morning, and this is more pronounced in the wet season. The diurnal variation of ozone is mainly due to photochemical reactions in sunlight. Therefore, O_3 concentrations increase from 9:00 am local time to a peak at around 15:00 pm local time. The O_3 concentrations are lowest at night.

The hourly behaviour of $PM_{2.5}$ and PM_{10} is broadly similar, showing as being low between 0:00 am and 7:00 am and rising from 9:00 am to 15:00 pm local time.

Figure 8.80 Photochemical smog over Mexico City.

Activity

Figure 8.81 shows data for air quality in Delhi, India. The scale represents the air quality index, with values of 0–25 being the best air quality and more than 400 being the worst.

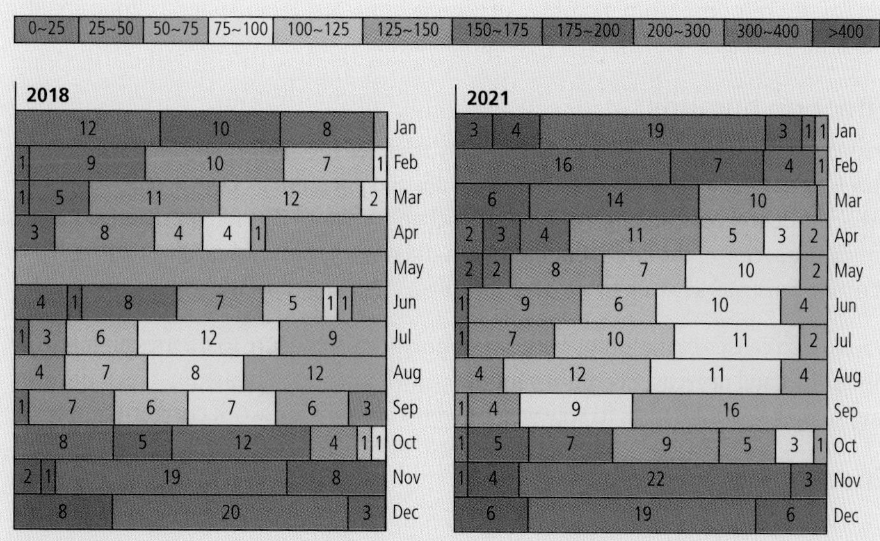

Figure 8.81 Air quality in Delhi, India in 2018 and 2021.

1. Using the data in Figures 8.81 a and b, state the modal* air quality index for October 2018 and October 2021.
   (*The mode is the most common value in a range of values.)
2. Identify the median* air quality index for October 2018 and October 2021.
   (*The median is the middle value when all the readings are placed in ascending or descending order.)

Table 8.17 shows the air quality categories for October 2018 and October 2021.

Air quality index	50–75	75–100	100–125	125–150	150–175	175–200
Mid-point	62.5	87.5	112.5	137.5	162.5	187.5
Frequency October 2018	1	1	4	12	5	8
Frequency October 2021	1	3	5	9	7	1

Table 8.17 Air quality categories.

3. Using the mid-point for each air quality category, calculate the mean air quality index for October 2018 and October 2021.

8.3.10 Direct impacts of tropospheric ozone

HL

The direct impacts of tropospheric ozone can be both biological and physical. Tropospheric ozone damages plants (crops and forests), irritates eyes, creates respiratory illnesses and damages fabrics and rubber materials. It is also the main pollutant in smog.

Tropospheric ozone is highly reactive and damaging to plants and animals.

Effects on vegetation

The impacts of tropospheric ozone on vegetation include a reduction in crop and timber yields leading to economic loss and a reduction in the production of roots, seed and fruit.

Tropospheric ozone has also been suggested as a cause of dieback of German forests, although this had previously been linked with acid rain.

Air pollution makes it more difficult for fruit flies to mate as females are unable to recognize a male's scent. Increased levels of ozone reduce the ability of males to release their characteristic odour. Male fruit flies in the areas with the highest ozone levels emitted fewer pheromones, which are chemicals released by insects or mammals that

Research in Hong Kong examined the impact of air pollution, especially ozone pollution, on plants and the environment. The average ozone levels have been increasing in Hong Kong over the past 20 years. Ozone reduces photosynthesis, reduces gas exchange from plants and reduces growth in both natural vegetation and crops. As vegetation plays an important role in regulating the environment, ozone-induced damage in plants may increase environmental degradation, with severe consequences for human health.

can cause a response from members of the same species. Tropospheric ozone could therefore be a cause of fruit flies' population decline.

Effect on humans

Ozone can harm lung tissues, impair the body's defense mechanisms, increase respiratory tract infections and aggravate asthma, bronchitis and pneumonia. Even at relatively low levels, incidences of coughing, choking and sickness increase. The long-term effects include premature ageing of the lungs. Children born and raised in areas where there are high levels of ozone can experience up to a 15% reduction in their lung capacity.

Ozone also causes irritation of eyes. Even short-term exposure to ozone can intensify discomfort and decrease secretions for people with dry-eye disease, in which the eyes cannot make enough tears to stay wet, or whose eyes do not work correctly.

Effects on materials

High levels of ozone can damage fabrics and rubber materials. Photochemical smog damages aesthetic and functional properties and shortens life spans of rubber products when stressed, folded or bent. Cracking, loss of elasticity and loss of resilience (strength) occur in rubber affected by ozone, especially in outdoor areas. The life of vehicle tyres has been shown to be reduced in areas that experience high levels of ground-level ozone. They may lose their grip or braking ability as they are worn down. Ozone has also been linked with the corrosion of aluminium, especially when it is damp or wet.

HL

8.3.11 Indirect impacts of tropospheric ozone

1.3 Sustainability

Economic losses caused by urban air pollution can be significant.

The indirect impacts of tropospheric ozone include societal costs and lost economic output.

Economic losses include absenteeism from work, reduced productivity, decreased crop productivity, the cost of healthcare, the cost of replacing materials and the cost of clean-up strategies.

The Clean Air Fund suggests that the cost of air pollution to India is worth nearly 3% of the country's GDP. Two cities in northern India lost at least 13% of their GDP in 2020 due to air pollution, namely Lucknow 14% and Delhi 13%. Much of this was due to lost labour productivity. Air pollution has a major impact on deaths and economic losses in large cities (Table 8.18). IQ Air (a Swiss air quality technology company) showed that four cities accounted for over 120,000 deaths and over US$ 66 billion of losses in 2022. In Los Angeles, USA around 14,000 deaths were caused by air pollution in 2020, and economic losses were estimated at around US$ 32 billion. Urban air quality is predicted to be the top environmental cause of death by 2050. However, in cities where ozone levels decrease, death rates due to air pollution decline and worker productivity increases.

Table 8.18 Deaths and economic losses due to air pollution in selected cities, 2022.

City	Deaths to air pollution	Economic losses (US$ billion)
Tokyo	40,000	43
Delhi	54,000	8.1
Mexico City	15,000	8
Sao Paulo	15,000	7
Total for all four cities	124,000	66.1

A study by the Environmental Protection Agency (EPA) in the USA found that exposure to ground level ozone is related to increased risk of death among all age groups but slightly higher for those with respiratory or cardiovascular problems. The increased risk of death increased even below the clean air standards set by the EPA.

A number of studies have examined how the impacts of tropospheric ozone affect different communities. One study found that communities that lived in areas with higher volumes of traffic were more exposed to ozone. These were often poorer communities whereas more wealthy communities were associated with quieter environments, better access to healthcare, lower stress and more exercise. Long-term studies in the USA revealed that mortality due to ozone was less in younger people than in older people, mortality was higher for the unemployed or those with low occupational status and mortality was higher for women than for men. The study found 'weak evidence' for racial or ethnic differences in vulnerability. Other studies, however, suggested that Black Americans, in particular, were more at risk from particle pollution than white Americans. This was believed to be due to residential segregation, with Black Americans more likely to live in areas where there was greater exposure to pollution. Other factors influencing increased risk were higher unemployment and greater use of public transport. Another survey found that people who smoked, whether currently or previously, were more susceptible to the respiratory effects of ozone exposure.

Exercise

Q22. Briefly **explain** why lichens can be used as an indicator species for air pollution.
Q23. **Distinguish** between primary and secondary pollutants.
Q24. **Outline** how growing trees, green walls and/or natural screens can improve air quality.
Q25. **Explain** the formation of acid rain.
Q26. **Outline** the impacts of acid rain on trees.
Q27. **Outline** the three main methods of pollution management strategies.

HL

Q28. HL **Suggest** why urban air pollution is worse during calm weather.
Q29. HL Briefly **explain** why particulate matter can be harmful to human health.
Q30. HL **Describe** diurnal variations in air quality in large cities, such as Mexico City.
Q31. HL **Outline** the formation of tropospheric (ground level) ozone.

HL end

Engagement

- Investigate the causes and consequences of urban air pollution in an environment local to you. Investigate and consider strategies that could be used to reduce pollution in that environment. Make a poster to illustrate the causes and potential solutions to urban air pollution near you.
- With the help of your teacher, start a citizen science air quality project in your school. Publicize your results on a department noticeboard, in the Common Room and in any school publications.
- With the help of your teacher, organize a meeting to call for better walking and cycling options to get to school. This might include, for example, more cycle racks being provided or the provision of reflective armbands or jackets.

Practice questions

1. Figure 8.82 shows seasonal variations in air quality in Delhi, India.

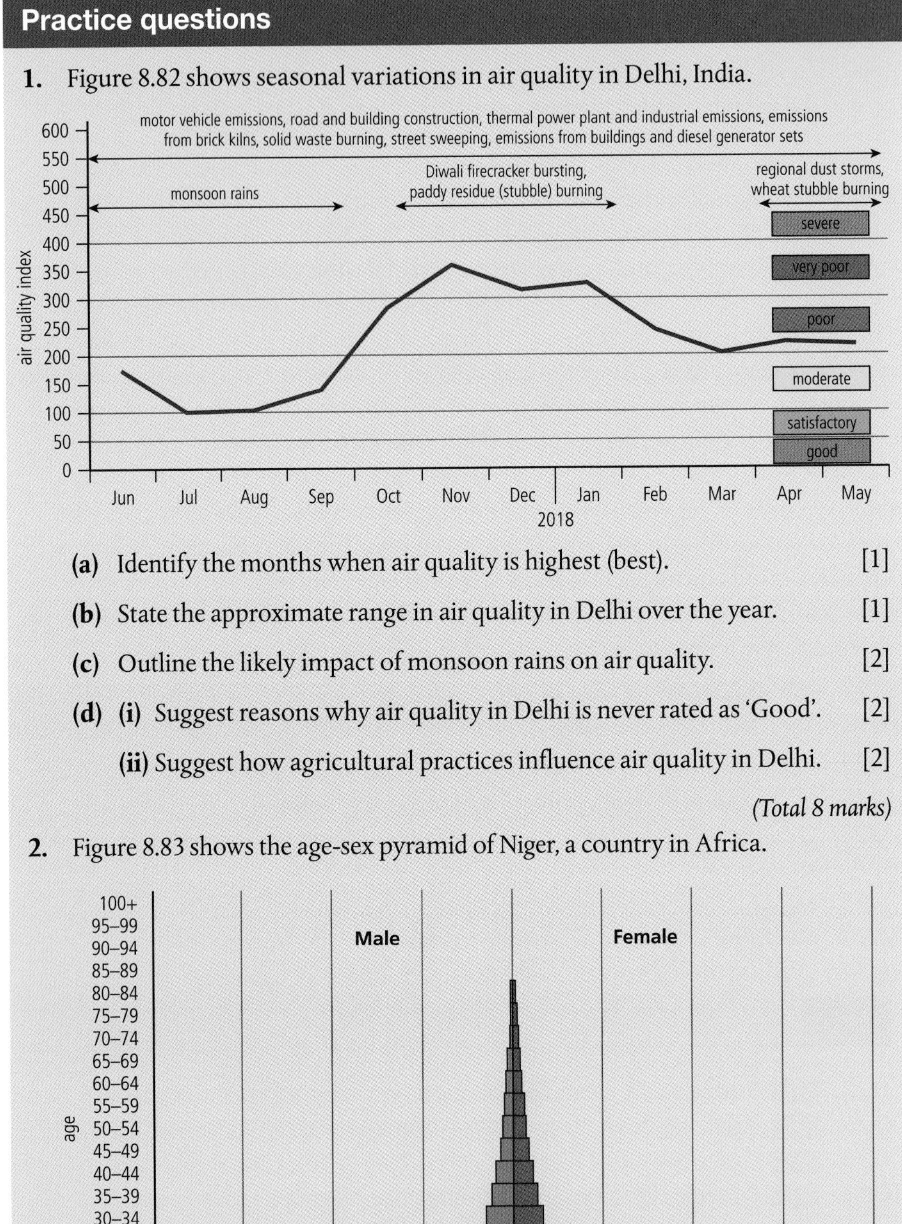

Figure 8.82 Seasonal variations in air quality in Delhi, India.

(a) Identify the months when air quality is highest (best). [1]

(b) State the approximate range in air quality in Delhi over the year. [1]

(c) Outline the likely impact of monsoon rains on air quality. [2]

(d) **(i)** Suggest reasons why air quality in Delhi is never rated as 'Good'. [2]

(ii) Suggest how agricultural practices influence air quality in Delhi. [2]

(Total 8 marks)

2. Figure 8.83 shows the age-sex pyramid of Niger, a country in Africa.

Figure 8.83 Age-sex pyramid for Niger, Africa.

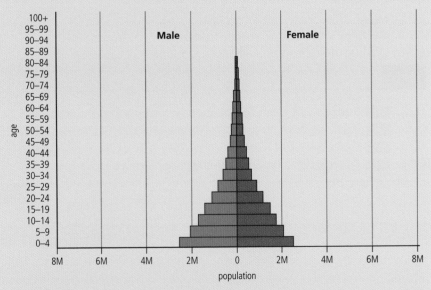

(a) Describe the main characteristics of Niger's population pyramid. [3]

(b) Suggest reasons why some countries have high death rates. [3]

(c) Explain why some HICs have low birth rates. [2]

(d) Identify the stage in the demographic transition model in which Niger is found. [1]

(Total 9 marks)

3. Table 8.19 shows projected megacity (cities with a population of over 10 million people) growth for selected cities between 2022 and 2050.

Table 8.19 Projected megacity growth for selected cities.

City and country	Population in 2022 (rounded to nearest million)	Projected population in 2030 (rounded to nearest million)
London, UK	9.5	10.2
Luanda, Angola	9.0	12.1
Dar es Salaam, Tanzania	7.4	10.8
Tehran, Iran	9.4	10.2
Ahmedabad, India	8.5	10.2
Chengdu, China	9.5	10.7
Nanjing, China	9.4	11.0
Seoul, South Korea	10.0	10.2
Ho Chi Minh City, Vietnam	9.0	11.0

(a) Identify the city with:

(i) the greatest projected percentage growth, between 2022 and 2050 [1]

(ii) the greatest projected absolute growth, between 2022 and 2050. [1]

(b) Analyse the potential impact of urban growth on natural ecosystems. [2]

(c) Explain how urban planning can improve the sustainability of cities. [4]

(Total 8 marks)

4. Evaluate the use of dependency ratios. [9]

(Total 9 marks)

5. Explain the impact of urban and suburban development on the natural environment. [9]

(Total 9 marks)

6. Examine the view that population growth in LICs creates more stress on the Earth's systems than population growth in HICs. [9]

(Total 9 marks)

7. To what extent is the human impact on urban air quality sustainable and ethical. [9]

(Total 9 marks)

HL

8. HL Explain the formation of temperature inversions and their significance for air pollution. [9]

(Total 9 marks)

9. HL Analyse how urban planning influences social justice. [9]

(Total 9 marks)

HL end

HL lenses

HL.a Environmental law

Guiding question

How can environmental law help ensure the sustainable management of Earth systems?

HL a.1 Laws are rules that govern human behaviour and are enforced by social or governmental authority.
HL a.2 Environmental law refers specifically to the rules about how human beings use and impact natural resources, with the aim of improving social and ecological sustainability.
HL a.3 Environmental laws can have an important role in addressing and supporting environmental justice, but they can be difficult to approve due to lobbying.
HL a.4 Environmental law is built into existing legal frameworks, but its success can vary from country to country.
HL a.5 Environmental constitutionalism refers to the introduction of environmental rights and obligations into the constitution.
HL a.6 Environmental laws can be drafted at the local, national or international level.
HL a.7 International law provides an essential framework for addressing transboundary issues of pollution and resource management.
HL a.8 UN conferences produce international conventions (agreements) that are legally binding, and protocols that may become legally binding, to all signatories.
HL a.9 International agreements can generate institutions or organizations to aid their implementation.
HL a.10 The application of international environmental law has been examined within international courts and tribunals.
HL a.11 There are an increasing number of laws granting legal personhood to natural entities in order to strengthen environmental protection.
HL a.12 Both legal and economic strategies can play a role in maintaining sustainable use of the environment.

HL.a.1 Laws

Laws are rules that govern human behaviour and are enforced by social or governmental authority. There are penalties if laws are broken. Laws determine the rules of conduct of a community. All members of the society must recognize and adhere to the laws if the community is to function without instability and conflict.

Laws are rules, usually made by a government, that state how people may and may not behave in a society. Laws are made and enforced by social or governmental authority.

The key concepts underpinning the rule of law include equality, fairness, liberty and justice.

Activity

Humans are a species of great ape (the other species are gorilla, chimpanzee, bonobo and orangutan). Humans rely on laws to regulate their activities, but the other species of great ape do not. Why is this? What features of human societies are different to those of the other great apes? How do the other great apes regulate their societies? Have human societies always been regulated by laws?

1. Create a Venn diagram, with two intersecting circles – one for the characteristics of human societies and the second for characteristics of the other great apes. Great ape societies vary, but are there any features that they have in common? In the intersecting area, think of any features that human societies have in common with those of the other species of great ape.

What happens without law? All activities in human societies are regulated and controlled by laws. Think of a specific example and then think what would happen if there were no laws regulating it. What would be the outcome? Are there any other alternatives to regulation and control of human societies?

2. Draw a mind map to show the role of law in regulating a particular human activity and what would happen without the rule of law.

HL.a.2 Environmental law

▲ **Figure HL 1** Environmental law.

Environmental law refers specifically to the rules about how human beings use and impact natural resources. The aim of environmental law is to improve social and ecological sustainability.

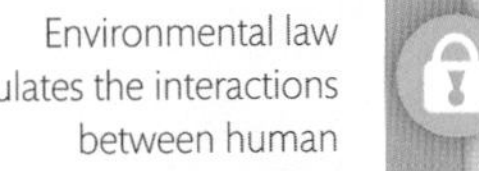

Environmental law regulates the interactions between human activities and the natural environment. It covers a wide range of topics, including pollution management, conservation of natural capital and conservation of biodiversity.

Environmental law (Figure HL 1) regulates interactions between human activities and the natural environment. It is used to address a range of issues such as:

- the unsustainable use of natural capital
- air, water and soil pollution
- land degradation
- deforestation
- climate change
- species extinction.

It is used to prevent and mitigate the negative impacts of human activities on the environment. It does this by setting out rules and regulations that individuals, businesses and governments must follow. These regulations minimize damage to the environment and promote sustainable development.

Environmental law can be divided into two main categories.

- **Domestic environmental law**, which addresses specific national or regional issues.
- **International environmental law**, which addresses issues on a global scale by determining the actions of countries and regions (territories) and organizations.

Environmental law may cover the management of:

- natural resources, such as fisheries, forests and minerals
- hazardous waste management
- air quality
- water quality

- land or soils
- conservation of biodiversity, by producing a legal framework to determine the conservation status of species
- construction and development projects using environmental impact assessments.

Strengths and limitations of environmental law

Environmental laws have both strengths and limitations.

Strengths of environmental law:

- Protecting natural resources, such as wetlands, forests and oceans, which in turn maintains biodiversity and ecological equilibrium. By doing so, environmental law can ensure the sustainability of Earth systems.
- Establishing sustainable practices, such as the conservation of water resources, sustainable agriculture and the development of renewable energy. Environmental law can add incentive for the sustainable use of natural resources and reduce the impact of human activities on the environment.
- Setting limits of pollution, such as the greenhouse gases that contribute to climate change. Regulation of technological, industrial and agricultural practices can lead to a reduction of pollution and protection of Earth systems.
- Holding polluters accountable by, for example, establishing fines and penalties for individuals or companies that do not keep to environmental regulations. By holding polluters accountable in this way, environmental law can discourage damaging activities and promote responsible behaviour for a sustainable future.

Limitations of environmental law:

- Limited scope of environmental laws, such as water or air pollution, may lead to broader issues not being addressed, for example, biodiversity loss or climate change.
- Earth systems are interconnected, and a law that addresses an environmental issue in one country may not help deal with global problems that require a more holistic approach.
- Conflicting interests, such as economic development or water, food and energy security, can hinder the development and implementation of environmental law. Support for environmental laws may be difficult to obtain if there are conflicting issues that stand in the way of sustainable development.
- Enforcement of environmental law may be difficult to achieve. For example, holding poachers of wildlife to account in extensive protected areas that are difficult to police. In some cases, such as the illegal pet trade, it may be difficult to identify the people that are responsible.
- Many environmental problems are global in nature, whereas environmental laws often operate at a local or national level. Jurisdictional challenges therefore exist in addressing global problems such as climate change.
- Political systems in many countries operate on a short-term basis, with regular elections that can lead to frequent changes in political leadership. These changes can result in shifts in environmental policy and a lack of continuity in the implementation of environmental regulations. These systems can result in a short-term view of political priorities, with issues that require long-term solutions, such as climate change, not receiving the urgency and priority that they require. Environmental laws ultimately need political will to drive progress and where this is lacking, there can be a lack of commitment to solving environmental problems.

Environmental law can be divided into two main categories: **domestic environmental law**, which focuses on specific national or regional issues, and **international environmental law**, which governs the actions of countries, regions (territories) and organizations on a global scale.

Environmental law plays an essential role in promoting environmental *sustainability*. It does this by establishing regulations, protecting natural resources, encouraging sustainable practices and holding polluters accountable for their actions.

You can use the strengths and limitations listed here to evaluate different laws you study during the ESS course. This can provide opportunities for debate and discussion of whether laws are effective in establishing regulations, protecting natural resources and promoting sustainability.

1.1 Perspectives
1.3 Sustainability
3.2 Human impact on biodiversity
3.3 Conservation and regeneration
4.3 Aquatic food production systems
4.4 Water pollution
6.3 Climate change – mitigation and adaptation
7.1 Natural resources – uses and management
7.3 Solid waste
8.2 Urban systems and urban planning
8.3 Urban air pollution

Environmental impact assessments

An **environmental impact assessment (EIA)** is a detailed study that examines the environmental impact of a major development such as new housing, new energy supplies or new transport links. The purpose of an EIA is to assess the impact of the project on the environment and to develop sustainable management guidelines (Topic 7, Sections 7.1.14–7.1.16). It predicts possible impacts on habitats, species and ecosystems, and helps decision-makers to decide whether the development should go ahead. An EIA also addresses the mitigation of potential environmental impacts associated with the development. An EIA suggests appropriate monitoring before, during and after the development and should include a **baseline study**. The report should also provide a non-technical concluding summary so that members of the public and the media can easily understand the implications of the study.

Possible methods that could be used to collect data for a baseline study during an EIA include:

- Evaluating species' abundance:
  - identify sample points through random coordinates or along transects to cover the area of development
  - employ sampling methods appropriate for given species, for example, quadrats, traps, mist nets and so on
  - calculate the total abundance from sample numbers, for example, through extrapolation of sample size using the Lincoln index method (mark–release–recapture).
- Evaluating ecological significance/diversity:
  - use a survey area to obtain a comprehensive list of species
  - identify any species that are of special interest, for example, those with Red List status, or those present in local breeding or feeding grounds
  - use abundance data and species richness to calculate diversity index, for example, using Simpsons Reciprocal Index
  - quantify the current status of ecosystems using a biotic index.
- Evaluating abiotic variables:
  - identify abiotic variables most relevant to the study, that is, those most likely to be impacted by the development, including pollutant levels, water temperature and soil qualities
  - design a sampling regime to cover the relevant area, considering seasonal variations, diurnal variations and maximum–minimum ranges
  - select appropriate instrumentation for recording abiotic factors, such as temperature probes, pH meters and atmospheric particle collectors.
- Evaluating social factors:
  - distribute questionnaires in the local community to assess opinions regarding the development
  - set up community meetings including people from different constituencies, for example, developers, commercial businesses, residents and environmentalists
  - carry out research to establish current economics, employment, land ownership and any land use issues associated with the proposed area.

The aims of an EIA are:

- to prevent or limit the environmental impact of a project
- to provide a baseline assessment of the environmental, social and economic impacts of a project
- to predict and evaluate possible impacts of a project
- to decide whether a project will be sustainable
- to suggest mitigation strategies for potential problems caused by a project
- to provide a tool for planning decisions about a proposed project.

The stages of an EIA include:

- a **baseline study**
- assessment of possible impacts
- proposals for mitigation of impact
- monitoring of change during development
- monitoring of change after development.

Possible limitations of an EIA include:

- EIAs are time-consuming, so may effectively prevent valuable development or not be completed in time to prevent development
- a wide variety of skills are needed to collect appropriate data, which implies extensive education
- there may be conflicts of interest as developers pay for the EIA, which may bias findings
- monitoring post development is often not completed and so their usefulness is limited
- the recommendations of an EIA may not be followed, and in some countries corruption may influence decisions rather than EIA.

Criticisms of EIAs include the lack of a standard practice or training for practitioners, the lack of a clear definition of system boundaries and the lack of inclusion of indirect impacts.

7.1 Natural resources – uses and management

Example – Qatar's Qetaifan Island North

With growing populations and limited area, many countries are seeking to create more land in coastal areas using the process of 'land reclamation'. In this process, rock can be used as a base that is then filled with clay and soil until the land is raised above sea level. The new areas of land created can be used for new housing, industrial and commercial areas, agriculture, tourism and to meet other demands of urban centres.

Qatar, in the Arabian Gulf, has experienced economic and population growth since 1971. This has led to coastal areas along the eastern shoreline of Doha being developed for urban expansion. The marine ecosystems along Qatar's coastline include coral reef, seagrass and mangrove. The integrity of these ecosystems is likely to be affected by reclamation and excavation works. Therefore, EIAs are needed to establish the potential impacts of such works, as well as being used to propose ways of mitigating impacts and preserving the biodiversity of coastal and marine ecosystems.

Lusail is the second-largest city in Qatar and is located on the coast 23 km north of Doha, near the West Bay Lagoon. Here, land reclamation is being used for artificial island development, to create Qetaifan Island (QI) North (Figure HL 2).

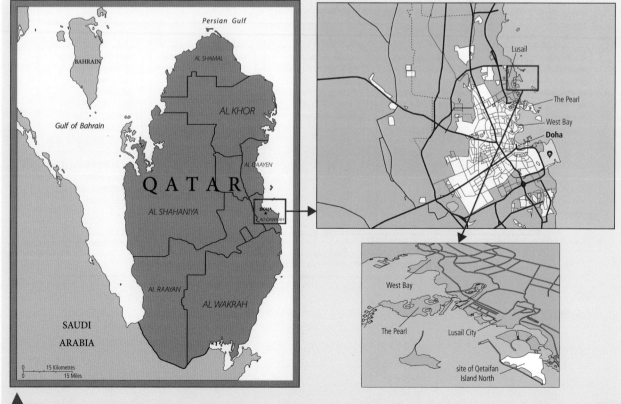

Figure HL 2 Location of Qetaifan Island North.

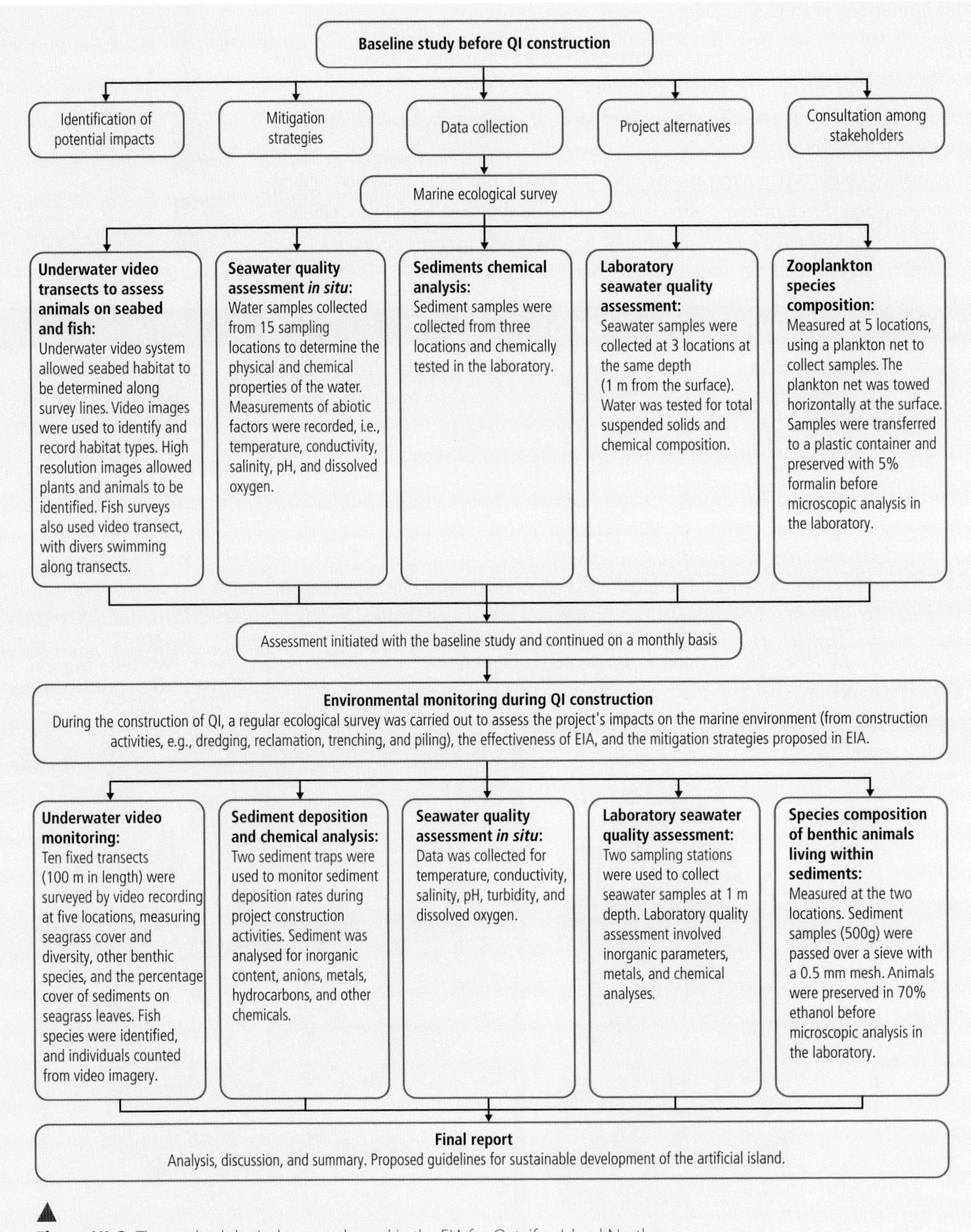

Figure HL 3 The methodological approach used in the EIA for Qetaifan Island North.

The main ecosystem across the survey area was seagrasses. Seagrass beds are the breeding grounds and essential food source for several marine species, such as fish, waterfowl, sea turtles and invertebrates.

Given the potential consequences of construction to the coast and in marine habitats, a detailed EIA assessment was carried out to build Qetaifan Island North (Figure HL 3).

Potential impacts of construction of the artificial island included:

- increased suspension of sediment in water leading to increased turbidity
- redistribution of sediment particle size
- construction dust settling in water, increasing water turbidity
- contamination of water by pollution
- construction activities and noise affecting bird habitats
- loss of fish habitat
- suspended particles due to dredging affecting fish
- noise affecting fish and marine mammals
- artificial light affecting fish and birds
- particles and dust affecting plankton communities
- dredging operations affecting benthic habitat and communities.

Some of the key findings of the EIA were:

- The sediment quality analysis of sediment from the seabed showed slightly higher levels of selenium (Se) and barium (Ba) before the island construction began. However, during construction of the island, analysis showed that these levels were within acceptable limits.
- There is likely to be sufficient circulation of the water within the area of the artificial island development to maintain good water quality.
- Animal communities play a key role in marine ecosystems because they maintain nutrient cycles and provide habitat and food sources, especially for organisms that live on the seabed (benthic communities).
- Despite rigorous mitigation measures proposed in the EIA, project activities still resulted in high turbidity and reduced the diversity of animals that live within the bottom sediments, which should have been managed during the pre-construction assessment stage.
- By taking appropriate mitigation measures during the EIA study, overall adverse environmental impacts were significantly reduced during the construction phase.

Read more about the EIA for Qetaifan Island North in this article:

Afzal, M.S, Tahir, F & Al-Ghamdi, S.G. (2023) The role of environmental impact assessment in the sustainable artificial island development: A Qatar's Island case study. *Cleaner Environmental Systems*, Vol 9, Article 100111

Details of the EIA and proposed mitigation measures are shown in Table 7, page 13 of the research paper.

There are further examples of EIAs on the website of the International Institute for Sustainable Development (search for 'iisd eia case studies').

A template for an EIA can be found here:

Challenge yourself

Find your own example of an EIA. What were the conclusions of the study? Were the recommendations followed?

Examples of EIAs that lead to good discussion due to their controversial elements include:

- the Dakota access pipeline (impact on sacred sites and water sources of the Standing Rock Sioux Tribe)
- the Keystone XL pipeline
- palm oil plantations
- fracking.

How does the social context of scientific work affect the methods and findings of science?

EIAs provide decision-makers with information to consider the environmental impact of a project. There is not necessarily a requirement to implement an EIA's proposals, and many socioeconomic factors influence the decisions made.

Both social *sustainability* and environmental sustainability are key components of environmental law. Social sustainability involves the survival of societies and their cultures and may include consideration of the continued use of language, belief or spiritual practices in a society. Environmental sustainability concerns the use and management of natural resources that allows replacement of the resources, along with the recovery and regeneration of ecosystems.

HL.a.3 Environmental laws and environmental justice

Environmental laws can have an important role in addressing and supporting environmental justice, but they can be difficult to approve due to lobbying.

1.3 Sustainability

Environmental justice means the fair treatment and meaningful involvement of all people with respect to the development, implementation, and enforcement of environmental laws, regulations and policies (Topic 1, Section 1.3.9). Environmental laws support environmental justice. They aim to prevent overexploitation and degradation of natural resources for the short-term interests of a minority above the long-term interests of the common good.

Prevention of overexploitation of resources can be limited by powerful lobbying of some stakeholders.

Economic systems can cause environmental and social harm (this topic, Sections HL.b.3, HL.b.12 and HL.b.13), but laws can support or ensure ethical behaviour to counteract such damaging activities. Despite best intentions, however, it can be difficult to get environmental laws passed due to political lobbying of economically powerful stakeholders (see Example below).

Example – The grey wolf

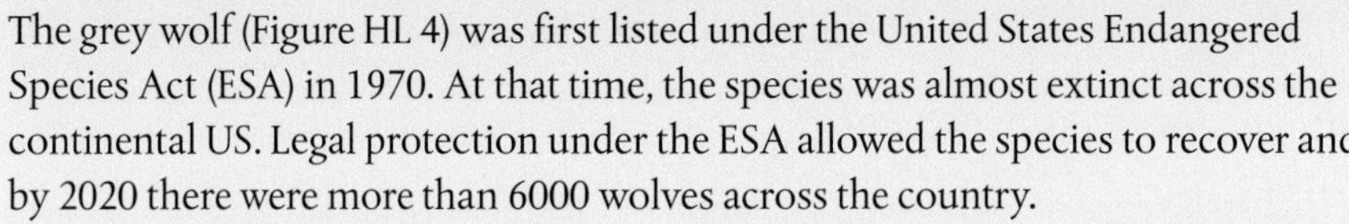

Figure HL 4 Two grey wolves, *Canis lupus*.

The grey wolf (Figure HL 4) was first listed under the United States Endangered Species Act (ESA) in 1970. At that time, the species was almost extinct across the continental US. Legal protection under the ESA allowed the species to recover and by 2020 there were more than 6000 wolves across the country.

The United States Fish and Wildlife Service, under the Trump administration, campaigned to delist the grey wolf, in order to manage wolf populations to protect livestock. In 2020 a rule was made that removed the wolf from the ESA. The National Rifle Association (NRA) is a powerful lobbying group representing gun owners in the US. It has been accused of lobbying against laws protecting endangered species, including the grey wolf, and for laws that would allow hunting in protected areas.

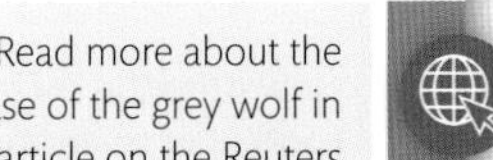

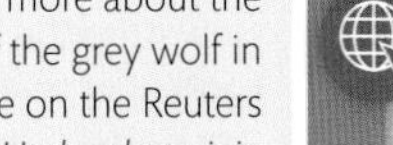

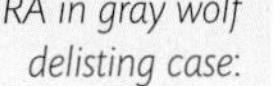

Read more about the case of the grey wolf in this article on the Reuters website: *Utah asks to join U.S., NRA in gray wolf delisting case*.

Environmental groups filed several lawsuits that challenged the delisting and the idea that the grey wolf population no longer required federal protection. Following a court order in February 2022, grey wolves were again protected under the ESA as threatened in Minnesota and endangered in the remaining states.

HL.a.4 Legal frameworks

A **legal framework** is set out in a system of legal documents that outline the rules, rights and obligations of companies, governments and citizens. A legal framework includes a country's constitution, legislation, policy, regulations and contracts. A legally binding contract is a voluntary agreement reached between parties and is enforceable in law. Legal documents that cover broad principles, such as the constitution, are generally more difficult to change. More specific documents, like laws and contracts, can often be more easily amended.

Environmental law requires effective enforcement of laws through strong administrative and legal institutions, and general acceptance by society. Adequate funding is also needed to support the environmental protection measures required by law.

Environmental law is built into existing **legal frameworks**, but its success can vary from country to country. Environmental law requires strong enforcement but may be limited by political will or other needs.

HL.a.5 Environmental constitutionalism

Environmental constitutionalism refers to the introduction of environmental rights and obligations into the constitution of individual countries. Internationally, there is a growth of environmental constitutionalism as more and more cases are effectively addressed by nations' constitutions. Climate change issues are increasingly being addressed in this way.

There are many key terms you need to know in the HL lenses and other HL content. Use the worksheet in the eBook to help you write your own glossary of these terms.

Example – Constitution of the Republic of South Africa

An example of a national constitution that has successfully addressed environmental issues is the Constitution of the Republic of South Africa.

In 1996, South Africa addressed environmental issues in its constitution. The South African Constitution:

- recognizes the right to a healthy environment as a basic human right
- provides for the protection and preservation of the environment as a fundamental duty of the state.

The Constitution has been used to support several environmental laws in South Africa, including those related to waste management, air quality, water resource management and the conservation of biodiversity. It plays a crucial role in shaping the country's environmental policies and promoting sustainable development.

One of the issues addressed by the South African Constitution is the right of access to sufficient water. However, there are limitations in its effectiveness:

- There is a lack of clarity in the definition of the term 'sufficient water'. This has made it difficult to establish clear standards for the equal distribution of freshwater.
- A lack of effective enforcement mechanisms. There are complex legal and bureaucratic structures that govern water management and allocation. Because of these complexities, the right to water is often violated, especially in rural and marginalized communities.
- Issues of implementation and resource allocation. The provision of water and sanitation services requires significant financial and administrative resources, which the government has struggled to provide to all citizens, especially in rural areas.

Overall, while the South African Constitution includes a right of access to sufficient water, there are significant challenges in ensuring that this right is effectively realized for all citizens.

Read more about the Constitution of South Africa on the LawGlobal Hub website:

Activity

1. Think about ways in which the environment affects your daily life. In which ways does a healthy environment improve your overall well-being? Reflect on ways in which legislation could make these factors more available and equally available for all.
2. Consider an example of an environmental issue in South Africa, such as climate change. Analyse the issue and discuss in small groups how it relates to the right to a healthy environment as recognized by the South African Constitution.

   Now propose solutions for the issue that align with the Constitution's fundamental duty of protecting and preserving the environment. Compare your example with others in your class. Which issues did they find out about and what solutions did they propose?
3. Find out about a local example of a national constitution or legislation that successfully addressed environmental issues. Produce a fact sheet that summarizes your findings.

HL.a.6 Environmental laws at local, national or international level

Environmental laws can be drafted at the local, national or international level.

Laws made at national or international levels supersede those made at local levels. For example,

- local councils can have laws about recycling and waste disposal
- countries create environmental laws about air and water quality standards
- international environmental agreements exist regarding fisheries, atmospheric pollution, trade in endangered species and climate change.

Local (domestic) legal systems have:

- a **legislature**, which is a body that makes law
- an **executive**, which is a body that carries out the laws, including government departments
- a **judiciary**, which is a hierarchy of courts that hears cases and settles disputes.

By contrast, the international legal system, has:

- no legislature – the UN General Assembly passes resolutions, but these are not legally binding
- no executive – the UN Security Council should fill this role, but five countries have the power to veto any decision (UK, USA, Russia, China and France) and so it generally fails to fulfil this role
- no judiciary – the International Court of Justice in the Hague, The Netherlands, can hear cases but only when both sides agree and there is no way to enforce its judgements (this topic, Section HL.a.10).

Activity

What are the differences between local (national) and international law? Use the video from the QR code, or other resources, to produce a table summarizing the differences. Produce a second table showing the strengths and limitations of each type of law.

Local (domestic) laws govern the behaviour and conduct of individuals within a nation. International laws govern the conduct and behaviour of nations in the international system.

International laws or bilateral agreements, that is, agreements between two parties, may be created and applied in transboundary environmental issues related to pollution and resource management.

Major international agreements include:

- the Montreal Protocol on Substances that Deplete the Ozone Layer (1987)
- the Basel Convention on the Control of Transboundary Movements of Hazardous Wastes and their Disposal (1989)
- the UN Framework Convention on Climate Change (UNFCCC) (1992)
- the Convention on Biological Diversity (CBD) (1992)
- the Kyoto Protocol (1997)
- the Paris Agreement (2015).

Example – The Nile River dispute

Figure HL 5 The Nile River flowing through Cairo, Egypt.

International law can play an important role in resolving conflicts between countries and regions (territories) with shared water sources. The Nile River in eastern Africa (Figure HL 5) raises issues of water security for countries that border the river (Topic 4, Sections 4.2.2 and 4.2.10).

1.1 Perspectives

4.2 Water access, use and security

Activity

1. Use Google Earth to list all the countries that have access to the Nile River.
2. What issues of water scarcity and security does Egypt face? What national environmental laws have been put in place to manage Egypt's water sustainably?
3. What are the issues surrounding the building of the Grand Ethiopian Renaissance Dam? Read the article and watch the Water crisis in Egypt video.

Article: The Nile Dispute: Beyond Water Security

Video: The Nile River: Water crisis in Egypt

Video: The Nile Agreements

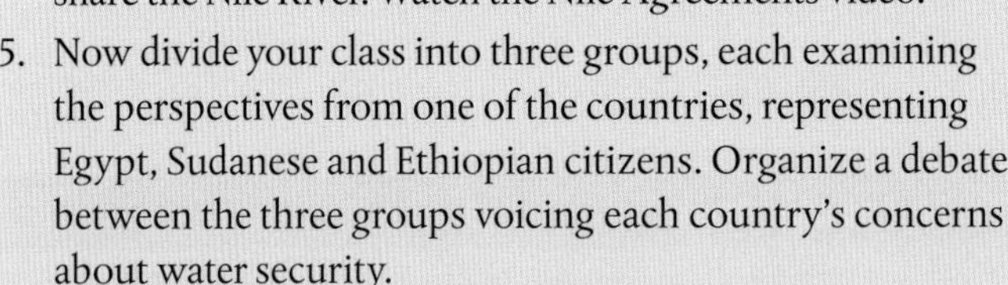

4. In small groups, discuss the problems posed by the dam for Egypt and Sudan and discuss the potential solutions and what common ground exists between the countries that share the Nile River. Watch the Nile Agreements video.
5. Now divide your class into three groups, each examining the perspectives from one of the countries, representing Egypt, Sudanese and Ethiopian citizens. Organize a debate between the three groups voicing each country's concerns about water security.
6. Now answer the following questions:
   - What role do environmental laws play in controlling access to the Nile River at local, national or international levels?
   - What are the limitations of international law? (For example, even when there are rules in places, arguments can still occur.)
   - How may climate change worsen the tensions between the countries that share access to the Nile River?

International law provides an essential framework for addressing transboundary issues of pollution and **resource management**.

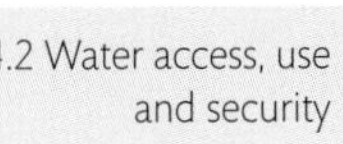

4.2 Water access, use and security

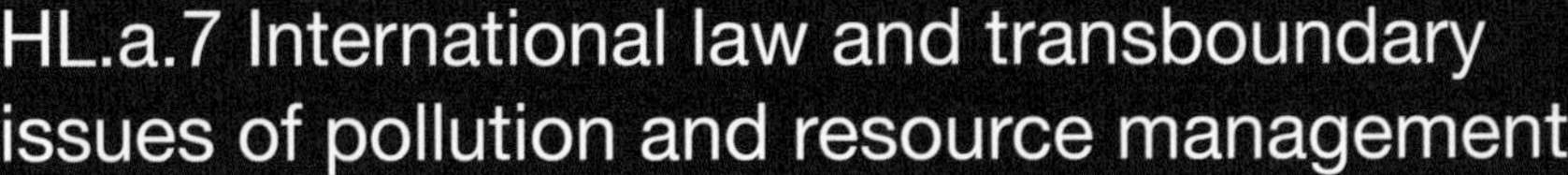

HL.a.7 International law and transboundary issues of pollution and resource management

Several environmental issues cross the boundaries between different countries (this topic, Section HL.a.6), and so are known as transboundary problems. These environmental issues therefore require transboundary solutions. There are two types of agreement:

- those addressing transboundary pollution, such as the Association of South-East Asian Nations (ASEAN) Agreement on Transboundary Haze Pollution
- those addressing transboundary **resource management**, such as the Food and Agriculture Organization (FAO) International Plan of Action to Prevent, Deter and Eliminate Illegal, Unreported and Unregulated Fishing.

Example – The Association of South-East Asian Nations

The Association of South-East Asian Nations (ASEAN) is a group of nations including Indonesia, Brunei Darussalam, Cambodia, Laos, Malaysia, Myanmar, the Philippines, Singapore, Thailand and Vietnam. Land and forest fires have become an increasing problem in the region including these nations, with smoke and haze resulting from fires spreading to other countries often at some distance from the original source.

For example, in 1997, forest fires burning in the Indonesian part of Borneo affected the neighbouring countries of Malaysia (Figure HL 6) and Singapore, spreading thick clouds of smoke and haze. These fires had been caused by illegal slash-and-burn agriculture in the region and were made worse by peat deposits catching fire. A prolonged dry season meant there was no rain to extinguish them. As well as destroying forests and releasing large quantities of carbon dioxide (CO_2) into the atmosphere, the air pollution caused respiratory illnesses and death. This led the countries of ASEAN to seek a solution.

Figure HL 6 Haze in Kuala Lumpur, Malaysia, October 2015, caused by smoke from forest fires in neighbouring Indonesia.

The ASEAN Agreement on Transboundary Haze Pollution (AATHP) was signed on 10 June 2002 in Kuala Lumpur, Malaysia. AATHP is an agreement in which signatories undertake individual and joint action to assess the origin, causes, nature and extent of land and/or forest fires and the resulting haze. Countries agree to prevent and control the sources of land and/or forest fires and the resulting haze by applying environmentally sound policies, practices and technologies. Countries also seek to strengthen national and regional capabilities and cooperation in assessment, prevention, mitigation and management of land and/or forest fires and the resulting haze.

Initially, only seven of ASEAN's ten member states had ratified the June 2002 agreement, with Cambodia joining in 2006, the Philippines in 2010 and Indonesia in 2014.

Activity

The key objective of the ASEAN Agreement on Transboundary Haze Pollution is to 'prevent and monitor transboundary haze pollution as a result of land and/or forest fires which should be mitigated, through concerted national efforts and intensified regional and international cooperation'.

1. Read more about the issues on these websites.

Search online to read the ASEAN Agreement on Transboundary Haze Pollution in full.

Obstacles to a regional solution:	Overview of ASEAN environment, Transboundary Haze Pollution Agreement and public health:	Effectiveness of transboundary haze pollution in handling of smoke haze cases in South-East Asia:

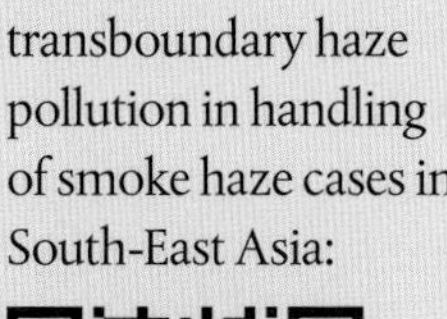

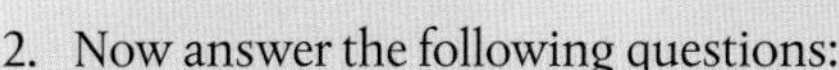

2. Now answer the following questions:
   - Why would international agreement be needed in these cases?
   - What are the limitations of involving international parties at these meetings?
   - To what extent has the agreement been successful?

United Nations (UN) conferences produce international conventions (agreements) that are legally binding, and protocols that may become legally binding, to all signatories.

HL.a.8 UN conferences produce international conventions and protocols

United Nations (UN) conferences (Figure HL 7) bring most countries from around the world together to discuss major environmental issues and their solutions. International agreements and protocols can be challenging and slow to develop. Challenges include:

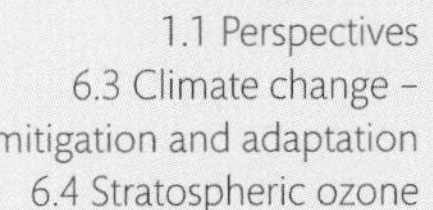

1.1 Perspectives
6.3 Climate change – mitigation and adaptation
6.4 Stratospheric ozone

- the complexity of the agreements
- rapidly evolving scientific knowledge
- pressures on individual governments from internal stakeholders with differing interests
- conflicts between countries over 'differentiated responsibilities' (for example, in discussions on climate change, developing countries have the perspective that developed countries should take more of the responsibility and cost of addressing the issue, because they were the ones that initially caused the problem through fossil fuel combustion in industrial revolutions)
- financing commitments of developed countries towards developing countries
- general geopolitical conflicts
- potential economic impact of agreements.

Figure HL 7 UN conferences involve meetings with most nations.

The Montreal Protocol

Ozone (O_3) is a gas that has a vital role in absorbing ultraviolet (UV) radiation from the Sun (Topic 6, Sections 6.4.2 and 6.4.3). Under natural conditions, O_3 exists in a steady state or dynamic equilibrium, constantly forming and being destroyed. However, human activities may alter the balance of the equilibrium.

Ozone-depleting substances (ODSs) are industrial products or byproducts and include halogenated organic gases such as chlorofluorocarbons (CFCs), hydrochlorofluorocarbons (HCFCs), halons and methyl bromide (bromomethane).

CFCs were traditionally used in aerosols, gas-blown plastics, pesticides, flame retardants and refrigerants. Increasing measurements of CFCs correlate with declining O_3 levels (Topic 6, Sections 6.4.7 and 6.4.8).

There are now ozone layer holes at both the North and South poles, with the one over Antarctica stretching as far as Argentina. The balance of formation and destruction of stratospheric O_3 is seriously affected by ODSs, notably those containing the halogens chlorine, fluorine and bromine.

Most ODSs do not occur naturally. They are usually very stable compounds and can persist in the atmosphere for decades as they travel upwards to the stratosphere. However, once they are in the stratosphere, and under the influence of UV radiation, they break down and release halogen atoms. The halogen atoms act as catalysts for the reactions that destroy O_3 molecules. Thus, ODSs greatly accelerate the rate of O_3 destruction.

The UN Environment Programme (UNEP) has played a key role in providing information, and in creating and evaluating international agreements for the protection of stratospheric O_3. The **Montreal Protocol** on Substances that Deplete the Ozone Layer (1987), along with subsequent updates, is an international treaty for the reduction of use of ODSs, signed under the direction of the UNEP (Topic 6, Section 6.4.8). National governments complying with the agreement made national laws and regulations to decrease the consumption and production of halogenated organic gases such as CFCs.

The use of ozone-depleting substances (ODSs) led to the creation of a 'hole' in the ozone layer over Antarctica, with levels of O_3 falling from 1965 (Topic 6, Sections 6.4.6 and 6.4.7).

6.1 Introduction to the atmosphere

6.4 Stratospheric ozone

7.1 Natural resources – uses and management

To see a time line showing milestones of the Montreal Protocol, search online for the Green Cooling Initiative's Milestones of the Montreal Protocol poster.

Activity

Search for 'Countries subscribed to the Montreal Protocol' on the Our World in Data website to see when countries joined the Montreal Protocol:

Data can be viewed via a table or map. Go to the map (click on tab at top left of screen). Slide the bar on the 'Play time-lapse' to show when countries joined the Protocol, from its inception to up to 2022.

Which countries joined first? Why was this? Which were the later countries to join? Discuss in small groups reasons for the timing of countries' signing of the Protocol. Briefly summarize your ideas and exchange these with other groups in your class.

The Montreal Protocol is regarded as the most successful example yet of international cooperation in management and intervention to resolve a significant environmental issue, as the production and consumption of ODSs has reduced by more than 95% compared to 1986. However, illegal trade in ODSs has developed. It is believed that India and the Republic of Korea account for approximately 70% of the total global production of CFCs. Countries in the region with a high consumption of CFCs include India, Malaysia, Pakistan and the Philippines (Topic 6, Sections 6.4.8 and 6.4.9).

The most widely used ODSs are CFCs and these were often replaced with HCFCs. Although HCFCs are greenhouse gases, and have ozone-depleting properties, their global warming potential (GWP) is less than that of CFCs. However, they still have damaging effects on the environment and so were subsequently replaced by hydrofluorocarbons (HFCs), which do not deplete O_3. But due to further developments in scientific understanding, HFCs were also discovered to be greenhouse gases with GWP. As a result, in 2016, Parties to the Montreal Protocol adopted the **Kigali Amendment** to phase down production and consumption of HFCs worldwide. Richer countries agreed to provide financial assistance for poorer countries to phase out HFCs. This is made possible because technological development has found alternatives to HFCs (Topic 6, Section 6.4.12).

The Kyoto Protocol

Figure HL 8 The Kyoto Protocol.

The effect of climate change, in terms of sustainable development and its effect on the planet, was discussed at a UN conference in Kyoto in 1997. Agreements were made to reduce emissions of greenhouse gases and gave participants of developed countries legally binding targets for cuts in emissions from the 1990 level. The **Kyoto Protocol** (Figure HL 8) stipulated that these targets should be reached by the year 2012.

The meetings that followed the UN Framework Convention on Climate Change (UNFCCC) (Topic 1, Section 1.1.10 and Topic 6, Section 6.3.7) meeting at Copenhagen in 2009 worked towards finding a successor to the Kyoto Protocol. At the 2011 Durban conference, in South Africa, the debate about a legally binding global agreement was reopened. Countries were given until 2015 to decide how far and how fast to cut their carbon emissions. Before the Durban conference, most countries were going to follow national targets for carbon emissions after 2012, which would be voluntary and not legally binding. The **Durban Agreement** differs from the Kyoto Protocol in that it includes both developed and developing countries, rather than just developed countries. And it differs from other summits in that it works towards a legally binding treaty.

The Paris Agreement

Figure HL 9 The Paris Agreement.

In December 2015, the Paris Agreement (Figure HL 9) was signed. This is a legally binding international treaty, adopted by 196 Parties at the UNFCCC COP21 in Paris, France. It entered into force on 4 November 2016. The goal of the Paris Agreement is to hold 'the increase in the global average temperature to well below 2 °C above pre-industrial levels' and pursue efforts 'to limit the temperature increase to 1.5 °C above pre-industrial levels.'

COP27 of the UNFCCC, at Sharm el-Sheikh, Egypt, 2022, produced a breakthrough agreement to provide 'loss and damage' funding for vulnerable countries hard hit by climate disasters. At COP27, countries reaffirmed their commitment to limit global temperature rise to 1.5 °C above pre-industrial levels, although this would require global greenhouse gas emissions to peak before 2025 at the latest and be reduced by 43% by 2030.

It is true that countries can break these agreements and there is little the international community can do about this. Moreover, summits may not achieve their initial goals. However, they do act as important catalysts in changing the attitudes of governments, organizations and individuals.

The Intergovernmental Panel on Climate Change (IPCC) publishes reports that assess information concerning climate change (Topic 6, Sections 6.2.9, 6.3.1, and 6.3.5). In 2023, the IPCC produced a short report that summarized the scientific findings of the larger report. The shorter version of the report aimed to make the findings more accessible to policymakers and provide a clear account of the scientific underpinning for global climate action. The report stated that the 1.5 °C limit to rises in global temperature is set to be missed by a wide margin and that an estimated 3.6 billion people are already climate-vulnerable. The report stated that there is a risk of 'catastrophic consequences' for people around the world. This suggests that the international conventions and protocols on climate change are failing to prevent further planetary warming.

Activity

The Montreal Protocol has been successful in reversing stratospheric O_3 depletion, whereas the UNFCCC has failed to stop global warming, with average temperatures heading towards an increase of 2 °C.

Why was the Montreal Protocol successful and what can the implementors of the Paris Agreement learn from this success?

Discuss this issue in small groups. Write lists showing the strengths and limitations of each agreement.

- Which features of the Montreal Protocol enabled it to meet its objectives? How can the same ideas be applied to the climate change crisis?
- Are there particular issues that climate change raises that make addressing the causes, and implementing change, more difficult? What are the solutions?

Now meet up as a whole class and exchange ideas. What advice would you give to the politicians at the next COP for climate change?

Read more about why the Montreal Protocol was successful and what climate change treaties can learn from it in the news article *What The Ozone Layer Teaches Us About Climate Action* on the UNFCCC website:

HL.a.9 International agreements can generate institutions or organizations

International agreements lead to institutions or organizations being set up to aid their implementation.

There are a range of conventions and organizations covered in the course, for example, the Convention on International Trade in Endangered Species (CITES) and the International Union for the Conservation of Nature (IUCN).

3.3 Conservation and regeneration

The Convention on International Trade in Endangered Species

The Convention on International Trade in Endangered Species (CITES) is an international agreement aimed at preventing trade in endangered species of both plants and animals (Topic 3, Section 3.3.2). The convention was set up by the International Union for the Conservation of Nature (IUCN).

CITES offers varying degrees of protection to 35,000 species of animals and plants with species under threat from extinction being protected under 'Appendix I'. Commercial trade in wild-caught specimens of these species is illegal and permitted only in exceptional licensed circumstances. The wildlife species in trade that are not endangered are listed under 'Appendix II'. CITES aims to ensure that trade of Appendix II species remains sustainable and does not endanger wild populations. This would safeguard these species for the future.

Example – African elephants

Figure HL 10 A herd of African elephants.

African elephants (Figure HL 10) were listed under Appendix I by CITES in 1990 (Topic 3, Section 3.3.2). This banned the international trade of ivory. Since then, elephant populations have increased in several African countries, indicating that the ban has been effective in reducing poaching and illegal trade.

African elephants were reclassified under Appendix II in South Africa in 2000. Delisting may have led to increased ivory poaching and a decline in several wild elephant populations. African elephants provide an example of the effect of reclassification on wild populations (Topic 3, Section 3.3.2).

An example of how CITES supports the conservation of African elephants is given in the CITES national ivory action plan. This tool is being used by a number of parties to strengthen their controls of the trade in ivory and ivory markets and help combat the illegal trade in ivory.

Example – Vicuña

Vicuña (*Vicugna vicugna*) (Figure HL 11), also known as vicugna, are the smallest member of the camel family and are the wild ancestor of the alpaca. They can be found in Chile, Ecuador, Peru, Argentina and Bolivia. They live on high, mountainous grasslands. The species forms a usable natural resource particularly because of its fleece, which can be sold as a rare and valuable wool. This is of major economic and social importance to the rural communities in the areas that are inhabited by the vicuña.

Figure HL 11 A group of vicuña grazing.

In 1975, CITES declared the vicuña 'most endangered' and listed it under Appendix I. This placed a ban on all international commerce of vicuña products. However, despite the ban, the continued demand for vicuña products, especially its wool, led to an increase in poaching and their population declined further. The ban was also difficult to enforce because patrols were difficult in the remote and extensive areas across which the animal was found. In 1994, the species was downgraded from Appendix I to II, to allow local communities to use it as a resource. In 2008, the vicuña was further downgraded to 'least concern' on the list of threatened species.

Read more about the delisting of the vicuña in the BBC Travel article *The rarest fabric on Earth*.

Activity

Allowing trade in specific species perhaps seems challenging and counterintuitive, but the example of the vicuña shows the positive impact that wildlife trade can have on certain species.

Discuss this example in small groups and answer the following questions:

- How do you feel about permitting trade in specific species?
- What are the pros and cons of downgrading the conservation status of the vicuña? (For example, pros may include increased legal trade in vicuña wool, which could provide economic benefits to local communities and incentivize conservation efforts. Cons may include the risk of overexploitation and poaching if trade is not well regulated.)
- Are there other examples you can find where this has had a positive effect on a species? Are there examples of species where it has had a negative effect?

Discuss these questions within your group and then share your answers with the rest of the class.

1.1 Perspectives
3.2 Human impact on biodiversity
3.3 Conservation and regeneration

The International Union for the Conservation of Nature

The International Union for the Conservation of Nature (IUCN) brings governments and NGO member organizations together (Topic 1, Section 1.1.9 and Topic 3, Section 3.3.10). It is concerned with the importance of conservation of resources for sustainable economic development. The IUCN has three areas of focus:

- maintaining ecological processes
- preserving genetic diversity
- using species and ecosystems in a sustainable fashion.

Read more about the IUCN on their website:

In 1980, the IUCN established the World Conservation Strategy (WCS) along with the UNEP and the World Wildlife Fund for Nature (WWF). The WCS outlined a series of global priorities for action. It recommended that each country prepare a national strategy as a developing plan that would consider the conservation of natural resources for long-term human welfare. The strategy also drew attention to a fundamental issue – the importance of giving the users of natural resources the role of guardians. Local communities are dependent on the careful management of natural resources and conservation strategies cannot succeed without their support and understanding.

History of the IUCN

The IUCN was founded in 1948. Its full name is the 'International Union for the Conservation of Nature and Natural Resources', but this is abbreviated to the 'International Union for the Conservation of Nature'. Between 1990–2008, it was also known as the World Conservation Union.

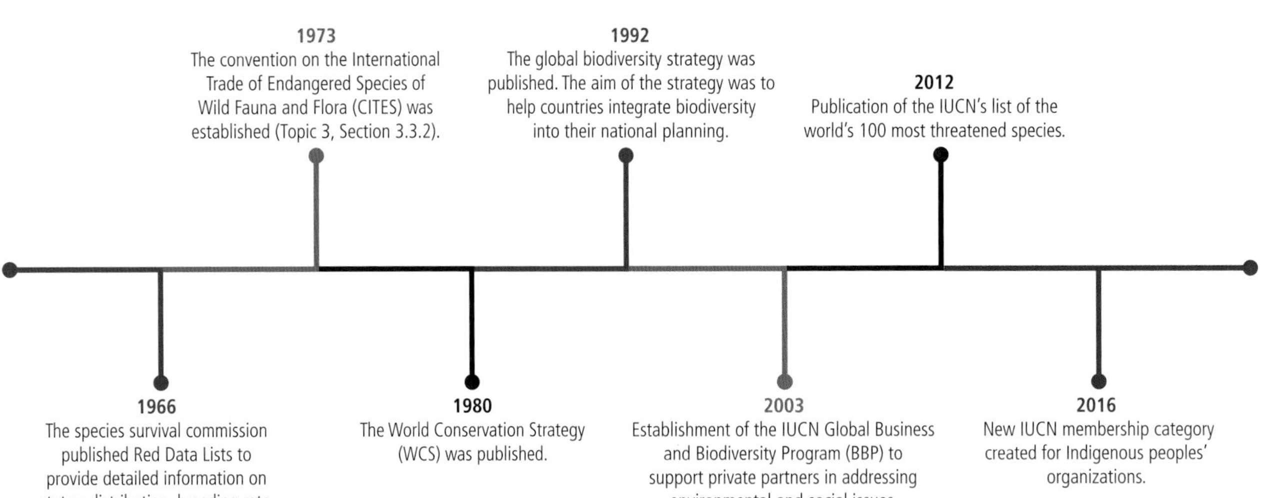

1966
The species survival commission published Red Data Lists to provide detailed information on status, distribution, breeding rate, causes of decline and proposed protective measures for all endangered species (Topic 3, Section 3.2.4).
1973
The convention on the International Trade of Endangered Species of Wild Fauna and Flora (CITES) was established (Topic 3, Section 3.3.2).
1980
The World Conservation Strategy (WCS) was published.
1992
The global biodiversity strategy was published. The aim of the strategy was to help countries integrate biodiversity into their national planning.
2003
Establishment of the IUCN Global Business and Biodiversity Program (BBP) to support private partners in addressing environmental and social issues.
2012
Publication of the IUCN's list of the world's 100 most threatened species.
2016
New IUCN membership category created for Indigenous peoples' organizations.

For more than four decades, the IUCN has published documents called the Red Data Books. These assess the conservation status of particular species in order to highlight species threatened with extinction and to promote their conservation (Topic 3, Section 3.2.4). The Red List is an inventory of all threatened species. The genetic diversity represented by the plants and animals in the Red List is an irreplaceable resource that the IUCN is looking to conserve through increased awareness. Many of these species also represent key building blocks of ecosystems (Topic 2, Section 2.1.23). Information on their conservation status provides the basis for making informed decisions about conserving biodiversity at local, national and global levels.

HL.a.10 The application of international environmental law

The application of international environmental law has been examined within international courts and tribunals.

Examples of bodies involved in the development of international environmental law include:

- The International Court of Justice (ICJ) (Figure HL 12)
  - This is the principal judicial body of the UN. The court's role is to settle legal disputes submitted to it by countries, following international law. The court decides disputes between countries, based on the voluntary participation of the countries concerned. If a country agrees to participate in a proceeding, it is obligated to comply with the court's decision. The court also gives advisory opinions on legal questions referred to it by authorized UN bodies and specialized agencies.
  - One of the limitations of the ICJ is lack of accessibility. Individuals, corporations, parts of states, NGOs, self-determination groups, and even UN bodies, cannot be parties because only countries ('states') are allowed to be parties in cases that are brought before it.
  - Another limitation is that the ICJ only has jurisdiction based on consent and does not have compulsory jurisdiction. This means that if there is a dispute between two states, and one of the states has not consented to ICJ jurisdiction by treaty, the ICJ cannot hear the case.
  - A third limitation of the ICJ is that, although it can make judgements, these are not legally binding so there is no way to enforce its judgements.
- The International Tribunal for the Law of the Sea
  - An independent judicial body that was established by the UN Convention on the Law of the Sea (1982). It has jurisdiction over any dispute concerning the Convention. Disputes relating to the Convention may concern navigation, demarcation of maritime zones, conservation and management of living resources of the sea, protection and preservation of the marine environment and marine scientific research.
- The European Court of Justice
  - Ensures that European Union (EU) law is interpreted and applied in the same way in every EU country. This ensures that EU countries and EU institutions abide by EU law.

▲ **Figure HL 12** Peace Palace, International Court of Justice, the Hague, the Netherlands.

One of the difficulties faced by international judiciary bodies is how to evaluate appropriate compensation and damages for infringements of environmental law.

Find out more at the following websites.

International Court of Justice:

International Tribunal for the Law of the Sea:

The Court of Justice of the European Union in the list of EU Institutions on the European Union website:

Activity

Research one of the bodies listed above. How are they involved with the development of international environmental law?
Produce a fact sheet on your findings.

There are an increasing number of laws granting legal personhood to natural entities in order to strengthen environmental protection.

HL.a.11 Laws granting legal personhood to natural entities

Environmental personhood recognizes that nature has rights, and that those rights should be enforced by law. The granting of such bio rights to 'natural entities', such as animals, can result in stronger environmental protection. For example, in 2019 Bangladesh was the first country to grant all its rivers the same legal status as humans, so that all its rivers would be treated as living entities in a court of law. This is an ecocentric viewpoint rather than an anthropocentric one.

Granting legal personhood to natural entities is similar to the long-established granting of legal personhood to corporations, where a corporation has the same rights as a person to hold property, enter into contracts and to sue or be sued. Corporate personhood is the ethical and legal concept according to which corporations may be treated, morally or legally, as entities independent of the human beings associated with them.

Several indigenous knowledge systems do not recognize the distinction between humans and nature, and so granting legal personhood to natural entities connects to these worldviews.

Read about the legal personhood of rivers in Bangladesh in the NPR online news article *Should Rivers Have Same Legal Rights As Humans? A Growing Number Of Voices Say Yes.*

Example – The Whanganui River, New Zealand

The Whanganui River (Figure HL 13), which flows from Tongariro to the sea, is the longest navigable river in New Zealand. The Māori, the Indigenous people in the area, have lived in settlements along the Whanganui River for hundreds of years. They consider the river as an ancestor – it was 'their source of food, their single highway, their spiritual mentor,' according to a 1999 report on Māori rights to the Whanganui River.[1]

1.1 Perspectives

In the 1800s, British colonizers began settling in New Zealand, including around Whanganui. The colonizers did not treat the river as a single entity, but as a patchwork of legally separate parts, each controlled by different laws. This conflicted with the Māori worldview that the river was a single and indivisible entity and not something that could be owned. The Europeans also treated the river as a resource to be exploited, by releasing trout into the river for fishing, operating a steamer for tourists, extracting the river's gravel and destroying the old fishing weirs where Māori had fished for generations. Māori settlements were pushed back from the river to make way for new developments.

[1]Whanganui River Report: https://ngatangatatiaki.co.nz/assets/Uploads/Important-Documents/Whanganui-River-Report-1999.pdf

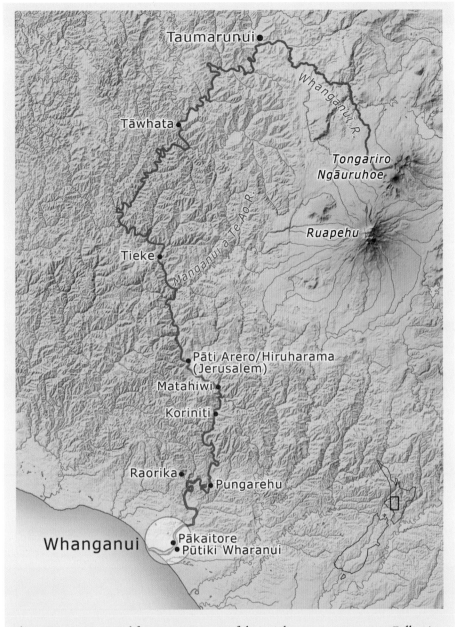

Figure HL 13 Map of the Whanganui River, in the southwestern part of the North Island of New Zealand.

The Māori campaigned for reinstatement of their rights over many years. Following a change in national government in 2008, discussion began about treating the river as one indivisible being that had rights, just like a person. The Whanganui River Claims Settlement Act was passed by the New Zealand Parliament in 2017 and granted legal personhood to the Whanganui River, making it the first river in the world to be considered as a legal person. The river is recognized as a legal entity with its own rights and interests. The act also established:

- a fund for the restoration and protection of the river
- a river strategy group to develop and implement a strategy for the long-term management of the river.

The act is a significant development in the recognition of bio rights and the granting of legal personhood to natural entities.

Read more in the article *When A River Becomes A Legal Person: A Short Journey Down New Zealand's Whanganui River* in the International Rivers archive:

Activity

1. Find out about sites of environmental, historical and spiritual significance to the Māori people of the Whanganui River, and locate these key environmental and cultural features on Figure HL 13.
   - Which areas are protected under the Whanganui River Claims Settlement Act?
   - Why were these areas designated in this way?

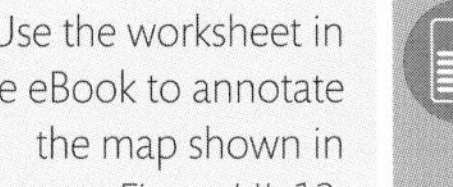

Use the worksheet in the eBook to annotate the map shown in Figure HL 13.

2. Now summarize your findings, adding annotations to a copy of the map shown in Figure HL 13. What is the importance of the river to the Māori people and how does the settlement aim to protect and preserve the river's cultural and natural heritage for future generations?
3. Now research a different indigenous society. Summarize how the value systems relate to the society and environment of the group. How do the knowledge and value systems compare with those of the Māori people (e.g. Do they have a concept of bio rights? Are there similarities? What are the differences?) Draw a mindmap showing similarities and differences between the two societies, and link these to the historical and environmental features of the time and place in which each society exists.

HL.a.12 Legal and economic strategies

Both legal and economic strategies can play a role in maintaining sustainable use of the environment. There are different contributions to sustainable management that can be achieved by the two strategies. Both have their own challenges:

- there is the challenge in economics of attaching economic value to ecosystem services and degradation (this topic, Section HL.b.10)
- there is the challenge in law of achieving agreement between stakeholders and the enforcement of compliance (this topic, Section HL.a.7; Topic 4, Section 4.3.14; Topic 6, Section 6.3.6).

The most successful outcomes may come from an integration of the two approaches, for example, laws imposing fines for illegal dumping or oil spills.

Exercise

Q1. **Define** the term *environmental law*.

Q2. **Explain**, using an example, why environmental laws can be difficult to approve due to lobbying.

Q3. **List** three factors that are required to effectively enforce environmental laws.

Q4. **Describe** an example of a national constitution that was successfully involved in addressing environmental issues.

Q5. **Outline** how environmental laws can be drafted at the local, national or international level.

Q6. **Describe** an example of an international law that provides an essential framework for addressing a transboundary issue of pollution or resource management.

Q7. **Compare** and **contrast** the Montreal Protocol and Paris Agreement, in terms of their aims, objectives and outcomes.

Q8. **List** three bodies involved in the development of international environmental law.

Q9. **Describe**, using an example, how laws granting legal personhood to natural entities can be used to strengthen environmental protection.

HL.b Environmental economics

Guiding questions

How can environmental economics ensure sustainability of the Earth's systems?
How do different perspectives impact the type of economics governments and societies run?

HL b.1 Economics studies how humans produce, distribute and consume goods and services, both individually and collectively.
HL b.2 Environmental economics is economics applied to the environment and environmental issues.
HL b.3 Market failure occurs when the allocation of goods and services by the free market imposes negative impacts on the environment.
HL b.4 When the market fails to prevent negative impacts, the polluter-pays principle may be applied.
HL b.5 'Greenwashing' or 'green sheen' is where companies use marketing to give themselves a more environmentally friendly image.
HL b.6 The tragedy of the commons highlights the problem where property rights are not clearly delineated and no market price is attached to a common good, resulting in overexploitation.
HL b.7 Environmental accounting is the attempt to attach economic value to natural resources and their depletion.
HL b.8 In some cases, economic value can be established by use, but this is not the case for non-use values.
HL b.9 Ecological economics is different from environmental economics in that it views the economy as a subsystem of Earth's larger biosphere and the social system as being a subcomponent of ecology.
HL b.10 While the economic valuation of ecosystem services is addressed by environmental economics, there is an even greater emphasis in ecological economics.
HL b.11 Economic growth is the change in the total market value of goods and services in a country over a period and is usually measured as the annual percentage change in GDP.
HL b.12 Economic growth is influenced by supply and demand and may be perceived as a measure of prosperity.
HL b.13 Economic growth has impacts on environmental welfare.
HL b.14 Eco-economic decoupling is the notion of separating economic growth from environmental degradation.
HL b.15 Ecological economics supports the need for degrowth, zero growth or slow growth, and advocates planned reduction in consumption and production, particularly in high-income countries.
HL b.16 Ecological economists support a slow/no/zero growth model.
HL b.17 The circular economy and doughnut economics models can be seen as applications of ecological economics for sustainability.

Economics studies how humans produce, distribute and consume goods and services, both individually and collectively.

HL.b.1 Economics

Economics is a social science. It is concerned with how individuals and groups of human beings make decisions to meet their needs by managing and exploiting limited resources. These resources include natural, human and financial resources (such as land, labour, capital and entrepreneurship). Economics focuses on the supply and demand of resources and the outcomes of market interaction.

Economic systems involve the provision of markets, households, firms and the state. Thus, the study of economics can be used to meet and assess social and ecological goals. It can also be used to assess human impacts on the environment.

Make sure you are familiar with the terms microeconomic and macroeconomic before you read the rest of this topic. Make your own summaries of the definitions to help you learn their meaning.

Terminology

Economics is studied on two different scales:

- **microeconomic**: small/individual
- **macroeconomic**: large/national/international.

Opportunity cost is the value or benefit of an alternative choice compared to the value of what is chosen. For example, if a business is deciding whether to purchase new solar panels, the opportunity cost of not doing so would be the potential revenue and profitability lost by not being able to take on another project. Opportunity cost is therefore the choice not taken, that is, the benefit foregone. The concept of opportunity cost is used in decision-making to help individuals and organizations make better choices, primarily by considering the alternatives.

Decisions refer to choices made regarding opportunity costs. Any decision requires a choice between two or more competing alternatives. When the decision is made, economists analyse the benefits foregone. This means that economists analyse the benefit that the unsuccessful choice would have given. For example, the government of a country has an investment decision to make and makes the decision to offer subsidies to open a new coal-fired power station rather than subsidizing a firm to develop a wind farm. In this case, the benefits foregone are the opportunity costs that would have resulted from developing wind farms rather than giving subsidies for a coal-fired power station.

The market refers to monetary exchanges between households and businesses. A market economy is a system in which economic decisions, such as the pricing of goods and services, are directed by the interactions between individual citizens and businesses. **Allocating systems** describe how resources are distributed to the people who require the resource, using capital (money), land (natural resources), labour (people) and **entrepreneurship** (using creativity and original ideas to create an original path for a new business). Entrepreneurship creates a space for both environmental and ecological economic activity.

The commons refer to natural resources that are shared by people. Commons include forests, fisheries or groundwater resources. The commons connect humans to the natural world. The common resource is any scarce or finite resource, such as water or pasture, that provides users with noticeable benefits but which nobody in particular owns or has exclusive claim to.

HL.b.2 Environmental economics

Environmental economics (Figure HL 14) studies the relationship between the economy and the environment. It addresses **market failures** (this topic, Sections HL.b.3 and b.4), promotes sustainable development by valuing natural resources and ecosystem services and analyses the costs and benefits of environmental policies.

The existing economic system, where the economy is a closed linear system (Topic 1, Section 1.3.21; this topic, Section HL.b.12) isolated from nature, reinforces the belief that humans will develop new science and technology (for example, using engineering, chemistry, genetics or microbiology) to solve the current environmental issues. This is known as the technocentric approach (Topic 1, Section 1.1.8).

Ecological economics aims to integrate both ecological and economic principles (this topic, Section HL.b.9). It emphasizes the importance of well-being, sustainability and equity and looks to achieve a mutually beneficial and resilient relationship between humans and the natural environment by exploring interdependencies between ecosystems and the economy.

Socio-ecological economics is a multidisciplinary approach to economics that includes both environmental and societal perspectives. Ecological economics is the strand of socio-ecological economics that deals mainly with the natural world.

People who support ecological economics believe that solutions to the current environment problems can be achieved through a fundamental change in human ways. This belief is leading to a developing movement of ecological economics.

Environmental economics is economics applied to the environment and environmental issues.

Figure HL 14 The concept of environmental economics.

The *perspectives* of environmental economists focus on how finite natural resources can be used and managed in a way that serves the human population while meeting concerns about environmental impact.

If you study IB DP Economics, you will be exposed to different schools of thought. This section presents ideas concerning socio-ecological economics. The IB Economics syllabus, however, does not examine socio-ecological economics, and so some of the ideas in this HL lens may be new to you.

The terms 'environmental economics' and 'ecological economics' sound similar, but actually represent two different schools of thought. They both look at similar end effects on the environment and the planet, but ecological economics is more inclusive and cross-disciplinary, and adopts a more holistic approach than environmental economics.

Activity

Electric cars function less well in cold climates because the lithium-ion batteries do not work as well at very low temperatures. Scientists are working to develop a battery that works well in cold conditions.

1. Read more about Lithium-Ion Batteries That Work In The Cold on the CleanTechnica website:
   How does this report support the idea that science and technology will enable environmental solutions to work within the current economic framework, rather than one framed by environmental or socio-ecological economics?
   How would an ecocentric approach differ from this technocentric one?
2. Discuss these issues with another person in your class, then exchange your ideas with other groups.

Technocentrics have the *perspective* that science and technology will enable environmental economics to work within the current economic framework. More ecocentric perspectives tend to value the more innovative approach of ecological economics.

HL.b.3 and HL.b.4 Market failure

Market failure occurs when the allocation of goods and services by the free market imposes negative impacts on the environment.

Market failure refers to examples when economics fails to deliver the best solutions. This can lead to damaging outcomes. In these cases, the outcome of markets is not satisfactory from the point of view of society. In terms of environmental economics, market failure occurs when the allocation of goods and services by the free market imposes negative impacts on the environment. A global example of market failure is climate change, due to the inability of organizations to account for the release of greenhouse gases into the atmosphere during production and consumption processes. A local or national example would be a factory that, during the production of goods, causes pollution that creates a net welfare loss on society at no cost to the factory (Figure HL 15).

Figure HL 15 Factory pollution.

Externalities are situations where the action of a company or individual has consequences for someone else not directly involved. Externalities are also called third party effects or spillover effects. Externalities can be negative or positive.

- **Negative externalities,** for example, pollution:
  - Motorists causing noise and air pollution that damages the quality of life and health of people who live in an urban environment. The market economy does not require motorists to take such externalities into account when planning their journeys.
  - Toxic effluent from a factory, discharged into a river, may harm the livelihood of someone who fishes the river and sells the catch for income. The loss of income for the individual, due to reduced catch, is not considered by the polluting factory when they are calculating profits or making business decisions.
- **Positive externalities**, for example, the maintainence of bees by a beekeeper. The beekeeper enjoys this activity and is provided with regular harvests of honey. The bees pollinate surrounding crop trees such as fruit trees in nearby orchards.

Externalities can lead to market failure. For example, the production process that generates pollution to the environment means that the market is performing inefficiently and leading to harm, which causes a market failure.

When the market fails to prevent negative impacts, the **polluter-pays principle** may be applied.

The polluter-pays principle

The **polluter-pays principle** means that the costs of stopping, managing and cleaning up the pollution are covered by the polluter. Environmental economics has provided solutions to address this issue, such as quotas, fines, taxes, tradeable permits and carbon neutral certification to ensure the polluter pays and limits the burden to society.

Some international policies are aimed directly at protection. Access the RFA news website for more information on the first-ever global ocean treaty:

Government intervention strategies and policies are designed to prevent externalities and have an impact on the polluter. The polluter-pays principle can be applied to businesses that emit greenhouse gases, such as oil and gas companies, through a 'carbon price'. Carbon pricing (or CO_2 pricing) imposes a charge on the emission of greenhouse gases. This charge is equivalent to the corresponding potential cost caused through future climate change, that is, the externalities involved. The cost forces emitters to take on or 'internalize' the cost of their pollution. This additional cost encourages polluters to reduce the combustion of coal, oil and gas.

Activity

Select a real-world example of the polluter-pays principle. Draw up a table outlining the pros and cons of this principle in relation to your example. Now examine a second example. Do the same pros and cons apply? Finally, select a third example, and repeat the procedure. Do the same pros and cons apply in each case, or are there differences? Discuss your findings with someone else in your class. Do they agree with your conclusions?

Greenwashing or **green sheen** refers to the use of marketing by companies to give themselves a more environmentally friendly image.

HL.b.5 Greenwashing

Greenwashing is a form of misinformation when companies or organizations spend time and money on marketing themselves as being sustainable or environmentally friendly, rather than spending time or money on changing practices to become sustainable. An example of greenwashing is seen in oil companies who claim that they are undergoing transitions to clean energy.

Greenwashing reveals itself in several ways.

- A company that claims it is on track to reduce its polluting emissions and achieve net zero (i.e. where greenhouse gases entering the atmosphere are balanced by removal from the atmosphere – Topic 7, Section 7.1.11), but has no convincing plan in place.
- The use of vague or non-specific terminology by a company about their operations or materials used. For example, the use of vague terms such as 'climate positive' when it is unclear what they mean, or using a recycling symbol on packaging without saying which parts are or can be recycled.
- Not providing evidence to back up a claim. For example, a company that wants consumers to take their word without sharing the proof behind their claims. In these instances, the claims cannot be checked or certified independently by someone else.
- Applying intentionally misleading labels such as 'eco-friendly' or 'green', which do not have standard definitions and can be easily misinterpreted.
- Emphasizing a single positive environmental feature, while ignoring other negative impacts. For example, a fast-food company that promotes a change to recyclable paper straws from plastic ones, while still using meat suppliers that are responsible for deforestation and habitat loss.
- Claiming to avoid environmentally damaging practices that are not relevant to a product.
- Communicating the positive sustainability features of a product in isolation from the activities of the company that produces it. For example, promoting clothes that are made from recycled materials but which are produced in a factory that pollutes the air and nearby waterways. The opposite may also be true. For example, a company that highlights its environmentally friendly beliefs, while simultaneously producing environmentally damaging products.

Many international and national organizations call out greenwashing.

Greenpeace: We're living in a golden age of greenwash:

WWF: Guide to greenwashing

Earth.org: 10 Companies called out for greenwashing

The Sierra Club: Help tackle greenwashing and improve corporate performance on climate change

Green claims:

Screening of websites for greenwashing:

A survey conducted in the EU in 2020 found that 53% of green claims for environmentally-friendly products were 'vague, misleading or unfounded'.

Authorities suspected 42% of green product strategies of being 'false or deceptive' in another survey conducted the same year.

Activity

1. Look carefully at Figure HL 16. What message does this image suggest? Is it effective at the job it is trying to do?
   Design an image to promote the same issue.

Figure HL 16 The concept of greenwashing.

2. Find your own examples of greenwashing.
   Which companies or governments were involved and what were the signs that greenwashing was involved?
   Write summaries of the examples, listing the evidence you have found.

Environmental, social and corporate governance (ESG) considers the impact that a company has on its employees, customers and the communities. ESG evaluates and assesses how sustainable and ethical a company is by taking environmental issues, social issues and corporate governance issues into account. Since 2020, there have been accelerating incentives from the UN to connect ESG data with the Sustainable Development Goals (SDGs) (Topic 1, Section 1.3.18).

Critics claim that products linked to ESG have not had, and are unlikely to have, the intended impact of raising the cost of capital for polluting firms. These critics have accused the ESG movement of greenwashing.

Activity

How effective is ESG? Is it a practical and effective way to ensure sustainable development?

1. Write a short paragraph expressing your initial views.
2. Now read the following online articles.

HBR: An Inconvenient Truth About ESG Investing	Ethics.org: Top 6 ESG issues for companies to tackle	How brands are 'greenwashing' you into a false sense of sustainability

Have these articles changed your views on ESG or have they confirmed your initial thoughts? Add your reflections to your notes on ESG.

The tragedy of the commons highlights the problem where property rights are not clearly delineated and no market price is attached to a common good, resulting in overexploitation.

HL.b.6 The tragedy of the commons

An individual or firm can overexploit a common good despite the detriment to others. Overexploitation of the commons has led to the occurrence of what is described by the use of the term 'tragedy of the commons'.

Read more about common international waters, and a landmark high seas treaty agreed in 2023, at the World Wide Fund For Nature website:

The tragedy of the commons is a concept relating to the overexploitation of shared natural resources through human activity and the tension between individual self-interest and the shared benefits of sustainable development (Topic 3, Section 3.2.7). It describes the possible outcomes of shared unrestricted use of a resource, with implications for sustainability and impacts on biodiversity. The tragedy of the commons suggests, for example, that catastrophic climate change is likely unless there is international cooperation on an unprecedented scale (Topic 6, Section 6.3.14). Another example is seen in international waters, where international agreements are needed to restrict or control access to resources such as fish (Topic 4, Section 4.3.8).

3.2 Human impact on biodiversity

4.3 Aquatic food production systems

6.3 Climate change - mitigation and adaptation

This phenomenon highlights a limitation of free market economics in addressing environmental issues. This dilemma can be avoided, however, through alternative approaches (see the following Example).

Example – Governing the commons

Elinor Ostrom (1933–2012) (Figure HL 17) was a leading figure in investigating how the commons are viewed and can be shared within societies. Her work on cooperation in sharing resources is central to discussions and debates about how shared resources can be used sustainably. Ostrom documented how communities have developed ways to address the tragedy of the commons, by **governing the commons** in ways that assure their survival for present and future generations.

Figure HL 17 Elinor Ostrom, who won the Nobel Prize in Economic Sciences in 2009 for her work investigating how communities succeed or fail at managing common resources such as grazing land, forests and irrigation water.

Figure HL 18 Törbel, 1497 m above the town of Visp in Switzerland, was the location of Elinor Ostrom's best-known study.

A well-known example of Ostrom's work concerned shared pastures in Switzerland. The study took place in a Swiss village, Törbel, where farmers tended private plots for crops but shared a communal meadow to graze their cows (Figure HL 18). Ostrom found that, contrary to the tragedy of the commons theory, there were no problems with the overgrazing of shared land. This was because of a common agreement among villagers. This agreement, dating back to 1517, stated that an individual could not send more cows to the communal grazing area than they could look after during the winter. During the summer, there was sufficient grazing for all cattle. The cows also provided the community with milk for cheese-making, which supported the local economy. This innovative strategy of the local community resolves the issue of the tragedy of the commons. Ostrom documented similar effective examples of 'governing the commons' during her research in Guatemala, Kenya, Los Angeles, Nepal, Japan, the Philippines and Turkey. In her book *Governing the Commons,*[1] she examined these real examples of shared commons that had succeeded, along with examples of others that had failed.

Ostrom developed eight principles to be followed for commons to be governed sustainably and equitably within a community.

1. **Commons boundaries** There are clearly defined boundaries, with effective exclusion of people who do not have permission to access the commons.
2. **Social-ecological fit** Local needs and resources are matched with governance structures and rules.
3. **Participation in rulemaking** Decisions are made through collective choice, where people affected by the rules can take part in modifying the rules.
4. **External recognition** The rule-making rights of the community to self-govern are recognized by outside authorities.
5. **Self-monitoring** Rules are enforced by community members through effective monitoring of members' behaviour.
6. **Proportional and effective sanctions** Those who break the rules are punished with graduated (step-by-step and progressive) sanctions.
7. **Conflict resolution** Disputes are addressed with low-cost and easily accessible conflict resolution structures.
8. **Hierarchical systems** In the case of larger common resources, rules are arranged and enforced through multiple layers of nested operations (i.e. one placed inside another), from the lowest level up to the entire interconnected system.

Elinor Ostrom's theory stated that local communities are the best at managing their natural resources as they are the ones that use them. She also recommended that all regulation on the use of resources should be done at the local level, as opposed to a higher, central authority that does not have direct interaction with the resources.

In 2009, Elinor Ostrom became the first woman to win the Nobel Prize in Economic Sciences.

[1]Ostrom, E (1990) *Governing the commons: the evolution of institutions for collective action.* Cambridge University Press, UK.

Activity

Find out about another community that has found ways to avoid the tragedy of the commons, and which shares common resources in a sustainable way.

Write up the information you find as a fact sheet, which you can use as a further example of how the commons can be governed in the interest of all.

Find out more about environmental accounting by watching the following videos:

Can a new way of accounting save our planet?

How accountants can help fight climate change

How to value and account for ecosystems

HL.b.7 and HL.b.8 Environmental accounting

Environmental (or **green**) **accounting** is the attempt to attach economic value to natural resources and their depletion.

Environmental accounts provide a statistical system, which brings together economic and environmental information in a common framework to measure the contribution of the environment to the economy and the impact of the economy on the environment. The **system of environmental–economic accounting (SEEA)** is an international standard procedure for measuring these factors (this topic, Section HL.b.9).

Environmental accounting is problematic in achieving a consensus value for all stakeholders.

Use and non-use values

Natural resources are the raw materials and sources of energy that are used and consumed by societies (Topic 7, Section 7.1.1). Natural capital is the stock of natural resources available on Earth (Topic 7, Section 7.1.2), which has various values. We usually, rightly or wrongly, assess the worth of natural resources in monetary terms.

Economic value can be determined from the market price of the goods and services a resource produces. **Ecological values** have no formal market price. For example, soil erosion control, nitrogen fixation and photosynthesis are all essential for human existence but have no direct monetary value. Similarly, aesthetic values, such as the appreciation of a landscape for its visual attraction, have no market price. Ecological and aesthetic values do not provide easily identifiable commodities, so it is difficult to assess the economic contributions of these values using traditional methods of accounting. They are usually undervalued from an economic viewpoint (Topic 7, Section 7.1.7).

In some cases, **economic value** can be established by use, but this is not the case for **non-use values**.

The value of natural capital can be divided into 'use' and non-use' (Figure HL 19). **Use values** are ecosystem goods and services that are directly used by humans. Use values can be further subdivided into **direct values, indirect values** and **option values** (Figure HL 19).

use
non-use
direct values: outputs that can be consumed directly, such as timber, medicines, food, recreation, etc.
indirect values: ecological services, such as flood control, storm protection, carbon sequestration, climatic control, etc.
option values: the premium placed on maintaining resources for future direct and indirect uses, some of which may not be known now
existence values: the intrinsic value of resources, irrespective of their use, such as cultural, aesthetic, bequest significance, etc.
Harder and harder to quantify
More and more often ignored

Figure HL 19 Levels of difficulty in assessing the economic value of natural capital.

Non-use values include aesthetic and intrinsic values and are sometimes called existence values.

Non-use values (also known as existence values) may include the intrinsic value of a species, the potential for future use or the value it may have for forthcoming generations. They can be established by surveys on how much people would be willing to pay for a common good or how much compensation they would accept in return for its destruction.

There are attempts to acknowledge these diverse valuations of nature. For example, scientists can examine the importance of biodiversity for ecosystem functioning by looking at connections between species diversity and the integrity of ecosystem processes. An example here is the role of pollinators such as wasps and bees in maintaining flowering and fruiting in rainforest.

1.3 Sustainability
7.1 Natural resources – uses and management

Biodiversity also has value in its contribution to ongoing evolution and speciation, as well as a genetic resource. We need to find ways to value nature more rigorously against common economic values, such as gross domestic product (GDP) (Topic 1, Section 1.3.8, and this topic, Section HL.b.11). However, some people argue that such valuations are impossible to quantify or price realistically (Figure HL 19). Not surprisingly, much of the sustainability debate centres on the problem of how to weigh conflicting values in our treatment of natural capital.

Example – Valuing the oceans: the US$ 2 trillion question

Economists at the Stockholm Environment Institute have estimated that the cost of climate change on the oceans will amount to nearly US$ 2 trillion annually by 2100 or about 0.4% of global GDP. The estimate was based on five measures:

- loss of fisheries
- reduced tourism revenues
- the economic cost of rising sea levels
- the cost of increased storm activity
- ocean acidification.

The economists estimate that a rise in temperature of 4 °C by 2100 would come to a total cost of US$ 1.98 trillion, whereas if temperatures rise by only 2.2 °C, the total cost is estimated at US$ 612 billion.

Estimates of the world's GDP a century from now depend on too many variables to calculate with any precision. The same is true for the rise in temperature by 2100. The timescale is too great to be able to make an accurate prediction.

Example – Pollination of crops in the USA

There are 250,000 species of flowering plants that depend on bees for pollination. Many of these species are crucial to world agriculture. Without pollinators, crops would not grow, many fruits and vegetables would become scarce or prohibitively expensive, and other essential products, such as clothing (cotton is bee-pollinated), would be affected.

A recent study suggested that five out of seven crops in the USA showed evidence that a lack of pollinators was limiting current crop production (a condition known as 'pollinator limitation'). The crops studied were blueberry, apple, sweet cherry, tart cherry, almond, watermelon and pumpkin. The study showed that, in most crops, the overall contribution of wild bees to pollination was similar to (or higher than) that of honeybees. The study estimated that the nationwide annual production value of wild pollinators to the seven crops exceeded US$ 1.5 billion; the value of wild bee pollination of all pollinator-dependent crops would be much greater. The study[1] concluded that decline in the populations of pollinators could result directly in decreased yields for most of the crops studied, and that wild species contribute substantially to the pollination of most study crops in major crop-producing regions.

Activity

In 2023, there was a series of destructive wildfires across the world, covering regions of Asia, Europe and North America, including a devastating wildfire in Maui, Hawaii's second-largest island. These fires were started by lightning, land-clearance or human-caused accidents. Wildland fires are now burning more often and for longer, with climate change suggested as the main driving force. The fires in 2023 led to the destruction of infrastructure, properties and natural ecosystems, and to the loss of life (Figure HL 20).

- Which ecosystems were affected by the wildfires?
- What are the use values of the ecosystems affected? How can these be estimated?
- How could non-use values be estimated?
- Why is it important to assess both non-use and use values when determining the impact of an ecological disaster, such as wildfires? Can such values easily be quantified?

Write a short summary of your findings.

Figure HL 20 A wildfire burning through a forest ecosystem.

Read more about the 2023 fire season on Nasa's Earth Observatory website:

HL.b.9 Ecological economics vs environmental economics

Ecological economics is different from environmental economics. Ecological economics views the economy as a subsystem of Earth's larger biosphere and the social system as being a subcomponent of ecology. Environmental economics studies the relationship between the economy and the environment, addresses market failures (this topic, Section HL.b.3), promotes sustainable development by valuing natural resources and ecosystem services and analyses the costs and benefits of environmental policies (this topic, Section HL.b.2).

The ecological economist perceives the biosphere as a system with:

- inputs of solar energy sustaining natural energy
- material resources that enter the economic subsystem and then produce wastes
- an overall loss of low-grade thermal energy from the biosphere.

1.2 Systems

Ecological economics places emphasis on the sustainable use of natural capital, applying the precautionary principle to minimize environmental and social impacts and emphasizing the value of natural capital alongside physical, human and financial capital.

Natural capital can be accounted by recording and reporting status and trends and the ways in which people are using natural resources.

[1]Reilly, J.R. et al. (2020) Crop production in the USA is frequently limited by a lack of pollinators. *Proceedings of the Royal Society B*, Vol 287: 20200922.

Read more about the SEEA on the UN SEEA website:

The system of environmental–economic accounting (SEEA) provides information about the status and trends of the environment and natural resources, and how people are using them. It works within the **system of national accounts (SNA)**. The SNA is the internationally agreed standard set of recommendations on how to compile measures of economic activity. GDP is a measure that reflects economic activity in a country (Topic 1, Section 1.3.8 and this topic, Section HL.b.11). GDP works within the SNA but does not contain any data about how ecosystems are changing or the ecological capital on Earth. The SEEA was created to fill this gap. The development of the SEEA was coordinated by the UN statistics division in New York. The data generated by the SEEA is important because it provides reliable and accurate data to inform decisions about managing ecosystems better. The SEEA gathers data from countries that addresses the following questions:

- What is the extent of ecosystems?
- What are the conditions of ecosystems (e.g. quality of water and soil)?
- How is the environment changing?
- What are the ecosystem services and goods provided?
- What are the asset values of ecosystems? Are ecosystems regenerating to provide capital? How much of the natural resource is being used to generate capital?

The SEEA does not give values to all aspects of natural resources but aims to understand the contribution of ecosystems to economic activity, for example through production and consumption. Unlike the measures of economic activity previously discussed, such as GDP, SEEA makes extensive and novel use of spatial data from maps, because ecosystems are very diverse and complex. Spatial diversity between different areas of ecosystem needs to be captured in statistical data. Spatial information such as satellite images can be integrated with statistical data to generate information about land use. The emission of CO_2 can be calculated, including the actual costs of CO_2, even down to the field level on a farm.

Activity

Learn more about Natural Capital Accounting in this TED talk:

Produce a short presentation that summarizes the key ideas in this talk. Show your presentation to the rest of your class. Be prepared to answers questions at the end of your talk.

HL.b.10 Economic valuation of ecosystem services

While the economic valuation of ecosystem services is addressed by environmental economics, there is an even greater emphasis on this in ecological economics.

Ecosystems provide life-supporting ecosystem services, such as water replenishment, flood and erosion protection, pollution mitigation (e.g. reed beds in lakes provide a buffer that removes inorganic nutrients) and carbon sequestration (Topic 7, Section 7.1.5). These ecosystem services support all living things, including humans. Ecosystems and ecosystem services constantly change as a result of demographic, economic, social and cultural factors. For example, in Europe since the 1940s there has been intensification of agriculture at the expense of several habitats, including wetlands, forests and grasslands.

There are different types of ecosystem service (Topic 7, Section 7.1.5).

- **Supporting services** These are the essentials for life and include primary productivity, soil formation and the cycling of nutrients. All other ecosystem services depend on these.
- **Regulating services** These are a diverse set of services and include pollination, regulation of pests and diseases, and the production of goods such as food, fibre and wood. Other services include climate and hazard regulation and water quality regulation.
- **Provisioning services** These are the services people obtain from ecosystems such as food, fibre, fuel (peat, wood and non-woody biomass) and water from aquifers, rivers and lakes. Goods can be from heavily managed ecosystems (intensive farms and fish farms) or from semi-natural ones (hunting and fishing).
- **Cultural services** These are derived from places where people interact with nature, providing cultural goods and benefits. Gardens, parks, rivers, forests, lakes, the seashore and wilderness, all provide opportunities for outdoor recreation, learning, spiritual well-being and improvements to human health.

Resources become depleted when they are being used faster than they can be replenished. **Resource-depleted** countries have used up their resources to develop economically (Topic 4, Section 4.2.15). These resource-depleted, and usually developed countries, pay **resource-rich** developing countries to not deplete their natural assets. This can create tensions between countries (Topic 6, Section 6.3.1). For example, countries with depleted forests used for economic gain in the past, may pay countries with extensive forests to not remove them for economic growth. Forests are seen in ecological economics as having economic value beyond timber value. The ecological services, the aesthetic value for tourism and recreation, and the ethical value are all considered in ecological economics.

3.3 Conservation and regeneration
4.2 Water access, use and security
4.4 Water pollution
6.3 Climate change - mitigation and adaptation
7.1 Natural resources – uses and management

Find out more about ecological economics with this online article and video.

Yale Insights article: What is ecological economics?

Video: Ecological Economics Explained

HL.b.11 – HL.b.13 Economic growth

Economic growth is traditionally measured and internationally recognized by **GDP** (Topic 1, Section 1.3.8). Terms that are also used are rates of GDP growth (year on year) and GDP per capita (per person). **Per capita GDP** is a more accurate assessment of living standards but does not consider inequalities in the actual distribution of income.

Economic growth is the change in the total market value of goods and services in a country over a period of time, and is usually measured as the annual percentage change in GDP.

The full cost of energy, material inputs or loss of ecosystem services caused by economic activity are not recorded in the GDP indicator. The goal of economic growth has often resulted in regions overexploiting natural resources for certain kinds of economic activities, including agriculture, industrialization and transport, at the expense of equitable, sufficient and sustainable access of these resources for the general population.

Find out more about GDP in this video:

GDP only measures output that is paid for with money and recorded. It therefore reflects the limited scope of the circular-flow-of-income model in mainstream economics. This means that consumers, firms and governments are not making decisions based on a complete cost/benefit analysis (that is, the full cost of energy, material inputs or loss of ecosystem services caused by economic activity are not recorded), which leads to *unsustainable* use of the Earth's natural resources.

Economic growth is influenced by supply and demand and may be perceived as a measure of prosperity.

Supply and demand in a linear economy

Activity

Would you expect a strong positive correlation between CO_2 emissions and GDP per capita (income), with emissions rising as countries become wealthier? You could provide valid reasons for this argument. For example, with increased GDP, countries gain access to, and increase consumption of, energy-intensive goods such as electricity, heating, transport and other resources that require high outputs of energy. Countries with higher GDP therefore require increasing access to energy, but if fossil fuels are the dominant source of energy, their access to modern energy results in excessive carbon emissions.

Use this interactive map to explore the relationship between consumption-based CO_2 emissions per capita vs. GDP per capita:

Use the slider to see the changes between 1990 and 2021.

1. Carry out research to find if there is a relationship between CO_2 emissions and GDP. Use these research papers as a starting point:

Economic growth and CO_2 emissions: the ECM analysis

See Figure 11 in: Bouramdane A.-A. (2024) Morocco's Path to a Climate-Resilient Energy Transition

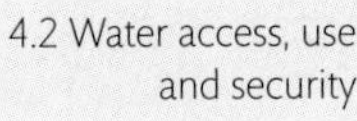

4.2 Water access, use and security

2. Is the relationship universal, or are there exceptions? Summarize your findings in a poster to show to the rest of your class.
3. The goal of economic growth has often resulted in regions overexploiting water resources for economic activities such as agriculture and industrialization. These activities can be at the expense of equitable, sufficient and sustainable water access for the general population.

   Consider examples from Topic 4:

   - Access to drinking water in Monterrey, Mexico (Section 4.4.16)
   - Bangladesh – water stress due to population pressure (Section 4.2.15)
   - Water stress and the Indian textile industry (Section 4.2.15).

(a) In these cases, to what extent has inequitable access occurred as a result of the prioritization of economic growth (of a sector or business) over the general health and well-being of a population? Add your conclusions to notes on these examples.

(b) Find your own example of where inequitable access to water has occurred because economic growth has been prioritized. Summarize your real-world example on one side of A4.

Traditional economic models such as GDP provide a linear economy. GDP does not usually consider waste, pollution and issues that lead to environmental degradation. A circular model is required to account for all of these factors (Figure HL 21). For further discussion of the circular model, see Topic 1 (Section 1.3.21), Topic 7 (Sections 7.2.6 and 7.3.9) and Topic 8 (Section 8.2.12).

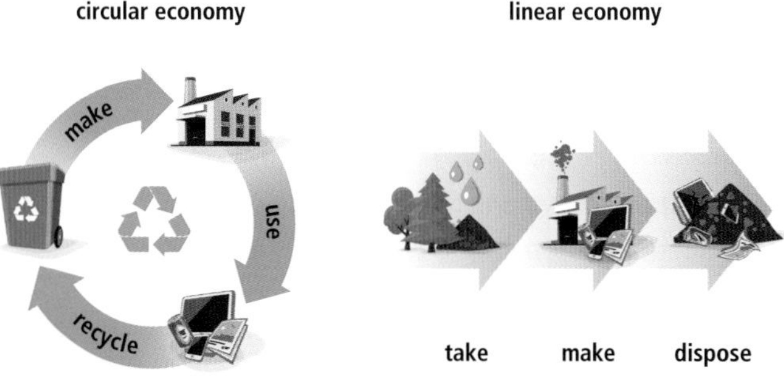

Figure HL 21 The circular and linear economies.

1.3 Sustainability
7.2 Energy sources – uses and management
7.3 Solid waste
8.2 Urban systems and urban planning

Economic growth has impacts on environmental welfare. In environmental welfare economics, the values of environmental goods such as biodiversity count on the 'benefit' side of net benefits. Damages to environmental quality from production and consumptive processes, such as pollution, count as 'costs'. Environmental welfare economics can help policymakers protect nature and conserve natural resources.

Impacts on environmental welfare

Economic growth and the resulting increase in incomes can have both positive and negative effects on the environment.

- Negative effects such as higher consumption of non-renewable resources, increased pollution levels, global warming and the loss of natural habitats.
- Positive effects such as providing resources to protect the environment and addressing environmental problems such as pollution.

However, this can be a complex issue because it raises questions about environmental justice for those who are impacted by increased consumption of natural resources (Topic 1, Section 1.3.9).

Economic growth impacts on society and the environment. Typically, these impacts are negative externalities, for example, pollution is a negative externality (this topic, Sections HL.b.3 and HL.b.4). These effects are a result of a market misallocation of resources or a market failure (this topic, Section HL.b.3).

Watch this video on Negative externalities: The hidden social costs.

HL.b.14 Eco-economic decoupling

Decoupling refers to economies that would be able to grow without corresponding increases in pressure on the environment. While some countries have claimed some success in decoupling CO_2 emissions from economic growth, it seems impossible that there should ever be absolute decoupling. Indefinite growth would seem to require infinite availability of resources. Some argue that technological development can make this possible. Relative decoupling may occur, where resource degradation is at least reduced, although this still allows for some degradation.

Clearly, a different economic model is needed, which combines social and environmental systems with economics.

Eco-economic **decoupling** is the notion of separating economic growth from environmental degradation.

Watch this video on decoupling economic growth from environmental resources.

HL.b.15 and HL.b.16 Ecological economics

Ecological economics supports the need for **degrowth**, zero growth or slow growth and advocates planned reduction in consumption and production, particularly in high-income countries (HICs). Degrowth is a concept where economies shrink, rather than grow, in order to use less of the world's resources and to use them sustainably.

Biocapacity is the capacity of a given biologically productive area to generate an on-going supply of renewable resources and to absorb the resulting wastes (Topic 1, Section 1.3.15).

An ecological footprint (EF) is the area of land and water required to sustainably provide all resources at the rate of consumption and assimilate all wastes at the rate of production by a given population (Topic 1, Section 1.3.13).

An ecological footprint lower than biocapacity suggests a population is living sustainably. Unsustainability occurs if the area's ecological footprint exceeds its biocapacity.

Example – Brazil

Figure HL 22 Ecological footprint and biocapacity of Brazil, 1961–2011.

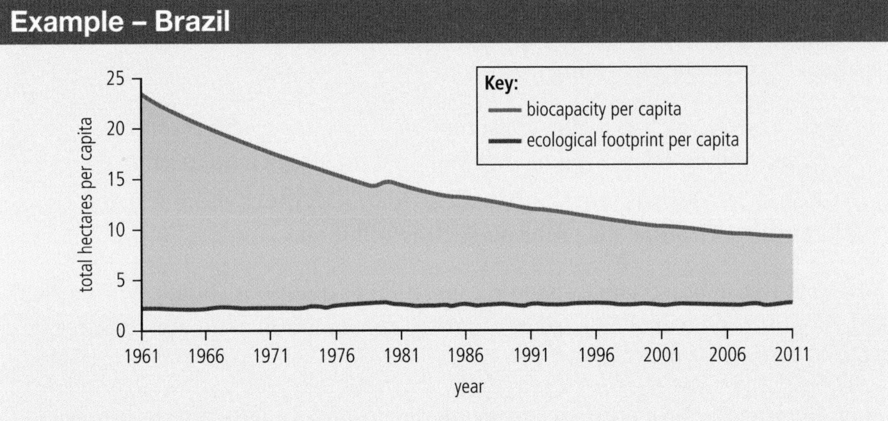

1.3 Sustainability

Several conclusions can be reached from Figure HL 22 regarding the sustainability of the Brazilian population over the period shown.

- The ecological footprint increased over the period, which suggested that Brazil had moved toward unsustainability.
- Biocapacity decreased over the period, which also suggested that Brazil had moved toward unsustainability. Brazil was living unsustainably by using resources at a rate that was not replenishable, resulting in a decline in the biocapacity.
- A meeting or crossing over of the lines for biocapacity and ecological footprint would suggest unsustainability.
- The rate of decrease in biocapacity was falling and stabilizing toward the end of period. This suggested that the country had remained, or was moving towards, becoming sustainable.
- The Brazilian population and government needed to reduce their ecological footprint to sustain biocapacity.

Balancing the ecological footprint of a country with its biocapacity leads to sustainability and this is the goal of ecological economics. However, there are inherent difficulties in dismantling deeply embedded economic systems and in objectively measuring social and environmental well-being.

Activity

An ecological reserve exists when the biocapacity of a region exceeds its population's ecological footprint. An ecological deficit occurs when the ecological footprint of a population exceeds the biocapacity of the area available to that population.

1. Click on Dive into Data! on the Global Footprint Network website and use the interactive map to assess whether a country is in ecological reserve or deficit.
2. Select two countries – one that is in reserve and one that is in deficit. How have the biocapacity and ecological footprints changed over time in each country?
3. Produce a fact sheet for each country, outlining how sustainability has changed over time and reasons for this.

Example – The challenges of sustainability: Costa Rica

7.1 Natural resources – uses and management

Costa Rica, in Central America, has tried to drive the biocapacity ecological footprint towards sustainability (Topic 7, Section 7.1.11). In the 1940s, 75% of the land in Costa Rica was covered by forests. Then, logging and unregulated exploitation destroyed large areas of Costa Rica's ecosystems, including tropical rainforests, with forests declining by approximately one half. This rapid deforestation was the result of an economic system that valued changing forest (termed then as 'unproductive land') to agricultural land ('productive land'). In the early 1990s, political leaders in Costa Rica realized the need for change, to significantly improve the environmental and social systems that the country's economy relied on. Investment policies were introduced to reverse the unsustainable situation. Costa Rica's government developed a plan to save their natural ecosystems, in which people were compensated to plant trees and restore ecosystems. This led to its forests doubling in size, with flora and fauna thriving, leading to a boom in ecotourism that has injected US$ 4 billion into the economy. Other policies established national parks, promoted ecotourism, encouraged organic farming, preserved the natural environment, improved societal well-being, health, educational access and support for a green culture, and the development of a plan to implement a circular (green) economy. A 'pay to throw' program charges residents according to the weight of garbage they generate. Successes of these strategies include:

- Costa Rica is 98% free of deforestation, which has lowered the country's carbon footprint and mitigated climate change.
- Costa Rica has set aside 28 national parks.
- Protected areas cover a quarter of the country's land surface (25–28% coverage).
- A significant increase in the rate of recycling (an increase of 469% between 2015 and 2017).
- Since 1997, Costa Rica has collected 3.5% tax on fossil fuels, generating US$ 26.4 million per year.

- Costa Rica generates approximately 99% of its electricity from renewable sources, including hydroelectric, geothermal, wind, and solar power. Due to the significant investments made in recent years, the majority (67.5%) of Costa Rica's energy comes from hydroelectric power.

More recently, the government of Costa Rica has developed plans to decarbonize the country's economy by 2050, in alignment with commitments of the Paris Climate Agreement and the UN SDGs. In 2019, Costa Rica was awarded the UN's Champions of the Earth award, which recognized the country's role in protecting nature and commitment to ambitious policies to combat climate change. Costa Rica's environmental credentials are known to be one of the best in the world, and the country is often described as a 'living Eden'.

Watch these videos:

Can our economies grow forever

Is capitalism saving or destroying us?

Since the early 1990s, loss of biocapacity in Costa Rica has slowed and has now levelled off (see Figure 1.70, Topic 1, Section 1.3.15). However, the country's ecological footprint has slowly increased, meaning that Costa Rica is in ecological deficit overall (Topic 1, Section 1.3.15). The increase in ecological footprint is due to several reasons. Energy use and related greenhouse gas emissions have increased over the last decade. Private cars are a major and growing source of emissions, which affects climate and air quality. Waste disposal still relies on landfill, and large quantities of wastewater remain untreated. Costa Rica's ecological footprint is, however, much lower than other developed countries (such as the USA), because of its green policies. With its ongoing commitment to tackling climate change and biodiversity loss, Costa Rica demonstrates both the challenges and rewards of achieving a sustainable future.

Ecological economists support a slow/no/zero growth model

Ecological economists address the extent to which the ecological footprint of a country is sustainably balanced by its biocapacity, which removes the focus on GDP.

Activity

How can we live better while producing less?

1. Watch the video, Degrowth: Is it time to live better with less?

Are the aims and objectives of the degrowth movement realistic? What are the pros and cons of degrowth? Does it provide the basis for future economic models?

2. Discuss these ideas with another person in your class. Now compare your ideas with others.

HL.b.17 The circular economy and doughnut economics models

The circular economy and doughnut economics models can be seen as applications of ecological economics for sustainability.

1.3 Sustainability

Traditional models of economic activity

A model of an economy is an overview of the system of resource/product creation and monetary exchanges between households and businesses (markets). There is a significant focus on markets as allocating (or provisioning) systems (land, labour, capital and entrepreneurship) to meet human needs and wants.

Circular flow models show how money flows through an economy. This system is studied via either the two-sector model (Figure HL 23) or the five-sector model (Figure HL 24). These models are not to be confused with the circular economy (Figure HL 27, p852).

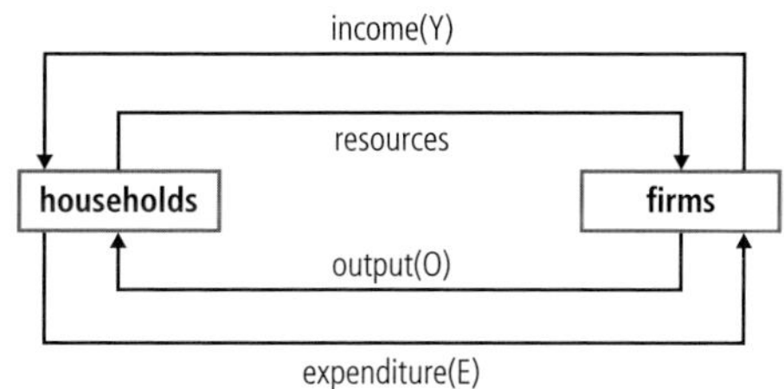

Figure HL 23 A simple two-sector closed model of the economy where there are only two economic agents/actors, namely households and firms. Households provide resources (factors of production) to firms, most notably labour. In return, households receive income from firms. Firms use the resources to create goods and services (output). Households spend money (expenditure) to buy these goods and services.

- income (Y) = wages, rent, dividends and profit
- resources = factors of production
- output (O) = goods and services
- expenditure (E) = consumer spending.

Economics assesses the impacts of parts of the circular flow model on society and the environment. Circular flow of income models show economic activity as separate from the natural world and society; nature is invisible in these models. These models consider society as exterior to nature, and nature as a resource system. This viewpoint has historically played a large role in the overexploitation and degradation of the natural environment.

Figure HL 23 shows the two-sector model of an economy (closed model).

Figure HL 24 shows a more complex, five-sector version of the circular flow model. Three additional economic agents/actors are included: government sector, financial sector (firms such as banks) and the overseas sector (international trade or foreign firms).

Each of these three additional sectors either provide money to (injections) or receive money from (leakages) the core exchange between households and firms. For example, both households and firms pay taxes to the government (leakage), but the government also spends money in the core economy (injection).

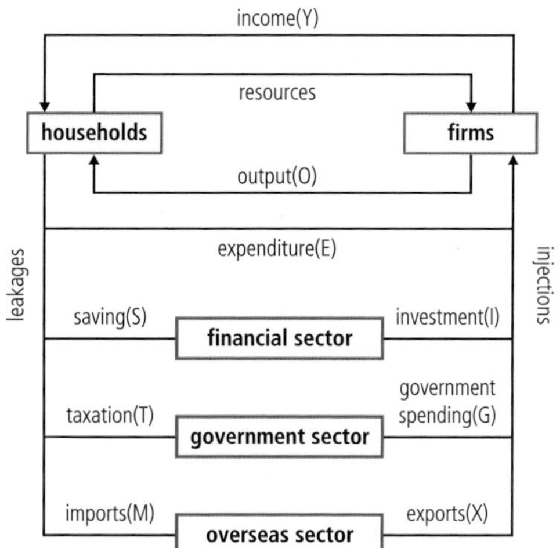

Figure HL 24 The five-sector model of an economy. Additional inputs and outputs in the five-sector model:

- savings (S) = income not spent but set aside for future use
- investment (I) = generates income or appreciation
- taxation (T) = raises revenue for government expenditure
- government spending (G) = finances government activities, e.g. healthcare and education
- imports (M) = money paid to foreign companies
- exports (X) = bring in money from international buyers from the foreign sector.

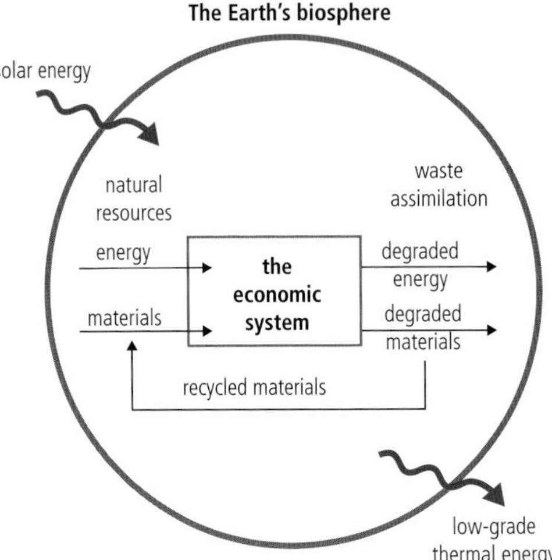

Figure HL 25 Diagram describing the flow of natural resources through the economy, developed by Herman Daly. Valuable resources are procured from nature at the input end of the economy. The resources flow through the economy, being transformed and manufactured into goods along the way. Non-valuable waste and pollution accumulate at the output end. Recycling of material resources is possible, but only by using up some energy sources as well as an additional amount of other material resources. Energy sources cannot be recycled and are dissipated as waste heat.

Socio-ecological economic models

In contrast to the closed model (Figure HL 23), socio-ecological economics uses an 'open' model of the economy (Figure HL 25). This **embedded model** was first introduced in the 1970s by the ecological economist Herman Daly. The model shows the input of solar energy and material resources, as well as heat loss and waste into Earth's sinks. The economy is embedded or contained within society and within the natural environment. Daly defined his concept of a steady-state economy as an economic system made up of a constant stock of physical wealth (capital) and a constant stock of people (population), both stocks to be maintained by a flow of natural resources through the system.

Figures HL 25 and HL 26 show circular flow diagrams of income models. You need to know what these diagrams include and what they exclude, along with the significance of these choices. You will not be required to draw these diagrams in examinations.

GDP has been the internationally recognized indicator of economic progress for many decades. GDP, however, only measures output that is paid for with money and is recorded, so the full cost of energy, material inputs or loss of ecosystem services caused by economic activity is not recorded. This can lead to development that is not sustainable, and is therefore harmful to Earth systems. In contrast, the open system model of ecological economics (which includes inputs of solar energy and matter, and shows waste and heat outputs) is a *sustainable* model for development.

The Doughnut Economics Action Lab (Figure HL 26) further developed the embedded model.

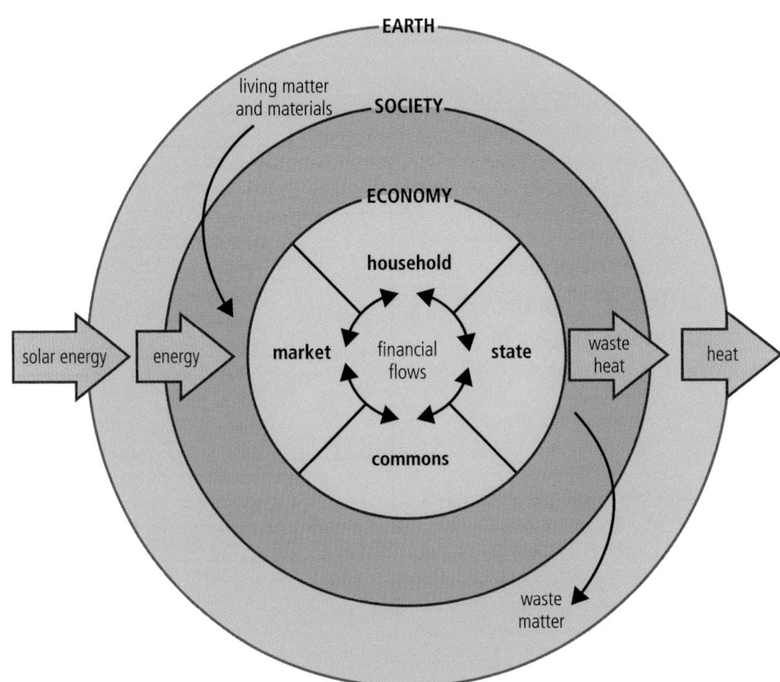

Figure HL 26 The embedded economy.

This model recognizes the dependency and integration of both society and the economy with the natural environment. Thus, any economic analysis using this model is more likely to have a holistic understanding of the interplay between the economy, society and the natural environment.

The embedded model includes more provisioning systems than the economics circular flow models. In the embedded economy model, markets and the state are joined by the household and the commons. The household in this model includes all the unpaid care work that is done in the home (primarily by women). The way the term 'household' is used in this model is different from households in the circular flow diagram, which focuses only on the role of providing labour to firms and consuming goods and services.

Mainstream economics and socio-ecological economics have different views on how to model the economy. Conventional economists use a closed *system* – the circular flow model – which only includes monetary and resource/product exchanges between households and firms (two-sector model) and the state, financial sector and firms abroad (five-sector model). Ecological economists use an open system model that includes inputs of solar energy and matter, and shows waste and heat outputs (embedded economy).

Example – Tipping points

Tipping points occur when a small alteration in one component produces large overall changes, resulting in a shift in equilibrium (Topic 1, Section 1.2.11; Topic 2, Section 2.1.22; Topic 3, Section 3.2.13; Topic 5, Section 5.1.21 and Topic 6, Sections 6.2.13 and 6.2.14). GDP growth puts strain on Earth systems through resource extraction, resulting in emission of pollutants and waste. These factors can increase the probability of tipping points occurring. Free market economics can be said to be myopic (short-sighted) to these risks because current established economic models assume linear and stable relationships between economic factors that can be quantified. In contrast, the socio-ecological economic model is more sensitive to the risks of tipping points. In socio-ecological economics, the economy is seen as a complex, adaptive system where storages and flows, feedback loops and delays, are likely to produce unpredictable tipping points (from financial crashes to climate breakdown). In this model, the economy is embedded in complex, adaptive social and ecological systems. Complex systems are more difficult to measure, predict and influence, so socio-ecological economics is more likely to propose stronger measures to limit or prevent ecological harm. With socio-ecological economics, people are more likely to take precautions (for example, plan for mitigation rather than adaptation) to avoid tipping points, because they understand the complexity and unpredictability of the systems involved.

The circular economy and doughnut models

The earlier models are incorporated in the circular economy (Figure HL 27, and Topic 1, Section 1.3.21). The circular economy:

- reduces material use
- redesigns materials, products and services to be less resource intensive
- recaptures waste as a resource to manufacture new materials and products.

Economist Kate Raworth explains the embedded economy in this short video:

What role do models play in the acquisition of knowledge in the human sciences?

There are contrasting models of the economy, each reflecting different perspectives and understanding. What is the significance of where system boundaries are drawn, and how does this relate to the sustainability of economic and environmental systems? How does the way we draw models influence the knowledge we gain from studying them?

1.2 Systems

2.1 Individuals, populations, communities, and ecosystems

3.2 Human impact on biodiversity

5.1 Soil

6.2 Climate change – causes and impacts

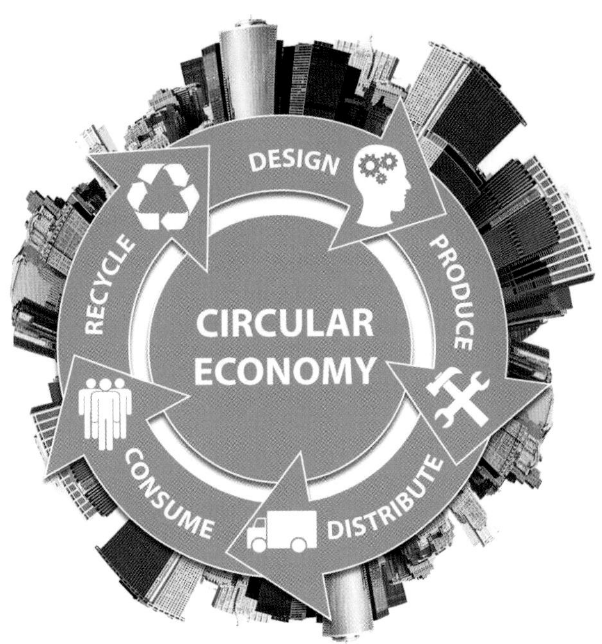

Figure HL 27 The circular economy.

Sustainability refers to the responsible maintenance of socio-ecological systems such that there is no diminishment of conditions for future generations. Tipping points occur when a small alteration in one component produces large overall changes, and they can occur as a result of unsustainable development. Socio-ecological economics is more sensitive to the risks of tipping points. This is because it assumes that the economy is a complex, adaptive system whose stocks and flows, feedback loops and delays are likely to produce unpredictable tipping points (such as climate breakdown).

These ideas are further developed in the doughnut economics model (Topic 1, Section 1.3.20). The doughnut economics model integrates social and planetary boundaries to define an environmentally safe and socially just space in which humanity can thrive. The doughnut model fundamentally attempts to address issues of inequality and injustice. There are attempts to quantify this model for different countries.

Exercise

Q10. **Define** the term *environmental economics.*

Q11. **Outline** the concept of market failure, including the role of negative externalities.

Q12. **Describe** the polluter-pays principle.

Q13. **Describe** the term *greenwashing*.

Q14. **Evaluate** the theory of the tragedy of the commons.

Q15. **Outline** how environmental accounting attempts to attach economic value to natural resources and their depletion.

Q16. **Compare** and **contrast** use and non-use values.

Q17. GDP has been the most important internationally recognized indicator of economic progress for several decades. **Evaluate** the use of GDP in market economies.

Q18. **Explain** the effects of economic growth on environmental welfare.

Q19. **Explain** how ecological economists assess the sustainability of a country using its ecological footprint and biocapacity.

Q20. **Distinguish** between circular flow models and the circular economy.

Q21. **Explain** how the circular economy and doughnut economics models can be seen as applications of ecological economics for sustainability.

HL.c Environmental ethics

Guiding questions

To what extent do humans have a moral responsibility towards the environment?
How does environmental ethics influence approaches to achieving a sustainable future?

HL c.1 Ethics is the branch of philosophy that focuses on moral principles and what behaviours are right and wrong.
HL c.2 Environmental ethics is a branch of ethical philosophy that addresses environmental issues.
HL c.3 A variety of ethical frameworks and conflicting ethical values emerge from differing fundamental beliefs concerning the relationship between humans and nature.
HL c.4 Instrumental value is the usefulness an entity has for humans.
HL c.5 Intrinsic value is the value one may attach to something simply for what it is.
HL c.6 The concepts of instrumental and intrinsic value are not exclusive.
HL c.7 An entity has 'moral standing' if it is to be morally considered with regard to how we ought to act towards it.
HL c.8 There are three major approaches of traditional ethics: virtue ethics, consequentialist (for example, utilitarian) ethics and rights-based (deontological) ethics.
HL c.9 Virtue ethics focuses on the character of the person doing the action. It assumes that good people will do good actions and bad people will do bad actions.
HL c.10 Consequentialist ethics is the view that the consequences of an action determine the morality of the action.
HL c.11 Rights-based ethical systems focus on the actions and whether they conflict with the rights of others. There is debate about what these rights might be.
HL c.12 Some people hold the view that whatever is natural is correct or good. This position is contentious and is described as the 'appeal to nature' fallacy.
HL c.13 Environmental movements and social justice movements have developed from separate histories but are increasingly seeking common goals of equitable and just societies.

Figure HL 28 Ethics focuses on moral principles and whether behaviours are right or wrong.

Throughout the ESS course, think about how you can apply the HL environmental ethics lens, and how ethical conclusions might be reached concerning content from throughout the course (Topics 1–8). These conclusions may form your own position on any particular issue. Make sure that you also explore how a range of ethical conclusions could be arrived at by different individuals and by using different ethical approaches.

Ethical *perspectives* vary across cultures and individuals.

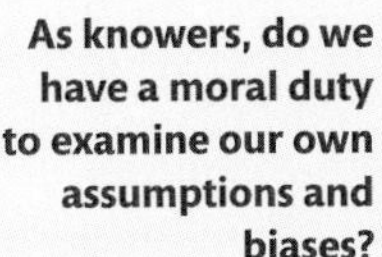

TOK

As knowers, do we have a moral duty to examine our own assumptions and biases?

What factors can influence an ethical stance? To what degree have those influences shaped your own ethics? Why do people have different ethical perspectives? Can any particular ethics be considered to be 'more correct' than any other?

HL.c.1 Ethics

Ethics (Figure HL 28) is the branch of philosophy that focuses on moral principles and whether behaviours are right or wrong.

Different cultures, traditions and individuals often have ethical codes that they have developed or adopted from influences that surround them. These influences include:

- formal ethical systems
- religion
- family values
- traditions
- books
- education
- media and technology
- your own thinking and reflections.

Activity

1. Consider the influences on your own ethical system.
   - What value do you attribute to the world, non-human organisms, humans and the ecosystems in it?
   - How do we decide what is morally right or wrong when the values that are attributed to the world, non-human organisms, humans and ecosystems conflict?

   Briefly summarize your ideas. You can refer to your summary and add to it as you learn about the way that ethics interconnects with ESS.
2. Continue to make notes as you explore the different topics in ESS.
   - How does the ethics lens allow you to reach ethical conclusions regarding different issues?
   - How can a range of ethical conclusions be arrived at by different individuals, using different ethical approaches?
3. Throughout the course, think about and reflect on the range of ethical positions that might exist and what reasons underpin these ethical conclusions.

HL.c.2 Environmental ethics

Environmental ethics is a branch of ethical philosophy that studies the moral relationship of human beings to the environment, and the value and moral status of other species. This branch of ethics arose in the 1960s and 1970s when environmental issues and awareness became well-known and widespread.

Western ethical traditions tend to focus on social actions and relationships between people. Environmental ethics was developed because traditional ethics did not adequately address the moral status of non-human or non-living environmental entities such as animals, plants and rivers.

Example – The problem of invasive species

Invasive alien species can reduce local biodiversity through competition for limited resources, predation and the introduction of diseases or parasites (Topic 3, Section 3.2.3). Environmental ethics poses interesting questions concerning the fate of such species. Some people may hold the ethical view that the alien species are not to blame as they were moved to new areas by human activity, and that humanity has a duty to leave these alien species in their new environment because their lives have value. The general view of conservation is that invasive species should be removed from ecosystems because they disrupt the ecological balance of these systems and can threaten the existence of endemic species. People that hold this view argue that humans have a duty to protect the local ecosystem and must therefore attempt to return it to the state it was in before the alien species was introduced. This can lead to attempts to kill or eradicate members of the alien species. Grey squirrels, for example, were introduced to Europe in the 19th century and management is currently done mainly through lethal control, namely poisoning, trapping and shooting. In the UK, a law was introduced in 2019 that made it illegal to treat grey squirrels in rescue centres, and so the public are unable to take orphaned or injured grey squirrels to wildlife rescue centres or vets. Others might argue that only when the alien species has a detrimental effect on human health should humans attempt to kill or remove the alien species.

For more information on the ethical response to invasive species, access the following articles:

- Inglis, M.I. Wildlife Ethics and Practice: Why We Need to Change the Way We Talk About 'Invasive Species'. *J Agric Environ Ethics* 33, 299–313 (2020).
- Perry, D. Animal Rights and Environmental Wrongs: The Case of the Grey Squirrel in Northern Italy. *Essays in Philosophy* Vol. 5: Iss. 2, Article 26, 2004.

Environmental ethics is the branch of philosophy that studies the moral relationship of human beings to the environment, and the value and moral status of other species.

Example – Red List species

The Red List assesses the conservation status of species in order to highlight plants and animals threatened with extinction and to promote their conservation (Topic 3, Section 3.2.4). Keystone species are especially important to conserve, because of their impact on the ecosystems in which they are found (Topic 2, Section 2.1.23). For example, the jaguar (*Panthera onca*) is the largest cat species in the Americas, playing a key role in forests and grasslands as an apex predator, hunting and eating other mammals such as deer, peccaries and capybaras. Without jaguars, its prey species would overpopulate, leading to extensive loss of vegetation. Resulting habitat loss would lead to the population collapse of many more species. Jaguar populations are increasingly under threat, with over 95% of its original range lost in Argentina and over 40% of its habitat lost in Panama, due to changing land use, including urbanization, agriculture and infrastructure projects, as well as human-jaguar conflict. As a result, the jaguar is considered 'Near Threatened' on the IUCN Red List.

2.1 Individuals, populations, communities, and ecosystems

3.2 Human impact on biodiversity

If moral claims conflict, does it follow that all views are equally acceptable?

Some conservationists hold the ethical perspective that humans have no obligation to species other than the human species. Others may hold the view that humans do have an ethical responsibility to sustain and preserve other species. A third ethical perspective may be that humans have a responsibility to conserve species that are declining only as a result of human activity. Can any of these perspectives be said to be correct?

This raises the question about whether humans have an ethical responsibility to manage ecosystems or whether humans should leave ecosystems to manage themselves. Environmental ethics promotes the moral status of non-human species, adding to the argument that species identified as under threat on the Red List should be protected not only because of the role they play in ecosystems (such as keystone species) but also because they have an intrinsic right to exist.

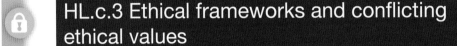

A variety of ethical frameworks and conflicting ethical values emerge from differing fundamental beliefs concerning the relationship between humans and nature.

HL.c.3 Ethical frameworks and conflicting ethical values

Different environmental value systems (EVSs) (Topic 1, Section 1.1.7), can result in different ethical frameworks. Because of fundamental differences between EVSs, conflicting ethical values emerge concerning the relationship between humans and nature.

1.1 Perspectives

A *perspective* is how a particular situation is viewed and understood by an individual. Ethical *perspectives* encourage individuals to act in ways that balance the demands of society with those of an individual. Different value systems can form different ethical frameworks. Conflict can emerge from differing ethical values.

Three environmental value systems

- **Ecocentric perspective.** If someone believes that humans are not significantly different from the rest of nature, they might conclude that all components of nature have intrinsic and equal rights. Ethical judgements will be made on that basis.
- **Anthropocentric perspective.** Someone may believe that the human species is part of nature but has a special responsibility of stewardship towards it. Such a belief may influence ethical judgements in favour of a compassionate, respectful, good steward approach to the natural world.
- **Technocentric perspective.** Where someone sees technology and science as a way to repair environmental damage rather than changing ethical perspectives on environmental issues. If someone believes that nature is separate from human society and exists to serve human needs, then they are likely to embrace a technocentric worldview.

HL.c.4 – HL.c.6 Values

Instrumental value is the usefulness an entity has for humans.

Instrumental value

Something has **instrumental value** when it has value for a reason other than what it is. This value may come from the use that thing has for humans. For example, it may provide:

- goods such as food and water
- services such as decomposers processing waste or erosion protection
- opportunities for human development, such as knowledge or creative inspiration
- aesthetic beauty and pleasure to humans.

When applied to the biosphere (Topic 2, Section 2.1.1), instrumental value gives a monetary focus to natural resources. If natural resources have instrumental value, then they can be used for monetary gain. Many people who believe that the world has instrumental value may still think the world should be protected or sustained because of that value. For example, if the world has value because it is good for humans, it should be preserved for humans. Others, though, might think that if the world is valuable only for humans, then humans can use natural resources as they wish.

Intrinsic value

Intrinsic value is the value one may attach to something simply for what it is. The value that it has does not come from any use it has. This concept can be applied to the biosphere because some people believe the planet has intrinsic value, that is, it has value in itself. Following on from this assumption, the biosphere should be protected and maintained for no other reason than its intrinsic value.

Intrinsic value is the value one may attach to something simply for what it is.

For example, non-living objects, such as rivers, may be valued because they are wild, culturally significant or beautiful. Living organisms may be valued because, like humans, they have parts, processes and behaviours that are organized to accomplish survival and reproduction. Therefore, we should respect their ongoing existence and well-being.

Intrinsic value is value for its own sake, whereas instrumental value is value for the end results gained from it.

The concepts of instrumental and intrinsic value are not exclusive

Instrumental values represent the value of ecosystems as merely a means to an end and are often measured in monetary terms. In contrast, intrinsic values refer to the value of ecosystems as ends in themselves and are often represented as moral duties.

What is the relationship between knowledge and culture?

How do different cultures, such as Indigenous people, value entities? What values and assumptions underpin the use of the term 'indigenous' knowledge? In these societies, do established values change in the face of new knowledge?

There are no reasons why something cannot have both intrinsic and instrumental value, depending on context and perspective. For example, whales may be considered to have intrinsic value based on their aesthetic appeal and they may be considered to have instrumental value as a tourist attraction.

HL.c.7 Moral standing

Environmental ethics examines the question of what kinds of organisms or entities can have **moral standing** in their own right. A being or entity with moral standing is one for which it is possible to give direct moral consideration and toward which people can have moral obligations.

An entity has **moral standing** if it is to be morally considered with regard to how we ought to act towards it.

Different environmental value systems have different views of moral standing.

- An ecocentric perspective suggests that all living things have moral standing because they have intrinsic value.
  - Some ecocentrists would extend this argument to non-living things in nature such as rivers, rocks and landscapes.
  - These ideas were developed by environmentalist Aldo Leopold (see Example – The land ethic, page 858).
- A person with an anthropocentric perspective may believe that only humans have moral standing or that morality should be centred on humans and that non-humans are of peripheral moral concern.
- A technocentric perspective focuses on technology and science as a way to repair any damage done to the environment, rather than changing ethical perspectives on environmental issues.

It is possible to consider the moral standing of future generations. For example, do humans alive today have obligations towards humans living in the future, irrespective of benefits to humans of today? This concept is known as **intergenerational equity**.

Intergenerational equity is a notion that views the human community as a partnership among all generations. Each generation has the right to inherit the same diversity in natural and cultural resources enjoyed by previous generations and to equitable access to the use and benefits of these resources. Read more about intergenerational equity in this article:

Example – The land ethic

Figure HL 29 Aldo Leopold.

Aldo Leopold (1887–1948) (Figure HL 29) was a conservationist, writer, philosopher, forester, educator and outdoor enthusiast. He is considered by many to be the father of wildlife ecology and the USA's wilderness system.

Ethics encourages all members of a community to treat each other with respect, for the mutual benefit of all. Leopold expanded the definition of community to include all parts of the Earth as well as humans. So, animals, plants, soil and water, or what Leopold called 'the land', are included. Leopold wrote his *Land Ethic* essay as the finale to his famous book *A Sand County Almanac*. It was published in 1949, as a call for moral responsibility to the natural world.

Read more about the land ethic at the Aldo Leopold Foundation website:

1.1 Perspectives

Leopold's *Land Essay* argues that 'a thing is right when it tends to preserve the integrity, stability and beauty of the biotic community. It is wrong when it tends otherwise.'

HL.c.8 – HL.c.11 Three major approaches of traditional ethics

There are three major approaches of traditional ethics. **Virtue ethics** focuses on the person's character, **consequentialist ethics** (for example, utilitarian) focuses on the consequences of their actions and **rights-based ethics** (deontological) focuses on the rights of the entities involved.

Virtue ethics

Virtue ethics focuses on the character of the person doing the action. It assumes that good people will do **good actions** and bad people will do **bad actions**.

A key debate within the virtue ethics approach is focused on the identification of the virtues that should be valued. If respect, compassion and responsibility are key virtues that are exhibited by ethical humans, then any environmental action that displays these virtues may be judged to be ethically correct.

Consequentialist ethics

Consequentialist ethics is the view that the consequences of an action determine the morality of the action.

In consequentialist ethics:

- actions with good consequences are good actions
- actions with bad consequences are bad actions.

Morally good actions are those that result in the greatest common good. The morality of the action is determined by its outcome, not the intention of the action.

How are decisions made about which consequences are good and which are bad?

Some ethicists argue that human happiness can be used to measure whether consequences are good or bad. This leads to the conclusions that:

- behaviours that affect the natural world and increase human happiness are ethically good
- behaviours that affect the natural world and decrease human happiness are ethically bad.

Making ethical conclusions about the environment and determining whether the consequences are positive or negative can be challenging. The scientific understanding of nature changes over time. Therefore, consequences that are initially seen as good may later be seen as bad as the understanding of the impact of the consequences develops.

In **consequentialist ethics**, actions with good consequences are good actions and actions with bad consequences are bad actions. Morally good actions are those that result in the greatest common good. The morality of the action is determined by its outcome, not by the intention of the action.

Rights-based ethics

Rights-based ethical systems focus on the action itself and whether it conflicts with the rights of others. Where those rights are protected or maintained, then an action could be said to be morally correct. If the rights are violated, then an action could be said to be morally incorrect or morally wrong.

There is disagreement about what the rights should be and who or what has rights.

For some people, only humans have rights. So then:

- actions that damage the ecosystem while maintaining human rights may be deemed to be ethically correct
- actions that damage the ecosystem and violate human rights are ethically incorrect.

Others may believe that humans, non-human organisms (such as plants and other animals) and the ecosystem all have rights. For these people, it would follow that:

- any kind of action that maintains the rights of humans, non-human organisms and/or the ecosystem would be morally correct
- any kind of action that violates the rights of humans, non-human organisms and/or the ecosystem would be morally wrong.

For example, consider someone who believes that a religious text provides ethical rules and the text states that animals have rights and killing animals is wrong. For this person, killing animals for food would be ethically incorrect because it conflicts with the rights of the animal.

Conclusions reached by the different approaches

Conclusions reached by the different approaches might be the same, but they are reached for different reasons. For example, both the rights-based approach and the virtue ethics approach might lead to the conclusion that air pollution should not be increased. A rights-based perspective would see it as ethically wrong to pollute the atmosphere because this is damaging to animals, plants and other organisms, whose rights should be respected and maintained. On the other hand, a virtue ethics approach would see it as ethically wrong to pollute the atmosphere because those who pollute the environment show a lack of compassion for other people.

2.2 Energy and biomass in ecosystems

Human populations do not tend to be limited by environmental factors, but human activity can adversely affect ecosystems and the planet. This might give rise to the ethical question of whether or not humans have an obligation to control or limit their population as a way to increase *sustainability*. Different *perspectives* on environmental and societal issues produce varied ethical standpoints. Some rights-based ethical approaches may determine that human life is more valuable than any other form of life and so human population growth should not be limited. Other rights-based ethical approaches might hold the opposing view because they value the ecosystem more than human life. Therefore, reducing the human population to sustain the ecosystem could be ethically justifiable to them.

Example – The release of non-biodegradable pollutants in ecosystems

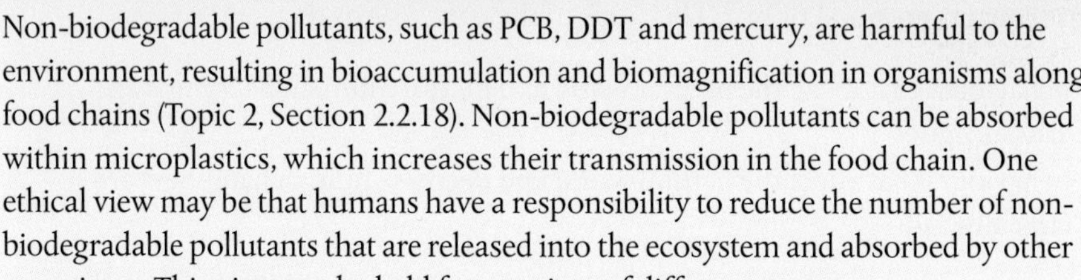

Non-biodegradable pollutants, such as PCB, DDT and mercury, are harmful to the environment, resulting in bioaccumulation and biomagnification in organisms along food chains (Topic 2, Section 2.2.18). Non-biodegradable pollutants can be absorbed within microplastics, which increases their transmission in the food chain. One ethical view may be that humans have a responsibility to reduce the number of non-biodegradable pollutants that are released into the ecosystem and absorbed by other organisms. This view can be held for a variety of different reasons.

- Advocates for rights-based ethics (deontologists) believe that we have a duty to protect ecosystems, and so might hold this view because human pollution is bad and should be reduced.
- Others may believe that releasing non-biodegradable pollutants shows a lack of respect, compassion and responsibility for ecosystems and the organisms that live in them, which in turn reflects badly on those that do it (the virtue ethics approach).
- Consequentialists, who judge the ethical value of an action based on the consequences, may think that non-biodegradable pollutants should be reduced because their absorption has negative consequences on the ecosystem, other organisms or humans.

Ethical conclusions and behaviour

Activity

1. How can ethical conclusions be translated into behaviour regarding the natural world? Think about one environmental issue and your ethical response to it. Discuss your ideas with another person.
2. Are there discrepancies between your ethical conclusions and behaviour? For example, you may think that increasing air pollution is ethically wrong, while still contributing to it by using transport that burns fossil fuels. Now think about the following questions.
   - Why might there be discrepancies between your ethical conclusions and your behaviour?
   - Should ethical conclusions lead to particular behaviours? These behaviours may be personal, individual behaviours or collective, community or international actions.
3. Now exchange your ideas in a small group. Do you all agree or have you developed contrasting ideas?

HL.c.12 The 'appeal to nature' fallacy

Some people hold the view that whatever is natural is correct or good. This position is contentious and is described as the **'appeal to nature' fallacy**.

People may assume that what is natural is also ethically good. The same people might also assume that what is unnatural or against nature is ethically bad. This could be an apparently good way to resolve ethical issues because it seems to give a clear criteria about how ethical conclusions are reached. For example, if deforesting destroys parts of nature and is unnatural then it is ethically bad. But the actual situation may be more complex.

Activity

It is contentious that all that is natural is a reliable ethical guide. There are two considerations to think about.

- What is considered natural is debatable. To extend the deforesting example above, is it natural that humans deforest in order to create houses to live in? Or is this unnatural?
- Humans might question the assumption that what is natural is good on the basis that some things that seem natural do not seem good, for example, predation, disease, drought or low food yields. Diseases are natural but not good – is it right to protect mosquitoes despite their spread of diseases such as malaria?

Discuss these ideas with a partner. Do you agree with the view that whatever is natural is correct or good, or does this depend on the context?

Many natural things are also good, but naturalness itself does not make something good or bad. A fallacy is a mistaken belief, based on unsound arguments. The appeal to nature concept is a logical fallacy because something is claimed to be good because it is perceived as natural or bad because it is perceived as unnatural. This is why this concept is known as the 'appeal to nature' fallacy.

HL.c.13 Environmental and social justice movements

Environmental movements and social justice movements have developed from separate histories but are increasingly seeking common goals of equitable and just societies.

Some people compare the misuse of nature to social injustices against particular racial groups, genders, sexual orientation or disability. These comparisons rest on the basis that people who hold most power in a society see themselves, and others like them, as superior to people who are different. This attitude of social superiority can be extended to nature. If someone's attitude is that humans are superior to nature or entities in nature, this can justify disregard of nature and entities within it. Both social justice and environmental justice movements can be seen as acting against attitudes of social superiority or superiority over nature.

1.3 Sustainability

Human superiority over nature is a parallel issue to other types of exploitation. For example, conflicts over the rights of disenfranchised social groups, issues of sexism, racism and equity with future generations.

Some people argue that environmental injustices may be based on economic inequality, sociopolitical exclusion and racial discrimination. These injustices are being addressed through environmental and social justice movements (Topic 1, Section 1.3.9).

Speciesism is the idea that humans discriminate against particular species. Some proponents of speciesism argue that it is morally wrong to discriminate on the grounds of the species that an organism belongs to. Other people argue that either speciesism itself is a problematic concept or that such discrimination in some cases is justified.

Activity

1. Look carefully at the image shown in Figure HL 30. What does the image suggest to you? How can the imbalances suggested in the image be addressed? Now develop and draw your own image of the issues you have explored.

Figure HL 30 The concept of environmental and social justice.

2. Imagine you are given the three picture tiles shown in Figure HL 31.

Figure HL 31 Building blocks towards sustainability.

(a) Create a narrative using these tiles to explain how sustainability can be achieved, using a specific environmental issue to illustrate your points.

(b) The rest of your class should carry out the same activity. Everyone in the class will have the same tiles, but they may well develop different narratives. Divide into small groups to discuss your different narratives/ideas. What can you learn from each other's ideas?

Exercise

Q22. Define the term *ethics.*

Q23. Explain why the discipline of environmental ethics was developed.

Q24. Outline how a variety of ethical frameworks and ethical values emerge from differing fundamental beliefs concerning the relationship between humans and nature.

Q25. Distinguish between instrumental value and intrinsic value.

Q26. Describe the concept of *moral standing.*

Q27. **Compare** and **contrast** virtue ethics, consequentialist ethics and rights-based ethics.

Q28. **Evaluate** the view that whatever is natural is correct or good.

Q29. **Describe** how environmental movements and social justice movements are seeking common goals of equitable and just societies.

Making connections with the HL lenses

Throughout the course, you need to think about and reflect on how the HL lenses connect to content and examples in Topics 1–8. As you proceed through the ESS course, consider the following guiding questions – these will help you to apply and make connections with the HL lenses.

HL.a Environmental law

- How does environmental law play an essential role in promoting environmental sustainability:
    - by establishing regulations?
    - protecting natural resources?
    - encouraging sustainable practices?
    - holding polluters accountable for their actions?
- How does environmental law prevent and mitigate the negative impacts of human activities on the environment?
- What are the strengths and limitations of a particular law?

HL.b Environmental economics

- What insights do the economics lenses provide on how and why human beings degrade ecological systems?
- What insights do the economics lenses provide on what we can do about ecological degradation?
- What role does economics play in human impacts on the environment and strategies to rectify environmental problems?

HL.c Environmental ethics

- What are the range of ethical positions that might exist and what reasons underpin these ethical conclusions?
- How do ethical approaches lead to conclusions about the issues explored in the ESS course?

The eBook has mapping documents to help you make connections between the HL lenses and Topics 1-8.

Practice questions

1. The hole in the ozone layer over Antarctica, discovered in the 1980s, was caused by chlorofluorocarbons (CFCs). The Montreal Protocol requires the use of hydrochlorofluorocarbons (HCFCs) or hydrofluorocarbons (HFCs) instead of CFCs (Figure HL 32). However, these two gases are also linked to environmental problems (Figure HL 33).

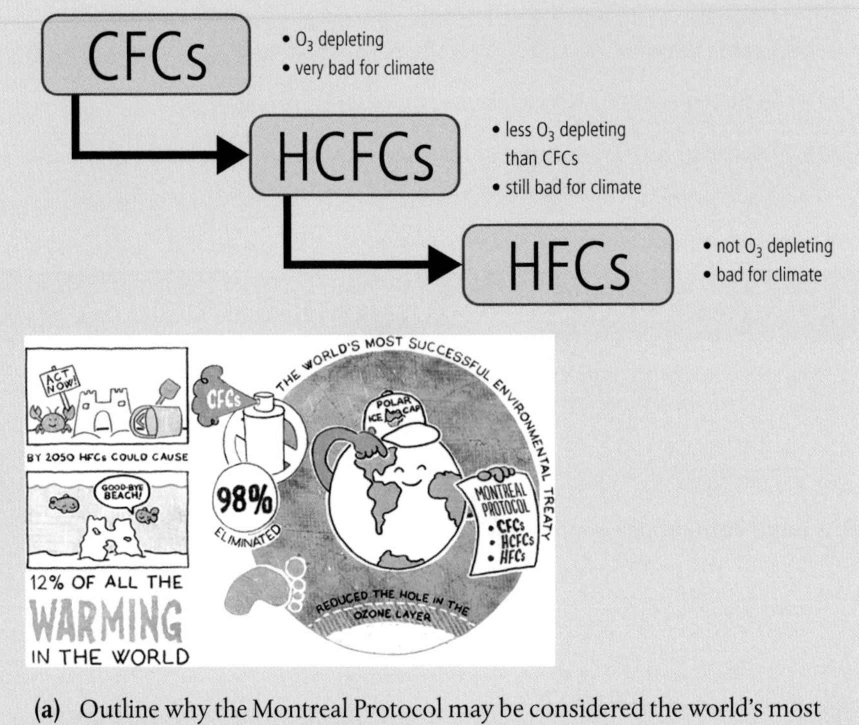

Figure HL 32 Comparison of the effects of CFCs, HCFCs and HFCs.

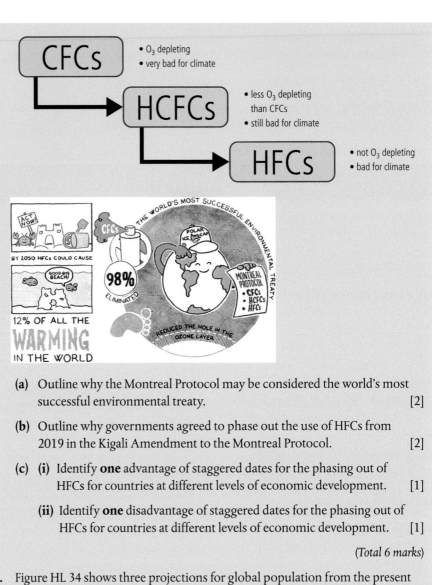

Figure HL 33 HCFCs and HFCs cause less damage than CFCs but still affect the environment.

(a) Outline why the Montreal Protocol may be considered the world's most successful environmental treaty. [2]

(b) Outline why governments agreed to phase out the use of HFCs from 2019 in the Kigali Amendment to the Montreal Protocol. [2]

(c) **(i)** Identify **one** advantage of staggered dates for the phasing out of HFCs for countries at different levels of economic development. [1]

(ii) Identify **one** disadvantage of staggered dates for the phasing out of HFCs for countries at different levels of economic development. [1]

(Total 6 marks)

2. Figure HL 34 shows three projections for global population from the present day to 2100. Use the data shown to answer questions **(a)** to **(d)**.

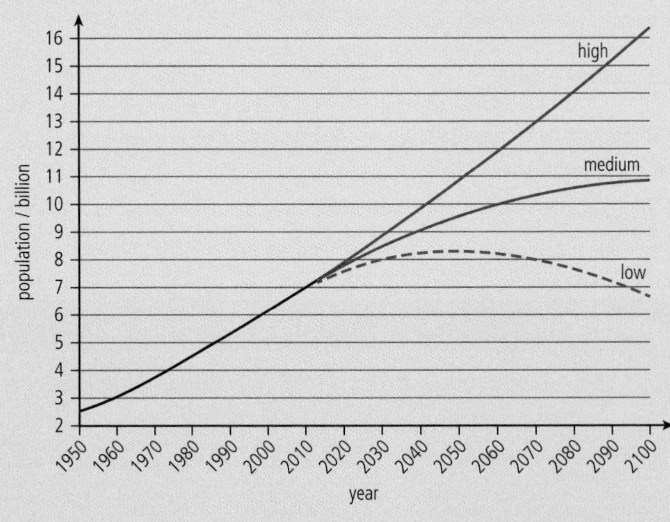

Figure HL 34 Three projections for world population from the present day to 2100. The three lines indicate the high, medium and low projections for population size.

(a) Calculate the range between the highest and lowest projected population size for 2100. [1]

(b) Identify **two** factors that could explain the variation in the projected population growth for the world. [2]

(c) Outline **one** economic implication of the highest projection for world population being realized. [1]

(d) (i) Outline **one** disadvantage of modelling future human population sizes. [1]

(ii) Outline **one** advantage of modelling future human population sizes. [1]

(iii) Outline **one** environmental implication of the highest projection for world population being realized. [1]

(e) Using a range of ethical perspectives, discuss whether humans have an obligation to control or limit the human population as a way to increase sustainability. [7]

(Total 14 marks)

3. Using examples, discuss how social, cultural, ethical and economic factors influence societies in their choice of food production systems. [9]

(Total 9 marks)

4. (a) Outline how pollution is an example of market failure. [4]

(b) Discuss the value of international agreements in addressing the issue of climate change. [7]

(c) To what extent have international agreements and environmental law been successful in solving atmospheric air pollution and climate change? [9]

(Total 20 marks)

5. Figure HL 35 shows data about the global capture from fisheries and aquaculture production from 1991 and projected to 2025. Use the data shown to answer questions **(a)** and **(b)**.

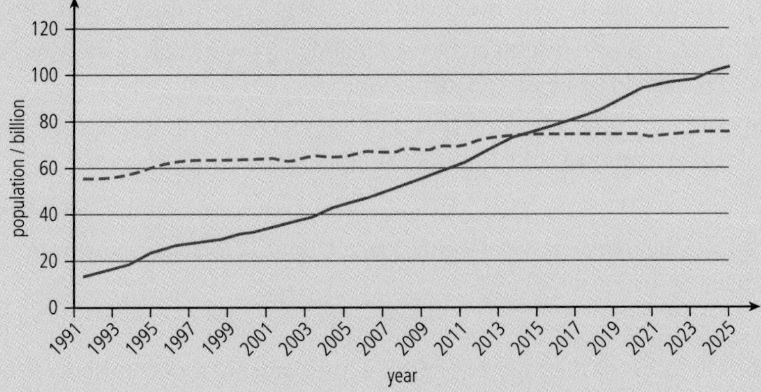

Figure HL 35 Global capture from fisheries and aquaculture production from 1991 and projected to 2025.

Key to graph:
- - - capture fisheries for human consumption
— aquaculture for human consumption

(a) (i) Using Figure HL 35, identify **one** reason for the trend shown in the curve for aquaculture. [1]

(ii) Using Figure HL 35, identify **one** reason for the trend shown in the curve for capture fisheries. [1]

(continued)

(b) Describe **two** strategies for the management of sustainable capture fisheries. [2]

(c) Outline legal and ethical issues concerning the sustainable management of fisheries. [7]

(Total 11 marks)

6. Discuss the impact of economic development on the ecological footprint of a human population. [7]

(Total 7 marks)

7. **(a)** Outline the factors that lead to different environmental value systems in contrasting cultures. [4]

(b) Explain why the harvesting of a named aquatic species may be controversial. [7]

(c) Referring to both circular flow and doughnut economic models, examine whether global sustainable economic development is achievable. [9]

(Total 20 marks)

8. Use the data in Figure HL 36 to answer questions **(a)** to **(d)**.

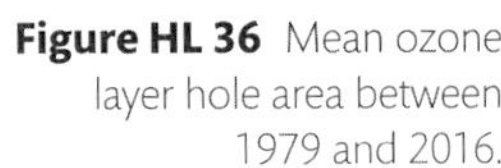

Figure HL 36 Mean ozone layer hole area between 1979 and 2016.

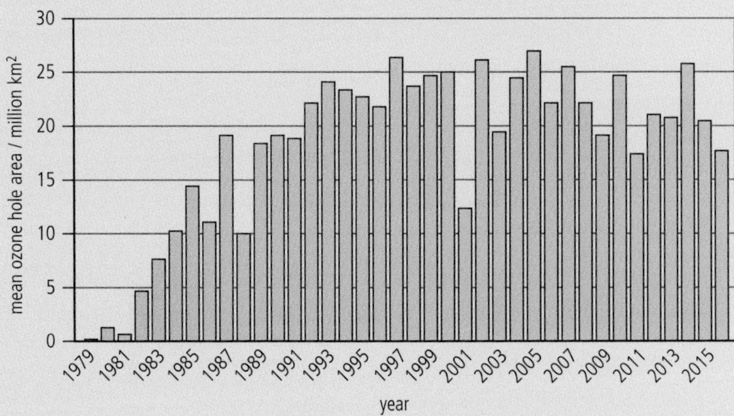

(a) State where the ozone hole is located. [1]

(b) Describe the changes in mean ozone hole area between 1979 and 2016. [2]

(c) Identify one possible reason for the changes shown during the 1980s. [1]

(d) Explain how the data can be used in judging the success of the Montreal Protocol in addressing O_3 depletion. [4]

(e) Discuss the relative success of the Montreal Protocol and Paris Agreement, along with their subsequent amendments and developments. [7]

(Total 15 marks)

9. Evaluate the role of national legislation and international agreements in achieving sustainability. [9]

(Total 9 marks)

10. **(a)** Outline how the concept of product stewardship may contribute to the sustainable use of resources. [4]

(b) Evaluate the strategies that have been used to protect stratospheric O_3. [7]

(c) Discuss how different ethical views regarding the relationship between humans and nature may influence approaches to conservation. [9]

(Total 20 marks)

Theory of knowledge and ESS

There are plenty of opportunities to explore the Theory of Knowledge (TOK) within Environmental Systems and Societies (ESS). The systems approach used throughout ESS is different from traditional models of scientific exploration. This allows us to compare the two approaches to understanding. Conventional science tends to use a **reductionist approach** to look at scientific issues, whereas the systems approach requires a **holistic approach**.

A **reductionist approach** divides systems into parts, or components, and studies each part separately. The reductionist approach often used in traditional science tends to look at the individual parts of a system, rather than the whole, so that the 'big picture' is missed. Although the individual parts of a complex system can be looked at using the reductionist approach, this ignores the way in which such a system operates. A system can also be studied as a whole, with patterns and processes described for the whole system: this is the **holistic approach**. A holistic approach is necessary to fully understand the way in which the parts of a complex system operate together and is used, for example, in modern ecological investigations.

While the systems approach is frequently quantitative in its representation of data, it also addresses the challenge of handling a wide range of qualitative data. This leads to questions about the value of qualitative versus quantitative data. There are many checks and guidelines used to ensure objectivity in quantitative data collection and handling in the purely physical sciences, but these standards of objectivity are more difficult to rigorously control in ecological and biological sciences. In addition, ESS is an interdisciplinary subject so the material addressed often crosses what may seem to be clear subject boundaries between, for example, geography, economics and politics.

Personal *perspectives* give rise to a wide range of different positions on environmental and social issues, and influence people's choices and actions (Figure TOK 1). TOK emphasizes comparisons and connections between areas of knowledge and encourages you to become more aware of your own perspectives and the perspectives of others.

Figure TOK 1 Thinking about the environment.

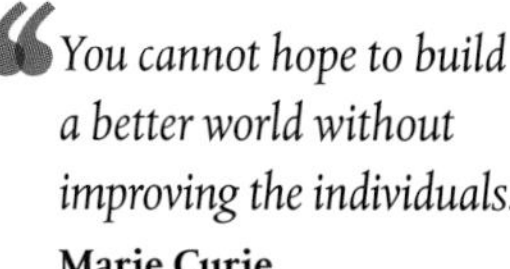

You cannot hope to build a better world without improving the individuals.
Marie Curie

We know what we are, but know not what we may be.
William Shakespeare

The systems approach allows comparisons to be made across disciplines. The values and issues surrounding this are discussed throughout the course and throughout this

Curiosity is probably one of the most important characteristics that people have who go into science.
Ellen Ochoa

Trust yourself. You know more than you think you do.
Benjamin Spock

Chance favours the prepared mind.
Louis Pasteur

TOK

What are the uses and limitations of models?
What is the significance of where we draw system boundaries?
How does the way we draw models influence the knowledge we gain from studying them?
How does a systems approach enhance our understanding of environmental issues?
How does knowledge of environmental systems progress?
What is the role of imagination and intuition in a systems approach?

book. In exploring and understanding an environmental issue, you must be able to integrate the hard, scientific, quantitative facts with the qualitative value-judgements of politics, sociology and ethics. All this makes particularly fertile ground for discussions related to the TOK.

Throughout this book, TOK boxes contain advice and information relating to this aspect of the course. This topic looks in more detail at ways in which TOK can be applied in specific parts of the syllabus. For each topic, stimulus questions (in TOK boxes) are given to promote further inquiry. We are going to consider every topic in turn.

Foundation

Topic 1, Foundation, covers the concepts that are central to the ESS course, namely the systems approach, perspectives and sustainability. Throughout Topic 1, relevant TOK ideas are raised at appropriate points in the text.

Environmental value systems (EVSs) are influenced by education, family, friends, culture and other inputs from the society we live in. These EVSs influence how we see the world and respond to it. The Foundation topic offers several opportunities to discuss the interaction between EVSs and societies' responses to the environmental issues covered in the course.

Several of the strategies proposed during the course to tackle environmental concerns have alternative options. Experts sometimes disagree about pollution management strategies. For example, how do we decide which strategy is best, and on what basis might we decide between the judgements of the experts if they disagree? How do we decide between alternative perspectives, and can any single management strategy be considered as final?

Example – Holism versus reductionism

The emphasis in this course is on understanding the sum of the parts of a system using a holistic approach, rather than considering the components separately. For example, James Lovelock's Gaia hypothesis is a model of the Earth as a single integrated system (Topic 1, Section 1.1.10) and shows how a holistic view of Earth's systems (Figure TOK 2) is needed to understand the functioning of Earth's systems. This contrasts with the reductionist approach of conventional science (Figure TOK 3). Data collection involves measuring the inputs and outputs of a system, and processing the data reveals an understanding of the processes within the system. The main difference between the systems approach and conventional science is that the former describes the patterns and models of the whole system, whereas the latter aims to explain the cause-and-effect relationships within it. Is one approach better than the other, or is it a matter of perspective as to which approach brings real benefits in understanding?

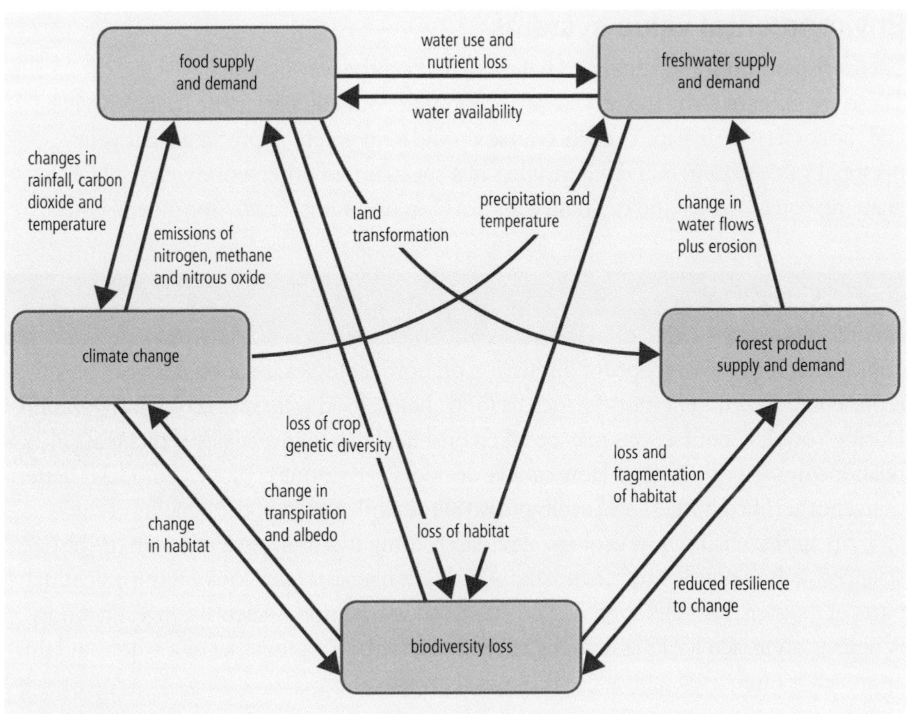

Figure TOK 2 Holism, such as the Gaia hypothesis, looks at the whole system.

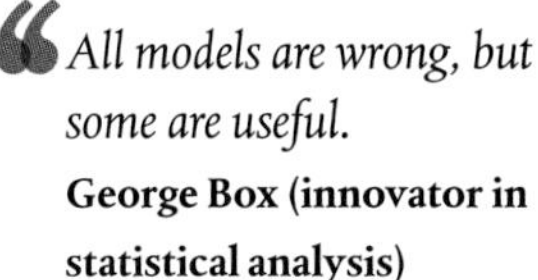

All models are wrong, but some are useful.
George Box (innovator in statistical analysis)

Figure TOK 3 Traditional science often uses a reductionist approach, where a system is broken down into its consituent parts and each part is studied separately.

Advantage of holism

The advantage of the holistic approach in environmental science is that it is used extensively in other disciplines, such as economics and sociology, and so allows integration of these different subjects in a way that would not be possible (or at least not so easy) in conventional science.

As systems are hierarchical, that is, arranged at different levels, what may be seen as the whole system in one investigation may be seen as only part of another system in a different study (Figure TOK 4). For example, a human could be seen as a whole system with inputs of food and water and outputs of waste, or as a part of a larger system such as an ecosystem or a social system. Difficulties may arise where the boundaries are placed and how this choice is made.

Shall I refuse my dinner because I do not fully understand the process of digestion?
Oliver Heaviside

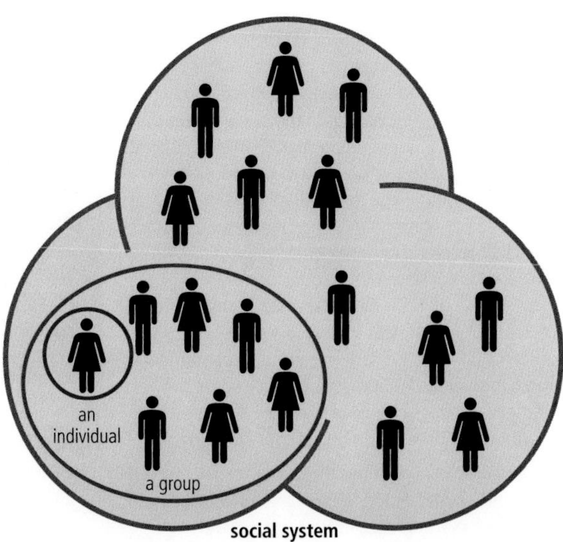

Figure TOK 4 Nested systems within social systems. One person is part of a larger community, that is a group of people, and social systems are formed from several interrelated communities.

The strongest arguments prove nothing so long as the conclusions are not verified by experience. Experimental science is the queen of sciences and the goal of all speculation.
Roger Bacon

To what extent do the names and labels that we use help or hinder the acquisition of knowledge?

TOK

Does the holistic approach really differ from conventional science, or is it just a matter of using different terminology?

If all mankind were to disappear, the world would regenerate back to the rich state of equilibrium that existed ten thousand years ago. If insects were to vanish, the environment would collapse into chaos.
Edward O Wilson

Figure TOK 5 Students on an ecology field trip are instructed on sampling techniques.

I often say that when you can measure what you are speaking about, and express it in numbers, you know something about it; but when you cannot measure it, when you cannot express it in numbers, your knowledge is of a meagre and unsatisfactory kind.
Lord Kelvin

Environmental value systems

There are assumptions, values and beliefs that affect the way in which we view the world. These are influenced by the way we are brought up, our education, the friends we have and the society we live in. The ESS course should help you to appreciate what your personal value system is and where it lies in a spectrum of other worldviews, while also enabling you to justify and evaluate your position on a range of environmental issues.

Ecology

Topic 2, Ecology, gives scope for discussion on how ecological relationships can be represented by different models, such as food chains, food webs and ecological pyramids. During your ESS course, you may be taken on a field trip to investigate ecological relationships (Figure TOK 5). How can we decide whether one ecological model is better than another? Ecosystems and ecology also allow exploration of the benefits of the systems approach and how ecological research compares to investigations in the physical sciences such as physics and chemistry. A reductionist approach looks at the individual parts of a system and this approach is often used in traditional scientific investigations. A holistic approach looks at how the parts of a system work together as a whole and this approach is often used in modern ecological investigations.

Ecological research applies techniques that aim to remove subjectivity. An example of this would be the randomized location of quadrats when studying the distribution of species in a habitat, which rules out site-selection by the researcher. The interpretation of data, however, is open to interpretation and personal judgement. It has been said that historians cannot be unbiased. Could the same be said of environmental scientists when making knowledge claims?

TOK

Through the use of specialized vocabulary, is the shaping of knowledge more dramatic in some areas of knowledge compared to others?

Feeding relationships can be represented by different models. How can we decide when one model is better than another?

When is quantitative data superior to qualitative data in giving us knowledge about the world?

TOK

How do our expectations and assumptions have an impact on how we perceive things?

Succession is the change in communities through time, where changes in the abiotic factors affect the type and composition of species found in an ecosystem. The changes in the biotic factors in turn affect the abiotic factors. Over time, several changes in the community take place. It is usually not possible to study succession in one fixed location through time due to the lengths of time involved. For example, climax communities can take centuries to develop. Therefore, changes along environmental gradients, where each part represents a different stage of the succession, can be studied instead. An example of this is the observable changes in a shingle ridge succession (Figure TOK 6). In studying succession, we can therefore use spatial changes to make inferences about temporal changes (i.e. changes through time). Should this be allowed? Is it possible to infer temporal changes by using spatial ones instead? What assumptions about changes in communities are being made?

Ecosystems, and changes in communities through time, are studied by measuring biotic and abiotic factors. How can you know in advance which of these factors are significant to the study?

Figure TOK 6 Setting up a transect to study succession on a shingle ridge.

Ecology provides many opportunities to explore issues regarding the reliability and validity of data and how it is collected. It also addresses the pros and cons of **subjective data** as opposed to **objective data**. Nevertheless, the interpretation of data, even objective data, is open to widely different viewpoints.

Subjective data is based on personal perspective or preferences, whereas **objective data** is verifiable information based on facts and evidence, independent of what anyone may believe to be true.

Ecology relies on the collection of both biotic and abiotic data. Abiotic data can be collected using instruments that avoid issues of objectivity as they directly record quantitative data. The measurement of the biotic (or living) component is often more subjective, relying on interpretation of different measuring techniques to provide data. For example, although measuring the diameter of trees at breast height (DBH) is a relatively objective measure to obtain information about the size and growth of trees, the choice of trees measured (e.g. only those above a specific diameter) can be subjective, and measurements may not reflect other tree characteristics such as canopy cover. The way in which the measurement is taken can also vary between different people (Figure TOK 7), with results also affected by difference in species and bark thickness. It is rare in environmental investigations to be able to provide ways of measuring variables that are as precise and reliable as those in the conventional, that is physical, sciences. Working in the field means that variables cannot be controlled, only measured, and fluctuations in environmental conditions can cause problems when recording data. Standards of acceptable margins of error are therefore different. Will this affect the value of the data collected and the validity of the knowledge? Applying the rigorous standards used in a physics investigation, for example, would render most environmental studies unworkable and we would miss gaining a useful understanding of the environment. A pragmatic approach is called for in ecological studies, but this leaves the subject open to criticism from physical scientists regarding the rigour with which studies are done. Is some understanding better than no understanding at all?

Science and everyday life cannot and should not be separated.

Rosalind Franklin

Figure TOK 7 Fieldworkers measuring the diameter of trees at breast height (DBH) to assess the recovery of tropical rainforest following logging in Borneo.

Now there is one outstandingly important fact regarding Spaceship Earth, and that is that no instruction book came with it.

Buckminster Fuller

Biodiversity and conservation

TOK

The term 'biodiversity' has replaced the term 'nature' in much literature on conservation issues – does this represent a paradigm shift?

A diversity index is not a measure in the true sense of a word, but is merely a number (index), as it involves a subjective judgement on the combination of two measures: proportion and richness. **Are there examples in other areas of knowledge of the subjective use of numbers?**

A loss of biodiversity may have long-term consequences. **Should people be held morally responsible for the long-term consequences of their actions?**

There are various approaches to the conservation of biodiversity. **How can we determine when we should be disposed to act on what we know?**

Topic 3, Biodiversity and conservation, offers the opportunity to discuss what is meant by the term 'diversity'. Diversity indices are not absolute measures in the same way that temperature is, for example. Diversity indices involve a subjective judgement on the combination of two measures – proportion and richness. Diversity measures are sometimes misread or confused with species richness (Topic 3, Section 3.1.7). This can have implications for the way in which the impacts of human disturbance are interpreted.

This topic also offers different perspectives on species and habitat conservation. Which strategy is best for conservation and how do societies decide the best approach? How do we know when critical points are reached, beyond which damage to ecosystems and biodiversity may become irreversible, such as leading to species extinction?

TOK

Is there a single 'scientific method'? Is the depiction of the 'scientific method' an accurate model of scientific activity?

Controlled laboratory experiments are often seen as a key principle of the scientific method but are not possible in fieldwork. To what extent is the knowledge obtained by observational natural experiment less scientific than the manipulated laboratory experiment?

What knowledge, if any, is likely to always remain beyond the capabilities of science to investigate or verify?

- Science concerns testable ideas.
- Science therefore focuses on recurrent, repeatable events.

Is this true for all science?

Is evolution by natural selection a testable theory? Are there organisms that are suitable for experimentation to see natural selection in operation?

"Facts do not cease to exist because they are ignored.

Aldous Huxley

Should the people who cause environmental damage be held morally responsible for the long-term consequences of their actions?

One further topic for discussion is the different views people have on the origin of life on Earth. The established scientific explanation is that all species have evolved through the process of natural selection, although there are alternative views.

Evolution versus creationism

What constitutes 'good science' and what makes a 'good theory'? Can we have confidence in scientific theories that rely on indirect evidence and that happen over such long periods of time as to make testability a problem?

In 1859, Charles Darwin's book *On the Origin of Species* revolutionized biology and the way it was studied. Despite this, some people still refute its claims. One such group is the creationists, who believe in the literal truth of the biblical Genesis story. What do their views say about the scientific method and what constitutes good science?

Creationist claims

The following points are made by creationists in support of their views.

1. **Is evolution scientific?**
   - Evolution within a species can be tested and is well established but doesn't explain the creation of species.
   - If evolution occurs over millions of years, it is untestable and therefore unscientific.
2. **Evolution contradicts physics**
   - Physics: The second law of thermodynamics states that the entropy, or disorder, in a system will always increase over time.
   - Evolution: Life appears from disorder, becoming increasingly ordered and increasingly complex over time.
3. **Counter-evidence**
   - Evidence of fossilized allegedly human tracks alongside dinosaur tracks, in the same rock layer (Figure TOK 8), was used to suggest that humans existed at the same time as dinosaurs.

(a) 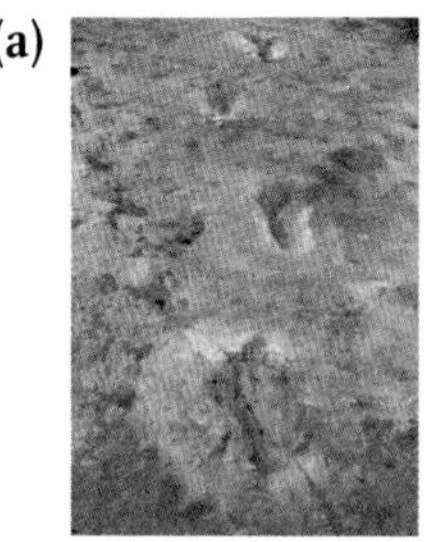

(b) 

Figure TOK 8 (a) These largely infilled metatarsal (heel-impressed) dinosaur tracks in the Cretaceous limestone of the Paluxy River, near Glen Rose, Texas, USA, were once considered by many creationists to be human tracks. **(b)** Infilled metatarsal tracks can be seen running from bottom to top of this photo, with other larger dinosaur tracks running from bottom to middle right. It was thought that this was evidence for humans and dinosaurs living together before Noah's flood. Other types of misidentified human tracks have also been involved in the controversy, including selectively highlighted erosion marks and carvings on loose blocks of rock.

   - Radioisotope dating is the basis for almost all estimates of evolutionary time. The method was applied in 1986 to establish the age of lava from Mt St Helens, which erupted in 1980 (Figure TOK 9). The results showed that the lava had been produced millions of years ago. Since the dating is almost a million times too old, dating of fossils must likewise be a million times too old.

- The key 'missing link' fossils, meaning the intermediates between major groups, are still missing.
- *Archaeopteryx,* the famously feathered reptile, may be a fake, along with Piltdown man and several others.

4. Key creationists in science

- Physics – Newton, Maxwell, Kelvin
- Chemistry – Boyle, Dalton, Ramsay
- Biology – Linnaeus, Mendel, Pasteur
- Astronomy – Copernicus, Galileo, Kepler, Herschel
- Mathematics – Pascal, Leibnitz.

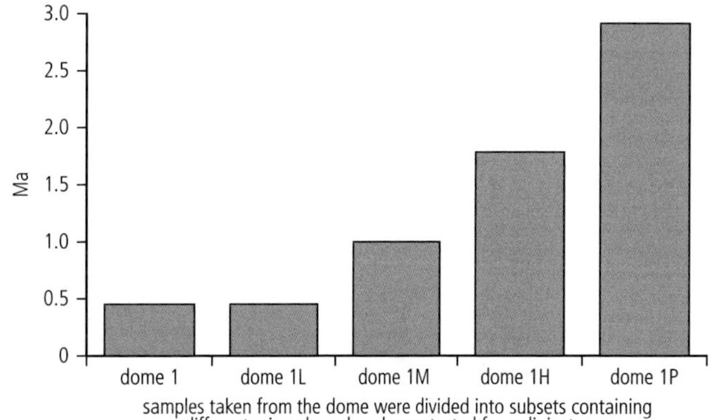

Figure TOK 9 Potassium/argon dating of the volcanic dome formed by lava at Mt St Helens.

5. Common sense

The idea that we were created via a purely random process of mutation...
... is statistically absurd
... contradicts the obvious signs of design all around us
... denies humanity: it allows no meaning for creativity, love or purpose
... just gives selfish people the justification to act without regard for morality.

Ignorance more frequently begets confidence than does knowledge: it is those who know little, not those who know much, who so positively assert that this or that problem will never be solved by science.
Charles Darwin

Neither science nor maths can ever be complete.
Kurt Gödel

Re-assessing the creationist argument

The following points assess the claims made by creationists, outlined above.

1. Distortion

- The second law of thermodynamics is true as quoted but it only applies to isolated systems. Life is part of a system in which entropy does increase overall.
- Mutation is indeed random, but natural selection is not, so it can work cumulatively to bring about apparent design.
- Evolution by natural selection can be demonstrated in organisms with short generations, such as MRSA bacteria.

2. Highly selective use of data

- For every creationist scientist mentioned previously there are hundreds, even thousands, of other scientists who are not creationists. Moreover, scientists who pre-date evolutionary theory cannot be called creationists since there was no creationist/evolutionist argument at that time.
- Areas of evolutionary data that have not been taken into account by the creationist arguments include:
  - homologous structures
  - biogeographical evidence
  - molecular evidence, such as DNA
  - embryological evidence.

3. Misinterpretation

- *Archaeopteryx* is widely accepted as authentic by the scientific community so there is no basis for saying that it is a fake (Figure TOK 10). Piltdown man was a famous fake, but it is incorrect to link authentic fossilized remains with it.

Figure TOK 10 *Archaeopteryx* – a link between reptiles and birds.

"Nothing in biology makes sense except in the light of evolution.
Theodosius Dobzhansky

- We now understand, from dedicated work in the 1980s, how the tracks at Paluxy River were formed (Figure TOK 8). Dinosaur footprints normally recognized as such were created by dinosaurs walking or running on their toes – these are the deep three-toed tracks called digitigrade tracks. Dinosaurs walking on their soles or heels (metatarsal bones) create different impressions called metatarsal tracks, which are longer than the digitigrade ones. Unlike digitigrade tracks, metatarsal tracks may look superficially like human tracks after erosion or if mud-movements followed the formation of the tracks.
- Many species living today are intermediates between other groups (see Richard Dawkins' book *The Greatest Show on Earth* for extensive evidence). It is not true that evidence for missing links is absent (see photos in Figure TOK 11).

Metatarsal impressions are not the only reasons for creationists misinterpreting the tracks at Paluxy River. Several other phenomena have also been mistaken for human tracks including erosional features and some carvings on loose stone blocks. To learn more about the Paluxy River site, search for Paluxy Man on the National Center for Science Education (NCSE) website:

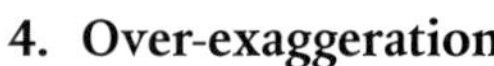

4. Over-exaggeration

- Some real concerns about isotope dating voiced by scientists are over-exaggerated to make the whole process appear void.
- Sensible explanations of anomalous results, such as those for the lava from Mt St Helens, are interpreted as 'desperate evolutionists patching up a defunct theory'.

Figure TOK 11 A 47-million-year-old fossil, named Ida, (top photo) seems to be a link in primate evolution and bridges the evolutionary split between higher primates such as monkeys, apes and humans and their more distant relatives such as lemurs (lower photo).

5. Learning to live with uncertainty

- There is much uncertainty in both science and faith. Doubt and questioning are creative.
- In science, uncertainty leads to new ideas.
- In faith, too, doubt can lead us to ask new questions and find new meaning.
- At the same time, you need to know what your core values are.

Conclusion

The assessment of creationists' claims indicates how good science can be distinguished from 'pseudo-science' claims that are incompatible with the scientific method as shown in Table TOK 1.

Table TOK 1 Learning to spot 'pseudo-science'.

Pseudo-science	Good science
shows fixed ideas (dogma)	shows willingness to change
selects favourable findings	accepts and attempts to explain all findings
does not have a peer-review process	has a ruthless peer-review process
is unable to predict	has predictive power
has unverifiable claims	is experimentally verifiable
has a hidden agenda	makes few assumptions
lacks consistency	is usually consistent

How can we know that current knowledge is an improvement upon past knowledge?

Archbishop James Ussher (1581–1656), Church of Ireland (Protestant) Bishop of Armagh, claimed to have established the date the Earth was formed as Sunday 23 October, 4004 BCE, whereas the evolutionist approach now puts the Earth as at least 4.5 billion years old.

Example – How should we decide what to protect?

Humans make judgements about the natural world and the ways in which it can be protected. Do species have an intrinsic right to exist even if they are of no economic value at the moment? **Intrinsic value** means having inherent worth, irrespective of economic considerations, such as the belief that all life on Earth has a right to exist. Should as much as possible of the environment be protected, or do we need more pragmatic approaches based on realistic expectations?

How do we justify the species we choose to protect?

Is there a focus on animals we find attractive? Is there a natural bias within the system? Sometimes the choices we make are based on emotion rather than reason (Figure TOK 12). Does this affect their validity? Do tigers have a greater right to exist than endangered and endemic species of rat? (Figure TOK 13).

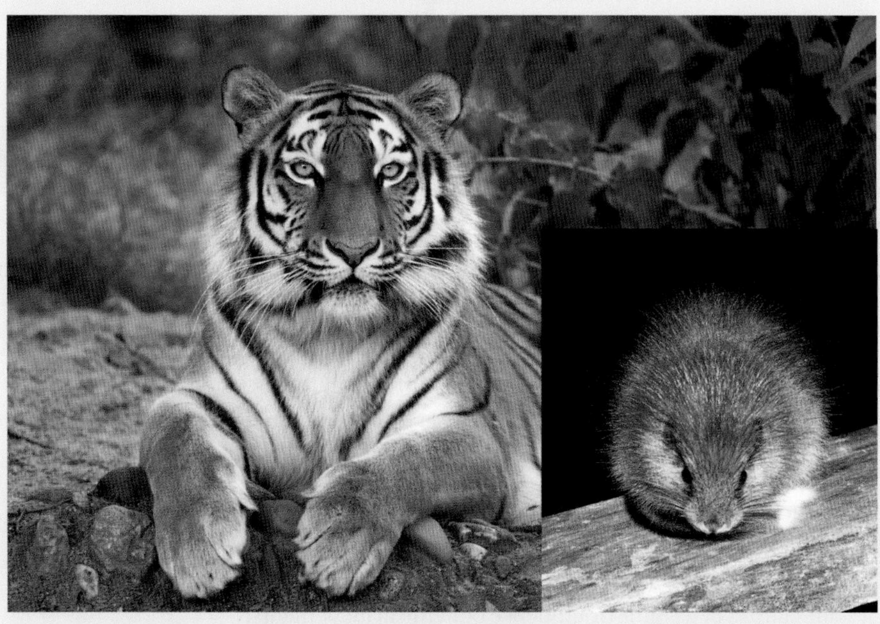

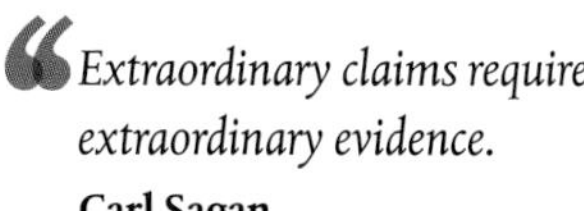

Extraordinary claims require extraordinary evidence.
Carl Sagan

Figure TOK 12 Cheetahs have a very small gene pool with little genetic variation. They are especially prone to changes in their environment or the outbreak of disease. Should we focus conservation on species that are more resilient and therefore more likely to survive into the future?

Figure TOK 13 Do conservation efforts focus on species that people empathize with, such as tigers, rather than species they find less attractive, such as critically endangered species of rodent. e.g. the red-crested tree rat (*Santamartamys rufodorsalis*).

Describing species

Historically, taxonomists (scientists who describe new species) focused on groups that interested them. These tended to be the larger more attractive groups such as mammals, birds and flowering plants. Is there a bias in the way in which species are described? What about small and more obscure groups such as nematodes, or smaller organisms that are difficult to collect and identify, or those organisms that have not attracted as much scientific attention as larger 'furry or feathery' animals (Figure TOK 14)? What impact does this have on estimations of the total number of species on the Earth? Can we reliably comment on species' extinction rates?

People are not going to care about animal conservation unless they think that animals are worthwhile.
David Attenborough

The nation behaves well if it treats the natural resources as assets which it must turn over to the next generation increased, and not impaired, in value.
Theodore Roosevelt

Figure TOK 14 Most of the species of animals on the planet are beetles. Do you think the number of described species reflect this? What type of organisms have scientists historically focused attention on?

Like the resource it seeks to protect, wildlife conservation must be dynamic, changing as conditions change, seeking always to become more effective.
Rachel Carson

A little knowledge that acts is worth infinitely more than much knowledge that is idle.
Kahlil Gibran

Water

Topic 4, Water, provides the opportunity to discuss the values and limitations of models. The hydrological cycle is represented as a systems model. To what extent can such models effectively reflect reality, given that they are based on limited observable features?

Water scarcity around the globe raises the issue of how aid agencies often use emotive advertisements to promote their cause. To what extent can emotion be used to manipulate EVSs and the actions that follow on from them? Do the ends justify the means?

Many societies have traditions of food production that may go against our own EVS. The Inuit people, for example, have an historical tradition of whaling (Figure TOK 15) – something that would go against the EVS of many, if not most, societies. To what extent does our culture determine or influence our ethical judgements?

TOK

The hydrological cycle is represented as a systems model. **To what extent can systems diagrams effectively model reality, given that they are only based on limited observable features?**

A wide range of parameters are used to test the quality of water, and judgements are made about causes and effects of water quality. **How can we effectively identify cause-and-effect relationships, given that we can only ever observe correlation?**

This topic also looks at how water quality can be tested. A wide range of parameters are used to test the quality of water, but to what extent can scientists be sure that they have correctly identified cause-and-effect relationships, such as stating that pollution directly affects species diversity in a stream, given that they can only ever observe correlation?

Figure TOK 15 Inuit whale hunting off the coast of Alaska.

Example – The tragedy of the commons

Renewable resources, such as fish, need not be depleted provided that the rate of use does not exceed maximum sustainable yield. In other words, if the rate of use is within the limit of natural replacement and regeneration. If resources become overexploited, then depletion and degradation will lead to scarcity (Figure TOK 16). If more than one nation is exploiting a resource, which is clearly the case in the fishing industry, resource degradation is often the result. Garrett Hardin (1968) suggested a metaphor, the '*Tragedy of the Commons*', to explain this tendency (Topic 3, Section 3.2.7). The *Tragedy of the Commons* describes situations where shared resources are overused, and are eventually depleted, with little control over the way the common resources are used and where the selfish acts of a few individuals can destroy the resource for others.

In any given ocean, a number of nations may be fishing. Apart from the seas close to land, where there is an Economic Exclusive Zone, no country owns the oceans, or the resources that they contain. Many countries may use the resources. If one country takes more fish from the oceans, their profit increases. However, other countries do not benefit from this. To maintain the same relative profitability, other countries may increase their catch, so that they are not losing out relative to their competitors. The 'tragedy' is that other countries feel compelled to increase their catch, to match the catch of the one that initially increased its catch. Thus, the rate of use may exceed maximum sustainable yield and the resources may become depleted.

Although simplistic, the *Tragedy of the Commons* does explain the tendency to over-exploit shared resources and the need for agreements over common management.

▲ **Figure TOK 16** Fishing net catch, North Sea.

Land

Topic 5, Land, raises issues concerning different methods of food production. Are the intensive methods of food production carried out in many middle-income countries (MICs) detrimental to the environment or are they, in reality, the best way to provide food for ever-growing populations? Do intensive farming methods, in fact, have environmental benefits? Intensive chicken farming (broiler production systems), for example, has been shown to produce a lower carbon footprint than free-range/organic methods. What ethical issues do different types of animal feed production raise?

This topic also provides points for discussion concerning our perception of time compared to the timescales that environmental systems operate under. Fertile soil can be considered as a non-renewable resource because once depleted, it can take significant time to restore the fertility. How does our perception of time influence our understanding of change?

TOK

The soil system may be represented by a soil profile. **Since a model is, strictly speaking, not real, how can it lead to knowledge?**

Consumer behaviour plays an important role in food production systems. **Are there general laws that can describe human behaviour?**

Our understanding of soil conservation has progressed in recent years. **What constitutes progress in different areas of knowledge?**

Example – Food deserts

A **food desert** is a geographic area where affordable and nutritious food is difficult to obtain, especially for those without a car (Figure TOK 17). The term 'food desert' can be defined as any census area where at least 20% of inhabitants are below the poverty line and 33% live more than a mile from a supermarket.

According to the US Department of Agriculture (USDA), 10% of the USA is a food desert. They claim that there are thousands of areas where low-income families have limited or no access to healthy fresh food. The concept of food deserts was originally identified in Scotland in the 1990s. They are associated with urban decay and are characterized by numerous fast-food restaurants and convenience stores serving junk food.

Figure TOK 17 Food deserts are areas without ready access to fresh, healthy and affordable food. These communities may have only fast-food restaurants and shops that offer few healthy, affordable food options. Such factors contribute to a poor diet and can lead to high levels of obesity, diabetes and cancer.

Figure TOK 18 shows the incidence of food deserts in the USA. The USDA links food deserts to a growing obesity problem. In the USA, childhood obesity has tripled in adolescents since 1990 and more than doubled in younger children. Obesity currently affects around 42% of adult Americans, according to data from the Centres for Disease Control and Prevention (CDC). Treating obesity costs the US healthcare system nearly US$ 173 billion a year.

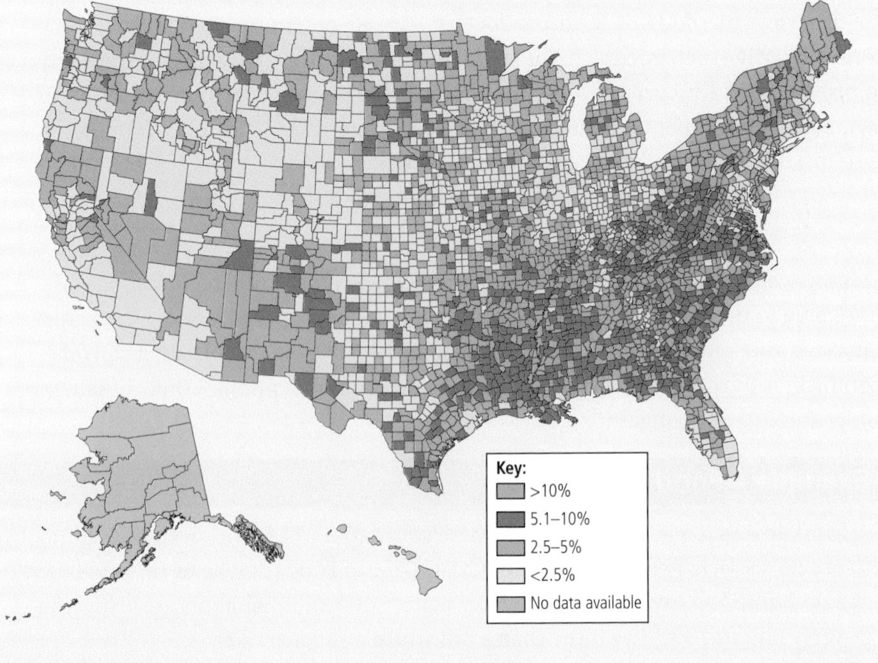

Figure TOK 18 The colours on this map of the USA indicate the percentage of families with no car and no supermarket within a mile.

Critics note that only about 15% of customers shop within their own census area and that the focus on supermarkets means that the USDA ignores tens of thousands of larger and smaller retailers, farmers' markets and roadside greengrocers.

An example of a food desert is found in the South Side district of Chicago. Though crisps, sweets and doughnuts are easy to come by, fresh fruit is a rare commodity. It sometimes takes only one shop to make a big difference. The Food-4-Less store in Englewood improved access to fresh food for over 40,000 people. Moreover, the opening of a decent grocery store can have a multiplier effect and lead to the arrival of other better-class shops in the area, which in turn can fuel a local economic revival.

A study published in 2018[1] showed that, while the number of grocery stores in Chicago had increased between 2007 and 2014, there was little change in communities that were already considered food deserts. In most cases, these were neighbourhoods of people with low-income, predominately Black, on Chicago's South Side. The study showed that although African Americans make up only around a third of Chicago's total population, almost 80% of African Americans live in low food-access areas.

8.3 Urban air pollution

Atmosphere and climate change

Topic 6, Atmosphere and climate change, examines the atmospheric systems that control and regulate climate systems. It also explores the effects that human societies have had on these systems (e.g. through pollution). International meetings have endeavoured to limit the emissions of pollutants that have an adverse effect on the atmosphere. To what extent have international agreements such as the UN-organized Montreal Protocol (Topic 6, Section 6.4) been successful? Unless treaties are legally binding, is there any point in countries signing up to them? Can a single group or organization decide what is best for the rest of the world?

TOK

The Montreal Protocol was an international agreement created by the UN. **Can one group or organization decide what is best for the rest of the world?**

Environmental problems are often emotive. **Under what circumstances should we maintain a detached relationship with the subject matter under investigation?**

To what extent does the recognition of the ethical responsibility of knowledge influence the further production or acquisition of knowledge?

Should we hold people responsible for the applications of technologies they develop/create?

Natural pollution

Are all forms of pollution human in origin? No. Many are natural. Some, like acidification, may be completely natural in some areas and anthropogenic in others. However, it is the case that acidification is largely related to human activity. It is a form of 'industrial ruination', which pays little heed to international boundaries. Many countries produce acidic pollutants, and some export them. Nevertheless, there are also natural causes of acidification. For example, bog moss secretes acid, heather increases soil acidity and conifer plantations acidify soils. Volcanoes are important sources of atmospheric pollution – especially sulfur dioxide and hydrogen sulfide (Figure TOK 19). For example, before the eruption of the Soufrière volcano, Montserrat had some of the finest cloud forest in the Caribbean, but by 1996 the vegetation loss from acid rain, gases, heat and dust was severe (Topic 8, Section 8.3.6, Figure 8.73). In 1996, the pH of the lake at the top of Chances Peak was recorded at a pH of 2.0, that is 1000 times more acidic than a pH of 5.0.

---

[1]https://www.sciencedirect.com/science/article/abs/pii/S1353829217302009

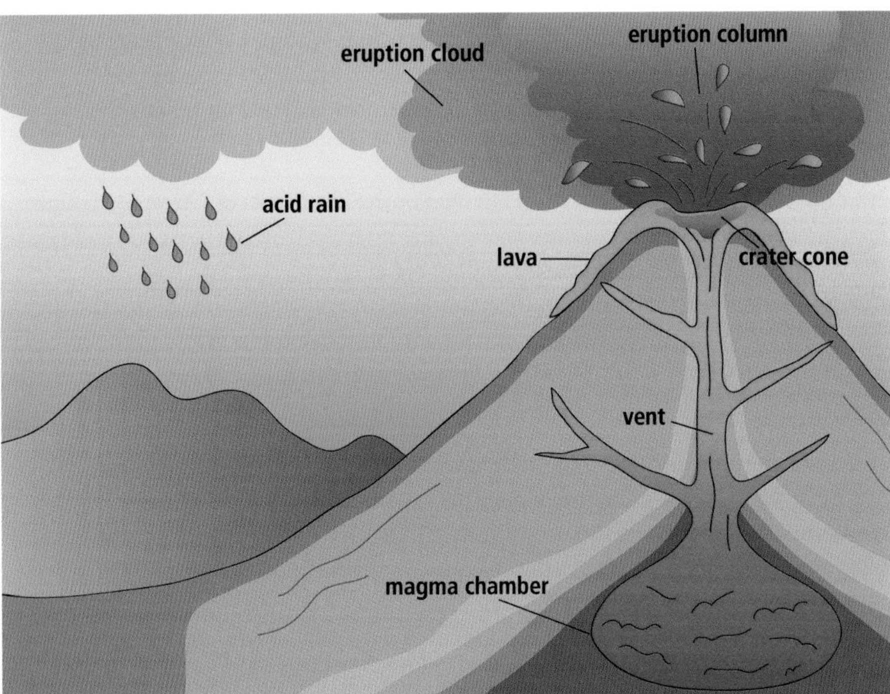

Figure TOK 19 Acid rain caused by volcanic eruption.

Figure TOK 20 Someone else's problem – atmospheric pollution in one country leads to harmful effects on the environment elsewhere.

> *If you don't read the newspaper, you are uninformed; if you do read the newspaper, you are misinformed.*
> **Mark Twain**

> *Some of the scientists, I believe, haven't they been changing their opinion a little bit on global warming? There's a lot of differing opinions and before we react I think it's best to have the full accounting, full understanding of what's taking place.*
> **George W Bush**

Example – Atmospheric pollution and the prisoners' dilemma

The 'prisoner's dilemma' (also known as the Nash equilibrium, after the mathematician who developed it) relates to scenarios where two people are concerned with maximizing their own payoff – given a situation which requires cooperation, each will defect in pursuit of their own interests – this collectively leads to a suboptimal solution. Solutions to the prisoner's dilemma are to improve benefits of cooperation (reduce risk/improve trust), reduce benefits of self-interest, or increase costs of self-interest. The prisoner's dilemma model can be used to explore the ethical issues involved in atmospheric pollution, and the ways in which these problems can be resolved. The model says that pollution such as that produced by the combustion of fossil fuels leading to global warming or acid rain, may mean that an individual polluting a common resource suffers little. Indeed, such an individual may even benefit from their disposal of pollutants. The non-polluting users of the resource are negatively affected by the pollution, and they do not benefit in any way. For example, atmospheric pollution produced in the UK and carried to Scandinavia has led to the destruction of freshwater ecosystems (fiords) there, but ecosystems in the UK have not been damaged. There is, therefore, no visible/direct incentive for those causing the pollution to change their actions. There is, therefore, a benefit for those who continue to pollute. This conundrum underlies several issues regarding the management of pollution, from local (e.g. a lake) to global (e.g. the atmosphere, Figure TOK 20). Not making the polluter pay for the damage caused by their actions can result in problems such as global warming and acid rain. This course explores ways in which solutions to the prisoners' dilemma can be found to solve both local and international issues of pollution. The ways in which legislation and public opinion can be used to address these problems is rich territory for TOK. Is a system of rules better than a programme that educates and informs the public?

Example – Bias and spin

Global warming challenges views of certainty within the sciences. In the popular perception, global warming is having a negative impact on the world. There is, however, some confusion in the public mind between global warming and the greenhouse effect. The greenhouse effect is a natural process, without which there would be no life on Earth. There is, however, an enhanced or accelerated greenhouse effect that is implicated in global warming. The enhanced greenhouse effect is largely due to human (anthropogenic) forces, although feedback mechanisms may also trigger some natural forces. Lobby groups and politicians may take views that suit their own economic and political ends – it is possible to hide other agendas behind the uncertainties around the causes, consequences and potential solutions for global warming. In the USA, the strength of the oil companies during the Bush administration was seen by many as an example of an economically powerful group, and the politicians it supported, choosing a stance that was not in the long-term environmental, social or economic interest of the world. However, there were short-term benefits for both the oil companies and the politicians they supported.

> *The warnings about global warming have been extremely clear for a long time. We are facing a global climate crisis. It is deepening. We are entering a period of consequences.*
> **Al Gore**

Figure TOK 21 Humans are leaving a massive footprint on the planet. Is this damage reversible?

Natural resources

Topic 7, Natural resources, examines the intrinsic values of nature, that is the aesthetic and indirect values, as opposed to the values that are measured on economic grounds. This exemplifies the problem of trying to give a value to, or quantify, factors that are qualitative in nature. The value of the systems approach is especially highlighted in this part of the course. The concepts of resource and carrying capacity are given a fresh look by using the systems approach and models of ecological footprint (Figure TOK 21) and natural capital/income bring a new moral and political perspective to these subjects.

The term 'natural capital' came from ecologically minded economists and brings with it a value-system that implies that resources must have an economic value. The baggage such terms come with encourages a particular view of the world. Terms can therefore influence the way we see the world. The term 'ecological footprint' considers the environmental threat of a growing population, whereas the term 'carrying capacity' allows us to see the same issues in terms of the maximum number a population can reach sustainably. Does such use of language affect our understanding of concepts and environmental issues? It has been claimed that historians cannot be unbiased – could the same be said of environmental scientists when they are making knowledge claims? The human-carrying capacity of the environment is difficult to quantify and contains elements of subjective judgement.

This topic also offers the opportunity to discuss the models and indicators that are employed to quantify human population dynamics – to what extent are the methods of the human sciences scientific? Do they offer a quantitative assessment or a qualitative one?

TOK

How does emotion impact on our perception and understanding of environmental issues?

As resources become scarce, we have to make decisions about how to use them. **To what extent should potential damage to the environment limit our pursuit of knowledge?**

Do scientists or the societies in which scientists operate exert a greater influence on what is ethically acceptable?

Sometimes the choices we make are based on emotion rather than reason: does this affect their validity?

> *Your descendants shall gather your fruits.*
> **Virgil**

Human populations and urban systems

Topic 8, Human populations and urban systems, allows you to explore the implications of population growth on society. Most people now live in cities and so the importance of sustainable development is now paramount.

TOK

Human carrying capacity is difficult to quantify and contains elements of subjective judgement. **It has been claimed that historians cannot be unbiased – could the same be said of environmental scientists when making knowledge claims?**

A variety of models and indicators are employed to quantify human population dynamics – to what extent can these methods be termed scientific?

Here are two opposing points of view:

- population growth is going to use up the world's resources
- population growth will stimulate the development of new resources.

Both of these views are valid. Which do you believe? It may depend on the timescale and spatial scale that you use. On a small timescale, there is evidence that population growth can lead to famine, such as that in Ethiopia in 1984. However, during the 1984 famine, Ethiopia was still exporting crops – not everyone had access to food and that is why there was famine. In addition, there was long-term drought. Human populations have so far managed to survive on Earth, despite massive increases in the size of the human population.

However, the population decline on Easter Island (Example below) suggests that environmental mis-management could lead to population crashes. Maybe we just have not experienced this on a global scale yet.

Figure TOK 22 Easter Island is famous for its statues (moais).

Example – Population crash on Easter Island

Easter Island was discovered by Europeans in 1722. The island is about 117 km^2 and situated about 3700 km west of the Chilean coast. It is one of the most remote inhabited islands in the world. It was colonized by Polynesian people in 700 CE and the population peaked at 12,000 in 1600 CE. The population of the island is now about 8700.

Pre-1600, the islanders had a diet of birds and fish. But after about 1600, palm forests disappeared and the supply of birds and fish ran out. There was social disintegration, starvation, hardship and conflict, with a Malthusian crisis in the post-1600 period. The cause of the crisis appears to be total deforestation related to the cult of statue building (Figure TOK 22). Trees were used to move the statues. Removal of the trees led to soil erosion, landslides, crop failures and famine. Thus, it appears to have been a human-made ecological disaster – namely the overuse of resources.

However, by 1722 when the island was discovered, there was no sign of such a crisis. The islanders had reorganized their society to regulate their use of resources and control their distribution (Boserup: 'necessity is the mother of invention'). But between 1722 and 1822, the arrival of Europeans led to the spread of disease and the death rate increased. In 1862, slave traders from Peru took 1500 slaves (a third of the population). Only 15 returned home and they brought smallpox with them. By 1877, the population had decreased to just 111 individuals. The population has now risen to 8700, largely as a result of migration. Easter Island is now struggling to cope with a new distinction. It was recently named by UNESCO as a World Heritage Site and the pressure caused by tourism is having a negative impact on resource availability for some of the islanders.

"There is a sufficiency in the world for man's need but not for man's greed.
Mohandas K Gandhi

"If facts are the seeds that later produce knowledge and wisdom, then the emotions and the impressions of the senses are the fertile soil in which the seeds must grow.
Rachel Carson

HL lenses

The HL lenses provide many opportunities for reflecting on the nature, scope and limitations of knowledge and the process of knowing through an exploration of knowledge questions. The following table shows how knowledge questions can be applied to the HL lenses, and how these can then be used to explore the nature of knowledge and the key TOK concepts in context.

	Knowledge question	Context
Environmental law	Do human rights exist in the same way that the laws of gravity exist?	Environmental constitutionalism refers to the introduction of environmental rights and obligations into the constitution. (HL.a.5)
	When exposed to numerous competing ideologies and explanations, what makes an individual settle on a particular framework?	Environmental law is built into existing legal frameworks, but its success can vary from country to country. (HL.a.4)
	Is the truth what the majority of people accept?	Laws are rules that govern human behaviour and are enforced by social or governmental authority. (HL.a.1)
	What constitutes a 'good reason' for us to accept a claim?	Environmental laws can have an important role in addressing and supporting environmental justice, but they can be difficult to approve due to lobbying. (HL.a.3)
	Given access to the same facts, how is it possible that there can be disagreement between experts on a legal issue?	The application of international environmental law has been examined within international courts and tribunals. (HL.a.10)
	To what extent is our perspective determined by our membership of a particular culture?	There are an increasing number of laws granting legal personhood to natural entities in order to strengthen environmental protection. (HL.a.11)
	Does a neutral position exist from which to make judgements about competing claims from different groups with different traditions?	International law provides an essential framework for addressing transboundary issues of pollution and resource management. (HL.a.7)
Environmental economics	In what ways do values affect the production of knowledge?	Environmental economics is economics applied to the environment and environmental issues. (HL.b.2)
	What criteria can we use to decide between contrasting knowledge claims?	Ecological economists support a slow/no/zero growth model (HL.b.16).
	What counts as a good justification for a claim?	Ecological economics supports the need for degrowth, zero growth or slow growth, and advocates planned reduction in consumption and production, particularly in high-income countries (HICs) (HL.b.15). Should we pursue green growth or degrowth to bring our societies and economies back within planetary boundaries?
	By what criteria could we decide whether activities are morally justifiable?	Economic growth has impacts on environmental welfare (HL.b.13). Many wealthy countries have polluted the environment in return for the economic benefits they gain (e.g. energy production), at the expense of other countries. Is this moral?
	Why do facts sometimes not change our minds?	Eco-economic decoupling is the notion of separating economic growth from environmental degradation (HL.b.14). To what extent can developed countries limit economic growth in order to pursue sustainable development?
	Do we tend to exaggerate the objectivity of scientific facts and the subjectivity of moral values?	In some cases, economic value can be established by use, but this is not the case for non-use values (HL.b.8). Should we put a price on nature?
	Can all disagreements be resolved with reference to empirical evidence?	The tragedy of the commons highlights the problem where property rights are not clearly delineated and no market price is attached to a common good, resulting in overexploitation. (HL.b.6)
	To what extent do established values change in the face of new knowledge?	The circular economy and doughnut economics models can be seen as applications of ecological economics for sustainability. (HL.b.17)

Environmental ethics	Does all knowledge impose ethical obligations on those who know it?	Ethics is the branch of philosophy that focuses on moral principles and what behaviours are right and wrong. (HL.c.1)
	Can moral disagreements be resolved with reference to empirical evidence?	Rights-based ethical systems focus on the actions and whether they conflict with the rights of others. There is debate about what these rights might be. (HL.c.11)
	Do scientists or the societies in which scientists operate exert a greater influence on what is ethically acceptable?	Environmental ethics is a branch of ethical philosophy that addresses environmental issues. (HL.c.2)
	To what extent are the methods used in the human sciences limited by the ethical considerations involved in studying human beings?	A variety of ethical frameworks and conflicting ethical values emerge from differing fundamental beliefs concerning the relationship between humans and nature. (HL.c.3)
	Do researchers have different ethical responsibilities when they are working with human subjects compared to when they are working with animals?	Intrinsic value is the value one may attach to something simply for what it is. (HL.c.5)
	Should scientific research be subject to ethical constraints or is the pursuit of all scientific knowledge intrinsically worthwhile?	There are three major approaches of traditional ethics: virtue ethics, consequentialist (for example, utilitarian) ethics and rights-based (deontological) ethics. (HL.c.8)
	In what ways have developments in science challenged long-held ethical values?	Consequentialist ethics is the view that the consequences of an action determine the morality of the action. (HL.c.10)

The TOK exhibition

The exhibition requires you to identify three objects and discuss them in relation to a response to one of the IA prompts. For this you will need to select three objects that can each act as a response to that prompt.

In TOK, you will complete an exhibition, which explores how TOK manifests in the world around us. The TOK exhibition is internally assessed by your teacher and externally moderated by the IB at the end of the course. The exhibition forms 33% of your final marks in TOK, with the TOK essay (see below) forming the other 67%.

For your exhibition, you will select three objects and write a commentary on each. In your commentary you will explain why those particular objects effectively represent an idea about how knowledge works in the real world. You need to justify your selection of objects. Your justifications will be persuasive if they are accurate, rational, balanced and objective. There is a list of 35 knowledge questions (also known as 'TOK Internal Assessment (IA) prompts'), and you will choose one of those as the basis for your exhibition. The TOK curriculum guide recommends that you complete your TOK exhibition with reference to the core theme or one of the optional themes.

An object does not have to be a physical object. It could be a tweet, online article, photo and so on.

An object needs to be pre-existing so you cannot make your own object.

An object needs to be specific rather than general, e.g. your diary rather than just any diary.

In creating your TOK exhibition, you need to interpret the significance of the three objects in terms of what they reveal about how knowledge functions in the real world. Imagine that you were creating an exhibition about 'the degree to which certainty is possible'. You will have to choose objects that will illustrate an answer, or several different answers, to that question. The best exhibitions explore the knowledge question by considering different points of view – each point of view could be represented by a different object.

Your exhibition should be no longer than 950 words. Title, header, captions, references, and so on, do not count toward the word count.

When you choose objects to put in your TOK exhibition, you will be looking for items that represent some belief or set of beliefs, rather than just what the object is. Many Indigenous communities, for example, create art or artefacts that have a particular meaning to them, one that is unknowable to others unless they take the time to learn. Even then, the significance might not be understood without being deeply embedded in that community.

When selecting objects, ask yourself the following questions:

- What is interesting about the particular object?
- Why have you picked this particular object rather than something else?
- Is there a more specific object that would be more suitable, or can you narrow this down to be a more specific part/instance of the object?

Once you have selected your objects, ask yourself the following questions to help write the commentary for each object:

- Why is the object interesting for the IA prompt you have chosen?
- What is the connection between the object and the IA prompt?
- Why did you pick this object?
- How is the object interesting or helping us to think about the question/prompt?
- What are the connotations?
- What does this tell us about the nature of knowledge?

The TOK essay

The essay is an extended piece of writing that draws on your knowledge and understanding of TOK. The essay engages you in a formal and sustained piece of writing in response to a title that focuses on the areas of knowledge. You choose one from a list of six prescribed titles (PTs) that change for each examination period. The PTs take the form of knowledge questions. The chosen title must be used exactly as given and must not be altered in any way. As well as the content of the essay, references and a bibliography are required.

The maximum number of words for the essay is 1600. Do not go over the word limit or you will lose marks.

It is suggested that 10 hours of teaching time should be dedicated to working on the TOK essay.

The TOK essay forms 67% of the marks in TOK. The assessment of the TOK essay, which is marked by an IB examiner, is underpinned by the following single driving question: 'Does the student provide a clear, coherent and critical exploration of the essay title?'

You can use PEEL to help structure your essay:

- **P**oint
- **E**vidence/Example
- **E**xplain why the example supports the point
- **L**ink back to the question.

Do this for each different point you are making.

You can take a side on the question, but you must also present at least some form of counterarguments or alternative points of view, for example:

- 'Some would argue that... because...'
- 'On the other hand, others would instead argue that... because...'
- 'While I agree with the claim, it is true that some would say that…'

You then need to evaluate these arguments, for example:

- 'The limitations of this argument are...'
- '[a specific example] would illustrate [a problem with an argument]'

Your argument must be supported by specific real-life situations (RLSs).

You must also draw implications from your arguments, for example:

- 'If we accept this argument, then [the implications for knowledge/the question are]...'
- 'However, if this is true, I would argue that this means we cannot know... because...'

At the end of your essay you should have a conclusion that makes a balanced assessment using evidence presented in the essay. Do you agree or disagree with the essay title and if so, why?

During the preparation and writing of the essay, you need to meet regularly with the teacher who is supervising your essay. Three *formal* recorded interactions between you and your teacher are required. These three interactions must be recorded on the TOK essay Planning and Progress Form (PPF), which is submitted to the IB along with your essay. Although the PPF is not used in the awarding of final marks, it forms important evidence that steps have been taken to help ensure the authenticity of work. It also plays an important role in terms of helping to ensure that all students receive an appropriate level of support when completing their essays.

Good luck with both your TOK essay and the exhibition!

Internal Assessment

The internal assessment (IA) involves the design, implementation and completion of an individual investigation of an environmental systems and societies (ESS) research question. The investigation is submitted as a written report. The purpose of the IA is to enable you to demonstrate skills and knowledge you have gained during the course and to pursue a topic that is of personal interest to you. The IA focuses on a particular environmental issue and explores tensions arising within a social context. Tensions can arise due to strain, imbalance, unrest or opposition between individuals, organizations or communities that have different perspectives or worldviews regarding strategies to solve environmental issues.

The IA for ESS is interdisciplinary. The focus should be on an environmental issue and the tensions that can impact environmental or societal issues.

The investigation may draw on methodologies and analytical techniques used in either experimental or human science studies, reflecting the interdisciplinary nature of ESS.

The investigation can be carried out at a local, regional or global level. There are several options for how the IA can be approached:

The individual investigation is an open-ended task in which you gather and analyse data in order to answer your own research question. The requirements are the same for both SL and HL.

- You can identify a global issue, carry out a related study on a local scale and then consider how your findings relate to the bigger issue.
- You can identify a global issue, and then carry out a small-scale study of one aspect of that global problem using secondary data that is available through databases or other secondary sources.
- You can use a local issue as the basis of your focused study, as not all environmental problems are global in nature.

Throughout the ESS course, you learn and practice skills that help you to investigate the subject. These skills include tools, such as experimental techniques, the use of technology (such as data loggers), mathematics and the application of systems and models. Skills also include the inquiry process, i.e. exploring and designing, collecting and processing data, concluding and evaluating. Figure IA 1 shows how these skills integrate within the ESS syllabus.

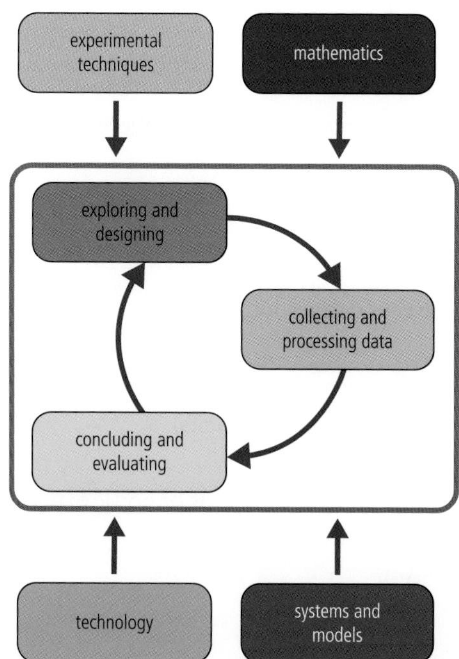

Figure IA 1 Skills for ESS.

The IA involves the completion of an individual investigation of an ESS research question that you have designed and implemented. The investigation is submitted as a written report. The IA needs to address specific assessment criteria (see pages 890–895). If you are also undertaking an ESS Extended Essay (EE), the essay must not be based on the research question of your ESS IA.

You are allowed 10 hours to carry out the IA. This includes time for initial discussions, planning, gathering data, and for the review, monitoring and support of progress.

You are allowed a total of 10 hours to complete the IA. The 10 hours include time for:

- initial explanation of the IA requirements by your teacher
- asking your teacher questions
- consultation with your teacher to discuss your research question before the investigation is carried out and throughout the execution of the IA
- developing the methodology and collecting data
- reviewing and monitoring progress.

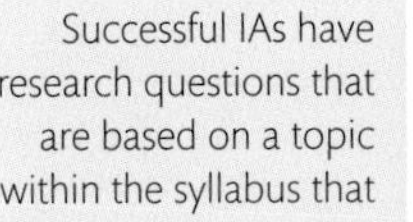

Successful IAs have research questions that are based on a topic within the syllabus that is of particular interest to you.

For your IA to be successful, your research question should be based on a topic within the syllabus that is of particular interest to you. Each person in your class needs to have a different research question. You need to make sure you carefully follow the IA criteria and hit the marking points that the IB are looking for. You should be aiming for the highest marks possible in your IA as good marks will give you confidence as you approach the exams and will help support your overall mark. At SL, the IA is worth 25% of your final ESS marks, and at HL it is worth 20%. A good performance in the IA can raise you to the next grade if you are at the borderline between two grades in your final assessments.

The weighting for the IA is different for SL and HL students. The IA contributes 25% to the final assessment in the SL course and 20% in the HL course.

The main problems students encounter with IAs revolve around design (especially suitable sample sizes and sampling techniques), proper treatment of data (this is closely linked to lack of data stemming from poor design), vigorous discussions of the data in a broader context and an analysis of strengths and weaknesses of design. Specific issues concerning each criterion are discussed below.

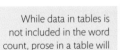

The IA report should be a maximum of 3000 words long.

You will need to write a report. The maximum overall word count for the report is 3000 words. External moderators (who check the marks given by your teacher) will not read beyond the word limit. Not included in the word count are:

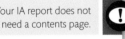

While data in tables is not included in the word count, prose in a table will be included.

- charts and diagrams
- data tables
- equations, formulae and calculations
- citations/references (whether parenthetical, numbered, footnotes or endnotes)
- bibliography
- titles and subheadings.

Your IA report does not need a contents page.

The following methodologies may be applied in your IA:

- values and attitude surveys or questionnaires
- interviews
- issues-based inquiries to inform decision-making
- observational fieldwork (natural experiments)
- field manipulation experiments
- ecosystem modelling (including mesocosms or bottle experiments)
- laboratory work
- models of sustainability

- use of systems diagrams or other valid holistic modelling approaches
- elements of environmental impact assessments
- secondary demographic, development and environmental data
- collection of both qualitative and quantitative data.

The following analytical techniques may be applied to data:

- estimations of NPP/GPP or NSP/GSP
- application of descriptive statistics (measures of spread and average) and inferential statistics (testing of null hypotheses)
- other complex calculations
- cartographic analysis
- use of spreadsheets or databases
- detailed calculations of footprints (including ecological, carbon or water footprints).

When presenting qualitative information as text only, remember the maximum word count for the IA.

Investigations may consist of appropriate qualitative work or quantitative work:

- Quantitative information is collected through measurement and may be processed using statistical and other techniques. The focus is on numbers and can be displayed through tables, graphs and maps.
- Qualitative information collected through observation and subjective judgement, is non-numerical and does not involve measurement. Qualitative information may be processed or quantified where appropriate, or it may be presented through images or as text.

You can convert qualitative data into quantitative data to help answer your research question. Some qualitative data can be used to set the scene for the quantitative data collection. For example, the weather on the day of fieldwork data gathering.

In some cases, these are descriptive approaches and may involve the collection of considerable qualitative data. In others, establishing cause and effect through inferential statistical analysis may be used.

Collaborative group work

Although it is possible to work collaboratively on the IA, in groups of three or less, you are required to develop a unique research question and methodology with unique data.

Collaborative work can be used to develop a methodology where each student within a group investigates their individual research question by manipulating one of the following:

- a different independent variable from those selected by other group members
- the same independent variable with a different dependent variable from those selected by other group members
- different data from those selected by other group members from within a larger communally acquired data set.

Group work can be useful for particular types of IA. Assisting each other in gathering data can be useful in extensive investigations such as ecological field studies.

Collaborative work is permitted on the understanding that the final report presented for assessment is that of an individual. A report by the group is not permitted. All authoring, including the description of the methodology, must be done individually.

Internal Assessment criteria

Table IA 1 shows the assessment criteria used for the IA. The number of marks allocated to each criterion is indicated in the table. The IA follows the same inquiry process that you have been exploring throughout your ESS course.

Table IA 1 Internal Assessment criteria.

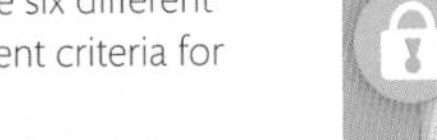

There are six different assessment criteria for the IA:

- research question and inquiry
- strategy
- method
- treatment of data
- analysis and conclusions
- evaluation.

The maximum number of marks for the IA is 30.

A. Research question and inquiry	**B. Strategy**	**C. Method**	**D. Treatment of data**	**E. Analysis and conclusions**	**F. Evaluation**	**Total**
4 (13.3%)	4 (13.3%)	4 (13.3%)	6 (20%)	6 (20%)	6 (20%)	30 (100%)

Criterion A: Research question and inquiry

This criterion assesses the extent to which you establish and explore an environmental issue (either local or global) for an investigation and develop this issue to state a relevant and focused research question.

Table IA 2 shows the achievement level descriptors for Criterion A.

Table IA 2 Achievement levels for Research question and inquiry.

Marks	**Level descriptor**
0	The report does not reach a standard described by the descriptors below.
1–2	The report: • **describes** a local or global environmental topic or issue but with errors or omissions showing a limited understanding • **states** a research question but there is a lack of focus, or it is not linked to the chosen environmental topic or issue.
3–4	The report: • **explains** a local or global environmental topic or issue with sufficient background to support the research question • **states** a focused research question that addresses the chosen environmental topic or issue.

Research questions such as *How does the loss of forest habitat in the grounds of St Edmund's School affect the diversity of insects in Montreal?* are not possible to answer within the timeframe and word limit of an IA. Such research questions would require an investigation of a possible causal link between the school site and the wider city – something not possible to do within the timeframe of an IA.

When clarifying your research question, you need to make sure that:

- the research question can be suitably addressed within the word limit (3000 words):
    - Is your investigation achievable in the timeframe available (a maximum of 10 hours, including initial planning and development)?
    - Are the necessary resources for your investigation available to you?
    - Do you have the necessary numerical and analytical skills to process and analyse the raw data?
- background research is sufficient, e.g. there is a literature review of the environmental issue, or consideration of a theory or model
- the citation of published materials is sufficiently detailed to allow sources of information to be traceable.

The best reports come from a personal connection between the student and their research question, especially if this includes some direct investigation (field, lab or survey).

If you quote broadly accepted facts or theories, citations are generally not needed. However, if a precise fact is quoted, a citation would be expected. For example, the fact that energy is lost through food chains can be considered general knowledge, but that energy is lost in a specific food chain in a particular location would require a citation.

Criterion B: Strategy

When addressing any environmental issue, there will be different opinions, or tensions, about the strategy that can best deal with the problem. Tensions can arise from actual or potentially conflicting goals, interests or needs. These tensions may arise as a result of, for example, differing economic, social, cultural, political or environmental perspectives.

In this criterion, you are assessed on the extent to which you understand how tensions between perspectives can impact the environmental or societal outcomes of a strategy. For example, the creation of a national park by a government to protect natural habitats may cause tension between the local community living within the new national park boundaries and the government. This criterion should include a review of the position of both parties. For example, in the example given here, why does the government want a park in the given location and why does the community want to keep living there? The reasons for and against the strategy from each worldview or perspective should also be included and both should be linked to the outcome of the strategy. The strategy should address an issue central to your investigation. This criterion allows you to show personal engagement in the issue.

Table IA 3 shows the achievement level descriptors for Criterion B.

Table IA 3 Achievement levels for Strategy.

Marks	Level descriptor
0	The report does not reach a standard described by the descriptors below.
1–2	The report: • **states** an existing or developing strategy that addresses an environmental issue linked to the research question • **describes** a tension between different perspectives (economic, social, cultural, political or environmental) that results from the strategy.
3–4	The report: • **describes** an existing or developing strategy that addresses an environmental issue linked to the research question • **explains** a tension between different perspectives (economic, social, cultural, political or environmental) that results from the strategy.

Example – Conversion of tropical rainforest to palm oil

An example of a tension between different perspectives is the clearance of rainforest in South-East Asia for palm oil production. Rainforests are one of the most biodiverse ecosystems on Earth and conservationists see their preservation as essential for maintaining global biodiversity. Countries that rely on the income from palm oil see land use as an economic argument. This illustrates the tension between national economies and global environmental sustainability.

In this criterion, you need to describe an existing or developing strategy and then discuss the tensions that different perspectives have with that strategy. It is not appropriate for you to devise your own strategy. The strategy does not have to be in direct relation to your individual investigation but must have a connection to the research question.

For example, if you carry out a study on the environmental issue of climate change and look at the efficiency of solar power, then the strategy could be providing more solar panels at your school. Installing more solar panels locally may create tensions with different perspectives within the local community – you should discuss at least one tension that could have, or has, been created.

Criterion C: Method

This criterion assesses the extent to which you have developed an appropriate and repeatable method to collect data that is relevant to the research question. This data could be primary or secondary, qualitative or quantitative in nature.

Primary data are data you obtain yourself during your investigation.

Secondary data are data collected by someone else, such as those found in published research papers.

Quantitative data are collected through measurement and may be processed using statistical and other techniques. The focus is on numbers, which can be displayed through tables, graphs and maps.

Qualitative data are non-numerical and are collected through observation and subjective judgement. Qualitative information may be processed or quantified where appropriate, or it may be presented through images or as text.

Table IA 4 shows the achievement level descriptors for Criterion C.

Table IA 4 Achievement levels for Method.

Marks	Level descriptor
0	The report does not reach a standard described by the descriptors below.
1–2	• The report **describes** a method that is not repeatable. • The method does not allow for sufficient data to be collected to address the research question.
3–4	• The report **describes** a repeatable method. • The method does allow for the collection of sufficient data to answer the research question.

A method that is repeatable should include sufficient details to allow another person to replicate the investigation. A descriptive, literature-based investigation that only reviews the literature cannot be considered a repeatable method.

The description of the method should include:

- the set-up and your contribution (if you have worked in a group)
- sampling or surveying techniques
- how data are collected.

Criterion D: Treatment of data

This criterion assesses the extent to which you have effectively communicated and processed your data in ways that are relevant to the research question. Data should be processed using techniques associated with the appropriate experimental or social science method of inquiry.

Table IA 5 shows the achievement level descriptors for Criterion D.

Table IA 5 Achievement levels for Treatment of data.

Marks	Level descriptor
0	The report does not reach a standard described by the descriptors below.
1–2	• The communication of raw and processed data is not clear. • The techniques used to process the raw data lead to findings that do not address the research question. • The raw data is processed with major errors.
3–4	• The communication of raw and processed data is clear. • The techniques used to process the raw data lead to findings that do not fully address the research question. • The raw data is processed with some minor errors.
5–6	• The communication of raw and processed data is clear and detailed. • The techniques used to process the raw data lead to findings that fully address the research question. • The raw data is processed correctly.

Data can be primary and/or secondary and qualitative and/or quantitative.

In the level descriptors in Table IA 5, 'clear' means that the presentation or method of processing can be understood easily, including appropriate details such as the labelling of graphs and tables or the use of units, decimal places and significant figures, where appropriate.

If there is a large amount of raw data (e.g. from survey results or data logging) this may be presented as a sample of the whole data, with the remaining data included within an appendix.

In the IA, there is particular emphasis on the treatment of data, the analysis and conclusion, and the evaluation. Each of these criteria is worth a maximum of 6 marks. These criteria require higher level thinking skills, which is why they have greater weighting.

Criterion E: Analysis and conclusion

In this criterion, you assess the extent to which you have interpreted the data in ways that are relevant to the research question. The patterns in the data should be highlighted and correctly interpreted to reach a valid conclusion.

A supported conclusion should include measures of bias, reliability, validity and uncertainty (which may indicate an appreciation of the strengths or weaknesses of the data).

Table IA 6 shows the achievement level descriptors for Criterion E.

Table IA 6 Achievement levels for Analysis and conclusion.

Marks	Level descriptor
0	The report does not reach a standard described by the descriptors below.
1–2	• The analysis **identifies** patterns or trends within the data that are relevant to the research question. • The conclusion either does not address the research question or is not supported by the analysis presented.
3–4	• The analysis **describes** patterns or trends within the data that are relevant to the research question, including (some) measures of bias, reliability, validity and uncertainty. • The conclusion addresses the research question and is partially supported by the analysis presented.
5–6	• The analysis **explains** all the patterns and trends within the data that are relevant to the research question, including measures of bias, reliability, validity and uncertainty. • The conclusion addresses the research question and is supported by the analysis presented.

Criterion F: Evaluation

Methodological and procedural limitations or weaknesses are evaluated in Criterion F. Table IA 7 shows the achievement level descriptors for Criterion F.

Table IA 7 Achievement levels for Evaluation.

Marks	Level descriptor
0	The report does not reach a standard described by the descriptors below.
1–2	The evaluation: • **states** generic methodological limitations or weaknesses that impact the conclusion • **states** improvements to the method that address the identified limitations or weaknesses • **states** generic unresolved questions that arise from the investigation.
3–4	The evaluation: • **describes** methodological limitations or weaknesses that impact the conclusion • **describes** improvements to the method that address the identified limitations or weaknesses • **outlines** unresolved questions that arise from the investigation.
5–6	The evaluation: • **evaluates** specific methodological limitations or weaknesses that impact the conclusion • **evaluates** improvements to the method that address limitations or weaknesses • **describes** unresolved questions that arise from the investigation as they impact the conclusion.

To score highly in this criterion, there should be:

- an evaluation of the relative impact of specific limitations or weaknesses of the methodology that affect the conclusion
- evidence supporting the identified limitations or weaknesses including measures of reliability, validity and uncertainty
- realistic and relevant improvements for specific weaknesses and limitations
- an evaluation of the suggested improvements (e.g. how realistic are they?)
- a description of realistic unresolved questions that may impact the conclusion
- a clear link to the method and environmental topic or issue, that extends the investigation beyond the original research question.

Methodological weaknesses need to consider both the issues in the methodology and their effect on the quality of the data. Methodological weaknesses can relate to issues regarding the control of variables or the precision of measurements.

Limitations refer to the fact that experiments will only go so far in answering the research question and drawing a conclusion. Limitations could refer to how the conclusion is limited in scope by the range of the data collected, the confines of the system or the applicability of assumptions made.

Advice for your IA

Read these pages carefully – they provide advice for carrying out the IA successfully and obtaining good marks.

Research question and inquiry

You need to ensure that the topic or issue, and your research question, are appropriate for an ESS IA. Investigations that focus on only human health, economics, or elements of biology or geography are often not suitable for an ESS investigation.

Your research question must contain variables. Most research questions will use independent and dependent variables, although derived variables may be stated or two variables compared/correlated. An experiment should have an independent variable that will be used to test the dependent or derived variable.

Strategy

The strategy can be a plan of action, a management option, or any other intervention that is designed to address the environmental issue.

You need to discuss how a developing or existing strategy addresses the environmental issue that is central to your investigation. You then need to explore how tensions between different perspectives can impact the environmental or societal outcomes of the strategy.

When writing this section, consider the following questions:

- Have I described a developing or existing strategy that addresses an environmental topic or issue linked to my research question?
- Does a tension (or do tensions) arise from the strategy when viewed from different perspectives? Have I discussed these?
- Does my discussion include at least two contrasting worldviews or perspectives on a stated tension?
- Does the discussion include the arguments used by each perspective? How does each worldview or perspective view the strategy?
- Have I discussed the potential impacts of the tension on the outcome of the strategy, both positive and negative?
- Have I included a personal perspective on the stated strategy? Have I stated a conclusion on the strategy, supported by a brief appraisal of the tensions discussed?

Tensions arise from unrest, strain, imbalance or opposition between individuals, organizations or communities that have different worldviews or perspectives regarding the strategy. Tensions can arise from actual or potentially conflicting goals, interests or needs.

The environmental issue or topic can be different to the one mentioned in the research question, but there must be a clearly stated connection to the research question. Most reports will probably use the same environmental issue or topic when describing and explaining the strategy and tensions.

The strategy might be based in the local context of the study itself, or be broader, depending on the nature of the environmental topic or issue. Local strategies could include distribution of essential information about the issue in leaflets, posters or brochures. For example, community-based action to save a local river or lake might be linked to a research question on water pollution and species loss.

Method

An **independent variable** is the variable that is changed in an investigation.

A **dependent variable** is the variable that is measured in an investigation.

A **control variable** is a variable that is kept the same in an investigation.

A **control** is an experiment where the independent variable is either kept constant or removed. This can be used to prove that any changes in the dependent variable are due to the independent variable rather than other factors.

Many students lose marks for not knowing the difference between independent, dependent and control variables. You need to clearly identify each of these variables in your report. The terminology is not compulsory and some students instead simply refer to the variables that they will manipulate, those variables that will respond, and those variables that will be held constant.

The terms **control** and **control variable** are often confused. Control variables are required for a fair test, where only one variable is changed (the **independent variable**) and the rest kept the same (the control variables). The **dependent variable** is the one you are measuring.

A control refers to an experiment where the independent variable is removed – this proves that the independent variable is the one having the effect rather than other factors. In ecological IAs it may not be possible to control other variables as you will be working outside, where conditions vary. In these investigations, you need to say that you will monitor other variables that may affect your dependent variable.

When explaining your sampling method, you must outline how those samples are to be selected, ensuring that there is no significant bias. **Bias** in an investigation can be defined as a preference, opinion, or inclination in support of, or counter to, a concept or result. Bias can result from an assumption or personal choice. You need to be able to develop a method that results in a 'fair' test or one in which reasonable attempts have been made to remove bias. For example, a practical that includes sampling of quadrats (Topic 2, Section 2.1.16) should include some description of how these are to be selected. It is not sufficient simply to state that quadrats were selected randomly – the method to ensure randomness should be outlined. If you are comparing germination of plants under different salinity conditions, for example, the method should indicate how temperature, moisture and other variables are being controlled in order to ensure that the results are comparable.

When carrying out ecological fieldwork, time constraints can be problematic and it is appreciated that in these cases you may need to collect fewer than five samples or transects. In such cases, three may be acceptable, but you need to explain in your report about the time constraints you encountered.

Most students succeed in obtaining data that are relevant to the question or topic that is being studied but may lose marks by collecting data that is insufficient in quantity. Normally, five is the minimum number of samples required per site, treatment, repetition and so on. For example, if you are measuring changes in rate of oxygen release in *Elodea* (pondweed) with respect to water quality (measured by quantity of suspended sediment), it would be expected that you would take at least five readings for each level of water quality. Lack of sufficient data can have knock-on effects for other marking criteria. For example, if only a single measurement is collected per treatment, the data does not lend itself for processing and, by extension, is not suitable for the presentation of processed data.

Treatment of data

When completing this section, ask yourself the following questions:

- Have I included qualitative observations (these may include correctly labelled pictures and drawings)?
- Have I concisely presented text, tables, calculations, graphs and other illustrations?
- Have I used the correct scientific units and their symbols?
- Have I correctly formatted my data, including units, uncertainties, consistent number of decimal places or significant figures?
- Does the raw and processed data address the research question?
- If I have included a calculation, have I included a sample calculation or used screenshots where appropriate?
- Are all graphs relevant and do they add value to the report, e.g. do they include lines or curves of best fit?

Students often **lose** marks for the following errors:

- Tables and graphs not being labelled correctly. Tables should have an adequate title and appropriate column headings. Axes of graphs should be labelled, with units included.
- Adding units in the cells of a table and not in the column or row headings where they should be.
- Reporting data to a varying number of decimal places within the same column or row. In a table, for example, the temperature data and dissolved oxygen data may have different numbers of decimal places, but all the temperature readings must have the same number of decimals.
- Collecting insufficient amounts of data. It is not possible to carry out a good analysis of data when the data are insufficient. If the design calls for one pH sample from each of five locations in a stream, then there is no significant analysis that can be carried out with these data and therefore you are likely to perform poorly. Five repeats at each site would have been necessary for good data analysis.
- Not processing the data correctly. It is expected that you will do some processing of your data (e.g. calculating indices, averages, standard deviations and so on). Statistical techniques such as chi squared, regressions, *t*-test can also be done. Although these techniques are not specifically required, they do provide a way to achieve full marks in this aspect. However, to achieve full marks the techniques must be used well.

Presentation of processed data usually takes the form of a scatter plot, pie chart, histogram, bar chart, or some other method of visually portraying the analysed data.

When processing data, accuracy is sometimes increased through mathematical means. Processed data should be to the same level of accuracy as raw data. If a mean is calculated from numbers with two decimal places, for example, the mean should not be reported to four decimal places.

Do not just plot unprocessed/raw data (e.g. if you take temperature readings at ten different sites on a river, do not just draw a graph of these – you should plot the mean values).

The data you collect must be recorded at the level of accuracy made possible by the precision of the equipment you are using. For example, if plant lengths are measured with a ruler that reports millimetres, the average of these data should not be reported to 8 decimal places in the data tables, but rather to the nearest millimetre. Similarly, if a light meter records two decimal places, then this is the level of accuracy that should be used when calculating mean values.

Analysis and conclusion

Your analysis needs to discuss all of the processed data. Where possible, the variability and reliability of the data, and its impact on the conclusion, should be explained. By referring to scientific literature, you can discuss whether other sources support or refute your data.

Variability is the spread or range of data in a sample. One way of measuring variability is standard deviation, which measures the variation from the mean of a set of values.

Reliable results are ones that are repeated so that any data that do not fit the overall pattern can be identified and mean results calculated. **Replicates** can improve the **reliability** of an investigation and enable anomalies to be identified.

Validity is a measure of confidence in a conclusion. It depends on the range and reliability of observations and measurements.

The best IA reports cite literature, indicate how close data is to what might be expected, contain discussion about why data did not support the theory and include comments about the relative reliability of the data. Calculation of standard deviations allows for discussion about the reliability of the data. Although it is not intended that the discussion should turn into a dissertation of several pages, there does need to be a critical look at the quality of the data and how it relates to what is known.

When completing this section, ask yourself the following questions:

- Have I included a valid discussion of trends, patterns or correlations in the results?
- Have I interpreted my data in a way that will lead to a valid conclusion?
- Is there a valid interpretation of the significance of statistical tests results, if used?
- Is there discussion of the impact of the uncertainties, as appropriate?
- Is there a discussion of the measures of bias, reliability and validity of the data (which may indicate an appreciation of the strengths or weaknesses of the data)?

A good analysis should identify patterns in the data (or comment on their absence), place the research in a context that relates it to theory and/or research and assess the quality of the data generated. This is much easier to do if the planning and results sections have been done well. If the research question is tightly focused, and there is sufficient data to address the question, then a discussion is more likely to produce interesting insight. For example, if you have carried out a study of the relationship between temperature and dissolved oxygen at sites above and below a pollution source, you should address the quality of the data. Is it reliable? Why or why not? This is where having means and standard deviations can be useful. Standard deviation (which can easily be worked out on a scientific calculator) shows the variation in the data. If there is a very large standard deviation, you would be expected to comment on this fact and interpret it (i.e. large variation means that the data are less reliable).

The analysis should be thought-provoking and will almost certainly be the most challenging (and perhaps longest) part of the report. Are there important differences among the data? Are there trends? Do these trends support/refute accepted theory?

Are the standard deviations in the data so huge as to make differences meaningless? Are there anomalies in the data? An **anomaly** can be identified as a data point that lies significantly outside the range of other data in an investigation, i.e. a point that does not fit the overall trend. These anomalies should be discussed, and if they are to be ignored or excluded from the analysis, a case for this decision should be made. Were the samples collected without significant bias? Are there literature values that can be used for comparison? If there are, these should be mentioned. If these are non-existent or unavailable, a note to this effect should be included.

An **anomaly** is a data point that does not fit the pattern of other data.

In the conclusion, marks are often lost by not being specific enough. You should cite your data in your conclusions (e.g. if you conclude that in a study of soil moisture along a slope, there is a trend towards increasing moisture down the slope, this should be illustrated with the actual data). There should be a brief explanation included as well. For example, 'The increase in soil moisture down the slope may be due to run-off and infiltration.'

Evaluation

When evaluating your investigation, ask yourself questions such as 'what might I have done differently?' or 'how confident am I of my findings and how could I increase my confidence level?'

You need to look at your method critically and offer improvements. Marks are generally lost by making suggestions for improvements that are either too simple or unrealistic, such as simply gathering more data or using scientific apparatus that is beyond the scope of school science investigations. Weaknesses and improvements must have sufficient discussion of their potential impacts on the investigation. Weaknesses that undermine the validity of the investigation (for example, assumptions on which the investigation is based or its design) are usually more significant than random or human errors. In the evaluation, data quality issues that may have been noted in the discussion should be addressed. Was the standard deviation very high? How can it be reduced? Is the data representative? If not, how can that be addressed? What improvements will address the issues that have been identified? All these questions should be answered in this section of the report.

Realistic unresolved questions in the Evaluation should be qualitatively different from the method undertaken. For example, in an ecological investigation, it is not sufficient just to say that more samples would be collected, whereas undertaking the field investigation in different seasons would be acceptable. Investigating a controlled variable in a survey, to see how that changes the results, would also be acceptable. If gender was investigated, then age or location could be discussed.

In this section, you also need to describe realistic unresolved questions that may impact the conclusion. These questions should follow on from your original investigation in a meaningful way and enhance understanding of the issue or research question. You should include potential questions that might bring the results closer to what you may have expected, based on published literature. These could be modifications to the weaknesses or limitations already mentioned or linked to research seen in literature. A clear link needs to be made to the method and environmental issue that extends the investigation beyond the original investigation.

Format of report

You must decide how to structure your IA report, which should be clear, concise, focused and demonstrate relevant scientific or social science skills. A clear and informative title reflecting the research question and inquiry should inform the reader what the investigation is about.

Make sure that your report is well structured and well organized. The report should make consistent use of appropriate terminology and be concise, follow a logical order and be clearly written.

The following details should be stated at the start of the report:

- title of the investigation
- IB candidate code (alphanumeric, for example, abc123)
- IB candidate code for all group members (if applicable)
- number of words.

There is no requirement to include a cover page or a contents page.

The individual investigation for your IA allows you to explore an environmental issue that is of particular interest to you and gives you an opportunity to implement the research and investigative skills you have learnt during your course. This should be a very rewarding experience. Good luck with your investigation!

Extended Essay

Note: The Extended Essay Guide is due to be updated by the IB in 2025. Visit the Pearson IB website for the most up-to-date information.

The Extended Essay is an in-depth study of a focused topic that promotes intellectual discovery, creativity and writing skills. It provides you with an opportunity to explore and engage with an academic idea or problem in your favourite IB DP subject. It will develop your research skills (something needed at universities and for further education in general) and provide you with the opportunity to produce an individualized and personal piece of work. The essay is a major piece of structured writing that is formally presented. Many students find the Extended Essay a valuable stimulus for discussion in interviews for university or employment. You are expected to spend approximately 40 hours on your essay, and the finished piece of work should be no more than 4000 words.

The essay should be no more than 4000 words. You are expected to spend approximately 40 hours on the essay.

You will have a supervisor for your essay, who will help you to decide on a suitable topic and check that you are keeping to the timing and regulations. You can meet with your supervisor for 3 to 5 hours over the course of your essay: a number of short meetings are recommended (e.g. once a fortnight for 20 minutes) rather than a few long ones, as this will help you and your supervisor to exchange ideas and feedback on a regular basis. Your supervisor will:

- give you a copy of the assessment criteria and subject specific details (available from the IB)
- give you advice on the skills of undertaking research
- support you in the use of the Researcher's reflection space (RRS) as an integral part of the Extended Essay process
- help you with shaping your research question and the subsequent structure and content of your essay
- give you examples of excellent Extended Essays
- read and comment on your work (but will not be able to edit it)
- give you advice on the format of the bibliography, the abstract and referencing
- conduct a short concluding interview (*viva voce*) with you once you have finished the essay.

To make the most of your Extended Essay, you need to make sure you:

- undertake the work agreed by you and your supervisor
- keep appointments and deadlines
- are honest about your progress and any problems you may be facing
- pace yourself so you do not have a lot of work at the last minute.

The maximum number of marks for the Extended Essay is 34. It is marked using five different assessment criteria. One of the five criteria relates to the Reflections on planning and progress form (RPPF).

The Extended Essay is marked according to certain assessment criteria. The maximum total number of marks you can receive is 34, and you can see from the criteria how many marks are allotted to each aspect of your Essay (there are five different marking criteria, pages 904–906).

The RPPF allows examiners to gain an insight into your thinking throughout the process of undertaking research and writing. It will allow for the application of criterion E (engagement).

Reflections on planning and progress form (RPPF)

Reflection is an important aspect of the DP Core, with both the Theory of Knowledge and the Extended Essay providing different kinds of reflection. In the Extended Essay, reflection focuses on your progress during the research, planning and completion of your essay. You are expected to consider the effectiveness of your choices, to re-examine ideas and decide whether changes are needed in order to complete the task.

You will have three mandatory reflection sessions with your supervisor. Your 3 to 5 hours of supervision time must include the three mandatory reflection sessions. The third and final mandatory reflection session is the *viva voce*, which is a concluding interview with your supervisor.

The RPPF allows examiners to gain an insight into your thinking throughout the process of undertaking your research and writing. You must complete this form after each of your mandatory reflection sessions. Your supervisor must sign after each reflection is completed and at the end of the process once the *viva voce* has taken place.

Bibliography (references)

A correctly referenced bibliography contributes to the quality of presentation. References need to contain the name of author, date of publication, title of source and page numbers as applicable. You should include the date for any web pages used to show when they were last accessed. The sources included in a bibliography should be arranged in alphabetical order according to author's surname. The bibliography should be included on a separate sheet of paper with a title at the top. You must make sure you consider whether any source you use is likely to be reliable; this is especially true for internet resources, where there are relatively few quality controls. References should be given to any text, audiovisual material, graphs and data published in print and electronic sources.

Detail specific to Environmental systems and societies

An Extended Essay in ESS will provide you with the opportunity to explore an environmental topic or issue of particular interest to you and your locality. As this is an interdisciplinary subject, you will need to integrate theory from the course with practical methodologies that are relevant to your topic. A systems approach is particularly effective and, as this is something emphasized throughout the course, this should be familiar to you. You will be expected to show appreciation and use of this approach in the analysis and interpretation of the data gathered.

The ESS course focuses on the interaction and integration of natural environmental systems and human societies, and your essay needs to achieve this as well. It should not deal exclusively with ecological processes or with societal activities, but instead should give significant (though not necessarily equal) weight to both these dimensions. For example, the ESS syllabus includes the study of pure ecological principles, but an Extended Essay would have to explore ecological principles within the context of some human interaction with an environmental system. A specific natural system needs to be studied, rather than general systems that have been covered in the course.

When selecting your Extended Essay, think carefully about the type of essay you want to write. If you aim to obtain largely descriptive or narrative data, of the type produced in the human sciences, an individuals and societies subject group essay may be more appropriate. If you want to collect quantitative data typical of the experimental sciences, then a sciences subject group essay may be more appropriate. An ESS essay *must* cover the criteria of both subject groups and be fully interdisciplinary in nature.

An ESS Extended Essay must integrate aspects of both the 'Sciences' group and 'Individuals and Societies' group.

A crucial feature of any suitable topic is that it must be open to analytical argument. For example, rather than simply describing a given nature reserve, you would need to evaluate its relationship with a local community, or compare its achievement with original objectives, or with a similar initiative elsewhere. The topic must leave room for you to be able to form an argument that you both construct and support, using analysis of your own data, rather than simply reporting analysed data obtained from other sources. Certain topics should be avoided for ethical or safety reasons (e.g. experiments likely to inflict pain on living organisms, cause unwarranted environmental damage, or put pressure on others to behave unethically). Experiments that pose a threat to health (e.g. using toxic or dangerous chemicals, or putting oneself at physical risk during fieldwork) should also be avoided unless adequate safety apparatus and qualified supervision are available.

Your research question must be open to analytical argument.

Your essay must adhere to the IB animal experimentation policy. You must familiarize yourself with this before undertaking an Extended Essay in ESS.

Focus

Essential to a successful Extended Essay is the focus of the topic chosen. If a topic is too broad, it can lead you into superficial treatment and it is unlikely you will be able to produce any fresh analysis, or novel and interesting conclusions of your own. So, for example, topics on the left of Table EE 1 are better than topics on the right.

An essay with a sharply-focused research question will be more successful than one that has a topic that is too broad.

Table EE 1 Focusing the topic of your essay.

Focused ✓	Unfocused ✗
How has the ecological recovery of worked-out bauxite quarries in Jarrahdale, Western Australia been achieved?	Environmental effects of mining
How does the energy efficiency of grain production in The Netherlands compare with that of Swaziland?	Efficiency of world food production
How does the importance/significance of different sources of carbon dioxide pollution in New York compare with that of Sacramento?	Impacts of global warming
How is the environmental impact of paper use at a Welsh college managed?	Paper recycling

Topics with a sharper focus enable you to channel your research to produce interesting and original conclusions and discussions. A short and precise statement outlining the overall approach of your investigation is also helpful in determining the focus of your essay and making sure you stick to it. For example, if your topic is an examination of the ecological footprint of your school canteen, the research question could be: *From the major inputs and outputs of the school canteen, what overall estimate of its environmental impact can be made in terms of an ecological footprint?* An approach could include an analysis of the records and practical measurements that assess the inputs and outputs of the canteen, and an analysis of data into a holistic environmental footprint model that

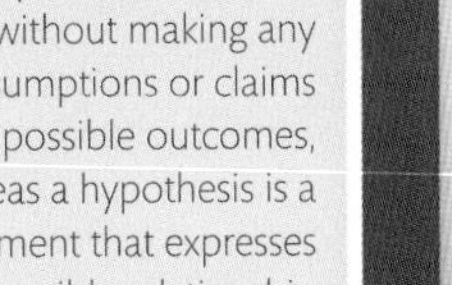

A research question explores the possible relationship between different factors (e.g. independent and dependent variables) without making any assumptions or claims about possible outcomes, whereas a hypothesis is a statement that expresses a possible relationship between variables based on existing knowledge or observations.

indicates environmental impact. For some investigations, particularly those that are experimental, a clearly stated hypothesis may be just as acceptable as, and possibly better than, a research question.

An Extended Essay in ESS may be investigated either through primary data collection (i.e. from fieldwork, laboratory experimentation, surveys or interviews) or through secondary data collection (i.e. from literature or other media). It may even involve a combination of the two. However, given the limited time available and the word limit for the essay, the emphasis should be clearly with one or the other to avoid the danger of both becoming superficial. Experience shows that data based on questionnaires and interviews are to be avoided, as such data is difficult to analyse and conclusions difficult to arrive at. Fieldwork and lab experiments are a more reliable way to gather data for your essay.

An Extended Essay in ESS may be investigated either through primary data collection (i.e. from fieldwork, laboratory experimentation, surveys or interviews) or through secondary data collection (i.e. from literature or other media).

If the essay is focused largely on the collection of primary data, you must check carefully with the literature to make sure you select the most appropriate method for obtaining valid quantitative data. You must ensure you reference these secondary sources of information in your bibliography. If the essay is focused on secondary data, you need to take great care in selecting sources, ensuring that there is a sufficient quantity and range and that they are all reliable. The internet and other media contain a great many unfounded and unsupported claims that you need to be wary of – checking information from several different sources will help you evaluate its value and accuracy. You must sort through your sources and use only those that have academic credibility. For an essay of this type, you are expected to produce a substantial bibliography and not limit yourself to just a few sources.

Once you have assembled your data, you must produce your own analysis and argue your own conclusions. This will happen more naturally if the essay is based on primary data since such data has not been previously analysed. A source of secondary data may come with its own analysis and conclusions. If you use secondary data, it is essential that you further manipulate it, or possibly combine it with other sources, so that there is clear evidence in the essay of your personal involvement in the analysis and drawing of conclusions. You are expected to be academically honest in your essay – plagiarism (direct copying) is a very serious matter, which the IB deals with severely.

The systems approach is a central theme in the ESS syllabus and this should also be reflected in an ESS Extended Essay. The essay should include an attempt to model the system or systems in question.

A central theme in the syllabus for ESS is the systems approach. This should be reflected to some degree in your essay, which should include an attempt to model, at least partially, the system or systems in question. The term *model* can be applied in its broadest sense to include, for example, mathematical formulae, maps, graphs and flow diagrams. Systems terminology (e.g. input, output, processes) should be used where appropriate.

Read the advice on these pages carefully. Check your essay to see that you have fulfilled all of the assessment criteria.

Assessment criteria

Your essay will be marked according to specific assessment criteria. There are five different criteria. The maximum total number of marks you can receive is 34. For each criterion, the number of marks allocated and the details that should be covered in relation to ESS are outlined below. In each case, details are presented as a series of questions to help you check you have fully met each one.

Criterion A: Focus and method (6 marks)

Clear communication of the topic:

- Do you have a sharply-focused research question clearly defining the purpose of the essay?
- Have you effectively identified and explained the research topic?
- Have you clearly communicated the purpose and focus of the research?
- Is your research focus appropriate?

Complete methodology of the research:

- Do you have an appropriate range of relevant source(s) and/or method(s) in relation to the topic and research question?
- Is there evidence of effective and informed selection of sources and/or methods?

Criterion B: Knowledge and understanding (6 marks)

Knowledge and understanding:

- Have you selected sources that are clearly relevant and appropriate to the research question?
- Are the sources used effectively and with understanding?
- Have you shown your knowledge of the topic/discipline(s)/issue clearly and coherently?

Use of terminology and concepts:

- Have you used the subject-specific terminology and concepts accurately and consistently?
- Does your use of terminology and concepts demonstrate effective knowledge and understanding?

Criterion C: Critical thinking (12 marks)

Research:

- Is your research appropriate to the research question?
- Have you applied the research question in a consistently relevant way?

Analysis:

- Have you analysed the research effectively?
- Is this analysis of the research clearly focused on the research question?
- Are your conclusions to individual points of analysis effectively supported by the evidence?

Discussion/evaluation:

- Have you developed an effective and focused reasoned argument from the research with a conclusion that is reflective of the evidence presented?
- Is your reasoned argument well-structured and coherent?
- Have you critically evaluated your research?

Criterion D: Presentation (4 marks)

This criterion assesses the extent to which the presentation follows the standard format expected for academic writing and the extent to which this aids effective communication.

- Is the structure of the essay clearly appropriate in terms of the expected conventions for the topic, the argument and subject in which the essay is registered?
- Have you used an appropriate layout?
- Do the structure and layout support the reading, understanding and evaluation of the extended essay?

Criterion E: Engagement (6 marks)

Criterion E will be assessed with the RPPF.

This criterion assesses your engagement with the research focus and the research process. After the final reflection session, the *viva voce*, your supervisor will add their own comments to your RPPF and then submit the form along with your essay, for the examiner to consider and assess as part of the Extended Essay.

- Are your reflections on decision-making and planning evaluative?
- Do your reflections show your capacity to consider actions and ideas in response to setbacks experienced in the research process?
- Do your reflections communicate a high degree of intellectual and personal engagement with the research focus and process of research?
- Do your reflections demonstrate authenticity, intellectual initiative and/or creative approach?

The extended essay gives you the opportunity to explore, in depth, an environmental issue that is of particular interest to you, and to develop academic research and writing skills. It is a major piece of formally presented, structured writing, and you should find the process extremely rewarding. Good luck with your extended essay!

Examination strategies

At the end of your ESS course, you will sit two exam papers: Paper 1 and Paper 2.

The duration, number of marks and weighting for each paper varies between SL and HL. Table 1 shows the differences between the two levels. The other assessed part of the course is the Internal Assessment (IA) (the Individual Investigation – see pages 887–900), which is marked by your teacher. The IA has a 25% weighting at SL and 20% at HL.

Weighting is the percentage of marks available from all assessment marks (including the IA).

Table 1 Differences between Paper 1 and Paper 2 at SL and HL.

	Paper 1		Paper 2	
	SL	HL	SL	HL
Duration	1 hour	2 hours	2 hours	2.5 hours
Number of marks	35	70	60	80
Weighting	25%	30%	50%	50%

All topics from the course need to be thoroughly revised for both papers. Here is some general advice for the exams:

There are two exam papers in ESS, for both SL and HL students: Paper 1 and Paper 2.

- The skills and applications listed in the ESS syllabus use specific command terms that let you know the approach needed in exams (e.g. evaluate, explain, outline, discuss) and the depth of treatment required. Make sure you have learned the command terms. Questions that use the command term 'compare and contrast' require you, for example, to relate the *similarities* as well as *differences* between two sets of data. If you are asked to 'discuss' you should identify and present at least two alternative views; if you are asked to 'list three factors' you will not gain any extra credit for listing more than three factors. There is a tendency to focus on the content in an exam question rather than the command term, but it is essential that your answer addresses what the command term is asking of you (command terms are listed on pages 912–913).
- Answer all required questions and do not leave gaps.
- Do not write outside the answer boxes provided to answer a question – if you do so, this work will not be marked. Your answers will be scanned and only the material within the boxes is sent to examiners. If you run out of room on the page, use continuation sheets and indicate clearly that you have done this at the end of the question box and on the cover sheet. (The fact that the answer continues on another sheet of paper needs to be clearly indicated in the text box provided.)
- Plan your time carefully before the exams – make sure you have time to revise all topics and to practice past papers.

Paper 1

Paper 1 includes an examination paper and a resource booklet. The resource booklet has information about a specific case study, which you use to answer questions in the examination paper.

Paper 1 follows the same format at both SL and HL and focuses on a case study. You will be given two booklets in this exam:

- An examination paper that contains the questions and space to write your answers.
- A resource booklet, containing information about a case study that will be unfamiliar to you.

There are plenty of case studies available from the ESS course (up to the 2016 examinations, these were part of Paper 2, with data again presented in a resource booklet) – practice as many of them as you can. Remember that because the case studies test knowledge from the whole course, you will not be able to properly tackle a full Paper 1 until you have completed the course.

You are expected to apply the knowledge and understanding gained during the course to this new scenario. The resource booklet will give you a range of data in various forms (e.g. maps, photos, diagrams, graphs and tables). You are required to answer a series of questions, which can involve a variety of command terms, by analysing and evaluating these data. All questions are compulsory.

In the exam, make sure you read the case study carefully. You will be given 5 minutes reading time before the exam begins – use this time to look through each figure and to read the questions.

Paper 2

Paper 2 contains short answers, data-based questions and structured essays. Questions cover the whole breadth of the syllabus.

Paper 2 consists of two sections: section A and section B. Section A includes both short answer and data-based questions, whereas section B includes essay questions.

Paper 2 consists of two sections, A and B:

- Section A is made up of short-answer and data-based questions.
- Section B contains structured essays. Each question is worth 20 marks and consists of three sections: a), b) and c).

Section A follows the same format at both SL and HL, but the requirements for Section B are different. SL students are required to write **one** structured essay from a choice of two, and HL students are required to write **two** structured essays from a choice of three (see below).

Advice for Section A

- The short answer section (Section A) is worth 40 marks, at both SL and HL. The questions cannot cover all aspects of the syllabus. However, it is essential that you thoroughly revise the whole syllabus so that you can tackle any question that comes up.
- Section A also asks you to answer data-based questions. Data-based questions present you with data in some form and ask you questions about it. Some questions will ask you to read the data displayed and some will ask you to draw conclusions from it. You are expected to use the data provided in the question. Try to get into the habit of using data when you practice data-based questions. This will make it natural to do the same when sitting the exam.
  Become familiar with unit expressions such as kJ m^{-2} yr^{-1} (read as kilojoules per metre squared per year). If you are not comfortable with the unit expressions you see in data-based questions, ask your teacher for help.
- The size of the answer boxes and the number of marks available give you an indication of the length of answer expected – make sure your answers are concise. If three marks are awarded, the examiner will be looking for three different points. Make sure you do not contradict yourself.

Paper 2 Section B – Standard Level

- Section B requires you to answer **one** structured essay question from a choice of two. The structured essay is worth 20 marks.
- The final part of each essay in Section B (9 marks) will be marked using mark-bands. Here are the descriptors for these mark-bands:

Marks	Description of details included in the answer
0	The work does not reach a standard described by the descriptors below.
1–3	The response contains: • minimal evidence of knowledge and understanding of ESS issues and concepts • fragmented knowledge statements that are poorly linked to the context of the question • some appropriate use of ESS terminology • no examples, where required, or examples with insufficient explanation/relevance • superficial analysis that amounts to no more than a list of facts/ideas • judgements/conclusions that are vague or not supported by evidence/argument.
4–6	The response contains: • some evidence of sound knowledge and understanding of ESS issues and concepts • knowledge statements that are effectively linked to the context of the question • largely appropriate use of ESS terminology • some use of relevant examples, where required, but with limited explanation • some clear judgements/conclusions that are supported by limited evidence/arguments.
7–9	The response contains: • substantial evidence of sound knowledge and understanding of ESS issues and concepts • a wide breadth of knowledge statements that are effectively linked to each other and to the context of the question • consistent, appropriate and precise use of ESS terminology • effective use of pertinent, well-explained examples, where required, showing some originality • thorough, well-balanced, insightful analysis • explicit judgements/conclusions that are well supported by evidence/arguments and that include some critical reflection.

Table 2 Mark-band descriptors for final part of essay in Section B, at SL.

The descriptors of these mark-bands suggest certain features that may be offered in response. The descriptors outline the kind of elements examiners will be looking for when deciding on the appropriate mark-band and the specific mark within that band.

The examiner will decide which band your answer fits best and whether it is at the top, middle, or bottom of the mark-band. Marks will be awarded accordingly.

Paper 2 Section B – Higher Level

- Section B requires you to answer **two** structured essay questions from a choice of three. Each question is worth 20 marks. The total number of marks available for Section B is therefore 40 marks,
- The final part of each essay in Section B (9 marks) will be marked using mark-bands. Here are the descriptors for these mark-bands:

Table 3 Mark-band descriptors for final part of essay in Section B, at HL.

Marks	Description of details included in the answer
0	The work does not reach a standard described by the descriptors below.
1–3	The response contains: • minimal evidence of knowledge and understanding of ESS issues, concepts or HL lens content • fragmented knowledge statements that are poorly linked to the context of the question • some appropriate use of ESS terminology • no examples, where required, or examples with insufficient explanation/relevance • superficial analysis that amounts to no more than a list of facts/ideas • judgements/conclusions that are vague or not supported by evidence/argument.
4–6	The response contains: • some evidence of sound knowledge and understanding of ESS issues, concepts and HL lens content • knowledge statements that are effectively linked to the context of the question • largely appropriate use of ESS terminology • some use of relevant examples, where required, but with limited explanation • some clear judgements/conclusions that are supported by limited evidence/arguments.
7–9	The response contains: • substantial evidence of sound knowledge and understanding of ESS issues, concepts and HL lens content • a wide breadth of knowledge statements that are effectively linked to each other and to the context of the question • consistent, appropriate and precise use of ESS terminology • effective use of pertinent, well-explained examples, where required, showing some originality • thorough, well-balanced, insightful analysis • explicit judgements/conclusions that are well supported by evidence/arguments and that include some critical reflection.

Advice for Paper 2

Make sure you plan your strategy for the paper before you sit it. How much time will you spend on Section A and how much time on the essays (Section B)? Practicing past papers will help you work out how much time you need to spend on each of the sections. This will vary from student to student, but here is some general advice.

- Some students will want to answer the structured essay(s) first and some will want to start with the short answer questions. Tackle the paper in whichever order suits you best.
- The structured essays need to be thought about carefully and planned – aim to spend a *minimum* of 35 minutes on an essay. At HL, where you need to write two structured essays, move on to the second one after 40 minutes, even if you haven't finished working on the first one.
- Choose your structured essay(s) carefully. Look at all sections of an essay before making your choice. There are three sections in a structured essay question, a), b) and c) – make sure you answer all parts and label the parts of your questions clearly, e.g. 1a, 1b, 1c.
- Look carefully at the number of marks available for each part of the question and adjust the amount of time you spend on that part accordingly. Writing a plan for your essays will help you.
- Each part of a structured essay should be subdivided into sections, not written as one long paragraph – examiners like this because it makes the paper easier to read and mark. Make sure you clearly label the different parts of your question ('a', 'b' and 'c').
- Leave at least one line between sections of an essay for clarity and note on your scripts if a continuation sheet has been used.

Using real-life examples you have learned during the course will help you answer Paper 2 structured essay question(s) (examples of 4, 7 and 9 mark questions, the usual mark allocation for a structured essay, are given in this book). You should use your real-life examples to answer the essay questions rather than taking ideas from the case study used in Paper 1.

In Paper 2, section B, ensure that you label the parts of your question.

Tips for exams

Remember these tips.

- Use the 5-minute reading time to look through the paper and assess the content.
- A calculator is required for both papers. Graphic display calculators (GDCs) are permitted (check with your teacher if you are not sure).
- The examiner does not know you. You must communicate fully what you know and not expect the examiner to do your thinking for you.
- State the obvious in your answers. Many of the items in a mark-scheme will be information that is very basic in relation to the question.
- Do not use abbreviations that may be unfamiliar to someone else. Always use the full words first and put the abbreviations in brackets. Be clear and concise with your choice of words.
- If your handwriting is very small or unclear, print your response. If the examiner cannot read your writing, you will not get any marks.
- Make sure to use extra paper if you need it.

During the exam, use your time appropriately:

- read each question twice before beginning to write
- plan your time – allocate time according to the number of marks per question
- if you have time at the end, re-read your answers and make sure you have said exactly what you want to say.

Remember that the written papers form only part of the overall assessment. The IA is graded by your teacher and moderated by an examiner.

Command terms

Command terms indicate the depth of treatment required for a given assessment statement.

Make sure you learn, and can apply, command terms. It is essential that you are familiar with these terms, for both Papers 1 and 2, so that you are able to recognize the type and depth of response you are expected to provide. Command terms are grouped according to the different assessment objectives: objectives 1 and 2 address simpler skills, and objectives 3 and 4 relate to higher-order skills.

Assessment objective 1

Define: Give the precise meaning of a word, phrase, concept or physical quantity.

Draw: Represent by means of a labelled, accurate diagram or graph, using a pencil. A ruler (straight edge) should be used for straight lines. Diagrams should be drawn to scale. Graphs should have points correctly plotted (if appropriate) and joined in a straight line or smooth curve.

Label: Add labels to a diagram.

List: Give a sequence of brief answers with no explanation.

Measure: Obtain a value for a quantity.

State: Give a specific name, value or other brief answer without explanation or calculation.

Assessment objective 2

Annotate: Add brief notes to a diagram or graph.

Apply: Use an idea, equation, principle, theory or law in relation to a given problem or issue.

Calculate: Obtain a numerical answer showing the relevant stages in the working.

Describe: Give a detailed account.

Distinguish: Make clear the differences between two or more concepts or items.

Estimate: Obtain an approximate value.

Identify: Provide an answer from a number of possibilities.

Interpret: Use knowledge and understanding to recognize trends and draw conclusions from given information.

Outline: Give a brief account or summary.

Assessment objective 3 and assessment objective 4

Analyse: Break down in order to bring out the essential elements or structure.

Comment: Give a judgement based on a given statement or result of a calculation.

Compare and contrast: Give an account of similarities and differences between two or more items or situations, referring to all of them throughout.

Construct: Display information in a diagrammatic or logical form.

Deduce: Reach a conclusion from the information given.

Demonstrate: Make clear by reasoning or evidence, illustrating with examples or practical application.

Derive: Manipulate a mathematical relationship to give a new equation or relationship.

Design: Produce a plan, simulation or model.

Determine: Obtain the only possible answer.

Discuss: Offer a considered and balanced review that includes a range of arguments, factors or hypotheses. Opinions or conclusions should be presented clearly and supported by appropriate evidence.

Evaluate: Make an appraisal by weighing up the strengths and limitations.

Examine: Consider an argument or concept in a way that uncovers the assumptions and interrelationships of the issue.

Explain: Give a detailed account including reasons or causes.

Justify: Give valid reasons or evidence to support an answer or conclusion.

Predict: Give an expected result.

Sketch: Represent by means of a diagram or graph (labelled as appropriate). The sketch should give a general idea of the required shape or relationship and should include relevant features.

Suggest: Propose a solution, hypothesis or other possible answer.

To what extent: Consider the merits or otherwise of an argument or concept. Opinions and conclusions should be presented clearly and supported with appropriate evidence and a sound argument.

Mathematical skills

You should be able to manipulate, interpret and evaluate data, including:

- execute basic arithmetic functions: addition, subtraction, multiplication and division
- perform calculations involving averages, decimals, fractions, percentages, ratios, approximations, frequencies and reciprocals
- calculate measures of central tendency: mean, median and mode
- use and interpret standard notation (e.g. 3.6×10^6)
- apply and use the International System of Units (SI units) for mass, time, length and their derived units, e.g. speed, area and volume or non-SI metric units
- use direct and inverse proportion
- plot graphs (with suitable scales and axes) including two variables that show linear and non-linear relationships, independent variable on the *x*-axis, dependent on the *y*-axis
- interpret graphs, including the significance of gradients, changes in gradients, intercepts and areas
- interpret data presented in various forms: scatter plot, point-to-point line, line of best fit, bar chart, stacked histogram, pie chart, box and whisker plot, kite diagram
- evaluate data through statistical tests and quantities, for example using standard deviation, correlation coefficient, Spearman's rank, analysis of variance (ANOVA), chi-squared test, t-test
- calculate indices from given formulae, for example Simpson's reciprocal index, Lincoln index
- calculate natural increase rates and population doubling times from given data.

There are usually several marks for mathematical analysis in both Paper 1 and Paper 2 (Section A). Make sure you bring an appropriate calculator to each exam (your teacher will tell you which type you are allowed to use).

Systems and models

You should be able to construct and interpret models and diagrams of systems, including:

- construct a systems/flow diagram from a given set of data showing transfers, transformations and stores
- construct and interpret systems diagrams representing, but not limited to, ecosystems, soil, biogeochemical cycles, urban systems
- interpret models representing, but not limited to, feeding relationships, population growth and interactions, demographic transition, atmospheric changes, climate graphs, yield/fishing effort curves, circular and doughnut economies
- calculate efficiency of energy transfer through a system (HL only)
- interpret cladograms (HL only).

These skills can be examined in both Paper 1 and Paper 2.

Organization of the United Nations & historical sources OurWorldInData.org/food-supply 545, Share of domestic wastewater that is safely treated, 2022, Our World in Data. https://ourworldindata.org/grapher/wastewater-safely-treated 437, UN Food and Agriculture Organization (FAO) OurWorldInData.org 493; **Overseas Development Administration:** ODA (1996). Manual of Environmental Appraisal. Overseas Development Administration. Revised July 1996. 131pp. 661; **Oxford University Centre for the Environment:** Centre for Research into Energy Demand Solutions, https://www.creds.ac.uk/creds-study-uncovers-best-ways-to-change-consumption-to-cut-carbon-footprint/ 063, **Oxford University Press:** Aldo Leopold (1949) A Sand County Almanac, and Sketches Here and There. New York: Oxford University Press. 858, Aristotle (1946) Politics. Oxford: Clarendon Press. 621, Climate change: A Very Short Introduction, Mark Maslin © 2021 Oxford University Press. "Reproduced with permission of the Licensor through PLSclear." 592, 605, Maslin, M., 2021, Climate change: a very short introduction, Oxford, Adapted from Table 1, p. 28 565, Nagle, G and Cooke, B., 2017, Geography Course Companion, Oxford, p. 34, Figure A36 461, Nagle, G. (2003) AS and A Level Geography for Edexcel Specification B. OUP, p. 65. 719; **Pearson Education:** Adapted from Brady, N and Well, R., 1999, The nature and properties of soil, 12th Edition, Pearson Education, USA 476; **Pew Research Center:** Survey of U.S. adults conducted Jan, 8-13, 2020. https://www.pewresearch.org/politics/2020/02/13/as-economic-concerns-recede-environmental-protection-rises-on-the-publics-policy-agenda/ 016; **PLOS One:** González-Maya, J.F., Víquez-R, L.R., Belant, J.L. and Ceballos, G, 2015. Effectiveness of Protected Areas for Representing Species and Populations of Terrestrial Mammals in Costa Rica. PLoS ONE 10(5): e0124480. doi: 10.1371/journal.pone.0124480 [online]. Available at: https://journals.plos.org/plosone/article?id=10.1371/journal.pone.0124480. This file is licensed under the Creative Commons Attribution 4.0 International (CC BY 4.0) https://creativecommons.org/licenses/by/4.0/ [Accessed 06 November 2019]. 328, Matsunami, M., et. al. (2016). Population structure and evolution after speciation of the Hokkaido salamander (Hynobius retardatus). Plos one, 11(6), e0156815, Figure 1. 325; **PopulationPyramid.net:** "Population Pyramids of the World from 1950 to 2100," PopulationPyramid.net. https://www.populationpyramid.net/japan/2025/ 734, Adapted from populationpyramid.net 741; **Proceedings of the National Academy of Sciences:** Steffen, W., et. al. (2018). Trajectories of the Earth System in the Anthropocene. Proceedings of the National Academy of Sciences, 115(33), 8252-8259. 556, From Christopher W. Tessum et al., Inequity in consumption of goods and services adds to racial–ethnic disparities in air pollution exposure. Social Sciences 116 (13), 6001-6006. https://doi.org/10.1073/pnas.1818859116 058; **PUB, Singapore's National Water Agency:** "NEWater," PUB. https://www.pub.gov.sg/watersupply/fournationaltaps/newater 371; **Rothamsted Research:** Broadbalk Wilderness Carbon Open Access Chart, https://www.era.rothamsted.ac.uk/metadata/rbk1w/BKWoc/Broadbalk_Wilderness_Carbon_Open_Access_Chart.png 209; **Royal Society:** Bushmeat hunting and extinction risk to the world's mammals. Available at: https://royalsocietypublishing.org/doi/10.1098/rsos.160498 535; **Sadalmelik:** 245; **Springer Nature:** "Used with permission of Springer Nature, from Biodiversity Hotspots Distribution and Protection of Conservation Priority Areas, Frank E. Zachos, Jan Christian Habel, © 2011; permission conveyed through Copyright Clearance Center, Inc." 287, "Used with the permission of Springer Nature from Fisheries: Does catch reflect abundance?, Pauly, D., Hilborn, R., & Branch, T. A., Nature, 494(7437), 303-306, © 2013; permission conveyed through Copyright Clearance Centre, Inc." 408, Gunaratne, M. S., Radin Firdaus, R. B., & Rathnasooriya, S. I. (2021). Climate change and food security in Sri Lanka: Towards food sovereignty. Humanities and Social Sciences Communications, 8(1), Figure 1. 665; **Stacker:** Lisa, A (April 14, 2023) How long it takes 50 common items to decompose. Stacker https://stacker.com/environment/how-long-it-takes-50-common-items-decompose 701; **Stockholm University:** Azote for Stockholm Resilience Centre, based on analysis in Wang-Erlandsson et al. 2022 068; **Taylor & Francis Group:** Park, C. (1997) The environment. Routledge, p. 291, Figure 9.15 337, Smithson, P., et al., 2002, Fundamentals of the Physical Environment, Routledge, p. 394, Figure 1 488; **TED Conferences:** Greta Thunberg "The disarming case to act right now on climate change," TEDxStockholm (November 2018). https://www.ted.com/talks/greta_thunberg_the_disarming_case_to_act_right_now_on_climate_change/transcript 579; **The Arizona Board of Regents:** Assumed population of St. Mathew Island, https://www.geo.arizona.edu/Antevs/nats104/00lect21crash2.gif 102, El Nino, La Nina and Walker Circulation Walker Circulation, https://library.scotch.wa.edu.au/earthandenvironmentalscience/year11/elninolaninawalkercirculatio/walkercirculation 193; **The Creative Learning Exchange:** Getting Started with Behavior Over Time Graphs: Four Curriculum Examples, retrieved from http: //static.clexchange.org/ftp/documents/x-curricular/CC1998-10GettingStartedBOTG.pdf 016; **The Economist:** "Used with permission of The Economist, from Either Ore, 9 July 2022, p. 51; permission conveyed through Copyright Clearance Center, Inc." 691; The **Guardian:** "Air conditioning: the benefits, problems and alternatives," The Guardian. https://www.theguardian.com/environment/2023/jul/29/air-conditioner-alternatives-benefit-environment 633, "Global temperatures have reached record seasonal highs," in Jonathan Watts, Julian Amani, Paul Scruton & Lucy Swan (3 Jul 2023) Will El Niño on top of global heating create the perfect climate storm? The Guardian. https://www.theguardian.com/environment/2023/jul/03/a-perfect-storm-scientists-ponder-if-climate-has-entered-a-new-erratic-era 557, "The risk of climate tipping points is rising rapidly as the world heats up," in Damian Carrington (8 Sep 2022) World on brink of five 'disastrous' climate tipping points, study finds. The Guardian. https://www.theguardian.com/environment/2022/sep/08/world-on-brink-five-climate-tipping-points-study-finds 577, The 36 most biologically rich yet threatened regions in Patrick Greenfield "The biodiversity crisis in numbers - a visual guide," The Guardian (6 Dec 2022). https://www.theguardian.com/environment/2022/dec/06/the-biodiversity-crisis-in-numbers-a-visual-guide-aoe. 287, The region of Latin America and the Caribbean has experienced the steepest decline in animal populations since 1970 in Patrick Greenfield "The biodiversity crisis in numbers - a visual guide," The Guardian (6 Dec 2022). https://www.theguardian.com/environment/2022/dec/06/the-biodiversity-crisis-in-numbers-a-visual-guide-aoe. 287, Thousands of animals are reported to have starved in Oostvaardersplassen, a 5, 000-hectare reserve home to red deer, horses and cattle in Patrick Barkham "Dutch rewilding experiment sparks backlash as thousands of animals starve," The Guardian (27 Apr 2018). https://www.theguardian.com/environment/2018/apr/27/dutch-rewilding-experiment-backfires-as-thousands-of-animals-starve 319; **The Intergovernmental Panel on Climate Change:** IPCC AR6 Climate Change 2021: The Physical Science Basis Press Conference Presentation Slides: https://www.ipcc.ch/report/ar6/wg1/downloads/outreach/IPCC_AR6_WGI_Press_Conference_Slides.pdf 610, 611, Figure PP-1 in Boyd, P.W., S. Sundby, and H.-O. **Pörtner, 2014:** Cross-chapter box on net primary production in the ocean. In: Climate Change 2014: Impacts, Adaptation, and Vulnerability. Part A: Global and Sectoral Aspects. Contribution of Working Group II to the Fifth Assessment Report of the Intergovernmental Panel on Climate Change [Field, C.B., V.R. Barros, D.J. Dokken, K.J. Mach, M.D. Mastrandrea, T.E. Bilir, M. Chatterjee, K.L. Ebi, Y.O. Estrada, R.C. Genova, B. Girma, E.S. Kissel, A.N. Levy, S. MacCracken, P.R. Mastrandrea, and L.L. White (eds.)]. Cambridge University Press, Cambridge, United Kingdom and New York, NY, USA, pp. 133-136. 407, Table SPM 1 in IPCC, 2021: Summary for Policymakers. In: Climate Change 2021: The Physical Science Basis. Contribution of Working Group I to the Sixth Assessment Report of the Intergovernmental Panel on Climate Change [Masson-Delmotte, V., P. Zhai, A. Pirani, S.L. Connors, C. Péan, S. Berger, N. Caud, Y. Chen, L. Goldfarb, M.I. Gomis, M. Huang, K. Leitzell, E. Lonnoy, J.B.R. Matthews, T.K. Maycock, T. Waterfield, O. Yelekçi, R. Yu, and B. Zhou (eds.)]. Cambridge University Press, Cambridge, United Kingdom and New York, NY, USA, pp. 3–32, doi: 10.1017/9781009157896.001 612; **The Jaguar Project:** The Jaguar Project 329; **The King's Centre for Visualization in Science:** "Climate Model Hindcasting: Hansen et al., 1988," The King's Centre for Visualization in Science. https://applets.kcvs.ca/

ClimateModelHindcasting/ 587, "Climate Model Hindcasting: Sawyer, 1972" The King's Centre for Visualization in Science. https://applets.kcvs.ca/ClimateModelHindcasting/ 586; **The National Archives:** Figure 3 in "Emissions of air pollutants in the UK – Particulate matter (PM10 and PM2.5)," GOV.UK. https://www.gov.uk/government/statistics/emissions-of-air-pollutants/emissions-of-air-pollutants-in-the-uk-particulate-matter-pm10-and-pm25#why-are-emissions-of-particulate-matter-estimated 784; **The National Science Foundation:** National Science Foundation 489; **The Smithsonian Institution:** Ocean Acidification Graph, https://ocean.si.edu/conservation/acidification/ocean-acidification-graph 573; **The Trustees of The Natural History Museum:** Trustees of the Natural History Museum, London 117; **The University Corporation for Atmospheric Research:** MetEd, The COMET Program, UCAR 586; **The World Air Quality Project:** "PM2.5 Y2018," in Pusa, Delhi past 72 months daily average AQI. World Air Quality Historical Database. https://aqicn.org/historical#!city: delhi/pusa 801, "PM2.5 Y2021," in Pusa, Delhi past 72 months daily average AQI. World Air Quality Historical Database. https://aqicn.org/historical#!city: delhi/pusa 801, Pusa, Delhi past 72 months daily average AQI. World Air Quality Historical Database. https://aqicn.org/historical#!city: delhi/pusa 801; **The World Bank:** "Global treatment and disposal of waste (percent)," in What a waste 2.0: a global snapshot of solid waste management to 2050. The World Bank. https://datatopics.worldbank.org/what-a-waste/trends_in_solid_waste_management.html 699, "Global waste composition (percent)," in What a waste 2.0: a global snapshot of solid waste management to 2050. The World Bank. https://datatopics.worldbank.org/what-a-waste/trends_in_solid_waste_management.html 698, "Projected waste generation, by region (millions of tonnes/year)," in What a waste 2.0: a global snapshot of solid waste management to 2050. The World Bank. https://datatopics.worldbank.org/what-a-waste/trends_in_solid_waste_management.html 698. "Waste collection rates, by income level (percent)," in What a waste 2.0: a global snapshot of solid waste management to 2050. The World Bank. https://datatopics.worldbank.org/what-a-waste/trends_in_solid_waste_management.html 697; **Timm Kekeritz:** Water Footprint, https://www.europenowjournal.org/wp-content/uploads/2018/12/Screenshot-333.png; **Data:** Mesfin Mekonnen & Arjen Hoekstra (2011). Design: Timm Kekeritz 064; **Timothy O'Riordan:** The pattern of environmentalist ideologies', adapted from Environmentalism, 2nd edition by Timothy O'Riordan, Figure 10.1, page 376, copyright © 1981 Pion Ltd 011; **U.S. Department of Commerce:** "Climate Modeling," Geophysical Fluid Dynamics Laboratory. https://www.gfdl.noaa.gov/climate-modeling/#What%20is%20a%20Global%20Climate%20Model 584, Antarctic ozone hole is 13th largest on record and expected to persist into November, https://www.noaa.gov/news/antarctic-ozone-hole-is-13th-largest-on-record-and-expected-to-persist-into-november 627, Rebecca Lindsey "Climate Change: Global Sea Level," Climate.gov (19 Apr 2022). https://www.climate.gov/news-features/understanding-climate/climate-change-global-sea-level 588, Ross J. Salawitch et. al. Twenty Questions and Answers About the Ozone Layer: 2022 Update, Scientific Assessment of Ozone Depletion: 2022, 75 pp., World Meteorological Organization, Geneva, Switzerland, 2023. 626; **U.S. Energy Information Administration:** "The mix of U.S. energy consumption and production has changed over time," in U.S. energy facts explained. U.S. Energy Information Administration. https://www.eia.gov/energyexplained/us-energy-facts/#: ~: text=In%202019%2C%20U.S.%20total%20annual, and%20consumption%20equaled%2097.33%20quads. 686; **U.S. Geological Survey:** 333, 691; **United Nations:** "Sustainable Development Goals Progress Chart 2022: Goal 12," United Nations. https://unstats.un.org/sdgs/report/2022/Progress-Chart-2022.pdf 656, "Ten countries with the highest share of remittances as a percentage of GDP and a policy to reduce the transfer costs of remittances, 2016," in International Migration Policies. United Nations. https://www.un.org/en/development/desa/population/publications/pdf/policy/international_migration_policies_data_booklet.pdf 726, "UN Secretary-General's Remarks at COP22 Press Conference," United Nations Secretary General (15 Nov 2016). https://www.un.org/sg/en/content/sg/press-encounter/2016-11-15/un-secretary-generals-remarks-cop22-press-conference 707, Brundtland Report, Our Common Future, produced by the UN World Commission 054, Figure III.4 in World Population Prospects 2022. United Nations. https://www.un.org/development/desa/pd/sites/www.un.org.development.desa.pd/files/wpp2022_summary_of_results.pdf 723, From "Rationale for current immigration policy, 2015," in International Migration Policies https://www.un.org/en/development/desa/population/publications/pdf/policy/international_migration_policies_data_booklet.pdf 725, From World Population Prospects: the 2015 Revision, by UN Department of Economic and Social Affairs, Population Division, ©2015 United Nations. 864, United Nations, Department of Economic and Social Affairs, Population Division (2018a). World Urbanization Prospects 2018. 751, United Nations. https://population.un.org/wpp/Download/Standard/Population/ 732; **United Nations Environment Programme:** "HFCs: a critical link in protecting climate and the ozone layer," UNEP. https://www.unep.org/resources/report/hfcs-critical-link-protecting-climate-and-ozone-layer 632, "The UN Environment Programme and the climate emergency," UNEP. https://www.unep.org/unga/our-position/unep-and-climate-emergency 615, "UNEP-WCMC, IUCN and NGS (2018). Protected Planet Report 2018. UNEP-WCMC, IUCN and NGS: Cambridge UK; Gland, Switzerland; and Washington, D.C., USA. Page 11, Figure 6. Map of Key Biodiversity Areas." 289; **United Nations Framework Convention on Climate Change:** "The Paris Agreement," United Nations Climate Change. https://unfccc.int/process-and-meetings/the-paris-agreement 596, The Paris Agreement, https://unfccc.int/process-and-meetings/the-paris-agreement#: ~: text=Its%20overarching%20goal%20is%20to, above%20pre%2Dindustrial%20levels.%E2%80%9D 822; **United Nations Office for the Coordination of Humanitarian Affairs:** Poverty in Haiti, United Nations Office for the Coordination of Humanitarian Affairs 651; **United States Department of Agriculture:** Global Carbon. Retrieved from https://www.fs.usda.gov/ccrc/topics/global-carbon 477; **United States Environmental Protection Agency:** Inventory of U.S. Greenhouse Gas Emissions and Sinks 1990-2020 (EPA, 2022) 566; **University of California Regents:** "Sea level rise," Understanding Global Change. https://ugc.berkeley.edu/background-content/sea-level-rise/ 568; **University of Chicago Press:** Sellers W. D. (1965) Physical climatology © 1965 by The University of Chicago 550; **University of Leeds:** University of Leeds 600; **University of Maryland Center for Environmental Science:** Boesch, D.F. (editor). 2008. Global Warming and the Free State: Comprehensive Assessment of Climate Change Impacts in Maryland. Report of the Scientific and Technical Working Group of the Maryland Commission on Climate Change. University of Maryland Center for Environmental Science, Cambridge, Maryland. 435; **Voice of America (VOA):** Lisa Schlein "Sahel Risks Becoming a Forgotten Crisis, UN Official Says," VOA News (8 Sept 2022). https://www.voanews.com/a/sahel-risks-becoming-a-forgotten-crisis-un-official-says/6736298.html 664; **Waitangi Tribunal:** "The Whanganui River Report," Waitangi Tribunal (1999). https://ngatangatatiaki.co.nz/assets/Uploads/Important-Documents/Whanganui-River-Report-1999.pdf 828; **Woods Hole Oceanographic Institution:** Hugh Powell "Dumping Iron and Trading Carbon," OCEANUS. https://www.whoi.edu/oceanus/feature/dumping-iron-and-trading-carbon/ 603; **World Health Organization:** World Health Organization 144; **World Parrot Trust:** Data from World Parrot Trust, 2019. https://www.parrots.org/projects/red-necked-amazon 227; **World Resources Institute:** Kuzma, S. (August 16, 2023). 25 Countries, Housing One-quarter of the Population, Face Extremely High Water Stress. World Resources Institute. https://www.wri.org/insights/highest-water-stressed-countries 378; **Yale Climate Connections:** Adapted and simplified from https://yaleclimateconnections.org/2021/06/talking-climate-with-those-holding-different-worldviews/ 620, **Yale Program on Climate Change Communication:** Yale Program on Climate Change Communication, http: //climatecommunication.yale.edu/wp-content/uploads/2019/06/Fig-3n.png 015; **Zenodo:** Intergovernmental Science. (2022). Summary for policymakers of the thematic assessment of the sustainable use of wild species of the Intergovernmental Science-Policy Platform on Biodiversity and Ecosystem Services (IPBES) (Version 1). Zenodo. https://doi.org/10.5281/zenodo.7411847 533

Acknowledgments are continued from Copyright page (iv)

Non-Prominent Text Credit(s):

Her Majesty the Queen in Right of Canada: An age-structured Bayesian population model for St. Lawrence Estuary beluga (Delphinapterus leucas), Canadian Science Advisory Secretariat (CSAS) Research Document 2013/127, Quebec Region. Fisheries and Oceans Canada. 223; **Hodder & Stoughton Limited:** Advanced Geography: Concepts & Cases by P. Guinness and G. Nagle (Hodder Education, 1999), p.247 466, Guinness, P., and Nagle, G. (2023) Geography for Pearson International IGCSE. Hodder, p. 247, Figure 7.3 664, The water and carbon cycles, Davis, A., & Nagle, G. © 2018 Hodder and Stoughton Educational Limited. "Reproduced with permission of the Licensor through PLSclear." 572; **IntechOpen:** Méndez-Astudillo, J., Caetano, E., & Pereyra-Castro, K. (2023). Air Quality in Mexico City after Mayor Public Policy Intervention. IntechOpen, Fig. 2. 799, Méndez-Astudillo, J., Caetano, E., & Pereyra-Castro, K. (2023). Air Quality in Mexico City after Mayor Public Policy Intervention. IntechOpen, Fig. 3. 800; **Inter IKEA Systems B.V.:** A zero waste mindset, https://www.ikea.com/us/en/this-is-ikea/climate-environment/becoming-a-circular-business-pub40dc71c0 608; **International Baccalaureate Organization:** 080, 226, 225, 326, 327, 330, 332; **International Energy Agency:** IEA (2020), Methane Tracker 2020, IEA, Paris https://www.iea.org/reports/methane-tracker-2020, License: CC BY 4.0 566; **International Organization for Migration:** International Organization for Migration (IOM), 2019. World Migration Report 2020. IOM, Geneva 717; **IOP Science:** Animesh K Gain et al. 2016 Measuring global water security towards sustainable development goals Environ. Res. Lett 11 (12) 124015, 1-13 (2016) https://iopscience.iop.org/article/10.1088/1748-9326/11/12/124015 360; **Jairam Ramesh:** Quoted by Jairam Ramesh 053; **John Englander:** "Chart of 420, 000 year history: temperature, CO2, sea level," John Englander. https://johnenglander.net/chart-of-420000-year-history-temperature-co2-sea-level/ 569; **John Wiley & Sons, Inc.:** "Used with the permission of John Wiley & Sons Inc from Survival rates and causes of mortality of Amur tigers on and near the Sikhote-Alin Biosphere Zapovednik, J. M. Goodrich et al., Journal of Zoology 276 (4), 323-329, © 2008; permission conveyed through Copyright Clearance Centre, Inc." 331, Biodiversity crisis or sixth mass extinction? https://www.ncbi.nlm.nih.gov/pmc/articles/PMC8728607/pdf/EMBR-23-e54193.pdf 118, Circular-Economy Framework for Automobiles: Closing Energy and Material Loops, https://onlinelibrary.wiley.com/doi/10.1111/jiec.13088; Figure 1 075, Jeffrey A. Maynard et al. Great Barrier Reef No-Take Areas Include a Range of Disturbance Regimes, Conservation Letters 9 (3), 191-199 403, Kerr, K. C. (2021). Zoo animals as "proxy species" for threatened sister taxa: Defining a novel form of species surrogacy. Zoobiology, 40(1), 65-75. 305, The Earth Through Time, Eighth Edition by Harold L. Levin. John Wiley & Sons. ISBN: 9780471697435. 2006. Chapter 14 Life of the Mesozoic. Graph: Diversity of marine animals through geologic time, as indicated by number of known fossil genera. Used with permission from Wiley. Permission conveyed through Copyright Clearance Center, Inc. 333; **Kate Raworth:** Adapted from https://www.kateraworth.com/doughnut/ 069, The Doughnut of social and planetary boundaries (2017), https://www.kateraworth.com/doughnut/ 070; **Mahatma Gandhi:** Quoted by Mahatma Gandhi 017; **Manatū Taonga Ministry for Culture and Heritage:** David Young, 'Whanganui tribes - Ancestors', Te Ara - the Encyclopedia of New Zealand, http: //www.TeAra.govt.nz/en/map/2174/map-of-the-whanganui-river 829; **McKinsey & Company:** Exhibit from "The decoupling of GDP and energy growth: A CEO guide", April 2019, McKinsey & Company, www.mckinsey.com. Copyright © 2024 McKinsey & Company. All rights reserved. Reprinted by permission. 674, Net-Zero Challenge, McKinsey 598; **MDPI:** Megahed, Y., et. al. (2015). Land cover mapping analysis and urban growth modelling using remote sensing techniques in Greater Cairo Region—Egypt. ISPRS International Journal of Geo-Information, 4(3), 1750-1769, Figure 4. 759; **Met Office:** Adapted from Met Office 562, Climate zones, https://www.metoffice.gov.uk/weather/climate/climate-explained/climate-zones 191; **Mongabay:** Morgan Erickson-Davis,"Timber company says it will destroy logging roads to protect tigers", Mongabay, 29 July 2015 331; **Mote Marine Laboratory:** Mote Marine Laboratory, 1993 701; **National Aeronautics and Space Administration:** "Carbon Dioxide," NASA Global Climate Change. https://climate.nasa.gov/vital-signs/carbon-dioxide/#: ~: text=Since%20the%20onset%20of%20industrial, ice%20age%2020%2C000%20years%20ago 635, NASA Ozone Watch 866; **National Oceanic and Atmospheric Administration:** Radiative forcing (warming influence) of long-lived atmospheric greenhouse gases has nearly doubled since 1979. https://gml.noaa.gov/aggi/aggi.html 552, Vertical Water Temperature in Southern Lake Michigan December 14, 2016 by Kaye LaFond. Retrieved from https://noaaglerl.blog/2016/12/14/vertical-water-temperature-in-southern-lake-michigan/ 355, What is upwelling? Retrieved from https://oceanservice.noaa.gov/facts/upwelling.html 355; **NatureScot:** © NatureScot 645; **Nelson:** Adapted from Baker, S., et al., 1995, Pathways in Senior Geography. Nelson, p. 39. 339; **New Scientist Ltd:** Hacking the planet: The only climate solution left? By Catherine Brahic 25 February 2009 New Scientist Ltd. 616; **Nilfanion:** Nilfanion, 2010. Muntjac deer at Dumbleton Hall. [image online] Available at: https://fr.wikipedia.org/wiki/Fichier: Muntjac_deer_at_Dumbleton_Hall.jpg Attribution-ShareAlike 3.0 Unported (CC BY-SA 3.0) https://creativecommons.org/licenses/by-sa/3.0/deed.en [Accessed 22 May 2020]. 220; **NOAA Ocean Acidification Program:** "What is Ocean Acidification?," NOAA Ocean Acidification Program. https://oceanacidification.noaa.gov/what-is-ocean-acidification/ 398; **Northwest Scientific Association:** Lewis, N. S., & Henkel, S. K. (2016). Characterization of ecosystem structure within transplanted and natural eelgrass (Zostera marina) beds. Northwest Science, 90(3), 355-375, Figure 3. 353; **Observer Research Foundation:** Chatterji, A. (2020), Air pollution in Delhi: filling the gaps, ORF Occasional Paper No. 291, Observer Research Foundation, Table 3 804; **One Grower Publishing:** For the most troublesome weed in rice, the winner is, https://www.ricefarming.com/departments/breaking-news/cultural-management-practices-can-affect-methane-emissions-in-rice/ 517; **Open University:** The Middle East, with major rivers: the Jordan, Euphrates and Tigris, from The Open University 382; **Organisation for Economic Co-operation and Development:** OECD, 2015. https://www.oecd.org/agriculture/topics/agricultural-productivity-and-innovation/documents/analysing-policies-to-improve-agricultural-productivity-growth-sustainably.pdf 640; **Our World in Data:** "Earth's Atmospheric ozone," Our World in Data. https://ourworldindata.org/ozone-layer 796, "Fertility rate: children per woman, 2022," Our World in Data. https://ourworldindata.org/grapher/children-born-per-woman?time=latest 720, "GDP per capita vs. energy use, 2015," Our World in Data. https://ourworldindata.org/grapher/energy-use-per-capita-vs-gdp-per-capita 675, "How is overfishing changing over time?," Our World in Data. https://ourworldindata.org/fish-and-overfishing#how-is-overfishing-changing-over-time 663, "Life expectancy, 2021," Our World in Data. https://ourworldindata.org/grapher/life-expectancy?tab=map 721, "The Demography of the World Population from 1950 to 2100," in Max Roser (18 Apr 2019) The global population pyramid: How global demography has changed and what we can expect for the 21st century. Our World in Data. https://ourworldindata.org/global-population-pyramid 742, By Getsnoopy - Own work based on File: BlankMap-World.svg, CC BY-SA 4.0 541, Food and Agriculture Organization of the United Nations and various historical sources; World Bank, OurWorldInData.org/food-supply 496, Food and Agriculture Organization of the United Nations OurWorldInData.org/land-use 494, Hannah Ritchie, Max Roser and Pablo Rosado (2022) "Fertilizers" Our World in Data. https://ourworldindata.org/fertilizers 669, Hannah Ritchie, Pablo Rosado and Max Roser. CO_2 and Greenhouse Gas Emissions. Our World In Data. https://ourworldindata.org/co2-and-greenhouse-gas-emissions. 599, Joseph Poore and Thomas Nemecek (2018). - Learn more about this data OurWorldInData.org/environmental-impacts-of-food 531, Max Roser and Hannah Ritchie (2023) - "How has world population growth changed over time?" Published online at OurWorldInData.org. Retrieved from: 'https://ourworldindata.org/population-growth-over-time' [Online Resource] 722, Our World in Data based on the Food and Agriculture